GALE ENCYCLOPEDIA OF AMERICAN LAW

3RD EDITION

GALE ENCYCLOPEDIA OF AMERICAN LAW

3RD EDITION

VOLUME 1

A TO BA

GALE
CENGAGE Learning

Detroit • New York • San Francisco • New Haven, Conn • Waterville, Maine • London

Gale Encyclopedia of American Law, 3rd Edition

Project Editor: Donna Batten

Editorial: Laurie J. Fundukian, Kristin Key, Jacqueline Longe, Kristin Mallegg, Jennifer Mossman, Brigham Narins, Andrew Specht, Jeffrey Wilson

Product Manager: Stephen Wasserstein

Rights Acquisition and Management: Dean Dauphinais, Leitha Ethridge-Sims, Barbara McNeil, Kelly Quin, Susan Rudolph

Editorial and Production Technology Support Services: Charles Beaumont, Luann Brennan, Grant Eldridge

Composition: Evi Abou-El-Seoud, Mary Beth Trimper

Product Design: Pamela A.E. Galbreath

Imaging: John Watkins

For product information and technology assistance, contact us at
Gale Customer Support, 1-800-877-4253.
For permission to use material from this text or product,
submit all requests online at **www.cengage.com/permissions**.
Further permissions questions can be emailed to
permissionrequest@cengage.com

While every effort has been made to ensure the reliability of the information presented in this publication, Gale, a part of Cengage Learning, does not guarantee the accuracy of the data contained herein. Gale accepts no payment for listing; and inclusion in the publication of any organization, agency, institution, publication, service, or individual does not imply endorsement of the editors or publisher. Errors brought to the attention of the publisher and verified to the satisfaction of the publisher will be corrected in future editions.

EDITORIAL DATA PRIVACY POLICY: Does this product contain information about you as an individual? If so, for more information about our editorial data privacy policies, please see our Privacy Statement at www.gale.cengage.com.

LIBRARY OF CONGRESS CATALOGING-IN-PUBLICATION DATA

Gale encyclopedia of American law. -- 3rd ed.
    p. ; cm.
    Rev. ed. of: West's encyclopedia of American law. 2nd ed. 2005.
    Includes bibliographical references and index.
    ISBN-13: 978-1-4144-3684-5 (set)
    ISBN-10: 1-4144-3684-X (set)
    ISBN-13: 978-1-4144-3685-2 (vol. 1)
    ISBN-10: 1-4144-3685-8 (vol. 1) [etc.]
    1. Law--United States--Encyclopedias. 2. Law--United States--Popular works.
I. West's encyclopedia of American law. II. Title: Encyclopedia of American law.

    KF154.W47 2011
    349.7303--dc22   2010045527

Gale
27500 Drake Rd.
Farmington Hills, MI, 48331-3535

ISBN-13: 978-1-4144-3684-5	ISBN-10: 1-4144-3684-X	(14 vol. set)
ISBN-13: 978-1-4144-3685-2	ISBN-10: 1-4144-3685-8	(vol. 1)
ISBN-13: 978-1-4144-3686-9	ISBN-10: 1-4144-3686-6	(vol. 2)
ISBN-13: 978-1-4144-3687-6	ISBN-10: 1-4144-3687-4	(vol. 3)
ISBN-13: 978-1-4144-3688-3	ISBN-10: 1-4144-3688-2	(vol. 4)
ISBN-13: 978-1-4144-3689-0	ISBN-10: 1-4144-3689-0	(vol. 5)
ISBN-13: 978-1-4144-3690-6	ISBN-10: 1-4144-3690-4	(vol. 6)
ISBN-13: 978-1-4144-3691-3	ISBN-10: 1-4144-3691-2	(vol. 7)
ISBN-13: 978-1-4144-3692-0	ISBN-10: 1-4144-3692-0	(vol. 8)
ISBN-13: 978-1-4144-3693-7	ISBN-10: 1-4144-3693-9	(vol. 9)
ISBN-13: 978-1-4144-3694-4	ISBN-10: 1-4144-3694-7	(vol. 10)
ISBN-13: 978-1-4144-3695-1	ISBN-10: 1-4144-3695-5	(vol. 11)
ISBN-13: 978-1-4144-3696-8	ISBN-10: 1-4144-3696-3	(vol. 12)
ISBN-13: 978-1-4144-3697-5	ISBN-10: 1-4144-3697-1	(vol. 13)
ISBN-13: 978-1-4144-3698-2	ISBN-10: 1-4144-3698-X	(vol. 14)

This title is also available as an e-book.
ISBN-13: 978-1-4144-4302-7   ISBN-10: 1-4144-4302-1
Contact your Gale, Cengage Learning, sales representative for ordering information.

Printed in Mexico
1 2 3 4 5 6 7 15 14 13 12 11

DEDICATION

*Gale Encyclopedia of American Law
(GEAL)* is dedicated to librarians
and library patrons throughout the
United States and beyond. Your
interest in the American legal
system helps to expand and fuel the
framework of our Republic.

—m—

CONTENTS

VOLUME 1

Preface ix

How to Use this Book xiii

Contributors xv

A–Ba 1

Abbreviations 539

VOLUME 2

Preface ix

How to Use this Book xiii

Contributors xv

Be–Col 1

Abbreviations 539

VOLUME 3

Preface ix

How to Use this Book xiii

Contributors xv

Com–Dor 1

Abbreviations 539

VOLUME 4

Preface ix

How to Use this Book xiii

Contributors xv

DOT–Fre 1

Abbreviations 555

VOLUME 5

Preface ix

How to Use this Book xiii

Contributors xv

Fri–I 1

Abbreviations 531

VOLUME 6

Preface ix

How to Use this Book xiii

Contributors xv

J–Ma 1

Abbreviations 507

VOLUME 7

Preface ix

How to Use this Book xiii

Contributors xv

Mc–Pl 1

Abbreviations 521

VOLUME 8

Preface ix

How to Use this Book xiii

Contributors xv

Po–San 1

Abbreviations 495

VOLUME 9

Preface ix

How to Use this Book xiii

Contributors xv

Sar–Ten 1

Abbreviations 511

VOLUME 10

Preface ix

How to Use this Book xiii

Contributors xv

Ter–Z 1

Abbreviations 499

VOLUME 11

Milestones in the Law

*Brown v. Board of Education of
   Topeka, Kansas* 1

District of Columbia v. Heller 167

Gideon v. Wainwright 305

Kelo v. City of New London 353

VOLUME 12

Milestones in the Law

Lawrence v. Texas 1

Mapp v. Ohio 95

Marbury v. Madison 139

Miranda v. Arizona 161

New York Times v. Sullivan 261

Roe v. Wade 407

VOLUME 13

Primary Documents

Foundations of U.S. Law 1

Civil Rights 139

Reflections on Law and
   Society 501

Legal Miscellany 597

VOLUME 14

Dictionary of Legal Terms 1

Cases Index 235

General Index 291

The U.S. legal system is admired around the world for the freedoms it allows the individual and the fairness with which it attempts to treat all persons. On the surface, it may seem simple, yet those who have delved into it know that this system of federal and state constitutions, statutes, regulations, and common-law decisions is elaborate and complex. It derives from the English common law, but includes principles older than England, along with some principles from other lands. The U.S. legal system, like many others, has a language all its own, but too often it is an unfamiliar language: many concepts are still phrased in Latin. The third edition of *Gale Encyclopedia of American Law (GEAL)*, formerly *West's Encyclopedia of American Law*, explains legal terms and concepts in everyday language. It covers a wide variety of persons, entities, and events that have shaped the U.S. legal system and influenced public perceptions of it.

MAIN FEATURES OF THIS SET

Entries

This *Encyclopedia* contains nearly 5,000 entries devoted to terms, concepts, events, movements, cases, and persons significant to U.S. law. Entries on legal terms contain a definition of the term, followed by explanatory text if necessary. Entries are arranged alphabetically in standard encyclopedia format for ease of use. A wide variety of additional features provide interesting background and supplemental information.

Definitions

Every entry on a legal term is followed by a definition, which appears at the beginning of

the entry and is italicized. The Dictionary of Legal Terms volume is a glossary containing all the definitions from *GEAL*.

Further Readings

To facilitate further research, a list of Further Readings is included at the end of a majority of the main entries.

Cross-References

GEAL provides two types of cross-references, within and following entries. Within the entries, terms are set in small capital letters—for example, LIEN—to indicate that they have their own entry in the *Encyclopedia*. At the end of the entries, related entries the reader may wish to explore are listed alphabetically by title.

Blind cross-reference entries are also included to direct the user to other entries throughout the set.

In Focus Essays

In Focus essays accompany related entries and provide additional facts, details, and arguments on particularly interesting, important, or controversial issues raised by those entries. The subjects covered include hotly contested issues, such as abortion, capital punishment, and gay rights; detailed processes, such as the Food and Drug Administration's approval process for new drugs; and important historical or social issues, such as debates over the formation of the U.S. Constitution.

Sidebars

Sidebars provide brief highlights of some interesting facet of accompanying entries. They complement regular entries and In Focus essays by adding informative details. Sidebar topics include trying juveniles as adults, the Tea Party Movement, and the branches of the U.S. armed services. Sidebars appear at the top of a text page and are set in a box.

Biographies

GEAL profiles a wide variety of interesting and influential people—including lawyers, judges, government and civic leaders, and historical and modern figures—who have played a part in creating or shaping U.S. law. Each biography includes a timeline, which shows important moments in the subject's life as well as important historical events of the period. Biographies appear alphabetically by the subject's last name.

ADDITIONAL FEATURES OF THIS SET

Enhancements Throughout *GEAL*, readers will find a broad array of photographs, charts, graphs, manuscripts, legal forms, and other visual aids enhancing the ideas presented in the text.

Appendixes

Four appendix volumes are included with *GEAL*, containing hundreds of pages of documents, laws, manuscripts, and forms fundamental to and characteristic of U.S. law.

Milestone Cases in the Law

Special Appendix volumes entitled Milestones in the Law, allows readers to take a close look at landmark cases in U.S. law. Readers can explore the reasoning of the judges and the arguments of the attorneys that produced major decisions on important legal and social issues. Included in each Milestone are the opinions of the lower courts; the briefs presented by the parties to the U.S. Supreme Court; and the decision of the Supreme Court, including the majority opinion and all concurring and dissenting opinions for each case.

Primary Documents

There is also an Appendix volume containing more than 60 primary documents, such as the English Bill of Rights, Martin Luther King Jr.'s Letter from Birmingham Jail, and several presidential speeches.

Citations

Wherever possible, *GEAL* entries include citations for cases and statutes mentioned in the text. These allow readers wishing to do additional research to find the opinions and statutes cited. Two sample citations, with explanations of common citation terms, can be seen below and opposite.

Miranda v. Arizona, 384 U.S. 436, 86 S.Ct. 1602, 16 L.Ed 2d 694 (1966)

      1   2 3   4   5   6   7

1. *Case title.* The title of the case is set in italics and indicates the names of the parties. The suit in this sample citation was between Ernesto A. Miranda and the state of Arizona.

2. *Reporter volume number.* The number preceding the reporter name indicates the reporter volume containing the case. (The volume number appears on the spine of the reporter, along with the reporter name).

3. *Reporter name.* The reporter name is abbreviated. The suit in the sample citation is from the reporter, or series of books, called *U.S. Reports,* which contains cases from the U.S. Supreme Court. (Numerous reporters publish cases from the federal and state courts.)

4. *Reporter page.* The number following the reporter name indicates the reporter page on which the case begins.

5. *Additional reporter page.* Many cases may be found in more than one reporter. The suit in the sample citation also appears in volume 86 of the *Supreme Court Reporter,* beginning on page 1602.

6. *Additional reporter citation.* The suit in the sample citation is also reported in volume 16 of the *Lawyer's Edition,* second series, beginning on page 694.

7. *Year of decision.* The year the court issued its decision in the case appears in parentheses at the end of the citation.

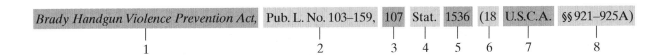

Brady Handgun Violence Prevention Act, Pub. L. No. 103–159, 107 Stat. 1536 (18 U.S.C.A. §§ 921–925A)

　　　　　　　1　　　　　　　　　　　　2　　　3　　4　　5　　6　　7　　　8

1. *Statute title.*

2. *Public law number.* In the sample citation, the number 103 indicates this law was passed by the 103d Congress, and the number 159 indicates it was the 159th law passed by that Congress.

3. *Reporter volume number.* The number preceding the reporter abbreviation indicates the reporter volume containing the statute.

4. *Reporter name.* The reporter name is abbreviated. The statute in the sample citation is from *Statutes at Large.*

5. *Reporter page.* The number following the reporter abbreviation indicates the reporter page on which the statute begins.

6. *Title number.* Federal laws are divided into major sections with specific titles. The number preceding a reference to the U.S. Code stands for the section called Crimes and Criminal Procedure.

7. *Additional reporter.* The statute in the sample citation may also be found in the *U.S. Code Annotated.*

8. *Section numbers.* The section numbers following a reference to the *U.S. Code Annotated* indicate where the statute appears in that reporter.

How to Use This Book

■ 1 ■ Article Title

■ 2 ■ Definition in italics with Latin translation provided

■ 3 ■ First-level subhead

■ 4 ■ Sidebar expands upon an issue addressed briefly in the article

■ 5 ■ Quotation from subject of biography

■ 6 ■ Biography of contributor to American law

■ 7 ■ Timeline for subject of biography, including general historical events and life events

■ 8 ■ In Focus article examines a controversial or complex aspect of the article topic

■ 9 ■ Further readings to facilitate research

■ 10 ■ Cross references at end of article

■ 11 ■ See reference

■ 12 ■ Full cite for case

■ 13 ■ Internal cross-reference to entry within GEAL

---

than $100,000. During the war, Catron continued to support the Union by broadly interpreting the federal government's war powers. In one case, he wrote an opinion refusing to release a prisoner if evidence showed that he was a Confederate sympathizer. After 1862, Catron also worked hard to keep order in the states forming his new circuit: Tennessee, Arkansas, Louisiana, Texas, and Kentucky. He stayed in close touch with President ABRAHAM LINCOLN and worked hard to keep the federal judiciary effective during the war.

On May 30, 1865, Catron, one of the last embodiments of Jacksonian democracy to leave the national scene, died in his adopted city of Nashville.

FURTHER READINGS

Anderson, Burnet. 1996. "John Catron." In The Supreme Court Justices: Illustrated Biographies, 1789–1995, 2d ed. Claire Cushman. Washington, D.C.: Congressional Quarterly.

Gatell, Frank O. 1995. "John Catron." In The Justices of the United States Supreme Court 1789–1969: Their Lives and Major Opinions, Volumes I–V. New York: Chelsea House.

Tennessee Dept. of State. "Catron, John (1786–1865) Papers 1833–[1833–1862]–1912." Nashville, TN: Tennessee State Library and Archives.

CROSS REFERENCES

Judicial Review; Native American Rights.

CAUSA MORTIS

[Latin, In contemplation of approaching death.] A phrase sometimes used in reference to a deathbed gift, or a gift causa mortis, since the giving of the gift is made in expectation of approaching death. A gift causa mortis is distinguishable from a gift inter vivos, which is a gift made during the donor's (the giver's) lifetime.

The donor of the gift of PERSONAL PROPERTY must expect to die imminently from a particular ailment or event. This has important consequences in terms of the donor's ability to revoke the gift.

For example, an elderly man is suffering from pneumonia and believes he is going to die as a result of the sickness. He tells his grandson that if he dies, he will give the grandson his pocket watch. If the man recovers and wants to retain his watch, he will be able to do so, because a gift causa mortis is effective only if made in CONTEMPLATION OF DEATH due to a known condition and the donor actually dies as a result of that condition.

A gift causa mortis is taxed under federal estate tax law in the same way as a gift bequeathed by a will.

CAUSE

A suit, litigation, or action. Any question, civil or criminal, litigated or contested before a court of justice.

Cause and Causality in American Law

If an individual is fired from a job at the bank for embezzlement, he or she is fired for cause—as distinguished from decisions or actions considered to be arbitrary or capricious.

In CRIMINAL PROCEDURE, PROBABLE CAUSE is the reasonable basis for the belief that someone has committed a particular crime. Before someone may be arrested or searched by a police officer without a warrant, probable cause must exist. This requirement is imposed to protect people from unreasonable or unrestricted invasions or intrusions by the government.

In the law of torts, the concept of causality is essential to a person's ability to successfully bring an action for injury against another person. The injured party must establish that the other person brought about the alleged harm. A defendant's liability is contingent upon the connection between his or her conduct and the injury to the PLAINTIFF. The plaintiff must prove that his or her injury would not have occurred but for the defendant's NEGLIGENCE or intentional conduct.

Actual, Concurrent, and Intervening Cause

The actual cause is the event directly responsible for an injury. If one person shoves another, thereby knocking the other person out an open window and he or she breaks a leg as a result of the fall, the shove is the actual cause of the injury. The IMMEDIATE CAUSE of the injury in this case would be the fall, since it is the cause that came right before the injury, with no intermediate causes. In some cases the actual cause and the immediate cause of an injury may be the same.

Concurrent causes are events occurring simultaneously to produce a given result. They are contemporaneous, but either event alone would bring about the effect that occurs. If one

---

The First Payments of Social Security

After the enactment of the Social Security Act of 1935 (42 U.S.C.A. § 301 et seq.) and the creation of the Social Security Administration (SSA), the federal government had a short time to establish the program before beginning to pay benefits. Monthly benefits were to begin in 1940. The period from 1937 to 1940 was to be used both to build up the trust funds and to provide a minimum period for participation for persons to qualify for monthly benefits.

From 1937 until 1940, however, Social Security paid benefits in the form of a single, lump-sum payment. The purpose of these one-time payments was to provide some compensation to people who contributed to the program but would not participate long enough to be vested for monthly benefits.

The first applicant for a lump-sum benefit was Ernest Ackerman, a Cleveland motorman who retired one day after the Social Security Program began. During his one day of participation in the program, five cents was withheld from Ackerman's pay for Social Security, and upon retiring, he received a lump-sum payment of seventeen cents.

Payments of monthly benefits began in January 1940. On January 31, 1940, the first monthly retirement check was issued to Ida May Fuller of Ludlow, Vermont, in the amount of $22.54. Fuller died in January 1975 at the age of one hundred. During her thirty-five years as a beneficiary, she received more than $20,000 in benefits.

---

pay into the Social Security system should be allowed to pay the funds into personal retirement accounts. Under this proposal, employees would have the option of converting these funds into other investments, such as stock. Bush did not push the issue hard during his first term, but in his second term he attempted to move it forward. However, the idea of privatizing Social Security went nowhere, and the precipitous decline in the STOCK MARKET beginning in the fall of 2007 provided fresh ammunition to the critics of the idea.

In 2009, the Social Security Administration predicted that OASDI tax income would fall short of outlays by 2016, and the OASDI trust fund was predicted to be exhausted by 2037 if no adjustments were made to the program. The total combined OASDI assets in 2008 amounted to $2.4 trillion.

FURTHER READINGS

Béland, Daniel 2007. Social Security: History and Politics from the New Deal to the Privatization Debate. Lawrence, Kan.: Univ. Press of Kansas.

Mitchell, Daniel J. B. 2000. Pensions, Politics, and the Elderly: Historic Social Movements and Their Lessons for Our Aging Society. Armonk, N.Y.: M.E. Sharpe.

Sass, Steven A. 1997. The Promise of Private Pensions: The First Hundred Years. Cambridge, Mass: Harvard Univ. Press.

Schieber, Sylvester J. 1999. The Real Deal: The History and Future of Social Security. New Haven, Conn.: Yale Univ. Press.

CROSS REFERENCES

Disability Discrimination; Elder Law; Health Care Law; Old Age; Survivors and Disability Insurance; Senior Citizens.

SOCIAL SECURITY ACT OF 1935

The Social Security Act (42 U.S.C.A. § 301 et seq.), designed to assist in the maintenance of the financial well-being of eligible persons, was enacted in 1935 as part of President FRANKLIN D. ROOSEVELT'S NEW DEAL.

In the United States, SOCIAL SECURITY did not exist on the federal level until the passage of the Social Security Act of 1935. This statute provided for a federal program of old-age retirement benefits and a joint federal-state venture of UNEMPLOYMENT COMPENSATION. In addition, it dispensed federal funds to aid development at the state level of such programs as vocational rehabilitation, public health services, and child welfare services, along with

■5■

240   ALITO, SAMUEL ANTHONY, JR.

Additionally, critics assailed the absence of alimony provisions in Texas FAMILY LAW as being unduly harsh. In a large number of divorces where neither spouse had acquired substantial assets during the marriage, Texas courts were powerless to compensate spouses who had sacrificed educational and career opportunities, since in such situations there were essentially no assets to divide in the first place. As a result, spouses who successfully pursued educational or career opportunities at the expense of their partner were allowed to walk away from the marriage "scot-free."

Despite the late twentieth-century universality of alimony laws in all the 50 states, lawmakers in some jurisdictions continued to propose legislation that would abolish it. In 1999 several Iowa legislators proposed a bill to abolish alimony, arguing that alimony laws provide incentive to get divorced. The bill never passed.

Because alimony is an award for support and maintenance that one spouse may be compelled to pay to another after DISSOLUTION of the marriage, it would seem to follow that no alimony could be awarded to a spouse following an ANNULMENT, which treats the marriage relationship as if it had never existed. In fact, alimony is not awarded to spouses under any conditions following the annulment of a marriage in most jurisdictions. However, in some jurisdictions the enforcement of a flat PROHIBITION of alimony awards to spouses whose marriages have been annulled has sometimes been found to impose unnecessary hardship on a spouse, usually the wife, especially where the parties have lived together for a considerable period of time. Consequently, judicial and legislative exceptions have been created to the basic rule of treating an annulled marriage as if it had never existed, for the purposes of determining whether an alimony award is appropriate. Under these exceptions, temporary as well as permanent alimony have been awarded.

FURTHER READINGS

"Alimony Strategies" 2003. Family Advocate 25, vol. 4 (spring).
American Law Institute. 2002. Principles of the Law of Family Dissolution: Analysis and Recommendation. Newark, NJ: Bender.
Sheldon, John C., and Nancy Diesel Mills. 1993. In Search of a Theory of Alimony. Orono, ME: Univ. of Maine School of Law 45.
Storey, Brenda L. 2003. "Surveying the Alimony Landscape: Origins, Evolution and Extinction." Family Advocate 25 (spring).

CROSS REFERENCES

A Mensa Et Thoro; Child Support; Damages; Divorce; Family Law; Husband and Wife; Marriage; No Fault Divorce; Sex Discrimination.

■6■

◊ ALITO, SAMUEL ANTHONY, JR.

SAMUEL ALITO is a conservative justice appointed to the U.S. Supreme Court in 2006. Upon his confirmation, he became the 110th associate justice in the Court's history and only the second Italian-American. He replaced Sandra Day O'Connor on the Court.

Alito was born on April 1, 1950, in Trenton, New Jersey. His father emigrated from Italy as a boy and became a high school teacher. His father later changed careers in the 1950s to work as the research director of a nonpartisan agency that analyzed legislation for state legislators. Alito's mother was an elementary school principal. Alito excelled as a student, deciding on a legal career after discovering a special affinity for in-depth research and finely honed argument on the high school debate team. He graduated as valedictorian of his class and headed off to Princeton University in 1968.

After receiving his undergraduate degree in 1972, Alito pursued a law degree at Yale Law School, where he graduated in 1975. At Yale he served as an editor of the Yale Law Journal and quickly became known as a traditionalist with a quick intellect. It was a reputation that he was to carry with him throughout his working life. In 1976 Alito was hired as a law clerk by Third CIRCUIT COURT of Appeals Judge Leonard I. Garth (who eventually became a colleague when Alito was named to the same bench). After clerking for Garth, Alito spent 1977 to 1981 as an assistant U.S. attorney in New Jersey. He then went to Washington, D.C., to work for the DEPARTMENT OF JUSTICE, first as an assistant to the SOLICITOR GENERAL from 1981 to 1985 and then as a deputy assistant attorney general from 1985 to 1987. In the former position, he argued several cases before the U.S. Supreme Court. By 1987 Alito returned to New Jersey as U.S. attorney, in which role he handled cases from ORGANIZED CRIME to CHILD PORNOGRAPHY.

Alito took a seat on the U.S. Court of Appeals for the Third Circuit in 1990. While his time there undisputedly marked him as a solidly conservative JURIST, it also showed a man unwilling to express his political views openly. He was widely respected by Democrats and

GALE ENCYCLOPEDIA OF AMERICAN LAW, 3RD EDITION

ALITO, SAMUEL ANTHONY, JR.   241

Republicans alike, and few saw him as either rigid or an ideologue. Still, one of Alito's controversial opinions was his lone DISSENT in a 1991 case that struck down a Pennsylvania law requiring married women seeking abortions to inform their husbands Planned Parenthood v. Casey, 947 F. 2d 682). He also concluded in a 1998 opinion that a holiday display that included secular symbols along with religious ones did not violate the FIRST AMENDMENT. By contrast, Alito voted with the majority to find a ban on late-term abortions unconstitutional where there is no exception considering the health of the mother. These, and the broad array of other published opinions stemming from 15 years on the bench, were to come under intense scrutiny when Alito was nominated to replace retiring U.S. Supreme Court Justice O'Connor in October 2005.

Alito's nomination came in the wake of the withdrawal of previous nominee Harriet E. Miers, whom many believed was unqualified for the position. It also came at a time when President GEORGE W. BUSH was lagging in the polls and there was increasing acrimony between parties in the Senate. The situation was further sharpened by O'Connor's pivotal role as a centrist justice on a fairly divided Court, thus making the stakes particularly high for both parties in finding a suitable replacement. In short, there was little doubt that Alito's confirmation hearings were destined to be difficult and time-consuming, with conservative and liberal agendas likely to take precedence.

Several groups, including the AMERICAN CIVIL LIBERTIES UNION, strongly opposed Alito's nomination. According to the ACLU, Alito had

Samuel Alito.
STEVE PETTEWAY, COLLECTION OF THE SUPREME COURT OF THE UNITED STATES

displayed a "willingness to support government actions that abridge individual freedoms." In reviewing Alito's professional qualifications, though, a committee of the AMERICAN BAR ASSOCIATION concluded that Alito was "well-qualified" to serve on the Court.

As expected, the ideological battle between the parties caused great friction and talk of filibustering the Alito nomination. Despite Democratic attempts to block a vote on the nomination by filibustering, a Senate closure motion ended debate by a 72-23 vote. The closure motion forced a vote on the nomination, and the Senate confirmed Alito by a 58-42 vote, the smallest margin since CLARENCE THOMAS

■7■

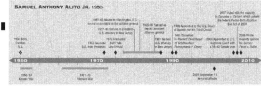

SAMUEL ANTHONY ALITO JR. 1950

GALE ENCYCLOPEDIA OF AMERICAN LAW, 3RD EDITION

---

272   SOCIAL SECURITY

■8■

THE FUTURE OF SOCIAL SECURITY

The payment of OLD-AGE, SURVIVORS, AND DISABILITY INSURANCE (OASDI) benefits has been a cornerstone of U.S. social welfare policy since the establishment of the Social Security Administration (SSA) in 1935. At the same time, the long-term financial stability of OASDI has been a constant worry. In the early 2000s, concerns about Social Security mounted as policy makers assessed the impact of the retirement of the "Baby Boom" generation. Many younger people raised the issue of "generation equity." They express doubt that Social Security benefits will be available when they retire and anger that they will be forced to pay, through payroll TAXES, for the baby boomers' retirement benefits.

Reform of the Social Security system has always been a politically charged subject. Retirees and those approaching retirement form a strong LOBBYING force, and they zealously protect their benefits. Employers and employees are equally vocal in their opposition to higher payroll taxes to fund OASDI. Thus, changes in Social Security required bipartisan support, which materialized in the face of an impending financial crisis. The 1982–1983 National Commission on Social Security Reform successfully secured from Congress the short-term financing of OASDI. As a result, Congress passed a series of laws meant to accumulate surpluses as a hedge against future burdens. The Social Security surplus is the amount by which revenue from the federal payroll tax exceeds

the amount of Social Security benefits paid out.

Shortly after these new laws went into effect, Social Security began running a surplus. Surplus Social Security revenue can be used to fund other government programs and to help retire the national debt. During the favorable economic climate of the late 1990s, Congress began to use the surplus to pay down the federal debt, hoping to better position the government to meet its obligations to future retirees. Also, in 2000, the federal government generated enough revenue so that the entire Social Security surplus was available for paying off debt.

In its 1996 report, the Social Security Administration's Advisory Council looked at various long-term financing options for OASDI. The council could not reach consensus on a specific long-term plan, but it did suggest several types of financing that represent a marked departure from previous efforts to fund Social Security. The council noted that past efforts have generally featured cutting benefits and raising tax rates on a "pay-as-you-go" basis. The council agreed that this approach must be changed and offered three ways of restoring financial solvency.

One approach, called Maintenance of Benefits (MB), calls for an increase in income taxes on OASDI benefits, a redirection of some revenue from other trust funds, and, most importantly, the investment of a portion of the trust fund assets directly in common stocks. Rates of returns on stocks have historically exceeded those on federal government bonds, where all Social Security funds are invested. If the returns

long-term solvency of the Social Security trust fund. Planners estimate that the income from the trust fund will exceed expenses each year until 2017. The trust fund balances will then start to decline as investments are exhausted to meet the increased expenses from a swelling retired workforce. The SSA estimates that beginning in 2041, payroll taxes would have to rise to 28 percent to cover the projected deficit.

The state of Social Security became a major campaign issue in the 2000 elections, with both Republicans and Democrats attempting to appear as though they were guardians of Social Security assets. Candidates from both parties promised to create a "lockbox," meaning that the Social Security surplus would be spent entirely on debt retirement. With the advent of fiscally lean years in the early 2000s, the lockbox approach was largely disregarded by politicians who advanced other ideas about what to do with Social Security surpluses. These ideas included using the surplus to help offset decreases in revenues brought about by tax cuts and using the surplus to fund new or expanded spending initiatives.

Analysts argue that the real issue often is clouded. It is not how to spend the surplus now, but how to maintain the

By the 1990s, however, concerns were again raised about the long-term financial viability of Social Security and Medicare. Various ideas and plans to ensure the financial stability of these programs were put forward. The budget committees in both the HOUSE OF REPRESENTATIVES and the SENATE established task forces to investigate proposals for Social Security reform. Other

legislative changes. The final bill, signed into law in 1983 (Pub. L. 98-21, 97 Stat. 65), made numerous changes in the Social Security and Medicare Programs; these changes included taxing Social Security benefits, extending Social Security coverage to federal employees, and increasing the retirement age in the twenty-first century.

GALE ENCYCLOPEDIA OF AMERICAN LAW, 3RD EDITION

114   NLRB V. JONES & LAUGHLIN STEEL CORP.

The Supreme Court, in a unanimous decision (Justice WILLIAM H. REHNQUIST recused himself because he had served in the Nixon administration), recognized for the first time the general legitimacy of executive privilege. Nevertheless, Chief Justice WARREN E. BURGER, writing for the Court, rejected Nixon's claim of "an absolute, unqualified Presidential privilege of IMMUNITY from judicial process under all circumstances." Burger found that [a]bsent a claim of need to protect military, diplomatic, or sensitive national security secrets," the need to protect the confidentiality of presidential communications must give way to a legitimate request by the courts for information vital to a criminal prosecution. Burger noted that the judge would review the subpoenaed tapes in private to determine what portions should be released to the prosecutors. This confidential review would prevent sensitive, but irrelevant, information from being disclosed.

Nixon obeyed the order and turned the tapes over to the district court. When relevant portions were released, they revealed that the president had been intimately involved with the attempt to cover up White House involvement in the Watergate burglary. Less than three weeks after the Court announced its decision, Nixon resigned the presidency, thereby avoiding IMPEACHMENT by Congress.

FURTHER READINGS

Gray, L. Patrick, and Gray, Ed. 2009 In Nixon's Web: A Year in the Crosshairs of Watergate. New York: Holt.
Jaworski, Leon. 1976. The Right and the Power: The Prosecution of Watergate. New York: Reader's Digest.
Johnson, Dawn. 1999. Executive Privilege Since United States v. Nixon: Issues of Motivation and Accommodation." Minnesota Law Review 83 (May).
Rozell, Mark J. 1999. "Executive Privilege and the Modern Presidents: In Nixon's Shadow." Minnesota Law Review 83 (May).

CROSS REFERENCES

Nixon, Richard Milhous; Watergate.

■9■

■10■

■11■   NLRB

See NATIONAL LABOR RELATIONS BOARD.

NLRB V. JONES & LAUGHLIN STEEL CORP.

From the 1870s through the mid-1930s the U.S. Supreme Court was generally hostile to federal legislation that sought to regulate business through the use of the Constitution's COMMERCE

CLAUSE. A conservative judiciary believed that the free market should govern economic activities; consequently laws that attempted to regulate labor relations were overturned. The Great Depression of the 1930s led to the presidential election in 1932 of FRANKLIN D. ROOSEVELT, who advocated an aggressive role for the federal government in national economic affairs. Congress consistently turned Roosevelt's legislative agenda into law yet the Supreme Court ruled these new laws unconstitutional. However, in the landmark case of NLRB v. Jones & Laughlin Steel Corp., 301 U.S. 1, 57 S. Ct. 615, 81 L. Ed. 893 (1937), the Court reversed course, paving the way for NEW DEAL legislation and a new judicial attitude toward the Commerce Clause.

For generations LABOR UNIONS had confronted a business community that was hostile to the concept of COLLECTIVE BARGAINING. Therefore, the passage of the National Labor Relations Act (NLRA or WAGNER ACT) of 1935 (29 U.S.C.A. § 151 et seq.) was a dramatic recognition of workers' rights. The law gave workers the right to organize unions and to require employers to negotiate with a certified union. An elaborate administrative process was also established, headed by the National Labor Relations Board (NLRB). The NLRB was create to review complaints about alleged violations of the law and issue administrative sanctions against union membership or organization activities. Employers vowed to test the constitutionality of the NLRA and the actions of the NLRB.

In July 1935, 13 employees of the Jones and Laughlin Steel Corporation plant in Aliquippa, Pennsylvania, were discharged for minor infractions of company rules. Most of these workers had been actively involved in a union. The union filed with the NLRB a charge of UNFAIR LABOR PRACTICES against the steel company, claiming that the discharges were because of union membership. At a subsequent NLRB hearing, Jones & Laughlin argued that the NLRA was unconstitutional because it regulated labor relations and not interstate commerce. Therefore, Congress had no authority to regulate labor relations. The NLRB rejected the argument and found that the company was the fourth largest steel producer in the United States and was clearly involved in interstate commerce. It ordered the workers reinstated and directed Jones & Laughlin to cease and

■12■

■13■

GALE ENCYCLOPEDIA OF AMERICAN LAW, 3RD EDITION

CONTRIBUTORS

Editorial Reviewers
Patricia B. Brecht
Matthew C. Cordon
Frederick K. Grittner
Halle Butler Hara
Scott D. Slick

Contributing Authors
Richard Abowitz
Paul Bard
Joanne Bergum
Michael Bernard
Gregory A. Borchard
Susan Buie
James Cahoy
Terry Carter
Stacey Chamberlin
Sally Chatelaine
Joanne Smestad Claussen
Matthew C. Cordon
Richard J. Cretan
Lynne Crist
Paul D. Daggett
Susan L. Dalhed
Lisa M. DelFiacco
Suzanne Paul Dell'Oro
Heidi Denler
Dan DeVoe
Joanne Engelking
Mark D. Engsberg
Karl Finley

Sharon Fischlowitz
Jonathan Flanders
Lisa Florey
Robert A. Frame
John E. Gisselquist
Russell L. Gray III
Frederick K. Grittner
Victoria L. Handler
Halle Butler Hara
Lauri R. Harding
Heidi L. Headlee
James Heidberg
Clifford P. Hooker
Marianne Ashley Jerpbak
David R. Johnstone
Andrew Kass
Margaret Anderson Kelliher
Christopher J. Kennedy
Anne E. Kevlin
John K. Krol
Lauren Kushkin
Ann T. Laughlin
Laura Ledsworth-Wang
Linda Lincoln
Theresa J. Lippert
Gregory Luce
David Luiken
Frances T. Lynch
Jennifer Marsh
George A. Milite
Melodie Monahan

Sandra M. Olson
Anne Larsen Olstad
William Ostrem
Lauren Pacelli
Randolph C. Park
Gary Peter
Michele A. Potts
Reinhard Priester
Christy Rain
Brian Roberts
Debra J. Rosenthal
Mary Lahr Schier
Mary Scarbrough
Stephanie Schmitt
Theresa L. Schulz
John Scobey
Kelle Sisung
James Slavicek
Scott D. Slick
David Strom
Linda Tashbook
Wendy Tien
M. Uri Toch
Douglas Tueting
Richard F. Tyson
Christine Ver Ploeg
George E. Warner
Anne Welsbacher
Eric P. Wind
Lindy T. Yokanovich

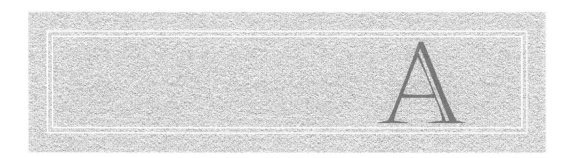

A FORTIORI

[Latin, With stronger reason.] *This phrase is used in logic to denote an argument to the effect that because one ascertained fact exists, therefore another which is included in it or analogous to it and is less improbable, unusual, or surprising must also exist.*

A MENSA ET THORO

[Latin, From table and bed, but more commonly translated as "from bed and board."] *This phrase designates a DIVORCE which is really akin to a SEPARATION granted by a court whereby a HUSBAND AND WIFE are not legally obligated to live together, but their MARRIAGE has not been dissolved. Neither spouse has the right to remarry where there is a divorce a mensa et thoro; only parties who have been awarded a divorce a* vinculo matrimonii, *the more common type of divorce, can do so.*

A POSTERIORI

[Latin, From the effect to the cause.] A posteriori *describes a method of reasoning from given, express observations or experiments to reach and formulate general principles from them. This is also called inductive reasoning.*

A PRIORI

[Latin, From the cause to the effect.] *This phrase refers to a type of reasoning that examines given general principles to discover what particular facts or real-life observations can be derived from them. Another name for this method is deductive reasoning.*

AB INITIO

[Latin, From the beginning; from the first act; from the inception.] *An agreement is said to be "void* ab initio*" if it has at no time had any legal validity. A party may be said to be a trespasser, an estate said to be good, an agreement or deed said to be void, or a marriage or act said to be unlawful,* ab initio. *Contrasted in this sense with* ex post facto, *or with* postea.

The illegality of the conduct or the revelation of the real facts makes the entire situation illegal *ab initio* (from the beginning), not just from the time the wrongful behavior occurs. A person who enters property under the authority of law but who then by misconduct abuses his or her right to be on the property is considered a trespasser *ab initio*. If a sheriff enters property under the authority of a court order requiring him to seize a valuable painting, but instead he takes an expensive marble sculpture, he would be a trespasser from the beginning. Because the officer abused his authority, a court would presume that he intended from the outset to use that authority as a cloak from under which to enter the property for a wrongful purpose. This theory, used to correct abuses by public officers, has largely fallen into disuse.

ABANDONMENT

The surrender, relinquishment, disclaimer, or cession of property or of rights. Voluntary relinquishment of all right, title, claim, and possession, with the intention of not reclaiming it.

In the case of children, abandonment is the willful forsaking or forgoing of parental duties. Desertion as a legal concept, is similar in this respect, although broader in scope, covering both real and constructive situations; abandonment is generally seen as involving a specific and tangible forsaking or forgoing.

Property That Can Be Abandoned

Various types of personal property—such as personal and household items—contracts, copyrights, inventions, and PATENTS can be abandoned. Certain rights and interests in real property, such as easements and leases, may also be abandoned. Suppose a ranch owner, for example, gives a shepherd an easement to use a path on her property so that the sheep can get to a watering hole. The shepherd later sells his flock and moves out of the state, never intending to return. This conduct demonstrates that the shepherd has abandoned the easement, because he stopped using the path and intends never to use it again. Ownership of real property cannot be obtained because someone else abandoned it but may be gained through ADVERSE POSSESSION.

Elements of Abandonment

Two things must occur for property to be abandoned: (1) an act by the owner that clearly shows that he or she has given up rights to the property; and (2) an intention that demonstrates that the owner has knowingly relinquished control over it.

Some clear action must be taken to indicate that the owner no longer wants his or her property. Any act is sufficient as long as the property is left free and open to anyone who comes along to claim it. Inaction—that is, failure to do something with the property or nonuse of it—is not enough to demonstrate that the owner has relinquished rights to the property, even if such nonuse has gone on for a number of years. A farmer's failure to cultivate his or her land or a quarry owner's failure to take stone from his or her quarry, for example, does not mean that either person has abandoned interest in the property.

A person's intention to abandon his or her property may be established by express language

to that effect or it may be implied from the circumstances surrounding the owner's treatment of the property, such as leaving it unguarded in a place easily accessible to the public. The passage of time, although not an element of abandonment, may illustrate a person's intention to abandon his or her property.

Parental Abandonment of Children

Parental abandonment of children is different from other cases of abandonment in that it involves a person rather than property. Abandonment of children is a criminal CAUSE OF ACTION under most state laws. In the civil context, it arises when a court decides to terminate the natural rights of the parent on the grounds of abandonment to allow ADOPTION.

In a criminal context, abandonment of children is defined as actually abandoning a child, or failing to provide necessities of living to a child. In California, for example, a parent is guilty of abandonment if they fail to provide "necessary clothing, food, shelter or medical attendance, or other remedial care for their child." A parent is required to accept their minor child into their home, or provide alternative shelter. Parents in California are also punished for "desertion with intent to abandon." These laws are typical of most states.

In the late 1990s the issue of baby abandonment in the United States came to a head as a result of several high profile cases. These cases prompted 38 states to pass so-called "safe haven laws." The laws decriminalize baby abandonment by allowing mothers to leave their unharmed babies at a designated "safe." location such as a hospital, fire station, or licensed child-placing agency. The laws include a time frame, beginning from the baby's birth, in which abandonment may take place; the time frame varies from state to state, ranging from 72 hours up to one year.

In a civil context, abandonment of a child is usually ruled on by a court to facilitate an adoption. State Courts employ various guidelines to determine if a child has been abandoned. In an action for adoption on the ground of abandonment, the PETITIONER generally must establish conduct by the child's natural parent or parents that shows neglect or disregard of parental duties, obligations, or responsibilities. They must also show an intent by the child's parent or parents to permanently avoid parental duties, obligations, or responsibilities. Some jurisdictions require an actual intention of the parents to relinquish their rights to find abandonment, but most allow a finding of abandonment regardless of whether the parents intended to extinguish their rights to the child.

FURTHER READINGS

Brunette, Stephen A. 2001. *Cause of Action for Adoption without Consent of Parent on Ground of Abandonment.* Causes of Action Series, 1st ser. Eagan, MN: West.

Magnusen, Debbie. 2001–02. "From Dumpster to Delivery Room: Does Legalizing Baby Abandonment Really Solve the Problem?" *Journal of Juvenile Law* 22.

Vassilian, Karen. 2000–2001. "A Band-Aid or a Solution? Child Abandonment Laws in California." *McGeorge Law Review* 32.

CROSS REFERENCE

Desertion.

ABATEMENT

A reduction, a decrease, or a diminution. The suspension or cessation, in whole or in part, of a continuing charge, such as rent.

With respect to estates, an abatement is a proportional diminution or reduction of the monetary legacies, a disposition of property by will, when the funds or assets out of which such legacies are payable are insufficient to pay them in full. The intention of the TESTATOR, when expressed in the will, governs the order in which property will abate. Where the will is silent, abatement occurs in the following order: INTESTATE property, gifts that pass by the RESIDUARY CLAUSE in the will, general legacies, and specific legacies.

In the context of TAXATION, an abatement is a decrease in the amount of tax imposed. Abatement of taxes relieves property of its share of the burdens of taxation after the ASSESSMENT has been made and the LEVY of the tax has been accomplished.

CROSS REFERENCES

Taxation; Will.

ABATEMENT OF AN ACTION

An entire overthrow or destruction of a suit so that it is quashed and ended.

The purpose of ABATEMENT is to save the time and expense of a trial when the plaintiff's suit cannot be maintained in the form originally presented. After an action abates, the PLAINTIFF is ordinarily given an opportunity to correct errors in his or her PLEADING. If the plaintiff still is unable to ALLEGE the facts necessary to state a legal CAUSE OF ACTION, then the action is terminated.

Not every possible reason for dissatisfaction with another person can be heard by a court. When the old COMMON LAW form of action governed the procedure followed by courts (as opposed to state and federal rules of procedure, which now do), only legal wrongs that fit exactly into one of the allowed categories could be pleaded in court. If the DEFENDANT believed that the plaintiff's complaint did not fit one of these forms, the defendant could respond with a PLEA IN ABATEMENT. A PLEA in abatement was called a DILATORY PLEA because it delayed the time when the court would reach the merits of the plaintiff's CLAIM, if ever.

The rigid formality of common law pleading became less satisfactory as legal disputes became more complicated. It has been replaced in each state by a procedure that allows the plaintiff to plead facts showing his or her right to legal relief. Modern systems of pleading retain a right for the defendant to seek abatement of the action when the plaintiff is not entitled to be in court. They allow a defendant to object to the court's jurisdiction, the venue of the trial, the sufficiency of process, or of the SERVICE OF PROCESS, the legal sufficiency of the plaintiff's claim, or the failure to include someone who must be a party. A plea in abatement is made either in the defendant's answer or by MOTION and order— that is, an application to the court for relief and an order that can grant it. Abatement is usually granted in the form of a dismissal of cause of action, and now the term *dismissal* is used more often than the term *abatement* for this procedure.

In the early twenty-first century, the word *abatement* is most often used for the termination of a lawsuit because of the death of a party. Under the common law, a lawsuit abated automatically whenever a party died. This rule was considered a part of the substance of the law involved and was not merely a question of procedure. Whether the cause of action abated depended on whether or not the lawsuit was considered personal to the parties. For example, contract and property cases were thought to involve issues separate from the parties themselves. They were not personal and did not necessarily abate on the death of a party.

PERSONAL INJURY cases were considered personal, however, and did abate at death. These included claims not only for physical ASSAULT or negligent injuries inflicted on the body, but also for other injuries to the person—such as libel, slander, and MALICIOUS PROSECUTION.

There are statutes that permit the REVIVAL OF AN ACTION that was pending when a party died. An executor or administrator is substituted for the deceased party and the lawsuit continues. A lawsuit may not be revived unless the underlying cause of action, the ground for the suit, continues to have a legal existence after the party's death. Revival statutes vary from state to state, but today most lawsuits do not abate.

This general rule does not apply to matrimonial actions. A lawsuit for DIVORCE or SEPARATION is considered entirely personal and therefore cannot be maintained after the death of a party. Different states do make exceptions to this rule in order to settle certain questions of property ownership. An action for the ANNULMENT of a MARRIAGE after the death of an innocent spouse may be revived by the deceased spouse's PERSONAL REPRESENTATIVE if it is clear that the marriage was induced by FRAUD and the PERPETRATOR of the fraud would inherit property to which he or she would otherwise not be entitled.

❖ ABBOTT, BENJAMIN VAUGHN

Benjamin Vaughn Abbott was born June 4, 1830, in Boston, Massachusetts. He graduated from New York University in 1850 and was admitted to the New York bar in 1852.

From 1855 to 1870 Abbott, in collaboration with his brother Austin, wrote a series of law treatises and reports, including *Digest of New York Statutes and Reports* (1860). The series led to *Abbott's New York Digest*, the most recent series of which has been renamed *West's New York Digest 4th*.

In 1864 Abbott became secretary of the New York Code Commission and was instrumental in the formulation of the New York PENAL Code, much of which is still in use.

From 1870 to 1872 he served as a commissioner to amend the statutes of the United States. Abbott died February 17, 1890, in Brooklyn, New York.

As an author, Abbott wrote several publications, including *Judge and Jury* (1880); *The Travelling Law School* (1884); and *Addison on Contracts* (1888).

ABDICATION

Renunciation of the privileges and prerogatives of an office. The act of a sovereign in renouncing and relinquishing his or her government or throne, so that either the throne is left entirely vacant, or is filled by a successor appointed or elected beforehand. Also, where a magistrate or person in office voluntarily renounces or gives it up before the time of service has expired. It differs from resignation, in that resignation is made by one who has received an office from another and restores it into that person's hands, as an inferior into the hands of a superior; abdication is the relinquishment of an office that has devolved by act of law. It is said to be a renunciation, quitting, and relinquishing, so as to have nothing further to do with a thing, or the doing of such actions as are inconsistent with the holding of it. Voluntary and permanent withdrawal from power by a public official or monarch.

The difference between abdicating a position and resigning one lies primarily in the irrevocability of abdication. Once an office or throne is abdicated, a return is not legally

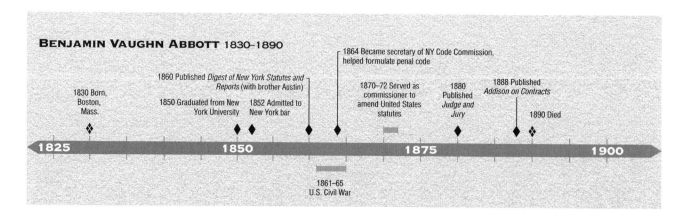

BENJAMIN VAUGHN ABBOTT 1830–1890

1830 Born, Boston, Mass.

1850 Graduated from New York University

1852 Admitted to New York bar

1860 Published *Digest of New York Statutes and Reports* (with brother Austin)

1864 Became secretary of NY Code Commission, helped formulate penal code

1870–72 Served as commissioner to amend United States statutes

1880 Published *Judge and Jury*

1888 Published *Addison on Contracts*

1890 Died

1825   1850   1875   1900

1861–65 U.S. Civil War

possible. Unlike resignation, abdication is not a matter of the relinquishment of a position to an employer or a superior. Instead, it is the ABSOLUTE and final RENUNCIATION of an office created specifically by an act of law. After an abdication, the office remains vacant until a successor is named by appointment or election.

An early example of royal abdication occurred in 305 A.D., when the Roman emperor Diocletian withdrew from power after suffering a serious illness. Another sovereign, King Louis Philippe of France (the Citizen King), abdicated on February 24, 1848, because of public hostility toward the monarchy.

Perhaps the most famous abdication of power occurred on December 11, 1936, when England's King Edward VIII (1894–1972) renounced his throne in order to marry Wallis Warfield Simpson (1896–1986). Simpson was a twice-divorced socialite whose rocky MARITAL history and American citizenship made her an unacceptable choice as wife of the British monarch. The affair between Edward and Simpson created an international scandal because it began well before her second DIVORCE was finalized. Edward's ministers pleaded with him to sever his relationship with the woman, whom his mother, Queen Mary, dismissed as "the American adventuress." Edward could not remain king and head of the Church of England if he married Simpson, because of the church's opposition to divorce. Unhappy with many of his royal duties and transfixed by Simpson, Edward chose to renounce the monarchy and marry her.

On December 11, 1936, Edward announced his decision at Fort Belvidere, his private estate six miles from Windsor Castle. There he signed an instrument of abdication and conducted a farewell radio broadcast in which he told his subjects that he relinquished the throne for "the woman I love." The 42-year-old royal, who had ascended the throne on January 20, 1936, upon the death of his father, King George V, was succeeded by his younger brother, the duke of York, who became King George VI, father of Queen Elizabeth II.

Edward and Simpson were married in Paris on June 3, 1937. Afterward, the former sovereign and his wife were addressed as the duke and duchess of Windsor. Except for a period during WORLD WAR II spent in colonial Bahamas, the couple resided in royal exile in Paris for most of their nearly 35-year MARRIAGE.

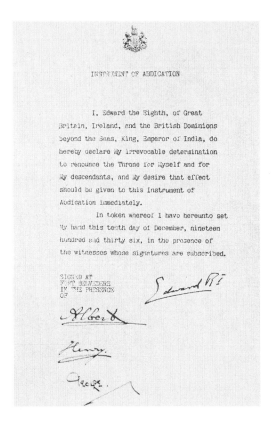

The abdication document signed on December 10, 1936, by King Edward VIII and his brothers, Albert, Henry, and George.

AP IMAGES

FURTHER READINGS

Thornton, Michael. 1985. *Royal Feud: The Dark Side of the Love Story of the Century.* New York: Simon & Schuster.

Warwick, Christopher. 1985. *Abdication.* London: Sidgwick & Jackson.

Williams, Douglas R. 2000. "Congressional Abdication, Legal Theory, and Deliberative Democracy." *Saint Louis Univ. Public Law Review* 19 (summer).

ABDUCTION

The act of restraining another through the use or threat of deadly force or through fraudulent persuasion. The requisite restraint generally requires that the abductor intend to prevent the liberation of the abductee. Some states require that the abductee be a minor or that the abductor intend to subject the abductee to prostitution or illicit sexual activity.

CROSS REFERENCE

Kidnapping.

❖ ABERNATHY, RALPH DAVID

In the long battle for CIVIL RIGHTS, few leaders have had as an important a role as Ralph David Abernathy. From the late 1950s until 1968, Abernathy was the right-hand man of MARTIN

Ralph Abernathy.
BETTMANN/CORBIS.

LUTHER KING Jr. Together in 1957 they founded the SOUTHERN CHRISTIAN LEADERSHIP CONFERENCE (SCLC), the organization chiefly responsible for the nonviolent PROTEST movement whose gains over the next decade included major legal and social reforms for black Americans. Abernathy often shared a place next to King in meetings, marches, and jail, yet despite his considerable contributions to the CIVIL RIGHTS MOVEMENT, he labored largely in King's shadow. Later becoming SCLC president, he watched the transformation of the movement as his influence weakened and his politics changed, until controversy ultimately divided him from its mainstream.

Born on March 11, 1926, in Marengo County, Alabama, Abernathy was the grandson of a slave.

His family members were successful farmers, and his father's leadership in the county's black community inspired him. Upon graduating from Linden Academy, he served in the army in WORLD WAR II. He was ordained as a Baptist minister in 1948. He earned a B.A. in mathematics from Alabama State College in 1950, an M.A. in sociology from Atlanta University in 1951, and later a law degree from Allen University in 1960.

The defining moment in Abernathy's life was meeting King. As a student in Atlanta, he had heard King preach in church. From there, they began a friendship that would shape both men's futures. In 1955, while both were pastors in Montgomery, Alabama, they began the first of many local protest actions against racial DISCRIMINATION. They organized a BOYCOTT of city buses by black passengers that led to the successful desegregation of local bus lines one year later. To build on this triumph, the pastors called a meeting of black leaders from ten southern states in January 1957 at an Atlanta church. This meeting marked the founding of the SCLC, which was devoted to the goal of furthering civil rights throughout the south. King was appointed the group's president, Abernathy its secretary-treasurer. The civil rights movement had begun.

Although the SCLC had committed itself to nonviolent protest, the forces they opposed were far from gun-shy. Segregationists bombed Abernathy's home and church. As opposition from individuals as well as government and law enforcement mounted, Abernathy continued to stress nonviolence. He said, "violence is the weapon of the weak and nonviolence is the weapon of the strong. It's the job of the state troopers to use mace on us. It's our job to keep marching. It's their job to put us in jail. It's our job to be in jail."

I DON'T KNOW WHAT THE FUTURE MAY HOLD, BUT I KNOW WHO HOLDS THE FUTURE.
—RALPH ABERNATHY

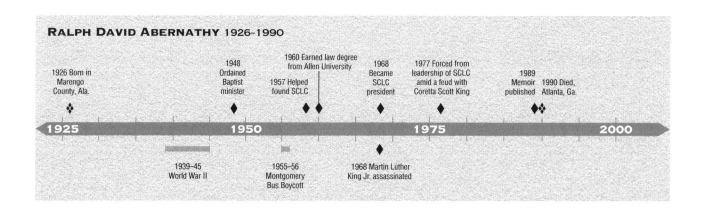

RALPH DAVID ABERNATHY 1926–1990

1926 Born in Marengo County, Ala.

1948 Ordained Baptist minister

1957 Helped found SCLC

1960 Earned law degree from Allen University

1968 Became SCLC president

1977 Forced from leadership of SCLC amid a feud with Coretta Scott King

1989 Memoir published

1990 Died, Atlanta, Ga.

1925 ◆ 1950 ◆ 1975 ◆ 2000

1939–45 World War II

1955–56 Montgomery Bus Boycott

1968 Martin Luther King Jr. assassinated

For nearly a decade, this philosophy was a clarion call answered by thousands. Through sit-down strikes, marches, arrests and jailings, and frequently at great personal danger, King and Abernathy led a mass of nonviolent protesters across the south, working together to devise strategy and put it into action. The enactment of federal civil rights LEGISLATION in 1964 marked a major success. But tragedy followed with King's ASSASSINATION in May 1968, after which Abernathy replaced him as SCLC president. He now added a new aggressiveness to the group's goals, notably organizing a week-long occupation of Potomac Park in Washington, D.C., by five thousand impoverished tent-dwellers in what was called the Poor People's Campaign. This effort to dramatize poverty was quickly crushed by federal law enforcement.

By the end of the 1960s, Abernathy's influence was in decline. The civil rights movement had splintered as younger, more militant members gravitated toward groups such as the Black Panthers and the Committee on Racial Equality (CORE). In 1977 Abernathy was forced from leadership of the SCLC amid a feud with King's widow, Coretta Scott King, and made an unsuccessful bid for Congress. In 1980, he supported the presidential campaign of conservative Republican RONALD REAGAN, which further divided him from former friends and associates. References to Martin Luther King Jr.'s MARITAL infidelities in Abernathy's 1989 memoir *And the Walls Came Tumbling Down* provoked more criticism. Politically and personally isolat-ed, Abernathy died one year later of a heart attack on April 17, 1990, at the age of 64. In death, however, the criticism faded and was replaced by praise for his contributions to civil rights.

CROSS REFERENCES

Civil Rights Movement; King, Martin Luther, Jr.; Southern Christian Leadership Conference.

ABET

To encourage or incite another to commit a crime. This word is usually applied to aiding in the commission of a crime. To abet another to commit a murder is to command, procure, counsel, encourage, induce, or assist. To facilitate the commission of a crime, promote its accomplish-ment, or help in advancing or bringing it about.

In relation to charge of aiding and abetting, term includes knowledge of the perpetrator's wrongful purpose, and encouragement, promotion or counsel of another in the commission of the criminal offense.

A French word, abeter—to bait or excite an animal.

For example, the manager of a jewelry store fails to turn on the store's silent alarm on the night she knows her cousin plans to rob the store. Her conduct is that of abetting the ROBBERY. If, however, she merely forgot to turn on the alarm, she would not have abetted the crime.

The word *abet* is most commonly used as part of the comprehensive phrase AID AND ABET.

ABETTOR

One who commands, advises, instigates, or encourages another to commit a crime. A person who, being present, incites another to commit a crime, and thus becomes a principal. To be an abettor, the accused must have instigated or advised the commission of a crime or been present for the purpose of assisting in its commission; he or she must share criminal intent with which the crime was committed.

A person who lends a friend a car for use in a ROBBERY is an abettor even though he or she is not present when the robbery takes place. An abettor is not the chief actor, the principal, in the commission of a crime but must share the principal's criminal intent in order to be prosecuted for the same crime.

ABEYANCE

A lapse in succession during which there is no person in whom title is vested. In the law of estates, the condition of a freehold when there is no person in whom it is vested. In such cases the freehold has been said to be in nubibus (in the clouds), in pendenti (in suspension); and in gremio legis (in the bosom of the law). Where there is a tenant of the freehold, the remainder or reversion in fee may exist for a time without any particular owner, in which case it is said to be in abeyance. A condition of being undeter-mined or in state of suspension or inactivity. In regard to sales to third parties of property acquired by county at tax sale, being held in abeyance means that certain rights or conditions are in expectancy.

For example, until an order of FORECLOSURE is granted by a court, a mortgagee does not have title to the property of a delinquent debtor that is the subject of a MORTGAGE in those jurisdictions that follow the LIEN theory of mortgages.

ABIDING CONVICTION

A definite conviction of guilt derived from a thorough examination of the whole case. Used commonly to instruct juries on the frame of mind required for guilt proved beyond a reasonable doubt. A settled or fixed conviction.

ABINGTON SCHOOL DISTRICT V. SCHEMPP

In 1963 the U.S. Supreme Court banned the Lord's PRAYER and Bible reading in public schools in *Abington School District v. Schempp,* 374 U.S. 203, 83 S. Ct. 1560, 10 L. Ed. 2d 844. The decision came one year after the Court had struck down, in ENGEL V. VITALE, a state-authored prayer that was recited by public school students each morning (370 U.S. 421, 82 S. Ct. 1261, 8 L. Ed. 2d 601 [1962]). *Engel* had opened the floodgates; *Schempp* ensured that a steady flow of anti-school prayer rulings would continue into the future. *Schempp* was in many ways a repeat of *Engel*: the religious practices with which it was concerned were nominally different, but the logic used to find them unconstitutional was the same. This time, the majority went one step further, issuing the first concrete test for determining violations of the First Amendment's Establishment Clause.

The *Schempp* RULING involved two cases: its namesake and *Murray v. Curlett,* 228 Md. 239, 179 A.2d 698 (Md. 1962). The *Schempp* case concerned a 1949 Pennsylvania law that forced public schools to start each day with a reading of ten Bible verses (24 Pa. Stat. § 15-1516). The law did not specify which version of the Bible should be used—for instance, it could be the Catholic Douay text or the Jewish version of the Old Testament. But local school officials only bought the Protestant King James Version. Teachers ordered students to rise and recite the verses reverently and in unison, or, as in the Abington School District, students in a BROADCASTING class read the verses over a public-address system. Teachers could be fired for refusing to participate, and pupils occasionally were segregated from others if they did not join in the daily reading.

The Pennsylvania law was challenged by the Schempps, whose three children also attended Unitarian Sunday school. In 1958 a special three-judge federal court heard the case. The father, Edward L. Schempp, testified that he objected to parts of the Bible. Leviticus, in particular, upset him, "where they mention all sorts of blood sacrifices, uncleanness and leprosy. ... I do not want my children believing that God is a lesser person than a human father." Although hardly the first lawsuit on this issue—Bible reading cases in state courts had yielded contradictory rulings since 1910—*Schempp* was the first to reach a federal court. The three-judge panel ruled that the Bible reading statute violated the First Amendment's Establishment Clause ("Congress shall make no law respecting an establishment of RELIGION ... ") and interfered with its Free Exercise Clause ("or prohibiting the free exercise [of religion]"). Local and state officials immediately appealed to the U.S. Supreme Court.

The Supreme Court agreed to hear *Schempp* along with *Murray* as a consolidated case. Madalyn Murray O'Hair and her 14-year-old son, William Murray, were atheists. They had challenged a 1905 Baltimore school board rule requiring each school day to start with Bible reading or the Lord's Prayer ("Our father, who art in heaven ... "), or both. An ATTORNEY herself, Murray brought the suit only after protesting to officials, stirring up media attention, and encouraging her son to PROTEST in a controversial strike that kept him out of school for 18 days. The suit said the rule transgressed the Establishment Clause by requiring compulsory religious education and violated the Free Exercise Clause by discriminating against atheists. The Murrays originally lost in state courts and on APPEAL.

When the U.S. Supreme Court heard oral arguments for the consolidated cases on February 27 and 28, the nation was still reacting to the previous year's ruling in *Engel.* An uproar over the *Engel* decision had produced 150 proposals in Congress to amend the CONSTITUTION. *Schempp* gave advocates of school prayer a chance to argue that the Court had been wrong in *Engel,* and this they did. Attorneys representing Pennsylvania and Baltimore officials denied that Bible reading or prayer had a religious nature, and claimed that it therefore did not violate the Establishment Clause—which, in any event, they maintained, was only designed to prevent an official state religion. Their true purpose, argued attorneys, was to keep order and provide a proper moral climate for students.

The Court stood by the *Engel* decision. In an 8–1 decision, it ruled that both Bible reading and the Lord's Prayer violated the Establishment Clause. Justice Tom C. Clark's majority opinion differed in a few respects from the previous year's ruling: It admonished prayer advocates for ignoring the law, spelled out in some detail the precedents involved, and laid out the Court's first explicit test for Establishment Clause questions. Founded on the idea of state NEUTRALITY, this test had a vital standard: Any law hoping to survive the prohibitions of the Establishment Clause must have "a secular purpose and a primary effect that neither advances nor inhibits religion."

The test clearly spelled out the limits. Study of the Bible or religion was acceptable, but only so long as "presented objectively as part of a secular program of education." Religious practices in public school were not allowed under the FIRST AMENDMENT. "While the Free Exercise Clause clearly prohibits the use of STATE ACTION to deny the rights of free exercise to anyone," Justice Clark observed, "it has never meant that a majority could use the machinery of the State to practice its beliefs."

Schempp produced three concurring opinions, notably a 74-page opinion by Justice William J. Brennan Jr. As in *Engel,* the sole dissent came from Justice POTTER STEWART. Again he disagreed with the majority's emphasis on the Establishment Clause's taking precedence over the Free Exercise Clause. For Stewart, the key factor was whether the states in the case had actually coerced students into praying or Bible reading. He did not think so.

Schempp concluded the initial round of the Supreme Court's prayer ban. However, the issue did not fade from public, political, and religious concern, and it came before the Supreme Court two decades later in WALLACE V. JAFFREE, 472 U.S. 38, 105 S. Ct. 2479, 86 L. Ed. 2d 29 (1985) (a one-minute period of silence for meditation or prayer had no secular purpose and was created with religious purpose).

The constitutionality of student-led prayers made its way to the Supreme Court in *Santa Fe Independent School District v. Doe,* 530 U.S. 290, 120 S. Ct. 2266, 147 L.Ed.2d 295 (2000). The Court held that a Texas public school district could not let its students lead prayers over the public-address system before its high school football games. The school district's sponsorship of the public prayers by

Edward L. Schempp, his wife, Sidney, and two of his three children, Roger and Donna, challenged a Pennsylvania law that made Bible reading in the state's schools compulsory.

AP IMAGES

elected student representatives was unconstitutional because the schools could not coerce anyone to support or participate in religion. The Establishment Clause barred student prayers as well as those conducted by clergy at school events such as graduation (LEE V. WEISMAN, 505 U.S. 577, 112 S. Ct. 2649, 120 L. Ed.2d 467 [1992]).

FURTHER READINGS

American Civil Liberties Union (ACLU). 2002. "The Establishment Clause and Public Schools: An ACLU Legal Bulletin."

Blanshard, Paul. 1963. *Religion and the Schools: The Great Controversy.* Boston: Beacon Press.

Brown, Steven P., and Cynthia J. Bowling. 2003. "Public Schools and Religious Expression: The Diversity of School Districts' Policies Regarding Religious Expression." *Journal of Church and State* 45, no. 2 (spring).

Davis, Derek H. 2003. "Moments of Silence in America's Public Schools: Constitutional and Ethical Considerations." *Journal of Church and State* 45, no. 3 (summer).

Drakeman, Donald L. 1991. *Church-State Constitutional Issues: Making Sense of the Establishment Clause.* Westport, CT: Greenwood.

Levy, Leonard W. 1994. *The Establishment Clause: Religion and the First Amendment.* 2d ed. Chapel Hill: Univ. of North Carolina Press.

"Religion and Schools." 1994. *Congressional Quarterly* (February 18).

CROSS REFERENCES

Constitutional Amendment; Religion; Schools and School Districts.

ABJURATION

A renunciation or abandonment by or upon oath. The renunciation under oath of one's citizenship or some other right or privilege.

ABODE

One's home; habitation; place of dwelling; or residence. Ordinarily means "domicile." Living place impermanent in character. The place where a person dwells. Residence of a legal voter. Fixed place of residence for the time being. For service of process, one's fixed place of residence for the time being; his or her "usual place of abode."

ABOLITION

The destruction, annihilation, abrogation, or extinguishment of anything, but especially things of a permanent nature—such as institutions, usages, or customs, as in the abolition of slavery.

In U.S. LEGAL HISTORY, the concept of abolition generally refers to the eighteenth- and nineteenth-century movement to abolish the SLAVERY of African Americans. As a significant political force in the pre-Civil War United States, the abolitionists had significant effect on the U.S. legal and political landscape. Their consistent efforts to end the institution of slavery culminated in 1865 with the RATIFICATION of the Constitution's THIRTEENTH AMENDMENT, which outlawed slavery. The abolitionist ranks encompassed many different factions and people of different backgrounds and viewpoints, including European and African Americans, radicals

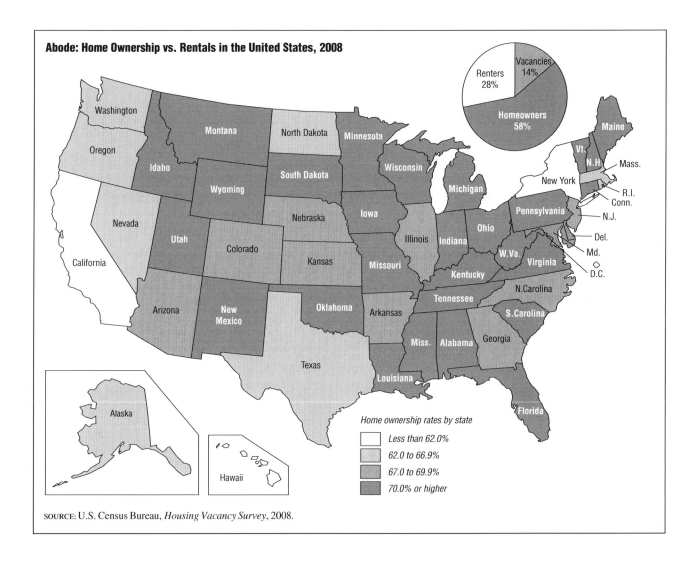

Abode: Home Ownership vs. Rentals in the United States, 2008

Home ownership rates by state

Less than 62.0%

62.0 to 66.9%

67.0 to 69.9%

70.0% or higher

SOURCE: U.S. Census Bureau, *Housing Vacancy Survey*, 2008.

and moderates. The motives of the abolitionists spanned a broad spectrum, from those who opposed slavery as unjust and inhumane to those whose objections were purely economic and focused on the effects that an unpaid Southern workforce had on wages and prices in the North.

Efforts to abolish slavery in America began well before the Revolutionary War and were influenced by similar movements in Great Britain and France. By the 1770s and 1780s, many antislavery societies, largely dominated by Quakers, had sprung up in the North. Early American leaders such as BENJAMIN FRANKLIN, ALEXANDER HAMILTON, JOHN JAY, and THOMAS PAINE made known their opposition to slavery.

The early abolitionists played an important role in outlawing slavery in Northern states by the early nineteenth century. Vermont outlawed slavery in 1777, and Massachusetts declared it INCONSISTENT with its new state CONSTITUTION, ratified in 1780. Over the next three decades, other Northern states, including Pennsylvania, New York, and New Jersey, passed gradual EMANCIPATION laws that freed all future children of slaves. By 1804, every Northern state had enacted some form of emancipation law.

In the South, where slavery played a far greater role in the economy, emancipation moved at a much slower pace. By 1800 all Southern states except Georgia and South Carolina had passed laws that eased the practice of private manumission—or the freeing of slaves by individual slaveholders. Abolitionists won a further victory in the early 1800s when the United States outlawed international trade in slaves. However, widespread SMUGGLING of slaves continued.

During the first three decades of the 1800s, abolitionists continued to focus largely on gradual emancipation. As the nation expanded westward, they also opposed the introduction of slavery into the western territories. Although abolitionists had won an early victory on this front in 1787, when they succeeded in prohibiting slavery in the Northwest Territory, their efforts in the 1800s were not as completely successful. The MISSOURI COMPROMISE OF 1820 (3 Stat. 545), for example, stipulated that slavery would be prohibited only in areas of the LOUISIANA PURCHASE north of Missouri's southern boundary, except for Missouri itself, which would be admitted to the Union as a slave state. Slavery in the territories remained

one of the most divisive issues in U.S. politics until the end of the CIVIL WAR in 1865.

Beginning in the 1830s, evangelical Christian groups, particularly in New England, brought a new radicalism to the cause of abolition. They focused on the sinfulness of slavery and sought to end its practice by appealing to the consciences of European Americans who supported slavery. Rather than endorsing a gradual emancipation, these new abolitionists called for the immediate and complete emancipation of slaves without compensation to slaveowners. Leaders of this movement included WILLIAM LLOYD GARRISON, founder of the abolitionist newspaper the *Liberator*; FREDERICK DOUGLASS, a noted African American writer and orator; the sisters Sarah Moore Grimké and Angelina Emily Grimké, lecturers for the American Anti-Slavery Society and pioneers for women's rights; Theodore Dwight Weld, author of an influential antislavery book, *American Slavery as It Is* (1839); and later, HARRIET BEECHER STOWE, whose 1852 novel *Uncle Tom's Cabin* was another important abolitionist tract.

In 1833 this new generation of abolitionists formed the American Anti-Slavery Society (AAS). The organization grew quickly, particularly in the North, and by 1840 had reached a height of 1,650 chapters and an estimated 130,000 to 170,000 members. Nevertheless, abolitionism remained an unpopular cause even in the North, and few mainstream politicians openly endorsed it.

To achieve its goals, the AAS undertook a number of large projects, many of which were

Members of the Pennsylvania Abolition Society (seated, far right, William Lloyd Garrison, founder of The Liberator, an abolitionist newspaper).
NATIONAL PORTRAIT GALLERY

A SLAVE FATHER SOLD AWAY FROM HIS FAMILY.

This frontispiece illustration, entitled "A Slave Father Sold Away from His Family," is from the Child's Antislavery Book (1860). The book was distributed by the Sunday School Union in an effort to alert children to the horrors of slavery.

CORBIS.

frustrated by Southern opposition. For example, the organization initiated a massive postal campaign designed to APPEAL to the moral scruples of Southern slaveowners and voters. The campaign flooded the South with antislavery tracts sent through the mails. Although a law that would have excluded antislavery literature from the mails was narrowly defeated in Congress in 1836, pro-slavery forces, with the help of President Andrew Jackson's administration and local postmasters, effectively ended the dissemination of abolitionist literature in the South. The AAS was similarly frustrated when it petitioned Congress on a variety of subjects related to slavery. Congressional gag rules rendered the many abolitionist petitions impotent. These rules of LEGISLATIVE procedure allowed Congress to table and effectively ignore the antislavery petitions.

By the 1840s the evangelical abolitionist movement had begun to break up into different factions. These factions differed on the issue of gradual versus radical change and on the inclusion of other causes, including women's rights, in their agendas. Some abolitionists decided to form a political party. The Liberty party, as they named it, nominated James G. Birney for U.S. president in 1840 and 1844. When differences later led to the dissolution of the Liberty party, many of its members created the FREE SOIL PARTY, which took as its main cause opposition to slavery in the territories newly acquired from Mexico. They were joined by defecting Democrats who were disgruntled with the increasing domination of Southern interests in their party. In 1848 the Free Soil party nominated as its candidate for U.S. president

MARTIN VAN BUREN, who had served as the eighth PRESIDENT OF THE UNITED STATES from 1837 to 1841, but Van Buren did not win. (ZACHARY TAYLOR won the election.)

After passage of the FUGITIVE SLAVE ACT OF 1850 (9 Stat. 462), which required Northern states to return escaped slaves and imposed penalties on people who aided such runaways, abolitionists became actively involved in the Underground Railroad, a secretive network that provided food, shelter, and direction to escaped slaves seeking freedom in the North. This network was largely maintained by free African Americans and is estimated to have helped 50,000 to 100,000 slaves to freedom. Harriet Tubman, an African American and ardent abolitionist, was one organizer of the Underground Railroad. During the 1850s she bravely traveled into Southern states to help other African Americans escape from slavery, just as she had escaped herself.

Whereas the vast majority of abolitionists eschewed violence, JOHN BROWN actively participated in it. In response to attacks led by pro-slavery forces against the town of Lawrence, Kansas, Brown, the leader of a Free Soil MILITIA, led a reprisal attack that killed five pro-slavery settlers in 1856. Three years later, he undertook an operation that he hoped would inspire a massive slave rebellion. Brown and 21 followers began by capturing the U.S. arsenal at Harpers Ferry, Virginia (now West Virginia). Federal forces under Robert E. Lee promptly recaptured the arsenal, and Brown was hanged shortly thereafter, becoming a martyr for the cause.

In 1854 abolitionists and Free Soilers joined with a variety of other interests to form the REPUBLICAN PARTY, which successfully stood ABRAHAM LINCOLN for president in 1860. Although the party took a strong stand against the introduction of slavery in the territories, it did not propose the more radical option of immediate emancipation. In fact, slavery ended as a result of the Civil War, which lasted from 1861 to 1865. Not a true abolitionist at the start of his presidency, Lincoln became increasingly receptive to antislavery opinion. In 1863 he announced the EMANCIPATION PROCLAMATION, which freed all slaves in areas still engaged in revolt against the Union. The PROCLAMATION served as an important symbol of the Union's new commitment to ending slavery. Lincoln later supported the ratification of the Thirteenth Amendment, which officially abolished slavery in the United States.

After the war, former abolitionists, including radical Republicans such as Senator CHARLES SUMNER (R-Mass.), continued to lobby for CONSTITUTIONAL amendments that would protect the rights of the newly freed slaves, including the FOURTEENTH AMENDMENT, ratified in 1868, which guaranteed citizenship to former slaves and declared that no state could "deprive any person of life, liberty, or property, without DUE PROCESS OF LAW; nor deny to any person ... the EQUAL PROTECTION of the laws." Former abolitionists also lobbied, albeit unsuccessfully, for land redistribution that would have given ex-slaves a share of their former owners' land.

FURTHER READINGS

Edwards, Judith. 2004. *Abolitionists and Slave Resistance: Breaking the Chains of Slavery.* Berkeley Heights, NJ: Enslow.

Greenburg, Martin H., and Charles G. Waugh, eds. 2000. *The Price of Freedom: Slavery and the Civil War.* Nashville: Cumberland House.

Hessler, Katherine. 1998. "Early Efforts to Suppress Protest: Unwanted Abolitionist Speech." *Boston Univ. Public Interest Law Journal* 7 (spring).

Klingaman, William K. 2001. *Abraham Lincoln and the Road to Emancipation, 1861–1865.* New York: Viking.

Merrill, Walter M. 1971. *Against the Wind and Tide: A Biography of William Lloyd Garrison.* Cambridge, MA: Harvard Univ. Press.

Tackach, James. 2002. *The Abolition of American Slavery.* San Diego: Lucent.

CROSS REFERENCES

Compromise of 1850; *Dred Scott v. Sandford*; Emancipation Proclamation; Fourteenth Amendment; Fugitive Slave Act of 1850; Lincoln, Abraham; Missouri Compromise of 1820; *Prigg v. Pennsylvania*; Slavery; Sumner, Charles; Thirteenth Amendment.

ABORTION

An abortion is the spontaneous or artificially induced expulsion of an embryo or fetus. As used in legal context, the term usually refers to induced abortion.

History

English COMMON LAW generally allowed abortion before the "quickening" of the fetus (i.e., the first recognizable movement of the fetus in the uterus), which occurs between the sixteenth and

eighteenth weeks of pregnancy. After quickening, however, common law was less clear as to whether abortion was a crime. In the United States, state legislatures did not pass abortion statutes until the nineteenth century. After 1880 abortion was criminalized by statute in every state of the Union, owing in large measure to strong anti-abortion positions taken by the AMERICAN MEDICAL ASSOCIATION (AMA). Despite the illegality, many thousands of women every year sought abortions. Under a heavy cloak of shame and secrecy, these abortions were performed in unsafe conditions, and many women died or suffered medical complications from the procedures.

The abortion laws developed in the late nineteenth century existed largely unchanged until the 1960s and 1970s, when a number of different circumstances combined to bring about a movement for their reform. Women's rights groups, doctors, and lawyers began an organized abortion reform movement to press for changes, in part because many of them had witnessed the sometimes deadly maternal complications resulting from illegal abortions. Women's organizations also began to see abortion reform as a crucial step toward the goal of equality between the sexes. They argued that women must be able to control their pregnancies in order to secure equal status. In addition, new concerns regarding explosive population growth and its effect on the environment increased public awareness of the need for BIRTH CONTROL. At the same time, many other countries developed far more permissive

Two police officers arrest one of many protestors partcipating in a pro-life sit-in during the 2008 Democratic National Convention in Denver, Colorado.
DOUG PENSINGER/GETTY IMAGES

laws regarding abortion. In Japan and Eastern Europe, abortion was available on demand, and in much of Western Europe, abortion was permitted to protect the mother's health.

Public awareness of the abortion issue also increased through two incidents in the early 1960s that caused a greater number of children to be born with physical defects. In 1961 the drug thalidomide, used to treat nausea during pregnancy, was found to cause serious birth defects. A three-year (1962–1965) German measles epidemic caused an estimated 15,000 children to be born with defects. Pregnant women who were affected by these incidents could not seek safe abortions because of the strict laws then in existence.

Reacting to these and other developments, and inspired by the successes of the CIVIL RIGHTS MOVEMENT of the 1950s and 1960s, women's rights organizations, including the NATIONAL ORGANIZATION FOR WOMEN (NOW), formed in 1966, sought to reform abortion laws through LEGISLATION and lawsuits. The organization hoped to educate a male-dominated legal and judicial profession about this important issue for women. This effort, supported by such groups as the AMERICAN CIVIL LIBERTIES UNION (ACLU), quickly began to have an effect.

Between 1967 and 1970, 12 states adopted abortion reform legislation. However, abortion activist groups began to see the abortion issue as a question of social justice and to press for more than reform. Under the rallying cry of "reproductive freedom," they began to demand an outright REPEAL of existing state laws and unobstructed access for women to legal abortion.

The increase in abortion-related cases before the courts eventually resulted in the need for clarification of the law by the Supreme Court. After considering many abortion-related appeals and petitions, on May 31, 1971, the Court accepted two cases, ROE V. WADE, 410 U.S. 113, 93 S. Ct. 705, 35 L. Ed. 2d 147 (1973) and *Doe v. Bolton,* 410 U.S. 179, 93 S. Ct. 739, 35 L. Ed. 2d 201 (1973), for hearing.

Roe v. Wade and Doe v. Bolton

Although the two cases before the Court appeared by their titles to involve the fates of two individuals, ROE and Doe, in reality both suits were brought by many people representing many different interests. *Roe v. Wade* was argued on behalf of all women of the state of Texas; in legal terminology, it was a CLASS ACTION suit. Thirty-six abortion reform groups filed briefs, or reports, with the Court on Roe's behalf. These included women's, medical, university, public health, legal, WELFARE, church, population control, and other groups. The anti-abortion side of the case included representatives from seven different anti-abortion groups and the attorneys general of five states.

Roe involved a person using the pseudonym Jane Roe—actually Norma McCorvey, who revealed her identity in 1984. Roe, an unmarried, pregnant woman from Texas, wanted to have an abortion, but an existing abortion statute prevented her from doing so. The Texas statute, originally passed in 1857, outlawed abortion except to save the mother's life. Roe filed a lawsuit in federal district court on behalf of herself and all other pregnant women. She sought to have the abortion statute declared unconstitutional as an invasion of her right to PRIVACY as protected by the First, Fourth, Fifth, Ninth, and Fourteenth Amendments in GRIS-WOLD V. CONNECTICUT, 381 U.S. 479, 513, 85 S. Ct. 1678, 14 L. Ed. 2d 510 (1965). She also sought to have an injunction, or court order, issued against the statute's enforcement so that she might go forward with the abortion. The abortion reform movement attached two other cases to Roe's in an attempt to represent a wider range of the interests involved in the issue. The physician James Hallford, who was being prosecuted under the statute for two abortions he had performed, also filed suit against the Texas law, as did a childless couple, the Does.

The three-judge district court combined Roe's case with the cases of Hallford and the Does, but later dismissed the suit brought by the Does on the grounds that neither had violated the law and the woman was not pregnant. The district court agreed with Roe that the law was unconstitutionally vague and violated her right to privacy under the NINTH AMENDMENT, which allows for the existence of rights, such as that of privacy, not explicitly named in the Constitution's BILL OF RIGHTS, and the FOURTEENTH AMENDMENT. It refused, however, to grant the injunction, allowing her to go ahead with the abortion. Roe then appealed the denial of the injunction to the U.S. Supreme Court.

Doe v. Bolton involved a 1968 Georgia statute that allowed abortion if necessary to save the mother's life, in the case of pregnancy resulting from RAPE or INCEST, or if the baby was likely to be born with serious birth defects (Ga. Crim. Code § 26-1202 a, b). However, the statute also created procedural requirements that effectively would have allowed few abortions. Those requirements included hospital accreditation, committee approval, two-doctor agreement, and state residency. The case concerned Mary Doe, who had sought an abortion at Grady Memorial Hospital in Atlanta. She claimed that she had been advised that pregnancy would endanger her health, but the hospital's Abortion Rights Committee denied her the abortion. She sought a DECLARATORY JUDGMENT, holding that the Georgia law unconstitutionally violated her right to privacy as well as her Fourteenth Amendment guarantees of due process and EQUAL PROTECTION. She also sought an injunction against the law's enforcement.

Roe and *Doe* were filed in March and April 1970, and the women's pregnancies would not have lasted through December 1970. The Court heard the cases in December 1971 and October 1972, and they were not resolved until January 1973, when the Court announced its decisions.

In *Roe*, the Court, on a 7–2 vote, found the Texas abortion statute unconstitutional. In its opinion, written by Justice HARRY A. BLACKMUN, the Court held that the law violated a right to privacy guaranteed by the due process clause of the Fourteenth Amendment. However, the Court further held that such a right is a "qualified" one and subject to regulation by the state. The state has "legitimate interests in protecting both the pregnant woman's health and the potentiality of human life" (i.e., the life of the fetus). To specify when the state's interests emerge, the Court divided pregnancy

On January 22, 2005, supporters of Roe v. Wade gather outside the Supreme Court building to commemorate the 33rd anniversary of the Court's decision to legalize abortion.

AP PHOTO/PABLO MARTINEZ MONSIVAIS

into twelve-week trimesters. In the first trimester, the state cannot regulate abortion or prevent a woman's access to it. It can only require that abortions be performed by a licensed physician and under medically safe conditions. During the second trimester, the state can regulate abortion procedures as long as the regulations are reasonably related to the promotion of the mother's health. In the third trimester, the state has a dominant interest in protecting the "potentiality" of the fetus's life. A state may prohibit abortions during this time except in cases where they are essential to preserve the life or health of the mother. The Court also cited judicial precedent in holding that the fetus is not a "person" as defined by the Fourteenth Amendment.

In *Doe,* the Court found the Georgia statute to be unconstitutional as well, holding that it infringed on privacy and personal liberty by permitting abortion only in restricted cases. The Court ruled further that the statute's four procedural requirements—hospital accreditation, hospital committee approval, two-doctor agreement, and state residency—violated the CONSTITUTION. The state could not, for example, require that abortions be performed only at certain hospitals, because it had not shown that such restrictions advanced its interest in promoting the health of the pregnant woman. Such a requirement interfered with a woman's right to have an abortion in the first trimester of pregnancy, which the Court in *Roe* had declared was outside the scope of state regulation.

After *Roe v. Wade*

After the Supreme Court decisions in *Roe v. Wade* and *Doe v. Bolton,* states began to liberalize their abortion laws. However, abortion quickly became a divisive political issue for Americans. Grassroots opposition to abortion—supported by such influential institutions as the Catholic Church—was strong from the start. By the early 1980s, the anti-abortion movement had become a powerful political force.

President RONALD REAGAN strongly opposed abortion and used his administration to try to change abortion rulings. He appointed a SURGEON GENERAL, C. Everett Koop, who opposed abortion, and Reagan made it a top priority of his JUSTICE DEPARTMENT to effect a reversal of *Roe.* Reagan even published a book on the subject in 1984, *Abortion and the Conscience of a Nation,* which contains many of the essential positions of the anti-abortion movement. Reagan argued that the fetus has rights equal to those of people who are already born. He also cited figures indicating that 15 million abortions had been performed since 1973, and he stated his belief that the fetus experienced great pain as a result of the abortion procedure. He quoted a statement by Mother Teresa, the famed nun who helped the poor of Calcutta: "The greatest misery of our time is the generalized abortion of children." Whereas abortion rights, or pro-choice, advocates argued that there were public health advantages of the new abortion laws, opponents of abortion, such as Reagan, referred to abortion as a "silent holocaust."

The anti-abortion, or pro-life, movement has challenged abortion in a number of different ways. It has sponsored CONSTITUTIONAL amendments that would effectively reverse *Roe,* as well as legislation that would limit and regulate access to abortion, including government financing of abortion procedures. Some anti-abortion groups have practiced CIVIL DISOBEDIENCE, attempting to disrupt and block abortion clinic activities. The most extreme opponents have resorted to violence and even MURDER in an attempt to eliminate abortion.

All these methods have resulted in a great deal of LITIGATION and added to the complexity of the abortion issue. Many of the subsequent cases have come before the Supreme Court. Observers have often expected the Court to overturn its *Roe* decision, particularly after the Reagan administration appointed three justices to the Court. However, although the Court allowed increasingly strict state regulation of abortion after *Roe,* it stuck to the essential finding in the case that women have a limited right to terminate their pregnancies. This entitlement is incorporated in the right of privacy guaranteed by the Fourteenth Amendment.

Constitutional Amendments Although amending the Constitution is the most direct way to reverse *Roe v. Wade,* neither Congress nor the states have passed a CONSTITUTIONAL AMENDMENT related to the issue of abortion. The anti-abortion forces have found it extremely difficult to achieve a public consensus on this divisive issue. However, at least 19 state legislatures have passed applications to convene a constitutional convention to propose an amendment that would outlaw abortions. Congressional representatives have also worked to bring such an amendment about. The many dozens of amendments that have been proposed can be grouped into two main categories: states' rights and the right to life. The former would restore to the states the same control over abortion that they exercised prior to *Roe*. The latter would designate the fetus as a person, entitled to all the privileges and rights guaranteed under the Fourteenth Amendment.

One unsuccessful attempt at changing the Constitution was the Hatch amendment of 1983, sponsored by Senator Orrin G. Hatch (R-Utah), which stated, "A right to abortion is not secured by this Constitution." It did not receive the two-thirds majority necessary in Congress to be submitted to the states for RATIFICATION.

Congress has also sponsored legislation that would effectively reverse *Roe*. For example, the Human Life Bill (S. 158), introduced by Senator JESSE HELMS (R-N.C.) in 1981, would have established that the fetus is a person, entitled to the full rights and privileges guaranteed by the Fourteenth Amendment. The bill did not pass, and it is doubtful whether Congress has the constitutional authority to overturn a Supreme Court precedent without violating the SEPARATION OF POWERS.

Federal Financing In 1976 Representative Henry J. Hyde (R-Ill.) sponsored an amendment to the FEDERAL BUDGET appropriations bill for the DEPARTMENT OF HEALTH AND HUMAN SERVICES (HHS). His amendment denied MEDICAID funding for abortion unless the woman's life is in danger or she is pregnant as a result of rape or incest, but only if the woman reports the incident at the time of its occurrence. Despite opposition from pro-abortion groups, Hyde attached this amendment every year to the same appropriations bill. The Supreme Court has upheld the constitutionality of the Hyde amendment (*Harris v. McRae*, 448 U. S. 297, 100 S. Ct. 2671, 65 L. Ed. 2d 784 [1980]; *McGowan v. Maryland*, 366 U.S. 420, 81 S. Ct. 1101, 6 L. Ed. 2d 393 [1961]). Evidence suggests that these federal actions have caused fewer women to have abortions.

In the late 1980s, with its composition having been changed by three Reagan appointees (Justices Sandra Day O'Connor, ANTONIN SCALIA, and ANTHONY M. KENNEDY), the Court issued a RULING related to federal financing of abortion that many perceived as a dramatic shift against abortion rights. In WEBSTER V. REPRODUCTIVE HEALTH SERVICES, 492 U.S. 490, 109 S. Ct. 3040, 106 L. Ed. 2d 410 (1989), the Supreme Court upheld a Missouri law prohibiting the use of public funds and buildings for abortion procedures and counseling, including a provision that required fetal testing for viability for abortions performed after the twentieth week of pregnancy (Mo. Rev. Stat. §§ 1.205.1, 1.205.2, 188.205, 188.210, 188.215). Scalia, appointed in 1986, argued in his concurring opinion that *Roe v. Wade* should be overruled and that the Court had missed an opportunity in not doing so in this case.

The *Webster* decision resulted in a flood of new state legislation related to abortion. Many states sought to reactivate old abortion laws that had never been taken off the books subsequent to *Roe*. Louisiana, for example, sought to reinstate an 1855 law making all abortions illegal and imposing a ten-year sentence on doctors and women violating it. However, in January 1990 a federal district court ruled that the 1855 law could not be reinstated and that subsequent laws allowing abortions in certain circumstances took precedence (*Weeks v. Connick*, 733 F. Supp. 1036 [E.D. La. 1990]). By mid-1991, Pennsylvania, Guam, Utah, and Louisiana had all enacted laws banning abortions except in limited circumstances. Pennsylvania became the first to approve new abortion restrictions when it amended its Abortion Control Act (Pa. Cons. Stat. Ann. § 3201) to create strict new regulations on abortion procedures (see the discussion of *Planned Parenthood of Southeastern Pennsylvania v. Casey* under "Other Major Abortion Regulations," later in this entry). In other states such as South and North Dakota, legislation that would have sharply restricted abortion was only narrowly defeated. However, some states, including Connecticut and Maryland, reacted to the *Webster* decision by passing legislation protecting women's rights to abortion.

Before the Court ruled on Pennsylvania's Abortion Control Act, it decided a major case relating to federal funding and regulation of family planning clinics. In *Rust v. Sullivan*, 500 U.S. 173, 111 S. Ct. 1759, 114 L. Ed. 2d 233 (1991), the Court upheld a series of regulations issued in 1988 by the Reagan administration's Justice Department affecting family planning clinics that receive funds through Title X of the PUBLIC HEALTH SERVICE Act of 1970, 42 U.S.C. §§ 300 to 300a-6. The regulations prohibited clinic personnel from providing any information about abortion, including counseling or referral. The regulations also required that the only permissible response to a request for an abortion or referral was to state that the agency "does not consider abortion an appropriate method of planning and therefore does not counsel or refer for abortion." This regulation became known to its detractors as the GAG RULE.

The regulations also prohibited Title X-funded family planning clinics from LOBBYING for legislation that advocated or increased access to abortion, and they required that such clinics be "physically and financially separate" from abortion activities. Although a family planning agency could still conduct abortion-related activities, it could not use federal money to fund such activities. Chief Justice WILLIAM H. REHNQUIST, who wrote the Court's opinion, disagreed with the contentions of the plaintiffs—several family planning agencies—that the federal regulations violated a woman's due process right to choose whether to terminate her pregnancy. He pointed out that the due process clause generally confers no affirmative right to government aid. The government has no constitutional duty to subsidize abortion and may validly choose to fund "childbirth over abortion." Rehnquist noted that a woman's right to seek medical advice outside a Title X-funded agency remained "unfettered."

Justice Blackmun, author of the *Roe* majority opinion, dissented, arguing that the regulations, because they restricted speech as a condition for accepting public funds, violated the First Amendment's free speech provision. The regulations, he wrote, suppressed "truthful information regarding constitutionally protected conduct of vital importance to the listener." Blackmun saw the regulations as improper government interference in a woman's decision to continue or end a pregnancy, and he claimed that they rendered the LANDMARK *Roe* ruling "technically" intact but of little substance.

On January 22, 1993, shortly after taking office, President BILL CLINTON signed a memorandum that revoked the gag rule, maintaining that it "endangers women's lives by preventing them from receiving complete and accurate medical information." On February 5, 1993, the secretary of HHS complied with the president's decision and declared that the department

would return to Title X regulations that were in effect before February 1988. Title X-funded clinics would again be able to provide nondirective counseling on all options to a patient and to refer her for abortion services if she chose. However, such clinics would still be prohibited from engaging in pro-choice lobbying or litigation.

Other Major Abortion Regulations

Among the first abortion regulations to be enacted after *Roe v. Wade* were requirements for the INFORMED CONSENT of the woman seeking an abortion. Although informed consent laws vary from jurisdiction to jurisdiction, it can generally be given only after a woman receives certain information from a doctor, medical professional, or counselor. This information can include the nature and risks of the abortion procedure, the risk of carrying the pregnancy to term, the alternatives to abortion, the probable age of the fetus, and specific government aid available for care of a child. Related to this issue are other types of consent, including parental and spousal consent, that states have sought to require before an abortion can be performed.

In 1976 the Court reviewed a Missouri statute requiring that the following provisions be met for an abortion to be performed: that a woman in the first twelve weeks of her pregnancy give written consent; that a wife obtain her husband's consent; and that a minor obtain her parents' consent, unless a medical necessity exists (Mo. Ann. Stat. § 188.010 et seq.). The statute also required that physicians and clinics performing abortions keep careful records of their procedures and that criminal and civil LIABILITY be imposed upon a physician who failed to observe standards of professional care in performing abortions. Planned Parenthood, a family planning organization, initiated a lawsuit to declare the law unconstitutional. The Supreme Court, in *Planned Parenthood v. Danforth,* 428 U.S. 52, 96 S. Ct. 2831, 49 L. Ed. 2d 788 (1976), upheld the requirement that the woman give written consent in the first trimester, as well as the requirement that records of abortion procedures be kept. However, the Court ruled that a woman need not inform her husband of an abortion performed in the first trimester, because the state may not interfere in the woman's private decision concerning her pregnancy during that period.

For the same reason, the Court struck down the law requiring a minor to obtain parental consent in the first trimester.

The Court clarified its position on parental consent in later rulings. In *Bellotti v. Baird*, 443 U. S. 622, 99 S. Ct. 3035, 61 L. Ed. 2d 797 (1979), it struck down a state law that required the consent of both parents or judicial approval—commonly called judicial bypass—before an unmarried minor could obtain an abortion. The Court found the law unconstitutional because it gave third parties—the child's parents or the court—absolute VETO power over the minor's ability to choose abortion, regardless of her best interests, maturity, or ability to make informed decisions. In *H.L. v. Matheson*, 450 U.S. 398, 101 S. Ct. 1164, 67 L. Ed. 2d 388 (1981), the Court upheld a Utah statute requiring that a physician notify the parents of a minor before performing an abortion on her (Utah Code Ann. § 76-7-304). Because the law required only notification rather than consent, the Court reasoned that it did not give any party veto power over the minor's decision. In *Hodgson v. Minnesota*, 497 U.S. 417, 110 S. Ct. 2926, 11 L. Ed. 2d 344 (1990), the Court upheld a parental notification statute because the statute's provision for judicial bypass took into account the best interests of the minor, her maturity, and her ability to make an informed decision. In *Ayotte v. Planned Parenthood of Northern New England*, 546 U.S. 320, 126 S. Ct. 961, 163 L. Ed. 2d 812 (2006), the Court reviewed another parental notification statute that did not contain an exception to allow a minor to obtain an abortion without notice to her parent when necessary to preserve the minor's health. The Court remanded the case to the lower federal courts to determine whether the statute as a whole had to be stricken or whether parts of the statute could remain intact.

In 1982 Pennsylvania passed the Abortion Control Act, which required that the woman give "voluntary and informed" consent after hearing a number of statements, including declarations of the following: the "fact that there may be detrimental physical and psychological effects" from the abortion; the particular medical risks associated with the abortion method to be employed; the probable gestational age of the fetus; the "fact that medical assistance benefits may be available" for prenatal care and childbirth; and the "fact that the father is liable to assist" in CHILD SUPPORT. The law also required a physician to report the woman's age, race, MARITAL status, and number of previous pregnancies; the probable gestational age of the fetus; the method of payment for the abortion; and the basis of determination that "a child is not viable."

When the Pennsylvania law came before the Court in the 1986 case *Thornburgh v. American College of Obstetricians & Gynecologists*, 476 U.S. 747, 106 S. Ct. 2169, 90 L. Ed. 2d 779, the Reagan administration's Justice Department specifically asked the Court to overturn *Roe*. In its brief, the department argued that the Court should "abandon" *Roe* because its textual and historical basis was "so far flawed" as to be a source of instability in the law. Instead, the brief urged, the Court should leave the state legislatures free to permit or prohibit abortion as they wish. However, by a 5–4 vote the Court found all the provisions of Pennsylvania's Abortion Control Act to be unconstitutional, thereby reaffirming its previous decisions upholding a woman's constitutional right to abortion. "The states," wrote Justice Blackmun in the Court's opinion, "are not free, under the guise of protecting maternal health or potential life, to intimidate women into continuing pregnancies." Pennsylvania defended itself by claiming that its procedures gave the pregnant woman information that would better inform her decision regarding abortion. Blackmun, although he agreed in principle with the idea of informed consent, found that the Pennsylvania procedures were designed not so much to inform as to encourage a woman to withhold her consent to an abortion.

The narrow margin of the Court's decision encouraged the anti-abortion movement. By the time the Court reached its next major abortion decision, in 1992 (*Planned Parenthood of Southeastern Pennsylvania v. Casey*, 505 U.S. 833, 112 S. Ct. 2791, 120 L. Ed. 2d 674), many expected it to finally reverse *Roe*. Again, it did not. *Casey*, the most important abortion decision since *Roe*, concerned amendments to the same Pennsylvania Abortion Control Act of 1982. The amendments prohibited abortions after 24 weeks except to save the woman's life or to prevent substantial and irreversible impairment of her bodily functions; required a woman to wait 24 hours after giving her informed consent before receiving an abortion;

allowed only a physician to give informed-consent information; required a woman to notify her spouse; and mandated that minors obtain informed consent from at least one parent or a court before receiving an abortion. The plaintiffs in the case, five family planning clinics and a physician provider of abortion services, asked the Court to declare the statutes invalid.

In a 5–4 decision, the Court again supported the basic provisions of *Roe* and upheld a woman's right to decide to obtain an abortion. The Court did, however, uphold all the Pennsylvania statutes except for the spousal notification provision, arguing that they did not present an "undue burden" to the woman's reproductive rights. Justices O'Connor, Kennedy, and DAVID H. SOUTER wrote the majority opinion, and Justices JOHN PAUL STEVENS and Blackmun wrote concurring opinions. Chief Justice Rehnquist and Justices Scalia, BYRON R. WHITE, and CLARENCE THOMAS all dissented.

Noting that the case marked the fifth time the Justice Department under the Ronald Reagan and George H. W. Bush administrations had filed a report with the Court making known its desire to overturn *Roe,* the Court's opinion defended the reasoning of the *Roe* decision. The Court characterized the *Roe* ruling as having three major provisions:

> First is a recognition of the right of the woman to choose to have an abortion before viability and to obtain it without undue interference from the state. ... Second is a confirmation of the State's power to restrict abortions after fetal viability, if the law contains exceptions for pregnancies which endanger a woman's life or health. And third is the principle that the State has legitimate interests from the outset of the pregnancy in protecting the health of the woman and the life of the fetus that may become a child.

In *Casey,* as in *Roe,* the Court found the constitutional basis of a woman's right to terminate her pregnancy in the due process clause of the Fourteenth Amendment. As the Court stated: "It is a promise of the Constitution that there is a realm of personal liberty which the government may not enter." The Court also invoked the legal doctrine of STARE DECISIS, the policy of a court to follow previously decided cases rather than OVERRULE them.

However, the Court emphasized, more than it had in *Roe,* "the State's important and legitimate interest in potential life," which is a quotation taken directly from *Roe.* The justices also sought to better define the "undue burden" standard, originally developed by Justice O'Connor, that the Court had used to assess the validity of any possible regulations of a woman's reproductive rights. The Court more precisely defined an undue burden as one whose "purpose or effect is to place a substantial obstacle in the path of a woman seeking an abortion before the fetus attains viability."

The dissenting justices in the case restated their opinion that *Roe* was decided wrongly because no FUNDAMENTAL RIGHT for a woman to choose to terminate her pregnancy was written into the U.S. Constitution and because U.S. society in the past permitted laws that prohibited abortion. They also gave different arguments for upholding the Pennsylvania statute's restrictions. Such provisions had only to show a "rational basis," and using that test, they would have upheld all the challenged portions of the Pennsylvania law. Chief Justice Rehnquist and Justice Scalia both argued that the Court had misused the notion of *stare decisis* in the case, because the Court did not uphold all aspects of *Roe.* Scalia also maintained that although the liberty to terminate a pregnancy may be of great importance to many women, it is not "a liberty protected by the Constitution."

The Court's decision in *Casey* was used to strike down other state laws that sharply restricted women's access to abortion. In September 1992, citing the *Casey* decision in *Sojourner v. Edwards,* 974 F.2d 27, the U.S. Court of Appeals for the Fifth Circuit struck down a Louisiana law that would have imposed stiff sentences on doctors performing abortions for reasons other than saving the life of the mother or in cases of rape or incest if the victim reported the crime (La. Rev. Stat. Ann. 14:87). The appeals court found the statute unconstitutional because it imposed an undue burden on women seeking an abortion before fetal viability. The Supreme Court later upheld this ruling without comment (*Sojourner,* 507 U.S. 972, 113 S. Ct. 1414, 122 L. Ed. 2d 785 [1993]).

After *Planned Parenthood v. Casey*

As a result of the Court's decision in *Planned Parenthood of Southeastern Pennsylvania v. Casey,* the battle over abortion moved beyond the question of whether *Roe v. Wade* would be overturned to focus on what conditions truly constitute an American woman's right to safe, legal abortion. After a number of violent incidents at abortion clinics, the abortion rights movement focused on lobbying for legislation and winning court cases guaranteeing access to abortion clinics. The anti-abortion movement, by contrast, continued to vigorously oppose abortion but became increasingly split between militant and moderate factions. Behind the split was an alarming increase in violent actions by militant anti-abortion protesters. During 1993 and 1994, five abortion providers were killed by anti-abortion militants. Although such killings undermined public support for the anti-abortion movement, they also damaged the morale of those who staff family planning clinics; some clinics even shut down. As a result, family planning services, including abortion, remain difficult to obtain for women in many parts of the United States, particularly in rural areas.

The Supreme Court decided a number of different cases surrounding the issue of anti-abortion protests, many of which made it more difficult for anti-abortion groups to disrupt the operations of family planning clinics. In *Madsen v. Women's Health Center,* 512 U.S. 753, 114 S. Ct. 2516, 129 L. Ed. 2d 593 (1994), the Court upheld a regulation barring abortion protesters within 36 feet of a Melbourne, Florida, clinic. In another 1994 decision, *National Organization for Women v. Scheidler,* 510 U.S. 249, 114 S. Ct. 798, 127 L. Ed. 2d 99, the Court upheld the use of the Racketeer Influenced and Corrupt Organizations (RICO) chapter of the ORGANIZED CRIME Control Act of 1970 (18 U.S.C.A. §§ 1961–1968) against militant anti-abortion groups. RICO, which was originally designed to combat Mafia crime, gives the government a potent tool to convict those involved in violence against abortion providers and their clinics.

In May 1994 President Clinton signed into law another tool to be used against anti-abortion militants, the Freedom of Access to Clinic Entrances Act (FACE), which allows for federal criminal prosecution of anyone who, "by force or threat of force or by physical obstruction, intentionally injures, intimidates, or interferes … with any person … obtaining or providing reproductive health services" (18 U.S.C.A. § 248). The law also makes it a federal crime to intentionally damage or destroy the property of any reproductive health facility, and

it permits persons harmed by those engaging in prohibited conduct to bring private suits against the wrongdoers. The law imposes stiff penalties as well for those found guilty of violating its provisions.

Ultimately, medical technology may have as much to do with the outcome of the abortion debate as politics. New drugs have been developed that induce abortion without a surgical procedure. The best known of these is RU-486, or mifepristone, developed by the French pharmaceutical company Roussel Uclaf. The drug blocks the action of the female hormone progesterone, preventing the implantation of a fertilized egg in the wall of the uterus. It is used with a second drug in pill form, prostaglandin, taken 48 hours later, which causes uterine contractions. The uterine lining is then sloughed off, along with any fertilized eggs. Widely used in Europe since the early 1990s, RU-486 is said to be 92 to 95 percent effective. In the early 2000s, the drug was also being tested as a possible treatment for breast cancer, endometriosis, brain tumors, and depression.

The FOOD AND DRUG ADMINISTRATION (FDA), under the Reagan and Bush administrations, banned the importation of RU-486 into the United States. However, in April 1993 the Clinton administration pressured Roussel Uclaf to license the drug for sale to the United States. Population Council, a New York-based NON-PROFIT organization, said it would conduct clinical tests in the United States. In 1994 the pharmaceutical company donated its U.S. PATENT of the drug to the council. By 1996 the Population Council had filed for FDA approval, and in September 2000, the FDA approved the "abortion pill." Danco Laboratories, a New York-based women's health pharmaceutical company which had been given the rights by the council to manufacture and distribute mifepristone, made the drug available to U.S. clinics by November. In the two years following its introduction, more than one hundred thousand women in the United States chose mifepristone as an abortion option. Abortion protesters quickly rallied and began to PETITION the FDA to RESCIND its approval of the drug, claiming that mifepristone is harmful to women.

The Pro-Life Movement and the Courts

Even before the Supreme Court's landmark 1973 abortion ruling in *Roe v. Wade,* anti-abortion groups were PICKETING and protesting at family planning clinics that perform abortions. Such groups had formed in response to an abortion reform movement that by 1970 had succeeded in liberalizing abortion laws in many states. From the start, most anti-abortion demonstrators modeled their protests on those of the CIVIL RIGHTS movement of the 1950s and 1960s. The anti-abortion movement was led by such people as Joan Andrews, a pacifist and HUMAN RIGHTS ADVOCATE who became a hero for the movement after she spent two-and-a-half years in a Florida jail for attempting to disengage a suction machine used in abortions. The movement advocated the nonviolent approach to civil disobedience pioneered by MOHANDAS K. GANDHI and MARTIN LUTHER KING Jr. By 1975, two years after *Roe,* Catholic groups had begun to conduct sit-ins at family planning clinics where abortions were performed. With time, evangelical Protestant groups joined the movement, and by the mid-1990s they accounted for a majority of anti-abortion activists.

Anti-abortion groups have labeled their activities as direct actions or rescues, believing that they are saving unborn children from murder, and their tactics have grown increasingly complex. Typical stratagems include bringing in dozens or hundreds of volunteers and blocking clinic entrances with their bodies, often chaining themselves to doors; shouting slogans, sometimes with bullhorns; attempting to intercept women leaving or entering the building and plying them with anti-abortion literature; displaying graphic pictures of fetuses; and trailing clinic employees to and from work while shouting such labels as "Baby killer!" Besides demonstrating, anti-abortion groups have sponsored pregnancy crisis centers, where they counsel pregnant women, with the intention of persuading them to carry their pregnancies to term. By the mid-1980s, activists had created national organizations and networks that promoted civil disobedience to stop the practice of abortion. One well-known organization is Operation Rescue, which was started in the 1980s by Randall Terry, an evangelical Christian.

The aggressive strategies of the anti-abortion movement prompted legal responses from women's and abortion rights organizations, resulting in a number of cases that have reached the Supreme Court. In several different rulings, the Court has attempted to clarify what is and is not allowed in anti-abortion demonstrations. In making these decisions, the Court has been careful to balance the rights of the demonstrators—particularly their right to free speech—with the rights of women seeking to use family planning clinic services. In 1988, for example, in *Frisby v. Schultz,* 487 U.S. 474, 108 S. Ct. 2495, 101 L. Ed. 2d 420, the Court upheld a Brookfield, Wisconsin, city ORDINANCE prohibiting pickets "focused on, and taking place in front of, a particular residence." The ordinance had been created in response to anti-abortion demonstrations targeting the private home of an obstetrician who performed abortions, a tactic used by the protesters after picketing at the physician's clinic had not stopped its operation. Justice Sandra Day O'Connor wrote in the Court's opinion, "There is simply no right to force speech into the home of an unwilling listener."

A later Supreme Court decision gave abortion clinics further protection: It supported the constitutionality of a court injunction prohibiting protesters from going within 36 feet of a clinic that had been a regular target of protests. In July 1994, in *Madsen v. Women's Health Center,* 512 U.S. 753, 114 S. Ct. 2516, 129 L. Ed. 2d 593, the High Court ruled 6–3 to let stand the 36-foot exclusion zone for the Melbourne, Florida, abortion clinic. However, the Court did strike down other provisions of the injunction, such as a 300-foot exclusion zone and restrictions on carrying banners and pictures. The ruling was considered a major defeat for the anti-abortion movement. Justice Antonin Scalia wrote a sharp dissent in which he claimed that the Supreme Court's position on abortion had claimed "its latest, greatest and most surprising victim: the First Amendment."

Increased Violence Changes the Debate

Violence has been a part of the heated debate surrounding abortion ever since the 1973 *Roe v. Wade* decision that guaranteed a woman's limited right to an abortion. Bombings, ARSON, and even murder have been committed by anti-abortion activists in the name of their cause. The National Abortion Federation counted more than three thousand violent or threatening incidents against abortion clinics between 1976 and 1994. In the 1990s the extremist wing of the anti-abortion movement turned even more violent, including murder as part of its tactics. Some extremists now view killing health care professionals who perform abortions as justifiable HOMICIDE.

Between March 1993 and the end of 1994, five staff workers at abortion clinics were murdered by anti-abortion zealots. Dr. David Gunn was fatally shot on March 10, 1993, outside an abortion clinic in Pensacola, Florida, by Michael Griffin, who was later sentenced to life in prison. In August 1994 Dr. John Bayard Britton, age 69, who had replaced Gunn as circuit-riding doctor in northern Florida, and his escort, James Barrett, age 74, were shot repeatedly in the face with a shotgun as their car pulled into the parking lot of the Ladies Clinic of Pensacola. Minutes later, police arrested Paul Hill, an anti-abortion extremist. President Bill Clinton called Britton's and Barrett's killings a case of domestic TERRORISM. Hill was executed in September 2003. In December 1994, in perhaps the most gruesome incident of all, John Salvi killed two people and wounded five more when he opened fire in two Boston-area family planning clinics. Salvi was sentenced to life in prison, where he later committed SUICIDE.

The government and abortion rights groups have responded to the increased violence in two ways: reviewing existing laws to find those that can be used to investigate and PROSECUTE violent groups and individuals, and creating new laws that specifically address access to abortion clinics. In 1993 women's rights groups attempted to use an existing civil rights law as precedence in *Bray v. Alexandria Women's Health Clinic*, 506 U.S. 263, 113 S. Ct. 753, 122 L. Ed. 2d 34 (1993). They were not successful. The Supreme Court ruled that a nineteenth-century federal civil rights law (42 U.S.C.A. § 1985[3]) aimed at protecting African Americans from the KU KLUX KLAN could not be used to prevent anti-abortion protesters from blockading abortion clinics. Originally enacted as part of the KU KLUX KLAN ACT of 1871, the law was specifically aimed at addressing mob violence and VIGILANTISM against African Americans.

In 1989 a lower-court ruling found that Operation Rescue had violated trespassing and public NUISANCE laws and had conspired to violate the right to interstate travel of women seeking abortions at clinics. The court banned Operation Rescue from trespassing on or obstructing access to abortion clinics (*NOW v.*

Operation Rescue, 726 F. Supp. 1483 [E.D. Va. 1989]). This decision was reversed by the Supreme Court in *Bray,* in a 6–3 ruling, when it held that women did not qualify as a class protected from DISCRIMINATION by the provisions of the Ku Klux Klan Act.

After *Bray,* congressional supporters of abortion rights, Representative Charles E. Schumer (D-N.Y.) and Senator EDWARD M. KENNEDY (D-Mass.), introduced the Freedom of Access to Clinic Entrances Act (FACE), which gives federal courts the authority to issue restraining orders against protesters blockading abortion clinics (18 U.S.C.A. § 248). Signed into law by President Clinton on May 26, 1994, the law allows for federal criminal prosecution of anyone who, "by force or threat of force or by physical obstruction, intentionally injures, intimidates, or interferes … with any person … obtaining or providing reproductive health services." The law also makes it a federal crime to intentionally damage or destroy the property of any reproductive health facility, and it permits persons harmed by those engaging in prohibited conduct to bring private suits against the wrongdoers. The penalties for violation of the act include IMPRISONMENT for up to one year and a fine of $10,000 for a first offense; for each subsequent offense, penalties can be up to three years' imprisonment and $25,000. FACE is patterned after existing civil rights laws, including 18 U.S.C.A. § 245(b), which prohibits force or threat of force to willfully injure, intimidate, or interfere with any person who is VOTING, engaging in activities related to voting, or enjoying the benefits of federal programs. Nevertheless, FACE is not identical to previous federal civil rights laws, particularly where it prohibits acts of physical obstruction.

FACE ignited immediate challenges by anti-abortion groups who claimed that it abridged their FIRST AMENDMENT right to FREEDOM OF SPEECH. Courts were unwilling to invalidate the law on this ground, reasoning that the law prohibits only conduct—as in "force," "threat of force," and "physical obstruction"—rather than speech (see *Council for Life Coalition v. Reno,* 856 F. Supp. 1422, No. 94-0843-1EG[CM], 1994 WL 363132 [S.D. Cal. 1994]).

Since the Freedom of Access to Clinic Entrances Act was passed, the Supreme Court has reviewed several laws restricting protests at clinics, with the goal of balancing the

THREE SIDES TO THE ABORTION DEBATE

To what extent does a woman have a right to obtain an abortion? And to what extent does a person have a right to PROTEST the practice of abortion? These two fundamental questions and two conflicting rights emerged in the decades following the U.S. Supreme Court's controversial decision in the 1973 case *ROE V. WADE* (410 U.S. 113, 93 S. Ct. 705, 35 L. Ed. 2d 147). With time, the conflict between those who differed on the answers to these questions, and the interpretation of these rights, became more intense and at times even violent. The question of access to abortion clinic property—whether to obtain clinic services or to protest them—became a pressing issue.

Three major points of view dominate the abortion debate: the pro-choice, or abortion rights, view; the moderate pro-life, or moderate anti-abortion, view; and the extremist (or militant) pro-life, or anti-abortion, view.

The pro-choice, or abortion rights, side of the debate is made up of a number of women's rights, family planning, and medical organizations, and other groups of concerned citizens and professionals. The groups include the NATIONAL ORGANIZATION FOR WOMEN (NOW), the Planned Parenthood Federation of America, the National Abortion Federation, and the National Abortion and Reproductive Rights Action League (NARAL). Many religious organizations have also taken positions that endorse the right of women to seek abortions in specific situations. Most of these pro-choice groups argue that a woman's decision to carry a pregnancy to term is a private choice that should not be interfered with by the state. They also maintain that abortion, although not a preferred family planning method, has always been used by women to gain control over their pregnancies. According to this view, women must have safe and legal access to abortion; without this access, women are likely to seek unsafe, illegal abortions that may result in their injury or death. Pro-choice advocates also maintain that giving women control over their reproductive functions—what they call their reproductive rights—is a fundamental requirement for achieving equality between men and women in U.S. society. Norma McCorvey, who sought anonymity as Jane Roe in *Roe* and who in 1995 switched sides on the abortion issue, spoke for the pro-choice position in a 1989 speech before a women's rally:

> Prior to *Roe v. Wade*, approximately one million women had illegal abortions each year. Approximately 5,000 of these women were killed. Another 100,000 were hospitalized from botched abortions.
>
> Obviously, abortion will continue whether it is legal or not. My concern is for the safety of millions of women should our freedom of choice be taken away from us. I want it clearly understood that I do not promote abortion. I promote personal choice.
>
> If we return to the antique methods of dealing with unwanted pregnancies that existed before *Roe v. Wade*, the women's movement will be taking an enormous step backward. We are on the verge of having our reproductive freedom taken away from us if we do not take a stand and let our voices be heard NOW.

Pro-choice groups remain committed to the CONSTITUTIONAL right to PRIVACY defined in *Roe*. They view anti-abortion demonstrations that prevent women from obtaining abortions as interfering with that right to privacy.

The pro-choice group also has a range of viewpoints within it. Whereas all persons who describe themselves as pro-choice support a general right to abortion, some oppose some kinds of abortions, such as late-term abortions.

The moderate pro-life movement consists of many different organizations, including the NATIONAL RIGHT TO LIFE COMMITTEE, HUMAN RIGHTS Review, and Feminists for Life of America. Although its members are extremely diverse, most come from religious groups such as the Catholic Church and evangelical

interests of protecting women seeking abortions with the freedom of speech interests of abortion clinic protesters. The Court has used an "intermediate scrutiny" standard to make its determinations. This standard analyzes the constitutionality of any regulation that infringes on speech to see whether it serves a legitimate STATE INTEREST, whether it is narrowly tailored to serve that interest, and whether alternative paths exist for protesters to communicate their message.

For example, in *Schenck v. Pro-Choice Network*, 519 U.S. 357, 117 S. Ct. 855 (1997), by an 8–1 vote, the Court invalidated a New York state court injunction that created a 15-foot "floating" buffer zone around any person or vehicle seeking access to or leaving an abortion clinic. The court majority held that

Protestant denominations. Generally, these groups believe that the fetus is a person with rights equal to those of other people, and some of these identify the unborn person as existing from the moment of conception or in the embryonic stage. Many are willing to allow abortion in certain cases, usually when pregnancy threatens the health of the mother or has resulted from RAPE or INCEST. Moderates in their manner of supporting changes in abortion laws and regulations differ from militants. Moderates emphasize using existing legal channels to bring about change.

Militant pro-life groups share many of the views of moderate groups, but they favor an activist use of CIVIL DISOBEDIENCE to prevent abortion procedures and to save or rescue the lives of the unborn. Randall Terry and Flip Benham, of the most well known anti-abortion group, Operation Rescue, represent the militant views. Terry is Operation Rescue's founder and leading figure; he participated in his first anti-abortion protest in 1984 and has served time in prison because of his demonstrations. As an evangelical Protestant Christian, Terry sees abortion as the work of the devil: "I believe that there is a devil, and here's Satan's agenda. First, he doesn't want anyone having kids. Secondly, if they do conceive, he wants them killed. If they're not killed through abortion, he wants them neglected or abused, physically, emotionally, sexually." Terry opposes abortion in all cases. His group's main tactics, he is quoted as saying, include "rescue missions, boycotts and protests."

A minority of the militant anti-abortion activists sanctions the use of physical force. A small number even regard the killing of abortion providers as

justifiable HOMICIDE. When asked to explain this increasing tendency toward violence, militant pro-life leader Joseph Scheidler, of the Pro-Life Action Network, blamed it on the 1994 Freedom of Access to Clinic Entrances Act (FACE) and buffer zone restrictions that kept protesters from conducting rallies at abortion clinics. Scheidler argued that making it tougher to have peaceful protests gave people a rationale for having violent protests. Benham, of Operation Rescue, condemned the anti-abortion killings. However, after John Salvi murdered two people and wounded others in an abortion clinic shooting in late 1994, Benham commented, "There is little that federal marshals or anyone else can do to halt this MURDER and violence. We will not have peace outside the womb until peace is restored within the womb." Added Terry, "We're involved in a cultural civil war." When Kansas obstetrician George Tiller was killed in May 2009, Terry called the doctor a "mass-murderer" and compared him to a Nazi war criminal. Scheidler and his group won a major victory in 2003 when the U.S. Supreme Court ruled 8–1 that the RICO statute was improperly used against the group and other pro-life activists, in the case brought against them by the National Organization for Women (*Scheidler v. Nat'l Organization for Women, Inc.,* 537 U.S. 393, 123 S. Ct. 1057, 154 L. Ed. 2d 991 [2003]).

It is possible the extremist position may have done more to hurt than to help the anti-abortion cause. The publicized violence of the movement, in combination with the new prosecutorial powers granted in FACE, served to ALIENATE many of the more moderate

individuals in pro-life groups, reducing the membership of those groups to a militant core and making those outside the groups less sympathetic to their cause. However, extremists have contributed to a climate in which access to abortion services has steadily become more difficult. The number of abortion providers declined by 2 percent between 2000 and 2005. By 2008, 87 percent of all U.S. counties lacked an abortion provider.

But as a positive result of the fallout, significant numbers from both sides tried to find common ground and an end to the mutual mistrust and ill will. Aptly calling themselves the Common Ground Network for Life and Choice, the alliance made its largest impact with the political issue of partial-birth abortions, when it began a campaign to ban the procedures. This more subtle collective voice of concerned citizens appeared to represent an important change in the direction of abortion debate. In specific, the committed extremists on both ends were being replaced with a new and more sophisticated national consensus concerning the acceptable limits of abortion rights. The Partial Birth Abortion Ban Act was enacted in 2003 and upheld by the Supreme Court in *Gonzales v. Carhart* (550 U.S. 124, 127 S. Ct. 1610, 167 L. Ed. 2d 480 [2007]).

FURTHER READING

Risen, James, and Judy L. Thomas. 1998. *Wrath of Angels: The American Abortion War.* New York: Basic Books.

CROSS REFERENCES

Civil Rights Acts; Schools and School Districts.

---

the floating buffer zone burdened "more speech than necessary to serve a relevant government interest." However, by a 6–3 vote, the Court upheld a provision creating a 15-foot "fixed" buffer zone outside abortion clinic doorways, driveways, and parking lots.

Three years later, the Court issued a more detailed decision involving restrictions on

abortion protests. In *Hill v. Colorado,* 530 U.S. 703, 120 S. Ct. 2480 (2000), the Court upheld by a 6–3 majority a Colorado statute that made it UNLAWFUL for any person within one hundred feet of the entrance to any abortion clinic (or other health facility) to knowingly approach within eight feet of another person without that person's consent, with the purpose of passing out a leaflet or handbill to, displaying a sign to, engaging in oral PROTEST with, or counseling said individual. The Court reasoned that the states' interest in protecting the health and safety of its citizens justified a special focus on unimpeded access to healthcare facilities and the avoidance of potential trauma to patients that could result from confrontational protests. In addition, the statute did not violate the First Amendment because it protected listeners from unwanted communication, was content-neutral, and served as a valid time, place, and manner restriction.

Abortion rights supporters suffered a more serious setback with the Court's decision in *Scheidler v. NOW & Operation Rescue v. NOW*, 123 S. Ct. 1057 (U.S. 2003). By a vote of 8–1, the Court determined that federal RACKETEERING laws, such as RICO, could not be used as the basis for criminal charges against anti-abortion protestors who demonstrate outside abortion clinics. The Court further found that the federal Hobbs Act was not violated by protestors who had not obtained property, attempted to obtain property, or conspired to obtain property from the abortion clinics. The Hobbs Act, 18 U.S.C.A. § 1951(b)(2), expanded the common-law definition of EXTORTION to include acts by private individuals. For purposes of the Hobbs Act requirement that property must be obtained for extortion to occur, the word *obtain* means to gain possession of. The extortion provision of the Hobbs Act requires not only the deprivation, but also the acquisition, of property. Women seeking access to the abortion clinic had argued that their right to seek medical services from the clinics, the clinic doctors' rights to perform their jobs, and the clinics' rights to conduct their business—constituted "property" for purposes of the Hobbs Act, and those rights had been "extorted" from them by abortion protestors.

The Supreme Court held that by interfering with, disrupting, and in some instances "shutting down" clinics that performed abortions, individual and corporate organizers of anti-abortion protest network did *not* "obtain" or attempt to obtain property from women's rights organization or abortion clinics, and so did not commit "extortion" under the Hobbs Act, as required for organization and clinics to establish RICO predicate offense; whereas organizers may have deprived or sought to deprive organizations and clinics of their alleged PROPERTY RIGHT of exclusive control of their business assets, they did not acquire any such property, nor did they pursue or receive something of value from organizations or clinics that they could exercise, transfer, or sell. The Court also ruled that an injunction obtained against the abortions protesters litigating this case on the basis of RICO was invalid.

The debate and litigation surrounding the issue of anti-abortion protests show little sign of waning, with pro-choice advocates attempting to limit protesters' efforts to demonstrate at abortion clinics, and anti-abortion protest groups challenging the laws regulating their activities, on the grounds that such laws abridge freedom of speech.

New Attempts to Restrict Abortion

Some state lawmakers have not ended their efforts to ban abortions. In 2006 the South Dakota LEGISLATURE approved a bill that would have banned most abortions. Pro-choice activists immediately announced that they would challenge the law, but the issue was eventually resolved by voters in the state. When the statute became subject to the general election in 2006, voters in the state defeated the proposal by a 55 to 45 percent margin.

The Supreme Court continues to be confronted with ongoing efforts to restrict abortion. In *Mazurek v. Armstrong*, 520 U.S. 968, 117 S. Ct. 1865 (1997), the Court upheld Montana's statute requiring that only licensed physicians perform abortions, ruling that physician-only requirements in general are constitutional. In another decision out of Montana, *Lambert v. Wicklund*, 520 U.S. 292, 117 S. Ct. 1169 (1997), the Court upheld a state statute requiring one-parent notification before a minor can have an abortion. The judicial bypass procedure in this case required a minor to show that parental notification was not in her best interest.

Perhaps the biggest controversy to erupt in the late 1990s involved the debate over what is termed *partial-birth* abortion. Anti-abortion activists succeeded in having legislation passed in 29 states that bans physicians from performing what doctors call dilation and extraction. It is used most commonly in the second trimester, between 20 and 24 weeks of pregnancy, when a woman suffers from a life-threatening medical condition or disease. In *Stenberg v. Carhart*, 530 U.S. 914, 120 S. Ct. 2597 (2000), by a 5–4 vote, the Court struck down Nebraska's ban on partial-birth abortion. The Court ruled the statute was invalid because it lacked any exception to protect a woman's health, noting that the state could promote but not endanger a woman's health when it regulates the methods of abortion. It also concluded that terms in the statute were unconstitutionally vague such that it would affect not only partial birth abortion but also other constitutionally protected second-trimester abortion methods.

In early 2003 the U.S. Congress passed the Partial Birth Abortion Ban Act, Pub. L. No. 108-105, 117 Stat. 1201, which contained a ban similar to the Nebraska law. The Congress had passed this law before, only to have Bill Clinton veto it. President GEORGE W. BUSH went on record as saying he would sign the bill if it reached his desk. When he did so, the Supreme Court was called upon to decide whether *Stenberg* applied. In *Gonzales v. Carhart*, 550 U.S. 124, 127 S. Ct. 1610, 167 L. Ed. 2d 480 (2007), the Court upheld the act, ruling that it did impose an undue burden on a woman's right to end a pregnancy. The two newest members of the Court, Chief Justice JOHN ROBERTS and Justice SAMUEL ALITO, voted in the majority, confirming that the recent appointees had solidified the conservative base on the Court. The decision also revealed a new interest in the mother's health and safety.

FURTHER READINGS

Drucker, Dan. 1990. *Abortion Decisions of the Supreme Court, 1973 through 1989: A Comprehensive Review with Historical Commentary.* Jefferson, N.C.: McFarland.

De Rosa, Melissa. 2002. "Partial-Birth Abortion: Crime or Protected Right?" *St. John's Journal of Legal Commentary* 16 (winter).

Edwards, Jaime. 2003. "*McGuire v. Reilly*: The First Amendment and Abortion Clinic Buffer Zones in the Wake of *Hill v. Colorado*." *U.C. Davis Law Review* 6 (February).

Mauro, Tony. 2003. "Weighing the Fate of *Roe v. Wade*: With Increased Fervor after the 30 Years of Legal and Social Turmoil It Spawned, Scholars Kick It, Probe It, Tear It Apart and Try to Rewrite It." *New Jersey Law Journal* 171 (January).

McCorvey, Norma. 1994. *I Am Roe.* New York: Harper-Collins.

Palmer, Louis J. 2009. *Encyclopedia of Abortion in the United States.* 2d ed. Jefferson, N.C.: McFarland.

Perry, Michael J. 2009. *Constitutional Rights, Moral Controversy, and the Supreme Court.* New York: Cambridge University Press.

Reagan, Ronald. 1984. *Abortion and the Conscience of a Nation.* Nashville: Nelson.

Rubin, Eva R. 1987. *Abortion, Politics, and the Courts: Roe v. Wade and Its Aftermath.* New York: Greenwood.

CROSS REFERENCES

Constitutional Amendment; Fetal Rights; Husband and Wife; Parent and Child; Privacy; Reproduction; "Roe v. Wade" (Appendix, Milestone); Wattleton, Alyce Faye; Women's Rights.

ABRAMS V. UNITED STATES

In *Abrams v. United States*, 250 U.S. 616, 40 S.Ct. 17, 63 L.Ed. 1173 (1919), the U.S. Supreme Court applied the CLEAR AND PRESENT DANGER test in upholding the conviction of five anti-war protestors, who had been charged with SEDITION for distributing pamphlets criticizing President WOODROW WILSON during WORLD WAR I. However, the case is remembered more for the lone dissenting opinion written by Justice Oliver Wendell Holmes Jr., architect of the original clear-and-present-danger test just eight months earlier. Holmes's dissent argued that FREEDOM OF SPEECH cases analyzed under the FIRST AMENDMENT to the U.S CONSTITUTION must be subjected to a heightened level of judicial scrutiny before LEGISLATION abridging free expression could be upheld, a level of scrutiny that was eventually adopted by a majority of the Court for the balance of the twentieth century.

The case began on August 23, 1918, when Jacob Abrams, a Russian immigrant and a professed anarchist, was arrested in New York City with four others. Abrams and his comrades admitted to writing, printing, and distributing two sets of leaflets, one in English and one in Yiddish, assailing President Woodrow Wilson as a "coward" and a "hypocrite" for sending troops to fight the Soviet Union during World War I. The Yiddish leaflet called for a general strike among all workers to protest against Wilson's policy.

Abrams and the other defendants were charged with violating the Sedition Act. This act made it a crime to "willfully utter, print, write, or publish any disloyal, profane, scurrilous, or abusive" language about the form of government in the United States or language that was intended to bring that form of government "into contempt, scorn, contumely, and disrepute," or language that was "intended to incite, provoke, and encourage resistance to the" U.S. war effort. The act also made it illegal to "willfully urge, incite, or ADVOCATE [the] curtailment" of manufacturing and production

Defendants in Abrams v. United States prior to their 1921 deportation to Russia. Clockwise from center, Molly Steimer, Samuel Lipman, Hyman Lachowsky, and Jacob Abrams.

efforts "necessary and essential to the prosecution of the war."

Whereas the five defendants in *Abrams* were released on BAIL during March 1919, the Supreme Court issued two decisions upholding the convictions of several other antiwar protestors. In the first case, the Court affirmed the convictions under the 1917 ESPIONAGE Act. SCHENCK V. UNITED STATES, 249 U.S. 47, 39 S. Ct. 247, 63 L.Ed. 470 (1919). In the other case, the Court affirmed the convictions under the 1918 Sedition Act. *Debs v. United States,* 249 U.S. 211, 39 S. Ct. 252, 63 L.Ed. 566 (1919) Both decisions were unanimous, and both decisions were written by Justice Holmes.

In *Schenck,* Holmes articulated what has become known as the "clear-and-present danger" doctrine, a doctrine by which the constitutionality of laws regulating subversive expression are evaluated in light of the First Amendment's guarantee of free speech. "The question in every case," Holmes wrote in *Schenck,* "is whether the words used are used in such circumstances and are of such a nature as to create a clear and present danger that they will bring about the substantive evils that

Congress has a right to prevent. It is a question of proximity and degree."

In *Schenck* Holmes concluded that the government did not run afoul of the Free Speech Clause in suppressing the protestors' antiwar expression, because Holmes said that when "a nation is at war many things that might be said in time of peace are such a hindrance to its effort that their utterance will not be endured so long as men fight and that no court could regard them as protected by any CONSTITUTIONAL right." Nor was Holmes's opinion in *Schenck* influenced by the possibility that the antiwar protests had no practical effect in changing the minds of passersby. "If the act (speaking, or circulating a paper,), its tendency and the intent with which it is done are the same," Holmes reasoned in *Schenck,* "we perceive no ground for saying that success alone warrants making the act a crime."

Writing for the majority in *Abrams,* Justice JOHN H. CLARKE echoed Holmes's reasoning from *Schenck.* The purpose of the pamphlets written by Abrams and his comrades was to "excite" riots, sedition, and disaffection with the war, Clarke wrote. Distributed at a time when World War I was at a "supreme crisis," Clarke continued, the pamphlets' call for a general strike among munitions workers would necessarily have hindered the U.S. war effort. As a result, Clarke concluded that Abrams's pamphlets created a clear and present danger of "defeating the military plans of the government in Europe."

Holmes dissented from the *Abrams's* majority's application of the same clear and present danger test Holmes himself had formulated just eight months earlier. Holmes still agreed that the government's power to SUPPRESS speech is greater in times of war than in times of peace, "because war opens dangers that do not exist at other times." But "nobody can suppose that the surreptitious publishing of a silly leaflet by an unknown man, without more, would present any immediate danger that its opinions would hinder the success of the government arms or have any appreciable tendency to do so," Holmes cautioned.

"To allow opposition by speech," Holmes now thought, "seems to indicate that you think the speech impotent, as when a man says that he has squared the circle." A CIVIL WAR veteran who had joined the Union Army in large part due to his support for the ABOLITION movement, Holmes reminded readers that "time has upset many fighting faiths," and, accordingly, "the ultimate good desired is better reached by free trade in ideas—that the best test of truth is the power of the thought to get itself accepted in the competition of the market, and that truth is the only ground upon which their wishes safely can be carried out. That at any RATE is the theory of our Constitution."

Holmes then moved to his application of the clear-and-present-danger test. In CIVIL LAW, Holmes observed that defendants may be held liable for all the foreseeable consequences of their negligent behavior. Not so in the CRIMINAL LAW, Holmes said, where a crime is not normally committed unless done "with intent to produce a consequence [and] that consequence is the aim of the deed." But intent alone is not the only factor critical to a court's First Amendment analysis, Holmes observed. Instead, a court must also evaluate the "success" of the speech "upon others." Unless the speech creates a "present danger of immediate evil," Holmes argued that Congress cannot punish the speaker without violating the federal constitution. In concluding that the "silly" leaflets distributed by Abrams and his co-defendants created no clear and present danger, Holmes said that "we should be eternally vigilant against attempts to check the expression of opinions that we loathe and believe to be fraught with death, unless they so imminently threaten immediate interference with the lawful and pressing purposes of the law that an immediate check is required to save the country."

Holmes's opinion in *Abrams* cemented his reputation for being one of the Supreme Court's exceptional writers of persuasive dissenting opinions. It also laid the building blocks for his reputation as a great defender of civil liberties. But most importantly, Holmes's dissenting opinion in *Abrams* changed the course of First Amendment law for the remainder of the twentieth century. In *Schenck* the clear-and-present-danger test had been applied with minimal scrutiny as to whether the antiwar pamphlets in question were likely to have any practical impact on those who might read them. Holmes's opinion in *Schenck* focused almost entirely on the gravity of the dangers created by the pamphlets, without paying much attention to whether those dangers were likely to result.

By contrast, Holmes's dissenting opinion in *Abrams* more carefully scrutinized the competing factors at work in evaluating whether the subversive speech sought to be punished does in fact create a clear and present danger of harm that Congress may prohibit. Holmes contended that the *Abrams*'s majority opinion should have more closely examined the intent of the pamphleteers. Additionally, Holmes believed that the majority opinion should not only have attempted to determine whether the pamphlets would have any effect on readers, but also urged the majority to allow the defendants to go unpunished unless by distributing the pamphlets the defendants had created a danger that was both clear and immediate.

Supreme Court scholars have spent much time trying to explain why Holmes modified his view of the Free Speech Clause in the eight months that separated his majority opinion in *Schenck* and his dissenting opinion in *Abrams*. There is evidence to suggest that Holmes was influenced by the anti-Communist and anti-radical hysteria that was sweeping much of the nation during those months, and the government–instituted repression of radicals that resulted. There is also evidence indicating that Holmes was influenced by correspondence he received from various acquaintances, including Harvard Law School professor ZECHARIAH CHAFEE, federal district judge Learned Hand, and political theorist Harold J. Laski, all of whom praised Holmes for articulating the clear-and-present-danger test but also encouraged the ASSOCIATE JUSTICE to apply it with more exacting scrutiny.

Some 50 years after Holmes first enunciated the clear-and-present-danger test in *Schenck,* the majority of the Supreme Court reformulated the doctrine in *Brandenburg v. Ohio,* 395 U.S. 444, 89 S. Ct. 1827, 23 L. Ed. 2d 430 (1969). In *Brandenburg,* the Court reversed the conviction of a KU KLUX KLAN leader under a state statute, Ohio Rev. Code Ann. § 2923.13, prohibiting ADVOCACY of crime and violence as a necessary means to accomplish political reform. The Court held that a state could not forbid or proscribe advocacy of the use of force, except where such advocacy is directed toward producing imminent lawless action and is likely to incite or produce such action. Though the Court's opinion fails to use the phrase "clear and present danger," many CONSTITUTIONAL LAW scholars have seen *Brandenburg* as a return to the Holmes immediacy test first set forth in *Abrams*.

FURTHER READINGS

Blasi, Vincent. 1997. "Reading Holmes through the Lens of Schauer: The Abrams Dissent." *Notre Dame Law Review* 72 (July).

Fagan, James F., Jr. 1991. "Abrams v. United States: Remembering the Authors of Both Opinions." *Touro Law Review* 8 (winter).

Polenberg, Richard. 1999. *Fighting Faiths: The Abrams Case, the Supreme Court, and Free Speech.* Ithaca, NY: Cornell Univ. Press.

CROSS REFERENCES

American Civil Liberties Union; Constitutional Amendment; Debs, Eugene Victor; Due Process of Law; Fourteenth Amendment; Privacy.

ABROGATION

The destruction or annulling of a former law by an act of the legislative power, by constitutional authority, or by usage. It stands opposed to rogation; *and is distinguished from derogation, which implies the taking away of only some part of a law; from subrogation, which denotes the substitution of a clause; from* dispensation, *which only sets it aside in a particular instance; and from* antiquation, *which is the refusing to pass a law.*

For example, the abrogation of the EIGHTEENTH AMENDMENT to the CONSTITUTION, which prohibited the manufacture or sale of intoxicating liquors, was accomplished by the enactment of the TWENTY-FIRST AMENDMENT. Implied abrogation takes place when a new law contains provisions that are positively contrary to a former law, without expressly abrogating such laws, or when the order of things for which the law has been made no longer exists.

ABSCOND

To go in a clandestine manner out of the jurisdiction of the courts, or to lie concealed, in order to avoid their process. To hide, conceal, or absent oneself clandestinely, with the intent to avoid legal process. To postpone limitations. To flee from arresting or prosecuting officers of the state.

ABSCONDING DEBTOR

One who absconds from creditors to avoid payment of debts. A debtor who has intentionally concealed himself or herself from creditors, or withdrawn from the reach of their suits, with intent to frustrate their just demands. Such act was formerly an act of bankruptcy.

A person who moves out of the state may be an absconding debtor if it is that person's intention to avoid paying money that he or she owes.

It is difficult or impossible for a creditor to serve an absconding debtor with a SUMMONS in order to start a lawsuit and collect his or her money. Where a court is convinced that a debtor has absconded, it may permit the creditor to begin the lawsuit in some way other than PERSONAL SERVICE of a summons.

For example, a franchisee bought a doughnut franchise and opened up a small shop. He also bought a house for his family. Unfortunately, the business failed after a year, and he turned all of the equipment and materials back to the franchisor. The franchisor claimed that additional money was owed to him and decided to SUE the former franchisee. A PROCESS SERVER was sent to take a summons to the apartment that was listed as the address in the original application for the franchise. The LANDLORD there told the process server that the former franchisee had moved and left no forwarding address. The franchisor applied to the court for permission to serve him as an absconding debtor. The court allowed the franchisor to publish notice of the lawsuit on three occasions in the legal section of the local newspaper. The franchisee did not see the notice and did not appear in court. The court entered a DEFAULT JUDGMENT against him without hearing his side of the story. After that, the franchisor began searching public records to see if the franchisee owned any property that could be seized to pay off the amount of the judgment. He discovered the recorded deed for the house and went back to court, seeking an order to have the house sold. This time the franchisee, who was served personally with the court papers, appeared with his ATTORNEY. He explained at the hearing that he had never intended to conceal himself or to avoid paying the money he owed. The court found that he had never been an absconding debtor who could be served merely by publication. The default judgment, therefore, could not be enforced, and the franchisor could not have the house seized and sold.

ABSENTEE

One who has left, either temporarily or permanently, his or her domicile or usual place of residence or business. A person beyond the geographical borders of a state who has not authorized an agent to represent him or her in legal proceedings that may be commenced against him or her within the state.

An absentee LANDLORD is an individual who leases REAL ESTATE to another but who does not reside in the leased premises.

An absentee corporation is one that conducts business within a state other than the place of its incorporation but has not designated an agent for purposes of SERVICE OF PROCESS, which might ensue from disputes involving its business transactions there.

ABSENTEE VOTING

Participation in an election by qualified voters who are permitted to mail in their ballots.

The Uniformed and Overseas Citizens Absentee Voting Act (42 U.S.C.A. § 1973ff et seq.) covers absentee VOTING in presidential ELECTIONS, but the states regulate absentee voting in all other elections. According to Article I, Section 4, of the U.S. CONSTITUTION, "The Times, Places and Manner of holding Elections for Senators and Representatives, shall be prescribed in each state by the LEGISLATURE thereof; but the Congress may . . . make or alter such Regulations, except as to the Places of ch[oo]sing Senators."

Originally created to accommodate overseas military service personnel in WORLD WAR I, absentee voting has since expanded to include all voters expecting to be absent from their precincts on election day. The right to vote, even by absentee ballot, is no trifling concern. A state may restrict it only to the extent that doing so serves a compelling STATE INTEREST such as preventing FRAUD.

State laws governing absentee voting are based on statutes. federal courts that have reviewed absentee ballot laws have established general principles regarding these laws. For instance, the Fifth Circuit determined that because Mississippi's absentee voting law was designed to protect the integrity of the absentee ballot, voters had to comply with the law strictly (*United States v. Brown*, 561 F.3d 420 [5th Cir. 2009]). In another example, the Ninth Circuit ruled that a state law that establishes different requirements for in-person voters than requirements applied to absentee voters did not violate the EQUAL PROTECTION rights of the in-person voters (*ACLU of N.M. v. Santillanes*, 546 F.3d 1313 [10th Cir. 2008]).

Although all states allow absentee voting, the procedures and qualifications vary from state to state. According to statistics as of 2008, compiled by the Early Voting Information Center at Reed College in Oregon, 32 states allow individuals to vote without having to provide an excuse. Under these state laws, individuals may vote early on a voting machine or submit absentee ballots in person. Conversely, 14 states require an excuse for in-person absentee voting. The majority of states allow voters to submit ballots by mail without excuse, whereas 22 states require an excuse. Oregon is the only state that requires all early voting to take place via mail.

The amount of time that an application for an absentee ballot must precede the election can vary. In Minnesota, it is one day (M.S.A. § 203B.04[1]). In Louisiana, it depends on the voter. For example, a voter who goes in person to apply for an absentee ballot must do so between 12 and 6 days before the election (LSA-R.S. 18:1309[a][1]); a voter who registers for an absentee ballot by mail must get the registration form to the registrar not more than 60 days and not less than 96 hours before the election (LSA-R.S. 18:1307[b]); military personnel must return the application not more than 12 months and not less than 7 days before election day (LSA-R.S. 18:1307[c]).

Many states allow absentee voters to vote again on election day if they are present in the state. If voters so choose, they may change their votes. Officials in states that allow this practice count the absentee ballots after the poll ballots have been counted, and any duplicate absentee ballots are simply disregarded. This is the case in Minnesota (M.S.A. § 203B.13[3a]). In Louisiana, however, a person who has voted by absentee ballot may not vote again on election day (LSA-R.S. 18:1305). In 1977 Louisiana amended its law to allow absentee voters to change their votes on election day, but in 1980 it changed the law again to prohibit the practice.

In any state, to cast an absentee ballot, citizens must be eligible voters and have a reason for being unable to vote at the polls. Between August 1, 1991, and November 30, 1992, Minnesota experimented with allowing

A sample absentee voting ballot application

ILLUSTRATION BY GGS CREATIVE RESOURCES. REPRODUCED BY PERMISSION OF GALE, A PART OF CENGAGE LEARNING.

Absentee Voting Ballot Application

Absentee Ballot Application Instructions

If you would like to have an absentee ballot mailed to you, PRINT legibly on the application below and sign where it says "Signature of Voter." All applications for an absentee ballot submitted by mail (or by a relative or guardian in person at the Election Board office) must be in the office of the Jackson County Board of Election Commissioners by 5:00 P.M. on the Wednesday prior to the election. Pursuant to Missouri law, (115.279) absentee ballots cannot be mailed if the application is received after this deadline.

For your application to be complete, you must have the following:

- The date of the election
- The date of the application
- If it is a primary election you must state which political party ballot you would like
- The applicant's daytime phone number
- The name of the applicant as registered
- The address at which the applicant is registered
- The reason for which an absentee ballot is needed
- The signature of the applicant

If you are going to be away from home and need a ballot mailed to a location other than your home address, fill out the section labeled "Mailing Address if different than Home Address."

Note: An Absentee Ballot Application may be forwarded to us by facsimile but must be followed by a hard copy with an original signature. If the original application is not in our office by 7:00 P.M. CST on the day of the election, the absentee ballot will NOT be counted. This application is good for the Jackson County Board of Election Commissioners only.

ABSENTEE BALLOT APPLICATION
(FOR REGISTERED VOTERS)

Election Date _____ Date of Application _____

Party Primary Election,
Indicate Party _____ Phone Number _____

Print Name _____
           FIRST   MIDDLE NAME / INITIAL   LAST

Registered
Address _____
     NUMBER   DIRECTION   STREET   APT   CITY   ZIP

OFFICE USE ONLY

Cert. # _____

OFFICE   Township
☐   Precinct _____

Style _____

MAILOUT Color _____
☐
Ballot # _____

I expect to be prevented from going to the poll on election day due to the following checked reason:

____ Absence on election day from the jurisdiction of the election authority in which I am registered;

____ Incapacity or confinement due to illness or physical disability, including caring for a person who is incapacitated or confined due to illness or disability;

____ Religious belief or practice;

____ Employment as an election authority or by an election authority at a location other than my polling place;

____ Incarceration, although I have retained all the necessary qualifications for voting.

MAILING ADDRESS IF DIFFERENT THAN HOME ADDRESS:

_____

_____

City   State   Zip

_____

Signature of Voter

Signature of Guardian or relative;   Relationship
or Witness, If signed with an "X" _____ to applicant _____

Mail This Application To:
JACKSON COUNTY ELECTION BOARD
POST OFFICE BOX 296
INDEPENDENCE, MISSOURI 64051

MISSOURI ELECTION LAW 115.279

No application for an absentee ballot submitted by mail or by a guardian or relative after 5:00 p.m. on the Wednesday immediately prior to the election shall be accepted by any election authority. No application for an absentee ballot submitted by the applicant in person after 5:00 p.m. on the day before the election shall be accepted by any election authority.

voters to cast absentee ballots without explanation, but this practice was discontinued on January 1, 1994. All states allow persons with permanent disabilities and military personnel to cast votes by absentee ballot. Other valid reasons for voting in absentia include illness, temporary DISABILITY, and religious observances or practices. In Louisiana, any person age 65 or older may vote by absentee ballot.

All states require that the application for an absentee ballot be requested before election day, but this rule has some exceptions. In Minnesota, for example, a health care patient who becomes a resident or patient in a health care facility on the day before the election may vote by absentee ballot on election day if she or he telephones the municipal clerk by 5:00 P.M. the day before the election (M.S.A. § 203B.04[2]). Each county enlists election judges to deliver absentee ballots to hospitalized voters (M.S.A. § 203B.11[3]).

Some people have had to fight for the right to vote by absentee ballot. In *Cepulonis v. Secretary of the Commonwealth*, 452 N.E.2d 1137, 389 Mass. 930 (Mass. 1983), Richard Cepulonis and Kevin Murphy, two Massachusetts residents and long-term prisoners in the Walpole Massachusetts Correctional Institution, asserted their right to vote by absentee ballot. Cepulonis, eligible for PAROLE in 1997, and Murphy, eligible for parole in 1985, attempted to vote from prison in 1982. City officials in Worcester told Cepulonis that he could not vote by absentee ballot without registering in person; officials in Boston told Murphy the same.

Cepulonis and Murphy filed suit together in superior court, asking for a CLASS ACTION on behalf of Massachusetts prisoners and a judicial declaration that the class of prisoners be declared eligible to vote by absentee ballot. The judge denied the requests, holding specifically that prisoners who did not register to vote prior to their IMPRISONMENT, and prisoners who are not imprisoned in the city of their domicile, may not register to vote by absentee ballot because they must register to vote in person. The absentee voting statutes of Massachusetts contained no provision for voter registration of Massachusetts prisoners through the postal service.

Cepulonis and Murphy asked the Massachusetts Supreme Judicial Court to review the case; on August 15, 1982, the court denied the request. On October 21, Cepulonis and Murphy moved for a court order allowing prisoners to vote in the November 2 elections; the Massachusetts high court denied this request as well. Cepulonis and Murphy then filed a MOTION for *injunctive relief*—a court order—with the U.S. Supreme Court. Justice William J. Brennan Jr. denied the motion WITHOUT PREJUDICE, which meant that Cepulonis and Murphy were free to bring the matter before the Court in the future. Justice JOHN PAUL STEVENS referred the case to the full bench of the Supreme Court, which, after consideration, refused to command Massachusetts to institute procedures enabling incarcerated residents to vote by absentee ballot.

Undaunted, Cepulonis and Murphy applied directly to the Massachusetts Supreme Judicial Court for review of the case; the court granted the application. On April 4, 1983, Cepulonis and Murphy argued that Massachusetts's failure to install an absentee registration procedure for incarcerated residents deprived those residents of their state the CONSTITUTIONAL right to vote in state elections. Although some states had chosen to prohibit convicted criminals from voting in elections, Massachusetts had not.

The court began the analysis in its opinion by discussing the CASE LAW of Massachusetts on the subject of voting. Without exception, the precedents held that voting laws should be interpreted to facilitate voting, and not to impair or defeat the right to vote. In light of this principle, the court announced that it agreed with Cepulonis and Murphy; the Massachusetts statutory scheme was denying deserving citizens a state constitutional right.

The court then examined the Massachusetts statutory scheme and observed that some eligible prisoners could vote, whereas others could not. The absentee voting laws of Massachusetts provided that prisoners incarcerated in the municipality of their domicile, if already registered, could vote by absentee ballot. However, registered voters incarcerated in a municipality other than their own could not register for absentee ballots. Furthermore, prisoners who were adult registered voters before they were incarcerated could vote, but prisoners reaching the AGE OF MAJORITY while incarcerated could not vote. These distinctions were arbitrary and, according to the court, unconstitutional.

The court then cited relevant case law that held that Massachusetts must prove the existence of a compelling state interest when it denies a FUNDAMENTAL RIGHT such as voting. The state argued that the registration laws existed in their present form to prevent voter fraud. The court countered by pointing out that Maine, New York, Vermont, Georgia, and Pennsylvania had all seen fit to permit prisoners domiciled in their states to register as absentee voters. This showed that it was possible to create a system allowing eligible prisoners to vote by absentee ballot.

The state also argued that prisoners not registered to vote had had the opportunity to register before INCARCERATION. Requiring the state to supply special absentee voting procedures to disinterested citizens seemed unnecessary. However, failure to register to vote before incarceration did not mean that prisoners who were otherwise eligible should be denied the right to vote, and, according to the court, no case law supported such a denial.

Ultimately, the court held that Massachusetts prisoners must be given the means to vote in state elections. The Massachusetts absentee voting statutes were unconstitutional to the extent that they prevented incarcerated, eligible Massachusetts voters from registering to vote. The court refrained from giving the vote to Cepulonis and Murphy, and instead left the job of revising the Massachusetts absentee voting laws to the legislature.

The issue of absentee voting became a particularly contested topic during the 2000 presidential election, when every vote was needed to determine the ultimate outcome. The seat of controversy was Florida, where a recount became necessary in several counties because the vote was so close. Between November and December, Democrat AL GORE and Republican GEORGE W. BUSH appealed to the state Supreme Court and even the U.S. Supreme Court (BUSH V. GORE, 531 U.S. 98 [2000]) over whether or not ballots should be recounted. For example, lawsuits filed by Florida's DEMOCRATIC PARTY involved the counting of absentee ballots in Seminole and Martin Counties (*Taylor v. Martin County Canvassing Board*, 773 So.2d 517 [2000]; *Jacobs v. Seminole County Canvassing Board*, 773 So.2d 519 [2000]). The party alleged that Republicans were allowed to correct mistakes in some voter absentee ballots, while Democrats were not given the same chance. In Seminole County, Republican officials added

missing voter identification numbers at the county election office, whereas in Martin County an election supervisor let Republican workers take home application forms and add missing voter identification numbers. The stakes were high because the 15,000 absentee votes in Seminole County and the 10,000 in Martin County contributed to Bush's razor thin majority over Gore.

The two state circuit judges who reviewed the issues decided that, despite irregularities, the ballots should be counted. On APPEAL, the Florida Supreme Court upheld these rulings. The court, although acknowledging that there were irregularities in the process, concluded that there was no evidence of fraud, GROSS NEGLIGENCE, or intentional wrongdoing.

The use of absentee ballots can complicate elections when a candidate resigns or dies during the last days of a campaign. The 2002 U.S. Senate elections in New Jersey and Minnesota illustrated these complications and led to LITIGATION over whether new absentee ballots could be issued to include a substitute candidate.

The New Jersey Republican candidate for the Senate asked the U.S. Supreme Court to overturn a state supreme court RULING that Democrat Frank Lautenberg's name could replace Senator Robert Torricelli on the November ballot. Torricelli, who had admitted to ethical violations and been censured by the Senate, dropped his reelection bid after public opinion polls indicated that he would lose decisively. New Jersey Republicans asked the Supreme Court to keep Torricelli's name on the ballot, arguing that there would be delays in delivering military ballots, which would violate the 1973 Uniformed and Overseas Citizens Absentee Voting Act. In addition, they contended that the state supreme court order violated the due process rights of military personnel and citizens who had already received ballots and voted. Unlike the 2000 presidential election controversy, the Supreme Court refused to intervene. Lautenberg went on to win the election.

The Minnesota elections in 2002 were thrown into turmoil when Democratic Senator Paul Wellstone was killed in a plane crash just 10 days before the election. An estimated 104,000 absentee ballots had been distributed and many had already been returned to county election officials before Wellstone's death. In reviewing the state's election laws, the SECRETARY

OF STATE concluded that county elections could not mail out new absentee ballots. This meant that thousands of absentee ballots that contained votes for Wellstone would not count for the substitute candidate, former VICE PRESIDENT Walter Mondale.

The state Democratic Party filed an emergency election appeal with the state supreme court, arguing that new ballots should be issued immediately and that Minnesota voters should be able to vote absentee using modern means such as fax and E-MAIL. The court held oral ARGUMENT on the Thursday before the election and issued an order later that day, ruling that voters could request new absentee ballots be mailed to them but they had to be returned to county voting officials by the following Tuesday. The court did not authorize any electronic means as suggested by the Democrats. County officials began to print ballots but the tight deadline made it certain that many voters, such as college students living far away, did not have time to request, receive, and return their ballots. In the end, Republican candidate Norm Coleman beat Mondale by a close but comfortable margin. The Minnesota absentee ballot case illustrates how absentee voters may risk having their vote not count if an unusual chain of events unfolds before an election.

Although commentators have expected development in the use of the INTERNET for absentee voting, the states as of 2009 have not moved to adopt this method. During the 2008 presidential election, the State of Florida experimented with Internet voting for about 700 U.S. soldiers stationed overseas. These soldiers voted at special kiosks set up in Germany, Japan, and the United Kingdom. Officials took a number of security precautions, such as removing the hard drives from the computers used for the voting, but commentators still expressed concerns about the integrity of this method of absentee voting.

FURTHER READINGS

Booth, Michael. 2002. "Republicans Sue in N.J. Federal Court to Block Senate Ballot Substitution." *New Jersey Law Journal* (October 7).

The Early Voting Information Center. Available online at http://earlyvoting.net (accessed May 21, 2009).

Federal Voting Assistance Program. Available online at http://www.fvap.gov (accessed May 21, 2009).

McCauley, William T. 2000. "Florida Absentee Voter Fraud: Fashioning an Appropriate Judicial Remedy." *Univ. of Miami Law Review* 54 (April).

"Supreme Court Asked to Block Lautenberg: N.J. Republican Candidate Files Appeal." 2002. *Washington Post* (October 5).

CROSS REFERENCES

Elections; Prisoners' Rights; Voting.

ABSOLUTE

Complete; perfect; final; without any condition or incumbrance; as an absolute bond in distinction from a conditional bond. Unconditional; complete and perfect in itself; without relation to or dependence on other things or persons.

Free from conditions, limitations or qualifications, not dependent, or modified or affected by circumstances; that is, without any condition or restrictive provisions.

Absolute can be used to describe DIVORCE, estates, obligation, and title.

ABSOLUTE DEED

A document used to transfer unrestricted title to property.

An absolute deed is different from a MORTGAGE deed, which transfers ownership back to the mortgagee when the terms of the mortgage have been fulfilled.

ABSTENTION DOCTRINE

The concept under which a federal court exercises its discretion and equitable powers and declines to decide a legal action over which it has jurisdiction pursuant to the Constitution and statutes where the state judiciary is capable of rendering a definitive ruling in the matter.

The abstention doctrine was adopted by the Supreme Court to allow the federal JUDICIARY to refrain from RULING on CONSTITUTIONAL questions. Because it has no explicit source in federal or state laws, it is the exception to the general rule that a litigant may SUE or be sued in federal court if the federal court has *jurisdiction,* or power to hear the case. A federal court has jurisdiction over several species of cases and controversies, such as those involving a federal constitutional question, a federal statute, or litigants of different states in a dispute totaling over $50,000 (in which case, the court's power to hear is called diversity jurisdiction). Federal courts have an obligation to hear the cases properly brought before them, so abstention is an extraordinary judicial maneuver.

Also known as the Pullman doctrine, the abstention doctrine was first fashioned by the Court in *Railroad Commission of Texas v. Pullman Co.*, 312 U.S. 496 61 S. Ct. 643, 85 L. Ed. 971 (1941). At issue in *Pullman* was a Texas Railroad Commission regulation that prevented the operation of sleeping cars on trains without a Pullman conductor. Before the regulation, Texas trains used only one sleeping car in areas of light passenger traffic. When only one sleeping car was used, the trains had only Pullman porters to watch over the sleepers. When more sleeping cars were used, the trains employed Pullman conductors, who supervised the porters. The regulation eliminated a practice that deprived conductors of wages, but it also effectively decreased the earnings and eliminated the autonomy of porters. This result introduced the issue of DISCRIMINATION, since, at the time, Pullman conductors were white and porters were black.

The Pullman Company and Texas railroads objected to the regulation, and together they brought suit in federal district court to keep the commission from enforcing the order. Pullman porters joined the Pullman Company and the railroads as complainants, and Pullman conductors joined the commission as defendants. The federal district court granted the request of the complainants, ruling that the commission did not have the authority to make such an order. The defendants appealed directly to the U.S. Supreme Court.

The complainants argued that the regulation violated constitutional rights, namely the protections provided under the Due Process and commerce clauses of the U.S. CONSTITUTION. The porters specifically asserted that the order was discriminatory against "negroes," and thus violated the FOURTEENTH AMENDMENT to the Constitution. The commission answered that its authority to order such a regulation was created by Texas law. Vernon's Texas Revised Civil Statutes Annotated, article 6445, provided in part that the commission was empowered to prevent "unjust discrimination ... and to prevent any and all other abuses" in the Texas railroad industry.

The Supreme Court acknowledged the sensitive nature of the porters' ALLEGATION of discrimination, but declared that the fate of the offending law should be decided first by the state courts. The Court then faced the question of whether a state RESOLUTION was possible.

The Supreme Court noted that a federal district court in the Fifth Circuit had ruled against the commission, but called the decision nothing more than a "forecast." According to the Court, the Texas state courts were more capable of interpreting Texas laws and determining how they should be applied. Federal courts were simply not competent to define the concept of discrimination and its prevention as understood in Texas.

Furthermore, deciding Texas law in a federal court was of little use when the ruling could later be displaced by the decision of a state court. The Court conceded that federal constitutional claims against state laws or regulations may be appealed to federal courts, but it emphasized the PUBLIC INTEREST in avoiding "needless friction with state policies." This meant that when a state had the means to resolve a constitutional issue, the first word on the meaning and constitutionality of the challenged law should be left to the state.

Texas law provided for JUDICIAL REVIEW of administrative orders in state court, so the complainants could have filed suit there. Likewise, the defendants could have brought suit in state court to enforce the order in the event of a railroad strike. Because these avenues existed and had not been traveled, the Supreme Court reversed the decision of the lower federal court and ordered the case held in the federal court pending the outcome of state proceedings.

The abstention doctrine has expanded since the *Pullman* case. The Supreme Court has identified three distinct types of cases from which a federal court should abstain: (1) If the meaning of a state law or regulation is claimed to be unconstitutional, and the meaning of the statute or regulation can be discovered in the state's court system, abstention is appropriate. (2) Abstention is also appropriate when a federal suit seeks to delay or upset an ongoing state proceeding, such as a criminal prosecution or the collection of state taxes. (3) Finally, a federal court should yield to state courts when a case PRESENTS a difficult policy question of vital importance to the state. This last justification for abstention breeds the most creative arguments.

One difficult issue of vital importance to states is domestic relations. DIVORCE, ALIMONY, and CHILD CUSTODY cases involve legitimate local policies concerning MARRIAGE and RELIGION. Until the 1990s, domestic relations abstention has been invoked by federal courts in virtually any case concerning family members. In *Ankenbrandt v. Richards,* 504 U.S. 689, 112 S. Ct. 2206, 119 L. Ed. 2d 468 (1992), the Supreme Court put a stop to this practice.

On September 26, 1989, Carol Ankenbrandt, on behalf of her daughters, sued Jon Richards and Debra Kesler in the U.S. District Court for the Eastern District of Louisiana. Ankenbrandt, a Missouri citizen, had been married to Richards, a Louisiana citizen. After the couple divorced, Richards became romantically involved with Kesler. In her suit, Ankenbrandt claimed that Richards and Kesler had sexually and physically abused Ankenbrandt's daughters. Ankenbrandt filed the suit in federal court under diversity jurisdiction; she was able to do so because she did not live in the defendants' home state and she was suing for over $50,000.

The federal court decided not to hear the merits of Ankenbrandt's case. The district court granted the defendants' earliest MOTION to dismiss, ruling that the case belonged in state court under the domestic relations exception to federal jurisdiction based on diversity. As an alternative to that holding, the court declared that its refusal to hear the case was also justified by the abstention doctrine. The court of appeals affirmed these holdings without a published opinion.

On APPEAL, the Supreme Court reversed the decision. The Court traced the origins of the domestic relations exception to federal diversity jurisdiction and concluded that the exception was valid. Nevertheless, the exception contemplated federal abstention only from cases such as divorce, alimony, and child custody. Ankenbrandt's action was a *tort action,* an action for monetary recovery based on the accusations of one individual against another. Ankenbrandt's previous marriage to Richards did not provide a permissible reason for the federal court to invoke the domestic relations exception.

The federal district court's alternative holding of abstention was equally erroneous. The district court had cited *Younger v. Harris,* 401 U.S. 37, 91 S. Ct. 746, 27 L. Ed. 2d 669 (1971), as support for its abstention. However, the *Younger* decision simply held that a federal court could not interfere with a pending state criminal prosecution. Here, no state proceeding was pending, and the defense had not alleged that any important STATE INTEREST existed, so

reliance on that particular reason for abstention was misplaced.

Although the ARGUMENT had not been raised by Richards or Kesler, the Supreme Court anticipated another reason for abstention, to foreclose the argument in future cases. The federal district court may have sought to abstain from the *Ankenbrandt* case because the suit seemed to present a difficult state policy question of vital importance to the public. The case seemed to involve a determination of the family status of the litigants, an area of state interest that could bring the case within the domestic relations exception. This basis for abstention was not supportable, though, because the familial status of the parties had already been determined in a divorce proceeding and a parental rights proceeding.

The Supreme Court further warned that the family status of the litigants had no bearing on the underlying case. In a CIVIL ACTION for monetary damages, where sexual and physical abuse is alleged, a federal court could not refuse to hear the case because the litigants had at one time been related. Ultimately, neither the domestic relations exception nor its close relative the abstention doctrine would deprive Ankenbrandt of the right to file her complaint in federal court.

Despite its expansion since *Pullman,* federal court abstention is very rare. A federal court may refuse to hear a case over which it has jurisdiction only in unusual circumstances. When a case poses federal constitutional questions, a federal court may abstain only when the challenged state law or regulation is unclear. In addition, the methods for determining the meaning of the law or regulation must exist in the state's court system, and these methods must not have been used. Then and only then may a federal court refrain from hearing a constitutional question. The boundaries of the abstention doctrine are continually tested and stretched, but in 1992 the Supreme Court sent notice through the *Ankenbrandt* case to the federal courts that its use is limited.

CROSS REFERENCES

Constitutional Law; Courts; Federal Courts.

ABSTRACT

To take or withdraw from; as, to abstract the funds of a bank. To remove or separate. To summarize or abridge.

An abstract comprises—or concentrates in itself—the essential qualities of a larger thing—or of several things—in a short, abbreviated form. It differs from a TRANSCRIPT, which is a verbatim copy of the thing itself and is more comprehensive.

CROSS REFERENCE

Abstract of Title.

ABSTRACT OF TITLE

A condensed history, taken from public records or documents, of the ownership of a piece of land.

An abstract of title, or title abstract, briefly summarizes the various activities affecting ownership of a parcel of land. When a person or business agrees to purchase REAL ESTATE, that person or business arranges for an examination of the history of the property's title. This examination is known as a TITLE SEARCH. A title search is conducted to determine that the seller of the property in fact owns the property and has a *free-and-clear* title. A free-and-clear title has no *clouds* on it, which means that no person or business other than the seller has an interest in, or CLAIM to, the property.

The process of determining the precise ownership of a piece of land by searching an abstract is complex and laborious. Often, the title abstract does not contain every transaction or proceeding that may affect ownership of the land. The search conductor, or *abstractor*, usually a trained professional, must verify that the abstract is complete by reviewing recent certifications that the abstract is correct, checking for gaps in dates and certification numbers, and ensuring that a proper legal description appears with each entry. The abstractor conducts a credit and finances check on all the names appearing in the abstract to see if any of the parties has filed for BANKRUPTCY or has incurred other debts that may have caused a creditor to file a LIEN against the property toward payment of the debt.

An abstractor must refer to many different sources to verify that the title to a parcel of land is true and correct. The abstractor verifies the original government survey, which should include gaps and overlaps in land ownership. Given improved technology, surveys have a margin of error of less than one foot. The abstractor must understand the various means of describing the exact BOUNDARIES of a piece of land and must recognize unacceptable methods.

Claims on the title to a property are subject to time limitations, but the limitations have certain exceptions. For example, the Forty-Year Law holds that no party with a potential claim that arose over 40 years before can claim an interest in a property of which one person or business has been the recorded owner for at least 40 years. Exceptions are made, however, for those holding mortgages or contracts with terms that span more than 40 years and also for prior interests claimed as school or school district lands, parkland dedications, or the property of religious CORPORATIONS or associations.

To perform a title search, the abstractor must obtain a copy of the abstract from the county recorder in the county in which the land is located. Then it takes time to make sense of the document. The accompanying sample abstract of title illustrates typical entries.

1. Entry 1 identifies the land in question. The sample abstract is for platted land, which is land described by lots and blocks. A platted parcel spans a certain number of feet, on a certain lot, within a certain block, within a certain city. Another method of identifying a parcel of land is by METES AND BOUNDS. For metes and bounds land, a parcel is identified by its boundaries according to their terminal points and angles. Platted descriptions are used in urban areas, and metes and bounds descriptions are used mostly in rural areas.

2. Entry 2 is the original entry. It states the time and place that the U.S. government first conveyed this tract of land to a private individual. The description follows a progression from small to large. The parcel is identified first by its location within a certain section, which is located within a certain township, which is located within a certain range. Each range spans six miles and several townships, and each township contains several sections, which in turn are divided into quarters, which can also be divided into quarters. The last two lines of the right-hand column might read, for example, "Land Office Records, page 100. North $\frac{1}{4}$ of Section 36, T. [Township] 32, R. [Range] 22." The original description of any parcel of land comes from the measurements of the original government survey of the nineteenth century.

3. Entry 3 is the land patent, or John Doe's title defense. The land patent is issued by the government to operate as proof of title for the first governmentally recognized owner of the land. The land patent shows the date of the land transfer, the date the patent was filed with the government, the particular book of deeds containing the patent, and the land parcel as described in the original entry.

4. Entry 4 reveals that John Doe platted his quarter of section 36—that is, he subdivided the land and dedicated it to the public for sale. The beginning of the entry might read, "Plat of Stoneybrook Addition to the City of New Heidelberg." Note that township 36 has become, or has been incorporated into, what is now New Heidelberg. The entry continues with the date John Doe received approval from the city of New Heidelberg, the date the subdivision was filed with the county, the particular book of plats in which the subdivision is entered, and the original description of the land. The subdivision is entered in the county's book of plats because New Heidelberg has chosen to identify its land parcels by plats, and not metes and bounds. Other means of identifying land parcels are sometimes employed. Land is sometimes identified by acres in rural areas, and by government lots for land adjacent to meandering lakes, but most of the land in the United States is identified by either plats or metes and bounds.

5. Entry 5 shows that John Doe sold a parcel of the subdivision to Richard ROE. Roe received a WARRANTY DEED, which serves as evidence of Doe's title. A warranty deed means that Doe has warranted to Roe that Doe is the rightful owner of the land. This type of deed has legal ramifications that benefit the purchaser, here Roe. There are other types of real ESTATE deeds. A purchaser receives a TAX DEED, for example, when he or she buys real estate sold for nonpayment of taxes, and this purchase involves procedures that differ from those of other land purchases. A sheriff's deed is given to the purchaser of land sold by court order such as in a MORTGAGE FORECLOSURE, and this transaction also has special legal ramifications for the purchaser. Because the land in the sample abstract is platted, the parcel is assigned a lot number, within a certain block, within the city of New Heidelberg—for example, this entry might read, "Lot 1, Block E, Stoneybrook Addition to City of New Heidelberg." The entry also contains information on when the warranty deed was signed and when it was filed with the county.

6. Entry 6 shows that Richard Roe and Ruth Roe have mortgaged their property to John Smith. With an interest in lot 1 of block E as COLLATERAL, Smith has paid for the Roes' property, and the Roes have undertaken to repay Smith. The entry shows the date the mortgage agreement was signed and the date the mortgage was filed with the county. The remainder might read, "Book 1 of Mortgages, page 10, to secure $10,000, due January 10, 1910. Lot 1, Block E, Stoneybrook Addition."

7. Entry 7 shows that John Smith has assigned the mortgage on lot 1, block E, to William White. In other words, Smith has sold to White his mortgagee interest in lot 1, block E. An assignment can occur for any number of reasons, but often it is a sale made to satisfy debts. This particular action is entered in the book of assignments in the county seat.

8. Entry 8 shows that Richard Roe and Ruth Roe have paid off, or *satisfied*, the mortgage (*et ux* is Latin for "and wife"). This entry is filed in the book of assignments in the county seat.

9. Entry 9 reveals that Richard Roe has died. This "Will and Probate" entry reports that, upon his death, Roe seeks to transfer ownership of lot 1, block E, in New Heidelberg, to his wife, Ruth Roe.

10. Entry 10 identifies Ruth Roe as the sole owner of the parcel. The PROBATE court, which tends to property matters surrounding the death of an individual, has approved the assignment of lot 1, block E, contained in Richard Roe's will.

11. Entry 11 shows that Ruth Roe has taken out a mortgage on lot 1, block E. She has borrowed money from Samuel Brown, using the real estate as collateral. The entry is identical to the first mortgage agreement with John Smith, entry 6.

A sample abstract of title

Abstract of Title

1. Abstract of Title to north __500__ feet, front and rear, of Lot __1__ , Block __2__ , in __NW__ Addition to the City of __New Heidelberg__ .

2. United States
   to
   John Doe.

   Entry No. __1__ .
   Dated __Jan. 1__ , 1889.
   Land Office Records, page __100__ .
   __North__ 1/4 of Section __36__ , T. __32__ , R. __22__ .

3. United States
   to
   John Doe

   Patent.
   Dated __Jan. 1, 1889__ .
   Filed __Jan. 1, 1889__ .
   Book __1__ of Deeds, Page __100__ .
   __North__ 1/4 of Section __36__ , T. __32__ , R. __22__ .

4. John Doe et al.
   to
   The Public.

   Plat of __Stoneybrook E__ Addition to the City of __New Heidelberg__ .
   Dated __Feb. 1, 1889__ .
   Filed __Feb. 1, 1889__ .
   Book __1__ of Plats, page __200__ .
   __North__ 1/4 of Section __36__ , T. __32__ , R. __22__ .

5. John Doe, unmarried,
   to
   Richard Roe.

   Warranty Deed.
   Dated __Feb. 1, 1890__ .
   Filed __Feb. 1, 1890__ .
   Book __3__ of Deeds, page __300__ .
   Lot __1__ , Block __E__ , __Stoneybrook__ Addition to City of __New Heidelberg__ .

6. Richard Roe and
   Ruth Roe, his wife,
   to
   John Smith.

   Mortgage.
   Dated __Feb. 1, 1890__ .
   Filed __Feb. 1, 1890__ .
   Book __1__ of Mortgages, page __10__ , to secure __$10,000__ , due __January 10, 1910__ .
   Lot __1__ , Block __E__ , __Stoneybrook__ Addition.

7. John Smith
   to
   William White

   Assignment of Mortgage No. 6.
   Dated __Jan. 1, 1895__ .
   Filed __Jan. 1, 1895__ .
   Book __5__ of Assignments, page __100__ .

8. William White
   to
   Richard Roe et ux.

   Satisfaction of No. 6.
   Dated __Jan. 1, 1910__ .
   Filed __Jan. 1, 1910__ .
   Book __3__ of Satisfactions, page __200__ .

9. Richard Roe
   to
   Ruth Roe

   Will and Probate.
   Dated __July 1, 1915__ .
   Probate __July 1, 1915__ .
   Filed __Aug. 1, 1915__ .
   Book __10__ of Miscellaneous, page __100__ .
   Testator leaves all of his property, real and personal, to his wife, Ruth Roe.

10. Richard Roe
    to
    Ruth Roe

    Final Decree.
    Probate Court, __Munich__ County.
    Dated __Aug. 1, 1915__ .
    Filed __Aug. 1, 1915__ .
    Book __10__ of Miscellaneous, page __300__ .
    Adjudged and decreed that Lot __1__ , Block __2__ , __NW__ . Addition is hereby assigned to Ruth Roe.

11. Ruth Roe, widow,
    to
    Samuel Brown.

    Mortgage.
    Dated __Jan. 1, 1920__ .
    Filed __Jan. 1, 1920__ .
    Book __10__ of Mortgages, page __100__ , to secure __$20,000__ , due __Jan. 1, 1930__ .
    Lot __1__ , Block __2__ , __NW__ Addition.

12. Ruth Roe, widow,
    by Sheriff of
    County,
    to
    Samuel Brown.

    Foreclosure of No. 11.
    Notice of sale, __Feb. 1, 1930.__
    Affidavit of publication, __Feb. 1, 1930__
    Proof of service, __Feb. 1, 1930.__
    Sheriff's certificate of sale, __March 1, 1930.__
    Filed __March 1, 1930.__
    Book __15__ of Miscellaneous, page __300__ .
    Lot __1__ , Block __2__ , __NW__ Addition, sold __March 1, 1930,__ to Samuel Brown, for __$10,000__ .

[continued]

Abstract of Title

13.	Samuel Brown and Sophy Brown, his wife, to James Jones.	Quitclaim Deed. Date __April 1, 1940__ . Filed __April 1, 1940__ . Book __27__ of Deeds, page __100__ . North __250__ feet, front and rear, of Lot __1__ , Block __2__ , __NW__ Addition.
14.	Taxes paid, except for year 1940, amounting to $15,000.	
15.	In re James Jones Bankruptcy No.	Petition of Debtor for arrangement under Chapter XI of the Bankruptcy Act, as amended (§ 301 et seq.) filed __Jan. 1, 1950__ in U.S. District Court for __the__ District of New Hampshire.

A sample abstract of title (continued)
ILLUSTRATION BY GGS CREATIVE RESOURCES. REPRODUCED BY PERMISSION OF GALE, A PART OF CENGAGE LEARNING.

12. Entry 12 reveals that Ruth Roe was unable to make her mortgage payments to Samuel Brown, and Brown has sought payment by exercising his right to force a sale of the property by foreclosing on the mortgage. The FORCED SALE was published in a newspaper. The dates of public notice, the publication AFFIDAVIT, and the service of notice to Roe are all entered in the abstract. The certificate of sale and the date the forced sale was filed with the county are also included. This entry shows that Brown has purchased lot 1 at the resulting sheriff's sale of the property. The amount Brown paid would depend on the value of the real estate and the amount of the mortgage. The "No. 11" following "Foreclosure of" simply refers to the court document number of the foreclosure.

13. Entry 13 shows that Samuel Brown and Sophy Brown have sold a part of lot 1 to James Jones by QUITCLAIM DEED. Generally, a quitclaim deed transfers title to property without warranties that the title is free and clear. Owing to Ruth Roe's financial troubles, the Browns are probably uncertain of their title's completeness, so they have chosen to sell parts of their lot by quitclaim deed instead of warranty deed. Jones now owns a northern piece of lot 1, block E, of Stoneybrook Addition.

14. Entry 14 shows the taxes paid on the property, except for the current year. An entry of taxes paid is listed every time a tax ASSESSMENT is made or paid in relation to the property of the abstract. Taxes listed in the abstract may include estate taxes, inheritance taxes, capital gains taxes, and local government property taxes. The abstract should include the current amount of these taxes and certification that they have been paid.

15. Entry 15 reveals that, to avoid financial disaster, James Jones has filed bankruptcy. The northern piece of lot 1, block E, Stoneybrook Addition, New Heidelberg, is now being used to secure protection from creditors. Jones has given to the bankruptcy court a TRUST DEED, which the court retains until Jones has fulfilled his obligations under the financial rehabilitation plan approved by the court. Should Jones default on this arrangement, the court could order a forced sale of the property, with proceeds going to Jones's creditors. The land covered by this particular abstract has now been defined; it is a certain northern piece of lot 1 of block E in the Stoneybrook Addition of New Heidelberg. The land to the south of this piece would have its own abstract, which would be identical to this abstract up to the point that lot 1 was divided up and part of it sold to Jones. Likewise, the abstract for the adjacent lot 2 on block E would have an abstract identical to this abstract up to the point that John Doe sold to Richard Roe the newly platted land of section 36 in township 32, range 22.

FURTHER READINGS

Galaty, Fillmore, Wellington J. Allaway, and Robert C. Kyle. 2002. *Modern Real Estate Practices*. 16th ed. Chicago: Dearborn Real Estate Education.

Jacobus, Charles J. 1998. *Real Estate Law*. 2d ed. Florence, KY: South-Western Education.

Koenig, R. Harry. 1991. *How to Lower Your Property Taxes*. New York: Fireside.

CROSS REFERENCES
Deed; Property Law; Real Property; Recording of Land Titles; Torrens Title System.

ABSTRACTION

Taking from someone with an intent to injure or defraud.

Wrongful abstraction is an unauthorized and illegal withdrawing of funds or an APPROPRI-ATION of someone else's funds for the taker's own benefit. It may be a crime under the laws of a state. It is different from embezzlement, which is a crime committed only if the taker had a lawful right to possession of the money when it was first taken.

ABUSE

Everything that is contrary to good order established by usage. Departure from reasonable use; immoderate or improper use. Physical or mental maltreatment. Misuse. Deception.

To wrong in speech, reproach coarsely, disparage, revile, and malign.

ABUSE EXCUSE

Description of efforts by some criminal defendants to negate criminal responsibility by showing that they could not tell right from wrong due to abuse by their spouses or parents. Although this defense is not specifically recognized in substantive criminal law, it has been used successfully in some cases to prove, for example, the insanity defense.

Using prior sexual or other physical abuse as evidence in a criminal defense is largely a result of research regarding mental disorders caused by such abuse. Psychologists and other researchers have identified disorders, including post-traumatic stress disorder and battered woman syndrome, as causes for severe emotional instability that can lead to violent acts by the victim against his or her abuser. Some writers have advocated more widespread use of such evidence to mitigate the PUNISHMENT of victims who commit violent acts.

Other scholars and writers disagree, noting that substantive CRIMINAL LAW does not recognize the ABUSE EXCUSE as a legitimate defense except in some limited circumstances, such as those involving the INSANITY DEFENSE. Harvard law professor ALAN DERSHOWITZ coined the term in his 1994 book, *The Abuse Excuse*, where he deems the studies regarding psychological

disorders caused by abuse as "psychobabble". Dershowitz and other critics disagree not only with the use of abuse as mitigating evidence of criminal intent, but also with the results of the studies themselves. According to these critics, especially Dershowitz, the abuse excuse fails to distinguish between the reasons why a person committed a crime and the responsibility for committing the crime.

In a few high profile cases during the late 1980s and 1990s, defendants sought to avoid criminal responsibility for their crimes by introducing evidence of prior abuse. In 1989 Lyle and Erik Menendez, ages 21 and 18 respectively, brutally killed their parents in the family's California home. At their first trial for MURDER in 1993, the brothers' defense team introduced evidence that the men's father, Jose Menendez, had sexually abused his sons for a number of years. Because of this abuse, Lyle and Eric, according to the defense, killed their parents out of fear. In raising the evidence of abuse, the defense sought to reduce the conviction from murder to voluntary MANSLAUGHTER. The defense won a victory of sorts when the first trial ended in a HUNG JURY because the jurors could not agree whether the brothers were killers or whether they acted out due to the years of alleged abuse they had suffered. In a second trial in 1995, however, the jury convicted the brothers of first-degree murder notwithstanding the evidence of abuse, and the judge sentenced them to life in prison without the possibility of PAROLE.

In 1993 Lorena Bobbitt was indicted for MALICIOUS wounding after cutting off her sleeping husband's penis during the middle of the night. At her trial, her defense team introduced evidence of a history of sexual and physical abuse committed by the husband, John, against Lorena. Unlike the Menendez case, where the defense conceded that the brothers were criminally responsible for their actions, Lorena's defense team used the evidence to prove the insanity defense. In 1994 a jury found her not guilty of the crime by reason of insanity.

Scholars have noted that the employment of the abuse excuse as a defense is more viable if it is used to prove insanity, which happened in the Lorena Bobbitt case. Commentators have also noted that evidence of prior abuse, whether substantiated or not, has been used in settings other than criminal defense. For instance, a wife may accuse a husband of SEXUAL ABUSE during

DIVORCE proceedings or an adult woman may SUE her father for sexual abuse that allegedly occurred when the woman was a child.

FURTHER READINGS

Arenella, Peter. 1996. "Demystifying the Abuse Excuse: Is There One?" *Harvard Journal of Law and Public Policy* 19.

Becker, Mary E. 1998. "The Abuse Excuse and Patriarchal Narratives." *Northwestern Univ. Law Review* 92, vol. 4.

Dershowitz, Alan M. 2000. "Review Essay: Moral Judgment: Does the Abuse Excuse Threaten Our Legal System?" *Buffalo Criminal Law Review* 3, vol. 2.

ABUSE OF DISCRETION

A failure to take into proper consideration the facts and law relating to a particular matter; an arbitrary or unreasonable departure from precedent and settled judicial custom.

Where a trial court must exercise discretion in deciding a question, it must do so in a way that is not clearly against logic and the evidence. An improvident exercise of discretion is an error of law and grounds for reversing a decision on APPEAL. It does not, however, necessarily amount to BAD FAITH, intentional wrong, or misconduct by the trial judge.

For example, the traditional standard of APPELLATE review for evidence-related questions arising during trial is the "abuse of discretion" standard. Most judicial determinations are made based on evidence introduced at LEGAL PROCEEDINGS. Evidence may consist of oral TESTIMONY, written testimony, videotapes and sound recordings, DOCUMENTARY EVIDENCE such as exhibits and business records, and a host of other materials, including voice exemplars, handwriting samples, and blood tests.

Before such materials may be introduced into the record at a legal proceeding, the trial court must determine that they satisfy certain criteria governing the admissibility of evidence. At a minimum, the court must find that the evidence offered is relevant to the legal proceedings. Evidence that bears on a factual or legal issue at stake in a controversy is considered relevant evidence.

The relevancy of evidence is typically measured by its PROBATIVE value. Evidence is generally deemed probative if it has a tendency to make the existence of any material fact more or less probable. Evidence that a MURDER DEFENDANT ate spaghetti on the day of the murder might be relevant at trial if spaghetti sauce was found at the murder scene. Otherwise such evidence would probably be deemed irrelevant

and could be excluded from trial if opposing counsel made the proper objection.

During many civil and criminal trials, judges rule on hundreds of evidentiary objections lodged by both parties. These rulings are normally snap judgments made in the heat of battle. Courts must make these decisions quickly to keep the proceedings moving on schedule. For this reason, judges are given wide latitude in making evidentiary rulings and will not be overturned on appeal unless the appellate court finds that the trial judge abused his or her discretion.

For example, in a NEGLIGENCE case, a state appellate court ruled that the trial court did not ABUSE its discretion by admitting into evidence a posed accident-scene photograph, even though the photograph depicted a model pedestrian blindly walking into the path of the driver's vehicle with the pedestrian's head pointed straight ahead as if she was totally oblivious to the vehicle and other traffic (*Gorman v. Hunt,* 19 S.W.3d 662 [Ky. 2000]). In upholding the trial court's decision to admit the evidence, the appellate court observed that the photograph was only used to show the pedestrian's position relative to the vehicle at the time of impact and not to blame the pedestrian for being negligent. The appellate court also noted that the LAWYER objecting to the photograph's admissibility was free to remind the jury of its limited relevance during CROSS-EXAMINATION and closing arguments.

An appellate court would find that a trial court abused its discretion, however, if it admitted into evidence a photograph without proof that it was authentic (*Apter v. Ross,* 781 N. E.2d 744 [Ind.App. 2003]). A photograph's authenticity may be established by a witness's personal observations that the photograph accurately depicts what it purports to depict at the time the photograph was taken. Ordinarily the photographer who took the picture is in the best position to provide such testimony.

FURTHER READINGS

Cohen, Ruth Bryna. 2000. "Superior Court Affirms Non Pros for Failure to Subpoena Own Witness; Trial Court Did Not Abuse Discretion in Its Application of Civil Procedure Rule 216." *Pennsylvania Law Weekly* (October 9).

Hamblett, Mark. 2001. "Circuit Panel Issues Recusal Guidelines; Says Rakoff Acted Properly In Not Stepping Down." *New York Law Journal* (February 26).

Riccardi, Michael A. 2002. "Polygraph Evidence OK to Prove Probable Cause, Circuit Judges Say; No Abuse of Discretion in Relying on 'Lie Detector' for Limited Purpose." *Pennsylvania Law Weekly* (April 29).

CROSS REFERENCES

Appeal; Bad Faith; Error; Evidence; Precedent; Probative; Relevancy.

ABUSE OF POWER

Improper use of authority by someone who has that authority because he or she holds a public office.

ABUSE OF POWER is different from usurpation of power, which is an exercise of authority that the offender does not actually have.

ABUSE OF PROCESS

The use of legal process to accomplish an unlawful purpose; causing a summons, writ, warrant, mandate, or any other process to issue from a court in order to accomplish some purpose not intended by the law.

For example, a grocer rents a small building but complains to the LANDLORD about the inadequate heating system, leaks in the roof, and potholes in the driveway. When the landlord fails to make the required repairs, the grocer decides the property is worth less and deducts $100 a month from his rent payments. The landlord starts a lawsuit to either recover the full amount of rent due or to oust the grocer and regain possession of the premises. The law in their state is fairly clear on the question: A tenant has no right to force a landlord to make repairs by withholding a portion of the rent. The landlord knows that she has a good chance of winning her case, but she also wants to teach the grocer a lesson. On the first three occasions that the case comes up on the court calendar, the grocer closes his store and appears in court, but the landlord does not show up. On the fourth occasion, the landlord comes to court and wins her case. The grocer, in a separate action for ABUSE OF PROCESS, claims that the landlord is using the court's power to order him to appear simply to harass him. The court agrees and awards him money damages for lost income and inconvenience.

Abuse of process is a wrong committed during the course of LITIGATION. It is a perversion of lawfully issued process and is different from MALICIOUS PROSECUTION, a lawsuit started without any reasonable cause.

ABUSIVE

Tending to deceive; practicing abuse; prone to ill-treat by coarse, insulting words or harmful acts.

Using ill treatment; injurious, improper, hurtful, offensive, reproachful.

Using ABUSIVE language, even though offensive, is not criminal unless it amounts to fighting words that, by their very utterance, tend to incite an immediate BREACH OF THE PEACE.

ABUT

To reach; to touch. To touch at the end; be contiguous; join at a border or boundary; terminate on; end at; border on; reach or touch with an end. The term abutting implies a closer proximity than the term adjacent.

When referring to real property, abutting means that there is no intervening land between the abutting parcels. Generally, properties that share a common boundary are abutting. A statute may require abutting owners to pay proportional shares of the cost of a street improvement project.

❖ ABZUG, BELLA SAVITSKY

Bella Savitsky Abzug served as a Democratic congresswoman in the 1970s and became one of the most outspoken advocates for women's rights in the United States. After she left Congress in 1976, she remained involved in political and social issues both nationally and internationally. With her raspy voice, New York accent, and trademark floppy hat, Abzug was one of the most recognizable public figures in recent U.S. history.

Bella Savitsky was born on July 24, 1920, in New York City and was raised in the Bronx. The daughter of Russian immigrant Jews, her father was a butcher who operated the "Live and Let Live" meat market. As a young girl, she raised and collected money on behalf of Zionism. After she graduated from high school, she attended Hunter College, where she was president of the student government. Following graduation in 1944, she attended Columbia Law School, where she was the editor of the LAW REVIEW and an outstanding student. In 1946 she married Martin Abzug, who would go on to become a successful stockbroker.

After graduating in 1947, Abzug concentrated her legal practice in the fields of LABOR LAW and CIVIL RIGHTS, while also becoming active in left-wing politics. As an ATTORNEY for the AMERICAN CIVIL LIBERTIES UNION, Abzug went to Mississippi in 1950 to argue the APPEAL of Willie McGee, an African American man who had been convicted of raping a white woman. She also defended individuals whom Senator JOSEPH R. MCCARTHY (R-Wisc.) had ACCUSED of Communist subversion. During the 1950s Abzug managed to juggle her legal and political careers, while being a mother to two daughters.

In the 1960s Abzug organized opposition to nuclear arms testing by founding Women's Strike for Peace. In 1970 she was elected as a Democratic congresswoman from New York City. She was an outspoken critic of the VIETNAM WAR and the policies of President RICHARD M. NIXON. After the WATERGATE scandals erupted in 1973, Abzug was the first public official to call for Nixon's IMPEACHMENT.

Although Abzug antagonized many of her male colleagues in Congress by insisting on gender equality inside and outside of the Capitol, in 1974 she served as an assistant whip to House Speaker Tip O'Neill (D-Mass.). She chaired a subcommittee on government information and individual rights and co-authored the FREEDOM OF INFORMATION ACT and the PRIVACY Act. Abzug also worked on behalf of the ill-fated EQUAL RIGHTS AMENDMENT, which failed to acquire the necessary number of states for RATIFICATION.

A national figure by the mid-1970s, Abzug sought the DEMOCRATIC PARTY nomination for the Senate in 1976. She lost a close race to Daniel Patrick Moynihan (D-N.Y.). Several campaigns for New York City mayor and Congress followed, but Abzug never served in elective office again. Despite these defeats, she remained active in efforts for women's rights. She was president of the National Commission on the Observance of International Women's Year, cofounder of the National Women's Political Caucus, and the

Bella Abzug.
AP PHOTOS.

WOMEN HAVE BEEN TRAINED TO SPEAK SOFTLY AND CARRY A LIPSTICK. THOSE DAYS ARE OVER.
—BELLA ABZUG

founder of the International Women's Environmental and Development Organization. In 1995 she played a major role in a world conference on women's issues, held in Beijing, China.

Abzug remained active in the women's movement despite numerous health problems that began in the mid-1980s. She died on March 31, 1998, in New York City following heart surgery.

FURTHER READINGS

Abzug, Bella S., with Mim Kelber. 1984. *Gender Gap: Bella Abzug's Guide to Political Power for American Women.* Boston: Houghton Mifflin.

Abzug, Bella S. 1972. *Bella! Ms. Abzug Goes to Washington.* New York: Saturday Review Press.

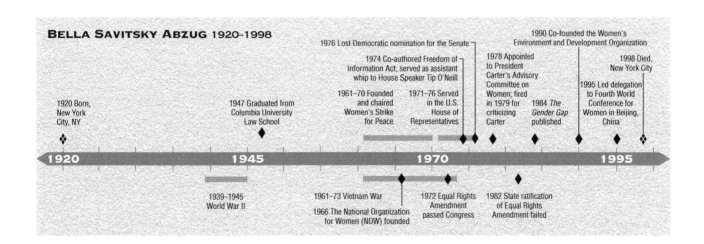

BELLA SAVITSKY ABZUG 1920–1998

1976 Lost Democratic nomination for the Senate

1990 Co-founded the Women's Environment and Development Organization

1974 Co-authored Freedom of Information Act; served as assistant whip to House Speaker Tip O'Neill

1978 Appointed to President Carter's Advisory Committee on Women; fired in 1979 for criticizing Carter

1998 Died, New York City

1920 Born, New York City, NY

1947 Graduated from Columbia University Law School

1961–70 Founded and chaired Women's Strike for Peace

1971–76 Served in the U.S. House of Representatives

1984 *The Gender Gap* published

1995 Led delegation to Fourth World Conference for Women in Beijing, China

1920   **1945**   **1970**   **1995**

1939–1945 World War II

1961–73 Vietnam War

1966 The National Organization for Women (NOW) founded

1972 Equal Rights Amendment passed Congress

1982 State ratification of Equal Rights Amendment failed

Faber, Doris. 1976. *Bella Abzug.* New York: Lothrop, Lee & Shepard.

Intimate Portrait: Bella Abzug (videotape). 1998. Lifetime Productions.

Rogers, Kathy. 1998. "Bella Abzug: ALeader of Vision and Voice." *Columbia Law Review* 98 (June) 1998.

CROSS REFERENCE

Equal Rights Amendment.

ACADEMIC FREEDOM

Academic freedom is the right to teach as one sees fit, but not necessarily the right to teach evil. The term encompasses much more than teaching-related speech rights of teachers.

Educational institutions are communities unto themselves with rules of their own, and when conflicts arise, often times the most common and compelling arguments involve freedom. As a result, the academic community energetically explores the nature of freedom in society at large, and it is often forced to confront its own concepts of freedom in the process.

The American Association of University Professors (AAUP) has long led efforts among educators to define the concept of ACADEMIC FREEDOM in U.S. COLLEGES AND UNIVERSITIES. In 1940 the AAUP, in conjunction with the Association of American Colleges (now the Association of American Colleges and Universities), drafted and approved the *Statement of Principles on Academic Freedom and Tenure.* The statement's purpose is to "promote public understanding and support of academic freedom and tenure and agreement upon procedures to ensure them in colleges and universities."

According to the statement, educational institutions should afford full freedom for teachers to conduct research and publish their results, subject to their adequate performance in other academic duties. Teachers should also have freedom in the classroom to discuss their subject, but they should be careful not to introduce controversial matter that has no relation to their subject. Institutions may place limitations on academic freedom because of religious or other aims of the institution, though these limitations should be stated clearly in writing at the time of the teacher's appointment.

Although the position of the AAUP is not binding upon colleges and universities, it has had an important impact on the tenure policies of these institutions. Tenure, according to the AAUP, promotes freedom of teaching, research, and other educational activities and also provides a "sufficient degree of economic security to make the profession attractive to men and women of ability." Tenure is based upon a contractual relationship between the educational institution and the teacher, and this agreement provides private rights between the two.

Academic freedom was first introduced as a judicial *term of art* (a term with a specific legal meaning) by Supreme Court Justice WILLIAM O. DOUGLAS. In *Adler v. Board of Education of City of New York* (342 U.S. 485, 72 S. Ct. 380, 96 L. Ed. 517 [1952]), the Supreme Court upheld a New York law (N.Y. Civ. Service Law § 12-a) that prohibited employment of teachers in public institutions if they were members of "subversive organizations." In a scathing dissent joined by Justice Hugo L. Black, Douglas argued that such LEGISLATION created a police state and ran contrary to the FIRST AMENDMENT guarantee of free speech.

Justice Douglas equated academic freedom with the pursuit of truth. If academic freedom is the pursuit of truth and is protected by the First Amendment, reasoned Douglas, then the New York law should be struck down because its potential effect was to produce standardized thought. According to Douglas's dissent, the New York law created an academic atmosphere concerned not with intellectual stimulation but with such questions as "Why was the history teacher so openly hostile to Franco's Spain? Who heard overtones of revolution in the English teacher's discussion of *The Grapes of Wrath*?" And "What was behind the praise of Soviet progress in metallurgy in the chemistry class?" Douglas conceded that the public school systems need not become "cells for Communist activities," but he reminded the court that the Framers of the CONSTITUTION "knew the strength that comes when the mind is free."

Shortly after the *Adler* decision, a similar case arose in New Hampshire that received very different treatment by the Supreme Court. On January 5, 1954, Paul M. Sweezy was summoned to appear before New Hampshire attorney general Louis C. Wyman for inquiries into Sweezy's political associations. Under a 1951 New Hampshire statute, the state ATTORNEY general was authorized to investigate "subversive activities" and determine whether "subversive persons" were located within the state (*Sweezy v. New Hampshire*, 354 U.S. 234, 77 S. Ct. 1203, 1 L. Ed. 2d 1311 [1957]). Wyman was especially interested in information on members of the PROGRESSIVE PARTY, an organization many politicians suspected of nurturing COMMUNISM in the United States.

Sweezy said he was unaware of any violations of the statute. He further stated that he would not answer any questions impertinent to the inquiry under the legislation and that he would not answer questions that seemed to infringe on his FREEDOM OF SPEECH. Sweezy did answer numerous questions about himself, his views, and his activities, but he refused to answer questions about other people. In a later inquiry by the attorney general, Sweezy refused to comment about an article he had written and about a lecture he had delivered to a humanities class.

When Sweezy persisted in his refusal to talk about others and about his lecture, he was held in contempt of court and sent to the Merrimack County Jail. The Supreme Court of New Hampshire affirmed the conviction, and Sweezy appealed.

The U.S. Supreme Court went on to reverse the decision. The basis for the reversal was the New Hampshire statute's improper grant of broad interrogation powers to the attorney general and its failure to afford sufficient criminal protections to an ACCUSED. The Court commented strongly upon the threat such a statute posed to academic freedom.

The principal opinion, written by Chief Justice EARL WARREN, questioned the wisdom of Wyman's LEGISLATIVE inquiry. With regard to the questions on Sweezy's lecture to the humanities class, Warren stated that "[t]o impose any strait jacket upon the intellectual leaders in our colleges and universities would imperil the future of our Nation."

Justice FELIX FRANKFURTER wrote a separate concurring opinion. To Frankfurter, the call of the Court was to decide the case by balancing the right of the state to self-protection against the right of a citizen to academic freedom and political PRIVACY. Frankfurter concluded that Wyman's reasons for questioning Sweezy on academics were "grossly inadequate" given "the grave harm resulting from governmental intrusion into the intellectual life of a university."

Neither of the PLURALITY opinions in *Sweezy* would have found all congressional inquiries into academia to be unconstitutional. However, both opinions helped free educators in later cases by

In 1954 Paul M. Sweezy, a New York magazine editor and former Harvard professor, refused to answer questions about his political associations from New Hampshire attorney general Louis C. Wyman. Sweezy was jailed for contempt of court but later won on appeal.

AP IMAGES

recognizing and emphasizing the danger of restricting academic thought. In *Keyishian v. BOARD OF REGENTS of the University of New York* (385 U.S. 589, 87 S. Ct. 675, 17 L. Ed. 629 [1967]), the Supreme Court finally awarded to teachers and professors the full complement of free speech and political privacy rights afforded other citizens. Political "loyalty oaths" required of New York State employees (including educators) under state CIVIL SERVICE laws were declared VOID, and New York education laws against "treasonable or seditious speech" were found to violate the First Amendment right to free speech. According to the *Keyishian* decision, "[A]cademic freedom ... is a special concern of the First Amendment, which does not tolerate laws that cast a pall of orthodoxy over the classroom."

The tension between academic oversight and academic freedom did not end with the *Keyishian* case. The Supreme Court has also held that if school authorities can show additional independent grounds for discharge, they may terminate a teacher for disruptive speech even if a substantial motivation for the termination was speech on issues of public concern (*Pickering v. Board of Ed. of Township High School Dist. 205, Will County*, 391 U.S. 563, 88 S. Ct. 1731, 20 L. Ed. 2d 811 [1968]; *Mt. Healthy City Bd. of Ed. v. Doyle*, 429 U.S. 274, 97

S. Ct. 568, 50 L. Ed. 2d 471 [1977]). This precedent seemed to give school authorities ample means to elude LIABILITY for unconstitutional terminations. However, neither of the principles helped City University of New York (CUNY) when it was sued by the chair of its black studies department.

Professor Leonard Jeffries specialized in black studies and the history of Africa, and his teaching style at CUNY was controversial. Some students felt that Jeffries discouraged classroom debate, whereas others applauded him for verbalizing the frustrations of many African Americans. Jeffries referred to Europeans as "ice people" and as "egotistic, individualistic, and exploitative." Africans, by contrast, were "sun people" who had "humanistic, spiritualistic value system[s]."

On July 20, 1991, Jeffries spoke at the Empire State Black Arts and Cultural Festival, in Albany, New York. In his speech, he assailed perceived Jewish power, asserting that Jews controlled CUNY and Hollywood and had financed the American slave trade. The speech attracted national attention and placed CUNY on the horns of a dilemma: Either it could punish Jeffries and risk running afoul of the First Amendment and academic freedom principles, or it could do nothing and risk losing expected income from offended school benefactors. For several months, the university wrestled with the problem. Then, in October, the board of trustees voted, without explanation, to limit Jeffries's current appointment as chair to one year instead of the customary three. On March 23, 1992, the CUNY Board of Trustees appointed Professor Edmund Gordon to the position of black studies chair. Jeffries filed suit in federal court on June 5, 1992.

Jeffries argued that the defendants violated his First Amendment free speech rights and his FOURTEENTH AMENDMENT due process rights when they denied him a full three-year term as chair of black studies. The jury agreed with Jeffries that a substantial motivating factor in his dismissal was his speech in Albany. The jury did find, however, that CUNY had reasonably expected the speech to have a detrimental effect on the school. Despite this seemingly justifiable excuse for the school's action, the jury finally found that CUNY had deprived Jeffries of property (the position of chair) without DUE PROCESS OF LAW. The district court judge held that Jeffries's First Amendment rights had been violated, and in August 1993 reduced Jeffries's recovery in damages by $40,000 but awarded him the black studies chair (*Jeffries v. Harleston*, 828 F. Supp. 1066 [S.D.N.Y., 1993]).

Upon APPEAL, the U.S. Supreme Court remanded the case to the Second Circuit with instructions to consider the Court's RULING in *Waters v. Churchill* (511 U. S. 661 [1994]). The CIRCUIT COURT reversed and remanded the case to the district court. The FINAL DECISION concluded that Jeffries's occupation did not afford him "greater protection from state interference with his speech than did the nurse in *Waters*." By taking away Jeffries's position as chair of the department, the university did not infringe on his ability to speak publicly or to teach in his own style, both of which could have been violations of his First Amendment rights (*Jeffries v. Harleston*, 52 F. 3d 9 [2d Cir. 1995]).

The Supreme Court has decided several cases that identified more precisely how much control school authorities may exercise over education. The Court held in *Board of Ed., Island Trees Union Free School Dist. No. 26 v. Pico* (457 U.S. 853, 102 S. Ct. 2799, 73 L. Ed. 2d 435 [1982]), that a school board can control curriculum and book selection, but it may not remove "objectionable" books from public school libraries solely in response to community pressure. Among the books that the Island Trees Union Free School District No. 26 in New York had banned in the mid-1970s were *Slaughterhouse Five*, by Kurt Vonnegut Jr.; *Black Boy*, by Richard Wright; *Naked Ape*, by Desmond Morris; and *The Fixer*, by Bernard Malamud.

School boards and state legislatures generally control public school curriculums, but their control is not complete. For instance, a state statute will be struck down if it requires public schools to also teach creationism if they teach evolution and vice versa. According to the Court in *Edwards v. Aguillard* (482 U.S. 578, 107 S. Ct. 2573, 96 L. Ed. 2d 510 [1987]), such a law undermines a comprehensive scientific education and impermissibly endorses RELIGION by advancing the religious belief that a supernatural power created human beings.

State legislatures have accommodated court rulings by drafting legislative language intended to create academic latitude without violating CONSTITUTIONAL rights. In July 2008 Louisiana governor Bobby Jindal signed into law the Louisiana Science Education Act, S.B. 733, which (according to the act's preamble) purported to "promote students' critical thinking skills and open discussion of scientific theories" in Louisiana classrooms. Section §285(B)(1) of the act states:

> The State Board of Elementary and Secondary Education, upon request of a city, parish, or other local public school board, shall allow and assist teachers, principals, and other school administrators to create and foster an environment within public elementary and secondary schools that promotes critical thinking skills, logical analysis, and open and objective discussion of scientific theories being studied including, but not limited to, evolution, the origins of life, global warming, and human cloning.

Section §285(C) provides that after teaching the material contained in a standard textbook supplied by the school system, a teacher may use supplemental textbooks and other instructional materials "to help students understand, analyze, critique, and review scientific theories in an objective manner."

Section §285(D) expressly states: "This Section shall not be construed to promote any religious doctrine, promote DISCRIMINATION for or against a particular set of religious beliefs, or promote discrimination for or against religion or non-religion."

The Louisiana Science Education Act was one of several similar bills introduced in state legislatures in 2008 and 2009, including those in Alabama (HB 300), Florida, Iowa (HF 183), Michigan, Missouri (HB 656), New Mexico (SB 433), Oklahoma (SB 320), South Carolina, and Texas (HB 224). Only Louisiana's was enacted in 2008. (Oklahoma's bill, the language of which closely paralleled that of Louisiana, was narrowly defeated by a 7-6 vote in the state's Senate Education Committee in early 2009.)

The question regarding whether the federal government can deny grants or funds to educational institutions which speak out against federal policies was the issue before the courts in *Rumsfeld v. F.A.I.R.* (*Forum for Academic and Institutional Rights, Inc.*) (547 U.S. 47, 126 S. Ct. 1297 [2006]). Congress had passed the SOLOMON AMENDMENT in 1994 (10 U.S.C. 983), which requires the U.S. DEPARTMENT OF DEFENSE (DOD) to deny federal funding to institutions of higher education that prohibit ACCESS to the institution for military representatives and/or deny or impede assistance for recruiting purposes.

The conflict arose over military policies regarding homosexuality. Since at least WORLD WAR I, the U.S. military maintained a policy of excluding service members based on evidence of homosexual conduct or orientation (10 U.S.C. 654). Unlike the military, many graduate schools (and law schools in particular) have, over the years, maintained formal policies expressly tolerant of expanded personal factors such as sexual orientation. Of particular import in this case was the prevalence of law school policies that withheld career services/career placement services from prospective employers who discriminated on the grounds of sexual orientation as well as the more traditional protected categories such as race, gender, religion.

In *F.A.I.R. v. Rumsfeld*, No. 03-4433 (3d Circuit Court of Appeals, 2004) the two conflicting policies over homosexuality faced-off in court, when a coalition of law schools and law faculty calling itself the Forum for Academic and Institutional Rights (F.A.I.R.) filed PETITION for PRELIMINARY INJUNCTION in the U.S. District Court for the District of New Jersey to enjoin enforcement of the Solomon Amendment. The Third Circuit Court of Appeals granted injunction against enforcement of the Solomon Amendment, holding that the law violated schools' First Amendment rights of expressive association, and forcing them to engage in the expressive act of recruiting. It reasoned that Congress could not require the FORFEITURE of a constitutional right as the basis for receiving federal funds. But the U.S. Supreme Court unanimously reversed, holding that the government could deny funds to schools that did not permit recruitment; indeed, said the Court, through the U.S. Constitution's "raise and support Armies" clause (Article I, Section 8), Congress could go so far as to force schools to allow recruiting without even threatening the withholding of funds. The Court continued that the Solomon Amendment neither denied the institutions the right to speak nor required them to say anything.

Though the concept of academic freedom has traditionally been applied only to teachers, it has affected lower-court opinions involving the rights of students. Several Supreme Court cases are cited in support of such rights. In *Healy v. James* (408 U.S. 169, 92 S. Ct. 2338, 33 L. Ed. 2d 266 [1972]), the Supreme Court held that a public university may deny campus access to provably disruptive groups, but it may not deny access based on the views the students wish to express. The Supreme Court ruled in *Hazelwood School District v. Kuhlmeier* (484 U.S. 260, 108 S. Ct. 562, 98 L. Ed. 2d 592 [1988]) that a public school may censor the content of a student newspaper if the newspaper is not an entirely public forum and the reason for CENSURE is related to a legitimate educational concern. In *Board of Education of Westside Community Schools (Dist. 66) v. Mergens* (496 U.S. 226, 110 S. Ct. 2356, 110 L. Ed. 2d 191 [1990]), the Court approved the establishment of a Christian student group in a public school. The Court also held in *Mergens* that a school's refusal to permit a religious student group to meet at school and use its facilities violates the federal Equal Access Act (Education for Economic Security Act § 802, 20 U.S.C.A. § 4071 et seq. [1984]) if the school provides such access to other extracurricular student groups. And in *Morse v. Frederick* (551 U.S. 393 [2007]), the Supreme Court held that a student's free speech rights were not violated when he was suspended for displaying a "Bong Hits 4 Jesus" banner during a school authorized event. The Court distinguished the constitutional rights of students in public schools from adults in other settings, finding that students' rights could be delineated "in light of the special characteristics of the school environment."

FURTHER READINGS

"Act No. 473 (Senate Bill No. 733)." Text available online at http://www.legis.state.la.us/billdata/streamdocument.asp?did=503483; website home page: http://www.legis.state.la.us (accessed July 10, 2009).

DeGeorge, Richard T. 1997. *Academic Freedom and Tenure: Ethical Issues.* Lanham, Md.: Rowman & Littlefield.

Finkin, Matthew W., and Robert C. Post. 2009. *For the Common Good: Principles of American Academic Freedom.* New Haven, Conn.: Yale Univ. Press.

Hamilton, Neil W. 2002. *Academic Ethics: Problems and Materials on Professional Conduct and Shared Governance.* Westport, Conn.: Praeger.

Hiers, Richard H. 2002. "Institutional Academic Freedom vs. Faculty Academic Freedom in Public Colleges and Universities: A Dubious Dichotomy." *Journal of College and Univ. Law* 29 (October): 35-109.

Rahdert, Mark C. July 2007. "The Roberts Court and Academic Freedom." *Chronicle of Higher Education* 53.

CROSS REFERENCES

Censorship; Douglas, William Orville; First Amendment; Frankfurter, Felix; Freedom of Speech; Loyalty Oath; Religion; Schools and School Districts; Tenure; Warren, Earl

ACADEMIC YEAR

That period of time necessary to complete an actual course of study during a school year.

SOCIAL SECURITY benefits may terminate at the end of an ACADEMIC YEAR, or a deferment from compulsory military service may continue only during an academic year.

ACADEMY OF CRIMINAL JUSTICE SCIENCES

The Academy of Criminal Justice Sciences (ACJS) was founded in 1963 to foster professionalism in the criminal justice system by advancing the quality of education and research programs in the field. The academy seeks to enrich education and research programs in institutions of higher learning, criminal justice agencies, and agencies in related fields by improving cooperation and communication, by serving as a clearinghouse for the collection and dissemination of information produced by the programs, and by promoting the highest ethical and personal standards in criminal justice research and education. To that end, the ACJS created an *ad hoc* committee in 1995 to adopt minimum standards for the improvement of quality in criminal justice higher education. The standards, reprinted in 2001, have been widely utilized in the curricular development of associate, undergraduate and graduate degree programs. The academy also PRESENTS numerous awards for outstanding contributions by individuals in the field. The members of the academy are individual teachers, administrators, researchers, students, and practitioners.

The academy publishes the *Journal of Criminal Justice* quarterly and a directory annually. It holds annual meetings in March.

FURTHER READINGS

Academy of Criminal Justice Sciences Web site. Available online at http://www.acjs.org (accessed July 2, 2009).

"J Journal: New Writing on Justice" New York: John Jay College of Criminal Justice. Available online at http://www.conference2004.jjay.cuny.edu/jjournal/index.asp; website home page: http://www.conference2004.jjay.cuny.edu/ (accessed August 28, 2009).

ACCEDE

To consent or to agree, as to accede to another's point of view. To enter an office or to accept a position, as to accede to the presidency.

ACCELERATION

A hastening; a shortening of the time until some event takes place.

A person who has the right to take possession of property at some future time may have that right accelerated if the present holder loses his or her LEGAL RIGHT to the property. If a LIFE ESTATE fails for any reason, the remainder is accelerated.

The principle of acceleration can be applied when it becomes clear that one party to a contract is not going to perform his or her obligations. ANTICIPATORY REPUDIATION, or the possibility of future breach, makes it possible to move the right to remedies back to the time of repudiation rather than to wait for the time when performance would be due and an actual breach would occur.

ACCELERATION CLAUSE

The provision in a credit agreement, such as a mortgage, note, bond, or deed of trust, that allows the lender to require immediate payment of all money due if certain conditions occur before the time that payment would otherwise be due.

The agreement may call for ACCELERATION whenever there is a default of any important obligation, such as nonpayment of principal or interest, or the failure to pay insurance premiums.

ACCEPTANCE

An express act or implication by conduct that manifests assent to the terms of an offer in a manner invited or required by the offer so that a binding contract is formed. The exercise of power conferred by an offer by performance of some act. The act of a person to whom something is offered or tendered by another, whereby the offeree demonstrates through an act invited by the offer an intention of retaining the subject of the offer.

In the law of contracts, acceptance is one person's compliance with the terms of an offer made by another. Acceptance occurs in the law of insurance when an insurer agrees to receive a person's application for insurance and to issue a policy protecting the person against certain risks, such as fire or THEFT. When a person who is offered a gift by someone keeps the gift, this indicates his or her acceptance of it.

Acceptance also occurs when a bank pays a check written by a customer who has a checking account with that bank.

In business dealings between merchants, which is governed by the law of sales, a buyer demonstrates his or her acceptance of goods that are not exactly what he or she had ordered from the seller by telling the seller that he or she will keep the goods even though they are not what was ordered; by failing to reject the goods; or by doing something to the goods inconsistent with the seller's ownership of them, such as selling the goods to consumers of the buyer's store.

Types of Acceptance

An acceptance may be conditional, express, or implied.

Conditional Acceptance A conditional acceptance, sometimes called a QUALIFIED ACCEPTANCE, occurs when a person to whom an offer has been made tells the offeror that he or she is willing to agree to the offer provided that some changes are made in its terms or that some condition or event occurs. This type of acceptance operates as a COUNTEROFFER. A counteroffer must be accepted by the original offeror before a contract can be established between the parties.

Another type of conditional acceptance occurs when a drawee promises to pay a draft upon the fulfillment of a condition, such as a shipment of goods reaching its destination on the date specified in the contract.

Express Acceptance An express acceptance occurs when a person clearly and explicitly agrees to an offer or agrees to pay a draft that is presented for payment.

Implied Acceptance An implied acceptance is one that is not directly stated but is demonstrated by any acts indicating a person's assent to the proposed bargain. An implied acceptance occurs when a shopper selects an item in a supermarket and pays the cashier for it. The shopper's conduct indicates that he or she has agreed to the supermarket owner's offer to sell the item for the price stated on it.

FURTHER READINGS

Chirelstein, Marvin A. 2006. *Concepts and Case Analysis in the Law of Contracts.* 5th ed. Eagan, MN: West.

Perillo, Joseph M. 2009. *Calamari and Perillo's Hornbook on Contracts.* 6th ed. Eagan, MN: West.

"Silence as Acceptance in Contracts Lawyers." 2009. *LegalMatch* Website. Available online at http://www.legalmatch.com/law-library/article/silence-as-acceptance-in-contracts.html; website home page: http://www.legalmatch.com (accessed August 28, 2009).

ACCESS

Freedom of approach or communication; or the means, power, or opportunity of approaching,

Acceleration Clause

PROMISSORY NOTE
INSTALLMENT - WITH ACCELERATION CLAUSE

_____
[city, state, date]

FOR VALUE RECEIVED, WE, THE UNDERSIGNED, jointly and severally promise to pay, in lawful money of the United States of America,

to the order of _____ at _____ ,
[name of lender] [address of lender]

(_____) Dollars in installments as follows:
[amount]

_____ on _____ , and _____ successive payments
[amount of payment] [date] [number]

of _____ beginning on _____ together with a delinquency charge on
[amount] [date of payment]

each installment in default for _____ days in an amount equal to _____ percent of such installment but not

less than $_____ .

In the event of default in the payment of any of the said installments or said interest when due as herein provided, time being of the essence hereof, the holder of this note may, without notice or demand, declare the entire principal sum then unpaid immediately due and payable.

The holder of this note may, with or without notice to any of us, cause additional parties to be added hereto, or release any party hereto, or revise, extend, or renew the note, or extend the time for making any installment provided for herein, or accept any installment in advance, all without affecting the liability of us, or any of us, hereon.

If suit be commenced on said note, the parties hereto jointly and severally agree to pay to the holder of said note a reasonable attorney fee.

The borrower agrees to pay a reasonable collection charge should collection be referred to a collection agency or to the payee`s collection facilities.

The parties hereto, jointly and severally, hereby waive presentment, demand, protest, notice of dishonor and/or protest and notice of nonpayment; the right, if any, to the benefit of, or to direct the application of, any security hypothecated to the holder until all indebtedness of the borrower to the holder shall have been paid; the right to require the holder to proceed against the borrower, or to pursue any other remedy in the holder's power; and agree that the holder may proceed against us directly and independently of the borrower, and that the cessation of liability of the borrower for any reason, other than full payment, or any revision, renewal, extension, forebearance, change of rate of interest, or acceptance, release or substitution of security, or any impairment or suspension of the holder's remedies or rights against the borrower, shall not in anywise affect the liability of any of the parties hereto.

The parties hereto hereby authorize _____ to date this note as of the day when the loan
[payee]

evidenced hereby is made and to complete this note in any other particular according to the terms of the said loan.

It is agreed that if the parties hereto, or any of them at any time fail in business or become insolvent, or commit an act of bankruptcy, or if any deposit account or other property of the parties hereto, or any of them, be attempted to be obtained or held by writ of execution, garnishment, attachment, or other legal process, or if any assessment for taxes against the parties hereto, or any of them, other than taxes on real property, is made by the federal or state government, or any department thereof, or if the parties hereto fail to notify you of any material change in their financial condition, then, and in such case all of the obligations of the parties hereto to you, or held by you, shall at your option immediately become due and payable without demand or notice.

Signatures   Address

_____   _____
Borrower

_____   _____
Co-Maker

communicating, or passing to and from. Sometimes importing the occurrence of sexual intercourse; otherwise as importing opportunity of communication for that purpose as between HUSBAND AND WIFE.

In real property law, the term access denotes the right vested in the owner of the land that adjoins a road or other highway to go and return from his own land to the highway without *obstruction. Access to property does not necessarily carry with it possession.*

For purposes of establishing element of access by defendant in COPYRIGHT *infringement action, access is ordinarily defined as opportunity to copy.*

Prisoners are entitled to have access to court. PRISON officials cannot prevent prisoners from filing papers or appearing in court even if they honestly think that such prevention would help them maintain discipline and good order.

Owners of real property are entitled to some means of access to their property from a road or highway. They do not necessarily need to own a corridor of land from their property to the nearest road, but they may claim an easement of access.

In a PATERNITY SUIT, access means the opportunity to have had sexual relations. When there is a question about who is the father of a certain child, it is appropriate for a court to determine which man had access to the mother around the estimated time of conception. A man charged with being the father of an illegitimate child may plead the defense of multiple access—that the mother had several lovers at the time of conception.

ACCESSION

Coming into possession of a right or office; increase; augmentation; addition.

The right to all that one's own property produces, whether that property be movable or immovable; and the right to that which is united to it by accession, either naturally or artificially. The right to own things that become a part of something already owned.

A principle derived from the CIVIL LAW, *by which the owner of property becomes entitled to all that it produces, and to all that is added or united to it, either naturally or artificially (that is, by the labor or skill of another) even where such addition extends to a change of form or materials; and by which, on the other hand, the possessor of property becomes entitled to it, as against the original owner, where the addition made to it by skill and labor is of greater value than the property itself, or where the change effected in its form is so great as to render it impossible to restore it to its original shape.*

Generally, accession signifies acquisition of title to PERSONAL PROPERTY *by bestowing labor on it that converts it into an entirely different thing or by incorporation of property into a union with other property.*

The commencement or inauguration of a sovereign's reign.

For example, a person who owns property along a river also takes ownership of any additional land that builds up along the riverbank. This right may extend to additions that result from the work or skill of another person. The buyer of a car who fails to make scheduled payments cannot get back his new spark plugs after the car is repossessed because they have become a part of the whole car. The principle of accession does not necessarily apply, however, where the addition has substantially improved the value and changed the character of the property, as when by mistake someone else's grapes were made into wine or someone else's clay made into bricks. In such cases, the original owner might recover only the value of the raw material rather than take ownership of the finished product.

In the context of a treaty, accession may be gained in either of two ways: (1) the new member nation may be formally accepted by all the nations already parties to the treaty; or (2) the new nation may simply bind itself to the obligations already existing in the treaty. Frequently, a treaty will expressly provide that certain nations or categories of nations may ACCEDE. In some cases, the parties to a treaty will invite one or more nations to accede to the treaty.

ACCESSORY

Aiding or contributing in a secondary way or assisting in or contributing to as a subordinate.

In CRIMINAL LAW, *contributing to or aiding in the commission of a crime. One who, without being present at the commission of an offense, becomes guilty of such offense, not as a chief actor, but as a participant, as by command, advice, instigation, or concealment; either before or after the fact or commission.*

One who aids, abets, commands, or counsels another in the commission of a crime.

In common law, an accessory could not be found guilty unless the actual PERPETRATOR was convicted. In most U.S. jurisdictions, however, an accessory can be convicted even if the principal actor is not arrested or is acquitted. The prosecution must establish that the accessory in some way instigated, furthered, or concealed the crime. Typically, PUNISHMENT for

Emergency workers attend to a woman involved in a single-car accident. Crashes such as this one are considered accidents unless a driver intentionally causes the crash.

AP IMAGES

a convicted accessory is not as severe as that for the perpetrator.

An accessory must knowingly promote or contribute to the crime. In other words, she or he must aid or encourage the offense deliberately, not accidentally. The accessory may withdraw from the crime by denouncing the plans, refusing to assist with the crime, contacting the police, or trying to stop the crime from occurring.

An *accessory before the fact* is someone behind the scenes who orders a crime or helps another person commit it. Many jurisdictions now refer to accessories before the fact as parties to the crime or even accomplices. This substitution of terms can be confusing because accessories are fundamentally different from accomplices. Strictly speaking, whereas an ACCOMPLICE may be present at the crime scene, an accessory may not. Also, an accomplice generally is considered to be as guilty of the crime as the perpetrator, whereas an accessory has traditionally received a lighter punishment.

An *accessory after the fact* is someone who knows that a crime has occurred but nonetheless helps to conceal it. In the early twenty-first century, this action is often termed obstructing justice or harboring a fugitive.

An infamous accessory after the fact was Dr. Samuel A. Mudd, the physician and Confederate sympathizer who set John Wilkes Booth's leg after it was broken when the assassin jumped from President Abraham Lincoln's box at Ford Theater. Despite Mudd's protestation of innocence, he was tried and convicted as an accessory after the fact in Lincoln's MURDER. He was sentenced to life IMPRISONMENT at Fort

Jefferson in the Dry Tortugas off Key West, Florida. President ANDREW JOHNSON pardoned Mudd in 1869, and the U.S. Congress gave him an official PARDON in 1979.

FURTHER READINGS

Berg, Alan. 1996. "Accessory Liability for Breach of Trust." *Modern Law Review* 59 (May).

Blakey, Robert G., and Kevin P. Roddy. 1996. "Reflections on Reves v. Ernst & Young: Its Meaning and Impact on Substantive, Accessory, Aiding Abetting and Conspiracy Liability under RICO." *American Criminal Law Review* 33.

Huett, Lisa. 2001. "Could You Be an Accessory? Uncertainty and Risk For Lawyers." *Law Institute Journal* 75 (March).

ACCIDENT

The word accident *is derived from the Latin verb* accidere, *signifying "fall upon, befall, happen, chance." In its most commonly accepted meaning, or in its ordinary or popular sense, the word may be defined as meaning: some sudden and unexpected event taking place without expectation, upon the instant, rather than something that continues, progresses or develops; something happening by chance; something unforeseen, unexpected, unusual, extraordinary, or phenomenal, taking place not according to the usual course of things or events, out of the range of ordinary calculations; that which exists or occurs abnormally, or an uncommon occurrence. The word may be employed as denoting a calamity, casualty, catastrophe, disaster, an undesirable or unfortunate happening; any unexpected personal injury resulting from any unlooked for mishap or occurrence; any unpleasant or unfortunate occurrence that causes injury, loss, suffering, or death; some untoward occurrence aside from the usual course of events. An event that takes place without one's foresight or expectation; an undesigned, sudden, and unexpected event.*

Accident is not always a precise legal term. It may be used generally in reference to various types of mishaps, or it may be given a technical meaning that applies when used in a certain statute or kind of case. Where it is used in a general sense, no particular significance can be attached to it. Where it is precisely defined, as in a statute, that definition strictly controls any decision about whether a certain event covered by that statute was in fact an accident.

In its most limited sense, the word *accident* is used only for events that occur without the intervention of a human being. This kind of accident also may be called an ACT OF GOD. It is an event that no person caused or could have prevented—such as a tornado, a tidal wave, or an ice storm. An accident insurance policy can by its terms be limited to coverage only for this type of accident. Damage by hail to a field of wheat may be considered such an accident.

A policy of insurance, by its very nature, covers only accidents and not intentionally caused injuries. That principle explains why courts will read some exceptions into any insurance policy, whether or not they are expressly stated. For example, life insurance generally will not compensate for a SUICIDE, and ordinary automobile insurance will not cover damages sustained when the owner is drag racing.

Accident insurance policies frequently insure not only against an act of God but also for accidents caused by a person's carelessness. An insured homeowner will expect coverage, for example, if someone drowns in his or her pool, even though the accident might have occurred because someone in the family left the gate open.

Not every unintended event is an accident for which insurance benefits can be paid; all the circumstances in a particular case must first be considered. For example, a policeman who waded into a surging crowd of forty or fifty fighting teenagers and then experienced a heart attack was found to have suffered from an accident. In another case, a man who was shot when he was found in bed with another man's wife was also found to have died in an accident because death is not the usual or expected result of ADULTERY. However, the family of another man was not allowed to collect insurance benefits when he was shot after starting a fight with a knife. In that case, the court ruled that DEADLY FORCE was a predictable response to a life-threatening attack, whether the instigator actually anticipated it or not.

Different states apply different standards when determining if an accident justifies payment of benefits under workers' compensation. Some states strictly limit benefits to events that clearly are accidents. They will permit payment when a sudden and unexpected strain causes an immediate injury during the course of work but they will not permit payment when an injury gradually results from prolonged assaults on the body. Under this approach, a worker who is asphyxiated by a lethal dose of carbon monoxide when he goes into a blast furnace to make repairs would be deemed to have suffered in an accident. However, a worker who

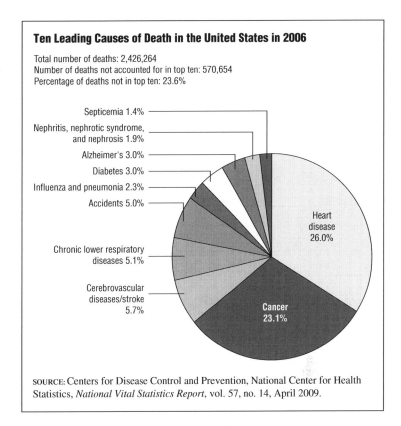

Ten Leading Causes of Death in the United States in 2006

Total number of deaths: 2,426,264
Number of deaths not accounted for in top ten: 570,654
Percentage of deaths not in top ten: 23.6%

Septicemia 1.4%
Nephritis, nephrotic syndrome, and nephrosis 1.9%
Alzheimer's 3.0%
Diabetes 3.0%
Influenza and pneumonia 2.3%
Accidents 5.0%
Chronic lower respiratory diseases 5.1%
Cerebrovascular diseases/stroke 5.7%
Heart disease 26.0%
Cancer 23.1%

SOURCE: Centers for Disease Control and Prevention, National Center for Health Statistics, *National Vital Statistics Report*, vol. 57, no. 14, April 2009.

contracts lung cancer after years of exposure to irritating dust in a factory could not CLAIM to have been injured in an accident. Because of the remedial purpose of workers' compensation schemes, many states are liberal in allowing compensation. In one state, a woman whose existing arthritic condition was aggravated when she took a job stuffing giblets into partially frozen chickens on a conveyor belt was allowed to collect workers' compensation benefits.

Insurance policies may set limits to the amount of benefits recoverable for one accident. A certain automobile insurance policy allowed a maximum of only $200 to compensate for damaged clothing or luggage in the event of an accident. When luggage was stolen from the insured automobile, however, a court ruled that the event was not an accident and the maximum did not apply. The owner was allowed to recover the full value of the lost property.

Sometimes the duration of an accident must be determined. For example, if a drunken driver hit one car and then continued driving until he or she collided with a truck, a court might have to determine whether the two victims will share the maximum amount of money payable under the driver's LIABILITY insurance policy or

ILLUSTRATION BY GGS CREATIVE RESOURCES. REPRODUCED BY PERMISSION OF GALE, A PART OF CENGAGE LEARNING.

whether each will collect the full maximum as a result of a separate accident.

CROSS REFERENCES

Automobiles "No-Fault Automobile Insurance" (In Focus); Automobiles "What to Do If You Are in an Auto Accident" (Sidebar); Insurance.

ACCIDENTAL DEATH BENEFIT

A provision of a life insurance policy stating that if the insured—the person whose life has been insured—dies in an accident, the beneficiary of the policy—the person to whom its proceeds are payable—will receive twice the face value of the policy.

The insurance company that is liable for the payment of such a benefit will conduct a thorough investigation into the cause of death of the insured person before paying the CLAIM.

Another name for an ACCIDENTAL DEATH BENEFIT is a DOUBLE INDEMNITY clause.

ACCIDENTAL KILLING

A death caused by a lawful act done under the reasonable belief that no harm was likely to result.

Accidental killing is different from INVOLUNTARY MANSLAUGHTER, which causes death by an UNLAWFUL act or a lawful act done in an unlawful way.

The COMMON LAW of crimes distinguished two types of accidental killings: (1) accidental killings resulting from unlawful acts of violence not directed at the victim were punishable as MANSLAUGHTER (killings resulting from unlawful acts directed at the victim were punishable as MURDER); and (2) accidental killings resulting from lawful acts of violence were excusable as HOMICIDE *by misadventure.*

For example, suppose that the DEFENDANT killed an innocent bystander while carrying out an ASSAULT, BATTERY, or other violent crime against the intended victim. The defendant told police that he intended to injure the victim by hitting him with a club but instead struck the bystander on the skull and killed him. The defendant could be prosecuted for manslaughter under the common law of crimes.

Now suppose that the defendant was lawfully defending himself or his property from attack, and in the process killed an innocent bystander. The defendant told police that lethal force was necessary to thwart an attack upon his person, and he tried to shoot the attacker but instead killed a nearby pedestrian, who had nothing to do with the attack. The common law would have treated the bystander's death as an excusable accidental killing, so long as reasonable grounds existed for the defendant's belief that lethal force was necessary for self-defense.

Although most states have abolished the common law of crimes, some of the concepts underlying the common law distinctions between manslaughter and accidental killings continue to appear in statutory classifications of manslaughter.

Most states recognize at least two classes of manslaughter, voluntary and involuntary. In these states voluntary manslaughter is defined as act of murder reduced to manslaughter because of EXTENUATING CIRCUMSTANCES such as adequate PROVOCATION (for example, murder committed in the *heat of passion*) or DIMINISHED CAPACITY. Involuntary manslaughter is defined in these states as a homicide that is committed with CRIMINAL NEGLIGENCE or during the commission of a crime that is not included within the FELONY-MURDER RULE but for which the prosecution has no proof that the defendant intended to kill the victim or do grievous bodily harm.

Accidental killings that do not result from the defendant's criminal NEGLIGENCE and do not occur during the commission of a crime are not criminal offenses in these jurisdictions. Some jurisdictions expressly classify accidental killings as excusable or justifiable homicides, such as the state of California, which provides that "[h]omicide is excusable . . . [w]hen committed by ACCIDENT and misfortune, or in doing any other lawful act by lawful means, with usual and ordinary caution, and without any unlawful intent" (CA PENAL § 195). Other states simply omit this class of homicide from their statutes defining prosecutable offenses.

CROSS REFERENCES

Common Law; Diminished Capacity; Homicide; Involuntary Manslaughter; Murder.

ACCIDENTAL VEIN

An imprecise term that refers generally to a continuous body of a mineral or mineralized rock filling a seam other than the principal vein that led to the discovery of the mining claim or location.

CROSS REFERENCES

Mine and Mineral Law.

ACCIDENTS OF NAVIGATION

Mishaps that are peculiar to travel by sea or to normal navigation; accidents caused at sea by the action of the elements, rather than by a failure to exercise good handling, working, or navigating of a ship. Such accidents could not have been avoided by the exercise of nautical skill or prudence.

CROSS REFERENCES

Admiralty and Maritime Law; Navigable Rivers.

ACCOMMODATION ENDORSEMENT

The act of a third person—the accommodation party—in writing his or her name on the back of a commercial paper without any consideration, but merely to benefit the person to whom the paper is payable or to enable the person who made the document—the maker—to obtain money or credit on it.

An accommodation endorsement is a loan of the endorser's credit up to the face amount of the paper.

ACCOMMODATION PAPER

A type of commercial paper (such as a bill or note promising that money will be paid to someone) that is signed by another person—the accommodation party—as a favor to the promisor—the accommodated party—so that credit may be extended to him or her on the basis of the paper.

An accommodation paper guarantees that the money lent will be repaid by the ACCOMMODATION PARTY on the date specified in the COMMERCIAL PAPER if the accommodated party fails to repay it. A lender often uses an accommodation paper when the person who is seeking a loan is considered a poor credit risk, such as a person who has a history of being delinquent in the payment of installment loans. By having a person who is a good credit risk cosign the PROMISSORY NOTE, the lender's financial interests are protected.

An accommodation bill and an accommodation note are two types of commercial papers.

ACCOMMODATION PARTY

One who signs a commercial paper for the purpose of lending his or her name and credit to another party to the document—the accommodated party—to help that party obtain a loan or an extension of credit.

A person wanting to obtain a car loan, for example, may offer a finance company a PROMISSORY NOTE for the amount of the requested

---

Accommodation Note

Agreement of an Accommodation Party to Modifications in an Accommodation Note

This agreement is made between _____ [*name of the holder of the note*] ("holder")

and _____ [*name of the accommodation party*] ("accommodation party").

On [*date of execution*], _____ [*name of maker*] ("maker"), of _____

_____ [*address of maker*] executed and issued a promissory note ("note") to the holder as payee,

by which the maker promised to pay to the order of the holder _____ [*amount*] [*include any other specific payment terms, including days after the date of execution*].

On [*date*], the accommodation party signed the note as co-maker in order to accommodate the maker at the request of the maker.

The accommodation party and the holder agree that the holder may modify the terms of the note without notice to or the consent of the accommodation party.

_____
[*Signature of holder*], holder

_____
[*Signature of Accommodation Party*], accommodation party

A sample accomodation note

loan, promising to repay the amount over a number of years. If the company does not consider the person a good credit risk (one who will be able to repay the loan), it will request that someone else sign the note to ensure that the company will be repaid. Such a person may be an accommodation endorser, because he or she endorses the note after it has been completed, or an accommodation maker, because he or she must sign the note with the accommodation party.

An accommodation party is liable to the person or business that extended credit to the accommodation party, but not to the accommodated party. The accommodation party is liable for the amount specified on the ACCOMMODATION PAPER. If an accommodation party repays the debt, he or she can seek reimbursement from the accommodated party.

ACCOMPANY

To go along with; to go with or to attend as a companion or associate.

A motor vehicle statute may require beginning drivers or drivers under a certain age to be accompanied by a licensed adult driver whenever operating an automobile. To comply with such a law, the licensed adult must supervise the beginner and be seated in such a way as to be able to render advice and assistance.

ACCOMPLICE

One who knowingly, voluntarily, and with common intent unites with the principal offender in the commission of a crime. One who is in some way concerned or associated in commission of crime; partaker of guilt; one who aids or assists, or is an accessory. One who is guilty of complicity in crime charged, either by being present and aiding or abetting in it, or having advised and encouraged it, though absent from place when it was committed, though mere presence, acquiescence, or silence, in the absence of a duty to act, is not enough, no matter how reprehensible it may be, to constitute one an accomplice. One is liable as an accomplice to the crime of another if he or she gave assistance or encouragement or failed to perform a legal duty to prevent it with the intent thereby to promote or facilitate commission of the crime.

An ACCOMPLICE may assist or encourage the principal offender with the intent to have the crime committed, the same as the chief actor.

An accomplice may or may not be present when the crime is actually committed. However, without sharing the criminal intent, one who is merely present when a crime occurs and stands by silently is not an accomplice, no matter how reprehensible his or her inaction.

Some crimes are so defined that certain persons cannot be charged as accomplices even when their conduct significantly aids the chief offender. For example, a businessperson who yields to the EXTORTION demands of a racketeer or a parent who pays ransom to a kidnapper may be unwise, but neither is a principal in the commission of the crimes. Even a victim may unwittingly create a perfect opportunity for the commission of a crime but cannot be considered an accomplice because he or she lacks a criminal intent.

An accomplice may supply money, guns, or supplies. In one case, an accomplice provided his own blood to be poured on selective service files. The driver of the getaway car, a lookout, or a person who entices the victim or distracts possible WITNESSES is an accomplice.

An accomplice can be convicted even if the person that he or she aids or encourages is not. He or she is usually subject to the same degree of punishment as the principal offender. In the 1982 decision of *Enmund v. Florida,* 458 U.S. 782, 102 S. Ct. 3368, 73 L. Ed. 2d 1140, the SUPREME COURT OF THE UNITED STATES ruled that the death PENALTY could not be constitutionally imposed upon an accomplice to a felony-murder, a crime leading to MURDER, if he or she had no intention to, or did not, kill the victim. Earl Enmund drove the getaway car from a ROBBERY that resulted in the murder of its victims, an elderly married couple. Although Enmund remained in the car during the robbery and consequent killings and the trial record did not establish that he intended to facilitate or participate in a murder, the trial court sentenced him to death, along with the persons who actually killed the victims, upon his conviction for robbery in the first degree. In overturning the decision, the Supreme Court reasoned that to condemn such a DEFENDANT to death violated the Eighth and Fourteenth Amendments to the CONSTITUTION, which prohibited CRUEL AND UNUSUAL PUNISHMENT in state prosecutions. The death penalty was an excessive punishment in light of the "criminal culpability" of this accomplice.

ACCOMPLICE WITNESS

A witness to a crime who, either as principal, accomplice, or accessory, was connected with the crime by unlawful act or omission on his or her part, transpiring either before, at time of, or after commission of the offense, and whether or not he or she was present and participated in the crime.

Generally, there can be no conviction solely on the basis of what is said by an accomplice witness; there must be evidence from an unrelated source to corroborate the witness's TESTIMONY.

ACCORD

An agreement that settles a dispute, generally requiring an obligee to accept a compromise or satisfaction from the obligor with something less than what was originally demanded. Also often used synonymously with treaty.

ACCORD AND SATISFACTION

A method of discharging a claim whereby the parties agree to give and accept something in settlement of the claim and perform the agreement, the accord *being the agreement and the* satisfaction *its execution or performance, and it is a new contract substituted for an old contract which is thereby discharged, or for an obligation or cause of action which is settled, and must have all of the elements of a valid contract.*

To constitute an accord and satisfaction, there must have been a genuine dispute that is settled by a meeting of the minds with an intent to compromise. Where there is an actual controversy, an ACCORD and satisfaction may be used to settle it. The controversy may be founded on contract or tort. It can arise from a collision of motor vehicles, a failure to deliver oranges ordered and paid for, or a refusal to finish constructing an office building, etc.

In former times, courts recognized an accord and satisfaction only when the amount of the controversy was not in dispute. Otherwise, the RESOLUTION had to be by COMPROMISE AND SETTLEMENT. The technical distinction is no longer made, however, and a compromise of amount can properly be part of an accord and satisfaction. The amount, whether disputed or not, is usually monetary, as when a pedestrian claims $10,000 in DAMAGES from the driver who struck him. The amount can be a variety of other things, however, as when a homeowner claims that she ordered a swimming pool thirty-six feet long rather than thirty-five feet or when an employee insists that he is entitled to eleven rather than ten days of vacation during the rest of the calendar year.

An accord and satisfaction can be made only by persons who have the legal capacity to enter into a contract. A SETTLEMENT is not binding on an insane person, for example; and an infant may have the right to disaffirm the contract. Therefore, a person, such as a guardian, acting on behalf of a person incapable of contracting for himself or herself may make an accord and satisfaction for the person committed to his or her charge, but the law may require that the guardian's actions be supervised by a court. An executor or administrator may bind an estate; a TRUSTEE can accept an accord and satisfaction for a trust; and an officer can negotiate a settlement for a corporation.

A third person may give something in satisfaction of a party's debt. In such a case, an accord and satisfaction is effected if the creditor accepts the offer and the debtor authorizes, participates in, or later agrees to, the transaction.

For example, a widower has an automobile accident but is mentally unable to cope with a lawsuit because his wife has just died. He gratefully accepts the offer of a close family friend to talk to the other driver, who has been threatening a lawsuit. The friend convinces the other driver that both drivers are at fault to some extent. The friend offers to pay the other driver $500 in damages in exchange for a written statement that she will not make any claim against the widower for damages resulting from the accident. The family friend and the other driver each sign a copy of the statement for the other, and when the payment is made, the accord and satisfaction is complete. If the other driver then sues the widower for more money on account of the accident, the widower could show that he agreed to let his friend negotiate an accord and satisfaction, and the court would deny relief.

An accord and satisfaction is a contract, and all the essential elements of a contract must be present. The agreement must include a definite offer of settlement and an

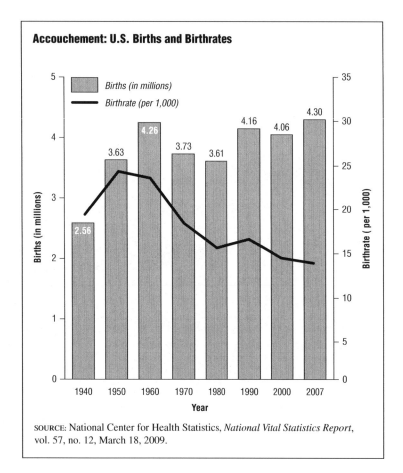

Accouchement: U.S. Births and Birthrates

Births (in millions)

Birthrate (per 1,000)

SOURCE: National Center for Health Statistics, *National Vital Statistics Report*, vol. 57, no. 12, March 18, 2009.

unconditional acceptance of the offer according to its terms. It must be final and definite, closing the matter it covers and leaving nothing unsettled or open to question. The agreement may call for full payment or some compromise and it need not be based on an earlier agreement of the parties. It does not necessarily have to be in writing unless it comes WITHIN THE STATUTE of frauds.

Unless there are matters intentionally left outside the accord and satisfaction, it settles the entire controversy between the parties. It extinguishes all the obligations arising out of the underlying contract or tort. Where only one of two or more parties on one side settles, this ordinarily operates to discharge all of them. The reason for this is the rule that there should be only one satisfaction for a single injury or wrong. This rule does not apply where the satisfaction is neither given nor accepted with the intention that it settle the entire matter.

An accord without satisfaction generally means nothing. With a full satisfaction, the accord can be used to defeat any further claims by either party unless it was reached by FRAUD, DURESS, or MUTUAL MISTAKE.

An accord and satisfaction can be distinguished from other forms of resolving legal disputes. A payment or performance means that the original obligations were met. A release is a formal relinquishment of the right to enforce the original obligations and not necessarily a compromise, as in accord and satisfaction. An ARBITRATION is a settlement of the dispute by some outside person whose determination of an award is voluntarily accepted by the parties. A COMPOSITION WITH CREDITORS is very much like an accord but has elements not required for an accord and satisfaction. It is used only for disputes between a debtor and a certain number of his or her creditors, while an accord and satisfaction can be used to settle any kind of controversy—whether arising from contract or tort—and ordinarily involves only two parties. Although distinctions have occasionally been drawn between an accord and satisfaction and a compromise and settlement, the two terms are often used interchangeably. A NOVATION is a kind of accord in which the promise alone, rather than full performance, is satisfaction, and is accepted as a binding resolution of the dispute.

FURTHER READINGS

Dolson, Andrew J. 1995. "Accord and Satisfaction under Article 3A of the UCC: A Trap for the Unwary." *Virginia Bar Association Journal* 21 (winter).

Floyd, Michael D. 1994. "How Much Satisfaction Should You Expect from an Accord? The U.C.C. Section 3-311 Approach." *Loyola Univ. of Chicago Law Journal* 26 (fall).

Veltri, Stephen C., Marina I. Adams, and Paul S. Turner. 2004. "Payments." *Business Lawyer* 59.

ACCOUCHEMENT

The act of giving birth to a child.

The fact of accouchement may be proved by the direct TESTIMONY of someone who was present, such as a midwife or a physician, at the time of birth. It may be significant in proving parentage; for example, where there is some question about who is entitled to inherit property from an elderly person who died leaving only distant relatives.

ACCOUNT

A written list of transactions, noting money owed and money paid; a detailed statement of mutual demands arising out of a contract or a fiduciary relationship.

An account can simply list payments, losses, sales, debits, credits, and other monetary transactions, or it may go further and show a balance or the results of comparing opposite transactions, like purchases and sales. Businesspersons keep accounts; attorneys may keep escrow accounts; and executors must keep accounts that record transactions in administering an estate.

ACCOUNT, ACTION ON

A civil lawsuit maintained under the common law to recover money owed on an account.

The *action on account* was one of the ancient FORMS OF ACTION. Dating back to the thirteenth century, it offered a remedy for the breach of obligations owed by fiduciaries. Originally, the action allowed lords to recover money wrongfully withheld by the bailiffs of their manors, whom they appointed to collect fines and rents. Later, statutes extended the right so that lawsuits could be brought against persons who were required to act primarily for someone else's benefit, such as guardians and partners. Eventually, the action withered away because its procedure was too cumbersome, and fiduciaries came under the jurisdiction of the special court of the king, called the CHANCERY.

An action on account is different from a modern-day ACCOUNTING, which is a settling of accounts or a determination of transactions affecting two parties, often when one party asks a court to order the other party to account.

ACCOUNT PAYABLE

A debt owed by a business that arises in the normal course of its dealings, that has not been replaced by a note from another debtor, and that is not necessarily due or past due.

Bills for materials received or obligations on an OPEN ACCOUNT may be accounts payable. This kind of LIABILITY usually arises from a purchase of merchandise, materials, or supplies.

ACCOUNT RECEIVABLE

A debt owed by a business that arises in the normal course of dealings and is not supported by a negotiable instrument.

The charge accounts of a department store are accounts receivable, but income from investments usually is not. Accounts receivable generally arise from sales or service transactions. They are not necessarily due or past due.

Insurance may be purchased to protect against the risk of being unable to collect on accounts receivable if records are damaged or lost.

ACCOUNT RENDERED

A statement of transactions made out by a creditor and presented to the debtor.

After the debtor has examined the account and accepted it, an account rendered becomes an ACCOUNT STATED.

ACCOUNT STATED

An amount that accurately states money due to a creditor; a debt arising out of transactions between a debtor and creditor that has been reduced to a balance due for the items of account.

A creditor agrees to accept and a debtor agrees that a specific sum is a true and exact statement of the amount he or she owes. The debtor may agree in words to pay the amount, or it may be understood that the debtor has accepted the account stated by failing to object within a certain period of time.

ACCOUNTANT

A person who has the requisite skill and experience in establishing and maintaining accurate financial records for an individual or a business. The duties of an accountant may include designing and controlling systems of records, auditing books, and preparing financial statements. An accountant may give tax advice and prepare tax returns.

A *public accountant* renders ACCOUNTING or auditing services for a number of employees, each of whom pays the accountant a fee for services rendered. He or she does more than just BOOKKEEPING but does not generally have all the qualifications of a certified public accountant.

A *certified public accountant* is one who has earned a license in his or her state that attests to a high degree of skill, training, and experience. In addition to passing an accounting examination, a candidate must have the proper business experience, education, and moral character in order to qualify for the license. The letters CPA are commonly used and generally recognized to be the abbreviation for the title Certified Public Accountant.

The practice of accounting is a highly skilled and technical profession that affects public WELFARE. It is entirely appropriate for the state to regulate the profession by means of a licensing system for accountants. Some states do not permit anyone to practice accounting except certified public accountants, but other states use the title to recognize the more distinguished skills of a CPA while permitting others to practice as public accountants. All states limit the use of the title and the initials to those who are licensed as certified public accountants.

All accountants are held to high standards of skill in issuing professional opinions. They can be sued for MALPRACTICE if performance of their duties falls below standards for the profession.

ACCOUNTING

Accounting is a system of recording or settling accounts in financial transactions and includes methods of determining income and expenses for tax and other financial purposes. Accounting is also one of the remedies available for enforcing a right or redressing a wrong asserted in a lawsuit.

Various accounting methods may be employed. The *accrual method* shows expenses incurred and income earned for a given period of time whether or not such expenses and income have been actually paid or received by that time. The *cash method* records income and expenses only when monies have actually been received or paid out. The *completed contract method* reports gains or losses on certain long-term contracts. GROSS INCOME and expenses are recognized under this method in the tax year in which the contract is completed. The *installment method* of accounting is a method used by regulated utilities to calculate DEPRECIATION for INCOME TAX purposes.

The *cost method* of accounting records the value of assets at their actual cost, and the *fair value method* uses the present MARKET VALUE for the recorded value of assets. *Price level accounting* is a modern method of valuing assets in a FINANCIAL STATEMENT by showing their current value in comparison to the gross national product.

Where a court orders an accounting, the party against whom judgment is entered must file a complete statement with the court that accounts for his or her administration of the affairs at issue in the case. An accounting is proper for showing how an executor has managed the ESTATE of a deceased person or

for disclosing how a partner has been handling PARTNERSHIP business.

An accounting was one of the ancient English remedies available in courts of equity. The regular officers of the CHANCERY, who represented the king in hearing disputes that could not be taken to courts of law, were able to serve as auditors and work through complex accounts when necessary. The chancery had the power to discover hidden assets in the hands of the DEFENDANT. Later, courts of law began to recognize and enforce regular contract claims, as actions in ASSUMPSIT, and the courts of equity were justified in compelling an accounting only when the courts at law could not give relief. A PLAINTIFF could ask for an accounting in equity when the complexity of the accounts in the case made it too difficult for a jury to resolve or when a TRUSTEE or other FIDUCIARY was charged with violating a position of trust.

In the early twenty-first century, courts in the United States generally have jurisdiction both at law and in equity. They have the power to order an accounting when necessary to determine the relative rights of the parties. An accounting may be appropriate whenever the defendant has violated an obligation to protect the plaintiff's interests. For example, an accounting may be ordered to settle disputes when a partnership is breaking up, when an HEIR believes that the executor of an estate has sold off assets for less than their FAIR MARKET VALUE, or when shareholders CLAIM that directors of a corporation have appropriated for themselves a business opportunity that should have profited the corporation.

An accounting may also be an appropriate remedy against someone who has committed a wrong against the plaintiff and should not be allowed to profit from it. For example, a bank teller who embezzles money and makes a huge profit by investing it in mutual funds may be ordered to account for all the money taken and the earnings made from it. A businessperson who sells a product as that of a more popular manufacturer might have to account for the entire profit made from it. A defendant who plagiarizes another author's book can be ordered to give an accounting and pay over all the profits to the owner of the copyrighted material. An accounting forces the wrongdoer to trace all transactions that flowed from the legal injury, because the plaintiff is in no position to identify the profits.

Arthur Andersen and Other Accounting Failures

The accounting profession, which is largely self-regulated, has suffered through a series of fiascoes since the late 1990s, resulting in a call for major changes in accounting standards. The Financial Accounting Standards Board (FASB) has served since 1973 as one of the organizations responsible for establishing standards of financial accounting and reporting. Although the FASB is a private organization, its standards are recognized as authoritative by the SECURITIES AND EXCHANGE COMMISSION (SEC) and the American Institute of Certified Public Accountants. In the late 1990s and early 2000s, debacles involving major accounting firms required the FASB and the SEC, as well as other regulatory organizations, to consider new rules designed to improve financial reporting. Between 1996 and 2002, investors lost an estimated $200 billion in earnings restatements and stock meltdowns following failures in auditing processes. A number of high-profile auditing failures decreased confidence in the accounting profession. Among these failures were incidents involving such companies as Bausch and Lomb, Rite Aid, Cendant, Sunbeam, Waste Management, Superior Bank, and Dollar General.

One of the most highly publicized accounting failures early in the new millennium involved Houston-based Enron Corporation and its ACCOUNTANT, Arthur Andersen, L.L.P. Enron suffered a collapse in the third quarter of 2001 that resulted in the largest BANKRUPTCY in U.S. history to date and numerous lawsuits alleging violations of federal securities laws. Thousands of Enron employees lost 401(k) retirement plans that held company stock. Enron reported annual revenues of about $101 billion between 1985 and 2000. On December 18, 2000, Enron's stock sold for $84.87 per share. Stock prices fell throughout 2001, however, and on October 16, 2001, the company reported losses of $638 million in the third quarter alone. During the next six weeks, company stock continued to fall, and by December 2, 2001, Enron stock dropped to below $1 per share after the largest single day trading volume for any stock listed on either the New York Stock Exchange or the NASDAQ.

Initial allegations focused on the role of Arthur Andersen. The company was one of the so-called Big Five accounting firms in the United States, and it had served as Enron's auditor for 16 years. Arthur Andersen also served as a consultant to Enron, thus raising serious questions regarding conflicts of interests between the two companies. According to court documents, Enron and Arthur Andersen had improperly categorized hundreds of millions of dollars as increases in shareholder equity, thereby misrepresenting the true value of the corporation. Arthur Andersen also did not follow GENERALLY ACCEPTED ACCOUNTING PRINCIPLES (GAAP) when it considered Enron's dealings with related partnerships. These dealings, in part, allowed Enron to conceal some of its losses.

Arthur Andersen was also ACCUSED of destroying thousands of Enron documents that included not only physical documents but also computer files and e-mail files. After investigation by the U.S. JUSTICE DEPARTMENT, the firm was indicted on OBSTRUCTION OF JUSTICE charges in March 2002. The government also charged the company with violating federal law, which criminalized the knowing and corrupt persuasion of others to withhold or alter documents.

After a six-week trial, Arthur Andersen was found guilty in June 2002. The company was placed on PROBATION for five years and was required to pay a $500,000 fine. Some analysts also questioned whether the company could survive after this series of incidents. However, the U.S. Supreme Court, in an unanimous opinion, later reversed the criminal conviction on the basis of faulty and improper jury instructions (*Arthur Andersen v. United States*, 544 U.S. 696 [2005]). The high court found nothing inherently corrupt about Arthur Andersen (the company) having ordered employees to destroy documents. The Court held that a conviction could be found only if prosecutors proved that company officials were aware that their conduct (in persuading the destruction of documents) was corrupt.

Civil FRAUD charges (relating to accounting and auditing) were also filed in a related CLASS ACTION lawsuit by Enron stockholders (including PENSION administrators for the University of California, the named plaintiffs) against several Wall Street investment banks, including Credit Suisse, Merrill Lynch, and JPMorgan Chase. The lawsuit charged that the banks essentially colluded with and assisted Enron officials with FRAUDULENT partnerships and transactions, manipulating the true status of Enron's financial health. This activity resulted in company officials presenting allegedly deceptive business reports to investors. In 2007 the Fifth Circuit Court of Appeals reversed the order certifying a class action (uniting plaintiff investors), finding that the defendants were under no fiduciary or other duty to disclose the nature of Enron transactions to investors. Therefore, there could not be a class-wide presumption of reliance on defendants by investors (an essential element to prove fraud or misrepresentation) (*Regents of the Univ. of Cal. v. Credit Suisse First Boston*, 482 F.3d 372 [5th Cir. 2007]). In January 2008, the U.S. Supreme Court denied review of the case (No. 06-1341, 2008 WL 169504, U.S. LEXIS 1120, 76 U.S.L.W. 3392).

The accounting issues in the Enron case extended beyond Enron and Arthur Andersen. In the wake of these and other major accounting/auditing scandals, Congress passed the anti-fraud SARBANES-OXLEY ACT OF 2002, P.L. 107-204, 116 Stat. 745 (codified in various chapters and sections of the U.S. CODE). Among other things, the act created a Public Company Accounting Oversight Board (PCAOB), to be paid for by fees collected on publicly traded companies, according to their size. The Board replaced the accounting industry's own internal regulators and had independent SUBPOENA power to facilitate its own regulation, oversight, and discipline of accountants and accounting firms. The Sarbanes-Oxley Act also provided for the SEC to appoint the chairman and four directors of the PCAOB. Another important provision in the act created greater financial disclosure mandates and increased the criminal penalties for securities fraud.

Later, the act itself came under criticism and CONSTITUTIONAL scrutiny when pro-business, anti-tax/fee plaintiffs brought suit alleging that the creation of the PCAOB violated the appointments clause of the U.S. CONSTITUTION (Article II, section 2, cl. 2) as well as the constitutionally mandated SEPARATION OF POWERS. A federal district court upheld the constitutionality of the act and the PCAOB, and its decision was affirmed by the U.S. District Court of Appeals for the D.C. Circuit in 2008 (*Free Enterprise Fund v. Public Company Accounting Oversight Board* 537 F.3d 667 [D.C. Cir. 2008]). (In May 2009 the U.S. Supreme Court granted review of that decision for its 2009–2010 term, 77 U.S.L.W. 3431.)

Despite these safeguards, one of the largest accounting and auditing frauds on record unfolded in 2008, when securities investment BROKER Bernard (Bernie) Madoff was formally charged in federal court in Manhattan, New York City, with SEC violations that cost investors at least $50 billion in false or nonexistent investments. In March 2009 Madoff pleaded guilty to creating false investment accounts and privately pocketing funds received from investors, periodically paying returns to some of them with money received from other prospective investors under a giant *Ponzi* scheme. In June 2009 he was sentenced to 150 years in prison. In connection with this case, the accounting firm of Friehling & Horowitz and partner David G. Friehling, C.P.A. were also charged with fraud and various SEC violations for falsely representing that they had conducted legitimate company audits of Madoff's investment firm over the years, when in fact they had not (*Securities and Exchange Commission v. David G. Friehling, C.P.A and Friehling & Horowitz, CPAs, P.C.* [S.D.N.Y. Civ. 09 CV 2467]).

FURTHER READINGS

Atvedlund, Erin. 2009. *Too Good to Be True: The Rise and Fall of Bernie Madoff.* New York: Portfolio Hardcover.

Meyer, Charles H. 2002. *Accounting and Finance for Lawyers in a Nutshell.* 2d ed. St. Paul, Minn.: West Group.

Rachlin, Robert, and Allen Sweeny. 1996. *Accounting and Financial Fundamentals for Nonfinancial Executives.* New York: AMACON.

SEC. 2009. "SEC Charges Madoff Auditors with Fraud." Press Release, March 18. Litigation Release No. 20959.

CROSS REFERENCES

Accrual Basis; Cash Basis; Income Tax.

ACCREDIT

To give official authorization or status. To recognize as having sufficient academic standards to qualify graduates for higher education or for professional practice. In international law: (1) To acknowledge; to receive as an envoy and give that person credit and rank accordingly. (2) To send with credentials as an envoy. This latter use is now the accepted one.

ACCREDITED LAW SCHOOL

A law school that has been approved by the state and the Association of American Law Schools (AALS), the American Bar Association (ABA), or both.

In certain states—for example, California—it is acceptable for a law school to be accredited by the state and not by either the AALS or the ABA. In most states, however, only graduates of AALS or ABA accredited law schools are permitted to take the state BAR EXAMINATION.

CROSS REFERENCE

Legal Education.

ACCRETION

The growth of the value of a particular item given to a person as a specific bequest under the provisions of a will between the time the will was written and the time of death of the testator— the person who wrote the will.

Accretion of land is of two types: (1) by alluvion, *the washing up of sand or soil so as to form firm ground; and (2) by* dereliction, *as when the sea shrinks below the usual watermark. The terms* alluvion *and* accretion *are often used interchangeably, but alluvion refers to the deposit itself while accretion denotes the act. Land uncovered by a gradual subsidence of water is not an accretion; it is a reliction.*

ACCRUAL BASIS

A method of accounting that reflects expenses incurred and income earned for income tax purposes for any one year.

Taxpayers who use the accrual method must include in their TAXABLE INCOME any money that they have the right to receive as payment for services, once it has been earned. Any expenses that they may take as deductions when computing taxable income must be due at the time the deduction is taken. For example, suppose a surgeon performed a tonsillectomy in October 2003, and on December 31, 2003, he received a bill for carpeting installed in the waiting room of his office. He was paid the surgical fee on January 3, 2004, the same day he paid for the carpeting. The surgical fee will be included in his taxable income for 2003, the year in which he earned it, regardless of the fact that he was not paid until the following year.

His expenses for the carpeting can be deducted from his 2003 income because once he received the bill, he was bound to pay it. The fact that he did not pay for the carpeting until the following year does not prevent him from taking the deduction in 2003.

The accrual method of ACCOUNTING differs from the CASH BASIS method, which treats income as only that which is actually received, and expense as only that which is actually paid out. If the cash method were used in the above

example, the payment of the surgical fee would be included as income for the 2004 tax year, the year in which it was received by the surgeon. The surgeon could deduct the cost of the carpeting only when he actually paid for it in 2004, although it had been installed in 2003.

Unearned income, such as interest or rent, is generally taxed in the year in which it is received, regardless of the accounting method that the taxpayer uses.

ACCRUE

To increase; to augment; to come to by way of increase; to be added as an increase, profit, or damage. Acquired; falling due; made or executed; matured; occurred; received; vested; was created; was incurred.

To attach itself to, as a subordinate or accessory claim or demand arises out of, and is joined to, its principal.

The term is also used of independent or original demands, meaning to arise, to happen, to come into force or existence; to vest, as in the sentence, "The right of action did not accrue *within six years." To become a present right or demand; to come to pass.*

Interest on money that a depositor has in a bank savings account accrues, so that after a certain time the amount will be increased by the amount of interest it has earned.

A CAUSE OF ACTION, the facts that give a person a right to judicial relief, usually accrues on the date that the injury to the PLAINTIFF is sustained. When the injury is not readily discoverable, the cause of action accrues when the plaintiff in fact discovers the injury. This occurs frequently in cases of fraud or MALPRACTICE. A woman, for example, has an appendectomy. Three years after the surgery, she still experiences dull pain on her right side. She is examined by another physician who discovers a piece of surgical sponge near the area of the operation. Although the injury had occurred at the time of surgery three years earlier, in this case the cause of action for MEDICAL MALPRACTICE accrues on the date that the sponge is discovered by the second doctor. This distinction is important for purposes of the running of the STATUTE OF LIMITATIONS, the time set by law within which a lawsuit must be commenced after a cause of action accrues. In cases involving injuries that cannot be readily discovered, it would be unfair to bar a plaintiff from bringing a lawsuit because he or she does not start the suit within the required time from the date of injury.

ACCUMULATED EARNINGS TAX

A special tax imposed on corporations that accumulate (rather than distribute via dividends) their earnings beyond the reasonable needs of the business. The accumulated earnings tax is imposed on accumulated taxable income in addition to the corporate income tax.

ACCUMULATION TRUST

An arrangement whereby property is transferred by its owner—the settlor—with the intention that it be administered by someone else—a trustee—for another person's benefit, with the direction that the trustee gather, rather than distribute, the income of the trust and any profits made from the sale of any of the property making up the trust until the time specified in the document that created the trust.

Many states have laws governing the time over which accumulations may be made.

ACCUMULATIVE JUDGMENT

A second or additional judgment against a person who has already been convicted and sentenced for another crime; the execution of the second judgment is postponed until the person's first sentence has been completed.

ACCUMULATIVE SENTENCE

A sentence—a court's formal pronouncement of the legal consequences of a person's conviction of a crime—additional to others, imposed on a defendant who has been convicted upon an indictment containing several counts, each charging a distinct offense, or who is under conviction at the same time for several distinct offenses; each sentence is to run consecutively, beginning at the expiration of the previous sentence.

A person must finish one sentence before being allowed to start the next one. Another name for ACCUMULATIVE SENTENCE is *cumulative* or *consecutive sentence*.

The opposite of an accumulative sentence is a CONCURRENT *sentence*—two or more prison sentences that are to be served simultaneously, so that the prisoner is entitled to be released at the end of the longest sentence.

ACCUSATION

A formal criminal charge against a person alleged to have committed an offense punishable by law, which is presented before a court or a magistrate having jurisdiction to inquire into the alleged crime.

The SIXTH AMENDMENT to the CONSTITUTION provides in part that a person ACCUSED of a crime has the right "to be informed of the nature and cause of the accusation." Thus in any federal criminal prosecution, the statute setting forth the crime in the ACCUSATION must define the offense in sufficiently clear terms so that an average person will be informed of the acts that come within its scope. The charge must also inform the accused in clear and unambiguous language of the offense with which he or she is being charged under the statute. An accused has the same rights when charged with violating state CRIMINAL LAW because the Due Process Clause of the FOURTEENTH AMENDMENT applies the guarantees of the Sixth Amendment to the states. The paper in which the accusation is set forth—such as an INDICTMENT, information, or a complaint—is called an *accusatory instrument*.

Most state constitutions contain language similar to that in the Sixth Amendment. In many state rules of CRIMINAL PROCEDURE, the accusatory instrument serves to protect the state CONSTITUTIONAL rights of the accused. In Louisiana, for example, the purpose of a bill of information is to inform a DEFENDANT of the nature and cause of the accusation against him or her as required by the Louisiana State Constitution (*State v. Stevenson*, 2003 WL 183998 [La. App. 2003]).

In order to QUASH a bill of information or other accusatory instrument, the accused must present DIRECT EVIDENCE not established by the record, showing the bill was insufficient. The accused generally has the BURDEN OF PROOF to demonstrate that the accusatory instrument was insufficient. The rules of evidence in a particular jurisdiction apply to the evidentiary determination of the sufficiency of the accusatory instrument.

CROSS REFERENCE

Criminal Law.

ACCUSATORY BODY

Body such as a grand jury whose duty it is to hear evidence to determine whether a person should be accused of (charged with) a crime; to be distinguished from a traverse or petit jury, which is charged with the duty of determining guilt or innocence.

ACCUSED

The generic name for the defendant in a criminal case. A person becomes accused *within the meaning of a guarantee of speedy trial only at the point at which either formal indictment or information has been returned against him or her, or when he or she becomes subject to actual restraints on liberty imposed by arrest, whichever occurs first.*

ACKNOWLEDGMENT

To acknowledge *is to admit, affirm, declare, testify, avow, confess, or own as genuine. Admission or affirmation of obligation or responsibility. Most states have adopted the Uniform Acknowledgment Act.*

The partial payment of a debt, for example, is considered an acknowledgment of it for purposes of tolling the statute of limitations—the time set by law for bringing a lawsuit—based on a person's failure to repay a debtor. State law usually gives a creditor six years from the date a debt is due, according to the creditor's contract with the debtor, to SUE for nonpayment. If, on the last day of the fifth year, the debtor repays any part of the loan, the STATUTE OF LIMITATIONS is tolled or suspended. The creditor then has another six years from the date of partial payment to sue the debtor for the balance of the loan. The debtor's partial payment indicates ACCEPTANCE of responsibility to pay the loan. If the debtor had not paid anything, he or she would have escaped LIABILITY six years after the date the loan was due.

An acknowledgment of PATERNITY means recognition of parental duties—such as financial support of an illegitimate child—by written agreement, verbal declaration, or conduct of the father toward the mother and child that clearly demonstrates recognition of paternity.

The requirement for acknowledgments on certain documents—such as deeds transferring the ownership of real property, wills giving the ownership of property to a decedent's heirs after death, or DOCUMENTARY EVIDENCE that is to be admitted in a legal proceeding—is established by state law. If such documents do not contain acknowledgments, they are ineffective and cannot be used in any LEGAL PROCEEDINGS.

Any or all of the parties to a document may be required to acknowledge it. Only those persons specified by law, a NOTARY PUBLIC, for example, may take an acknowledgment.

Usually, a person making an acknowledgment does not have to explain the contents of the document to the person taking the acknowledgment. A person who ordinarily takes an acknowledgment might be disqualified from doing so if that person stands to gain some benefit from or has a financial interest in the outcome of the transaction. For example, state law requires a person making a will, a TESTATOR, to make an acknowledgment to a certain number of WITNESSES that the document is the genuine expression of how that person wants his or her property disposed of upon his or her death.

Suppose the state requires two witnesses. If the people selected as witnesses have financial interests in the person's will, they will be disqualified for purposes of acknowledgment. This is done to deter dishonest people from fabricating a document that is beneficial to them. Such a will is legally ineffective; once the testator dies, his or her property will be transferred according to the laws of DESCENT AND DISTRIBUTION.

A certificate of acknowledgment, sometimes referred to as the acknowledgment, is evidence that the acknowledgment has been done properly. Although its contents may vary from state to state, the certificate must recite: (1) that acknowledgment before the proper officer was made by the person who completed the document; (2) the place where the acknowledgment took place; and (3) the name and authority of the officer. The certificate may be on the document itself or may be attached to it as a separate instrument.

ACQUIESCENCE

Conduct recognizing the existence of a transaction and intended to permit the transaction to be carried into effect; a tacit agreement; consent inferred from silence.

For example, a new beer company is concerned that the proposed label for its beer might infringe on the trademark of its competitor. It submits the label to its competitor's general counsel, who does not object to its use. The new company files an application in the PATENT AND TRADEMARK OFFICE to register the label as its trademark and starts to use the label on the market. The competitor does not file any objection in the PATENT Office. Several years later, the competitor sues the new company for infringing on its trademark and demands an

Examples of acknowledgments

Acknowledgments

Short forms of acknowledgment

The forms of acknowledgment set forth in this section may be used and are sufficient for their respective purposes under any law of this State. The forms shall be known as "Statutory Short Forms of Acknowledgment" and may be referred to by that name. The authorization of the forms in this section does not preclude the use of other forms. [1969, c. 364 (new).]

1. **Individual.** For an individual acting in his own right:

State of

County of

The foregoing instrument was acknowledged before me this (date) by (name of person acknowledged).

(Signature of person taking acknowledgment)

(Title or rank)

(Serial number, if any)

[1969, c. 364 (new).]

2. **Corporation.** For a corporation:

State of

County of

The foregoing instrument was acknowledged before me this (date) by (name of officer or agent, title of officer or agent) of (name of corporation acknowledging) a (state or place of incorporation) corporation, on behalf of the corporation.

(Signature of person taking acknowledgment)

(Title or rank)

(Serial number, if any)

[1969, c. 364 (new).]

3. **Partnership.** For a partnership:

State of

County of

The foregoing instrument was acknowledged before me this (date) by (name of acknowledging partner or agent), partner (or agent) on behalf of (name of partnership), a partnership.

(Signature of person taking acknowledgment)

(Title or rank)

(Serial number, if any)

[1969, c. 364 (new).]

4. **Principal.** For an individual acting as principal by an attorney in fact:

State of

County of

The foregoing instrument was acknowledged before me this (date) by (name of attorney in fact) as attorney in fact on behalf of (name of principal).

(Signature of person taking acknowledgment)

(Title or rank)

(Serial number, if any)

[1969, c. 364 (new).]

[continued]

Acknowledgments

5. Public officer. By any public officer, trustee or personal representative:

State of

County of

The foregoing instrument was acknowledged before me this (date) by (name and title of position).

(Signature of person taking acknowledgment)

(Title or rank)

(Serial number, if any)

[1969, c. 364 (new).]

Section History:
PL 1969, Ch. 364, § (NEW).

The Revisor's Office cannot provide legal advice or interpretation of Maine law to the public. If you need legal advice, please consult a qualified attorney.

Office of the Revisor of Statutes
7 State House Station
State House Room 108
Augusta, Maine 04333-0007

This page created on: 2003-03-13

Examples of acknowledgments (continued)
ILLUSTRATION BY GGS CREATIVE RESOURCES. REPRODUCED BY PERMISSION OF GALE, A PART OF CENGAGE LEARNING.

ACCOUNTING of the new company's profits for the years it has been using the label. A court will refuse the accounting, because by its acquiescence the competitor tacitly approved the use of the label. The competitor, however, might be entitled to an injunction barring the new company from further use of its trademark if it is so similar to the competitor's label as to amount to an infringement.

Similarly, the INTERNAL REVENUE SERVICE (IRS) may acquiesce or refuse to acquiesce to an adverse RULING by the U.S. TAX COURT or another lower federal court. The IRS is not bound to change its policies due to an adverse ruling by a federal court with the exception of the U.S. Supreme Court. The chief counsel of the IRS may determine that the commissioner of the IRS should acquiesce to an adverse decision, however, thus adopting the ruling as the policy of the IRS. The decision whether to acquiesce to an adverse ruling is published by the Internal Revenue Service as an Action on Decision.

Acquiescence is not the same as LACHES, a failure to do what the law requires to protect one's rights, under circumstances misleading or prejudicing the person being sued.

Acquiescence relates to inaction during the performance of an act. In the example given above, the failure of the competitor's general counsel to object to the use of the label and to the registration of the label as a trademark in the Patent and Trademark Office is acquiescence. Failure to SUE the company until after several years had elapsed from the first time the label had been used is laches.

ACQUIRED IMMUNE DEFICIENCY SYNDROME

A disease caused by the human immunodeficiency virus (HIV) that produces disorders and infections that can lead to death.

Acquired immune deficiency syndrome (AIDS), a fatal disease that attacks the body's immune system making it unable to resist infection, is caused by the human immunodeficiency virus (HIV), which is communicable in some bodily fluids and transmitted primarily through sexual behavior and intravenous drug use.

The United States struggled to cope with AIDS from the early 1980s until the late 1990s, when new drug therapies started to extend the length and quality of life for many people with

The AIDS quilt, on display in Washington, D.C., has become a well-known symbol of support for AIDS victims and their families. Families and supporters of AIDS victims create a panel to commemorate a person's life; each panel is then joined with others from around the country.

LEE SNIDER/CORBIS.

AIDS. Since the beginning, AIDS and its resulting epidemic in the United States have raised a great number of legal issues, which are made all the more difficult by the nature of the disease. AIDS is a unique killer, but some of its aspects are not: epidemics have been seen before; other sexually transmitted diseases have been fatal. AIDS is different because it was discovered in—and in the United States still predominantly afflicts—unpopular social groups: gay men and drug users. This fact has had a strong impact on the shaping of AIDS law. Law is often shaped by politics, and AIDS is a highly politicized disease. The challenge in facing an epidemic that endangers everyone is complicated by the stigma attached to the people most likely to be killed by it.

Epidemics have no single answer beyond a cure. Because no cure for AIDS exists, the law continues to grapple with a vast number of problems. The federal government has addressed AIDS in two broad ways: by spending money on research and treatment of the disease and by prohibiting unfairness to people with HIV or AIDS. It has funded medical treatment, research, and public education, and it has passed laws prohibiting DISCRIMINATION against people who are HIV-positive or who have developed AIDS. States and local municipalities have joined in these efforts, sometimes with federal help.

In addition, states have criminalized the act of knowingly transmitting the virus through sexual behavior or blood donation. The courts, of course, are the decision makers in AIDS law. They have heard a number of cases in areas that range from employment to education and from crimes to torts. Although a body of CASE LAW has developed, it remains relatively new with respect to most issues, and controversial in all.

AIDS and the Federal Government

Political attitudes toward AIDS have gone through dramatically different phases. In the early 1980s, it was dubbed "the gay disease" and as such was easy for lawmakers to ignore. No one hurried to fund research into a disease that seemed to be killing only members of a historically unpopular group. When it was not being ignored, some groups dismissed AIDS as a problem that homosexuals deserved, perhaps brought on them by divine intervention. Discriminatory action matched this talk as gay men lost jobs, housing, and medical care. AIDS activists complained bitterly about the failure of most U.S. citizens to be concerned. Public opinion only began to shift in the late 1980s, largely through awareness of highly publicized cases. As soon as AIDS had a familiar or more mainstream face, it became harder to ignore; when it became clear that heterosexuals were also contracting the disease, the epidemic acquired higher priority.

By the late 1980s much of the harshness in public debate had diminished. Both liberals and conservatives lined up to support LEGISLATIVE solutions. President RONALD REAGAN left office recommending increases in federal funding for medical research on AIDS. Already the amount spent in this area had risen from $61 million in 1984 to nearly $1.3 billion in 1988. President GEORGE H.W. BUSH took a more active approach and in 1990 signed two new bills into law. One was the Ryan White Comprehensive AIDS Resources Emergency (CARE) Act (Pub. L. No. 101-381, 104 Stat. 576), which provides much-needed money for states to spend on treatment. The other was the groundbreaking Americans with Disabilities Act (ADA) (42 U.S.C.A. §§ 12112–12117), which has proved to be the most effective weapon against the discrimination that individuals with the disease routinely suffer. Bush also hurried approval by the FOOD AND DRUG ADMINISTRATION for AIDS-related drugs. Though he supported Americans with the disease, Bush agreed to a controversial ban by Congress on travel and IMMIGRATION to the United States for people with HIV.

Like his predecessors, President BILL CLINTON called for fighting the disease itself, rather than the people afflicted with it. In 1993 he appointed the first federal AIDS policy coordinator. He fully funded the Ryan White Care Act, increasing government support by 83 percent, to $633 million, and also increased funding for AIDS research, prevention, and treatment by 30 percent. These measures met most of his campaign promises on AIDS. He reneged on one: despite vowing to lift the ban on HIV-positive ALIENS, he signed LEGISLATION continuing it. In addition, he met a major obstacle on another proposal: Congress failed to pass his health care reform package, which would have provided health coverage to all U.S. citizens with HIV, delivered drug treatment against AIDS, on demand, to intravenous drug users, and prohibited health plans from providing lower coverage for AIDS than for other life-threatening diseases.

President GEORGE W. BUSH also passed initiatives that allocated federal funds toward fighting the aids epidemic. In 2003 he announced the President's Emergency Plan for AIDS Relief (PEPFAR), in which he called upon congress to pass legislation that would appropriate $15 billion over five years to support international AIDS prevention and the purchase

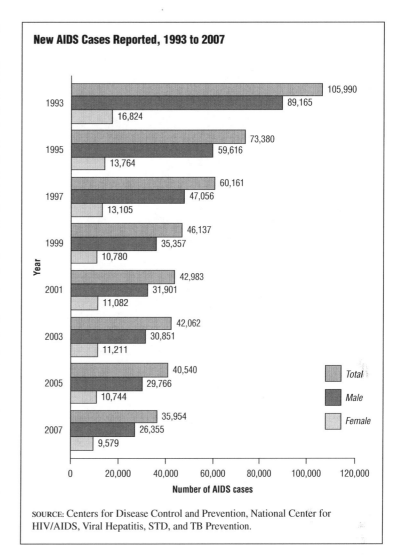

New AIDS Cases Reported, 1993 to 2007

Year		
1993	Total 105,990 / Male 89,165 / Female 16,824	
1995	Total 73,380 / Male 59,616 / Female 13,764	
1997	Total 60,161 / Male 47,056 / Female 13,105	
1999	Total 46,137 / Male 35,357 / Female 10,780	
2001	Total 42,983 / Male 31,901 / Female 11,082	
2003	Total 42,062 / Male 30,851 / Female 11,211	
2005	Total 40,540 / Male 29,766 / Female 10,744	
2007	Total 35,954 / Male 26,355 / Female 9,579	

Number of AIDS cases (0, 20,000, 40,000, 60,000, 80,000, 100,000, 120,000)

■ Total ■ Male ■ Female

SOURCE: Centers for Disease Control and Prevention, National Center for HIV/AIDS, Viral Hepatitis, STD, and TB Prevention.

ILLUSTRATION BY GGS CREATIVE RESOURCES. REPRODUCED BY PERMISSION OF GALE, A PART OF CENGAGE LEARNING.

of anti-viral drugs. The largest share of the money was contributed directly by the United States to other countries, such as through programs sponsored by the U.S. Agency for International Development. The proposal accounted for almost half the money in a global fund committed to fight HIV and AIDS. As the initial plan expired in the 2008 fiscal year, Congress approved, and President George W. Bush signed into law legislation that extended the plan another five years and authorized an additional $48 billion in funding. Specifically, the funds from PEPFAR are designated to help provide treatment to at least 3 million individuals with HIV, prevent approximately 12 million new infections, and provide care for 12 million people infected.

President BARACK OBAMA in his 2008 presidential campaign pledged to develop and implement a comprehensive national HIV/AIDS strategy designed to not only reduce HIV infections, but also to increase access to care and treatment and reduce HIV-related health disparities. He specifically pledged to expand funding for research and prevention of HIV, including a vaccine and a microbicide product for women to apply topically to prevent the transmission of HIV and other infections. He has further pledged to work toward improving the quality of life for those living with HIV and supports increased funding for adequate and safe housing for individuals living with HIV. In April 2009 President Obama's Administration announced it was implementing a five-year national communication campaign with the DEPARTMENT OF HEALTH AND HUMAN SERVICES (HHS) and the Centers for Disease Control and Prevention (CDC), known as Act Against AIDS, that would refocus the national attention of the HIV crisis in the United States. The campaign was in part a response to data released by the CDC in 2008, which estimated that approximately 56,000 Americans become infected with HIV each year and more than 14,000 Americans die with AIDS each year.

AIDS and Public Life

Having HIV is not a sentence to remove oneself from society. It does not limit a person's physical or mental abilities. Only later, when symptoms develop—as long as ten years from the time of infection—does the disease become increasingly debilitating. In any event, people who are HIV-positive and AIDS-symptomatic are fully able to work, play, and participate in daily life. Moreover, their rights to do so are the same as anyone else's. The chief barrier to a productive life often comes less from HIV and AIDS than from the fear, SUSPICION, and open hostility of others. Because HIV cannot be transmitted through casual contact, U.S. law has moved to defend the CIVIL RIGHTS of those individuals with the disease.

AIDS in the Workplace The workplace is a common battleground. Many people with AIDS have lost their jobs, been denied promotions, or been reassigned to work duties that remove them from public contact. During the 1980s this discrimination was fought through lawsuits based on older laws designed to protect the disabled. Plaintiffs primarily used the Rehabilitation Act of 1973 (29 U.S.C.A. § 701 et seq.), the earliest law of this type. But the Rehabilitation Act has a limited scope: it applies only to federally funded workplaces and institutions and says nothing about those who do not receive government money. Thus, for example, the law was helpful to a California public school teacher with AIDS who sued for the right to resume teaching classes (*Chalk v. United States district court*, 840 F.2d 701 [9th Cir. 1988]), but it would be of no use to a worker in a private business.

With passage of the ADA in 1990, Congress gave broad protection to people with AIDS who work in the private sector. In general, the ADA is designed to increase access for disabled persons, and it also forbids discrimination in hiring or promotion in companies with 15 or more employees. Specifically, employers may not discriminate if the person in question is otherwise qualified for the job. Moreover, they may not use tests to screen out disabled persons, and they must provide reasonable accommodation for disabled workers. The ADA, which took effect in 1992, quickly emerged as the primary means for bringing AIDS-related discrimination lawsuits. From 1992 to 1993, more than 330 complaints were filed with the U.S. EQUAL EMPLOYMENT OPPORTUNITY COMMISSION (EEOC), which investigates charges before they can be filed in court. Given the lag time needed for EEOC investigations, those cases started appearing before federal courts in 1994 and 1995.

AIDS and Health Care Closely related to work is the issue of health care. In some cases, the two overlap: HEALTH INSURANCE, SOCIAL SECURITY, and DISABILITY benefits for people with AIDS were often hard to obtain during the 1980s. Insurance was particularly difficult because employers feared rising costs, and insurance companies did not want to pay claims. To avoid the costs of AIDS, insurance companies used two traditional industry techniques: they attempted to exclude AIDS coverage from general policies, and they placed caps (limits on benefits payments) on AIDS-related coverage. State regulations largely determine whether these actions were permissible. In New York, for example, companies that sell general health insurance policies are forbidden to exclude coverage for particular diseases. Caps have hurt AIDS patients because their treatment can be as expensive as that for cancer or other life-threatening illnesses. Insurance benefits can be quickly exhausted—in fact, AIDS usually bankrupts people who have the disease. The problem is compounded when employers serve as their own health insurers. In *McGann v. H&H Music Co.*, 946, F.2d 401 (5th Cir. [1991]), a federal court ruled that such employers could legally change their policies to reduce coverage for workers who develop expensive illnesses such as AIDS.

In January 1995 the SETTLEMENT in a lawsuit brought by a Philadelphia construction worker with AIDS illustrated that the ADA could be used to fight caps on coverage. In 1992 the joint union-management fund for the Laborers' District Council placed a $10,000 limit on AIDS benefits, in stark contrast to the $100,000 allowed for other catastrophic illnesses. At that time, the fund said the cap on AIDS benefits was designed to curb all health costs. In 1993 the EEOC ruled that the fund violated the ADA, and, backed by the AIDS Law Project of Philadelphia, the worker sued. Rather than fight an expensive lawsuit, the insurance fund settled: under the agreement, it extended coverage for all catastrophic illnesses to $100,000. Hailing the settlement as a major blow against widespread discrimination in insurance coverage, the law project's executive director, Nan Feyler, told the *Philadelphia Inquirer,* "You can't single out someone based on a stereotype."

In other respects, health care is a distinct area of concern for AIDS patients and health professionals alike. Discrimination has often taken place. State and federal statutes, including the Rehabilitation Act, guarantee access to health care for AIDS patients, and courts have upheld that right. In the 1988 case of *Doe v. Centinela Hospital,* 57 U.S.L.W. 2034 (C.D. Cal.), for example, an HIV-infected person with no symptoms was excluded from a federally funded hospital residential program for drug and alcohol treatment because health care providers feared exposure to the virus. The case itself exposed the irrationality of such discrimination. Although its employees had feared HIV, the hospital argued in court that the lack of symptoms meant that the patient was not disabled and thus not protected by the Rehabilitation Act. A federal trial court in California rejected this ARGUMENT, RULING that a refusal to grant services based solely on fear of contagion is discrimination under the Rehabilitation Act.

Other actions during the 1990s have relied upon the ADA. In 1994 the U.S. DEPARTMENT OF JUSTICE reached a settlement in a lawsuit with the city of Philadelphia that ensures that city employees will treat patients with AIDS. The first settlement in a health care–related ADA suit, the case arose out of an incident in 1993, when an HIV-positive man collapsed on a Philadelphia street. Emergency medical workers not only refused to touch him but told him to get on a stretcher by himself. The man sued. In settling the case, the city agreed to begin an extensive training program for its 900 emergency medical technicians and 1,400 firefighters. In addition, officials paid the man $10,000 in COMPENSATORY DAMAGES and apologized. The Department of Justice viewed the suit as an important test of the ADA. Assistant Attorney General James Turner said the settlement would "send a clear message to all cities across the nation that we will not tolerate discrimination against persons with AIDS."

Health care professionals are not the only ones with concerns about HIV transmission. Patients may legitimately wonder whether their doctors are infected. During the early 1990s, the medical and legal communities debated whether HIV-positive doctors have a duty to inform their patients of the illness. According to the CDC, the risk of HIV transmission from health care workers to patients is very small when recommended infection-control procedures are followed, yet this type of transmission has occurred. The first cases of patients contracting HIV during a medical PROCEDURE were reported in 1991: Dr. David J. Acer, a Florida dentist with AIDS, apparently transmitted HIV to five patients. One was Kimberly Bergalis, age twenty-three, who died as a result. Before her death, Bergalis brought a CLAIM against the dentist's professional LIABILITY insurer, contending that it should have known that Acer had AIDS and effectively barred him from operating by refusing to issue him a MALPRACTICE insurance policy. Bergalis's claim was settled for $1 million. A second claim by Bergalis, against the insurance company that recommended Acer to her, was settled for an undisclosed amount.

Since the Bergalis case, many U.S. dentists, physicians, and surgeons with AIDS have begun disclosing their status to their patients. *Faya v. Almaraz,* 329 Md. 435, 620 A.2d 327 (Md. 1993), illustrates the consequences of not doing so. In *Faya* the court held that an HIV-positive doctor has the legal duty to disclose this medical condition to patients and that a failure to inform can lead to a NEGLIGENCE action, even if the patients have not been infected by the virus. The doctor's patient did not contract HIV but did suffer emotionally from a fear of having done so. The unanimous decision held that patients can be compensated for their fears. Although this case dealt specifically with doctor-patient relationships, others have concerned a variety of relationships in which the fear of contracting AIDS can be enough for a PLAINTIFF to recover damages.

Routine HIV-testing in healthcare facilities also raises legal issues. Most people who are HIV-positive want this information kept confidential. Facilities are free to use HIV testing to control the infection but in most states only with the patient's INFORMED CONSENT. Some states, such as Illinois, require written consent. The level of protection for medical records varies from state to state. California, for example, has broad protections; under its statutes, no one can be compelled to provide information that would identify anyone who is the subject of an HIV test. However, every state requires that AIDS cases be reported to the CDC, which tracks statistics on the spread of HIV. Whether the name of an HIV-infected person is reported to the CDC depends on state laws and regulations.

AIDS and Education Issues in the field of education include the rights of HIV-positive students to attend class and of HIV-positive teachers to teach, the confidentiality of HIV records, and how best to teach young people about AIDS. A few areas have been settled in court: for example, the right of students to attend classes was of greater concern in the early years of the epidemic and later ceased to be a matter of dispute.

Certain students with AIDS may assert their right to public education under the Education for All Handicapped Children Act of 1975 (EAHCA), but the law is only relevant in cases involving special education programs. More commonly, students' rights are protected by the Rehabilitation Act. Perhaps the most important case in this area is *Thomas v. Atascadero Unified School District*, 662 F. Supp. 376 (C.D. Cal. 1986), which illustrates how far such protections go. *Thomas* involved an elementary school student with AIDS who had bitten another youngster in a fight. Based on careful review of medical evidence, the U.S. District Court for the Central District of California concluded that biting was not proved

to transmit AIDS, and it ordered the school district to readmit the girl. Similarly, schools that excluded teachers with AIDS have been successfully sued on the ground that those teachers pose no threat to their students or others and that their right to work is protected by the Rehabilitation Act, as in *Chalk.*

Confidentiality relating to HIV is not uniform in schools. Some school districts require rather broad dissemination of the information; others keep it strictly private. In the mid-1980s the New York City Board of Education adopted a policy that no one in any school would be told the identities of children with AIDS or HIV infection; only a few top administrators outside the school would be informed. The policy inspired a lawsuit brought by a local school district, which argued that the identity of a child was necessary for infection control (*District 27 Community School Board v. Board of Education*, 130 Misc. 2d 398, 502 N.Y. S.2d 325 [N.Y. Sup. Ct. 1986]). The trial court rejected the argument on the basis that numerous children with HIV infection might be attending school, and instead noted that universal precautions in responding to blood incidents at school would be more effective than the revelation of confidential information.

Schools play a major role in the effort to educate the public on AIDS. Several states have mandated AIDS prevention instruction in their schools. But the subject is controversial: It evokes personal, political, and moral reactions to sexuality. Responding to parental sensitivities, some states have authorized excused absences from such programs. The New York State EDUCATION DEPARTMENT faced a storm of controversy over its policy of not allowing absences at parental discretion. Furthermore, at the local and the federal levels, some conservatives have opposed certain kinds of AIDS education. During the 1980s those who often criticized liberal approaches to sex education argued that AIDS materials should not be explicit, encourage sexuality, promote the use of contraceptives, or favorably portray gays and lesbians. In Congress lawmakers attached amendments to appropriations measures (bills that authorize the spending of federal tax dollars) that mandate that no federal funds may be used to "promote homosexuality." In response the CDC adopted regulations that prohibit spending federal funds on AIDS education materials that might be found offensive by some members of certain communities. Despite the controversy, some communities have taken radical steps to halt the spread of AIDS. In 1991 and 1992 the school boards of New York City, San Francisco, Seattle, and Los Angeles voted to make condoms available to students in their public high-school systems.

AIDS and Private Life

Although epidemics are public crises, they begin with individuals. The rights of people who have AIDS and those who do not are often in contention and seldom more so than in private life. It is no surprise that people with HIV continue having sex, nor is it a surprise that this behavior is, usually, legal. Unfortunately, some do so without knowing they have the virus. Even more unfortunately, others do so in full knowledge that they are HIV-positive but without informing their partners. This dangerous behavior has opened one area of AIDS law that affects individuals: the legal duty to warn a partner before engaging in behavior that can transmit the infection. Courts recognized a similar duty long before AIDS ever appeared, with regard to other sexually transmitted diseases.

A failure to inform in AIDS cases has given rise to both civil and criminal lawsuits. One such case was brought by Mark Christian, the lover of actor Rock Hudson, against Hudson's estate. Christian won his suit on the ground that Hudson had concealed his condition and continued their relationship, and the jury returned a multi-million-dollar VERDICT despite the fact that there was no evidence that Christian had been infected. Another case was brought in Oregon in 1991, when criminal charges were filed against Alberto Gonzalez for knowingly spreading HIV by having sex with his girlfriend. After Gonzalez pleaded NO CONTEST to third-degree ASSAULT (a felony) and to two charges of recklessly endangering others, he received an unusual sentence: the court ordered him to abstain from sex for five years and placed him under HOUSE ARREST for six months. Although such convictions are increasingly common, courts have also recognized that not knowing one has HIV can be a valid defense. In *C. A. U. v. R. L.*, 438 N.W.2d 441 (1989), for example, the Minnesota Court of Appeals affirmed a trial court's finding that the plaintiff could not recover damages from her former fiancé, who had unknowingly given her the virus.

State Legislation and the Courts To stem transmission of HIV, states have adopted several legal measures. Two states attempted to head off the virus at the pass: Illinois and Louisiana at one point required HIV blood testing as a prerequisite to getting a MARRIAGE license. Both states ultimately repealed these statutes because they were difficult to enforce; couples simply crossed state lines to be married in neighboring states. Several states have taken a less stringent approach, requiring only that applicants for a marriage license be informed of the availability—and advisability—of HIV tests. More commonly, states criminalize sexual behavior that can spread AIDS. Michigan law makes it a felony for an HIV- or AIDS-infected person to engage in sex without first informing a partner of the infection. Florida law provides for the prosecution of any HIV-positive person committing PROSTITUTION, and it permits RAPE victims to demand that their attackers undergo testing. Indiana imposes penalties on persons who recklessly or knowingly donate blood or semen with the knowledge that they are HIV-positive.

Older state laws have also been applied to AIDS. Several states have statutes that make it a criminal offense for a person with a contagious disease—including a sexually transmitted disease—to willfully or knowingly expose another person to it, and some have amended these laws specifically to include AIDS. In addition, in many states, it has long been a crime to participate in an act of SODOMY. The argument that punishing sodomy can stem HIV transmission was made in a case involving a Missouri sodomy statute specifically limited to homosexual conduct. In *State v. Walsh*, 713 S.W.2d 508 (1986), the Missouri Supreme Court upheld the statute after finding that it was rationally related to the state's legitimate interest in protecting public health. Other AIDS-related laws have been invalidated in court challenges: for example, in 1993 a U.S. district judge struck down a 1987 Utah statute that invalidated the marriages of people with AIDS, ruling that it violated the ADA and the Rehabilitation Act.

Sex is only one kind of behavior that has prompted criminal prosecution related to AIDS. Commonly, defendants in AIDS cases have been prosecuted for assault. In *United States v. Moor*, 846 F.2d 1163 (8th Cir., 1988), U.S. Court of Appeals for the Eighth Circuit upheld the conviction of an

IN FOCUS

READING, WRITING, AND AIDS

Teaching young people about AIDS is an enormously popular idea. Since the late 1980s, Gallup Polls have revealed that over 90 percent of respondents think public schools should do so. Agreement ends there, however. In the 1990s more angry debate focused on AIDS education than on any issue facing schools since court-ordered busing in the 1970s. The core question of the debate is simple: What is the best way to equip students to protect themselves from this fatal disease? The answers may be miles apart. For one side, "equipping" means advocating the only sure means of protection, sexual and drug abstinence. For the other, it means supporting abstinence along with knowledge of sexual practices, the use of clean drug needles, and the use of prophylactics (condoms), which are distributed in some schools. Between these positions lie a great many issues of disagreement that have bitterly divided school districts, provoked lawsuits, and cost high-ranking Washington, D.C., officials their jobs.

Sex is an old battleground in public education. Liberals and conservatives argued over it in the decade following the sexual revolution of the 1960s, initially over whether sexual issues should be discussed in schools. After all, earlier generations who went to public schools learned mainly about reproductive organs. As new classes began appearing in the late 1970s, children learned about the sexual choices people make. If liberals appeared to win

the "sex ed." debate, growing social problems helped: rises in teen pregnancies and sexually transmitted diseases secured a place for more explicit school health classes. The much greater threat of AIDS pushed state legislatures into action. By the mid-1990s AIDS prevention classes had been mandated in at least 34 states and recommended in 14. But the appearance of even more explicit teaching has reinvigorated the sex ed. debate.

Supporters of a comprehensive approach say AIDS demands frankness. Originating in comprehensive sex ed. theory, their ideas also came from pacesetting health authorities such as former SURGEON GENERAL C. Everett Koop. Arguing in the mid-1980s that AIDS classes should be specific and detailed and taught as early as kindergarten, Koop countered conservative arguments by saying, "Those who say 'I don't want my child sexually educated' are hiding their heads in the sand." This position holds that educators are obligated to teach kids everything that can stop the spread of the disease. "What is the moral responsibility?" Jerald Newberry, a health coordinator of Virginia schools, asked the *Washington Times* in 1992. "I think it's gigantic." Abstinence is a part of this approach, but expecting teens to refrain from having sex was considered by many to be unrealistic given some studies that show that nearly three out of four high school students have had sex before graduation. Thus, the

comprehensive curriculum might well include explaining the proper use of condoms, discussing homosexual practices, describing the STERILIZATION of drug needles, and so on.

Abstinence-only adherents think being less frank is being more responsible. They view sexuality as a moral issue properly left for parents to discuss with their children and one that lies beyond the responsibilities of schools. The conservative columnist Cal Thomas spoke for this viewpoint when he argued that parents "have lost a significant right to rear their children according to their own moral standards." Other objections come from religious conservatives who oppose any neutral or positive discussion of homosexuality. Koop, for example, was blasted for allegedly "sponsoring homosexually oriented curricula" and "teaching BUGGERY in the 3rd grade." In addition to voicing moral objections, critics say comprehensive sex ed. is generally a failure because it encourages a false sense of security among teens that leads to experimentation with sex or drugs. "We have given children more information presumably because we think it will change their behavior, and yet the behavior has gotten worse, not better," said Gary Bauer, president of the Family Research Council.

Each side accuses the other of deepening the crisis. Comprehensive approach supporters think abstinence-only backers are moral censors, indifferent to pragmatic solutions. The liberal

HIV-infected prisoner found guilty of assault with a deadly weapon—his teeth—for biting two prison guards during a struggle. Teeth were also the subject of a trial in *Brock v. State*, 555 So. 2d 285 (1989), but the Alabama Court of Criminal Appeals refused to regard them as a dangerous weapon. In *State v. Haines*, 545 N.E. 2d 834 (2d Dist. 1989), the Indiana Court of Appeals affirmed a conviction

of attempted MURDER against a man with AIDS who had slashed his wrists to commit SUICIDE; when police officers and paramedics refused to let him die, he began to spit, bite, scratch, and throw blood.

Civil Litigation TORT LAW has seen an explosion of AIDS-related suits. This area of law is

People for the American Way attacked "a growing wave of CENSORSHIP ravaging sexuality education" that promotes only "narrow" curricula. It mocked such abstinence-only programs as Teen Aid and Sex Respect, both of which have brought THREATS of legal action from the AMERICAN CIVIL LIBERTIES UNION and Planned Parenthood. The conservative American Enterprise Institute asserted that liberal programs only prod students toward bad choices: "There has been a transition from protection to preparation." Neither side can agree on any data, other than to point out that the problems of AIDS and teen sexuality have appeared to worsen.

Nowhere are the two sides more split than on the issue of condoms. Schools in at least 23 cities sought to distribute condoms during the mid- to late-1990s. The assumption was that since students will have sex anyway—despite warnings not to—they had better be protected. Conservatives see this position as a cop-out in two ways: it sells values short and it undermines parental authority. In 1992, in Washington, D.C., critics erupted over a decision by the Public Health Commission to hand out condoms in junior and senior high schools without parental consent. William Brown, president of the D.C. Congress of Parents and Teachers, complained: "We are looking to build and reinforce and establish family values where they have been lost, and here we have an agency of our government that totally ignores those things we are working for." Dr. Mary Ellen Bradshaw, the commission's chief, replied: "Our whole focus is to save the lives of these children, stressing abstinence as the only sure way to avoid [AIDS] and making condoms available only after intensive

education." In other cities, upset parents simply sued. By 1992, CLASS ACTION lawsuits had been brought against school districts in New York City, Seattle, and Falmouth, Massachusetts, arguing that condom distribution violated parents' right to PRIVACY.

AIDS education in schools is not merely a local issue. While most decisions are made by states and school boards the federal government plays two important roles. First, it funds AIDS prevention programs: abstinence-based programs receive funding under the Adolescent Family Life Act of 1981, and programs that promote contraceptive use among teenagers are supported through the Family Planning Act of 1970. How these funds are spent is a matter of local control, but conservatives have sought to put limits on program content. During the early 1990s, Senator JESSE HELMS (R-NC) twice tried to ban funding for programs that were perceived to promote homosexuality or that did not continuously teach abstinence as the only effective protection against AIDS. In response, one federal agency, the Center for Disease Control, adopted regulations that prohibited the use of funds on any materials that are found offensive by some members of communities.

The second role of the federal government is largely symbolic but no less controversial. It is to guide school efforts through advice, sponsorship, and public speeches, and primarily involves the offices of the surgeon general and of the federal AIDS policy coordinator. Koop, who was a Reagan appointee, roused a fair degree of controversy, yet it was nothing compared to the upheaval that greeted statements by appointees of the Clinton administration. AIDS policy

czar Kristine Gebbie and surgeon general M. Joycelyn Elders were forced from their posts after making statements that conservatives found appalling—Gebbie promoting attitudes toward pleasurable sex and Elders indicating a willingness to have schools talk about masturbation. Thereafter, the administration frequently stressed abstinence as its top priority for school AIDS programs.

Problems surrounding AIDS education are unlikely to go away. Communities frequently disagree on sex education itself, and compromise is often difficult on such a divisive issue of values. As the experience of the Clinton administration suggested, Washington, D.C., could easily exacerbate an already contentious area, with policy coordinators becoming lightning rods for criticism. On the matter of what to say to kids about AIDS, poll data have been misleading. U.S. citizens are of three minds: say a lot, say a little, and do not say what the other side thinks.

FURTHER READINGS

Kelly, Pat. 1998. *Coping When Your Friend Is HIV-Positive.* New York: Rosen Publishing Group.

National Commission on Acquired Immune Deficiency Syndrome. 1993. *National Commission on AIDS: An Expanding Tragedy: The Final Report of the National Commission on AIDS.* Washington, D.C.: National Commission on Acquired Immune Deficiency Syndrome.

World Health Organization. 1989. *Legislative Responses to AIDS.* Boston: Martinus Nijhoff Publishers.

CROSS REFERENCES

Civil Rights Acts; Schools and School Districts.

used to discourage individuals from subjecting others to unreasonable risks and to compensate those who have been injured by unreasonably risky behavior. The greatest number of AIDS-related liability lawsuits has involved the receipt of HIV-infected blood and blood products. A second group has concerned the sexual transmission of HIV. A third group involves

AIDS-related psychic distress. In these cases, plaintiffs have successfully sued and recovered damages for their fear of having contracted HIV.

Advances in Treatment Though the search for an AIDS vaccine has occupied many researchers, no significant breakthroughs have appeared. However, other researchers have concentrated on ways of controlling AIDS

What Causes AIDS—and What Does Not?

Since the first U.S. case was identified in 1981, acquired immune deficiency syndrome (AIDS) has grown into an epidemic that has, as of 2007, caused the death of 545,805 persons in the United States. The Joint United Nations Programme on HIV/AIDS estimates that at the end of 2007 there were 33 million people living with HIV/AIDS worldwide. During 2007, AIDS caused the deaths of an estimated 2 million people. At that time, women were increasingly affected by AIDS; it was estimated that women comprised approximately 50 percent of persons living with HIV or AIDS worldwide. No cure has been found, although existing treatment employing multiple drugs has made substantial gains in prolonging life and reducing pain. Despite the limits in medical treatment, however, much is known about the disease.

AIDS is caused by the human immunodeficiency virus (HIV). Transmitted by bodily fluids from person to person, HIV invades certain key blood cells that are needed to fight off infections. HIV replicates, spreads, and destroys these host cells. When the body's immune system becomes deficient, the person becomes AIDS-symptomatic, which means the person develops infections that the body can no longer ward off. Ultimately, a person with AIDS dies from diseases caused by other infections. The leading killer is a form of pneumonia.

Most of the fear surrounding AIDS has to do with its most common form of transmission: sexual behavior. The virus can be passed through any behavior that involves the exchange of blood, semen, or vaginal secretions. Anal intercourse is the highest-risk activity, but oral or vaginal intercourse is dangerous too. Thus, federal health authorities recommend using a condom, yet they caution that condoms are not 100 percent effective; condoms can leak, and they can break. Highly accurate HIV testing is widely available and often advisable, since infected people can feel perfectly healthy. Although the virus can be contracted immediately upon exposure to it, symptoms of full-blown AIDS may take up to ten years to appear.

In addition to sexual behavior, only a few other means of HIV transmission exist. Sharing unsterilized needles used in drug injections is one way, owing to the exchange of blood on the needle, and thus intravenous drug users are an extremely high-risk group. Several cities have experimented with programs that offer free, clean needles. These programs have seen up to a 75-percent reduction in new HIV cases. Receipt of donations of blood, semen, organs, and other human tissue can also transmit HIV, although here screening methods have proved largely successful. Childbirth and breast feeding are also avenues of transmission; thus, children of HIV-positive mothers may be at risk.

The medical facts about HIV and AIDS are especially relevant to the law. Unless exposed in one of a few very specific ways, most people have nothing to fear. Casual contact with people who are infected is safe. Current medical knowledge is quite strong on this point: no one is known to have caught the virus by sitting next to, shaking the hand of, or breathing the same air as an infected person. For this reason, U.S. law has moved to protect the civil rights of HIV-positive and AIDS-symptomatic persons. Section 504 of the Rehabilitation Act of 1973 (29 U.S.C. § 794 [1994]) prohibits discrimination against otherwise qualified disabled individuals, including individuals with a contagious disease or an infection such as HIV or AIDS.

The AIDS quilt, on display in Washington, D.C., has become a well-known symbol of support for victims of AIDS and their families. Families and supporters of victims of AIDS create a panel to commemorate that person's life and that panel is joined with others from around the country to create the quilt.

FURTHER READINGS

Barnett, Tony, and Alan Whiteside. 2006. *AIDS in the Twenty-First Century.* 2d ed. New York: Palgrave Macmillan.

Farmer, Paul. 2003. *Pathologies of Power: Health, Human Rights, and the New War on the Poor.* Berkeley: Univ. of California Press.

CROSS REFERENCES

Discrimination

through drug-treatment regimens that require individuals to consume many different types of medications at the same time. These anti-AIDS "cocktails" undergo constant study and modification as researchers learn more about the workings of HIV. The medications are from a family of drugs called "protease inhibitors."

Survival rates have dramatically improved for those individuals using protease inhibitors, but other problems have also arisen. Some persons do not respond to these medications, or the side effects from taking the drugs diminish the quality of life. Protease inhibitors, for many people, are intolerable because of nausea, diarrhea, vomiting, headache, kidney stones, and serious drug interactions with other medications. By 2003 researchers had found that serious side effects include increased risk of heart attack, abnormalities in fat distribution, an increased propensity toward diabetes, and abnormalities in cholesterol metabolism.

Cost is another concern associated with protease inhibitors. To be effective, protease inhibitors must be used in combination with at least two other anti-HIV drugs. Originally, annual costs for this treatment was estimated to be between $12,000 and $15,000 per person. However, in 2006 research was released that estimated that Americans who were diagnosed with the AIDS virus could have a life expectancy of 24 years and spend approximately $600,000 in healthcare costs during those years. The average cost of the drugs equated to $2,100 a month and $25,200 a year. The increase in cost from the original reports is due to improved and more costly HIV medications. Those persons without private health insurance must rely on public programs such as the AIDS Drug Assistance Program (ADAP), a federally funded initiative to provide AIDS-related drugs to people with HIV. Most ADAP programs, which are administered by states, have lacked the funding to enroll everyone in need.

International Issues By 2003 the international AIDS problem had become a crisis in Africa and parts of Asia. The situation is gravest in sub-Saharan Africa, where AIDS is the leading cause of death. Over 22 million adults and children live with HIV and AIDS, which accounts for more than two-thirds of all individuals worldwide living with AIDS. Approximately 1.7 million people die there each year from AIDS. This number is more than three-quarters of the global total number of AIDS-related deaths each year. These figures stand in stark contrast to those of North America, where fewer than one million people are living with HIV and AIDS.

The growth of AIDS in Africa and Asia has raised worries about global political and economic stability. Governments in these ravaged countries have not been able to afford the antiviral drugs. In 2002 pharmaceutical companies agreed to sell these drugs to these countries as generic drugs, thus dropping the cost from $12,000 to $300 per year per patient; yet, even at these prices, many governments would be hard pressed to purchase them.

The UNITED NATIONS (UN) and the World Health Organization (WHO) have worked together to address the issues of prevention and treatment. Although AIDS is among the most deadly infectious diseases in the world, the statistics reveal that, on a global basis, the number of individuals dying of AIDS-related causes has declined in recent years. In December 2002 a joint UN-WHO report disclosed that 42 million people in the world were living with HIV and AIDS. In 2002 five million people contracted HIV, and over three million people died of AIDS. In 2007 the reports indicated that the number of individuals living with HIV had dropped to 33 million people worldwide and that 2.7 million people were newly infected in that year. The total number of AIDS deaths decreased from five million to two million in 2007. This decline is due in large part to the increased availability of the antiretroviral treatment and improved prevention and care programs available worldwide.

FURTHER READINGS

ACLU. 1996. *The Rights of People Who Are HIV Positive.* Carbondale: Southern Illinois University Press.

———. 1995a. *AIDS and Civil Liberties.* Briefing paper no. 13.

———. 1995b. *Lesbian and Gay Rights.* Briefing paper no. 18.

———. 1994. *ACLU Wins Precedent-Setting Claim in AIDS Case; Federal Court Rules That ADA Covers AIDS Discrimination.* Press release, November 21.

———. 1993. *ACLU Files AIDS Discrimination Suit; Challenges South Carolina Insurance Risk Pool.* Press release, April 6.

"Fighting Aids." February 10, 2003. *PBS News Hour.* Available online at www.pbs.org (accessed Mar. 31, 2010).

Health and Human Services Department. Social Security Administration. 1991. *A Guide to Social Security and SSI Disability Benefits for People with HIV Infection.* Pub. no. 05-10020, September.

Jarvis, Robert M., et al., eds. 1996. *AIDS Law in a Nutshell.* 2d ed. Minneapolis, Minn.: West.

Rollins, Joe. 2002. "AIDS, Law, and the Rhetoric of Sexuality." *Law & Society Review* 36 (April).

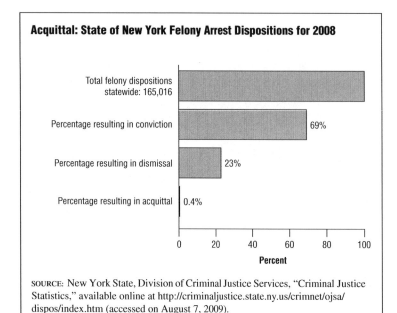

Acquittal: State of New York Felony Arrest Dispositions for 2008

SOURCE: New York State, Division of Criminal Justice Services, "Criminal Justice Statistics," available online at http://criminaljustice.state.ny.us/crimnet/ojsa/dispos/index.htm (accessed on August 7, 2009).

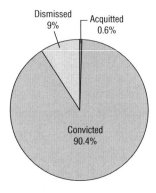

Results of Criminal Trials in 2007–2008[a]

[a]Refers to trials completed in U.S. District Courts from April 1, 2007, to March 31, 2008.

SOURCE: U.S. Courts, "Federal Judicial Caseload Statistics," available online at http://www.uscourts.gov/caseload2008/contents.html (accessed on August 12, 2009).

White House. Office of the Press Secretary. 1994. *Proclamation for World AIDS Day, November 30, 1994.* Press release.

———. 2009. *Obama Administration Announces New Campaign to Refocus National Attention on the HIV Crisis in the United States.* Press release, April 7, 2009; National Center for HIV/AIDS, Viral Hepatitis, STD and TB Prevention, Centers for Disease Control and Prevention.

"Barack Obama: Fighting HIV/AIDS Worldwide." Available online at http://www.barackobama.com/pdf/AIDSFactSheet.pdf; website home page: http://www.barackobama.com (accessed June 10, 2009).

Public Library of Science (Pl o S Medicine). 2007. The US Anti-Prostitution Pledge; First Amendment Challenges and Public Health Priorities. (Policy Forum)(United States Leadership Against Global HIV/AIDS, Tuberculosis, and Malaria Act of 2003).

"Global Summary of the AIDS Epidemic, December 2007." Available online at http://www.who.int/hiv/data/2008_global_summary_AIDS_ep.png; website home page: http://www.who.int (accessed June 10, 2009).

"AIDS Patients Will Spend $600K for care." Available online at http://www.msnbc.msn.com/id/15655257/print/1/displaymode/1098; website home page: http://www.msnbc.com (accessed June 8, 2009).

"The United States President's Emergency Plan for AIDS Relief (PEPFAR)." Available online at http://www.pepfar.gov/about/index.htm. (accessed June 7, 2009).

CROSS REFERENCES

Disability Discrimination; Discrimination; Food and Drug Administration; Gay and Lesbian Rights; Health Care Law; Patients' Rights; Physicians and Surgeons; Privacy.

ACQUISITION CHARGE

A fee imposed upon a borrower who satisfies a loan prior to the date of payment specified in the loan agreement.

Many home mortgages provide that if the persons who borrowed the money want to repay their MORTGAGE within two years, they must pay an ACQUISITION CHARGE of a small percentage of the outstanding balance of the mortgage. *Prepayment penalty* is another name for acquisition charge.

ACQUIT

To set free, release or discharge as from an obligation, burden or accusation. To absolve one from an obligation or a liability; or to legally certify the innocence of one charged with a crime.

ACQUITTAL

The legal and formal certification of the innocence of a person who has been charged with a crime.

Acquittals *in fact* take place when a jury finds a VERDICT of not GUILTY. Acquittals *in law* take place by OPERATION OF LAW such as when a person has been charged as an ACCESSORY to the crime of ROBBERY and the principal has been acquitted.

ACT

Something done; usually, something done intentionally or voluntarily or with a purpose.

The term encompasses not only physical acts—such as turning on the water or purchasing a gun—but also refers to more intangible acts such as adopting a decree, edict, law, judgment, award, or determination. An act may be a private act, done by an individual managing his or her personal affairs, or it may be a public act, done by an official, a council, or a court. When a bill is favorably acted upon in the process of LEGISLATION, it becomes an act.

ACT OF GOD

An event that directly and exclusively results from the occurrence of natural causes that could not have been prevented by the exercise of foresight or caution; an inevitable accident.

Courts have recognized various events as acts of God—tornadoes, earthquakes, death, extraordinarily high tides, violent winds, and floods. Many insurance policies for property damage exclude from their protection damage caused by acts of God.

ACTION

Conduct; behavior; something done; a series of acts.

A case or lawsuit; a legal and formal demand for enforcement of one's rights against another party asserted in a court of justice.

The term *action* includes all the proceedings attendant upon a legal demand, its ADJUDICATION, and its denial or its enforcement by a court. Specifically, it is the LEGAL PROCEEDINGS, while a CAUSE OF ACTION is the underlying right that gives rise to them. In casual conversation, *action* and *cause of action* may be used interchangeably, but they are more properly distinguished. At one time it was more correct to speak of actions at law and of proceedings or suits in equity. The distinction is rather technical, however, and not significant since the merger of law and equity. The term *action* is used more often for civil lawsuits than for criminal proceedings.

Parties in an Action

A person must have some sort of LEGAL RIGHT before starting an action. That legal right implies a duty owed to one person by another, whether it is a duty to do something or a duty not to do something. When the other person acts wrongfully or fails to act as the law requires, such behavior is a breach, or violation, of that person's legal duty. If that breach causes harm, it is the basis for a cause of action. The injured person may seek redress by starting an action in court.

Acts of God, which include hurricanes such as Hurricane Katrina, are sometimes excluded from insurance policies for property damage.

AP IMAGES

The person who starts the action is the PLAINTIFF, and the person sued is the DEFENDANT. They are the parties in the action. Frequently, there are multiple parties on a side. The defendant may assert a defense which, if true, will defeat the plaintiff's claim. A COUNTERCLAIM may be made by the defendant against the plaintiff or a CROSS-CLAIM against another party on the same side of the lawsuit. The law may permit joinder of two or more claims, such as an action for property damage and an action for personal injuries, after one auto ACCIDENT; or it may require consolidation of actions by an order of the court. Where prejudice or injustice is likely to result, the court may order a SEVERANCE of actions into different lawsuits for different parties.

Commencement of an Action

The time when an action may begin depends on the kind of action involved. A plaintiff cannot start a lawsuit until the cause of action has accrued. For example, a man who wants to use a parcel of land for a store where only houses are allowed must begin by applying for a variance from the local zoning board. He cannot bypass the board and start an action in court. His right to SUE does not ACCRUE until the board turns down his request.

Neither can a person begin an action after the time allowed by law. Most causes of action are covered by a STATUTE OF LIMITATIONS, which specifically limits the time within which to begin the action. If the law in a particular state says that an action for libel cannot be brought more than one year after publication of a defamatory statement, then those actions must be initiated within that statutory period. Where there is no statute that limits the time to commence a particular action, a court may nevertheless dismiss the case if the claim is stale and if LITIGATION at that point would not be fair.

A plaintiff must first select the right court, then an action can be commenced by delivery of the formal legal papers to the appropriate person. Statutes that regulate proper procedure for this must be strictly observed. A typical statute specifies that an action may be begun by delivery of a SUMMONS, or a WRIT on the defendant. At one time, common-law actions had to be pleaded according to highly technical FORMS OF ACTION, but now it is generally sufficient simply to serve papers that state facts describing a recognized cause of action. If this SERVICE OF PROCESS is done properly, the defendant has fair notice of the claim made against him or her and the court acquires jurisdiction over him or her. In some cases, the law requires delivery of the summons or writ to a specified public officer such as a U.S. marshal, who becomes responsible for serving it on the defendant.

Termination of an Action

After an action is commenced, it is said to be pending until termination. While the action is pending, neither party has the right to start another action in a different court over the same dispute or to do any act that would make the court's decision futile.

A lawsuit may be terminated because of dismissal before both sides have fully argued the merits of their cases at trial. It can also be ended because of COMPROMISE AND SETTLEMENT, after which the plaintiff withdraws his or her action from the court.

Actions are terminated by the entry of final judgments by the courts. A judgment may be based on a jury VERDICT or it may be a JUDGMENT NOTWITHSTANDING THE VERDICT. Where there has been no jury, judgment is based on the judge's decision. Unless one party is given leave—or permission from the court—to do something that might revive the lawsuit, such as amending an insufficient complaint, the action is at an end when judgment is formally entered on the records of the court.

CROSS REFERENCE

Civil Procedure.

ACTION ON THE CASE

One of the old common-law forms of action that provided a remedy for the invasion of personal or property interests.

ACTION ON THE CASE is also called TRESPASS on the case because it developed from the COMMON-LAW ACTION of trespass during the fifteenth century in England. Often it is simply called case.

Case differs from trespass in that it redresses more indirect injuries than the WILLFUL invasion of the plaintiff's property contemplated by trespass. It was designed to supplement the action of trespass. For example, a person struck by a log thrown over a fence could maintain an action in trespass against the thrower. If, instead, the wrongdoer tossed the log into the street and the PLAINTIFF were hurt by stumbling over it, the plaintiff could maintain an action on the case rather than in trespass.

In PLEADING an action on the case, the plaintiff sets forth the circumstances of the entire case. In pleading an action on the case, the complaint differed from the forms used in pleading other actions because other actions generally had highly stylized and rigid forms that had to be followed word for word. The plaintiff in the action on the case alleged facts to show that (1) the DEFENDANT had some sort of duty; (2) the defendant had violated that duty; and (3) the result was harm to the plaintiff or the plaintiff's property. Over the years this action developed into a remedy for a wide variety of wrongs that were not redressed by the other FORMS OF ACTION. For example, a plaintiff could SUE a defendant who maintained a NUISANCE in the neighborhood; who violated an easement or a RIGHT OF WAY; or who committed libel, slander, malicious prosecution, fraud, or deceit. Most importantly, the action on the case came into common use as the legal method for compensating victims of NEGLIGENCE. It thus became one of the most widely used forms of action in the common-law system and gave birth to the modern law of torts.

When ejectment was still considered a modern improvement on trespass in England, it already had been abandoned in New England because of its complicated technical requirements. One of the reasons for the American experience is that law books were scarce in the colonies, and many judges were laymen. The most rigid applications of technical formalities came during the first half of the nineteenth century after lawyers gained influence in the legal system.

Dissatisfaction with the technicalities of the forms soon began to peak. CODE PLEADING was then introduced to replace the prior forms of action. An attempt was made to reduce the number of writs to some basic few that would be adequate for all of the different requirements of modern LITIGATION. Attention was shifted from the form to the elements of a CAUSE OF ACTION. Courts asked only whether the plaintiff had stated a CLAIM on which relief could be granted. The objective was to decide whether the plaintiff was entitled to a remedy with as little procedural red tape as possible. When code pleading fell short of this goal, the modern law of CIVIL PROCEDURE developed the theory that there should be only one form of action, the CIVIL ACTION.

The old forms of action exist only as names for procedures based on them and as the foundation of much of the SUBSTANTIVE LAW. In Pennsylvania, for example, the word *trespass* is used for tort actions, and *assumpsit* for lawsuits based upon contracts.

ACTIONABLE

Giving sufficient legal grounds for a lawsuit; giving rise to a cause of action.

An act, event, or occurrence is said to be actionable when there are legal grounds for basing a lawsuit on it. For example, an ASSAULT is an actionable tort.

ACTIONABLE PER SE

Legally sufficient to support a lawsuit in itself.

Words are ACTIONABLE PER SE if they are obviously insulting and injurious to one's reputation. In lawsuits for libel or slander, words that impute the commission of a crime, a loathsome disease, or unchastity, or remarks that affect the plaintiff's business, trade, profession, calling, or office may be actionable per se. No special proof of actual harm done by the words is necessary to win monetary damages when words are actionable per se.

ACTUAL CASH VALUE

The fair or reasonable cash price for which a property could be sold in the market in the ordinary course of business, and not at forced sale.

The price it will bring in a fair market after reasonable efforts to find a purchaser who will give the highest price. What property is worth in money, allowing for depreciation. Ordinarily, actual cash value, fair market value, *and* market value *are synonymous terms.*

ACTUAL NOTICE

Conveying facts to a person with the intention to apprise that person of a proceeding in which his or her interests are involved, or informing a person of some fact that he or she has a right to know and which the informer has a legal duty to communicate.

When such notice has been given to someone personally, it is called *express actual notice* or *express notice.* If a tenant notifies a landlord that the elevator is broken, the landlord has express actual notice of the defect. Should the landlord fail to repair the elevator and another tenant is injured while riding it, the landlord would be liable for the tenant's injuries.

Actual notice can be presumed if an average person, having witness of the same evidence, should know that a particular fact exists. This is called *implied actual notice* or *implied notice.* If the landlord had been with the tenant when the tenant discovered the broken elevator, the landlord would be considered to have implied notice of the defect.

ACTUARY

A statistician who computes insurance and pension rates and premiums on the basis of the experience of people sharing similar age and health characteristics.

The profession also includes statisticians who provide expert data analysis on risk assessment and risk management for the financial services sector. Actuaries are most often employed within the insurance industry, but also prepare and assess data for commercial and investment banks, retirement and PENSION fund administrators, or are self-employed as consultants. Specific data prepared by actuaries is often presented in the form of actuarial tables (MORTALITY TABLES) that indicate the life expectancy of an individual. Such tables may be used as the bases for calculating estimated insurance premiums or monthly retirement annuities. When utilized by expert WITNESSES, actuarial tables are admissible in evidence to show life expectancy. Juries may award damages to plaintiffs for compromised life expectancy resulting from the alleged wrongdoing of tortfeasors (wrongdoers).

ACTUS REUS

[Latin, Guilty act.] *As an element of criminal responsibility, the wrongful act or omission that comprises the physical components of a crime. Criminal statutes generally require proof of both* actus reus *and* mens rea *on the part of a defendant in order to establish criminal liability.*

AD DAMNUM

[Latin, To the loss.] *The clause in a complaint that sets a maximum amount of money that the plaintiff can recover under a default judgment if the defendant fails to appear in court.*

It is a fundamental principle of due process that a DEFENDANT must be given fair notice of what is demanded of him or her. In a CIVIL ACTION, a PLAINTIFF must include in the complaint served on a defendant a clause that states the amount of the loss or the amount of money damages claimed in the case. This clause is the *ad damnum.* It tells a defendant how much he or she stands to lose in the case.

In some states, the *ad damnum* sets an absolute limit on the amount of damages recoverable in the case, regardless of how much loss the plaintiff is able to prove at trial. The reason for this rule is that a defendant should not be exposed to greater LIABILITY than the *ad damnum* just because he or she comes into court and defends himself or herself. In states that follow this rule, a plaintiff may be given leave to increase the amount demanded by amending the complaint if later circumstances can be shown to warrant this. For example, a plaintiff who sues for $5,000 for a broken leg may find out after the action has begun that she will be permanently disabled. At that point, the court may allow the plaintiff to amend her complaint and demand damages of $50,000.

In most states and in the federal courts, a plaintiff can collect money damages in excess of the *ad damnum* if proof can be made at trial to support the higher amount. A defendant may ask for more time to prepare the case in order not to be prejudiced at trial if it begins to look as though the plaintiff is claiming more money than the *ad damnum* demands. However, the defendant cannot prevent judgment for a higher amount.

AD HOC

[Latin, For this; for this special purpose.] *An attorney ad hoc or a guardian or curator ad hoc is one appointed for a special purpose, generally to represent the client, ward, or child in the particular action in which the appointment is made.*

An administrative agency, a legislature, or other governmental bodies may establish *ad hoc* committees to study particular problems. For example, a city government may establish an ad hoc committee to investigate and discuss the placement of a new stadium in the city. Likewise, an administrative agency in some jurisdictions may engage in *ad hoc* rulemaking, whereby the agency establishes specific procedures to promulgate a rule without necessarily adhering to formal rulemaking requirements.

AD HOMINEM

[Latin, To the person.] *A term used in debate to denote an argument made personally against an opponent, instead of against the opponent's argument.*

AD INTERIM

[Latin, In the meantime.] *An officer* ad interim *is a person appointed to fill a position that is temporarily open, or to perform the functions of a particular position during the absence or temporary incapacity of the individual who regularly fulfills those duties.*

AD LITEM

[Latin, For the suit; for the purposes of the suit; pending the suit.] *A guardian ad litem is a guardian appointed to prosecute or defend a suit on behalf of a party who is legally incapable of doing so, such as an infant or an insane person.*

AD VALOREM

According to value.

The term *ad valorem* is derived from the Latin *ad valentiam,* meaning "to the value." It is commonly applied to a tax imposed on the value of property. Real property taxes that are imposed by the states, counties, and cities are the most common type of *ad valorem* taxes. *ad valorem* taxes can, however, be imposed upon

PERSONAL PROPERTY. For example, a motor vehicle tax may be imposed upon personal property such as an automobile.

An article of commerce may be subjected to an *ad valorem* tax in proportion to its value, which is determined by assessment or appraisal.

Duties, taxes on goods imported or brought into this country from a foreign country, are either *ad valorem* or specific. An *ad valorem* duty is one in the form of a percentage on the value of the property, unlike a specific duty that is a fixed sum imposed on each article of a class, such as all Swiss wristwatches, regardless of their individual values.

CROSS REFERENCE

Taxation.

❖ ADAMS, JOHN

JOHN ADAMS achieved prominence on many levels—as JURIST, statesman, and as the second PRESIDENT OF THE UNITED STATES. Known for his sharp diplomatic skills, his flair for words, and his spirited activism, he was an instrumental figure in forging the fledgling nation that would become the United States of America.

Adams was born on October 30, 1735, in Braintree (now Quincy), Massachusetts, the son of a farmer. His parents encouraged him in his studies, and pushed him to enter Harvard College to study for the clergy. Upon graduation in 1755, the strong-willed Adams instead decided to teach and study law. He was admitted to the Boston bar in 1758 and established a prestigious legal practice. During the pre–Revolutionary War years, Adams spoke out strongly against many acts enforced by the British government, including the TOWNSHEND ACTS, which unjustly taxed items such as glass and tea. He also joined the Sons of Liberty—a

John Adams.
LIBRARY OF CONGRESS

group of lawyers, merchants, and businessmen who, in 1765, banded together to oppose the STAMP ACT.

From 1774 to 1778 Adams served as the Massachusetts representative to the CONTINENTAL CONGRESS. He entered the judiciary during this period and rendered decisions as chief justice of the Superior Court of Massachusetts from 1775 to 1777. In 1776 he signed the newly created DECLARATION OF INDEPENDENCE.

After the war, Adams entered the field of foreign service, acting as commissioner to France in 1777. In 1783 Adams went to Paris with JOHN JAY and THOMAS JEFFERSON to successfully negotiate the TREATY OF PARIS with Great Britain, which officially ended the Revolutionary War and established the United States as an

> FEAR IS THE FOUNDATION OF MOST GOVERNMENTS.
> —JOHN ADAMS

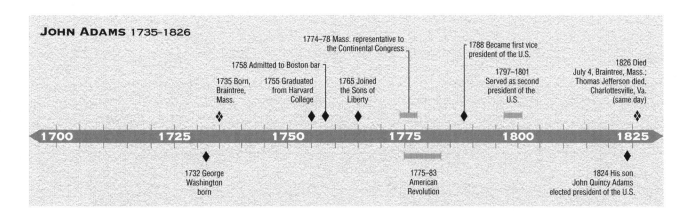

JOHN ADAMS 1735–1826

1774–78 Mass. representative to the Continental Congress

1788 Became first vice president of the U.S.

1758 Admitted to Boston bar

1735 Born, Braintree, Mass.

1755 Graduated from Harvard College

1765 Joined the Sons of Liberty

1797–1801 Served as second president of the U.S.

1826 Died July 4, Braintree, Mass.; Thomas Jefferson died, Charlottesville, Va. (same day)

1700   1725   1750   1775   1800   1825

1732 George Washington born

1775–83 American Revolution

1824 His son John Quincy Adams elected president of the U.S.

independent nation. In 1785 Adams became the first U.S. minister to Great Britain.

Adams returned to the United States in 1788 and began service to the new government with his election to the office of vice president of the United States. He was the first person to serve in this office and was reelected for a second term in 1792. In 1796 Adams was elected president of the United States. He was the second man to hold this position, following the retirement of the first president, GEORGE WASHINGTON. During his term of office, Adams advocated naval strength; approved the ALIEN AND SEDITION ACTS of 1798 (1 Stat. 566, 570, 577, 596), which increased the restrictions concerning ALIENS and imposed harsh penalties on any person who attempted to obstruct the government system; averted war with France; and selected the eminent JOHN MARSHALL as chief justice of the U.S. Supreme Court. In 1800 Adams ran for the presidency for a second term but was defeated by Thomas Jefferson.

Adams's political and personal JURISPRUDENCE was characterized by intense nationalism; some consider him the most influential designer of the new nation's government and identity. A Federalist and a realist who spoke his mind without consideration for political fallout, Adams believed that unchecked power created abuse even in the best of democracies. To that end, he was the most significant advocate for the creation of a balance of powers through a tripartite government: a bicameral legislature, a strong executive, and an independent judiciary. He also authored the state constitution for the Commonwealth of Massachusetts, which remains the oldest functioning written constitution in the world. Adams published a number of political treatises, including *Thoughts on Government* (1776) and *Defense of the Constitutions of the United States of America against the Attacks of Mr. Turgot* (1787).

John Adams sought a written constitution based on unwritten NATURAL LAW. He believed that the COMMON LAW was the source of unalienable, INDEFEASIBLE rights of men, the honor and dignity of human nature, the grandeur and glory of the public, and the universal happiness of individuals.

John Adams was also a devoted family man. His wife, Abigail, was a vivacious and witty first lady who openly commented on politics and issues of the day. There were five Adams children, including John Quincy, who served as the sixth president of the United States. John Adams died on July 4, 1826, in Braintree.

FURTHER READINGS

Allen, Brooke. 2002. "John Adams: Realist of the Revolution." *The Hudson Review* (spring) 55.

McCullough, David. 2001. *John Adams.* New York: Simon & Schuster.

Ryerson, Richard Alan, ed. 2001. *John Adams and the Founding of the Republic.* Boston: Massachusetts Historical Society.

Thompson, C. Bradley. 1998. *John Adams and the Spirit of Liberty.* Lawrence: Univ. Press of Kansas.

❖ ADAMS, JOHN QUINCY

John Quincy Adams was more than just the sixth PRESIDENT OF THE UNITED STATES. He was a child of the American Revolution, having witnessed the Battle of Bunker Hill. He was the son of the nation's second president, JOHN ADAMS. And he was a successful diplomat. Chosen president by the House after finishing second in the ELECTORAL COLLEGE, Adams became the first president to wear long trousers, rather than breeches, at his inauguration, on March 4, 1825. After one term as president, he went on to serve with distinction for 17 years in the House of Representatives.

Adams was born on July 11, 1767, in Braintree, Massachusetts (now Quincy, Massachusetts). As the son of one of the nation's founders, he had many opportunities not available to other young men. Before reaching the age when young people today graduate from high school, Adams had established himself as a diplomat. He accompanied his father on diplomatic missions to Europe in 1778 and 1780, where he studied in Paris, France, and in Amsterdam and Leiden, the Netherlands. In 1781, at the age of 14, Adams traveled with Francis Dana, the first American minister to Russia, as Dana's private secretary and French interpreter. In 1783 the young Adams joined his father in Paris, where he served as one of the secretaries to the American commissioners in the negotiations of the peace treaty that concluded the American Revolution. Fearing alienation from his own country, Adams returned home in 1785 and, by virtue of his earlier studies, was able to enroll as a junior at Harvard College, from which he graduated in 1787.

For three years Adams read law at Newburyport, Massachusetts, under THEOPHILUS PARSONS, and in 1790 he was admitted to the bar. While struggling to find clients, Adams engaged in political journalism. He wrote a series of 11 articles controverting some of the doctrines presented in Thomas Paine's *Rights of Man* (1791–92). In a second series of articles, he defended President George Washington's policy of neutrality in the war between France and England in 1793. His third series of articles attacked those who wanted the United States to join France in a war against Britain. These articles impressed Washington so much that he appointed Adams U.S. minister to the Netherlands in May 1794.

President Washington thought Adams one of the ablest officers in the foreign service. In 1796 he appointed Adams minister to Portugal. Before Adams's departure for that new post, however, his father became president. Both Adamses felt that it was undesirable for the son of a president to hold a post in the father's administration, but Washington urged that the younger Adams remain in the diplomatic corps, calling him the most valuable public person abroad. President Adams then appointed his son minister to Prussia.

Before taking up his new post in Prussia, Adams was married, in London, to Louisa Catherine Johnson (1775–1852), daughter of the U.S. counsel in London.

In September 1801, with new president THOMAS JEFFERSON in the White House, Adams was called back from Prussia. In 1802 he was elected to the Massachusetts senate. One year later the state senate elected him to the U.S. Senate. (Prior to the passage of the SEVENTEENTH AMENDMENT in 1913, U.S. senators were elected by the senates of the individual states.)

Adams had always considered himself a political independent, and he was given a

John Quincy Adams.
LIBRARY OF CONGRESS

chance to prove this in the U.S. Senate. After his election, he was set upon by forces opposed to the FEDERALIST PARTY, of which Adams was considered a member, and political enemies of his father. Instead of accepting his fate as a powerless and unpopular member of an unpopular political minority, Adams asserted his political independence. He began to vote with President Jefferson and the opposition Democratic-Republicans, and broke with his party completely in 1807 by supporting the EMBARGO ACT (46 App. U.S.C.A. § 328). This act, backed by Jefferson, placed an embargo on all

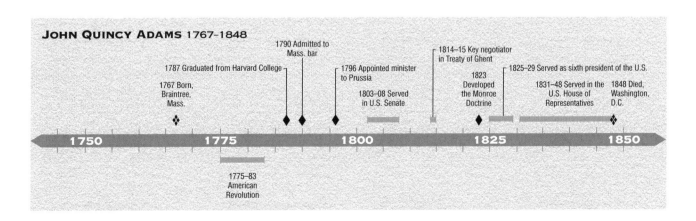

JOHN QUINCY ADAMS 1767–1848

1790 Admitted to
Mass. bar

1787 Graduated from Harvard College

1767 Born,
Braintree,
Mass.

1796 Appointed minister
to Prussia

1803–08 Served
in U.S. Senate

1814–15 Key negotiator
in Treaty of Ghent

1823
Developed
the Monroe
Doctrine

1825–29 Served as sixth president of the U.S.

1831–48 Served in the
U.S. House of
Representatives

1848 Died,
Washington,
D.C.

1750   1775   1800   1825   1850

1775–83
American
Revolution

foreign commerce. The act was opposed by the Federalists and the New England states, who wanted to encourage trade with the British. They feared that the Embargo Act would stifle New England's economy. Adams voted for the Embargo Act, against the wishes of his party and region, believing that it benefited the nation as a whole.

Adams paid the price for breaking with his party. Federalist leaders in Massachusetts—who felt that Adams had betrayed them—elected another man to the Senate several months before the 1808 elections. Adams resigned, and later that year, in a move indicative of his political independence, attended a Democratic-Republican congressional caucus meeting, where JAMES MADISON was nominated for president, thus allying himself with that party.

Adams attempted to retire from public life and devote himself to a teaching position at Harvard College, but the lure of public service was too strong. In 1809 President Madison persuaded him to accept an appointment as minister to Russia. In 1814 and 1815 Adams played a key role in the negotiations resulting in the Treaty of Ghent, with the British, ending the WAR OF 1812. The negotiations helped Adams gain respect as a diplomat.

In 1817 President JAMES MONROE called Adams back to the United States to serve as his SECRETARY OF STATE. Adams's most important achievement in this office was the development of the MONROE DOCTRINE. It was Adams who made the first declaration of that policy in July 1823, several months before Monroe formally announced it in his annual message to Congress, on December 2, 1823. At that time, the United States feared that Russia intended to establish colonies in Alaska and, more important, that the continental European states would intervene in Central and South America to help Spain recover its former colonies, which had won their independence in a series of wars in the early nineteenth century. Adams believed that the Americas were no longer subject to any European colonial establishment and that they should make their own foreign policies. The Monroe Doctrine set forth three basic policy statements aimed at protecting the Western Hemisphere from European intervention: North and South America were closed to further European colonization; the United States would not intervene in wars in Europe and would not interfere with European colonies and dependencies in the Americas; and the United States would regard any intervention by a European power in the independent states of the Western Hemisphere as the manifestation of an unfriendly disposition toward the United States.

Adams served as secretary of state for the entire eight years under President Monroe. When the presidential election of 1824 came around, Adams was considered a favorite; after all, the previous two presidents, Madison and Monroe, had also served as secretaries of state. But 1824 was no normal year for politics in the United States. All four candidates were members of the same political party, the DEMOCRATIC-REPUBLICAN PARTY, and party affiliation had given way to sectionalism. Secretary of the Treasury William Harris Crawford, of Georgia, who had recently suffered a paralytic stroke, was nominated by a congressional caucus. The Tennessee legislature nominated ANDREW JACKSON, and the Kentucky legislature nominated HENRY CLAY. Adams was nominated by an eastern faction of the party in Boston. On Tuesday, November 9, 1824, voters went to the polls and cast 153,544 votes for Jackson, 108,740 for Adams, 46,618 for Clay, and 47,136 for Crawford. (Figures from Kane, *Facts about the Presidents*; figures in other sources differ.) The electoral vote results were as follows: Jackson, 99; Adams, 84; Crawford, 41; and Clay, 37. As no candidate received a majority of the electoral votes, the House of Representatives was called upon to choose the president, as set forth under Article II, Section 1, Clause 3, of the Constitution. After Clay gave his support to Adams, the House elected Adams the sixth president in February 1825.

For one who had led so accomplished a life, Adams must have viewed his presidency as a failure. He got off to a rocky start when Jackson's supporters in Congress decried what they called a corrupt bargain between Adams and Clay. Only days after the House selected Adams president, Clay was offered the office of secretary of state, which he accepted. This deal split the Democratic-Republican Party, and Adams's group became known as the National Republicans. Jackson's group fought with Adams for the next four years.

Adams threw all his energies into the presidency. In his inaugural address, he called for an ambitious program of national improvements including the construction of highways, canals, weather stations, and a national university. He urged Congress to use the powers of government for the benefit of all people. Congress disagreed. Many of the programs advocated by Adams were not realized until after his death.

Despite his best efforts, Adams felt worn down by the burdens and demands of the presidency. His personal reserve, austerity, and coolness of manner prevented him from appealing to the imagination and affections of the people. He had not even tried to defend himself against the attacks of Jackson and his followers, feeling that it was below the dignity of the president to engage in political debate. Throughout Adams's presidency, Jackson gained in popularity, so much so that in the elections of 1828, he defeated Adams by 178 electoral votes to 83. Jackson won a popular vote proportionally larger than that of any other presidential candidate during the rest of the 1800s.

Once again Adams sought to retire from public life, but the people of Massachusetts called him back. In 1830 he defeated two other candidates and was elected to the U.S. House of Representatives, representing a district from Plymouth. When it was suggested to him that his acceptance of this position would degrade a former president, Adams replied that no person could be degraded by serving the people as a representative in Congress, or, he added, as a selectman. Indeed, Adams said that his election as president was not half so gratifying as his election to the House.

Adams shone brightly from 1831 to his death in 1848. He remained independent of party politics, and held important posts in Congress, serving at times as chairman of the Foreign Affairs Committee and of the Committee on Manufactures. Adams was conspicuous as an opponent of the expansion of SLAVERY and was at heart an abolitionist, though he never became one in the political sense of the word. He took center stage during debates over the gag rules, which resulted when abolitionists sent many petitions to Congress urging that slavery be abolished in the District of Columbia and the new territories. Southern members of Congress who did not want to discuss slave issues passed a series of rules, known as the gag rules, that kept the abolitionists' petitions from being read on the House floor, effectively blocking any discussion of slavery. Adams fought the gag rules as violations of the right of free speech and the right of citizens to petition their government as guaranteed in the FIRST AMENDMENT. As the leading opponent of the gag rules, Adams became the person abolitionists sent their petitions to. He, in turn, tried to have the House consider those petitions, only to run up against the gag rules. For several years Adams tried unsuccessfully to have the rules repealed, but he was able to win supporters to his side each time he tried, and in 1844 he finally succeeded in having the rules abolished.

Another contribution of Adams to the antislavery cause was his championing of Africans on the slave ship Amistad. The slaves had mutinied off the coast of Cuba, capturing their masters. The slaves, unfamiliar with navigation, asked their captives to help them sail to a country where slave trade was illegal. The former masters took advantage of the slaves' navigational inexperience and directed the ship into U.S. waters near Long Island, hoping to find sympathetic U.S. authorities. Adams was one of two attorneys who argued the case of the Africans before the U.S. Supreme Court, defending the blacks as free people. President MARTIN VAN BUREN had taken the position that the slaves must be returned to their masters and to their inevitable death. Adams helped win their freedom (*United States v. Libellants of Schooner Amistad*, 40 U.S. [15 Pet.] 518, 10 L. Ed. 826 [1841]).

Adams's support of the arts and sciences was evident in his battle to uphold the dying wishes of an eccentric Englishman named James Smithson. Smithson was the illegitimate son of the first duke of Northumberland. At his death in 1829, he bequeathed his entire estate to his nephew. His will further provided that if the nephew were to die without heirs, which he did in 1835, the entire estate was to be given to the U.S. government to found what Smithson asked be called the Smithsonian Institution, an establishment for the increase and diffusion of knowledge. Adams led a ten-year fight for acceptance of the endowment, which was valued at $508,000 in 1835, and the Smithsonian Institution was established on August 10, 1846.

On November 19, 1846, Adams suffered a stroke, from which he never fully recovered. He continued to serve in Congress until he suffered a second stroke and collapsed in the House of Representatives. He was carried from his seat to the Speaker's room, where he lay until his death two days later, on February 23, 1848.

FURTHER READINGS

Kane, Joseph N. 2001. *Facts about the Presidents: A Compilation of Biographical and Historical Information.* 7th ed. New York: Wilson.

Nagel, Paul C. 1997. *John Quincy Adams: A Public Life, A Private Life.* New York: Knopf.

Parsons, Lynn H. 1998. *John Quincy Adams.* Madison, Wis.: Madison House.

Remini, Robert Vincent. 2002. *John Quincy Adams.* New York: Times Books.

ADAPTATION

The act or process of modifying an object to render it suitable for a particular or new purpose or situation.

In the law of patents—grants by the government to inventors for the exclusive right to manufacture, use, or market inventions for a term of years—adaptation denotes a category of patentable inventions, which entails the application of an existing product or process to a new use, accompanied by the exercise of inventive faculties. Federal law provides: "Whoever invents or discovers any new and useful process, machine, manufacture, or composition of matter, or any new and useful improvement thereof, may obtain a PATENT therefore, subject to the conditions and requirements of this title." 35 U.S.C.A. §101.

The adaptation of a device to a different field can constitute an invention if inventiveness exists in the conception of new use and with modifications necessary to render the device applicable in the new field. The progressive adaptation of well-known devices to new, but similar, uses is merely a display of an expected technical proficiency, which involves only the exercise of common reasoning abilities upon materials furnished by special knowledge ensuing from continual practice. It, therefore, does not represent a patentable invention. Ingenuity beyond the mere adaptation of teachings as could be done by a skilled mechanic is required to achieve a patentable invention; inventive talent, rather than skill in adaptation, must be manifested. To entitle a party to the benefit of the patent statute, the device must not only be new; it must be inventively new. The readaptation of old forms to new roles does not constitute invention where there is no significant alteration in the method of applying it or in the nature of the result obtained. No invention will be recognized if the new form of the result has not previously been contemplated and, irrespective of the remoteness of the new use from the old, if no modifications in the old device are necessary to adapt it to the new use.

Invention is generally not involved where an old process, device, or method is applied to a new subject or use that is analogous to the old or to a new use or the production of a new result in the same or analogous field. If the new use is so comparable to the old that the concept of adapting the device to the new use would occur to a person proficient in the art and interested in devising a method of changing the intended function, there is no invention even though significant alterations have been made. The application of an old device to a new use is normally patentable only if the new use is in a different field or involves a completely novel function. In addition, the physical modifications need not be extensive, as long as they are essential to the objective.

In the law of copyrights the exclusive right of the author of a literary project to reproduce, publish, and sell his or her work, which is granted by statute, adaptation refers to the creation of a derivative work, which is protected by federal COPYRIGHT laws.

A derivative work involves a recasting or translation process that incorporates preexisting material capable of protection by copyright. An adaptation is copyrighted if it meets the requirement of originality, in the sense that the author has created it by his or her own proficiency, labor, and judgment without directly copying or subtly imitating the preexisting material. Mere minor alterations will not suffice. In addition the adapter must procure the consent of the copyright owner of the underlying work if he or she wants to copy from such work. The copyright in a derivative work, however, extends only to the material contributed by the adapter and does not affect the copyright protection afforded to the preexisting material.

The rise in the use of digital media has caused new dilemmas in the area of copyright law with respect to adaptations. Even average technology users may make copies and adapt the original works to their needs. Issues in this area have focused upon INTELLECTUAL PROPERTY rights in the context of the INTERNET and computer programs.

Even average computer users are capable of copying digital music files and modifying them through the use of software. The Internet enables these users to prepare these modifications and distribute them to a wide audience using the Web, E-MAIL, and other methods of distribution. The Copyright Act of 1976 continues to protect the copyright holders, generally requiring those who prepared derivative works to obtain permission from the copyright holder (17 U.S.C.A. § 114(b) [1996]). However, enforcement of these provisions has proven difficult and led to a number of efforts, including those by the Recording Industry Association of America, to find new methods for protecting the rights of the copyright holders.

A second cause of concern among copyright owners is the ability of computer users to make copies of computer programs and adopt these programs to serve the users' purposes. The Copyright Act provides an exclusive right to the copyright holders of computer programs and allows owners of copies of these programs to make additional copies only in limited circumstances (17 U.S.C.A. § 117 [1996]). Like sound recordings, protection of these copyrights has proven difficult, leading lawmakers to consider a number of new options to protect these rights.

In the law of real property, with respect to fixtures (articles that were PERSONAL PROPERTY but became part of the realty through annexation to the premises), adaptation is the relationship between the article and the use that is made of the realty to which the article is annexed.

The prevailing view is that the adaptation or appropriation of an article affixed to real property for the purpose or use to which the premises are devoted is an important consideration in ascertaining its status as a fixture. According to this theory, if the article facilitates the realization of the purpose of the real property, the annexor presumably intends it to be a permanent accession. Numerous other cases, however, allude to the adaptation of an item to the use to which the premises are designated, as merely one of the tests or factors that should or must be evaluated in determining that it constitutes real property. Other cases view the character of the use of the article annexed as significant.

The special construction or fitting of an article for location and use on certain land or in a particular building, which mitigates against

use in another location, indicates that is was intended to constitute a part of the land.

The adaptability of an annexed article for use in another location is sometimes viewed as demonstrating the retention of its character as personalty (personal property), but this characteristic is not conclusive. Articles not designed to comprise the realty retain their character as personalty.

FURTHER READINGS

Benn, Marvin N., and Richard J. Superfine. 1994. "§ 117— The Right to Adapt into the Fourth Generation and the Source Code Generator's Dilemma." *John Marshall Journal of Computer and Information Law* 12 (spring).

Miller, Arthur R., and Michael H. Davis. 2007. *Intellectual Property: Patents, Trademarks, and Copyright in a Nutshell.* 4th ed. Eagan, MN: West.

Plotkin, Mark E., ed. 2003. *E-Commerce Law & Business.* Frederick, MD: Aspen.

ADD-ON

A purchase of additional goods before payment is made for goods already purchased.

An add-on may be covered by a clause in an installment payment contract that allows the seller to hold a security interest in the earlier goods until full payment is made on the later goods.

❖ ADDAMS, JANE

Jane Addams, a pioneer in social reform, founded Hull House, the first SETTLEMENT house in the United States, to serve the immigrant families who came to Chicago at the beginning of the industrial revolution. For nearly 50 years, Addams worked relentlessly for improved living and working conditions for America's urban poor, for women's suffrage, and for international PACIFISM.

Addams was the youngest of eight children, born on September 6, 1860, to John H. and Sarah Addams. Her mother died when she was two years old, and her teenage sisters, Mary, Martha, and Alice, took over her upbringing. Her family followed the Quaker faith, and valued hard work and change through peaceful efforts. Addams idolized her father, whom she described as a man of great integrity. He remained a pivotal figure in her life until his death in 1881.

Addams's first exposure to urban poverty occurred when she was six years old, during a trip with her father to Freeport, Illinois. Upon seeing the city's garbage-filled streets and slum

Jane Addams.
LIBRARY OF CONGRESS.

graduating from high school in 1877, she attended nearby Rockford Female Seminary, one of the oldest institutions for female education in the area. Rockford encouraged its students to become missionaries, but Addams, who struggled with her religious beliefs all her life, refused to consider that vocation. While at Rockford, she met Ellen Gates Starr, who would later help her found Hull House. Reflecting Addams's emerging concern about the place of women in America, she and Starr attempted to convince the seminary to offer coursework equivalent to that of men's colleges. Eventually, the seminary did become Rockford College.

Addams graduated from Rockford in 1881. Several months later, she was devastated when her father died of a ruptured appendix while on a family vacation in Wisconsin. His death left her a wealthy woman, and she decided to fulfill her plan to attend the Women's Medical College of Philadelphia. Addams began her studies that fall, but almost immediately the back pain she had suffered all her life flared up, forcing her to undergo back surgery.

During her lengthy recovery, Addams toured Europe with her stepmother, Anna Haldeman Addams. Throughout her trip, Addams was struck by the poverty of the industrialized countries she visited. At a fruit and vegetable auction in London, she watched as starving men and women fought over decayed and bruised produce. As she wrote in her autobiography, her impression was of "myriads of hands, empty, pathetic, nerveless and workworn, . . . clutching forward for food that was already unfit to eat." She was also appalled at the lack of concern for poor people shown by better-off Europeans.

housing, she asked her father why the people lived in such horrid houses. After her father told her the people were too poor to have nicer homes, she announced that she would buy a big house when she was grown, where poor children could come and play whenever they liked.

Addams suffered throughout her life from a painful curved spine that caused her to walk pigeon-toed. As a result, she was always self-conscious about her appearance. She was a good student and often helped classmates who were having difficulties with their studies. After

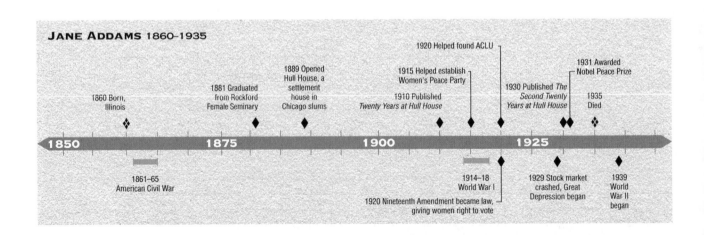

JANE ADDAMS 1860–1935

- 1860 Born, Illinois
- 1881 Graduated from Rockford Female Seminary
- 1889 Opened Hull House, a settlement house in Chicago slums
- 1910 Published *Twenty Years at Hull House*
- 1915 Helped establish Women's Peace Party
- 1920 Helped found ACLU
- 1930 Published *The Second Twenty Years at Hull House*
- 1931 Awarded Nobel Peace Prize
- 1935 Died

1850 1875 1900 1925

- 1861–65 American Civil War
- 1914–18 World War I
- 1920 Nineteenth Amendment became law, giving women right to vote
- 1929 Stock market crashed, Great Depression began
- 1939 World War II began

On her return home in 1885, Addams found herself exhausted, depressed, and unsure of her life's purpose. On a second trip to Europe, she visited Toynbee Hall, an experimental Oxford-based project in London's poverty-stricken East End. Educated young men had moved into the area and were offering literacy classes, art lessons, and other activities to residents. Because the men actually settled in the area and lived with the residents, Toynbee was called a settlement house.

Addams decided to use Toynbee as a model and establish a similar facility in the slums of Chicago. With over a million residents, that city was home to hundreds of thousands of immigrants—from Germany, Ireland, Sweden, Italy, Russia, Greece, and many other countries. These desperate people were a ready source of cheap labor for the Chicago factories, and their poor wages forced them to live in overcrowded, rat-infested tenements, surrounded by filthy, garbage-filled streets. Journalist Lincoln Steffens described the Chicago of that time as violent, foul smelling, and lawless.

Addams enlisted the aid of her former schoolmate, Starr, in her new venture. The women first had to overcome the adamant objections of friends and relatives who were horrified that two educated, unmarried women would consider living in the city's slums. But Addams and Starr soon found a house where they could begin their work, the former mansion of Charles J. Hull. Once a stately country home, the house was now surrounded by rundown, noisy city tenements. In the beginning, Addams was able to rent only a few rooms in the house, but eventually, Hull's heir, Helen Culver, gave her the entire house and some surrounding land.

After several months of cleaning and refurbishing, Addams and Starr opened Hull House in September 1889. Initially the two were met with great suspicion by the area's residents. Local priests warned their parishioners the women might try to convert them to a new RELIGION, and street children threw garbage and rocks at the house. But Addams and Starr continued to greet their neighbors in a friendly manner, and the residents soon discovered that the women were concerned about their well-being. They also found that the women would sell them nourishing food for just a few pennies, and they soon came to depend on Hull House.

In the first few years of the settlement house, Addams established a kindergarten, a women's boarding house, the nation's first public playground, and a day care center for mothers forced to leave their children alone for as long as ten hours each day in order to work. Hull House offered evening college extension courses, English and art classes, a theater group, and books and magazines for children and adults. Observing the long hours and dangerous working conditions that the neighborhood children were forced to endure, Addams and her friends soon began working for state regulation of child labor, and went on to lobby in Washington, D.C. At home, when city garbage collectors continually ignored overflowing garbage bins, Addams applied for and was appointed to the position of ward garbage inspector, and forced the trash collectors to remove the filth.

Addams described her work at Hull House as an effort to conserve and push forward the best of the community's achievements. She strove to respect and preserve the immigrants' cultures, and the holidays of their various nations were always celebrated at Hull House.

Among the volunteers who flocked to Hull House to work with Addams were several women who later brought about important social reform. Julia C. Lathrop helped establish Chicago's first juvenile court. Dr. Alice Hamilton worked in industrial medicine and conducted studies that helped improve factory conditions. Florence Kelley investigated sweatshops for the Illinois State Bureau of Labor and helped establish CHILD LABOR LAWS. Although Addams developed a wide circle of influential supporters because of her work, such as socialist EUGENE V. DEBS and journalist Steffens, she also occasionally lost admirers for the same reason. Addams never wavered in her belief that the same activities that caused her to lose some supporters would help her to gain others.

In the first decade of the twentieth century, Addams established herself as a prolific writer, publishing *Democracy and Social Ethics* (1902), *Newer Ideals for Peace* (1907), *The Spirit of Youth and the City Streets* (1909), and the best-selling first volume of her autobiography, *Twenty Years at Hull House* (1910). During these years, she began to turn her attention more and more to women's issues—particularly the right to vote. In 1913, seven years before the NINETEENTH AMENDMENT to the U.S. Constitution

PRIVATE BENEFICENCE IS TOTALLY INADEQUATE TO DEAL WITH THE VAST NUMBERS OF THE CITY'S DISINHERITED.
—JANE ADDAMS

granted women the right to vote in all elections, she helped secure the vote for women in Chicago.

Addams's work continued to expand beyond Hull House and women's rights. In 1909 she supported the founding of the National Association for the Advancement of Colored People (NAACP) and served on its executive committee. In 1915 she helped establish the Women's Peace Party, and traveled to Europe to attend the International Women's Peace Conference in the Netherlands and carry the message of peace to the countries fighting in WORLD WAR I. Addams continued to hold to her pacifist views even when the United States entered the war in 1917, and she was blacklisted as a result. The Daughters of the American Revolution, a group that had once honored Addams for her colonial ancestry, expelled her, and she was shunned by many other supporters. She continued her humanitarian work during the war, however, helping the U.S. Department of Food Administration to distribute food to European allies.

Following the war, Addams also worked to have food sent to the starving civilians in the defeated countries, setting off yet another round of criticism. In 1920, in response to increasing attempts to stifle unpopular opinion in the United States, Addams helped found the AMERICAN CIVIL LIBERTIES UNION, dedicated to protecting the individual's right to believe, write, and speak whatever he or she chooses.

By the 1930s the public's bitterness toward Addams had abated. In 1931 she was awarded the Nobel Peace Prize, an achievement that Addams felt justified her pacifist work to the world. Frederick Stang, of the Nobel Committee in Norway, said Addams had clung to her idealism during a difficult time in which peace was overshadowed. Addams went on to receive fourteen honorary degrees, among them one from Yale, the first honorary degree that school had ever awarded to a woman.

In 1930 Addams completed her autobiography with the publication of *The Second Twenty Years at Hull House*. A few years later, surgery revealed that Addams was suffering from advanced cancer. She died in May 1935. Shortly before her death, Addams was honored at an event marking the twentieth anniversary of the Women's International League for Peace and Freedom. In response to the many tributes

she received, she said she was driven by the fear that she might give up too soon and fail to make the one effort that might save the world.

FURTHER READINGS

Addams, Jane. 2002. *Democracy and Social Ethics.* Urbana: Univ. of Illinois Press.

Davis, Allen Freeman. 2000. *American Heroine: The Life and Legend of Jane Addams.* Chicago, Ill.: Ivan Dee.

Deegan, Mary Jo. 1988. *Jane Addams and the Men of the Chicago School, 1892–1918,* New Brunswick, N.J.: Transaction Books.

Linn, James Weber. 2000. *Jane Addams: A Biography.* Urbana: Univ. of Illinois Press.

Polikoff, Barbara Garland. 1999. *With One Bold Act: The Story of Jane Addams.* Chicago: Boswell Books.

ADDICT

Any individual who habitually uses any narcotic drug so as to endanger the public morals, health, safety, or welfare, or who is so drawn to the use of such narcotic drugs as to have lost the power of self-control with reference to his or her drug use.

Addiction to narcotics is not a crime in itself, but that does not excuse violation of related statutes. It may be an offense to be under the influence of an illegal drug in a public place, even though being an addict is not illegal. While such a statute is intended to protect society from the dangers of drug abuse and the antisocial conduct of drug abusers, it generally is not necessary for conviction to prove that the DEFENDANT was disturbing the peace when arrested.

CROSS REFERENCES

Drugs and Narcotics.

ADDITIONAL EXTENDED COVERAGE

A provision added to an insurance policy to extend the scope of coverage to include further risks to dwellings.

The provision may cover water damage from the plumbing or heating systems, VANDALISM or MALICIOUS MISCHIEF, glass breakage, falling trees, damage from ice or snow storms, or additional risks not otherwise covered by the LIABILITY policy.

ADDITIONAL INSTRUCTIONS

A charge given to a jury by a judge after the original instructions to explain the law and guide the jury in its decision making.

A man and woman inject themselves with heroin. Though addiction to narcotics is not a crime in itself, addicts are not excused from the violation of narcotics-related statutes.

AP IMAGES

Additional instructions are frequently needed after the jury has begun deliberations and finds that it has a question concerning the evidence, a point of law, or some part of the original charge.

ADDITUR

The power of the trial court to assess damages or increase the amount of an inadequate award made by jury verdict, as a condition of a denial of a motion for a new trial, with the consent of the defendant whether or not the plaintiff consents to such action. This is not allowed in the federal system.

Damages assessed by a jury may be SET ASIDE when the amount is shocking to the judicial conscience—so grossly inadequate that it constitutes a miscarriage of justice—or when it appears that the jury was influenced by prejudice, corruption, passion, or mistake.

For example, a 61-year-old woman was mugged in a hallway of her apartment building after the landlord failed to replace a broken lock on the back service entrance. She sustained a broken shoulder, a broken arm, and numerous cuts and bruises. Her medical bills amounted to more than $2,500. She sued the landlord for his negligent maintenance of the building, and the jury returned a VERDICT in her favor but awarded damages of only $2,500. Her attorney immediately moved for a new trial on the ground that the verdict was shockingly inadequate. The trial judge ruled that the jury could not possibly have calculated compensation for the woman's pain and suffering, an item that should have been included under state law. The trial judge, therefore, awarded an ADDITUR of $15,000. The effect of this order was to put the DEFENDANT on notice that he must either pay the $15,000 in addition to the verdict of $2,500 or a new trial would be held. The defendant weighed the disadvantages of investing time and money in a new trial and the risk of an even higher award of monetary damages by a sympathetic jury. He consented to the additur.

An additur is not justified solely because the amount of damages is low. For example, damages of $10,000 certainly will not compensate the family of a forty-four-year-old man who had been steadily employed as a plumber until he was permanently disabled in an auto accident. In such a case, however, the jury could have found that the plaintiff's NEGLIGENCE contributed to the cause of the accident and reduced the damages proportionately, as is permitted in most states.

An award of additur is not permitted in every state, nor is it allowed in the federal courts. Under the rules that govern procedure in the federal courts, a trial judge has the power to set aside a verdict for a PLAINTIFF on the ground that the damages awarded are clearly inadequate, but then the judge's only RECOURSE is to grant a new trial.

CROSS REFERENCES

Civil Procedure; Trial.

ADDUCE

To present, offer, bring forward, or introduce.

For example, a BILL OF PARTICULARS that lists each of the plaintiff's demands may recite that it contains all the evidence to be adduced at trial.

ADEMPTION

The failure of a gift of personal property—a bequest—or of real property—a devise—to be distributed according to the provisions of a decedent's will because the property no longer belongs to the testator at the time of his or her death or because the property has been substantially changed.

There are two types of ademption: by extinction and by satisfaction.

Extinction

Ademption by extinction occurs when a particular item of PERSONAL PROPERTY or specially designated real property is substantially changed or not part of the testator's estate when he or she dies. For example, a TESTATOR makes a will giving her farm to her nephew and a diamond watch to her niece. Before she dies, she sells the farm and loses the watch. The proceeds of the sale of the farm are traced to a bank account. After the testator's death, the nephew claims the proceeds from the sale and the niece claims that the executor of the estate should pay her the value of the diamond watch. Neither claim will be upheld. Once the farm is sold, the specific devise is adeemed by extinction. The proceeds from its sale are not its equivalent for INHERITANCE purposes. In some states, however, if all of the proceeds had not yet been paid, the nephew would be entitled to receive the unpaid balance.

Because the testator no longer owns the diamond watch when she dies, that specific bequest is also adeemed by extinction.

Satisfaction

Ademption by satisfaction takes place when the testator, during his or her lifetime, gives to his or her heir all or a part of the gift he or she had intended to give by his or her will. It applies to both specific bequests and devises as well as to a general bequest or legacy payable from the general assets of the testator's estate. If the subject of the gift made while the testator is alive is the same as the subject of a provision of the will, many states presume that it is in place of the TESTAMENTARY gift if there is a parent-child or grandparent-grandchild relationship. Otherwise, an ademption by satisfaction will not be found unless there is independent evidence, such as express statements or writings, that the testator intended this to occur. A father makes a will leaving his ski house to his daughter and $25,000 to his son. Before death, he gives the daughter the deed to the ski house and he gives the son $15,000 with which to complete medical school. After the father's death, the daughter will get nothing, while the son will get $10,000.

After the son received the $15,000 from his father, there was an ademption by satisfaction of the GENERAL LEGACY of $25,000 to the extent of the size of the lifetime gift, $15,000. The son is entitled to receive the remaining $10,000 of the original general legacy. Because there was a parent-child relationship, there was no need for independent proof that the $15,000 gift was intended to adeem the gift under the will.

FURTHER READINGS

Lundwall, Mary Kay. 1993. "The Case against the Ademption by Extinction Rule: A Proposal for Reform." *Gonzaga Law Review* 29 (fall).

McEowen, Roger. 2009. "Court Decides Ademption Case." *AgDM Whole Farm Legal and Taxes Recent Iowa Opinions* (May). Available online at http://www.extension.iastate.edu/agdm/articles/mceowen/McEowOpinionsMay07a.html; website home page: http://www.extension.iastate.edu (accessed August 28, 2009).

Volkmer, Ronald R. 2000. "Doctrine of Ademption in the Law of Wills." *Estate Planning* 27 (March-April).

ADEQUATE

Sufficient; equal to what is required; suitable to the case or occasion.

A law that requires PUBLIC UTILITIES to provide adequate service does not create a right for customers to sue the electric company whenever the meat in their freezers spoils because of a power outage in the absence of NEGLIGENCE. Service does not have to be perfect in order to meet a standard of adequacy.

ADEQUATE REMEDY AT LAW

Sufficient compensation by way of monetary damages.

Courts will not grant equitable remedies, such as SPECIFIC PERFORMANCE or injunctions, where monetary damages can afford complete legal relief. An EQUITABLE REMEDY interferes much more with the defendant's freedom of action than an order directing the DEFENDANT to pay for the harm he or she has caused, and it is much more difficult for a court to supervise and enforce judgments giving some relief other than money. Courts, therefore, will compensate an injured party whenever possible with monetary damages; this remedy has been called the remedy at law since the days when courts of equity and courts at law were different.

ADHESION CONTRACT

A type of contract, a legally binding agreement between two parties to do a certain thing, in which one side has all the bargaining power and uses it to write the contract primarily to his or her advantage.

An example of an ADHESION CONTRACT is a standardized contract form that offers goods or services to consumers on essentially a "take it or leave it" basis without giving consumers realistic opportunities to negotiate terms that would benefit their interests. When this occurs, the consumer cannot obtain the desired product or service unless he or she acquiesces to the form contract.

There is nothing unenforceable or even wrong about adhesion contracts. In fact, most businesses would never conclude their volume of transactions if it were necessary to negotiate all the terms of every CONSUMER CREDIT contract. Insurance contracts and residential leases are other kinds of adhesion contracts. This does not mean, however, that all adhesion contracts are valid. Many adhesion contracts are UNCONSCIONABLE; they are so unfair to the weaker party that a court will refuse to enforce them. An example would be severe PENALTY provisions for failure to pay loan installments promptly that are physically hidden by small print located in the middle of an obscure paragraph of a lengthy loan agreement. In such a case a court can find that there is no meeting of the minds of the PARTIES to the contract and that the weaker party has not accepted the terms of the contract.

ADJACENT

Lying near or close to; neighboring.

Adjacent means that objects or parcels of land are not widely separated, though perhaps they are not actually touching; but adjoining implies that they are united so closely that no other object comes between them.

ADJECTIVE LAW

The aggregate of rules of procedure or practice. Also called adjectival law, as opposed to that body of law that the courts are established to administer (called substantive law), it means the rules according to which the substantive law is administered, e.g., Rules of Civil Procedure. That part of the law that provides a method for enforcing or maintaining rights, or obtaining redress for their invasion. Pertains to and prescribes the practice, method, procedure, or legal machinery by which substantive law is enforced or made effective.

CROSS REFERENCE

Civil Procedure.

ADJOINING LANDOWNERS

Those persons, such as next-door and backyard neighbors, who own lands that share common boundaries and therefore have mutual rights, duties, and liabilities.

The RECIPROCAL rights and obligations of ADJOINING LANDOWNERS existed at COMMON LAW but have been modified by various state laws and court decisions.

Rights, Duties, and Liabilities

Landowners are expected to use their property reasonably without unduly interfering with the rights of the owners of contiguous land. Anything that a person does that appropriates adjoining land or substantially deprives an adjoining owner of the reasonable enjoyment of his or her property is an unlawful use of one's property. A man buys a house in a residentially zoned area and converts it into an office building. He paves the backyard for a parking lot but encroaches two feet beyond his property into the lot of the adjoining landowner. His use of the property is unlawful for a number of reasons. He has appropriated his neighbor's land and substantially interfered with his neighbor's right to use it. His neighbor may sue him in a tort action for the NUISANCE created and, if successful, the neighbor will be awarded damages and an INJUNCTION to stop the unlawful use of the land. In addition, the purchaser has violated zoning laws by using residential property for commercial purposes without seeking a VARIANCE.

Property owners have the right to grade or change the level of their land or to build foundations or embankments as long as proper precautions are taken, such as building a retaining wall to prevent soil from spilling upon adjoining land. If permitted by law, landowners may blast on their own property but will be liable for damages caused by debris thrown onto adjoining land.

Lateral Support A landowner has a legally enforceable right to LATERAL SUPPORT from an adjoining landowner. Lateral support is the right to have one's land in its natural condition held in place from the sides by the neighboring land so that it will not fall away. Land is considered in its natural condition if it has no artificial structures or buildings on it. A landowner can enforce the right to lateral support in court. A lawsuit for the removal of lateral support accrues when the damage occurs, not when the excavation is done.

An adjoining landowner who excavates close to his or her boundary line has a duty to prevent injury arising from the removal of the lateral support of a neighbor's property. Because the right to lateral support is considered an absolute PROPERTY RIGHT, an adjoining landowner will be liable for damages to the natural condition of the land regardless of whether or not he or she acted negligently.

When, however, a landowner has erected buildings on the land, his or her right to recover for deprivation of the lateral support is different. Because additional weight has been placed on the land, thus increasing the burden on the lateral support, the landowner can be awarded damages for injuries to the building caused by excavation only if his or her neighbor has been negligent. Sometimes local ordinances require that persons planning to excavate on their own property give notice to neighboring adjoining landowners so that neighbors may take preventive measures to protect their property. The failure of landowners who receive notice to take precautions does not necessarily absolve the excavator of LIABILITY for NEGLIGENCE. If, however, the excavator does not notify neighboring landowners, courts have treated this failure as negligence, and the excavator will be responsible for damages even though the excavating itself was not done negligently.

When evidence establishes that an adjoining landowner has removed the lateral support of a neighbor's land, the neighbor will recover damages in the amount of either the cost of restoring the property to its value before its support was removed or the cost of restoring the land to its former condition, whichever is less. An injunction prohibiting further excavation may be granted if it poses a clear danger to contiguous lands and if it will cause irreparable damage.

Subjacent Support A landowner is entitled to subjacent support, the absolute right to have one's land supported from beneath its surface. If one person owns the surface of the land while another owns the subjacent surface, the owner of the surface is entitled to have it remain in its natural condition without subsidence caused by

the subsurface owner's withdrawal of subjacent materials. An adjoining landowner who, during excavation, taps a subterranean stream, causing the soil of the neighbor's land to subside, will be liable for any injuries that result. The surface owner's right to sue the subsurface owner for deprivation of subjacent support arises when the land actually subsides, not when the excavation is made.

The construction of buildings on the surface of the land does not lessen a person's right to subjacent support. It does, however, change the circumstances under which that person may recover for the removal of subsurface support. If such buildings are damaged, their owner must show that the removal of the support was done negligently.

Light, Air, and View No landowner has an absolute right to light and air from or passing over adjoining property or to a view over adjoining lands. Zoning laws imposed by localities may, however, require that any construction undertaken by an individual not deprive an adjoining landowner of adequate air, light, and view. Similarly, many agreements such as restrictive covenants in deeds or easements affect a person's duty toward his or her next-door neighbor's right to air, light, and view. In the absence of zoning laws or agreements, therefore, a person may build on his or her own property without regard to the fact that he or she is depriving the next-door neighbor of the light, air, and view that was enjoyed before the building was erected. An exception is a structure that blocks air, light, and view for the sole purpose of injuring a neighbor—such as a "spite" fence—and which is of no BENEFICIAL USE or pleasure to the owner. Courts will generally not permit such structures.

Encroachments An ENCROACHMENT is an intrusion upon the property of another without that person's permission. No person is legally entitled to construct buildings or other structures so that any part, regardless of size, extends beyond that person's property line and intrudes upon adjoining lands. An encroaching owner can be required to remove the eaves of a building that overhang an adjoining lot. If he or she refuses to do so, the owner of the contiguous lot may personally remove as much of the encroachment that deprives him or her of the complete enjoyment of his or her land, but if negligent, he or she will be liable for damages. Should any expenses be incurred in the removal of the encroachment from the adjoining land, the person whose property was encroached upon can sue the owner to recover damages.

The person whose property has been encroached upon may sue the encroacher under either the theory of nuisance or the theory of TRESPASS to obtain monetary damages, or instead, may seek an injunction against continuation of the encroachment or to force its removal.

Trees and Shrubs Landowners should not permit trees or hedges on their property to invade the rights of adjoining landowners. If an individual knows, for example, that a tree on his or her property is decayed and may fall and damage the property of another, that individual has a duty to eliminate the danger. A tree on the boundary line of contiguous land belongs to both adjoining landowners. Each owner has an interest identical with the portion standing on his or her land. Each can sever intruding tree branches or roots at the boundary line of his or her property, whether or not any injuries have been sustained by the intrusion, but reasonable care must be exercised so as not to kill the entire tree.

FURTHER READINGS

Barlow, John R. II, and Voncannon Barlow. 1997. *Skelton on the Legal Elements of Boundaries & Adjacent Properties* 2d ed. New York: LexisNexis.

Jex, Thomas D. 1998. "Alcaraz v. Vece: If You Mow or Water Your Next-Door-Neighbor's Yard, You Might Be Liable for Anyone Injured There." *BYU Journal of Public Law* 13 (winter).

Merrill, Karen R. 2002. *Public Lands and Political Meaning: Ranchers, the Government, and the Property between Them.* Berkeley: Univ. of California Press.

Perin, Constance. 1977. *Everything in Its Place: Social Order and Land Use in America.* Princeton, NJ: Princeton Univ. Press.

Stephens, Ana Boswell. 1999. "Prospecting for Oil at the Court House: Recovery for Drainage Caused by Secondary Recovery Operations." *Alabama Law Review* 50 (winter).

CROSS REFERENCE

Land-Use Control.

ADJOURNED TERM

A continuance of a previous or regular court session that results from postponement.

When a term is adjourned, it is actually prolonged due to a temporary putting off of the business being conducted.

ADJOURNMENT

A putting off or postponing of proceedings; an ending or dismissal of further business by a court, legislature, or public official—either temporarily or permanently.

If an adjournment is final, it is said to be SINE DIE, "without day" or without a time fixed to resume the work. An adjournment is different from a RECESS, which is only a short break in proceedings.

In legislatures, adjournment officially marks the end of a regular session. Both state and federal lawmakers vote to determine when to adjourn. The exact timing depends upon multiple factors such as work load, election schedules, and the level of comity among lawmakers. Because a session can end with unfinished legislative business, adjournment is commonly used as a means of political leverage in securing or delaying action on important matters. In the U.S. Congress, where the single annual legislative session usually ends in the fall, the president may call an adjournment if the House and Senate cannot agree upon a date.

FURTHER READINGS

Baumann, David, and Kirk Victor. 2001. "Congress: Pitfalls to Adjournment." *National Journal* (November 10).

"Of Adjournment." 2009. *ChestofBooks.com.* Available online at http://chestofbooks.com/business/meetings/Rules-Order-Conduct/Of-Adjournment.html; website home page: http://chestofbooks.com (accessed August 28, 2009).

Robert, Henry M. 2000. *Robert's Rules of Order,* Newly Revised. Cambridge, MA: Perseus.

CROSS REFERENCES

Congress of the United States; Legislature.

ADJUDGE

To determine by a judge; to pass on and decide judicially.

A person adjudged guilty is one who has been convicted in court.

ADJUDICATION

The legal process of resolving a dispute. The formal giving or pronouncing of a judgment or decree in a court proceeding; also the judgment or decision given. The entry of a decree by a court in respect to the parties in a case. It implies a hearing by a court, after notice, of legal evidence on the factual issue(s) involved. The equivalent of a determination. It indicates that the claims of all

Justice Charles Tejada listens to arguments during a New York State Supreme Court proceeding. The adjudicative process is governed by formal rules of evidence and procedure.

AP IMAGES

the parties thereto have been considered and set at rest.

Three types of disputes are resolved through adjudication: disputes between private parties, such as individuals or corporations; disputes between private parties and public officials; and disputes between public officials or public bodies. The requirements of full adjudication include notice to all interested parties (all parties with a legal interest in, or LEGAL RIGHT affected by, the dispute) and an opportunity for all parties to present evidence and arguments. The adjudicative process is governed by formal rules of evidence and procedure. Its objective is to reach a reasonable SETTLEMENT of the controversy at hand. A decision is rendered by an impartial, passive fact finder, usually a judge, jury, or administrative tribunal.

The adjudication of a controversy involves the performance of several tasks. The trier must establish the facts in controversy, and define and interpret the applicable law, or, if no relevant law exists, fashion a new law to apply to the situation. Complex evidentiary rules limit the presentation of proofs, and the Anglo-American tradition of STARE DECISIS, or following precedents, controls the outcome. However, the process of applying established rules of law is neither simple nor automatic. Judges have considerable latitude in interpreting the statutes or CASE LAW upon which they base their decisions.

An age-old question that still plagues legal theorists is whether judges "make" law when they adjudicate. SIR WILLIAM BLACKSTONE believed that judges do nothing more than maintain and expound established law (*Commentaries on*

the Laws of England); other writers vehemently disagree. Some legal analysts maintain that the law is whatever judges declare it to be. Echoing those sentiments, President THEODORE ROOSEVELT asserted that "the chief lawmakers in our country may be, and often are, the judges, because they are the final seat of authority. Every time they interpret ... they necessarily enact into law parts of a system of social philosophy; and as such interpretation is fundamental, they give direction to all lawmaking" (Message to Congress [Dec. 8, 1908]). Supreme Court Justice BENJAMIN N. CARDOZO, writing in *The Nature of the Judicial Process*, argued that the law is evolutionary and that judges, by interpreting and applying it to specific sets of facts, actually fashion new laws.

Whether judges are seen as making law or merely following what came before, they are required to operate within narrow strictures. Even when they are deciding a case of FIRST IMPRESSION (a question that has not previously been adjudicated), they generally try to analogize to some existing PRECEDENT. Judges often consider customs of the community; political and social implications; customs of the trade, market, or profession; and history when applying the law. Some, such as Justice Oliver Wendell Holmes and Justice Cardozo, thought that considerations of social and PUBLIC POLICY are the most powerful forces behind judicial decisions.

A hearing in which the parties are given an opportunity to present their evidence and arguments is essential to an adjudication. Anglo-American law presumes that the parties to the dispute are in the best position to know the facts of their particular situations and develop their own proofs. If the hearing is before a court, formal rules of procedure and evidence govern; a hearing before an administrative agency is generally less structured.

Following the hearing, the decision maker is expected to deliver a reasoned opinion. This opinion is the basis for review if the decision is appealed to a higher tribunal (a court of appeals). It also helps ensure that decisions are not reached arbitrarily. Finally, a well-reasoned opinion forces the judge to carefully think through his or her decision in order to be able to explain the process followed in reaching it.

Adjudication of a controversy generally ensures a fair and equitable outcome. Because courts are governed by evidentiary and procedural rules, as well as by stare decisis, the adjudicative process assures litigants of some degree of efficiency, uniformity, and predictability of result.

FURTHER READINGS

Cardoza, Benjamin N. 2009. *The Nature of the Judicial Process (1921)*. Whitefish, MT: Kessinger.

Lewis, William D., ed. 2007. *Commentaries on the Laws of England*. Clark, NJ: Lawbook Exchange.

Lucy, William. 1999. *Understanding and Explaining Adjudication*. New York: Oxford Univ. Press.

Roosevelt, Theodore. 1908. *Eighth Annual Message to Congress*. In The American Presidency Project [online], compiled by John T. Woolley and Gerhard Peters. Santa Barbara, CA: Univ. of California. Available online at http://www.presidency.ucsb.edu (accessed July 3, 2009).

CROSS REFERENCES

Blackstone, Sir William; Cardozo, Benjamin Nathan; Holmes, Oliver Wendell, Jr.; Judiciary.

ADJUDICATIVE FACTS

Factual matters concerning the parties to an administrative proceeding as contrasted with legislative facts, which are general and usually do not touch individual questions of particular parties to a proceeding. Facts that concern a person's motives and intent, as contrasted with general policy issues. Those facts that must be found BEYOND A REASONABLE DOUBT by the trier of fact before there can be a conviction.

Adjudicative facts, *of which a trial court may take notice if a fact is not subject to reasonable dispute, are those to which law is applied in the process of adjudication; they are facts that, in a jury case, normally go to the jury.*

The role of a U.S. court is to resolve the dispute that has brought the parties before it. Determining what happened to whom, when and how it happened, and what the result is or will be, is part of the adjudicative process by which the court reaches that RESOLUTION. These determinations establish the ADJUDICATIVE FACTS of the dispute.

Adjudicative facts differ from ordinary facts in that they are considered facts only if the court recognizes and accepts them. For example, a witness may TESTIFY that she saw the defendant's car parked at a specific place at a specific time. These are the facts as she recalls them. However, the court may reject her account and instead accept another witness's TESTIMONY that the DEFENDANT was driving that same car in another part of town at the same time. The second witness's account will therefore become part of the adjudicative facts of the case, and the first witness's recollection will be considered IMMATERIAL.

Adjudicative facts are specific and unique to a particular controversy. For this reason, the fact determination in one case is not controlling in other similar cases, even if all the cases arose from the same incident. Adjudicative facts differ from LEGISLATIVE FACTS, which are general and can be applied to any party in a similar situation. For example, the facts used by a court to determine the legality of a tax increase levied against a single taxpayer would be adjudicative facts particular to that taxpayer's case. By contrast, the facts used to determine the legality of a general tax increase levied against all the residents of a city would be legislative in nature. Because facts can be perceived and interpreted differently by different people, the skillful lawyer is careful about what facts to present and how to present them at trial.

Adjudicative facts re-create the course of events that led to the dispute. They may also predict what will happen as a result. For example, where one party is suing another for PERSONAL INJURY, adjudicative facts will determine what happened, who was at fault, and what redress is appropriate for pain and suffering. Adjudicative facts will further establish what lasting consequences, such as lost future wages, the PLAINTIFF is likely to suffer and what compensation is fitting.

Adjudicative facts found by the court are final and will not be reviewed on appeal except in cases where it can be shown that the findings were made on insubstantial evidence or were clearly erroneous.

FURTHER READINGS

Carp, Robert A., and Ronald Stidham. 1993. *The Judicial Process in America*. 2d ed. Washington, D.C.: Congressional Quarterly.

Fraher, Richard M. 1987. "Adjudicative Facts, Non-evidence Facts, and Permissible Jury Background Information." *Indiana Law Journal* 62 (spring).

"Section 201. Judicial Notice of Adjudicative Facts." Available online at http://www.mass.gov/courts/sjc/guide-to-evidence/201.htm; website home page: http://www.mass.gov/ (accessed August 28, 2009).

ADJUNCTION

Attachment or affixing to another. Something attached as a dependent or auxiliary part.

Under the CIVIL LAW system that prevails in much of Europe and Latin America, adjunction is the permanent union of a thing belonging to one person to something that belongs to someone else.

A branch agency, for example, is an adjunct of the main department or administrative agency.

ADJURATION

A swearing; taking an oath to be truthful.

To adjure is to command solemnly, warning that penalties may be invoked.

ADJUST

To settle or arrange; to free from differences or discrepancies. To bring to a satisfactory state so that parties are agreed, as to adjust amount of loss by fire or controversy regarding property or estate. To bring to proper relations. To determine and apportion an amount due. The term is sometimes used in the sense of pay, when used in reference to a liquidated claim. Determination of an amount to be paid to insured by insurer to cover loss or damage sustained.

ADJUSTED GROSS INCOME

The term used for income tax purposes to describe gross income less certain allowable deductions such as trade and business deductions, moving expenses, alimony paid, and penalties for premature withdrawals from term savings accounts, in order to determine a person's taxable income.

The rules for computing ADJUSTED GROSS INCOME for federal INCOME TAX may differ from the rules in a state that imposes a state income tax.

ADJUSTER

A person appointed or employed to settle or arrange matters that are in dispute; one who determines the amount to be paid on a claim.

An insurance adjuster determines the extent of the insurance company's LIABILITY when a claim is submitted. A public adjuster is a self-employed person who is hired by litigants to determine or SETTLE the amount of a claim or debt.

ADJUSTMENT SECURITIES

Stocks and bonds of a new corporation that are issued to stockholders during a corporate reorganization in exchange for stock held in the original corporation before it was reorganized.

ADMINISTER

To give an oath, as to administer the oath of office to the president at the inauguration. To direct the transactions of business or government. Immigration laws are administered largely by the Immigration and Naturalization Service. To take care of affairs, as an executor administers the estate of a deceased person. To directly cause the ingestion of medications or poisons. To apply a court decree, enforce its provisions, or resolve disputes concerning its meaning.

School teachers generally are not authorized to administer medicines that pupils take to school, for example.

When divorced parents cannot agree on how to administer a visitation provision in a judgment granting CHILD CUSTODY to one of them, they might have to return to court for clarification from the judge.

ADMINISTRATION

The performance of executive duties in an institution or business. The Small Business Administration is responsible for administration of some disaster-relief loans. In government, the practical management and direction of some department or agency in the executive branch; in general, the entire class of public officials and employees managing the executive department. The management and distribution of the estate of a decedent performed under the supervision of the surrogate's or probate court by a person duly qualified and legally appointed. If the decedent made a valid will designating someone called an executor to handle this function, the court will issue that person letters testamentary as authority to do so. If a person dies intestate or did not name an executor in his or her will, the court will appoint an administrator and grant him or her letters of administration to perform the duties of administration.

An executor or administrator must carry out the responsibilities of administration, including collection and preservation of the decedent's assets; payment of debts and claims against the estate; payment of estate tax; and distribution of the balance of the estate to the decedent's heirs.

ADMINISTRATION, OFFICE OF

The OFFICE OF ADMINISTRATION was established within the Executive Office of the President (EOP) by REORGANIZATION PLAN 1 of 1977

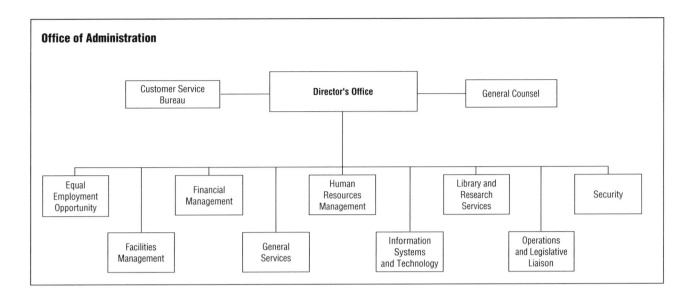

Office of Administration

(implemented by EXECUTIVE ORDER 12,028, 42 Fed. Reg. 62, 895 [1977], issued on December 12, 1977, by President JIMMY CARTER). The office was created to help centralize the activities of all EOP offices into a single agency. The director of the Office of Administration, who is appointed by, and reports directly to, the president, is responsible for, according to Executive Order 12,028, "ensuring that the Office of Administration provides units within the Executive Office of the President common administrative support and services."

The Office of Administration provides administrative support services to all EOP offices in the White House, including services that are in direct support of the president. The services provided by the Office of Administration include personnel management; financial management; data processing; and office operations, including the handling of mail (except for presidential mail), messenger service, printing and duplication, graphics, word processing, procurement, and supply. The office also oversees three libraries (not open to the general public): a general reference library in the New Executive Office Building, and a reference library and a law library in the Old Executive Office Building.

The Office of Administration consists of nearly two hundred full- and part-time employees who maintain accounts for all EOP offices; recruit employees (except for those who will staff the Office of Policy Development and the White House, all of whom are political appointees); and maintain official records, including those of the White House. In addition

to the director and an assistant director, the office is managed by three deputy assistant directors, who provide supervision in the areas of general services, information management, and resources management.

The Office of Administration also manages the Preservation Office, which has initiated and overseen several restoration projects, such as the award-winning restoration of the slate and cast iron roof and the restoration of the three Department libraries originally occupying the Eisenhower Executive Office Building that currently houses the Office of Administration. In all the projects that are completed, the work is monitored to ensure consistency with preservation criteria. In 1988 Congress enacted legislation to allow the Office of Administration to accept gifts and loans for preservation activities so as to shift the expense to public and private partnerships.

FURTHER READING

Administration Office Website. Available online at www. whitehouse.gov/oa (accessed September 22, 2009).

CROSS REFERENCE

President of the United States.

ADMINISTRATIVE ACTS

Whatever actions are necessary to carry out the intent of statutes; those acts required by legislative policy as it is expressed in laws enacted by the legislature.

If a city commission votes to create the position of park superintendent, that is a legislative act that can take effect only if the commission follows all the steps required for formal legislation. When the same commission votes to rezone a parcel of real property from single-family residential to business uses, however, that is an administrative act that does not require the same formality as legislation. It is administrative because it is carrying out the zoning laws already in effect.

ADMINISTRATIVE ADJUDICATION

The process by which an administrative agency issues an order, such order being affirmative, negative, injunctive, or declaratory in form.

Most formal proceedings before an administrative agency follow the process of either rule making or adjudication. Rule making formulates policy by setting rules for the future conduct of persons governed by that agency. Adjudication applies the agency's policy to the past actions of a particular party, and it results in an order for or against that party. Both methods are strictly regulated by the law of administrative procedure.

CROSS REFERENCES

Administrative Law and Procedure.

ADMINISTRATIVE AGENCY

An official governmental body empowered with the authority to direct and supervise the implementation of particular legislative acts. In addition to agency, *such governmental bodies may be called commissions, corporations (e.g., Federal Deposit Insurance Corporation), boards, departments, or divisions.*

Administrative agencies are created by the federal Constitution, the U.S. Congress, state legislatures, and local lawmaking bodies to manage crises, redress serious social problems, or oversee complex matters of governmental concern beyond the expertise of legislators. Although Article I, Section 1, of the federal Constitution plainly states that "[a]ll legislative Powers herein granted shall be vested in a Congress of the United States," the "necessary-and-proper" clause, in the eighth section of the same article, states that Congress shall have power "[t]o make all Laws which shall be necessary and proper for carrying into Execution the foregoing Powers, and all other Powers ... in any Department or Officer thereof." With this language, many have argued that the Framers of the Constitution expected,

indeed encouraged, the creation of powerful administrative agencies. This argument prevailed, and courts therefore have allowed the U.S. Congress—and other legislative bodies—to make laws that delegate limited lawmaking authority to administrative agencies. The substance of an administrative agency's powers must be intelligible, and a system of controls must be in place to limit those powers, but courts almost always find that administrative agencies meet these requirements.

Administrative agency rules and regulations often have the force of law against individuals. This tendency has led many critics to charge that the creation of agencies circumvents the constitutional directive that laws are to be created by elected officials. According to these critics, administrative agencies constitute an unconstitutional, bureaucratic fourth branch of government with powers that exceed those of the three recognized branches (the legislative, executive, and judiciary). In response, supporters of administrative agencies note that agencies are created and overseen by elected officials or the president. Agencies are created by an ENABLING STATUTE, which is a state or federal law that gives birth to the agency and outlines the procedures for the agency's rule making. Furthermore, agencies include the public in their rule-making processes. Thus, by PROXY, agencies are the will of the electorate.

Supporters of administrative agencies note also that agencies are able to adjudicate relatively minor or exceedingly complex disputes more quickly or more flexibly than can state and federal courts, which helps preserve judicial resources and promotes swift resolutions. Opponents argue that swiftness and ease at the expense of fairness are no virtues, but while the debate continues, administrative agencies thrive.

Governmental representation in an administrative capacity of any kind can be considered administrative agency. The president is an administrative agent whose enabling statute is the federal Constitution. The 13 executive departments reporting to the president are administrative agencies. For example, the DEPARTMENT OF JUSTICE is a cabinet-level executive department, but it functions as the administrative agency that addresses the legal concerns of the U.S. government and its people. The departments housed within the Department of

Justice, such as the DRUG ENFORCEMENT ADMINISTRATION and the FEDERAL BUREAU OF INVESTIGATION, are also administrative agencies, and they have procedures and rules of their own.

An administrative agency that falls under the direction of the EXECUTIVE BRANCH is referred to as an executive agency. However, an enabling statute may establish an independent agency, commission, or board, which does not fall under the direction of the president. The primary distinction between an executive agency and an independent agency is that the statute creating an independent agency typically precludes the president from removing the head of the agency without cause. By contrast, a head of an executive agency generally serves at the pleasure of the president. The U.S. Supreme Court on several occasions has considered whether independent agencies are constitutional. In *Humphrey's Executor v. United States,* 295 U.S. 602, 55 S. Ct. 869, 79 L. Ed. 1611 (1935), the Court held the President FRANKLIN D. ROOSEVELT could not remove the commissioner of the FEDERAL TRADE COMMISSION (FTC) without cause. The statute that created the commission permitted removal of the commissioner only for inefficiency, neglect of duty, or MALFEASANCE of office. Roosevelt purported to remove FTC Commissioner William E. Humphrey, who had been nominated by President HERBERT C. HOOVER to a seven-year term in 1931, in order to replace Humphrey with an individual of Roosevelt's own selection. The Court held that because Humphrey was not an executive officer, the president could not remove him from office except for the causes set forth in the statute.

Many of the administrative agencies that affect everyday activities are independent agencies. Among the numerous examples of independent agencies are the CENTRAL INTELLIGENCE AGENCY, ENVIRONMENTAL PROTECTION AGENCY, the NATIONAL LABOR RELATIONS BOARD, and the SECURITIES AND EXCHANGE COMMISSION. Because the president is generally able to appoint the chairs or fill vacancies within these agencies, the president is often able to influence their activities, notwithstanding the limitation on the removal of the heads of the agencies.

Administrative agencies are made up of experts in the field in which the agency operates. For example, the Maritime Administration employs experts in the areas of sea commerce and navigation to set its rules on

The National Recovery Administration was created in the 1930s to ensure fair market competition. It was one of numerous agencies created by Congress during the Great Depression in an effort to regulate the production and marketing of goods.

AP IMAGES

merchant marine activities. Many agencies have the power to assess fines or otherwise deprive persons of liberty in hearings conducted by their own judicial bodies, or administrative boards. Given the specialized knowledge within administrative agencies, administrative law judges (ALJs), who hear agency claims and disputes, are loath to overturn the legal conclusions reached by administrative boards. Determinations and sanctions made by ALJs are subject to review by state or federal courts, but a party must exhaust all appeals within the agency before suing in civil court.

An agency's actions must be in accordance with its enabling statute, and courts will examine the agency records to determine whether the agency exceeded its lawmaking or judicial powers. Rigorous judicial oversight of agencies would defeat a cherished feature of administrative agency by eliminating agency flexibility in resolving conflicts. To avoid this outcome, most enabling statutes are worded vaguely, in such a way as to allow the agencies broad discretion in determining their rules and procedures. To keep agencies from wielding unbridled power, the Administrative Procedure Act of 1946 (APA) (5 U.S.C.A. § 551 [1982]) sets standards for the activities and rule making of all federal regulatory agencies. The APA provides federal courts with a framework for reviewing the rules made and procedures used by administrative agencies. Individual states have similar statutes to guide their own courts.

History of Administrative Agency

The first administrative agency was created by Congress in 1789 to provide pensions for wounded Revolutionary War soldiers. Also in the late 1700s, agencies were created to determine the amount of duties charged on imported goods, but it was not until 1887 that the first permanent administrative agency was created. The INTERSTATE COMMERCE COMMISSION (ICC), created by the INTERSTATE COMMERCE ACT (49 U.S.C.A. § 10101 et seq. [1995]), was enacted by Congress to regulate commerce among the states, especially the interstate transportation of persons or property by carriers. The ICC was designed to ensure that carriers involved in interstate commerce provided the public with fair and reasonable rates and services. To buttress the Interstate Commerce Act, the Federal Reserve System was established by the Federal Reserve Act of 1913 (12 U.S.C.A. § 221) to serve as the United States' central bank and execute U.S. monetary policy. One year later, the Federal Trade Commission was established by Congress to promote free and fair competition in interstate commerce by preventing unfair methods of competition.

In 1908 the Federal Bureau of Investigation (FBI) was established to investigate violations of federal laws not assigned to other federal agencies. The FBI is charged with solving crimes such as KIDNAPPING, ESPIONAGE, SABOTAGE, bank ROBBERY, extortion, interstate transportation of stolen property, CIVIL RIGHTS violations, interstate gambling violations, FRAUD against the government, and the ASSAULT or killing of a federal officer or the president. As an agency concerned with criminal apprehension, the FBI is considered an arm of the government, and its directorship is subject to presidential approval. However, the FBI carries out its investigations independent of political influence. It can, for example, probe the actions of presidents and legislators, the very persons responsible for its existence.

Administrative agencies are usually created in response to a felt public need. Some older agencies, for example, were created after the Civil War to address economic matters critical to the United States' expanding government. After the STOCK MARKET crash of October 1929, and during the Great Depression of the 1930s, Congress created numerous agencies in an effort to regulate the production and marketing of goods. Agencies such as the SOCIAL SECURITY Administration (created by the SOCIAL SECURITY ACT OF 1935 [42 U.S.C.A. § 301 et seq.]), the Federal Savings and Loan Insurance Corporation (established by a 1933 amendment to the Federal Reserve Act, 12 U.S.C.A. § 264, and now codified at 12 U.S.C.A. §§ 1811–1831) helped provide financial security for many Americans. The National Industrial Recovery Act (NIRA) (15 15 U.S.C.A. §§ 701 et seq., 40 U.S.C.A. § 401 et seq.) created the NATIONAL RECOVERY ADMINISTRATION to ensure fair market competition. However, the NIRA gave the president limitless authority to impose sanctions, and it was declared invalid by the Supreme Court in the "Sick Chicken" case, SCHECHTER POULTRY CORP. V. UNITED STATES, 295 U.S. 495, 55 S. Ct. 837, 79 L. Ed. 1570 (1935). The National Labor Relations Board (created by the National Labor Relations Act of 1935 [29 U.S.C.A. § 151 et seq.], later amended by acts of 1947 and 1959) also helped to ease the devastating effects of the depression, by protecting employees' rights to organize, preventing unfair labor practices, and promoting COLLECTIVE BARGAINING between employers and labor unions.

Congress installed the Federal Radio Commission (FRC) in 1927 after entrepreneurs discovered the commercial potential of radio airwaves. In 1934 the FRC was merged into the FEDERAL COMMUNICATIONS COMMISSION (FCC), which was created by the Communications Act of 1934 (47 U.S.C.A. § 151 et seq.) to tackle the myriad issues presented by the sudden widespread use of radio waves. In the wake of television's popularity, the Communications Satellite Act of 1962 (47 U.S.C.A. §§ 701–744) was enacted by Congress to broaden the FCC's powers to include regulation of television broadcasting; telephone, telegraph, and cable television operation;

two-way radio and radio operation; and satellite communication.

When the United States entered WORLD WAR II, more agencies were created or enlarged to mobilize human resources and production and to administer price controls and rationing. The social upheaval of the 1960s spawned agencies designed to improve urban areas, provide opportunities for people who were historically disadvantaged and marginalized, and promote artistic endeavors. In the 1970s, 1980s, and 1990s, pressing issues such as human and environmental health were addressed through the creation of agencies such as the ENVIRONMENTAL PROTECTION AGENCY and a new, enlarged DEPARTMENT OF ENERGY.

Federal Administrative Agencies

On the federal level, business and individual matters are addressed by such agencies as the FARM CREDIT ADMINISTRATION, SMALL BUSINESS ADMINISTRATION, COMMODITY FUTURES TRADING COMMISSION, FEDERAL TRADE COMMISSION, FEDERAL DEPOSIT INSURANCE CORPORATION, OFFICE OF THRIFT SUPERVISION, INTERNAL REVENUE SERVICE, DEPARTMENT OF COMMERCE, INTERSTATE COMMERCE COMMISSION, and SECURITIES AND EXCHANGE COMMISSION.

Governmental money matters are overseen and assisted by the GENERAL ACCOUNTING OFFICE, OFFICE OF MANAGEMENT AND BUDGET, Office of the Comptroller of the Currency, TREASURY DEPARTMENT, GENERAL SERVICES ADMINISTRATION, CONGRESSIONAL BUDGET OFFICE, and FEDERAL RESERVE BOARD.

Public services are handled by administrative agencies that include the DEPARTMENT OF EDUCATION, DEPARTMENT OF TRANSPORTATION, Environmental Protection Agency, FOOD AND DRUG ADMINISTRATION, DEPARTMENT OF HEALTH AND HUMAN SERVICES, DEPARTMENT OF HOUSING AND URBAN DEVELOPMENT, DEPARTMENT OF INTERIOR, IMMIGRATION and NATURALIZATION service, and National Highway Traffic Safety Administration.

Work-related administrative agencies include the TENNESSEE VALLEY AUTHORITY, Office of Technology Assessment, Occupational Safety and Health Administration, Occupational Safety and Health Review Commission, National Labor Relations Board, Mine Safety and Health Administration, Mine Safety and Health Review Commission, MERIT SYSTEMS PROTECTION BOARD, DEPARTMENT OF LABOR, EQUAL EMPLOYMENT OPPORTUNITY COMMISSION, and Office of Personnel Management.

Police and military functions are served by the Central Intelligence Agency, DEPARTMENT OF DEFENSE, Department of Justice, Department of Veterans Affairs, Federal Bureau of Investigation, and NATIONAL SECURITY COUNCIL.

The administrative agency that directly affects the most U.S. citizens is the Social Security Administration (SSA). The SSA collects contributions from workers and pays out cash benefits when a worker retires, dies, or becomes disabled.

As the needs of the nation change, Congress continues to establish new agencies and abolish existing agencies. The Interstate Commerce Commission, for instance, was established in 1887 to regulate carriers engaged in the transportation of interstate and foreign commerce in the United States. Over time, many of the commission's functions were transferred to other agencies or otherwise abandoned, and Congress abolished the commission in 1995. A more recent example of the development of an administrative agency is the creation of HOMELAND SECURITY DEPARTMENT in 2002 to prevent terrorist attacks in the United States and to reduce the country's vulnerability to TERRORISM in the aftermath of the SEPTEMBER 11TH ATTACKS.

State and Local Administrative Agencies

State and local administrative agencies often mirror federal agencies. Thus, the individual states have agencies that control transportation, public health, public assistance, education, natural resources, labor, law enforcement, agriculture, commerce, and revenue. Any regulation established by such an agency that conflicts with a federal regulation will not be legally valid, but this fact does not keep state agencies from developing regulations that differ from those promulgated by their federal counterparts. In the spirit of administrative agency, state and local governments also create agencies that help address compelling, peculiarly local concerns.

Just like federal agencies, state and local administrative agencies are often empowered to hold hearings. These hearings are conducted by their administrative boards, which are obligated to represent the PUBLIC INTEREST. By contrast, courts must remain impartial to the two parties before them. A PAROLE board, for example, holds informal hearings during which prisoners are allowed to offer evidence of their suitability for early release from INCARCERATION. The strict rules observed in a courtroom do not apply to these hearings, and the board's decisions must account for the public interest as well as the rights of the prisoners.

FURTHER READINGS

Aman, Alfred C., Jr., and William T. Mayton. *2001 Aman and Mayton's Hornbook on Administrative Law*. 2d ed. Eagan, MN: West.

Barksdale, Yvette M. 1993. "The Presidency and Administrative Value Selection." *American Univ. Law Review* 42.

Diver, Colin S. 1987. "The Uneasy Constitutional Status of the Administrative Agencies, Part II: Presidential Oversight of Regulatory Decisionmaking: Commentary: Presidential Powers." *American Univ. Law Review* 36.

Pierce, Richard J. 2002 (updated 2008). *Administrative Law Treatise*. 4th ed. Frederick, MD: Aspen.

U.S. Government Manual Web site. Available online at http://www.gpoaccess.gov/gmanual/index (accessed July 3, 2009).

CROSS REFERENCES

Administrative Conference of the United States; Administrative Law and Procedure; Bureaucracy; National Industrial Recovery Act of 1933; *Schechter Poultry Corp. v. United States*. See also entries for specific federal agencies (e.g., Food and Drug Administration).

ADMINISTRATIVE BOARD

A comprehensive phrase that can refer to any administrative agency but usually means a public agency that holds hearings.

An administrative board is usually obligated to represent the PUBLIC INTEREST; courts, in contrast, must remain impartial between the two parties before them. A PAROLE board, for example, holds informal hearings where prisoners are allowed to offer evidence of their suitability for early release from prison. The strict rules observed in a courtroom do not apply to board hearings like these, and the board's decision must take into account the public's interest as well as the prisoner's rights.

ADMINISTRATIVE CONFERENCE OF THE UNITED STATES

Created in 1968, the Administrative Conference of the United States (ACUS) was a federal independent agency and advisory committee chartered for the purpose of ensuring the fair and efficient administration of various federal agencies. The ACUS studied administrative processes and recommended improvements in the procedures by which federal agencies administered regulatory, benefit, and other government programs. It had no power to enact its recommendations into law, or to enforce them once they were enacted, but it did carry great weight in the formulation of procedures and policies of federal administrative agencies.

The ACUS consisted of heads of administrative agencies, private lawyers, university professors, various federal officials, and other experts in administrative law and government. These experts collectively conducted continuing studies of selected problems that existed in the procedures of federal administrative agencies. The specific charge of ACUS was to harness the experience and judgment of the administrative agency specialists to improve the fairness and effectiveness of administrative procedures and functions.

From 1968 to 1995 the ACUS issued approximately two hundred recommendations, the majority of which were at least partially implemented. In 1995 Congress terminated funding for the ACUS, and it ceased operation.

FURTHER READINGS

"Administrative Conference of the United States" (Symposium). 1998. *Arizona State Law Journal* 30 (spring).

Funk, William. "R.I.P. A.C.U.S." ABA Network: Administrative & Regulatory Law News. Available online at www.abanet.org/adminlaw/news/vol21no2/acus_rip.html (accessed Mar. 31, 2010).

"Recommendations of the Administrative Conference of the United States." ABA Administrative Procedure Database. Available online at www.law.fsu.edu/library/admin/acus/acustoc.html (accessed Mar. 31, 2010).

CROSS REFERENCES

Administrative Agency; Administrative Law and Procedure.

ADMINISTRATIVE DISCRETION

The exercise of professional expertise and judgment, as opposed to strict adherence to regulations or statutes, in making a decision or performing official acts or duties.

A discretionary action is informal and, therefore, unprotected by the safeguards inherent in formal procedure. A public official, for example, has ADMINISTRATIVE DISCRETION when he or she has the freedom to make a choice among potential courses of action. ABUSE OF DISCRETION is the failure to exercise reasonable judgment or discretion. It might provide a CAUSE OF ACTION for an unconstitutional invasion of rights protected by the Due Process Clause of the Constitution.

ADMINISTRATIVE LAW AND PROCEDURE

Administrative law is the body of law that allows for the creation of public regulatory agencies and contains all of the statutes, judicial decisions, and regulations that govern them. It is created by administrative agencies to implement their powers and duties in the form of rules, regulations, orders, and decisions. Administrative procedure constitutes the methods and processes before administrative agencies, as distinguished from judicial procedure, which applies to courts.

The Administrative Procedure Act (5 U.S.C. §§ 551-706) governs the practice and proceedings before federal administrative agencies. The procedural rules and regulations of most federal agencies are set forth in the CODE OF FEDERAL REGULATIONS (CFR).

The fundamental challenge of administrative law is in designing a system of checks that will minimize the risks of bureaucratic arbitrariness and overreaching, while preserving for the agencies the flexibility that they need in order to act effectively. Administrative law thus seeks to limit the powers and actions of agencies and to fix their place in U.S. scheme of government and law. It contrasts with traditional notions that the three branches of the U.S. government must be kept separate, that they must not delegate their responsibilities to bureaucrats, and that the formalities of due process must be observed.

Separation of Powers

The U.S. Constitution establishes a three-part system of government, consisting of the Legislative Branch, which makes the laws; the EXECUTIVE BRANCH, which carries out or enforces the laws; and the Judicial Branch, which interprets the laws. This system of checks and balances is designed to keep any one branch from exercising too much power. Administrative agencies do not fit neatly into any of the three branches. They are frequently created by the legislature and are sometimes placed in the Executive Branch, but their functions reach into all three areas of government.

For example, the SECURITIES AND EXCHANGE COMMISSION (SEC) administers laws governing the registration, offering, and sale of securities, such as stocks and bonds. The SEC formulates laws like a legislature does by writing rules that spell out what disclosures must be made in a PROSPECTUS that describes shares of stock that will be offered for sale. The SEC enforces its rules in the way that the Executive Branch of government does, by prosecuting violators. It can bring disciplinary actions against broker-dealers, or it

The Securities and Exchange Commission administers laws governing the actions of these traders on the floor of the New York Stock Exchange. The SEC is an independent agency that enforces its rules without need for approval from Congress or the executive branch of the government.

AP IMAGES

can issue stop orders against corporate issuers of securities. The SEC acts as judge and jury when it conducts adjudicatory hearings to determine violations or to prescribe punishment. Although SEC commissioners are appointed by the president subject to the approval of the Senate, the SEC is an independent agency. It is not part of Congress, nor is it part of any executive department.

Combining the three functions of government allows an agency to tackle a problem and to get the job done most efficiently, but this combination has not been accepted without a struggle. Some observers have taken the position that the basic structure of the administrative law system is an unconstitutional violation of the principle of the SEPARATION OF POWERS.

Delegation of Authority

The first issue that is encountered in the study of administrative law concerns the way in which Congress can effectively delegate its legislative power to an administrative agency. Article I, Section I, of the U.S. Constitution provides that all legislative power is vested in Congress. Despite early resistance, the U.S. Supreme Court gradually accepted the delegation of legislative authority so long as Congress sets clear standards for the administration of the duties in order to limit the scope of agency discretion. With this basic principle as their guide, courts have invalidated laws that grant too much legislative power to an administrative agency. President FRANKLIN D. ROOSEVELT learned just how far the Court would go in allowing the delegation of authority, in two cases that stemmed from his administrative-agency actions to support his NEW DEAL program.

The National Industrial Recovery Act (15 U.S.C.A. § 701 et seq., 40 U.S.C.A. § 401 et seq. [1933]) authorized the president to prohibit interstate shipments of oil that had been produced in violation of state board rules that attempted to regulate crude-oil production to match consumer demand. The Panama Refining Company sued to prevent federal officials from enforcing the prohibition, known as the "hot oil" law (*Panama Refining Co. v. Ryan,* 293 U.S. 388, 55 S. Ct. 241, 79 L. Ed. 446 [1935]). The U.S. Supreme Court found the law to be unconstitutional. Congress could have passed a law prohibiting interstate shipments of hot oil,

but it did not do so; instead, it gave that power to the president. This instance has been called a case of delegation run amok because the law had no clear standards defining when and how the president should use the authority that the statute delegated to him.

Four months later, the Court invalidated a criminal prosecution for violation of the Live Poultry Code, an unfair-competition law that President Roosevelt had signed in 1934 pursuant to another section of the National Industrial Recovery Act. This was the case of *Schechter Poultry v. United States,* 295 U.S. 495, 55 S. Ct. 837, 79 L. Ed. 1570 (1935). The problem in this case was not that the delegation of authority was ill-defined, but that it seemed limitless. The president was given the authority to "formulate codes of fair competition" for any industry if these codes would "tend to effectuate the policy" of the law. Comprehensive codes were created, establishing an elaborate regulation of prices, minimum wages, and maximum hours for different kinds of businesses. But there were no procedural safeguards from arbitrariness or abuses by enforcement agencies. Someone who was charged with a violation was not given the right to notice of the charges, the right to be heard at an agency hearing, or the right to challenge the agency's determination in a lawsuit. The Court struck this law down, stating that the unfair procedures helped strong industrial groups to use these codes to improve their commercial advantage over small producers.

As a result of *Panama Refining* and *Schechter Poultry,* when Congress delegates authority to agencies, it also sets out important provisions detailing procedures that protect against arbitrary administrative actions.

Resolving Conflicts of Authority

On some occasions, the courts have to determine which agency is the proper body to exercise authority over a certain action. For instance, in *Coeur Alaska, Inc. v. Southeast Alaska Conservation Council,* No. 07-984, 2009 WL 1738643 (2009), the Supreme Court reviewed a case involving the issuance of a permit that would allow a company to dump rock materials into a lake. The U.S. Army Corps of Engineers originally issued the permit, but a citizens' group argued that the ENVIRONMENTAL PROTECTION AGENCY was the proper body to issue the permit. The Court determined that the

CLEAN WATER ACT, 33 U.S.C. § 1251 et seq., had delegated authority in the specific instance presented by the case to the Corps of Engineers.

Due Process of Law

The Fifth and Fourteenth Amendments guarantee that the federal government and the state governments, respectively, will not deprive a person of his or her life, liberty, or property without DUE PROCESS OF LAW. An administrative agency thus may not deprive anyone of life, liberty, or property without providing that person with a reasonable opportunity, appropriate under the circumstances, to challenge the agency's action. People must be given fair warning of the limits that an agency will place on their actions, federal courts routinely uphold very broad delegations of authority. When reviewing administrative agency actions, courts ask whether the agency afforded those under its jurisdiction due process of law as guaranteed by the U.S. Constitution.

The U.S. Supreme Court has held it improper for a state agency to deny welfare benefits to applicants who meet the conditions for entitlement to those benefits as defined by the legislature. The state must afford due process (in these cases, an oral hearing) before it can terminate benefits (*Goldberg v. Kelly,* 397 U.S. 254, 90 S. Ct. 1011, 25 L. Ed. 2d 287 [1970]). Likewise, when a state grants all children the right to attend public schools and establishes rules specifying the grounds for suspension, it cannot suspend a given student for alleged misconduct without affording the student at least a limited prior hearing (*Goss v. Lopez,* 419 U.S. 565, 95 S. Ct. 729, 42 L. Ed. 2d 725 [1975]).

Political Controls over Agency Action: Legislative and Executive Oversight

Government institutions that set and enforce PUBLIC POLICY must be politically accountable to the electorate. When the legislature delegates broad lawmaking powers to an administrative agency, the popular control provided by direct election of decision makers is absent, but this does not mean that administrative agencies are free from political accountability. In many areas, policy oversight by elected officials in the legislature or the Executive Branch is a more important check on agency power than is JUDICIAL REVIEW.

Federal agencies are dependent upon Congress and the president for their budgets and operating authority. An agency that loses the support of these bodies or oversteps the bounds of political acceptability may be subjected to radical restructuring. In the 1970s the Atomic Energy Commission (AEC) took the politically unpopular position of promoting NUCLEAR POWER, while underemphasizing safety and environmental protection. It paid the price when some of its promotional functions were transferred to a newly created DEPARTMENT OF ENERGY, and the AEC was restructured into the NUCLEAR REGULATORY COMMISSION, which was responsible for the former agency's regulatory duties.

Federal administrative agencies must be responsive to legislative and executive oversight mechanisms. During the 1970s many members of Congress began to feel that the normal process of legislation was too cumbersome for effective control of administrative action. They devised a solution called the legislative VETO. Legislative vetoes took a variety of forms, but most of them directed agencies to transmit final administrative rules to Congress for review before they became effective. Just as this approach was gaining in popularity and use, the U.S. Supreme Court declared the legislative veto unconstitutional. This ruling involved the IMMIGRATION and Nationality Act (8 U.S.C. § 1101 et seq.), which allowed either house of Congress to nullify a decision by the attorney general suspending DEPORTATION of an alien. Jagdish Rai Chadha brought suit when the House of Representatives exercised this power in his case. The Court held, in *INS v. Chadha,* 462 U.S. 919, 103 S. Ct. 2764, 77 L. Ed. 2d 317 (1983), that the legislative veto was essentially a one-house veto, and therefore it violated Article I, Section 7, of the Constitution, which states that no legislation is valid unless passed by both houses of Congress and signed by the president (or, if the president vetoes it, repassed by two-thirds of each house). The Court said that in *Chadha,* the House veto of the attorney general's decision was a legislative action, and therefore Article I, Section 7, applied. The *Chadha* decision invalidated all of the nearly 200 legislative-veto provisions that were on the books.

Another important legislative-oversight mechanism is the annual appropriations process.

Congress determines the budget and appropriates money for the various administrative agencies. An administrative agency that angers Congress, or a key member of either house, could find itself with less money to work with in the next year, or could even see certain programs eliminated. A legislature may also enact a SUNSET PROVISION, which provides for automatic termination of an agency after a stated time unless the legislature is convinced that the need for the agency continues. Sometimes, a sunset provision is written into the statute that creates a particular agency, but a general sunset law may terminate any agency that cannot periodically demonstrate its effectiveness. A useful agency can always be revived or retained by the enactment of a new statute.

Like Congress, the president uses a variety of powers and techniques to oversee and influence the operations of administrative agencies. The Appointments Clause of the Constitution (art. II, §2, cl. 2) states that the president may generally appoint all "officers of the United States," with the ADVICE AND CONSENT of the Senate. Under the authority of this provision, presidents often appoint agency heads who share their political agenda. The president's power to remove an agency head depends on whether the agency is an independent agency or a cabinet department. Independent agencies tend to be multimember boards and commissions, such as the Securities and Exchange Commission, FEDERAL COMMUNICATIONS COMMISSION (FCC), and NATIONAL LABOR RELATIONS BOARD (NLRB), which are run by officials who are appointed for a fixed period that does not correspond to the president's term of office. There also may be statutes protecting the commissioners from arbitrary removal during their terms of office. The heads of cabinet-level agencies, called secretaries, serve at the pleasure of the president and may be removed at any time. Appointments of cabinet secretaries must be confirmed by the Senate.

The president also reviews agency budgets, through the OFFICE OF MANAGEMENT AND BUDGET (OMB). A president's disapproval of agency initiatives can block appropriations in Congress. The president may also use an EXECUTIVE ORDER, a formal directive, to direct federal agencies or officials. One technique that has been used frequently is the president's authority to modify the organizational structure of the BUREAUCRACY. Under the Executive Reorganization Act (5 U.S.C. §§ 901-912), the president may submit a REORGANIZATION PLAN to Congress, transferring functions from one department to another. This law recognizes that although responsibility for the organization and structure of the Executive Branch is vested in Congress, the president needs flexibility to carry out executive duties.

Public opinion is another forceful weapon against unbridled agency action. Some jurisdictions of the United States have created special public offices to investigate complaints about administrative misconduct. Investigators holding these offices, called ombudsmen, usually have broad authority to evaluate individual complaints, to intercede on behalf of beleaguered victims of red tape, and to make reports or recommendations.

The Development of Administrative Procedure Law

Administrative agencies were established to do the government's work in a simpler and more direct manner than the legislature could do by enacting a law or the courts could do by applying that law in various cases. Because they pursue their actions less formally, agencies do not follow the CIVIL PROCEDURE that is set up for courts. Instead, the law of administrative procedure has developed to ensure that agencies do not abuse their authority even though they use simplified procedures.

Although administrative agencies have existed since the founding of the United States, the early twentieth century saw a growth in the number of agencies that were designed to address new problems. During the Great Depression, a host of new agencies sprang up to meet economic challenges. Antagonism toward bureaucracy increased as existing dissatisfactions were multiplied by the number of new bureaucrats. In 1939 President Roosevelt appointed a committee to investigate the need for procedural reform in the field of administrative law. Although the comprehensive and scholarly report of that committee was not enacted into law, a later version of it was enacted in 1946 when Congress unanimously passed the Administrative Procedure Act (5 U.S. C.A. §§ 551-706) (APA). The statute made agencies' methods fairer so that there would be less reason to object to them. It also limited the power of the courts to review agency actions and to overturn them.

Judicial review of agency action furnishes an important set of controls on administrative behavior. Unlike the political oversight controls, which generally influence entire programs or basic policies, judicial review regularly operates to provide relief for the individual person who is harmed by a particular agency decision. Judicial review has evolved over a period of years into a complex system of statutory, constitutional, and judicial doctrines that define the proper BOUNDARIES of this system of oversight. The trend of judicial decisions and the Administrative Procedure Act is to make judicial review more widely and easily available.

How far can a court go in examining an agency decision? The reviewing court may be completely precluded from testing the merits of an agency action, or it may be free to decide the issues DE NOVO, that is, without deference to the agency's determination. In general, administrative agencies make either formal or informal decisions, and courts have different standards for reviewing each type.

Informal Agency Action Most of the work done by agencies is accomplished with informal procedures. For example, a person who applies for a driver's license does not need or want a full trial in court in order to be found qualified. So long as the motor vehicle department follows standard, fair procedures, and processes the application promptly, most people will be happy. Agencies take informal action in a variety of settings. The SOCIAL SECURITY Administration reviews over four million claims for benefits annually, holding hearings or answering challenges to their decisions in only a small number of cases. Most transmitter applications before the Federal Communications Commission are approved or disapproved without any formal action. The INTERNAL REVENUE SERVICE processes most tax returns without formal proceedings. It also will provide informal opinions to help people avoid making costly mistakes in their financial planning.

Anyone who objects to the informal decisions made by a government agency can invoke more formal procedures. Someone may believe that standards are unclear and that they should be promulgated through formal agency rule making. Or someone may feel that the decision in a particular case is unfair and may demand a

Employees of the Internal Revenue Service process tax returns using informal procedures that make their jobs easier and less time-consuming. If a taxpayer objects to a decision made in this way, he or she may initiate more formal review procedures.

AP IMAGES

formal adjudicatory hearing. If one of these formal procedures does not satisfy a party, the agency's decision may be challenged in court.

Formal Agency Action Most formal action taken by administrative agencies consists of rule making or adjudication. Rule making is the agency's formulation of policy that will apply in the future to everyone who is affected by the agency's activities. Adjudication is for the agency what a trial is for the courts: It applies the agency's policies to some act that already has been done, so that an order is issued for or against a party who appears for a decision. Rule making looks to the future; adjudication looks at the past. Where either of these formal procedures is used, the agency will usually give interested or affected persons notice and an opportunity to be heard before a final rule or order is issued.

Rule making Administrative agencies promulgate three types of rules: procedural, interpretative, and legislative. Procedural rules identify the agency's organization and methods of operation. Interpretative rules are issued to show how the agency intends to apply the law. They range from informal policy statements announced in a press release to authoritative rules that bind the agency in the future and are issued only after the agency has given the public an opportunity to be heard on the subject. Legislative rules are like statutes enacted by a legislature. Agencies can promulgate legislative rules only if the legislature has given them this authority.

The Administrative Procedure Act sets up the procedures to be followed for administrative rule making. Before adopting a rule, a federal agency generally must publish advance notice in the FEDERAL REGISTER, the government's daily publication for federal agencies. Most states have similar publication requirements. This practice gives those who have an interest in, or are affected by, a proposed rule the opportunity to participate in the decision making by submitting written data or by offering views or arguments orally or in writing. Before a rule is adopted in its final form, and 30 days before its effective date, the agency must publish it in the *Federal Register*. Formally adopted rules are published in the *Code of Federal Regulations*, a set of paperback books that the government publishes each year so that rules are readily available to the public.

Adjudication The procedures that administrative agencies use to adjudicate individual claims or cases are diverse. Like trials, these hearings resolve disputed questions of fact, determining policy in a specific factual setting and ordering compliance with laws and regulations. Although often not as formal as courtroom trials, administrative hearings are extremely important. Far more hearings are held before agencies every year than are trials in courts. Adjudicative hearings concern a variety of subjects, such as individual claims for worker's compensation, welfare, or Social Security benefits, in addition to multimillion-dollar disputes about whether business mergers will violate antitrust rulings. These proceedings may be called hearings, adjudications, or adjudicatory proceedings. Their final disposition is called an administrative order.

Many administrative proceedings appear to be just like courtroom trials. Most are open to the public and are conducted in an orderly and dignified manner. Typically, a proceeding begins with a complaint filed by the agency, much as a civil trial begins with a complaint prepared by the PLAINTIFF. After the RESPONDENT answers, each side may conduct discovery of the other's evidence and prehearing conferences. A HEARING EXAMINER, sometimes called an administrative law judge (ALJ), presides over the hearing, giving rulings in response to a party's applications for a particular type of relief. The agency presents its evidence, usually

through counsel, either by a written report or in the question-and-answer style of a trial, and then the respondent offers his or her case. WITNESSES may be called and cross-examined. The examiner gives a decision, usually with written findings and a written opinion, shortly after the hearing.

The Executive Branch of the federal government employs federal ALJs. When Congress originally enacted the APA, it addressed concerns about the relationship between ALJs and their respective agencies by providing independence to the ALJ. The U.S. Office of Personnel Management (OPM) makes most of the decisions regarding the tenure and compensation of ALJs, and ALJs are exempted from many of the performance reviews that apply to other CIVIL SERVICE employees. An agency may remove an ALJ only for cause and after a hearing conducted by the MERIT SYSTEMS PROTECTION BOARD.

Because administrative hearings do not use juries, an ALJ makes both factual determinations and legal decisions based upon the evidence presented and the law governing the dispute. The specific duties of an ALJ in an individual agency depend upon the powers delegated to the agency in the respective ENABLING STATUTE and procedural regulations promulgated by the agency. For instance, the Office of Inspector General is empowered to impose civil penalties against a person who makes false statements or representations with respect to Social Security benefits. Under regulations promulgated by the Social Security Administration (20 C.F.R. § 498.204 [2009]), the ALJ may make a number of decisions regarding the submission of evidence or the examination of witnesses; rule on motions and other procedural matters; and render a SUMMARY JUDGMENT where appropriate. However, the ALJ may not rule as invalid a federal statutory or regulatory provision, enjoin agency officials, or review discretionary acts by the inspector general.

An ALJ's decision is often subject to review by a board or commission of the entire agency before parties may appeal the decision to a federal court. For example, labor disputes governed by the National Labor Relations Act are first heard by ALJs of the National Labor Relations Board (NLRB). The ALJ's decision may be appealed to the five members of the NLRB for review. Only after review by the NLRB, upon which it renders a decision and issues an opinion, may a party appeal the decision to a U.S. court of appeals.

Unlike a trial, an administrative hearing has no jury. The hearing examiner, or administrative law judge, is usually an expert in the field involved and is likely to be more concerned with overall policies than with the particular merits of one party's case. The Administrative Procedure Act affords parties who appear in administrative hearings involving federal agencies the right to notice of the issues and proceedings, the RIGHT TO COUNSEL, and the right to confront and cross-examine witnesses.

Judicial Review of Agency Actions

When individuals believe that they have been the victim of administrative error or wrongdoing and seek to have the actions of the responsible agency reviewed in a court of law, the reviewing court is faced with two principal issues: (1) the court must determine whether it has a right to review the agency action, and (2) if the court does, the court must determine the scope of that court's review.

The Right to Have a Court Review an Agency's Decision Whether someone has the right to ask a court to review the action taken by an agency depends on the answers to several questions. The first question is whether the person bringing the action has standing (i.e., the LEGAL RIGHT) to bring the suit. Section 702 of the Administrative Procedure Act allows court review for any person who is adversely affected or aggrieved by agency action within the meaning of a relevant statute. When the U.S. Supreme Court reviewed section 702 in *Association of Data Processing Service Organizations v. Camp*, 397 U.S. 150, 90 S. Ct. 827, 25 L. Ed. 2d 184 (1970), the Court said that for the plaintiff to have standing to seek judicial review of administrative action, two questions must be answered affirmatively: (1) Has the complainant alleged an "injury in fact"?; and (2) Is the interest that the complainant seeks to protect "arguably within the zone of interests to be protected or regulated by the statute or constitutional guarantee in question"?

Even though an agency's decision is reviewable and the plaintiff has standing to litigate, the plaintiff still may be unable to obtain judicial review if he or she has brought the action at the wrong time. The aggrieved person must exhaust all other avenues of relief before the dispute is ripe for judicial determination. The doctrines of EXHAUSTION OF REMEDIES and RIPENESS require a person who deals with an agency to follow patiently all of the available steps within the agency's procedures before resorting to court action. These rules are essential to prevent overloading the courts with questions that might not even be disputes by the time the agencies determine what their final orders or rulings will be.

The Scope of a Court's Review If an AGGRIEVED PARTY can convince a court that he or she has standing, that all available administrative remedies have been exhausted, and that the case is ripe for judicial review, the court will hear the case, but the scope of its review is limited. The law seeks to give agencies enough freedom of action to do their work, while ensuring that individual rights will be protected. The Administrative Procedure Act provides that courts may not second-guess agencies when the agencies are exercising discretion that has been granted to them by statute. A court is generally limited to asking whether the agency went outside the authority granted to it; whether it followed proper procedures in reaching its decision; and whether the decision is so clearly wrong that it must be SET ASIDE. The court also may set aside an agency decision that is clearly wrong.

The court usually will accept the agency's findings of fact, but it is free to determine how the law will be applied to those facts. It will look at the whole record of the administrative proceeding and will take into account the agency's expertise in the matter. The court will not upset agency decisions for harmless errors that do not change the outcome of the case. If the question at issue has been committed to agency discretion, the court may consider whether the agency has exercised its discretion. If the agency has not done so, then the court may order the agency to look at the situation and make a decision. The Administrative Procedure Act allows courts to OVERRULE an agency action that is found to be "arbitrary, capricious, an ABUSE OF DISCRETION, or otherwise not in accordance with law."

FURTHER READINGS

Aman, Alfred C., and William Mayton. 2001. *Administrative Law*. 2d ed. St. Paul, Minn.: West Group

Beerman, Jack M. 2006. *Administrative Law*. New York: Aspen.

Lubbers, Jeffrey S., ed. 2003. *Developments in Administrative Law and Regulatory Practice* (annual). Chicago, Ill.: Section of Administrative Law and Regulatory Practice, American Bar Association.

Mezines, Basil J., Jacob A. Stein, and Jules Gruff. 2009. *Administrative Law.* New York: Matthew Bender & Co.

Rosenbloom, David H. 1997. *Public Administration and Law.* 2d ed. New York: M. Dekker.

Weaver, Russell L., and William D. Araiza. 2006. *Administrative Law.* St. Paul, Minn.: Thomson/West.

CROSS REFERENCES

Administrative Conference of the United States; Administrative Discretion; Federal Budget; Veto; See also entries for specific federal agencies (e.g., Food and Drug Administration).

ADMINISTRATIVE OFFICE OF THE UNITED STATES COURTS

The Administrative Office of the United States Courts is the administrative headquarters of the federal court system. It was created by congressional act on August 7, 1939 (28 U.S.C.A. § 601), and since November 6, 1939, it has tended to the nonjudicial business of the U.S. courts. The Administrative Office helps Congress monitor the state of affairs within the federal judiciary. The Administrative Office arranges clerical and administrative support to federal district courts and their subdivisions, and it provides for the various benefits available to the federal judiciary. Furthermore, by gathering and analyzing statistics and data and reporting the findings to Congress and the JUDICIAL CONFERENCE OF THE UNITED STATES, the Administrative Office plays an important part in determining the extent and character of the very support it provides.

The Director

The director of the Administrative Office is the administrative officer of all the federal courts except the Supreme Court. The Judicial Conference of the United States—the federal agency charged with overseeing federal judicial matters—supervises and guides the director's work. The director and the deputy director are appointed by the SUPREME COURT OF THE UNITED STATES.

The director is required to perform a variety of tasks. First and foremost, the director must supervise all administrative matters relating to the offices of clerks and other clerical and administrative personnel of the federal courts. These administrative matters can range from performance policies and pay scales to guidelines on clerical procedures.

The director is charged with providing many reports to various governmental bodies. With the aid of the deputy director and the Audit Office and other operatives, the director must examine court dockets, determine the needs of the various courts, and report the results four times per year to the chief judges of the circuits. These reports allow the federal courts to analyze and plan for their own clerical and administrative costs. This information is also used when the director prepares and submits to Congress the budget of the federal courts.

The director must submit a report of the Administrative Office to the annual meeting of the Judicial Conference of the United States. At least two weeks before the conference, the director prepares an overview of the activities of the Administrative Office and the state of the business of the courts, together with certain statistical data submitted to the chief judges of the circuits. This report also contains the director's recommendations on administrative efficiency. The director submits the report, data, and recommendations to Congress and makes all these materials available to the public.

The director is responsible for many financial matters of the federal courts. The director must fix the compensation of employees of the courts whose compensation is not otherwise fixed by law, regulate and pay annuities to the surviving spouses and dependent children of judges, disburse monies appropriated for the maintenance and operation of the federal courts, examine accounts of court officers, regulate travel of judicial personnel, and provide accommodations and supplies for the courts and their clerical and administrative personnel.

The director must also establish and maintain programs for the certification and utilization of court interpreters and the provision of special interpretation services in the courts. Other duties may be assigned to the director by the Supreme Court or the Judicial Conference of the United States.

As of 2009, a total of seven individuals have served as director of the Administrative Office. James C. Duff took over the position in 2006 from Leonidas Ralph Meachum after the latter had served as director for 21 years.

Probation Officers

The Probation Division of the Administrative Office supervises the accounts and practices of the federal probation offices. However, primary control of probation practices and procedures is left to the district courts served by the probation offices. The Probation Division establishes pretrial services in the federal district courts according to the Pretrial Services Act of 1982 (18 U.S.C.A. § 3152). The pretrial service offices report to their respective courts with information on the pretrial release of persons charged with federal offenses. These offices also supervise criminal defendants released to their custody.

With the Bureau of Prisons of the DEPARTMENT OF JUSTICE, the Administrative Office publishes the magazine *Federal Probation*. The magazine, issued four times per year, is a journal "of correctional philosophy and practice."

Bankruptcy Act

The Administrative Office has special responsibility for BANKRUPTCY courts. The Bankruptcy Amendments and Federal Judgeship Act of 1984 (28 U.S.C.A. § 152) established bankruptcy judges as distinct units of the federal district courts. Under the Bankruptcy Amendments Act, all cases under Title 11 of the United States Code and all proceedings related to federal statute 28 U.S.C.A. § 1334 are to be brought before federal district courts. Such a case arises when a person seeks to discharge his or her debts through judicial proceedings. When a suit is filed under Title 11, the federal district court will refer the case to its bankruptcy judges, as authorized by 28 U.S.C.A. § 157.

Bankruptcy judges are appointed by the federal courts of appeals and serve a 14-year term as judicial officers of the district courts. The number of bankruptcy judges is controlled by Congress, but the bankruptcy courts are overseen by the Administrative Office.

The director of the Administrative Office has specific duties related to the bankruptcy courts. The director must make recommendations to the Judicial Conference on logistical concerns such as the geographic placement of bankruptcy courts. The director must consider whether additional bankruptcy judges should be recommended to Congress; the director is also in charge of determining the staff needs of bankruptcy judges and clerks.

Federal Magistrates

Under the Federal Magistrates Act as amended in 1979 (28 U.S.C.A. § 631), the director of the Administrative Office must answer to Congress and the Judicial Conference on the affairs of federal magistrates. Federal magistrates are appointed by federal district court judges, and their job is to reduce each case to its essence before it reaches the district courts. Federal proceedings are expensive; by ruling on pretrial motions and issuing various orders at the pretrial stage, federal magistrates help preserve judicial resources.

Federal magistrates do not have the full range of judicial powers available to other federal judges. For example, they cannot preside over FELONY trials. Federal magistrates may conduct civil or MISDEMEANOR criminal trials, but they normally conduct pretrial proceedings in both criminal and civil cases. Owing to their special function, federal magistrates operate separately from the district courts and maintain a separate budget.

With the guidance of the Judicial Conference, the director supervises the administrative matters of federal magistrates through the Magistrate Division of the Administrative Office. The director prepares legal and administrative manuals for the use of the magistrates. In addition, the Administrative Office must conduct surveys of the federal judiciary to ask questions on court conditions. With these surveys, the director makes recommendations as to the number, location, and salaries of magistrates. The expansion of magistrate offices depends significantly on the availability of funds appropriated by Congress.

The director of the Administrative Office compiles and evaluates information on the magistrate offices and reports the findings to the Judicial Conference. The director must also report to Congress every year on the general affairs of federal magistrates.

Federal Defenders

The Administrative Office also assists and oversees the offices of federal public defenders. Under the Criminal Justice Act (18 U.S.C.A. § 3006A [1964]), the federal district courts are required to appoint counsel to criminal defendants who are unable to afford adequate representation. The act also authorizes the district courts to establish federal PUBLIC DEFENDER and federal community defender organizations. Establishing these organizations can be done in districts where at least 200 persons annually require the appointment of counsel. Two adjacent districts may be combined to reach this total.

Each defender organization submits to the director of the Administrative Office an annual report of its activities along with a proposed budget. Because they rely on grants and not regular funding, community defender organizations submit grant proposals to the Administrative Office for the coming year. The director then submits the proposed budgets and grants to the Judicial Conference of the United States for approval. After budgets are determined, the director pays the defender organizations. The director also compensates private counsel appointed to defend individuals charged in federal court.

In wake of the SEPTEMBER 11TH ATTACKS in 2001, the Administrative Office relied on its newly created Office of Emergency Preparedness. This office worked with courts around the United States to develop crisis response plans to deal with emergency evacuations, relocations, and the continuation of court business. The office also arranged for the testing of courthouses for hazardous materials.

FURTHER READINGS

Administrative Office of the U.S. Courts Website. Available online at http://www.uscourts.gov/adminoff.html (accessed June 25, 2009).

U.S. Government Manual Website. Available online at http://www.gpoaccess.gov/gmanual/ (accessed June 25, 2009).

CROSS REFERENCES

District Court; Federal Courts; Justice Department; Magistrate.

ADMINISTRATIVE PROCEDURE ACT OF 1946

Since its original enactment in 1946, the Administrative Procedure Act (APA), 5 U.S.C.A. §§ 501 et seq., has governed the process that federal administrative agencies follow. The statute applies to all federal agencies except for those that are expressly exempted from its provisions. Despite the broad nature of the act, however, it allows flexibility among the various agencies in carrying out their responsibilities.

Although a number of administrative agencies were created during the nineteenth and early twentieth centuries, no federal law at the time governed the conduct of these agencies. Legislation that was enacted during the NEW DEAL era of the 1930s established a new series of administrative agencies. In 1936 President FRANKLIN D. ROOSEVELT established the President's Committee on Administrative Management. The committee's report found that agencies were "irresponsible" and that they had been given "uncoordinated powers." Moreover, the report characterized administrative agencies as a "headless 'fourth branch' of government."

The committee found that the laws that created administrative agencies failed to distinguish between the legislative and executive functions of those committees. It recommended that each of the existing administrative agencies be moved into the EXECUTIVE BRANCH of the government and that the judicial powers of the agencies be limited. Members of Congress and many commentators at the time disagreed with the committee's findings. At the center of the debate was the need to maintain a SEPARATION OF POWERS with respect to the work of federal agencies.

In 1939 President Roosevelt established the Attorney General's Committee on Administrative Procedure. The committee was charged with the responsibility of reviewing criticisms of the federal administrative processes and formulating recommendations for improvement in these processes. The committee issued its recommendations in 1941 in a detailed report of almost 500 pages. Legislation was drafted based upon the recommendations of the 1941 report, but the U.S. entrance into WORLD WAR II interrupted the enactment of the statute. After the war, the legislation was reintroduced, and following a series of compromises, Congress enacted the Administrative Procedure Act in 1946.

In 1947 the DEPARTMENT OF JUSTICE issued the *Attorney General's Manual on the Administrative Procedure Act.* This document explains how the act can be applied and remains valuable as a research tool in the early 2000s. Some of the information in this manual provides analysis that the courts had not considered as of 2009.

The purpose of the APA is to provide minimum procedural standards that federal administrative agencies must follow. It distinguishes between two major forms of administrative functions: agency rulemaking and agency adjudication. Administrative rulemaking is analogous to LEGISLATIVE ACTS, whereas ADMINISTRATIVE ADJUDICATION is analogous to judicial decision. This distinction contained in the APA has long been the subject of scholarly debate. Some argue that such a dichotomy is unnecessarily rigid and that it might not always allow for the most appropriate procedures for a particular agency. Supporters of the distinction between rulemaking and adjudication contained in the APA note that this distinction best represents the basic functions of administrative agencies.

The rulemaking provisions of the APA are more detailed than those governing adjudications. Most agencies engage in notice-and-comment rulemaking, which is required as the minimum rulemaking procedure under the APA. Under notice-and-comment rulemaking, agencies are required to give the public advance notice of the contents of a proposed rule and to offer citizens an opportunity to express their views of the proposed rule before the agency. Some agencies are required by the statutes that created them to follow more stringent standards, whereby all of the agency's actions during rulemaking are conducted "on the record." This latter type of rulemaking is known as *formal rulemaking.*

The APA defines and governs only those types of adjudications that are required by statute to be conducted "on the record after opportunity for an agency hearing." If an agency is required to conduct such a formal adjudication under the APA, it must engage in a proceeding that resembles a trial. However, if the agency is not required to conduct such a hearing, the APA remains silent. Accordingly, an agency may adopt its own procedure for an informal adjudication, so long as the agency otherwise does not violate the U.S. Constitution or other law.

Other provisions of the APA govern JUDICIAL REVIEW of agency actions and public access to agency-created law and information emanating from agencies. The judicial-review provisions under the APA have given rise to the greatest amount of scholarship regarding federal administrative law, although these provisions are contained in only six sections of the APA. Courts have similarly grappled with judicial review of agency actions. For instance, *Chevron U.S.A., Inc. v. National Resources Defense Council, Inc.* (467 U.S. 837, 104 S. Ct. 2778, 81 L. Ed. 2d 694 [1984]) has been cited more often than any other decision in the history of the U.S. Supreme Court. In *Chevron,* the U.S. Supreme

Court held that interpretive decisions of administrative agencies are entitled to substantial judicial deference. In doing so, it enhanced the efficacy of administrative bodies in mitigating the transition costs of legislative law.

The APA was designed to increase access to agency law by allowing the public to participate in agencies' decision-making process. In 1966 Congress enacted the FREEDOM OF INFORMATION ACT, Pub. L. No. 89-487, 80 Stat. 250 (codified as amended at 5 U.S.C.A. § 552), which greatly increased the amount of government information that is available to the public. Congress later enacted similar laws designed to make governmental decisions open to the public, including the PRIVACY ACT OF 1974, Pub. L. No. 93-579, 88 Stat. 1896 (codified as amended at 5 U.S.C.A. § 552a); the Government in the Sunshine Act of 1976, Pub. L. No. 94-409, 90 Stat. 1241 (codified at 5 U.S.C.A. § 552b); and the Electronic Freedom of Information Act of 1996, Pub. L. No. 104-231, 110 Stat. 2422 (codified as amended at 5 U.S.C.A. § 552).

In 2005 the Judiciary Committee of the House of Representatives began collaborative research under the Administrative Law, Process and Procedure Project, intended to review the efficacy of federal ADMINISTRATIVE LAW AND PROCEDURE. Several studies were commenced, including the solicitation of comments from public agencies, law schools, the AMERICAN BAR ASSOCIATION, and several other organizations. One important study, conducted by the CONGRESSIONAL RESEARCH SERVICE (CRS) analyzed the outcome of cases appealed to all 12 U.S. Circuit Courts of Appeal over a ten-year period that challenged administrative agencies or their rulemaking. An interim report was presented in a hearing before the Judiciary Committee's Subcommittee on Commercial and Administrative Law in November 2006. The report, which contained more than 1,400 pages, summarized various recommendations and the proposed adoption of several of them. Most addressed a perceived need for more standardization of procedures. Following this, various federal agencies published notices in the *Federal Register,* outlining proposed changes and soliciting comment, ultimately making changes as warranted.

In November 2008, then-Democratic presidential candidate BARACK OBAMA campaigned on a platform promising more transparency in the federal government and more access by the public to governmental records and policy-making efforts. As one of his first official acts, President Barack Obama signed EXECUTIVE ORDER 13489 on January 21, 2009, which revoked the previous Executive Order 13233 from the Bush administration that had severely restricted release to the public of presidential records. At that time, Obama signed two other memoranda focusing on transparency and openness. One directed the attorney general to issue new guidelines to agencies for complying with the letter and spirit of the FOIA. In the other, Obama asked three senior officials to produce an "open government" directive within the first 120 days of the administration. Said Obama, "[T]he old rules said that if there was a defensible argument for not disclosing something to the American people, then it should not be disclosed. That era is now over. Starting today, every agency and department should know that this administration stands on the side not of those who seek to withhold information but those who seek to make it known."

FURTHER READINGS

Allen, William H. 1986. "The Durability of the Administrative Procedure Act." *Virginia Law Review* 235.

Bonfield, Arthur Earl. 1986. "The Federal APA and State Administrative Law." *Virginia Law Review* 297.

"Executive Order 13489 of January 21, 2009." Presidential Documents, *Federal Register,* Vol. 74, No. 15, January 26, 2009. Also available at http://edocket.access.gpo.gov/2009/pdf/E-9-1712.pdf

Funk, William F., and Richard H. Seamon. 2009. *Administrative Law: Examples and Explanations.* 3d ed. New York: Aspen Publishers, Inc.

Obama, Barack H. 2009. Remarks to White House Senior Staff with the signing of Executive Order 13,489, January 21. Available at http://www.gpoaccess.gov/presdocs/2009/DCPD200900012.htm.

Prepared Testimony of the Administrative Law, Process and Procedure Project, Before the Subcommittee on Commercial and Administrative Law of the Committee on the Judiciary, House of Representatives, 109th Congress. November 14, 2006. Available online at http://commdocs.house.gov/committees/judiciary/hju 30838.000/hju30838_0.htm; website home page: http://judiciary.house.gov (accessed August 5, 2009).

Stein, Jacob A., et al. 2003. *Administrative Law.* New York: LexisNexis/Matthew Bender.

ADMINISTRATOR

A person appointed by the court to manage and take charge of the assets and liabilities of a decedent who has died without making a valid will.

When such a person is a male, he is called an administrator, whereas a woman is called an administratrix. An administrator c.t.a. (*cum testamento annexo,* Latin for "with the will annexed") is appointed by the court where the TESTATOR had made an incomplete will without naming any executors or had named incapable persons, or where the executors named refuse to act. A public administrator is a public official designated by state law to perform the duties of administration for persons who have died INTESTATE.

An executor differs from an administrator in that he or she is named in the decedent's will to manage the estate. If an executor dies while performing these duties, a court will appoint an administrator *de bonis non cum testamento annexo* (Latin for "of the goods not [already] administered upon with the will annexed") to complete the distribution of the decedent's estate. This term is often abbreviated: administrator d.b.n.c.t.a.

ADMIRALTY AND MARITIME LAW

A field of law relating to, and arising from, the practice of the admiralty courts (tribunals that exercise jurisdiction over all contracts, torts, offenses, or injuries within maritime law) that regulates and settles special problems associated with sea navigation and commerce.

History of Admiralty and Maritime Law

The life of the mariner, spent far away from the stability of land, has long been considered an exotic one of travel, romance, and danger. Stories of pirates, mutinies, lashings, and hasty trials—many of them true—illustrate the peculiar, isolated nature of the maritime existence. In modern times, the practice of shipping goods by sea has become more civil, but the law still gives maritime activities special treatment by acknowledging the unique conflicts and difficulties involved in high-seas navigation and commerce.

The roots of maritime law can be traced as far back as 900 B.C., which is when the Rhodian Customary Law is believed to have been shaped by the people of the island of Rhodes. The only concept in the Rhodian Laws that still exists is the law of jettison, which holds that if goods must be thrown overboard (*jettisoned*) for the safety of the ship or the safety of another's property, the owner of the goods is entitled to compensation from the beneficiaries of the jettison.

Admiralty law concerns personal injuries or loss of cargo suffered during accidents such as this one, in which the freighter Republic of Colombia was struck by the Trans Hawaii.
BETTMAN/CORBIS.

Codes enacted by medieval port cities and states have formed the current U.S. maritime law. The eleventh-century Amalphitan Code, of the Mediterranean countries; the fourteenth-century Consolato del Mare, of France, Spain, and Italy; the twelfth-century Roll of Oleron, from England; and the thirteenth-century Law of Visby all drew on the customs of mariners and merchants to create the unique SUBSTANTIVE LAW of admiralty that still exists in the early twenty-first century. Procedural differences existed between maritime cases and other civil proceedings until 1966, when the U.S. Supreme Court approved amendments to the Federal Rules of CIVIL PROCEDURE that brought admiralty and maritime procedural rules into accord with those used in other civil suits. The substantive maritime law, however, has remained intact.

Admiralty and Maritime Law in the Early 2000s

The terms *admiralty* and *maritime law* are sometimes used interchangeably, but *admiralty* originally referred to a specific court in England and the American colonies that had jurisdiction over torts and contracts on the high seas, whereas substantive maritime law developed through the expansion of admiralty court jurisdiction to include all activities on the high seas and similar activities on NAVIGABLE WATERS.

Because water commerce and navigation often involve foreign nations, much of the U.S. maritime law has evolved in concert with the maritime laws of other countries. The federal statutes that address maritime issues are often customized U.S. versions of the convention resolutions or treaties of international maritime law. The UNITED NATIONS organizes and prepares these conventions and treaties through branches such as the International Maritime Organization and the International Labor Organization, which prepares conventions on the health, safety, and well-being of maritime workers.

The substance of maritime law considers the dangerous conditions and unique conflicts involved in navigation and water commerce. Sailors are especially vulnerable to injury and sickness owing to a variety of conditions, such as drastic changes in climate, constant peril, hard labor, and loneliness. Under the Ship-owners' LIABILITY Convention (54 Stat. 1693 [1939]), a shipowner may be liable for the maintenance and cure of sailors injured on ship and for injuries occurring on land. Courts have construed accidents occurring during leave as being the responsibility of the shipowner because sailors need land visits in order to endure the long hours of water transportation.

Assigning responsibility for onboard NEGLI-GENCE was a long-standing problem, but the JONES ACT of 1920 (46 U.S.C.A. § 688 et seq.) solidifies the right of sailors to recover from an employer for injuries resulting from the negligence of the employer, a master, or another crew member. The 1920 Death on High Seas Act (46 App. U.S.C.A. § 761 et seq.) allows recovery by the beneficiaries of a sailor's estate when the sailor dies by negligence, default, or wrongful act on the high seas "beyond a marine league from the shore of any state [territory or dependency]." A marine league is one-twentieth of a degree of latitude, or three miles.

Accidents suffered by nonmaritime persons on docks, piers, wharfs, or bridges do not qualify for the application of maritime law principles. However, personal injuries suffered while individuals were aboard a ship or as a result of an air-to-water airplane crash are considered within the jurisdiction of admiralty law.

The Longshoremen's and Harbor Workers' Compensation Act (33 U.S.C.A. § 901 et seq. [1927]) sets up a federal system to compensate injured maritime workers who do not sail. Through the Federal Office of Workers' Compensation Programs, employees such as *steve-dores* (workers who load and unload ships) and ship service operators can receive compensation for injuries suffered in the course of their employment. U.S. sailors benefit from Title 46 of the U. S. Code, which sets a schedule for sailors' earnings and the conditions of their contracts. Title 46 also lists the qualifications for sailor employment (§§ 7301 et seq.), the hours and conditions of the employment (§§ 8104 et seq.), and the living conditions that must be provided (§§ 11101 et seq.).

Federal laws also address the problems that beset ships and the life-or-death decisions made by carriers. The Carriage of Goods by Sea Act (46 U.S.C.A. §§ 1300–1315 [1936]) regulates the rights, responsibilities, liabilities, and immunities regarding the relationship between shippers and carriers of goods. The Salvage Act (46 U.S. C.A. §§ 727–731 [1912]) provides for compensation to persons who help save a ship or cargo from danger or help recover a ship or cargo from actual loss. To qualify for salvage remuneration, a person must not be acting in service of the ship or in performance of a contract, and the help given must have contributed at least in part to a wholly or partially successful salvage of the ship or goods.

The CASE LAW of the United States is rich in the areas of sailors' rights respecting the unseaworthiness of vessels, compensation for vessel suppliers and servicers, and the liabilities arising from collisions, towage, pilotage, and groundings. The MARITIME LIEN Act (46 U.S.C.A. §§ 31341–31343 [1920]) gives a LIEN to any person who, upon the order of the shipowner, furnishes repairs, supplies, towage, use of dry dock or marine railway, or other necessaries to any vessel, without allegation or proof that credit was given. The Ship Mortgage Act (46 U. S.C.A. §§ 31301–31330 [1920]) regulates the mortgages on ships registered in the United States, and also provides for enforcement of the maritime liens obtained through the Maritime Lien Act.

In case of collision or other damage to a vessel, an IN REM proceeding is often used to recover DAMAGES. An in rem action is a lawsuit brought against an offending thing (in admiralty, usually the ship), whereas an IN PERSONAM action is a suit brought against a person. Rule C of the Supplemental Rules for Certain Admiralty and Maritime Claims (1985) provides necessary details for the SEIZURE of an offending owner's vessel or property if a DEFENDANT vessel owner does not live in the state in which a suit is brought. The practical effect of Supplemental Rules B to E is to make it easier for a PLAINTIFF to bring actions against out-of-state and foreign vessel owners and to provide for the attachment and GARNISHMENT of the offending vessel.

An important consideration in any lawsuit is venue. Under Article III, Section 2, of the U.S. Constitution, federal courts have the power to try "all Cases of admiralty and maritime Jurisdiction" (art. III, SEC. 2). However, state courts can also hear admiralty and maritime cases by virtue of the "saving-to-suitors" clause of 28 U.S.C.A. § 1333(1). This clause allows a plaintiff to sue in state court through an ordinary CIVIL ACTION when the court's COMMON LAW is competent to give a remedy. In such actions, the state court must apply the federal law of admiralty to the admiralty claims. Nevertheless, if a plaintiff believes he or she will fare better before a local tribunal, the option is available.

When no applicable federal statute exists, the governing law of a maritime case will be the uniform laws as expounded by the U.S. Supreme Court and applicable to all torts and contracts, whether the case is tried in federal or state court. Maritime case law—not the general common law—will govern a contract dispute only if the subject matter of the contract pertained to water commerce. Maritime precedents will govern a tort claim only if the negligent or reckless actions involved commercial activity on navigable waters.

Charter parties are often a topic of concern in maritime law. A *charter party,* or *charter,* is an agreement among a shipowner, a crew (the charterer), and the owner of the goods to be transported. Charter parties come in three types: time, voyage, and demise. A *time charter* is the lease of a ship to a charterer for a specified period of time. A *voyage charter* is the lease of a ship for a specific number of voyages. A *demise charter* (so called because the shipowner effectively relinquishes ownership for a certain period, causing a "demise" in ownership interest) is usually a bareboat charter, which means that the charterer supplies the master and crew for the ship. Other demise charters provide that the shipowner's master and crew take charge of the vessel.

In contrast to the usual contract practice of providing risk-of-loss insurance for one party, charters utilize what is called a general average. *General average* is the traditional, primitive form of maritime risk allocation whereby all participants in a charter agree to share any damages resulting from an unsuccessful voyage. Most parties to a charter obtain insurance to cover their portion of risk. However, because a charter involves multiple parties, and because insurance policies are subject to interpretation, insurance coverage does not always prevent disputes over damages.

Risk of loss is sometimes decided according to a BILL OF LADING. This document confirms a carrier's receipt of goods from the owner (*consignor*), verifies the voyage contract, and shows rightful ownership of the goods. In *Lekas & Drivas, Inc. v. Goulandris,* 306 F.2d 426 (2d Cir. 1962), the SS *Ioannis P. Goulandris* had chartered to carry olive oil, cheese, and tobacco from the western Greek port of Piraiévs to the United States via the Strait of Gibraltar. On October 28, 1940, with the *Ioannis* docked in Piraiévs, Italy attacked Greece, and the *Ioannis* was requisitioned by the Greek government for a military mission.

On November 10, 1940, the *Ioannis* finally set sail with its cargo for the United States via the Suez Canal and the Red Sea, and around Cape Horn. After an arduous journey that included two crossings of the equator, hull damage, and lengthy repairs, the *Ioannis* came into port at Norfolk, Virginia, on May 3, 1941. En route, the tobacco had been damaged, much of the olive oil had leaked from its drums, and the cheese was "'[m]elted with a terrible stench, and worthless.'"

Despite the *Ioannis*'s brave participation in wartime activities, the intended recipients (*consignees*) of the tobacco and olive oil sued the *Ioannis* and were able to recover for the losses suffered as a result of the damage. However, on the subject of the cheese, the court refused to allow recovery by Lekas and Drivas, which had consigned the cheese to itself.

Lekas argued that the crew of the *Ioannis* was negligent in storing the cheese in the structure at the stern above the main deck, known as the poop. According to Lekas, it was inappropriate for the cheese to be in the poop. The poop lacked ventilation, and it was not refrigerated. However, according to the bill of lading between Lekas and the *Ioannis,* special cooling was not necessary and had not been contracted for. The cheese was also stored on *lighters* (large, flat-bottomed barges used for loading and unloading ships) during the 35 days needed for repairs of the *Ioannis,* and Lekas claimed that this storage was improper. But because wartime conditions were responsible for the length of repairs and the lack of proper storage space for the cheese, the court ultimately held that the *Ioannis* was not negligent in its handling of the cheese.

In addition to the state and federal governments, municipalities can affect the private enjoyment of maritime activity. In *Beveridge v. Lewis,*

939 F.2d 859 (9th Cir. 1991), appellants Richard Beveridge, Peter Murray, Gregory Davis, and Peter Eastman challenged a Santa Barbara city ordinance (Santa Barbara Municipal Code § 17.13.020) that prohibited the anchoring or mooring of boats within 300 feet of Stearns Wharf from December to March. Santa Barbara had acquired ownership of Stearns Wharf in 1983, passed the ordinance in 1984, and started issuing citations for noncompliance shortly thereafter. Beveridge, Murray, Davis, and Eastman all owned boats moored or anchored within 300 feet of Stearns Wharf, and the four, represented by Eastman, brought suit against the city in 1989, seeking injunctive relief against enforcement of the ordinance.

At trial, Eastman argued that the Santa Barbara ordinance conflicted with the Ports and Waterways Safety Act of 1972 (PWSA) (33 U.S. C.A. §§ 1221 et seq.), a federal act designed to reduce the loss of vessels and cargo, protect marine environment, prevent damage to structures on or adjacent to navigable waters, and ensure compliance with vessel operation and safety standards. The trial court dismissed the case, reasoning that the ordinance was neither preempted by, nor in conflict with, the federal statute.

On appeal, the Ninth CIRCUIT COURT of Appeals agreed that the Santa Barbara ordinance was not in conflict with the PWSA, because the federal act was not intended to limit a municipality's control over its local shores. The appeals court also rejected the proposition that the enactment of the PWSA implicitly foreclosed the enactment of similar ordinances by municipalities, and Santa Barbara's control over the Stearns Wharf was complete.

Admiralty and maritime matters will always deserve laws carefully crafted to suit the complexity and urgency of maritime endeavors. The international nature of high-seas navigation and its attendant perils demand no less. Federal, state, and local control of navigable waters can affect everyone from the largest charter party to a private boat owner.

FURTHER READINGS

Healy, Nicholas J., and David J. Sharpe. 2006. *Cases and Materials on Admiralty*. 4th ed. Eagan, MN: West.

Lucas, Jo Desha. 2003. *Admiralty: Cases and Materials*. 5th ed. New York: Foundation.

Robertson, David W. 2008. *Admiralty and Maritime Law in the United States: Cases and Materials*. 2d ed. Durham, NC: Carolina Academic.

Schoenbaum, Thomas J. 2004. *Admiralty and Maritime Law*. 4th ed. Eagan, MN: West.

CROSS REFERENCES

Carriers; Environmental Law; Navigable Rivers; Piracy; Salvage; Shipping Law; Territorial Waters.

ADMISSIBLE

A term used to describe information that is relevant to a determination of issues in any judicial proceeding so that such information can be properly considered by a judge or jury in making a decision.

Evidence is admissible if it is of such a character that the court is bound to accept it during the trial so that it may be evaluated by the judge or jury. Admissible evidence is the foundation of the deliberation process by which a court or jury decides upon a judgment or VERDICT.

The FEDERAL RULES OF EVIDENCE regulate the admissibility of evidence in federal courts. State rules of evidence determine evidence that is admissible in state court proceedings.

ADMISSION

A voluntary acknowledgment made by a party to a lawsuit or in a criminal prosecution that certain facts that are inconsistent with the party's claims in the controversy are true.

In a lawsuit over whether a DEFENDANT negligently drove a car into the PLAINTIFF pedestrian, the defendant's apology to the plaintiff and payment of the plaintiff's medical bills are admissions that may be introduced as evidence against the defendant.

An admission may be express, such as a written or verbal statement by a person concerning the truth, or it may be implied by a person's conduct. If someone fails to deny certain assertions which, if false, would be denied by any REASONABLE PERSON, such failure indicates that the person has accepted the truth of the allegations.

An admission is not the same as a confession. A confession is an acknowledgment of guilt in a criminal case. Admissions usually apply to civil matters; in criminal cases they apply only to matters of fact that do not involve criminal intent.

Admissions are used primarily as a method of discovery, as a pleading device, and as evidence in a trial.

Once a complaint is filed to commence a lawsuit, the parties can obtain facts and information about the case from each other to assist their preparation for the trial through the use of discovery devices. One type of discovery tool is a request for admission: a written statement submitted to an opposing party before the trial begins, asking that the truth of certain facts or the genuineness of particular documents concerning the case be acknowledged or denied. When the facts or documents are admitted as being true, the court will accept them as such so that they need not be proven at trial. If they are denied, the statements or documents become an issue to be argued during the trial. Should a party refuse to answer the request, the other party can ask the court for an order of preclusion that prohibits denial of these facts and allows them to be treated as if they had been admitted.

By eliminating undisputed facts as issues in a case, requests for admissions expedite trials. Matters that are admitted are binding only for the pending case and not for any other lawsuit.

Judicial admissions—made in court by a party or the party's attorney as formal acknowledgments of the truth of some matter, or as stipulations—are not considered evidence that may be rebutted but are a type of pleading device. Averments in a pleading to which a RESPONSIVE PLEADING is required are admitted if they are not denied in the responsive pleading. If a party has made an admission in a pleading that has subsequently been amended, the pleading containing the admission will be admissible as evidence in the case. In civil actions any offers to SETTLE the case cannot be admitted into evidence.

A plea of guilty in a criminal case may usually be shown as an admission in a later civil or criminal proceeding, but it is not conclusive. The defendant may explain the circumstances that brought it about, such as a PLEA BARGAINING deal. Any admissions or offers to plead guilty during the plea-bargaining process are INADMISSIBLE as evidence. Many courts refuse to admit a guilty plea to a traffic offense as evidence because many people plead guilty to avoid wasting their time and money by appearing in traffic court. A guilty plea that has subsequently been withdrawn and followed by a plea of not guilty cannot be used as an admission in either a criminal or civil case. It is considered an unreliable admission that has a potentially prejudicial effect on the opportunity of the defendant to get a fair trial.

Admissions are used as a type of evidence in a trial to bolster the case of one party at the expense of the other, who is compelled to admit the truth of certain facts. They may be made directly by a party to a lawsuit, either in or out of court; or implicitly, by the conduct of a party or the actions of someone else which bind the party to a lawsuit. When an admission is made out of court, it is hearsay because it was not made under OATH and not subject to CROSS-EXAMINATION. Although hearsay cannot be used as evidence in a trial because of its unreliable nature, admissions can be introduced as evidence because they are considered trustworthy. An admission by a party can be used only to prove the existence of the fact admitted and to IMPEACH the credibility of the party. An admission by a witness can be introduced as evidence only to discredit the witness's TESTIMONY.

An admission against interest is a statement made by a party to a lawsuit, usually before the suit, that contradicts what he or she is now alleging in the case. Because the statements tend to establish or disprove a material fact in the case, they are considered admissions against interest. The truth of such statements is presumed because people do not make detrimental statements about themselves unless they are true. Such an admission is considered an exception to the hearsay rule and, therefore, can be used as evidence in a lawsuit.

ADMISSION TO THE BAR

The procedure that governs the authorization of attorneys to practice law before the state and federal courts.

Statutes, rules, and regulations governing admission to practice law have been enacted to protect the PUBLIC INTEREST, in terms of preventing the victimization of clients by incompetent practitioners. The courts have inherent power to promulgate reasonable rules and regulations for ADMISSION TO THE BAR. Although this authority is vested exclusively in the courts, the legislature can, subject to constitutional

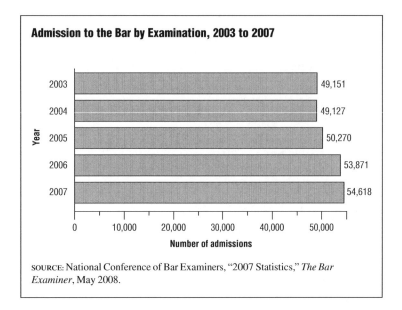

Admission to the Bar by Examination, 2003 to 2007

Year	Number of admissions
2003	49,151
2004	49,127
2005	50,270
2006	53,871
2007	54,618

SOURCE: National Conference of Bar Examiners, "2007 Statistics," *The Bar Examiner*, May 2008.

ILLUSTRATION BY GGS CREATIVE RESOURCES. REPRODUCED BY PERMISSION OF GALE, A PART OF CENGAGE LEARNING.

limitations, issue reasonable rules and regulations governing bar admission provided they do not conflict with judicial pronouncements.

The highest state court administers the admission of applicants to the state bar, usually requiring successful completion of a bar examination and evidence of good moral character. With respect to admission to the federal bar, federal district courts are empowered to issue requirements for admission separately from those of the state courts. If, however, a federal district court, pursuant to a rule, derivatively admits to its bar those admitted to the state bar, it cannot arbitrarily deny admission to an applicant who is a member in good standing of the state bar. In most instances, the federal district courts have considerable latitude in establishing requirements for admission to practice before them, but their rules must not contravene federal law.

In terms of the federal bar, an attorney is also eligible for admission to the bar of a court of appeals, if he or she has been admitted to practice before the Supreme Court or the highest court of a state or another federal court and if the lawyer is of good moral and professional character. The attorney must comply with the procedural requirements and take and subscribe to the following OATH: "I, [name], do solemnly swear (or affirm) that I will demean myself as an attorney and counselor of this court, uprightly and according to law; and that I will support the Constitution of the United States."

In order to gain admission to the bar of the Supreme Court, an attorney must have practiced for three years in the highest court of a state, territory, district, commonwealth, or possession. The person must be of good character in terms of both his or her private and professional lives and complete the specified procedures, including taking or subscribing the following oath: "I, [name], do solemnly swear (or affirm) that as an attorney and as a counselor of this court I will conduct myself uprightly, and according to law, and that I will support the Constitution of the United States."

In some instances, a particular board is empowered to promulgate rules pertaining to applicants seeking to practice before it as attorneys. For example, the SECURITIES AND EXCHANGE COMMISSION has implied authority under its general statutory power to determine qualifications for attorneys practicing before it. Under federal law, the commissioner of PATENTS and trademarks, subject to the approval of the secretary of commerce, can promulgate regulations governing the recognition and conduct of attorneys appearing before the U.S. PATENT AND TRADEMARK OFFICE.

Qualifications for admission to the bar must be rationally related to the applicant's fitness to practice law; therefore, a state cannot prevent a person from practicing law for racial, political, or religious reasons. Good moral character is a prerequisite to the right to admission to practice law and, at a minimum, consists of honesty. Lack of good moral character is demonstrated by an immutable dishonest and corrupt nature and not by radical political beliefs or membership in lawful, but controversial, political parties.

In regard to the effect of criminal conduct upon the evaluation of an applicant's character, a conviction for the commission of a FELONY is not, per se, sufficient to demonstrate a lack of good moral character. It will be incumbent upon the applicant, however, to prove complete rehabilitation. Although a conditional PARDON is insufficient to remove objections to bar admission, a felony conviction will not prevent an applicant from practicing law if he or she has received a full pardon and is otherwise qualified.

MISDEMEANOR convictions do not necessarily result in a finding of lack of good moral character, but mere conduct that does not culminate in a conviction might present an insurmountable obstacle to admission if it indicates a lack of moral fitness. In some cases, an applicant has been rejected for want of good moral character because he or she has made false statements or concealed material facts in the application for admission or in other legal documents. In other cases, the withholding or falsification on the application of minor matters has been viewed as having no effect on an evaluation of character; the same principle applies to unintentional concealment of information.

Admission to the bar cannot be denied because the applicant is not a United States citizen, but the states can impose reasonable residency requirements upon all applicants prior to, or during, the time a license is sought. This requirement enables the state examining authority to investigate the character of the applicant, but it must be rationally related to the attainment of this objective. While a majority of states have some form of residency requirement for admission to the bar, the emerging trend is to nullify durational residency requirements that mandate that an attorney live in a state for a prescribed period as a prerequisite to certification to practice law.

Applicants for admission to practice law must take a bar examination, unless they are exempted from this requirement by statute or court rule. According to the National Conference of Bar Examiners, 80,319 applicants took a bar examination in 2008, of which 70,172 were first-time takers. Overall, 71 percent, or 56,915 examinees, passed. However, among first-time takers from AMERICAN BAR ASSOCIATION (ABA)-approved law schools, 85 percent passed, whereas repeat-takers had a 43 percent pass rate. The examination can be taken more than once. In rare cases, an attorney who has been disbarred or suspended can take a special bar examination for reinstatement. In 2008 only 20 disbarred or suspended attorneys across the U.S. took a reinstatement exam (seven, or 35 percent, passed).

Attorneys from other states can be admitted to practice in the state without examination upon providing the required proof of practice in another state that has reciprocity provisions, pursuant to which an attorney licensed in one state can be admitted to the bar of another state, if the first state grants RECIPROCAL rights to attorneys admitted to practice in the other state. Under the device of PRO HAC VICE, an attorney can be admitted to practice in a jurisdiction without having to take the bar examination, but

only on a limited basis and only for a particular case. Such an attorney must be a member in good standing of a bar of other states or countries.

In order to practice law, an attorney must obtain a certificate or license, which is a privilege rather than a PROPERTY RIGHT. Attorneys must also comply with the court rules or statutes governing the registration system, which is used to maintain a current list of all attorneys authorized to practice law in the state. Generally, admission by court order constitutes sufficient registration, but in some states, attorneys sign the roll or file a certificate with the clerk of the court to establish that they have been duly admitted to practice.

An applicant for admission to the bar is entitled to notice of, and a hearing on, the grounds for rejection either before the committee on character and fitness or the court. The courts can review the decision of bar examiners who deny an applicant admission to the bar, and the courts can ascertain whether the examiners acted after a fair investigation and hearing, exercised their discretion impartially and reasonably, and conducted their proceedings in compliance with the requirements of procedural due process.

The legal profession has tried in recent years to diversify the population of attorneys. First-year law student statistics compiled by the American Bar Association show that for the 2008–2009 academic year, out of 49,414 students, 23,407 (roughly 47 percent) were women. A steady supply of new attorneys continue to enter the profession each year. According to the National Council of Bar Examiners, in 2008, 56,357 persons were admitted to state bars by examination; 7,888 by court motion, and 468 by diploma privilege.

FURTHER READINGS

American Bar Association (ABA), 2009. "Legal Education and Bar Admissions 2008 Statistics." Available online at http://www.abanet.org/legaled/statistics/charts/stats%20-%201.pdf; website home page: http://www.abanet.org/ (accessed August 5, 2009)

American Bar Association Publishing Company. 2009. *Rules for Admission to the Bar in the Several States and Territories of the United States.* Charleston, SC: BibioLife LLC.

Glen, Kristin Booth. 2002. "When and Where We Enter: Rethinking Admission to the Legal Profession." *Columbia Law Review* 102 (October): 1696–1740.

Moeser, Erica. 2002. "Bar Admission in the United States 2001: Framing the Discussion for Response to

Globalization." *South Texas Law Review* 43 (spring): 499–505.

National Conference of Bar Examiners (NCBE), 2009. "2008 Statistics." *The Bar Examiner*, May 2009. Text available online at http://www.ncbex.org/fileadmin/mediafiles/downloads/Bar_Admissions/2008_Stats.pdf; website home page: http://www.ncbex.org/bar-admissions/stats/ (accessed August 5, 2009).

Ritter, Matthew A. 2002. "The Ethics of Moral Character Determination: An Indeterminate Ethical Reflection Upon Bar Admissions." *California Western Law Review* 39 (fall): 1–52.

CROSS REFERENCES

Attorney; Bar Association; Bar Examination; "Bradwell v. Illinois" (Appendix, Primary Document); Courts; Federal Courts; Residency.

ADMONITION

Any formal verbal statement made during a trial by a judge to advise and caution the jury on their duty as jurors, on the admissibility or nonadmissibility of evidence, or on the purpose for which any evidence admitted may be considered by them. A reprimand directed by the court to an attorney appearing before it cautioning the attorney about the unacceptability of his or her conduct before the court. If the attorney continues to act in the same way, ignoring the admonition, the judge will find him or her in contempt of court, punishable by a fine, imprisonment, or both. In criminal prosecution, before the court receives and records the plea of the accused, a statement made by a judge informing the accused on the effect and consequences of a plea of guilty to criminal charges.

ADOPT

To accept, appropriate, choose, or select, as to adopt a child. To consent to and put into effect, as to adopt a constitution or a law.

CROSS REFERENCE

Adoption.

ADOPTION

A two-step judicial process in conformance to state statutory provisions in which the legal obligations and rights of a child toward the biological parents are terminated, and new rights and obligations are created between the child and the adoptive parents.

Adoption involves the creation of the parent-child relationship between individuals who are not naturally so related. The adopted child is given the rights, privileges, and duties of a child and heir by the adoptive family.

Because adoption was not recognized at COMMON LAW, all adoption procedures in the United States are regulated by statute. Adoption statutes prescribe the conditions, manner, means, and consequences of adoption. In addition, they specify the rights and responsibilities of all parties involved.

DE FACTO adoption is a voidable agreement to adopt a child pursuant to a state's statutory proceeding. This agreement becomes lawful when the petition to adopt is properly presented.

The law treats equitable adoption, sometimes referred to as *virtual adoption,* as final for certain purposes in spite of the fact that it has not been formally executed. When adoption appears to comply with standards of fairness and justice, some states will grant a child the rights of one who has been adopted even though the adoption procedure is incomplete. The court might enforce an equitable adoption for the benefit of a child in order to determine INHERITANCE rights, for example. Similarly, adoption by ESTOPPEL is the equitable adoption of a child by promises and acts that prevent the adoptive parents and their estates from denying the child adoptive status.

Who May Adopt

To be entitled to adopt a child, an individual must meet qualifications under applicable state law, because the state has sole power to determine who may become an adoptive parent. Unless otherwise provided by state statute, U.S. citizenship is not a prerequisite for adoption.

A child may be jointly adopted by a HUSBAND AND WIFE. If not contrary to statutory provision, either may adopt without being joined by the other. Unmarried people may adopt unless prohibited by law.

One growing issue is whether adoption by a child's grandparents is a viable alternative. Such adoption might be considered to be in the child's best interests if the natural parents die or if the custodial parent is found to be unfit. A legal guardian may adopt a child but is not ordinarily given preference in the court proceedings.

The best interests of the child are of paramount importance in policy considerations toward adoption. Although legislative policy prefers such conditions as adoption by people of the same RELIGION as the prospective adoptee, an interfaith adoption is allowed when it does not adversely affect the welfare of the child.

Elements in determining who will be suitable adoptive parents include race, religion, economic status, home environment, age, and health. Most of these criteria are taken into consideration in placements by agencies or in private placements where state law requires that adoptive parents be investigated.

Who May Be Adopted

Because the status of an adopted person is regulated by state statutes that authorize the adoption, state law determines whether an individual is a proper candidate for adoption. In addition, to be subject to adoption in a particular state, the individual must be living within that state.

Children may be adopted in situations where their natural parents are living, dead, or unknown, or where the children have been abandoned. An adoption will not be prevented by the fact that a child has a legal guardian.

Some statutes expressly limit adoption to minors, and others expressly provide for adoption of adults. The adoption of adults is regarded by statutes and the courts in a manner similar to the adoption of children. Practically, however, the adoption of adults differs greatly, because it serves different purposes and creates few of the difficulties arising out of the adoption of children. In most cases, the purpose of adult adoption is to facilitate a device for inheritance. One may designate an heir by adopting an adult. Generally, the adoptee would not otherwise be entitled to INHERIT but for the adoption.

Social Considerations

In the past, adoption was viewed primarily as a means for a childless married couple to "normalize" their relationship. The focus has switched, however; adoption has come to be seen as an institution that exists to help place children into improved environments.

Since the 1990s, a number of states have enacted statutes that permit subsidization of adoptions. The adoption procedure has thereby become a social instrument for the improvement of the lives of underprivileged children. Subsidized adoption tends to encourage adoption of children by suitable individuals who would otherwise be unable to afford it. This type of adoption has a significant effect upon placement of children deemed to be hard to place. Such children, who are frequently either physically or mentally handicapped, might have no other alternative except protracted institutionalization.

State law may require that the adopting parent have custody of a child for a certain period before obtaining an adoption decree. This requirement is designed to prevent premature action and to establish whether the best interests of the child will be furthered by the adoption.

Transracial Adoption The issue of transracial adoption (adoption of children who are not the same race as the adoptive parents) has come under close scrutiny by courts, legislatures, and the public. Americans are sharply divided on this issue. Is it a positive way to create stable families for needy children and well-meaning adults? Or is it an insidious means of co-opting members of racial minorities and confusing their sense of identity?

In 1972, when the number of African American children adopted annually by white families rose to 15,000, the National Association of Black Social Workers (NABSW) issued its opinion on the subject. Igniting a furious national debate that continued in the mid-1990s, the association equated transracial adoption with cultural GENOCIDE for African Americans.

The NABSW and other minority groups opposed to the adoption of African American children by whites claim that the children are deprived of a true appreciation and understanding of their culture. Their childhood is skewed toward white values and assimilation. Without a sense of racial identity and pride, these children cannot truly belong to the African American community; yet, by the same token, racism prevents their full inclusion in the white world.

Despite these arguments, some African Americans applaud the unconditional love and permanence offered by transracial adoptions. Transracial adoption supporters argue that it is much worse to grow up without any family at all than to be placed with parents of a different race. Because a disproportionate number of African American children are placed in foster care, mixed-race adoptions may be necessary to

A sample petition for adoption

State of Michigan Petition for Adoption

Approved, SCAO

JIS CODE: APF

STATE OF MICHIGAN JUDICIAL CIRCUIT–FAMILY DIVISION COUNTY	PETITION FOR ADOPTION ❑ Stepparent ❑ Related Within 5th Degree ❑ Other (Excluding Direct Adoption)	FILE NO.

In the matter of _____ ,adoptee
         Full name of child

❑ I, _____ , join with my spouse in this petition for adoption (applicable to stepparent adoption only)
   Name

	Name and Social Security Number	Relationship to Adoptee	Address, City, State, Zip	Date and Place of Birth
Adopting Mother	Maiden:			
Adopting Father				

Each adopting petitioner states:

❑ 1. An action within the jurisdiction of the family division of circuit court involving the family or family members of the minor has been

previously filed in _____ Court, Case Number _____ , was

assigned to Judge _____ , and ❑ remains ❑ is no longer pending.

2. I desire to adopt _____
         Full name of child   Birth date and time

         City, county, and state of birth

         Present residential address (if known)

3. The adoptee will be my heir at law.

4. The adoptee's name will ❑ not be changed.
                 ❑ be changed to _____
                         First   Middle   Last

5. The adoptee's property is _____

6. The adoptee's parents are:

Father's name Birth date	Mother's name (and maiden name) Birth date
Address	Address
City, state, zip	City, state, zip

❑ unknown because the rights of the parents have been terminated by a court of competent jurisdiction and parental rights are vested in

_____ .

Name and address of court or agency

(PLEASE SEE OTHER SIDE)

Do not write below this line– For court use only

PCA 301 (9/07) **PETITION FOR ADOPTION**   MCL 710.24, MCL 710.26, MCL 710.45, MCL 710.46, MCL 710.52, MCL 710.56

---

ensure permanent homes for some African American children. Transracial adoption may also be viewed as an opportunity to achieve integration on the most basic level.

Controversies involving transracial adoption soon found their way to the courts. In 1992 the Minnesota Supreme Court upheld a district court's order to transfer a three-year-old African

State of Michigan Petition for Adoption

☐ 7. The adoptee's court appointed guardian and/or conservator is (attach copy of letters of authority):

Name   Address

City, state, zip

☐ 8. The adoptee has been living in the home of and with the petitioners for _____ months before the filing of this petition.

☐ 9. (Applies only to stepparent adoptions) The noncustodial parent has failed to provide support or comply with a support order and failed to visit or contact the adoptee for a period of 2 years or more. (Attach form PCA 302, Supplemental Petition and Affidavit to Terminate Parental Rights of Noncustodial Parent)

☐ 10. I have been unable to obtain the required consent to adopt the child from the court, Michigan Department of Human Services, or child placing agency having permanent custody or from the persons to whom the child was released. A motion alleging that the decision to withhold consent was arbitrary and capricious is attached.

I REQUEST:

11. Termination of all existing parental rights inconsistent with the order of adoption, entry of an order approving placement of the child

with me, and entry of an order of adoption with the adoptee's name recorded as _____.

☐ 12. The adoption be completed immediately because: _____

_____

_____

☐ 13. The court to waive the required investigation because the adoptee has been placed in foster care with me for at least 12 months and a foster family study was completed or updated within the last 12 months.

I declare that this petition has been examined by me and that its contents are true to the best of my information, knowledge, and belief.

Attorney/Agency signature   Date

Attorney/Agency name (type or print)   Bar no.   Signature of petitioner mother

Address   Signature of petitioner father

City, state, zip   Telephone no.   Petitioner telephone no.

IT IS ORDERED:

14. _____

Court agent or employee, child placing agency, or Michigan Department of Human Services

is directed to fully investigate and report its findings in writing to this court, within 3 months of this order, in accordance with the provisions of MCL 710.46.

☐ 15. The full investigation is waived. The petitioner(s) shall file a copy of the most recent foster family study as updated and supplemented.

Date   Judge   Bar no.

A sample petition for adoption (continued)
ILLUSTRATION BY GGS CREATIVE RESOURCES. REPRODUCED BY PERMISSION OF GALE, A PART OF CENGAGE LEARNING.

American girl from her suburban Minneapolis foster home to her maternal grandparents' home in Virginia (*In re Welfare of D. L.*, 486 N.W.2d 375 [Minn. 1992]). Referred to as Baby D in court records, the child had been raised since birth by white foster parents who had been married for 24 years and had already raised three grown children. Baby D's birth mother placed her in foster care almost immediately after delivery and had not seen the child since. When no relatives could be found to claim the child, the foster parents decided to adopt the girl, whom they had grown to love.

When Baby D's grandparents learned that their daughter had delivered a baby, they set out to find their grandchild and to obtain custody. (The couple were already raising their daughter's three other children.) When the foster parents' petition to adopt Baby D surfaced, the grandparents vigorously opposed it.

The Minnesota Minority Heritage Preservation Act mandated a preference for placing children with relatives and adoptive parents of the same race (Minn. Stat. Ann. § 259.57(2)). An intermediate appeals court and the Minnesota Supreme Court agreed with the lower court that, under the law, the Virginia grandparents must be granted custody. Despite the white foster parents' argument that they had provided security and loving care for the child, the grandparents' claim to Baby D was superior. Although many African Americans applauded the decision, some critics questioned the constitutionality of a law favoring same-race adoption.

A similar case in Lexington, Texas, produced a different result in 1995. Two foster parents, Scott Mullen and Lou Ann Mullen, who were white and Native American, respectively, applied to adopt two African American boys in their care. Initially, social workers for the Texas Department of Protective and Regulatory Services denied the Mullens' request, stating that departmental policy required them to seek adoptive parents of the same race as the children.

A civil liberties group called the Institute for Justice filed suit against the department on behalf of the Mullens. The group also filed suits in other states, arguing that adoption decisions based on race are unconstitutional. The Texas department reconsidered and allowed the Mullens to adopt the boys despite race differences.

Another statute affecting transracial adoptions is the INDIAN CHILD WELFARE ACT of 1978 (25 U.S.C.A. § 1901 et seq.) (ICWA), a federal law giving special preference to family and tribal adoptions of Native American children. Prior to its enactment, nearly one-quarter of all Native American children were removed from their parents' care and placed in foster care, through which some were adopted. ICWA's sponsors argued that the adoption of Native American children by white parents was not necessarily in the children's best interests and was unquestionably harmful to tribal membership. The law was intended to preserve Native American culture and to support an Indian child-rearing philosophy that relies heavily upon the extended family. Under the 1978 law, tribes have jurisdiction over the proposed adoption of any Native American child living on a reservation. Extended families or tribal placements are given automatic priority over all other applicants.

Another law covering transracial adoptions is the Multiethnic Placement Act of 1994 (42 U.S.C.A. §§ 622, 5115a, 5115a note). Sponsored by Senator Howard M. Metzenbaum (D-Ohio), the law prevents federally assisted child welfare agencies from screening prospective adoptive parents on the basis of race, color, or national origin. Although agencies may still consider the cultural or racial identity of children when making permanent placements, the law is intended to prevent DISCRIMINATION and to speed the adoption process. The intention of the law is to give thousands of minority foster children who are eligible for adoption a greater chance of finding permanent homes.

Same Sex Adoption Several jurisdictions have laws on the books that permit second-parent adoptions by same-sex couples, including California, Colorado, Connecticut, the District of Columbia, Illinois, Massachusetts, New York, New Jersey, and Vermont. In 17 other states, trial courts have granted second-parent adoptions to same-sex couples. In other words, these states do not have laws permitting adoptions statewide, but adoptions may be granted in county family courts on a case-by-case basis. These states are Alabama, Alaska, Delaware, Georgia, Hawaii, Indiana, Iowa, Louisiana, Maryland, Michigan, Minnesota, Nevada, New Mexico, Oregon, Rhode Island, Texas, and Washington. In states where there is no statewide law permitting second-parent adoptions, the odds of a trial court granting an adoption vary from county to county. Many of the courts that approve these adoptions are located in metropolitan areas where judges may be more liberal than their rural counterparts.

Whereas the majority of states do not specifically prohibit gays and lesbians from adopting children, three states prohibit the practice. Florida's law is considered the nation's toughest, because it prohibits adoptions not only by gay couples, but also by gay individuals. However, in May 2009 a Florida court of appeals in *Embry v. Ryan* Florida App. No. 2D08-1323 (May 13, 2009) reversed a trial court's ruling that had refused to recognize an adoption judgment by a same-sex couple that was previously entered in the State of Washington. The appellate court held that because Florida law specifically provides for the recognition of adoption decrees from other states, the court ruled that Embry was entitled to the same rights as any other adoptive parent in Florida, despite whether the trial court believed that the Washington adoption violated an established PUBLIC POLICY in Florida, which prohibits adoption by gay individuals. In 2008 an Arkansas law was passed that prohibited gays and lesbians from becoming foster parents. Mississippi also has legislation barring gay couples from adopting children.

Consent

Virtually all statutes make parental consent to adoption an indispensable condition. Most statutes set forth detailed requirements for the form and procedure of such consent. Ordinarily, statutes dispense with the parental consent requirement only when a parent has reached a serious level of unfitness that would be so significant as to terminate parental rights, or when such rights have already been judicially terminated.

In addition to parental consent, most states require a child to consent to the adoption if the child has reached a certain age, generally between 10 and 14 years.

The increasing number of divorces has resulted in de-emphasis of the necessity of consent to adoption by noncustodial parents, the purpose being to ease integration of children of a former MARRIAGE into the family created by a subsequent marriage. Some statutes allow adoption without the consent of the noncustodial parent if that parent has been unable to or has failed to contribute to the support of a child for a certain period of time. Courts are more inclined to find abandonment—a common ground for termination of parental rights—in cases involving noncustodial divorced parents.

Unmarried Father's Consent Historically, if a child was illegitimate, most jurisdictions required only the consent of the child's natural mother to the adoption of the child. The right to grant or withhold such consent was not extended to the fathers of illegitimate offspring, because they were not considered to have sufficient interest in the benefits and obligations of raising a child to determine whether the child should be released for adoption.

In 1979 this trend was reversed in *Caban v. Mohammed*, 441 U.S. 380, 99 S. Ct. 1760, 60 L. Ed. 2d 297 (1979). The key issue was whether the consent of an unwed biological father need be obtained before an adoption could be finalized.

In *Caban*, a mother of illegitimate children and her husband filed a petition for adoption. The children's natural father filed a cross petition to adopt. The New York Surrogate's Court granted the mother's petition, and the natural father appealed. The decision was affirmed by the New York Supreme Court, Appellate Division, and subsequently affirmed by the New York Court of Appeals.

On appeal, the U.S. Supreme Court ruled that a law depriving all unwed fathers of the right to decide against adoption, whether they actually took care of the children in question or not, was unconstitutional and a form of SEX DISCRIMINATION. The unwed father in *Caban* had lived with the mother of the children for five years prior to the birth of the children. The Court held that he had the right to block their adoption by a man who subsequently married the mother.

Consents that are signed by the parents either immediately before or after the birth of the child may be particularly subject to challenge by the natural mother. Owing to the mother's weakened physical and mental condition, findings of involuntary consent frequently have been handed down in such cases.

A parent can forfeit the right to give or deny consent for the adoption of his or her child in certain instances. *Abandonment,* the nonperformance of the natural obligations of caring for the child, including support, is one such case. Courts will ordinarily keep the PARENT AND CHILD together when the parent exhibits a continuing interest in the child's welfare.

A finding of abandonment may terminate a parent's rights and free the child for adoption with or without parental consent. A parent's rights may also be severed in cases of serious CHILD ABUSE or neglect. Some statutes provide that a custodial parent cannot VETO an adoption; however, that parent is generally entitled to be heard when a court considers the case, especially when the parent has established some kind of family tie with the child, either by having been married to, or having lived with, the custodial parent or by taking the child into his or her home.

State law may require that if a child has been placed in the custody of an agency, the agency's consent is a prerequisite for an adoption. Similarly, consent of a guardian who has custody of a child is necessary. The consent of the natural mother's parents may also be required if she is under 18 years of age and unwed.

Invalid Consent If coercion or deception plays any part in the decision to terminate parental rights, the birth parents' consent may be ruled invalid. In the wake of the highly publicized battle over "Baby Jessica," it appears that regardless of the length of time or quality of a child's placement, the consent rights of the birth parents outweigh the best interests of the child.

Many U.S. families pursue the adoption of children from foreign countries. Byron and Cathy Nehls of Wisconsin are pictured with their adopted children, Carissa, from India; Marco Tulio, from Guatemala; Hannah, from South Korea; and Lucas, from Brazil.

AP IMAGES

In an agonizing case that divided the adoption community, Michigan couple Roberta DeBoers and Jan DeBoers lost custody in 1993 of Jessica, the two-and-a-half-year-old child they had raised from birth (*In re Clausen,* 442 Mich. 648, 502 N.W.2d 649 [1993]). Courts in both Iowa and Michigan concluded that the necessary consent by Iowa birth parents Cara Schmidt and Daniel Schmidt was flawed. After a protracted legal battle, Jessica was ordered to return to Iowa to live with her biological parents.

Shortly after Jessica's birth on February 8, 1991, the DeBoers filed a petition in Iowa juvenile court to adopt her. The couple, who for 10 years had tried to conceive or adopt a child, were named her temporary guardians and custodians. When Jessica was less than four weeks old, however, birth mother Cara Clausen sued to have her maternal rights restored. The biological father, Dan Schmidt, also sought custody.

Unmarried at the time, Clausen had signed a release-custody form, terminating her parental rights, approximately 40 hours after giving birth to Jessica. (Iowa law requires a 72-hour waiting period before waiving parental rights.) The man Clausen identified as the child's father—not Schmidt—also signed a release form. Seventeen days later, Clausen informed Schmidt that she had lied on the release form and that Schmidt was actually the father.

On March 6, 1991, Clausen sought to revoke the custody agreement, naming Schmidt as the child's father. Upon learning that he was the baby's father, Schmidt filed an AFFIDAVIT of PATERNITY and asked for a court intervention to prevent the adoption proceedings. Clausen and Schmidt were married shortly thereafter.

The district court and subsequent courts determined that Dan Schmidt was indeed the biological father and that he had not agreed to have his parental rights terminated. Because he had not abandoned the baby, it was not clearly in the best interests of Jessica to remain with the DeBoers. Also, the parental rights WAIVER signed by Cara Schmidt was invalid because the statutorily imposed waiting period had not been observed. Therefore, early in the legal skirmish, the court ordered the baby returned to the Schmidts.

The DeBoers continued to fight Jessica's removal from their custody. With the legal maneuvering and delays, the case stretched out over a 29-month period. By the end, the DeBoers had developed a close bond with Jessica, even though they knew from the time Jessica was an infant that their claim to her might not hold up in court. But with the passage of time, the DeBoers could make a powerful claim that Jessica needed them more than the Schmidts. After all, they were the only parents she knew. The DeBoers argued that it was in Jessica's best interests to remain with them, or she could face possible emotional and psychological damage.

After Iowa courts refused to change position on the custody, the DeBoers took their case to Michigan, hoping that the best-interests-of-the-child argument would be persuasive. However, Michigan courts also agreed that Jessica should be returned to her Iowa birth parents. She was delivered to the Schmidts on August 2, 1993, and renamed Anna.

Methods of Adoption

There are several types of adoption-placement procedures. Foreign adoptions are affected by the policies and procedures of the adoptees' countries. Agency placement and independent placement are governed by statute, as is adoption by contract or by deed. Some people adopt through illegal purchase of a child or arrange to have a child by a surrogate mother.

Foreign Adoption Because of the scarcity of healthy babies for adoption in the United States, many U.S. citizens pursue adoption of orphaned and abandoned babies from foreign countries.

Most U.S. parents with children in foster care do not relinquish their parental rights. Foster children in the U.S. may also be difficult to place because many are older and carry the emotional scars of physical or SEXUAL ABUSE.

Since the 1950s, U.S. couples have adopted thousands of children from other countries. Originally a majority of the international adoptions came from Korea. However, children from a wide array of countries are now being adopted by U.S. citizens. In 2008, the United States DEPARTMENT OF STATE reported that 17,438 children were adopted by U.S. couples. This number is approximately 5,500 fewer international adoptions than occurred in 2004. Guatemala, China, Russia, Ethiopia, and South Korea are the five leading countries for the number of children adopted by U.S. couples. Yet, in March 2009, because Guatemala failed to comply with certain international laws regarding adoption, the U.S. Department of State advised families and adoption agencies to stop initiating adoptions from that country.

Each country has different adoption policies regarding the age, income level, and marital status of prospective parents. Often, foreign adoptions are handled privately. Countries may allow children to be escorted to the United States or may require adoptive parents to come and stay for days or even months to complete the adoption paperwork. The costs of adoption also vary from nation to nation.

Agency Placement In agency placement of a child, the arrangements are made by a licensed public or private agency. Such agencies exist solely for the placement of children, and part of their responsibility involves a thorough investigation of the suitability of the potential adoptive parents. Such an investigation is ordinarily quite detailed and takes into consideration the background of both the child and the prospective parents.

Statutes generally provide for agencies that are operated or licensed by the government to act in an intermediary role between natural and adoptive parents. The method by which a child is transferred to an adoption or placement agency is through the execution of a formal surrender agreement that the natural parents sign. By surrendering a child to an agency, the parent relinquishes all rights to the child. The agency is then given complete authority to arrange for adoption. In arranging for an adoption, agencies must take into consideration

such issues as whether a particular child is a proper subject for adoption, whether the proposed home is a suitable one, and whether the adoption is in the child's best interests.

Agency placement has three basic advantages: (1) It minimizes such risks as the adoption of nonhealthy children, the discovery of the adoptive parents' identity by the natural mother, and the natural mother's changing her mind about the adoption. (2) The suitability of adoptive parents is determined by a stringent investigation, which minimizes the risk that a child will be adopted by unfit parents. (3) Adoption through an agency minimizes fees incidental to the adoption.

One essential disadvantage of agency placement is that it involves a long, detailed process. The adoptive parents might be forced to wait for many months while they are being investigated as to their suitability. A second disadvantage of agency placement is that only a limited number of children are available for adoption through agencies.

Independent Placement In independent placement, or private adoption, a child is directly transferred from the natural mother, or her representative, to the parents seeking to adopt. This type of placement is ordinarily arranged by the natural mother's family or doctor. Generally, neither the natural nor the adoptive parents are thoroughly investigated. The adoptive parents often arrange to pay all medical bills incidental to the pregnancy and birth, in addition to legal expenses. Private adoptions are lawful in most states.

Like agency placement, independent placement has both advantages and disadvantages. Private placement facilitates the adoption of a child by parents who might otherwise be forced to endure an extended waiting period or who might be unable to find a child through agency channels because of stringent requirements or mere non-availability of adoptable children. As with all adoptions, there is an inherent risk that the natural mother might change her mind and never complete the adoption procedure. With some private adoptions, the natural mother remains anonymous. With others, her identity is known to the adoptive parents at the outset.

Independent placement aids mothers who do not have financial resources, by arranging for the payment of medical expenses by the adoptive parents. Such a procedure can, however, lead to a black market if not carefully monitored.

Other disadvantages of private placements are the risks of adoption of an unhealthy child or of nonsuitability of the adoptive parents.

Some states prohibit lawyers from obtaining babies for adoption by clients under any circumstances. Attorneys, however, are ordinarily permitted to accept fees for handling the legal aspects of adoption.

Surrogate Motherhood During the 1980s many infertile couples turned to SURROGATE MOTHERHOOD as an alternative to traditional adoption. A surrogate mother was paid a fee to bear a child conceived through ARTIFICIAL INSEMINATION. Once the child was born, the surrogate mother agreed to terminate her parental rights in favor of the sperm donor, typically the husband of the woman unable to have children. For public policy reasons, paid surrogate motherhood has been denounced as an unacceptable means of buying and selling babies.

The wrenching "Baby M" case proved to be the ultimate downfall of surrogate motherhood contracts. In *In re Baby M*, 109 N.J. 396, 537 A.2d 1227 (1988), Mary Beth Whitehead entered a written agreement to bear the child of William Stern, whose wife, Elizabeth Stern, was unable to have children. Whitehead was to be paid $10,000 for her services. When the baby girl was born in 1985, Whitehead refused to give her up and fled with the infant to Florida. Four months later, she was apprehended by authorities, who gave the baby over to the Sterns.

Despite Whitehead's efforts to regain the child, the New Jersey Superior Court stripped her of parental and VISITATION RIGHTS and allowed the Sterns to adopt the baby, whom they had named Melissa. The decision had little to do with adoption policy but centered primarily on contract enforcement. The court ruled that Whitehead was obligated to honor her contract with the Sterns.

The New Jersey Supreme Court reversed the lower-court decision, declaring that surrogate motherhood contracts are unenforceable because they violate public policy. The Sterns were allowed to maintain custody of Baby M, although the adoption was voided, and some of Whitehead's parental and visitation rights were restored. After the decision, most states passed legislation to prohibit surrogate motherhood contracts altogether.

Adoption by Contract or Agreement Generally, an adoptive relationship cannot be formed by private contract, either express or implied. Although adoption contracts are not usually considered to be injurious to public welfare, they are discouraged on the basis of the principle that a parent should not be permitted to trade away his or her child.

A court may, however, choose to treat a contract of adoption as an agreement to be enforced, with the outcome being equivalent to a formal adoption. The courts have upheld contracts between parents and institutions. In addition, in a number of states, an adoption contract between a natural parent and an institution that provides that the parent is not to be informed of the child's location is enforceable.

Because courts are not eager to deprive natural parents of the right to care for a child, adoption contracts are not enforced when they are in conflict with the welfare of the child. Some states provide that a contract made by one parent alone, absent a showing of clear consent by the other, is not valid. The procedure for adoption by a written declaration or deed is permitted in some states. Ordinarily, it must be properly recorded before the adoption will be valid.

Revocation A court will allow an agreement for the adoption of a child to be broken by a natural parent if the circumstances warrant it, such as when a parent was forced into an adoption agreement.

The court has discretion over whether to permit revocation of an adoption agreement. In such cases, the court will scrutinize the circumstances under which the parent gave consent as well as the parent's reasons for revoking the contract.

Consequences of Adoption

Adoption ordinarily terminates the rights and responsibilities of the natural parents to the child. The death of an adoptive parent does not restore the rights of the natural parents.

Adoption creates the same rights and responsibilities between a child and adoptive parents that existed between natural parent and child. An adopted child is entitled to the same rights as a natural child. When an adult is adopted, however, the adoptive parent does not assume the usual duty of support.

State law governs whether the name of a child will be affected by adoption or not. When a minor child is adopted, his or her LEGAL RESIDENCE is changed from that of the natural parent to that of the adoptive parent.

Inheritance A state legislature has the authority to impart or remove inheritance rights of adopted children or adoptive parents. Statutes usually provide that adopted children can inherit from adoptive parents in the same capacity as natural children and, conversely, adoptive parents can inherit the property of an adopted child who predeceases them.

Revocation of Adoption

If an adoption decree is acquired by FRAUD, it may be revoked. In addition, in the absence of the requisite consent of all concerned parties, an order of adoption is void. After a decree is revoked, a child assumes the status he or she had prior to the adoption proceedings.

Summary of Adoption Procedure

The formal steps in adoption of a child are generally uniform in all states.

Notice Notice of adoption proceedings is given to all parties who have a legal interest in the case except the child. In the case of ILLEGITIMACY, both natural parents should be given notice if they can be located.

Some statutes provide that a parent who has failed to support a child is not entitled to notice. However, a parent who has lost custody of a child in a DIVORCE or separation case is normally entitled to notice. Similarly, an adoption agency that has custody of the child is entitled to notice.

Petition The parents seeking to adopt must file a petition in court that supplies information about their situation as well as the situation of the child. The filing of a proper petition is ordinarily a prerequisite to the court's jurisdiction.

The petition indicates the names of the adoptive parents, the child, and the natural parents, if known. In addition, the child's gender and age are stated, and some states mandate that a medical report on the child must also accompany the petition.

Consent Written consent of the adoption agency or the child's natural parents accompanies the petition for adoption. Consent of the natural parents is not required if their parental rights have been involuntarily terminated as a result, for example, of abandonment or abuse of the child.

Hearing A hearing is held so that the court may examine the qualifications of the prospective parents and either grant or deny the petition. There must be an opportunity for the parties to present TESTIMONY and to examine WITNESSES at such a hearing. Adoption proceedings are confidential, so the hearing is conducted in a closed courtroom.

Ordinarily, the records of an adoption hearing are available for inspection only by court order. Confidentiality is thought to promote a sense of security for the child with his or her new family.

Probation Most states require a period of PROBATION in adoption proceedings. During this period, the child lives with the adoptive parents, and the appropriate state agency monitors the development of the relationship. The agency's prime concern is the ability of the adoptive parents to properly care for the child. If the relationship is working well for all concerned parties, the state agency will request that the court issue a permanent decree of adoption. If the relationship is unsatisfactory, the child is either returned to his or her previous home or is taken care of by the state.

Decree An adoption decree is a judgment of the court and is given the same force and effect as any other judgment.

Birth Certificate Following the adoption proceedings, a certificate of adoption is issued for the adopted child, to replace the birth certificate. It lists the new family name, the date and place of the child's birth, and the ages of the adoptive parents at the time the child was born.

Generally, the certificate of adoption does not indicate the names of the child's natural parents or the date and place of adoption. A child might never know that he or she was adopted unless the adoptive parents reveal the information, because the old birth certificate is sealed and may be opened only by court order.

Right to Information on Natural Parents

Ordinarily, all information concerning an adopted child's origins is sealed in compliance with the court adoption proceedings. However, many states ask the birth parents whether they are willing to have their identity disclosed to the adopted child once he or she becomes an adult.

A majority of the state statutes provide for the release of identifying information when the birth parents have consented to such release. One method that states use to organize such consents is a mutual consent registry, which is a system whereby individuals involved in the adoptions can indicate whether they will allow for their identifying information to be disclosed. Approximately 29 states have devised some type of registry. Other states have in place a type of search-and-consent system, which allows for the adoption agency to assist a party in locating birth family members if the birth family members consent to the release of the information.

Most state statutes deny adoptees access to records that disclose identifying information about the natural parents in situations where the consent of the birth parents is not on record. The natural parents often make their consent to the adoption contingent upon the condition that no information about them ever be revealed. Yet, many states now have instituted procedures for which a party to an adoption may obtain non-identifying information. Non-identifying information may include, but is not limited to, the following: the date and place of the adopted person's birth and the birth parents' age, physical description, race, ethnicity, religion, and medical history. Some states are more restrictive than others regarding the release of information from the adoption records. For example, New York, Oklahoma, and Rhode Island require that any person seeking non-identifying information must first register with the state adoption registry prior to receiving such information.

Because of a growing PUBLIC INTEREST in tracing ethnic and family backgrounds, many adoptees, as adults, have been calling for the right to obtain access to sealed adoption records, which includes identifying information. The adult adoptees recognize that a disclosure of this kind of information could be traumatic to minor adoptees, but they contend that lack of access could cause serious psychological trauma to them as adults. In addition, they cite medical problems or misdiagnoses that could be caused by absence of genetic history, as well as fear of unwitting INCEST.

Adult adoptees contend that most adoption statutes do not draw a distinction between adoptees as minors and later as adults, which causes the adults to be deprived of the right to trace their background. In addition, the adults allege that they have been denied EQUAL PROTECTION of law because their status precludes them from receiving medical information readily available to non-adoptees.

Various approaches are being used to resolve this problem. One approach involves the enactment of a legislative requirement that public and private adoption agencies be required to open their records, upon request, to adults who were adopted as children, with certain limitations. For example, if the child had been placed by the natural parents prior to the effective date of the legislation, the natural parents could prevent the adoptee from seeing the records.

The issue of right to access to adoption records by adoptees when they reach adulthood also encompasses the legal consideration of the natural parents' right to privacy, which could be violated if free access to sealed court records were given to adult adoptees. The adult adoptees' right to know must be balanced against their natural parents' right to privacy. The way to achieve such a balance, however, has never been clearly determined.

In September 1999 Tennessee's Supreme Court overturned the Tennessee Court of Appeals ruling in *Doe v. Sundquist,* 2 S.W.3d 919 (Tenn., Sep 27, 1999) (NO. 01-S-01-9901-CV00006), which challenged a law passed in 1995 that unsealed both adoption records and original birth certificates to adult adoptees. Earlier, the U.S. Court of Appeals for the 6th CIRCUIT COURT had ruled in favor of the state and opined, much to the dismay of sealed records advocates: "A birth is simultaneously an intimate occasion and a public event—the government has long kept records of when, where, and by whom babies are born. Such records have myriad purposes, such as furthering the interest of children in knowing the circumstances of their birth," *Doe v. Sundquist,* 106 F.3d 702, 65 USLW 2527, 1997 Fed.App. 0051P (6th Cir. (Tenn.) Feb 11, 1997) (NO. 96-6197). The U.S. Supreme Court, however, elected not to hear the Tennessee case.

FURTHER READINGS

"Access to Adoption Records, State Statutes Series." Available online at http://www.childwelfare.gov/system wide/laws_policies/statutes/infoaccessap.cfm; website home page: http://www.childwelfare.gov (accessed June 11, 2009).

Carp, E. Wayne, ed. 2002. *Adoption in America: Historical Perspectives.* Ann Arbor: University of Michigan Press.

DuPrau, Jeanne. 1990. *Adoption.* Englewood Cliffs, N.J.: Messner.

Embry v. Ryan Florida App. No. 2D08-1323 (May 13, 2009).

Marshner, Connaught, ed. 1999. *Adoption Factbook III.* Washington, D.C.: National Council for Adoption.

Manian, Maya. 2009. "The Irrational Woman: Informed Consent and Abortion Decision-Making". *Duke Journal of Gender Law and Policy.* August.

Melosh, Barbara. 2002. *Strangers and Kin: The American Way of Adoption.* Cambridge, Mass.: Harvard University Press.

Rundberg, Gayle D. 1988. *How to Get Babies through Private Adoption.* Bend, Ore.: Maverick.

Sloan, Irving J. 1988. *The Law of Adoption and Surrogate Parenting.* London: Oceana.

"Total Adoptions to the United States." Available online at http://adoption.state.gov/news/total_chart.html; website home page: http://adoption.state.gov (accessed June 11, 2009).

Van Alstyne, William. 2009. "The Unbearable Lightness of Marriage in the Abortion Decisions of the Supreme Court: Altered States in Constitutional Law." *William and Mary Bill of Rights Journal.* October.

CROSS REFERENCES

Child Custody; Child Support; Children's Rights; Family Law; Illegitimacy; Infants; Parent and Child; Surrogate Motherhood.

ADULT

A person who by virtue of attaining a certain age, generally eighteen, is regarded in the eyes of the law as being able to manage his or her own affairs.

The age specified by law, called the legal AGE OF MAJORITY, indicates that a person acquires full legal capacity to be bound by various documents, such as contracts and deeds, that he or she makes with others and to commit other legal acts such as voting in elections and entering MARRIAGE. The age at which a person becomes an adult varies from state to state and often varies within a state, depending upon the nature of the action taken by the person. Thus, a person wishing to obtain a license to operate a motor vehicle may be considered an adult at age sixteen, but may not reach adulthood until age eighteen for purposes of marriage, or age twenty-one for purposes of purchasing intoxicating liquors.

Anyone who has not reached the age of adulthood is legally considered an infant.

ADULTERATION

Mixing something impure with something genuine, or an inferior article with a superior one of the same kind.

Adulteration usually refers to mixing other matter of an inferior and sometimes harmful quality with food or drink intended to be sold. As a result of adulteration, food or drink becomes impure and unfit for human consumption. The federal FOOD AND DRUG ADMINISTRATION prohibits transportation of adulterated foods, drugs, and cosmetics in interstate commerce, as provided under the Food, Drug and Cosmetic Act (21 U.S.C.A. § 301 et seq. [1938]). State and local agencies, acting under the authority of local laws, do the same to ban the use of such impure goods within their borders.

ADULTERY

Voluntary sexual relations between an individual who is married and someone who is not the individual's spouse.

Adultery is viewed by the law in many jurisdictions as an offense injurious to public morals and a mistreatment of the MARRIAGE relationship.

Statutes attempt to discourage adultery by making such behavior punishable as a crime and by allowing a blameless party to obtain a DIVORCE against an adulterous spouse.

Although adultery has been historically regarded as a legal wrong, it has not always been considered a crime. In Europe during the fifteenth and sixteenth centuries, adultery was punishable solely in courts created by the church to impose good morals. In the ECCLESIASTICAL COURTS, adultery was any act of sexual intercourse by a married person with someone not his or her spouse. The act was considered wrongful regardless of whether the other person was married. At COMMON LAW, adultery was wrongful intercourse between a married woman and any man other than her husband.

Criminal Laws

Several state legislatures statutorily prohibit adultery as a crime. Under some statutes, both parties to an adulterous relationship are guilty of a crime if either of them is married to someone else. Other statutes provide that the act is criminal only if the woman is married.

Under the law of many states, a single act of adultery constitutes a crime, whereas in others, there must be an ongoing and notorious relationship. The punishment set by statute may be greater for an individual who engages in repeated acts of adultery than for one who commits an isolated act.

Defenses An individual who has been charged with committing adultery may have a valid legal defense, such as the failure or physical incapacity to consummate the sex act.

A woman is not guilty of adultery if the sex act resulted from RAPE. Some states recognize ignorance of the accused regarding the marital status of his or her sexual partner as a defense. In a few jurisdictions only the married party can be prosecuted for adultery. If the other party to the relationship is not married, he or she may be prosecuted for fornication instead of adultery.

Initiation of Criminal Proceedings Under some statutes, a prosecution for adultery can be brought only by the spouse of the accused person although technically the action is initiated in the name of the state. Other states provide that a husband or wife is precluded from commencing prosecution for adultery since those states have laws that prohibit a husband or wife from testifying against his or her spouse. In such states, a complaint can be filed by a husband or wife against the adulterous spouse's lover.

Evidence Customary rules prescribe the types of evidence that can be offered to prove guilt or innocence. There must be a showing by the PROSECUTOR that the accused party and another named party had sexual relations. Depending on state statutes, the prosecutor must show that either one or both parties to the adultery were wed to someone else at the time of their relationship.

Evidence that the DEFENDANT had the chance to have sexual relations coupled with a desire, or *opportunity* and *inclination,* might be sufficient to prove guilt. Photographs or TESTIMONY of a witness who observed the couple having sexual intercourse is not necessary. The fact that a married woman accused of adultery became pregnant during a time when her husband was absent might be admissible to demonstrate that someone other than her spouse had the opportunity of engaging in illicit sex with her.

Letters in which the accused parties have written about their amorous feelings or clandestine encounters may be introduced in court to support the assertion that the parties had the inclination to engage in sexual relations. CHARACTER EVIDENCE indicating the good or bad reputation of each party may be brought before the jury. Evidence of a woman's sexual relationships with men other than the party to the adultery generally cannot be used; however, if her reputation as a prostitute can be demonstrated, it may be offered as evidence.

Suspicious activities and incriminating circumstances may be offered as CIRCUMSTANTIAL EVIDENCE.

Enforcement of Statutes

Although the District of Columbia and approximately half of the states continue to have laws on the books criminalizing adultery, these laws are rarely invoked. Traditionally, states advanced three goals in support of their adultery laws: (1) the prevention of disease and illegitimate children; (2) the preservation of the institution of marriage; and (3) the safeguarding of general community morals.

Courts in the jurisdictions still prohibiting adultery have openly questioned whether adultery laws in fact serve these goals. The Florida Supreme Court, for example, found that adultery statutes bear no rational, much less compelling relationship to disease prevention. The court said that the risk of contracting disease is already a greater deterrent to extramarital sex than criminal punishment. The court also noted that the fear of prosecution prevents infected people from voluntarily seeking treatment (*Purvis v. State,* 377 So. 2d 674, 677 [Fla.1979]).

At the same time, many prosecutors began to realize that once the act of adultery is committed, the harm to the marriage is for the most part complete, especially if the infidelity is disclosed or discovered. In other words, after a spouse has been unfaithful, there is little the judicial system can offer to undo the act and reverse the damage. Thus, prosecutors have increasingly questioned whether prosecuting the adulterer will do much if anything to preserve the marriage.

Finally, judges, prosecutors, and other state officials have increasingly realized that prosecutions for adultery have had little practical effect in "safeguarding the community morals." Opinion polls consistently show that significant numbers of spouses admit to cheating on their partners during marriage. In light of the growing evidence that adultery laws no longer serve their three underlying purposes, most state prosecutors have made a conscious decision against wasting their scarce resources on prosecuting alleged adulterers.

In states that still have adultery laws on the books, but have failed to PROSECUTE anyone under them recently, courts have ruled that the mere lack of prosecution under the adultery statute does not result in that statute becoming invalid or judicially unenforceable. Courts have also rejected the argument that prosecutions for adultery are inconsistent with the right to privacy guaranteed by state and federal constitutions (*Commonwealth v. Stowell*, 389 Mass 171, 449 NE2d 357 [Mass 1983]).

As a Defense

Occasionally, adultery has been successfully asserted as a defense to the crime of MURDER by an individual charged with killing his or her spouse's lover. Courts are loath, however, to excuse the heinous crime of murder on the ground that the accused party was agitated about a spouse's adulterous activities. However, individuals who kill their spouse after catching him or her committing adultery may be able to rely on a HEAT OF PASSION defense, and thereby face prosecution or conviction for MANSLAUGHTER, rather than first degree murder.

Divorce

Based on the state's interest in the marital status of its residents, all legislatures had traditionally assigned statutes enumerating the grounds on which a divorce would be granted. These grounds, listed separately in the laws of each jurisdiction, generally included DESERTION, NON-SUPPORT, and adultery.

The basis of adultery as a ground for divorce has been discussed in various cases. There is an overriding PUBLIC POLICY in favor of preserving the sanctity of marital relationships and family unity and a fear that adultery will serve to undermine these societal objectives.

Late twentieth-century changes in divorce laws, primarily the enactment of no-fault divorce statutes in many states, have made it easier for couples seeking divorce to end their marriages without having to prove adultery or any other ground. In the past many unhappy couples resorted to trickery to attempt to obtain a divorce through staging the discovery of allegedly adulterous conduct.

Nonetheless, adultery still may be relevant to divorce proceedings in which ALIMONY is an issue. In twenty-seven states plus Puerto Rico and the District of Columbia, fault is one factor which courts will consider in deciding whether to AWARD alimony. If the spouse seeking an alimony award committed adultery, he or she will have a more difficult time convincing the court that he or she is entitled to alimony than if he or she had not been unfaithful.

FURTHER READINGS

Duhaime, Lloyd. "Adultery." *Duhaime.org* Web site. Available online at http://www.duhaime.org/Legal Dictionary/A/Adultery.aspx; website home page: http://www.duhaime.org (accessed August 28, 2009).

Friedman, Lawrence M. 2000. "A Dead Language: Divorce Law and Practice before No-fault." *Virginia Law Review* 86 (October).

Haggard, Melissa Ash. 1999. "Adultery: A Comparison of Military Law and State Law and the Controversy This Causes under Our Constitution and Criminal Justice System." *Brandeis Law Journal* 37 (spring).

CROSS REFERENCES

Circumstantial Evidence; Common Law; Divorce; Ecclesiastical Courts; Family Law; Fornication; Husband and Wife; Marriage; Privacy; Rape.

ADVANCE

To pay money or give something of value before the date designated to do so; to provide capital to help a planned enterprise, expecting a return from it; to give someone an item before payment has been made for it.

ADVANCE SHEETS

Pamphlets containing recently decided opinions of federal courts or state courts of a particular region.

Cases appearing in advance sheets are subsequently published in bound volumes containing several past pamphlets, usually with the same volume and page numbers as appeared in the advance sheets. Sometimes a court will publish an individual opinion soon after it has been rendered by the court. This is called a slip opinion, which later may appear in an advance sheet.

Advance Sheets in the National Reporter System

The National Reporter System, published by the West Group, St. Paul, Minnesota, is the most comprehensive collection of the decisions of the appellate courts of the states and each of the courts of the United States. Eighteen reporters comprise the National Reporter System. Eight units cover federal courts, including the

Supreme Court Reporter (cited as S. Ct.); the *Federal Reporter*, in its third series; the *Federal Supplement*, in its second series; the *Federal Rules Decisions* (cited as F.R.D.); the *Military Justice Reporter* (cited as M.J.); and the *Bankruptcy Reporter*.

Ten reporters cover the 50 states and the District of Columbia. These reporters, each of which is in its second or third series, include the following: *Atlantic Reporter* (A., A.2d); *North Western Reporter* (N.W., N.W.2d); *Pacific Reporter* (P., P.2d, P.3d); *South Eastern Reporter* (S.E., S.E.2d); *Southern Reporter* (So., So. 2d); *South Western Reporter* (S.W., S.W.2d, S.W.3d); *California Reporter* (Cal. Rptr.); *Illinois Decisions* (Ill. Dec.); and *New York Supplement* (N.Y.S., N.Y.S.2d).

Advance sheets in the National Reporter System are published 50 times each year (weekly, except for the last week of September and first week of October) for the regional units reporting state cases. Three units report federal cases 52 times per year. The remaining units are published biweekly, monthly, or semi-monthly, depending on how many cases are issued by the courts covered by the various reporters.

CROSS REFERENCES

Opinion; Reporter.

ADVANCEMENT

A gift of money or property made by a person while alive to his or her child or other legally recognized heir, the value of which the person intends to be deducted from the child's or heir's eventual share in the estate after the giver's death.

An advancement is not the same as a gift or a loan because the person intends that the "advance" of the heir's share of the estate be applied against what the heir would normally INHERIT. Although sometimes used to describe situations involving both people who have died INTESTATE (without leaving a valid will) and people who have left a will, the term *advancement* should be used only when there is no valid will. The laws of DESCENT AND DISTRIBUTION regulate the distribution of an intestate's property. The term ademption applies to lifetime gifts that reduce a beneficiary's share under a will.

ADVERSARY PROCEEDING

Any action, hearing, investigation, inquest, or inquiry brought by one party against another in *which the party seeking relief (initiating the action) has given legal notice to the other party and provided that party with an opportunity to contest the claims being made against him or her. A court trial is a typical example of an adversary proceeding.*

CROSS REFERENCE

Adjudication.

ADVERSARY SYSTEM

The scheme of American jurisprudence wherein a judge or jury renders a decision in a controversy between or among parties who assert contradictory positions during a judicial examination such as a trial, hearing, or other adjudication.

U.S. courtrooms have often been compared to battlefields or playing fields. The adversary system by which legal disputes are settled in the United States promotes the idea that legal controversies are battles or contests to be fought and won using all available resources.

The contemporary Anglo-American adversary system has gradually evolved, over several hundred years. Early English jury trials were unstructured proceedings in which the judge might act as inquisitor, or even PROSECUTOR, as well as fact finder. Criminal defendants were not allowed to have counsel, to call WITNESSES, to conduct CROSS-EXAMINATION, or to offer affirmative defenses. All types of evidence were allowed, and juries, although supposedly neutral and passive, were actually highly influenced by the judge's remarks and instructions. In fact, before 1670 jurors could be fined or jailed for refusing to follow a judge's directions.

The late 1600s saw the advent of a more modern adversarial system in England and its American colonies. Juries took a more neutral stance, and appellate review, previously unavailable, became possible in some cases. By the eighteenth century, juries assumed an even more autonomous position as they began functioning as a restraint on governmental and judicial abuse and corruption. The Framers of the Constitution recognized the importance of the jury trial in a free society by specifically establishing it in the SIXTH AMENDMENT as a right in criminal prosecutions. The Eight Amendment also established the right to a jury in noncriminal cases: "In Suits at COMMON LAW, where the value in controversy shall exceed twenty dollars, the right of trial by jury shall be preserved, and no fact tried by a jury, shall be otherwise reexamined in any Court of the United States, than according to the rules of the common law."

The independent judiciary was somewhat slower in developing. Before the 1800s, English judges were still biased by their ties with the Crown, and U.S. judges were often politically partisan. U.S. Supreme Court Chief Justice JOHN MARSHALL, who served from 1801 to 1835, established the preeminence and independence of the high court with his opinion in MARBURY V. MADISON, 5 U.S. (1 Cranch) 137, 2 L. Ed. 60 (1803). *Marbury* established "the basic principle that the federal judiciary is supreme in the exposition of the law of the Constitution" (*Cooper v. Aaron*, 358 U.S. 1, 78 S. Ct. 1401, 3 L. Ed. 2d 5 [1958]). By the early 1800s, attorneys had risen to prominence as advocates and presenters of evidence. Procedural and evidentiary rules were developed, and they turned the focus of LITIGATION away from arguments on minute points of law and toward the RESOLUTION of disputes. The basic parameters of the United States' modern legal system had been established.

In the Anglo-American adversary system, the PARTIES to a dispute, or their advocates, square off against each other and assume roles that are strictly separate and distinct from that of the decision maker, usually a judge or jury. The decision maker is expected to be objective and free from bias. Rooted in the ideals of the American Revolution, the modern adversary system reflects the conviction that everyone is entitled to a DAY IN COURT before a free, impartial, and independent judge. Adversary theory holds that requiring each side to develop and to present its own proofs and arguments is the surest way to uncover the information that will enable the judge or jury to resolve the conflict.

In an adversary system, the judge or jury is a neutral and passive fact finder, dispassionately examining the evidence presented by the parties with the objective of resolving the dispute between them. The fact finder must remain uninvolved in the presentation of arguments so as to avoid reaching a premature decision.

The Anglo-American requirement of an impartial and passive fact finder contrasts with the requirements of other legal systems. For example, most European countries employ the INQUISITORIAL SYSTEM, in which a judge investigates the facts, interviews witnesses, and renders a decision. Juries are not favored in an inquisitorial court, and the disputants are minimally involved in the fact-finding process. The main emphasis in a European court is the search for truth, whereas in an Anglo-American courtroom, truth is ancillary to the goal of reaching the fairest resolution of the dispute. It has been suggested that the inquisitorial system, with its goal of finding the truth, is a more just and equitable legal system. However, proponents of the adversary system maintain that the truth is most likely to emerge after all sides of a controversy are vigorously presented. They also point out that the inquisitorial system has its own deficiencies, including abuse and corruption. European judges must assume all roles in a trial, including those of fact finder, evidence gatherer, interrogator, and decision maker. Because of these sometimes conflicting roles, European judges might tend to prejudge a case in an effort to organize and dispose of it. Inquisitorial courts are far less sensitive to individual rights than are adversarial courts, and inquisitorial judges, who are government bureaucrats (rather than part of an independent judicial branch), might identify more with the government than with the parties. Critics of the inquisitorial system argue that it provides little, if any, check on government excess and that invites corruption, BRIBERY, and ABUSE OF POWER.

The parties to an Anglo-American lawsuit are responsible for gathering and producing all of the evidence in the case. This challenge forces them to develop their arguments and to present their most compelling evidence, and it also preserves the neutrality and passivity of the fact finder. The adversary process is governed by strict rules of evidence and procedure that allow both sides equal opportunity to argue their cases. These rules also help to ensure that the decision is based solely on the evidence presented. The structure of this legal system naturally encourages zealous advocacy by lawyers on behalf of their clients, but the code of ethics governing the conduct of lawyers is designed to curb the tendency to attempt to win by any means.

The adversary system has staunch defenders as well as severe critics. The image of the courtroom as a battleground or playing field where contestants vie for victory is evident in the news media's preoccupation with who is "winning" or "losing" or "scoring points" in such highly visible cases as the 1995 trial of

IN FOCUS

THE ADVERSARY SYSTEM: WHO WINS? WHO LOSES?

The legal system in the United States is known as an adversary system. In this system, the parties to a controversy develop and present their arguments, gather and submit evidence, call and question WITNESSES, and, within the confines of certain rules, control the process. The fact finder, usually a judge or jury, remains neutral and passive throughout the proceeding.

Critics pose some disturbing questions about the adversary system: Is justice served by a process that is more concerned with resolving controversies than with finding the ultimate truth? Is it possible for people with limited resources to enjoy the same access to legal services as wealthy people do? Does a system that puts a premium on winning encourage chicanery, manipulation, and deception?

The 1995 trial of O.J. SIMPSON, an actor, sportscaster, and professional football player accused of murdering his former wife and her friend, cast unprecedented scrutiny on the criminal justice system and left many people wondering whether truth or justice plays any role in its operation. Each day for over a year, the trial was televised in the homes of millions of people, most of whom had never seen the inside of a courtroom.

They were fascinated and repelled by prosecutors and defense attorneys who argued relentlessly about seemingly trivial points. Even more disturbing to some viewers was the acrimonious name-calling that went on between the two sides as each attempted to discredit the other's evidence and witnesses. Likewise, the inability of federal prosecutors to convict reputed mob boss John Gotti Jr. after four trials in five years ended in hung juries (the last in 2009) bewildered some observers. Defense attorneys are quick to point out that the Constitution guarantees that the accused is innocent unless found guilty in a court of law, and it is impossible to protect the innocent without occasionally protecting the guilty. Lawyers are obligated to challenge the evidence against their clients, even if that means impugning the police or attacking a victim's or witness's character. It is their job to win an ACQUITTAL by whatever legal and ethical means lies within their power.

Disparaging the legal system has become something of a national pastime. Indeed, criticism of the system comes from all corners of the landscape, including the top of the system itself. The late Chief Justice WARREN E. BURGER

was outspoken in his lambasting of the system and of lawyers, asserting that they are too numerous and too zealous, that they file too many frivolous lawsuits and motions, and that there is general failure within the system to encourage out-of-court settlements. Burger was a vocal proponent of ALTERNATIVE DISPUTE RESOLUTION (ADR). He advocated the use of nonlitigious solutions such as MEDIATION or ARBITRATION as a means of reducing court congestion. Supporters of the adversary system point out that it is not clear that the savings reaped from ADR always outweigh the costs. In situations where the parties are not at equal bargaining strength, questions arise as to whether settlements are extracted through duress. Some attorneys and litigants have noted that ADR is often as adversarial in nature as LITIGATION, with evidence presented and slanted by counsel. They further complain that there is no guarantee that an arbitrator will be informed about the subject matter of the dispute and, therefore, no guarantee of a fair outcome.

One criticism of the adversary system is that it is slow and cumbersome. The judge, acting as a neutral fact finder, can do little to accelerate a trial, and

O. J. SIMPSON, an actor, sportscaster, and former professional football player who was tried for killing his former wife, Nicole Brown Simpson, and her friend Ronald Goldman.

The emphasis on "winning at all costs" without commensurate concern for truth-seeking dismays some U.S. citizens, and a growing number are demanding reforms in the legal system. During the 1980s and 1990s, the use of alternative forms of dispute resolution such as MEDIATION and ARBITRATION grew dramatically. However, defenders of the adversary system note that these alternatives have been used all along, in the form of SETTLEMENT conferences, minitrials, and summary jury trials, and that

the vast majority of lawsuits are already settled before the parties ever appear in court.

When a dispute cannot be resolved without a trial, the adversary system is the established method of adjudication in the United States. Indeed, the organized bar remains committed to the notion that vigorous advocacy by both sides of a legal controversy ultimately leads the judge or jury to the facts needed for a fair resolution and that it is the process that is best calculated to elicit the truth and to protect individual rights. Although many concede that the adversary system is imperfect and that it may be subject to abuse and manipulation, the majority still believe that, by giving all parties and their

procedural and evidentiary rules further slow the process. Likewise, the wide availability of appellate review means that a final determination can take years. However, at least one study has shown that in courts where adversarial trials were discouraged and settlements actively encouraged, litigants still encountered substantial delays in RESOLUTION. Moreover, supporters of the adversary system maintain that a methodical, albeit cumbersome, system is necessary for protection of individual rights.

It is fair to challenge the ethics of a legal system that places a higher value on winning than on truth seeking. At least one commentator has characterized the system as one in which lawyers spend more time avoiding truth than seeking it. But proponents argue that the vigorous clash of opposing viewpoints eventually yields the truth and that allowing the sides to fight it out under specific rules that guarantee fair play allows the truth to surface on its own.

Many other complaints have been leveled against the U.S. adversary system. Some feel that because the parties control the litigation, they are encouraged to present only the evidence that is favorable to them and to suppress evidence that is unfavorable. Criticism of attorneys abounds. Some feel that the lawyers' ethics code encourages zealous representation at the expense of truth, making attorneys, in the words of Burger, "hired guns" (*In re Griffiths*, 413 U.S. 717, 93 S. Ct. 2851, 37 L. Ed. 2d 910 [1973]). Others complain that lawyers file too many frivolous lawsuits and have become too dominant in the adversary process. Some even say that the rules of evidence, designed to guarantee fairness to all parties, actually work against fairness by preventing important information from being presented to the fact finder.

Defenders of the adversary system are quick to refute each criticism lobbed at it. They contend that it is necessary for the parties to control the litigation in order to preserve the neutrality of the judge and jury. They point out that lawyers, although as susceptible to corruption as any other group, are governed by a code of ethical conduct that, when enforced, deals effectively with instances of overreaching. Plus, while conceding that evidentiary rules may be subject to manipulation, they vigorously maintain that such rules are the only means by which to ensure fairness and prevent judicial abuse.

The criticism of the U.S. legal system that may be most difficult to refute has to do with accessibility. It cannot be plausibly argued that an average criminal DEFENDANT has the same access to LEGAL REPRESENTATION as O.J. Simpson or John Gotti Jr. had, nor can it be argued that an injured PLAINTIFF in a civil suit is in an equal bargaining position with a huge corporation. Yet supporters of the adversary system counter that unequal access to legal services is the result of economic and social conditions, not the structure of the legal system and that changing the way legal services are delivered would do nothing to address the root causes of the disparity. They also point out that the much criticized contingency fee arrangement, by which an attorney is paid a percentage of the award her or his client receives, opens the courts to members of the population who could not otherwise afford legal representation.

Many legal experts agree that, in the long run, the adversary system results in societal benefits that outweigh its inherent shortcomings. By allowing all sides of a controversy to be heard, the system protects against ABUSE OF POWER and forces those with the most at stake to focus on the issues in dispute. At its worst, it can be manipulated to the benefit of those least deserving, but at its best, it offers every injured party a forum for relief, sometimes against powerful odds. No doubt the arguments about whether and how to change the system will persist well into the twenty-first century. This system, which has evolved over three hundred years, will probably undergo some changes. But the basic values at its heart, such as PRESUMPTION OF INNOCENCE, the right to trial by jury, and protection of individual rights, appear to be firmly cemented as the cornerstones of U.S. JURISPRUDENCE.

advocates the opportunity to present evidence and arguments before an impartial judge, it promotes a free and pluralistic society with the best available means of settling disputes.

FURTHER READINGS

Burger, Warren E. 1993. "Essays: The State of the Adversary System 1993." *Valparaiso Univ. Law Review* 27 (spring).

Doyle, Stephen, and Roger Haydock. 1991. *Without the Punches: Resolving Disputes without Litigation*. Minneapolis: Equilaw.

Kagan, Robert A. 2003. *Adversarial Legalism: The American Way of Law*. Cambridge, MA: Harvard Univ. Press.

Landsman, Stephan. 1984. *The Adversary System: A Description and Defense*. Washington, D.C.: American Institute for Public Policy Research.

———. 1988. *Readings on Adversarial Justice: The American Approach to Adjudication*. Eagan, MN: West.

Olson, Walter K. 1991. *The Litigation Explosion*. New York: Truman Talley.

CROSS REFERENCES

Alternative Dispute Resolution; Civil Law; Common Law; Inquisitorial System; Judge; Judiciary; Jury.

ADVERSE INTEREST

The legal right or liability of a person called to testify as a witness in a lawsuit that might be lost or impaired if the party who called him or her to testify wins the case.

This interest against the interest of the party calling a witness to the stand makes him or her an adverse or HOSTILE WITNESS. Although usually the party calling a witness to TESTIFY cannot IMPEACH that person's credibility, if the person has an adverse interest, the TESTIMONY may be discredited by the party who called that witness to the stand.

ADVERSE POSSESSION

A method of gaining legal title to real property by the actual, open, hostile, and continuous possession of it to the exclusion of its true owner for the period prescribed by state law. Personal property may also be acquired by adverse possession.

Adverse possession is similar to prescription, another way to acquire title to real property by occupying it for a period of time. Prescription is not the same, however, because title acquired under it is presumed to have resulted from a lost grant, as opposed to the expiration of the statutory time limit in adverse possession.

Real Property

Title to land is acquired by adverse possession as a result of the lapse of the STATUTE OF LIMITATIONS for ejectment, which bars the commencement of a lawsuit by the true owner to recover possession of the land. Adverse possession depends upon the intent of the occupant to claim and hold real property in opposition to all the world and the demonstration of this intention by visible and hostile possession of the land so that the owner is or should be aware that adverse claims are being made.

The legal theory underlying the vesting of title by adverse possession is that title to land must be certain. Because the owner has, by his or her own fault and neglect, failed to protect the land against the hostile actions of the adverse possessor, an adverse possessor who has treated the land as his or her own for a significant period of time is recognized as its owner.

Title by adverse possession may be acquired against any person or corporation not excepted by statute. Property held by the federal government, a state, or a MUNICIPAL CORPORATION cannot be taken by adverse possession. As long as the property has a public use, as with a highway or school property, its ownership cannot be lost through adverse possession.

Anyone, including corporations, the federal government, states, and municipal corporations, can be an adverse possessor.

Elements In order that adverse possession ripen into LEGAL TITLE, nonpermissive use by the adverse claimant that is actual, open and notorious, exclusive, hostile, and continuous for the statutory period must be established. All of these elements must coexist if title is to be acquired by adverse possession. The character, location, present state of the land, and the uses to which it is put are evaluated in each case. The adverse claimant has the burden of proving each element by a preponderance of the evidence.

Actual Adverse possession consists of actual occupation of the land with the intent to keep it solely for oneself. Merely claiming the land or paying taxes on it, without actually possessing it, is insufficient. Entry on the land, whether legal or not, is essential. A TRESPASS may commence adverse possession, but there must be more than temporary use of the property by a trespasser for adverse possession to be established. Physical acts must show that the possessor is exercising the dominion over the land that an average owner of similar property would exercise. Ordinary use of the property—for example, planting and harvesting crops or cutting and selling timber—indicates actual possession. In some states acts that constitute actual possession are found in statute.

Open and Notorious An adverse possessor must possess land openly for all the world to see, as a true owner would. Secretly occupying another's land does not give the occupant any legal rights. Clearing, fencing, cultivating, or improving the land demonstrates open and notorious possession, while actual residence on the land is the most open and notorious possession of all. The owner must have actual knowledge of the adverse use, or the claimant's possession must be so notorious that it is generally known by the public or the people in the neighborhood. The notoriety of the possession puts the owner on notice that the land will be lost unless he or she seeks to recover possession of it within a certain time.

Exclusive Adverse possession will not ripen into title unless the claimant has had exclusive possession of the land. Exclusive possession means sole physical occupancy. The claimant must hold the property as his or her own, in opposition to the claims of all others. Physical improvement of the land, as by the construction of fences or houses, is evidence of exclusive possession.

An adverse claimant cannot possess the property jointly with the owner. Two people may, however, claim title by adverse possession as joint tenants if they share occupancy of the land. When others or the general public have regularly used or occupied the land with the adverse claimant, the requirement of exclusive possession is not satisfied. Casual use of the property by others is not, however, inconsistent with exclusive possession. Generally, easements do not affect the exclusive possession by an adverse possessor. In some jurisdictions easements exercised by the public or railroad rights of way will destroy exclusive possession.

Hostile Possession must be hostile, sometimes called adverse, if title is to mature from adverse possession. Hostile possession means that the claimant must occupy the land in opposition to the true owner's rights. There need not be a dispute or fighting over title as long as the claimant intends to claim the land and hold it against the interests of the owner and all the world. Possession must be hostile from its commencement and must continue throughout the statutory period.

One type of hostile possession occurs when the claimant enters and remains on land under COLOR OF TITLE. Color of title is the appearance of title as a result of a deed that seems by its language to give the claimant valid title but, in fact, does not because some aspect of it is defective. If a person, for example, was suffering from a legal DISABILITY at the time he or she executed a deed, the grantee-claimant does not receive actual title. But the grantee-claimant does have color of title because it would appear to anyone reading the deed that good title had been conveyed. If a claimant possesses the land in the manner required by law for the full statutory period, his or her color of title will become actual title as a result of adverse possession.

Continuous Adverse possession must be continuous for the full statutory period if title is to vest. Continuity means regular, uninterrupted occupancy of the land. Mere occasional or sporadic use is not enough. Continuity is sometimes explained as the daily control of the land by the adverse claimant for the length of the statutory period. If a person has continuously occupied only a part of all the land claimed under adverse possession, he or she will acquire title only to the occupied portion.

While continuous possession is required for the acquisition of title by adverse possession, it is not necessary that only one person hold the land continuously for the statutory period. The time periods that successive adverse occupants have possessed the land may be added together to meet the continuity requirement if PRIVITY exists between the parties. The addition of these different periods is called tacking. Privity refers to the giving of possession of the land from one owner to the next so that it is continuously occupied by a possessor. Privity exists between different persons whose interests are related to each other by a sale or INHERITANCE of the land or by OPERATION OF LAW, as possession by a TRUSTEE in BANKRUPTCY.

Tacking is permitted only when the possession by the prior occupant had been adverse or under color of title. If any time lapses between the end of one owner's possession and the start of another's occupation, there is no continuity, so tacking will not be allowed.

Interruption of continuous possession deprives the adverse possessor of the legal effect of his or her prior occupancy. The statute of limitations will begin to run again from the time he or she starts actual, open, hostile, notorious, and exclusive possession. The length of the interruption is insignificant as long as it disturbs continuous possession. At that time the law restores constructive possession of the land to the true owner.

The commencement of a lawsuit by the owner against the occupant over the right of ownership and possession of the land is one way to interrupt continuous possession. It may be an action to quiet title, for trespass, for an INJUNCTION involving possessive rights, or to file a petition for registration of land title. Such lawsuits will destroy the continuity of possession only if successfully pursued to final judgments. If the owner chooses to abandon or SETTLE a suit or if a court dismisses it, the continuity of possession is not breached.

The entry of the owner upon the land with the intent to repossess it is a clear exercise of ownership that disturbs possession. A survey of the land made at the request of the true owner does not interrupt possession unless the purpose is to help the true owner take possession. The owner's actions must be notorious and open so there can be no doubt as to what is intended.

An accidental, casual, secret, or permissive entry is ineffective. While the entry must be notorious, it must also be peaceable to prevent violence and warfare, which might otherwise result.

The payment of REAL ESTATE taxes by the owner, while demonstrating that he or she has not abandoned land, is not considered to have any impact on continuous possession.

The adverse claimant may destroy his or her continuous possession by abandoning the land or giving it to someone else, even the owner, before the time at which title to it would vest. It does not matter how long or brief the abandonment is as long as it was intentional. A temporary absence from the land is not the same as an abandonment and has no effect on the occupancy, provided it is for a reasonable period of time.

Statutory Period The time period of the statute of limitations that must expire before title can be acquired by adverse possession varies from state to state. No statute will begin to run until the adverse claimant actually possesses the property in question under color of title or claim of right, where necessary. As of that time, the landowner is entitled to bring a lawsuit against the possessor to recover the property.

The adverse possessor must occupy the property for the full statutory period. In jurisdictions that also require color of title, it must coexist with possession for the complete period.

If the statute of limitations has been suspended—for example, because there is a lawsuit pending between the owner and the claimant or the owner is insane, an infant, or serving in the armed services—that amount of time will not be counted toward the time necessary for the acquisition of title.

Acquired Title

Once adverse possession is completed, the claimant has full legal title to the property. The expiration of the statutory period eliminates any CAUSE OF ACTION or LIABILITY for ejectment or trespass regarding the new owner's prior UNLAWFUL possession of the property. Once the time period is satisfied, the adverse possessor is considered the original owner of the land. He or she may use the land any way he or she sees fit provided it is lawful.

Personal Property

Ownership of PERSONAL PROPERTY may be acquired by adverse possession if the same requisites are met. The claimant must possess the property actually, openly, notoriously, exclusively, hostilely, under claim of right, and uninterrupted for the statutory period.

FURTHER READINGS

Berger, Lawrence. 1999. "Unification of the Doctrines of Adverse Possession and Practical Location in the Establishment of Boundaries." *Nebraska Law Review* 78 (winter).

Bloch, David S., and James Parton III. 2001. "The Intent Theory of Extinguishment Under California Law." *Southwestern Univ. Law Review* 30 (winter).

Gonski, Dennis M. 2001. "Disrupting More Than a Half Century of Accepted Law." *New Jersey Law Journal* (June 18).

Latovick, Paula R. 1998. "Adverse Possession of Municipal Land: It's Time to Protect This Valuable Asset." *Univ. of Michigan Journal of Law Reform* 31 (winter).

Spitler, William Hayden. 2000. "Over a Century of Doubt and Confusion: Adverse Possession in Arkansas, Intent to Hold Adversely and Recognition of Superior Title in Fulkerson v. Van Buren." *Arkansas Law Review* 53 (spring).

Stake, Jeffrey Evans. 2001. "The Uneasy Case for Adverse Possession." *Georgetown Law Journal* 89 (August).

CROSS REFERENCES

Cause of Action; Color of Title; Easement; Real Property; Statute of Limitations; Title; Trespass.

ADVICE AND CONSENT

The authority given by the U.S. Constitution to the Senate to ratify treaties and confirm presidential cabinet, ambassadorial, and judicial appointments.

Article II, Section 2, of the Constitution gives the president the right to negotiate foreign treaties and to nominate individuals to high-ranking government positions, including cabinet members, ambassadors, and federal judges. However, these powers are conditioned upon the advice and consent of the Senate. Section 2 requires the Senate to approve treaties by a two-thirds majority, while presidential appointments require a simple majority. The advice and consent requirement is an example of one of the checks and balances built into the Constitution. The provision seeks to limit presidential power.

The Senate has used the treaty RATIFICATION authority to extract changes in negotiated treaties and, in some cases, to reject an international agreement. The most famous rejection involved President WOODROW WILSON'S desire to have the United States join the newly created LEAGUE OF NATIONS after WORLD WAR I.

The Senate, hostile to the concept of international government, refused to ratify the treaty in 1919, which severely weakened the organization. In contrast, the Senate ratified the UNITED NATIONS Charter in 1945.

The advice and consent power has drawn the most public attention when the Senate has rejected presidential nominations to the cabinet and to federal judgeships. The Senate voted down the 1987 Supreme Court nomination of Robert Bork by President RONALD REAGAN, leading to charges that the Senate had politicized the confirmation process. CLARENCE THOMAS was confirmed as Supreme Court justice in 1991, but only after a bruising confirmation struggle that was nationally televised. In 2002, the Senate rejected several judicial nominations by President GEORGE W. BUSH, again leading to charges of partisan politics.

ADVISE

To give an opinion or recommend a plan or course of action; to give notice; to encourage, inform, or acquaint.

Advise does not mean the same as instruct or persuade. If a statute authorized a trial court to acquit, the court has no power to instruct the jury to acquit. The court can only counsel, and the jury is not bound by the advice.

ADVISEMENT

Deliberation; consultation.

A court takes a case *under advisement* after it has heard the arguments made by the counsel of opposing sides in the lawsuit but before it renders its decision.

ADVISORY JURY

A jury that makes recommendations to a judge but does not render final judgment.

Advisory juries are authorized by Rule 39(c) of the Federal Rules of CIVIL PROCEDURE (FRCP). This provision states that in all actions where the PLAINTIFF does not have the right to a jury trial, the court may authorize an advisory jury if a party requests it or the judge concludes independently that it is appropriate. The "verdict" the advisory jury renders is not binding on the judge. Advisory juries are typically used when the federal government is the sole DEFENDANT in a civil lawsuit and when

the claims at issue are particularly sensitive. In addition, OBSCENITY trials sometimes employ an advisory jury to determine whether the material in question is OBSCENE based on community standards. Because the FRCP serves as the model for state rules of procedure, most states also authorize advisory juries.

The advisory jury originated in English courts of equity, in which the chancellor (the name for an equity court judge) heard cases without a jury but had discretion to appoint a jury to advise him. In modern law a judge has great discretion in determining how much weight an advisory jury VERDICT will bear on a final judgment. Some judges adopt advisory jury findings unless they are clearly erroneous while other judges consider the findings an additional piece of evidence to be weighed in deciding the case.

After the government siege of the Branch Davidian compound in Waco, Texas, in 1993, an advisory jury was used in a lawsuit against the federal government filed by the survivors of the fire that ended the siege, and relatives of those who died in the fire. The survivors' WRONGFUL DEATH action asked for $675 million in damages. Under the FEDERAL TORT CLAIMS ACT the survivors did not have a right to a jury trial but the federal judge concluded that an advisory jury was needed. In July 2000, the jury ruled in favor of the federal government on all counts and the judge endorsed these findings in a final judgment.

FURTHER READINGS

Spielbauer, T. "Practice and Potential of the Advisory Jury."1987. *Harvard Law Review* 100 (April).
Wisenberg, Solomon. 2000. "What the Waco Advisory Jury Did Not Hear." *CNN.com: Law Center.* Available online at http://edition.cnn.com/2000/LAW/07/columns/fl. wisenberg.waco.07.20; website home page: http:// edition.cnn.com (accessed July 3, 2009).

ADVISORY OPINION

An opinion by a court as to the legality of proposed legislation or conduct, given in response to a request by the government, legislature, or some other interested party.

Advisory opinions are issued in the absence of a CASE OR CONTROVERSY. Although they are not binding and carry no precedential value, they are sometimes offered as persuasive evidence in cases where no PRECEDENT exists.

Federal courts will not issue advisory opinions. This rule, based on the constitutional guarantee of SEPARATION OF POWERS, was established in 1793 when JOHN JAY, the first chief justice of the Supreme Court, refused to provide legal advice in response to requests by President GEORGE WASHINGTON and Treasury Secretary ALEXANDER HAMILTON. Washington asked the Court for advice relating to his Neutrality Proclamation in regard to the French Revolution. Hamilton asked Jay for an opinion on the constitutionality of a RESOLUTION passed by the Virginia House of Representatives. In both instances, the Court diplomatically but firmly refused to supply an opinion.

The Supreme Court has steadfastly resisted subsequent efforts to elicit advisory opinions, even when these efforts appear under the guise of an actual lawsuit. Thus, in *Muskrat v. United States*, 219 U.S. 346, 31 S. Ct. 250, 55 L. Ed. 246 (1911), the Court struck down an act of Congress that authorized the plaintiffs to sue the United States to determine the validity of certain laws. The Court found the lawsuits authorized by the act to be thinly veiled attempts to obtain advisory opinions, since the constitutional requirements of justiciability and an actual case or controversy were not satisfied. Justice WILLIAM R. DAY, writing for the Court, predicted that if the justices rendered a judgment in the case,

> the result will be that this court, instead of keeping within the limits of judicial power and deciding cases or controversies arising between opposing parties, as the Constitution intended it should, will be required to give opinions in the nature of advice concerning legislative action, a function never conferred upon it by the Constitution.

Echoing the convictions expressed in *Muskrat*, Supreme Court Justice FELIX FRANKFURTER, writing on advisory opinions, stated, "Every tendency to deal with constitutional questions abstractly, to formulate them in terms of barren legal questions, leads to ... sterile conclusions unrelated to actualities."

Unlike their federal counterpart, a number of state constitutions authorize their courts to issue advisory opinions. However, even in those states, courts usually restrict advisory opinions to pending legislation and refuse requests for opinions on abstract or theoretical questions of law. In any event, the opinions are not BINDING AUTHORITY in future cases.

Whereas courts are typically limited in issuing advisory opinions, the attorney general of the United States and state attorneys general frequently issue opinions that are advisory in nature. By statute, the president or head of an executive department may require from the U.S. attorney general an opinion on questions of law arising from the administration of that office or department (28 U.S.C.A. §§ 511-512 [1993]). Most states charge attorneys general with similar responsibilities. Although advisory opinions issued by attorneys general are not typically binding in nature, in some circumstances the opinions may bind the authorities that request them.

Advisory opinions have their greatest effect as guides to policy making for the executive and legislative branches of state government. They are most often sought in the areas of intergovernmental relations, TAXATION, and finance.

Advisory opinions contrast with declaratory judgments, which determine the rights of litigants in an actual controversy and involve specific individuals who are at least nominally adverse to each other. Declaratory judgments are allowed by courts at both the federal and state levels. Although the line between advisory opinions and declaratory judgments is a fine one, the Supreme Court has consistently reiterated the necessity of keeping it intact. In *Ashwander v. Tennessee Valley Authority*, 297 U.S. 288, 56 S. Ct. 466, 80 L. Ed. 688 (1936), the justices insisted that the Federal DECLARATORY JUDGMENT Act, which gives federal courts the power to issue declaratory judgments, "does not attempt to change the essential requisites for the exercise of judicial power." An actual, not theoretical, case or controversy between specific parties must still be shown. In another case, the Court stated specifically that the Declaratory Judgment Act cannot be invoked to "obtain an advisory decree upon a hypothetical state of facts" (*Electric Bond & Share Co. v. Securities & Exchange Commission*, 303 U.S. 419, 58 S. Ct. 678, 82 L. Ed. 936 [1938]).

FURTHER READINGS

Bonsignore, John J., et al. 2006. *Before the Law: An Introduction to the Legal Process.* 8th ed. Florence, KY: Cengage Learning.

Schaper, Todd. 1998. "The Advisory Opinion Process: True Safe Harbors or More Rocky Coastlines?" *New Jersey Law Journal* 154 (December 14).

CROSS REFERENCES
Attorney General; Declaratory Judgment; Evidence; Hamilton, Alexander; Justiciable; Precedent; Separation of Powers; Washington, George.

ADVOCACY

The act of pleading or arguing a case or a position; forceful persuasion.

ADVOCATE

To support or defend by argument; to recommend publicly. An individual who presents or argues another's case; one who gives legal advice and pleads the cause of another before a court or tribunal; a counselor. A person admitted to the practice of law who advises clients of their legal rights and argues their cases in court.

AERONAUTICS

Aeronautics is the science and art of flight, encompassing the functioning and ownership of all aircraft vehicles from balloons to those that travel into space.

Aviation is travel by means of an aircraft that is heavier than air. *Aerospace* is a term used in reference to the atmosphere and the area beyond. The *aerospace industry* is involved with the planning and building of vehicles operating in both air and space.

Airspace is the region that extends above real property. *Air transportation,* as set forth by federal statute, refers to interstate and distant conveyance of people, cargo, and mail by U.S. and foreign aircraft vehicles.

Airspace Rights

The federal government has jurisdiction over airspace within its domain, and each state has authority over the space above the ground within its borders except in places within the domain of federal regulation. An aircraft is subject to the authority of the federal government and to the authority of a particular state while traveling over it. Landowners have air rights that extend upward beyond their property, the BOUNDARIES of which are delineated by local zoning ordinances. These air rights

The Federal Aviation Administration has responsibility for air traffic control. Air traffic controllers have a duty to keep aircraft from colliding with each other by guiding their path.
AP IMAGES

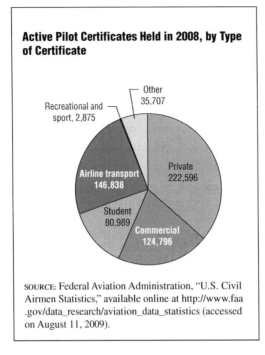

Active Pilot Certificates Held in 2008, by Type of Certificate

SOURCE: Federal Aviation Administration, "U.S. Civil Airmen Statistics," available online at http://www.faa.gov/data_research/aviation_data_statistics (accessed on August 11, 2009).

ordinarily may be used to the extent that they are connected to the enjoyment of the property.

Because the general public has the right to freedom of travel in the navigable airspace of the United States, an aircraft may have legal access to airspace above private property. A landowner might have a civil CAUSE OF ACTION for trespass or NUISANCE, however, where an aircraft enters the landowner's airspace in such manner as to constitute an INFRINGEMENT on the landowner's right to the use and possession of the property. In some instances the landowner is entitled to an INJUNCTION to prohibit unlawful intrusion of his or her airspace.

Air Transportation Regulation

The FEDERAL AVIATION ADMINISTRATION (FAA) is the agency with the authority to govern air commerce. The intent of such regulation is to advance the growth and safety of air travel while satisfying national defense needs. The director of the FAA has the power to engage in, or monitor, work and testing that will bring about the production of advanced aircraft; to set forth prescribed rules and regulations for the planning and servicing of airplanes; and to administer stringent sanctions if the regulations are not observed. The FAA is also responsible for air traffic control at airports. The NATIONAL TRANSPORTATION SAFETY BOARD (NTSB) is charged with

investigating the circumstances surrounding, and the causes of, accidents involving aircraft.

Certificate Requirements

An airplane must have a valid airworthiness certificate in order for it to be lawfully operated. The airworthiness of a plane is determined by an inspector authorized by the FAA. The inspector may neither delegate this duty to inspect the aircraft nor depart from procedures for inspection that have been prescribed by the administrator of the FAA.

The FAA administrator is empowered to create minimum standards for the inspection, maintenance, and repair of air carrier equipment as well as for safe operation of the vehicle. Another important function of the administrator is to issue certificates to eligible aeronautical personnel, which includes pilots; navigators; and people who inspect, maintain, overhaul, and repair aircraft. The administrator specifies the particular function that each of these individuals is qualified to perform.

Certain prerequisites exist for an airline PILOT rating, including a high degree of technical skill, medical fitness, care, judgment, and emotional stability. If public safety is endangered, the FAA administrator will either revoke or suspend a pilot's license. A pilot is entitled to notice and a FAIR HEARING before the revocation or suspension of his or her certification, absent an emergency that warrants immediate action. The pilot may appeal the order of suspension or revocation to the NTSB, and subsequent appeals may be brought to the usual appellate channels of federal courts ordinarily beginning in a U.S. district court.

Regulation on the State and Local Level

A state or municipality has the authority to regulate the air traffic that affects it; this power, however, is limited by the condition that the regulation must not interfere or conflict with either interstate commerce or federal restraints. State or municipal regulations on noise precipitated by aircraft engines may not, for example, conflict with federal rules governing noise pollution.

Airport Operation

Most federal law affecting airports and air carriers can be found under 49 U.S.C. 401, et seq., and Titles 14 and 49 of the CODE OF FEDERAL

REGULATIONS (C.F.R.). The Airline Deregulation Act of 1978, P.L. 95-504 (as amended 49 U.S.C.A. 41713 [2007]) provides that states may not enact or enforce a law relating to pricing, routing, or service of an air carrier.

However, the state can give a local legislature the power to regulate airports and their connected facilities. States may join together to form a regional airport authority to operate an airport. An airport may also be built and maintained by a private party or a corporation, subject to the requirement that use and enjoyment of neighboring landowners' property is not unreasonably disrupted. Airports that are not properly constructed and operated might amount to nuisances. A private homeowner can sue for damages in the event that an improperly run airport constitutes a nuisance and can attempt to have the court suspend its operation pursuant to the provisions of an injunction. Notice must be given to the municipality before such a cause of action may be commenced against it.

The creation and maintenance of airports are subject to zoning regulations. In certain jurisdictions a public agency is empowered by the state to adopt zoning laws that limit the use of adjacent property. Such ordinances are designed to reduce interference with the operation of the airport.

In considering the need for intervention concerning the building and operation of airports, courts examine the interests of the concerned parties in light of prevailing PUBLIC POLICY in favor of encouraging quiet use and enjoyment of one's land compared to the interests of society in accessible and convenient air travel.

For example, in *Clark County, Nevada v. Vacation Village* (497 F.3d 209 [9th Cir. 2007]), PLAINTIFF landowners fought local county ordinances imposing airspace restrictions that affected their property. (The ordinances created airport runway protection zones and imposed land-use limitations, including restrictions on the height of buildings on property located within those zones.) This adversely affected plaintiffs' intended use of the property for vacation resort condominium development. The lawsuit alleged that the restrictions were tantamount to a *taking* of the property under state EMINENT DOMAIN law (inverse condemnation), which would require the county to pay compensation to the landowners. The Nevada Supreme Court found that the airport zoning

and height-restrictions amounted to a taking of airspace under the Nevada Constitution. It had already so concluded in a similar previous case, *McCarran International Airport v. Sisolak* (cert. denied by the U.S. Supreme Court, 06-658, February 2007), finding that a landowner had a property interest in the airspace above his land up to 500 feet. On appeal, the Ninth CIRCUIT COURT of Appeals, while disagreeing with the Nevada high court, found that it had no choice, in the absence of federal preemption, except to apply *McCarran* and find Clark County liable for a taking under the Nevada Constitution. In 2008, the U.S. Supreme Court denied review of the case (No. 07-373, June 2008).

The owner of a public airport may arrange leases for its use, and a municipality that owns an airport may charge reasonable fees for the right to do business there. A public airport owner has the power to govern its ground transportation, to give qualified individuals and companies exclusive privileges to transport passengers to and from the airport, and to run an automobile rental company on airport grounds.

Use and Ownership of Aircraft Vehicles

The legality of the sale or conveyance of an aircraft is regulated by the statute of the jurisdiction where the document of conveyance or sale is transferred.

Federal law mandates the registration of aircraft and the proper recording of any paper that affects its title, such as a mortgage. Such recording must take place at the administration and records branch of the FAA. In addition, documents creating security interests in the aircraft must be recorded to provide notice to prospective purchasers of prior claims to the vehicle.

General principles of contract law govern aircraft rental, and parties to the agreement are ordinarily bound by its terms. The renter of a defective vehicle might, however, have the right to terminate the contract since the individual offering the aircraft for rent is obligated to provide a vehicle in satisfactory operating condition.

Duties in Aircraft Operation

An individual who is injured as a result of the operation of an aircraft usually has a legally enforceable right to damages for any injuries or losses sustained.

Manufacturers A manufacturer must exercise reasonable care and proficiency in the design, production, and assembly of an aircraft vehicle. LIABILITY for a departure from this duty may be extended to the manufacturer regardless of whether that company was directly involved in the manufacture of the parts. The law will imply a warranty of proper design and manufacture of an aircraft. A manufacturer of parts will also be held responsible for damage caused by the product and must use a high degree of care in their production, although they need not be made accident-proof. A manufacturer is not relieved of a continuing obligation to improve the component parts of an air vehicle when there is continuing risk to safe travel.

Pilots The pilot of a private aircraft is subject to ordinary NEGLIGENCE standards in the absence of a special law. The pilot is required to exercise ordinary, but not extreme, care and caution regarding its operation. Negligence rules, however, impose a greater standard of care when applied to aviation, because of the severity and magnitude of potential harm posed by improper operation of an aircraft.

Owners Generally ownership of an aircraft vehicle is insufficient to render a person liable for damage resulting from its unreasonable operation by another. In certain jurisdictions, however, an owner who lends a plane to an individual he or she knows to be reckless or incompetent will be held responsible. Similarly, the federal or state government cannot evade liability for damage arising from the improper operation of its aircraft by government employees.

Passengers Passengers in a private aircraft have the obligation to exercise reasonable care for their own well-being. They must subscribe to the reasonable-person standard and refrain from going on a particular flight that would be an obvious danger, such as a flight during a hurricane.

Passengers on AIRLINES and other air common carriers must observe safety precautions by obeying instructions of flight attendants, such as by fastening their seatbelts.

Airport Operators An airport operator has the duty to exercise ordinary care in protecting aircraft on its premises and the people who use airport facilities. Neglecting to maintain the airport premises in a reasonably safe condition results in tort liability for resulting injuries to anyone present.

Air Traffic Control

The federal government has responsibility for air traffic control. Air traffic controllers have a duty to keep aircraft from colliding by guiding their paths. Liability can be extended to the federal government for the negligence of its air traffic controllers. Contributory negligence by the individual harmed might, however, prevent recovery against the United States for damage caused only partially by the negligence of controllers.

The FAA has broad authority for the regulation of U.S. air space and air traffic control. In early 2008 it issued a final rule aimed at addressing the air traffic congestion at New York and New Jersey airports. The rule specifically limited the number of scheduled aircraft arrivals at JOHN F. KENNEDY International and LaGuardia airports in New York and Liberty International Airport in New Jersey during peak hours. In conjunction with that ruling, the FAA declared that the available space (called *slots*) created by the limitations was agency property, which the FAA then declared it would auction off on an annual basis. The Air Transport Association (ATA) then sued the FAA to invalidate the *slot auction* rules, challenging the preemption amendment of the Airline Deregulation Act (*ATA v. FAA* 08-1333, D.C. Cir.). In May 2009 the FAA proposed RESCISSION of those rules (*Federal Register* 74: 22714 and 22717).

Airlines

An airline has the duty to employ the greatest degree of care possible to protect its passengers. Liability might be imposed for harm to a passenger resulting from wrongful behavior of its employees. It must also take steps to guard passengers against misconduct of fellow passengers.

Companies that accept goods for air transport must exercise a high degree of care to properly handle and deliver such goods. Liability for LOSS or damage may be restricted to a prearranged amount, which must be listed on the passenger's ticket in the case of baggage or on the BILL OF LADING regarding the goods shipped.

Flying Schools

A flying school that maintains facilities that interfere with the customary use and enjoyment of property by neighboring landowners can be liable for nuisance or trespass. A student pilot flying with a flight instructor is considered legally to be a passenger, and, therefore, the school owes the same duty of care to the student as a commercial airline owes to its passenger. A trainee, however, assumes certain risks while being taught to fly, and the school can successfully assert the defense of assumption of the risk in tort cases. A member of a flight club, as an owner of an airplane that belongs to the club, may be held personally liable for accidents that might occur while he or she is piloting the craft. Statutes that govern the liability of a flight club member explain liability issues.

Following the September 11, 2001, terrorist attacks on the United States, Congress moved to tighten regulations on flying schools. It was believed that terrorists who hijacked and crashed airplanes into the World Trade Center and the Pentagon had trained at flying schools in the United States. The goal of the post-September 11 reform is to make information about foreign flight school enrollees more readily accessible to law enforcement agencies (49 CFR 1552).

Under the USA PATRIOT ACT OF 2001, flying schools are one of several types of educational institutions required to participate in the Student and Exchange Visitor Information System (SEVIS) implemented by the U.S. IMMIGRATION and Naturalization Service. Exempt from federal privacy restrictions, SEVIS is a database of information about foreign students, such as identification, visa status, and criminal data. Flying schools failing to participate in SEVIS may lose their ability to enroll international students. Under broadened powers granted by the PATRIOT Act, the U.S. attorney general may make use of such information to seize educational records, conduct surveillance, bypass certain SEARCH WARRANT requirements, and take into custody ALIENS whose visa status is in violation. Some parts of the PATRIOT Act had a sunset clause for December 31, 2005, but President GEORGE W. BUSH signed the act into law after much congressional debate in March 2006. As late as 2009, many people in and outside government urged repeal of this act, arguing its intrusion in personal liberties. Others believed terrorist threats to the United States warranted keeping the PATRIOT Act.

Air Piracy

Aircraft piracy or an attempt to hijack an airplane is a federal offense, punishable by either life imprisonment or death. Airlines can deny an individual passage on an airplane if a magnetometer (an instrument used to measure magnetic intensity) indicates the presence of a metal object, such as a weapon, on that person and the person refuses to surrender to the appropriate officials any metal object that might have triggered the instrument.

Aerospace

The National Aeronautics and Space Administration (NASA) was established by Congress to organize, direct, and carry out research into difficulties attached to flight within and beyond the atmosphere of the Earth and to facilitate the development and functioning of aeronautical vehicles.

FURTHER READINGS

Banner, Stuart. 2008. *Who Owns the Sky?: The Struggle to Control Airspace from the Wright Brothers On.* Cambridge, Mass.: Harvard Univ. Press.

Fixel, Rowland W. 1999. *The Law of Aviation.* Holmes Beach, Fla.: Gaunt.

Hamilton, J. Scott. 2001. *Practical Aviation Law.* 3d ed. Ames: Iowa State Univ. Press.

Institute of Air & Space Law. Available online at http://www.mcgill.ca/iasl/ (accessed September 26, 2009).

Journal of Air Law and Commerce Overview. Available online at http://smu.edu/lra/Journals/JALC/Overview.asp (accessed September 26, 2009).

Rollo, Vera A. Foster. 2000. *Aviation Law: An Introduction.* 5th ed. Lanham, Md.: Maryland Historical Press.

Transportation Research Board, Airport Cooperative Research Program (ACRP). 2008. *Legal Research Digest 1.* January 2008.

CROSS REFERENCES

Airlines; Carriers; Eminent Domain; Federal Aviation Administration; Hijacking; National Transportation Safety Board; Pilot; Terrorism.

AFFIDAVIT

A written statement of facts voluntarily made by an affiant under an oath or affirmation administered by a person authorized to do so by law.

Distinctions

An affidavit is voluntarily made without any CROSS-EXAMINATION of the affiant and, therefore, is not the same as a DEPOSITION, a record of an examination of a witness or a party made either voluntarily or pursuant to a SUBPOENA, as if the party were testifying in court under cross-examination. A pleading—a request to a court to exercise its judicial power in favor of a party that contains allegations or conclusions of facts that are not necessarily verified—differs from an affidavit, which states facts under OATH.

Affidavit

STATE OF _____ COUNTY OF _____

BEFORE ME, the undersigned authority, _____ [name and capacity of officer before whom affidavit is sworn],

on this _____ [day of month] day of _____ [month], 20____, personally appeared

_____ [name of affiant], known to me to be a credible person and of lawful age, who being by me first duly sworn,

on _____ [his or her] oath, deposes and says: _____ [set forth statement of facts].

_____ [signature of affiant]

_____ [typed name of affiant]

_____ [address of affiant]

Subscribed and sworn to before me, this _____ [day of month] day of _____ [month], 20____.

[Seal]   _____ [signature of officer]

              _____ [typed name of officer]

              _____ [title of officer]

              My commission expires: _____, 20____

Basis

An affidavit is based upon either the personal knowledge of the affiant or his or her INFORMATION AND BELIEF. Personal knowledge is the recognition of particular facts by either direct observation or experience. Information and belief is what the affiant feels he or she can state as true, although not based on firsthand knowledge.

The Affiant

Any person having the intellectual capacity to take an oath or make an affirmation and who has knowledge of the facts that are in dispute may make an affidavit. There is no age requirement for an affiant. As long as a person is old enough to understand the facts and the significance of the oath or affirmation he or she makes, the affidavit is valid. A criminal conviction does not make a person incapable of making an affidavit, but an adjudication of INCOMPETENCY does.

Someone familiar with the matters in question may make an affidavit on behalf of another, but that person's authority to do so must be clear. A guardian may make an affidavit for a minor or insane person incapable of doing so. An attorney may make an affidavit for a client if it is impossible for the client to do so. When necessary to the performance of duties, a PERSONAL REPRESENTATIVE, agent, or corporate officer or partner may execute an affidavit that indicates the capacity in which the affiant acts. A court cannot force a person to make an affidavit, because by definition, an affidavit is a voluntary statement.

The Taker of the Affidavit

Any public officer authorized by law to administer oaths and affirmations—such as city recorders, court clerks, notaries, county clerks, commissioners of deeds, and court commissioners—may take affidavits. Justices of the peace and magistrates are sometimes authorized to take affidavits. Unless restricted by state law, judges may take affidavits involving controversies before them.

An officer cannot take affidavits outside of the particular jurisdiction in which he or she exercises authority. The source of this authority must appear at the bottom of the affidavit. A notary, for example, would indicate the county in which he or she is commissioned and the expiration date of the commission. An official seal is not essential to the validity of the affidavit but may be placed on it by the proper official.

The Oath or Affirmation

Unless otherwise provided by statute, an oath is essential to an affidavit. The statement of the affiant does not become an affidavit unless the proper official administers the oath. When religious convictions prevent the affiant from taking an oath, he or she may affirm that the statements in the affidavit are true.

Contents

There is no standard form or language to be used in an affidavit as long as the facts contained within it are stated clearly and definitely. Unnecessary language or legal arguments should not appear. Clerical and grammatical errors, while to be avoided, are inconsequential.

The affidavit usually must contain the address of the affiant and the date that the statement was made, in addition to the affiant's signature or mark. Where the affidavit has been made is also noted. When an affidavit is based on the affiant's information and belief, it must state the source of the affiant's information and the grounds for the affiant's belief in the accuracy of such information. This permits the court to draw its own conclusions about the information in the affidavit.

An affiant is strictly responsible for the truth and accuracy of the contents of the affidavit. If false statements are made, the affiant can be prosecuted for PERJURY.

Functions

Affidavits are used in business and in judicial and administrative proceedings.

Business Generally affidavits are used in business whenever an official statement that others might rely upon is needed. Statements of the financial stability of a corporation, the pedigree of animals, and the financial conditions of a person applying for credit are examples of affidavits used in the commercial world.

Judicial Proceedings Affidavits serve as evidence in civil actions and criminal prosecutions in certain instances. They are considered a very weak type of evidence because they are not taken in court, and the affiant is not subject to cross-examination. Their use is usually restricted to times when no better evidence can be offered. If a witness who has made an affidavit is not available to TESTIFY at a trial, his or her affidavit may be admitted as evidence. If the witness is present, his or her affidavit is INADMISSIBLE except when used to IMPEACH the witness's TESTIMONY, or to help the witness with past recollection of facts.

Affidavits are also used as evidence in EX PARTE proceedings such as a hearing for the issuance of a TEMPORARY RESTRAINING ORDER or an order to SHOW CAUSE. The expeditious nature of such proceedings is considered to substantially outweigh the weak PROBATIVE value of the affidavits. In addition, there is normally a subsequent opportunity in the course of LITIGATION for the opposing party to refute the affidavits or cross-examine the affiants.

An affidavit based on the knowledge of the affiant is accorded more weight than one based on information and belief. When admissible, affidavits are not conclusive evidence of the facts stated therein.

Administrative Proceedings Affidavits are frequently used in administrative and QUASI-JUDICIAL proceedings as evidence when no objection is made to their admission and there is an opportunity for cross-examination.

AFFILIATION PROCEEDING

A court hearing to determine whether a man against whom the action is brought is the father of an illegitimate child and thus legally bound to provide financial support for the child.

Formerly referred to as bastardy actions or proceedings in many jurisdictions, as of 2003 these are called paternity or filiation proceedings. In several states, these proceedings are governed in part by the Uniform Parentage Act, first adopted by the Commissioners on Uniform Laws in 1973. The purpose of the act is to identify natural fathers through a paternity test so that a court may order child support obligations against them.

CROSS REFERENCES

Commissioners on Uniform Laws; DNA Evidence; Paternity; Paternity Suit.

AFFINITY

The relationship that a person has to the blood relatives of a spouse by virtue of the marriage.

The doctrine of affinity developed from a maxim of CANON LAW that a HUSBAND AND WIFE were made one by their MARRIAGE. There are three types of affinity. *Direct affinity* exists between the husband and his wife's relations by blood, or between the wife and the husband's relations by blood. *Secondary affinity* is between a spouse and the other spouse's relatives by marriage. *Collateral affinity* exists between a spouse and the relatives of the other spouse's relatives. The determination of affinity is important in various legal matters, such as deciding whether to PROSECUTE a person for INCEST or whether to disqualify a juror for bias.

AFFIRM

To ratify, establish, or reassert. To make a solemn and formal declaration, as a substitute for an oath, that the statements contained in an affidavit are true or that a witness will tell the truth. In the practice of appellate courts, to declare a judgment, decree, or order valid and to concur in its correctness so that it must stand as rendered in the lower court. As a matter of pleading, to allege or aver a matter of fact.

A judgment, decree, or order that is not affirmed is either remanded (sent back to the lower court with instructions to correct the irregularities noted in the appellate opinion) or reversed (changed by the appellate court so that the decision of the lower court is overturned).

AFFIRMANCE

A declaration by an appellate court that a judgment, order, or decree of a lower court that *has been brought before it for review is valid and will be upheld.*

AFFIRMATION

A solemn and formal declaration of the truth of a statement, such as an affidavit or the actual or prospective testimony of a witness or a party that takes the place of an oath. An affirmation is also used when a person cannot take an oath because of religious convictions.

AFFIRMATIVE ACTION

Employment programs required by federal statutes and regulations designed to remedy discriminatory practices in hiring minority group members; i.e., positive steps designed to eliminate existing and continuing discrimination, to remedy lingering effects of past discrimination, and to create systems and procedures to prevent future discrimination; commonly based on population percentages of minority groups in a particular area. Factors considered are race, color, sex, creed, and age.

The idea of affirmative action was foreshadowed as early as the Reconstruction Era, which followed the U.S. CIVIL WAR. When that conflict ended, the former slave population throughout the South owned virtually nothing and had only a limited set of skills with which they could make a living. To help these newly emancipated citizens sustain a minimal economic base, the victorious

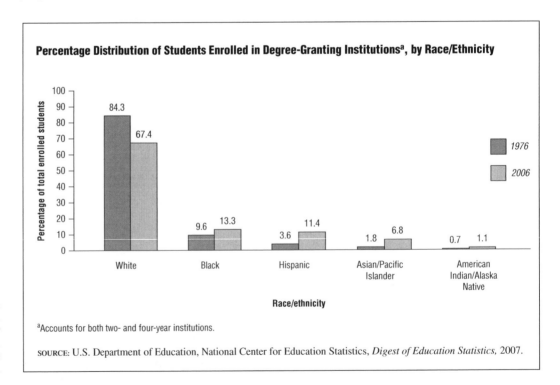

Percentage Distribution of Students Enrolled in Degree-Granting Institutions[a], by Race/Ethnicity

[a]Accounts for both two- and four-year institutions.

SOURCE: U.S. Department of Education, National Center for Education Statistics, *Digest of Education Statistics,* 2007.

General William T. Sherman proposed to divide up the land and goods from the sizable plantations of southeastern Georgia that were under his command and grant to each family of color "40 acres and a mule." The proposal ran into powerful political opposition, however, and it was never widely adopted.

Nearly a century later, this idea of assisting whole classes of individuals to gain access to the goods of U.S. life reemerged in U.S. law and society through a series of court decisions and political initiatives interpreting the CIVIL RIGHTS guarantees within the EQUAL PROTECTION Clause of the FOURTEENTH AMENDMENT. These decisions and initiatives came to be known as affirmative action.

The term itself refers to both mandatory and voluntary programs intended to *affirm* the civil rights of designated classes of individuals by taking positive *action* to protect them from, in the words of Justice William J. Brennan Jr., "the lingering effects of pervasive discrimination" (*Local 28 of the Sheet Metal Workers' International Association v. EEOC*, 478 U.S. 421, 106 S. Ct. 3019, 92 L. Ed. 2d 344 [1986]). A law school, for example, might voluntarily take affirmative action to find and admit qualified students of color. An employer might recruit qualified women where only men have worked before, such as businesses that operate heavy equipment.

Affirmative action developed during the four decades following the decision in *Brown v. Board of Education*, 347 U.S. 483, 74 S. Ct. 686, 98 L. Ed. 873 (1954). In *Brown*, the Supreme Court held that public school SEGREGATION of children by race denied minority children equal educational opportunities, rejecting the doctrine of "separate but equal" in the public education context. During the 1960s and early 1970s, the CIVIL RIGHTS MOVEMENT as well as the VIETNAM WAR inspired members of minorities and women to advocate collectively for increased equality and opportunity within U.S. society. These groups appealed for equal rights under the Fourteenth Amendment, and they sought opportunity in the public arenas of education and employment. In many ways, they were successful. As affirmative action grew, however, it drew increasing criticism, often from men and whites, who opposed what they viewed as "reverse discrimination."

While the *Brown* decision declared segregated schools unlawful, it did not create affirmative action to remedy discriminatory practices. A decade after *Brown*, little had changed to integrate the nation's schools. The Court acted ahead of business executives and legislatures when it mandated, in *Green v. County School Board*, 391 U.S. 430, 88 S. Ct. 1689, 20 L. Ed. 2d 716 (1968), that positive actions must be taken to integrate schools. There followed the adoption of an array of devices such as redistricting, majority-to-minority transfers, school pairings, magnet schools, busing, new construction, and abandonment of all-black schools.

The first major legal setback for voluntary affirmation action was the decision in *Regents of the University of California v. Bakke*, 438 U.S. 265, 98 S. Ct. 2733, 57 L. Ed. 2d 750 (1978), in which the Supreme Court struck down an admissions plan at the University of California, Davis, medical school. The plan, which had SET ASIDE 16 places for minority applicants, was challenged by white applicant Allan Bakke, who had been refused admission even though he had higher test scores than some of the minority applicants. The Court held that by setting aside a specific number, or quota, of places by race, the school had violated Bakke's civil rights. By denying the "set-aside" practice of an affirmative action plan, the decision seemed to threaten the principle underlying affirmative action as well.

The following year, however, the Court found in *United Steelworkers v. Weber*, 443 U.S. 193, 99 S. Ct. 2721, 61 L. Ed. 2d 480 (1979), that the voluntary plan of Kaiser Aluminum Company to promote some of its black workers into a special training program ahead of more senior white workers did *not* violate the latter's civil rights when it did not involve quotas. The Court also found in *Local 28 of Sheet Metal Workers' International Association v. EEOC*, 478 U.S. 421, 106 S. Ct. 3019, 92 L. Ed. 2d 344 (1986), that rights were not being violated by a court-ordered membership goal of 29.23 percent minorities. Writing for the PLURALITY, Justice Brennan said Title VII of the Civil Rights Act of 1964 does not prohibit courts from ordering "affirmative race-conscious relief as a remedy for past discrimination" in appropriate circumstances. Such circumstances might include "where an employer or LABOR UNION has engaged in persistent or egregious DISCRIMINATION, or where necessary to dissipate the lingering effect of pervasive discrimination."

The Court later found, in *City of Richmond v. J.A. Croson Co.*, 488 U.S. 469, 109 S. Ct. 706, 102 L. Ed. 2d 854 (1989), that the Minority Business

HOW MUCH AFFIRMATIVE ACTION IS ENOUGH AFFIRMATIVE ACTION?

In the combustive debate over affirmative action, fairness is the hottest issue of all. Most people agree that employers should hire and promote people fairly. Does affirmative action make this happen? Americans disagree sharply: A July 1995 Associated Press poll found that 39 percent think it does, but 48 percent said giving preference to women and minorities produces even greater unfairness. These numbers barely scratch the surface of the antagonisms in a debate now more than 30 years old. Proponents argue that the benefits of affirmative action policies are TANGIBLE, deserved, and necessary. Opponents reply that these benefits hide the real harm done by affirmative action: rewarding the wrong people, devaluing the idea of merit, and punishing white men. The two sides disagree on what should be done, yet there is no shortage of ideas. In the 1990s a flurry of arguments came from politicians, academics, CIVIL RIGHTS leaders, and reformers that are aimed at preserving, modifying, or ending affirmative action.

History has drastically rewritten the terms of this debate. In the years of great advances in federal civil rights, Presidents JOHN F. KENNEDY and LYNDON B. JOHNSON could easily frame the issue as a purely moral one. Johnson put it this way in 1965:

> Freedom is not enough.... You do not take a man who for years has been hobbled by chains, liberate him, bring him to the starting line of a race, saying, "you are free to compete with all the others," and still justly believe you have been completely fair. Thus it is not enough to open the gates of opportunity.

Thirty years later, Senate majority leader Bob Dole (R-Kan.) made this widely quoted attack: "The race-counting game has gone too far." Polls indicate that both Johnson and Dole spoke for a majority of citizens of their time. Johnson captured the essence of a nation willing to move beyond the legacy of JIM CROW LAWS. Dole summoned the resentment of white males who had seen the affirmative action net expand to hold not only minorities but also women and immigrants. But white men are hardly the only complainers: According to a March 1995 *Washington Post*-ABC News poll, 79 percent of middle-class white women oppose preferences for women.

For affirmative action's strongest supporters, explaining the new harshness in the policy's politics is a matter of going back to the beginning. They point out that affirmative action was never supposed to be painless. Making room for groups that have historically suffered DISCRIMINATION means that the very group that did not suffer—white males—now has to do so. This can be characterized as the sins-of-the-fathers argument, illustrated in a 1995 briefing paper from the AMERICAN CIVIL LIBERTIES UNION (ACLU): "[W]hile it's true that white males in any given era may not all have been responsible for excluding people of color and women, all white males have benefited unjustly from that historical exclusion ... [thus enjoying] privileged status and an unfair advantage." This position is supported by statistics: in 1995 white males held nearly 95 percent of senior management positions in major corporations, earned 25 to 45 percent more than women and minorities, and held well over 80 percent of the seats in Congress. On the other hand, from 1973 to 1993, black poverty increased from 31.4 to 33.1 percent. Without doubt, discrimination continues; from the perspective of supporters of affirmative action, the sins of the fathers are far from paid for.

Utilization Plan of Richmond, Virginia, violated the rights of private contractors. The plan, which required 30 percent of all subcontracts to be awarded to minority-owned companies, was struck down because this municipality had failed to show compelling STATE INTEREST for such a measure. The Court applied the compelling interest test after holding that race-based action by state and local government was subject to STRICT SCRUTINY. The Court extended this to the federal government in *Adarand Constructors, Inc. v. Pena*, 115 S. Ct. 2097, 132 L. Ed. 2d 158 (1995).

In *Johnson v. Transportation Agency*, 480 U.S. 616, 107 S. Ct. 1442, 94 L. Ed. 2d 615 (1987), the Court ruled that a county agency had not violated Title VII of the Civil Rights Act when, as part of an affirmative action plan, it took a female employee's gender into account in promoting her ahead of a male employee with a slightly higher test score. The Court held that a "manifest imbalance" existed in this workforce because of an underrepresentation of women, and that the employer had acted properly in using a "moderate, flexible, case-by-case approach to effecting a gradual improvement in the representation of minorities and women."

At issue in affirmative action cases is whether the Equal Protection Clause of the Fourteenth Amendment can be employed to advance the welfare of one class of individuals

Because equality still eludes the beneficiaries of affirmative action, supporters dismiss attacks on the policies as part of a backlash. Three decades of advances for affirmative action's beneficiaries have meant diminished dominance for white men, a group whose income has been falling in real terms since 1973. But, supporters say, the reason white men earn less today than their fathers did is not the fault of affirmative action. They point to long-term changes in the U.S. economy and job market as the real explanations for stagnating incomes, diminishing buying power, and decreasing job security. Yet affirmative action gets the blame. "We are the ultimate scapegoat for whatever goes wrong," Mary Frances Berry, chairwoman of the U.S. COMMISSION ON CIVIL RIGHTS, told the *Boston Globe* in 1995. Dwindling support from middle-class white women also draws the ire of affirmative action's advocates. "In the 1970s and 80s, white women had no problem hitching up to the affirmative action banner of 'women and minorities,'" journalist Derrick Z. Jackson wrote. "If they now want to rip down the banner, it will confirm the dirtiest little secret of all about affirmative action"— that white women supported it only to the extent that it benefited themselves.

Dismissing these explanations as excuses, critics of affirmative action denounce it as "reverse discrimination." They either reject outright the idea that historical wrongs can be redressed through contemporary means, or believe that the cost to those who must pay for such redress is too high. Conservative think tanks such as the Institute for Justice and the HERITAGE FOUNDATION regularly lead this prong of the attack. Clint Bolick, the Institute for Justice's vice president, told *Congressional Quarterly*, "If you add up the number of people who have encountered reverse discrimination in college admissions, scholarships, public school magnet programs, government contracts and jobs in the private and public sectors, you have a pretty sizable population." The charge strikes the strongest advocates of affirmative action as insupportable. According to the research of law professor Alfred Blumrosen, of Rutgers University, only a few dozen such cases reached the federal courts in the early 1990s, and in most, the PLAINTIFF failed. Other advocates see the reverse discrimination argument as sour grapes; the ACLU goes so far as to call it a smoke screen "for retention of white male privilege."

Critics frequently argue that affirmative action does an injustice to the idea of merit. Organizations representing police officers and firefighters, such as the national Fraternal Order of Police, complain that qualifications and standards have fallen to accommodate affirmative action candidates. This criticism is popular not only with whites, who have long claimed that better qualified candidates lose out as a result of affirmative action, but also with two leading conservative African American critics. "What we've had to do for 25 years to pull off affirmative action," the author Shelby Steele said, "is demean the idea of merit." The economist Thomas Sowell advances much the same argument in his claim that the policy hurts African Americans. Like other conservatives, Sowell ties the rise of affirmative action in the 1970s to the development of the black economic underclass. Steele and Sowell have argued that affirmative action sets up its beneficiaries for failure, corrupting the value of achievement for blacks and reinforcing racist stereotypes for whites. Viewing affirmative action as antidemocratic, they conclude that individual qualities alone should determine who is hired or accepted into an academic program.

Advocates are highly suspicious of the merit argument. In the first place, they deny that creating opportunities ignores the value of personal merit. Voluntary affirmative action merely gives people who traditionally have been excluded a leg up, they assert; and when it is court ordered to redress a pattern of workplace discrimination, the question of merit misses the point. More crucially, supporters think the merit line is superficial. Political commentator Michael E. Kinsley quipped that critics "seem to imagine that everyone in America can be ranked with scientific precision, from No. 1 to No. 260,000,000, in terms of his or her qualification for any desirable career opportunity." He and other

for compelling social reasons even when that advancement may infringe in some way upon the life or liberty of another. The continuing existence of affirmative action laws and programs suggests that, so far, the Supreme Court's answer has been yes.

Affirmative action plans may be undertaken voluntarily, as in the case of a private school's admissions goals; imposed by the courts to protect civil rights; or required by law to qualify for federal contracts. Plans required to qualify for federal contracts are enforced by the Office of Federal Contract Compliance Programs (OFCCP), an agency of the U.S. LABOR DEPARTMENT. The OFCCP defines its mission with its critics in mind: "Affirmative action is not preferential treatment. Nor does it mean that unqualified persons should be hired or promoted over other people. What affirmative action does mean is that positive steps must be taken to provide equal employment opportunity" (EEOC, U.S. Labor Department, Pub. No. 2850, *Making EEO and Affirmative Action Work* 8 [1993]). One ranking OFCCP administrator defended the program even more sharply by saying, "Affirmative action is not about goals and has nothing to do with preferences. It is about inclusion versus exclusion: people who have been excluded from participation in the process for years are now to be included."

HOW MUCH AFFIRMATIVE ACTION IS ENOUGH AFFIRMATIVE ACTION?
(CONTINUED)

supporters consider the argument specious in a society in which merit is often the last reason for success and other variables that give advantages to certain groups are deemed perfectly natural—the children of the rich attend the best schools regardless of their abilities, for example, and military veterans receive preferences whether or not they have personally sacrificed anything for the nation. The United States was never a meritocracy, asserts Laura Murphy Lee, director of the ACLU's national legislative office: "Affirmative action didn't come along to taint a process that never existed."

Proposals for reforming affirmative action became increasingly popular in the mid-1990s. At one extreme, politicians have called for dumping it altogether. This idea has been urged in Congress chiefly by ultraconservative Republicans such as Senators Phil Gramm (R-Tex.) and JESSE HELMS (R-N.C.). Although no action has been taken on the congressional level, similar proposals in the states of California and Florida have gained ground. California reformers scored two victories in the mid-1990's: First, in 1995, regents of the University of California, *Regents of Univ. of Cal. v. Bakke*, 438 U.S. 265, 98 S. Ct. 2733, 57 L. Ed. 2d 750

(1980) dropped gender- and race-based admissions, hiring, and contracting. Then, reformers succeeded in passing an anti-affirmative action referendum—the California Civil Rights Initiative, a measure that would outlaw gender- and race-based preferences in government programs—in 1996. A similar REFERENDUM passed in Washington State in 1998.

Less radical and perhaps more politically feasible, another proposal calls for preserving affirmative action while shifting its emphasis. The idea would abandon race and gender as yardsticks and match preferences solely with economic need. Conservatives again lead this campaign, but it draws some support even from moderates: President BILL CLINTON, declaring that his administration was against quotas and guaranteed results, ordered a review of federal employment policies in 1995 to ensure that they were being applied fairly. Critics of affirmative action believe that this kind of reform would ensure opportunity for disadvantaged people while ending what they see as egregious abuses, such as the awarding of contracts to rich minority-owned businesses. Traditional supporters agree that affirmative action benefits do not always help the people who

most need them. But they believe that substantial gains should not be reversed, and that any need-based measurement should only augment—not replace—existing policies.

The journey of affirmative action from its heyday to the present reflects great changes in the United States. Between the administration of President Johnson and the Republican-controlled Congress elected in 1994 lies a thirty-year experience with GREAT SOCIETY initiatives that has left many citizens soured on the idea of government assistance. Radical changes in the nation's economy and workforce have surely not made the journey any easier. Bridging this gap seems unlikely, given the vastly different history of white males on the one hand, and women and people of color on the other. From these two poles of experience, two opposing ideas of necessity emerge. Critics say the time is ripe to overhaul affirmative action, a well-intentioned policy gone bad. Supporters, perceiving a playing field that is still far from level, maintain that the real work of affirmative action has scarcely begun.

In the early 2000s, the battlefield for affirmative action has shifted from

Affirmation action plans are subject to mandatory compliance procedures, which may include monitoring by review, conciliation of disputes, exclusion from federal contract work, or even suit by the DEPARTMENT OF JUSTICE.

Criticism of affirmative action has been constant since the Supreme Court first articulated its views. By the 1990s, opponents began to press the Court to reverse its precedents both in employment and in higher education admission policies. Supporters of affirmative action openly worried that the Court would severely restrict affirmative action. For example, in 1997,

the Court was scheduled to hear an appeal involving a New Jersey schoolteacher who claimed she had suffered discrimination because of an improper affirmative action plan (*Taxman v. Piscataway Township Board of Education*, 91 F.3d 1547 [3d. Cir. 1996]). Weeks before oral argument, supporters of affirmative action made the schoolteacher a financial SETTLEMENT in return for her dismissing the case. They admitted that this was hardly a victory, but supporters pointed to troubling developments.

One of these developments was the Supreme Court's refusal to review a decision that struck

the workplace to education. Higher education—the arena that gave birth to *Bakke*, the first significant Supreme Court decision endorsing affirmative action—has more recently produced a mishmash of court decisions and laws that have called into question the future of affirmative action. There were arguments not just how *Bakke* should be applied, but whether it should be applied at all.

Higher education has been a particularly contentious area on affirmative action for many reasons. Because many higher education institutions are public, there is an issue of whether taxpayer money should be going to institutions supporting affirmative action. The public status of colleges and universities also ensures that affirmative action debates will be conducted out in the open. Also, the quality and prestige of a college or university is often seen as determining where someone will end up on the socioeconomic scale after graduation, making the affirmative action stakes at such institutions high.

In a reversal of the way they tolerated discrimination through most of the twentieth century, many colleges and universities now seem anxious to employ affirmative action to increase the diversity of their campuses. Court cases litigating affirmative action in higher education are brought by disgruntled white students and parents claiming "reverse discrimination." It has been the courts and the

legislatures, not the colleges and the universities, that have shown willingness to put the brakes on affirmative action.

The battle over *Bakke* and its effects on higher education swung into focus in 1996, when the 5th CIRCUIT COURT of Appeals struck down affirmative action in college admissions in their decision *Hopwood v. Texas*, 78 F.3d 932, 5th Cir. (Tex. 1996). The decision covered institutions in the states of Texas, Louisiana, and Mississippi. Within a year of that ruling, enrollments by minorities in higher education institutions dropped in all three states.

In response, the state of Texas guaranteed a place in a state university or college to anyone who had graduated in the top 10 percent of their class. This gave more minorities a chance, and as a result minority enrollment at higher education institutions in the state was higher in 2001 than it was in the year before *Hopwood*. Several other states, including California and Florida, have adopted versions of Texas' "10 percent" solution. Critics have charged that these programs are inadequate, failing to ensure that minorities are represented at the most prestigious institutions even when they do boost enrollment in state university systems overall.

The affirmative action focus in higher education has shifted over to the University of Michigan. White applicants to both the undergraduate school and the

law school at the University of Michigan sued on reverse discrimination grounds. One U.S. district judge in Michigan upheld the undergraduate program, and another struck down the law school program. A divided Sixth Circuit Court of Appeals ruled in favor of the program in *Grutter v. Bollinger*, 288 F.3d 732, 6th Cir. (Mich. 2002) and the U.S Supreme Court agreed to hear the appeal of that decision. The Court upheld its decision in 2003.

The administration of GEORGE W. BUSH filed a brief opposing Michigan's affirmative action program. "The method used by the University of Michigan to achieve this important goal is fundamentally flawed," said President Bush in statement. Defending the policy, Michigan President Mary Sue Coleman said the President "misunderstands how our admission process works" and denied it was unconstitutional. Who the Supreme Court decides is right may decide the future of affirmative action in America.

FURTHER READINGS

Buchanan, Sidney. 2002. "Affirmative Action: The Many Shades of Justice." *Houston Law Review* 39 (summer).

"Coloring the Campus." 2001. *Time Magazine* (September 17).

Goldstein, Amy, and Dana Milbank. 2003. "Bush Joins Admissions Case Fight; U-Mich. Use of Race Is Called 'Divisive'." *Washington Post* (January 16).

down a university admission plan that used race as one factor for acceptance. In *Hopwood v. Texas*, 78 F. 3d. 932 (5th Cir. 1996), the U.S. Court of Appeals for the Fifth Circuit ruled that the practice of providing preferential treatment to minorities in a public university's admissions policy was repugnant to the Constitution.

The University of Texas Law School implemented an admissions policy in which the standards for admission were lowered for minorities. The school employed an index (called the Texas Index, or TI) that combined standardized test scores with grade-point averages. A minimum score for acceptance was ten points higher for whites than for non-whites. The appeals court

found problems with the structure of the TI. While minorities, specifically African Americans and Mexican Americans, earned scores sufficient to be categorized as "presumptive admits" (i.e.,-certain to be accepted), whites who received the same scores were categorized as "presumptive denials" (i.e., certain to be rejected). The court invalidated the admissions policy, concluding that using race as a criteria for admissions is as arbitrary as using one's blood type.

In *Grutter v. Bollinger*, 539 U.S. 306, 123 S. Ct. 2325, 156 L.Ed.2d 304, the U.S. Supreme Court narrowly endorsed the use of race in choosing students for America's top universities and the concept of racial diversity as a compelling governmental interest. In a LANDMARK decision with wide-ranging implications for affirmative action programs across the United States, the Court ruled that it does not violate the Equal Protection Clause to give some preferential treatment to disadvantaged minorities, calling the diversity that minorities bring to education, business, and the military necessary for the cultivation of "a set of leaders with legitimacy in the eyes of the citizenry." In that case, the Court held that promoting racial diversity on campuses not only serves a compelling government interest, but also that the law school's admissions program was narrowly tailored and focused on each applicant as an individual as opposed to being a member of a particular racial group. However, the victory for affirmative action was conditional, as the Court emphasized that racial preferences should be a temporary, rather than permanent, fixture in American society, and called for "periodic reviews" and "sunset provisions" for race-conscious admissions.

In the 5–4 decision, written by Justice Sandra Day O'Connor and joined by joined by Justices JOHN PAUL STEVENS, DAVID SOUTER, RUTH BADER GINSBURG, and STEPHEN BREYER, the Court ruled that attaining a diverse student body is at the heart of a law school's proper institutional mission, and that GOOD FAITH on the part of a university in pursuing diversity should be presumed absent a showing to the contrary.

The Supreme Court emphasized that the law school sought to enroll a "critical mass" of minority students, not simply to ensure that its student body had some specified percentage of a particular group. In concluding that the law school's admissions policy was narrowly tailored, the Supreme Court stated that the policy did not operate as a quota, but used race as a "plus" factor, such that the policy was flexible enough to ensure that each applicant was evaluated as an individual.

The PLAINTIFF was a white Michigan resident whose application was rejected by the law school. She alleged that her application was denied because the law school used race as a "predominant factor." A district court agreed with the plaintiff, but the U.S. Court of Appeals for the Sixth Circuit reversed.

In *Gratz v. Bollinger*, a separate 6–3 decision handed down the same day as *Grutter v. Bollinger*, the Court struck down a separate University of Michigan undergraduate-admissions process based on a point system that rated students and awarded additional points to minorities. Because the admissions process made race a "decisive" factor, rather than just one of many in determining who was admitted, the Court ruled that the formulaic approach was unconstitutional. *Gratz v. Bollinger*, 539 U.S. 244, 123 S. Ct. 2411, 156 L. Ed.2d 257. The opinion was delivered by Chief Justice WILLIAM REHNQUIST, who was joined by Justices O'Connor, ANTONIN SCALIA, ANTHONY KENNEDY, and CLARENCE THOMAS.

This point-system ruling is expected to force state schools that use similar numerical methods to revise them, and it could cause companies to rethink their reliance on quantitative evaluations of job applicants and employees. Although Michigan is a public university, the decision is considered likely to apply to selective private universities as well, because they receive government funding. It also will affect admissions practices at selective public high schools where affirmative action has also been eliminated or curtailed.

Distaste for affirmative action also led opponents to attack the policy at the state level through ballot initiatives and referendums. In November 1998 the California electorate passed Proposition 209 (54 to 46 percent), which banned many of the affirmative action programs in California. The REFERENDUM was promoted by the nonprofit Center for Individual Rights, which was also instrumental in building opposition to the University of Texas admissions policy that was struck down in *Hopwood*. The proposition has remained a controversial topic, with supporters arguing that state and local officials have avoided dismantling affirmative action. These same supporters continue to call on state officials to enforce the law. Officials, however, have pointed out that under the proposition, when federal laws mandate affirmative action to qualify for federal monies, the state law must give way.

In 1998 Washington State passed Initiative 200 and became the second state to abolish state affirmative action measures. The initiative is similar to that of California's Proposition 209.

In 2000 Florida became the first state to voluntarily end affirmative action in higher education and state contracts. Public universities put into place new college admissions policies that prohibit affirmative action. One new component was the Talented 20 Plan, which mandates that students who graduate in the top 20 percent of their class and who complete a college preparatory curriculum must be admitted into one of the ten state universities. These changes were designed to increase opportunity and diversity while ending racial preferences and set-asides.

On June 28, 2007, the Supreme Court issued a landmark decision in two joined cases involving race and public school systems. In *Meredith v. Jefferson County Board of Education*, and *Parents Involved in Community Schools v. Seattle School District No. 1*, the Court ruled that race cannot be a factor in assigning children to a particular public school. In both cases, the school districts used race as the primary factor in determining which school the students would attend in order to maintain some level of racial integration in the school districts. Chief Justice JOHN ROBERTS, writing for the majority, argued that racial integration does not justify assigning students to a school based on the racial category under which they fall. He further stated that "the way to stop discrimination on the basis of race is to stop discriminating on the basis of race."

The fate of affirmative action in this country is unclear. In November 2008 two states, Nebraska and Colorado, had ballot measures proposing to ban affirmative action preferences by public entities. The ban passed in Nebraska with more than 50 percent of the vote, whereas Colorado voters rejected the ban.

FURTHER READINGS

"Affirmative Action." 1995. *CQ Researcher*. April 28.

American Civil Liberties Union. 1995. *Affirmative Action*. Briefing paper no. 17, March 22.

American Civil Liberties Union. 1995. *The Case for Affirmative Action*. July 1.

Clinton, President Bill. 1995. Speech at the National Archives, July 31.

Coyle, Marcia. 2003. "The Fallout Begins: In Its Final Week of the Term, the Supreme Court Hands Down Landmark Rulings That Give Legal Backing to Two Kinds of Diversity; Affirmative Action and Gay Rights." *The National Law Journal* 25 (July 7).

Curry, George E., and Cornel West, eds. 1996. *The Affirmative Action Debate*. New York: Perseus.

Landsberg, Brian K. 2003. "Affirmative-Action Decision Indicated Shifts in Position." *The Los Angeles Daily Journal* 116 (June 30).

Marin, Patricia, and Catherine L. Horn, eds. 2008. *Realizing Bakke's Legacy: Affirmative Action, Equal Opportunity, and Access to Higher Education*. Sterling, VA: Stylus Publishing.

Rubio, Philip F. 2001. *A History of Affirmative Action, 1619–2000*. Oxford: University Press of Mississippi.

Schmidt, Peter. "Supreme Court Leaves Affirmative-Action Precedents Intact in Striking Down School-Integration Plans." The Chronicle of Higher Education. Available online at http://chronicle.com/cgi2-bin/printable.cgi?article=http://chronicle.com/free/2007/06/2007062901n.htm; website home page: http://chronicle.com (accessed July 7, 2009).

Mears, Bill. "Divided Court rejects school diversity plans." Available online at http://cnn.com/2007/LAW/06/28/scouts.race/index.html (accessed July 7, 2009).

Brunner, Borga. "Timeline of Affirmative Action Milestones." Available online at http://www.infoplease.com/spot/affirmativetimeline1.html; website home page: http://www.infoplease.com (accessed July 7, 2009).

CROSS REFERENCES

Civil Rights Acts; Equal Employment Opportunity Commission; Seniority; Sex Discrimination.

AFFIRMATIVE DEFENSE

A new fact or set of facts that operates to defeat a claim even if the facts supporting that claim are true.

A PLAINTIFF sets forth a claim in a CIVIL ACTION by making statements in the document called the complaint. These statements must be sufficient to warrant relief from the court. The DEFENDANT responds to the plaintiff's claims by preparing an answer in which the defendant may deny the truth of the plaintiff's allegations or assert that there are additional facts that constitute a defense to the plaintiff's action. For example, a plaintiff may demand compensation for damage done to his or her vehicle in an automobile accident. Without denying responsibility for the accident, the defendant may claim to have an affirmative defense, such as the plaintiff's contributory NEGLIGENCE or expiration of the STATUTE OF LIMITATIONS.

An affirmative defense is also allowed under rules of CRIMINAL PROCEDURE. For example, a defendant accused of ASSAULT may claim to have been intoxicated or insane, to have struck out in SELF-DEFENSE, or to have had an alibi for the night in question. Any one of these affirmative defenses must be asserted by showing that there are facts in addition to the ones in the INDICTMENT or information charging the defendant and that those additional facts are legally sufficient to excuse the defendant.

The rules that govern pleading in most courts require a defendant to raise all affirmative defenses when first responding to the civil claim or criminal charges against him or her. Failure to do so may preclude assertion of that kind of defense later in the trial.

AFFRAY

A criminal offense generally defined as the fighting of two or more persons in a public place that disturbs others.

The offense originated under the COMMON LAW and in some jurisdictions has become a statutory crime. Although an agreement to fight is not an element of the crime under the common-law definition, some statutes provide that an affray can occur only when two or more persons agree to fight in a public place.

An affray is a type of DISORDERLY CONDUCT and a BREACH OF THE PEACE since it is conduct that disturbs the peace of the community. It is punishable by a fine, IMPRISONMENT, or both.

AFORESAID

Before, already said, referred to, or recited.

This term is used frequently in deeds, leases, and contracts of sale of real property to refer to the property without describing it in detail each time it is mentioned; for example, "the aforesaid premises."

AFORETHOUGHT

In criminal law, intentional, deliberate, planned, or premeditated.

MURDER in the first degree, for example, requires MALICE AFORETHOUGHT; that is, the murder must have been planned for a period of time, regardless how short, before it was committed.

AFTER-ACQUIRED PROPERTY CLAUSE

A phrase in a mortgage (an interest in land that furnishes security for payment of a debt or performance of an obligation) that provides that any holdings obtained by the borrower subsequent to the date of the loan and mortgage will automatically constitute additional security for the loan.

AFTER-ACQUIRED TITLE

A legal doctrine under which, if a grantor conveys what is mistakenly believed to be good title to land that he or she did not own, and the grantor later acquires that title, it vests automatically in the grantee.

AFTER-BORN CHILD

A child born after a will has been executed by either parent or after the time in which a class gift made according to a trust arrangement expires.

The existence of an after-born child has significant legal ramifications upon gifts made under wills and trusts. Under the law of wills, the birth of an after-born child after the parent makes a will does not revoke it but has the effect of modifying its provisions. Generally, the after-born child must be given the share of the parent's estate that the child would have been entitled to if the parent had died without leaving a will, according to the law of DESCENT AND DISTRIBUTION. The beneficiaries of the will must contribute a proportionate share of what they inherited to make up the after-born child's share.

Under the law of trusts, a gift to a class is one in which the creator of the trust, the SETTLOR, directs that the principal of the trust should be distributed to a specifically designated group of persons, such as to grandchildren, who are alive at a certain time, such as at the settlor's death. Any child born after this time would not be entitled to a proportionate share of the trust

---

Security Agreement with an After-Acquired Property Clause

This Security Agreement is made on this_____day of _____, 20 _____

between _____ , _____ , _____

[*name and address of the debtor*] ("Debtor"), and _____ , _____ ,

_____ [*name and address of secured party*] ("Secured Party").

　1.　**SECURITY INTEREST**. Debtor grants to Secured Party a security interest in all inventory, equipment, appliances, furnishings, and

fixtures placed upon the premises known as _____ , located at _____ ,

_____ (the "Premises") or used in connection therewith and in which Debtor now has or hereafter acquires any right and the proceeds therefrom. The security interest of Secured Party extends to all collateral of the kind which is the subject of this agreement which the debtor may acquire at any time during the continuation of this agreement. The Security Interest shall

secure the payment and performance of Debtor's promissory note of even date herewith in the principal amount of _____
[*amount of payment*] Dollars and the payment and performance of all liabilities and obligations of Debtor to Secured Party of every kind and description, direct or indirect, absolute or contingent, due or to become due now existing or hereafter arising.

[Portions omitted for purposes of illustration]

An example of how an after-acquired property clause might be used

ILLUSTRATION BY GGS CREATIVE RESOURCES. REPRODUCED BY PERMISSION OF GALE, A PART OF CENGAGE LEARNING.

principal unless conceived before the settlor died. An after-born child born eleven months after the settlor's death, therefore, would not share in the principal, since the class had closed nine months after the settlor's death.

AGE DISCRIMINATION

Prejudicial treatment or denial of rights based on age.

As the baby boom generation, the largest demographic group in U.S. history, reached middle age and looked toward retirement, laws governing the treatment of older U.S. citizens took on greater importance than ever before. Between 1970 and 1991, the number of workers over the age of 40 in the U.S. workforce rose from 39,689,000 to 53,940,000. It is no surprise, then, that major developments, both legislative and judicial, occurred in the area of age discrimination in employment.

Congress outlawed DISCRIMINATION by employers against employees or applicants over the age of 40, with the Age Discrimination in Employment Act of 1967 (ADEA) (29 U.S.C.A. § 621 et seq.). Amendments to the act in 1974, 1978, and 1986 (29 U.S.C.A. § 623 et seq.) raised and then eliminated the mandatory retirement age for most workers and extended the act's coverage to most employers. The ADEA does permit employers to set maximum age limits for employees if the employer can show that age is a bona fide occupational qualification (BFOQ) and is reasonably necessary for the operation of the business. Although the ADEA did not originally apply to government employers, Congress extended the act to cover federal, state, and local governments in 1974. However, it no longer applies to state governments.

The EQUAL EMPLOYMENT OPPORTUNITY COMMISSION (EEOC) is charged with enforcing the ADEA. Complainants must first file a claim with the EEOC or their state's employment or HUMAN RIGHTS commission before pursuing a lawsuit. The EEOC attempts to resolve the dispute through voluntary compliance on the part of the employer, conciliation, or other persuasive measures. If the EEOC decides to bring an action against the employer, the employee's right to sue is extinguished. However, the employee need not exhaust his or her administrative remedies—that is, wait for a final determination from the EEOC—before filing suit. In fact, on February 27, 2008, the Supreme Court in *Federal Express Corp. v. Holowecki*, 552 U.S. ___, 128 S. Ct. 1147, addressed the issue of whether the intake questionnaire, or the specific complaint form that aggrieved employees are required to file with the EEOC prior to filing a lawsuit against their

Employers may not require the retirement of a worker unless they can demonstrate that the employee's age is relevant to the operation of the business.

AP IMAGES

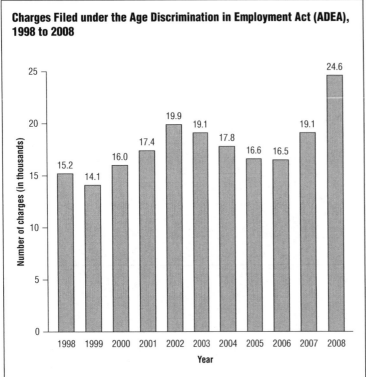

Charges Filed under the Age Discrimination in Employment Act (ADEA), 1998 to 2008

SOURCE: U.S. Equal Employment Opportunity Commission, "Enforcement Statistics and Litigation," available online at http://www.eeoc.gov/stats/enforcement.html (accessed on August 12, 2009).

ILLUSTRATION BY GGS CREATIVE RESOURCES. REPRODUCED BY PERMISSION OF GALE, A PART OF CENGAGE LEARNING.

employers, can serve as a "charge" or basis for a lawsuit under the ADEA. Under the ADEA, the employees are required to wait 60 days after filing their formal complaint with the EEOC before they can file a lawsuit. In this case, the PLAINTIFF filed her intake questionnaire and had attached to it a six-page sworn AFFIDAVIT outlining her allegations of discrimination. Then, after the 60-day waiting period, she filed her lawsuit with the court. Federal Express moved to dismiss her case, arguing that her intake questionnaire was not a formal "charge" alleging discrimination under the ADEA; and thus she filed her lawsuit prematurely, prior to the expiration of the 60-day waiting period. In a ruling for the plaintiff, the Supreme Court held that the formal intake questionnaire constituted a formal charge of discrimination under the ADEA.

Landmark Discrimination Cases

A number of LANDMARK cases have interpreted the ADEA since its passage. *Western Air Lines v. Criswell,* 472 U.S. 400, 105 S. Ct. 2743, 86 L. Ed. 2d 321 (1985), set out the guidelines for defending an age limit based on the BFOQ exception. Western required flight engineers,

who are members of the flight crew but generally do not operate flight controls, to retire at age 60. When this policy was challenged, the airline maintained that the age limit was a BFOQ necessary to ensure safety. The Supreme Court disagreed and in a unanimous decision announced a two-pronged test to be applied when evaluating a BFOQ based on safety: (1) whether the age limit is reasonably necessary to the overriding interest in public safety; and (2) whether the employer is justified in applying the age limit to all employees rather than deciding each case on an individual basis.

In another case the same year, the Supreme Court found TWA guilty of age discrimination for refusing to transfer pilots to the position of flight engineer after they reached age 60, the Federal Aviation Administration's (FAA's) mandatory retirement age for pilots (*Trans World AIRLINES v. Thurston,* 469 U.S. 111, 105 S. Ct. 613, 83 L. Ed. 2d 523 [1985]). TWA had allowed younger pilots who had become disabled to transfer automatically to the position of flight engineer, but did not allow pilots and copilots past the age of 60 to do the same. The Court held that the airline must give the same opportunity to retiring pilots and copilots as it had given to younger disabled pilots. However, the Court denied the pilots' request for double damages, which are allowed in cases of "willful violation" of the ADEA, stating that a violation is willful only if the employer knew that its conduct was prohibited by the ADEA or showed a "reckless disregard" for whether the act applied.

Older workers seeking redress under the ADEA received mixed opinions in 1989. *Public Employees Retirement System of Ohio v. Betts,* 492 U.S. 158, 109 S. Ct. 2854, 106 L. Ed. 2d 134 (1989), overturned a series of courts of appeals decisions as well as EEOC and LABOR DEPARTMENT regulations that required employers to justify any age-based distinctions in employee benefit plans by showing a "substantial business purpose." *Betts* shifted the BURDEN OF PROOF to the plaintiff to show that the disputed plan was a "subterfuge" for discrimination.

Congressional response to *Betts* was a compromise between employee advocates and business interests. A 1990 amendment to the ADEA, known as the Older Workers Benefit Protection Act (OWBPA) (29 U.S.C.A. § 626), prohibits discrimination against older employees in the provision of fringe benefits unless the benefit differences are due to age-based differences in cost.

Shortly after the *Betts* decision, the Supreme Court relaxed the procedural rules governing class actions alleging age discrimination, in *Hoffmann-LaRoche v. Sperling*, 493 U.S. 165, 110 S. Ct. 482, 107 L. Ed. 2d 480 (1989). The *Sperling* decision made it easier for plaintiffs to join a CLASS ACTION suit against an employer after the suit has been filed.

Waiver Controversy

During the late 1980s and early 1990s, businesses trying to survive in a sluggish economy began reducing their workforces, a practice known as "downsizing." When layoffs or early retirements affected older workers disproportionately, age discrimination claims escalated.

Many companies offered attractive early-retirement packages in return for an employee's WAIVER of rights to any legal claims. During the 1980s, courts generally allowed such waivers as long as the employee's acceptance was knowing and voluntary and the employee received VALUABLE CONSIDERATION in return. In *Cirillo v. Arco Chemical Co.*, 862 F.2d 448 (1988), for example, the U.S. Court of Appeals for the Third Circuit held that because the plaintiff had knowingly and voluntarily signed a waiver of his right to sue, and in return had received a higher-than-average SEVERANCE package, the waiver did not violate the ADEA. Likewise, in *Lancaster v. Buerkle Buick Honda Co.*, 809 F.2d 539, *cert. denied*, 482 U.S. 928, 107 S. Ct. 3212, 96 L. Ed. 2d 699 (1987), the U.S. Court of Appeals for the Eighth Circuit found that the plaintiff, by virtue of his years of business experience, was well equipped to understand the waiver he signed. Similar reasoning prevailed in *Runyan v. National Cash Register Corp.*, 787 F.2d 1039 (6th Cir. 1986) (EN BANC), *cert. denied*, 479 U.S. 850, 107 S. Ct. 178, 93 L. Ed. 2d 114 (1986), where the court upheld a waiver because the employee who signed it was an experienced labor lawyer.

The ADEA specifically recognizes the validity of waivers in the OWBPA and establishes strict guidelines for employers to follow in executing them. The waiver must use simple, understandable language that clearly delineates the terms of the agreement and leaves no question that the employee is giving up any right to pursue a lawsuit (29 U.S.C.A. § 626[f]). Several cases in 1993 and 1994 that invalidated waiver agreements illustrate how important it is for an employer to follow the guidelines to the letter. *Oberg v. Allied Van Lines, Inc.*, 11 F. 3d 679 (7th Cir. 1993), held that a waiver agreement that did

not meet the requirements of the OWBPA was void and could not be ratified even though the employee accepted and retained the severance package offered in exchange for the waiver. The same reasoning applied to invalidate the waiver agreement in *Soliman v. Digital Equipment Corp.*, 869 F. Supp. 65 (D. Mass. 1994).

The Supreme Court has also upheld that employers must follow the LETTER OF THE LAW when asking employees to waive their rights to file an age discrimination complaint in return for severance pay. In *Oubre v. Entergy Operations, Inc.*, 522 U.S. 422, 118 S. Ct. 838, 139 L.Ed.2d 849 (1998), the worker accepted a severance package and signed a release that stated she would not sue the company for any reason related to her termination. She accepted the severance payments but soon after filed an age discrimination lawsuit. The company argued that the release was valid and that she had not attempted to return her severance payments.

The Supreme Court ruled that the company had failed to meet the minimum notice requirements set out in the OWBP. Specifically, the employer had not given the worker enough time to consider her options; it had failed to give her seven days after she signed the release to change her mind; and the release made no specific reference to claims under the ADEA.

ADEA is Further Clarified

Several cases further clarified the application of the ADEA. In *Gilmer v. Interstate/Johnson Lane Corp.*, 500 U.S. 20, 111 S. Ct. 1647, 114 L. Ed. 2d 26 (1991), the Supreme Court upheld compulsory ARBITRATION under the ADEA. When Robert Gilmer was hired by Interstate/Johnson Lane Corporation, he was required to register with the New York Stock Exchange, which compelled him to agree to arbitrate any controversy regarding employment or termination. He was fired at age 62 and filed a complaint with the EEOC. He then filed an age discrimination suit against Interstate, which moved to compel arbitration of the dispute.

In a decision that seems to reflect the Court's growing encouragement of ALTERNATIVE DISPUTE RESOLUTION, Justice BYRON WHITE dismissed Gilmer's arguments that compulsory arbitration was inconsistent with the purposes of the ADEA and that he was in an unequal bargaining position with Interstate. The Court held that an ADEA claim can be subjected to compulsory arbitration without triggering any "inherent conflict" with the ADEA's

AGE DISCRIMINATION: DISPARATE IMPACT

In 1967 Congress passed the Age Discrimination in Employment Act (ADEA), which protects workers age 40 or older from employment DISCRIMINATION based on their age. Anyone who employs 20 or more people is subject to ADEA; it covers hiring, firing, compensation and benefits, training, job assignments, promotions, and layoffs.

Since ADEA's passage, however, there has been a difference of opinion among legal experts about exactly what types of action constitute "discrimination."

There are two approaches that a PLAINTIFF may take when filing an age discrimination suit, *disparate treatment* and DISPARATE IMPACT. In disparate treatment cases, the plaintiff must prove that there was a SPECIFIC INTENT to discriminate based on age. An example would be an employee whose supervisor keeps saying in front of other staffers, "Are you sure you're still able to do this work?" or "Don't you think it's time you retired?" Disparate impact cases require the plaintiff to prove that an employment decision disproportionately affects members of a protected group (in this case, those over 40). In other words, in a disparate impact case, the discriminatory effect is what matters, even if the employer's intent was not discriminatory. In cases applying the disparate impact argument in age discrimination cases, companies often must prove "business necessity." For example, if a disproportionate number of employees affected by a layoff are over 40, the company will have to prove that those people were let go because their salaries were disproportionately high and that the company would face financial hardship if they were allowed to stay on.

In other forms of employment discrimination, the disparate impact argument has been used successfully.

For example, employers who require prospective employees to have a certain educational background can be liable for a disparate impact charge if it turns out that those educational requirements rule out certain racial groups. The case of *Griggs v. Duke Power* (401 U. S. 424, 88 P.U.R. 3d 90, 91 S. Ct. 849, 28 L. Ed. 2d 158 [1971]) was the first racial discrimination case to recognize disparate impact. In age discrimination cases, disparate impact was met with skepticism by some courts. In fact, the U.S. federal circuit courts could not agree about whether disparate impact claims were allowable. The Supreme Court finally resolved the issue in *Smith v. City of Jackson* (544 U.S. 228, [2005]), ruling that disparate impact arguments could be applied to age discrimination cases.

Proponents of disparate impact claims for age discrimination cases had argued that employers should not be

---

underlying purposes. The Court further pointed out that Gilmer was a professional businessman who signed the arbitration agreement voluntarily and with full knowledge.

Federal and State Employees *Stevens v. Department of the Treasury,* 500 U.S. 1, 111 S. Ct. 1562, 114 L. Ed. 2d 1 (1991), clarified the statutory time limits for federal employees to file an age discrimination claim. Charles Z. Stevens III, an INTERNAL REVENUE SERVICE (IRS) employee, filed an age discrimination complaint with the IRS's administrative unit. His complaint was rejected because it had not been filed within 30 days of the alleged discriminatory conduct. His subsequent complaint filed with the TREASURY DEPARTMENT was also dismissed, and the EEOC affirmed that dismissal. Stevens filed suit in U.S. district court, only to have his suit dismissed on the ground that it was not timely, a decision that was affirmed by the U.S. Court of Appeals for the Fifth Circuit. The Supreme

Court disagreed with the lower courts' interpretation of the statute and held that the ADEA requires federal employees to give the EEOC notice of intent to sue *not less than* 30 days before the suit is filed, rather than *within* 30 days, and within 180 days of the alleged discriminatory conduct. These small, but significant, clarifications of statutory interpretation made it easier for federal employees to seek redress under the ADEA.

The legal landscape for age discrimination complaints became more challenging for plaintiffs who work for state government after the Supreme Court decided *Kimel v. Florida Board of Regents,* 528 U.S.62, 120 S. Ct. 631, 145 L.Ed.2d 522 (2000). In this case, a group of Florida university professors and librarians who were over age 40 alleged that the university system had failed to compensate them adequately as compared to younger employees. The plaintiffs sued under the ADEA and a state CIVIL RIGHTS act.

allowed to make employment decisions that disproportionately affect those over 40. In support of their position they pointed to employers who try to get around the claims so that they can demote or lay off their older workers. Often, those older workers are among the most highly paid and have the most expensive benefits in the company. From the company's point of view, getting rid of such an expensive workforce in favor of a younger and cheaper staff can generate significant savings, which is the reason the company will give for laying off a disproportionate number of older workers during a round of cost-cutting measures. This, said proponents of disparate impact claims, is clearly age discrimination because it singles out people over a certain age. The fact that a company uses cost savings or some other reason for taking the action does not diminish the adverse impact that action has on older workers.

Opponents of age-based disparate impact claims used the same example to make their case. The employer may indeed have laid off older workers to save money. But saving money is not the same as practicing age discrimination. From a business perspective, the employer has a legitimate financial concern for the future of the company. The fact that a particular action affects one group more than another is not adequate ground for protection in such cases. If a company's only viable options are laying off high-salary employees or closing, it does not have the luxury of protecting workers who are over 40.

It should be noted that opponents of the disparate argument are not necessarily opposed to protection against age discrimination. The U.S. CHAMBER OF COMMERCE, which had filed *amicus* briefs in such cases on numerous occasions, has stated its position clearly: "Reliance on age stereotypes about the abilities of older workers should not be tolerated. Due to natural job progression, however, age affects job terms such as compensation, PENSION, and SENIORITY. In this context … imposing a burden on employers to justify the business necessity of routine and uniform job standards that statistically impact older workers is unjustified." Few would argue that employers should be forced to tolerate poor workers simply because they are past a certain age. The question is whether disparate impact actually forces them to do so.

There is no doubt companies that have legitimate financial difficulties may be forced to lay off a disproportionate number of older workers. A company that does so and then makes do with fewer staffers is not the same as a company that turns around and hires younger people at salaries comparable to what the older workers were making. Likewise, an employee who is demoted because his or her work has measurably deteriorated in quality is different from an employee who is demoted for some vague reason upon reaching age 40 or 50.

FURTHER READINGS

Falk, Ursula Adler, and Gerhard Falk. 1997. *Ageism, the Aged, and Aging in America: On Being Old in an Alienated Society.* Springfield, Ill.: Charles C. Thomas.

Posner, Richard A. 1995. *Aging and Old Age.* Chicago: Univ. of Chicago Press.

CROSS REFERENCE

Civil Rights Acts.

The state of Florida, instead of litigating the merits of the lawsuit, challenged the constitutionality of the ADEA as applied to state governments. It argued that, under the ELEVENTH AMENDMENT, it was immune from federal age discrimination lawsuits. Prior court decisions had found that Congress had validly exercised its power under the Constitution's COMMERCE CLAUSE to enact the ADEA. However, this power did not extend to lawsuits filed by private individuals. Instead, Congress could abrogate a state's SOVEREIGN IMMUNITY by invoking the FOURTEENTH AMENDMENT as its authority.

The Supreme Court concluded that Congress had not demonstrated that the Fourteenth Amendment authorized the application of the ADEA to state governments. States could lawfully discriminate on the basis of age if the discrimination is "rationally related to a legitimate state interest." In addition, the Court found no facts in the record to show that Congress needed to act against state governments for age discrimination.

In light of this ruling, state employees must use state civil rights laws involving age discrimination to press their claims.

Hazen Paper v. Biggins In 1993 the Supreme Court clarified the standards by which a business decision will be found to be a "pretext" for discrimination, and what conduct constitutes "willful" violation of the ADEA. In *Hazen Paper Co. v. Biggins,* 507 U.S. 604, 113 S. Ct. 1701, 123 L. Ed. 2d 338 (1993), a 62-year-old employee, Walter Biggins, sued his employer and its two owners, alleging age discrimination in the decision to fire him after almost ten years of employment. Biggins sought relief by claiming "disparate treatment" because of his age. In a claim of disparate treatment, the employee must prove that the employer intended to discriminate against the employee based on an impermissible criterion, his or her age. Biggins alleged that, because the firing had occurred just weeks before his ten-year anniversary, when he would have been fully vested in the company's

PENSION plan, the dismissal was due to his age. The company maintained that Biggins's outside activities created a risk of exposing trade secrets and that his refusal to sign a nondisclosure, noncompetition agreement prompted its decision to fire him.

The Supreme Court attempted to address several questions presented by the case. Did Biggins prove a case of disparate treatment based on age? Is discrimination based on pension status necessarily equivalent to discrimination based on age? What constitutes willfulness under the ADEA?

On the first issue, the Court found that the element of intent to discriminate because of age, necessary to prove a claim of disparate treatment, was absent. A decision to fire Biggins because he was close to vesting in the pension plan did not satisfy the proof requirements because it was not motivated by the prohibited presumptions about older workers, namely, that they are less productive and less competent than younger employees. Biggins failed to show that these stereotypes "had a determinative influence" on Hazen's decision.

Next, the Court found that Biggins did not prove that Hazen's reason for terminating him was a pretext for age discrimination. Justice Sandra Day O'Connor, writing for a unanimous Court, stated that "an employer does not violate the ADEA just by interfering with an older employee's pension benefits that would have vested by virtue of the employee's years of service." The Court found that pension status is not the same as age under the ADEA and that employers may make business decisions based on an employee's years of service without necessarily violating the ADEA. Biggins did prove that his firing was a pretext for discrimination because of his pension status. It did not follow, however, that he was fired because of his age. Age and pension status, according to the Court, are "analytically distinct" factors in determining a claim under the ADEA. The Court concluded that proof of discrimination based on an employee's pension status is not, absent further evidence, the legal equivalent of proof of discrimination based on age.

Addressing the question of whether Hazen had acted willfully so as to incur LIQUIDATED DAMAGES under the ADEA, the Court reaffirmed its position that a violation is willful only if the employer knew or showed reckless disregard for whether its actions violated the act. Using this test, the employer will not incur liquidated damages if it makes an age-based decision that it believes, in GOOD FAITH and nonrecklessly, is permitted.

Other Noteworthy Supreme Court Rulings

Biggins made it more difficult for an ADEA plaintiff to prevail. Under *Biggins* the plaintiff had to show DIRECT EVIDENCE of age discrimination. Indirect, empirical correlations, such as pensions and SENIORITY, were not enough to prove the claim.

However, the Supreme Court took a different direction in its holding in *Smith v. City of Jackson* 544 U.S. 228, on March 30, 2005. In that case, the Court held that a plaintiff could prove discrimination under the ADEA by using a DISPARATE IMPACT theory. Specifically, an employee could prevail when proving that an employer, or prospective employer, used a neutral business practice that was not motivated by discriminatory intent, but had an adverse impact on people 40 years of age or older. In sum, the plaintiff was no longer required to establish that the employer had intended to discriminate. The Supreme Court continued to follow the same reasoning as it did in *Smith* in the case of *Meacham v. Knolls Atomic Power Laboratory* 128 S. Ct. 2395 (2008). In that case, the Knolls Atomic Power Laboratory had laid off thirty-one employees, and of those, thirty were over the age of 40. The Court in a 7-1 decision held that when an employer practice places a disproportionate burden on older workers, then the employer has both the burden of proof and persuasion of showing that its employment action was based on reasonable factors other than age.

Previously, in situations where an employee could show that age was a motivating factor for the employer's decision, courts of appeals throughout the country held that the BURDEN OF PERSUASION then shifted to the employer to show that it had other reasons for its employment decision. However, the Supreme Court addressed this issue in the case of *Gross v. FBL Financial Services, Inc.* On June 18, 2009, the Court issued its 5–4 decision holding that a plaintiff who brings a disparate-treatment claim under the ADEA must prove, by a preponderance of the evidence, that age was the "but-for" reason of the adverse employment action. The Court further held that the burden of persuasion does not shift to the employer to show that it would have taken such action despite the age of the plaintiff, even in situations when the plaintiff had produced some evidence that age was one of the motivating factors for the employment decision.

Reverse Age Discrimination?

Age discrimination is not limited to the workplace, nor is it experienced only by those over age 40. In 1994, the state of New York successfully sued five car-rental agencies for refusing to rent vehicles to licensed drivers between the ages of 18 and 25 (*People by Koppell v. Alamo Rent A Car, Inc.,* 162 Misc. 2d 636, 620 N.Y.S.2d 695 [1994]). A few months earlier, New York City had become the first city in the United States to prohibit discrimination against the young in public places; a violation of the new law could bring a fine of up to $100,000.

In January 1994, coverage of the ADEA was extended to tenured faculty at colleges and universities. The result was that many tenured professors continued to teach after the age of 70, the typical mandatory retirement age before ADEA. With enrollments shrinking and fewer faculty positions opening up, younger people found it more and more difficult to obtain teaching positions in higher education, raising the specter of a "reverse discrimination" challenge.

FURTHER READINGS

Beyer, James R. 1993. "*Biggins* Leaves ADEA Issues Unresolved." *National Law Journal* (July 19).

Bodensteiner, Jill R. 1994. "Post OWBPA Developments in the Law Regarding Waivers to ADEA Claims." *Washington University Journal of Urban and Contemporary Law* 46 (summer).

Fick, Barbara. 1997. *American Bar Association Guide to Workplace Law.* New York: Times Books.

Gregory, Raymond F. 2001. *Age Discrimination in the American Workplace: Old at a Young Age.* Piscataway, N.J.: Rutgers Univ. Press.

Johns, Roger J., Jr. 1994. "Proving Pretext and Willfulness in Age Discrimination Cases after *Hazen Paper Company v. Biggins.*" *Labor Law Journal* 45 (April).

Kulatz, Karen. 1993. "Trading Substantive Values for Procedural Values: Compulsory Arbitration and the ADEA." *University of Florida Journal of Law and Public Policy* 5 (spring).

Lawrence, Emily J. 1992. "Clarifying the Timing Requirements for Federal Employees' Age Discrimination Claims." *Boston College Law Review* 33 (March).

Payton, Janet G. 2003. "Age Discrimination Checklist." *Corporate Counsel's Quarterly* 19 (January): 78–81.

Sullivan, Charles and Lauren M. Walter. 2008. *Employment Discrimination: Law and Practice.* 4th ed. New York: Aspen Publishers.

CROSS REFERENCES

Affirmative Action; Discrimination; Seniority.

AGE OF CONSENT

The age at which a person may marry without parental approval. The age at which a female is legally capable of agreeing to sexual intercourse, so that a male who engages in sex with her cannot be prosecuted for statutory rape.

A person below the age of consent is sometimes called an infant or minor.

AGE OF MAJORITY

The age at which a person, formerly a minor or an infant, is recognized by law to be an adult, capable of managing his or her own affairs and responsible for any legal obligations created by his or her actions.

A person who has reached the age of majority is bound by any contracts, deeds, or legal relationships, such as MARRIAGE, which he or she undertakes. In most states the age of majority is 18, but it may vary depending upon the nature of the activity in which the person is engaged. In the same state the age of majority for driving may be 16 while that for drinking alcoholic beverages is 21.

Another name for the age of majority is LEGAL AGE.

AGE OF REASON

The age at which a child is considered capable of acting responsibly.

Under COMMON LAW, seven was the age of reason. Children under the age of seven were conclusively presumed incapable of committing a crime because they did not possess the reasoning ability to understand that their conduct violated the standards of acceptable community behavior. Those between the ages of seven and fourteen were presumed incapable of committing a crime, but this presumption could be overcome by evidence, such as the child having possession of the gun immediately after the shooting. The REBUTTABLE PRESUMPTION for this age group was based on the assumption that, as the child grew older, he or she learned to differentiate between right and wrong. A child over the age of 14 was considered to be fully responsible for his or her actions. Many states have modified the age of criminal responsibility by statute.

All states have enacted legislation creating juvenile courts to handle the adjudication of young persons, usually under 18, for criminal conduct rather than have them face criminal prosecution as an adult. However, a child of 13 who commits a violent crime may be tried as an adult in many jurisdictions.

AGE REQUIREMENT FOR HOLDING OFFICE

The Framers of the CONSTITUTION OF THE UNITED STATES as well as the drafters of constitutions for most of the individual states set a minimum age for a person to be eligible for elective office. As a result, voters may not always be able to evaluate and elect candidates for public office on whatever criteria they choose, or on no criteria at all.

With respect to the states, the minimum age required to serve as a house representative ranges from 18 to 25, with about half the states requiring a minimum age of 21. Only about a third of the states allow 18-year-olds to serve in the state senate, and 20 have set a minimum age of 25. In five states, the minimum age required to serve as a state senator is 30.

For governor, most states require a minimum age of 30. Oklahoma has a minimum age of 31, six states have no age qualification, three allow a minimum age of 18, and six specify a minimum age of 25.

Although many states, over the years, have voluntarily changed their age qualification laws to allow more people to run for elective office, court challenges to these statutes have largely failed. In 1971 the SUPREME COURT OF THE UNITED STATES held that the TWENTY-SIXTH AMENDMENT to the U.S. Constitution, which forbids the states to deny the vote to anyone 18 years or older, had no effect on the constitutionality of age requirements for holding office. Those challenging age restrictions have argued that such laws deny people under the required age EQUAL PROTECTION of the law. These challenges have not been successful. Courts have found that holding office is not a FUNDAMENTAL RIGHT that states may not restrict. They have determined that age is a reasonable basis of DISCRIMINATION to ensure that those serving in government possess the necessary maturity, experience, and competence to perform as effective representatives.

The Framers of the U.S. Constitution set forth a number of reasons for requiring a minimum age for election to office, beliefs that are still held in the early 2000s. JAMES MADISON successfully argued that a minimum age of 30 should be required to serve in the U.S. Senate. He cited as his reason "the Senatorial trust," requiring a "stability of character" that could only be realized with age (*Federalist* No. 62). GEORGE MASON, of Virginia, suggested that 25 be set as the minimum age for the House of Representatives, a proposal that was adopted. He maintained that 21-year-olds did not possess sufficient maturity to serve in the House, as their political beliefs were "too crude and erroneous to merit an influence on public opinions" (1 Records of the Federal Convention of 1787). JAMES WILSON, a drafter from Pennsylvania, countered, unsuccessfully, that age requirements would "damp the effects of genius and of laudable ambition" and added that there was "no more reason for incapacitating youth than age" (1 Records of the Federal Convention of 1787). In the mid-1990s, the average member of Congress was in her or his mid-fifties, but the number of younger members elected to serve was on the increase.

The Framers also considered the minimum age that should be required for individuals seeking the presidency of the United States, and settled on 35—the highest age qualification for any office in the United States. JOHN F. KENNEDY, who became president at the age of 43, was the youngest person to be elected to that office.

Although the Framers of the U.S. Constitution and the individual states were careful to set minimum age requirements for office, upper age limits have not been established. President RONALD REAGAN was the oldest individual to assume the office of president; he was almost 70 when he was sworn in, and served two terms before leaving office at nearly 78.

FURTHER READINGS

Cooke, Jacob E., ed. 1982. *The Federalist (Alexander Hamilton, James Madison, and John Jay. 1787–88).* Middletown, CT: Wesleyan Univ. Press.

Council of State Governments. 2009. *The Book of the States.* Lexington, KY: Council of State Governments.

Records of the Federal Convention of 1787. Rev. ed. Vol. 1. 2008. Charleston, SC: BiblioLife.

CROSS REFERENCES

Constitution; Constitution of the United States; Discrimination.

AGENCY

A consensual relationship created by contract or by law where one party, the principal, grants authority for another party, the agent, to act on behalf of and under the control of the principal to deal with a third party. An agency relationship is fiduciary in nature, and the actions and words of an agent exchanged with a third party bind the principal.

An agreement creating an agency relationship may be express or implied, and both the agent and principal may be either an individual or an ENTITY, such as a corporation or partnership.

Under the law of agency, if a person is injured in a traffic accident with a delivery truck, the truck driver's employer may be liable to the injured person even if the employer was not directly responsible for the accident. That is because the employer and the driver are in a relationship known as principal-agent, in which the driver, as the agent, is authorized to act on behalf of the employer, who is the principal.

The law of agency allows one person to employ another to do her or his work, sell her or his goods, and acquire property on her or his behalf as if the employer were present and acting in person. The principal may authorize the agent to perform a variety of tasks or may restrict the agent to specific functions, but regardless of the amount, or scope, of authority given to the agent, the agent represents the principal and is subject to the principal's control. More important, the principal is liable for the consequences of acts that the agent has been directed to perform.

A voluntary, GOOD FAITH relationship of trust, known as a FIDUCIARY relationship, exists between a principal and an agent for the benefit of the principal. This relationship requires the agent to exercise a duty of loyalty to the principal and to use reasonable care to serve and protect the interests of the principal. An agent who acts in his or her own interest violates the fiduciary duty and will be financially liable to the principal for any losses the principal incurs because of that breach of the fiduciary duty. For example, an agent who accepts a bribe to purchase only the goods from a particular seller breaches his fiduciary duty by taking the money, because it is the agent's duty to work only for the best interests of the principal.

An agency relationship is created by the CONSENT of both the agent and the principal; no one can unwittingly become an agent for another. Although a principal-agent relationship can be created by a contract between the parties, a contract is not necessary if it is clear that the parties intend to act as principal and agent. The intent of the parties can be expressed by their words or implied by their conduct.

Perhaps the most important element of a principal-agent relationship is the concept of control: the agent agrees to act under the control or direction of the principal. The extent of the principal's control over the agent distinguishes an agent from an INDEPENDENT CONTRACTOR, over whom control and supervision by the principal may be relatively remote. An independent contractor is subject to the control of an employer only to the extent that she or he must produce the final work product that she or he has agreed to provide. Independent contractors have the freedom to use whatever means they choose to achieve that final product. When the employer provides more specific directions, or exerts more control, as to the means and methods of doing the job—by providing specific instructions as to how goods are to be sold or marketed, for example—then an agency relationship may exist.

The agent's authority may be actual or apparent. If the principal intentionally confers express and implied powers to the agent to act for him or her, the agent possesses *actual authority.* When the agent exercises actual authority, it is as if the principal is acting, and the principal is bound by the agent's acts and is liable for them. For example, if an owner of an apartment building names a person as agent to lease apartments and collect rents, those functions are express powers, since they are specifically stated. To perform these functions, the agent must also be able to issue receipts for rent collected and to show apartments to prospective tenants. These powers, because they are a necessary part of the express duties of the agent, are implied powers. When the agent performs any or all of these duties, whether express or implied, it is as if the owner has done so.

A more complicated situation arises when the agent possesses *apparent authority.* In this case, the principal, either knowingly or even mistakenly, permits the agent or others to assume that the agent possesses authority to carry out certain actions when such authority does not, in fact, exist. If other persons believe in good faith that such authority exists, the principal remains liable for the agent's actions and cannot rely on the defense that no actual authority was granted. For instance, suppose the owner of a building offers it for sale and tells prospective buyers to talk to the rental agent. If a buyer enters into a purchase agreement with the agent, the owner may be liable for breaching that contract if she later agrees to sell the building to someone else. The first purchaser relied on the apparent authority of the agent and will not be penalized even if the owner maintains that no authority was ever given to the agent to enter into the contract. The owner remains responsible for acts done by an agent who was exercising apparent authority.

The scope of an agent's authority, whether apparent or actual, is considered in determining an agent's liability for her or his actions. An agent is not personally liable to a THIRD PARTY for a contract the agent has entered into as a representative of the principal so long as the agent acted within the scope of her or his authority and signed the contract as agent for the principal. If the agent exceeded her or his authority by entering into the contract, however, the agent is financially responsible to the principal for violating her or his fiduciary duty. In addition, the agent may also be sued by the other party to the contract for FRAUD. The principal is generally not bound if the agent was not actually or apparently authorized to enter into the contract.

With respect to liability in tort (i.e., liability for a civil wrong, such as driving a car in a negligent manner and causing an accident), the principal is responsible for an act committed by an agent while acting within his or her authority during the course of the agent's employment. This legal rule is based on RESPONDEAT SUPERIOR, which is Latin for "let the master answer." The doctrine of respondeat superior, first developed in England in the late 1600s and adopted in the United States during the 1840s, was founded on the theory that a master must respond to third persons for losses negligently caused by the master's servants. In more modern terms, the employer is said to be *vicariously liable* for injuries caused by the actions of an employee or agent; in other words, liability for an employee's actions is imputed to the employer. The agent can also be liable to the injured party, but because the principal may be better able financially to pay any judgment rendered against him or her (according to the "deep-pocket" theory), the principal is almost always sued in addition to the agent.

A principal may also be liable for an agent's criminal acts if the principal either authorized or consented to those acts; if the principal directed the commission of a crime, she or he can be prosecuted as an accessory to the crime. Some state and federal laws provide that a corporation may be held criminally liable for the acts of its agents or officers committed in the transaction of corporate business, since by law a corporation can only act through its officers.

An agent's authority can be terminated only in accordance with the agency contract that first created the principal-agent relationship. A principal can revoke an agent's authority at any time but may be liable for DAMAGES if the TERMINATION violates the contract. Other events—such as the death, insanity, or BANKRUPTCY of the principal— end the principal-agent relationship by OPERATION OF LAW. (Operation of law refers to rights granted or taken away without the party's action or cooperation, but instead by the application of law to a specific set of facts.) The rule that death or insanity terminates an agent's authority is based on the policy that the principal's estate should be protected from potential fraudulent activity on the part of the agent. Some states have modified these common-law rules, allowing some acts of the agent to be binding upon other parties who were not aware of the termination.

FURTHER READINGS

Gregory, William A., and Harold Gill Reuschlein. 2001. *The Law of Agency and Partnership.* 3d ed. Eagan, MN: West.

Hynes, J. Dennis, and Mark J. Loewenstein. 2001. *Agency, Partnership, and the LLC in a Nutshell.* 4th ed. Eagan, MN: West.

Reuschlein, Harold G., and William A. Gregory. 2001. *Hornbook on the Law of Agency and Partnership.* Eagan, MN: West.

CROSS REFERENCES

Contracts; Fiduciary; Good Faith; Imputed; Liability; Master and Servant; Respondeat Superior; Vicarious Liability.

AGENT

One who agrees and is authorized to act on behalf of another, a principal, to legally bind an individual in particular business transactions with third parties pursuant to an agency relationship.

AGGRAVATED ASSAULT

A person is guilty of aggravated assault if he or she attempts to cause serious bodily injury to another or causes such injury purposely, knowingly, or recklessly under circumstances manifesting extreme indifference to the value of human life; or attempts to cause or purposely or knowingly causes bodily injury to another with a deadly weapon. In all jurisdictions statutes punish such aggravated assaults as assault with intent to murder (or rob or kill or rape) and assault with a dangerous (or deadly) weapon more severely than "simple" assaults.

AGGRAVATION

Any circumstances surrounding the commission of a crime that increase its seriousness or add to its injurious consequences.

Such circumstances are not essential elements of the crime but go above and beyond them. The aggravation of a crime is usually a result of intentional actions of the PERPETRATOR. Such crimes are punished more severely than the crime itself. One of the most common crimes that is caused by aggravation is AGGRAVATED ASSAULT.

AGGRESSION

Unjustified planned, threatened, or carried out use of force by one nation against another.

The key word in the definition of aggression is "unjustified"—that is, in violation of INTERNATIONAL LAW, treaties, or agreements. It was the basic charge leveled against Nazi Germany at the NUREMBERG TRIALS in 1946.

AGGRESSIVE COLLECTION

Various legal methods used by a creditor to force a debtor to repay an outstanding obligation.

Attachment of the debtor's property and GARNISHMENT of his or her salary are common kinds of AGGRESSIVE COLLECTION.

AGGRIEVED PARTY

An individual who is entitled to commence a lawsuit against another because his or her legal rights have been violated.

A person whose financial interest is directly affected by a DECREE, judgment, or statute is also considered an AGGRIEVED PARTY entitled to bring an action challenging the legality of the decree, judgment, or statute.

AGOSTINI V. FELTON

See RELIGION "Agostini v. Felton" (sidebar).

AGREEMENT

A meeting of minds with the understanding and acceptance of reciprocal legal rights and duties as to particular actions or obligations, which the parties intend to exchange; a mutual assent to do or refrain from doing something; a contract.

The writing or document that records the meeting of the minds of the parties. An oral compact between two parties who join together for a common purpose intending to change their rights and duties.

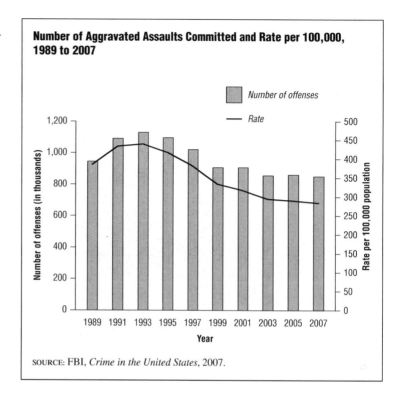

Number of Aggravated Assaults Committed and Rate per 100,000, 1989 to 2007

SOURCE: FBI, *Crime in the United States*, 2007.

An agreement is not always synonymous with a contract because it might lack an essential element of a contract, such as consideration.

AGRICULTURAL LAW

The body of law governing the cultivation of various crops and the raising and management of livestock to provide a food and fabric supply for human and animal consumption.

The law as it relates to agriculture is concerned with farmers, ranchers, and the consuming public. AGRICULTURAL LAW is designed to ensure the continued, efficient production and distribution of foods and fibers. Through a vast system of regulations that control the various aspects of agricultural practice, federal and state governments are able to provide for the needs of both agriculturalists and consumers.

History of Agricultural Law

Agricultural law is a relatively new phenomenon. Farmers have always been subject to established contract, real property, and estate laws. State regulations concerning the inspection, promotion, and improvement of farm production were in place at the United States's infancy, but the federal government's first foray into the promotion of farming was the HOMESTEAD ACT OF 1862 (ch. 75, 12 Stat. 392

[repealed 1976]). This act encouraged the westward expansion of European Americans by selling federally owned lands for farming. Another method of sale was *land debt,* a financial arrangement in which farmers agreed to pay the federal government a certain amount from their yearly profits in exchange for the land. Congress passed subsequent legislation concerning land ownership for farming purposes, but federal lands were eventually exhausted, and in 1976 these late-nineteenth- and early-twentieth-century acts became unnecessary and were repealed.

The colonial and pioneer families who practiced farming generally raised a variety of animals and crops, depending on what the soil would yield. This seminal arrangement came to be known as the "family farm." The family farm community was rich in resources derived from land, not money, and from this unique prosperity grew a lifestyle with a status all its own. Expendable income was not a priority for farm families. The values attached to their way of life placed a higher premium on plentiful food, vast land ownership, and a spiritual fulfillment derived from farming. Farmwork was difficult, and the farmer was different from the rest of society; it

was against this backdrop that federal and state legislators began to work when addressing the pressing issues that farmers would come to face.

The years following the Civil War were especially fruitful for farming communities. WORLD WAR I saw an increase in the value of farm products, and in the Roaring Twenties, robust prices were maintained by a general public capable of buying food and clothing. However, in the months before the STOCK MARKET crash of October 1929, the value of farmland and its products began to decrease. This was due in part to high tariffs on manufacturing equipment essential to farming, which allowed U.S. manufacturers to price farming equipment without foreign competition. It was also due in part to a new emphasis on mass productivity inspired by the Industrial Revolution. The ability of farmers to increase production on less land led to lower prices and, eventually, fewer family farms.

The Great Depression of the 1930s eliminated many family farms. As the general public became less able to buy such basic farm products as food and clothing, food prices dropped drastically, and farmers found themselves without the profits they needed in order to pay their mortgages. Foreclosures became routine. Farm

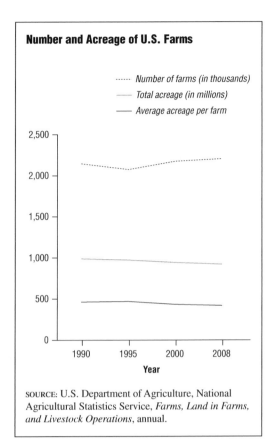

Number and Acreage of U.S. Farms

······ Number of farms (in thousands)
—— Total acreage (in millions)
—— Average acreage per farm

SOURCE: U.S. Department of Agriculture, National Agricultural Statistics Service, *Farms, Land in Farms, and Livestock Operations*, annual.

ILLUSTRATION BY GGS CREATIVE RESOURCES. REPRODUCED BY PERMISSION OF GALE, A PART OF CENGAGE LEARNING.

families considered foreclosures a breach of the government's promise to allow productive farm families to keep their land, and vast numbers of farmers organized to withhold food from their markets in an effort to force product prices higher. A smaller number of farmers resorted to violence to prevent other farmers from delivering their goods to market. Several foreclosures were also prevented by force.

The unrest of the early 1930s in the Great Plains states eventually led to widespread state legislation that limited the rights of banks to foreclose on farms with undue haste. Action was also taken on the federal level. To avoid a national farmers' strike planned for May 13, 1933, President FRANKLIN D. ROOSEVELT signed the Agricultural Adjustment Act (7 U.S.C.A. § 601 et seq.) on May 12. This act was the first in a series of federal laws that provided COMPENSATION to farmers who voluntarily reduced their output. Parts of the act were declared unconstitutional by the Supreme Court in 1936, in part because the Court considered agriculture a matter of local concern. Congress and President

Roosevelt continued to press the issue, with the amended Agricultural Adjustment Act of 1938, which contained more federal control of production, benefit payments, loans, insurance, and soil conservation.

The TEST CASE for the new Agricultural Adjustment Act was *Wickard v. Filburn*, 317 U.S. 111, 63 S. Ct. 82, 87 L. Ed. 122 (1942). In *Wickard*, Ohio farmer Roscoe C. Filburn sued Secretary of Agriculture Claude R. Wickard over the part of the act concerning wheat acreage allotment. Under the act, the U.S. DEPARTMENT OF AGRICULTURE (USDA) had designated 11.1 acres of Filburn's land for wheat sowing and established a normal wheat yield for this acreage. Filburn defied the department's directive by sowing wheat on more than 11.1 acres and exceeding his yield. This constituted farm marketing excess, and Filburn was penalized $117.11 by the department. When Filburn refused to pay the fine, the government issued a LIEN against his wheat, and the Agriculture Committee denied him a marketing card. This card was necessary to protect Filburn's buyers from LIABILITY for the fine, and to protect buyers from the government's lien on Filburn's wheat.

Filburn sued to invalidate the wheat-acreage-allotment provision, arguing in part that it was beyond the power of the federal government to enforce such farming limitations. Even though Filburn did not intend to sell much of the wheat, the Supreme Court reasoned that because all farm product surplus had a substantial effect on interstate COMMERCE, it was within the power of the U.S. Congress to control it. This decision affirmed the power of Congress to regulate all things agrarian, and the U.S. farmer, for better or worse, was left with a meddlesome lifetime friend in the federal government.

As the United States enjoyed economic prosperity through the 1950s and 1960s, the number of family farms remained relatively stable. Farm families learned to work with the federal government and its dizzying stream of agencies, regulations, and paperwork. Nevertheless, the mid-1980s saw another farm crisis. Widespread financial difficulty led to the loss of more family farms and prompted further federal action.

In response to this crisis, Congress passed an extensive credit-relief package in 1985, over the PROTEST of President Ronald Reagan's agriculture secretary, John R. Block. The various bills in this package provided for additional federal monies for loan guarantees, reduction of lender interest rates, and loan advancements.

This farm crisis was triggered by a combination of natural disasters, market shifts, lower prices, and production improvements. Furthermore, the onset of *corporate farming,* which involves mass production of farm products, forced farm families to consistently reckon with the harsh realities of the financial world.

Dissatisfaction with federal farm laws and policy led Congress in 1996 to pass the Federal Agriculture Improvement and Reform Act, which came to be known as the Freedom to Farm Act (Pub.L. 104–127, Apr. 4, 1996, 110 Stat. 888). The law, which conservatives trumpeted as the means to end 60 years of federal farm subsidies and to reinvigorate the free market, reduced regulatory burdens on farmers and ended requirements that farmers idle land to qualify for crop subsidies. However, the central part of the law consisted of "market transition payments"—the USDA paid farmers to compensate them for the possibility that farm subsidies might end in six years. This departed from the traditional federal practice whereby support payments were inversely related to crop prices—the higher the crop prices, the lower the support payments.

In 1996 and 1997 the Freedom to Farm Act gave farmers more than three times as much in cash subsidies as they would have received under the previous five-year farm bill. Even with these payouts, farm income began to fall in 1998, leading Congress to reverse course and authorize billions of dollars in farm relief. By 2002 Congress had abandoned the idea that the federal government should not subsidize farmers. It passed the Farm Security and Rural INVESTMENT Act of 2002 (Farm Bill 2002), Pub.L. 107–171, May 13, 2002, 116 Stat. 134, which set agricultural policy for the next six years. It is estimated that the total subsidies paid out over this period will reach $200 billion.

While government involvement in farming continues, the face of U.S. farming is evolving. Most farmers are now trained in business and keep abreast of farming trends, technological and manufacturing improvements, and the stock market. Many family farms have adapted by specializing in the mass production of one or two particular foods or fibers, like corporate farms do. Other farmers have formed what is called a "cooperative," a group of farmers dedicated to the most profitable sale of their products. By pooling their resources and producing a variety of goods, cooperative farmers are able to weather low-price periods and postpone sales until a product price reaches a high level.

Agriculture has become a powerful LOBBYING group in state capitals across the country, and the political issues are myriad. The industry itself is split into competing special interests, according to product. Family farms and cooperatives are often at odds, although sometimes they join forces against massive corporate farming. Farming interests are frequently opposed by advocates for the environment and food purity. The government does not always seem to act in the best interests of farmers, and farmers and their creditors continually struggle for leverage. Federal and state regulations seek to provide some predictability for the players in these struggles.

Federal Law

According to the *Wickard* case, the U.S. Congress has the power to regulate agricultural production under Article I, Section 8, of the federal Constitution, and Congress has left virtually nothing to chance. The numerous programs and laws that promote and regulate farming are overseen by the secretary of agriculture, who represents the USDA in the president's cabinet. The USDA is the government agency that carries out federal agricultural policy, and it is the most important legal entity to the farmer.

Usually, some two dozen agencies are housed within the USDA, all charged with carrying out the various services and enforcing the numerous regulations necessary for the efficient, safe production of food and fiber. Other administrative agencies can affect a farmer's legal rights, such as the FOOD AND DRUG ADMINISTRATION (FDA), the INTERIOR DEPARTMENT, and the TREASURY DEPARTMENT, but the USDA is the single department to which every farmer must answer.

The 2008 Farm Bill

In April 2008 Congress finally enacted the massive Food, Conservation, and Energy Act of 2008, P.L. 110–246, more commonly referred to as the Farm Bill. The entire law incorporated a $288 billion, five-year agricultural policy bill that essentially continued the 2002 Farm Bill. Specific initiatives were aimed at increased Food Stamp benefits, research money for new pest and disease control in crops, and support for the production of cellulosic ethanol (an alternative energy).

Other major provisions included the Average Crop Revenue Election (ACRE), which will allow farmers to chose between continued subsidies or revenue-based market oriented protections; funding for local food programs, including farmers' market programs; and funds for conservation and working land programs.

Section 9003 provides for grants of up to 30 percent of costs for developing and building biorefineries demonstratively capable of producing biofuels (all fuels not produced by corn kernel starch). Section 15321 establishes a new tax credit for producers of cellulosic biofuels (produced from wood, grasses, or the non-edible parts of plants). Section 9010 authorizes the COMMODITY CREDIT CORPORATION (CCC) to purchase sugar from U.S. producers and sell it to bioenergy producers. Section 9011 creates the Biomass Crop Assistance Program supporting the establishment and production of biomass crops. Two other sections, 9009 and 9013, create rural energy self-sufficiency initiatives to develop community-wide renewable energy systems.

The Farm Bill also created the National Institute of Food and Agriculture for federal sector agricultural research. For fiscal years 2009 to 2012, the bill granted $78 million for organic agricultural research; $230 million for specialty crops; and $118 million for biomass research and development.

The Agricultural Adjustment Acts establish and maintain prices for crops by preventing extreme fluctuations in their availability. These acts empower the secretary of agriculture to allot a certain amount of farmland for the production of a specific crop, and to apportion the land among the states capable of producing the crop. State agricultural committees then assign a certain amount of the land to various counties, and the counties in turn assign the land to local farms. This system guards against crop surpluses and shortages, and preserves economic stability by preventing extreme fluctuations in crop prices.

The COMMODITY Credit Corporation (CCC) exists within the USDA to further the goal of stabilizing food prices and farmers' incomes. The CCC provides DISASTER RELIEF to farmers, and it controls prices through an elaborate system of price support. Loans to farmers and governmental buyouts of farm products allow the CCC to maintain reasonable price levels. The secretary of the CCC is also authorized to issue

subsidies, or governmental grants, to farmers as another means of controlling prices by maintaining farmers' incomes. By encouraging or discouraging the production of a particular food or fiber through financial reward, subsidies promote price stability in the markets.

Several federal programs help serve the same purpose of price stability. The secretary of agriculture may set national quotas for the production of a certain farm product. *Set-aside conditions,* also established by the secretary of agriculture, require farmers to withhold production on a certain amount of cropland during a specified year. *Diversion payments* are made to farmers who agree to divert a percentage of their cropland to conservation uses, and the Payment in Kind Program allows farmers to divert farmland from production of a certain commodity in exchange for a number of bushels of the commodity normally produced on the diverted land. Federal CROP INSURANCE, emergency programs, and INDEMNITY payment programs protect farmers against unforeseen production shortfalls. The FARM CREDIT ADMINISTRATION, established by Congress as an independent agency in the EXECUTIVE BRANCH of government, provides funds for farmers who are unable to purchase feed for livestock or seed for crops.

Also in place are federal programs and regulations that provide for the coordination of farm cooperatives, standardization of marketing practices, quality and health inspections, the promotion of market expansion, the reporting of farm statistics, and the administration of soil conservation efforts. For example, the Soil Conservation and Domestic Allotment Act (16 U.S.C.A. §§ 590 et seq. [1936]) directs the secretary of agriculture to help farmers and ranchers acquire the knowledge and skill to preserve the quality of their soil. The federal Food Stamp Program helps to support domestic food consumption and economic stability for consumers and farmers alike by subsidizing the food purchases of people with low incomes.

Under Title VII of the United States Code, the secretary of agriculture is charged with coordinating educational outreach services. The Morrill Act (7 U.S.C.A. §§ 301–05, 307, 308), passed by Congress in 1863, granted public land to institutions of higher education for the purpose of teaching agriculture. In 1887 the HATCH ACT (7 U.S.C.A. § 361a et seq.) created agricultural experiment stations for colleges of agriculture, and in 1914 the Smith-Lever Act (7 U.S.C.A. § 341 et seq.) created the Extension Service, which allowed agriculture colleges to educate farmers not enrolled in school.

In the Extension Service, agents are hired by an agriculture college to help farmers address a variety of farming issues, and to promote progress in farming by providing farmers with information on technological advances. Many farm families have been helped by the land-grant programs, but some critics have argued that this college system too often emphasizes increased productivity and frenzied technological advancement at the exclusion of small-scale farm operations. In the mid-1990s the Extension Service began to branch out. The Minnesota Extension Service, for example, began to address such issues as teen drug abuse and child neglect. This use of agricultural monies for social services has disappointed some and pleased others.

One high-profile controversy involves the Bovine Somatatropin (BST) bovine growth hormone. The BST hormone increases the milk output of dairy cows. The Milk Labeling Act bills passed by Congress in April 1993 regulate the use of the drug by requiring the secretary of agriculture to conduct a study of its economic effect on the dairy industry and on the federal price support program for milk. The act also requires the producers of the milk from cows treated with BST to keep records on its manufacture and sale. Proponents of the drug praise its production benefits, but opponents argue that increasing productivity is less important than ensuring food purity.

HOMESTEAD protection is another form of federal relief, which helps keep farms out of FORECLOSURE. To qualify for homestead protection, farmers must show that they have received a gross farm income that is comparable to that of other local farmers, and that at least 60 percent of their income has come from farming. A 1993 case challenged the definition of this type of relief. *Schmidt v. Espy*, 9 F.3d 1352 (8th Cir. 1993) was a suit brought by the Schmidt family to stop the FmHA from calling in the Schmidts' farm loan. The USDA had ruled that because the Schmidts' farm had suffered net losses, it could not qualify for homestead protection. The Schmidts took their case to the U.S. district court, which affirmed the USDA's decision.

The Eighth CIRCUIT COURT of Appeals reversed the decision. According to the appeals court, the statutory definition of income for purposes of homestead protection is GROSS INCOME, not gross profits. The court reasoned that because homestead protection is normally sought by financially distressed farmers, limiting the protection to profitable farmers would run contrary to the purpose of homestead protection.

State Law

The TENTH AMENDMENT grants states the right to pass laws that promote the general safety and well-being of the public. Because courts have found that agricultural production and consumption directly affect public health and safety, states are free to enact their own agricultural laws, provided those laws do not conflict with federal laws and regulations.

Many state laws provide for financial assistance to farmers. By issuing loans or providing emergency aid, states are able to ensure the survival of family farms and continued agricultural production. The states also have the power to impose agricultural liens, which are claims upon crops for unpaid debts. If a farmer is unable to make timely payments on loans for services or supplies, the state may sue the farmer to gain a security interest in the farmer's crops. States also enact laws to supervise the inspection, grading, sale, and storage of grain, fertilizer, and seed.

Municipalities can also set regulations that ostensibly control agricultural production. The subject of wetlands, for example, is within the jurisdiction of local governing bodies. In *Ruotolo v. Madison Inland Wetlands Agency*, No. CV 93-0433106, 1993 WL 544699 (Conn.Super., Dec. 23, 1993), Michael Ruotolo, a farmer in Madison, Connecticut, challenged a MUNICIPAL regulation that prevented him from filling in wetlands located on his property. Ruotolo wanted to plant nursery stock on the area after moving earth to raise the ground level, but the Madison Wetlands Regulation precluded the filling in of any wetlands. According to a state statute, however, farming was permitted on some wetlands of less than three acres.

Ruotolo asserted a right to farm, and argued that because the state law and the local regulation were in conflict, the state law should prevail. However, in previous proceedings between Ruotolo and the Madison Inland Wetlands Agency, the agency had found that the wetlands on Ruotolo's property had "continual flow," and were therefore subject to more protection than standing-water wetlands. Because the state statute prevented even farmers with less than three acres from filling in wetlands with continual flow, Ruotolo was prevented from farming the wetlands on his own property.

FURTHER READINGS

Barnes, Richard L. 1993. "The U.C.C.'s Insidious Preference for Agronomy over Ecology in Farm Lending Decisions." *University of Colorado Law Review* 64.

Commodity Credit Corporation. Available online at www.fsa.usda.gov/ccc/default.htm (accessed May 29, 2003).

Daniels, Tom, and Deborah Bowers. 1997. *Holding Our Ground: Protecting America's Farms and Farmland.* Washington, D.C.: Island Press.

Department of Agriculture. 2009. "Food, Conservation, and Energy Act of 2008." Available online at http://www.usda.gov/wps/portals; website home page: http://www.usda.gov/ (accessed September 10, 2009)

Farm Credit Administration. Available online at www.fca.gov (accessed May 29, 2003).

Gardner, Bruce L. 2002. *American Agriculture in the Twentieth Century: How It Flourished and What It Cost.* Cambridge, Mass.: Harvard Univ. Press.

Hamilton, Neil D. 1993. "Feeding Our Future: Six Philosophical Issues Shaping Agricultural Law." *Nebraska Law Review* 72.

———. 1990. "The Study of Agricultural Law in the United States: Education, Organization, and Practice." *Arkansas Law Review* 43.

Kimbrell, Andrew. 2002. *Fatal Harvest: The Tragedy of Industrial Agriculture.* Washington, D.C.: Island Press.

Looney, J. W. 1994. *Agricultural Law: Principles and Cases.* 2d ed. New York: McGraw-Hill.

Meyer, Keith G., et al. 1985. *Agricultural Law: Cases and Materials.* St. Paul, Minn.: West.

Prim, Richard. 1993. "Saving the Family Farm: Is Minnesota's Anti–Corporate Farm Statute the Answer?" *Hamline Journal of Public Law and Policy* 14.

Sumner, Daniel A., ed. 1995. *Agricultural Policy Reform in the United States.* Washington, D.C.: AEI Press.

CROSS REFERENCES

Agriculture Department; Agriculture Subsidies; Environmental Law; Land-Use Control; Zoning.

AGRICULTURE DEPARTMENT

The U.S. DEPARTMENT OF AGRICULTURE (USDA) is an executive, cabinet-level department in the federal government. It is directed by the secretary of agriculture, who reports to the PRESIDENT OF THE UNITED STATES. The USDA's primary concern is the nation's agriculture industry, and the department addresses this concern through numerous economic, regulatory, environmental, and scientific programs. The USDA provides financial aid to farmers through loans, grants, and a system of price supports. The USDA's international efforts promote domestically grown products abroad.

The department regulates the quality and output of the grain, meat, and poultry industries. Through various conservation programs, the department helps protect soil, water, forests, and other natural resources. The USDA also administers the federal Food Stamp Program, one of the WELFARE system's largest services.

The USDA has a long history. As early as 1838, farmers had urged Congress to create a federal AGRICULTURE DEPARTMENT, but it took more than 20 years before the idea gained widespread support. On May 15, 1862, President ABRAHAM LINCOLN signed the Department of Agriculture Organic Act (12 Stat. 387, now codified at 7 U.S.C.A> § 2201), which created the department. The creation of the USDA coincided with several other major events, including the middle of the Civil War. Within days of signing the act that created the USDA, Lincoln also signed the HOMESTEAD ACT OF 1862, which was vital in the development of family farms in the western United States.

The USDA was administered by a COMMISSIONER of agriculture until 1889 (25 Stat. 659). In 1889, Congress enlarged the department's powers and duties (7 U.S.C.A. §§ 2202, 2208). It made the USDA the eighth executive department in the federal government, and the commissioner became the secretary of agriculture. Federal lawmakers have tinkered with the department ever since. Notably, programs providing economic aid to farmers were established during the Great Depression, and these programs have since become a firmly entrenched part of federal law. Important contemporary reforms have included federal welfare services such as the Food Stamp Program, administered through the Food and Nutrition Service since the 1970s, and the Food, Agriculture, Conservation, and Trade Act of 1990 (7 U.S.C.A. §§ 1421 note et seq.), enacted to maintain the income of farmers. Several federal statutes have established the department's central role in administering subsidy programs. These statues include: the Federal Agriculture Improvement and Reform Act of 1996 (Freedom to Farm Act) (Pub. L. No. 104–127, Apr. 4, 1996, 110 Stat. 888), the Farm Security and Rural INVESTMENT Act of 2002 (2002 Farm Bill) (Pub. L. No. 107–171, May 13, 2002, 116 Stat. 134), and the Food, Conservation, and Energy Act of 2008 (2008 Farm Bill) (Pub. L. No. 110–246, 122 Stat. 1651).

The secretary of agriculture presides over an elaborate BUREAUCRACY. The deputy secretary

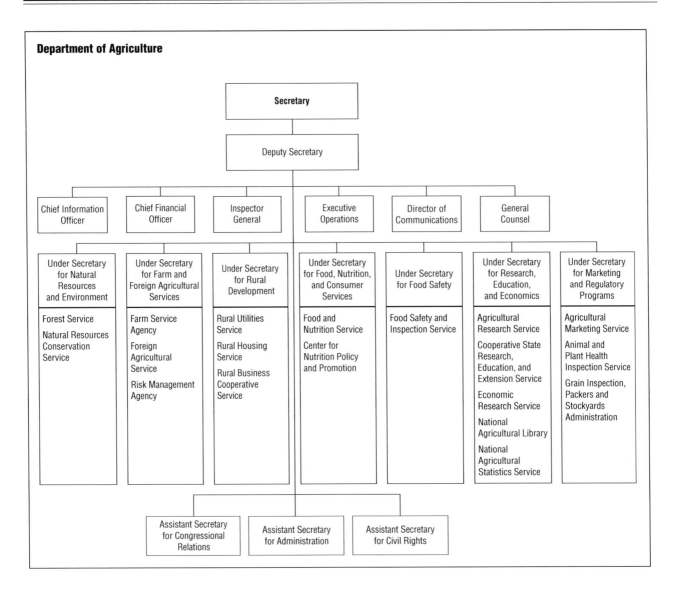

Department of Agriculture

- Secretary
  - Deputy Secretary
    - Chief Information Officer
    - Chief Financial Officer
    - Inspector General
    - Executive Operations
    - Director of Communications
    - General Counsel

- Under Secretary for Natural Resources and Environment
  - Forest Service
  - Natural Resources Conservation Service

- Under Secretary for Farm and Foreign Agricultural Services
  - Farm Service Agency
  - Foreign Agricultural Service
  - Risk Management Agency

- Under Secretary for Rural Development
  - Rural Utilities Service
  - Rural Housing Service
  - Rural Business Cooperative Service

- Under Secretary for Food, Nutrition, and Consumer Services
  - Food and Nutrition Service
  - Center for Nutrition Policy and Promotion

- Under Secretary for Food Safety
  - Food Safety and Inspection Service

- Under Secretary for Research, Education, and Economics
  - Agricultural Research Service
  - Cooperative State Research, Education, and Extension Service
  - Economic Research Service
  - National Agricultural Library
  - National Agricultural Statistics Service

- Under Secretary for Marketing and Regulatory Programs
  - Agricultural Marketing Service
  - Animal and Plant Health Inspection Service
  - Grain Inspection, Packers and Stockyards Administration

- Assistant Secretary for Congressional Relations
- Assistant Secretary for Administration
- Assistant Secretary for Civil Rights

ILLUSTRATION BY GGS CREATIVE RESOURCES. REPRODUCED BY PERMISSION OF GALE, A PART OF CENGAGE LEARNING.

runs day-to-day operations, serving as the secretary's principal adviser. Reporting to the secretary and deputy secretary are six officers: chief financial officer, general counsel, inspector general, executive of operations, director of communications, and chief information officer. These officers and their staffs coordinate a number of operations, including: the USDA's personnel management program; equal opportunity and CIVIL RIGHTS activities; safety and health activities; management improvement programs; media relations; accounting, fiscal, and financial activities; automated data processing administration; procurement and CONTRACTS; and management of real and PERSONAL PROPERTY.

Various branches of the USDA handle the department's legal affairs. The judicial officer, rather than the secretary, serves as the final deciding officer, in regulatory proceedings and appeals of a QUASI-JUDICIAL nature where a hearing is required by law. Two quasi-judicial agencies, the Office of Administrative Law Judges and the Board of Contract Appeals, adjudicate cases and decide contract disputes. Additional input to the secretary comes from the general counsel, who is both the principal legal adviser and the chief law officer of the department. All audits and investigations are conducted by the Office of the Inspector General, established by the Inspector General Act of 1978 (5 U.S.C.A. §§ 2 et seq.). The Office of Congressional Relations informs Congress of administrative policy.

Also reporting to the secretary and deputy secretary are seven under secretaries who oversee major divisions. These divisions include Rural Development; Marketing and Regulatory

Programs; Food, Nutrition, and Consumer Services; Food Safety; Farm and Foreign Agriculture Service; Natural Resources and Environment; and Research, Education, and Economics. The USDA also runs a graduate school.

Rural Development

The Rural Development division includes three programs that provide financial help to farmers and rural communities. The Rural Business-Cooperative Service (RBS) provides and guarantees loans to public entities and private parties who cannot obtain credit from other sources. Loans are made to help finance industry and business and to provide jobs in rural areas. The Rural Housing Service (RHS) provides affordable rental housing, home ownership opportunities, and essential community facilities. It also provides loans to buy, operate, and improve farms, and guarantees loans from commercial lenders. The Rural Utilities Service (RUS) is a credit agency that helps rural electric and telephone utilities obtain financing.

As part of the farm bills passed in 2002 and 2008, the Rural Development division has issued grants and loans to promote energy efficiency and use of renewable energy. Those eligible to receive these loans include individual farms as well as rural businesses. Many of these loans are awarded for the production of energy-efficient grain dryers, but some farms and businesses receive funds for other purposes, such as replacement of farming equipment.

Marketing and Regulatory Programs

The Marketing and Regulatory Programs division oversees three major programs. The Agricultural Marketing Service (AMS) administers standardization, grading, inspection, market news, marketing orders, research, promotion, and regulatory programs. The Animal and Plant Health Inspection Service conducts programs pertaining to quarantine, environmental protection, the humane treatment of animals, and the reduction of crop and livestock losses. The Grain Inspection, Packers, and Stockyards Administration regulates grain, meat, and poultry industries, in addition to other commodities. It also enforces antitrust laws to ensure fair competition in the meat industry.

Food, Nutrition, and Consumer Services

The Food, Nutrition, and Consumer Services division includes two social welfare programs and one consumer information service. The Food and Nutrition Service administers federal assistance programs to needy people, including the Food Stamp Program, special nutrition programs, and supplemental food programs. The Center for Nutrition Policy and Promotion (CNPP) conducts research to improve professional and public understanding of diets and eating, and develops the national Dietary Guidelines for Americans. The CNPP also focuses on consumer advocacy by helping USDA policy makers, representing the department before Congress, monitoring USDA programs, and conducting consumer outreach.

Food Safety

The Food Safety division administers the Food Safety Inspection Service (FSIS). Established in 1981, the FSIS conducts federal meat and poultry inspections on cattle, swine, goats, sheep, lambs, horses, chickens, turkeys, ducks, geese, and guineas used for human food. It also inspects the production of egg products. The service monitors meat and poultry products in storage, distribution, and retail channels.

In the wake of the terrorist attacks of September 11, 2001, the USDA emphasized the need to protect the nation's food supply. The department's primary focus was on bioterrorist threats and working to establish an infrastructure that provides better food safety. For example, additional Import Surveillance Liaison (ISL) inspectors were hired to focus on specific points of entry across the United States, and to re-inspect meats and poultry imported from other countries. The USDA also increased resources at universities and laboratories where research into biological agents and food safety analysis were taking place. Such initiatives ultimately benefit the overall integrity of the nation's food supply.

In 2005 the USDA and several other federal agencies announced the formation of the Strategic Partnership Program Agroterrorism (SPPA) Initiative. This program requires collaboration between the federal government, the states, and private industry to ensure that the nation's food supply would be protected in the event of a terrorist attack. Other federal agencies involved in this initiative include the FOOD AND DRUG ADMINISTRATION, HOMELAND SECURITY DEPARTMENT, and the FEDERAL BUREAU OF INVESTIGATION.

Farm and Foreign Agricultural Service

The Farm and Foreign Agricultural Service division administers three programs that help maintain a stable market for farm commodities, thus ensuring a steady income for farmers. The Farm Service Agency (FSA) administers programs of the COMMODITY CREDIT CORPORATION (CCC). These programs include so-called price supports: farmers who agree to limit their production of specially designated crops can sell them to the CCC or borrow money at support prices. The FSA also furnishes emergency financial aid to farmers, operates a grain reserve program, provides milk producers refunds of the reduction in the price received for milk during a calendar year, and provides payments to dairy farmers if their milk is removed from the market because of contamination. It has responsibility for plans relating to food production and conservation in preparation for a national security emergency, and provides incentives for preserving and protecting agricultural resources. The Risk Management Agency (RMA) provides CROP INSURANCE to farmers to protect them against unexpected production losses caused by natural causes.

The division also has an international focus. The Foreign Agricultural Service (FAS) has primary responsibility for the USDA's overseas market information, access, and development programs. It maintains a worldwide agricultural intelligence and reporting system, and also administers the USDA's export assistance and foreign food assistance programs. The Office of International Cooperation and Development (OICD) helps other USDA agencies and U.S. universities enhance U.S. agricultural competitiveness globally. Utilizing the technical expertise of the U.S. agricultural community, it seeks to increase income and food availability in developing nations.

Natural Resources and Environment

Two programs in the Natural Resources and Environment division address environmental resources. The Forest Service oversees the national forests. It manages 155 national forests, 20 national grasslands, and eight land-utilization projects on more than 191 million acres in 44 states, the Virgin Islands, and Puerto Rico. It provides national leadership as well as financial and technical assistance to owners and operators of nonfederal forestland, processors of forest products, and urban forestry interests. The Natural Resources Conservation Service has responsibility for developing and carrying out a national soil and water conservation program

in cooperation with landowners, developers, communities, and federal, state, and local agencies. It also assists in agricultural POLLUTION control, environmental improvement, and rural community development.

Research, Education, and Economics

The Research, Education, and Economics division administers four major programs. The Agricultural Research Service (ARS) conducts studies in the United States and overseas to improve farming. The Cooperative State Research, Education, and Extension Service administers acts of Congress that authorize federal appropriations for agricultural research carried out by the State Agricultural Experiment Stations. The Extension Service is the educational agency of the USDA. The National Agricultural Statistics Service provides information services to everyone from research scientists to the general public, and maintains the electronic Agricultural Online Access (AGRICOLA) database available over the INTERNET and on compact disc. It prepares estimates and reports on production, supply, price, and other economic information. The Economic Research Service (ERS) analyzes economic and other social science data in order to improve agricultural performance and rural living. It makes analyses of recommendations by USDA agencies, task forces, and study groups to be used as a basis for short-term agricultural policy.

One of the units within the ARS is the National Agricultural Library, which is one of four national libraries in the United States. The library houses one of the largest collections of agricultural information in the world. It has two locations: Washington, D.C. and Beltsville, Maryland. The library helps to fund the National Agricultural Law Center based at the University of Arkansas School of Law. This center studies a wide range of legal issues affecting agriculture.

USDA Graduate School

The Graduate School, U.S. Department of Agriculture, is a continuing education school offering career-related training to adults. Not directly funded by Congress or the USDA, it is self-supporting, with a mostly part-time faculty drawn from government and industry. The graduate school is administered by a director and governed by a general administration board appointed by the secretary of agriculture. The school was established on September 2, 1921, pursuant to the act of May 15, 1862 (7 U.S.C.A. § 2201); JOINT RESOLUTION of April 12, 1892 (27 Stat. 395); and the Deficiencies APPROPRIATION Act of March 3, 1901 (20 U.S.C.A. §. 91).

FURTHER READINGS

Agriculture Department. Available online at http://www.usda.gov (accessed May 3, 2009).

Drummond, H. Evan, and John W. Goodwin. 2000. *Agricultural Economics.* New York: Prentice Hall.

Ellis, Seth L. 2008. "Disestablishing 'The Last Plantation': The Need for Accountability in the United States Department of Agriculture." *Journal of Food Law and Policy.* Spring.

Hallberg, Milton C. 1992. *Policy for American Agriculture: Choices and Consequences.* Ames: Iowa State Univ. Press.

The United States Senate Committee on Agriculture, Nutrition, and Forestry, 1825–1998. Available online at http://www.access.gpo.gov/congress/senate/sen_agriculture/

U.S. Government Manual Website. Available online at http://www.gpoaccess.gov/gmanual (accessed May 3, 2009).

CROSS REFERENCES

Agricultural Law; Agriculture Subsidies; Consumer Protection; Environmental Law.

AGRICULTURE SUBSIDIES

Payments by the federal government to producers of agricultural products for the purpose of stabilizing food prices, ensuring plentiful food production, guaranteeing farmers' basic incomes, and generally strengthening the agricultural sector of the national economy.

Proponents of AGRICULTURE SUBSIDIES point to several reasons why they are necessary. They claim that the country's food supply is too critical to the nation's well-being to be governed by uncontrolled market forces. They also contend that in order to keep a steady food supply, farmers' incomes must be somewhat stable, or many farms would go out of business during difficult economic times. These premises are not accepted by all lawmakers and are the subject of continual debate. Critics argue that the subsidies are exceedingly expensive and do not achieve the desired market stability.

The U.S. government first initiated efforts to control the agriculture economy during the Great Depression of the 1930s. During this period, farm prices collapsed, and farmers became increasingly desperate in attempts to salvage their livelihood, sometimes staging violent protests. President HERBERT HOOVER made several failed attempts to shore up prices and stabilize the market, including the disastrous Smoot-Hawley TARIFF Act of 1930, 6 U.S.C.A.

§ 1, 19 U.S.C.A. § 6 et seq., which created a limited tariff to protect farmers from competition from foreign products. The tariff set in motion a worldwide wave of protective tariffs, greatly exacerbating the global economic panic and resulting in drastically decreased export markets for U.S. commodities.

After the Hawley-Smoot Tariff Act of 1930, tariffs were not a widely supported method of subsidizing most agricultural products. The model for post–Smoot-Hawley farm subsidies is the Agricultural Adjustment Act of 1933 (AAA), 7 U.S.C.A. § 601 et seq., passed by President FRANKLIN D. ROOSEVELT and the NEW DEAL Congress. The AAA implemented some ideas that became staples of agriculture subsidy programs to the present day, including provisions allowing the government to control production by paying farmers to reduce the number of acres in cultivation; purchasing surplus products; regulating the marketing for certain crops; guaranteeing minimum payments to farmers for some products; and making loans to farmers using only their unharvested crops as COLLATERAL.

The government also has attempted to stabilize agricultural markets by subsidizing the export of U.S. agricultural products and by signing international agreements designed to promote agricultural exports. In the 1950s and 1960s the government took major steps to increase exports, including the adoption of the Agricultural Trade Development and Assistance Act of 1954, 7 U.S.C.A. § 1427 et seq., and the GENERAL AGREEMENT ON TARIFFS AND TRADE (GATT). Such measures resulted in widened markets for U.S. agricultural products.

The GATT, a multination agreement intended to reduce international trade impediments and decrease the potential for tariff-based trade wars, has undergone several revisions during its history. Agriculture subsidies and tariffs have often been a source of great debate in these revisions. During the Uruguay round of modifications, GATT members could not agree on this issue. The stalemate nearly resulted in a renewed tariff war and the abandonment of the agreement during the 1980s and 1990s. At one point, farmers in France staged violent demonstrations when that country agreed to lower its subsidies and open its markets to imports.

Some export-based policies have had drawbacks. In 1972 the Nixon administration announced a monumental agreement with the Soviet Union whereby the Soviet Union would purchase virtually all surplus grain produced in the United States. U.S. grain and food prices escalated rapidly owing to this new demand, causing great public skepticism about the deal, except in the rural United States, where farm values and incomes escalated.

Another method used by the government to subsidize agricultural products is the combination of target prices, deficiency payments, and mandatory acreage reduction. This approach is used primarily for corn and wheat, the main U.S. grain crops. Under this method, the government sets an ideal price, or *target price,* for a COMMODITY. If the market price falls below that target price, the government pays the farmer the difference—that is, makes a *deficiency payment* to the farmer. This prevents the farmer from being forced to sell the product at a price the government deems unfairly low, and supports the farmer's income during difficult economic periods. Programs using this method are not mandatory, so the farmer must enlist in one to be involved. In return for a guaranteed minimum income and price stability, the farmer normally is required to take a specified portion of land out of production—that is, make a *mandatory acreage reduction*—at least for program commodities.

In any given year, it is impossible to predict how expensive the deficiency payment programs will be, because weather conditions and uncontrolled market forces often greatly affect prices. These types of agriculture subsidies often have been quite expensive, especially during years when market prices are low owing to high production and low exports. To reduce the government's cash payments to farmers during one particularly disastrous market swing, the Reagan administration implemented the Payment in Kind (PIK) Program in 1983. Under the PIK Program, instead of paying farmers with cash, the government paid them with certificates good for federal surplus grain. Farmers could then exchange the certificates for actual grain or trade them like stock certificates. PIK, combined with a drought in 1983, succeeded in reducing the cash cost of the deficiency payment programs and the excessive grain surplus.

In the dairy industry, the government subsidizes milk production by agreeing to purchase milk from processors at a predetermined price.

Dairy farmers receive no direct deficiency payments; rather, they receive from their processor a milk check that includes the federal money.

The international community often attacks the U.S. dairy subsidy programs as predatory, although similar and even greater subsidies are given to many dairy farmers in European countries. U.S. dairy producers claim that until the other producing nations drop their subsidies, it would be economic SUICIDE for the United States to lower subsidies.

The government also subsidizes agriculture through *nonrecourse loans.* With this type of subsidy, the government loans money to farmers using the farmers' future harvest as collateral. The government sets a per-bushel loan rate at which farmers can borrow money prior to harvest, so that they can hold their crops for later sale when the market price rises. The government determines how much a farmer can borrow by multiplying the loan rate (which is usually equal to the government target price for the crop) by the farmer's base acreage (which is determined by calculating the number of acres the farmer planted of a target crop over several years, and multiplying that total by the farmer's average yield). The crop is the collateral for the loan, and the farmer can either repay the loan in cash and sell the crop, or default and FORFEIT the crop to the government. If the market price is lower than the loan rate or target price, or if the farmer's actual production rate is below the farmer's base acreage rate, the government's only RECOURSE for recouping part of its loan is to take the collateral crop. This subsidy is used primarily for corn and wheat, with a modified form of the program applying to soybeans, rice, and cotton.

The government still enforces restrictive tariffs to subsidize certain domestic crops, especially sugar, for which the U.S. tariff virtually eliminates all foreign imports. The tariff protects U.S. sugar producers and costs the government little, but opponents argue that the cost of this domestic MONOPOLY is passed on to consumers, who are forced to pay sugar prices almost four times higher than the world market rates, to the benefit of a few large sugar manufacturers.

For peanuts and TOBACCO, the government allows legal monopolies for a few government-licensed growers and imposes large tariffs on imports of these products. Cigarette companies are allowed to help determine the price of tobacco and the volume of foreign imports, creating a dual-monopoly relationship between tobacco growers and the cigarette industry.

Supporters of subsidies attribute the relatively low cost of food and the stability of food production to the assistance of the federal government. They argue that if agriculture subsidies did not exist, food prices would vary wildly from year to year, and that many farmers would be unable to support themselves through market lows and weather catastrophes. Supporters often state that government support for family farms keeps farm monopolies from dominating production and raising prices. They also cite the great advances in PER CAPITA production since the New Deal revisions in farm policy as evidence of the success of agriculture subsidies.

In addition, supporters point out that the government has encouraged soil conservation through subsidies. They point to laws such as the Soil Conservation and Domestic Allotment Act of 1936, 7 U.S.C.A. § 608-1 et seq., 16 U.S.C.A. § 590 et seq., which required that farmers who received income subsidies plant soil-conserving crops like legumes rather than soil-depleting crops such as corn, and that farmers use contour crop-stripping methods to hinder soil erosion resulting from water runoff.

Opponents of agriculture subsidies say the farm economy is overly dependent on government, and that market forces would be a more efficient and inexpensive method of regulating production and market price. They contend that in the 1970s and 1980s, up to 30 percent of farmers' incomes were made up of government payments, primarily during years when guaranteed deficiency payments ballooned, and that farm programs have become the third largest federal program expense, behind SOCIAL SECURITY and MEDICARE.

Another primary criticism of farm commodity programs, especially corn and wheat programs, is that they encourage farmers to expand their operation in order to acquire more base acres and higher guaranteed government payments. Opponents believe that this leads to a concentration of production in the hands of fewer and fewer farm CORPORATIONS, and actually undermines the concept of family farms. Opponents also state that although a primary goal of agriculture subsidies always has been to control production, most programs have had little success in doing so because farmers who are paid

to keep part of their land out of production tend to remove the least productive acres.

The Republican Congress of 1994–95 proposed large cuts in farm subsidies as a means to reduce the federal DEFICIT. In March 1996 Congress passed the Federal Agriculture Improvement and Reform Act, which came to be known as the Freedom to Farm Act (Pub.L. 104–127, Apr. 4, 1996, 110 Stat. 888). This act threatened to spell the end of agriculture subsidies, as it set out a plan to phase out subsidies by 2003. The six-year period, however, contradicted the avowed purpose of the 1996 act. The law sought to soften the blow to farmers by increasing subsidies through the use of *market transition payments.* These payments differed from traditional subsidies because they were not tied to commodity prices, so even if the market prices rose, the farmers would receive payments. In addition, the payment schedules were almost three times higher than the amounts paid out in previous farm bills.

Advocates of a free market without subsidies were angered as Congress started to back away from the basic concept of the Freedom to Farm Act. As farm incomes started to fall in 1998, members of both political parties agreed to authorize additional funds for farm subsidies. This process continued through 2001 as farmers cited bad weather, natural disasters, and other forces for a decline in farm income.

In addition, the 1996 law authorized a dairy "compact" for six New England states. This provision sets a minimum farm price for milk consumed in the six New England states. When federally regulated milk prices drop below the compact price, processors are required to pay farmers the difference. Midwest dairy farmers have argued this is unfair because the compact erects a trade barrier and encourages New England farmers to overproduce milk.

The Farm Security and Rural INVESTMENT Act of 2002 (Farm Bill 2002), Pub. L. 107–171, May 13, 2002, 116 Stat. 134, set agriculture policy through 2008. Some in Congress lamented the retreat from the Freedom to Farm Act, but others faced the political reality that agribusiness and family farmers are a potent LOBBYING force that few congressional representatives want to frustrate. The 2002 Farm Bill made clear that subsidies would not wither away. In fact, the law outlined an increase in subsidy payments by 74 percent over a ten-year period. In addition, the law added new crops to be included in the subsidies, and it established a new price-guarantee scheme called the "counter-cyclical" program. Under this program, farmers with an eligible historical production of covered commodities (wheat, corn, grain sorghum, barley, oats, upland cotton, rice, soybeans, oilseeds, dry peas, lentils, and chickpeas) and peanuts, are able to enroll annually to receive payments from the federal government when the commodity's effective price is lower than the target price. The effective price of a commodity is the direct payment rate, plus the higher of either the national commodity loan rate or the national average farm price for that year. The purpose of the counter-cyclical payments is to support and stabilize farm income in the years when market prices fall.

In 2008 Congress enacted law the Food, Conservation, and Energy Act (2008 Farm Act). The act governs the majority of federal agriculture and agriculture-related programs through 2012. Many of the commodity programs that were introduced in previous farm legislation were continued in this act, as well as the implementation of a new average crop revenue election program. In addition, the 2008 Farm Act introduced a permanent disaster-assistance program. Another major change in the act, which reflected the changes and trends of the United States in the move towards buying organic products, was the establishment of new programs to support agricultural producers who were transitioning to organic agriculture. The act, also provided funding to increase research into organic agriculture.

Not only did the 2008 Farm Act implement new programs, but it also improved some of the existing programs. For example, in 2007 a congressional committee hearing disclosed that billions of dollars of waste, FRAUD, and abuse were prevalent in the then-existing Federal CROP INSURANCE Program. Specifically, the TESTIMONY at the hearing revealed that over 40 percent of the program's funding, more than $10 billion, never reached the farmers whom it was intended to assist. Additionally, billions of dollars in excess subsidies for the private insurers that administered the program were also disclosed. The changes in the 2008 Farm Act included substantial reforms to the Crop Insurance Program that significantly reduced excessive subsidies for insurance and provided new funding for the

enforcement of that program as well as other programs that had significant waste and abuse by farmers and insurers. The changes were estimated to save over $3.4 billion over ten years.

Many environmentalists oppose farm subsidies, such as corn and wheat programs, for different reasons. These groups claim that the base acreage and deficiency-payment system encourage farmers to produce soil-depleting and erosion-prone crops such as corn year after year, even if the market offers a better price for a different crop. Soil depletion and the need to increase average yields lead to heavy use of chemical fertilizers, which in turn add to soil and WATER POLLUTION, they argue. Others who oppose farm subsidies argue that the subsidies redistribute wealth by transferring the taxpayer's money to a small group of well-off farm businesses and landowners. Another argument against farm subsidies is that it DAMAGES the economy by causing overproduction, overuse of marginal farmland, and price inflation. Other opponents contend that the subsidies not only damage the United States' trade relations, but also that agriculture in the United States would still thrive without the subsidies.

FURTHER READINGS

Cochrane, Willard, and Mary Ryan. 1976. *American Farm Policy, 1948–1973.* Minneapolis: Univ. of Minnesota Press.

"Congress Passes Farm Legislation Cutting Crop Insurance Waste by $3.4 Billion." Committee on Oversight and Government Reform. Available online at http://oversight .house.gov/story.asp?ID=2231; website home page: http:// oversight.house.gov (accessed September 16, 2009).

Edwards, Chris. *Agricultural Subsidies* Downsizing the Federal Government. Available online at http://www. downsizinggovernment.org/print/agriculture/subsidies; website home page: http://www.downsizinggovernment.org (accessed September 15, 2009).

"Farm and Commodity Policy: Program Provisions: Counter-Cyclical Payments." United States Department of Agriculture, Economic Research Service, Briefing Rooms. Available online at http://www.ers.usda.gov/ Briefing/FarmPolicy/countercyclicalpay.htm;website home page: http://www.ers.usda.gov(accessed September 18, 2009).

Helmberger, Peter G. 1991. *Economic Analysis of Farm Programs.* New York: McGraw-Hill.

Rapp, David. 1988. *How the United States Got into Agriculture: And Why It Can't Get Out.* Washington, D.C.: Congressional Quarterly Press.

Rehka, Mehra. 1989. "Winners and Losers in the U.S. Sugar Program." *Resources* 94 (winter).

"2008 Farm Bill Side-by-Side." United States Department of Agriculture, Economic Research Service. Available online at http://www.ers.usda.gov/FarmBill/2008/Overview.htm;

website home page: http://www.ers.usda.gov (accessed September 16, 2009).

U.S. Department of Agriculture. Available online at www.usda.gov (accessed May 29, 2003).

Wuerthner, George, and Mollie Matteson, eds. 2002. *Welfare Ranching: The Subsidized Destruction of the American West*. Washington, D.C.: Island Press.

CROSS REFERENCES

Agricultural Law; Agriculture Department; General Agreement on Tariffs and Trade.

AID AND ABET

To assist another in the commission of a crime by words or conduct.

The person who aids and abets participates in the commission of a crime by performing some OVERT ACT or by giving advice or encouragement. He or she must share the criminal intent of the person who actually commits the crime, but it is not necessary for the aider and abettor to be physically present at the scene of the crime.

An aider and abettor is a party to a crime and may be criminally liable as a principal, an accessory before the fact, or an accessory after the fact.

AID AND COMFORT

To render assistance or counsel. Any act that deliberately strengthens or tends to strengthen enemies of the United States, or that weakens or tends to weaken the power of the United States to resist and attack such enemies is characterized as aid and comfort.

Article 3, section 3, clause 1 of the U.S. Constitution specifies that the giving of AID AND COMFORT to the enemy is an element in the crime of TREASON. Aid and comfort may consist of substantial assistance or the mere attempt to provide some support; actual help or the success of the enterprise is not relevant.

In the wake of the September 11, 2001, terrorist attacks, there was a great deal of concern expressed about terrorist "sleeper cells" in the United States. Sleeper cells can be individual terrorists or groups of terrorists who blend in with society at large; they remain inactive, even for years, until they receive orders to carry out their mission. Some of the perpetrators of the September 11 attacks belonged to such sleeper cells.

Widespread concern over terrorist sleeper cells fueled suspicion that some U.S. citizens were knowingly providing aid and comfort to terrorist cells located in the United States. Aid and comfort was allegedly provided by shielding the identities of terrorists from U.S. authorities, and providing funds, transportation, and other forms of assistance to terrorists who plotted against U.S. interests.

In the subsequent U.S. military action against the Taliban government in Afghanistan and members of the al Qaeda terrorist organization located there, which started in October 2001, U.S. forces captured John Walker Lindh, a 20-year-old American citizen who was trained by and was fighting for the Taliban against the U.S. government. The Walker Lindh case garnered enormous coverage in the press, with many claiming that Walker Lindh's role as a combatant for the Taliban was tantamount to treason as it gave aid and comfort to enemies of the United States.

AIDING THE ENEMY ACTS

The outbreak of war normally ends all forms of normal relations between belligerent states. In support of the war effort MUNICIPAL laws may be implemented to prevent citizens and other persons within a belligerent state's jurisdiction from assisting an enemy state through trade or other forms of contact. In the United States, for example, the Trading with the Enemy Act (40 Stat. 411 as amended [1917]) suspends all forms of trade or communication with persons in enemy TERRITORY. The statutory or executive restrictions imposed under the Trading with the Enemy Act are limited to formal periods of war, although other authority exists permitting the president to impose restrictions on trade or communications with a country without a DECLARATION of war.

Because the Trading with the Enemy Act and similar statutes apply specifically to other nations in times of war, their provisions do not apply easily to dealings between citizens of the United States and members of terrorist organizations. After the SEPTEMBER 11TH ATTACKS were perpetrated by terrorist organizations against the United States, Congress enacted the Uniting and Strengthening America by Providing Appropriate Tools Required to Intercept and Obstruct TERRORISM (USA PATRIOT Act) (Pub. L. No. 107-56, 115 Stat. 277) in order to strengthen the ability of the United States to protect itself from terrorist activities. The USA PATRIOT Act amended the existing statutory provisions permitting the president to restrict transactions and other transfers with foreign countries, organizations, and persons in order to respond to unusual and extraordinary threats against the United States.

The current statutory provisions allowing the president to impose economic sanctions against a nation that the president deems to be a threat against the United States are provided by the International Emergency Economic Powers Act (IEEPA), Pub. L. No. 95-223, 91 Stat. 1626 (50 U.S.C.A. §§ 1701–1702). Under this act, the president may, with respect to any person or property subject to the jurisdiction of the United States, investigate, regulate, or prohibit transactions in foreign exchange; transfers of credit or payments by or to any banking institute; or importation or exportation of SECURITIES or currency. The president and the federal government may also confiscate property owned by certain foreign countries, organizations, or nationals.

Violation of an EXECUTIVE ORDER issued pursuant to the IEEPA prohibiting trade with a foreign nation or organization may result in criminal sanctions. During the Gulf War in 1991, President GEORGE HERBERT WALKER BUSH issued an executive order prohibiting citizens of the United States from traveling to or dealing with the government of Iraq. Arch Trading Company, Inc., a corporation based in Virginia, violated this DECREE by completing a contract with Iraq. The U.S. government brought criminal charges against the company for conspiring to commit an offense against the United States in violation of 18 U.S.C.A. § 371 (2000). Despite arguments by the company that violation of the order was not an "offense" under federal law, the U.S. Court of Appeals for the Fourth Circuit held that the company could be properly charged (*United States v. Arch Trading Co.*, 987 F.2d 1087 [4th Cir. 1993]).

FURTHER READINGS

Bordwell, Percy. 2008. *The Law of War between Belligerents: A Commentary (1908)*. Whitefish, MT: Kessinger.

Green, Leslie C. 1999. *Essays on the Modern Law of War*. 2d ed. Ardsley, NY: Transnational.

Williams, Nathan. 2001. "How Has the Onset of War Coincided with Limitations on Press Freedom Throughout Our Nation's History?" *George Mason Univ.'s History News Network* Web site. Available online at http://hnn.us/articles/392.html; website home page: http://hnn.us (accessed August 29, 2009).

CROSS REFERENCES

Rules of War; War.

AIDS

See ACQUIRED IMMUNE DEFICIENCY SYNDROME.

AIR POLLUTION

Air pollution has plagued communities since before the Industrial Revolution. Airborne pollutants, such as gases, chemicals, smoke particles, and other substances, reduce the value of, and ability to enjoy, affected property and cause significant health and environmental problems. Despite the long history and significant consequences of this problem, effective legal remedies only began to appear in the late nineteenth and early twentieth centuries. Though some U.S. cities adopted air quality laws as early as 1815, air POLLUTION at that time was seen as a problem best handled by local laws and ordinances. Only as cities continued to grow, and pollution and health concerns with them, did federal standards and a nationwide approach to air quality begin to emerge.

The earliest cases involving air pollution were likely to be brought because of a noxious smell, such as from a slaughterhouse, animal herd, or factory, that interfered with neighboring landowners' ability to enjoy their property. These disputes were handled through the application of the nuisance doctrine, which provides that possessors of land have a duty to make a reasonable use of their property in a manner that does not harm other individuals in the area. A person who polluted the air and caused harm to others was liable for breaching this duty and was required to pay DAMAGES or was enjoined (stopped through an INJUNCTION issued by a court) from engaging in the activities that created the pollution. In determining whether to enjoin an alleged polluter, courts balanced the damage to the PLAINTIFF landowner's property against the hardship the DEFENDANT polluter would incur in trying to eliminate, or abate, the pollution. Courts often denied injunctions because the economic damage suffered by the defendant—and, by extension, the surrounding community if the defendant was essential to the local economy—in trying to eliminate the pollution often outweighed the damage suffered by the plaintiff. Thus, in many cases, the plaintiff was left only with the remedy of money damages—a cash payment equal to the estimated monetary value of the damage caused by the pollution—and the polluting activities were allowed to continue.

Using a nuisance action to control widespread air pollution proved inadequate in other ways as well. At COMMON LAW, only the attorney general or local PROSECUTOR could sue to abate a *public nuisance* (one that damages a large number of persons) unless a private individual could show "special" damage that was distinct from, and more severe than, that suffered by the general public. The private plaintiff with SPECIAL DAMAGES had the necessary standing (legally protected interest) to seek injunctive relief. In some states, the problem of standing has been corrected through laws that allow a private citizen to sue to abate public nuisances such as air pollution, though these laws are by no means the norm. Moreover, with the nuisance doctrine the plaintiff has the burden of showing that the harm he or she has experienced was caused by a particular defendant. However, because pollutants can derive from many sources, it can be difficult, if not impossible, to prove that a particular polluter is responsible for a particular problem. Last, nuisance law was useful only to combat particular polluters; it did not provide an ongoing and systematic mechanism for the regulation and control of pollution.

Early in the nineteenth century, a few U.S. cities recognized the shortcomings of common law remedies and enacted local laws that attempted to address the problem of air pollution. Pittsburgh, in 1815, was one of the first to institute air-quality laws. Others, such as Chicago and Cincinnati, passed smoke-control ordinances in 1881, and by 1912, 23 U.S. cities with populations of more than 200,000 had passed smoke-abatement laws.

Though the early court cases usually addressed polluted air as an interference with the enjoyment of property, scientists quickly discovered that air pollution also poses significant health and environmental risks. It is believed to contribute to the incidence of chronic diseases such as emphysema, bronchitis, and other respiratory illnesses and has been linked to higher mortality rates from other diseases, including cancer and heart disease.

The shortcomings associated with the common law remedies to control air pollution and increasing alarm over the problem's long-range effects finally resulted in the development of state and federal legislation. The first significant legislation concerning air quality was the Air Pollution Control Act, enacted in 1955 (42 U.S.

Drivers in downtown Phoenix are advised to utilize public transportation in order to help reduce the area's high levels of air pollution.
© JACK KURTZ/ZUMA/ CORBIS.

C.A. § 7401 et seq. [1955]). Also known as the CLEAN AIR ACT, it gave the Secretary of Health, Education, and Welfare the power to undertake and recommend research programs for air-pollution control. Amendments passed during the 1960s authorized federal agencies to intervene to help abate interstate pollution in limited circumstances, to control emissions from new motor vehicles, and to provide some supervision and enforcement powers to states trying to control pollution. By the end of the 1960s, when it became clear that states had made little progress in combating air pollution, Congress toughened the Clean Air Act through a series of new laws, which were known as the Clean Air Act Amendments of 1970 (Pub. L. No. 91-604, 84 Stat. 1676 [Dec. 31, 1970]).

The 1970 amendments greatly increased federal authority and responsibility for addressing the problem of air pollution. They provided for, among other things, uniform national emissions standards for the hazardous air pollutants most likely to cause an increase in mortality or serious illness. Under the amendments, each state retained some regulatory authority, having "primary responsibility for assuring air quality within the entire geographic area comprising such state." Thus, states could not "opt out" of air pollution regulation and, for the first time, were required to attain certain air-quality standards within a specified period of time. In addition, the amendments directed the administrator of the ENVIRONMENTAL PROTECTION AGENCY (EPA), which was also established in 1970, to institute national standards regarding ambient air quality for air pollutants

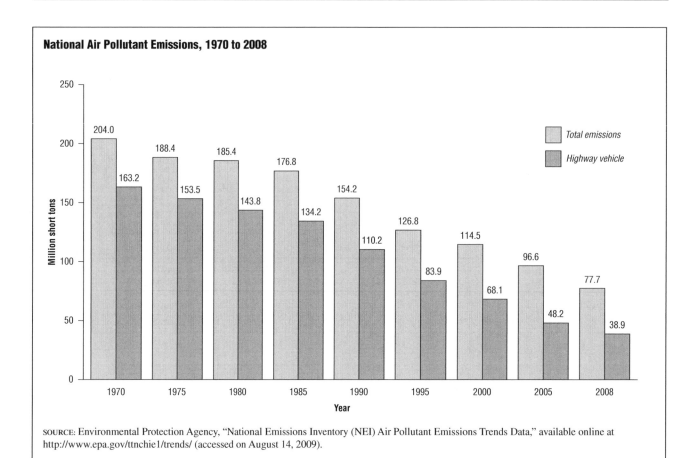

National Air Pollutant Emissions, 1970 to 2008

SOURCE: Environmental Protection Agency, "National Emissions Inventory (NEI) Air Pollutant Emissions Trends Data," available online at http://www.epa.gov/ttnchie1/trends/ (accessed on August 14, 2009).

endangering public health or welfare, in particular sulfur dioxide, carbon monoxide, and photochemical oxidants in the atmosphere. The EPA was also granted the authority to require levels of harmful pollutants to be brought within set standards before further industrial expansion would be permitted.

Despite the ambitious scope of the 1970 legislation, many of its goals were never attained. As a result, the Clean Air Act was extensively revised again in 1977 (Pub. L. No. 95-95, 91 Stat. 685 [Aug. 7, 1977]). One significant component of the 1977 amendments was the formulation of programs designed to inspect, control, and monitor vehicle emissions. The 1977 revisions also sought to regulate parking on the street, discourage automobile use in crowded areas, promote the use of bicycle lanes, and encourage employer-sponsored carpooling. Unlike the goals of several of the 1970 amendments, many of the 1977 reforms were achieved. Many states, with the help of federal funding, developed programs that require AUTOMOBILES to be tested regularly for emissions problems before they could be licensed and registered. The 1977

amendments also directed the EPA to issue regulations to reduce "haze" in national parks and other wilderness areas. Under these regulations the agency sought to improve air quality in a number of areas, including the Grand Canyon in Arizona.

During the 1980s and 1990s, several environmental issues, including acid rain, global climate change, and the depletion of the ozone layer, gave rise to further federal regulation. Acid rain, which has caused significant damage to U.S. and Canadian lakes, is created when the sulfur from fossil fuels, such as coal, combines with oxygen in the air to create sulfur dioxide, a pollutant. The sulfur dioxide then combines with oxygen to form sulfate, which, when washed out of the air by fog, clouds, mist, or rain, becomes acid rain, with potentially catastrophic effects on vegetation and ground water. Amendments to the Clean Air Act in 1990 (Pub. L. No. 101-549, 104 Stat. 2399 [Nov. 15, 1990]) sought to address the challenges posed by acid rain by commissioning a number of federally sponsored studies, including an analysis of Canada's approach to dealing with acid rain and an investigation of the use of buffering and neutralizing agents to restore lakes and streams. The 1990 laws also directed the EPA to prepare a report on the feasibility of developing standards related to acid rain that would "protect sensitive and critically sensitive aquatic and terrestrial resources." In addition, the amendments provided for a controversial system of "marketable allowances," which authorize industries to emit certain amounts of sulfate and which can be transferred to other entities or "banked" for future use.

The problem of global climate change is linked to the accumulation of gases, including carbon dioxide and methane, in the atmosphere. The 1990 amendments implemented a number of strategies to address changes in the global climate, including the commissioning of studies on options for controlling the emission of methane. The amendments also contained provisions to deal with the depletion of the ozone layer, which shields the earth from the harmful effects of the sun's radiation. Though the long-term consequences were hard to determine in the early 2000s, damage had already been seen in the form of a "hole" in the ozone layer over Antarctica. The destruction of the ozone layer was believed to be caused by the release into the atmosphere of chlorofluorocarbons (CFCs) and other similar substances. The 1990 laws included a ban on "nonessential uses" of ozone-depleting chemicals, and the placement of conspicuous warning labels on certain substances, indicating that their use harms public health and the environment by destroying the ozone in the upper atmosphere.

Regulatory interpretation of the Clean Air Act shifted between the late 1990s and early 2000s. Under President WILLIAM J. CLINTON, the Environmental Protection Agency sought to close loopholes in the law's enforcement through the New Source Review (NSR) program. Essentially, these rules used an industrial facility's age to determine when higher pollution emissions would require the facility to go through a permitting process and install pollution-control equipment. The agency sued some 50 companies in an effort to hold them to the highest pollution-control standards. But the EPA shifted direction under President GEORGE W. BUSH, who favored less stringent regulations. Under its so-called Clear Skies initiative, the Bush administration proposed issuing individual utilities pollution credits, which would allow the utility to lawfully generate a fixed amount of pollution, and if unused, any remaining credits could be sold to other utilities exceeding their permitted limit ("cap and trade system"). Environmentalists criticized the proposals for gutting protections, while industry embraced them as flexible cost-savings measures.

Greenhouse Gases

Meanwhile, in 1999, various environmental groups filed an administrative "rule-making" PETITION asking the EPA to establish standards for motor vehicle "greenhouse gas" emissions (primarily carbon dioxide and other heat-trapping gases). The EPA announced a review of the Clinton-era policy, then issued proposed rule changes in December 2002 that would relax requirements governing pollution levels and mandatory equipment upgrades. The EPA stated that it lacked authority to regulate such gases. It argued, in part, that carbon dioxide and other greenhouse gases were naturally occurring substances in the atmosphere and therefore did not constitute "air pollutants" within the meaning of the Clean Air Act.

In *Massachusetts v. Environmental Protection Agency (EPA)*, 549 U.S 497 (2007), the U.S. Supreme Court was asked to determine whether the EPA had the statutory authority to regulate greenhouse gas emissions from new motor vehicles; and if so, whether EPA's stated reasons for declining to act were consistent with the statute. The Court narrowly decided, in a 5–4 landmark decision, that gases that cause global warming were pollutants under the federal Clean Air Act. The Court further held that EPA did indeed have the statutory authority to regulate them, and that it had acted arbitrarily and capriciously in refusing to exercise that authority.

The long-winded controversy centered on Section 202(a)(1) of the Clean Air Act, specifically, 42 USC §7521(a)(1), which states in relevant part:

> The [EPA] Administrator shall by regulation prescribe (and from time to time revise) in accordance with the provisions of this section, standards applicable to the emission of any air pollutant from any class or classes of new motor vehicles or new motor vehicle engines, which in his judgment cause, or contribute to, air pollution which may reasonably be anticipated to endanger public health or welfare . . . The Act defines air pollutants to include "any air pollution agent . . . including any physical, chemical . . . substance . . . emitted into . . . the ambient air." [§7602(g)].

Tobacco Smoke

Although the trend has been toward adoption of smoking bans, advocates and opponents have fought pitched battles. Advocates point to successes such as stringent statewide bans in New York, California, and Delaware, along with an estimated 400 bans in cities such as Boston and Dallas, according to the American Non-smokers' Rights Foundation. They also cited evidence presented at the American College of Cardiology's annual meeting in 2002 showing that the city of Helena, Montana, enjoyed dramatically reduced heart attack rates the year following enactment of its ban. Ironically, enforcement was subsequently halted while a court battle was waged over the ban. By 2008 a clear majority of states (more than 30) had implemented state-wide smoking bans in public places, but legal challenges at the local level continued across the country.

Opposition to indoor smoking bans has come from the bar, restaurant, and TOBACCO industries. Commercial groups argue that bans result in revenue loss, burdensome COMPLIANCE regulation, and even a diminished labor force. They have achieved some success. Some city councils rejected proposed ordinances after heavy LOBBYING, such as in Eden Prairie, Minnesota, and the city of Pueblo, Colorado, was forced to suspend its ordinances following a successful public signature drive calling for a public REFERENDUM in 2003.

FURTHER READINGS

Findley, Roger W., and Daniel A. Farber. 2008. *Environmental Law in a Nutshell.* 7th ed. St. Paul, Minn.: Thomson/West.

Jackson, Ted. 2003. "Activists Fret President's Plan Hurts Effort on FPL Emissions." *Palm Beach Post* (February 28).

Kaiser Family Foundation. 2008. "Public Place Smoking Bans-Kaiser State Health Facts." February 2008. Text available online at http://www.statehealthfacts.org/comparetable.jsp?ind=86&cat=2 (accessed August 25, 2009).

Menell, Peter S., ed. 2002. *Environmental Law.* Aldershot, England; Burlington, Vt.: Ashgate/Dartmouth

Natural Resources Defense Council (NRDC). 2008. "Solving Global Warming: Your Guide to Legislation." January 2008. Text available online at http://www.nrdc.org/legislation/factsheets/leg_07032601a.pdf; website home page: http://www.nrdc.org/policy (accessed August 5, 2009).

Rodgers, William H., Jr. 1986. *Environmental Law: Air and Water.* Vol. 2. St. Paul, Minn.: West.

Stagg, Michael K. 2001. "The EPA's New Source Review Enforcement Actions: Will They Proceed?" *Trends* 33 (November-December).

CROSS REFERENCES

Automobiles; Environmental Law; Environmental Protection Agency; Pollution; Surgeon General; Tobacco.

AIRLINES

In 1978 the airline industry, which had been heavily regulated and controlled, was liberated from government oversight and released to the vagaries of the marketplace. As a result, the industry underwent significant change during the 1980s and 1990s. At the same time, several major air disasters took place, including the 1996 Valujet and TWA 800 aircraft crashes. In response to the post-accident events, Congress passed the Aviation Disaster Family Assistance Act (ADFAA) the same year. The terrorist attacks of September 11, 2001, wrought further change on the airline industry. Just weeks after the attacks, President GEORGE W. BUSH signed the Air Transportation Safety and System Stabilization Act (ATSSSA). According to a statement released by President Bush on September 22, 2001, the act was intended to ensure passenger safety and to "assure the safety and immediate stability of the nation's commercial airline system." It also created financial turmoil for nearly all the major carriers. What followed was a period of evolution and metamorphosis that changed the nature of flying considerably.

Deregulation

When the first commercial airlines appeared after WORLD WAR I, fewer than 6,000 passengers per year traveled by air. By the 1930s the Big Four—Eastern Air Lines, United Air Lines, American Airlines, and Trans World Airlines (TWA)—dominated commercial air transport. These companies had garnered exclusive rights from the federal government to fly domestic airmail routes, and Pan American (Pan Am) held the rights to international routes. The hold of these four airlines on their lucrative CONTRACTS went virtually unchallenged until deregulation in 1978. Even after the formation of the Civil Aeronautics Board (CAB) in 1938, formed to license new airlines, grant new routes, approve mergers, and investigate accidents, the Big Four and Pan Am continued to be guaranteed permanent rights to these routes. In fact, no new major scheduled airline was licensed for the next four decades.

In October 1978 Congress passed the Airline Deregulation Act (49 U.S.C.A. § 334 et seq.), ending the virtual MONOPOLY held by the Big

Four and Pan Am. The government's goal was to promote competition within the industry. The act gave airlines essentially unrestricted rights to enter new routes without CAB approval. The companies could also exit any market and raise and lower fares at will.

The immediate effect of deregulation was a drop in fares and an increase in passengers. New cut-rate, no-frills airlines, such as People Express Airlines and New York Air, offered travelers the lowest fares ever seen in the industry. Forced to compete to fill their planes, the larger companies lowered their prices as well. Then the oil-producing countries in the Middle East formed a cartel and raised the price of jet fuel 88 percent in 1979 and an additional 23 percent in 1980. Combined with tumbling fares and increased passenger loads, the higher cost of jet fuel caused airline profits to drop.

Labor strife also affected the industry in the early days following deregulation. In 1981, after years of working under stressful conditions made worse by deregulation, the Professional Air Traffic Controllers Organization (PATCO) called a strike, demanding shorter working hours and higher pay. The union expected support and cooperation from the Reagan administration because of a sympathetic letter that President RONALD REAGAN had sent to PATCO when he was campaigning for the presidency. In the letter, he pledged to do whatever was necessary to meet PATCO's needs and to ensure the public's safety. But Reagan ordered the strikers to return to work within three days or be fired. Most did not return. The FEDERAL AVIATION ADMINISTRATION (FAA) ordered all carriers to temporarily reduce their number of flights by one-third. Newer and smaller carriers found themselves increasingly unable to gain access to lucrative routes. Rebuilding the air traffic controller force took years, during which landing slots at the largest airports remained restricted, and small carriers, unable to compete, simply abandoned their attempts to break into the larger markets.

To some extent, competitive pricing actually had the opposite effect of what the deregulators intended. When the small "upstart" companies offered extremely low fares, the larger companies responded aggressively. For example, in 1983, People Express announced a $99 round-trip fare between Newark, New Jersey, and Minneapolis–St. Paul. Northwest Airlines, which had always

Passengers preparing to board an airplane must discard all liquids weighing more than 3 ounces, a limit enacted by the U.S. Transportation Security Administration in 2006 after an alleged liquid bomb plot was exposed in the United Kingdom.

GEORGE RIZER-POOL/ GETTY IMAGES

dominated the Twin Cities market, undercut People by instituting a $95 fare for the same destination and scheduling extra departures. As a result, People decided it could not compete and withdrew from the market. Passengers enjoyed the benefit of lower fares, but only for a short time before the competitive effect faded and high fares returned.

When deregulation brought competitive pricing, the large carriers began to realize that it was not profitable for them to do business the way they had in the past. The first major change they made was to abandon the practice of criss-crossing the continent with nonstop flights to many different cities. Instead, the major airlines scheduled most of their flights into and out of a central point, or "hub," where passengers might need to change to a different flight to complete their journey. One airline controlled most of the reservation desks and gates at a particular hub— for example, United in Chicago, Northwest in Minneapolis–St. Paul, American in Dallas–Fort Worth, and Delta in Atlanta. For this reason, and because passengers tend to dislike changing carriers in the middle of a trip, the dominant company in a hub had a tremendous advantage over the competition in influencing what carrier a passenger would choose. By 1990 two-thirds of

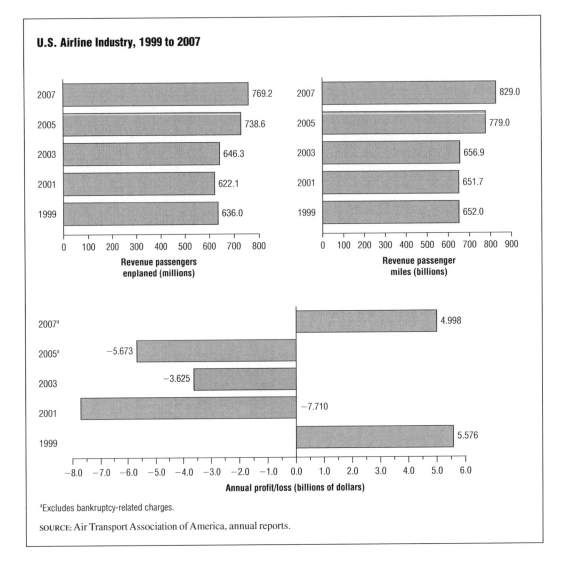

U.S. Airline Industry, 1999 to 2007

Revenue passengers enplaned (millions)

Year	Value
2007	769.2
2005	738.6
2003	646.3
2001	622.1
1999	636.0

Revenue passenger miles (billions)

Year	Value
2007	829.0
2005	779.0
2003	656.9
2001	651.7
1999	652.0

Annual profit/loss (billions of dollars)

Year	Value
2007[a]	4.998
2005[a]	−5.673
2003	−3.625
2001	−7.710
1999	5.576

[a]Excludes bankruptcy-related charges.

SOURCE: Air Transport Association of America, annual reports.

all domestic passengers traveled through a hub city before arriving at their final destination. Of those passengers, eight out of ten remained on the same airline throughout their journey. By 1992, there were at least 12 "fortress hubs," or airports where one airline controlled more than 60 percent of the traffic. Passengers who flew out of these hubs paid over 20 percent more than they would have for a comparable trip out of an airport that was not a hub.

After deregulation, the airlines also came to realize that they needed a more efficient way to book reservations and issue tickets. It is difficult to imagine, in these days of highly sophisticated computers and split-second communications, that until the late 1970s and early 1980s, airline schedules were contained in large printed volumes, reservations were taken over the telephone and tallied manually at the end of each day, and tickets

were written by hand. To streamline this process, the large companies initially proposed a joint computer system, listing schedules and fares. The DEPARTMENT OF JUSTICE objected on the grounds that such a system would be anticompetitive and would violate the SHERMAN ANTI-TRUST ACT (15 U.S.C.A. § 1 et seq. [1890]). Instead, each airline developed its own computer system and entered data in a manner that unfairly biased travel agents' choices in favor of the carrier that owned the system. Through skillful manipulation of the data, the airlines were able to put competitors at a disadvantage. For example, the airline that owned the system might enter the data so that all its flights to a particular destination appear on the screen before any flights of a competitor.

In a further attempt to win loyalty from passengers, the large airlines instituted frequent-flyer programs, which awarded free tickets to travelers after they logged a certain number of miles flown with the company. The combination of hubs, central computer reservation systems, and frequent-flier programs made the major airlines almost invulnerable in large markets.

Deregulation also brought a period of financial upheaval and an epidemic of "merger fever." A number of companies ceased doing business between 1989 and 1992, and still others merged with stronger, more aggressive companies. Among the companies that disappeared from the skies were Eastern, Pan Am, Piedmont, and Midway Airlines. Continental and TWA sought the shelter of Chapter Eleven BANKRUPTCY reorganization. USAir and Northwest required cash infusions through cooperative arrangements with foreign airlines. Even financially strong carriers such as United and American laid off employees and abandoned plans to purchase new aircraft, which added to the burdens on the depressed aerospace industry.

The mergers and buyouts of the 1980s were often accomplished in an atmosphere of hostility and distrust. Charges of predatory pricing and other unfair business practices were leveled by one carrier against another. During the 1980s the Justice Department's Antitrust Division made a number of GRAND JURY investigations into alleged anticompetitive activity by the major airlines, but no indictments were handed down. However, the companies that survived did not emerge unscathed. Many of the acquisitions were highly leveraged buyouts that left the reconstituted companies heavily in debt. With profits insufficient to cover their enormous debt loads, the companies frantically competed for business, engaging in fare wars that produced a dizzying array of pricing plans with equally numerous and confusing restrictions. Some of the tactics were questionable, but, again, not clearly illegal. In 1993 American Airlines was sued by Continental and Northwest for alleged predatory pricing during a 1992 fare war. The jury took just over two hours to return a VERDICT in favor of American.

By 1993 the industry began to rebound. Continental Airlines and TWA emerged from bankruptcy, and a few small carriers, such as Kiwi International, formed by former Eastern pilots, responded to the public's demand for low fares and began to make incursions into the established markets, although they generally shied away from directly challenging the giants.

Older carriers, for the most part, chose to stay with their hub-and-spoke systems, whereas several, including Northwest and United, came up with a creative new solution to their financial situation.

Northwest avoided bankruptcy when its unions agreed to wage concessions in return for part ownership of the airline. Then in 1994, after seven years of negotiating, employees of United gained majority control of their company in return for deep pay and benefits cuts. Secretary of Labor Robert B. Reich commented that other financially troubled companies would undoubtedly follow suit: "From here on in, it will be impossible for a BOARD OF DIRECTORS to not consider employee ownership as one potential business strategy." However, some industry analysts doubted that employee ownership would be effective in the long run because of inherent conflicts between labor and management, or between different labor groups. "It can't work," declared former Chrysler chairman Lee A. Iacocca. "What do you think will happen when it's a choice between employee benefits and capital investment?"

Safety

One troubling criticism of deregulation is that aggressive competition has forced airlines to cut corners, resulting in safety lapses. In 1990 Eastern Airlines was handed a 60-count federal INDICTMENT charging it with shoddy and dishonest maintenance practices. The indictments came after years of complaints by the financially troubled airline's mechanics, who claimed that pressures to cut costs led to maintenance shortcuts and falsification of maintenance records. In January 1991 Eastern ceased operation.

Critics contend that Eastern was hardly alone in its cavalier approach to safety. They charge that the FAA is understaffed and poorly managed and that money shortages have caused all the airlines to relax safety standards. They point not only to increased pressures on the labor force but also to companies' reluctance to replace their aging fleets, the congestion of airspace caused by increased air travel, crowded hub airports that create security risks, and overworked and sometimes poorly trained air traffic controllers. Yet, statistically, passengers are no more likely to die in a plane crash since deregulation than they were before it. Still, critics maintain that, despite the airlines' and the government's efforts to assure the traveling public to the contrary, air safety is in need of substantial improvements.

Many critics feel that at least part of the problem lies in the dual role of the FAA. Charged simultaneously with promoting the economic health of the aviation industry and fostering safety, the agency is often at odds with itself. In addition, the FAA's budget was cut, and the number of inspectors reduced in the 1980s, the same period during which the number of passengers multiplied and the number of air traffic controllers was reduced. Furthermore, unions, which stand to benefit from the increased scrutiny and higher standards imposed by the FAA, continue to be major instigators for change. However, even neutral commentators have suggested that it is time to impose some degree of regulation on the industry in the form of stronger FAA oversight. In fact, the FAA has been accused of suffering from a "tombstone mentality" that causes the agency to delay acting on safety concerns until negative publicity generated by a crash forces the issue. Even after safety measures are recommended by the NATIONAL TRANSPORTATION SAFETY BOARD (NTSB), the agency charged with investigating accidents, the FAA has been criticized for not always following through.

Aging aircraft became a major concern during the late 1980s and early 1990s. In 1988 an Aloha Airgroup Boeing 737-200, purchased in 1969, lost the top of its fuselage while flying at 24,000 feet. A flight attendant was immediately sucked out of the plane. The plane made a harrowing emergency landing, but not before 65 passengers suffered injuries, some serious. Congress responded in 1991 by passing the Aging Aircraft Safety Act (49 App. U.S.C.A. 1421 note), which requires airlines to demonstrate that their older planes are airworthy. Critics claim that enforcement of the law has been lax and that it ignores other compelling reasons to replace aging aircraft, such as the availability of newer fire-retardant seat materials and of updated seats designed to be more resistant to the impact of a crash.

Concerns over airline safety became even more acute in the early 1990s with a series of fatal crashes. The Boeing Company, a major producer of aircraft, predicted that the number of jet crashes worldwide could double by 2010 if accident rates of the early 1990s continue. However, according to David R. Hinson, former

FAA administrator, flight safety "is not a simplistic science that lends itself to easy solutions." Flight safety experts point out that all the most obvious causes of crashes have been addressed with technological advances that include such safeguards as early warning systems for wind shear.

Many experts feel that not enough research has been devoted to the study of the human elements that contribute to crashes. Boeing reports that flight crews have been the primary cause in more than 73 percent of jet crashes since 1959. In 1990 a federal jury in Minneapolis convicted three Northwest Airlines crewmen—a flight captain, a copilot, and a flight engineer—of flying a jet aircraft while under the influence of alcohol. Although this was the first flying-while-intoxicated CONVICTION involving professional pilots, many claim that the problem of alcohol and drug abuse among flight crews is widespread and well hidden. Yet it is difficult to convince companies to focus on the issue of human elements that contribute to accidents.

In 1994 five fatal crashes, three involving commuter airlines, brought safety concerns to light once again. After the fifth crash, Secretary of Transportation Federico Peña ordered a safety AUDIT of the entire airline industry. As a result, commuter airlines, which had previously been held to a lower standard of safety than major carriers, were placed under new operating rules that required them to bring their safety standards up to those of the other companies by the end of 1996. Industry experts said the elimination of the two-tier safety standards was "the most important decision affecting the industry since it was deregulated in 1978."

Several other safety and health issues have been publicized. Some have questioned the quality of air aboard an airplane. As a result of intense LOBBYING by passenger groups and flight attendants, federal law prohibits smoking on all domestic flights and on many international flights as well. Air quality was again questioned in 1993 when it was revealed that, as a cost-saving measure, many airlines were circulating fresh air into their aircraft less frequently than they had in the past. This led to complaints by passengers and crew of headaches, nausea, and the transmission of respiratory illnesses. Although the FAA conceded that circulating more fresh air would be beneficial, it backed off from requiring airlines to do so, because of the cost involved.

The safety of babies and toddlers on airplanes was investigated after it was shown that a number of them suffered injuries, some serious or fatal, during incidents that did not injure their parents. Unlike adults and their luggage, children under age two are not required to be secured on an airplane but rather may be held on an adult's lap. These "lap babies" are often ripped from the adult's grasp during turbulence or crashes. In 1994 Representatives Jolene Unsoeld (D-Wash.) and Jim Ross Lightfoot (R-Iowa) introduced a bill that would have required the use of child safety restraints on commercial flights. However, the measure, which was supported by the Association of Flight Attendants, NTSB, Air Transport Association, Aviation Consumer Action Project, and Air Line Pilots Association, was opposed by the FAA and eventually defeated. An FAA spokesperson, testifying in opposition to the bill, said the FAA's research indicated that if all children who needed them were placed in child safety seats, the airlines would save approximately one life over a ten-year period, and families would save $2.5 billion in added fares and costs over the same timespan. In contrast to the FAA's findings, a study conducted at Harvard Medical School estimated that one infant per year could be saved through the use of safety seats. The sponsors of the bill vowed to continue to press for more stringent safety standards for babies.

Another major concern is delayed and/or cancelled flights. On Valentine's Day in February 2007, an ice storm hit the Northeast and resulted in many delayed and/or grounded flights. At New York area airports, passengers were grounded on the runway in planes for three to ten hours without water, food, and other basic needs. The air inside the planes became stale, and the restrooms on board were inadequate and/or malfunctioning. Following that disaster, in June 2007 the state of New York became the first in the nation to enact a Passenger BILL OF RIGHTS [N.Y. Gen. Bus. Law §251(g)(1)]. The law, which took effect in January 2008, was short-lived. The Air Transport Association of America (ATA) filed suit, arguing that the new legislation regulated a "service" provided by air carriers. Accordingly, the ATA argued, this meant that it was preempted by the federal Airline Deregulation Act, the scope of which extended to anything "related to a price, route, or service of an air carrier." (49 U.S.C. §41713). The U.S. Court of Appeals for the Second Circuit agreed. *Air Transportation Assn v. Cuomo*, 520 F.3d 218 (2d Cir. 2008). In the INTERIM between legislation and court decision, nine other states had proposed similar legislation relating to lengthy ground delays and likely faced similar challenges. As of August 2009, uniform federal legislation was pending in both House and Senate congressional bills, folded into the FAA re-authorization package.

Safety concerns will continue to plague the airline industry, even though the FAA assures the flying public that, statistically, at least, flying a major airline in the United States is far safer than driving on an interstate highway. Questions persist about the FAA's effectiveness in overseeing air safety. And financially strapped airlines, which posted $12.8 billion in losses from 1990 to 1994, must make difficult risk-benefit analyses when contemplating new safety measures.

Some critics, such as RALPH NADER, who initially supported deregulation, are now calling for limited government intervention to ensure safety. However, experts warn that the U.S. airline system, which is already extremely safe, probably can never be completely without risk. According to Stuart Matthews, president of the Flight Safety Foundation, "If the public absolutely demands that flying be totally safe, you are going to have to ban flying." Given the choice between taking a calculated risk and not flying at all, Americans, who take their lives into their hands each time they drive, will probably continue to trust the statistics and take their chances.

The ADFAA and September 11, 2001

In 1996, to address concerns that the families of airline crash victims were not receiving timely information, Congress passed the Aviation Disaster Family Assistance Act (ADFAA) (49 USCA § 1136; 49 USCA § 41113). The act requires airlines to submit a plan to the National Transportation Safety Board that would address the needs of the families of passengers who are involved in any aircraft accident that results in a major loss of life. Once approved, the carrier must make a GOOD FAITH effort to carry out the plan.

Plans approved under the ADFAA have some minimum requirements for notification and care of families affected by an airline crash. Among them are that the airline carrier must set up, publicize, and staff a toll-free telephone line that passengers' families can call for information. The carrier must also cooperate with the independent, NTSB-appointed NONPROFIT (i.e., the Red Cross) to provide an appropriate level of aid and support. In addition, the carrier must assist a passenger's family in traveling to the crash site, as well as provide for their physical needs while at the accident location. Finally, the carrier must respect a family's wishes for burial, a memorial, or a religious ceremony, and obtain the input of all families before any memorial is erected in memory of the passengers.

The ADFAA provides limitations on the LIABILITY of airline carriers for passenger lists. The act states that a carrier may not be liable for DAMAGES in preparing or providing a passenger list, unless the conduct of the air carrier was grossly negligent or constituted intentional misconduct. Further limiting airline liability, the ADFAA provides that no unsolicited communication concerning a potential action for PERSONAL INJURY or WRONGFUL DEATH may be made by an attorney or any potential party to the LITIGATION to an individual injured in an airplane accident, or to a relative of an individual involved in the accident, before the 45th day following the date of the accident.

The provisions of the ADFAA became crucial on September 11, 2001—the day that four domestic airplanes were hijacked by terrorists and crashed into the World Trade Center in New York City, the Pentagon outside Washington, D.C., and a field in Pennsylvania. In the aftermath of that tragedy, the government built on the ADFAA by passing the Air Transportation Safety and System Stabilization Act (ATSSSA) (Pub.L. 107-42, Sept. 22, 2001, 115 Stat. 230). This act took into consideration the devastation wrought on U.S. airlines on September 11 and enacted measures to try to ensure their survival.

In addition to compensating airlines for direct losses incurred as a result of September 11, the ATSSSA established a framework for computing the maximum grant that an airline could claim as COMPENSATION. To streamline efforts, it set up the Air Transportation Stabilization Board to review the prospective loan applications. The act attempted to protect the insurance industry, as well as the aviation industry, by limiting the claims that could be made upon them. It also established the September 11th Victim Compensation Fund of 2001 to deal directly with the needs of families who were victims of the SEPTEMBER 11TH ATTACKS. The fund provided direct financial assistance to families so

they would not have to endure lengthy court battles. Liability for all third-party losses was transferred from the airlines to the U.S. government, and a WAIVER system was established so that families could not sue the airlines for damages as a result of the terrorist attack at any future date.

Security measures for airlines have also been upgraded since September 11. The government took over security at airports from private companies through the creation of the Transportation Security Administration (TSA) under the DEPARTMENT OF HOMELAND SECURITY. In addition, cockpit doors were reinforced, passengers were limited in what they could bring on to flights, luggage screening was upgraded, and pilots were allowed to carry guns to protect themselves on flights. In 2007 President George W. Bush signed into law the Implementing the 9/11 Commission Recommendation Act (the 9/11 Act), P.L. 110-53, requiring the Secretary of Homeland Security to establish a system that would ultimately result in the screening of 100 percent of cargo transported on passenger aircraft. The new law was to be sequentially implemented within three years, with full COMPLIANCE by 2010. Further, the Narrow Body Screening Amendment became effective in October 2008, requiring 100 percent screening of all cargo on narrow body aircraft.

Despite the ATSSSA and the increased security measures, the September 11 attacks had a disastrous effect on U.S. airlines. A little over a year later, two major airlines, U.S. Airways and United Airlines, were in bankruptcy, with a good chance that others would follow. And the threat of low-cost airlines, such as Southwest, combined with a widespread decline in flying, made the business plans of most major airlines inviable. Following a few mergers and reorganizations, the airlines appeared to be more stable by 2009.

FURTHER READINGS

Dempsey, Paul Stephen. 2003. "Aviation Security: The Role of Law in the War against Terrorism." *Columbia Journal of Transnational Law* (spring): 649-733.

Schroeder, Kristin Buja. 2002. "Failing to Prevent the Tragedy, but Facing the Trauma: The Aviation Disaster Family Assistance Act of 1996 and the Air Transportation Safety and System Stabilization Act of 2001." *Journal of Air Law and Commerce* 67 (winter).

Schwieterman, Joseph. 2002. "From Consolidation to Crisis: The Airline Industry in Transition. (Terrorism, Security, and Competition: The Future of the Airline Industry)." *DePaul Business Law Journal* 14 (spring): 269-277.

Sheth, Jagdish N., and Fred C Allvine. 2007. *Deregulation and Competition: Lessons from the Airline Industry.* Thousand Oaks, Calif.: Sage Publications.

Stempel, Jeffrey W. 2002. "The Insurance Aftermath of September 11: Myriad Claims, Multiple Lines, Arguments over Occurrence Counting, War Risk Exclusions, the Future of Terrorism Coverage, and New Issues of Government Role." *Tort and Insurance Law Journal* 37 (spring).

Transportation Security Administration. 2009. "TSA: Programs and Initiatives." Available online at http://www.tsa.gov/what_we_do/tsnm/air_cargo/programs.shtm; website home page: http://www.tsa.gov/ (accessed September 10, 2009)

CROSS REFERENCES

Aeronautics; Carriers; Federal Preemption; Homeland Security; Labor Union; National Transportation Safety Board; Sherman Anti-Trust Act; Unfair Competition.

❖ AKERMAN, AMOS TAPPAN

Amos Tappan Akerman, born in 1821 in New Hampshire, served as attorney general of the United States from 1870 to 1872 under President ULYSSES S. GRANT.

A graduate of Dartmouth College, Akerman was admitted to the bar in 1841. He opened his first practice at Elberton, Georgia, in 1850. He was a well-established attorney by the outbreak of the Civil War. Akerman supported Georgia's decision to secede from the Union in 1861, and he served the Confederate government in the quartermaster's department during the war. (A quartermaster is charged with procuring and dispensing uniforms, WEAPONS, and other supplies for the troops.) After the war, Akerman developed ties with the REPUBLICAN PARTY and the Reconstructionists. He was appointed DISTRICT ATTORNEY for Georgia in 1866. Four years later, he was named attorney general of the United States.

Amos Tappan Akerman.

Akerman's TENURE as attorney general coincided with the Grant administration's early attempts to enforce CIVIL RIGHTS laws in the South during RECONSTRUCTION. Initially, Akerman believed prosecutions for violations of criminal CIVIL RIGHTS ACTS should be left to state and local authorities. However, he soon changed his mind and advocated a more aggressive federal role in the prosecution of crimes related to civil rights.

His change of mind can be attributed to the growth of the KU KLUX KLAN in the South, and the results of a congressional investigation. Investigators found that state and local legal systems in

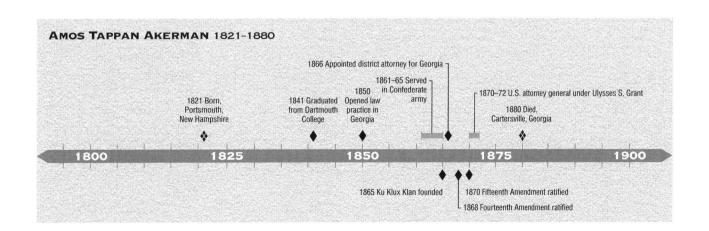

AMOS TAPPAN AKERMAN 1821–1880

1866 Appointed district attorney for Georgia

1861–65 Served in Confederate army

1850 Opened law practice in Georgia

1821 Born, Portsmouth, New Hampshire

1841 Graduated from Dartmouth College

1870–72 U.S. attorney general under Ulysses S. Grant

1880 Died, Cartersville, Georgia

1800   1825   1850   1875   1900

1865 Ku Klux Klan founded

1870 Fifteenth Amendment ratified

1868 Fourteenth Amendment ratified

the South were inadequate to protect the rights of free blacks or to PROSECUTE the increasingly violent actions of the Klan.

Akerman agreed that the federal government should step in, and he wrote extensively on the subject. In his opinion, some Southerners would never acknowledge the rights of free blacks and government attempts to "conciliate by kindness" were a waste of time. He noted that Southern klansmen and other malcontents "take all kindness ... as evidence of timidity, and hence are emboldened to lawlessness by it." He concluded that the federal government should "command their respect by the exercise of its powers."

With Akerman's leadership—and his successful effort to obtain a financial commitment from Congress—attorneys from the newly created DEPARTMENT OF JUSTICE worked with local U.S. attorneys to bring hundreds of indictments under the Enforcement Act of 1870 (16 Stat. 140 [codified as amended at 42 U.S.C.A. § 1981 et seq.]) and the KU KLUX KLAN ACT of 1871 (§ 2, 17 Stat. 13 [current version at 42 U.S.C.A. § 1985(3) (Supp. V 1976)]).

Together, these government officials prosecuted, convicted, and imprisoned hundreds of Klan members from 1870 to 1872, and, for a short time, criminal civil rights acts were successfully enforced in the South. Though he "rejoiced" at the suppression of the Klan, Akerman wrote, "I feel greatly saddened by this business. It has revealed a perversion of moral sentiment among the Southern whites, which bodes ill to that part of the country for this generation."

Akerman was also saddened—and frustrated—by fiscal circumstances that combined to slow his efforts. Concerned by the growing financial burden of the actions, and pressured to allocate funds for other priorities, Congress and the Grant administration eventually brought Akerman's prosecutions to a standstill. The violence resumed, and Akerman resigned.

Akerman's resignation as attorney general can also be attributed to his discouragement with the pace of federal civil rights enforcement, and to political issues as well. Akerman had angered President Grant by refusing to execute a deed conveying western lands to the railroads, and he had antagonized many congressional Republicans with his lack of support for other business and railroad projects.

IT CONCERNS US MORE TO ASCERTAIN WHAT IS THE CONSTITUTIONAL RULE THAN TO LEARN WHETHER THAT RULE HAS ALWAYS BEEN OBSERVED. NINETEEN VIOLATIONS OF THE CONSTITUTION DO NOT JUSTIFY A TWENTIETH.
—AMOS TAPPAN AKERMAN

After his resignation, Akerman returned to private life and the PRACTICE OF LAW. He died in 1880.

FURTHER READINGS

Baker, Nancy V. 1992. *Conflicting Loyalties: Law and Politics in the Attorney General's Office, 1789–1990.* Lawrence: Univ. Press of Kansas.

Kousser, J. Morgan, and James M. McPherson. 1982. *Region, Race, and Reconstruction.* New York: Oxford Univ. Press.

Sobel, Robert. 1990. *Biographical Directory of the United States Executive Branch. 1774–1989.* Westport, CT: Greenwood.

CROSS REFERENCES

Civil Rights Acts; Grant, Ulysses Simpson; Ku Klux Klan Act; Railroad.

ALASKA BOUNDARY DISPUTE

During the late 1800s and early 1900s, a dispute erupted between the United States and Canada regarding the legal boundaries of Alaska, which the United States had purchased from Russia in 1867. The primary point of contention in the dispute related to a several thousand mile long strip to the west of British Columbia and to the southeast of the Alaska TERRITORY. Although the dispute was resolved by way of a treaty signed in 1903, it caused a severe threat to U.S.-Canadian relations.

Russia was the first nation to claim the Alaska territory after it was discovered by Vitus Bering, a Danish explorer who received a commission from Peter the Great to lead Russian sailors on a expedition of Siberia on August 20, 1741. Russia named the land Russian-America, and Russian whalers and fur traders established settlements in the region. Russia and Canada, then a colony of Great Britain, disagreed as to the proper boundaries, and in 1825 Russia and Great Britain signed the Anglo-Russian treaty. Under this treaty, the Russian and Canadian territory was divided by the 141st Meridian, though at the time, much of this land had not been surveyed. Russia lost much of the land it had claimed under the treaty, though the specific boundaries were still unclear.

As fur-trading from Russian-America began to decline, Russia lost interest in the territory. The United States in 1867 agreed to purchase the territory for $7,200,000 and renamed the territory Alaska. The continental nation of Canada formed during the same year, encompassing the Province of Canada, Nova Scotia, and New Brunswick.

The United States maintained that it had taken over the territory that appeared on Russian maps at the time of the purchase. However, the Russian maps indicated that Russia had owned more of the land than had been stipulated in the 1825 treaty. As early as 1872, British Columbia petitioned the United States for an official survey of the boundaries between Alaska and western Canada, but the United States refused due to the costs that would have been involved. Both the United States and Canada conducted surveys of particular areas in the region in the 1870s and 1880s, but no widespread survey was conducted during that time.

The dispute regarding the proper boundaries between Alaska and western Canada heated up during the 1880s after gold was discovered in the area. Between the 1880s and 1890s, an estimated 100,000 fortune seekers moved to the Klondike region in search of gold. Though only a fraction of these miners and prospectors actually discovered gold, more than $100 million was eventually extracted from the region. Although the Klondike gold rush was not a direct factor in the ALASKA BOUNDARY DISPUTE, it almost certainly focused more attention on that region.

In 1898 the United States and Great Britain formed a Joint High Commission to resolve the boundary dispute. The goal of the commission was to order the survey and marking of the 141st Meridian and to reach a compromise between the United States and Canada. The commission agreed to a convention that would have resulted in the survey and marking of the territory, but the western states of the United States objected to the commission's work, and the United States Senate refused to ratify the convention.

Five years later, in January 1903, the United States and Great Britain agreed to appoint an Alaskan Boundary TRIBUNAL, which consisted of six IMPARTIAL judges, three from each side, to resolve the dispute. U.S. President THEODORE ROOSEVELT appointed Senator HENRY CABOT LODGE, Secretary of War Elihu Root, and former senator George Turner. Great Britain appointed Lord Chief Justice of England Baron Alverstone and two officials from Canada, Sir Louis A. Jette and Allen B. Aylesworth. Although Canada believed that Great Britain would support Canadian interests, Great Britain largely sided with the United States because it needed the latter's assistance in an arms race between Great Britain and Germany. After three weeks of discussion, the PANEL of judges voted in favor the United States' position.

The tribunal established an International Boundary Commission to mark the official boundaries between Alaska and Canada. The commission was made permanent by a treaty between the United States and Great Britain in 1908. Another treaty in 1925 required the commission to maintain a 20-foot wide demarcated line along the border. The boundary is several thousand miles long and spread over mountains and through rivers, marshes, and forests.

Although the Alaska Boundary Dispute has fallen beyond the American consciousness, it remains a point of contention among some Canadians. The United States and Canada have had several disagreements regarding the proper land and water division in parts of the area. Moreover, environmentalists decry the clearing of timber along the border because of the potential for destroying biological diversity of plant and animal life. The Alaskan boundary remains, however, exactly how it appeared in the 1903 agreement, and the 1925 treaty remains intact.

FURTHER READINGS

Carroll, F. M. 1987. "Robert Lansing and the Alaska Boundary Settlement." *International History Review* 9.

Munro, John A., ed. 1970. *The Alaska Boundary Dispute.* Toronto: Copp Clark.

Penlington, Norman. 1972. *The Alaska Boundary Dispute: A Critical Reappraisal.* New York: McGraw-Hill Ryerson.

CROSS REFERENCES

Boundaries; International Law.

❖ ALBRIGHT, MADELEINE KORBEL

Madeleine Korbel Albright served from 1997 to 2001 as U.S. SECRETARY OF STATE, the government's highest-ranking foreign relations officer. She has the distinction of being the first woman to serve in this position. Albright, who has also taught international affairs, has had a long association with DEMOCRATIC PARTY presidential candidates, advising them on foreign policy.

Albright was born on May 15, 1937, in Prague, Czechoslovakia, the daughter of a Czech diplomat. In 1939 her family left Czechoslovakia for London, arriving shortly before the outbreak of WORLD WAR II. After the war ended in 1945, the family returned to their homeland but left again in 1948 following the Communist takeover of the Czech government. The family settled in the United States in 1949.

WE UNDERSTAND THAT TRUE DEMOCRACY IS NEVER ACHIEVED; IT IS ALWAYS A PURSUIT. AND WE KNOW THAT IF WE WHO LOVE LIBERTY GROW WEARY, THOSE WHO LOVE ONLY POWER WILL ONE DAY SWEEP US AWAY.
—MADELEINE ALBRIGHT

Madeleine Albright.
AP IMAGES

Albright earned a bachelor's degree in political science from Wellesley College in 1959 and then studied at the School of Advanced International Studies at Johns Hopkins University. She then entered the graduate program at Columbia University, receiving her master's degree and doctorate from the university's Department of PUBLIC LAW and Government. While working on her advanced degrees, Albright served in the diplomatic corps, acting as counselor for economic affairs at the U.S. embassy in Belgrade, Yugoslavia, from 1969 to 1972. She also worked for the Export-Import Bank.

After receiving her doctorate in 1976, Albright joined the staff of Democratic Senator Edmund S. Muskie of Maine, serving as his chief legislative assistant until 1978. She became a staff member of the NATIONAL SECURITY COUNCIL in 1978, serving President JIMMY CARTER until he left office in 1981.

Albright shifted her focus in 1981 to academia. She was awarded a fellowship at the Woodrow Wilson International Center for Scholars at the Smithsonian (1981–82), following an international competition in which she wrote about the role the press played in the political changes that occurred in Poland during the early 1980s. Her findings were published in *Poland, the Role of the Press in Political Change* (1983). Albright also served as a senior fellow in Soviet and Eastern European Affairs at the Center for Strategic and International Studies, conducting research in developments and trends in the Soviet Union and Eastern Europe. From 1982 to 1993 Albright taught at Georgetown University's School of Foreign Service, lecturing on international affairs, U.S. foreign policy, Russian foreign policy, and Central and Eastern European politics. She was also responsible for developing and implementing programs designed to enhance women's professional opportunities in international affairs. From 1989 to 1993 Albright was president of the Center for National Policy, a NONPROFIT research organization formed in 1981 by representatives from government, industry, labor, and education to promote the study and discussion of domestic and international issues.

Albright began working with Democratic presidential candidates in 1984 when she advised Walter F. Mondale on foreign policy. She served in a similar role for 1988 nominee Michael Dukakis and did the same for BILL CLINTON in 1992. After he was elected president, Clinton named Albright chief U.S. representative to the UNITED NATIONS, a cabinet-level position.

After President Clinton was reelected in 1996, he made changes in his cabinet. In

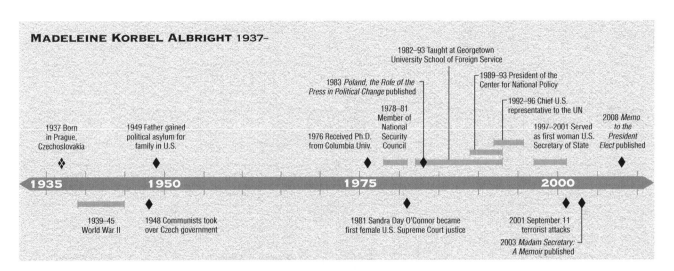

MADELEINE KORBEL ALBRIGHT 1937–

1982–93 Taught at Georgetown
University School of Foreign Service

1983 *Poland, the Role of the
Press in Political Change* published

1989–93 President of the
Center for National Policy

1992–96 Chief U.S.
representative to the UN

1978–81
Member of
National

2008 *Memo
to the
President
Elect* published

1937 Born
in Prague,
Czechoslovakia

1949 Father gained
political asylum for
family in U.S.

1976 Received Ph.D.
from Columbia Univ.

Security
Council

1997–2001 Served
as first woman U.S.
Secretary of State

1935   1950   1975   2000

1939–45
World War II

1948 Communists took
over Czech government

1981 Sandra Day O'Connor became
first female U.S. Supreme Court justice

2001 September 11
terrorist attacks

2003 *Madam Secretary:
A Memoir* published

December 1996 Clinton nominated Albright as secretary of state. After being unanimously confirmed by the U.S. Senate, she was sworn in as secretary of state on January 23, 1997.

The outspoken and dynamic Albright reinforced U.S. alliances, promoted American trade and business, and sought to establish international standards on trade and HUMAN RIGHTS. Albright advocated for the expansion and modernization of NATO and helped coordinate NATO's successful campaign to end ethnic cleansing in Kosovo. She helped to promote peace in Northern Ireland, the Middle East, and the Balkans.

Albright sought the expansion of democracy in Europe, Africa, Asia, and Latin America; she traveled to China to promote trade with the United States and also to address human rights issues. In June 2000, Albright and representatives from all over the world convened the first ever Conference of the Community of Democracies. Albright also led the fight to reverse a decade-long drop in funding for U.S. embassies and overseas operations by helping to persuade Congress to increase funding by 17 percent.

In May 2001 Albright returned to Georgetown University where she accepted an endowed chair in the School of Foreign Service. She lectures at colleges and universities and has appeared on numerous television news commentary programs since leaving the STATE DEPARTMENT. In 2006 her book *The Mighty and the Almighty: Reflections on America, God, and World Affairs*, was published. In 2008 *Memo to the President Elect: How to Restore America's Reputation and Leadership*, HarperCollins (New York, NY) was published. She continues her work with The Albright Group (global strategy firm), of which she is founder and principal, and Albright Capital Management LLC (INVESTMENT advisory firm), which she chairs and is principal.

FURTHER READINGS

Albright, Madeleine. 2003. *Madam Secretary: A Memoir.* New York: Miramax.

Blackman, Ann. 1998. *Seasons of Her Life: A Biography of Madeleine Korbel Albright.* New York: Scribner.

Blood, Thomas. 1997. *Madam Secretary: A Biography of Madeleine Albright.* New York: St. Martin's Press.

Dobbs, Michael. 1999. *Madeleine Albright: A Twentieth-Century Odyssey.* New York: Henry Holt.

Georgetown University. Available online at www.georgetown.edu (accessed August 24, 2009).

Hirsh, Michael. 2000. "The Lioness in Winter." *Newsweek* (July 10).

Lippman, Thomas W. 2000. *Madeleine Albright and the New American Diplomacy.* New York: Westview.

Special Libraries Association. Available online at www.sla.org (accessed August 24, 2009).

ALCOHOL

Alcohol is the active principle of intoxicating drinks, produced by the fermentation of sugars.

> A Congressman was once asked by a constituent to explain his attitude toward whiskey. "If you mean the demon drink that poisons the mind, pollutes the body, desecrates family life, and inflames sinners, then I'm against it," the Congressman said. "But if you mean the elixir of Christmas cheer, the shield against winter chill, the taxable potion that puts needed funds into public coffers to comfort little crippled children, then I'm for it. This is my position, and I will not compromise."

The LEGAL HISTORY of alcohol in the United States closely parallels the economic and social trends that shaped the country. The libertarian philosophy that ignited the WHISKEY REBELLION was born in the American Revolution. Shifting concerns about morality and family harmony that were characteristic of the Industrial Revolution inspired the TEMPERANCE MOVEMENT and brought about PROHIBITION, which began with the 1919 passage of the EIGHTEENTH AMENDMENT to the Constitution and ended with its repeal in 1933. The return of legalized drinking in the United States led to renewed discussion of the many health and safety issues associated with alcohol consumption. Over the following decades, the states addressed these issues through a variety of laws, such as those dealing with a minimum age for the purchase or consumption of alcohol, the labeling of alcoholic beverages, and drunk driving. Private litigants have expanded protections against harm from alcohol through tort actions, and various groups, both national and local, continue to lobby for increased legislation and higher penalties for alcohol-related acts that lead to injury.

Historical Background of Alcohol in the United States

> Drink is in itself a good creature of God,
> and to be received with thankfulness,
> but the abuse of drink is from Satan,
> the wine is from God, but the Drunkard is
>   from the Devil.
> (Increase Mather, Puritan clergyman, *Wo to Drunkards* [1673])

Alcoholic beverages have been consumed in the United States since the days of Plymouth Rock.

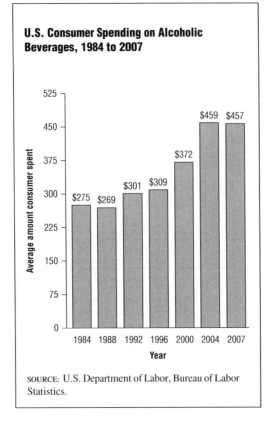

U.S. Consumer Spending on Alcoholic Beverages, 1984 to 2007

SOURCE: U.S. Department of Labor, Bureau of Labor Statistics.

In fact, beer and wine were staples on the ships carrying settlers to the New World. In colonial times, water and milk were scarce and susceptible to contamination or spoilage, and tea and coffee were expensive. The Pilgrims turned to such alternatives as cider and beer, and, less frequently, whiskey, rum, and gin. In 1790 PER CAPITA consumption of pure alcohol, or absolute alcohol, was just under six gallons per year. (Pure alcohol constitutes only a small percentage of an alcoholic drink. For example, if a beverage contains 10 percent alcohol by volume, one would have to drink ten gallons of it to consume one gallon of pure alcohol.)

Although the majority of the colonists drank alcohol regularly, strong community social strictures curbed any tendency toward immoderation. Drunken behavior was dealt with by emphasizing the need to restore community harmony and stability, rather than by imposing punishment.

Alcohol consumption continued without much controversy until after the Revolutionary War when whiskey and other distilled spirits became valuable commercial commodities. When Congress imposed an excise tax on the farmers who produced liquor in the 1790s, they resisted paying the tax. Their resistance became

known as the Whiskey Rebellion, a PROTEST movement of farmers who felt the tax placed an undue burden on their commercial activities.

Before the nineteenth century, farming was the predominant occupation, and, although it involved grueling work, it did not demand precision or speed. The Industrial Revolution brought millions of workers into factories where efficiency, dexterity, and rigid scheduling were necessary. With these economic changes came a shift in societal attitudes toward alcohol. Gone was the time when people considered the midday liquor break a benign DIVERSION.

The Temperance Movement

'Mid pleasures and palaces, though we may roam,
Be it ever so humble, there's no place like home.
But there is the father lies drunk on the floor,
The table is empty, the wolf's at the door,
And mother sobs loud in her broken-back'd chair,
Her garments in tatters, her soul in despair.
(Nobil Adkisson, *Ruined by Drink* [c. 1860])

As the United States entered the Industrial Age, attitudes about alcohol consumption gradually changed. A moralistic and punitive view of alcohol replaced the laissez-faire attitudes of earlier times. What had been the "good creature of God" in the eighteenth century became the "demon rum" of the nineteenth.

The U.S. temperance movement emerged around 1826 with the formation of the American Society for the Promotion of Temperance, later called the American Temperance Society. In the 1840s the society began crusading for complete abstinence from alcohol. Dissemination of the temperance message caused a fall in per capita consumption of pure alcohol from a high of more than seven gallons per year in 1830 to just over three in 1840, the largest ten-year drop in U.S. history. By the outbreak of the Civil War, 13 states, beginning with Maine in 1851, had adopted some form of prohibition as law.

Other temperance organizations became prominent during the middle to late 1800s. In 1874 the Woman's Christian Temperance Union (WCTU) was founded. The only temperance organization still in operation, the WCTU has worked continuously since its inception to educate the public and to influence policies that discourage the use of alcohol and other drugs. In

1990 the group was nominated for a Nobel Peace Prize.

In 1869 the anti-alcohol movement created its own political party—the National Prohibition party—devoted to a single goal: to inspire legislation prohibiting the manufacture, transportation, and sale of alcoholic beverages. The party made modest showings in state elections through the 1860s and 1870s and reached its peak of popular support in 1892 when John Bidwell won almost 265,000 votes in his bid for the presidency. The Prohibition party's main effect was its influence on PUBLIC POLICY. It succeeded in placing Prohibition planks into many state party platforms and was a potent impetus behind passage of the Eighteenth Amendment.

One of the most powerful forces in the Prohibition movement was the Anti-Saloon League, a nonpartisan group founded in 1893 by representatives of temperance societies and evangelical Protestant churches. The Anti-Saloon League, unlike the PROHIBITION PARTY, worked within established political parties to support candidates who were sympathetic to the league's goals. By 1916 the league, with the help of the Prohibition party and the WCTU, had sent enough sympathetic candidates to Congress to ensure action on a Prohibition amendment to the Constitution.

Prohibition

Prohibition is an awful flop.
We like it.
It can't stop what it's meant to stop.
We like it.
It's left a trail of graft and slime.
It don't prohibit worth a dime.
It's filled our land with VICE and crime.
Nevertheless, we're for it.
(Franklin P. Adams, quoted in *Era of Excess*)

In December 1917 the temperance movement achieved its goal when Congress approved the Eighteenth Amendment, which prohibited the manufacture, sale, transportation, importation, or exportation of intoxicating liquors from or to the United States or its territories. The amendment was sent to the states, and by January 1919 it was ratified. In January 1920 the United States officially became dry.

The demand for liquor did not end with Prohibition, however. Those willing to violate the law saw an opportunity to fill that demand and become wealthy in the process. Illegal stills produced the alcohol needed to make "bathtub

gin." Rum and other spirits from abroad were commonly smuggled into the country from the east and northwest coasts, and illegal drinking establishments, known as speakeasies or blind pigs, proliferated. The illicit production and distribution of alcohol, called bootlegging, spawned a multibillion-dollar underworld business run by a SYNDICATE of criminals.

Perhaps the most famous of the bootleggers was Al Capone, who ran liquor, PROSTITUTION, and RACKETEERING operations in Chicago, one of the wettest of the wet towns. At the height of his power in the mid-1920s, Capone made hundreds of millions of dollars per year. He employed nearly a thousand people and enjoyed the cooperation of numerous police officers and other corrupt public officials who were willing to turn a blind eye in return for a share of his profits. For years, Capone and others like him evaded attempts to shut down their operations. Capone's reign finally ended in 1931 when he was convicted of income TAX EVASION.

Historians differ about the success of Prohibition. Some feel that the effort was a ludicrous failure that resulted in more severe social problems than had ever been associated with alcohol consumption. Others point to ample evidence that Prohibition, although never succeeding in making the country completely dry, dramatically changed U.S. drinking habits. Per capita consumption at the end of Prohibition had fallen to just under a gallon of pure alcohol per year, and accidents and deaths attributable to alcohol had declined steeply.

Although Prohibition enjoyed widespread popular support, a substantial minority of U.S.

The 1888 Prohibition Party presidential candidate, Clinton Bowen Fisk, and his running mate, John A. Brooks, received close to 250,000 votes. Despite the party's meager showings in presidential elections, it was successful in influencing public policy and became an important player in the passage of the Eighteenth Amendment.

CORBIS.

citizens simply ignored the law. Also, although Prohibition unquestionably fostered unprecedented criminal activity, many people were concerned that the government's enforcement efforts unduly intruded into personal privacy. In cases such as *Carroll v. United States,* 267 U.S. 132, 45 S. Ct. 280, 69 L. Ed. 543 (1925), the Supreme Court indicated its willingness to stretch the limits of POLICE POWER to enforce Prohibition. In *Carroll,* the Court held that federal agents were justified in conducting a warrantless search of an automobile, because they had PROBABLE CAUSE to believe it contained illegal liquor.

Concerns over diminished liberties led to feelings that Prohibition was too oppressive a measure to impose upon an entire nation. This sentiment was bolstered by arguments that the production and sale of alcohol were profitable enterprises that could help boost the nation's depressed economy. By the beginning of the 1930s, after little more than a decade as law, Prohibition lost its hold on the U.S. conscience. The promise of jobs and increased tax revenues helped the anti-Prohibition message recapture political favor. The TWENTY-FIRST AMENDMENT, repealing Prohibition, swept through the necessary 36-state RATIFICATION process, and the "noble experiment" ended on December 5, 1933.

Post-Prohibition Regulation and Control

The repeal of Prohibition forced states to address once more the dangers posed by excessive alcohol consumption. The risks are well documented. The National Highway Traffic Safety Administration (NHTSA) estimated that in 2001 alcohol was involved in 41 percent of all fatal crashes (more than 17,000 fatalities). NHTSA also estimates that three out of ten Americans will be involved in an alcohol-related crash sometime during their lives. Alcohol is the most widely used drug among teenagers and is linked to juvenile crime, health problems, SUICIDE, date RAPE, and unwanted pregnancy. Alcohol-related traffic accidents are the leading cause of death among 15- to 24-year-olds.

In the face of rising concerns about liquor consumption and PERSONAL INJURY, many states chose to regulate alcohol through dramshop laws. A dramshop is any type of drinking establishment where liquor is sold for consumption on the premises. Dramshop statutes impose LIABILITY on sellers of alcoholic beverages for injuries caused by an intoxicated patron. Under

such statutes, a person injured by a drunk patron sues the establishment where the patron was served. The purpose of dramshop laws is to hold responsible those who enjoy economic benefit from the sale of liquor, thereby ensuring that a loss is not borne solely by an innocent victim (as when the intoxicated person who caused the injuries has no assets and no insurance).

The first dramshop law, enacted in Wisconsin in 1849, required saloons or taverns to post a bond for expenses that might result from civil lawsuits against their patrons. Many states followed Wisconsin's lead, and dramshop laws were prominent until the 1940s, 1950s, and 1960s, when most were repealed. However, the 1980s brought renewed concern over the consequences of overindulgence in alcohol, and public pressure led to the passage of new dramshop statutes. As of 2009, 42 states as well as the District of Columbia had imposed some form of liability on purveyors of alcoholic beverages for injuries caused by their customers.

All states and the District of Columbia also regulate the sale of liquor to minors or to individuals who are intoxicated. Challenges to the age restriction on EQUAL PROTECTION grounds have been unsuccessful.

Along with statutory measures, most courts have also recognized a common-law CAUSE OF ACTION against alcohol vendors for the negligent sale of alcohol. In *Rappaport v. Nichols,* 156 A.2d 1 (N.J. 1959), the court held that a tavern could be held liable for the plaintiff's husband's death after the tavern served an intoxicated minor who caused the accident that killed the man. The court relied on the public policy concerns underlying liquor control laws. Such laws are intended to protect the general public as well as minors or intoxicated persons, the court reasoned, and therefore the tavern should be held liable if its NEGLIGENCE was a substantial factor in creating the circumstances that led to the husband's death. Under *Rappaport,* serving as well as consuming alcohol can be construed to be the PROXIMATE CAUSE of an injury. A majority of jurisdictions later followed the *Rappaport* court's reasoning.

In determining the extent of an alcohol vendor's liability, a growing number of courts apply comparative negligence principles. Comparative negligence assesses partial liability to a PLAINTIFF whose failure to exercise reasonable care contributes to his or her own injury. In *Lee v. Kiku Restaurant,* 603 A.2d 503 (N.J. 1992), and *Baxter v.*

Noce, 752 P.2d 240 (N.M. 1988), the plaintiffs sued under dramshop statutes for injuries suffered when they rode with drunk drivers. The courts in both cases recognized the importance of dramshop statutes in protecting innocent victims of drunk behavior. However, they also recognized the need to hold individuals responsible to some degree for their own safety. Under comparative negligence, which divides liability among the parties in accordance with each party's degree of fault, both goals are achieved.

A few courts have extended liability for injuries to social hosts who serve a minor or an intoxicated guest. In *Kelly v. Gwinnell*, 476 A.2d 1219 (N.J. 1984), the New Jersey Supreme Court found both the host and the guest jointly liable when the guest had an accident after drinking at the host's house. The court based the host's liability on his continuing to serve alcoholic beverages to the guest when he knew the guest was intoxicated and likely to drive a car. Similarly, in *Koback v. Crook*, 366 N.W.2d 857 (Wis. 1985), the Wisconsin Supreme Court held that a social host was negligent for serving liquor to a minor guest at a graduation party. The guest was later involved in a motorcycle accident in which the plaintiff was injured. However, the Ohio Supreme Court refused to extend liability to the social host in *Settlemyer v. Wilmington Veterans Post No. 49*, 464 N.E.2d 521 (Ohio 1984). The court in *Settlemyer* held that assigning liability to a social host is a matter better left to the legislature.

All states and many local governments regulate the sale of alcohol through the issuance of licenses. These licenses limit the times and locations where liquor sales can take place. The government also regulates alcohol through TAXATION. Current taxes on liquor serve the same dual purpose as did the first excise tax on liquor when it was proposed by ALEXANDER HAMILTON in 1791: They provide a source of revenue for the government and, theoretically, discourage overindulgence. Enforcement of the laws regulating alcohol and taxing it is carried out by the BUREAU OF ALCOHOL, TOBACCO, FIREARMS, AND EXPLOSIVES (ATF), an agency of the U.S. JUSTICE DEPARTMENT, and the Tax and Trade Bureau (TTB), an agency of the TREASURY DEPARTMENT, respectively. The collection of alcohol revenues is important to the federal government: In 2005, liquor taxes exceeded $8.9 billion.

Since the 1980s, public awareness of the dangers of alcohol has led to a number of changes in the law. Specifically, special interest groups such as MOTHERS AGAINST DRUNK DRIVING (MADD) and Students Against Drunk Driving (SADD) urged state legislatures to greatly increase enforcement and penalties for driving while intoxicated (DWI). Criminal statutes make DWI a MISDEMEANOR offense. Historically, few persons served JAIL time unless they were repeat offenders. Moreover, prosecutors often reduced DWI charges to lesser charges, such as reckless driving, so defendants could avoid the stain of a DWI CONVICTION on their driving records.

MADD was formed by mothers of children who had been killed by drunk drivers. They were outraged at the way the criminal justice system treated DWI crimes. A major focus in the 1990s for MADD was convincing state legislatures to reduce the blood alcohol count needed to constitute a DWI offense. Specific blood-alcohol concentration (BAC) limits varied from state to state, but during the 1990s, a measure of .10 percent BAC usually qualified as driving while intoxicated.

The debate moved to the national level in 1998 when Congress first rejected and then enacted legislation that requires all states to lower the drunken driving arrest threshold to .08 percent. States that failed to change their laws would FORFEIT millions of dollars in federal highway construction funds. Although states were initially reluctant to do so, every state since the end of 2002 has used the .08 percent standard.

An increased knowledge about the consequences of alcohol consumption also had an effect on the makers of alcohol. Concerned individuals felt that liquor manufacturers had the duty to warn consumers that their product may be hazardous. Before 1987, manufacturers of alcoholic beverages were immune from civil liability for injuries resulting from the use of liquor. *Garrison v. Heublein, Inc.*, 673 F.2d 189 (7th Cir. 1982), held that the DEFENDANT did not have a duty to warn the plaintiff of the dangers of its product. The court stated that the dangers inherent in the use of alcohol are "common knowledge to such an extent that the product cannot objectively be considered to be unreasonably dangerous."

Garrison was followed by other jurisdictions until 1987 when *Hon v. Stroh Brewery*, 835 F.2d 510 (3d Cir. 1987), signaled a shift in judicial sentiment. In *Hon*, the plaintiff's 26-year-old husband died of pancreatitis attributable to his

DRINKING ON CAMPUS: A RITE OF PASSAGE OUT OF CONTROL?

Alcohol has had its advocates and its critics, particularly on college campuses, where the desires of students to enjoy the rights and freedoms of adults collide with the concerns of parents, university officials, and the police. Although some widely publicized studies from the late 1980s and early 1990s indicated that student drinking was at an all-time high, threatening students' health and academic careers, others indicated that the problem of student drinking was overblown and on the decline. By 2009, however, it was clear that over-consumption of alcohol, especially in episodes of binge drinking, remained a national problem. An Associated Press study found that 157 college-age people, age 18 to 23, drank themselves to death between 1999 and 2005. Attempts to curb drinking on campus have met with little success, as enforcement of underage drinking laws has proved ineffective, if nonexistent. In 2008 the presidents of 100 major universities and colleges threw up their hands and proposed lowering the drinking age from 21 to 18. They hoped that this might diminish the lure of alcohol as a forbidden fruit.

During the 1980s and 1990s attention focused increasingly on alcohol use by college students. An article published in the December 7, 1994, issue of the *Journal of the American Medical Association* reported the findings of a study conducted by Henry Wechsler, director of the Alcohol Studies Program at the Harvard School of Public Health. Wechsler and his team surveyed more than 17,000 students, first-year students to seniors, at 140 colleges in 40 states. They concluded that college students were drinking more than ever before.

In Wechsler's study, 44 percent of the students surveyed reported binge drinking, defined as having five consecutive drinks in a row for men or four in a row for women, on at least one occasion in the two weeks before the survey. (Wechsler defined binge drinking at a lower level of consumption for women because women's bodies take longer to metabolize alcohol, causing them to be affected by lesser amounts in a given time period.) Nineteen percent of all the surveyed students were found to be frequent binge drinkers, meaning they had at least three recent binges.

Similar findings were reported in 1994 by the Commission on Substance Abuse at Colleges and Universities, a group established by the Center on Addiction and Substance Abuse at Columbia University. Its report, titled *Rethinking Rites of Passage: Alcohol Abuse on America's Campuses,* stated that white males were the biggest drinkers on campus. However, the commission noted a sharp rise in the percentage of college women who drank to get drunk, from 10 percent in 1977 to 35 percent in 1994. Unlike female students in earlier studies, those in 1994 reported that they felt little or no social stigma attached to their drinking. At the same time, they felt pressure to succeed, and consuming alcohol was one way they CHOSE to relieve some of that pressure.

College administrators were not surprised by the findings of the two studies. The Harvard study reported that an overwhelming majority of the supervisors of security, deans of students, and directors of health services at the colleges surveyed considered heavy alcohol use a problem on their campuses. Plus, a survey by the Carnegie Foundation revealed that college presidents considered alcohol abuse their most pressing challenge.

College presidents and administrators have had practical reasons to be concerned about student drinking. Reports of drunken brawls, sexual assaults, even deaths attributable to alcohol create public relations nightmares for schools competing for students. There has also been the issue of LIABILITY: Is a college responsible for injuries inflicted by a drunk student? In addition, much of the drinking on campus has been done illegally by students who are under age.

moderate consumption of alcohol over a six-year period. The plaintiff alleged that the defendant's products were "unreasonably dangerous" because consumers were not warned of the lesser-known dangers of consumption. The court, relying on the Restatement (Second) of Torts § 402A, held that a product is defective if it lacks a warning sufficient to make it safe for its intended purpose. Because the general public is unaware of all the health risks associated with liquor consumption, the court found the defendant liable for failing to warn the plaintiff.

The reasoning in *Hon* has been followed in other cases, including *Brune v. Brown-Forman Corp.,* 758 S.W.2d 827 (Tex. App. 1988), where the court found that the defendant's product was unreasonably dangerous because it bore no warning about the dangers of excessive consumption. The plaintiff's daughter, a college student, died after consuming 15 shots of tequila over a short period of time.

The duty of liquor manufacturers to warn consumers of the hazards of drinking was codified when Congress passed the Alcoholic

Academic administrators have found particularly disturbing the increases in drinking among women. According to female students, the desire to compete with men in all arenas, including social, is one reason they feel the need to demonstrate their equality by drinking as much as or more than their male peers. A study conducted by Virginia's College of William and Mary indicated that the number of women at the college who had five or more drinks at one sitting increased from 27 percent to 36 percent during the early 1990s.

Both men and women students have cited intense peer pressure to join the partying that takes place on college campuses, which may begin as early as Wednesday or Thursday night and last through the weekend. At some schools, alcohol-centered gatherings can readily be found any night of the week. Administrators acknowledge that partying may have been just as hearty in the past but note that before the late 1980s, it was generally confined to the weekend.

The fallout from uncontrolled drinking has been felt throughout campus life. According to the report issued by the Commission on Substance Abuse at Colleges and Universities, 95 percent of violent crimes and 53 percent of injuries on campus are alcohol related. In 90 percent of all campus rapes, the assailant, the victim, or both had been drinking. Sixty percent of college women who acquire sexually transmitted diseases, including herpes and AIDS, report that they were drunk at the time they were infected. The financial costs are high as well. Students

spend $5.5 billion on alcohol each year, more than they spend on books, coffee, tea, sodas, and other drinks combined. Although athletes might be expected to take fewer risks with their health than other students, the commission concluded that they were equally affected by alcohol abuse.

The commission also found that students who belong to fraternities and sororities drink three times more than their non-Greek counterparts, averaging 15 drinks per week. Indeed, fraternity drinking has been blamed in several disciplinary actions and at least one death. In July 1994 the national office of Alpha Tau Omega (ATO) announced it was closing 11 of its chapters for violating rules against hazing and alcohol abuse. ATO had already closed its chapter at Wittenberg University, in Springfield, Ohio, after a newly recruited pledge was hospitalized in January 1994 for alcohol poisoning. Similarly, the national office of Beta Theta Pi (BTP) announced in 1994 that it would intensify enforcement of rules against hazing and alcohol use in its chapters. According to Erv Johnson, director of communications for the national office, BTP was concerned not only about the legal issues involved but also about the image of the fraternity and the national office's desire to emphasize that the primary purpose of going to college is to learn.

Excessive drinking has a direct effect on academic performance. Students with an A average generally have 3.6 drinks per week, C students average 9.5 drinks per week, and D and F students consume almost 18 drinks per week. According to college officials, alcohol is implicated in almost half of all

academic problems and is an issue for more than one-fourth of dropouts.

Excessive drinking has obvious negative consequences for the students who engage in it, but it also affects those who do not partake. During the early 1990s some students and school officials began to speak out against the damage and disorder that binge drinkers cause. Just as nonsmokers brought awareness of the effects of secondhand smoke, moderate and nondrinking students called attention to the results of "secondhand bingeing." Likewise, administrators, who had traditionally tried to downplay the severity of the problem, began to acknowledge it and tried several approaches to controlling it. One method involved having peer counselors educate students about the dangers of excessive drinking and about the effects of their actions on others. Another program provided students with recreational options that did not include alcohol. Some schools offered houses or sections of dorms where residents pledged not to drink or smoke. However, most administrators stopped short of preaching abstinence, acknowledging that most students have begun to drink before they enter college.

Concern over binge drinking on college campuses continued to rise at the beginning of the twenty-first century. In 2002 the Task Force on College Drinking of the National Institute on Alcohol Abuse and Alcoholism (NIAAA) released a study indicating that 1,400 college students died and another 500,000 were injured per year as a result of alcohol abuse. The study also found that more than 600,000 college

Beverage Labeling Act of 1988 (27 U.S.C.A. § 215). The act requires all alcoholic beverage containers to bear a clear and conspicuous label warning of the dangers of alcohol consumption.

The United States' long history of ambivalence toward the consumption of alcoholic beverages shows no sign of abating. At the same time that manufacturers are required to warn consumers about the health risks inherent in liquor, some medical studies indicate that certain health benefits may be associated with moderate imbibing.

FURTHER READINGS

Alcoholics Anonymous World Services (AAWS). *Twelve Steps and Twelve Traditions.* New York: AAWS.

Bartell, Donald J., and Anne D. ImObersteg. 2007. *Attacking and Defending Drunk Driving Tests.* Santa Anna, Cal.: James.

Blocker, Jack S., ed. 1979. *Alcohol, Reform and Society.* Westport, Conn.: Greenwood Press.

Boyd, Steven R., ed. 1985. *The Whiskey Rebellion.* Westport, Conn.: Greenwood Press.

Cochran, Robert F., Jr. 1994. "'Good Whiskey,' Drunk Driving, and Innocent Bystanders: The Responsibility of Manufacturers of Alcohol and Other Dangerous Hedonic Products for Bystander Injury." *South Carolina Law Review* 45 (winter).

DRINKING ON CAMPUS: A RITE OF PASSAGE OUT OF CONTROL?
(CONTINUED)

students were assaulted annually by another student who had been drinking, and more than 70,000 were victims of alcohol-associated sexual assaults or date rapes.

Also in 2002, the Harvard School for Public Health College Alcohol Study issued its fourth and final report on college drinking. It put the number of binge drinkers on college campuses at 44 percent—the same amount as in the school's 1994 report. This indicated that almost a decade of trying to combat binge drinking by colleges and universities had not succeeded in driving down the number of binge drinkers. Indeed, the 2002 survey found an increase in binge drinking among several groups, including binge drinkers at women's colleges, which rose from 24 percent to 32 percent of the population.

The 2002 College Alcohol Study found the number of frequent binge drinkers, defined as students who binged three or more times over a two-week period, had also remained steady at 20 percent. These frequent binge drinkers accounted for 70 percent of all alcohol consumption on campus. Drinking rates were highest among incoming freshmen, males, members of fraternities or sororities, and athletes. Students who attended two-year institutions, religious schools, commuter schools, or predominantly or historically black colleges and universities drank the least.

In response to the failure to bring down binge drinking rates, colleges and universities tried innovative approaches to tackle the problem. One was the use of "social norms" advertising, telling students that drinking on colleges was less prevalent than they thought, to convince students that most students do not binge drink, and that it is socially acceptable to abstain. Critics pointed out, however, that social norms advertising might simply send the wrong message to administrators and other policy makers—that drinking on campus was no big deal.

Other universities tried harsher enforcement policies, banning alcohol from college-run housing, even eliminating sororities and fraternities. Some colleges also tried to curb alcohol related advertising on campus, refusing to allow sponsorship of university activities by beer producers and asking bars and taverns near campus to limit promotions to college students. Several reinstated Friday and Saturday morning classes as a way to encourage students not to drink on weekends.

College administrators have had mixed results after tackling the problem. Former Middlebury College president John McCardell formed the @Amethyst Initiative in 2007 for the sole purpose of starting a debate on lowering the drinking age. By 2008, he had recruited 100 college presidents to agree that a discussion begin about lowering the drinking age to 18

in hopes of reducing binge drinking. (Changing state laws would first require Congress to repeal a federal highway law that requires states to maintain the drinking age at 21 or lose all federal highway funding.) McCardell believed the current laws were routinely evaded and that they discriminated against young people. Organizations such as Mother Against Drunk Driving oppose the lowering of the drinking age and complain that colleges refuse to enforce campus policies as well as state law. Other college presidents disagree with the lowering of the drinking age. It is clear that the idea of allowing 18-year-olds to drink legally remains a volatile issue.

FURTHER READINGS

College Drinking: Changing the Culture. National Institute on Alcohol Abuse and Alcoholism website: http://www.college drinkingprevention.gov (accessed Mar. 31, 2010)

Okie, Susan. 2002. "Study Cites Alcohol Link in Campus Deaths; 1,400 Die Yearly in Accidents." *Washington Post* (April 10).

Russell, Jenna. 2002. "Little Improvement Seen in College Binge Drinking." *Boston Globe* (March 25).

Sullivan, Michelle. 2002. "Students at Risk Due to 'Culture of Drinking.'" *Clinical Psychiatry News* (June 1).

CROSS REFERENCES

Alcohol "Alcoholics Anonymous" (Sidebar).

Cordes, Renee. 1992. "Alcohol Manufacturer Held Partially Liable for Student's Death." *Trial* 28 (December).

Goldberg, James M. 1992. "Social Host Liability for Serving Alcohol." *Trial* 28 (March).

Gorski, Terence T. 1989. *Understanding the Twelve Steps.* New York: Prentice-Hall/Parkside.

Jacobs, James B. 1989. *Drunk Driving: An American Dilemma.* Chicago, Ill.: Univ. of Chicago Press.

Khoury, Clarke E. 1989. "Warning Labels May Be Hazardous to Your Health: Common-Law and Statutory Responses to Alcoholic Beverage Manufacturers' Duty to Warn." *Cornell Law Review* 75.

Kyvig, David E., ed. 1985. *Law, Alcohol, and Order.* Westport, Conn.: Greenwood Press.

Lender, Mark. 1987. *Drinking In America: A History.* New York: Free Press.

Moore, Pamela A. 1993. "*Lee v. Kiku Restaurant:* Allocation of Fault between an Alcohol Vendor and a Patron—What Could Happen after Providing 'One More for the Road'?" *American Journal of Trial Advocacy* 17: 1.

Smith, Christopher K. "State Compelled Spiritual Revelation: The First Amendment and Alcoholics Anonymous as a Condition of Drunk Driving Probation." 1992. *William and Mary Bill of Rights Journal* 1 (fall).

Taylor, Lawrence, and Steve Oberman. 2006. *Drunk Driving Defense.* New York: Aspen.

Alcoholics Anonymous

The courts have long struggled with the problem of what sanctions to impose on people who violate the law while under the influence of liquor. Punishing these offenders fails to address the root cause of the behaviors, the uncontrolled consumption of alcohol. Many judges order offenders to undergo alcohol-dependency treatment or counseling as part of a sentence or as a condition of probation.

One of the most popular programs for treating alcoholism is Alcoholics Anonymous (AA). AA was founded in 1935 by New York stockbroker Bill Wilson and Ohio surgeon Robert Smith. Wilson and Smith recognized their inability to control their drinking and were determined to overcome their problem. They developed the Twelve Steps, on which AA is based and which have become the foundation for similar self-help and recovery programs. AA comprises ninety thousand local groups in 141 countries. Participation is voluntary, and there are no dues or other requirements. Members attend meetings run by nonprofessionals, many of whom are recovering alcoholics. The meetings offer fellowship, support, and education to those with a desire to stop drinking.

Participants in AA declare that they cannot control their drinking alone, and invoke a higher power to help them overcome their dependence on alcohol. AA's Twelve Steps require a fundamental change in personality and outlook. Members admit their powerlessness over alcohol to themselves, to God, and to their friends and families. They attempt to make amends for any wrongs they have committed because of alcohol abuse. Finally, through prayer, meditation, and daily self-evaluation, AA members strive for a radical transformation or spiritual awakening, which results in changed perceptions, thought processes, and actions. Finally, participants share their experiences with others.

Although AA's Twelve Steps speak of God, a higher power, and spiritual awakening, AA maintains that it is not a religious organization. However, the group's religious underpinnings and the tone of its meetings, which may begin with the Serenity Prayer and generally end with group recitation of the Lord's Prayer, are objectionable to some. Courts have split over the issue of whether forced participation in AA violates the First Amendment religion clauses.

CROSS REFERENCES

First Amendment; Religion.

Vartabedian, Ralph. 2002. "Some States Resist Lower Alcohol Limits." *Los Angeles Times* (December 30).

Wagenaar, Alexander C., and Traci L. Toomey. 2000 "Alcohol Policy: Gaps Between Legislative Action and Current Research." *Contemporary Drug Problems* 27 (winter).

CROSS REFERENCES

Alcohol, Tobacco, Firearms, and Explosives, Bureau of; Automobile Searches; Blue Laws; Organized Crime; Product Liability.

ALCOHOL, TOBACCO, FIREARMS, AND EXPLOSIVES, BUREAU OF

For more than 80 years, the Bureau of Alcohol, Tobacco, and Firearms was an agency of the U.S. DEPARTMENT OF THE TREASURY. The Homeland Security Act of 2002, Pub. L. No. 107-296, 116 Stat. 2135, divided the agency into two bureaus: the Bureau of Alcohol, Tobacco, Firearms, and Explosives (still referred to as ATF) and the Tax and Trade Bureau (TTB). Effective January 24, 2003, the ATF became part of the JUSTICE DEPARTMENT, while the TTB remained part of the TREASURY DEPARTMENT. The move of the ATF to the Justice Department would allow ATF agents and inspectors to partner with traditional law enforcement agencies, such as the FEDERAL BUREAU OF INVESTIGATION. With this change, the TTB became responsible for revenue collection and regulation of legitimate alcohol and tobacco industries.

The ATF itself was established on July 1, 1972, but it traces its roots to the days of PROHIBITION. The legendary Eliot Ness and his Untouchables, famous U.S. revenue agents remembered for their dramatic surprise raids on illegal alcohol operations, were predecessors of twenty-first century ATF agents. The Untouchables earned their name

Three Bureau of ATF agents display firearms outside an ATF office in Maryland. The ATF is an agency of the U.S. Justice Department.

AP IMAGES

because of their reputation for high moral integrity and resistance to corruption.

Before the division of the bureau in 2002, the ATF had a long and somewhat complex history. With the passage of the EIGHTEENTH AMENDMENT, the manufacture, sale, transportation, importation, and exportation of "intoxicating liquors" from or to the United States or its territories became illegal. This amendment ushered in Prohibition, an era of ORGANIZED CRIME and underworld syndicates that controlled an illicit liquor business with violence and intimidation. In an attempt to stanch the flow of WEAPONS to these criminals, Congress passed several laws to regulate the firearms and ammunition industries. Originally, the Bureau of Prohibition was responsible for administering these laws. In 1942 the Alcohol Tax Unit (ATU), a forerunner of the ATF, formally took over the bureau's job when the bureau was disbanded following repeal of the Eighteenth Amendment. In 1952 the ATU added enforcement of tobacco tax laws to its list of responsibilities and changed its title to the Alcohol and Tobacco Tax Division (ATTD) of the INTERNAL REVENUE SERVICE (IRS).

During the 1960s Congress recognized the need to control destructive devices other than firearms. The Omnibus Crime Control and Safe Streets Act of 1968 and the Gun Control Act of 1968, 18 U.S.C.A. § 921 et seq., superseded earlier firearms control laws and placed bombs and other explosives as well as firearms under the strict control of the government. The ATTD was given jurisdiction over the criminal use of explosives and was renamed the Alcohol, Tobacco, and Firearms Division (ATFD) of the IRS.

In 1970 the Organized Crime Control Act, 18 U.S.C.A. 841-848, which included the Explosives Control Act, 18 U.S.C.A. § 842, provided for close regulation of the explosives industry and designated certain arsons and bombings as federal crimes. With the additional responsibility of enforcing these new laws, the ATFD redefined its mission in order to distinguish itself from the IRS. On July 1, 1972, the ATFD was given full bureau status within the Treasury Department and acquired the name, the Bureau of Alcohol, Tobacco and Firearms.

The ATF and TTB are responsible for enforcing and ensuring COMPLIANCE with the following laws:

- Federal Alcohol Administration Act, 27 U.S.C.A. § 201 et seq. (1935);
- Internal Revenue Code of 1954, as it relates to distilled spirits, tobacco products, and firearms (26 U.S.C.A. §5001 et seq.);

- Gun Control Act of 1968, as amended, 18 App. 26 U.S.C.A. § 5801 et seq.;
- Title XI of the Organized Crime Control Act (1970) (Explosives Control Act) (22 U.S.C. §2778);
- Portions of the Arms Export Control Act (1976);
- Trafficking in Contraband Cigarettes Act (1978) 18 U.S.C.A. 2341–2346;
- Anti-Arson Act of 1982 (amended title XI of the Organized Crime Control Act), 18 U.S.C.A. §§ 841 note, 844;
- Armed Career Criminal Act of 1984, 18 App. U.S.C.A. §§ 1201, 1202.

In the area of alcohol and tobacco regulation, as of 2003, the TTB controls production, labeling, advertising, and the relationships between producers, wholesalers, and retailers. The responsibility was previously under the PURVIEW of the ATF. TTB efforts are directed mainly at protecting consumers against products that are impure or mislabeled or otherwise potentially harmful.

During the 1980s alcohol-related activities of the ATF focused on the promulgation and enforcement of labeling regulations. For example, in March 1994, the Miller Brewing Company replaced an advertisement for one of its beers in response to concerns raised by ATF officials. The advertisement showed the beer's label, which listed the product's alcohol content, a violation of the Federal Alcohol Administration Act (FAAA), 27 U.S.C.A. § 201 et seq., one of the laws the ATF enforces. However, the strength of that act was diluted later by a 1995 Supreme Court decision declaring the restriction unconstitutional. In *Rubin v. Coors Brewing Co.*, 514 U.S. 476, 115 S. Ct. 1585, 131 L. Ed. 2d 532 (1995), the Court held that the subsection of the act that prohibits brewers from advertising the alcohol content of their beers was unnecessarily broad and violated the FIRST AMENDMENT. The Court stated further that the government's legitimate interest in preventing manufacturers from competing by increasing the alcohol content of their beers could be accomplished through less restrictive means, such as by directly limiting the alcohol content of beer or by banning the advertisement of alcohol content of high-alcohol brews.

During the 1980s and 1990s, ATF enforcement duties were increasingly focused on firearms as alcohol and tobacco regulation became mainly a matter of TAXATION. As of 1991, an estimated 270,000 dealers, importers, and manufacturers of firearms, ammunition, and explosives were licensed in the United States. Approximately 140 million to 200 million firearms were in circulation. The ATF must oversee enforcement of the laws regulating these items.

The ATF functioned with relative anonymity until February 28, 1993, when it became involved in an ill-fated raid that tainted its reputation and called its future into question. Acting on reports of stockpiled weapons and explosives at the headquarters of a religious sect, the Branch Davidians of Waco, Texas, ATF agents executed a military-style raid of the compound. The agents proceeded with the raid even after discovering that the Branch Davidians had been tipped off by an informant. In the ensuing gunfight, four ATF agents were killed and fifteen wounded. The Davidians refused to surrender, and the agents refused to back down. The standoff continued until April 19, when ATF agents again moved to take the compound by force. The raid turned into a shoot-out and conflagration in which 85 members of the cult, including 17 children, perished.

The bureau was widely criticized for its actions at Waco. A report on the incident issued by the Treasury Department concluded that the decision to proceed was wrong and that those in charge of the operation knew it was a mistake to proceed with the raid because the element of surprise was missing. The bureau's director, Stephen E. Higgins, retired early from his position, and two agents, Phillip J. Chojnacki and Charles D. Sarabyn, were suspended for their roles in the botched raid. Chojnacki and Sarabyn appealed their suspensions, and, in December 1994, they were reinstated with full back pay and benefits, although they were demoted. In addition, the incident was removed from their personnel files.

The incident at Waco aroused the ire of many U.S. citizens, particularly right-wing MILITIA groups who saw the raid as an example of government intrusion upon their right to keep and bear arms. The NATIONAL RIFLE ASSOCIATION sent out membership solicitation letters in 1995 described ATF agents as "jack-booted government thugs." Some believe that an April 1995 bombing of a federal building in Oklahoma City, which took place exactly two years after Waco, was planned in retaliation for the ATF raid on the Branch Davidians.

Controversy continues to surround the ATF. Some critics say that its agents are not sufficiently trained to carry out the types of operations its administrators seem to favor. Others contend that it lacks a coherent mission and that many of its duties, such as enforcement of alcohol regulations, are better suited to other agencies. The move toward a complete split between the agencies was expected to take some time. Information on the ATF is available online at www.aft.gov.

FURTHER READINGS

Bureau of Alcohol, Tobacco, Firearms, and Explosives Web site. "History of ATF from Oxford Univ. Press, Inc. 1789–1998 U.S." Available online at http://www.atf. gov/about/atfhistory.htm; website home page: http:// www.atf.gov (accessed December 9, 2009).

Reavis, Dick J. 1998. The Ashes of Waco: An Investigation. New York: Syracuse Univ. Press.

U.S. Government Printing Office Web site. Available online at http://www.gpoaccess.gov (accessed July 4, 2009).

CROSS REFERENCES

Alcohol; Branch Davidian Raid; Explosives; Gun Control; Weapons.

ALDERMAN OR ALDERWOMAN

A public officer of a town or city council or a local legislative body who is elected to the position by the persons he or she represents.

ALEATORY CONTRACT

A mutual agreement between two parties in which the performance of the contractual obligations of one or both parties depends upon a fortuitous event.

The most common type of aleatory contract is an insurance policy in which an insured pays a premium in exchange for an insurance company's promise to pay DAMAGES up to the face amount of the policy in the event that one's house is destroyed by fire. The insurance company must perform its obligation only after the fortuitous event, the fire, occurs.

✧ ALEXANDER, JAMES

James Alexander, born in 1691 in Scotland, was an eminent lawyer who became famous for his support of FREEDOM OF THE PRESS.

In 1715 Alexander immigrated to America, and began a career of public service to New York and New Jersey. He performed the duties of surveyor general for the Province of New Jersey in 1715, and three years later served as recorder of Perth Amboy.

Alexander participated in the Council of New York from 1721 to 1732 but continued to be active in New Jersey. He was admitted to the New Jersey Provincial bar in 1723, and joined the Council of New Jersey in that same year, serving until 1735. From 1723 to 1727 Alexander performed the duties of New Jersey attorney general.

In 1735 journalist John Peter Zenger was on trial, accused of libelous attacks on the administration of New York Governor William Cosby. Alexander served as codefense lawyer at this trial, and ALEXANDER HAMILTON pleaded the case. Zenger was acquitted, and the success of this defense was a triumph for the principles of a free press.

Alexander died in Albany, New York, on April 12, 1756.

ALIAS

[Latin, Otherwise called.] *A term used to indicate that a person is known by more than one name.*

Alias is a short and more popular phrase for *alias dictus.* The abbreviation a.k.a., *also known as,* is frequently used in connection with the description of a person sought by law

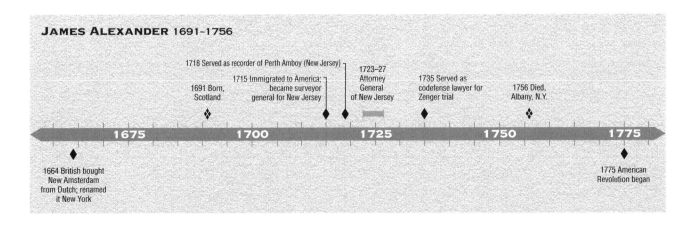

JAMES ALEXANDER 1691–1756

1718 Served as recorder of Perth Amboy (New Jersey)

1715 Immigrated to America; became surveyor general for New Jersey

1691 Born, Scotland

1723–27 Attorney General of New Jersey

1735 Served as codefense lawyer for Zenger trial

1756 Died, Albany, N.Y.

1675   1700   1725   1750   1775

1664 British bought New Amsterdam from Dutch; renamed it New York

1775 American Revolution began

enforcement officers to disclose the names that the person has been known to use. A fictitious name assumed by a person is popularly termed an alias.

ALIAS WRIT

A second writ, or court order, issued in the same case after an earlier writ of that kind has been issued but has not been effective.

ALIEN AND SEDITION ACTS

In 1798 the Federalist-controlled Congress passed four acts to empower the president of the United States to expel dangerous aliens from the country; to give the president authority to arrest, detain, and deport resident aliens hailing from enemy countries during times of war; to lengthen the period of naturalization for immigrants; and to silence Republican criticism of the Federalist Party. Also an act passed by Congress in 1918 during World War I that made it a crime to disrupt military recruiting or enlistments, to encourage support for Germany and its allies or disrespect for American war efforts, or to otherwise bring the U.S. government, its leaders, or its symbols into disrepute.

The Alien and Sedition Acts of 1798

Passions over the French Revolution split early American politics. Having endured Shays's Rebellion and the WHISKEY REBELLION, Federalists saw much to fear in the French Revolution. On the other hand, Democratic-Republicans, led by THOMAS JEFFERSON, proudly supported the French Revolution as the progeny of the American Revolution. Democratic-Republicans still viewed Britain as an enemy, while the Federalists regarded Britain as a bulwark against French militancy.

In early 1798 JOHN QUINCY ADAMS, son of President JOHN ADAMS and the U.S. ambassador to Prussia, advised his father that France intended to invade America's western frontier. Jonathon Dayton, speaker of the U.S. House of Representatives, speculated publicly that troops already massed in French ports were destined for North America. Federal officials feared parts of America were rife with French agents and sympathizers who might rise up in support of an invasion. George Tucker, professor of Law at the College of William and Mary, predicted that 100,000 U.S. inhabitants, including himself, would join a French invading army. Former president GEORGE WASHINGTON, summoned from retirement to lead the U.S. Army against a

possible French invasion, expressed concerns that France would invade the southern states first, "because the French will expect from the TENOR of the debates in Congress to find more friends there."

Congress responded to these concerns by enacting the Alien and Sedition Acts, the popular names for four laws passed in 1798. On June 18 Congress passed the NATURALIZATION Act, which extended from five to 14 years the period of residence required for alien immigrants to become full U.S. citizens (1 Stat. 566). On June 25 Congress passed the Alien Act, which authorized the president to expel, without a hearing, any alien the president deemed "dangerous to the peace and safety" of the United States or whom the president suspected of "treasonable or secret" inclinations (1 Stat. 570). On July 6 Congress passed the Alien Enemy Act, which authorized the president to arrest, imprison, or banish any resident alien hailing from a country against which the United States had declared war (1 Stat. 577).

None of these first three acts had much practical impact. The Naturalization Act contained a built-in window period that allowed resident ALIENS to become U.S. citizens before the fourteen-year requirement went into effect. President Adams never invoked the Alien Act, and the passing of the war scare in 1789 rendered the Alien Enemies Act meaningless.

However, the Sedition Act deepened partisan political positions between the FEDERALIST PARTY and the DEMOCRATIC-REPUBLICAN PARTY. The Sedition Act made it a high MISDEMEANOR, punishable by fine, IMPRISONMENT, or both, for citizens or aliens (1) to oppose the execution of federal laws; (2) to prevent a federal officer from performing his or her duties; (3) to aid "any INSURRECTION, RIOT, UNLAWFUL ASSEMBLY, or combination"; or (4) to make any defamatory statement about the federal government or the president (1 Stat. 596).

Because the Federalists controlled Congress and the White House, Republicans believed these laws were aimed at silencing Jeffersonian critics of the Adams administration and its laws and policies. Eighteen people were indicted under the Sedition Act of 1798; 14 were prosecuted, and 10 convicted, some of whom received prison sentences.

The validity of the Sedition Act was never tested in the U.S. Supreme Court before it expired in 1801. But Congress later passed a law that repaid all fines collected under it, and Jefferson, after becoming president in 1801, pardoned all those convicted under the act.

Before becoming president, Jefferson joined Madison in voicing opposition to the Sedition Act by drafting the Virginia and Kentucky Resolutions. Jefferson was responsible for drafting the two Kentucky Resolutions, while Madison penned the one Virginia RESOLUTION. The Virginia and Kentucky Resolutions condemned the Sedition Act as a violation of the Free Speech Clause to the FIRST AMENDMENT of the U.S. Constitution. The resolutions also argued that Congress had exceeded its powers by passing the law in the first place, because Congress may only exercise those powers specifically delegated to it, and nowhere in Article I of the Constitution is authority given to the legislative branch to regulate political speech. The Kentucky state legislature passed its two resolutions on November 16, 1798, and November 22, 1999, whereas Virginia passed its one resolution on December 24, 1798.

Sedition Act of 1918

Concern over disloyalty during wartime provided the backdrop for the second Sedition Act in U.S. history. In April 1917 the United States entered WORLD WAR I when Congress declared war against Germany and its allies. A month later, the Selective Service Act reinstated the military draft. Both the draft and U.S. entry into the war were met with PROTEST at home. Worried that anti-war protestors might interfere with the prosecution of the war, Congress passed the Sedition Act of 1918.

An amendment to the ESPIONAGE ACT OF 1917, the Sedition Act of 1918 made it a FELONY (1) to convey false statements interfering with American war efforts; (2) to willfully employ "disloyal, profane, scurrilous, or abusive language" about the U.S. form of government, the Constitution, the flag, or U.S. military or naval forces; (3) to urge the curtailed production of necessary war materials; or (4) to advocate, teach, defend, or suggest the doing of any such acts. Violations were punishable by fine, imprisonment, or both. The law was aimed at curbing political DISSENT expressed by socialists, anarchists, pacifists, and certain labor leaders.

The U.S. Supreme Court upheld the Sedition Act of 1918 over free speech objections made by civil libertarians. However, in a famous dissenting opinion that shaped First Amendment law for the rest of the twentieth century, Associate Justice Oliver Wendell Holmes Jr. encouraged courts to closely scrutinize prosecutions under the Sedition Act to make sure that only those individuals who created a "clear and present danger" of immediate criminal activity were convicted (ABRAMS V. UNITED STATES, 250 U.S. 616, 1180, 40 S. Ct. 17, 63 L. Ed. 1173 [1919]).

FURTHER READINGS

Miller, John Chester. 1951. *Crisis in Freedom: The Alien and Sedition Acts.* Boston: Little, Brown.

Moore, Wayne D. 1994. "Reconceiving Interpretive Autonomy: Insights from the Virginia and Kentucky Resolutions." *Constitutional Commentary* 11 (fall).

Smith, James Morton. 1967. *Freedom's Fetters: The Alien and Sedition Laws and American Civil Liberties.* Ithaca, NY: Cornell Univ. Press.

CROSS REFERENCES

Aliens "Aliens and Civil Rights" (Sidebar); Espionage; Freedom of Speech.

ALIEN ENEMY

In international law, a foreign-born citizen or subject of a nation or power that is hostile to the United States.

An alien enemy is an individual who, due to permanent or temporary allegiance to a hostile power, is regarded as an enemy in wartime. Under federal law, an alien enemy is a native, citizen, or subject of a foreign nation, state, or sovereign with which the United States is at war. Such a person is considered an alien enemy as long as the United States remains at war as determined through PROCLAMATION by the president or RESOLUTION by Congress. 8 C.F.R. § 331.1 (2002). During times of declared war, Congress has permitted the president to order the apprehension, restraint, and DEPORTATION of alien enemies. 50 U.S.C.A. § 21 (2003).

A citizen or subject of an enemy country, residing in the United States, under license or permission of the U.S. Government, express or tacit, and peacefully carrying on his or her ordinary vocation, is not under disability in the civil courts, and may institute an action to enforce his or her rights during the continuance of the war, or PROSECUTE such an action already instituted before the war. A resident alien enemy is precluded from bringing suit in the courts of this country only so far as this preclusion is necessary to prevent the use of

During World War II, the U.S. government moved thousands of Japanese Americans to detention camps because it considered them alien enemies while the country was at war with Japan.

NATIONAL ARCHIVES AND RECORDS ADMINISTRATION

the courts to accomplish a purpose that might hamper the war effort or give aid to the enemy.

The term *alien enemy*, as it is defined by federal law, does apply easily to individuals who belong to organizations that are not affiliated with a foreign sovereign. Nevertheless, the treatment of such ALIENS mirrors treatment permitted by federal law for aliens who are citizens of foreign nations. In the wake of the SEPTEMBER 11TH ATTACKS, Congress passed the Authorization for the Use of Military Force JOINT RESOLUTION, Pub. L. No. 107-40, 115 Stat. 224, permitting the president to use force to detain and try non-citizens in the WAR ON TERRORISM. On November 13, 2001, President GEORGE W. BUSH issued a military order [66 Fed. Reg. 57,831–57,836 (2001)] setting forth the military's policy for the treatment of non-citizens in the war on TERRORISM. The order applies to individuals who are or were members of the terrorist organization al Qaeda; have engaged in, aided or abetted, or conspired to commit acts of international terrorism; or have harbored such a non-citizen.

FURTHER READINGS

Green, Leslie C. 1999. *Essays on the Modern Law of War.* 2d ed. Ardsley, N.Y.: Transnationals.

Fehlings, Gregory. 2002. "Storm on the Constitution: The First Deportation Law." *Tulsa Journal of Comparative and International Law* 63.

Levie, Howard S. 1993. *Terrorism in War: The Law of War Crimes.* Dobbs Ferry, N.Y.: Oceana.

Schmidt, Michael N., and Leslie C. Green. 1997. *Levie on the Law of War.* Newport, R.I.: Naval War College.

ALIENABLE

The character of property that makes it capable of sale or transfer.

Absent a restriction in the owner's right, interests in real property and tangible personal property are generally freely and fully alienable by their nature. Likewise, many types of intangible personal property, such as a patent or trademark, are alienable forms of property. By comparison, constitutional rights of life, liberty, and property are not transferable and, thus, are termed inalienable. Similarly, certain forms of property, such as employee security benefits, are typically not subject to transfer on the part of the owner and are inalienable forms of property.

ALIENATE

To voluntarily convey or transfer title to real property by gift, disposition by will or the laws of descent and distribution, or by sale.

For example, a seller may alienate property by transferring to a buyer a parcel of the seller's land containing a house, in exchange for cash. The seller is said to have alienated her rights in that parcel, such as the right to modify or even demolish the house on the parcel of land, to the buyer. Those rights now belong to the buyer.

ALIENATION CLAUSE

A provision in a document permitting or forbidding a person from transferring property that is the subject of the document.

In a fire insurance policy, an ALIENATION CLAUSE prohibits the alienation of the insured premises while the policy is in effect. If the insured violates this provision, the policy is void.

ALIENATION OF AFFECTION

The removal of love, companionship, or aid of an individual's spouse.

Historically, ALIENATION OF AFFECTION furnished grounds for an action against the individual who interloped in a marital relationship. The harm caused was viewed as a deprivation of an individual's rights of consortium.

The elements of the action generally included wrongful conduct by the interfering party with the complainant's spouse, the loss of affection or consortium, and a nexus between the conduct of the DEFENDANT and the impairment or loss of consortium, which included a deprivation of such rights a services, assistance, and sexual relations. In the early twenty-first century, the action has fallen into disuse and no longer constitutes a ground for a lawsuit in most states.

ALIENS

Foreign-born persons who have not been naturalized to become U.S. citizens under federal law and the Constitution.

The federal IMMIGRATION laws determine whether a person is an alien. Generally, a person born in a foreign country is an alien, but a child born in a foreign country to parents who are U.S. citizens is a U.S. citizen. The term *alien* also refers to a native-born U.S. citizen who has relinquished U.S. citizenship by living and acquiring citizenship in another country. Aliens are categorized in several ways: resident and nonresident, immigrant and nonimmigrant, documented and undocumented ("illegal").

Overview

The United States welcomes a large number of aliens every year. Millions of foreign-born persons travel, work, and study in the country, and hundreds of thousands more choose to immigrate and become U.S. citizens. All of them are subject to federal immigration law. At the simplest level, the law serves as a gatekeeper for the nation's borders: It determines who may enter, how long they may stay, and when they must leave. In totality, of course, its scope far exceeds this simple purpose. Immigration law is concerned not only with borders but with what goes on inside them. It has much to say about the legal rights, duties, and obligations of aliens in the United States, which, in some respects, are different from those of citizens. Ultimately, it also provides the means by which certain aliens are naturalized as new citizens with all the rights of citizenship.

Congress has total authority over immigration. In the legislative branch of government, this power has no equal. The U.S. Supreme Court has determined that "over no conceivable subject is the legislative power of Congress more complete" (*Fiallo v. Bell*, 430 U.S. 787, 97 S. Ct. 1473, 52 L. Ed. 2d 50 [1977]). With a few notable exceptions concerning the right of aliens to constitutional protections, the courts have rarely intruded. Presidents have no inherent say; their influence is limited to policies on REFUGEES. Moreover, congressional authority preempts all state laws and regulations and even addresses the rights of aliens during wartime. In practical terms, these circumstances mean that immigration law is entirely the domain of federal lawmakers, whose say is usually final. Congress alone decides who will be welcomed or turned away, as well as what aliens may and may not do in the United States.

This authority has a long and controversial past. The first laws date to 1875, and their history is rife with discrimination. Lawmakers have always created barriers that favor some aliens over others. At one time, Chinese were not wanted; at others, Japanese; the list goes on and on. Only in the latter half of the twentieth century were these widely divergent policies codified under a primary federal statute, the Immigration and Nationality Act (INA) (Pub. L. No. 414, ch. 477, 66 Stat. 163, codified as amended in scattered sections of 8 U.S.C.A., 18 U.S.C.A., 22 U.S.C.A., 49 U.S.C.A., 50 App. U.S. C.A.), since 1952 the basic source of immigration law. For decades, the INA was easily tinkered with through amendments and bills. A dazzling number of political reasons made Congress create a patchwork of preferences, exceptions, and quotas, each reflecting who was wanted and who was not. Although somewhat less frequently toward the end of the twentieth century, national origin has often decided whether the United States admitted an alien.

Modern legislation has introduced significant changes. Reform has followed two distinct lines of thought: the need to stem illegal immigration, and the desire to make the law more fair for legal immigrants. Congress tackled the first issue in the Immigration Reform and Control Act of 1986 (IRCA) (Pub. L. No. 99-603, 100 Stat. 3359, codified as amended in scattered sections of the U.S.C.A.). The IRCA toughened criminal sanctions for employers who hire illegal aliens, denied these aliens federally funded WELFARE benefits, and legitimized some aliens through an amnesty program. Related legislation, the Immigration MARRIAGE FRAUD Amendments of 1986, 8 U.S. C.A. § 1101 note et seq., cracked down on the popular illegal practice of marrying to obtain citizenship. Fairness issues helped influence the

second major reform, the Immigration Act of 1990, Pub. L. No. 101-649, 104 Stat. 4978 (codified in scattered sections of the U.S.C.A.). Thoroughly revamping the INA, the 1990 act allocated visas more evenly among foreign nations, eliminated archaic rules, and increased the level of worldwide immigration by 35 percent, to an annual level of 675,000.

The September 11th terrorist attacks on the United States led to a reorganization of the agencies responsible for carrying out the nation's immigration laws, as well as to several revisions in the immigration laws themselves. In 2002 Congress abolished the Immigration and NATURALIZATION Service (INS), replacing it with the Bureau of Citizenship and Immigration Services (BCIS), a part of the DEPARTMENT OF HOMELAND SECURITY (DHS). The move became effective March 1, 2003. The attacks also led to the enactment of a number of statutes that seek both to improve the immigration system and to help protect the United States from illegal aliens who may engage in terrorist activities on its soil. The goals of the new statutes were to accelerate immigration processes related to citizenship

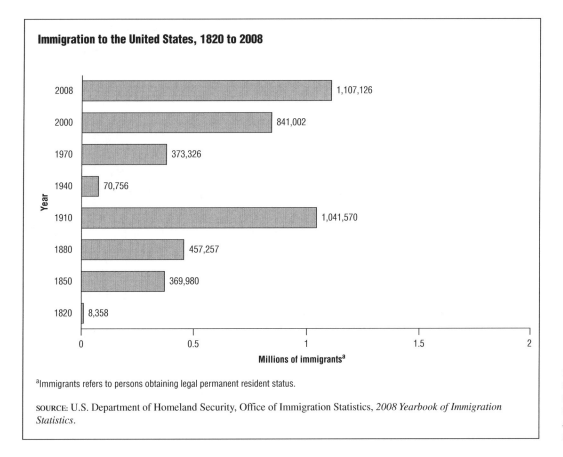

Immigration to the United States, 1820 to 2008

Year	Millions of immigrants[a]
2008	1,107,126
2000	841,002
1970	373,326
1940	70,756
1910	1,041,570
1880	457,257
1850	369,980
1820	8,358

[a]Immigrants refers to persons obtaining legal permanent resident status.

SOURCE: U.S. Department of Homeland Security, Office of Immigration Statistics, *2008 Yearbook of Immigration Statistics*.

ILLUSTRATION BY GGS CREATIVE RESOURCES. REPRODUCED BY PERMISSION OF GALE, A PART OF CENGAGE LEARNING.

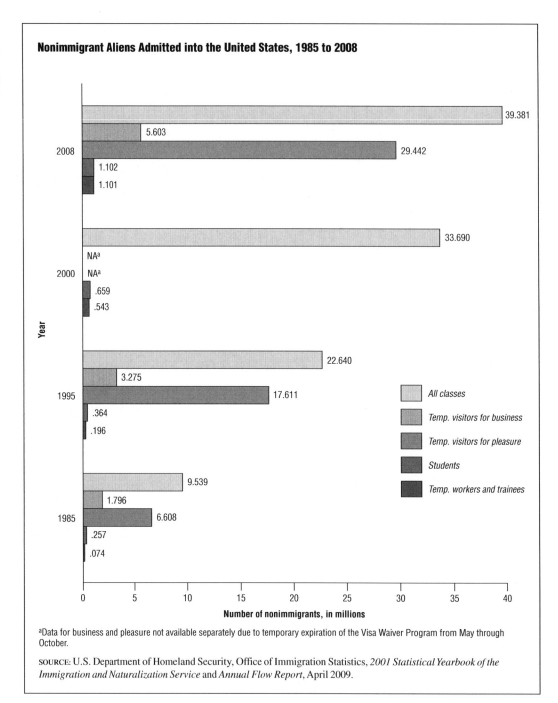

Nonimmigrant Aliens Admitted into the United States, 1985 to 2008

2008: 39.381 / 5.603 / 29.442 / 1.102 / 1.101

2000: 33.690 / NAª / NAª / .659 / .543

1995: 22.640 / 3.275 / 17.611 / .364 / .196

1985: 9.539 / 1.796 / 6.608 / .257 / .074

Year

Number of nonimmigrants, in millions

All classes

Temp. visitors for business

Temp. visitors for pleasure

Students

Temp. workers and trainees

ªData for business and pleasure not available separately due to temporary expiration of the Visa Waiver Program from May through October.

SOURCE: U.S. Department of Homeland Security, Office of Immigration Statistics, *2001 Statistical Yearbook of the Immigration and Naturalization Service* and *Annual Flow Report*, April 2009.

and benefits, to strengthen border patrol and enforcement, and to ensure DETENTION and removal of illegal aliens.

Administrative Implementation of Immigration and Naturalization Laws

For many years the INS was responsible for implementing many of the nation's immigration and naturalization laws. The terrorist attacks on September 11, 2001, along with a number of other incidents, led to harsh criticism of the agency. According to a number of lawmakers and other commentators, the INS was the worst-managed agency in the federal government. Calls for reforming the agency led in 2002 to a call to abolish the agency. When Congress passed the Homeland Security Act of 2002, Pub. L. No. 107-296, 116 Stat. 2135 (codified as amended in scattered sections of 6 U.S.C.A.), it eliminated the agency and created the BCIS. The primary mission of the DHS is to prevent terrorist attacks, reduce the vulnerability of the United States to TERRORISM, and minimize any damage and assist in any recovery should terrorist attacks occur in the country.

The BCIS does not possess all of the powers that the INS once had. It focuses exclusively on immigration and citizenship issues regarding aliens in the United States. Among the agency's primary responsibilities are the review of petitions by aliens for entry or retention in the country, ADJUDICATION of asylum and processing of refugees, implementation of naturalization procedures, and issuance and renewal of documents. Many of the law enforcement powers that the INS held have been removed from the BCIS, however.

Under the Homeland Security Act, a number of new agencies were created to carry out several other functions. Many of the responsibilities for preventing entry of terrorists into the United States, carrying out immigration enforcement functions, and other issues relating to the protection of U.S. borders were delegated to the Undersecretary for Border and Transportation Services. Other enforcement powers were given to the Bureau of Border Security Enforcement, which is responsible for the detention, investigation, and inspection of aliens under federal law.

Admission Procedures

Normally, aliens wishing to enter the United States first apply for a VISA at one of the over 200 U.S. consulates and embassies abroad. Visas are documents required for travel to most nations in the world. For example, U.S. citizens may not simply cross the borders of Germany or Zaire without a visa. Aliens, likewise, may not simply cross the borders into the United States; they have no inherent right to enter the country. A visa is the only legal means of entry. In a larger sense, it is the key to understanding the goals and practices of immigration law.

Two types of visas exist: immigrant visas and nonimmigrant visas. It is much easier to obtain nonimmigrant visas, which are primarily issued to tourists and temporary business visitors. In 1993 the INS admitted 21,447,000 nonimmigrants to the United States. Nonimmigrant visas are divided into 18 main categories ranging from vacationers and diplomatic personnel to athletes, temporary workers, and students. Most categories do not have any numerical limitation. The reasoning is simple: Nonimmigrants generally spend a short time and a lot of money in the United States, with obvious benefits for the nation's economic, social, and cultural life, and relatively few demands on its resources. The most significant issue in nonimmigrant visas is whether the alien may work in the United States without violating the terms of the visa.

Immigrants find visas much harder to obtain. Millions of aliens want to live and work in the United States and enjoy the benefits of U.S. citizenship, but only a fraction of them can. Congress sets numerical limits on most types of immigrant visas, under the theory that the country can realistically absorb only so many new people. The 1995 annual ceiling was 675,000, with flexibility for some categories. In addition, many immigrant visas are subject to per-country caps—roughly 25,000 per country, though some countries receive special allowances.

In law, aliens granted visas are said to have obtained *entry*. The term *entry* has a special meaning that is different from a mere "physical presence in the United States." An alien might cross the border but still be determined by authorities not to have entered the country. Entry means legal admittance and the freedom from official restraint. Its benefits are tangible: generally, aliens recognized by law to have gained entry have more rights than those who have not gained entry.

Denial of entry is called *exclusion*. Dating from the earliest attempts to control immigration, this controversial concept holds that it is not in the national interest to admit some persons. Far-reaching grounds bar applicants for reasons related to health, crime, national security, and other variables. As part of the process for reviewing visa applications, consular officials decide whether any ground for exclusion applies. If the officials decide that none does, a visa may be granted, but entry is still not certain. The Bureau of Border Security Enforcement can decide otherwise when the alien actually attempts to cross the border. In practice, exclusion occurs every day.

Excluded aliens can argue their case in an *exclusion hearing*. This procedure differs greatly from a DEPORTATION *hearing*, which involves an alien who has already entered the United States. Deportation hearings are actually more advantageous: unlike exclusion proceedings, deportation hearings only follow from specific allegations, and aliens subject to deportation have more forms of legal relief. In an exclusion hearing, the burden is always on the alien to prove his or her right to enter the United States. The alien is entitled to many attributes of procedural due process, and aliens who lose may also seek asylum (refuge or protection, usually for political reasons) in some instances.

Excluded applicants seeking to cross the border may be kept in detention facilities until their hearings have been held. In some cases, officers may choose to release an alien on PAROLE pending further review. Parole allows an alien to travel away from the border and detention facilities temporarily, for reasons such as preventing the separation of families. As a limited right, parole is not equivalent to entry.

Nonimmigrant Visas

Each applicant for a nonimmigrant visa must demonstrate that he or she has no intention of immigrating. Generally, the application requires detailed information about the alien's native residence, place of employment, reason for traveling to the United States, and destination. Most nonimmigrant visas do not have annual numerical limits, but the INA does restrict those for professionals to 65,000; temporary agricultural workers to 66,000; and performing athletes, artists, and entertainers to 25,000.

Nonimmigrant aliens apply for a visa from one of 18 categories, each assigned a letter, as follows:

A. Career diplomats;

B. Temporary visitors for business and pleasure;

C. Aliens in transit;

D. Crew members;

E. Treaty traders and investors;

F. Students;

G. International organization representatives;

H. Temporary workers;

I. Foreign media representatives;

J. Exchange program visitors;

K. Fiancées, fiancés, or children of U.S. citizens;

L. Intracompany transferees;

M. Students in nonacademic institutions;

N. Parents and children of special immigrants;

O. Aliens with extraordinary abilities;

P. Entertainers;

Q. Participants in cultural exchange programs;

R. Religious workers. The visas are further categorized by numbers—for example, A-1, A-2, and so forth.

Aliens use specific procedures for the particular visa sought. Broadly speaking, these fall into three classes: (1) applications that do not require contact with anyone in the United States (visas A, B, C, D, E, G, I, and O); (2) applications that require proof of acceptance in an authorized program (visas F, J, M, and Q, and visas for special education trainees); and (3) applications that require approved petitions, which provide the basis for the alien's presence in the United States (visas H, K, L, P, and R). More than half of all visas require supporting documents at the time of application. For example, an alien hoping to work temporarily in the United States as a registered nurse needs an employer's PETITION to obtain an H-1A visa. Similarly, an alien planning to study at a university must present proof of acceptance at the university for an F-1 visa. An alien engaged to a U.S. citizen will never see a K visa—let alone get married—unless the citizen has filed a petition. In all cases, consular officials make the final decision. Generally, no JUDICIAL REVIEW is available.

Once admitted into the United States, aliens are inspected by Bureau of Border Security Enforcement officers, who give them a form I-94 indicating the length and terms of their stay. Most aliens ultimately return to their country of origin. Some wish to stay and immigrate. Generally, all nonimmigrant visa holders who are in the United States may apply to have their visa status adjusted to permanent-resident status, with the exception of crew member visa (visa D) holders. To qualify, the alien must have been inspected and admitted or paroled into the United States and must meet standard eligibility requirements for obtaining an immigrant visa, and an immigrant visa must be immediately available at the time the application is filed. In addition, the alien must not have been in an UNLAWFUL status or, with few exceptions, have accepted any unauthorized employment.

Immigrant Visas

Immigrant visas come in two main categories: visas subject to numerical limitation and visas not subject to numerical limitation. The term *numerical limitation* means several things. First, it refers to the overall limits set by Congress on immigrants. Second, it involves the use of per-country caps. Third, and most important, numerically limited visas are organized along a system of preferences that favors certain aliens over others. Every immigrant wants the best chance to obtain a visa, but qualifying for the easiest category—visas not subject to numerical limitation—is quite difficult. Congress has reserved this category for immediate relatives of U.S. citizens, resident aliens returning from temporary visits abroad, and former U.S. citizens. Consequently, for the vast majority of aliens who want to immigrate, demand is much higher than the relatively short supply prescribed by law.

Though having no numerical limitation makes it easier to obtain, the immediate-relative visa still carries strict limitations. Generally, the term *immediate relatives* means children, spouses, and parents, but unique rules apply to children and spouses. To qualify as a child, the person must be unmarried and under 21 years of age. The law is also concerned with how the parent came to have the child, and it applies special age restrictions to legitimate and illegitimate children, stepchildren, adopted children, and orphans. Spouses of U.S. citizens must pass the most demanding tests. The law requires the alien to have a "valid and subsisting marriage" with the citizen under the laws of the country where the marriage took place, and it considers a wide variety of marriages insufficient for granting the visa. This severity is an answer to the common abuse of marriage to obtain citizenship. The Immigration Marriage Fraud Amendments of 1986 impose criminal penalties for violations. The Fraud Amendments also impose a two-year conditional residency requirement before alien spouses and their sons and daughters may petition for permanent-resident status.

Three categories exist for visas subject to numerical limitation: family sponsored, employment related, and so-called diversity immigration. The last is a special category created to reverse the drastic reductions in immigration from European countries, particularly Ireland. Effective after 1995, a formula was used to determine whether in the previous five years a country had been "underrepresented." If so, an alien from that country is eligible for one of 55,000 visas annually allocated to diversity immigrants. Aliens may apply once per year in a lottery, making this a highly uncertain way to obtain a visa. Not everyone is eligible; applicants must generally have a high-school education and two years of work experience. Different goals make more visas available to Hong Kong: because of uncertainty over the transfer of the country to China, the law allotted 20,000 visas annually to certain Hong Kong citizens who were employees of U.S. businesses, their spouses, and their children.

The primary types of numerically limited visas—family-sponsored and employment-related—are organized into PREFERENCE categories. Preference means that the law allocates visas to certain aliens over others in order to promote such goals as preserving families, protecting U.S. jobs, and admitting immigrants most likely to benefit the nation. How the law ranks aliens can be seen from the numerical limits on each category. Families are allotted 226,000 visas annually, with a somewhat flexible maximum of 480,000 in four preference categories. Only 140,000 employment-related visas are allotted, in five preference categories. Unused visas from higher preference categories are reallocated to the lower categories.

Preference in family-sponsored visas is decided by the nature of an alien's relationship to the petitioner:

First preference: Unmarried sons and daughters of U.S. citizens, who are too old to qualify (age 21 or older) for the nonnumerically limited immediate-relative visa: 23,400 visas plus any unused visas from the other family-sponsored preference classes.

Second preference: Spouses, children, and unmarried sons and daughters of aliens who are lawful permanent residents: minimum of 114,200 visas. Spouses and children are allocated 77 percent of the visas; unmarried sons and daughters (at least 21 years old), 23 percent.

Third preference: Married sons and daughters of U.S. citizens: 23,400 plus any unused visas from the first- and second-preference classes.

Fourth preference: Brothers and sisters of U.S. citizens, if the citizen is at least 21 years old:

65,000 plus any unused visas from the three higher classes.

Employment-related preferences are not based on any familial relationship. They focus on educational attainment and stress occupations that are highly specialized. Their levels are set as percentages of the worldwide maximum of 140,000.

First preference: Priority workers are allotted 28.6 percent. These are persons of "extraordinary ability" in the sciences, arts, education, business, or athletics; outstanding professors and researchers; and multinational executives and managers.

Second preference: Professionals holding advanced degrees or persons of exceptional ability in the sciences, arts, or business are allotted 28.6 percent.

Third preference: Skilled workers in short supply, professionals holding baccalaureate degrees, and other workers in short supply are allotted 28.6 percent.

Fourth preference: Certain special immigrants: 7.1 percent. These are mainly religious workers, as well as former employees of the U.S. government and international organizations.

Fifth preference: Employment creation immigrants are allotted 7.1 percent. These are investors who will create at least ten U.S. jobs by investing in a new commercial enterprise benefiting the U.S. economy, especially in areas of low employment. Generally, the minimum required INVESTMENT is $1 million.

Though all potential immigrants face rigorous application requirements, certain categories are more exacting. Petitions are needed for visas based on the immediate-relative, family-sponsored, and employment-related preference categories. These must be filed in the United States by citizens or resident aliens on behalf of the applicant and then approved by the BCIS. (Under a significant exception, anyone may petition on behalf of Amerasian children of U.S. service members.) Many of the employment-related preference categories also need an employer's petition. As a safeguard intended to protect U.S jobs, the employer is first required to seek an official form of permission called *labor certification*. This is approved only if (a) sufficient qualified workers are not available, and (b) employment of the alien will not adversely affect wages or working conditions of similarly employed U.S. workers. The DEPARTMENT OF LABOR defines the occupations for which employers may seek certification in two groups: the professions and unskilled labor. Only rarely is an unskilled labor application approved. Furthermore, the job for which the employer seeks labor certification must also be permanent in nature.

After APPROVAL of the labor certification or preference petition, or both, the actual visa application process begins for an alien who resides outside the United States. This process takes place at the appropriate U.S. consulate, where authority to approve or deny an application belongs exclusively to consular officials. If eligible, the alien must submit considerable documentation. The required documents include biographical reports; police, court, prison, and military records; birth and marriage certificates; passports; photographs; and evidence that the alien will not become a public charge while in the United States. The alien gives the consul these documents and the results of a medical examination. If all is in order, the applicant signs a formal application under OATH.

The consul usually rules on the application the same day. The principal consular officer reviews any refusal to issue a visa, but no formal review is available after that. The STATE DEPARTMENT has only limited authority over visa denials. The applicant has one year to overcome the objection to the visa on which a refusal was based, or the entire visa application process must be started anew. The BURDEN OF PROOF is always on the applicant to establish eligibility. If the applicant passes, the consul issues an immigrant visa. Under certain circumstances, immigrants unable to travel immediately may receive new visas later.

Once the immigrant actually arrives in the United States, an immigration officer again independently examines the alien's visa eligibility. This officer may exclude the alien in spite of the visa. In that case, the alien may be temporarily detained, either aboard the vessel of arrival or in the United States pending a ruling. If the officer finds the visa in order and admits the alien, the visa is retained by the BCIS as a permanent record of admission. The alien is then issued a form I-151, commonly known as a "green card" (even though its color is now off-white), and becomes a permanent-resident alien. Although it is most often thought of as an employment permit, the GREEN CARD was originally designed to serve as evidence of the alien's status as a permanent resident of the United States. In 2008, 1,107,126 individuals became legal permanent residents of the United States. Sixty-five percent of those individuals were granted such status based on a family relationship with a U.S. citizen or a permanent resident of the United States.

Rights of Aliens

Aliens enjoy many of the rights afforded to citizens. They can claim general protections under the Constitution and the BILL OF RIGHTS. However, aliens cannot vote or hold federal elective office—rights belonging solely to citizens. Further legal rights depend on an alien's status: use of the courts, ownership of land, obtaining a public education, and qualifying for federal welfare benefits are each, to varying degrees, restricted to lawful resident aliens. Similarly, the LIABILITY of an alien to pay taxes depends on resident or nonresident status. Resident aliens pay taxes in much the same way that citizens do; nonresident aliens may qualify for special exemptions. Aliens can also be required to obtain a so-called exit permit to ensure that all taxes owed are paid before leaving the country.

In addition to following laws generally, aliens also have special duties. Some visas impose additional requirements such as notifying the BCIS of changes of address and refraining from engaging in paid employment. Criminal penalties apply to some misconduct of aliens and citizens who abet them, including MISREPRESENTATION or fraud in obtaining immigration status, unlawful entry, and transporting or concealing an undocumented alien. For aliens who violate the law, the PENALTY is commonly deportation. Citizens who bring aliens into the country illegally may face a fine, IMPRISONMENT for up to five years, or both, for each alien they have illegally transported.

Although the Supreme Court has held that Congress alone makes immigration law, historically states have placed harsh restrictions on aliens. However, in *Graham v. Richardson*, 403 U.S. 365, 91 S. Ct. 1848, 29 L. Ed. 2d 534, the Supreme Court held that aliens could not be denied state welfare benefits. Most important, the Graham decision struck a blow against state discrimination in general: It said that equal protection cases involving aliens would be subject to the same STRICT SCRUTINY applied in

racial discrimination cases. In a series of decisions that followed, the Court removed numerous state barriers—laws that barred all aliens from competitive CIVIL SERVICE employment, engineering licenses, and licenses to practice law. Nonetheless, through the late 1970s and 1980s, it backed away from the strict scrutiny standard: It upheld New York's limitations on the certification of alien public school teachers (*Ambach v. Norwick*, 441 U.S. 68, 99 S. Ct. 1589, 60 L. Ed. 2d 49 [1979]), for example, and California's restriction of peace officer jobs to citizens (*Cabell v. Chavez-Salido*, 454 U.S. 432, 102 S. Ct. 735, 70 L. Ed. 2d 225 [1982]). One key exception was *Plyler v. Doe*, 457 U.S. 202, 102 S. Ct. 2382, 72 L. Ed. 2d 786 (1982), granting the children of undocumented aliens the right to attend public schools.

Naturalization and Citizenship

Resident aliens become citizens through naturalization. To apply for naturalization, most aliens must meet several requirements. They must (1) reside continuously in the United States for five years as lawfully admitted permanent residents (or three years for spouses of United States' citizens); (2) be physically present in the United States for at least half of the time before filing the petition for naturalization; and (3) reside for at least three months within the district in which the petition is filed. Aliens must generally be at least 18 years of age, although parents who are citizens can file on behalf of younger children. Literacy and educational standards must be met: unless physically unable to do so, aliens must be able to speak, understand, read, and write simple English. They have to show "good moral character"—an ambiguous term that includes not being a drunkard, gambler, or CONVICT jailed for 180 days or more. They must exhibit an attachment to constitutional principles, essentially proved through a belief in representative democracy, the Bill of Rights, and political processes.

To ascertain an applicant's fitness for naturalization, a naturalization examiner conducts an informal hearing. The examiner questions the applicant and WITNESSES who can TESTIFY on her or his behalf and then renders a decision. If denied, the applicant may reapply with LEGAL REPRESENTATION; in some cases, federal district courts may determine naturalization or remand the matter to the BCIS with instructions. Finally, if approved, the applicant is granted citizenship at a

Resident aliens become citizens through naturalization. Karwinder Singh (left) and Ranjit Kaur take an oath of citizenship during a naturalization ceremony in Seattle.

AP IMAGES

government free rein "to terminate hospitality" (*Harisiades v. Shaughnessy*, 343 U.S. 580, 72 S. Ct. 512, 96 L. Ed. 586 [1952]). Deportation provisions apply to all aliens whether they have legally or illegally entered the country, with several specific exceptions ranging from ambassadors to employees of international organizations such as the UNITED NATIONS. Citizens cannot be deported, but denaturalization proceedings can be brought against a naturalized citizen and can then lead to deportation.

Five major broad categories of grounds for deportation cover (1) being excludable at the time of entry or adjustment of status; (2) committing criminal offenses; (3) failing to register and falsifying documents; (4) posing a security risk and related grounds; and (5) becoming a public charge of the state. Many more grounds for deportation follow from these; the first category alone establishes nine classes of aliens excludable at the time of entry. Since the Technical Amendments Act of 1991, these grounds have expanded with the addition of attempting or conspiring to commit a crime. Deportation is far-reaching in additional ways: Frequently the BCIS applies the statutes retroactively, so that aliens may be deported for conduct that was not a ground for deportation at the time they committed the act. Many of the provisions also depend on when the alien entered the United States, and still others make aliens deportable for acts they committed prior to entry.

The mechanism of deportation involves broad official powers. Officers of the Bureau of Border Security Enforcement have considerable power to investigate without search warrants, arrest, and detain suspects within 100 miles of the U.S. border. Aliens then receive a deportation hearing conducted by an immigration judge. They are entitled to legal counsel—though not at government expense—and the basic rights of due process, as well as the rights to examine evidence, present new evidence, and cross-examine witnesses. If the judge finds an alien deportable, various avenues of relief are available, including administrative and judicial appeals. Furthermore, several forms of discretionary relief may entitle the alien to leave voluntarily, claim suspension of deportation, apply for an adjustment of status, seek asylum as a refugee, or pursue numerous other options.

Deportation often causes the U.S. citizen children of aliens to leave the United States.

hearing in OPEN COURT after taking an oath of ALLEGIANCE to the United States. Between 2006 and 2008 naturalizations grew at a record pace, reaching a total of 2.4 million immigrants who became new United States citizens.

Deportation

Deportation is the expulsion of an alien from the United States. In theory, it is a civil proceeding rather than a punishment, though those who are deported may certainly see it as a punishment. It is designed to remove undesirables as defined under the INA. As in most aspects of immigration law, the Supreme Court has left total authority over deportation to Congress. Merely allowing aliens to enter the country "is a matter of permission and tolerance," the Court has said, leaving the

These children are not technically deported and may ultimately choose to return.

Deportation Remedies

Aliens generally want to avoid deportation at all costs. Even if an immigration judge rules that an alien is deportable, the alien may still fight the deportation order. This is called "seeking relief from deportation." Broadly speaking, two kinds of options exist: filing an appeal and seeking "discretionary" relief. Whichever method the alien chooses, time is of the essence. He or she usually must seek relief before the BCIS begins executing the deportation order.

Appeals from deportation rulings operate on three levels. First, the alien's attorney may file a *motion to reopen* the case, also called a "motion to reconsider." It is used chiefly to present new evidence, and strict rules govern its usage. Courts frown on such motions because of the potential for unnecessarily delaying deportation, and the judge may deny the motion if the alien has previously failed to establish a sufficient case. In any event, the motion will not stop a pending deportation order. Second, aliens may go to the higher authority of the Board of Immigration Appeals (BIA). Filing a so-called *administrative appeal* with the BIA automatically delays the execution of a pending deportation order. The BIA decision to uphold the deportation order, throw it out, or send the case back to the immigration judge is final. Within six months, however, the alien may appeal a decision of the BIA to a federal court for *judicial review*. Courts may hear the case if there have been violations of the alien's constitutional rights.

As the name implies, discretionary relief is granted at the discretion of a judge. If granted, it will eliminate or postpone the execution of a deportation order. Generally, the alien must apply for discretionary relief during the deportation hearing, although some forms of relief may be sought before the hearing begins. In a two-part process, the judge first determines whether the alien is eligible under statutory requirements and then at the judge's discretion decides whether to grant it. Mere eligibility is not a guarantee of relief.

Several forms of discretionary relief exist. One very popular form is *voluntary departure*, which permits the alien to leave the United States under his or her own power, seek a destination, and even return to the selected country immediately, thus avoiding the stigma and penalties of deportation.

Suspension of deportation helps the alien who has been in the United States for a long period of time and for whom deportation would result in harsh consequences. Qualifying for suspension relief is difficult: The alien must have been continuously present in the United States for seven to ten years, depending on the nature of the conduct that rendered the alien deportable—for example, overstaying a visa versus committing a FELONY; must have been a person of good moral character during that time; and must demonstrate that he or she or the alien's U.S. citizen spouse, parent, or child would suffer extreme hardship (under the seven-year rule) or exceptional and extremely unusual hardship (under the ten-year rule) if the alien were deported. Another form of relief, *adjustment of status*, is available to an alien whose status would otherwise let him or her remain in the United States: If an alien is admissible for permanent residence, he or she may seek this relief to avoid having to go abroad while an immigrant visa is processed.

Asylum, available only to aliens who qualify as refugees, differs from other forms of discretionary relief. First, it does not guarantee an alien permanent residence but merely grants the right to reside and work in the United States temporarily, for as long as the alien is entitled to refugee status. Under the INA, a refugee is an alien who is unwilling or unable to return to his or her nation because of a well-founded fear of persecution on the ground of race, RELIGION, nationality, membership in a particular social group, or political opinion, or an alien whose nationality has been given refugee status by the PRESIDENT OF THE UNITED STATES. Asylum may be sought at any time during a deportation or exclusion hearing and can sometimes lead to the granting of permanent residence within one year.

Closely related to asylum is *withholding of deportation*. Although the grounds for withholding are similar to those for asylum, this form of relief may only be sought during a deportation hearing, and its duration is always temporary. Aliens who are granted asylum or withholding of deportation may qualify for adjustment of status and thereby become lawful permanent residents or citizens.

Finally, a few kinds of discretionary relief are used in exceptional circumstances. A *stay of deportation* is a temporary hold on a deportation order, commonly used in connection with a motion to reopen a case or pending an application

WELFARE AND IMMIGRATION

In 1875 the United States passed the first of many restrictive laws intended to keep out certain aliens. A powerful force behind federal legislation has always been widespread hostility toward certain new arrivals. Disliking everything from skin color to habits of speech, appearance, and worship, citizens have consistently opposed certain immigrants: the Irish in the 1800s, Jews and Slavs in the early twentieth century, and Southeast Asians subsequently. Illegal aliens have upset many U.S. citizens for decades. Since the late 1980s, a new theme has entered public discussion: opposing WELFARE benefits to legal immigrants.

Opponents of providing welfare for immigrants usually voiced such opposition within a general context of opposition to the welfare system. The influential conservative author George Will argued that aliens are brainwashed, in much the same way as poor U.S. citizens, into believing that welfare is a normal way of life. "Today immigrants are received in a welfare culture that encourages an entitlement mentality," Will wrote. The notion of an "entitlement mentality" is well-established in the anti-welfare camp, where it is believed that government has erred by creating a mindset of CASUAL acceptance among recipients of benefits. This view does not discriminate between citizens and aliens. It holds that welfare is equally wrong for both because it creates dependence over several generations and leads, as the prominent critic Charles Murray has asserted, to social ills such as crime, drug addiction, and illegitimate children. Moderates embrace this analysis to a degree, yet remain less inclined than conservatives to support eliminating welfare completely.

Welfare is a jumping-off point for a broader attack on federal IMMIGRATION law. If welfare is a mistaken policy, it follows that any immigration policy that creates new dependents is itself flawed. Does U.S. policy create new dependents? The major emphasis of the 1990 Immigration Act (Pub. L. 101–649, Nov. 29, 1990, 104 Stat. 4978) was on family unification: It stressed immigration by relatives of U.S. citizens and resident aliens, the majority of whom were generally granted visas as long as they did not become "public charges," that is, welfare recipients. Immigrants were supposed to meet this requirement by having a sponsor family that would help feed, clothe, and care for them. Despite this requirement, federal data suggested that many immigrants became public charges anyway.

To the most outspoken critics, the United States was clearly welcoming the wrong immigrants. Instead of opening its doors to just anyone, they argued, the nation should be more selective. "Today's laws," *Investor's Business Daily* editorialized in 1995, "perversely favor immigrants from the Third World over others with higher skills and greater understanding of Western culture." The newspaper bemoaned this "low-skilled tide" for "push[ing] down the wages of poorer Americans." Not only did the conservative financial press make this argument; the left-wing magazine of opinion, *The Nation*, also repeated it, with a slightly different emphasis on race. Immigrants have "pushed blacks out of the marketplace altogether," the writer Wanda Coleman asserted in 1993. The economist Simon Kuznets and the author Peter Brimelow have tied the relative economic progress of African Americans to the dramatic decline in immigration between 1920 and 1965.

Some advocates of immigration reform went farther. The American Enterprise Institute, a neo-conservative think tank, called for dumping the family-reunification goal for a system based on "designer immigration": admitting better-educated immigrants. This case is made in detail in *The Immigration Wave: A Plea to Hold It Back* (1995) by Brimelow, himself an immigrant from England. Brimelow contended that the future is bleak: By the year 2050, the U.S. population will be nearly 400 million, and more than one-third of it will be low-skilled immigrants who arrived after 1970. Unlike the one-third of the immigrant population that came during the great wave between 1890 and 1920 and then returned home, these men, women, and children will have stayed because of the welfare system. "The failures are no longer winnowed out," Brimelow wrote. "Instead, they are encouraged to stay—at the expense of the American taxpayer." Only a designer approach can prevent a "bureaucratically regulated racial spoils system."

Of course, there was another side to the debate. Reviewing *The Immigration Wave,* the author Richard Bernstein criticized Brimelow for ignoring "the genuinely moving spectacle of millions of people making better lives for themselves in this country than they could in the countries they came from." Writing in the *New York Times,* Nathan Glazer expressed regret over an increasingly agitated tone in the debate: "[W]e will all have to keep our heads and remember that we all came from someplace else." Such sentiments have long informed arguments in favor of immigration—namely, that it is generous and humanitarian.

Sharper attacks on the reformers came from the political left. In 1993, the *New Left Review* defended immigration by blasting public selfishness in the form of "the fiscal constraints on public spending imposed by conservative, suburban voters." Instead of restricting immigration, the *Progressive* magazine urged President BILL CLINTON to "try to ease the economic deprivations and political persecutions the United States has fostered around the globe, which themselves have propelled much of the immigration to this country."

This debate set the stage for the changes in welfare for legal immigrants that were made in the 1990s. The reform efforts began in California: In 1994 nearly two-thirds of the state's voters passed Proposition 187 (CA Prop. 187 [1994], 1994 Cal. Legis. Serv. Prop. 187 [WEST]), a law intended to deny education and public assistance to illegal aliens. The biggest appeal of Proposition 187 was saving tax dollars. Although the proposition was not aimed at legal immigrants, its success with voters prompted some observers to regard it as a symptom of increasing intolerance toward immigration in general. However, a federal district court decision in 1995, *League of United Latin American Citizens v. Wilson* (908 F. Supp. 755, C.D. Cal [1995]), prevented it from going into effect, by ruling that most of the law was preempted by federal immigration law.

In 1996 the federal government passed the far-reaching welfare reform act known as the Personal Responsibility and Work Opportunity Reconciliation Act of 1996 (PRWORA) (Pub. L. 104–193 Aug. 22, 1996, 110 Stat. 2105). The new welfare law particularly affected immigrants. Under the law, immigrants who entered the United States legally after August 22, 1996, were prohibited for at least five years from receiving federal, non-emergency, means-tested benefits, including MEDICAID and the services funded by federal block grants. Additionally, immigrants were barred from two other programs, Supplemental Security Income (SSI) and food stamps, until they either became U.S. citizens or worked in the country for 40 qualifying quarters (8 USCA § 1601 et. seq.).

The reforms did not stop there. After the five-year ban expired, it was up to the states to determine what welfare to give new immigrants. States had the option of denying non-emergency Medicaid to most new arrivals even after the five-year ban was over. States could also bar immigrants from participating in any of the benefit programs financed by Title XX block grants, such as CHILD CARE, in-home assistance for disabled persons, and support services for abused and neglected children. Finally, states could exclude most current and future immigrants from other state-funded benefits, including Temporary Assistance for Needy Families.

Three groups of noncitizens were exempted from disqualification: (1) REFUGEES, asylum seekers, and aliens granted withholding of DEPORTATION during the first five years after receiving the immigration benefit; (2) permanent resident aliens if they have worked 40 qualifying quarters as defined by the SOCIAL SECURITY Act; and (3) an alien and his or her family if the alien lawfully resides in the United States and is on active duty in the military or has received an honorable discharge. Proponents suggested a variety of reasons for enacting these reforms, most embodied in the arguments against welfare for immigrants listed above. Some also alluded to a monetary factor: The immigrant restrictions accounted for almost half the total federal savings from the welfare reform law.

The provisions of the PRWORA that deal with immigrants were generally seen as the harshest part of the act and were opposed by a wide variety of groups. President Clinton, who signed the PRWORA into law, made it clear he disagreed with its provisions for cutting immigrant benefits and campaigned against them in the 1996 election. Immigrant rights groups filed CLASS ACTION lawsuits, and the state of Florida filed its own lawsuit, worried that its taxpayers would end up supporting immigrants who had been cut off from federal benefits.

As a result, Congress modified some of the harsher aspects of the law. As part of the Balanced Budget Act of 1997, the law restored SSI to those immigrants who were receiving SSI as of August 22, 1996. It also allowed immigrants residing in the United States on August 22, 1996, to be eligible for SSI if they became disabled in the future. New immigrants were still not eligible for SSI nor would earlier immigrants be eligible in the future based on their age.

Then in 1998, Congress decided to partially restore food stamps by reinstating eligibility for legal immigrant children and elderly persons who were legal immigrants as of August 22, 1996. This action readmitted approximately 250,000 immigrants who were excluded under the 1996 law. In addition, some states, such as Washington, have attempted to restore at least partial food stamp benefits to immigrants who were not covered by the 1998 legislation.

But other attempts to restore benefits at the federal level have failed. As of 2008, 40 percent of legal immigrants had entered the United States after 1996, making them ineligible for federally funded assistance. Some states have replaced federal benefits by subsidizing programs with state funds. Congress addressed healthcare for immigrant children and pregnant women in the Children's Health Insurance Program Reauthorization Act of 2009 (PUBLIC LAW No. 111-3, 2009). This law provides states with the opportunity to provide affordable health coverage to many immigrant children and pregnant women through Medicaid and the Children's Health Insurance Program. The law was based on earlier legislation entitled the Immigrant Children's Health Improvement Act, which was first proposed in 2005.

FURTHER READINGS

Camarota, Steven A. 2003. "Back Where We Started: An Examination of Trends in Immigrant Welfare Use since Welfare Reform." *Center for Immigration Studies* (March).

Dodson, Marvin E. 2001. "Welfare Generosity and Location Choices among United States Immigrants." *International Review of Law and Economics* 21 (March).

McCurdy, Thomas, and Margaret O'Brien-Strain. 1998. "Reform Reversed? The Restoration of Welfare Benefits to Immigrants in California." *Public Policy Institute of California*.

CROSS REFERENCE

Welfare.

Aliens and Civil Rights

Since the attacks on the United States on September 11, 2001, the status of aliens physically within the United States or its territories has been decidedly more tenuous. Aliens (noncitizens owing political allegiance to another country) are generally afforded certain fundamental rights and protections under the U.S. Constitution. For example, the due process clause of the Fourteenth Amendment states, in relevant part, that "no person shall be deprived of life or liberty without due process of law." But other constitutional provisions reserve certain fundamental rights to citizens only; for example, the Fifteenth and Nineteenth Amendments guarantee the right "of citizens of the United States" to vote.

International law uses the term "alien enemy" to indicate a person who is the subject or citizen of a nation hostile to, or at war with, the nation in which the alien is found. The significance is that the person becomes, in time of war, impressed with the character of the enemy. However, the problem for many aliens in the United States is that, while their homeland may not be in a declared war with the United States, it may harbor terrorists or contribute to terrorism in a manner that renders the distinction moot. How, then, does the United States treat aliens from those countries? As author Roberta Smith noted in her 1997 law journal article, "America Tries to Come to Terms with Terrorism: The United States Anti-Terrorism and Effective Death Penalty Act of 1996 v. British Anti-Terrorism Law and International Response":

> The Fundamental question facing the United States, a democratic society ... is how can they constrain terrorism without jeopardizing their value systems (e.g., protecting constitutional and civil rights such as prohibitions against unreasonable searches and seizures, and protection of free speech).

Prior to 2001, alleged terrorist attacks on the United States or on U.S. property included the 1993 bombing of the World Trade Center in New York City; the 1995 bombing of the Murrah Federal Building in Oklahoma City; the 1998 bombings of U.S. embassies in Kenya and Tanzania; the 1999 rocket shelling of U.S. buildings in Islamabad, Pakistan; and the 2000 attack on the U.S.S. *Cole*. Mostly in response to the Oklahoma bombing, Congress in 1996 passed the Antiterrorism and Effective Death Penalty Act (AEDPA), P.L. 104-132 (codified in scattered sections of 18 U.S.C.), and the Illegal Immigration and Reform and Immigration Responsibility Act (IIRIRA), P.L. 104-208 (codified as amended at 8 U.S.C. 1101). The AEDPA amended immigration laws and streamlined deportation procedures for aliens charged with terrorism.

Before these acts were passed, excludable aliens (those whose right to enter the United States was questioned by the Immigration and Naturalization Service [INS] prior to entry) were distinguished from deportable aliens (those whose entry into the United States was found to be illegal, or whose right to stay in the United States had terminated), and different correlative rights were attached to each. That distinction closely paralleled the terms of distinction between nonimmigrant aliens and illegal aliens. However, the AEDPA and IIRIRA muddied those distinctions, granting power to act against both illegal and immigrant aliens who fell under the acts' criteria.

For aliens, the distinction between punishable acts of terrorism and the constitutionally protected rights of association with, or support for, groups that historically advocate or engage in violence, was becoming increasingly nebulous. The AEDPA and IIRIRA permitted terrorism charges to be brought against an alien for any alleged association with an organization designated as terrorist by the secretary of state. Moreover, charges of terrorism could rest entirely on confidential reports not disclosed to the subject alien. Likewise, the IIRIRA limited judicial review in deportation cases, even when the challenge to deportation rested on First or Fourteenth Amendment constitutional grounds.

Nonetheless, the U.S. Supreme Court, in *Reno v. Arab Anti-discrimination Committee* (525 U.S. 471, 119 S. Ct. 936, 142 L. Ed. 2d. 940 [US 1999]), allowed the challenged AEDPA to stand. The Court again confronted AEDPA issues in *Zadvydas v. Davis* (533 U.S. 678, 121 S. Ct. 249, 150 L. Ed. 2d. 653 [US 2001]),

where a narrow majority ruled that deportable aliens with criminal records could not be detained indefinitely when their countries of nationality refused their return. The decision reaffirmed that due process clause protections still existed for this narrowly defined class of persons who faced deportation.

In the wake of the September 2001 attacks, Congress passed the all-encompassing USA PATRIOT Act (formally, the Uniting and Strengthening America by Providing Appropriate Tools Required to Intercept and Obstruct Terrorism Act), H.R. 3162 (October 2001). More than 100 pages long, the act contains more than 150 sections under ten titles. The act was reauthorized by Congress in 2006 with most of its original provisions unchanged. Of significance to aliens, Section 412 of the act provides for mandatory detention of suspected aliens. Aliens are suspect under the act for any of seven enumerated causes for detention. Further, certain aliens may be held for seven days without being charged and might possibly be detained indefinitely if deemed not removable. The section provides for limited judicial review of such detentions.

The act also requires enhanced communications and sharing of data between the FBI, the Justice Department, and the State Department, theoretically making it easier to watch and track individuals. The Immigration and Naturalization Service (INS) feeds information into the FBI's crime database, particularly concerning aliens who have received final deportation orders but failed to show for their exit trip. Any subsequent entry of that person's name or data in any other legal system, even for minor traffic offenses, will trigger arrest and deportation. In 2002 the Justice Department announced that younger Middle Eastern men from nations with active Al-Qaida cells who have ignored deportation orders would be expelled first.

Another key provision of the act was the implementation of an electronic tracking system affecting foreign students. It also began intense review of visa applications of scientists, engineers, and students in technical fields. Many foreign students accepted into scientific or academic programs were ultimately denied visas. The PATRIOT Act also prohibited illegal aliens, among others, from having access to "select agents" that could be used for harmful purposes.

Following the release of information that seven of the 19 terrorists who boarded planes on September 11, 2001, held drivers' licenses from the Commonwealth of Virginia (although they were illegal aliens), many states began enacting laws to limit the issuance of drivers' licenses to those aliens whose immigration status was legal. Congress followed suit by enacting the Real ID Act of 2005, which imposes rigorous standards on states when issuing driver's licenses. Most states have complained that the document verification requirements are a bureaucratic nightmare and have refused to comply. Congress delayed implementation of the law, and by late 2009 it was unclear when or if the act would go into effect.

A 2003 U.S. Justice Department report by its inspector general was critical of the detainment of several aliens in the wake of the September 2001 attacks. The 198-page report cited major delays in informing the detainees of the reasons for their detention and criticized the unwritten "no bond" policy of detention. The report also mentioned harsh conditions of confinement and instances of verbal and physical abuse.

FURTHER READINGS

American Library Association. USA Patriot Act Analyses, Website: www.ala.org/ala/aboutala/offices/oif/ifissues/usapatriotactanalyses.cfm (accessed Mar. 31, 2010).

"Arab Americans, Civil Rights Leaders Criticize Deportation Initiative." 2002. Press Release. KnightRidder Washington Bureau.

"Being on the Front Lines against Terrorism." 2003. *National Law Journal* 25.

Cohen, Adam. 2002. "Immigration." *Time* 158, 159.

"Licenses Denoting Noncitizens Criticized." 2002. *State Government News* 45.

Martin, David A. 2001. "Graduated Application of Constitutional Protections for Aliens: The Real Meaning of *Zadvydas v. Davis.*" *Supreme Court Review.*

Mukerjee, Madhusree. 2003. "Boxed Out." *Scientific American* 288.

Ross, Susan Dente. 2001. "In the Shadow of Terror: The Illusive First Amendment Rights of Aliens." *Communication Law and Policy.* 6.

"U.S. Report Critical of 9/11 Detainee Treatment." CNN. Available online at http://www.cnn.com/2003/LAW/06/02/detainees/ (accessed Mar. 31, 2010).

for permanent residence. *Registry*, available only to aliens who entered the United States before January 1, 1972, is used to create a lawful record of admission when no record is available. Further relief includes *deferred action status*, a nonstatutory guideline contained within BCIS instructions to district directors; it amounts to an indefinite hold on any deportation action based on sympathetic factors. Rarely used is *estoppel*, in which courts stop deportation orders because of government misconduct.

Treatment of Aliens after September 11, 2001

Since the SEPTEMBER 11TH ATTACKS, reforms in the immigration system have sought to accomplish two broad, yet competing, goals. On the one hand, many of the new laws relating to aliens have sought to accelerate the processes pertaining to the citizenship and naturalization benefits. The former INS was heavily criticized for its inefficiency in carrying out the provisions of the IRA, and the new agencies that replaced the INS have been charged with the responsibility of improving this system.

On the other hand, the new laws have sought to improve immigration procedures to identify potential terrorists and other illegal aliens. The first statute among several that enhanced law enforcement procedures for dealing with terrorist attacks was the USA PATRIOT ACT OF 2001, Pub. L. No. 107-56, 115 Stat. 272. This legislation and the subsequent revisions through statute and regulation have sought to improve procedures for identifying known terrorists and suspected criminals at the various ports of entry.

The dual concerns of immigration policy—that is, expediting the applications of aliens who wish to enter the United States lawfully versus the protection of the country from those who wish to inflict harm—were also present when the INS possessed powers both to implement immigration services and to enforce the immigration policies. The extensive background checks of aliens caused a backlog of applications, slowing the process that was perceived to be inaccurate and inefficient even prior to the attacks. Processing of immigrant applications took as long as three years in some cases. In 2002 the administration of President GEORGE W. BUSH sought to mandate a six-month standard for the processing of these applications when it launched a five-year $500 million initiative to achieve and maintain a universal six-month processing time standard. However, only some of the money was allocated for the application process, while other monies were diverted to be used for other purposes. By 2004 the Bush Administration had pushed back the deadline for the six-month processing goal to 2006. By the end of 2007 the application processing backlog was back to approximately 16 to 18 months. Several reasons for the backlog existed. In 2007 the fees to become a United States citizen increased by eighty percent. The announcement of the prospective fee increase encouraged many individuals to take the necessary steps to apply for naturalization prior to the effective date of the new fees. As a result a huge spike in the naturalization applications occurred in the summer of 2007. In addition, during this time period, a hostile immigration debate was present throughout the country concerning the rights of immigrants. Therefore, many immigrants moved toward becoming a citizen in an attempt to be able to vote and have a stronger voice in order to protect themselves.

Protection of U.S. citizens and land within the country was a primary concern under the Bush administration, and many observers noted that improved screening of aliens could have prevented the terrorist attacks. By the end of the Bush administration, reforms in the immigration system had not solved all of the problems.

When President BARACK OBAMA became president, his goals for immigration reform included strengthening border control by investing in additional personnel, infrastructure, and technology on the border and at the ports of entry. He also stands behind fixing the immigration BUREAUCRACY with the intention of enabling legal immigration so that families will be able to remain together. His administration is also focused on removing incentives for individuals to enter the United States illegally by preventing employers from hiring illegal immigrants. In addition, President Obama's initiative includes implementing a system that would allow for undocumented immigrants who are in good standing to pay a fine, learn English, and go to the "end of the line" for the opportunity to become a United States citizen, as opposed to deportation. Finally, the Obama administrated pledged to promote economic development in Mexico in an attempt to reduce the number of illegal immigrants from Mexico due to their desire to avoid economic desperation. As of August 2009, President Obama had signed the "Children's HEALTH INSURANCE Program Reauthorization Act," which provided quality healthcare to 11 million children and removed barriers that had prevented legal immigrant children from being covered. In addition, a portion of the American Recovery and Reinvestment Act provided funds to strengthen both security and the infrastructure for the United States ports of entry on the Southwest Border.

A number of state lawmakers have expressed concern about the federal government's response to the problem of illegal immigration. In April 2010, the Arizona Legislature enacted what would be the toughest immigration law in the nation. The law would render the failure to carry an immigration document a crime, and the legislation extended broad powers to police to detain a person suspected of being in the country illegally. Although the vast majority of other states had enacted immigration legislation during the latter half of the 2000s, no state had gone as far as Arizona did in terms of requiring aliens to carry documentation. Obama immediately decried Arizona's passage of the bill, and in July 2010, a federal district judge temporarily enjoined the bill from taking effect. As of October 2010, the case was still pending.

FURTHER READINGS

Baker, Bryan C.: *Trends in Naturalization Raters: 2008 Update, Fact Sheet, June 2009.* Available online at http://www.dhs.gov/xlibrary/assets/statistics/publications/ois_natzstrends_Fs_2008.pdf; website home page: http://www.dhs.gov (accessed September 19, 2009).

Cole, David. 1999. "Supreme Court Denies First Amendment Rights to Legal Aliens." *Legal Times* 21 (March): 19.

Illegal Aliens in the U.S. 1995. Upland, Pa.: Diane Publishing Company, 1995.

Immigration Legal Resource Center. 2001. *A Guide for Immigration Advocates.* San Francisco: Immigrant Legal Resource Center.

McWhirter, Robert James. 2001. *The Criminal Lawyer's Guide to Immigration Law: Questions and Answers.* Chicago: American Bar Association.

Monger, Randall and Rytina, Nancy; *U.S. Legal Permanent Residents: 2008, Annual Flow Report, March 2009* Department of Homeland Security, Office of Immigration Statistics. Available online at http://www.dhs.gov/xlibrary/assets/statistics/publications/lps_fr_2008.pdf; website home page: http://www.dhs.gov (accessed September 19, 2009).

"Out of Focus: The Hidden Crisis of the Latest Backlogs in Naturalization Processing." August 2008. Available online at http://www.immigrationforum.org/images/ ... / OutofFocus_BacklogReport.pdf; website home page: http://www.immigrationforum.org (accessed September 19, 2009).

Raskin, Jamin B. 1993. "Legal Aliens, Local Citizens: The Historical, Constitutional and Theoretical Meanings of Alien Suffrage." *Univ. of Pennsylvania Law Review* 141 (April): 1391–1470. http://www.whitehouse.gov/issues/immigration.

CROSS REFERENCES

Amnesty; Asylum; Citizens; Deportation; Immigration and Naturalization; Parole; Refugees; Visa.

ALIMONY

Payment that a family court may order one person in a couple to make to the other person when that couple separates or divorces.

The purpose of alimony is to avoid any unfair economic consequences of a DIVORCE, even after property is divided and CHILD SUPPORT, if any, is awarded. Courts set few specific guidelines to attaining this broad goal: instead of telling judges how and when to award alimony, most courts simply grant them broad discretion to decide what is fair in each case.

For example, suppose two individuals who married in 1985 agree in 1995 to divorce. At the time of the divorce, the husband earns $63,000 per year, after seven years at a large company where the top pay for his specialty is $80,000. When the couple married, he was in graduate school and the wife was earning $22,000. The wife worked for three more years, supporting the husband while he completed his coursework and graduated.

When their first child was born, they agreed that the wife would care for the child at home. At the time of divorce, the wife had been working full-time for one year since the couple's children, ages seven and six, had entered school. She was earning $23,000 per year and would have custody of the children.

A judge in this case would certainly award child support and would probably divide marital property equally between the couple. But it might not seem fair to the judge to allow the husband to leave the MARRIAGE with the sole possession of the couple's most valuable asset—his earning potential—when the wife contributed to his education by supporting him.

Unlike the family's home or station wagon, the husband's earning power has not yet reached its full value, but it promises to grow. It seems especially unfair for the wife not to receive a share of it since after helping the husband attain his education she agreed to FORFEIT her earning power to invest time in the family. The several years she spent out of the workforce continue to handicap her earnings. Alimony is the only means available to the court to avoid a potentially unjust division of assets.

The judge in this case may award alimony or may award a token amount—such as $1 a year—so that the wife has the option to request an increase later on (modifying an award is easier than winning one after the divorce). Or the judge may award no alimony; judges are not required to award alimony.

The HUSBAND AND WIFE in this example are unlikely to find a single solution they both consider equitable. In trying to reach an order that is fair, judges must balance spouses' contributions and sacrifices during the marriage with their needs after the divorce. Although the result may not match both spouses' ideas of what is fair, one of alimony's biggest virtues is its flexibility: it can always be changed.

Alimony can be modified or eliminated as the former spouses' needs change, if those needs are the result of decisions they made as a married unit. Awards and increases in alimony are meant to address only needs that are caused by the divorce itself, not unrelated needs. If the wife's elderly mother becomes ill and dependent on her after the divorce, for example, the wife's need increases, but the increase is unrelated to the divorce and will not increase her eligibility for alimony. However, a significant change in circumstances—such as a rise in the recipient's income or a drop in the payer's income—can cause the court to reduce or end alimony. Occasionally, courts increase alimony to keep up with inflation.

Many courts have indicated that situations such as maltreatment are not VALID triggers for alimony. Courts have clarified that allegations of physical or other harm done by one spouse must be brought in a civil lawsuit, to be heard and decided by a jury. In successful cases, compensatory and PUNITIVE DAMAGES would be awarded, not alimony.

Even in less egregious cases, alimony is not awarded as a punishment, especially in states that have adopted no-fault divorce laws—that is, laws providing that neither spouse has to prove wrongdoing on the part of the other.

Gaps in earning power that tend in general to favor men over women create another situation that many courts believe they cannot resolve using alimony. Such gaps are often the reason married couples decide that if it is appropriate for only one spouse to be the wage earner, it should be the husband. But courts do not base individual alimony awards on this trend alone, in part because an individual spouse cannot be held responsible for social injustices.

In fact, state laws specifying the gender of the paying spouse and of the receiving spouse have been ruled unconstitutional. In deciding *Orr v. Orr* 440 U.S. 268, 99 S. Ct. 1102, 59 L. Ed. 2d 306 (1979), the U.S. Supreme Court ruled that Alabama state law, which specified that husbands may be ordered to pay support to wives, but not vice versa, violated the EQUAL PROTECTION Clause of the FOURTEENTH AMENDMENT. The case arose when William Orr, who had been ordered to pay alimony, was taken to court by his ex-wife for failure to pay. Orr's defense included a motion requesting that the Alabama alimony statute be declared unconstitutional. Although Orr was not seeking alimony from his ex-wife, he argued that the award to her would decrease if his circumstances were considered in addition to hers. The Supreme Court decision supporting Orr meant that gender could not be considered in awarding alimony (although even in 1990s very few alimony awards are made in favor of men).

Modern underpinnings for alimony have little to do with gender, but this was not always so. The U.S. model of alimony is based on ecclesiastical law (guidelines of the Christian RELIGION), dating from a time in England's history when divorce did not exist. Unhappily married couples could live separately, but the husband was still obliged to support the wife financially. This arrangement was known as a divorce A MENSA ET THORO ("from bed and board," in Latin), and was not really a TERMINATION of the marriage. This limited divorce did not allow the parties to remarry, for example, and did not affect INHERITANCE rules. The wife remained her husband's dependent, and alimony was seen as his ongoing marital obligation to her.

When full divorce became available, the idea of alimony continued, but with some important differences. In the early 2000s, alimony awards were being made based not on men's and women's roles, but on relative needs arising from decisions made during the marriage. Alimony is not an aspect of marriage, as it was in divorce *a MENSA ET THORO*, but only becomes necessary—and available—from the time of divorce. Because the considerations that enter into a divorce award are sometimes complex, courts usually clarify the award's purpose and may place a time limit on it.

No mathematical guidelines exist to tell courts how to calculate alimony. In addition, each state legislature sets its own policy regarding whether and when alimony may be awarded. The Uniform Marriage and Divorce Act (UMDA), which many states use as a model, recommends that courts consider the following factors: the financial condition of the person requesting alimony; the time the recipient would need for education or job training; the standard of living the couple had during the marriage; the length of the marriage; the age, physical condition, and emotional state of the person requesting alimony; and the ability of the other person to support the recipient and still support himself or herself.

Courts have at times awarded alimony when an unmarried couple separates, if the relationship closely resembled marriage or in other circumstances, such as in keeping with the couple's intentions and verbal agreements. Awards of this type are informally called palimony. Private separation agreements negotiated between divorcing individuals also can contain alimony provisions. For these reasons, it is difficult to estimate accurately the size and frequency of awards through the most common method, U.S. census data.

If awards are hard to estimate, COMPLIANCE with awards is nearly impossible to gauge. Alimony enforcement is unlike child support enforcement, which has the "teeth" of wage GARNISHMENT, liens, and other mechanisms. Returning to court with contempt-of-court charges is usually the only option a would-be recipient has to enforce an existing alimony order.

If the divorce DECREE does not specify an ending date, an order to pay alimony usually remains effective until the court that awarded it changes or ends it. Alimony usually ends when the recipient remarries; this is known as terminable alimony. In the case of the recipient's remarriage, the payer sometimes must return to court to have the court change the alimony order, but often the termination is automatic.

The payer's death is not necessarily enough to end payments: some orders allow the recipient to inherit funds from the payer's estate or require the payer to maintain a life insurance policy that will continue to support the recipient after the payer's death. These provisions, when made, often involve a recipient whose age or health makes it too difficult for the recipient to enter or reenter the workforce.

On September 1, 1995, Texas became the last state in the country to authorize the award of alimony payments in divorce proceedings. TX FAMILY § 8.001. Until then, Texas courts had ruled that the state constitution prohibited alimony awards because alimony was not marital property existing at the time of the divorce. Instead, Texas courts said that alimony awards necessarily involved calculations based solely on the future, post-divorce earnings of the ex-spouse who would be making the alimony payments.

Texas courts also observed that spouses who sacrificed educational or career opportunities during the marriage to raise children so their spouses could pursue educational or career opportunities of their own could be adequately compensated for their sacrifice by receiving a larger share of the marital property than spouses who had not made such a sacrifice. In other words, Texas courts believed that since they had the power to give one spouse a larger share of the marital property to compensate for any career or educational sacrifices that spouse made during the marriage, there was no need to award alimony too. Courts also questioned why ex-spouses should be under any obligation to support each other after divorce, when the whole purpose of divorce is to end the costs and benefits of marriage.

But judges, lawyers, and scholars increasingly criticized the Texas statutory scheme as being unrealistic. For example, before 1995 Texas courts routinely ordered ex-spouses to pay child support from their so-called post-divorce "future earnings," and these orders survived scrutiny under the state constitution. Critics of Texas law saw no reason why state courts could not order ex-spouses to also pay alimony out of wages and salary they earned after the marriage terminated.

Additionally, critics assailed the absence of alimony provisions in Texas FAMILY LAW as being unduly harsh. In a large number of divorces where neither spouse had acquired substantial assets during the marriage, Texas courts were powerless to compensate spouses who had sacrificed educational and career opportunities, since in such situations there were essentially no assets to divide in the first place. As a result, spouses who successfully pursued educational or career opportunities at the expense of their partner were allowed to walk away from the marriage "scot-free."

Despite the late twentieth-century universality of alimony laws in the all 50 states, lawmakers in some jurisdictions continued to propose legislation that would abolish it. In 1999 several Iowa legislators proposed a bill to abolish alimony, arguing that alimony laws provide incentive to get divorced. The bill never passed.

Because alimony is an award for support and maintenance that one spouse may be compelled to pay to another after DISSOLUTION of the marriage, it would seem to follow that no alimony could be awarded to a spouse following an ANNULMENT, which treats the marriage relationship as if it had never existed. In fact, alimony is not awarded to spouses under any conditions following the annulment of a marriage in most jurisdictions. However, in some jurisdictions the enforcement of a flat PROHIBITION of alimony awards to spouses whose marriages have been annulled has sometimes been found to impose unnecessary hardship on a spouse, usually the wife, especially where the parties have lived together for a considerable period of time. Consequently, judicial and legislative exceptions have been created to the basic rule of treating an annulled marriage as if it had never existed, for the purposes of determining whether an alimony award is appropriate. Under these exceptions, temporary as well as permanent alimony have been awarded.

FURTHER READINGS

"Alimony Strategies" 2003. *Family Advocate* 25, vol. 4 (spring).

American Law Institute. 2002. *Principles of the Law of Family Dissolution: Analysis and Recommendations.* Newark, NJ: Bender.

Sheldon, John C., and Nancy Diesel Mills. 1993. *In Search of a Theory of Alimony.* Orono, ME.: Univ. of Maine School of Law 45.

Storey, Brenda L. 2003. "Surveying the Alimony Landscape: Origin, Evolution and Extinction." *Family Advocate* 25 (spring).

CROSS REFERENCES

A Mensa Et Thoro; Child Support; Damages; Divorce; Family Law; Husband and Wife; Marriage; No Fault Divorce; Sex Discrimination.

❖ ALITO, SAMUEL ANTHONY, JR.

SAMUEL ALITO is a conservative justice appointed to the U.S. Supreme Court in 2006. Upon his confirmation, he became the 110th associate justice in the Court's history and only the second Italian-American. He replaced Sandra Day O'Connor on the Court.

Alito was born on April 1, 1950, in Trenton, New Jersey. His father emigrated from Italy as a boy and became a high school teacher. His father later changed careers in the 1950s to work as the research director of a nonpartisan agency that analyzed legislation for state legislators. Alito's mother was an elementary school principal. Alito excelled as a student, deciding on a legal career after discovering a special affinity for in-depth research and finely honed argument on the high school debate team. He graduated as valedictorian of his class and headed off to Princeton University in 1968.

After receiving his undergraduate degree in 1972, Alito pursued a law degree at Yale Law School, where he graduated in 1975. At Yale he served as an editor of the *Yale Law Journal* and quickly became known as a traditionalist with a quick intellect. It was a reputation that he was to carry with him throughout his working life. In 1976 Alito was hired as a law clerk by Third CIRCUIT COURT of Appeals Judge Leonard I. Garth (who eventually became a colleague when Alito was named to the same bench). After clerking for Garth, Alito spent 1977 to 1981 as an assistant U.S. attorney in New Jersey. He then went to Washington, D.C., to work for the DEPARTMENT OF JUSTICE, first as an assistant to the SOLICITOR GENERAL from 1981 to 1985 and then as a deputy assistant attorney general from 1985 to 1987. In the former position, he argued several cases before the U.S. Supreme Court. By 1987 Alito returned to New Jersey as U.S. attorney, in which role he handled cases from ORGANIZED CRIME to CHILD PORNOGRAPHY.

Alito took a seat on the U.S. Court of Appeals for the Third Circuit in 1990. While his time there undisputedly marked him as a solidly conservative JURIST, it also showed a man unwilling to express his political views openly. He was widely respected by Democrats and Republicans alike, and few saw him as either rigid or an ideologue. Still, one of Alito's controversial opinions was his lone DISSENT in a 1991 case that struck down a Pennsylvania law requiring married women seeking abortions to inform their husbands *Planned Parenthood of Southeastern Pennsylvania v. Casey*, 947 F. 2d 682). He also concluded in a 1998 opinion that a holiday display that included secular symbols along with religious ones did not violate the FIRST AMENDMENT. By contrast, Alito voted with the majority to find a ban on late-term abortions unconstitutional where there is no exception considering the health of the mother. These, and the broad array of other published opinions stemming from 15 years on the bench, were to come under intense scrutiny when Alito was nominated to replace retiring U.S. Supreme Court Justice O'Connor in October 2005.

Alito's nomination came in the wake of the withdrawal of previous nominee Harriet E. Miers, whom many believed was unqualified for the position. It also came at a time when President GEORGE W. BUSH was lagging in the polls and there was increasing acrimony between parties in the Senate. The situation was further sharpened by O'Connor's pivotal role as a centrist justice on a fairly divided Court, thus making the stakes particularly high for both parties in finding a suitable replacement. In short, there was little doubt that Alito's confirmation hearings were destined to be difficult and time-consuming, with conservative and liberal agendas likely to take precedence.

Several groups, including the AMERICAN CIVIL LIBERTIES UNION, strongly opposed Alito's

Samuel Alito.
STEVE PETTEWAY, COLLECTION OF THE SUPREME COURT OF THE UNITED STATES

nomination. According to the ACLU, Alito had displayed a "willingness to support government actions that abridge individual freedoms." In reviewing Alito's professional qualifications, though, a committee of the AMERICAN BAR ASSOCIATION concluded that Alito was "well-qualified" to serve on the Court.

As expected, the ideological battle between the parties caused great friction and talk of filibustering the Alito nomination. Despite Democratic attempts to block a vote on the nomination by filibustering, a Senate closure motion ended debate by a 72-25 vote. The closure motion forced a vote on the nomination, and the Senate confirmed Alito by a 58-42 vote, the smallest margin since CLARENCE THOMAS

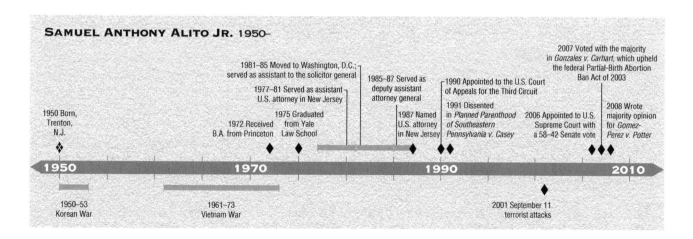

SAMUEL ANTHONY ALITO JR. 1950–

1950 Born, Trenton, N.J.

1972 Received B.A. from Princeton

1975 Graduated from Yale Law School

1977–81 Served as assistant U.S. attorney in New Jersey

1981–85 Moved to Washington, D.C.; served as assistant to the solicitor general

1985–87 Served as deputy assistant attorney general

1987 Named U.S. attorney in New Jersey

1990 Appointed to the U.S. Court of Appeals for the Third Circuit

1991 Dissented in *Planned Parenthood of Southeastern Pennsylvania v. Casey*

2006 Appointed to U.S. Supreme Court with a 58–42 Senate vote

2007 Voted with the majority in *Gonzales v. Carhart*, which upheld the federal Partial-Birth Abortion Ban Act of 2003

2008 Wrote majority opinion for *Gomez-Perez v. Potter*

1950   1970   1990   2010

1950–53 Korean War

1961–73 Vietnam War

2001 September 11 terrorist attacks

was confirmed in 1991. Alito was sworn in on January 31, 2006.

Since his confirmation, Alito has generally voted with the Court's conservative block, though he has voted differently in some cases from other conservative justices, including ANTONIN SCALIA. During his second year on the Court, Alito voted with the majority in *Gonzales v. Carhart* (550 U.S. 124, 127 S. Ct. 1610, 167 L. Ed. 2d 480 [2007]), where the Court upheld a challenge to the federal Partial-Birth ABORTION Ban Act of 2003. This marked the first abortion case the Court heard since Alito and Chief Justice JOHN ROBERTS became members of the Court. Alito and Roberts joined the majority opinion of Justice ANTHONY KENNEDY, along with Scalia and Thomas.

In 2008 Alito wrote the majority opinion in *Gomez-Perez v. Potter* (128 S. Ct. 29, 168 L. Ed. 2d 806), where the Court held that a federal employee could assert a claim for retaliation resulting from the employee's filing of a complaint for AGE DISCRIMINATION. Significantly, the more liberal justices on the Court joined Alito's majority, while Roberts, Scalia, and Thomas dissented.

Alito is married to the former Martha-Ann Bomgardner, and they have two children.

FURTHER READINGS

Babington, Charles. 2006. "Alito Is Sworn in on High Court." *Washington Post.* February 1.

Davis, Elliott M. 2007. "The Newer Textualism: Justice Alito's Statutory Interpretation." *Harvard Journal of Law and Public Policy.* 30 (Summer).

ALL FOURS

Identical; similar.

All fours specifically refers to two cases or decisions that have similar fact patterns and raise identical legal issues. Because the circumstances leading to their individual determinations are virtually the same, the decision rendered by the court in each case will be similar. Such cases or decisions are said to be on *all fours* with each other.

ALLEGATION

The assertion, claim, declaration, or statement of a party to an action, setting out what he or she expects to prove.

If the allegations in a plaintiff's complaint are insufficient to establish that the person's legal rights have been violated, the DEFENDANT can make a motion to the court to dismiss the complaint for failure to state a CAUSE OF ACTION. If the allegations in the defendant's answer do not contradict the allegations in the complaint, the PLAINTIFF can make a motion for SUMMARY JUDGMENT.

ALLEGE

To state, recite, assert, or charge the existence of particular facts in a pleading or an indictment; to make an allegation.

ALLEGIANCE

In English law, the duty of loyalty and obedience owed by all persons born within the king's realm that attaches immediately upon their birth and that they cannot be relieved of by their own actions.

In U.S. law, allegiance is the obligation of fidelity and obedience that is owed by native born and naturalized U.S. citizens to the United States that cannot be relinquished without the consent of the government expressed by a statutory enactment.

The act of swearing allegiance to the country, its laws, and its government is a bedrock requirement of U.S. citizenship reflected in both state and federal law. Before foreign citizens may lawfully immigrate to the United States, they must take an OATH renouncing their allegiance to all foreign sovereigns and swearing their allegiance to the laws and constitution of the U.S. government (8 USCA § 1448). The U.S. Constitution itself requires state and federal legislators, judicial officers, and EXECUTIVE BRANCH officials to take an oath or affirmation to support its provisions (Article 6, clause 3).

Swearing allegiance to the government is not always the most important value recognized by U.S. law. Having won its independence and liberty from England through a bloody revolution, the United States has a long history of respecting FREEDOM OF SPEECH, freedom of RELIGION, and the right to DISSENT in its participatory democracy. In fact, one reason many Americans remain steadfastly loyal to the United States is that U.S. laws protect their right to dissent, PROTEST, demonstrate, and criticize the government.

Public school children in many states learn to recite the Pledge of Allegiance. Slightly fewer than half of the states plus the TERRITORY of Guam require public school teachers to recite the Pledge of Allegiance in class. The majority of states make recitation discretionary.

The U.S. Supreme Court, in striking down a state law that compelled public school students to recite the Pledge of Allegiance, drew upon this history when it wrote that if "there is any fixed star in our constitutional constellation, it is that no official, high or petty, can prescribe what shall be orthodox in politics, nationalism, religion, or other matters of opinion or force citizens to confess by word or act their faith therein" (*West Virginia State Board of Education v. Barnette*, 319 U.S. 624, 63 S. Ct. 1178, 87 L. Ed. 1628 [U.S. 1943]).

After the Supreme Court announced its decision in *Barnette*, neither the state nor federal government could lawfully compel public school children to recite the pledge, though they could require school teachers and administrators to lead the pledge, so long as they allowed students the right to abstain from reciting it themselves. But the *Barnette* decision did not end the controversy over the Pledge of Allegiance. In 1954 Congress changed the official version of the pledge to include a statement that the United States is "one nation under God" (4 USCA § 4).

The reference to a deity in the pledge prompted several constitutional challenges. Many of these challenges were raised under the establishment clause of the FIRST AMENDMENT, which generally forbids the state and federal governments from "establishing" an official religion within their jurisdiction.

In 2002, one day after a three-judge PANEL for the Ninth CIRCUIT COURT of Appeals released a decision holding that recitation of the Pledge of Allegiance in public schools was unconstitutional, the full court voted to stay the decision pending further consideration. However, on February 28, 2003, the full court reinstated its holding that a school district's policy of requiring teacher-led recitations of the Pledge of Allegiance violated the establishment clause of the First Amendment by impermissibly coercing a religious act (*Newdow v. U.S. Congress*, 328 F.3d 466 [9th Cir. 2003]). At the same time, in its amended opinion, the Ninth Circuit declined to rule on the constitutionality of the words "under God" in the federal statute. U.S. Solicitor General Theodore Olson filed a PETITION for WRIT of certiorari on April 30, 2003, asking the U.S. Supreme Court to overturn the Ninth Circuit decision.

Children in a California elementary school recite the Pledge of Allegiance. In June 2002, a Ninth Circuit U.S. Court of Appeals panel ruled that the phrase "under God," as contained in the pledge, violated the Establishment Clause.

AP IMAGES

Indeed, the Supreme Court reversed the Ninth Circuit in *Elk Grove Unified School District v. Newdow* (9542 U.S. 1 [2004]). However, the Court did not address the constitutional merits of the case. Instead, it reversed on a procedural technicality, ruling that Sacramento, California, atheist and divorced parent Michael Newdow lacked the legal standing to sue on behalf of his daughter because he did not have legal custody of her, such custody having been granted to the mother. (*Standing* is a legal requirement that the PLAINTIFF must have been injured or threatened with injury by the action complained of and focuses on the question of whether the plaintiff is the proper party to bring the lawsuit.) In 2005 Newdow, to avoid the standing issue, joined with three other anonymous parents/families and again filed legal challenges. In these cases, defendants included the Rio Linda Union School District and the United States as a defendant-intervenor, along with John Carey (the captioned DEFENDANT), who sought to preserve the current wording of the Pledge. This time around, the Ninth Circuit consolidated the three defendants' cases on appeal for oral arguments in December 2007. As of late 2009, it had not issued its opinion (*Newdow v. Carey*, Nos. 05-17257, 05-17344, and 06-15093).

Also in 2009, the U.S. Court of Appeals for the Eleventh Circuit denied rehearing of its 2008 decision to let stand a Florida law that required public school students to recite the Pledge of Allegiance unless excused by a note from their parents (*Frazier v. Alexandre*, 535 F.3d 1279 [2008]). However, the appellate court struck a provision within the same law that required students and other civilians to stand during recitation. In *Croft v. Perry* (N.D. Tex., March 26, 2009), a federal district court threw out an establishment challenge to the Texas Pledge of Allegiance, which reads, in relevant part, "Honor the Texas flag; I pledge allegiance to thee, Texas, one state under God, one and indivisible."

FURTHER READINGS

Bergman, Jerry. 1997. "The Modern Religious Objection to Mandatory Flag Salute in America: A History and Evaluation." *Journal of Church and State* 39 (spring): 215–36.

Canipe, Lee. 2003. "Under God and Anti-communist: How the Pledge of Allegiance Got Religion in Cold-War America." *Journal of Church and State* 45 (spring): 305–23.

Ellis, Richard J. 2007. *To the Flag: The Unlikely History of the Pledge of Allegiance.* Lawrence, Kansas: Univ. Press of Kansas.

Sanford, Bill W., Jr. 2003. "Separation v. Patriotism: Expelling the Pledge from School." *St. Mary's Law Journal* 34 (winter): 461–502.

CROSS REFERENCES

Citizens; Dissent; Establishment Clause; First Amendment; Freedom of Speech; Immigration and Naturalization.

ALLOCATION

The apportionment or designation of an item for a specific purpose or to a particular place.

In the law of trusts, the allocation of cash dividends earned by a stock that makes up the principal of a trust for a BENEFICIARY usually means that the dividends will be treated as income to be paid to the beneficiary. The allocation of stock dividends generally means that such dividends will be added to the shares of stock held as principal, thereby increasing its size.

ALLOCUTION

The formal inquiry by a judge of an accused person, convicted of a crime, as to whether the person has any legal cause to show why judgment should not be pronounced against him or her or as to whether the person has anything to say to the court before being sentenced.

ALLODIAL

Free; not subject to the rights of any lord or superior; owned without obligation of vassalage or fealty; the opposite of feudal.

A description given to the outright ownership of land that did not impose upon its owner the performance of feudal duties.

CROSS REFERENCE

Feudalism.

ALLOGRAPH

A writing or signature made by one person for another.

When a principal gives his or her agent the power to pay creditors, the checks written by the agent are allographs for the principal.

An autograph is the opposite of an allograph.

ALLONGE

Additional paper firmly attached to commercial paper, such as a promissory note, to provide room to write endorsements.

An allonge is necessary when there is insufficient space on the document itself for the endorsements. It is considered part of the commercial paper as long as the allonge remains affixed thereto.

ALLOTMENT

A portion, share, or division. The proportionate distribution of shares of stock in a corporation. The partition and distribution of land.

❖ ALLRED, GLORIA

Gloria Allred, born July 3, 1941, in Philadelphia, is a flamboyant, widely recognized lawyer, feminist, activist, and radio talk show host. Though her critics dismiss her as a publicity monger and a dilettante, Allred has received praise from others who believe that she is a master at using the power of the news media to draw attention to the day-to-day struggles of ordinary people.

Born Gloria Rachel Bloom, Allred grew up in Philadelphia with her parents, Morris Bloom, a door-to-door salesman, and Stella Davidson Bloom, a homemaker. Her conventional middle-class childhood gave no hint of the outspoken activist to come. Allred graduated with honors from the University of Pennsylvania in 1963 with a bachelor's degree in English. She moved to New York to pursue a master's degree in teaching at New York University. While there, she became interested in the CIVIL RIGHTS MOVEMENT, which was beginning to gain momentum. After earning her master's degree in 1966, she returned to Philadelphia to teach at a high school with a predominantly black enrollment.

Allred says that her interest in the struggle for equal rights arose from personal experiences. While she was in college, she married, gave birth to a daughter, and divorced. Unable to collect CHILD SUPPORT from her former husband, she was forced to return to her parents' home. She also recalls being paid less than a man for what she considered equal work. The reason given was that the man had a family to support, but at the time, Allred as the single mother also had a dependent to support. Perhaps the experience that most galvanized her commitment to equal rights was being raped and then having to undergo an ABORTION at a time when the operation could not legally be performed by a doctor. She nearly died after the operation. According to Allred, the experience made her realize the need for safe and legal abortions and precipitated her lifelong commitment to the fight for reproductive freedom.

Allred moved to Los Angeles and married again in 1968, this time to Raymond Allred; they were divorced in 1987. Allred taught in the turbulent Watts section of Los Angeles and became the first full-time female staff member in United Teachers of Los Angeles, the union representing Los Angeles's teachers. The

Gloria Allred.
AP PHOTOS.

experience stirred her interest in CIVIL RIGHTS and COLLECTIVE BARGAINING and prompted her to go to law school. She received her law degree, with honors, from Loyola Marymount University, Los Angeles, Law School in 1974. Soon after, she entered a law firm partnership with her classmates Nathan Goldberg and Michael Maroko. Allred, Maroko, Goldberg, and Ribakoff grew during the 1970s and 1980s into a firm with annual revenues exceeding $2.5 million. The firm's caseload has ranged from family and CONSTITUTIONAL LAW to business LITIGATION and PERSONAL INJURY suits. The firm has won national

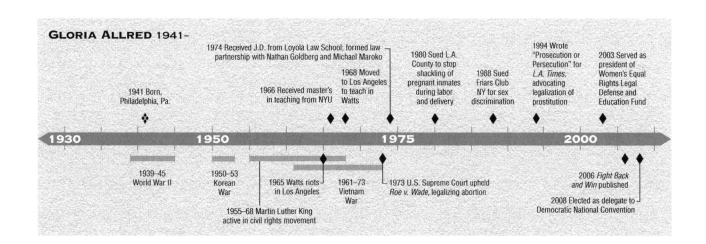

GLORIA ALLRED 1941–

1974 Received J.D. from Loyola Law School; formed law partnership with Nathan Goldberg and Michael Maroko

1968 Moved to Los Angeles to teach in Watts

1980 Sued L.A. County to stop shackling of pregnant inmates during labor and delivery

1994 Wrote "Prosecution or Persecution" for *L.A. Times,* advocating legalization of prostitution

2003 Served as president of Women's Equal Rights Legal Defense and Education Fund

1941 Born, Philadelphia, Pa.

1966 Received master's in teaching from NYU

1988 Sued Friars Club NY for sex discrimination

1930   1950   1975   2000

1939–45 World War II

1950–53 Korean War

1965 Watts riots in Los Angeles

1961–73 Vietnam War

1973 U.S. Supreme Court upheld *Roe v. Wade,* legalizing abortion

1955–68 Martin Luther King active in civil rights movement

2006 *Fight Back and Win* published

2008 Elected as delegate to Democratic National Convention

prominence through many precedent-setting cases over the course of more than 30 years, working on such high profile cases including those involving O.J. Simpson, Michael Jackson, Scott Peterson, and Robert Blake, as well as one of the earliest SEXUAL ABUSE suits against the Catholic Church.

Allred has been perhaps the most flamboyant and well known member of her firm. She has achieved notoriety and name recognition through staged press conferences and demonstrations publicizing and dramatizing the causes she has championed at various times. She has also accepted controversial cases that naturally attract media attention. During her years in practice, she has successfully sued Los Angeles County to stop the practice of shackling and chaining pregnant inmates during labor and delivery; put a halt on the practice by the city of El Segundo of quizzing job applicants about their sexual histories (*Thorne v. City of El Segundo*, 802 F.2d 1131 [9th Cir. 1986]); represented a client who was turned down for a job as a police officer after a six-hour lie detector exam that included questions about her sex life; and sued a dry cleaning establishment for discrimination because it charged more to launder women's shirts than men's. Allred also successfully sued on behalf of two lesbians who had been denied entrance to the "romance booth" at a Los Angeles restaurant (*Rolon v. Kulwitsky*, 153 Cal. App. 3d 289, 200 Cal. Rptr. 217 [Cal. App. 2 Dist. 1984]). The OWNER of the restaurant vowed to close the booth if Allred's clients won. They did, and he made good on his promise.

Allred relishes confrontation, and her showy tactics have earned her both praise and criticism. Defending what many have called self-promoting publicity stunts, Allred says she is aware of the impression she makes and contends that it is exactly the effect she wants. She tries to use the few moments she is in the spotlight to make her point as forcefully as possible. Her detractors say that she wastes her time and energy on trivial issues that do not advance any worthwhile cause and deflect attention away from serious issues. Yet, she points out, she is often stopped on the street by people who recognize her and want to thank her for taking on the small fights that no one else wants. Allred contends that what she is really doing is tackling issues that are symbolic of the day-to-day struggles people face. It is her way of educating the public and the legal establishment to move beyond stereotypes.

Asked whether she is an activist or a lawyer, Allred replied that she is an "activist lawyer." She added that she believes in seeking change and winning rights through the legal process but that she does not shrink from utilizing the political process when legal remedies prove inadequate. She once held a press conference in the office of California governor Jerry Brown to cast media attention on his threat to VETO a bill authorizing payroll deductions for child support payments. When the news media arrived, Allred and a group of women and children had hung diapers across the governor's office. Brown reversed his position and signed the bill. In another case that drew media attention, Allred held a press conference at the door of the all-male Friars Club of New York to dramatize her lawsuit challenging the club's policy of not allowing women members and not allowing women to enter, even as guests, before 4:00 p.m. She won her suit on the grounds that the club did not meet the "substantially private" requirement under New York law that would have allowed it to legally exclude women. Possibly her most famous politically motivated demonstration was presenting California state senator John Schmitz (R-Corona del Mar) with a chastity belt at a hearing on a bill to limit abortion and BIRTH CONTROL. Schmitz retaliated in a press release in which he called Allred "a slick butch lawyeress." Allred sued for libel and won a damage award and an apology.

Allred has earned a reputation as a champion of those who have been sexually victimized. She represented a woman who won a $5 million civil suit against an accused rapist the DISTRICT ATTORNEY declined to PROSECUTE; represented a boy who claimed to have been sexually abused by a famous rock singer (although she abruptly and without explanation withdrew from the case before it was settled); and tackled the thorny issue of clergy sexual abuse. She says she wants people to know that, even if the criminal justice system fails them, they are entitled to file a civil suit.

Allred is an ardent feminist who believes that all attorneys and all judges should be feminists, because she feels anyone who is not a feminist is a bigot. Some critics say she is all show and no substance. She has been compared to legal showmen such as Melvin M. Belli ("the King of Torts") and Marvin Mitchelson, who gained notoriety through a series of celebrity palimony suits. However, even Mitchelson, not one to shrink from publicity himself, describes her style as rough. But Allred has many supporters as well. Among them is Justice Joan Dempsey Klein of the California COURT OF APPEAL who credits Allred with moving women's issues forward. Klein also points out that Allred saves her dramatics for outside the courtroom and always observes proper decorum while before the bench. According to Klein, Allred is always well-prepared and, for that reason, is quite successful.

In 1994 Allred wrote an editorial for the December 6 issue of the *Los Angeles Times,* titled "Prosecution or Persecution," in which she asserted that laws prohibiting PROSTITUTION are sexist and victimize women. She advocated legalization and regulation of the sex trade in order to reduce sexually transmitted diseases and drug abuse. According to Allred, "Unprotected, uninsured sex workers are the real victims who deserve legal status and an end to government-funded harassment."

In the 1990s Allred, whose law firm partners were both the children of Holocaust survivors, sued an organization that had promised a monetary award to an Auschwitz survivor for proving the existence of the Holocaust and then reneged on the award. Allred won a six-figure judgment that ultimately bankrupted the organization. In 1995 Allred sued the Boy Scouts of America (BSA) over the organization's refusal to let a girl join the troop to which her twin brother belonged. The trial judge's decision that the BSA was not a business organization and was not subject to the state Civil Rights Act was upheld by the Court of Appeals. The case was appealed to California's Supreme Court, but, when that court upheld two similar cases, the PLAINTIFF withdrew her appeal.

In early 2003 Allred served as president of the Women's Equal Rights Legal Defense and Education Fund, an organization she founded. She hosted her own radio talk show on a Los Angeles radio station and was selected as one of the 25 most important talk show hosts by *USA Today.* She has also been a columnist for the *National Law Journal* and has been nominated three times for television's Emmy award for her commentaries on KABC-TV.

During the early twenty-first century, Allred's career achievements include being elected as a delegate to the 2008 Democratic National Convention and receiving the Distinguished Alumna Achievement Award from New York University's Steinhardt School of Culture, Education, and Human Development in May 2009. Allred's most recent case garnering media attention involved Nadya Suleman, the so-called "Octo-mom," who gave birth to eight babies in 2009. Allred asked for an investigation into what she alleged were violations of labor laws and regulations in the filming of the babies. California State Labor officials issued numerous citations for violations of the law as a result of the investigation.

Dressed in her trademark reds and electric blues, Allred is a combination of scholarship and theatrics. Her intelligence and shrewd understanding of the power of the media have made her a contemporary success story in the world of law and politics. Gloria Allred has her own Web site: www.gloriaallred.com.

FURTHER READINGS

Allred, Gloria (with Deborah Caulfield Rybak). 2006. *Fight Back and Win: My Thirty-Year Fight against Injustice and How You Can Win Your Own Battles.* New York: Harper Collins.

Berry, Dawn Bradley. 1996. *The 50 Most Influential Women in American Law.* Los Angeles: Contemporary Books.

Drachman, Virginia G. 1998. *Sisters in Law: Women Lawyers in Modern American History.* Cambridge: Harvard Univ. Press.

Gloria Allred. Available online at <www.gloriaallred.com> (accessed August 12, 2009).

ALLUVION

See TERRITORY.

ALTER EGO

A doctrine used by the courts to ignore the corporate status of a group of stockholders, officers, and directors of a corporation in reference to their limited liability so that they may be held personally liable for their actions when they have acted fraudulently or unjustly or when to refuse to do so would deprive an innocent victim of redress for an injury caused by them.

A corporation is considered the alter ego of its stockholders, directors, or officers when it is used merely for the transaction of their personal business for which they want IMMUNITY from individual LIABILITY. A parent corporation is the alter ego of a SUBSIDIARY corporation if it controls and directs its activities so that it will have limited liability for its wrongful acts.

The alter ego doctrine is also known as the INSTRUMENTALITY RULE because the corporation becomes an instrument for the personal advantage of its parent corporation, stockholders, directors, or officers. When a court applies it, the court is said to pierce the corporate veil.

Courts have not traditionally applied the alter ego doctrine to other business forms, such as partnerships and limited partnerships, because partners generally do not enjoy the same form of limited liability as corporate stockholders, officers, and directors. By comparison, however, owners of limited liability companies may structure their business in a manner similar to a corporation so that members and managers are shielded from personal liability for the debts of the LIMITED LIABILITY COMPANY (LLC). Several courts have determined that the alter ego doctrine may also apply to LLCs. For instance, in *Kaycee Land & Livestock v. Flahive*, 46 P.3d 323 (Wyo. 2002), the Wyoming Supreme Court held that the equitable doctrine of piercing the veil was an available remedy under the Wyoming Limited Liability Company Act.

CROSS REFERENCES

Corporations; Immunity; Liability.

ALTERATION

Modification; changing a thing without obliterating it.

An alteration is a variation made in the language or terms of a legal document that affects the rights and obligations of the parties to it. When this occurs, the alteration is material and the party who did not CONSENT to the change can be released from his or her duties under the document by a court.

When an essential part of a writing has been cut, torn, burned, or erased, the alteration is also known as a mutilation. The alteration of a document by someone other than a party to it is called a spoliation.

ALTERATION OF INSTRUMENTS

A change in the meaning or language of a legal document, such as a contract, deed, lease, or commercial paper, that is made by one party to the document without the consent of the other after it has been signed or completed.

If such a change is made by a THIRD PARTY without the CONSENT of either party to the instrument, it is called a SPOLIATION or mutilation.

Method

The face of an instrument is changed by its alteration. A difference in handwriting, a change in words or figures, an erasure, and the striking out of particular words are some methods used to alter an instrument. Since there must be a change in the meaning or language of a document, retracing an original writing—as when a figure written in pencil is retraced in ink—is not an alteration.

Material Changes

The alteration of an instrument materially changes it. The document no longer reflects the terms that the parties originally intended to serve as the basis of their legal obligation to each other. To be material, the change must affect an important part of the instrument and the rights of the parties to it. Any material alteration relieves the nonconsenting party of any obligation to perform according to the terms of the instrument. If the altered instrument is a contract, then the original contract is void. The nonconsenting party cannot be legally obligated by the new contract since he or she never agreed to it. A document that has been materially altered does not regain its original validity if it is restored to its original form by erasing or deleting unauthorized words.

The date of an instrument is often considered a material provision when it establishes the time within which the parties to a document must perform their obligations under it. An unauthorized change of date that shortens the time of payment or extends the time of performance so that more interest will become due is a material alteration.

An alteration of a signature that changes the legal effect of an instrument is material. Erasing words that show that the signer is acting as an agent, for example, changes the signer's LIABILITY under the instrument and, therefore, is a material alteration. However, when a signature that was improperly placed on a document is erased, there is no material alteration since the legal meaning of the document is not changed.

Any change in the terms of the instrument that affects the obligations of the parties is material. In a contract to sell land on commission, a change in the rate of commission is material. A change in a description in a deed so that it transfers a smaller piece of land, a change in the name of a purchaser in a sales contract, or an alteration in the terms of financing set forth in a MORTGAGE is also material.

Time of Alteration

A modification in a document before its completion is not an alteration. The parties are bound to review the document and to have agreed upon its terms before executing it. In order for an alteration to nullify the legal effect of an instrument, the change must be made after its completion.

Intention

A material change must be intentionally made. The motive behind the alteration is unimportant. If a mistake or accident causes a change, this is not considered a material alteration, but the document may be reformed or rescinded.

The Person Making the Change

The change to the instrument must be made by a party or someone authorized by him or her to do so. No change made by a third person without the consent of either party to the document will invalidate it if its original terms can be learned. When a material alteration is made by a party to COMMERCIAL PAPER, such as a check or PROMISSORY NOTE, the paper will be enforced as originally written against the party who made the changes.

Consensual Alteration

A change in an instrument made with the consent of the parties is binding upon them. Such CONSENSUAL ALTERATION is usually evidenced by the signing by each party of his or her initials and the date that the agreement to the changes to the instrument was reached.

ALTERNATIVE DISPUTE RESOLUTION

Procedures for settling disputes by means other than litigation; e.g., by arbitration, mediation, or minitrials. Such procedures, which are usually less costly and more expeditious than litigation, are increasingly being used in commercial and labor disputes, in divorce actions, in resolving motor vehicle and medical malpractice tort claims, and in other disputes that would likely otherwise involve court litigation.

In the late 1980s and early 1990s, many people became increasingly concerned that the traditional method of resolving legal disputes in the United States, through conventional LITIGATION, had become too expensive, too slow, and too cumbersome for many civil lawsuits (cases between private parties). This concern led to the growing use of ways other than litigation to resolve disputes. These other methods are commonly known collectively as "alternative dispute resolution" (ADR).

As of the early 2000s, ADR techniques were being used more and more, as parties and lawyers and courts realized that these techniques could often help them resolve legal disputes quickly and cheaply and more privately than could conventional litigation. Moreover, many people preferred ADR approaches because they saw these methods as being more creative and more focused on problem solving than litigation, which has always been based on an adversarial model.

To some degree, the term *alternative dispute resolution* is a misnomer. In reality, fewer than 5 percent of all lawsuits filed go to trial; the other 95 percent are settled or otherwise concluded before trial. Thus, it is more accurate to think of *litigation* as the alternative and ADR as the norm. Despite this fact, the term *alternative dispute resolution* has become such a well-accepted shorthand for the vast array of non-litigation processes that its continued use seems assured.

Although certain ADR techniques are well established and frequently used—for example, mediation and arbitration—alternative dispute resolution has no fixed definition. It includes a wide range of processes, many with little in common except that each is an alternative to full-blown litigation. Litigants, lawyers, and judges are constantly adapting existing ADR processes or devising new ones to meet the unique needs of their legal disputes. The definition of alternative dispute resolution is constantly expanding to include new techniques.

ADR techniques have not been created to undercut the traditional U.S. court system. Certainly, ADR options can be used in cases where litigation is not the most appropriate route. However, they can also be used in conjunction with litigation when the parties want to explore other options but also want to remain free to return to the traditional court process at any point.

Of the many litigation alternatives to resolve a legal dispute, mediation, arbitration, mediation-arbitration, minitrial, early neutral evaluation, summary jury trial, and collaborative law are the most common.

Alternative Dispute Resolution Information Form

NAME OF COURT: _____

ADR Information Form

*This form should be filled out and returned,
within 10 days of the resolution of the dispute, to:*

1. Case name: _____ No. _____

2. Type of civil case: ☐ PI/PD-Auto ☐ PI/PD-Other ☐ Contract ☐ Other (*specify*): _____

3. Date complaint filed _____   Date case resolved _____

4. Date of ADR conference _____   5. Number of parties _____

6. Amount in controversy: ☐ $0–$25,000 ☐ $25,000–$50,000 ☐ $50,000–$100,000 ☐ over $100,000 (*specify*)_____

7. ☐ Plaintiff's Attorney ☐ Cross Complainant's Attorney   8. ☐ Defendant's Attorney ☐ Cross Defendant's Attorney

NAME _____   NAME _____

ADDRESS _____   ADDRESS _____

(____)_____   (____)_____
TELEPHONE NUMBER   TELEPHONE NUMBER

9. Please indicate your relationship to the case:

   ☐ Plaintiff   ☐ Plaintiff's attorney   ☐ Defendant   ☐ Defendant's attorney

   ☐ 3rd party defendant   ☐ 3rd party defendant's attorney   ☐ Other (*specify*): _____

10. Dispute resolution process:

    ☐ Mediation   ☐ Arbitration   ☐ Neutral case evaluation   ☐ Other (*specify*): _____

11. How was case resolved?

    a. ☐ As a direct result of the ADR process.

    b. ☐ As an indirect result of the ADR process.   c. ☐ Resolution was unrelated to ADR process.

12. Check the closest dollar amount that you estimate you saved (attorneys fees, expert witness fees, and other costs) by using this dispute resolution process compared to resolving this case through litigation, whether by settlement or trial.

    ☐ $0   ☐ $250   ☐ $500   ☐ $750   ☐ $1,000   ☐ more than $1,000 (*specify*): $ _____

13. If the dispute resolution process caused a net increase in your costs in this case, check the closest dollar amount of the *additional* cost:

    ☐ $0   ☐ $250   ☐ $500   ☐ $750   ☐ $1,000   ☐ more than $1,000 (*specify*): $ _____

14. Check the closest number of court days that you estimate the court saved (motions, hearings, conferences, trial, etc.) as a result of this case being referred to this dispute resolution process:

    ☐ 0   ☐ 1 day   ☐ more than 1 day (*specify*): _____

15. If the dispute resolution process caused a net increase in court time for this case, check the closest number of *additional* court days:

    ☐ 0   ☐ 1 day   ☐ more than 1 day (*specify*): _____

16. Would you be willing to consider using this dispute resolution process again?   ☐ Yes   ☐ No

Form Adopted by the
Judicial Council of California
ADR-101 [New March 1, 1994]

WEST GROUP
Official Publisher

Mediation

Mediation—also known as "conciliation"—is the fastest-growing ADR method. Unlike litigation, mediation provides a forum in which parties can resolve their own disputes, with the help of a neutral THIRD PARTY.

Mediation depends upon the commitment of the disputants to solve their own problems. The mediator, also known as a "facilitator," never imposes a decision upon the parties. Rather, the mediator's job is to keep the parties talking and to help move them through the more difficult points of contention. To do this, the mediator typically takes the parties through five stages.

First, the mediator gets the parties to agree on procedural matters, such as by stating that they are participating in the mediation voluntarily, setting the time and place for future sessions, and executing a formal confidentiality agreement. One valuable aspect of this stage is that the parties, who often have been unable to agree on anything, begin a pattern of saying yes.

Second, the parties exchange initial positions, not by way of lecturing the mediator but in a face-to-face exchange with each other. Often, this is the first time each party hears the other's complete and uninterrupted version. The parties may begin to see that the story has two sides and that it may not be so unreasonable to compromise their initial positions.

Third, if the parties have agreed to what is called a "caucusing procedure," the mediator meets with each side separately in a series of confidential, private meetings and begins exploring SETTLEMENT alternatives, perhaps by engaging the parties in some "reality testing" of their initial proposals. This process, sometimes called *shuttle diplomacy,* often uncovers areas of flexibility that the parties could not see or would have been uncomfortable putting forward officially.

Fourth, when the gap between the parties begins to close, the mediator may carry offers and counteroffers back and forth between them, or the parties may elect to return to a joint session to exchange their offers.

Finally, when the parties agree upon the broad terms of a settlement, they formally reaffirm their understanding of that settlement, complete the final details, and sign a settlement agreement.

Mediation permits the parties to design and retain control of the process at all times and, ideally, eventually strike their own bargain. Evidence suggests that parties are more willing to comply with their own agreements, achieved through mediation, than with adjudicated decisions, which are imposed upon them by an outside party such as a judge.

One additional advantage is that when the parties reach agreement in mediation, the dispute is over—they face no appeals, delays, continuing expenses, or unknown risks. The parties can begin to move forward again. Unlike litigation, which focuses on the past, mediation looks to the future. Thus, a mediated agreement is particularly valuable to parties who have an ongoing relationship, such as a commercial or employment relationship.

Arbitration

Arbitration more closely resembles traditional litigation in that a neutral third party hears the disputants' arguments and imposes a final and binding decision that is enforceable by the courts. The difference is that in arbitration, the disputants generally agreed to the procedure before the dispute arose; the disputants mutually decide who will hear their case; and the proceedings are typically less formal than in a court of law. One extremely important difference is that, unlike court decisions, arbitration offers almost no effective appeal process. Thus, when an arbitration decision is issued, the case is ended.

Final and binding arbitration has long been used in labor-management disputes. For decades, unions and employers have found it mutually advantageous to have a knowledgeable arbitrator—whom they themselves have chosen—resolve their disputes in this cheaper and faster fashion. One primary advantage for both sides has been that taking disputes to arbitration has kept everyone working by providing an alternative to strikes and lockouts and has kept everyone out of the courts. Given this very successful track record, the commercial world has become enthusiastic about arbitration for other types of disputes as well.

A new form of arbitration, known as "court-annexed arbitration," has emerged. Many variations of court-annexed arbitration have developed throughout the United States. One can be found in Minnesota, where, in the mid-1990s, the Hennepin County district court adopted a program making civil cases involving less than $50,000 subject to mandatory non-binding arbitration. The results of that experimental program were so encouraging that legislation was later enacted expanding the arbitration program statewide. Most cases were channeled through an ADR process before they could be heard in the courts. A growing number of other federal and state courts were adopting this or similar approaches.

Mediation-Arbitration

As its name suggests, mediation-arbitration, or "med-arb," combines mediation and arbitration. First, a mediator tries to bring the parties closer together and help them reach their own agreement. If the parties cannot compromise, they then proceed to arbitration—before that same third party or before a different arbitrator—for a final and binding decision.

Minitrial

The minitrial, a development in ADR, is finding its greatest use in resolving large-scale disputes involving complex questions of mixed law and fact, such as PRODUCT LIABILITY, massive construction, and antitrust cases. In a minitrial, each party presents its case as in a regular trial, but with the notable difference that the case is "tried" by the parties themselves, and the presentations are dramatically abbreviated.

In a minitrial, lawyers and experts present a condensed version of the case to top management of both parties. Often, a neutral adviser—sometimes an expert in the subject area—sits with management and conducts the hearing. After these presentations, top management representatives—by now more aware of the strengths and weaknesses of each side—try to NEGOTIATE a resolution of the problem. If they are unable to do so, they often ask for the neutral adviser's best guess as to the probable outcome of the case. They then resume negotiations.

The keys to the success of this approach are the presence of both sides' top officials and the exchange of information that takes place during the minitrial. Too often, prelitigation work has insulated top management from the true strengths and weaknesses of their cases. Minitrial presentations allow them to see the dispute as it would appear to an outsider and set the stage for a cooperative settlement.

Early Neutral Evaluation

An early neutral evaluation (ENE) is used when one or both parties to a dispute seek the advice of an experienced individual, usually an attorney, concerning the strength of their cases. An objective evaluation by a knowledgeable outsider can sometimes move parties away from unrealistic positions, or at least provide them with more insight into their cases' strengths and weaknesses. Of course, the success of this technique depends upon the parties' faith in the fairness and objectivity of the neutral third-party, and their willingness to compromise.

Summary Jury Trial

Summary jury trials have been used primarily in the federal courts, where they provide parties with the opportunity to "try" their cases in an abbreviated fashion before a group of jurors, who then deliberate and render an ADVISORY OPINION.

Like an early neutral evaluation, an advisory opinion from a summary jury trial can help the parties assess the strengths and weaknesses of their cases and sometimes can facilitate the settlement of the dispute. Another advantage of the summary jury trial, which it has in common with the minitrial, is that it can be scheduled much sooner than a trial. When early evaluations help the parties SETTLE their cases, the parties typically avoid much of the delay, expense, and anxiety that occurs in litigation.

Collaborative Law

Collaborative Law, sometimes referred to as "collaborative practice" or "collaborative divorce," is a form of alternative dispute resolution used for DIVORCE or legal FAMILY LAW disputes. In this process, the goal is to resolve the conflict outside of the courtroom by entering into a series of joint sessions with the two parties, their lawyers, and neutral experts. The primary focus of the meetings or joint sessions is to settle the dispute by identifying the priorities, goals, needs, and interests of the parties and helping them work together toward a settlement that is consistent with such goals and needs. Unlike mediation, in the collaborative law process the parties agree at the beginning of the dispute to settle the case outside of court. In addition, while going through the process, the attorneys facilitate the negotiations, and the parties are fully informed of the law and any legal consequences regarding their various decisions and options. As of September 2009, California, North Carolina, and Texas had implemented statutes regarding collaborative divorce. Other courts have implemented local court rules regarding the collaborative law process for their jurisdiction. In addition, the National Conference of Commissioners on Uniform State laws, on July 15, 2009, adopted the Uniform Collaborative Law Act, which will be presented to state legislatures for enactment.

ADR by Statute and Regulation

Since the late 1980s, Congress has recognized that ADR provides a cost-efficient alternative to traditional methods for dispute resolution. In 1988, Congress enacted the Judicial Improvements and Access to Justice Act, 28 U.S.C.A. § 652 (1993 & Supp. 2003), which permitted U.S. district courts to submit disputes to arbitration. Congress amended this statute with the enactment of the Alternative Dispute Resolution Act of 1998, Pub. L. No. 105-315, 112 Stat. 2994 (28 U.S.C.A. § 652), which requires each district court to require, by local rule, that litigants in all civil cases consider using an ADR process at the appropriate state of litigation.

Local rules of U.S. district courts typically provide a wide array of ADR methods. For example, the U.S. District Court for the Western District of Texas recognizes early neutral evaluation, mediation, minitrial, moderated settlement conference, summary jury trial, and arbitration as acceptable forms of ADR. According to these rules, the court may order ADR on the motion of a party, on agreement of both parties, or on its own motion. Most other district courts have adopted similar rules. Congress has also included ADR provisions in a number of statutes to resolve a variety of disputes. For example, the Board of Directors of the Office of Compliance, which reviews complaints brought by employees of Congress, may order counseling or mediation, in addition to holding a board hearing or initiating a CIVIL ACTION in federal court. 2 U.S.C.A. § 1401 (1997). Similar statutes apply to such conflicts as labor disputes and claims by individuals with disabilities.

State legislatures have similarly provided for ADR in many of their statutes. Judges in Florida, for example, possess authority to submit most types of cases to mediation or arbitration in lieu of litigation. Fla. Stat. § 44.1011 (1997). The COMMISSIONERS ON UNIFORM LAWS have approved several uniform laws, which may be adopted by the various states, related to ADR proceedings. Versions of the Uniform Arbitration Act, first approved in 1956, have been adopted by 49 states. Likewise, the Uniform Mediation Act, drafted in conjunction with the American Bar Association's Section on Dispute Resolution in 2001, provides rules on the issues of confidentiality and privileges in mediation.

ADR has had an impact on administrative agencies as well. Congress amended the Administrative Procedure Act in 1990 to authorize and encourage administrative agencies to submit administrative disputes to ADR (5 U.S.C.A. § 572 [1996]). ADR often takes the form of mediation in disputes involving labor and employment relations and equal employment opportunity. Several federal agencies provide guides about ADR proceedings to prospective complainants and other constituents.

Courts frequently uphold decisions made during ADR proceedings. In *Major League Baseball Players Association v. Garvey*, 532 U.S. 504, 121 S. Ct. 1724, 149 L. Ed. 2d 740 (2001), the U.S. Supreme Court reviewed a decision in which the U.S. Court of Appeals for the Ninth Circuit had reversed a decision of an arbitration panel regarding a complaint by former baseball player Steve Garvey about a contract dispute. The Ninth Circuit then remanded the case to the arbitration panel with instructions to enter an award in favor of the player for the amount he claimed. Noting that JUDICIAL REVIEW of labor arbitration decisions is limited, the Supreme Court reversed the Ninth Circuit's decision, holding that it was not the place of a court of appeals to resolve the dispute on its merits.

In 2008 the Supreme Court issued additional decisions pertaining to its role of reviewing arbitration decisions. In *Hall Street Associates, L.L.C. v. Mattel, Inc.,* the Court held that parties who enter into an agreement to arbitrate cannot contractually change the statutory grounds for modifying or vacating the arbitration award. It noted that the grounds for vacating an arbitration award under the Federal Arbitration Act are exclusive and could not be expanded to include either evidentiary or legal review. Thus, the decision further upheld the limited role of judicial review of an arbitrator's decision. In the 8–1 decision written by Justice RUTH BADER GINSBURG in *Preston v. Ferrer,* the Court held that the question of whether a contract is unenforceable under California's Talent Agencies Act is a question that must be decided by an arbitrator rather than the court. Specifically Justice Ginsburg wrote in the decision that when the parties have a contract that includes an arbitration clause, the Federal Arbitration Act supersedes state laws that provide for a specific forum to resolve the dispute. In that case, the Court held that the decision to determine whether the contract was enforceable was for the arbitrator rather than the state's labor commissioner.

Pete Peterson, the first U.S. ambassador to Vietnam since the end of the Vietnam War, presents his diplomatic credentials to the vice president of Vietnam, Nguyen Thi Binh, in Hanoi on May 14, 1997.
AP IMAGES

FURTHER READINGS

International Academy of Collaborative Professionals. Home page: http://www.collaborativepractice.com (accessed on September 21, 2009).

Meek, Susan B. 1996. *Alternative Dispute Resolution.* Tucson, Az.: Lawyers and Judges.

National Conference of Commissioners on Uniform State Laws. Home page: http://www.nccusl.org (accessed on September 21, 2009).

Nolan-Haley, Jacqueline M. 2008. *Alternative Dispute Resolution in a Nutshell* St. Paul, Minn.: West Group.

Ware, Stephen J. 2001. *Alternative Dispute Resolution.* St. Paul, Minn.: West Group.

ALTERNATIVE RELIEF

Remedies sought in a lawsuit in various forms or in the alternative, such as a demand for specific performance of a contract or monetary damages to compensate for the failure to perform the obligation, or both.

Modern rules governing PLEADING in courts specifically permit a party to demand relief in the alternative. This eliminates the harsh consequences of the rule of COMMON-LAW PLEADING that required a party to make one demand for one type of relief and to lose the case if a different remedy were more appropriate. A party can ask for alternative forms of relief and recover what is later proved to be most appropriate at trial.

ALTERNATIVE WRIT

An order, issued originally by the king in England but more recently by a court, commanding a person to do a specific thing or to appear and explain why he or she should not be compelled to do it.

Under the COMMON LAW, the writs of PROHIBITION and MANDAMUS were alternative writs. In modern systems of court procedure, an order to SHOW CAUSE serves the same purpose. It commands a person to do something or come into court and show cause why he or she should not be made to do it.

AMBASSADORS AND CONSULS

An ambassador *is the foreign diplomatic representative of a nation who is authorized to handle political negotiations between his or her country and the country where the ambassador has been assigned. A* consul *is the commercial agent of a nation, who is empowered only to engage in business transactions, and not political matters in the country where he or she is stationed.*

The president with the CONSENT of the Senate appoints ambassadors and consuls whereas the SECRETARY OF STATE appoints staff officers and other subordinate employees.

Powers and Duties

The powers of an ambassador are specified in his or her credentials, or documents of introduction, which the ambassador submits to the foreign government. In addition to responsibility for political negotiations, an American ambassador may initiate LEGAL PROCEEDINGS on behalf of the United States and defend suits instituted against it. A foreign ambassador in the United States has similar duties regarding his or her government.

In general, a consul is authorized to safeguard the legal rights and property interests of the citizens of his or her country and to appear in court to ascertain that the laws of the nation where he or she is assigned are administered impartially to all of the ambassador's compatriots. A U.S. citizen who has legal difficulties in a foreign country should consult the United States consul.

CONSULS are also empowered and obligated to protect the estates of their countrymen and -women who die within their consular districts. This duty terminates when the decedent's heirs are represented by an attorney.

Diplomatic Immunity

The development of harmonious international relations and protection against arrest, harassment, or other unjustified actions taken against diplomatic representatives constitute the objectives of DIPLOMATIC IMMUNITY. The Vienna Convention on Diplomatic Relations, which became effective as part of the federal law in 1972, governs diplomatic IMMUNITY by granting various degrees of immunity from civil and criminal LIABILITY to the members of diplomatic missions.

Diplomatic Agents The supervisor of a mission, such as an ambassador, and members of the mission staff who possess diplomatic rank are DIPLOMATIC AGENTS. Such an agent is immune from criminal liability in the nation in which he or she serves, but the commission of a crime may result in a recall request to the ambassador's country. His or her expulsion may ensue upon the refusal of any such request.

In addition, a diplomatic agent is immune from civil lawsuits, except for actions involving estates, when he or she is the executor, administrator, or BENEFICIARY; actions concerning real property held by the diplomatic agent for personal, not official functions; and actions relating to professional or business activities that are beyond the scope of diplomatic duties. A diplomatic agent is not required to TESTIFY as a witness; and the family members living in the agent's household enjoy the same immunities.

Due to the hardship imposed on the victims of motor vehicle accidents in the United States caused by foreign diplomats who have diplomatic immunity, federal law mandates that mission members and their families insure their personal motor vehicles, boats, and airplanes. If the mission has similar vehicles registered in its name, it also must purchase liability insurance. An action for DAMAGES for property loss, personal injuries, or WRONGFUL DEATH can be maintained directly against the diplomat's insurance company and is tried by the court, presiding without a jury.

Staff Members The administrative and technical staffs and families and household members of the mission are completely immune from criminal liability, but are immune from civil liability only for official acts. Similar rules apply to members of the service staff employed as domestics, but their families and private servants employed by staff members are not so protected against liability.

Consuls Consuls are not diplomatic agents and, therefore, they are usually amenable to civil lawsuits and criminal prosecution in the country where they are assigned. Federal law, however, extends immunity to consuls from all suits and proceedings in state courts. This prevents any embarrassment to foreign nations that might ensue from such proceedings.

Other Exemptions Diplomatic agents in the United States and the members of their households are generally exempt from federal, state, and MUNICIPAL taxes. They are responsible, however, for indirect taxes that are part of the price of goods, taxes on property inherited from a citizen, taxes on any real property they own privately, or capital gains taxes on profits from personal investments. Diplomatic agents have no obligation to serve in the U.S. armed forces. These exemptions also apply to the administrative and technical staffs of the mission and their families. The service staff and private servants are exempt from taxes on wages received from their employment with the mission or its members.

FURTHER READINGS

Keeley, Robert V., ed. 2000. *First Line of Defense: Ambassadors, Embassies, and American Interests Abroad.* Washington, D.C.: American Academy of Diplomacy.

Lehman, Daniel J. 2002. "The Federal Republic of Germany v. The United States of America: The Individual Right to Consular Access." Law & *Inequality: A Journal of Theory and Practice* 20, vol. 2 (summer).

Pittman, Andrew B. 2001. "Ambassadorial Waiver of Foreign State Sovereign Immunity to Domestic Adjudication in United States Courts." *Washington and Lee Law Review* 58 (spring).

CROSS REFERENCES

Diplomatic Agents; Diplomatic Immunity; International Law; State Department.

AMBER ALERT

A national law enforcement early warning plan designed to help find missing or abducted children by broadcasting information over radio, television, the Internet, and roadside signs as quickly as possible.

The ABDUCTION of a child by a relative or stranger requires immediate action by law enforcement officials. Beginning in the 1990s, some states and communities developed early warning plans that informed the public immediately about a missing child by using the electronic news media and roadside signs. These plans, which have come to be known as AMBER Alerts, have proved popular, though some researchers question their true effectiveness. Congress enacted a law in 2003 that gave the federal government a role in coordinating such plans.

The 1996 KIDNAPPING and MURDER of Amber Hagerman in Texas triggered the first early warning plan. The Dallas/Fort Worth Association of Radio Managers worked with local law enforcement officials in north Texas to establish what they called the AMBER Alert plan. Though named after Amber Hagerman, AMBER also served as an acronym for America's Missing: Broadcast Emergency Response. The first AMBER plan called on broadcasters to provide information over radio and television as soon as possible. This information included descriptions and pictures of the missing child, the suspected abductor, a suspected vehicle, and any other information that could prove helpful in locating the child.

The AMBER Alert concept spread quickly around the United States. By 2002, 18 states had enacted such plans and local communities in other states set up their own AMBER Alert plans. Proponents claimed that the alerts had proved effective and urged Congress to enact a law that would make AMBER Alerts a national program. Congress responded by including an AMBER Alert provision in the Prosecutorial Remedies and Other Tools to end the Exploitation of Children Today (PROTECT) Act of 2003 (Pub. L. No. 108-21, 117 Stat. 650). Under the statute, the DEPARTMENT OF JUSTICE, in cooperation with the DEPARTMENT OF TRANSPORTATION and the FEDERAL COMMUNICATIONS COMMISSION (FCC), appoints a National AMBER Alert coordinator to oversee the communication network. The coordinator works with states, broadcasters, and law enforcement agencies to set up and coordinate AMBER plans. Grants are provided to help set up AMBER Alert programs.

The federal government does not mandate that each state follow one type of plan. Instead, each state AMBER Alert plan has its own criteria for issuing AMBER Alerts. The national coordinator does issue minimum standards for AMBER Alerts that states can adopt voluntarily. Most states have followed these criteria. The key criteria are as follows:

- Law enforcement must confirm that an abduction has taken place.
- The child must be at risk of serious injury or death.

- There is sufficient descriptive information of child, captor, or captor's vehicle to issue an alert.
- The child must be 17 years old or younger.
- Immediate entry of AMBER Alert data is entered in FBI's National Crime Information Center.

Many states have also formal memorandums of understanding with other states. By 2009 there were 28 regional plans as well. If law enforcement believes that the child has been taken across state lines, the AMBER state coordinator asks that state to issue an alert. Even if there is no formal agreement between states, many have informal arrangements to issue AMBER Alerts upon request.

The federal AMBER coordinator issues an annual report that analyzes the number of alerts issued, the various classifications of abductions, and their RESOLUTION. There are four classifications: family abduction; nonfamily abduction; lost, injured, or otherwise missing; and endangered runaway. A family abduction occurs when an individual between birth and 17 years of age is abducted from his or her custodial parent or legal GUARDIAN by a noncustodial family member who is related to the child by blood or MARRIAGE. A nonfamily abduction occurs when a child, age 17 or younger, is abducted by someone who is unknown to the child or his or her family, an acquaintance, or someone who is unidentifiable as either. The classification of lost, injured, or otherwise missing refers to any missing child where there are insufficient facts to determine the cause of a child's disappearance as well as any child age 10 or younger who is missing on his or her own accord. An endangered runaway is any missing child between 11 and 17 years of age, who is missing on his or her own accord without permission from his or her parent or legal guardian.

The 2008 report disclosed that in 2008, 194 AMBER Alert cases were issued in the United States involving 256 children in 36 states; 166 cases resulted in recovery, but only 40 were the direct result of an AMBER Alert. Of these alerts, 50 percent were statewide alerts, 40 percent were regional alerts, and 18 percent were local. Out of the 194 alerts, 6 percent were found to be hoaxes and 7 percent were eventually determined to be unfounded. Girls constituted 58 percent of the alerts, with more than half of all the children under the age of five. Of the 162 abductors, 118 had previous relationships with the children. Most significantly, 67 percent of the children were recovered on the same day the alert was issued.

Critics of AMBER Alerts have expressed concerns about *alert fatigue*. If the citizens are constantly presented with alerts, they may eventually tune out the information that is presented. A study of the 233 Amber Alerts issued in 2004 also revealed that stranger abductions, which are the most publicized cases, constituted only 30 percent of the alerts. Family abductions accounted for 50 percent of the alerts, and 20 percent were hoaxes or unfounded. Another study challenged the claim that the alerts saved as many lives as claimed. Successful recovery is most likely when the victim is abducted by a parent, who rarely harms the child.

FURTHER READINGS

AMBER Alert, Office of Justice Programs, DOJ, www. amberalert.gov (accessed December 21, 2009).

Fass, Paula. 2006. *Kidnapped: Child Abduction in America.* New York: Oxford Univ. Press.

CROSS REFERENCES

Child Molestation; Kidnapping.

AMBIGUITY

Uncertainty or doubtfulness of the meaning of language.

When language is capable of being understood in more than one way by a REASONABLE PERSON, ambiguity exists. It is not the use of peculiar words or of common words used in a peculiar sense. Words are ambiguous when their significance is unclear to persons with competent knowledge and skill to understand them.

There are two categories of ambiguity: LATENT and PATENT. Latent ambiguity exists when the language used is clear and intelligible so that it suggests one meaning but some extrinsic fact or evidence creates a need for interpretation or a choice among two or more possible meanings. In a classic case, *Raffles v. Wichelhaus,* 159 Eng. Rep. 375 (Ex. 1864), a contract was made to sell 125 bales of cotton that were to arrive on a ship called Peerless that sailed from Bombay, India. Unknown to the parties to the contract, two ships of the same name were to arrive from the same port during different months of the same year. This extraneous fact necessitated the interpretation of an otherwise clear and definite term of the contract. In such cases, extrinsic or PAROL EVIDENCE may be admitted to explain what was meant or to identify the property referred to in the writing.

A patent ambiguity is one that appears on the face of a document or writing because uncertain or obscure language has been used.

In the law of CONTRACTS, ambiguity means more than that the language has more than one meaning upon which reasonable persons could differ. It means that after a court has applied rules of interpretation, such as the plain meaning, COURSE OF DEALING, COURSE OF PERFORMANCE, or TRADE USAGE rules to the unclear terms, the court still cannot say with certainty what meaning was intended by the parties to the contract. When this occurs, the court will admit as evidence extraneous proof of prior or contemporaneous agreements to determine the meaning of the ambiguous language. Parol evidence may be used to explain the meaning of a writing as long as its use does not vary the terms of the writing. If there is no such evidence, the court may hear evidence of the subjective intention or UNDERSTANDING of the parties to clarify the ambiguity.

Sometimes, courts decide the meaning of ambiguous language on the basis of who was responsible or at fault for the ambiguity. When only one party knew or should have known of the ambiguity, the unsuspecting party's subjective knowledge of the meaning will control. If both parties knew or should have known of the uncertainty, the court will look to the subjective understanding of both. The ambiguity no longer exists if the parties agree upon its meaning. If the parties disagree and the ambiguous provisions are material, no contract is formed because of lack of mutual assent.

Courts frequently interpret an ambiguous contract term against the interests of the party who prepared the contract and created the ambiguity. This is common in cases of adhesion contracts and insurance contracts. A drafter of a document should not benefit at the expense of an innocent party because the drafter was careless in drafting the agreement.

In CONSTITUTIONAL LAW, statutes that contain ambiguous language are void for vagueness. The language of such laws is considered so obscure and uncertain that a reasonable person cannot determine from a reading what the law purports to command or prohibit. This statutory ambiguity deprives a person of the notice requirement of DUE PROCESS OF LAW, and, therefore, renders the statute unconstitutional.

AMBIT

A boundary line that indicates ownership of a parcel of land as opposed to other parcels; an exterior or enclosing line. The limits of a power or jurisdiction. The delineation of the scope of a particular subject matter.

AMBULANCE CHASER

A colloquial phrase that is used derisively for a person who is hired by an attorney to seek out NEGLIGENCE cases at the scenes of accidents or in hospitals where injured parties are treated, in exchange for a percentage of the damages that will be recovered in the case.

Also used to describe attorneys who, upon learning of a personal injury that might have been caused by the negligence or the wrongful act of another, immediately contact the victim for consent to represent him or her in a lawsuit in exchange for a contingent fee, a percentage of the judgment recovered.

AMBULATORY

Movable; revocable; subject to change; capable of alteration.

An *ambulatory court* was the former name of the Court of King's Bench in England. It would convene wherever the king who presided over it could be found, moving its location as the king moved.

An *ambulatory disposition* is a judgment, DECREE, or sentence that is subject to change, amendment, or revocation.

A will is considered ambulatory because as long as the person who made it lives, it can always be changed or revoked.

AMENDMENT

The modification of materials by the addition of supplemental information; the deletion of unnecessary, undesirable, or outdated information; or the correction of errors existing in the text.

In practice, a change in the pleadings—statements of the allegations of the parties in a lawsuit—may be achieved if the parties agree to the amendment or if the court in which the proceeding is pending grants a motion for the amendment made by one party. A judgment may be altered by an amendment if a motion to do so is made

within a certain time after its entry and granted by the court. The amendment of pleadings and judgments is regulated by state codes of CIVIL PROCEDURE and the rules of federal civil procedure.

A constitution or a statute may be changed by an amendment.

A will, trust, corporate charter, and other legal documents are also subject to amendment.

CROSS REFERENCE

Constitutional Amendment.

AMERICAN ASSOCIATION FOR JUSTICE

The American Association for Justice (AAJ) (formerly the Association of Trial Lawyers of America, or ATLA) is a NONPROFIT organization that represents the interests of PERSONAL INJURY attorneys. The AAJ is the world's largest trial bar organization, with more than 56,000 members worldwide. AAJ's goals are to safeguard the interests of people who seek redress for injury and to protect individuals from abuses of power. Any person who is licensed to practice law in any country, state, or jurisdiction, who is committed to the ADVERSARY SYSTEM, and who, for the most part, does not represent the defense in personal injury LITIGATION is eligible for membership. In 1946, a group of plaintiffs' attorneys involved in workers' compensations litigation founded the National Association of Claimants' COMPENSATION Attorneys (NCACCA). In 1972 NACCA became ATLA, and in 1977, the organization moved its headquarters from Boston to Washington, D.C. The association changed its name once again in 2006 to the AAJ.

AAJ comprises a network of U.S. and Canadian affiliates involved in diverse areas of trial advocacy. It provides lawyers with the information and professional assistance needed to serve clients successfully and protect the civil justice system. AAJ is governed by its membership through a board of governors and national officers who are elected at the organization's annual convention. AAJ committees help to set policies in critical areas, make recommendations to the board of governors, and oversee staff implementation of AAJ objectives. The AAJ has 155 staff members, including approximately 30 attorneys. It publishes the monthly magazine *Trial*, *AAJ Law Reporter*, and *AAJ Advocate*.

AAJ's sections, each of which encompasses an area of litigation practice, include admiralty, aviation, CIVIL RIGHTS, products LIABILITY, insurance, FAMILY LAW, and workers' compensation law. Services of the sections include the publication of annual directories and periodic newsletters and information exchange. AAJ also has organized litigation groups, which are voluntary networks of AAJ members sharing an interest in a particular type of case, many of which involve hazardous products. The groups share timely documents and information, much of it obtained from discovery in similar cases. The litigation groups organize programs that educate members about recent developments in their special areas.

AAJ has been a leading opponent of state and federal legislative efforts to restrict the amount of DAMAGES a PLAINTIFF can recover for MEDICAL MALPRACTICE or for injuries caused by a defective product. Two major areas of litigation that emerged during the early 2000s were related to asbestos and toxic mold. For many years, the organization has lobbied against tort reform bills, rebutting arguments that too many lawsuits have led to excessive costs and delays and that juries can no longer be trusted to render fair verdicts. The election of GEORGE W. BUSH as president in 2000 and the gain of Republican seats in both the House and Senate in 2002 brought the issue to the forefront. Although some commentators expected a significant number of states to approve tort reform measures, the proposals in most of these states failed. As Democrats regained control of Congress during the mid- to late-2000s, focus on the tort reform issue became less intense. Tort reform was not a major issue during the presidential campaign of 2008.

In addition to its LOBBYING efforts, AAJ provides a specialization certification program for trial skills and statistical compilation, as well as a placement service. It also conducts seminars and conferences across the country.

During the 2000s, members of the ATLA expressed concern about negative reactions to the reference to trial lawyers in the association's name. In 2006 the members agreed to change the name to the American Association for Justice. Membership is not limited to trial lawyers and instead extends to attorneys, law professors, paralegals, and law students.

Web site: http://www.justice.org

FURTHER READINGS

American Association for Justice. Available online at http://www.justice.org (accessed May 12, 2009).

Bogus, Carl T. 2001. *Why Lawsuits Are Good for America: Disciplined Democracy, Big Business, and the Common Law.* New York: New York Univ. Press.

Orey, Michael. 1999. *Assuming the Risk: The Mavericks, the Lawyers, and the Whistle-Blowers Who Beat Big Tobacco.* Boston: Little, Brown.

AMERICAN ASSOCIATION OF RETIRED PERSONS

The American Association of Retired Persons (AARP) is a NONPROFIT, nonpartisan organization dedicated to helping older Americans achieve lives of independence, dignity, and purpose. Founded in 1958 by Dr. Ethel Percy Andrus, AARP is the oldest and largest organization of older Americans, with a membership of 40 million. The National Retired Teachers Association (NTRA), which was founded in 1947, is a division of AARP. Membership in AARP is open to anyone age 50 or older, working or retired. More than one-third of the association's membership is in the workforce. The AARP headquarters are in Washington, D.C. By the early 2000s, AARP had fulfilled its goal of having staffed offices in all 50 states, as well as the District of Columbia, Puerto Rico, and the U.S. Virgin Islands. AARP has an extensive network of local AARP chapters, its National Community Service Programs and NTRA members to involve members, volunteers, the media, community partners, and policymakers in carrying out its objectives. The organization is led by a 21-member BOARD OF DIRECTORS and has an administrative staff that carries out the group's day-to-day activities. The organization is funded almost entirely by annual membership dues.

The AARP has been an effective advocate for issues involving older persons, in part because of its large membership and its ability to mobilize its members to lobby for its positions before Congress and government agencies. The organization has concentrated much of its LOBBYING effort on SOCIAL SECURITY, MEDICARE, and long-term care issues. The AARP has fought zealously to protect the Social Security benefits of retired citizens and has resisted efforts by Congress to change the system itself. Its Advocacy Center for Social Security develops policy proposals and lobbies Congress.

The AARP Advocacy Center for Medicare seeks to ensure the availability of affordable, quality health care for older individuals and persons with disabilities. In the early 2000s, it worked to develop ways of maintaining the short-term SOLVENCY of the Hospital Insurance Trust Fund and was preparing for the long-term needs of the aging baby boomers. With the dramatic growth in managed health care plans, the AARP has sought to educate its members about this new way of providing services and to empower older people by telling them what their rights are under this system. However, AARP lost a significant and protracted court battle in 2008 when the U.S. Supreme Court denied review of the AARP challenge to a proposed rule from the EQUAL EMPLOYMENT OPPORTUNITY COMMISSION (EEOC), which created a new exemption to the AGE DISCRIMINATION in Employment Act (ADEA) (*AARP v. EEOC*, 2008 WL 754343, ___ U.S. ___ [2008]). The new exemption allows employers to reduce retiree health benefits for anyone 65 or older (i.e., eligible for Medicare). The Third CIRCUIT COURT of Appeals sided with EEOC in finding that Congress had delegated to the EEOC complete authority to create exemptions under ADEA (*AARP v. EEOC*, 489 F.3d 558 [3rd Cir. 2008]).

The association also has been actively involved in voter education. A major, nonpartisan component of the association's legislative program is AARP/VOTE, a voter education program designed to inform the public about important PUBLIC POLICY issues and the positions of candidates for public office. Through issue and candidate forums and voter guides, AARP/VOTE works to promote issue-centered campaigns and a more informed electorate.

The organization also provides many benefits to its members. The AARP licenses the use of its name for selected services of chosen providers. For example, it offers members a choice of insurance plans. Because most of the plans are neither age-rated nor medically underwritten, the association can make HEALTH INSURANCE available to many of its members who otherwise would be unable to obtain coverage because of pre-existing conditions. The association receives an administrative allowance or a royalty from the providers and the income realized from these services is used for the general purposes of the association and its members.

AARP operates a nationwide volunteer network that helps older citizens. Programs include information and support for grandparents who are raising their grandchildren, legal hotlines, and INCOME TAX preparation. These and other programs are funded, in part, by federal grants.

The association produces two national radio network series and publishes a monthly magazine, *AARP The Magazine*; a monthly newspaper, the *AARP Bulletin*; and a quarterly Spanish-language newspaper, *Segunda Jeventud*. As older adults have gained computer skills, the organization's Web site has become increasingly popular.

Outreach programs launched by AARP in the early 2000s include a collaborative national effort to help prepare people for independent living, long-term care, and end-of-life care, as well as a pilot program to promote physical activities for healthy aging.

FURTHER READINGS

American Association of Retired Persons. Available online at www.aarp.org (accessed September 26, 2009).

Kimbol, Anne. 2008. "Medicare and Retiree Benefits: The Impact of AARP v. EEOC." *Health Law Perspectives,* University of Houston Law Center, April 2008. Text available online at http://www.law.uh.edu/healthlaw/perspectives/homepage.asp; website home page: http://www.law.uh.edu/ (accessed August 5, 2009)

Morris, Charles R. 1996. *The AARP: America's Most Powerful Lobby and the Clash of Generations.* New York: Times Books.

Van Atta, Dale. 1998. *Trust Betrayed: Inside the AARP.* Chicago: Regnery.

CROSS REFERENCES

Age Discrimination; Elder Law; Senior Citizens; Senior Citizens: How to Avoid Being Defrauded; Senior Citizens "Scamming the Elderly" (In Focus).

AMERICAN BANKERS ASSOCIATION

The American Bankers Association (ABA) is composed of banks and other financial institutions. It seeks to promote the strength and profitability of the banking industry by LOBBYING federal and state governments, building industry consensus on key issues, and providing products and services, including public affairs support and legal services, to its member banks. Membership in the ABA includes community, regional, and money-center banks (the nation's major banks) and holding companies, as well as savings associations, trust companies, and savings banks. The ABA, which was founded in 1875, is the largest banking trade association in the United States. The organization includes more than 95 percent of the commercial banking industry as members. As of 2009 these members employ more than two million people and have more than $13 trillion in assets. The ABA's headquarters are in Washington, D.C.

The ABA places great emphasis on representing the interests of banks before Congress and state legislatures. The association takes stands on banking and bank-related bills as they move through Congress, attempts to influence the interpretations of laws and regulations by banking regulators, and is actively involved in state LITIGATION that has implications for the banking industry. Throughout the 1990s and 2000s, ABA representatives frequently testified before Congress, filed official letters of comment, and sponsored trips by state associations to the nation's capital. During this time, BankPac, the banking industry's POLITICAL ACTION COMMITTEE and one of the strongest committees nationwide, raised and distributed millions of dollars for congressional elections. The ABA fought legislative efforts to regulate the fees banks charge customers to use automated teller machines (ATM) and has challenged in court the membership policies used by credit unions to gain customers. ABA also became involved in such issues as ATM accessibility for blind persons, predatory lending practices, SOCIAL SECURITY reform, and MONEY LAUNDERING.

In 2001 the ABA established the ABA Mortgage Solutions program, which assists member banks in the secondary mortgage market. When a lender initially makes a loan, it has a choice to keep the loan as part of its portfolio or to sell the loan on the secondary mortgage market. The ABA's program became the most widely used in the banking industry. By 2009, the total amount of mortgages sold through this program surpassed $100 billion. Several major banks and organizations are involved in this program, including the Federal Home Loan Mortgage Corporation (Freddie Mac) and FEDERAL NATIONAL MORTGAGE ASSOCIATION (Fannie Mae).

The ABA operates the American Institute for Banking (AIB), which is the largest provider of banking education. The AIB teaches more than 100,000 students annually. In addition, the ABA sponsors approximately 24 residential schools with 3,700 students covering specialty areas within banking and the prestigious Stonier Graduate School of Banking. New technology has provided new opportunities as well. American Financial Skylink is a satellite TELECOMMUNICATIONS network that delivers news, information, and training directly to banks through regular telecasts.

Other ABA affiliates include the following: ABA eCom, which facilitates electronic banking and COMMERCE over the INTERNET; the ABA Education Foundation, which provides resources for consumer education; and the ABA Marketing Network (ABAMN), which informs and educates banks in the marketing of their products and services. The ABA SECURITIES Association assists sections of the banking industry that are competing in the securities business.

Since the early twentieth century the ABA has produced the *ABA Banking Journal,* a monthly magazine that focuses on news and analysis of the financial services industry. The journal is published for the ABA by Simmons-Boardman Publishing Corp.

Though the ABA is a NONPROFIT organization, it operates the for-profit Corporation for American Banking (CAB). CAB was created to facilitate group buying of services, allowing participating banks to receive CAB-arranged discounts on long-distance telephone service, overnight package delivery, office products, and copying products.

FURTHER READINGS

ABA Banking Journal. Available online at http://www.ababj. com/ (accessed May 3, 2009).

American Bankers Association. Available online at http:// www.aba.com (accessed May 3, 2009).

Lovett, William A. 2005. *Banking & Financial Institutions Law in a Nutshell,* 6th ed. St. Paul, MN: Thomson/ West.

Malloy, Michael A. 2003. *Principles of Banking Regulation,* 2d ed. St. Paul, MN: West Group.

AMERICAN BAR ASSOCIATION

The American Bar Association (ABA) is a nationwide organization to which qualified attorneys voluntarily belong. With more than 413,000 members, the ABA is the largest voluntary professional organization in the world.

The ABA was founded in 1878 to improve LEGAL EDUCATION, to set requirements to be satisfied for admittance to the bar, and to facilitate the exchange of ideas and information among its members. Over the years, the ABA has been largely responsible for the further development of American jurisprudence; the establishment of formal education requirements for persons seeking to become attorneys; the formulation of ethical principles that govern the PRACTICE OF LAW; and the creation of the American Law Institute (ALI) and the Conference of Commissioners on Uniform State Laws, both of which advance the fair administration of justice through encouraging uniformity of statutes and judicial decisions whenever practicable. For several years, the ABA has been prominently involved in the recommendation and selection of candidates for the federal JUDICIARY, the accreditation of law schools, and the refinement of rules of legal and judicial ethics.

Applicants for membership in the ABA must meet certain criteria. They must be members in good standing of the bar of a state, TERRITORY, or possession of the United States. They must also have good moral character and pay the designated dues. Law students qualify to be members of the Law Student Division of the ABA if they attend an ABA-approved law school and pay the specified dues. The ABA continues to put great emphasis on promoting diversity within its membership and has initiated several programs designed to bring more women and racial and ethnic minorities into the profession.

The ABA provides various forums through which attorneys continue their legal education during their careers. The association's national institutes are held frequently in areas of law that have become topical or have undergone sweeping reform. In conjunction with the ALI, the ABA holds seminars in order to continue the professional education of interested members.

Within the ABA, members may participate in the activities of numerous sections, which range in size from about 2,300 members to more than 70,000 and are organized according to specialized areas of law. Various committees exist that deal with such topics as judicial selection, PROFESSIONAL RESPONSIBILITY and discipline, lawyer referral services, and the UNAUTHORIZED PRACTICE of law. Other committees are concerned with topical areas, such as prepaid legal services, MALPRACTICE, legal problems of the elderly, and public-interest law. The ABA employs more than 750 professional staff members to assist committees, sections, and individual members.

The ABA is involved in the political process through its seven-person Governmental Affairs Office (GAO), a LOBBYING effort that serves as the "eyes, ears and voice" of the organized bar at the seat of the national government in Washington, D.C. The GAO staff is housed with about 170 other ABA staffers in the ABA's Washington, D.C. office. (The ABA's main offices are in Chicago, with more than 500 staff members.) The lobbying group in Washington, D.C., headed by the ABA's associate executive director, testifies on Capitol Hill more often

than any other trade association. The ABA's lobbyists offer detailed information and analysis on various technical issues, such as tax or antitrust legislation. On issues such as ABORTION, which many ABA members and leaders consider as having an EFFECT on the legal system, the ABA offers its voice along with those of other interested groups.

Another influential ABA committee is the Standing Committee on the Federal Judiciary. This committee consists of 15 members, including one representative for each federal circuit, two representatives for the Ninth Circuit, and one at-large member. The President of ABA selects members based on professional competence, integrity, and devotion to public service. The committee rates each judicial nominee as "well qualified," "qualified," or "not qualified." The committee lists these ratings with the initials WQ, Q, and NQ. For example, when President GEORGE W. BUSH nominated JOHN ROBERTS to serve as Chief Justice of the Supreme Court in 2005, the ABA committee rated Roberts as WQ.

Equal access for all to the justice system has become an increasingly important theme in the ABA's mission. The association has sought for a number of years to increase and improve free legal services to needy persons by practicing lawyers. These lawyers donate some of their work PRO BONO *publico* (for the good of the public). In 1981, the ABA created the Private Bar Involvement Project, now called the Pro Bono Project, which acts as a national clearinghouse of information and resources for various pro bono programs around the United States. When it began, there were 66 organized projects nationwide; by 1995 there were more than 950.

The ABA actively supports several major legislative priorities on topics that have been in the forefront of American political and governmental affairs. The ABA has called for a MORATORIUM on the death PENALTY until certain procedures and policies are put into effect that mandate fair and IMPARTIAL administration of CAPITAL PUNISHMENT. The Death Penalty Moratorium Implementation Project had produced a number of reports focusing on specific states, including California, Maryland, New Jersey, and Illinois. These reports typically demonstrate flaws in capital punishment procedures used in those states.

Since the SEPTEMBER 11TH ATTACKS in 2001, the ABA has stepped up its opposition to laws requiring extra verification of citizenship for immigrants. Additionally, the ABA has urged that U.S. citizens and legal residents detained as "enemy combatants" be afforded due process rights and that military tribunals authorized to conduct trials of suspected terrorists be used in limited circumstances. The ABA has also announced its opposition to the incommunicado DETENTION of nationals held in undisclosed locations by IMMIGRATION officials or the HOMELAND SECURITY DEPARTMENT. The ABA continued to PROTEST detentions of nationals in such locations as Guantanamo Bay during the early 2000s.

The ABA holds annual conventions and midyear meetings to discuss designated legal topics and ABA matters. It publishes the monthly *American BAR ASSOCIATION Journal*, an annual directory, and various journals and newsletters reporting the work of its sections and committees. The ABA also supports the activities of affiliated organizations, such as the American Bar Foundation, which sponsors research activities in law.

The ABA provides a social outlet for its members through which members meet to freely exchange ideas and experiences that add to the human dimension in the practice of law.

The ABA has eleven goals:

1. Promote improvement in the U.S. system of justice

2. Promote meaningful access to LEGAL REPRE-SENTATION and the U.S. system of justice for all persons regardless of their economic or social condition

3. Provide ongoing leadership in improving the law to serve the changing needs of society

4. Increase public understanding of and respect for the law, the legal process, and the role of the legal profession

5. Achieve the highest standards of professionalism, competence, and ethical conduct

6. Serve as the national representative of the legal profession

7. Provide benefits, programs, and services that promote professional growth and enhance the quality of life of the members

8. Advance the rule of law in the world

9. Promote full and equal participation in the legal profession by members of minorities and women

10. Preserve and enhance the ideals of the legal profession as a common calling and its dedication to public service

11. Preserve the independence of the legal profession and the judiciary as fundamental to a free society

FURTHER READINGS

ABA Standing Committee on the Judiciary. Available online at http://www.abanet.org/scfedjud/roster.html

American Bar Association Website. Available online at http://www.abanet.org/home.html (accessed May 11, 2009).

Hobson, Wayne K. 1986. *The American Legal Profession and the Organizational Society, 1890–1930.* New York: Garland.

AMERICAN CIVIL LIBERTIES UNION

Since 1920 the American Civil Liberties Union (ACLU) has fought energetically for the rights of individuals. This private, nonprofit organization is a multipurpose legal group with 300,000 members committed to the freedoms in the Bill of Rights. Although these liberties—such as free speech, equality, due process, privacy—are guaranteed to each citizen, they are never completely secure. Governments and majorities can easily weaken them or even take them away. The ACLU has had enormous success fighting such cases: Many of the most important Supreme Court decisions have been won with its involvement, and the ACLU continues to fight thousands of lawsuits in state and federal courts each year. The ACLU also lobbies lawmakers and speaks out on a wide variety of civil liberties and civil rights issues. Its devotion to these concerns makes it highly controversial.

The origins of the ACLU date to WORLD WAR I, a dark era for civil liberties. War fever gripped the United States, and official hostility toward DISSENT ran high. Attorney General A. MITCHELL PALMER orchestrated much of this hostility from Washington, D.C., by ordering crackdowns on protesters, breaking strikes, prosecuting conscientious objectors, and deporting thousands of immigrants. One group in particular stood up to him: the American Union against Militarism (AUAM), led by social reformers and radicals. Among its founders was the pacifist ROGER BALDWIN, a former sociology teacher. In 1917, as the United States prepared to enter the war, Baldwin gave the group a broader mission by transforming it into the Civil Liberties Bureau, dedicated to the defense of those the government saw fit to crush and corral. Anti-Communist hysteria worsened the civil liberties picture

The ACLU's involvement in the 1925 Scopes Monkey Trial brought the organization national attention. Pictured is the Scopes defense team: (l-r) Clarence Darrow, Arthur Garfield hays, Dudley Field Malone, George Rappelyea, John Neal, and Miss McClosky.

BETTMANN/CORBIS.

between 1919 and 1920, and the upstart bureau had its hands full as Palmer, and his assistant, J. EDGAR HOOVER, staged massive police raids that netted thousands of alleged subversives at a time.

In 1920 the Civil Liberties Bureau became the ACLU. Joining Baldwin in launching the new organization were several distinguished social leaders, including the author Helen A. Keller, the attorney and future Supreme Court Justice FELIX FRANKFURTER, and the socialist clergyman Norman Thomas. The ACLU quickly joined the U.S. Congress and the AMERICAN BAR ASSOCIATION in denouncing Attorney General Palmer for his raids—and the outcry helped end his tyrannical career. In the first annual ACLU report, Baldwin weighed the effectiveness of public activism, noting, "[T]he mere public assertion of the principle of freedom ... helps win it recognition, and in the long run makes for tolerance and against resort to violence." In its weekly "Report on Civil Liberties Situation," the group watched over a torrent of abuses: a mob forcing a Farmer-Labor party delegation in Washington State to salute the U.S. flag; a Russian chemist being arrested in Illinois for distributing "inflammatory" handbills; and the LYNCHING and burning of six black men in Florida after a black man attempted to vote.pi tp

From the beginning, strict political neutrality was the ACLU rule. The group did not oppose political candidates and declared itself

neither liberal nor conservative. This position had an important consequence: The ACLU would defend the civil liberties of all people, including those who were weak, unpopular, and despised, without respect to their views. This principle made for strange bedfellows. The *Boston Globe* recalled the following in its eulogy for Baldwin:

> [A]t one point Mr. Baldwin was engaged simultaneously in defending the rights of the KU KLUX KLAN to hold meetings in Boston, despite the orders of a Catholic mayor; of Catholic teachers to teach in the schools of Akron, despite the opposition of the Ku Klux Klan; and of Communists to exhibit their film, "The Fifth Year," in Providence, despite the opposition of both the Catholics and the Ku Klux Klan.

Consequently, while carving out a unique place for the ACLU in U.S. law, these defenses also won the organization enemies.

Within a few years, the ACLU was widely known. Its first victory before the Supreme Court came in the landmark 1925 case *Gitlow v. New York* (268 U.S. 652, 45 S. Ct. 625, 69 L. Ed. 1138), in which the Court threw out the defendant's CONVICTION under New York's "criminal anarchy" statute (N.Y. Penal Law §§ 160, 161, Laws 1909, ch. 88; Consol. Laws 1909, ch. 40), for advocating the overthrow of the U.S. government in a printed flyer. *Gitlow* established that the FOURTEENTH AMENDMENT, which applies to the states, includes FREEDOM OF SPEECH in its liberty guarantee. By 1926 the ACLU was involved in the debate over church-state separation. It joined the so-called SCOPES MONKEY TRIAL, arguing against a Tennessee law that forbade teaching the theory of evolution in public schools (*Scopes v. State*, 152 Tenn. 424, 278 S.W. 57 [1925]; 154 Tenn. 105, 289 S.W. 363 [1927]). Besides bringing the group to national and worldwide attention, *Scopes* set it on a course from which it never veered: fighting government interference in religious matters. It staged this fight with equanimity, opposing official help and hindrance to RELIGION, and it soon backed the Jehovah's Witnesses in a series of key Supreme Court cases. This involvement laid the groundwork for the Supreme Court's ruling, in a 1962 challenge originally brought by the ACLU, that school PRAYER is unconstitutional *ENGEL V. VITALE*, 370 U.S. 421, 82 S. Ct. 1261, 8 L. Ed. 2d 601).

Between the 1930s and the mid-1990s the ACLU won (as counsel) or helped to win (through amicus briefs) several Supreme Court cases that profoundly changed U.S. law and life. Among these were BROWN V. BOARD OF EDUCATION (347 U.S. 483, 74 S. Ct. 686, 98 L. Ed. 873 [1954]) (declaring racially segregated schools unconstitutional); MAPP V. OHIO (367 U.S. 643, 81 S. Ct. 1684, 6 L. Ed. 2d 1081 [1961]) (severely limiting the power of police officers and prosecutors to use illegally obtained evidence); GRISWOLD V. CONNECTICUT (381 U.S. 479, 85 S. Ct. 1678, 14 L. Ed. 2d 510 [1965]) (invalidating a state law that banned contraceptives and, for the first time, recognizing the concept of privacy in the BILL OF RIGHTS); MIRANDA V. ARIZONA (384 U.S. 436, 86 S. Ct. 1602, 16 L. Ed. 2d 694 [1966]) (requiring the police to advise suspects of their rights before interrogation); Loving v. Virginia (388 U.S. 1, 87 S. Ct. 1817, 18 L. Ed. 2d 1010 [1967]) (striking down the laws of Virginia and 15 other states that made interracial MARRIAGE a criminal offense); Brandenburg v. Ohio (395 U.S. 444, 89 S. Ct. 1827, 23 L. Ed. 2d 430 [1969]) (invalidating state SEDITION laws aimed at radical groups); and ROE V. WADE (410 U.S. 113, 93 S. Ct. 705, 35 L. Ed. 2d 147 [1973]) (recognizing a woman's constitutional right to an ABORTION).

Rarely did these victories endear the ACLU to its opponents. Liberals often—though not always—applauded the effort and the result. They praised, for instance, the ACLU fight against the Customs Bureau for banning James Joyce's novel *Ulysses*, and its battle to secure publication of the Pentagon Papers during the VIETNAM WAR. Conservatives often found the ACLU meddlesome and the results of its meddling ruinous. Southerners denounced its war on SEGREGATION, antiabortion groups blamed it for the legalization of abortion, and Vice President GEORGE H. W. BUSH even labeled it "the criminal's lobby" for its insistence on combating police illegality. At times, the organization outraged nearly everyone, as when it went to court to win the right of Nazis to march in Skokie, Illinois. Yet throughout its many controversies, the ACLU seldom seemed to go against its charter. Especially in the early 1990s, it did not avoid cases even when taking them on meant clashing with such traditional allies as feminists and university professors over its support of the freedom to publish PORNOGRAPHY and opposition to campus speech codes.

The ACLU is often called the nation's foremost advocate of individual rights. With dozens of Supreme Court cases and thousands of state and federal rulings behind it, the organization is a firmly established force in U.S. law. Its reach goes beyond the courts. Watchful of lawmakers, it frequently issues public statements on pending national, state, and local legislation, campaigning for and against laws. It also pursues special projects on women's rights, reproductive freedom, children's rights, CAPITAL PUNISHMENT, prisoners' rights, national security, and civil liberties. In these areas, its goal is both to defend existing liberties and to expand them into quarters where they are not generally enjoyed.

The election of GEORGE W. BUSH as president in 2000 and the gain of Republican seats in both the House and Senate in 2002 gave increased urgency to the ACLU advocacy for civil liberties. In addition to supporting the right to partial-birth abortion, the ACLU has fought for the rights of library patrons to view unrestricted INTERNET sites as well as AFFIRMATIVE ACTION programs for colleges and universities throughout the country. The ACLU opposed numerous initiatives of the Bush administration, in particular, federal funding for faith-based drug treatment programs and the attempts to give sweeping new powers to domestic law enforcement and intelligence agencies after the SEPTEMBER 11TH ATTACKS in 2001.

The ACLU has likewise advocated in favor of GAY AND LESBIAN RIGHTS. In 2004, the ACLU became involved in LITIGATION in California challenging the state's refusal to grant marriage licenses to same-sex couples. The California Supreme Court eventually heard the case, and in *In re Marriage Cases* (183 P.3d 384 [Cal. 2008]), the court ruled that the state could not constitutionally prohibit same-sex couples from marrying. The decision was later effectively overruled with the passage of Proposition 8, a CONSTITUTIONAL AMENDMENT in California that defines marriage as a union of a man and a woman.

The ACLU supported BARACK OBAMA in his bid for the presidency, and with his election, Democrats gained control of both houses of Congress as well as the White House. In 2009, the ACLU continued to advocate its agenda; for instance, the ACLU in March 2009 submitted a letter to Obama asking him to withhold support for funding for programs the support abstinence until marriage. According to the ACLU, the money going toward those programs should be devoted to teen education about safer sex practices.

WHOSE CIVIL LIBERTIES, ANYWAY? THE ACLU AND ITS CRITICS

Since 1920 the American Civil Liberties Union (ACLU) has stood at the forefront of nearly every great legal battle over personal freedom in the United States. The *C* in *ACLU* might easily stand for *Controversial*. Although the ACLU's role as a major institution in U.S. law is indisputable, its effect on the law and on the lives of citizens is frequently in dispute. Political debate over the group yields very little middle ground and a great amount of passionate disagreement. Supporters agree with its self-styled epithet, "the guardian of liberty." To them, the ACLU is often all that stands between freedom and tyranny. Opponents think the organization is simply a liberal establishment bent on imposing its views on society. They fault its reading of the law, despise its methods, and rue its results. At the heart of this debate is a fascinating question: how does an organization that fights for the very foundations of the nation's commitment to liberty inspire so much conflict?

Even from the start, the idea of a group devoted to defending liberty (the right of each person to be free from the despotism of governments or majorities) made some observers angry. In 1917 members of the Civil Liberties Bureau, which was soon renamed the ACLU, got this welcome from the *New York Times* editorial page: "Jails Are Waiting for Them." Although WORLD WAR I was a period of governmental heavy-handedness, the *Times* proved to be both right and wrong. In the next 75 years the ACLU became a powerful force in shaping law, and it won many more enemies than friends. By the 1988 presidential election, candidate GEORGE H. W. BUSH could make political hay in campaign speeches by attacking the ACLU as "the criminal's lobby." Other critics said the ACLU was anti-God, anti-American, anti-life, and so on. In the end, no jails held ACLU members (at least not for long), but no small number of people would have liked to lock them away.

The case against the ACLU is actually many cases. Every time the organization goes into court, it naturally has to displease someone; LITIGATION is hardly about making friends. Although the organization has one mandate, the abstract ideal of freedom, it must oppose the will of specific individuals if this mandate is to be carried out. Take, for example, one of the ACLU's civil liberties battles: religious freedom. For some, religious freedom means the First Amendment's guarantee that "Congress shall make no law respecting an establishment of religion"; in other words, that people will be free from government-imposed religious worship. For many others, religious freedom implies just the opposite FIRST AMENDMENT assurance, that Congress shall not prohibit the free exercise of RELIGION. In a 1962 court battle, the ACLU won a point for the former, an end to PRAYER in public schools, a victory that polls indicate was unwanted and unsupported by most U.S. citizens (ENGEL V. VITALE, 370 U.S. 421, 82 S. Ct. 1261, 8 L. Ed. 2d 601). Equally stymied by ACLU activism are people who want to display Christian crèches on government property at Christmastime. They have their holiday hopes dashed every time the ACLU wins a court order blocking such a display on First Amendment grounds. Each victory for the organization in such cases may be another disaster in local public relations.

In response, scorn heaped on the ACLU seldom fails to question its motives. The ACLU's "yuletide work" was attacked by the conservative commentator John Leo in an essay in the *Washington Times* entitled "Crushing the Public Crèche:" "While others frolic, the grinches of the ACLU tirelessly trudge out each year on yet another crèche-patrol, snatching Nativity scenes from public parks and rubbing out religious symbols." Leo's point is shared by many conservatives: The government,

far from remaining neutral in religious matters, is actually engaging in hostility toward religion, at the behest of ACLU "zealots." In this view, the defense of an abstract principle has taken hold of the senses of its defenders; they have become inflexible absolutists. The conservative attorney and author Bruce Fein took this complaint much further, discovering something insidious: "A partial sketch of the ACLU's vision of America reveals a contempt for individual responsibility, economic justice and prosperity and moral decency." Fein meant that the ACLU defends welfare.

Ascribing suspicious aims to the ACLU moves the debate into a more complicated area. The ACLU is not opposed simply because it has fought to block government-sanctioned religious displays, causing local upset and anger.

Similarly, it is not opposed merely because it defends the rights of some of society's most unpopular groups, Nazis, for example. The deeper issue is civil liberties themselves. Here people face a new question: Why does an organization that fights for the very foundations of the nation's commitment to liberty even have to exist?

The ACLU's answer is rather simple. Civil liberties, it argues, exist only when everyone enjoys them. In other words, there is no such thing as freedom for some without freedom for all, including those individuals whom the majority may hate or whom the government seeks to silence. Loren Siegel, ACLU director of public education, wrote that the United States

> was founded upon not one, but two great principles. The first, democracy, is the more familiar: The majority rules. The second principle, liberty, is not as well understood. Even in our democracy, the majority's rule is not unlimited. There are certain individual rights and liberties, enshrined in the BILL OF RIGHTS,

that are protected from the "tyranny of the majority." Just because there are more whites than blacks in this country does not, for example, mean that whites can vote to take the vote away from blacks. And just because there are more heterosexuals than homosexuals should not mean that the majority can discriminate with impunity against the minority.

But civil liberties "are not self-enforcing," Siegel adds. Moreover, NADINE STROSSEN, former ACLU president, points out that victories in civil liberties need to be continually re-won. It is not the habit of enemies to grant their opponents the same constitutional rights that they themselves enjoy; plainly, it is the habit of enemies to ignore, restrict, or even crush those rights. Not by accident, the government or a majority of voters can do this; the weak and the few cannot. Thus, the ACLU's commitment is precisely to those whose purchase on freedom is slim—not because the ACLU is necessarily in favor of their cause, but because it is in favor of upholding their rights.

That argument sounds nice on paper, opponents say, but it is neither practical nor sensible at all times in real life. Indeed, they ask, what about the majority—why must it suffer to please the few in its midst who cause trouble, such as criminals? This is the point that Bush wanted to make with his famous "criminal's lobby" blast: The civil liberties of criminals should not be upheld at the expense of the civil liberties of law-abiding citizens. Bush, like other critics, turned this charge into a broader INDICTMENT of the ACLU: In his 1988 campaign for the presidency, he accused Democratic presidential candidate Michael Dukakis of being a "card-carrying member of the ACLU." The term *card-carrying* resonates in U.S. political history; it comes from the era of anti-Communist witch hunts and implies anti-Americanism. Ira Glasser, the ACLU's executive director at the time, indignantly replied to Bush in the *Boston Globe*: "The vice president feels it is politically expedient to beat up on us, and if the only way that he can carry it off is by engaging in McCarthyism and distorting our record, then he is willing to do it."

Despite the conservative claim that the ACLU is a liberal group, the political left also has taken shots at it. In the 1980s and 1990s, some feminists opposed the ACLU's absolute defense of free speech. These critics were particularly distressed by the organization's support of the speech rights of pornographers. Others on the left, notably academics, resent the ACLU's opposition to so-called hate-speech codes that colleges and universities have imposed on campuses to protect members of minorities from others' abusive expression. Such issues have caused DISSENT even among the ranks of the ACLU itself, leading some to argue that the organization should emphasize CIVIL RIGHTS over civil liberties, that is, jettison its traditional mission in order to focus more specifically on the rights of women and racial minorities. In the ACLU's annual report (1992–1993), Strossen dismissed this argument. Liberty and equality, she wrote, are not mutually exclusive. "How can individual liberty be secure if some individuals are denied their rights because they belong to certain societal groups? How, on the other hand, can equality for all groups be secure if that equality does not include the exercise of individual liberty?"

Critics contend, however, that making individual rights paramount can produce results that clash with community values. They note that the ACLU has fought the implementation of the Children's Internet Protection Act, including a provision that requires public libraries receiving federal technology funds to install filters on their computers or risk losing aid. With the First Amendment seemingly protecting most forms of Internet PORNOGRAPHY, the act seeks to prevent access on public library computers, so as to prevent children from seeing disturbing images as they walk by. The act even permits adults to ask the librarians to turn off the filters. Nevertheless, the ACLU persuaded a federal court in 2002 that the law violated the First Amendment. Critics of the ACLU cite this as just one more example of blind devotion to an absolutist view of free expression.

In the aftermath of the SEPTEMBER 11TH ATTACKS of 2001, the ACLU exposed itself to more criticism over its objections to new federal laws and orders. It objected to proposed provisions of the USA PATRIOT ACT in October 2001, at a time when very few voices were raised about protecting the right to privacy and preventing the government from gaining more police powers. It lobbied again when the act was reauthorized in 2006, and in 2009 advocated that three provisions of the law be allowed to sunset at the end of the year. It has challenged the indefinite DETENTION of ALIENS who are suspected of terrorist activities and ties, and questioned the invasion of email and phone traffic by federal agencies tasked with fighting TERRORISM.

The ACLU promises to remain on the forefront of the debate over the scope of the Bill of Rights and the desire of citizens to be protected by their government. The WAR ON TERRORISM that began in September 2001 has generated many legal challenges by the ACLU as the federal government asserted new-found powers to monitor, investigate, and detain suspected terrorists. The ACLU will continue to find itself isolated at times as it battles for its vision of a free society.

FURTHER READINGS

American Civil Liberties Union. Available online at www.aclu.org (accessed July 11, 2003).

Hershkoff, Helen. 1997. *The Rights of the Poor: The Authoritative ACLU Guide to Poor People's Rights.* Carbondale, Ill.: Southern Illinois Univ. Press.

Schulhofer, Stephen J. 2002. *The Enemy Within: Intelligence Gathering, Law Enforcement, and Civil Liberties in the Wake of September 11.* New York: Twentieth Century Fund.

Strossen, Nadine. 2001. *Defending Pornography: Free Speech, Sex, and the Fight for Women's Rights.* New York: New York Univ. Press.

Walker, Samuel. 1999. *In Defense of American Liberties: A History of the ACLU.* New York: Oxford Univ. Press.

CROSS REFERENCES

Bill of Rights; Liberty; Right.

The ACLU national headquarters is in New York City. The group maintains a legislative office in Washington, D.C., and a regional office in Atlanta, along with chapters in each state. These state chapters follow the decisions of the national executive board yet are also free to pursue cases on their own.

FURTHER READINGS

ACLU. *ACLU's Seventy-Five Most Important Supreme Court Cases.* Briefing paper.

———. *The ACLU Today.* Briefing paper.

———. *Church and State.* Briefing paper.

———. *Guardian of Liberty.* Briefing paper.

American Civil Liberties Union. Available online at www. aclu.org (accessed September 17, 2009)

Hershkoff, Helen. 1997. *The Rights of the Poor: The Authoritative ACLU Guide to Poor People's Rights.* Carbondale: Southern Illinois Univ. Press.

Walker, Samuel. 1999. *In Defense of American Liberties: A History of the ACLU.* New York: Oxford Univ. Press.

CROSS REFERENCES

Baldwin, Roger Nash; Bill of Rights; Civil Rights; Frankfurter, Felix; Palmer, Alexander Mitchell; Strossen, Nadine M.

AMERICAN FARM BUREAU FEDERATION

The American Farm Bureau Federation (AFBF) is a NONPROFIT, nonpartisan organization dedicated to promoting, protecting, and representing the interests of U.S. farmers. More than five million members in 50 states and Puerto Rico belong to the AFBF, making it the largest U.S. farm organization. The AFBF is a federation of 2,800 county farm organizations, which elect representatives to state farm bureaus. The organization maintains its general headquarters in Park Ridge, Illinois, and has an office in Washington, D.C. From these offices the AFBF staff offers many services and programs for state and county farm bureaus and members. As of 2009 the AFBF held more than $14 billion in assets.

The first county farm bureau was formed in Broome County, New York, in 1911. The word *bureau* in farm bureau is used because the first organization was formed as a "bureau" of the local chamber of COMMERCE. Missouri was the first state to form a statewide organization of farm bureaus in 1915. The AFBF was founded in 1919 when a small group of farmers from 30 state bureaus gathered in Chicago, Illinois. The AFBF soon became a voice for agriculture at the national level, LOBBYING Congress for passage of legislation favorable to farmers.

The AFBF relies on its 2,800 county bureaus for direction and support. Thousands of volunteer leaders serve on county farm bureau boards and committees. Members organize social outings, educational workshops, political action and community forums, and other programs and services for farm families.

State bureaus adopt policies and name delegates to represent them at the AFBF annual meeting. Policies adopted by VOTING delegates govern the federation. These policies deal with many issues, including the use of natural resources, TAXATION, property rights, services to the farm community, trade, food safety and quality, and other issues that affect rural America.

The AFBF has historically been a conservative organization, favoring flexible price supports for crops and a minimum of government regulation and oversight. Its government relations division employs a number of registered lobbyists who are specialists on farm policy, trade, budget and taxes, farm credit, labor, transportation, conservation, and the environment. These individuals maintain daily contact with Congress and regulatory agencies and appear before congressional committees.

The AFBF's PUBLIC POLICY division is responsible for research, education, and policy support for AFBF and the state farm bureaus. Staff members engage in research projects on a variety of current issues, including property rights, health care, clean water, endangered species, animal welfare, farm programs, and dairy policy.

One of the hottest issues that began in the 1990s and continues into the 2000s concerns the current and future role of biotechnology in agriculture. Biotechnology and other technological developments such as computers, lasers, and robots are also issues closely followed by AFBF and the county and state farm bureaus. Additionally, the AFBF has sought to play a major role in such areas as the continuing development of renewable fuels and international trade. The division coordinates several special farm bureau activities, including COMMODITY advisory committees, annual crop surveys, and various national seminars and conferences on policy issues.

The federation's communication division operates a computerized marketing, news, and weather system that delivers the latest news, market information, U.S. DEPARTMENT OF AGRICULTURE news, and agricultural weather reports to subscribers by satellite.

The American Farm Bureau Foundation for Agriculture, founded in 1967, funds research on agricultural issues. The foundation is funded by gifts from individuals, county and state farm bureaus, CORPORATIONS, and foundations. The foundation has funded research on animal waste management, pesticide use, new methods of helping endangered species, and animal welfare education. The foundation is also active in numerous educational outreach programs including "Educating About Agriculture," awards and contests, farm tours and field days, garden and planting projects, mobile classroom units, newsletters, books, and videos. The AFBF sponsors scholarships for teachers as well as a number of grants.

FURTHER READINGS

American Farm Bureau. Available online at http://www.fb. org (accessed May 11, 2009).

Howard, R. P. 1982. *James R. Howard and the Farm Bureau.* Ames, IA: Iowa State Univ. Press.

Woell, Melvin. 1990. *Farm Bureau Architects: Through Four Decades.* Dubuque, IA: Kendall-Hunt.

CROSS REFERENCE

Farm Credit Administration.

AMERICAN FEDERATION OF LABOR— CONGRESS OF INDUSTRIAL ORGANIZATIONS

The American Federation of Labor-Congress of Industrial Organizations (AFL-CIO) is a voluntary federation of 56 national and international labor unions. It comprises 65 national union affiliates, 45,000 local unions, 51 state federations (including Puerto Rico), 570 central labor councils, and a membership of more than 10 million workers. The organization, which has had enormous political influence since the 1930s, is headquartered in Washington, D.C. However, the AFL-CIO's influence was weakened during the mid-2000s when two major national labor unions withdrew from the AFL-CIO.

The AFL was formed in 1886 as a loose confederation of 25 autonomous national trade unions with more than 316,000 members. Renouncing identification with any political party or movement, the AFL concentrated on pursuing achievable goals, such as higher wages and shorter work hours. Members were encouraged to support politicians who were friendly to labor, no matter their party affiliation.

During the 1930s the AFL became embroiled in internal conflict. The trade unions that dominated the AFL were composed of skilled workers who opposed organizing the unskilled or semiskilled workers on the manufacturing production line. Several unions rebelled at this refusal to organize and formed the Committee for Industrial Organization (CIO). The CIO aggressively organized millions of workers who labored in automobile, steel, and rubber plants. In 1938, unhappy with this effort, the AFL expelled the unions that formed the CIO. The CIO then formed its own organization and changed its name to the Congress of Industrial Organizations. By the 1950s, the leadership of both the AFL and CIO realized that a unified labor movement was necessary. In 1955, the AFL and the CIO merged into a single organization, the AFL-CIO.

The AFL-CIO is primarily concerned with influencing legislative policies that affect unions. Its staff members conduct research, set policy, and TESTIFY before congressional and state legislative committees. More importantly, the organization provides funds and volunteers to labor-endorsed political candidates. Although the AFL-CIO is a nonpartisan organization, it traditionally has supported DEMOCRATIC PARTY candidates.

With the 1995 election of John J. Sweeney as president, the AFL-CIO has made increased union membership its highest priority. Although Sweeney was subsequently reelected three times, membership in U.S. trade unions has continued to fall over the last several decades as the manufacturing sector of the U.S. economy has steadily declined. Union membership in 1954 comprised 34.7 percent of the workforce. By 2000, this number had declined to 13.4 percent, and by 2007, only 12.1 percent of the workforce were union workers.

Sweeney pushed the organization to recruit women, minorities, low-paid workers, and white-collar workers. In 2001 the AFL-CIO launched the New Alliance Initiative with the purpose of restructuring unions at the state and local levels. However, Sweeney was not popular with everyone associated with the AFL-CIO. In 2005, two major unions—the International Brotherhood of Teamsters and the Service Employees International Union—each voted unanimously to withdraw from the AFL-CIO. Heads of both unions cited concerns with the

American Indian activist Glenn Morris leads a protest against the annual Colombus Day parade in Denver, Colorado.

AP IMAGES

AFL-CIO's direction as reasons for leaving the organization. Total membership in the AFL-CIO fell from more than 13 million in 2001 to less than 11 million in 2009.

The day-to-day work of the federation is carried out by 11 programmatic departments including the Organizing Department; Field Mobilization Department; Civil, Human and Women's Rights Department; and the International Affairs Department. Topics of major importance to the AFL-CIO include manufacturing, CIVIL RIGHTS, the global economy, health care, immigrant workers, minimum-wage issues, pensions, and SOCIAL SECURITY.

FURTHER READINGS

AFL–CIO Website. Available online at http://www.aflcio.org/ (accessed May 11, 2009).

Edsall, Thomas B. 2005. "Two Top Unions Split from AFL-CIO." *Washington Post.*

AMERICAN INDIAN MOVEMENT

Founded in 1968, the American Indian Movement (AIM) is an organization dedicated to the Native American CIVIL RIGHTS MOVEMENT. Its main objectives are the SOVEREIGNTY of Native American lands and peoples, preservation of their culture and traditions, and enforcement of all treaties with the United States.

Despite the straightforwardness of its stated objectives, AIM's reputation was seriously harmed by well-publicized and controversial incidents of law-breaking, VANDALISM, and violence, resulting in the organization's peak and decline within a few years. Significant historical events include AIM's hostile occupation of Alcatraz Island (1969); the "Trail of Broken Treaties" march on Washington, D.C. (1971); occupation of Wounded Knee (1973); and the Pine Ridge shootout of 1975, which resulted in the controversial arrest and IMPRISONMENT of the most famous AIM member, Leonard Peltier. Following these events, the organization's visibility and viability as a political force greatly declined.

History

Prior to the formation of AIM, issues involving U.S. Indian–non-Indian relations had largely faded away. Starting in the 1950s, the U.S. government embarked on a serious policy plan to terminate its responsibilities to Native Americans pursuant to extant treaties and agreements. This action included the relocation of thousands of reservation Indians to urban areas and the TERMINATION of federal duties to two major tribes, the Menominee of Wisconsin and the Klamath of Oregon. (Federal rights were restored to both a few years later.) However, by the 1970s, relocation as well as termination policies were all but abandoned.

A number of problems arose when Native Americans left the reservations and intermingled with local towns. Native Americans allegedly caused and/or became parties to local disturbances or crimes. Moreover, after WORLD WAR II and the KOREAN WAR, many Native Americans who had served in the armed forces no longer wanted to return to stereotypical Indian lifestyles. As more intermingling and merging occurred, other Native Americans became increasingly intent on searching for their cultural roots and maintaining their ethnic identities. They vowed not to be assimilated and their views paralleled the ideals of other CIVIL RIGHTS movements of the era. The most radical elements to emerge from these militant Native American groups ultimately formed the AIM, which was intended as an indigenous version of the BLACK PANTHER PARTY.

During the summer of 1968, about 200 members of the Native American community in urban Minneapolis, Minnesota, met to discuss various issues, including slum housing, alleged police brutality, unemployment, and alleged discriminatory policies involving the local county's WELFARE system. The group had been impressed with media coverage of the Black Panther policy of monitoring routine police interrogations or arrests and adopted similar tactics.

From the beginning, the group stirred controversy in seeking attention. Mobilizing in different cities and gaining momentum, it employed increasingly negative tactics such as holding an "anti-birthday party" for the United States atop Mt. Rushmore on the Fourth of July; painting Plymouth Rock bright red on Thanksgiving Day 1970, and seizing the Mayflower replica. All of these actions served to alienate many would-be sympathizers. However, AIM did get the media attention it desired, which seemed only to spawn further controversy. When the group organized a hostile occupation of Alcatraz Island off the coast of California, AIM finally became a force to be reckoned with, just briefly.

Alcatraz

On November 9, 1969, a group of Native American supporters, led by Mohawk Richard Oakes, chartered a boat and set out to symbolically claim the island of Alcatraz for "Indians of all tribes." By November 20 the gesture had turned into a full-scale occupation that ultimately became the longest prolonged occupation by Native Americans of a federal facility or federal property.

Early use of Alcatraz Island by indigenous peoples is difficult to reconstruct. Ancient oral histories seem to support the view that at one time Alcatraz was used as a place of isolation for tribal members who had violated some tribal law or taboo and were exiled or ostracized for punishment. Earlier or concurrently, the island changed hands several times during Spanish and Portuguese explorations, but ultimately it became federal property and in time became the site of the infamous federal prison once operated there.

Many of the Indian occupiers of November 1969 were students recruited by Oakes from UCLA, who returned with Oakes to Alcatraz and began to live on the island in old federal buildings. They ran a school and daycare center, and began delivering local radio broadcasts that could be heard in the San Francisco Bay area.

Initially the federal government placed an effective barricade around the island and

insisted that the group leave; the government did, however, agree to an Indian demand for formal negotiations. The talks accomplished nothing, as the Indian group insisted on a deed and CLEAR TITLE to the island. The group continued occupation and the federal government insisted they depart but took no aggressive action to remove them. Officially, the government adopted a position of non-interference and hoped that support for the occupation would fade. The FBI and Coast Guard were under strict orders to remain clear of the island and media attention began to dwindle.

The occupation continued all through 1970, but by this time, internal problems among the indigenous group caused the occupation to lose momentum. Student recruits left to return to classes at UCLA and were replaced by urban recruits, many of whom had been part of the San Francisco drug and hippie culture of the time. Several rose in opposition to Oakes's leadership on the island, and Oakes ultimately left after his teenaged stepdaughter fell to her death in a building stairwell.

After several months of hostile occupation, the federal government shut off electric power to the island and removed the water barge that had been supplying fresh water to the occupiers. A fire broke out, and both sides blamed the other for the loss of several historic buildings. Splintered leadership on the island resulted in the loss of a common voice with which to NEGOTIATE with the government. When the occupiers began stripping the remaining buildings of copper wiring and tubing, the press turned on them and began publishing stories of assaults, drugs, violence, and the trial of three Indians found guilty of selling 600 pounds of copper.

With government patience growing thin, then-president RICHARD NIXON finally approved a peaceful removal plan, to be conducted with as little force as possible and when the least number of people were on the island. On June 10, 1971, FBA agents, armed federal marshals, and special forces police removed five women, four children, and six unarmed men from the island.

Trail of Broken Treaties

In November 1971 AIM organized what it called the Trail of Broken Treaties, a march on Washington, D.C., involving approximately 1,000 angry Native Americans. It ended with the occupation of the Bureau of Indian Affairs

(BIA) headquarters. After taking over the offices, AIM protesters seized large numbers of files from the BIA offices and caused more than $2 million in DAMAGES to the trashed building. They also presented President Nixon with 20 demands for immediate action. The Nixon administration provided $66,000 in transportation monies in return for a peaceful end to the takeover. It also agreed to appoint a Native American to a BIA post. Again, the real success for AIM was in getting some media attention and in heightening public awareness of unresolved Indian issues.

Wounded Knee

The tiny village of Wounded Knee, South Dakota, is the historic site of an infamous 1890 massacre of Native Americans (the last) by the U.S. Cavalry. The original site and burial ground became part of the Pine Ridge Indian reservation in that state.

In 1973 about 200 members of the local Oglala Lakota Indians, led by AIM members, seized the village of Wounded Knee (a Catholic church, trading post, and post office) and declared it to be an independent nation. Their single demand was the return of the Great Sioux Nation (a sovereign parcel of REAL ESTATE comprising the entire western half of South Dakota) allegedly promised to them by the United States in the Fort Laramie Treaty of 1868.

Just prior to this development, on the nearby Pine Ridge reservation, tribal council president Dick Wilson (a Native American) had secured a tribal council order prohibiting AIM members from attending or speaking at reservation meetings or public gatherings. He considered AIM members to be lawless misfits bent on agitating the populace. AIM members, in return, accused Wilson of nepotism, corruption, and mismanagement of tribal monies. A group of Wilson supporters, locally referred to as the "goon squad," began harassing and threatening AIM members. The Lakota Indians invited AIM to meet with their group, and both decided to take a stand at Wounded Knee. At this point, the federal government, including the BIA, remained neutral, claiming the stand-off was an internal tribal dispute.

When AIM occupiers built fortifications and took up arms and munitions, both Wilson and the federal government (FBI, U.S. marshals, and BIA police) moved in. In the well-publicized 71-day occupation that followed, two AIM members were killed. Ultimately, AIM leaders negotiated a "peace pact" with the government stipulating that the activists would be treated fairly and that the federal government would conduct a fair review of several treaties.

Although the immediate stand-off was defused, tensions between Wilson's goon squad and AIM members continued over the next several years. Dozens of AIM members, including early founding members Russell Means and DENNIS BANKS, were indicted on dozens of charges related to the Wounded Knee standoff. The charges were ultimately dropped when a federal judge acknowledged spurious activity and involvement by the FBI.

Pine Ridge

Wilson's tribal leadership at the Pine Ridge reservation was reportedly federally sanctioned and supported. Allegations arose at the trials of AIM members that goon squad members were paid with BIA monies and that many of the members were in fact off-duty BIA police. Several murders occurred on the reservation and were never fully investigated. For its part, the FBI maintained that it was an investigatory rather than enforcement agency, a position that further exacerbated the regional tension and fear.

In June 1975 two FBI agents in an unmarked car and clad in civilian clothes chased a pickup truck into an isolated area near an AIM encampment. During the resulting shootout, the two FBI agents were shot and killed, along with one Indian activist. Over the next several days, more than 300 FBI agents swarmed the reservation, followed by officers making dozens of arrests and prosecutions. Ultimately, AIM activist Peltier was tried and convicted for his role in the FBI killings, receiving two life sentences. His trial and CONVICTION remained shrouded with allegations of suppressed evidence, coerced WITNESSES, and a fabricated MURDER weapon.

Later Years

Following the Pine Knee incident, AIM declined rapidly in both leadership and momentum. It held its last national unified event in 1978 and the following year dismantled as a national organization in favor of independent regional chapters. Means and Banks were in and out of court for years defending their leadership roles in the 1973 and 1975 shootouts. Eventually, both were acquitted of all significant charges. Banks went on to found another Indian organization, the Sacred Run, devoted to spiritual renewal and environmental issues. In 2007, Means made news when he announced that the Lakota Indian tribe would withdraw from treaties with the United States. However, several other tribal leaders opposed Means' stance.

Peltier remained in prison. As of 2003, the FBI refused to release nearly 500 documents on Peltier, being withheld on grounds of "national security." In 2009 Peltier's family reported that the 64-year-old had been beaten by a gang of inmates at the U.S. PENITENTIARY in Lewisburg, Pennsylvania. Some called for President BARACK OBAMA to PARDON Peltier.

In 1978 Congress passed the American Indian Religious Freedom Act (AIRFA)(42 U.S. C.A. § 1996), designed to review and update federal policies regarding such matters as Native Americans' right to access sacred grounds and legal rights to practice their traditional religions. Reviews and recommendations were made. Pursuant to this action, Congress passed the Native American Graves Protection and Repatriation Act, Public L. No. 101-601, 104 Stat. 3048, in 1990 but in that same year, the U.S. Supreme Court reiterated its 1988 ruling that AIRFA was a policy statement and not law. As such, there was no LEGAL RIGHT to the protection of sacred sites or the religious use of peyote in the Native American RELIGION. *Lyng v. Northwest Indian Cemetery Protection Association,* 483 U.S. 439, 107 S. Ct. 2924, 97 L. Ed. 2d 364 (1988). New sacred land protection legislation was again introduced in 2002, but the legislation died in committee.

FURTHER READINGS

American Indian Movement Website. Available online at http://www.aimovement.org/ (accessed May 11, 2009).

Churchill, Ward. June 1997. "A Force, Briefly, To Reckon With." *Progressive.*

Johnson, Troy. "We Hold the Rock: The American Indian Occupation of Alcatraz Island." *Indians of North America.* Long Beach: California State Univ. Press.

Marshall, Joseph M., III, and Sicangu Lakota. 2000. "Wounded Knee Takover, 1973." *Encyclopedia of North American Indians.* Houghton Mifflin.

Oswalt, Wendell H., and Sharlotte Neely. 1994. *This Land Was Theirs.* 5th ed. Mountain View, CA: Mayfield.

Singer, Daniel. July 18, 1994. "Free Peltier!" *Nation.*

CROSS REFERENCES

Native American Graves Protection and Repatriation Act of 1990; Native American Rights.

AMERICAN ISRAEL PUBLIC AFFAIRS COMMITTEE

The American Israel Public Affairs Committee (AIPAC) is a national advocacy group that lobbies for U.S. support to the nation of Israel. Founded in 1951, AIPAC has grown into a 100,000-member organization that is recognized as one of the most influential foreign policy groups in the United States. AIPAC has lobbied Congress for U.S. foreign aid to Israel since 1951, when it helped defeat several efforts to cut aid for the resettling of hundreds of thousands of Holocaust REFUGEES in Israel. In addition, AIPAC has lobbied for U.S. military aid to Israel and has helped preserve the special relationship that has existed between the United States and Israel since the United States recognized the nation of Israel in 1948.

AIPAC is headquartered in Washington, D.C. Members of its staff maintain an active presence in the halls of Congress, attending committee sessions and reviewing legislation that may affect the relationship between the United States and Israel. AIPAC estimates that it monitors 2,000 hours of congressional hearings annually. Research staff members analyze periodicals and documents in five different languages, amassing a large archive of information on hundreds of issues, including foreign aid, antiterrorism initiatives, and programs that promote United States-Israel strategic cooperation. AIPAC staff members also work with key officials in developing legislation and policy, presenting concepts and information that are moved into the legislative process. AIPAC lobbyists hold 1,000 meetings annually with congressional offices.

AIPAC also works with aspiring politicians. During the 1994 elections, representatives of AIPAC met with 600 congressional candidates. Since 1990, AIPAC has worked to educate these new legislators about the relationship between the United States and Israel and the key issues critical to maintaining that relationship. AIPAC staff frequently meets with every freshman representative. Likewise, AIPAC representatives meet with members of new presidential administrations, including the administration of President BARACK OBAMA in 2009.

AIPAC regional staff members travel to more than 600 communities a year to train AIPAC members to be effective advocates for United States-Israel relations. AIPAC works in every congressional district, especially those districts with little or no Jewish population. AIPAC conducts small meetings and statewide workshops, giving its members the opportunity to become involved in grassroots LOBBYING.

The influence of AIPAC remains strong. The United States has appropriated billions of dollars to support Israel, and AIPAC has been influential in building and maintaining support for the Jewish state. Additional funds have been appropriated to help SETTLE Jewish refugees in Israel. AIPAC has also maintained congressional support for Israel's position in the Middle East peace process, arguing that attempts to distance the United States from Israel's position only encourage its Arab neighbors to ask for unilateral concessions. AIPAC believes that the peace process will only achieve results if the close working relationship between the United States and Israel continues.

Following the SEPTEMBER 11TH ATTACKS in 2001, AIPAC has stepped up its agenda to make sure that the United States continues to ensure Israel's security by working with Congress to isolate and financially constrict such groups as Hamas, Hezbollah, and Palestinian Islamic Jihad. AIPAC has continued to support U.S. efforts to isolate and pressure Palestinian authority chairman Yasir Afarat to stop bombings and SUICIDE missions within Israel. Through its Web site, the organization keeps members updated on protective measures taken by the Israeli people as the United States initiated war with Iraq in 2003. More recent efforts have focused on tensions with Iran, which has sought to develop a nuclear program. AIPAC has supported dozens of bills related to Iran, including the Iran Freedom Support Act, Pub. L. No. 109-293, 120 Stat. 1344 (2006), which renewed sanctions.

FURTHER READINGS

American Israel Public Affairs Committee. Available online at http://www.aipac.org (accessed May 12, 2009).

Bass, Warren. 2003. *Support Any Friend: Kennedy's Middle East and the Making of the U.S. Israel Alliance.* New York: Oxford Univ. Press.

Wright, John R. 1995. *Interest Groups and Congress: Lobbying, Contributions, and Influence.* New York: Addison-Wesley.

AMERICAN LEGION

The American Legion is a wartime veterans' organization chartered by Congress in 1919. The American Legion has almost three million members in nearly 15,000 American Legion posts worldwide. These posts are organized into 55 departments, one each for the 50 states, the District of Columbia, Puerto Rico, France, Mexico, and the Philippines. The American Legion's national headquarters is in Indianapolis, Indiana, with additional offices in Washington, D.C. Though volunteer members do most of the work of the American Legion, the national organization has a regular full-time staff of about 300 employees.

Eligibility in the American Legion is based on honorable service in the U.S. armed forces during WORLD WAR I, WORLD WAR II, the KOREAN WAR, the VIETNAM WAR, and military operations in Lebanon (1982–84); Grenada (1982–84); Panama (1989–90); and the Gulf Wars (1990–). Membership is based on the period of service, not the place of service, so an individual does not have to be stationed in a combat zone to be eligible. Members may participate in a low-cost life insurance program and may receive discounts on moving expenses, car rentals, hotel and motel rentals, eyewear, and prescription drugs. American Legion service officers provide free advice and guidance to veterans who need to deal with the Department of Veterans Affairs (VA) about benefits and other issues.

The American Legion sponsors many community activities and programs. Students showing the highest qualities of citizenship are recognized with an American Legion School Medal Award. More than 30,000 students in elementary, junior high, and senior high schools are recognized annually for their COMMITMENT to honor, courage, scholarship, leadership, and service. The organization also awards 10 national college scholarships each year. At the state level, 49 departments host Boys State programs each summer for outstanding high school juniors. Local posts sponsor nearly 28,000 young men each year to attend the week-long government education program. Two outstanding leaders from each of these Boys State programs are selected to attend the American Legion Boys Nation in Washington, D.C. The American Legion Auxiliary conducts parallel programs for young women through Girls State and Girls Nation.

Many local posts sponsor Junior Shooting Clubs, which provide training in gun safety and marksmanship for students ages 14 through 20. However, the American Legion is probably best known for its sponsorship of youth baseball programs. The American Legion spends millions each year to sponsor more than 4,800 baseball teams representing more than 89,000 players. Champions from the state level meet on the national level in the American Legion World Series tournament.

The American Legion has always been a strong advocate for U.S. veterans, appearing before congressional committees to submit information and viewpoints on pending legislation. The Veterans Affairs and Rehabilitation Commission (VAR) is a cornerstone of the American Legion, overseeing federally mandated programs provided by the VA for veterans and their dependents. VAR services include assistance with medical care, claims and appeals, insurance programs, burial benefits, and veterans' employment. Staff members also communicate with administrators of state veterans' affairs programs.

American Legion volunteers give more than one million hours of service to disabled veterans annually. Field representatives from the American Legion's Washington office systematically visit VA medical centers, nursing homecare units, and outpatient clinics to evaluate their programs and facilities. The field representatives report resource needs and areas for improvement to the VA headquarters in Washington, D.C.

For a number of years the Legion and other members of the Citizens Flag Alliance have continued to lobby Congress for a CONSTITUTIONAL AMENDMENT that would impose penalties for desecration of the U.S. flag. The Legion has also been active in LOBBYING for mandatory recitation of the Pledge of Allegiance in public schools. After the SEPTEMBER 11TH ATTACKS in 2001, the Legion established the American Legion September 11 Memorial Scholarship to help defray college costs for children of deceased military personnel.

FURTHER READINGS

American Legion. Available online at http://www.legion.org (accessed May 12, 2009).

Moley, Raymond. 1975. *The American Legion Story.* Westport, CT: Greenwood.

Rumer, Thomas. 1990. *The American Legion: An Official History, 1919–1989.* New York: Evans.

AMERICAN MEDICAL ASSOCIATION

The American Medical Association (AMA) is a federation of state and territorial medical associations. The AMA seeks to promote the art and science of medicine, the medical profession, and the betterment of public health. Its purposes include obtaining, synthesizing, integrating, and disseminating information about health and medical practice; setting standards for medical ethics, practice, and education; and being an influential advocate for physicians and their patients.

The AMA was founded in 1847. At its organizing convention, the AMA adopted the first code of ethics in the United States, a detailed document that addressed the obligations of physicians to patients and to each other and the duties of the profession to the public at large. The delegates also adopted the first national standards for medical education through a RESOLUTION establishing prerequisites for the study of medicine. Since that time, the AMA has grown into a large organization with great influence over issues involving health care and medicine. It is headquartered in Chicago, Illinois.

The AMA speaks out on issues important to the medical community. AMA policy on such issues is decided through a democratic process, at the center of which is the AMA House of Delegates. The house is comprised of physician delegates from every state, the national medical specialty societies, the SURGEON GENERAL of the United States, and sections representing organized medical staffs, young physicians, resident physicians, medical students, and medical schools.

Before the opening of the House of Delegates, which meets twice per year, individual committees consider resolutions and reports in hearings open to all AMA members. Each committee prepares recommendations for the delegates. The house then votes on these recommendations, deciding the AMA's formal position and future action on an issue.

The AMA has been active in numerous healthcare initiatives that affect the U.S. populace as a whole. In the 1990s the AMA launched a campaign against family violence and violence in schools and called on TOBACCO companies to refrain from engaging in advertising practices that target children. The AMA also launched a national campaign against so-called "drive-through" baby deliveries that ended with the passing of legislation requiring insurance companies to provide appropriate hospitalization and maternity stays.

James Barr Ames.
LIBRARY OF CONGRESS

In 2000 the AMA announced the first stage of its health literacy campaign that was aimed at increasing patient comprehension of basic healthcare communications such as prescription instructions and insurance forms. The AMA also began an initiative to reduce under-age drinking. In a more controversial area, the AMA has been active in medical LIABILITY reform efforts in several states. The AMA has maintained the position that the problems of rising healthcare costs are due to the costs of MEDICAL MALPRACTICE suits and has vigorously supported medical liability reform legislation.

The AMA opposed the creation of MEDICARE in the 1960s and during the 2000s has remained opposed to national healthcare insurance. In the late 2000s, the AMA advocated for reforms in Medicare payment programs. The AMA also called on Congress to end Medicare cuts caused by economic downturns. In 2009, the AMA opposed congressional proposals for a public insurance plan. However, as Congress appeared closer to passing a health care reform bill in December 2009, the AMA expressed support for the proposal.

The AMA is the world's largest publisher of scientific medical information. The *Journal of the American Medical Association* (JAMA) is printed in 12 languages and reaches physicians in 42 countries worldwide, making it the world's most widely read medical journal. The AMA also publishes nine monthly medical specialty journals as well as a newspaper of social and economic health news, *American Medical News.*

Web site: http://www.ama-assn.org/

FURTHER READINGS

American Medical Association. Available online at http://www.ama-assn.org/ (accessed June 13, 2009).

Kirkpatrick, David D. 2009. "Groups Back Health Reform, but Seek Cover." *New York Times.* September 11.

Pear, Robert. 2009. "Doctors' Group Opposes Public Insurance Plan." *New York Times.* June 10.

CROSS REFERENCES

Health Care Law; Medicare.

AMERICAN PARTY

See KNOW-NOTHING PARTY.

AMERICANS WITH DISABILITIES ACT

See DISABILITY DISCRIMINATION.

❖ AMES, JAMES BARR

James Barr Ames was born June 22, 1846, in Boston. He achieved prominence as an educator and concentrated his career efforts at Harvard University.

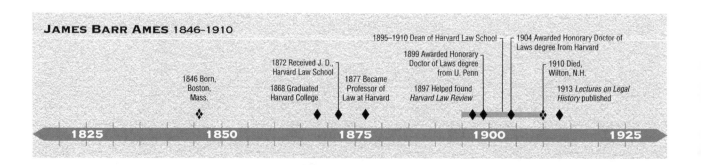

JAMES BARR AMES 1846–1910

1846 Born, Boston, Mass.

1868 Graduated Harvard College

1872 Received J. D., Harvard Law School

1877 Became Professor of Law at Harvard

1895–1910 Dean of Harvard Law School

1897 Helped found *Harvard Law Review*

1899 Awarded Honorary Doctor of Laws degree from U. Penn

1904 Awarded Honorary Doctor of Laws degree from Harvard

1910 Died, Wilton, N.H.

1913 *Lectures on Legal History* published

1825　1850　1875　1900　1925

A graduate of Harvard College in 1868, Ames earned a master of arts degree in 1871 and attended Harvard Law School in 1872. He received several doctor of laws degrees from various universities, including the University of Pennsylvania in 1899, Northwestern University in 1903, and Harvard in 1904.

In 1868 Ames began his teaching career as an instructor for a private school in Boston. Three years later he began his professional association with Harvard, acting as a tutor in French and German until 1872 and continuing as an instructor in medieval history for the next year. From 1873 to 1877 he was an associate professor of law; in 1877, he became a professor of law. From 1895 to 1910 he performed the duties of dean of the law school. In 1897 he participated in the establishment of the *Harvard Law Review*.

Ames distinguished himself as a teacher of law by utilizing the CASE METHOD introduced by legal educator and former Harvard Dean CHRISTOPHER COLUMBUS LANGDELL. Langdell's approach presented principles of law in relation to actual cases to which they were applied. By studying the cases, a student of law was given an accurate example of the law at work.

Ames extended his talents to the field of legal literature. He is the author of *Lectures on Legal History,* which was published in 1913. He died January 8, 1910, in Wilton, New Hampshire.

CROSS REFERENCE

Legal Education.

❖ AMES, SAMUEL

Samuel Ames was born September 6, 1806. He graduated from Brown University in 1823 and was admitted to the Rhode Island bar in 1826.

Samuel Ames.
LIBRARY OF CONGRESS

From 1841 to 1851 Ames represented Providence in the Rhode Island general assembly. During his TENURE, he was a prominent supporter of state authority in the "Dorr Rebellion." This INSURRECTION occurred in 1842 as a PROTEST against the limited VOTING rights that existed in Rhode Island. The protest resulted in a more liberal interpretation of the right to SUFFRAGE.

Beginning in 1856 Ames served as chief justice of the Rhode Island Supreme Court. In 1861 he was the representative from Rhode Island during a series of unsuccessful negotiations to effect a peace between the North and South during the Civil War. Ames died December 20, 1865, in Providence, Rhode Island.

CROSS REFERENCE

Dorr, Thomas Wilson.

IT IS DIFFICULT TO DRAW AND APPLY THE PRECISE LINE SEPARATING THE DIFFERENT POWERS OF GOVERNMENT.
—SAMUEL AMES

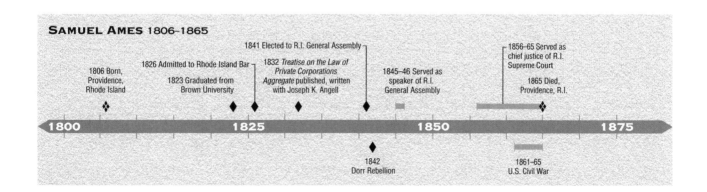

SAMUEL AMES 1806–1865

1806 Born, Providence, Rhode Island

1823 Graduated from Brown University

1826 Admitted to Rhode Island Bar

1832 *Treatise on the Law of Private Corporations Aggregate* published, written with Joseph K. Angell

1841 Elected to R.I. General Assembly

1845–46 Served as speaker of R.I. General Assembly

1856–65 Served as chief justice of R.I. Supreme Court

1865 Died, Providence, R.I.

1800   1825   1850   1875

1842 Dorr Rebellion

1861–65 U.S. Civil War

AMICABLE ACTION

An action commenced and maintained by the mutual consent and arrangement of the parties to obtain a judgment of a court on a doubtful question of law that is based upon facts that both parties accept as being correct and complete.

The action is considered amicable because there is no dispute as to the facts but only as to the conclusions of law that a judge can reach from consideration of the facts. An amicable action is considered a JUSTICIABLE controversy because there is a real and substantive disagreement between the parties as to the appropriate relief to be granted by the court.

Other names for an amicable action are a CASE AGREED ON, a CASE STATED, or a FRIENDLY SUIT.

AMICUS CURIAE

Literally, friend of the court. A person with strong interest in or views on the subject matter of an action, but not a party to the action, may petition the court for permission to file a brief, ostensibly on behalf of a party but actually to suggest a rationale consistent with its own views. Such amicus curiae briefs are commonly filed in appeals concerning matters of a broad public interest; e.g., civil rights cases. They may be filed by private persons or the government. In appeals to the U.S. courts of appeals, an amicus brief may be filed only if accompanied by written consent of all parties, or by leave of court granted on motion or at the request of the court, except that consent or leave shall not be required when the brief is presented by the United States or an officer or agency thereof.

An amicus curiae educates the court on points of law that are in doubt, gathers or organizes information, or raises awareness about some aspect of the case that the court might otherwise miss. The person is usually, but not necessarily, an attorney, and is usually not paid for her or his expertise. An amicus curiae must not be a party to the case, nor an attorney in the case, but must have some knowledge or perspective that makes her or his views valuable to the court.

The most common arena for amici curiae is in cases that are under appeal (are being reconsidered by the court) and where issues of public interest—such as social questions or civil liberties—are being debated. Cases that have drawn participation from amici curiae are those involving CIVIL RIGHTS (such as 1952's BROWN V. BOARD OF EDUCATION), CAPITAL PUNISHMENT, environmental protection, gender equality, infant ADOPTION, and AFFIRMATIVE ACTION. Amici curiae have also informed the court about narrower issues, such as the competency of a juror; or the correct procedure for completing a deed or WILL; or evidence that a case is collusive or fictitious—that is, that the parties are not being honest with the court about their reasons for being there.

The privilege that friends of the court are granted to express their views in a case is just that: amici curiae have no right to appear or to file briefs. Unless they represent the government, amici curiae must obtain leave (permission) to do so from the court, or CONSENT of all parties in the case, before filing. No court is obligated to follow or even to consider the advice of an amicus curiae, even one it has invited.

The principle that guides the appropriate role of a FRIEND OF THE COURT is that he or she should serve the court without also acting as "friend" to either of the parties. Rules of court and CASE LAW (past court decisions) have attempted to spell out the sometimes tricky specifics of how an amicus curiae should—and should not—participate in a case.

For example, Missouri's supreme court in 1969 distinguished the role of amicus curiae from the normal role of the attorney in assisting the court. In this case, the court requested the attorney who had formerly represented the parties in the case to help elicit TESTIMONY and cross-examine WITNESSES. The lawyer also made objections and argued objections against the city, which was defending the lawsuit over zoning. In seeking the payment of attorney fees for his services, the attorney argued that he had served as amicus curiae due to his acting at the court's request. The supreme court found that "in the orderly and intelligent presentation of the case, he rendered assistance to the court, the same as any attorney who contributes to the orderly presentation of a case. He was appearing, however, not as an adviser to the court but as a representative of private litigants ... advancing their partisan interests ... and is not entitled to have the fee for his admittedly valuable and competent professional services taxed as costs" (*Kansas City v. Kindle*, 446 S.W.2d 807 [Mo. 1969]).

The amicus curiae walks a fine line between providing added information and advancing the cause of one of the parties. For instance, she or he cannot raise issues that the parties themselves do not raise, because that is the task of the parties and their attorneys. If allowed by the court, amici curiae can file briefs (called *briefs amicus curiae* or *amicus briefs*), argue the case, and introduce evidence. However, they may not make most motions, file pleadings, or manage the case.

Whether participating by leave or by INVITATION, in an appearance or with a brief amicus curiae, a friend of the court is a resource person who has limited capacity to act.

FURTHER READINGS

Hollis, Duncan B. 2002. "Private Actors in Public International Law: Amicus Curiae and the Case for the Retention of State Sovereignty." *Boston College International and Comparative Law Review* 25, vol. 2 (spring).

Jost, Kenneth. 2001. "The Amicus Industry." *California Lawyer* 40 (October).

Robbins, Josh. 2003. "False Friends: Amicus Curiae and Procedural Discretion in WTO Appeals under the Hotrolled Lead/Asbestos Doctrine." *Harvard International Law Journal* 44, vol. 1 (winter).

AMISTAD MUTINY

In 1839 a group of Africans were kidnapped from their homeland and transported to Cuba as slaves. While being transported from one port in Cuba to another, the Africans revolted, killed the captain and cook, and steered for the coast of Africa. The ship was eventually boarded by U.S. authorities in U.S. waters, and the Africans were imprisoned. Fierce legal battles ensued regarding ENTITLEMENT to the Africans and the ship's cargo. In 1997 Steven Spielberg's company, DreamWorks, released a movie based upon the uprising. The movie *Amistad* engendered its own legal furor amid charges that the screenplay had been plagiarized a 1989 novel.

The Ship and Slavery

On August 26, 1839, the ship anchored off Long Island and was discovered by the U.S. brig *Washington*. The vessel, the cargo, and the Africans were taken into the District of Connecticut.

Ship owners Montes and Ruiz filed suit in federal court to recover some of the cargo and

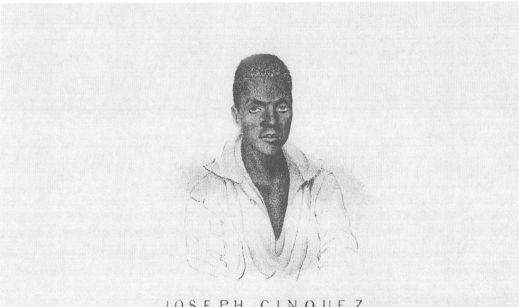

JOSEPH CINQUEZ.
The brave Congolese Chief, who prefers death to Slavery, and who now lies in Jail in Irons at New Haven Conn. awaiting his trial for daring for freedom.

SPEECH TO HIS COMRADE SLAVES AFTER MURDERING THE CAPTAIN &C. AND GETTING POSSESSION OF THE VESSEL AND CARGO

"Brothers we have done that which we purposed, our hands are now clean, for we have striven to regain the precious heritage we received from our fathers. We have only to persevere, where the Sun rises there is our home, our brethern, our fathers. Do not seek to defeat my orders, if so I shall sacrifice any one who would endanger the rest; when at home we will kill the Old Man, the young one shall be saved, he is kind and gave you bread, we must not kill those who give us water. Brothers, I am resolved that it is better to die than be a white mans slave, and I will not complain if by dying I save you. Let us be careful what we eat that we may not be sick. The deed is done and I need say no more."

This portrait of Joseph Cinque, one of the leaders of the slave revolt on board the Amistad, appeared in an 1839 edition of the New York Sun newspaper.

the Africans, asserting ownership of the Africans as their slaves. The U.S. DISTRICT ATTORNEY for the District of Connecticut appeared on behalf of the Spanish government and demanded that the Africans be handed over for trial in Cuba on MURDER and PIRACY charges.

Rallying on behalf of the Africans, New York abolitionists hired attorney ROGER SHERMAN Baldwin. Baldwin argued that because Spain had outlawed the African slave trade, the Africans could use whatever means possible to attain freedom after their illegal KIDNAPPING and enslavement. The abolitionists sought a WRIT of HABEAS CORPUS relief to free the Africans pending charges of piracy or murder that might be brought. The writ was denied and the Africans remained in custody but were not indicted on any criminal charges.

The trial proceeded in the U.S. district court of New Haven, Connecticut, with the litigants disputing what should be done with the Africans, the cargo, and the ship. Anticipating that U.S. District Judge Andrew Judson would order the Africans turned over for criminal proceedings in Cuba, President MARTIN VAN BUREN ordered that the *U.S.S. Grampus* wait in the New Haven harbor to transport the Africans to Cuba immediately upon such a ruling.

The *U.S.S. Grampus* waited in vain. Judge Judson ordered that the kidnapping and enslavement had been illegal and that the United States must return the Africans to their homeland. The United States, now acting on behalf of the Spanish government and the claims of Montes and Ruiz, appealed to the U.S. CIRCUIT COURT, where Judge Judson's ruling was upheld. The United States appealed again, to the U.S. Supreme Court.

JOHN QUINCY ADAMS, a member of the U.S. House of Representatives on behalf of Massachusetts, former U.S. president, and sympathetic to the abolitionist movement, joined Baldwin in representing the Africans before the Supreme Court. Adams and Baldwin contended that the Africans should be granted their freedom because they had exercised their natural rights in fighting to escape illegal enslavement. The U.S. Supreme COURT OPINION, delivered by Justice JOSEPH STORY, affirmed the rulings by the lower courts, but instead of ordering the United States to return the Africans to Africa, declared them to be free and ordered them to be immediately discharged from custody (*United States v. Amistad*, 40 U.S. [15 Pet.] 518, 10 L. Ed. 826 [1841]).

While the *Amistad* case essentially presented questions of INTERNATIONAL LAW and did not involve any legal attacks on U.S. SLAVERY, it was important in U.S. history because of the attention and support it garnered for the abolitionist movement.

The Movie and Plagiarism

The 1997 movie by Steven Spielberg and his company, DreamWorks SKG, is a fictitious rendering of the real events that ensued between 1839 and 1841. But before the movie was released, an author who had written a historical novel about the uprising attempted to halt the film's release, charging the moviemakers with COPYRIGHT INFRINGEMENT. Filing suit in October 1997, Barbara Chase-Riboud sought $10 million in DAMAGES and screenwriting acknowledgment, based upon alleged PLAGIARISM of her novel, *Echo of Lions*. In December a federal district judge declined to delay the movie's opening, ruling that the similarities between the movie and the novel did not establish a probability of success for Chase-Riboud but did raise serious questions for trial.

The plagiarism suit took a strange turn in December 1997 when the *New York Times* reported that Chase-Riboud had plagiarized several passages of her 1986 book, *Valide: A Novel of the Harem*, from a nonfiction book published 50 years earlier. Chase-Riboud admitted to the *New York Times* that she had used material for *Valide* without attribution. DreamWorks also charged that Chase-Riboud had taken passages for *Echo of Lions* from a 1953 novel, *Slave Rebellion*, by William A. Owens, the book optioned by *Amistad* producers for the movie.

In early 1998 Chase-Riboud and DreamWorks settled the lawsuit for an undisclosed amount. In dropping the lawsuit, Chase-Riboud stated that she and her attorneys had concluded that neither Spielberg nor DreamWorks had done anything improper.

FURTHER READINGS

Chase-Riboud, Barbara. 1989. *Echo of Lions*. New York: Morrow.

Genovese, Eugene D. 1992. *Rebellion to Revolution: Afro-American Slave Revolts in the Making of the Modern World*. Baton Rouge, LA: Louisiana State Univ. Press.

Linder, Douglas O. 2000. "Salvaging Amistad." *Journal of Maritime Law and Commerce* 31, vol. 4 (October).

Weissman, Gary A. 1998. "The Legal Case behind the Movie Amistad" *The Hennepin Lawyer* 67 (August): 28–30.

CROSS REFERENCES

Abolition; Adams, John Quincy; Copyright; International Law; Kidnapping; Slavery; Story, Joseph; Van Buren, Martin.

AMNESTY

The action of a government by which all persons or certain groups of persons who have committed a criminal offense—usually of a political nature that threatens the sovereignty of the government (such as sedition or treason)—are granted immunity from prosecution.

Amnesty allows the government of a nation or state to "forget" criminal acts, usually before prosecution has occurred. Amnesty has traditionally been used as a political tool of compromise and reunion following a war. An act of amnesty is generally granted to a group of people who have committed crimes against the state, such as TREASON, rebellion, or desertion from the military. The first amnesty in U.S. history was offered by President GEORGE WASHINGTON in 1795, to participants in the WHISKEY REBELLION, a series of riots caused by an unpopular excise tax on liquor; a conditional amnesty, it allowed the U.S. government to forget the crimes of those involved, in exchange for their signatures on an OATH of loyalty to the United States. Other significant amnesties in U.S. history were granted on account of the Civil and Vietnam Wars.

Because there is no specific legislative or constitutional mention of amnesty, its nature is somewhat ambiguous. Its legal justification is drawn from Article 2, Section 2, of the Constitution, which states, "The President ... shall have Power to grant Reprieves and Pardons for Offences against the United States, except in Cases of Impeachment." Because of their common basis, the difference between amnesty and PARDON has been particularly vexing. In theory, an amnesty is granted before prosecution takes place, and a pardon after. However, even this basic distinction is blurry—President GERALD R. FORD, for example, granted a pardon to President RICHARD M. NIXON before Nixon was charged with any crime. Courts have allowed the two terms to be used interchangeably.

The earliest examples of amnesty are in Greek and ROMAN LAW. The best documented case of amnesty in the ancient world occurred in 403 b.c. A long-term CIVIL WAR in Athens was

With a portrait of Abraham Lincoln as a background, President Gerald Ford announces his order of conditional amnesty for thousands of Vietnam-era draft evaders and military deserters.

BETTMANN/CORBIS.

ended after a group dedicated to reuniting the city took over the government and arranged a general political amnesty. Effected by loyalty oaths taken by all Athenians, and only later made into law, the amnesty proclaimed the acts of both warring factions officially forgotten.

In other nations in which amnesties are accepted parts of the governing process, the power to grant amnesty sometimes lies with legislative bodies. In the United States, granting amnesties is primarily a power of the EXECUTIVE BRANCH, though on some occasions Congress may also initiate amnesties as part of legislation. The Immigration Reform and Control Act of 1986 (100 Stat. 3359, 8 U.S.C.A. § 1101) attempted to reduce the number of ALIENS illegally entering the United States by punishing employers who knowingly hired them. However, because of concerns voiced by both employers and immigrant community leaders, the act compromised: it contained provisions for an amnesty giving citizenship to illegal immigrants who had been residents for a set period of time.

Though the Supreme Court has given the opinion that Congress can grant an independent amnesty, it has never expressly ruled on the issue. However, the president's power to grant amnesty autonomously has never been in serious question. The president always has RECOURSE to the pardoning powers granted the office by the Constitution.

During the Civil War period, President ABRAHAM LINCOLN offered a series of amnesties without congressional assent to Union deserters, on the condition that they willingly rejoin their regiments. After the war, Lincoln issued a PROCLAMATION of amnesty for those who had participated in the rebellion. Though Congress protested the leniency of the plan, it was helpless to alter or halt it. Lincoln's amnesty was limited, requiring a loyalty oath and excluding high-ranking Confederate officers and political leaders. Lincoln hinted at but never offered a broader amnesty. It was not until President Andrew Johnson's Christmas amnesty proclamation of 1868 that an unconditional amnesty was granted to all participants in the Civil War. Amnesty used in this way fosters reconciliation—in this case, by fully relinquishing the Union's criminal complaints against those participating in the rebellion.

Amnesty was used for a similar purpose at the conclusion of the VIETNAM WAR. In 1974, President Ford attempted RECONCILIATION by declaring a conditional amnesty for those who had evaded the draft or deserted the armed forces. The terms of the amnesty required two years of public service (the length of a draft term), and gave evaders and deserters only five months to return to the fold. Many of those whom the amnesty was designed to benefit were dissatisfied, viewing the required service as punishment. On the other hand, many U.S. citizens agreed with President Nixon that *any* amnesty was out of the question. It was left to President JIMMY CARTER, in 1977, to issue a broad amnesty to draft evaders. Carter argued the distinction that their crimes were forgotten, not forgiven. This qualification makes clear the purpose of an amnesty: not to erase a criminal act, nor to condone or forgive it, but simply to facilitate political reconciliation.

Though an amnesty can be broad or narrow, covering one person or many, and can be seriously qualified (as long as the conditions are not unconstitutional), it cannot grant a license to commit future crimes. Nor can it forgive crimes not yet committed.

FURTHER READINGS

Barcroft, Peter. 1993. "The Presidential Pardon—A Flawed Solution." *Human Rights Law Journal* 14 (December).

Damico, Alfonso J. 1975. *Democracy and the Case for Amnesty.* Gainesville: Univ. Presses of Florida.

Hagan, John. 2001. *Northern Passage: American Vietnam War Resisters in Canada.* Cambridge, MA: Harvard Univ. Press.

Kane, Joseph N. and Janet Podell 2009. *Facts about the Presidents.* New York: Wilson.

Norton, Mary Beth, et al., eds. 1991. *A People and a Nation.* 6th ed. Boston: Houghton Mifflin.

Slye, Ronald C. 2002. "The Legitimacy of Amnesties under International Law and General Principles of Anglo-American Law: Is a Legitimate Amnesty Possible?" *Virginia Journal of International Law* 43 (fall).

Young, Gwen K. 2002. "Amnesty and Accountability." *U.C. Davis Law Review* 35 (January).

AMNESTY INTERNATIONAL

Amnesty International (AI) is a NONPROFIT, independent international organization that works zealously to protect HUMAN RIGHTS around the world. Since its inception in 1961, Amnesty International has coordinated research, information, and education campaigns in order to focus world attention on such issues as freedom of conscience and expression, freedom from discrimination, and the cessation of physical and mental abuse and torture suffered by the victims of human rights violations.

With a membership of more than 2.2 million people and supporters and donors in more than 150 countries and regions, Amnesty International is the world's largest grassroots human rights organization. The organization was started by a British lawyer, Peter Benenson, who in a 1961 article in *The Observer* posited that the pressure of public opinion could be brought to bear on those who were imprisoning, torturing, and killing people based on their political opinions. Benenson wrote in support of several political prisoners whom he termed "prisoners of conscience" because they had been imprisoned for expressing their beliefs in a peaceful manner. The term came to encompass all men, women, and children who have been imprisoned because of their political or religious beliefs.

Amnesty International carries out its struggle for human dignity for all human rights victims by mobilizing public opinion throughout the world to pressure government officials and other influential persons to stop human rights abuses. Violations of human rights include the following: torture of a person and/ or his or her family members by mental or physical means, the "disappearance" of persons considered to be enemies of the state, the imposition by governments of the death PENALTY, the death of those held in custody or being detained, and the forcible return of persons to countries where they face torture or death. Amnesty International describes "disappeared persons" as persons who are taken into custody, kept hidden and unable to communicate with others, and whose whereabouts are denied by the government agents who arrested them. The prisoners are often tortured. If they are not murdered, they can be held incommunicado for years while the government agents responsible routinely deny that they have custody of these prisoners or knowledge of their fates and often suggest that the prisoners have "disappeared" of their own volition.

Amnesty International's primary goals include the following: (1) stopping violence against women; (2) defending the rights and dignity of individuals trapped in poverty; (3) abolition of the death penalty, torture, and other degrading punishment; (4) ending EXTRAJUDICIAL executions and "disappearances" (5) freeing prisoners of conscience; (6) protecting the rights of REFUGEES and migrants; (7) regulating the global arms trade and (8) working to ensure that the perpetrators of human rights abuses are brought to justice in accordance with international standards. Over time, Amnesty International has expanded its scope to cover human rights abuses committed by non-governmental bodies and private individuals, including armed political groups. The organization has also begun to focus on human rights abuses in homes or communities where governments have permitted such abuses or failed to take action to stop them.

Amnesty International does not accept government funding and remains independent of governmental, economic, or political interests. It has no religious affiliations. Members include people of various religious, political, and societal points of view who share the common goals mentioned above. Financial support for the organization comes from individual members and groups as well as trusts, foundations, and companies that are committed to support the cause of human rights worldwide.

The central body of Amnesty International is the International Secretariat, which is located in London. The organization has more than 350 staff members and more than 100 volunteers from more than 50 countries around the world.

Amnesty International is a democratic, self-governing body that is led by a nine-member International Executive Committee (EIC). The International Council that represents the sections elects committee members every two years. The organization consists of more than 7,800 groups representing local activists, youths, specialists, and professionals in more than 100 countries and territories. The organization has nationally organized sections in 80 countries.

Amnesty International members and supporters "wage peace" in numerous ways ranging from writing individual letters of support to participating in public demonstrations. The organization raises public awareness through educational information for school children and other groups, training programs for teachers, the encouragement of training programs for government officials and security personnel, INTERNET communications, and fund-raising concerts. In addition to reporting on human rights issues and LOBBYING members of government both privately and publicly, the organization works with other nongovernmental organizations (NGOs) as well as community organizations and human rights activists to secure its goals. Advocacy efforts range from targeted appeals for support of a single individual to worldwide campaigns concerning specific countries or issues. Each year, the organization highlights a particular country or human rights issue and mobilizes its members and supporters to focus global opinion to achieve change.

In nearly 50 years of work, Amnesty International delegates have visited numerous countries and territories and met with human rights victims, observed trials, and interviewed local activists and officials.

Under the auspices of Amnesty International, research teams focus on particular countries in which they investigate reports of human rights abuses. The organization strives to be rigorous in its investigations, checking and cross-checking information and trying to get corroboration from as many sources as possible. Information comes from interviews and meetings with prisoners and their families, lawyers, and journalists, as well as persons working for other human rights organizations, humanitarian agencies, and local community groups. Investigators also monitor the information contained in newspapers, journals, and Web sites. In addition, whenever possible, investigators observe trial proceedings and meet with government officials. Where reports of abuses arise in countries that deny access to Amnesty International, the organization relies on outside sources such as reports from news media and interviews with refugees, diplomats, and other sources.

To ensure accuracy and impartiality, the organization's International Secretariat approves the text of all organization statements or reports. If information is alleged rather than based on observable facts, the organization notes that the statements are based on allegations. If a statement or report contains errors, Amnesty International is quick to acknowledge its mistakes. As a result, the organization has a worldwide reputation for accuracy and reliability. In 1977 Amnesty International was awarded the Nobel Peace Prize, and in 1978 the organization received a UNITED NATIONS Human Rights Award.

The organization's specialist networks include the following: Lawyers' Network, which helped with RATIFICATION of legislation to establish the INTERNATIONAL CRIMINAL COURT; the Military Security and Police Network, which continues to campaign for the control of electroshock WEAPONS and other arms used to commit human rights abuses; the Company Approaches Network, which works with companies to help them develop policies that are compatible with human rights standards; the Children's Network, which lobbies states to help prohibit the involvement of "children soldiers" in armed conflicts; the Women's Network and the Lesbian, Gay, Bisexual, and Transgender Network, which have campaigned on numerous issues concerning torture and ill-treatment based on gender and/or sexual orientation; and the Medical Network, which consists of doctors, nurses, psychologists, and other health professionals who have provided aid to victims of torture and other types of abuse.

The organization developed its first global campaign against torture in 1973, and in 1984 the United Nations (UN) passed the Convention Against Torture, which called for governments to punish those who committed torture within their jurisdictions and which took effect in June of 1987. As of 2008, 146 of the 192 UN member nations had ratified the Convention.

In 2001 Amnesty International continued its focus on the torture and abuse of women, children, ethnic minorities, and persons discriminated against based on sexual orientation including homosexual, bisexual, and transgendered persons. At year's end, more than 35,000 persons from 188 countries had signed up at AI's Web site, www.stoptorture.org, indicating their willingness to send E-MAIL appeals regarding urgent cases. In the same year, Amnesty International supporters took action on behalf of more than 2,813 persons who were identified as being the victims of human rights abuses.

The Internet has been extremely useful to Amnesty International in reaching members to quickly organize campaigns and to mobilize for other purposes. Via its Web site, e-mail, and other methods of communication, the organization issues "Urgent Actions," Rapid Response Actions, and special campaign appeals. Over time, Amnesty International has proven that a steady stream of letters, faxes, e-mails, and other communications sent to government officials and others regarding the fate of a particular person or group of persons, has a tangible effect. Torture and mistreatment have been stopped and, in a number of cases, the subjects of the letter campaigns have been released. AI members and supporters are also encouraged to send positive letters and other communications to governments that have released prisoners or taken other steps to alleviate human rights abuses in order to reinforce the importance to the global community of these cases.

Amnesty International has been a major factor in a number of victories, including an international agreement to ban torture, an increasing number of countries that reject CAPITAL PUNISHMENT, and, in 2003, the inauguration of the International Criminal Court in the Hague, Netherlands. In December 2006 Amnesty International also helped with the United Nation's adoption of the International Convention for the Protection of All Persons from Enforced Disappearance. This treaty is considered to be one of the strongest human rights treaties ever adopted by the United Nations. The goal of the convention is to prevent enforced disappearance from taking place and to punish the perpetrators as well as provide reparations to the victims and their families. Amnesty International has been working to urge countries to ratify the convention and have it implemented. In 2003 Amnesty International established the "Control Arms" campaign, which calls for a legally binding international Arms Trade Treaty that help control arms by having governments take action on international arms control. Since its inception in 2003, the Control Arms campaign has more than one million supporters worldwide. In addition, in December 2006 the United Nations General Assembly had 153 countries vote for a RESOLUTION to start the process for a global Arms Trade Treaty.

Despite its successes, the organization continues to face many obstacles. Although torture has been banned by international agreement, it continues secretly in many countries. Moreover, the governments and political organizations of numerous countries still permit or participate in the wrongful IMPRISONMENT and the disappearance of political prisoners as well as other human rights abuses.

FURTHER READINGS

Amnesty International Website. Available online at http://www.amnesty.org. (accessed September 23, 2009).

Clark, Anne Marie. 2001. *Diplomacy of Conscience: Amnesty International and Changing Human Rights Norms.* Princeton, N.J.: Princeton University Press.

Schulz, William. 2002. *In Our Own Best Interests: How Defending Human Rights Benefits Us All.* Boston: Beacon.

CROSS REFERENCES

International Court of Justice; International Law; Prisoner of War; Prisoners' Rights.

AMORTIZATION

The reduction of a debt incurred, for example, in the purchase of stocks or bonds, by regular payments consisting of interest and part of the principal made over a specified time period upon the expiration of which the entire debt is repaid. A mortgage is amortized when it is repaid with periodic payments over a particular term. After a certain portion of each payment is applied to the interest on the debt, any balance reduces the principal.

The allocation of the cost of an intangible asset, for example, a patent or copyright, over its estimated useful life that is considered an expense of doing business and is used to offset the earnings of the asset by its declining value. If an intangible asset has an indefinite life, such as good will, it cannot be amortized.

Amortization is not the same as depreciation, which is the allocation of the original cost of a tangible asset computed over its anticipated useful life, based on its physical wear and tear and the passage of time. Amortization of intangible assets and depreciation of tangible assets are used for tax purposes to reduce the yearly income generated by the assets by their decreasing values so that the tax imposed upon the earnings of assets is less. Amortization differs from depletion, which is a reduction in the book value of a natural resource, such as a mineral, resulting from its conversion into a marketable product. Depletion is used for a similar tax purpose as amortization and depreciation—to reduce the yearly income generated by the asset by the expenses involved in its sale so that less tax will be due.

AMOTION

Putting out; removal; taking away; dispossession of lands.

Amotion essentially means the deprivation of possession. The term has been used to describe a wrongful SEIZURE of personal chattels.

The most common legal use of the word is in corporation law. In that context, amotion is the ousting of an officer from his or her post in the corporation prior to the end of the term for which the officer was appointed or elected, without taking away the person's right to be a member of the corporation. It can be distinguished from DISFRANCHISEMENT, which is the total expulsion of a corporation's officer or official representative.

AMOUNT IN CONTROVERSY

The value of the relief demanded or the amount of monetary damages claimed in a lawsuit.

Some courts have jurisdiction, or the power to hear cases, only if the amount in controversy is more or less than an amount specified by law. For example, federal district courts can hear lawsuits concerning questions of federal law and controversies between citizens of different states, but they can do this only if the amount in controversy is more than $50,000. Some lower-level state courts, such as those that hear small claims, have no authority to hear controversies involving more than certain maximum amounts.

When the amount in controversy determines the court's authority to hear a particular case, it may also be called the jurisdictional amount.

ANALOGY

The inference that two or more things that are similar to each other in some respects are also similar in other respects.

An analogy denotes that similarity exists in some characteristics of things that are otherwise not alike.

A sample legal form involving amortization

Amortization Provision with an Acceleration Clause

MORTGAGE

THIS INDENTURE, made as of the _____ day of _____, 20__, by and between _____, (Mortgagor), and _____, (Mortgagee).

AMOUNT OF LIEN:

WHEREAS, Mortgagor is justly indebted to Mortgagee in the sum of _____ dollars ($ ____) and has agreed to pay the same, with interest thereon, according to the terms of a certain note (Note) given by Mortgagor to Mortgagee, which is attached hereto as Exhibit A.

DESCRIPTION OF PROPERTY SUBJECT TO LIEN:

NOW, THEREFORE, in consideration of the premises and the sum set forth above, and to secure the payment of the Secured Indebtedness as defined herein, Mortgagor by these presents does grant, bargain, sell and convey unto Mortgagee the property located at _____,

more particularly described as:

Together with all buildings, structures and other improvements now or hereafter located on, above or below the surface of the property; and,

Together with all the common elements appurtenant to any parcel, unit or lot which is all or part of the Premises; and,

ALL the foregoing encumbered by this Mortgage being collectively referred to herein as the Premises;

TO HAVE AND TO HOLD the Premises hereby granted to the use, benefit and behalf of the Mortgagee, forever. Conditioned, however, that if Mortgagor shall promptly pay or cause to be paid to Mortgagee, at its address listed in the Note, or at such other place, which may hereafter be designated by Mortgagee, its successors or assigns, with interest, the principal sum of _____ dollars ($_____) with final maturity, if not sooner paid, as stated in said Note unless amended or extended according to the terms of the Note executed by Mortgagor and payable to the order of Mortgagee, then these presents shall cease and be void, otherwise these presents shall remain in full force and effect.

COVENANTS OF MORTGAGOR

Mortgagor covenants and agrees with Mortgagee as follows:

Secured Indebtedness. This Mortgage is given as security for the Note and also as security for any and all other sums, indebtedness, obligations and liabilities of any and every kind arising, under the Note or this Mortgage, as amended or modified or supplemented from time to time, and any and all renewals, modifications or extensions of any or all of the foregoing (all of which are collectively referred to herein as the Secured Indebtedness), the entire Secured Indebtedness being equally secured with and having the same priority as any amounts owed at the date hereof.

Performance of Note, Mortgage, Etc. Mortgagor shall perform, observe and comply with all provisions hereof and of the Note and shall promptly pay, in lawful money of the United States of America, to Mortgagee the Secured Indebtedness with interest thereon as provided in the Note, this Mortgage and all other documents constituting the Secured Indebtedness.

Extent Of Payment Other Than Principal And Interest. Mortgagor shall pay, when due and payable, (1) all taxes, assessments, general or special, and other charges levied on, or assessed, placed or made against the Premises, this instrument or the Secured Indebtedness or any interest of the Mortgagee in the Premises or the obligations secured hereby; (2) premiums on policies of fire and other hazard insurance covering the Premises, as required herein; (3) ground rents or other lease rentals; and (4) other sums related to the Premises or the indebtedness secured hereby, if any, payable by Mortgagor.

Care of Property. Mortgagor shall maintain the Premises in good condition and repair and shall not commit or suffer any material waste to the Premises.

Prior Mortgage. With regard to the Prior Mortgage, Mortgagor hereby agrees to: (1) Pay promptly, when due, all installments of principal and interest and all other sums and charges made payable by the Prior Mortgage; (2) Promptly perform and observe all of the terms, covenants and conditions required to be performed and observed by Mortgagor under the Prior Mortgage, within the period provided in said Prior Mortgage; (3) Promptly notify Mortgagee of any default, or notice claiming any event of default by Mortgagor in the performance or observance of any term, covenant or condition to be performed or observed by Mortgagor under any such Prior Mortgage. (4) Mortgagor will not request nor will it accept any voluntary future advances under the Prior

Mortgage without Mortgagee's prior written consent, which consent shall not be unreasonably withheld.

[continued]

Amortization Provision with an Acceleration Clause

DEFAULTS

Default. The occurrence of any one of the following events which shall not be cured within _____ days after written notice of the occurrence of the event, if the default is monetary, or which shall not be cured within _____ days after written notice, if the default is non-monetary, shall constitute an Event of Default: (1) Mortgagor fails to pay the Secured Indebtedness, or any part thereof, or the taxes, insurance and other charges, as herein before provided, when and as the same shall become due and payable; (2) Any material warranty of Mortgagor herein contained, or contained in the Note, proves untrue or misleading in any material respect; (3) Mortgagor materially fails to keep, observe, perform, carry out and execute the covenants, agreements, obligations and conditions set out in this Mortgage, or in the Note; (4) Foreclosure proceedings (whether judicial or otherwise) are instituted on any mortgage or any lien of any kind secured by any portion of the Premises and affecting the priority of this Mortgage.

Upon the occurrence of any Event of Default, the Mortgagee may immediately do any one or more of the following: (1) Declare the total Secured Indebtedness, including without limitation all payments for taxes, assessments, insurance premiums, liens, costs, expenses and attorney's fees herein specified, without notice to Mortgagor (such notice being hereby expressly waived), to be due and payable at once, by foreclosure or otherwise; (2) In the event that Mortgagee elects to accelerate the maturity of the Secured Indebtedness and declares the Secured Indebtedness to be due and payable in full at once as provided for herein, or as may be provided for in the Note, then Mortgagee shall have the right to pursue all of Mortgagee's rights and remedies for the collection of such Secured Indebtedness, whether such rights and remedies are granted by this Mortgage, any other agreement, law, equity or otherwise, to include, without limitation, the institution of foreclosure proceedings against the Premises under the terms of this Mortgage and any applicable state or federal law.

MISCELLANEOUS PROVISIONS

Prior Liens. Mortgagor shall keep the Premises free from all prior liens (except for those consented to by Mortgagee).

Notice, Demand and Request. Every provision for notice and demand or request shall be deemed fulfilled by written notice and demand or request delivered in accordance with the provisions of the Note relating to notice.

Severability. If any provision of this Mortgage shall, for any reason and to any extent, be invalid or unenforceable, the remainder of the instrument in which such provision is contained, shall be enforced to the maximum extent permitted by law.

Governing Law. The terms and provisions of this Mortgage are to be governed by the laws of the State of _____. No payment of interest or in the nature of interest for any debt secured in part by this Mortgage shall exceed the maximum amount permitted by law.

Descriptive Headings. The descriptive headings used herein are for convenience of reference only, and they are not intended to have any effect whatsoever in determining the rights or obligations of the Mortgagor or Mortgagee and they shall not be used in the interpretation or construction hereof.

Attorneys' Fees. As used in this Mortgage, attorneys' fees shall include, but not be limited to, fees incurred in all matters of collection and enforcement, construction and interpretation, before, during and after suit, trial, proceedings and appeals. Attorneys' fees shall also include hourly charges for paralegals, law clerks and other staff members operating under the supervision of an attorney.

Exculpation. Notwithstanding anything contained herein to the contrary, the Note which this Mortgage secures is a non-recourse Note and such Note shall be enforced against Mortgagor only to the extent of Mortgagor's interest in the Premises as described herein and to the extent of Mortgagor's interest in any personalty as may be described herein.

IN WITNESS WHEREOF, the Mortgagor has caused this instrument to be duly executed as of the day and year first above written.

_____
Mortgagor

STATE OF)
COUNTY OF)

Subscribed and sworn before me this the _____ day of _____, 20_____.

Witness my hand and seal.

_____ My commission expires:
Notary Public

Warning:

These forms are provided AS IS. They may not be any good. Even if they are good in one jurisdiction, they may not work in another. And the facts of your situation may make these forms inappropriate for you. They are for informational purposes only, and you should consult an attorney before using them.

In a legal argument, an analogy may be used when there is no PRECEDENT (prior CASE LAW close in facts and legal principles) in point. Reasoning by analogy involves referring to a case that concerns unrelated subject matter but is governed by the same general principles and applying those principles to the case at hand.

ANARCHISM

The theory espousing a societal state in which there is no structured government or law or in which there is resistance to all current forms of government.

Anarchists promote the absence of rules, which leads to the absence of any identifiable social structure beyond that of personal autonomy. When anarchy becomes defined by one anarchist, other anarchists may feel bound to change it.

Anarchism thus means different things to different believers. Anarchists do not hold common views on subjects such as desirable levels of community cooperation and the role of large industry in society. Another matter of continuing debate is whether anarchy is an end unto itself or simply the best means to a better government. To all anarchists, though, anarchy is the best refuge from political dogma and authority. Moreover, many anarchists agree that anarchism begins with the notion that people are inherently good, or even perfect, and that external authority—laws, governments, institutions, and so forth—limits human potential. External authority, they suggest, brings a corruption of the innocent human spirit and a ceiling on achievement.

Commentators on anarchism differentiate between "classical" theories of anarchy and more modern movements. Classical anarchists focused more heavily on the opposition to state control and capitalist society. Their strongest opposition was directed at government and the church. Many of the early anarchists were essentially socialists, and anarchist theories played a significant part in the socialist movements during the early twentieth century.

Beginning in about the 1960s, anarchism shifted its focus to a more general opposition to public and private hierarchy and domination of the working class. Modern anarchists tend to focus upon such issues as those related to patriarchy, racism, nature, and technology, and the effects these concepts have on society. One camp of anarchist theorists advocates a theory of anarcho-syndicalism, and those that subscribe to this theory promote a massive, leaderless movement of the working class intended to take control from those with public and private authority.

Modern anarchists directed their opposition against such pro-capitalist and quasi-governmental entities as the World Trade Organization, the WORLD BANK, and the INTERNATIONAL MONETARY FUND. Anarchists became the focus of national attention in the late 1990s and early 2000s when they staged massive protests against World Trade Organization meetings in such U.S. cities as Seattle, Washington, and Eugene, Oregon. Although anarchists claim these protests were peaceful until law enforcement officers disrupted them, others consider these anarchists to be violent and unruly revolutionaries.

William Godwin (1756–1836) is widely regarded as the first to give anarchy a comprehensive intellectual foundation. Godwin, the son of a Calvinist minister, argued that the state and its laws were enslaving people instead of freeing them. According to Godwin, government was necessary only to prevent injustice and external invasion. With every person educated in sincerity, independence, self-restraint, and seriousness, any more governmental activity would be unnecessary.

Godwin opposed the rise of liberal democracy in the late 1700s. In the wake of the American and French Revolutions, he observed, "electioneering is a trade so despicably degrading, so eternally incompatible with moral and mental dignity that I can scarcely believe a truly great mind capable of the dirty drudgery of such vice." Godwin's observations and proposals were largely ignored during his lifetime, but they informed anarchists several decades later, when the brutal working conditions and "wage slavery" of industrialism began to present new reasons for revolt.

Two well-known anarchists, EMMA GOLDMAN (1869–1940) and Alexander Berkman (1870–1936), gained recognition in the 1890s. Goldman, the daughter of Jewish merchants, immigrated to the United States from Russia in 1885 at the age of 16. In Rochester, New York, Goldman worked in a sweat shop—a large, unsafe factory that paid low wages and demanded long hours. The experience radicalized Goldman, and with her natural flair for public speaking, she soon became a spokeswoman for anarchism. Goldman worked extensively for the INDUSTRIAL WORKERS OF THE WORLD (IWW), an organization dedicated to *anarcho-syndicalism,* which seeks to use the INDUSTRIAL UNION as the basis for a reorganization of society. Goldman's cross-country lecture tours, in which she addressed a broad range of social topics in German and English, earned her a reputation as a witty speaker and provocative thinker. A voracious reader and a magazine publisher, Goldman gave voice to ideas on sexuality, free love, BIRTH CONTROL, and family structures that shocked members of her generation, including fellow anarchists.

Like many devout anarchists, Goldman had trouble with the law. She was imprisoned for a year for allegedly inciting a RIOT during a New York City hunger demonstration in 1893. Goldman also served a two-week sentence for distributing illegal birth control information. She was jailed on suspicion of complicity in the ASSASSINATION of President WILLIAM MCKINLEY, in 1901. In 1917 she was arrested with Berkman for participating in antiwar protests, and both were charged with violating the Selective Service Act of 1917 (40 Stat. 76) by inducing young men to resist the draft. Goldman and Berkman were convicted, and, despite appeals to the U.S. Supreme Court, both served prison terms. Upon release in 1919, they were deported to Russia.

Berkman, Goldman's ally, shared Goldman's passion for breaking social barriers and inspiring creative thought. He also possessed a violent streak. In 1892 he was arrested for attempting to assassinate steel magnate HENRY CLAY Frick during a steel strike. After serving a 14-year prison sentence, Berkman devoted the rest of his life to freeing imprisoned political radicals and promoting workers' rights. He remained a close companion of Goldman until his death in 1936.

Goldman and Berkman cut dashing figures as romantic, intellectual anarchists, and they played no small part in a modest rise of anarchism in the early 1900s. Although anarchism still gains followers in colleges and universities and among self-styled intellectuals, it has been mostly dormant as a social force since the Great Depression of the 1930s.

Many anarchists have suffered the bemusing fate of being convicted for breaking laws in which they do not believe. However, the justice system does occasionally protect the anarchist. In *Fiske v. Kansas,* 274 U.S. 380, 47 S. Ct. 655, 71 L. Ed. 1108 (1927), Harold B. Fiske was charged in Rice County, Kansas, with violating the Kansas Criminal Syndicalism Act (Laws Sp. Sess. 1920, c. 37). Fiske had been arrested for promoting the Workers' Industrial Union (WIU), an organization devoted in part to establishing worker control of industry and the abolition of the wage system.

Under the syndicalism statute in Kansas, any person advocating "the duty, necessity, propriety or expediency of crime, criminal syndicalism, or SABOTAGE . . . is guilty of a felony" (1920 Kan. Sess. Laws ch. 37, § 3). Criminal syndicalism was defined as the advocation of crime, physical violence, or destruction of property "as a means of effecting industrial or political revolution, or for profit" (§ 1). Kansas authorities charged Fiske with criminal syndicalism, citing only the PREAMBLE to the constitution of the IWW, the parent organization of Fiske's WIU. This preamble stated, in part, that "a struggle must go on until the workers of the World organize as a class, take possession of the earth, and the machinery of production and abolish the wage system" (*Fiske*).

The U.S. Supreme Court found insufficient evidence against Fiske to WARRANT CONVICTION of criminal syndicalism. According to the Court, there was no suggestion that "getting possession of the machinery of production and abolishing the wage system, was to be accomplished by other than lawful means." The Court confirmed that a state may enact legislation to protect its government from INSURRECTION, but it may not be arbitrary or unreasonable in policing its citizens who advocate changes in the social order.

FURTHER READINGS

Brailsford, Henry N. 2007. *Shelley, Godwin, and their Circle (1919).* Whitefish, MT: Kessinger.

Goldman, Emma. 1970. *Living My Life.* 2 vols. Reprint. New York: Dover.

Joll, James. *1979 The Anarchists.* 2d ed. Boston: Little, Brown.

Nozick, Robert. 1977. *Anarchy, State and Utopia.* New York: Basic.

Sonn, Richard D. 1992. *Anarchism.* New York: Twayne.

CROSS REFERENCES

Chicago Eight; Freedom of Speech; Goldman, Emma; Industrial Workers of the World; Rousseau, Jean Jacques.

ANCIENT LIGHTS

A doctrine of English common law that gives a landowner an easement or right by prescription to the unobstructed passage of light and air from adjoining land if the landowner has had uninterrupted use of the lights for twenty years.

Once a person gains the right to ancient lights, the OWNER of the adjoining land cannot obscure them, such as by erecting a building. If the neighbor does so, he or she can be sued under a theory of nuisance, and DAMAGES could be awarded.

The doctrine of ancient lights has not been adopted in the United States because it would greatly hinder commercial and residential growth and the expansion of towns and cities.

ANCIENT WRITING

An original document affecting the transfer of real property, which can be admitted as evidence in a lawsuit because its aged condition and its location upon discovery sufficiently establish its authenticity.

Under COMMON LAW, an ancient writing, sometimes called an ancient document, could be offered as evidence only if certain conditions were met. The document had to be at least thirty years old, the equivalent of a generation. It had to appear genuine and free from suspicion. For example, if the date of the document or the signatures of the parties to it appeared to have been altered, it was not considered genuine. When found, the document must have been in a likely location or in the possession of a person who would logically have had access to it, such as a deed found in the office of the county clerk or in the custody of the attorney for one of the parties to the writing. An ancient writing must also have related to the transfer of real property, for example, a will, a deed, or a mortgage. When all these requirements were met, an ancient writing was presumed to be genuine upon its presentation for admission as evidence without any additional proof.

In the early twenty-first century, various state rules of evidence and the FEDERAL RULES OF EVIDENCE have expanded the admissibility of ancient writings. An ancient writing can now be offered as evidence if its condition does not suggest doubt as to its authenticity, if it is found in a likely place, and if it is at least twenty years old at the time it is presented for admission into evidence.

Some states still adhere to the requirement that a document be at least thirty years old before it comes within the ancient writing exception to the HEARSAY rule. A few states recognize ancient documents only if, in addition to these basic requirements, the person seeking the admission of the ancient writing has taken possession of the property in question.

An ancient writing is admissible in a trial as an exception to the rule that prohibits hearsay from being used as evidence in a trial. In a case where no other evidence exists, the legitimacy of the writing must be considered if the case is to be determined on its merits. The probability that such a document is trustworthy is determined by its condition and location upon discovery. These factors permit a court and a jury to presume the authenticity of an ancient writing.

ANCILLARY

Subordinate; aiding. A legal proceeding that is not the primary dispute but which aids the judgment rendered in or the outcome of the main action. A descriptive term that denotes a legal claim, the existence of which is dependent upon or reasonably linked to a main claim.

For example, a PLAINTIFF wins a judgment for a specified sum of money against a DEFENDANT in a NEGLIGENCE action. The defendant refuses to pay the judgment. The plaintiff begins another proceeding for a WRIT of attachment so that the judgment will be satisfied by the sale of the defendant's property seized under the writ. The attachment proceeding is ancillary, or subordinate, to the negligence suit. An ancillary proceeding is sometimes called an ancillary suit or bill.

A claim for ALIMONY is an ancillary claim dependent upon the primary claim that there are sufficient legal grounds for a court to grant a DIVORCE.

ANCILLARY ADMINISTRATION

The settlement and distribution of a decedent's property in the state where it is located and which is other than the state in which the decedent was domiciled.

Ancillary administration occurs in a state to enable an executor or administrator to collect assets or to commence LITIGATION on behalf of the estate in that jurisdiction.

ANIMAL RIGHTS

Originally referring to the protection of animals from cruel and inhumane treatment, the concept of animal rights has expanded to keep pace with scientific research confirming that many species are sentient beings (capable of emotion and feeling, as distinguished from perception and thought). This awareness has led not only to a greater appreciation and protection of animals, but also to a correlative expansion of animal rights, even to the point of acknowledging, but not as of 2009 fully embracing, the concept of animals as fellow creatures with independent rights to an unfettered existence. Despite this growing awareness, the focus of animal rights laws remains in the early 2000s directed toward proscribing certain forms of inhumane and merciless treatment in medical and scientific research and in the transportation, handling of, and slaughter of animals in the meat and poultry industries and for human consumption.

By the end of the twentieth century, membership in animal advocacy organizations had reached more than 10 million people in the United States and opposition to the use of animals in laboratory experiments was rapidly growing. Some 76 medical schools claimed that demonstrations and break-ins by animal rights advocates had cost them more than $4.5 million, according to a report from the Association of American Medical Colleges.

As the conflict between animal rights activists and medical and scientific researchers has grown, federal and state regulation of activities involving animal research has also expanded. At the federal level, the Animal Welfare Act (7 U.S.C.A. § 2131 et seq. [1994]) regulates the treatment of animals used in federally funded research. Under amendments added to the act in 1985, the secretary of agriculture was required to PROMULGATE standards to govern the humane handling, care, treatment, and transportation of animals by dealers, research facilities, and exhibitors. These

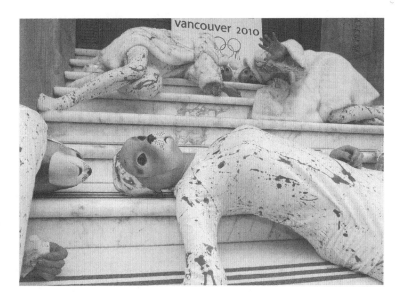

Members of People for the Ethical Treatment of Animals (PETA) protest seal hunting. The group has had a significant impact on the use of animals in medical and scientific research.

JENNY/WIREIMAGE/
GETTY IMAGES

standards were to include minimum requirements for housing, feeding, watering, sanitation, ventilation, shelter from extremes of weather and temperature, adequate veterinary care, and separation by species where necessary; for exercise of dogs, as determined by an attending veterinarian; and for a physical environment adequate to promote the psychological well-being of primates. In addition, the standards were to include requirements for animal care, treatment, and practices in experimental procedures in research facilities.

In 1991 the Secretary of Agriculture issued final regulations under the act (56 Fed. Reg. 6426; 9 C.F.R. § 3). Shortly thereafter, two animal rights organizations, the Animal Legal Defense Fund and the Society for Animal Protective Legislation, along with several individuals, sued the U.S. DEPARTMENT OF AGRICULTURE (USDA), claiming that the final regulations were arbitrary and capricious, in violation of the Administrative Procedure Act (APA) (5 U.S.C. A. § 551 et seq. [1994]). Under the APA, a court can compel agency action that is unlawfully withheld or unreasonably delayed and can set aside agency action that is arbitrary and capricious, an ABUSE OF DISCRETION, or otherwise in violation of the law.

The plaintiffs challenged the USDA on several grounds, including the lack of minimum requirements regarding exercise for dogs and the psychological well-being of primates; the amount of delay permitted under the regulations in complying with new cage requirements; and the loophole in the regulations' provision for special cage designs, which permitted facilities to evade the existing minimum requirements for cage sizes.

In February 1993 a federal district court found that the USDA treatment of laboratory animals waiting to be used in biomedical experiments violated federal statutes providing for the humane treatment of such animals. In *Animal Legal Defense Fund v. Secretary of Agriculture* (813 F. Supp. 882 [1993]), the U.S. District Court for the District of Columbia ruled that the regulations enacted by the secretary of agriculture and the USDA failed to comply with the mandate of Congress to ensure the well-being and humane treatment of animals.

The defendants appealed the district court's decision. In *Animal Legal Defense Fund v. Espy* (29 F.3d 720 [1994]), the U.S. Court of Appeals for the District of Columbia Circuit ruled that the animal rights organizations and other plaintiffs did not have standing to challenge the USDA. (*Standing* is a legal requirement that the PLAINTIFF must have been injured or threatened with injury by the action complained of and focuses on the question of whether the plaintiff is the proper party to bring the lawsuit.) Because the plaintiffs lacked standing, the court ordered that the case be dismissed.

The act was again amended (7 U.S.C.A. § 2132(g)) by P.L. 107–171 to expand the definition of *animal* to include any warm-blooded animal, but expressly excluded birds, rats of the genus Rattus, and mice of the genus Mus; horses not used for research purposes, and other farm animals. These exclusions have been the subject of controversy and LITIGATION. Although the statute required the National Research Council to submit to the House and Senate Agricultural committees a report summarizing the implications of including the above-excluded species in the definition, as of 2008, the CONGRESSIONAL RESEARCH SERVICE had not indicated that any existed.

Whereas the Animal Welfare Act governs the general treatment of research animals, other federal statutes govern the testing procedures that may be used on animals in the course of scientific and commercial research and in product testing. The Toxic Substances Control Act (15 U.S.C.A. § 2601 et seq. [1994]) authorizes the use of two procedures that have been particularly controversial: the Draize test and the lethal dose 50 (LD50) test.

The Draize test measures the irritancy of a substance such as a cosmetic or pesticide by applying it to the eyes of live rabbits for 24 hours. The LD50 test is used to calculate the median lethal dose of a substance by feeding it to a defined population of animals until 50 percent of them die. Some product manufacturers, such as Avon Products, Revlon, Faberge, Amway Corporation, Mary Kay Cosmetics, and Noxell Corporation, have discontinued some or all animal testing as a result of continued protests over the use of these tests.

The FEDERAL BUREAU OF INVESTIGATION reported numerous incidents of VANDALISM annually at research facilities and attacks on researchers themselves. In response, the U.S. Congress and numerous state legislatures enacted protective legislation. In August 1992 Congress passed the Animal Enterprise Protection Act (18 U.S.C.A. § 43 [1994]), which provides, in part, that anyone who "intentionally causes physical disruption to the functioning of an animal enterprise by intentionally stealing, damaging, or causing the loss of any property (including animals or records) used by the animal enterprise, and thereby causes economic damage exceeding $10,000 to that enterprise, or conspires to do so shall be fined under this title or imprisoned not more than one year, or both."

If serious bodily injury or death to another person occurs in the course of the prohibited activity, the statute provides for IMPRISONMENT up to a life term. The act defines an animal enterprise as "(A) a commercial or academic enterprise that uses animals for food or fiber production, agriculture, research, or testing; (B) a zoo, aquarium, circus, rodeo, or lawful competitive animal event; or (C) any fair or similar event intended to advance agricultural arts and sciences."

By 1995 the following states had passed similar legislation: Alabama, Arizona, Arkansas, Colorado, Georgia, Idaho, Illinois, Louisiana, Massachusetts, Minnesota, Missouri, Montana, Nebraska, New York, North Carolina, North Dakota, Oregon, South Carolina, Tennessee, Virginia, Washington, and Wisconsin.

Several states also regulate the use of animals kept in pounds for use in research. Maine prohibits the use of pound animals for any research (Me. Rev. Stat. Ann. tit. 17, § 1025 [West 1994]). California requires that any pound or animal regulation department where animals are turned over to a research facility post a sign stating "Animals Turned in to This Shelter May Be Used for Research Purposes," in a clearly visible place (Cal. Civ. Code § 1834.7 [West 1994]). In Oklahoma, pounds are required to supply unclaimed animals to research institutions, unless the OWNER of an animal bringing it to the pound specifies it is not to be used in research (Okla. Stat. Ann. tit. 4, § 394 [West 1994]).

At least three states regulate the sale of animals to research facilities. Minnesota law prohibits the transfer of a dog or cat by a person other than the owner to a research animal dealer, the possession of a dog or cat by a dealer without the owner's permission, or the transfer of a dog or cat by a dealer to an institution without the owner's permission (Minn. Stat. Ann. § 346.55 [West 1994]). California law provides that anyone who steals an animal for purposes of sale, medical research, or other commercial use, or who knowingly defrauds another person of any animal for purposes of medical research or slaughter, may be imprisoned for up to one year (Cal. Penal Code § 487g [West 1994]). New York law prohibits the selling or giving away of a dog to a research institution without the written permission of its owner (N.Y. Agric. & Mkts. Law § 366-a [McKinney 1994]).

On the federal level, the Animal Welfare Act was amended in 1990 to regulate the use of pound animals in research. A new section titled "Protection of Pets" provides that dogs and cats acquired by a pound, Humane Society, or similar entity or research facility must be held for not less than five days before being sold to dealers, so as to allow their recovery by their owners or their ADOPTION by other individuals (7 U.S.C.A. § 2158 [1994]).

An important development in the progress of investigation into research projects using dealer-sourced animals was the publication, in May 2009, of the National Research Council's report to Congress, *Scientific and Humane Issues in the Use of Random Source Dogs and Cats in Research*. The scathing report asserted that, despite new enforcement guidelines and intensified inspections, the USDA could not assure that stolen or lost pets would not enter research laboratories via the Class B dealer system. (Class A dealers sell dogs and cats specifically bred for the purpose of research. Class B dealers possess an operating license from the U.S. Department of Agriculture (USDA) that allows them to obtain dogs and cats from public animal shelters, auctions, private individuals, and other "random sources.")

The report further advised that undercover investigators had documented Class B dealers buying pets from unlicensed persons who had stolen animals from farms, backyards, and/or had represented themselves as prospective adoptive parents to animal shelters or "free to good home" advertisers. As of 2009, 11 Class B dealers were registered with the USDA, two of whom were under investigation. The published report was in response to a request by Congress, through the National Institutes of Health (NIH), for an assessment of the need to use random source dogs and cats from Class B dealers in NIH-funded research. (The Office of Laboratory Animal Welfare [OLAW] is maintained under an NIH grant.) Both House and Senate had approved amendments banning Class B dealers in a previous congressional session, but these provisions had been stripped from the final version of the Farm Bill. An updated legislative version, incorporating the report's findings, was expected to be reintroduced by Senator Daniel Akaka (D-HI) and Representative Mike Doyle (D-PA) in the 111th Congress (2009–2010).

The use of animals in scientific, medical, and commercial research is expected to remain controversial. In her book *The Monkey Wars*, Deborah Blum advocated that animal rights activists and researchers share their viewpoints together in education programs to achieve a realistic understanding of the issues. According to Blum, such an understanding could end the two sides' long and bitter standoff.

The largest and most active animal rights group is PEOPLE FOR THE ETHICAL TREATMENT OF ANIMALS (PETA), originally founded in 1980 in Norfolk, Virginia. Since its founding, PETA has claimed a certain level of success in curbing unethical treatment of animals. Its self-proclaimed successes include the closing of the largest horse slaughterhouse in the United States, the closing of a military laboratory where animals were shot, and the end of the use of cats and dogs in wound laboratories. PETA not only details its "victories" on its Web site, it also provides "action alerts" that identify instances that the group believes constitute animal cruelty.

Although PETA has had a significant impact on the use of animals in medical and scientific

WELCOME TO THE MONKEY LAB: THE BATTLE OVER ANIMAL RESEARCH

In May 1981 Alex Pacheco, cofounder of an animal rights organization called PEOPLE FOR THE ETHICAL TREATMENT OF ANIMALS (PETA), went to work as a volunteer at the Institute for Behavioral Research, a private research center in Silver Spring, Maryland. Pacheco told the institute's chief research scientist, Edward Taub, that he was fascinated by animal research. Taub's research involved the surgical crippling of monkeys using a procedure called deafferentation, in which the spinal cord is opened and various nerves leading to arms and legs are sliced away, causing numbness.

At the time Pacheco joined his lab, Taub had performed the procedure on 17 macaques, attempting to show that function could be restored to limbs by forcing new nerve growth. He had destroyed the nerves to only one arm on some of the monkeys, and then used straitjackets, binding up the good arms to force the animals to use their damaged arms, and had also applied electric shock to restrained monkeys if they did not move their numbed limbs. Taub planned to kill the monkeys after a year in order to determine whether this forced movement had stimulated nerve growth.

After receiving permission from Taub to work at night, Pacheco set to work documenting the filthy, cramped conditions of the lab, and the stressed behavior of the monkeys, many of which were chewing their numbed limbs open. With his PETA cofounder, Ingrid Newkirk, stationed outside with a walkie-talkie, Pacheco took photographs and brought in sympathetic veterinarians and scientists to provide affidavits about the lab conditions. Several months later, he took his documentation to the local police department, which seized the lab's monkeys and filed 17 charges of animal cruelty against Taub, under state law. The scientist was convicted on all the charges, but an appellate court decided that a federally-funded researcher was not required to comply with state laws. Eventually, Taub's lab lost its federal funding and discontinued animal research.

Many participants in the debate over animal rights view the 1981 SEIZURE of the Silver Spring monkeys as a turning point for the animal rights movement in the United States, heading it in a more combative and less compromising direction.

Animal welfare has long been an issue in the United States. As early as the mid-1600s the Puritans prohibited cruelty toward animals, and by the nineteenth century groups such as the American Society for the Prevention of Cruelty to Animals and the American Anti-Vivisection Society had been organized. Animal experimentation has been controversial not only between the animal rights movement and the scientific and medical research communities but also between the activist groups themselves.

Supporters of the use of animals in research are as adamant in their advocacy of the use of animals in research as animal rights activists are in their opposition to such use. Supporters of the use of animals in research point out that virtually every major advancement in medicine during the past century has been made possible by the use of animals in research. Researchers point out that, with the use of animals as subjects, scientists may be capable of curing or reducing the death and disability rates caused by such diseases as kidney and liver failure, birth defects, cancer, and AIDS. Former U.S. Surgeon General Jocelyn Elders said, "The use of animals in biomedical research and testing has been, and will continue to be, absolutely critical to the progress against AIDS and a wide range of other applications in both humans and animals."

The biomedical research industry has responded vigorously to criticisms of animal research. A 1988 study by the National Research Council, the research arm of the National Academy of Sciences, acknowledged the controversy over animal testing, stating that although animal research has saved human lives, it has caused suffering and death for the animals involved. Nevertheless, the study concluded that such experimentation has contributed significantly to the increase in human life expectancy since 1900 and that animals have been critical to research on most antibiotics and other drugs. Frankie Trull, executive director of the National Association for Biomedical Research, has argued that animal testing is necessary to sustain the human race.

Supporters of animal research frequently direct attack towards animal rights activists, often labeling animal rights groups as "extremists." Joseph Murray, who in 1990 won the Nobel Prize for medicine in recognition of his work on organ transplants, said, "None of this could have been done without animal experimentation. It's a tragedy and a waste of resources that scientists have to combat the anti-vivisectionists," referring to animal rights groups. Animal research supporters often argue that the tactics employed by animal rights groups impede the progress being made in the medical community through the use of animals in research.

The supporters of animal research and the animal rights activists have clashed in both the courts and in the legislatures. Concerned that animal rights activists would cause the dismantling of all animal research, the biomedical research community lobbied successfully for years against the passage of all legislation restricting such research. But in the early 1950s Christine Stevens founded the Animal Welfare Institute and the Society for Animal Protective Legislation, which successfully worked against passage of state laws that would require pounds to turn their dogs and cats over to researchers. Stevens then began working for passage of federal legislation that would also protect laboratory animals. In 1966, Congress enacted the Animal Welfare Act (7 U.S.C.A. § 2131 et seq. [1994]), which regulates the treatment of animals in federally funded research. Congress charged the U.S. DEPARTMENT OF AGRICULTURE (USDA) with overseeing the inspection of laboratories for COMPLIANCE.

In 1985, after Stevens documented continuing inhumane laboratory conditions, the Animal Welfare Act was amended to strengthen standards for the humane handling, treatment, and transportation of animals by dealers, research facilities, and exhibitors. In 1991 the secretary of agriculture issued regulations implementing the amended act.

During this period, the animal protection movement continued to expand. By the early 1990s PETA had grown to more than 400,000 members and had an annual budget of nearly $10 million. More than 400 animal rights groups had been organized in the United States, claiming a total membership of 10 million. Although each of these groups can be said to support the humane treatment of animals, their philosophies vary dramatically.

The most radical group is the Animal Liberation Front (ALF), an underground organization formed in 1982 with an estimated worldwide membership of several hundred as of the mid-1990s. ALF opposes the use of all animals in medical and scientific research, including psychological and surgical experimentation on living animals; ALF also opposes using animals for testing new drugs and cosmetics, for instructional purposes in biology and medical school classes, and for food, clothing, sports, circuses, and pets. ALF claimed responsibility for more than 75 attacks in the United States between 1979 and 1995, including stealing animals from labs in Arizona, California, Florida, Maryland, Oregon, Pennsylvania, and Washington, D.C.; burning and vandalizing the University of Arizona's veterinary lab and a new $3 million veterinary diagnostic center for farm animals at the University of California, Davis; vandalizing offices of researchers and stealing their research animals in Michigan and Texas; and starting small fires in four of Chicago's largest department stores to PROTEST the sale of furs. Although most of ALF's targets have been scientific research labs, the group claimed responsibility for bombing the cars of two research scientists in England in June 1990. ALF has also conducted raids in more than a dozen other countries.

By 1988, in response to raids by ALF and other groups, more than 20 states had enacted protective legislation prohibiting interference with animal research and agricultural facilities. In August 1992, citing the inability of state and local law enforcement agencies to conduct interstate or international investigations, Congress passed comparable federal legislation. The Animal Enterprise Protection Act of 1992 (18 U.S.C.A. § 43 [1994]) prohibits the disruption of "animal enterprises" such as research facilities and zoos by intentionally stealing or damaging property including animals or records.

Many scientists believe that ALF is a thinly disguised division of PETA. PETA denies any connection between the two groups but has expressed its admiration for ALF's activities and often publicizes the group's raids. Both ALF and PETA share a common goal of ending all animal research, a philosophy that represents a fundamental split from other animal rights organizations such as Stevens's Animal Welfare Institute and the Humane Society of the United States, which accept animal experimentation but work for the humane treatment of animals in that and other contexts.

Supporters of animal research debunk many of the claims of animal rights activities as pure myths. For instance, animal rights activists often direct their attention towards the use of such animals as dogs, cats, and non-human primates in medical research, but scientists point out that the use of such animals accounts for less than 1 percent of the total number of animals used in research. The vast majority of animals used in research, according to these scientists, are rodents, including mice and rats bred specifically for the purpose of testing them. Similarly, these scientists refute animal rights advocates' claims that alternatives to animal research exist in the form of computer models and tissue cultures but that the scientific community refuses to accept them. Scientists claim that even the most sophisticated technological model cannot replicate the genetic and physiological systems of humans as those found in live animals. According to the Foundation for Biomedical Research, the limitations in the use of computer models and other alternatives may overcome the need for animals in research, but these alternative methods serve only as adjuncts to basic animal research.

In a nationwide survey conducted in December 1993 by the *Los Angeles Times,* respondents were asked whether they agreed with the following statement by PETA's Newkirk: "Animals are like us in all important things—they feel pain, act with altruism, they talk and suffer fear. They value their lives, even if we don't understand those lives." Of the 1,612 adults polled, 47 percent agreed with Newkirk's statement and 51 percent disagreed. The survey also found that 54 percent opposed hunting for sport and 50 percent opposed the wearing of fur. Forty-six percent said the laws protecting animals from inhumane treatment were satisfactory, whereas 30 percent said the laws did not go far enough, and 17 percent said the laws went too far. Animal rights leaders expressed surprise that so many Americans agreed with some of the principle tenets of the animal protection movement.

A new wrinkle in the Animal Rights movement has been the attempt to gain the recognition of legal rights for animals. Animal rights advocates in both PETA and ALF had spoken for years about the need for animals to have legal rights under U.S. law. But this theory remained abstract until the end of the twentieth century.

Then in 2000 Stephen Wise published an influential animal rights book. *Rattling the Cage: Toward Legal Rights for Animals* took a legalistic approach in arguing that at least two human-like species, chimpanzees and bonobos, and perhaps other species that were similarly developed, should be considered

WELCOME TO THE MONKEY LAB: THE BATTLE OVER ANIMAL RESEARCH
(CONTINUED)

"persons". The book was reviewed in such noted publications as the *Yale Law Journal* and the *Harvard Law Review*. Among those legal scholars discussing the book were RICHARD POSNER, eminent professor at the University of Chicago law school and judge for the U.S. Court of Appeals for the Ninth Circuit, and Lawrence Tribe, professor of CONSTITUTIONAL LAW at Harvard University.

Tribe seemed especially taken with the book's arguments. "Broadening the circle of rights-holders, or even broadening the definition of persons, I submit, is largely a matter of acculturation," said Tribe in a speech in Boston in support of the book. "It is not a matter of breaking through something, like a conceptual sound barrier. With the aid of statutes like those creating corporate persons, our legal system could surely recognize the personhood of chimpanzees, bonobos, and maybe someday of computers that are capable not just of beating Gary Kasparov but feeling sorry for him when he loses."

In 2002 Wise published a book called *Drawing the Line: Science and the Case for Animal Rights*, in which he expanded his rights arguments to include other species. But the arguments remained very similar. "On what nonarbitrary ground," he asks, "could a judge find [that a] little girl has a common-law right to bodily integrity that forbids her use in terminal biomedical research but that Koko [a gorilla with an IQ equal to that of a 4- or 5-year-old child] shouldn't have that right, without violating basic notions of equality?" What influence this nascent movement for the legal rights of animals has on the general animal rights movement promised to be interesting to observe.

Many legal commentators have been supportive or, at least, sympathetic toward the views of Wise and writers with similar opinions. Other legal scholars, on the other hand, have pointed out that granting broad rights to animals conflicts with some of the basic assumptions of the U.S. legal system, as well as the legal system elsewhere. Even where laws provide heightened protection for animals against abuse, the animals are still treated as a special form of property. If the law were to extend recognition of animals as holders of certain legal rights, their status as something greater than property raises difficult questions. For instance, when would these rights conflict with recognized HUMAN RIGHTS, and could the right of an animal in a certain case be greater than a right enjoyed by a human? Likewise, how can society merge the recognition of animal rights with the traditional, and in some cases, fundamental uses of animals, including their functions as sources of food and as goods and services that may be bartered? Scholarship and debate by legal experts continues to grow regarding these questions.

FURTHER READINGS

Carbone, Larry. 2004. *What Animals Want: Expertise and Advocacy in Laboratory Animal Welfare Policy*. New York: Oxford Univ. Press.

Monamay, Vaughn. 2000. *Animal Experimentation: A Guide to the Issues*. New York: Cambridge Univ. Press.

CROSS REFERENCES

Cruelty.

research, as well as other uses, its tactics have created an equal level of controversy. For instance, according to PETA president Ingrid Newkirk, human beings should not drink milk produced by cows, eat turkey meat, or wear fur because of the practices involved in preparing these goods. PETA's protests have ranged from vandalizing fur coats sold at a Macy's outlet in Boston to advocating the bombing of a New Jersey laboratory that uses animals for research. PETA claims that it does not support TERRORISM, but it did fund, for example, the legal defense of an arsonist that set fire to a Michigan research lab.

PETA has been active in the court system, with various levels of success. In one case, PETA sought entry into a public art event held in 2000 in New York City called "CowParade." One of PETA's entries showed a cow divided into sections that resembled a butcher's chart. On each of the sections was a statement or quotation "concerning the health and ethical problems associated with the killing of cows for food." The committee responsible for the parade rejected the entry as too harsh and inappropriate for the parade. PETA brought suit in the U.S. District Court for the Southern District of New York, but the trial court granted SUMMARY JUDGMENT in favor of the parade organizers, and the U.S. Court of Appeals for the Second Circuit affirmed the summary judgment (*People for the Ethical Treatment of Animals v. Giuliani*, 18 Fed. App. 35 [2d Cir. 2001]).

In 2004 and 2005 PETA engaged in an illegal undercover investigation of a Virginia research facility run by pharmaceutical giant Covance. It then published heart-wrenching videos of monkeys allegedly suffering in Covance laboratories. Covance sued PETA in 2005, alleging breach of employment contract (regarding the undercover employee) and CONSPIRACY to harm the company's business. It also sought a GAG ORDER against the publication of the videos, photographs, and statements. A SETTLEMENT was reached in 2005, in which PETA agreed not to infiltrate Covance facilities and Covance tendered a monetary settlement amount (*Covance Laboratories Inc. v. People for the Ethical Treatment of Animals,* No. CH-2005-2590, CIRCUIT COURT for the County of Fairfax, Virginia [2005]).

FURTHER READINGS

Bekoff, Marc. 2009. *Encyclopedia of Animal Rights and Animal Welfare.* 2d ed. Westport, CT.: Greenwood Press.

Blum, Deborah. 1995. *The Monkey Wars.* Don Mills, ON, Canada: Oxford Univ. Press.

Congressional Record. 1990. 136 (July).

Congressional Research Service (CRS). 2008. Brief Summaries of Federal Animal Protection Statutes. 94-731. Washington, D.C.: National Academies Press.

Humane Society of the United States. 2009. "Class B. Dealer System Unnecessary and Unenforceable, According to National Academies Report." May 29. Text available online at http://www.hsus.org/ . . . /class_b_dealer_system_unnecessary_052909.html; website home page: http://www.hsus.org/ (accessed August 5, 2009)

Kistler, John M. 2000. *Animal Rights: A Subject Guide, Bibliography, and Internet Comparison.* Westport, Conn.: Greenwood.

National Research Council. 2009. *Scientific and Humane Issues in the Use of Random Source Dogs and Cats in Research.* Washington, DC: National Academies Press.

Sherry, Clifford J. 1994. *Animal Rights: A Reference Handbook.* Santa Barbara, Calif.: ABC-CLIO.

Singer, Peter. 1975. *Animal Liberation: A New Ethics for Our Treatment of Animals.* New York: Avon.

CROSS REFERENCES

Agriculture Department; Criminal Action; Cruelty; People for the Ethical Treatment of Animals.

ANIMUS

[Latin, Mind, soul, or intention.] *A tendency or an inclination toward a definite, sometimes unavoidable, goal; an aim, objective, or purpose.*

When *animus* is used in conjunction with other words of Latin origin, its most common meaning is "the intention of." For example, *animus revocandi* is the intention of revoking; *animus possidendi* is the intention of possessing.

Animo, meaning "with intent," may be employed in a manner similar to *animus.* For example, *animo felonico* means with felonious intent.

ANNEXATION

The act of attaching, uniting, or joining together in a physical sense; consolidating.

The term is generally used to signify the connection of a smaller or subordinate unit to a larger or principal unit. For example, a smaller piece of land may be annexed to a larger one. Similarly, a smaller document may be annexed to a larger one, such as a CODICIL to a will.

Although physical joining is implied, actual contact is not always necessary. For example, an annexation occurs when a country acquires new TERRITORY even though the new territory is not immediately adjacent to the existing country.

In the law of real property, annexation is used to describe the manner in which a chattel is joined to property.

CROSS REFERENCE

Fixture.

ANNOTATION

A note, summary, or commentary on some section of a book or a statute that is intended to explain or illustrate its meaning.

An annotation serves as a brief summary of the law and the facts of a case and demonstrates how a particular law enacted by Congress or a state legislature is interpreted and applied. Annotations usually follow the text of the statute they interpret in annotated statutes.

ANNUAL PERCENTAGE RATE

The actual cost of borrowing money, expressed in the form of a yearly measure to allow consumers to compare the cost of borrowing money among several lenders.

The Federal Truth-in-Lending Act (15 U.S.C.A. § 1601 et seq. [1968]) mandates the complete disclosure of this rate in addition to other credit terms.

CROSS REFERENCE

Truth in Lending Act.

ANNUAL REPORT

A document published by public corporations on a yearly basis to provide stockholders, the public,

*and the government with financial data, a
summary of ownership, and the accounting
practices used to prepare the report.*

Annual reports measure a corporation's
financial health. They focus on past and present
financial performance, and make predictions
about future prospects. By law, any corporation
that holds an annual meeting for stockholders
or security holders is required to issue an annual
report. Regulations set down by the SECURITIES
AND EXCHANGE COMMISSION (SEC) specify in detail
what information the report must include about
the corporation's finances, markets, and management. The rules are strict: the SEC can levy
stiff penalties if corporations fail to comply.

Traditionally a rather dry and factual document, the annual report has acquired a larger
audience in recent years as corporations increasingly treat it as not merely a legal obligation but
also a public relations opportunity. Yet even as
annual reports take on the appearance of glossy
magazines, promote corporate public relations,
and make political arguments, they remain
bound by legal concerns about completeness
and accuracy, and sometimes expose corporations to lawsuits when they fall short.

Although federal law governing the financial
industry is quite old, its application to annual
reports grew in complexity from the mid-1970s
to the mid-1990s. This authority derives from
two laws: the Securities Act of 1933 (15 U.S.C.A. §
77a et seq.) and the Securities Exchange Act of
1934 (15 U.S.C.A. § 78a–78jj). The 1933 law
requires issuers of securities to file financial
information with the federal government; the
1934 law authorizes the SEC to act as a regulatory
body over the financial industry. In 1974 the
SEC tightened requirements on annual reports
by specifying a broad range of information that
must be provided, and it frequently amended
them in subsequent years. Corporations have
consequently made greater efforts to scrutinize
their reports for compliance with the law,
increasing the role of lawyers in producing what
was once the work of accountants.

These requirements address financial and
general information. An annual report must
include a balance sheet reflecting changes in the
corporation's financial worth, an income and
cash flow statement, and other relevant documentation, all of which must be reviewed first
by outside auditors. A statement by management must analyze past performance as well as

discuss prospects for the following years; if
circumstances change, corporations have a duty
to issue corrected information. In addition, they
must make public details about products and
services, domestic and foreign markets, and the
backgrounds of directors and executive officers.

Corporations that fail to comply with all the
requirements can face enforcement proceedings. In such cases, the commission has the
power to invalidate the election of directors and
decisions made at the shareholders' meeting,
which can necessitate issuing a revised annual
report. Administrative remedies also exist.
Under the Securities Enforcement Remedies
and Penny Stock Reform Act of 1990 (15 U.S.C.
A. § 77g et seq.), the SEC can use violations of
any securities laws to force corporations to
make full disclosures in their reports. Corporations that are in the process of registering for
the first time with the SEC are particularly
scrutinized for overly optimistic projections.

Besides federal penalties, wishful thinking in
annual reports can lead to lawsuits. Hoping to put
the best spin possible on their achievements and
prospects, corporations sometimes attract CLASS
ACTION suits from shareholders who allege that the
corporations have exaggerated or misled the
public. One of many examples is a suit brought
against Pizza Time Theatre (*In re Pizza Time
Theatre,* 112 F.R.D. 15 [N.D. Cal. 1986]). Its 1982
annual report had cartoon characters bragging,
"We're going full speed ahead!" And so they were:
Nine months later, Pizza Time Theatre declared
BANKRUPTCY. Shareholders brought a class action
suit against the corporation and its directors,
citing the report's overly optimistic tone, but the
suit was discharged in bankruptcy.

Beyond requiring that annual reports meet
financial and general information regulations,
the law says nothing about the rest of their
contents. Corporations are free to package their
reports as they please, and the form itself is
constantly evolving: current annual reports
borrow from the flashy graphic styles of magazines, can be released on videodisc and computer
disk, and sometimes even include gifts. Particularly interesting is a trend toward using these
reports—usually via the president's letter—to
address political issues. As powerful forces in the
body politic, corporations rarely refuse an
opportunity to make their influence felt on
government, especially when pending legislation
may affect their interests. In the early 1990s, for

example, some annual reports from the medical industry targeted the ill-fated health care reform proposals of the Clinton administration.

Annual reports became a source of widespread PUBLIC INTEREST after the sudden collapse in 2002 of Enron, the seventh largest U.S. corporation. Within a few months other major corporations disclosed major financial difficulties, which came as a surprise to shareholders and regulators that had relied on upbeat financial information contained in these corporations' annual reports. The credibility and legitimacy of corporate financial data quickly became a topic of political debate.

The collapse of Enron was predicated on fraudulent accounting practices that concealed the amount of debt the corporation had accumulated. Federal prosecutors accused the major accounting firm of Arthur Anderson of aiding Enron's corporate officers in this enterprise and successfully won a conviction against the firm for its actions, including the destruction of documents. A careful review of Enron's annual reports revealed that certain transactions were buried in obscure footnotes or were not reported at all.

During 2002 the SEC and Congress examined the shortcomings of annual reports and other corporate reporting practices. In a bipartisan effort, Congress passed and President GEORGE W. BUSH signed the Sarbanes-Oxley Act, also known as the Accounting Industry Reform Act, in July 2002 (Pub.L. 107-204, 116 Stat. 745, [2002]). The act seeks to address CORPORATE FRAUD by, among other things, requiring chief executive and chief financial officers to personally certify the accuracy of the financial information contained in quarterly and annual reports. The certification must state that the officers have read the report, and must confirm it contains no misstatements or omissions and that it is a fair presentation. An officer who knowingly makes a false certification will be subject to fines of up to $5 million and a prison sentence of up to 20 years. In addition, officers will be forced to repay bonuses that were based on inaccurate financial earnings.

The SEC also responded by demanding that all major U.S. corporations recertify the accuracy of their 2002 annual reports or risk prosecution. A number of corporations took the opportunity to change their financial statements. In the wake of the 2002 scandals, the expectation is that annual reports will be more accurate in detailing the financial health of corporations.

FURTHER READINGS

Malveaux, Suzanne. July 31, 2002. "Bush Signs Bill to Stop 'Book Cooking'." *CNN.com: Inside Politics.* Available online at http://www.archives.cnn.com/2002/ALLPOLI-TICS/07/30/bush.corporate.reform; website home page: http://www.archives.cnn.com (accessed July 4, 2009).

Monks, Robert A. G., and Nell Minow, eds. 2008. *Corporate Governance.* 4th ed. Indianapolis: Wiley.

Practising Law Institute. 1994a. *The Annual Report to Shareholders.* Corporate Law and Practice Course Handbook Series, January–February.

Stough, Brooks, and L.C. Lau. 1997. *Annual Reports to Securityholders and Disclosure in Annual Reports.* Practising Law Institute (October–November).

Winkler, Carol. 2002. "Weighing SEC Ability to Fight Fraud." *Boston Globe* (December 26).

CROSS REFERENCES

Board of Directors; Financial Statement.

ANNUITY

A right to receive periodic payments, usually fixed in size, for life or a term of years that is created by a contract or other legal document.

The most common form of an annuity is akin to a savings account. The annuitant, the person who creates an annuity for his or her own benefit, deposits a sum of money, the principal, with an individual, business, or insurance company to be invested so that the principal will earn income at a certain percentage, usually specified by the terms of the annuity. This income is used by the company to pay the annuitant. Each payment received by the annuitant, sometimes called the primary BENEFICIARY, represents a partial return of the principal and a portion of the income generated by its investment. Such annuities are employed frequently to provide a source of income to persons upon their retirement. A group annuity contract supplies periodic payments to a retired individual member of a group of employees covered by their employer's master contract. A retirement annuity is a policy paid to the annuitant after retirement. If the annuitant dies prior to the expiration of the annuity or wants to surrender the policy, an amount specified in the terms of the annuity is returned to the annuitant's estate or designated beneficiary.

Classification

Annuities are classified according to the nature of the payment and the duration of time for payment. A *fixed annuity* requires payment in a specified amount to be made for the term of the annuity regardless of economic changes due to inflation or the fluctuation of the ventures in which the principal is invested. A *variable annuity* provides for payments that fluctuate in size contingent upon the success of the investment of the principal. Such variation offsets the effect of inflation upon the annuitant. If, however, the investment has fared poorly, the size of the payments decreases.

A *straight annuity* is a contract by an insurance company to make variable payments at monthly or yearly intervals. A *life* or *straight life annuity* is payable to an annuitant only during the annuitant's lifetime and ceases upon his or her death. The size of the periodic payment is usually fixed based upon actuarial charts that project the expected life span of a person based upon age and physical condition. This type of annuity often contains provisions that promise payment to be made to a secondary beneficiary, named by the annuitant to receive benefits in case of the annuitant's death, or to the annuitant's heirs for a period of time even if the annuitant has died before the expiration of the designated period. A *deferred annuity* is one in which payments start at a stipulated future date only if the annuitant is alive at that time. Payment of the INCOME TAX due on the income generated is delayed until payments start. A deferred annuity is used primarily by a person who does not want to receive payments until he or she is in a lower tax bracket, such as upon retirement.

A *refund annuity*, sometimes called a *cash refund annuity*, is a policy that promises to pay a set amount annually during the annuitant's life. In case the annuitant dies before receiving payments for the full amount of the annuity, his or her estate will receive a sum that is the difference between the purchase price and the sum paid during the annuitant's lifetime.

A *joint annuity* is one that is payable to two named persons but upon the death of one, the annuity terminates. A *joint and survivorship annuity* is a policy payable to the named annuitants during their lives and continues for the benefit of the surviving annuitant upon the death of the other.

Tax Aspects

When an annuity is paid to an annuitant, he or she receives a portion of the principal and part of the return it has earned. For federal and state income tax purposes, only the amount attributable to the income generated by the principal, not the principal itself, is considered TAXABLE INCOME. The INTERNAL REVENUE CODE provides an exclusion ratio to determine the amount of taxable income paid to the annuitant. Special tax rules apply to annuities that are qualified employee retirement plans.

The annuity payments made to the estate of a decedent might be subject to estate and gift tax as an asset of the decedent's GROSS ESTATE. Federal and state laws governing estate tax must be consulted to determine the liability for such taxes.

CROSS REFERENCE

Pension.

ANNULMENT

A judgment by a court that retroactively invalidates a marriage to the date of its formation.

An annulment differs from a DIVORCE, a court order that terminates a MARRIAGE, because it is a judicial statement that there was never a marriage. A divorce, which can only take place where there has been a valid marriage, means that the two parties are no longer HUSBAND AND WIFE once the decree is issued. An annulment means that the individuals were never united in marriage as husband and wife.

Various religions have different methods for obtaining a church divorce, or annulment, but these procedures have no legal force or effect upon a marriage that complied with the requirements of law. Such a marriage must be legally annulled.

History

English COMMON LAW did not provide for annulment. Prior to the mid-nineteenth century, the only courts in England with the power to annul an invalid marriage, when fairness mandated it, were the ECCLESIASTICAL COURTS. There was no statute that provided relief of this kind.

Northeastern American colonies passed laws enabling courts or legislatures to grant annulments, while other colonies adhered more closely to English traditions. The American tradition of keeping church and state separate precluded the establishment of ecclesiastical courts in the United States. Following the American Revolution, the civil courts in a majority of states never assumed that they had the authority to hear annulment cases.

A number of states eventually enacted laws authorizing annulment in recognition of the belief that it is unfair to require people to fulfill marital duties when a marriage is invalid.

Currently most states have annulment statutes. In states that do not, courts declare that no marriage exists if the laws regulating marriage have not been observed.

An annulment declares that a marriage, which appears to be valid, is actually invalid. Two kinds of invalid marriages exist: *VOID marriages* and *voidable marriages*. A void marriage is one that was invalid from its very beginning and, therefore, could never lawfully exist in any way. The major grounds for a void marriage are INCEST, bigamy, and lack of consent. Once these grounds are established, the court will grant a decree of annulment.

A voidable marriage is one that can be declared illegal but that continues as valid until an annulment is sought. The annulment takes effect only from the time a court renders its decision.

Grounds

State law governs the grounds for annulling a voidable marriage. Couples should not be obligated by the serious duties incident to marriage if both parties did not genuinely intend to be married.

FRAUD is the most prevalent ground for annulment. The MISREPRESENTATION, whether by lies or concealment of the truth, must encompass something directly pertinent to the marriage, such as religion, children, or sex, which society considers the foundation of a marital relationship.

Physical or emotional conditions may also be grounds for annulment, particularly when they interfere with sexual relations or procreation.

Other health conditions providing grounds for annulment include alcoholism, incurable insanity, and epilepsy. The mere existence of one of these conditions is a sufficient ground for an annulment in some states, whereas in others, an annulment may be obtained for fraud if such a condition was concealed.

Courts may also annul marriages that involved lack of consent, mistake, or duress. Lack of consent might arise if one party were senile, drunk, underage, or suffering from serious mental illness, or if there was no genuine intent to marry. A mistake as to some essential element of the marriage may also justify an annulment, for example, if the couple mistakenly believed that one party's insanity or impotence had been cured. Duress arises when one party compels the other to marry against his or her will.

Consequences

State law governs the consequences of an annulment. Customarily, an annulment was a court declaration that no marriage had ever existed, but this created various problems. If a marriage was dissolved by divorce, the children of the marriage were legitimate and the parent awarded custody could be awarded ALIMONY. No such provisions, however, were made in an annulment. A majority of states have rectified this situation by statutory provisions. In most states, children of voidable, and sometimes void, marriages are legitimate. In addition, some states provide for alimony and property settlements upon the granting of an annulment. Several other jurisdictions allow their courts to devise a fair allocation of property where necessary and equitable.

FURTHER READINGS

The Diocese of Saint Cloud Web site. 2008. "The Annulment Process." The Roman Catholic Diocese of Saint Cloud, MN. Available online at http://www.stcdio.org/annulment.htm; websie home page: http://www.stcdio.org (accessed August 28, 2009).

Escalera, Steve. 2000. "California Marital Annulments." *The Journal of Contemporary Legal Issues* 11 (spring).

Nelson, William T. 2000. *A Treatise on the Law of Divorce and Annulment of Marriage: Including the Adjustment of Property Rights upon Divorce, the Procedure in Suits for Divorce, and the Validity and Extraterritorial Effect of Decrees of Divorce.* Holmes Beach, FL: Gaunt.

ANON.

An abbreviation for anonymous, nameless, or name unknown.

ANSWER

The first responsive pleading filed by the defendant in a civil action; a formal written statement that admits or denies the allegations in the complaint and sets forth any available affirmative defenses.

The answer gives the PLAINTIFF notice of the issues the DEFENDANT will raise as the case progresses and enables the plaintiff to adequately prepare a case. In most jurisdictions, the answer must be filed within 20 days after receipt of the SUMMONS and complaint, although local rules and customs may dictate different filing times.

The answer begins with a caption, which identifies the location of the action, the court, the docket or file number (assigned by the court), and the title of the case (comprising the names of the parties, e.g., *Smith v. Jones*).

A sample answer and counterclaim

Answer and Counterclaim

United States District Court
Southern District of Texas
Corpus Christi Division

DirecTV, Inc.

vs.

John Bettiga, et al.

No. C-02-507
[Jury Requested]

Answer and Counterclaim

TO THE HONORABLE COURT:

John Bettiga ("Bettiga") respectfully files this Answer and Counterclaim.

Admissions and Denials

Preliminary Statement

1. **Paragraph 1.** Denied.
   - Bettiga purchased **standard electronic components** useful for a wide variety of lawful purposes. The components are not illegal. The components are not designed to intercept and decrypt protected satellite communications.
   - Bettiga never used any illegal device for any illegal purpose.
   - Bettiga never possessed any illegal device.
   - Bettiga never viewed Satellite TV for free.
   - Bettiga never distributed any illegal device.

DirecTV's Business Operations

2. **Paragraph 2.** Admit
3. **Paragraph 3.** Admit all except final sentence which is denied.
   - The primary basis of this dispute is DirecTV is on a fishing expedition harassing the purchasers of **standard electronic components** based on a mere possibility that the standard electronic components were used for an unlawful purpose.
4. **Paragraph 4.** Admit.
5. **Paragraph 5.** Admit.
6. **Paragraph 6.** Denied except Betigga is a resident of Texas.
   - Betigga never purchased or used any illegal pirate device. He purchased **standard electronic components** useful for a wide variety of lawful purposes.
   - Betigga never purchased or used any device designed to permit viewing of DirecTV's programming without authorization or payment to DirecTV.

DirecTV Obtained Evidence

7. **Paragraphs 7-10.** Bettiga does not have sufficient information to form a belief as to the truth of most of these paragraphs. However, Bettiga denies that DirecTV obtained evidence that he purchase an unlawful pirate device. At most, it obtained evidence of his purchase of lawful **standard electronic components** usable for a wide variety of lawful purposes. Further, Bettiga never possessed or used any pirate device. Further, he never manufactured, assembled, or used any pirate device. He merely purchased **standard electronic components**. He merely tinkered and experimented with these components. His tinkering did not result in a device capable of decrypting anything. It was capable only of converting a signal from one form to another.

DirecTV Obtained Records

8. **Paragraph 11.** Denied. Bettiga did not violate any federal or state statute or common law. He merely purchased **standard electronic components**. Bettiga never manufactured or assembled or obtained or possessed or purchased any unlawful pirate device. His tinkering did not result in a device capable of decrypting anything. It was capable only of converting a signal from one form to another. The device could not accomplish and was not designed to accomplish decryption of DirecTV's signal without additional components and decryption software or device.

Jurisdiction, Venue, and Parties

9. **Paragraphs 12-16.** Denied except subject matter jurisdiction, personal jurisdiction, and venue are all admitted. Bettiga never violated any right of DirecTV anywhere.
10. **Paragraph 17.** Admit except Bettiga does not have sufficient information to admit or deny the State of Incorporation of DirecTV.
11. **Paragraph 18.**
    - Admit that Bettiga resides in Corpus Christi, Texas.
    - Denied that Bettiga purchased any Pirate Access Device. He purchased **standard electronic components** useful for a wide variety of lawful purposes.
    - Bettiga did not purchase anything designed specifically to permit the surreptitious interception of DirecTV Satellite Programming.
    - Bettiga purchased capacitors, transisters, and an RS-232 Transceiver. These are all electronic components with completely lawful uses. These components are not sufficient without more to create any Pirate Access or Decryption Device.
12. **Paragraphs 19-21.** Bettiga does not have sufficient information to admit or deny any of the allegations relative to the other Defendants.
13. **Paragraphs 22-24.** Denied. Bettiga did not import any illegal device. He merely purchased standard electronic components useful for a wide variety of lawful purposes. Bettiga never viewed DirecTV programming without authorization or without payment. Bettiga was never capable of viewing DirecTV programming without authorization or without payment.
14. **Paragraph 25.** Denied. Bettiga never engaged in an enterprise to distribute or resell illegal pirate devices whether for profit or not. He never even possessed such a device. His tinkering and experimentation did not result in a device capable of decrypting anything. It was capable only of converting a signal from one form to another.

[continued]

Answer and Counterclaim

Discovery

15. **Paragraph 26.** Denied. DirecTV never discovered Bettiga's involvement in pirating Satellite Programming because he is and never was involved in that. He merely purchased completely lawful **standard electronic components** and engaged in some tinkering and experimentation. His tinkering and experimentation did not result in a device capable of decrypting anything. It was capable only of converting a signal from one form to another.

47 U.S.C. 605(e)(3)(C)

16. **Paragraphs 27-28.** Denied
    - Bettiga did not effect unauthorized interception and receipt of Satellite Programming through the use of an illegal Satellite decoding device or otherwise.
17. **Paragraph 29.** Denied.
    - Bettiga did not violate federal law.
    - Bettiga did not intercept, receive, or exhibit DirecTV without authorization.
    - Bettiga did not publish or divulge the existence, substance, etc. of the contents of DirecTV programming without authorization.
    - Bettiga did not use DirecTV programming for his own benefit or the benefit of others without authorization.
18. **Paragraphs 30-32.** Denied.
19. In general, Bettiga did not intercept or receive DirecTV's programming without authorization. He did not assemble a device primarily of assistance in unauthroized decryption of satellite programming. Thus, he did not violate 47 U.S.C. 605.
20. Bettiga did engage in experimentation and tinkering. The device he constructed was not capable of unauthorized decryption of satellite programming at all. It was merely capable of converting a signal into a different form (not decrypting the signal).

18 U.S.C. 2511

22. **Paragraphs 33-36.** Denied. Bettiga did not intercept, endeavor to intercept, or procure or otherwise to intercept electronic communications. He did not disclose or endeavor to disclose to others the contents of intercepted electronic communications. He did not use or endeavor to use intercepted communications. Further, the statute does not apply in some respects as DirecTV asserts because the statute in some respects is limited to "oral" communications.

18 U.S.C. 2512

23. **Paragraphs 37-40.** Denied. Bettiga did not assemble or possess any device primarily useful for surreptitous interception of DirecTV's programming. Bettiga did not assemble a device capable of doing that. The device was not capable of decrypting the DirecTV signal. It was merely a device built from standard components capable of transforming the signal from one form to another (not decrypting it). The device was never sent through the mail and never was going to be sent through the mail. It was not received by mail (**standard electronic components** were).

47 U.S.C. 605(e)(4)

24. **Paragraphs 41-44.** Denied. The device constructed by Bettiga was not capable of decrypting anything. It merely transformed a signal from one form to another (not decrypted it). Bettiga did not program or reprogram access cards. There is not even a place to put a card. The device was not capable of unlawful interception or receiving of DirecTV's signal. It was capable only of transforming a signal from one electronic form to another (not decrypting it).

Conversion

25. **Paragraphs 45-48.** Denied. Bettiga never viewed DirecTV programming without authorization. He did not convert anything.

Tex. Civ. P. Rem. Code 123.001, et seq.

26. **Paragraphs 49-51.** Denied. Bettiga did not intercept or attempt to intercept DirecTV's programming. He did not divulge intercepted programming.

Injunction

27. **Paragraphs 53-56.** Denied. There has been no illegal conduct to restrain. There is no showing of imminent irreparable injury or even any probability at all of illegal conduct to restrain.

Counterclaim

Factual Background

28. Bettiga has on more than one occasion been working on his computer when an advertisement for DirecTV appeared or "popped up" on his screen without his consent or request. In fact, this DirecTV advertisement "popped up" on the screen of his attorney's computer while working on this answer and counterclaim. This consumes computer resources and more importantly the time of the computer user to delete the unauthorized "pop up." No consent was ever given to these pop-up advertisements whether express or implicit.
29. This amounts to an unauthorized "trespass" on the computer. **See America Online vs. IMS**, 46 F.Supp. 444 (E.D. Va. October 29, 1998) (Court awards AOL summary judgment against a spammer finding that the sending of unauthroized junk e-mail to AOL subscribers constituted an actionable trespass to AOL's computer network); **CompuServe Incorporated v. Cyber Promotions, Inc. and Sanford Wallace**, Case No. C2-96-1070 (S.D. Ohio, Feb. 3, 1997) (Graham, J.) (Court issued preliminary injunction enjoining the defendants from sending unsolicited advertisements via E-mail to any CompuServe subscribers. The court held that by sending junk e-mail, defendants had committed the tort of trespass on personal property by utilizing without permission the computer system which supports CompuServe's e-mail facilities).
30. On information and belief, DirecTV commits this trespass through a third-party service provider not directly. However, DirecTV knows what its agent is doing and thus is responsible for the spam by its agent. Bettiga is entitled to actual and exemplary damages.
31. Further, DirecTV violated 18 U.S.C. 1030. Bettiga's computer is a "protected" computer in that it is used in interstate commerce and communication. 18 U.S.C. 1030)(e)(2)(B). DirecTV knowingly and with intent to defraud accessed this protected computer without authorization or exceeded authorized access and by means of such access defrauded him by appropriating his time and attention without authorization and use of his computer resources (not only this).
32. As a result, Bettiga has suffered loss. DirecTV intentionally accessed a protected computer without authorization and as a result recklessly caused damage. 18 U.S.C. 1030(a)(5)(ii). Bettiga has a private right of action. 18 U.S.C. 1030(g) for damages and "loss." Further, he has an action for injunctive and other equitable relief. Each pop-up causes distraction of work in process and attention. Bettiga is entitled to recover his attorneys' fees.

[continued]

Answer and Counterclaim

33. Even computer users who have successfully installed an effective "popup killer" program are damaged by illegal popups, because they have generally spent money for the "popup killer" program and have always expended time and effect directly or indirectly to find and install the "popup killer" program. Further, the "popup killer" program consumes computer resources.

34. Further, on information and belief, all prerequisites to a class action exist. The Court should promptly after appropriate discovery certify both a Plaintiff class and a Defendant Class. The Plaintiff class consists of all users of "protected" computers anywhere who have been victimized by an unauthorized "popup advertisement" within the last 2 years and the Defendant Class consists of all Corporations and other business entities who have either directly or indirectly caused "popup" advertisements to appear on "protected" computers. The Court should award appropriate relief to all Plaintiff Class Members against all Defendant Class Members. The Court should allow appropriate discovery on the identities of all Defendant Class Members and Plaintiff Class Members. It should award appropriate compensation to the class attorney.

Conditions Precedent

35. All conditions precedent have been performed or have occurred.

Conclusions

36. The Court should deny DirecTV damages. The Court should certify a class. The Court should grant actual and exemplary damages for trespass and for violation of 18 U.S.C. 1030.

Respectfully submitted,

_____

David A. Sibley
Attorney at Law
P.O. Box 9610
719 N. Upper Broadway (78401)
Corpus Christi, Texas 78469-9610
(361) 882-2377 - Telephone
(877) 582-7477 - Telecopier
david@davidsibley.com - E-mail
davidsibley.law - Home Page
State Bar No. 18337600
Federal I.D. 10053
Attorney-in-charge for Bettiga

Certificate of Service

On Sunday, January 5, 2002, I served this as follows:

Via Telecopier
Joe C. Fulcher
Attorney At Law

_____

David A. Sibley

Following the caption, the main body of the answer sets forth admissions or denials that respond to each allegation made in the complaint. In federal court and in jurisdictions that follow the Federal Rules of CIVIL PROCEDURE, denials must be unambiguous and stated in concise language that clearly identifies the allegations being denied (Fed. R. Civ. P. 8(b)). For example, if the complaint alleges that the defendant was driving an automobile that struck the plaintiff on Addison Street in Chicago on March 11, an answer stating that the defendant was in Milwaukee on March 11 is unclear and ambiguous because it avoids the question of whether the defendant was also in Chicago at a different time on the same day.

The answer may plead any form of denial that is truthful and made in GOOD FAITH. Although general denials that deny the truth of every fact in the complaint or of every element of a charge are sometimes used, they are not considered a sufficient response. Courts discourage general denials because they fail to respond to specific allegations and do not give the plaintiff sufficient basis to prepare a case. If the defendant lacks the knowledge or information needed to respond to the truth or falsity of a charge, rule 8(b) and similar rules in other jurisdictions allow the defendant to state such in the answer. This has the effect of a denial (rule 8 (b)). If the defendant fails to respond to an allegation by either denying it or by stating he or she does not have the information necessary to admit or deny it, it is considered admitted under rule 8(d).

Following the admissions and denials, the answer outlines any affirmative defenses available to the defendant. Affirmative defenses, which are grounded in SUBSTANTIVE LAW, state that an allegation may or may not be true, but that even if it is true, the law provides a legal defense that defeats the plaintiff's claim. The defendant must determine if the law allows an AFFIRMATIVE DEFENSE to a charge, and must allege sufficient facts to support the defense. For example, in a NEGLIGENCE action, the defendant might respond to an allegation that a duty of care was owed to the plaintiff by stating that, even if the allegation is true, the plaintiff assumed the risk of the activity that led to the injury. The defendant must then state the facts that support the defense. It is critical to the defendant's case that all applicable affirmative defenses are asserted. In most jurisdictions, affirmative defenses not raised in a timely manner in the defendant's RESPONSIVE PLEADING are deemed to have been waived.

The answer, like the complaint, ends with a "wherefore" clause that summarizes the defendant's demands, such as demands for a jury trial and judgment in the defendant's favor. Only one wherefore clause is generally needed, although local practice may dictate that each denial and each affirmative defense have its own wherefore clause.

Counterclaims and cross-claims sometimes appear in the answer. A COUNTERCLAIM arises when the defendant's response includes a claim against the plaintiff. A counterclaim may come from the same circumstances as the plaintiff's claim or from a different set of facts. A CROSS-CLAIM may be filed when one party to a suit charges another party with responsibility for the plaintiff's injuries or damages. Under Federal Rules of Civil Procedure rule 13(g), a cross-claim must arise out of "the transaction or occurrence that is the subject matter either of the original action or of a counterclaim therein or relating to any property that is the subject matter of the original action." A cross-claim may also be filed separately from the answer. Because counterclaims and cross-claims raise new issues and initiate a separate CAUSE OF ACTION, they must meet the procedural requirements of a complaint.

FURTHER READINGS

James, Fleming, Jr., Geoffrey C. Hazard, Jr., and John Leubsdorf. 2001. *Civil Procedure.* Eagan, MN: West.

McCord, James W.H. "Drafting the Complaint: Defending and Testing the Lawsuit." *Practising Law Institute* 447.

Witus, Morley. "What Is the Answer? New Guidelines on How to Draft the Answer and Affirmative Defenses." *Michigan Bar Journal* 7.

CROSS REFERENCE

Civil Procedure.

ANTARCTIC TREATY OF 1959

According to this treaty, Antartic Treaty, Dec. 1, 1959, 12 U.S. T. 794, 402 U.N.T.S. 71. Antarctica—the land adjacent to the South Pole—is considered "international" territory, like that of the high seas; it is not under the jurisdiction of any single nation. Its legal status, therefore, is governed by INTERNATIONAL LAW.

ANTE

[Latin, Before.] *A reference to a previous portion of a report or textbook.*

Ante is synonymous with *supra.*

ANTECEDENT DEBT

A legally enforceable obligation, which has been in existence prior to the time in question, to reimburse another with money or property.

Principles of contract law vary from jurisdiction to jurisdiction regarding whether an antecedent debt constitutes good consideration since the debtor does not incur any new detriment at the time that he or she enters a contract with another party. COMMERCIAL PAPER that has been given in exchange for an antecedent debt is deemed by the UNIFORM COMMERCIAL CODE to be supported by adequate consideration.

Under statutes governing BANKRUPTCY, a transfer of property made by a debtor because of an antecedent debt might be considered a voidable preference, depending upon the length of time between the creation of the debt and the filing of the petition for bankruptcy. A bankruptcy court may set aside a voidable preference since it gives one creditor a better right to payment than other creditors who are similarly situated.

❖ ANTHONY, SUSAN BROWNELL

People no longer are surprised when an American woman works outside the home, keeps her own bank account, maintains custody of her children after a divorce, or votes in a presidential election. Yet, not too long ago, these practices were uncommon, if not illegal, in the United States. Due in large part to the efforts of the remarkable Susan Brownell Anthony and other pioneers of feminism, women in the United

Susan B. Anthony.
LIBRARY OF CONGRESS

States enjoy rights and opportunities that are simply taken for granted today.

Anthony was born on February 15, 1820, during an era when most women got married, produced children, and deferred completely to their husbands. Daniel Anthony, her father, belonged to the Society of Friends (better known as Quakers), a religious group that recognized the equality of men and women. Daniel encouraged his daughter to think independently and to speak her mind. He supported her educational pursuits and emphasized self-sufficiency.

Although Anthony's father was an admirable man and progressive for his time, her mother, Lucy Anthony, found little pleasure in her restricted, duty-bound life. She appeared overwhelmed by eight pregnancies and exhausted from running the household while keeping boarders and raising six surviving children. Historians believe that the withdrawn, careworn Lucy became a symbol to Anthony of the unfair burdens of marriage. The institution seemed weighted against women, even those with kind and liberal-minded husbands. Anthony concluded that marriage was necessary only when a strong emotional bond existed between two people. This view put her at odds with most women of her generation, who considered matrimony a requirement for social and economic security. True to her principles, Anthony—who once referred to marriage as SLAVERY and "a blot on civilization"—rejected several suitors' offers and remained single throughout her long life.

Anthony was an intelligent young girl who received the best education available at the time. Although she attended a well-regarded boarding school in Philadelphia, she did not enroll in college. In the 1830s only one college in the United States, Ohio's Oberlin College, accepted women. Even with a college education, Anthony would have faced a limited number of employment opportunities. As a woman, her only options were to become a seamstress, a domestic, or a teacher. Anthony chose teaching, and in 1838, began the first of several teaching jobs. In 1846, she became headmistress at Canajoharie Academy in New York. There, she discovered

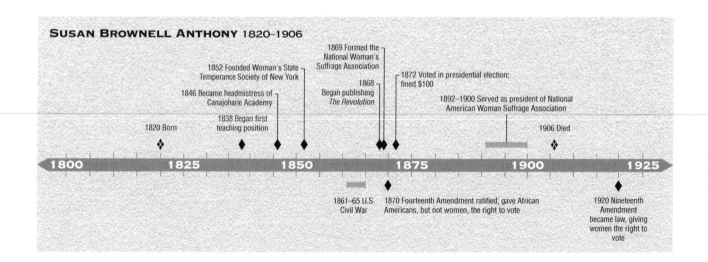

SUSAN BROWNELL ANTHONY 1820–1906

1852 Founded Woman's State Temperance Society of New York

1869 Formed the National Woman's Suffrage Association

1872 Voted in presidential election; fined $100

1846 Became headmistress of Canajoharie Academy

1868 Began publishing *The Revolution*

1892–1900 Served as president of National American Woman Suffrage Association

1838 Began first teaching position

1820 Born

1906 Died

1800　1825　1850　1875　1900　1925

1861–65 U.S. Civil War

1870 Fourteenth Amendment ratified; gave African Americans, but not women, the right to vote

1920 Nineteenth Amendment became law, giving women the right to vote

that male teachers were paid $10.00 per week, whereas she received $2.50. Frustrated with the low pay and a lack of respect for her work, Anthony decided to devote her energies to social reform.

Although Anthony is best known for her fight for women's suffrage, she also crusaded for other causes. In 1852 Anthony became active in the TEMPERANCE MOVEMENT, a national campaign to ban the sale and consumption of alcohol. When it became clear that women were not allowed full leadership in the existing temperance organizations, Anthony helped form the Woman's State Temperance Society of New York.

Like her father, Anthony also was a fervent abolitionist. She became friends with FREDERICK DOUGLASS and attended her father's antislavery meetings in the family home. Before and during the U.S. CIVIL WAR, Anthony devoted her organizational skills to the cause. As head of the Anti-Slavery Society of New York, she planned lecture schedules and spoke publicly against the evils of the Southern system and of the discriminatory practices in the North. During this time, she joined forces with another abolitionist, ELIZABETH CADY STANTON, who was the acknowledged leader of the fledgling women's rights movement.

After the war, Anthony and Stanton continued to work together for social reform. They were bitterly disappointed when their fellow abolitionists refused to support their strategy for constitutionally mandating voting rights for women. A golden opportunity for female suffrage had arisen with the drafting of the FIFTEENTH AMENDMENT to the U.S. Constitution. This amendment was necessary to grant voting rights to the former slaves who were liberated by President Abraham Lincoln's EMANCIPATION PROCLAMATION. However, the abolitionists supported the Fifteenth Amendment only to the extent that it gave African American males the right to vote. They were not concerned about the amendment's exclusion of women. With that defeat, Anthony focused her sights on a separate CONSTITUTIONAL AMENDMENT to grant women the franchise.

In 1868 Anthony began publishing *The Revolution,* a weekly newsletter advocating suffrage and equal rights for women. In 1869 Anthony and Stanton formed the National Woman's Suffrage Association. An indefatigable worker, Anthony became a fixture on the lecture circuit and headed national petition drives to establish support for female voting rights.

In 1872 Anthony decided to test the legality of voting laws that allowed only white and African American males to go to the polls. She registered and voted in the 1872 presidential election in Rochester, New York. Anthony was prosecuted for the offense and fined $100, but she refused to pay. Her defiance rallied supporters of women's rights across the nation. In time, Anthony merged her suffrage organization with another one, to form the National American Woman Suffrage Association. She served as president of this association from 1892 to 1900.

Not surprisingly, Anthony fought hard for the liberalization of laws for married women. During most of the nineteenth century, a wife had very little protection under the law. Any income she produced automatically belonged to her husband, as did any inheritance she received. Her husband could apprentice their children without her permission and was designated sole guardian of their children, no matter how unfit he might be. A husband even had the right to pass on his guardianship of the children by will. In Anthony's home state of New York, her petition drives and lectures were instrumental in convincing the legislature to pass laws giving married women power over their incomes and guardianship of their children.

Anthony was not afraid to flout social conventions to achieve her goals. For a time she wore bloomers, a controversial garment named after Amelia Jenks Bloomer, the woman who popularized it. Bloomers were loose-fitting trousers gathered at the ankle and worn underneath a knee-length skirt. The costume was intended as a protest against the tight-fitting corsets and unwieldy petticoats popularly worn by women at the time. Although she withstood ridicule to make her point, Anthony stopped wearing bloomers when she concluded that they were diverting attention from the more serious issues facing women.

Anthony's message of equality often met resistance, and not just from men. Many women in the nineteenth century were frightened by or skeptical of change. In 1870 Anthony lamented their wariness when she wrote, "The fact is, women are in chains, and their servitude is all the

MEN THEIR RIGHTS AND NOTHING MORE; WOMEN THEIR RIGHTS AND NOTHING LESS.
—SUSAN ANTHONY

more debasing because they do not realize it." She urged women to recognize the inequities they faced and to speak and act for their own freedom.

When Anthony died in 1906, women did not yet have the right to vote in presidential elections. When the NINETEENTH AMENDMENT to the U.S. Constitution finally became law in 1920, it was called the Anthony amendment in recognition of her valiant efforts to gain suffrage.

Anthony was also honored in 1979 and 1980, when the U.S. Mint issued one dollar coins bearing her likeness. She became the first woman to be pictured on a U.S. coin in general circulation.

FURTHER READINGS

Barry, Kathleen. 1988. *Susan B. Anthony: A Biography of a Singular Feminist.* New York: New York Univ. Press.
Cooper, Ilene. 1984. *Susan B. Anthony.* New York: Watts.
Gurko, Miriam. 1974. *The Ladies of Seneca Falls: The Birth of the Woman's Rights Movement.* New York: Macmillan.
Wells, Ida B. 1970. *Crusade for Justice: The Autobiography of Ida B. Wells.* Ed. Alfreda M. Duster. Chicago: Univ. of Chicago Press.

CROSS REFERENCES

Fifteenth Amendment; Nineteenth Amendment; Stanton, Elizabeth Cady; Temperance Movement; Women's Rights.

ANTI-BALLISTIC-MISSILE TREATY OF 1972

The Anti-Ballistic-Missile Treaty of 1972 (ABM Treaty) limited the number of defensive anti-ballistic missile (ABM) systems that the United States and the former Soviet Union could use in preparation for nuclear war (23 UST 3435: TIAS 7503; 944 UNTS 13, U.S. DEPARTMENT OF STATE, *Treaties in Force*, 1993). Restrictions on ballistic missile defenses (BMDs), military warning systems designed to alert and protect a nation, composed the bulk of the treaty's articles. The treaty limited each country's supply of remote-controlled, long-range nuclear rockets, or intercontinental ballistic missiles (ICBMs). Following the breakup of the Soviet Union in 1991, the Russian Federation continued to adhere to the agreement. In 2001, however, the United States announced that it would no longer abide by the pact.

On May 26, 1972, at the U.S.-Soviet summit in Moscow, President RICHARD M. NIXON of the United States and President Leonid Brezhnev of the Soviet Union signed, in conjunction with the Strategic Arms Limitation Talks of 1969–72 (SALT I), the ABM Treaty. The treaty limited each party to two ABM sites, with no more than one hundred ABM launchers and interceptors at each site. One of these sites could protect an ICBM silo deployment area, and the second could protect the national capital. The treaty prohibited the development, testing, or deployment of sea-based, air-based, space-based, or mobile land-based ABM systems. Furthermore, it excluded the transfer or deployment of ABM systems to or in other nations. The 15 articles of the treaty were of unlimited duration and would come up for renewal every five years.

The principles of the treaty explicitly reflected the policy of mutual assured destruction (MAD)—the belief that the best way to control nuclear arms is to allow both sides enough power to ensure the destruction of both nations in the event of war. As stated in Article I of the treaty, each side agreed "not to deploy ABM systems for a defense of the territory of its country and not to provide a base for such a defense, and not to deploy ABM systems for defense of an individual region" (Durch 1988). Article II defines an ABM system as "a system to counter strategic ballistic missiles or their elements in flight trajectory, currently consisting of ABM interceptor missiles ... ABM launchers [and] ... ABM radars." Article III reiterates the ban on ABM deployment, excepting, for each side, one deployment area around the national capital and one around an ICBM launcher deployment area. This provision was later reduced, in 1974, to just one deployment area for each country, allowing "no more than 100 ABM interceptor missiles at launch sites." Articles IV to XV outline provisions for, among other issues, nuclear testing, radar deployment, amendments to the treaty, and the terms of treaty withdrawal.

After the ABM Treaty was ratified by the U.S. Congress, legislators refused to authorize funds for building an ABM site outside Washington, D.C. In early 1975, the United States deployed its single permitted system near the Minuteman Fields at Grand Forks Air Force Base in North Dakota. Within a year, however, Congress deactivated the system on the ground that it was not very cost-effective. The Soviets, meanwhile, used their ABM deployments to protect Moscow.

Despite attempts to follow the principles of SALT I, continued limitations on strategic arms fell apart with the SALT II Treaty of 1979. The

U.S. President Richard Nixon and Soviet President Leonid Brezhnev sign the Anti-Ballistic-Missile Treaty in Moscow on May 26, 1972.

AP IMAGES

U.S. Congress refused to ratify the treaty, which had been signed by Presidents JIMMY CARTER and Leonid Brezhnev. SALT II went on to draw heavy fire in the 1980s from the newly empowered Reagan administration. Whereas the Soviets generally adhered to a strict interpretation of the ABM Treaty, President RONALD REAGAN advocated "peace through strength" and pushed for new WEAPONS programs and policies. Reagan reinterpreted the treaty liberally, putting it to its most serious test. His proposal to render nuclear ballistic missiles ineffective and obsolete, with the Strategic Defense Initiative (SDI), a space-based BMD system popularly known as Star Wars, caused great debate at home and considerable alarm in the Soviet Union.

Like Reagan, opponents of the ABM Treaty believed that its limits were based on one-way accommodation, that is, allowing the Soviets to retain their numerical superiority, as seen in SALT II. The Soviets had previously established numerical superiority in ICBM deployment, and the ABM Treaty supposedly held back the development of further U.S. weapons

technology. Especially troublesome to some was the Soviet's Krasnoyarsk radar system in western Siberia. According to Article VI of the ABM Treaty, an early-warning radar with this orientation should have been located on the Pacific coast or in the outer Arctic reaches of Siberia. Many believed that Moscow was cheating on its end of the deal, and thus that the treaty should go.

In the 1980s tensions between the United States and the Soviet Union flared. In October 1985 the Reagan administration announced a new interpretation of the ABM Treaty, under which the development and testing of "exotic" ABM systems (those not spelled out in the treaty itself, e.g., Star Wars) would have no limit. In 1986, with the Strategic Arms Reduction Treaty (START) talks in full swing, the United States and the Soviet Union treated the ABM Treaty as a central bargaining chip. Moscow looked to maintain the treaty for at least another decade, with tight constraints on space testing. Washington, meanwhile, looked to abide by the treaty for, at most, another decade and expected lessened constraints on the space testing of exotic technologies.

The ensuing events of the late 1980s and early 1990s caught everyone by surprise. Although the United States' interest in the SDI continued into the George H. W. Bush administration years, and persisted through the eventual breakup of the Soviet Union, both the United States and the Soviet Union showed interest in pursuing at least the spirit of the ABM Treaty. True arms-reduction talks developed with the Soviet demise. In 1991 Soviet nuclear forces were split up among four countries—Russia, Ukraine, Belarus, and Kazakhstan—and spokespersons on both sides saw revision of the ABM Treaty as necessary. The START agreements of 1992 shed new light on older concessions. As the chief U.S. architect of the original ABM Treaty, HENRY KISSINGER now joined others in declaring it obsolete in the new era of disarmament. As a gesture of GOOD FAITH, the Soviets demolished their controversial Krasnoyarsk radar system; a shoe factory now occupies the site.

In the years that followed, the United States and Russia both worked together and strayed from the MAD doctrine. They also turned their attention elsewhere, mainly to the developing world. New nations on the list of nuclear powers included Israel, India, Pakistan, Algeria, Egypt, Iran, Iraq, Libya, North Korea, and Syria, none of which had any formal attachment to the ABM Treaty. U.S. and former Soviet strategists went from analyzing BMD research provisions set forth in the ABM Treaty to setting up safeguards against attack from other powers.

In December 2001, however, the United States announced that it would no longer follow the ABM treaty. The withdrawal came after months of failed negotiations with Russia to jointly abandon the ABM treaty and to craft a new pact based on the current world situation. The formal announcement by President GEORGE W. BUSH set in motion a six-month period for ending the pact. He stated that the ABM Treaty "hinders our government's ability to develop ways to protect our people from future terrorist or rogue state missile attacks."

On June 13, 2002, the United States officially withdrew from the ABM Treaty. In response to the United States withdrawal, the following day Russia announced that it would no longer be bound by the START II Strategic Arms Reduction Treaty that was signed by both President GEORGE H.W. BUSH and Russian President Boris Yeltsin on January 3, 1993. However, Russia's decision to pull out from START II had no real impact, as the terms of that treaty had been superseded by the Strategic Offensive Reductions Treaty (SORT). SORT was entered into by President George W. Bush and Russian President Vladimir Putin on May 24, 2002, and was ratified on June 1, 2003. Under that treaty, both countries agreed to reduce their strategic nuclear warheads by 2012. Although Putin expressed regret at the United States' decision to withdraw from the ABM Treaty, he did not signal a move to build a competing system.

Putin was not the only person to express regret. President George W. Bush's decision to withdraw from the ABM Treaty was met with criticism by members of the United States House of Representatives. Thirty-two members of the House of Representatives, led by Ohio Representative Dennis Kucinich, filed a lawsuit against President George W. Bush, charging that he did not have the authority to unilaterally withdraw the United States from the ABM treaty without congressional approval. The district court dismissed the case and ruled that the members of the House of Representatives did not have any standing to challenge President Bush's decision, because they were not personally injured by the president's act, and because the issue of a treaty termination is a "political question" that cannot be resolved by the courts.

The Bush administration made it clear that the United States' withdrawal from the treaty was motivated by the desire to build and deploy a long-range missile defense system that would protect the nation from attacks by rogue nations such as North Korea and Iran. The deployment of the missile shield system was set for 2004 and was planned to have a missile radar system placed in the Czech Republic as well as 10 long-range missile interceptors in Poland. On September 17, 2009, however, President Barack Obama's administration announced that it was eliminating the original plans of the Bush Administration's long-range missile defense system to implement a system that favors more flexible, short-range systems that will counter potential short- or mid-range European missile THREATS from Iran.

FURTHER READINGS

American-Soviet Treaty on the Limitation of Anti-Ballistic Missile Systems. May 26, 1972. Moscow.

Assembly of Western European Union. 1993. Anti-Missile Defence for Europe, Symposium, Rome, April 20–21.

Blackwill, Robert D., and Albert Carnesale, eds. 1993. *New Nuclear Nations.* New York: Council on Foreign Relations.

Boese, Wade. "U.S. Withdraws from ABM Treaty; Global Response Muted." Arms Control Association. Available online at http:// www.armscontrol.org/print/1071 website home page: http://www.armscontrol.org (accessed September 24, 2009).

Durch, William J. 1988. *The ABM Treaty and Western Security.* Cambridge, Mass.: Ballinger.

———. 1987. *The Future of the ABM Treaty.* London: International Institute for Strategic Studies.

Greenville, J.A.S., and Bernard Wasserstein. 1987. *The Major International Treaties Since 1945.* London: Methuen.

Joint Chiefs of Staff. 1994. *Doctrine for Joint Theater Missile Defense.* Joint pub. no. 3-01.5, March 30.

"Judge Allows Bush's Withdrawal from ABM Treaty to Stand: Leaves Open Possibility of Future Congressional Role in Treaty Termination." Lawyers Committee on Nuclear Policy. Available online at http://lcnp.org/ disarmament/ABMlawsuit/ABMdecisionpr.pdf website home page: http://www.lcnp.org (accessed September 24, 2009).

Kartchner, Kerry M. 1992. *Negotiating START.* New Brunswick, N.J., and London: Transaction.

Martinez, Luis, Raddatz, Martha, Compton, Ann. September 17, 2009. "Obama: New European Missile Plan will Strengthen U.S. Defenses." ABCNews.com. Available online at http://abcnews.go.com/print?id=8599260. Website home page: http://abcnews.go.com (accessed September 24, 2009).

Mazarr, Michael J., and Alexander T. Lennon, eds., 1994. *Toward a Nuclear Peace.* New York: St. Martin's Press.

Perez-Rivas, Manuel. December 14, 2001. "U.S. Quits ABM Treaty." CNN.com: Inside Politics. Available online at www.cnn.com/2001/ALLPOLITICS/12/13/rec.bush. abm/index.html (accessed May 30, 2003).

Voas, Jeanette. 1990. *Soviet Attitudes towards Ballistic Missile Defence and the ABM Treaty.* London: International Institute for Strategic Studies.

CROSS REFERENCES

Arms Control and Disarmament; Bush, George Herbert Walker; International Law

ANTI-DEFAMATION LEAGUE

The Anti-Defamation League (ADL) is an agency of B'snai B'srith, an international Jewish service organization. The ADL combats anti-Semitism, religious and racial intolerance, and all forms of organized discrimination based on stereotypical beliefs. The ADL also is a strong advocate of the state of Israel, LOBBYING Congress in support of legislation that benefits the Jewish State. It has its headquarters in New York City and has regional and satellite offices throughout the United States. The ADL also has offices in Jerusalem and Vienna.

Sigmound Livingston founded the ADL in 1913 with the support of B'snai B'srith. Livingston, a Chicago attorney, stated that the mission of the league was "to stop, by appeals to reason and conscience, and if necessary, by appeals to law, the DEFAMATION of the Jewish people . . . to secure justice and fair treatment to all citizens alike . . . [and] put an end forever to unjust and unfair discrimination against and ridicule of any sect or body of citizens."

The ADL first gained recognition by taking steps to eradicate negative stereotypes of Jews in print and their stereotyping on stage and in film. By the early 1920s, objectionable references to Jews in the national press had virtually disappeared. However, popular culture was filled with negative stereotypes of Jews. The rise of the KU KLUX KLAN in the 1920s was based as much on anti-Semitism as racial intolerance. The ADL responded by circulating pamphlets that challenged hatred of Jews and demanded apologies from prominent citizens, such as automobile manufacturer Henry Ford, for endorsing anti-Semitic views.

With the rise of Nazism in the 1930s, the ADL fought U.S. supporters of Hitler who endorsed his anti-Semitic policies. During this decade, the ADL began to collect information on extremist individuals and organizations and to monitor and investigate fascist groups in the United States. These fact-finding and monitoring activities have remained a central part of the ADL's work.

Since the 1940s, the ADL has lobbied for CIVIL RIGHTS legislation, filed briefs in courts supporting the SEPARATION of church and state, and educated succeeding generations in religious tolerance. Since the creation of Israel in 1948, the ADL has also defended Israel's right to exist and has fought against anti-Zionism. In the 1990s, the organization began monitoring the INTERNET for evidence of anti-Semitism and right-wing extremism. In 2000 the ADL issued a report titled "Combating Extremism in Cyberspace," a review of legal issues raised by hate groups using the Internet. The ADL's monitoring of the Internet and other forms of communication took on new urgency in light of the events surrounding the SEPTEMBER 11TH ATTACKS of 2001 on the United States. In addition to the many other issues concerning the ADL including school vouchers and President George W. Bush's "Faith Based Initiative" to allow certain charities to receive federal funds, the ADL Internet site features a "Terrorism Update." The ADL has also created a handbook with suggestions for keeping Jewish institutions safe from terrorist attacks.

The ADL is divided into numerous groups and departments. The Civil Rights Division is the most prominent wing of the organization, as it has investigated and exposed anti-Semitism and bigotry. The division's research department has become a central source of information on organized bigotry, collecting and analyzing racist, anti-Semitic, terrorist, and extremist literature. The department issues an annual *Audit of Anti-Semitic Incidents* that serves as a reliable measurement tool of anti-Semitic trends. The Civil Rights Division's fact-finding department uses investigative journalists to track the activities of extremist groups. For example, this department tracked neo-Nazi skinhead activity in 33 countries and issued the first major survey on this movement.

The Civil Rights Division's legal affairs department serves as the ADL's advocate in court and before legislatures. The department's attorneys file briefs, analyze proposed bills and regulations, draft model laws, and prepare TESTIMONY and legal reports for ADL staff. The department's model hate crimes law has been adopted by almost four-fifths of the states and has been upheld as constitutional by the U.S. Supreme Court in *State v. Mitchell,* 508 U.S. 476, 113 S. Ct. 2194, 124 L.Ed.2d 436 (1993). In addition, the department works with local attorneys in the ADL's thirty regional offices.

The ADL's Braun Holocaust Institute, established in 1977, serves as a centralized information center on the Holocaust. The institute encourages public and religious schools to teach about the Holocaust by providing curricula for elementary and high school students. It has also organized teacher-training workshops and seminars to help teachers incorporate Holocaust studies into mainstream disciplines. The institute's collection of Holocaust-related materials is recognized as one of the best in the world. In addition, the institute publishes *Dimensions: A Journal of Holocaust Studies*, a general interest magazine on the Holocaust, and resource guides, catalogs, and background primers.

The Government and National Affairs Office in Washington, D.C., serves as the ADL's lobbyist, promoting the legislative agenda of the organization. The office worked with Congress to establish a congressional task force against anti-Semitism. The ADL has also led a broad coalition of civil rights, religious, and law enforcement groups in support of federal HATE CRIME initiatives. In addition, the ADL has fought against federal school voucher programs and has sought to increase workplace protection for employees who wish to observe their religious duties.

The ADL's commitment to the state of Israel includes maintaining an office in Jerusalem. This office provides information on current issues to ADL staff and members, and it communicates the U.S. Jewish community's concerns to the Israeli government. The Jerusalem office also introduces visiting Americans, such as government officials and journalists, to the people and politics of Israel. The ADL has endorsed the need for a just peace between Israelis and Palestinians but has been an adamant defender of Israel and opponent of TERRORISM.

FURTHER READINGS

Anti-Defamation League Web site. Available online at http://www.adl.org (accessed July 4, 2009).

Levin, Jack, and Jack McDevitt. 2002. *Hate Crimes Revisited.* New York: Westview.

Stern-Larosa, Caryl, and Ellen Hoffheimer-Bettmann. 2001. *Anti-Defamation League's Hate Hurts: How Children Learn and Unlearn Prejudice.* New York: Scholastic.

CROSS REFERENCES

Hate Crime; Hate Crime: "Do Hate Crime Laws Restrict First Amendment Rights?" (In Focus); Libel and Slander.

ANTICIPATION

The performance of an act or obligation before it is legally due. In patent law, the publication of the existence of an invention that has already been patented or has a patent pending, which are grounds for denying a patent to an invention that has substantially the same structure and function as the earlier invention.

In the law of NEGLIGENCE, anticipation refers to the knowledge that there is a reasonable probability that the consequences of particular conduct of one individual will result in injury to others.

The anticipation of an invention also occurs if the later invention is merely an ADAPTATION of an earlier patent, which would be obvious to a skilled person who need only exercise some mechanical skill to develop the same adaptation.

ANTICIPATORY REPUDIATION

The unjustifiable denial by a party to a contract of any intention to perform contractual duties, which occurs prior to the time performance is due.

This form of breach, also known as anticipatory breach of contract, occurs when one party positively states that he or she will not substantially perform a contract. The mere assertion that the party is encountering difficulties in preparing to perform, is dissatisfied with the bargain, or is otherwise uncertain whether performance will be rendered when due is insufficient to constitute a REPUDIATION. Another type of anticipatory breach consists of any VOLUNTARY ACT by a party that destroys, or seriously impairs, that party's ability to perform the contract.

The remedies available to the nonrepudiating party upon an anticipatory repudiation entail certain obligations. If the nonrepudiating party chooses to ignore the repudiation and proceeds with his or her performance, the duty to mitigate damages—which imposes on the injured party an obligation to exercise reasonable effort to minimize losses—mandates that the nonrepudiating party not perform if the consequence of performance would be to increase the damages. In addition, this duty requires, where applicable, the procurement of a substitute performance.

If the nonrepudiating party implores or insists that the other party perform, this demand, in and of itself, does not divest the nonrepudiating party's right to damages. The presence or absence of a breach of contract depends solely upon the repudiating party's actions. The prevailing view is that the non-repudiating party may pursue any remedy for breach of contract, even though he or she has informed the repudiating party that he would await the latter's performance.

The nonrepudiating party also possesses the option to do nothing and to commence an action for breach after the time for performance. Under the majority view, such an action can be instituted without tendering the non-repudiating party's performance or even alleging or proving that the party was ready, willing, and able to perform. The nonrepudiating party must demonstrate, however, that he or she would have been ready, willing, and able to perform but for the repudiation.

In regard to the law of sales, the UNIFORM COMMERCIAL CODE (UCC), a body of law governing commercial transactions by the states, provides that anticipatory repudiation entails the right of one party to a contract to sue for breach before the performance date when the other party communicates the intention not to perform. The repudiation can, however, be retracted before the performance date if the nonrepudiating party has not acted on the basis of the repudiation. Some jurisdictions direct the injured party to await the performance date before instituting an action.

ANTILAWYER MOVEMENT

Throughout early U.S. history, legal practitioners were the subject of ambivalence on the part of the general public. The attitude against lawyers reached its peak after the Revolutionary War and remained hostile until the beginning of the nineteenth century.

During the early days of the colonies, the system for the administration of justice was based on arbitration and religious principles, and lawyers specially educated and skilled in the law were presumably not needed and were often restricted or prohibited from practicing. Judges were ordinary men who used unpolished methods of questioning to determine the facts of each case; defendants were their own lawyers. This system remained successful as long as the population of each community remained small and manageable, and the people were clear about their rights and obligations to their neighbors and the community.

By the end of the seventeenth century, the colonies experienced a period of growth, and the original judicial system became unsatisfactory. Formal PLEADING and skilled lawyers began to replace the primitive methods of earlier colonial times.

After the Revolutionary War, Americans sought a new form of jurisprudence to interact with their newly gained freedoms. Laws were less confining, due to the belief that moral fiber was more important to satisfactory conduct than legislation.

During this period, the antilawyer movement gained momentum. Historians speculate that it evolved as a result of former prejudices and conflicts toward the legal profession. Although lawyers in the past had not been viewed favorably, they achieved prominence and esteem as strong proponents of freedom from England during the Revolutionary War. After the war, lawyers were once again an important part of the legal system but were used

A wood engraving from an 1884 Harper's Monthly shows Daniel Shays and his comrades occupying a Massachusetts courthouse to prevent the court from directing legal action at debt-ridden farmers in 1786.

BETTMANN/CORBIS.

common people of some of their hard-won freedoms. Although the fears were exaggerated, they were true to some degree, for lawyers did earn a living from the ramifications that legislation had upon the general public.

Two remedies were recommended to reconcile the proponents of the antilawyer sentiment and lawyers. The first suggestion was an updated version of the early colonial justice system, which prohibited lawyers from practicing. A judge representing the interests of the community would preside over the court and instruct the jury. Judges were educated aristocrats who could be impeached if their conduct so warranted. If a LEGAL REPRESENTATIVE was deemed necessary, a friend of the DEFENDANT could participate in the arbitration.

The second suggestion provided for a small group of professional lawyers to practice as public servants. Their salaries and actions would be controlled by the state, and their chief function would be to clarify legal principles of each case for the jury.

The conflicting feelings toward lawyers culminated in several incidents, the most noteworthy of which was known as Shays's Rebellion. The rebellion began in 1786 when Massachusetts voters elected a majority of nonlawyers to the General Court. This action led to a RIOT, and hostile agrarian mobs overran the courthouses, closing them down. The governor dispatched the state army, which successfully quelled the agitators.

Shays's Rebellion did not stop the people of Massachusetts from electing lawyers to political positions. The very tactics they feared in the courtroom were highly desirable in politics to control government officials; in spite of their conflicting feelings, voters were still attracted to legal skills.

The new methods of justice proved to be inefficient. Arbitration was fruitless, and laymen were fallible as lawyers. By 1790, most cases were again tried by lawyers, and the antilawyer movement began to wane.

CROSS REFERENCE

Shays's Rebellion.

ANTINOMY

An expression in law and logic to indicate that two authorities, laws, or propositions are inconsistent with each other.

primarily by the wealthy. As a result, they were often in conflict with those who were poor and could not pay their debts, which led to a resurrection of the old negative attitudes against them.

Lawyers were regarded with suspicion. They were accused of initiating unnecessary lawsuits, impeding the justice system, and prolonging trials to secure additional fees from unsuspecting clients. They were also criticized for the use of legal jargon, causing simple matters to seem complicated.

Despite these attacks, lawyers managed to attain political power. They were regarded as conspirators, however, for people could not accept the idea that lawyers who served as politicians made the laws by which they secured a living as legal practitioners. It was also feared that lawyers, judges, and legislators would band together to control society, depriving the

ANTITRUST LAW

Antitrust law refers to legislation enacted by the federal and various state governments to regulate trade and commerce by preventing unlawful restraints, price-fixing, and monopolies; to promote competition; and to encourage the production of quality goods and services at the lowest prices, with the primary goal of safeguarding public welfare by ensuring that consumer demands will be met by the manufacture and sale of goods at reasonable prices.

Antitrust law seeks to make enterprises compete fairly. It has had a serious effect on business practices and the organization of U.S. industry. Based on the belief that free trade benefits the economy, businesses, and consumers alike, the law forbids several types of RESTRAINT OF TRADE and monopolization. These fall into four main areas: agreements between or among competitors, contractual arrangements between sellers and buyers, the pursuit or maintenance of monopoly power, and mergers.

The Sherman Anti-Trust Act of 1890 (15 U.S.C.A. § 1 et seq.) is the basis for U.S. antitrust law, and many states have modeled their own statutes upon it. As weaknesses in the Sherman Act became evident, Congress added amendments to it at various times through 1950. The most important are the CLAYTON ACT of 1914 (15 U.S.C.A. § 12 et seq.) and the ROBINSON-PATMAN ACT of 1936 (15 U.S.C.A. § 13 et seq.). Congress also created a regulatory agency to administrate and enforce the law, under the FEDERAL TRADE COMMISSION Act of 1914 (15 U.S.C.A. §§ 41–58). In an ongoing analysis influenced by economic, intellectual, and political changes, the U.S. Supreme Court has played the leading role in shaping the ways in which these laws are applied.

Enforcement of antitrust law depends largely on two agencies: the Federal Trade Commission (FTC), which may issue cease-and-desist orders to violators, and the Antitrust Division of the U.S. DEPARTMENT OF JUSTICE (DOJ), which can litigate. Private parties may also bring civil suits. Violations of the Sherman Act are felonies carrying fines of up to $10 million for corporations, and fines of up to $350,000 and prison sentences of up to three years for persons. The federal government, states, and individuals may collect treble (i.e., triple) the amount of damages that they have suffered as a result of injuries.

During a December 1998 news conference in Washington, D.C., Bill Gates, founder of Microsoft, answers questions, via closed-circuit television, about the antitrust lawsuit filed against the company.

AP IMAGES

Origins

Antitrust law originated in reaction to a public outcry over *trusts,* which were late-nineteenth-century corporate monopolies that dominated U.S. manufacturing and mining. Trusts took their name from the legal device of business incorporation called trusteeship, which consolidated control of industries by transferring stock in exchange for trust certificates. The practice grew out of necessity. Twenty-five years after the Civil War, rapid industrialization had blessed and cursed business. Markets expanded and productivity grew, but output exceeded demand, and competition sharpened. Rivals sought greater security and profits in cartels (mutual agreements to fix prices and control output). Out of these arrangements sprang the trusts. From sugar to whiskey to beef to tobacco, the process of merger and consolidation brought entire industries under the control of just a few powerful people. Oil and steel, the backbone of the nation's heavy industries, lay in the hands of the corporate giants John D. Rockefeller and J. P. Morgan. The trusts could fix prices at any level. If a competitor entered the market, the trusts would sell their goods at a loss until the competitor went out of business, and then they would raise prices again. By the 1880s, abuses by the trusts brought demands for reform.

History gave only contradictory direction to the reformers. Before the eighteenth century,

This political cartoon depicts President Theodore Roosevelt resurrecting the Sherman Anti-Trust Act. Roosevelt's administration filed 44 antitrust lawsuits in eight years.

COMMON LAW concerned itself with contracts, combinations, and conspiracies that resulted in restraint of free trade, but it did little about them. English courts generally let restrictive contracts stand because the courts did not consider themselves to be suited to judging adequacy or fairness. Over time, courts looked more closely into both the purpose and the effect of any restraint of trade. The turning point came in 1711 with the establishment of the basic standard for judging close cases, "the rule of reason." Courts asked whether the goal of a contract was a general restraint of competition (a *naked restraint*) or particularly limited in time and geography (an *ancillary restraint*). Naked restraints were unreasonable, but ancillary restraints were often acceptable. Exceptions to the rule grew as the economic philosophy of *laissez-faire* economics (meaning "let the people do what they please") spread its doctrine of non-interference in business. As rival businesses formed cartels to fix prices and to control output, the late-eighteenth-century English courts often nodded in approval.

By the time the U.S. public was complaining about the trusts, common law in U.S. courts was somewhat tougher on restraint of trade. Yet it was still contradictory. The courts took two

basic views of cartels: tolerant and condemning. The first view accepted cartels as long as they did not stop other merchants from entering the market. This view used the rule of reason to determine this, and it put a high premium on the freedom to enter into contracts. Businesses and contracts mattered. Consumers, who suffered from price-fixing, were irrelevant; the wisdom of the market would protect them from exploitation. The second view was that cartels are thoroughly bad. It reserved the rule of reason only for judging more limited ancillary restrictions. Given these competing views, which varied from state to state, no comprehensive common law could be said to exist. But one approach was destined to win.

The Sherman Act and Early Enforcement

In 1890, Congress took aim at the trusts with passage of the SHERMAN ANTI-TRUST ACT, named for Senator JOHN SHERMAN (R-Ohio). It went far beyond the common law's refusal to enforce certain offensive contracts. Clearly persuaded by the more restrictive view that saw great harm in restraint of trade, the Sherman Act outlawed trusts altogether. The LANDMARK law had two sections. Section 1 broadly banned group action in agreements, forbidding "every contract, combination in the form of trust or otherwise, or conspiracy," that restrained interstate or foreign trade. Section 2 barred individuals from monopolizing or trying to monopolize. Violations of either section were punishable by a maximum fine of $50,000 and up to one year in jail. The Sherman Act passed by nearly unanimous votes in both houses of Congress.

Although sweeping in its language, the Sherman Act soon revealed its limitations. Congress had wanted action even though it did not know what steps to take. Historians would later dispute what its precise aims had been, but clearly the lawmakers intended for the courts to play the leading role in promoting competition and attacking monopolization: Judges would make decisions as cases arose, slowly developing a body of opinions that would replace the confusing precedents of state courts. For a public that expected overnight change, the process worked all too slowly. President Grover Cleveland's Department of Justice, which disliked the Sherman Act, made little effort to enforce it.

Initial setbacks also came from the U.S. Supreme Court's first consideration of the statute, in *United States v. E. C. Knight Co.,* 156 U.S. 1, 15 S. Ct. 249, 39 L. Ed. 325 (1895). Rejecting a challenge to a sugar trust that controlled more than 98 percent of the nation's sugar-refining capacity, the Court held that manufacturing was not interstate commerce. This was good news for trusts. If manufacturers were exempt from the Sherman Act, then they would have little to worry about from federal antitrust regulators. The Court only began strongly supporting the use of the law in the late 1890s, starting with cases against railroad cartels. By 1904 some 300 large companies still controlled nearly 40 percent of the nation's manufacturing assets and influenced at least 80 percent of its vital industries.

After the turn of the twentieth century, federal enforcement intensified. President Theodore Roosevelt's announcement that he was a "trustbuster" foreshadowed one important aspect of the future of antitrust enforcement: It would depend largely on political will from the Executive Branch of government. Roosevelt and his successor, President WILLIAM HOWARD TAFT, responded to public criticism over the rapid merger of even more industries by pursuing more vigorous legal action. Steady prosecution in the first decade of the twentieth century brought the downfall of trusts.

In 1911 the U.S. Supreme Court ordered the dissolution of the Standard Oil Company and the American Tobacco Company in landmark rulings that brought down two of the most powerful industrial trusts. But these were ambiguous victories. In *Standard Oil Co. of New Jersey v. United States,* 221 U.S. 1, 31 S. Ct. 502, 55 L. Ed. 619, for example, the Court dissolved the trust into 33 companies, but held that the Sherman Act outlawed only restraints that were anticompetitive—subject, furthermore, to a rule of reason. Critics of all stripes jumped on this decision. Some feared that conservative judges would now gut the Sherman Act; others predicted a return to lax enforcement; and businesses worried that in the absence of specific unlawful restraints, the rule of reason gave courts too much freedom to read the law subjectively.

Congressional Reform up to 1950

Dissatisfaction brought new federal laws in 1914. The first of these was the Clayton Act, which answered the criticism that the Sherman Act was too general. It declared four practices to be illegal but not criminal: (1) price discrimination—selling a product at different prices to similarly situated buyers; (2) tying and exclusive-dealing contracts—sales on condition that the buyer stop dealing with the seller's competitors; (3) corporate mergers—acquisitions of competing companies; and (4) interlocking directorates—boards of competing companies, with common members.

Quick to hedge its bets, the Clayton Act qualified each of these prohibited activities. They were only illegal where the effect "may be substantially to lessen competition" or "might tend to create a monopoly." This language was intentionally vague. Despite specifying different tests for violations, Congress still wanted the courts to make the difficult decisions. One important limitation was added: The Clayton Act exempted unions from the scope of antitrust law, refusing to treat human labor as a commodity.

The second piece of federal legislation in 1914 was the Federal Trade Commission Act. Without attaching criminal penalties, the law provided that "unfair methods of competition in or affecting commerce, and unfair or deceptive acts or practices in or affecting commerce are hereby declared illegal." This was more than a symbolic attempt to buttress the Sherman Act. The law also created a regulatory agency, the Federal Trade Commission (FTC), to interpret and enforce it. Lawmakers who feared judicial hostility to the Sherman Act saw the FTC as a body that would more closely follow their preferences. Originally, the commission was designed to issue prospective decrees and to share responsibilities with the Antitrust Division of the Department of Justice. Later court rulings would allow it greater latitude in attacking Sherman Act violations.

These laws helped to satisfy the short-term demand for tougher, more explicit action from Congress. Before long, antitrust enforcement would shift with the mood of the country. As WORLD WAR I and the 1920s reversed the outlook of previous years, antitrust policy was characterized by the hands-off policies of President CALVIN COOLIDGE, who declared, "The chief business of the American people is business." Economic trends created and supported this attitude; prosperity seemed a worthwhile reward. In this era, the DOJ gave more attention to promoting fairness than it did to attacking restrictive practices and monopoly power. Although activities such as price-fixing still came under attack, other kinds of business cooperation flourished and even received official encouragement during the early years of the NEW DEAL. This pattern lasted for a good 15 years, intensifying after the STOCK MARKET crash of 1929.

Following what historians called the era of neglect, antitrust made a resurgence. In 1935 the U.S. Supreme Court struck down President Franklin D. Roosevelt's National Industrial Recovery Act, which coordinated industry-wide output and pricing, in *ALA Schechter Poultry Corp. v. United States,* 295 U.S. 495, 55 S. Ct. 837, 79 L. Ed. 1570. The decision radically affected New Deal–era policy. The following year, Congress passed the Robinson-Patman Act in an attempt to make sense of the Clayton Act's bans on price discrimination. The Robinson-Patman Act explicitly forbade forms of price discrimination, in order to protect small producers from extinction at the hands of larger competitors. By 1937, economic decline brought federal antitrust enforcement back with a vengeance, as Roosevelt's administration began an extensive investigation into monopolies. The effort resulted in more than 80 antitrust suits in 1940 alone.

One federal court case in this period, *United States v. Aluminum Co. of America,* 148 F.2d 416 (2d Cir. 1945) (*Alcoa*), changed antimonopoly law for years to come. Since the 1920s, the U.S. Supreme Court had looked skeptically on the role of a business's size in judging monopoly cases. In *United States v. United States Steel Corp.,* 251 U.S. 417, 40 S. Ct. 293, 64 L. Ed. 343 (1920), it said, "[T]he law does not make mere size an offense, or the existence of unexerted power an offense. It, we repeat, requires overt acts." The decision weakened the monopoly ban of the Sherman Act. Rather than focus on abusive business conduct, *Alcoa* emphasized the role of market power. Judge Learned Hand wrote for the Court: "Many people believe that possession of unchallenged economic power deadens initiative, discourages thrift and depresses energy; that immunity from competition is a narcotic, and rivalry is a stimulant, to industrial progress; that the spur of constant stress is necessary to counteract an inevitable disposition to let well enough alone." The standard that emerged from this decision applied a two-part test for determining illegal monopolization: The DEFENDANT (1) must possess

monopoly power in a relevant market; and (2) must have improperly used exclusionary acts to gain or protect that power.

Congress added its last piece of important legislation in 1950 with the Celler-Kefauver Antimerger Act, addressing a weakness in the Clayton Act. Because only anticompetitive stock purchases had been forbidden, businesses would circumvent the Clayton Act by targeting the assets of their rivals. U.S. Supreme Court decisions had also undermined the law by allowing businesses to transfer stock purchases into assets before the government filed a complaint. The Celler-Kefauver amendment closed these loopholes.

The U.S. Supreme Court and Evolving Doctrine

Vigorous enforcement of antitrust legislation created an immense body of CASE LAW. After 1950, U.S. Supreme Court decisions did more than anything else to shape antitrust doctrine. Two competing outlooks emerged. One regarded markets as fragile, easily distorted by private firms, and readily correctable through public intervention. Economic efficiency mattered less, in this view, than the belief in the antitrust doctrine's ability to meet social and political goals. Opponents saw business rivalry as being generally healthy. They doubted that public intervention could cure defects, and they emphasized the self-correcting ability of markets to erode private restraints and private power. This outlook opposed the use of antitrust measures except to stop behavior that clearly harms the efficiency of business.

The most aggressive doctrine was developed under Chief Justice EARL WARREN. The WARREN COURT often saw the need for decentralized social, political, and economic power, a goal that it put ahead of the ideal of economic efficiency. In 1962, its first ruling on the Celler-Kefauver Act, *Brown Shoe Co. v. United States,* 370 U.S. 294, 82 S. Ct. 1502, 8 L. Ed. 2d 510, held that a merger between two firms that accounted for only 5 percent of total industry output violated the principal antimerger provision of the antitrust laws. *Brown Shoe* also reflected the Court's hostility toward *vertical restraints* (i.e., restrictions imposed in contracts by the seller on the buyer, or VICE versa) at that time.

This aggressive approach peaked in 1967 in *United States v. Arnold, Schwinn & Co.,* 388 U.S. 365, 87 S. Ct. 1856, 18 L. Ed. 2d 1249. *Arnold* concerned *nonprice vertical restraints* (i.e., territorial or customer restrictions on the resale of goods). The majority ruled that such restraints were per se illegal, in other words, so harmful to competition that they need not be evaluated. In ensuing years, respected antitrust experts, such as Chief Judge RICHARD POSNER of the U.S. Court of Appeals for the 7th Circuit, criticized the Court's use of "per se" tests to invalidate vertical price agreements between competitors or between sellers and buyers, arguing that such agreements can be efficient.

The U.S. Supreme Court heeded this criticism in *State Oil Co. v. Khan*, 522 U.S. 3, 118 S. Ct. 275, 139 L. Ed. 2d 199 (U.S. 1997). Relying heavily on an appellate opinion penned by Judge Posner, the high court overruled a 29-year-old precedent that declared all vertical maximum price-fixing arrangements to be per se violations of the Sherman Act. Vertical maximum price-fixing arrangements, like the majority of commercial arrangements that are subject to antitrust laws, should be evaluated under the rule of reason, the Court wrote. The rule-of-reason analysis will effectively identify those situations in which vertical maximum price-fixing amounts to anticompetitive conduct, by allowing courts to evaluate a variety of factors, according to the Court. These factors include specific information about the relevant business; the condition of the business before and after the restraint was imposed; and the history, nature, and effect of the restraint.

By the mid 1970s the U.S. Court backed off its robust interventionism. Two pivotal decisions came in 1977, including the most important since WORLD WAR II, *Continental TV v. GTE Sylvania*, 433 U.S. 36, 97 S. Ct. 2549, 53 L. Ed. 2d 568. In a decisive departure from the previous decade's rulings, the Court abandoned its hostility toward efficiency. Now, for evaluating nonprice vertical restraints, it returned to the use of a rule of reason. Per se rules would remain influential, but economic analysis would be the primary tool in formulating and applying antitrust rules. The second powerful change in doctrine was *Brunswick Corp. v. Pueblo Bowl-O-Mat*, 429 U.S. 477, 97 S. Ct. 690, 50 L. Ed. 2d 701. In the *Brunswick* decision, the Court wrote that antitrust laws "were enacted for the 'protection of competition, not competitors.'" The irony was addressed to private antitrust litigants. If they wanted to SUE, the Court wrote, they would have

to prove "antitrust injury." This decision discarded the old view that the demise of individual firms was plainly bad for competition. Replacing it was the view that adverse effects to businesses are sometimes offset by gains in reduced costs and increased output. Increasingly, after *Brunswick*, the U.S. Supreme Court and lower courts accepted economic efficiency as a justification for dominant firms to defend their market positions. By 1986 efficiency-based analysis was widely accepted in federal courts.

Even against this restrictive background, explosive change occurred. The early 1980s saw the dramatic conclusion of a historic monopoly case against the telephone giant American Telephone and Telegraph (AT&T) (*United States v. American Telephone & Telegraph Co.*, 552 F. Supp. 131 [D.D.C. 1982], *aff'd in Maryland v. United States*, 460 U.S. 1001, 103 S. Ct. 1240, 75 L. Ed. 2d 472 [1983]). DOJ settled claims that AT&T had impeded competition in long-distance telephone service and telecommunications equipment. The result was the largest divestiture in history: A federal court severed the Bell System's operating companies and manufacturing arm (Western Electric) from AT&T, thus transforming the nation's telephone services. But the historic settlement was an exception to the political philosophy and the level of enforcement that characterized the decade. As the 1980s were ending, the DOJ dropped its 13-year suit against International Business Machines (IBM). This lengthy battle had sought to end IBM's dominance by breaking it up into four computer companies. Convinced that market forces had done the work for them, prosecutors gave up.

Throughout the 1980s, political conservatism in federal enforcement complemented the U.S. Supreme Court's doctrine of non-intervention. The administration of President RONALD REAGAN reduced the budgets of the FTC and the DOJ, leaving them with limited resources for enforcement. Enforcement efforts followed a restrictive agenda of prosecuting cases of output restrictions and large mergers of a *horizontal* nature (i.e., those involving firms within the same industry and at the same level of production). Mergers of companies into conglomerates, by contrast, were looked on favorably, and the years 1984 and 1985 produced the greatest increase in corporate acquisitions in the nation's history.

As the U.S. Supreme Court strengthened requirements for evidence, injury, and the right to bring suit, antitrust cases became harder for plaintiffs to win. Most decisions during this period narrowed the reach of antitrust. A few rare exceptions, such as *Aspen Skiing Co. v. Aspen Highlands Skiing Corp.*, 472 U.S. 585, 105 S. Ct. 2847, 86 L. Ed. 2d 467 (1985), which condemned a monopolist's unjustified refusal to deal with a rival, faintly recalled the tough outlook of the Warren Court. Non-intervention, however, took precedence. In the strongest example, *Matsushita Electrical Industrial Co. v. Zenith Radio Corp.*, 475 U.S. 574, 106 S. Ct. 1348, 89 L. Ed. 2d 538 (1986), the majority dismissed allegations that Japanese television manufacturers had engaged in a 20-year pricing conspiracy that was designed to drive U.S. electronics equipment manufacturers out of business. The Court discouraged claims that rested on ambiguous CIRCUMSTANTIAL EVIDENCE or lacked "economic rationality," suggesting that lower courts settle these by SUMMARY JUDGMENT.

Litigation since the 1980s

Once again proving that antitrust law never remains static, the late 1980s and early 1990s brought more changes in enforcement, economic analysis, and court doctrine. At the state level in the late 1980s, governments attacked mergers and restraints. The U.S. Supreme Court gave these efforts support in *California v. American Stores Co.*, 495 U.S. 271, 110 S. Ct. 1853, 109 L. Ed. 2d 240 (1990), upholding the ability of state governments to break up illegal mergers. Another trend came again from academia, where for years critics of the Chicago School had been re-evaluating its highly influential efficiency model. They concluded that a proper analysis of efficiency goals showed that efficiency demanded tighter antitrust controls, not stubborn non-intervention.

An important 1992 U.S. Supreme Court case seemed to support this view. *Eastman Kodak Co. v. Image Technical Services*, 504 U.S. 451, 112 S. Ct. 2072, 119 L. Ed. 2d 265 (hereinafter *Kodak*), concerned *tying arrangements* (i.e., contracts between buyer and seller that restrict competition) in the sale and service of photocopiers. Kodak sold replacement parts only to buyers who agreed to have Kodak exclusively service the machines, and the restriction prompted a lawsuit from 18 independent service organizations (ISOs). The company defended itself by arguing that even

if it did monopolize the market, it lacked the necessary market power for a Sherman Act violation. The Court rejected the idea that this was enough to create a legal rule that equipment competition precluded any finding of monopoly power in the parts and services industry. In declaring Kodak's arrangement to be illegal, Justice HARRY A. BLACKMUN warned about the dangers of relying on economic theory as a substitute for "actual market realities"—in this case, the harm done to ISOs who were shut out of the service market.

After the Reagan years, antitrust attitudes sharpened in Washington, D.C. The administration of President George H. W. Bush adopted a slightly more activist approach, which was reflected in joint guidelines on mergers, issued in 1992 by the FTC and DOJ. In following the trend away from strict Chicago School efficiency standards, the guidelines looked more closely at competitive effects and tightened requirements. But understaffed government attorneys generally lost court cases. President BILL CLINTON took this activism further. Anne K. Bingaman, his appointee to head DOJ's Antitrust Division, strengthened the division's staff with 61 new attorneys, declaring her organization to be the competition agency. The Antitrust Division filed 33 civil suits in 1994, roughly three times the annual number that had been brought under Reagan and Bush. It won some victories without going to court, in one instance compelling AT&T to keep a subsidiary private, but it lost a major lawsuit in which it had claimed that General Electric had conspired with the South African firm of DeBeers to fix industrial diamond prices.

Congress continued to address monopolies in legislation passed during the 1990s. Congress passed the Telecommunications Act of 1996, Pub. L. No. 104-104, 110 Stat. 56, to increase competition within the telecommunications industry and to end state-sanctioned monopolies. The act required regional telephone companies (known as the Baby Bells) to share their networks with a new generation of telecommunications companies. Dozens of new companies began as a result of the 1996 act, and disputes emerged. During the early 2000s, LITIGATION arose accusing a local exchange carrier, Verizon Communications, of violating the antitrust provisions of the Sherman Act. The Supreme Court, however, determined that these types of claims did not fall under the Sherman Act

(*Verizon Communications, Inc v. Law Offices of Curtis V. Trinko*, 540 U.S. 398, 124 S. Ct. 872, 157 L. Ed. 823 [2004]).

Under President Clinton, the most important antitrust actions involved federal probes of the computer microprocessor giant Intel Corporation and the computer software giant Microsoft Corporation. In 1999 the FTC settled a year-old lawsuit against Intel by entering a CONSENT DECREE under which Intel agreed to cease retaliating against customers during INTELLECTUAL PROPERTY disputes over microprocessor technology. In its 1998 lawsuit, the FTC claimed that Intel had illegally cut off shipments of its microprocessor chips and withheld technical information regarding microprocessors, to coerce its competitors (Intergraph Corp., the former Digital Equipment Corp., and Compaq Computer Corp., which acquired Digital in 1998) to give up their microprocessor technology. Intel did not dispute most of the facts underlying the allegations, but it insisted that it had acted legally.

However, the Microsoft probe, in its potential for far-reaching action, was the biggest antitrust case since those involving AT&T and IBM. Competitors complained that Microsoft had been using illegal arrangements with buyers to ensure that its Windows operating system would be installed in nearly 80 percent of the world's computers. In-depth investigations by the FTC and DOJ followed. In July 1994, under threat of a federal lawsuit, Microsoft entered a consent decree that was designed to increase competitors' access to the market. The following year, Microsoft launched its popular Windows 95 operating system with an upgraded version of its INTERNET Explorer Web browser, two products that the software maker said were integrally related.

Over the next two years, the federal government received fresh complaints that Microsoft was again resorting to anti-competitive practices. The DOJ responded by suing Microsoft in the U.S. district court for the District of Columbia, alleging that the software maker had violated the 1994 consent decree by forcing computer makers to install its Internet Explorer Web browser as a pre-condition to the computer makers having the right to sell their PCs with the Windows 95 operating system included. Two months later U.S. District Judge Thomas Penfield Jackson issued a PRELIMINARY INJUNCTION

forcing Microsoft to stop, at least temporarily, requiring manufacturers who sell the Windows operating system to install Microsoft's Internet Explorer, an arrangement that he called an illegal tying agreement (*United States. v. Microsoft Corp.*, 980 F. Supp. 537 [D.D.C. 1997]). Fueled in part by Jackson's ruling, the DOJ joined 20 state attorneys general in May 1998 to bring suit against Microsoft, charging that the software maker's illegal bundling of Internet Explorer with Windows 95 violated federal antitrust laws and state unfair-competition statutes. The following month, a three-judge panel for the U.S Court of Appeals for the District of Columbia overturned the preliminary injunction that Judge Jackson had issued to enforce the consent decree, thus making way for the parties to resolve their dispute in the joint suit brought by DOJ and the state attorneys general (*United States v. Microsoft Corp.*, 147 F.3d 935 [D.C. Cir. 1998]).

On October 19, 1998, trial began in the antitrust suit against Microsoft. Less than a month later, Judge Jackson had issued a preliminary finding that Microsoft was exercising illegal monopoly power in the operating-system market and that the software maker had been using that power to promote its Web browser and to stifle competition through illegal bundling of the two products (*United States v. Microsoft Corp.*, 84 F.Supp.2d 9 [D.D.C. 1999]). Jackson issued his FINAL DECISION in April 2000. The judge reiterated his preliminary findings and also concluded that the same facts that demonstrated that Microsoft had unlawfully leveraged its operating-system monopoly to push rival Web browsers out of the market in violation of federal law also established Microsoft's liability under analogous state antitrust provisions (*United States v. Microsoft Corp.*, 97 F. Supp. 2d 59 [D.D.C. 2000]).

Later that month, the court proceeded to the remedy phase of the trial. DOJ and 18 state attorneys general (two attorneys general had since dropped out of the suit) asked the judge to break the company into two parts: one company to develop and market the Windows operating system, and the other to develop Microsoft's software, including its Web browser. On June 7, 2000, Judge Jackson granted the requested remedy, and Microsoft appealed. The court of appeals reversed, finding that Jackson had erroneously applied a *per se* analyses in making his findings instead of the appropriate "rule of reason" standard (*United States v. Microsoft Corp.*, 253 F.3d 34 [D.C. Cir. 2001]). The appellate court then remanded the matter for further proceedings, but ordered Judge Jackson removed from the case after he made extra-judicial comments to the press in violation of ethical canons forbidding judges from commenting on the merits of a pending case. Upon remand, Judge Colleen Kollar-Kotelly was selected to replace Jackson.

In September 2001 the DOJ announced that it would no longer seek a breakup of Microsoft and agreed to commence negotiations to settle the lawsuit. Those negotiations bore fruit in October 2001, when the DOJ and nine states announced that they had reached a tentative settlement with Microsoft. Ultimately approved by Judge Kollar-Kotelly on November 1, 2002, the settlement prevents Microsoft from participating in exclusive deals that could hurt competitors; requires Microsoft to offer uniform contract terms to PC makers; and obliges the software giant to release some technical information so that software developers can write programs for Windows that work as well as Microsoft's own products do. The settlement agreement also compels Microsoft to give manufacturers and customers a way to remove certain Microsoft icons from the Windows desktop. In the court's order approving the settlement, the judge expressly reserved the right to reopen the case herself if she ever suspects Microsoft of violating the settlement's terms *United States v. Microsoft*, 231 F. Supp. 2d 144 [D.D.C. 2002]). To demonstrate its GOOD FAITH, Microsoft immediately unveiled several business and product changes to comply with the settlement, including Windows functionality that gives users the ability to hide Microsoft programs like its Web browser and only see competing products.

In the early 2000s the Supreme Court was called upon several times to review provisions of the federal antitrust statutes. For instance, in *Leegin Creative Leather Products v. PSKS*, 551 U.S. 877, 127 S. Ct. 2705, 168 L. Ed. 2d 623 (2007), the Court reviewed a case involving vertical price restraints. In 1911 the Court had reviewed these types of restraints and concluded that the restraints were *per se* violations of the Sherman Act (*Dr. Miles Medical Co. v. John D. Park & Sons Co.*, 220 U.S. 373, 31 S. Ct. 376, 55 L. Ed. 502). In *Leegin Creative Leather Products*,

the Court concluded that the rule of reason should govern these types of restraints.

FURTHER READINGS

American Bar Association, Section of Antitrust Law. 2008. *State Antitrust Enforcement Handbook.* 2d ed. Chicago: American Bar Association, Section of Antitrust Law.

Dabbah, Maher M. 2003. *The Internationalisation of Antitrust Policy.* New York: Cambridge Univ. Press.

Evans, David S., ed. 2002. *Microsoft, Antitrust and the New Economy: Selected Essays.* Boston: Kluwer Academic.

Fundamentals of Antitrust Law (serial). New York: Aspen Law & Business.

Hylton, Keith N. 2003. *Antitrust Law: Economic Theory and Common Law.* New York: Cambridge Univ. Press.

Posner, Richard A. 2001. *Antitrust Law.* 2d ed. Chicago: Univ. of Chicago Press.

CROSS REFERENCES

Bork, Robert; Chicago School; Clayton Act; Corporations; Justice Department; Mergers and Acquisitions; Monopoly; Posner, Richard Allen; Restraint of Trade; Robinson-Patman Act; Sherman Anti-Trust Act; Unfair Competition.

APPARENT

That which is clear, plain, and evident.

In the law of agency, an agent has *apparent authority* to represent the person, or principal, for whom he or she acts, when the principal acts in such a manner toward the agent that a REASONABLE PERSON would plainly assume that the agent was acting for the principal.

APPEAL

Timely resort by an unsuccessful party in a lawsuit or administrative proceeding to an appropriate superior court empowered to review a final decision on the ground that it was based upon an erroneous application of law.

A person who initiates an appeal—the appellant, sometimes called the PLAINTIFF IN ERROR, must file a notice of appeal, along with the necessary documents, to commence appellate review. The person against whom the appeal is brought, the appellee, then files a brief in response to the appellant's allegations.

There are usually two stages of review in the federal court and in many state court systems: an appeal from a trial court to an intermediate appellate court and thereafter to the highest appellate court in the jurisdiction. Within the appellate rules of administrative procedure, there might be several levels of appeals from a determination made by an administrative agency. For example, an appeal of the decision of an administrative law judge may be heard by a reviewing body within the agency, and from that body, the appeal may go to a trial court, such as a federal district court. Thereafter, the appeal might travel the same route as an appeal taken from a judicial decision, going from an intermediate to a superior appellate court, or it might go directly to a superior appellate court for review, bypassing the intermediate stage. The rules of appellate procedure applicable to a particular court govern its review of cases.

Right to Appeal

There is no absolute right of appeal for all decisions rendered by a lower court or administrative agency. Federal and state constitutions and statutory provisions create appellate courts and prescribe the types of cases that are within their jurisdiction. An appeal may be granted as a matter of right, such as from a trial court to an intermediate appellate court or only at the discretion of a superior appellate court, for example, by a grant of CERTIORARI by the Supreme Court. If the decision presented does not meet the statutory requirements for review, the appellate court is powerless to hear the appeal and review is denied.

The right to appeal a decision is limited to those parties to the proceeding who are aggrieved by the decision because it has a direct and adverse effect upon their persons or property. In addition, an actual CASE OR CONTROVERSY must exist at the time of review. Issues that have become MOOT while the appeal is pending and cases that have been settled during that time are not reviewable.

Final Decision

A final judgment or order must have been reached by the trial court in order for a case to be appealable. A judgment is considered final for purposes of appeal when it ends the action in the court in which it was brought and nothing more is to be decided. This rule is intended to prevent the piecemeal LITIGATION of a lawsuit, to avoid delay resulting from INTERLOCUTORY appeals, and to give the trial court the opportunity to render a decision in the case to the satisfaction of both parties, thereby obviating the need for appeal. The consideration of INCIDENTAL matters, such as the computation of interest, attorneys' fees, or court costs, does not prevent a judgment or order from being appealed.

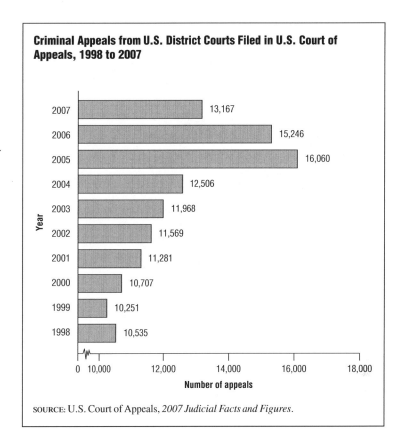

Criminal Appeals from U.S. District Courts Filed in U.S. Court of Appeals, 1998 to 2007

Year	Number of appeals
2007	13,167
2006	15,246
2005	16,060
2004	12,506
2003	11,968
2002	11,569
2001	11,281
2000	10,707
1999	10,251
1998	10,535

SOURCE: U.S. Court of Appeals, *2007 Judicial Facts and Figures.*

Grounds

Error is the basis for review of a FINAL DECISION rendered by a court or administrative agency. Error is called to the attention of a court through the use of objections, protests made during the course of a proceeding that an action taken by the opposing side in a controversy is unfair or illegal. Decisions rendered in favor of one party at trial level are presumed by an appellate court to be correct unless objections have been made to the issues in question during the trial. Failure to do so will preclude their review on appeal. An objection must be made as promptly and specifically as possible for each act to which it is directed so that the court may make an intelligent decision regarding its merits. The trial judge rules on the objection, and the decision is included in the trial record. If the attorney for either party disagrees with the ruling, he or she may take an exception, an objection taken to a decision of a court on a MATTER OF LAW, which is noted in the trial record to be preserved for purposes of appeal. Appellate jurisdiction is limited only to a review of actions taken by an INFERIOR COURT. No new objections can be raised before an appellate court for its consideration unless exceptional circumstances exist to justify the appellate court raising the issues SUA SPONTE, on its own motion. Exceptional circumstances mean the presence at trial of plain error, a mistake in the proceedings that substantially affects the rights of the party against whom the decision has been made and undermines the fairness and integrity of the judicial system, causing a MISCARRIAGE OF JUSTICE.

Time of Appeal

Appeals must be made within the time prescribed by statute or by the governing rules of the appellate court. Such statutes begin to run only after a final decision has been made. The timely filing of the notice of appeal with the clerk of the appellate court and the appellee completes, or perfects, the procedure. If the appeal is not taken and perfected within the time set by statute, the right to appeal is foreclosed. Extensions of time for the filing of an appeal may be granted, however, if EXTENU-ATING CIRCUMSTANCES exist, such as if either party is adjudicated incompetent or dies.

Notice of Appeal

A notice of appeal—a written document filed by the appellant with the court and a copy of which is sent to the appellee—is the initial step in the appeals process. It informs the court and the party in whose favor a judgment or order has been made that the unsuccessful party seeks a review of the case. Failure to file a notice of appeal according to the statutory requirements will preclude appeal.

Bonds

An appeal bond, a promise to pay a sum of money, must often be posted by an appellant to secure the appellee against the costs of the appeal, if the appellee is successful and the appellant fails to pay. Its amount is determined by the court itself or by statute. The imposition of such a bond discourages frivolous appeals. If successive appeals are taken from an intermediate appellate court to a superior one, a new bond is usually required.

Record on Appeal

The function of the appellate court is limited to a review of the trial record sent up from the lower court and the briefs filed by the appellant and appellee. AMICUS CURIAE briefs, if permitted by the appellate court, also become part of the record on appeal. The trial record, sometimes called the record proper, must show the pleadings that initiated the case, the complete transcript (in cases of jury trial) of lower court proceedings, the VERDICT, and the ENTRY of the final judgment or order. The appellant must clearly demonstrate that the grounds for review had been raised and unsuccessfully decided upon at the trial level and, therefore, prejudicial error exists to warrant the reversal of the decision of the lower court.

In some jurisdictions, a bill of exceptions—a written statement of the objections made by a party to the ruling, decision, charge, or opinion of the trial judge—must be submitted to the appellate court to provide a history of the trial proceedings. It should not include matters that belong in the record proper but, instead, should state those points concerning questions of law raised by the exceptions taken during the trial. The appellant's attorney prepares the bill and presents it to the trial judge for settlement, an agreement between the trial judge and the appellant that the bill contains a truthful account of the events of the trial. If there is disagreement, the judge returns the bill to the appellant with an explanation. The appellee must be given notice of the time and place of the settlement of the bill of exceptions in order to object to or approve its contents. The settled bill of exceptions becomes part of the trial transcript, which is part of the record on appeal. The appellant must submit a complete un-abridged transcript of the trial that is prepared by the clerk of the trial court.

The entire trial record is printed and filed with the appellate court, and a copy is also sent to the appellee.

Assignment of Errors

A statement by the appellant of the errors alleged to have been committed in the lower court is an assignment of errors, a type of appellate PLEADING used to point out to the appellate court the grounds for review. It controls the scope of an appeal because if a ground for review is not contained in it, it will not ordinarily be considered by the court. The assignment of errors is usually part of the notice of appeal, the bill of exceptions, the transcript of the record, or the brief, although in some jurisdictions, it is a separate document.

Appellate Brief

The appellant and appellee must file individual briefs to aid the appellate court in its consideration of the issues presented. Failure to do so results in a dismissal of the appeal. The facts of the case, the grounds for review, and the arguments relating to those questions must be concisely stated. Any statements referring to the trial record must be supported by an appropriate reference to it.

The appellant's brief must specifically discuss the alleged errors that entitle the appellant to a reversal and discuss why each ruling of the lower court was wrong, citing authority, such as a case in which a similar point of law has been decided or a statute that applies to the particular point in issue. Disrespectful or abusive language directed against the lower court, the appellate court, the parties, WITNESSES, or opposing counsel cannot be used. If it is, it will be stricken from the brief, and the costs of the brief that might have been awarded are disallowed.

Review

Appellate courts have jurisdiction to decide only issues actually before them on appeal and nothing else. They cannot render opinions on controversies or declare principles of law that have no practical effect in settling the rights of the litigants.

Only conclusions of law, not findings of fact made by a lower court, are reviewable.

Harmless Error The appellate court must decide whether the errors alleged to have been made by the trial court are harmless or prejudicial. An error that substantially injures the rights of one party is called a prejudicial or reversible error and warrants the reversal of the final judgment or order. However, an error that is technical or minimally affects the rights of the parties or the outcome of the lawsuit is considered a HARMLESS ERROR, insufficient to require a reversal or modification of the decision of the lower court.

Hearing

The clerk of the appellate court schedules on the court calendar the date of the hearing on which each side may present an oral argument. Oral arguments, usually ten to fifteen minutes for each side, help the court understand the issues argued in the brief and persuade the court to rule in favor of the arguing party. During the arguments of appellant and appellee, it is not unusual for the appellate judge to interrupt with questions on particular issues or points of law.

The appellant's argument briefly discusses the facts on which the CAUSE OF ACTION is based and traces the history of the case through the lower courts. It includes the legal issues raised by the exceptions taken to the allegedly erroneous rulings of the trial judge. Thereafter, the appellee's counsel presents arguments in favor of affirming the original decision.

Determination

An appellate court has broad powers over the scope of its decision and the relief to be granted. After reviewing the controlling issues in an action, it may affirm the decision of the inferior tribunal, modify it, reverse it, or remand the case for a new trial in the lower court pursuant to its order.

When a decision is affirmed, the appellate court accepts the decision of the lower court and rejects the appellant's contention that it was erroneously made. The modification of a decision by an appellate court means that, while it accepts part of the trial court's decision, the appellant was correct that the decision was partly erroneous. The trial court's decision is then modified accordingly.

A reversal of a decision means that the appellate court agrees with the appellant that the decision was erroneously made. The party who lost the case at the trial level becomes the winning party in appellate court.

In some cases, a decision might be reversed but the lawsuit is still unresolved. The appellate court then orders the reversal with the direction that the case be remanded to a lower court for the determination of the issues that remain unsettled.

If a judgment or order is reversed in an intermediate appellate court, the losing party may file an appeal with a superior appellate court for relief, and the appellate process begins again. The decision rendered by a superior appellate court cannot ordinarily be reviewed. In state cases involving issues based on federal statutes or the Constitution, however, an appeal may be brought in the federal court system on those questions that are within its jurisdiction.

FURTHER READINGS

Lynn, Richardson R. 1993. *Appellate Litigation*. 2d ed. Maryland: Austin & Winfield.

Magen, Barbara S. 2003. "Let's Twist Again: Getting Reargument and Reconsideration on Appeal." *Pennsylvania Law Weekly* 26 (April).

Wood, Jefri. 2002. *Guideline Sentencing: An Outline of Appellate Case Law on Selected Issues.* Washington, D.C.: Federal Judicial Center.

CROSS REFERENCES

Appellate Advocacy; Appellate Court; Federal Courts; Remand.

APPEAR

To come before a court as a party or a witness in a lawsuit.

APPEARANCE

A coming into court by a party to a suit, either in person or through an attorney, whether as plaintiff or defendant. The formal proceeding by which a defendant submits to the jurisdiction of the court. The voluntary submission to a court's jurisdiction.

In a criminal prosecution, an appearance is the initial court proceeding in which a DEFENDANT is first brought before a judge. The conduct of an appearance is governed by state and federal rules of CRIMINAL PROCEDURE. The rules vary from state to state, but they are generally consistent. During an appearance, the judge advises the defendant of the charges and of the defendant's rights, considers bail or other conditions of release, and schedules a PRELIMINARY HEARING. If the crime charged is a MISDEMEANOR, the defendant may sometimes, depending on the local rules of court, enter a PLEA of guilty or not guilty at the initial appearance; if the crime is a FELONY, the defendant usually enters the plea at a later court proceeding. A criminal defendant may have an attorney present and may confer with the attorney during the appearance.

In some situations, a defendant may not need to appear in court in person and may even make an appearance by mail. For example, when individuals receive traffic tickets they may choose to send in a check for the amount of the fine.

Many state statutes permit appearances to be made by two-way, closed-circuit television. For instance, North Carolina's rule on video appearances reads:

> A first appearance in a noncapital case may be conducted by an audio and video transmission between the judge and

defendant in which the parties can see and hear each other. If the defendant has counsel, the defendant shall be allowed to communicate fully and confidentially with his attorney during the proceeding (N.C. Gen. Stat. § 15A-601(a1) [1994]).

An appearance is also a coming into court as a party to a civil lawsuit. Although an appearance can be made by either the PLAINTIFF (the one who has sued) or the *defendant* (the one being sued), the term most often refers to the action of the defendant.

The subject of appearance is closely related to the subject of PERSONAL JURISDICTION, which is the court's authority over an individual party. An appearance is some OVERT ACT by which the defendant comes before the court to either submit to or challenge the court's jurisdiction.

Any party can appear either in person or through an attorney or a duly authorized representative; the party need not be physically present. In most instances, an attorney makes the appearance. An appearance can also be made by filing a notice of appearance with the clerk of the court and the plaintiff, which states that the defendant will either submit to the authority of the court or challenge its jurisdiction. In a lawsuit involving multiple defendants, an appearance by one is not an appearance for the others. Valid SERVICE OF PROCESS is not required before an appearance can be made.

Historically, appearances have been classified with a variety of names indicating their manner or significance. A *compulsory* appearance is compelled by process served on the party. A *conditional* appearance is coupled with conditions as to its becoming or being taken as a GENERAL APPEARANCE (defined later in this article). A *corporal* appearance indicates that the person is physically present in court. A *de bene esse* (Latin, "of well being," sufficient for the present) appearance is provisional and will remain good only upon a future contingency. A *gratis* (Latin, "free" or "freely") appearance is made by a party to the action before the service of any process or legal notice to appear. An *optional* appearance is entered by a person who is intervening in the action to protect his or her own interests, though not joined as a party. A *subsequent* appearance is made by a defendant after an appearance has already been entered for him or her by the plaintiff. Finally, a *voluntary* appearance is entered by a party's own will or consent, without service of process, although process might be outstanding.

The two most common categories of appearances are general and special.

General Appearance

Any action by which the defendant recognizes the jurisdiction of the court constitutes a general appearance. This is an unqualified submission to the court's personal jurisdiction over the defendant and is treated as the equivalent of a valid service of process.

By making a general appearance, the defendant agrees that the court has the power to bind her or him by its actions and waives the right to raise any jurisdictional defects (e.g., by claiming that the service of process was improper). The defendant also waives the objection that the case is brought in the wrong VENUE. The defendant does not, however, WAIVE any substantive rights or defenses, such as the claim that the court lacks jurisdiction over the subject matter of the case or authority to hear the particular type of case (e.g., a BANKRUPTCY court will not hear PERSONAL INJURY cases).

Special Appearance

A SPECIAL APPEARANCE is one made for a limited purpose. It can be made, for example, to challenge the sufficiency of the service of process. But most often, a special appearance is made to challenge the court's personal jurisdiction over the defendant. It prevents a DEFAULT JUDGMENT from being rendered against the defendant for failing to file a PLEADING. (A default judgment is an automatic loss for failing to answer the complaint properly.)

When a defendant makes a special appearance, no other issues may be raised without that appearance's becoming a general appearance. If a party takes any action dealing with the merits of the case, the party is deemed to have made a general appearance and submitted to the jurisdiction of the court.

If a challenge is successful and the court agrees that it does not have personal jurisdiction over the defendant, it will dismiss the action. If the court finds against the defendant on that issue, that decision can later be appealed.

The right to make a special appearance is almost universally recognized, except where abolished by statute. As a rule, leave of court (permission) must be obtained before a special

A defendant, accompanied by his court-appointed lawyer, appears before the judge in a Tacoma, Washington, courtroom. In a criminal prosecution, an appearance is the initial court proceeding in which the defendant is advised of the charges, bail is considered, and a preliminary hearing is set.

AP IMAGES

appearance can be made, but this is not always the case.

Federal Rules

Federal courts and states that have adopted the Federal Rules of CIVIL PROCEDURE have eliminated the distinction between a general and a special appearance. Instead of challenging the court's personal jurisdiction in a special appearance, a defendant can do so by use of a pretrial motion to dismiss the CAUSE OF ACTION, or in an answer to the complaint. A removal proceeding, in which a defendant asks to have the case moved from state court to federal court, is regarded as a special appearance.

Limited Appearance

In a number of states, a defendant in a lawsuit based on QUASI IN REM JURISDICTION may make a *limited* appearance. *Quasi in rem* is a Latin phrase for a type of jurisdiction in which the court has power over the defendant's property because it lies within the geographic boundaries of the court's jurisdiction. The presence of the property gives the court jurisdiction over the person of the defendant. To invoke *quasi in rem* jurisdiction, the court must find some connection between the property and the subject matter of the lawsuit.

A limited appearance enables a defendant to defend the action on the merits, but should the defendant lose, he or she will be held liable only up to the value of the identified property and not for all possible damages. A defendant who makes a limited appearance and wins the case can be sued again by the same plaintiff in a different court.

In states that have no provision for a limited appearance, a defendant can avoid being subject to the personal jurisdiction of the court by refusing to appear, thereby causing a default and a consequent FORFEITURE of the property. Or the defendant can submit to the court's personal jurisdiction, defend the case on its merits, and face the possibility of full liability. The defendant must decide which course of action is best, after comparing the value of the seized property with the damages being sought by the plaintiff and considering the likelihood of winning the case at trial.

The Federal Rules of Civil Procedure do not provide for limited appearances in federal court but instead defer to state law on that issue. A slightly greater number of courts permit limited appearances than do not. The law of the jurisdiction in which the action is brought must be consulted to determine whether limited appearances are permitted.

Withdrawal

If an appearance has been entered through FRAUD or mistake or after the plaintiff's complaint has been materially amended, the discretion of the court may permit the appearance to be withdrawn. A proper withdrawal is treated as if no appearance at all had been entered in the case. A defendant who has withdrawn a general appearance may ask the court for leave to file a special appearance to challenge the court's jurisdiction.

If someone makes an unauthorized appearance on behalf of the defendant, it may be stricken or set aside by a motion of any party with an interest in the proceeding.

Delay or Failure to Appear

A defendant who fails to appear in court pursuant to a service of process might have a default judgment entered against her or him and be held in contempt of court. A failure to appear does not, however, result in a WAIVER of objections to the court's jurisdiction.

If a defendant fails to make an appearance in the time allotted by statute or court rules, he or she may lose certain rights. But if the circumstances warrant it, a court may extend the time of appearance.

FURTHER READINGS

McKinney, William Mark, and Burdett Alberto Rich. 1914. *Ruling Case Law.* Northport, NY: Edward Thompson.

Weinreb, Lloyd L. 2006. *Criminal Process: Cases, Comments, Questions.* 7th ed. Eagan, MN: Foundation.

Yeazell, Stephen C. 1998. *Federal Rules of Civil Procedures: With Selected Statutes and Cases.* Frederick, MD: Aspen.

CROSS REFERENCE

Civil Procedure.

APPELLANT

A person who, dissatisfied with the judgment rendered in a lawsuit decided in a lower court or the findings from a proceeding before an administrative agency, asks a superior court to review the decision.

An appellant, sometimes called the petitioner, must demonstrate sufficient grounds for appeal, which are usually specified by statute, in order to challenge the judgment or findings. Whether a party was a PLAINTIFF or DEFENDANT in the lower court has no bearing on his or her status as an appellant.

APPELLATE

Relating to appeals, which are reviews by superior courts of decisions made by inferior courts or administrative agencies.

APPELLATE ADVOCACY

Appellate advocacy is the legal representation by an attorney before any state or federal court of intermediate or final appeal.

The U.S. COURTS OF APPEALS were created by the Evarts Act of 1891 (28 U.S.C.A. § 43) and are divided into 13 judicial circuits (see the accompanying table). The central location of each court is determined by statute (28 U.S.C.A. § 41 [1995]). In addition, a court may sit any place within its circuit and is required by statute to sit in certain locations other than its central location (28 U.S.C.A. § 44 [1995]). Appeals are heard and decided by panels of three judges that are selected randomly, by the CIRCUIT COURT EN BANC (in its entirety), or by a division established to perform the court's en BANC function in larger circuits.

The circuit courts' ORIGINAL JURISDICTION included all matters not exclusively reserved for the district trial courts. The circuit courts also had appellate jurisdiction to review district trial court decisions in civil cases in which the AMOUNT IN CONTROVERSY exceeded $50 and in admiralty cases in which the amount in controversy exceeded $300. They have jurisdiction to review final decisions of the federal district trial courts, both civil and criminal. Their jurisdiction extends only to matters authorized by Congress. An appellate court has no discretion in deciding whether to consider the merits of an appeal over which it has no jurisdiction. The most common basis for appellate jurisdiction is an appeal from a final district court judgment (324 U.S. 229, 28 U.S.C.A. § 1291 [1995]). When a judgment is entered that "ends the LITIGATION on the merits and leaves nothing for the court to do but execute the judgment," a case is completed (*Catlin v. United States,* 65 S. Ct. 631 [1945]).

Congress has progressively limited the Supreme Court's power to directly review trial court decisions without a hearing in the courts of appeals. Because Supreme Court review is usually discretionary in the overwhelming majority of cases, a court of appeals is the highest federal tribunal where a litigant or DEFENDANT can receive a hearing on the merits.

The Appeals Process

An unsuccessful party in a lawsuit or administrative proceeding may file a timely appeal to an appropriate SUPERIOR court empowered to review a FINAL DECISION, on the ground that it was based upon an erroneous application of law. The person who initiates the appeal, called the appellant, must file a notice of appeal, along with other necessary documents, to commence appellate review. The person against whom the appeal is brought, the appellee, then files a brief in response to the appellant's allegations.

Usually, review in the federal and state courts goes through two stages: an appeal from a trial court to an intermediate appellate court and then to the highest appellate court in the jurisdiction. An appeal may be granted as a matter of right or as a matter of CERTIORARI (at the discretion of a superior appellate court). For example, a party may appeal from a federal district trial court to a U.S. court of appeals as a matter of right, but may appeal to the U.S. Supreme Court only by a grant of certiorari. An appellate court may hear an appeal only if the decision presented meets the statutory requirements for review.

The right to appeal is limited to the parties to the proceedings who are aggrieved by the decision because it has a direct and adverse effect upon them or their property. Also, an actual CASE OR CONTROVERSY must exist at the time of review. Issues that have become MOOT while the appeal is pending and cases that have been settled are not reviewable.

For a case to be appealable, a final judgment or order must have been reached by a trial court. A judgment is considered final for purposes of appeal when the action is ended in the court where it was brought and nothing more is to be decided.

An appeal must be made within the time prescribed by statute or by the rules governing the appellate court. The time for filing an appeal begins to run once a final decision has been made by the trial court. The appellant must file a notice of appeal with the clerk of the appellate court in order to begin the appeal and send a copy to the appellee. If the appeal process is not begun within the time set by statute, any right to appeal is lost. If EXTENUATING CIRCUMSTANCES exist, an extension of time for filing the appeal may be granted.

The appellate court can review only the trial court record and the briefs filed by the appellant and appellee. If permitted by the appellate court, AMICUS CURIAE briefs may also become part of the record on appeal. (*Amicus curiae* means "friend of the court." A person who is not a party to the action may petition the court for permission to file such a brief.) The briefs must contain the facts of the case, the grounds for review, and arguments relating to the issues raised.

The appellant's brief must specifically discuss the alleged errors that entitle the appellant to a reversal of the trial court's decision and discuss why each ruling was wrong, citing authority such as a case or statute that applies to the particular point at issue. The appellee may file a brief containing arguments against reversal and explaining why the trial court's ruling was correct. Only conclusions of law, not findings of fact, made by a lower court are reviewable. Appellate courts can decide only issues actually before them on appeal.

The appellate court must decide whether the errors alleged to have been made by the trial court are harmless or prejudicial. If an error substantially injures the rights of the appellant, it is called a *prejudicial error,* or reversible error, and warrants the reversal of the final judgment or order. If the appeals court determines that the error is technical or minimally affects the rights of the parties or the outcome of the lawsuit, it is considered a HARMLESS ERROR and insufficient to require a reversal or modification of the decision of the trial court.

The appellate court may hear oral arguments from each side. These arguments, which usually last 10 to 15 minutes for each side, are intended to help the court understand the issues and to persuade the court to rule in favor of the arguing party. During the arguments, the appellate judge or judges may interrupt with questions on particular issues or points of law.

After reviewing the appeal, the appellate court may affirm the decision of the lower court, modify it, reverse it, or remand the case for a new trial in the lower court. When a decision is *affirmed,* the appellate court accepts the decision of the lower court and rejects the appellant's contention that the decision was erroneous. When the appellate court *modifies* the lower court's decision, it accepts part of the trial court's decision and determines that the appellant was partly correct in saying that the decision was erroneous. The trial court's decision is then modified accordingly. In *reversing* a decision, the appellate court indicates that it agrees with the appellant that the lower court's decision was erroneous. The party who lost the case at the trial court level then becomes the winning party in appellate court. Occasionally, a decision will be reversed, but the lawsuit is still unresolved. In such cases, the appellate court orders that the case be *remanded* (returned) to the lower court for the determination of issues that remain unresolved.

Federal Criminal Appellate Advocacy

The SIXTH AMENDMENT to the U.S. Constitution guarantees a criminal defendant the right to a jury trial and the right to an attorney. The FOURTEENTH AMENDMENT says states must provide criminal defendants with these same guarantees. The U.S. Supreme Court has repeatedly held that a person found guilty in a criminal proceeding has no constitutional right to appeal. A federal criminal defendant's right to appeal, therefore, is based on an act of Congress.

Prior to 1776 and the founding of the United States, many colonial legislatures allowed, by special act, new trials of criminal defendants. But generally, criminal appeals did not exist when the U.S. Constitution was drafted, and the JUDICIARY ACT OF 1789 (ch. 20, 1 Stat. 73) did not provide for appellate review of criminal cases. Thus, history does not support a constitutional right to criminal appeal. The issue was left to Congress.

Between 1855 and 1860 Congress refused to provide for federal criminal appellate jurisdiction, although several bills were introduced. Finally in 1879, Congress authorized the federal circuit courts to issue writs of error in criminal cases on a discretionary basis. In 1889 Congress gave defendants sentenced to death the right of direct appeal to the U.S. Supreme Court. In 1891 it extended the Supreme Court's jurisdiction for review to all "cases of conviction of a capital or otherwise infamous crime" (26 Stat. 827, quoted in 775 S. Ct. 1332 [1957]). Because of the burden on the Supreme Court of hearing a large number of criminal appeals, in 1897 Congress transferred jurisdiction over noncapital appeals to the circuit courts of appeals. In 1911 Congress abolished the right of direct appeal to the Supreme Court in capital cases, and the circuit courts became the appellate courts for all criminal cases.

In 1894, in *McKane v. Durston* (153 U.S. 684, 14 S. Ct. 913, 38 L. Ed. 867), a unanimous Supreme Court determined that no matter how serious the offense, a criminal defendant had no constitutional right to appeal her or his conviction.

The Criminal Justice Act (18 U.S.C.A. § 3006A [1995]) is an outgrowth of the Sixth Amendment RIGHT TO COUNSEL. The act requires courts to develop and implement plans to furnish representation for defendants charged with felonies or misdemeanors, other than petty offenses, who are financially unable to obtain an attorney. Although the act is directed primarily to proceedings at the trial court level, it provides that any person for whom counsel is appointed shall be represented at every stage of the criminal proceedings, from the defendant's initial appearance through the appeal process.

State Criminal Appellate Advocacy

All U.S. states provide defendants some form of appeal from a criminal conviction. Appeals were well-established elements of state criminal proceedings throughout the nineteenth century.

They probably developed earlier in state court systems because state governments had primary responsibility for enforcing criminal laws from the founding of the nation through the 1800s, since very few federal statutory offenses existed during this period.

Because states decided that criminal appeals were necessary to protect the innocent, the Supreme Court determined that appellate procedures must comply with the federal constitutional guarantees of due process and EQUAL PROTECTION (*Griffin v. Illinois,* 351 U.S. 12, 76 S. Ct. 585, 100 L. Ed. 891 [1956]). In *Douglas v. California* (372 U.S. 353, 83 S. Ct. 814, 9 L. Ed. 2d 811 [1963]), the Supreme Court held that a state violates a defendant's constitutional protections when it forces an indigent, who has a statutory right to appeal, to attempt the appeal without the assistance of an attorney. The Supreme Court reasoned that without an attorney, an appeal constituted nothing more than a "meaningless ritual." Therefore, a state must provide counsel to a defendant who wants to exercise the right to appeal but cannot afford to hire a lawyer.

In 2009 the Supreme Court faced a novel question regarding the reaches of appointed appellate counsel in *Harbison v. Bell* (No. 07-8521, 556 U.S. ___ [2009]). The question before the Court was whether Harbison, a death-row inmate who had exhausted all his state court and federal habeas appeals, could request a federally appointed (and funded) attorney (who had represented him in filing the federal WRIT of HABEAS CORPUS) to represent him (if no other attorney was available) to prepare a last-ditch petition for state CLEMENCY proceedings. The Court, by a 7–2 decision, said yes.

Tennessee law no longer authorized the appointment of state public defenders for clemency proceedings. Therefore, Harbison's federally appointed habeas attorney had requested the district court to expand the scope of her representation to include the state clemency proceedings, relying on 18 USC §3599 (which provides for the appointment of federal counsel) for authority. Section §3599 (a) 2 expressly refers to the federal habeas statute sections §2254 and §2255, providing for the appointment of counsel in "both state and federal post-conviction proceedings." Section §3599 (e) in relevant part, states that counsel is available to any defendant sentenced to death in "proceedings for executive or other clemency as may be available to the defendant." Despite the language, there had been a split in the federal circuit courts as to whether Section §3599 provided for federally funded attorney only in executive clemency proceedings from the president or also clemency from state governors or pardon boards. The Supreme Court found that both were covered under Section §3599.

Ineffective Appellate Representation

In 1985 the Supreme Court held that a defendant has the right to the effective assistance of appellate counsel. The Court concluded that a defendant whose counsel does not provide effective representation is "in no better position than one who has no counsel at all" (*Evitts v. Lucey,* 469 U.S. 387, 105 S. Ct. 830, 83 L. Ed. 2d 821 [1985]). However, in *Ross v. Moffitt* (417 U.S. 600, 94 S. Ct. 2437, 41 L. Ed. 2d 341 [1974]), the Supreme Court held that a criminal defendant does not have a constitutional right to appointed counsel on a discretionary review.

In *Roe v. Flores-Ortega* (528 U.S. 470, 120 S. Ct. 1029, 145 L. Ed. 2d 985 [2000]), the Court considered whether a defense lawyer must always consult with a defendant regarding an appeal of the conviction. In this case, the defendant (Flores-Ortega) alleged ineffective counsel because his attorney did not file an appeal within the 60-day time period dictated by the judge in his original case. The Court rejected a *bright-line rule* (a strict rule with no ability to use discretion) that would have mandated such a consultation, ruling that each case must be analyzed using a set of standards.

The Court in *Roe* held that a defendant claiming ineffective assistance of counsel must show that the attorney's representation "fell below an objective standard of reasonableness" and that the attorney's deficient performance prejudiced the defendant. The Court used a test set out in *Strickland v. Washington* (466 U.S. 668, 104 S. Ct. 205, 80 L. Ed. 2d 674 [1984]) to determine if Flores-Ortega's attorney was constitutionally ineffective for failing to file a notice of appeal. It directed that an inquiry should begin by asking whether the attorney in fact consulted with the defendant about the appeal. Such a consultation meant advising the defendant on the pros and cons of taking an appeal and making a reasonable effort to discover the defendant's wishes. However, the defendant would still have to show that there was a reasonable probability that, but for his attorney's conduct, he would have filed a timely appeal.

In *Glover v. United States* (531 U.S. 198, 121 S. Ct. 696, 148 L. Ed. 2d 604 [2001]), the Supreme Court ruled that defendants are entitled to a hearing to prove that they received ineffective counsel on an appeal. In this case, the defendant argued that his appellate attorney failed to appeal his sentence, which he claimed had been miscalculated under federal SENTENCING guidelines. This failure would mean serving between six and 21 months longer in prison. An appeals court held that the increase in his sentence was not serious enough to merit a review of his ineffective counsel claim. The Supreme Court disagreed, ruling that any amount of jail time justified a hearing into the issue.

The Supreme Court considered another claim of ineffective appellate counsel in *Mickens v. Taylor* (535 U.S. 162, 122 S. Ct. 1237, 152 L. Ed. 2d 291 [2002]), but this one involved trial counsel. However, the rule announced in *Mickens* could be made applicable to claims of ineffective appellate counsel. The defendant had been convicted of MURDER and sentenced to death. During the course of his death penalty appeals, his appellate attorney discovered that the defendant's trial attorney had represented the murder victim shortly before his murder. This was not disclosed to the defendant during his trial. The defendant argued that this tainted his trial, as there was no way the defense attorney could have been objective.

The Supreme Court disagreed, in a decision that signaled a departure from its death penalty jurisprudence. Because of the finality of a death sentence, the Court previously required less hard evidence of prejudice from ineffective counsel. In *Mickens,* the Court stated that the general rule for ineffective counsel should also be applied to capital murder cases. Under this standard the defendant must show that "but for" the lawyer's conduct, the result of the trial would have been different. The Court will presume an adverse effect "where assistance of counsel has been denied entirely or during a critical stage of the proceeding." In *Mickens,* however, the Court found that the trial attorney had done an acceptable job in representing the defendant, so no adverse effect could be presumed. Because the defendant could not show that the outcome of his trial would have been any different but for the actions of his attorney, his appeal was rejected (see also *Schriro v. Landrigan aka Hill* No. 05-1575, 550 U.S.___ [2007]).

FURTHER READINGS

Arkin, Marc M. 1992. "Rethinking the Constitutional Right to a Criminal Appeal." *University of California at Los Angeles Law Review* 39.

———. 1990. "Speedy Criminal Appeal: A Right without a Remedy." *Minnesota Law Review* 74.

Beazley, Mary Beth. 2002. *A Practical Guide to Appellate Advocacy.* New York: Aspen.

Berry, Carole C. 2009. *Effective Appellate Advocacy: Brief Writing and Oral Argument.* 4th ed. St. Paul, Minn.: West Group.

Frederick, David C. 2002. *Supreme Court and Appellate Advocacy.* St. Paul, Minn.: West Group.

Junkin, Federick D. 1988. "The Right to Counsel in 'Frivolous' Criminal Appeals: A Reevaluation of the Guarantees of *Anders v. California.*" *Texas Law Review* 67.

Klonoff, Robert H. and Gregory Castanias. 2008. *Federal Appellate Practice and Procedure in a Nutshell.* St. Paul, Minn.: Thomson/West.

Knibb, David G. 1990. *Federal Court of Appeals Manual.* 2d ed. St. Paul, Minn.: West.

National Conference of Bar Examiners (NCBE), 2009. "2008 Statistics." *The Bar Examiner,* May 2009. Text available online at http://www.ncbex.org/fileadmin/mediafiles/downloads/Bar_Admissions/2008_Stats.pdf; website home page: http://www.ncbex.org/bar-admissions/stats/ (accessed August 5, 2009)

Rubin, Alvin B. 1989. *Advocacy in the Court of Appeal.* American Law Institute-American Bar Association. No. C380.

CROSS REFERENCES

Criminal Law; Federal Courts; Habeas Corpus; Supreme Court of the United States.

APPELLATE COURT

An appellate court has jurisdiction to review decisions of a trial-level or other lower court.

An unsuccessful party in a lawsuit must file an appeal with an appellate court in order to have the decision reviewed. In the United States, appellate courts exist at both the federal and the state levels, and generally they consist of a panel of two or more judges. On the federal level, decisions of the U.S. district courts, where civil and criminal matters are tried, can be appealed to the U.S. court of appeals for the circuit covering the district court. Eleven numbered federal judicial circuits have been established. Each circuit comprises a number of states that are usually, though not always, in close geographic proximity. For example, the Eighth Circuit includes Arkansas, Iowa, Minnesota,

Missouri, Nebraska, and North and South Dakota, and the Sixth Circuit is made up of Kentucky, Michigan, Ohio, and Tennessee. Washington, D.C., has two U.S. COURTS OF APPEALS: the District of Columbia CIRCUIT COURT of Appeals, which hears appeals arising out of decisions of the Federal District Court for the District of Columbia, and the U.S. Court of Appeals for the Federal Circuit, which has exclusive and nationwide jurisdiction in appeals from U.S. district court decisions in patent, copyright, trademark, and other specialized areas.

A decision of a U.S. court of appeals may be appealed to yet another appellate court, the Supreme Court of the United States. An appeal to the Supreme Court is made by filing a *petition for CERTIORARI* (a document requesting a review of court records). The Supreme Court has broad discretion in determining whether to review decisions. The Court receives thousands of petitions per year, but can only review about one hundred cases in that span of time. It most often denies certiorari and hears only cases that raise important and unsettled constitutional questions or in which the federal appellate courts have reached conflicting decisions on the same issue.

On the state level, a decision of a state trial court—usually a district or other local court—can be appealed to a state appellate court for review. In most states, a case must first be appealed to an intermediate appellate court. If it receives an unfavorable ruling at the intermediate level, the case can then be appealed to the highest appellate court in the state, usually the state supreme court. Like the Supreme Court of the United States, a state's highest court usually has the discretion to decide whether to review a decision reached by the intermediate court. Some cases decided by the highest court in a state also can be appealed to the U.S. Supreme

Court, though again the U.S. Supreme Court will hear only appeals of major significance.

In both state and federal matters, in general, an appeal can be brought only after a FINAL DECISION, or final judgment, in the ACTION has been entered. A judgment is final for the purposes of an appeal when nothing more is to be decided in the action, and it concludes all rights that were subject to LITIGATION. This rule is based in part on the desire for judicial economy: It is more efficient for all matters to be heard in one appeal than for a case to be conducted "piecemeal" (in several appeals) before it is finally resolved. However, both state and federal courts will in some instances hear an INTERLOCUTORY appeal, which is an appeal of a matter that does not decide the entire case but must be addressed before the case can be decided on its merits. In other instances, whether an interlocutory appeal will be granted depends on the issue at hand. If the issue concerns whether the lawsuit should go forward at the trial level, it is more likely to be heard, since it may avoid an unnecessary trial. For example, an interlocutory appeal may be permitted from an order granting or denying an injunction, even though the main issues in the case have yet to be tried.

The proceedings in the federal and state appellate courts are quite different from those that take place in a trial court. At the trial level, WITNESSES are called to TESTIFY and a jury is often present to hear evidence and reach a VERDICT. At the appellate level, the trial court record and briefs prepared by both parties are reviewed, and oral arguments may be heard; witnesses are not called and no jury is convened. The *trial court record* usually contains the pleadings that first initiated the case, a complete transcript of the court proceedings, materials admitted into evidence, and documents indicating the final judgment.

An appellate court differs from a trial court in another important respect: Only the trial court determines the factual issues in a case. In its review, the appellate court does not try factual issues. Instead, it determines only whether there is sufficient evidence to support the findings of the trial court and whether the trial court correctly applied the law.

Both the appellant (the party appealing the lower-court ruling) and the appellee (the party against whom the appeal has been brought) file written briefs with the appellate court. The *briefs*—which recite the facts of the case, the arguments being raised on appeal, and the applicable law—help the court decide whether the trial court erred in its decision.

The appellate court may also hear *oral arguments* in the case. During oral argument, each party has 10 to 15 minutes to persuade the appellate court to rule in its favor. If numerous issues have been raised, a party may choose to use most of this time to cover the issues that are most crucial to the decision to be made. The court is free to interrupt an oral argument with questions concerning the facts of the case or the particular areas of law involved. The appellate court, at its discretion, may determine that oral argument is not necessary and may decide the case based only on the trial court record and the written briefs.

In making its decision, the appellate court may *affirm* the trial court, meaning that it accepts the decision of the lower court, or may *reverse* it, thus agreeing with the appellant's contention that the trial court's decision was erroneous. It may also *modify* the decision; in this instance, the court may accept part of the trial court's decision while ruling that other issues were erroneously decided.

The appellate court usually issues its decision in the form of a written opinion stating its reasons for the decision. The opinion will discuss the relevant facts and apply the law to those facts. Appellate court opinions are usually published, thus forming a body of law, known as precedent, that attorneys and judges can consult for guidance in resolving similar legal questions.

FURTHER READINGS

Cohen, Jonathan Matthew. 2002. *Inside Appellate Courts: The Impact of Court Organization on Judicial Decision Making in the United States Courts of Appeals.* Ann Arbor: Univ. of Michigan Press.

Klein, David E. 2002. *Making Law in the United States Courts of Appeals.* New York: Cambridge Univ. Press.

Klonoff, Robert H. 2008. *Federal Appellate Practice and Procedure in a Nutshell.* 1st ed. Thomson West.

Smithburn, J. Eric. 2009. *Appellate Review of Trial Court Decisions.* Durham, N.C.: Carolina Academic Press.

Sunstein, Cass R., David Schadke, Lisa M. Ellman, and Andres Sawicki. 2006. *Are Judges Political?* Washington, D.C.: Brookings Institution Press.

Wisotsky, Steven. 2009. *Professional Judgment on Appeal: Bringing and Opposing Appeals.* Durham, N.C.: Carolina Academic Press.

CROSS REFERENCES

Appeal; Appellate Advocacy; Courts; Federal Courts.

APPELLEE

A party who has won a judgment in a lawsuit or favorable findings in an administrative proceeding, which judgment or findings the losing party, the appellant, seeks to have a higher court reverse or set aside.

The designation as appellee is not related to a person's status as PLAINTIFF or DEFENDANT in the lower court.

Another name for *appellee* is respondent.

CROSS REFERENCE

Appeal.

❖ APPLETON, JOHN

JOHN APPLETON was a prominent nineteenth-century Maine lawyer and judge. He served as a justice and chief justice of the Maine Supreme Judicial Court from 1852 to 1883. During his long tenure he came to be recognized for his opposition to state laws that granted loans or tax exemptions to businesses. His belief in free market capitalism translated into minimal government regulation of business and no government breaks for business. In addition Appleton concerned himself with rethinking COMMON LAW rules of evidence.

Appleton was born on July 12, 1804, in New Ipswich, New Hampshire. He graduated from Bowdoin College—where his uncle, Jesse Appleton, was president—in 1822 and then apprenticed himself to a New Hampshire lawyer to gain the knowledge needed to become a member of the bar. Appleton was admitted to

the bar in 1826 and moved to Sebec, Maine, to start a private practice. Maine had been admitted to the Union in 1820 and was a growing, prosperous state. Appleton moved again to Bangor in 1838 and continued his PRIVATE LAW practice. A great reader of philosophy and law, Appleton was attracted to the utilitarian philosophy of JEREMY BENTHAM. An interest in the law from a purely intellectual viewpoint led him to pursue a judgeship.

In 1841 he was appointed the reporter of decisions for the Maine Supreme Judicial Court, the state's highest court. In this capacity Appleton edited the opinions of the justices, which gave him valuable insights into the workings of an appellate court. His diligence and intellectual esteem led to his appointment as a justice of the court in 1852. Eleven years later he was elevated to chief justice, a position he held for the next 31 years. Apart from his judicial opinions, Appleton published in 1860 a treatise entitled *The Rules of Evidence, Stated and Discussed*.

Appleton's opinions from the early 1870s on the proper relationship between government and business have come to be regarded as groundbreaking expressions of laissez-faire constitutionalism. After the Civil War state governments had rushed to give railroads and other businesses tax exemptions, loans, and property easements. When the town of Jay sought legislative authority to loan $10,000 to private entrepreneurs to move their mill and factory to the town, the legislature sought an ADVISORY OPINION from Maine's supreme court. In a bluntly worded opinion, Appleton declared that the legislature had no authority to help private businesses through gifts or loans. When

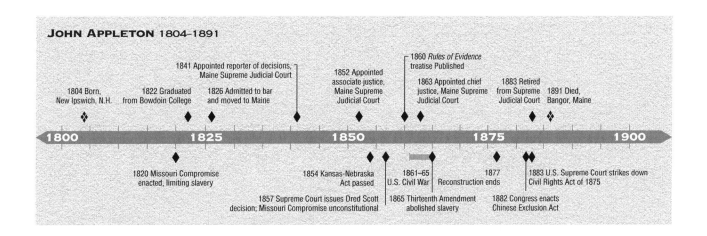

JOHN APPLETON 1804–1891

		1841 Appointed reporter of decisions, Maine Supreme Judicial Court	1852 Appointed associate justice, Maine Supreme Judicial Court	1860 *Rules of Evidence* treatise Published	
1804 Born, New Ipswich, N.H.	1822 Graduated from Bowdoin College	1826 Admitted to bar and moved to Maine		1863 Appointed chief justice, Maine Supreme Judicial Court	1883 Retired from Supreme Judicial Court 1891 Died, Bangor, Maine

1800   1825   1850   1875   1900

1820 Missouri Compromise enacted, limiting slavery

1854 Kansas-Nebraska Act passed

1857 Supreme Court issues Dred Scott decision; Missouri Compromise unconstitutional

1861–65 U.S. Civil War

1865 Thirteenth Amendment abolished slavery

1877 Reconstruction ends

1882 Congress enacts Chinese Exclusion Act

1883 U.S. Supreme Court strikes down Civil Rights Act of 1875 the legislature ignored this opinion and authorized the funding, Appleton issued an opinion ruling the act unconstitutional. Appleton's analysis foreshadowed the SUBSTANTIVE DUE PROCESS doctrine that the U.S. Supreme Court employed to strike down government regulations of business.

Appleton finally retired in 1883. He died on February 7, 1891, in Bangor, Maine.

FURTHER READINGS

Gold, David M. 1990. *The Shaping of Nineteenth-Century Law: John Appleton and Responsible Individualism.* Westport, Conn.: Greenwood.

———. 2000. "The Tradition of Substantive Judicial Review: A Case Study of Continuity in Constitutional Jurisprudence." *Maine Law Review*, 52.

Karsten, Peter. 1997. "Supervising the 'Spoiled Children of Legislation': Judicial Judgments Involving Quasi-Public Corporations in the Nineteenth-Century United States." *American Journal of Legal History*, 41.

Witt, John Fabian. 1999. "Making the Fifth: The Constitutionalization of American Self-Incrimination Doctrine." *Texas Law Review*, 77.

APPOINT

To designate, select, or assign authority to a position or an office.

Although sometimes used interchangeably, elect and appoint do not have the same meaning. Election refers to the selection of a public officer by the qualified voters of the community, and *appointment* refers to the selection of a public officer by one authorized by law to do so.

APPOINTMENT, POWER OF

A power that is conferred upon a donee to dispose of the donor's property by nominating and selecting one or more third-parties to receive it. The property may consist of tangible items such as cars, boats, and household items, or it may consist of an intangible interest in property, such as the right to receive dividend income from stocks.

A POWER OF APPOINTMENT may be transferred only in writing, such as by deed, trust, or will. Donees who receive an oral promise to be given a power of appointment, however, may bring an action for PROMISSORY ESTOPPEL if they have relied to their detriment on that promise. In no case will a court find that a power of appointment had been created unless the donor's intent to create the power is demonstrated; the person who would hold the power is indicated; the circumstances under which the power could be exercised are identified; and the property that is subject to the power is specified.

No particular semantic formula is necessary for the creation of a power of appointment. Any written expression, however informal, will suffice so long as it clearly indicates an intention to create such a power. Thus, a power of appointment may be created by implication. For example, a devise or bequest of property to a person as he or she may designate to receive it or subsequently transfer it gives that person a power of appointment. A TESTAMENTARY gift to a donee for life, to be at his or her disposal, or with a right to dispose of it at the donor's death, concers a power of appointment. For example, if a donor gives the donee an automobile to use as the donee sees fit during the donee's lifetime, the donor has given the donee a power of appointment over the automobile. Similarly, if a donor gives the donee authority to dispose of the automobile upon the donor's death, the donor has given the donee a power of appointment over the automobile.

There are three classes of powers of appointment. General powers of appointment give donees the power to dispose of the property in any way they see fit. Limited powers of appointment, also known as special powers of appointment, give donees the power to transfer the property to a specified class of persons identified in the instrument creating the power. Testamentary powers of appointment are powers of appointment that typically are created by wills.

APPORTIONMENT

Apportionment is the process by which legislative seats are distributed among units entitled to representation; determination of the number of representatives that a state, county, or other subdivision may send to a legislative body. The U.S. Constitution provides for a census every ten years, on the basis of which Congress apportions representatives according to population; each state, however, must have at least one representative. Districting is the establishment of the precise geographical boundaries of each such unit or constituency. Apportionment by state statute that denies the rule of one-person, one-vote violates the equal protection of laws.

Apportionment is also the allocation of a charge or cost such as real estate taxes between two parties, often in the same ratio as the respective times that the parties are in possession or ownership of

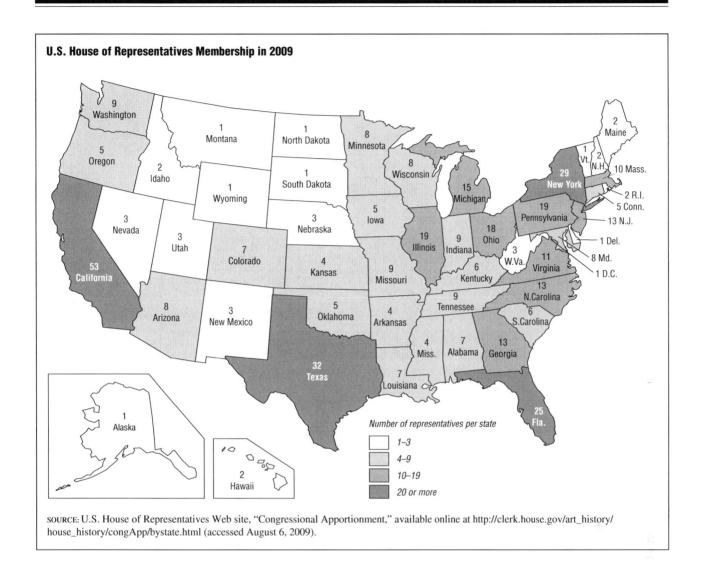

U.S. House of Representatives Membership in 2009

Number of representatives per state

- 1–3
- 4–9
- 10–19
- 20 or more

SOURCE: U.S. House of Representatives Web site, "Congressional Apportionment," available online at http://clerk.house.gov/art_history/house_history/congApp/bystate.html (accessed August 6, 2009).

property during the fiscal period for which the charge is made or assessed.

JAMES MADISON and his fellow founders of the United States of America had many objectives as they framed the U.S. Constitution. One was equal representation in a government run by members of Congress on behalf of citizens of the United States. To ensure that equal representation occurred, the founders proposed that the U.S. population be counted at regular intervals with a census. They later agreed in the Great Compromise of 1787 that congressional representation should be assigned—in other words, *apportioned*—to various regions of the country based on a total population standard.

Both Article 1, Section 2, Clause 3, and Amendment 14, Section 2, of the Constitution provide that representatives shall be apportioned among the states according to their respective numbers and that a population count will be taken by census every ten years. Apportionment requires that each state's total population be divided by the population of "the ideal district" to determine the appropriate number of representatives. The population of an ideal district, for purposes of federal apportionment, is defined as the total population of the state (as determined by census) divided by one hundred (for the House of Representatives), or by 50 (for the Senate).

In the centuries that followed the adoption of the U.S. Constitution, apportionment for the federal Congress has been based on total population—with the exception that a slave, until the Civil War, was considered property and thus counted only as three-fifths of a white person. Efforts to limit federal congressional apportionment to only people who are citizens or voters have been defeated, because the exclusion of groups such as illegal aliens, nonvoters, and children could significantly affect some areas of the country, because some states have large populations of these groups. Shifting political power away from an area means fewer legislators to demand a fair share of government resources for that area.

One such effort to exclude these groups occurred during the 1866 debates over the passage of the FOURTEENTH AMENDMENT and ultimately led to a congressional vote to continue basing apportionment on total population and to count the "whole number of persons in each state." In contrast, state legislatures have only been required to be based substantially on population since 1964 (*Reynolds v. Sims*, 377 U.S. 533, 84 S. Ct. 1362, 12 L. Ed. 2d 506). In 1968, the U.S. Supreme Court extended this requirement to municipal governments (*Avery v. Midland County*, 390 U.S. 474, 88 S. Ct. 1114, 20 L. Ed. 2d 45).

Apportionment is related to, but is not the same as, the electoral system and the districting process: *Apportionment* is the manner in which representation is distributed; the *electoral system* is the way an individual representative is elected; and the *districting process* establishes the precise electoral boundaries of a representative's district. Apportionment for the U.S. Congress, which consists of the Senate and the House of Representatives, has always been determined by the Constitution. Each state is assigned two senators, who were originally elected by state legislatures but since the adoption of the SEVENTEENTH AMENDMENT in 1913 have been chosen by direct voter election.

Membership in the House of Representatives is also assigned to the states and is apportioned according to population, with each state being constitutionally guaranteed at least one representative. The House of Representatives grew proportionally with the population of the United States until 1912, when the House froze its size at 435 members. Since 1941 the Census Bureau has used the system of *equal proportions* to determine how many of the 435 representatives each state is entitled to have. This method, developed in 1920 by Edward V. Huntington of Harvard University, establishes the smallest possible difference between the representation of any two states, because a

state's fair share of representatives will rarely be a whole number. The 1941 federal statute 2 U.S.C.A. §§ 2a and 2b provides that

> under the equal proportions method, the priority list of states or counties among which Representatives in excess of one per state or county are to be allocated is obtained by dividing the population of each state or county by the geometric mean of successive numbers of Representatives.

Congress must decide how to treat the fractional components whenever it reapportions congressional seats based on new census data. This decision affects the distribution of only a few seats in Congress and the ELECTORAL COLLEGE, but in closely contested elections, such as the presidential election of 1876, those seats could mean the difference between victory and defeat. (The electoral college is the body of electors of each state chosen to elect the president and VICE PRESIDENT. Apportionment affects the electoral college because it influences the number of electoral votes coming from various areas of the country.) Each state legislature is responsible for establishing the district boundaries of the congressional seats apportioned to the state by the federal government.

From 1842 to 1911 Congress required that all congressional districts be of compact and connecting territory. That stipulation was not continued after 1912, and by the 1960s the districts within some states differed greatly in size. These disparities were caused in some cases by gerrymandering, which is the process of drawing boundaries for election districts so as to give one party a greater political advantage. Large disparities led a group of urban Tennessee voters to bring suit against their state's electoral commission on the ground that the apportionment of the legislature was unfair. The Supreme Court's March 1962 decision in favor of the voters in *Baker v. Carr* (369 U.S. 186, 82 S. Ct. 691, 7 L. Ed. 2d 663) established the rule that a citizen may bring suit against legislative malapportionment when it deprives that citizen of EQUAL PROTECTION under the law as guaranteed by the Fourteenth Amendment. Previously, in *Colegrove v. Green* (328 U.S. 549, 66 S. Ct. 1198, 90 L. Ed. 1432 [1946]), the Court had refused to accept jurisdiction in apportionment cases.

Although the Supreme Court's decision in *Baker* was limited, it did rule that if a system other than one based on population is used for apportionment, the resulting districts must not be arbitrary or irrational in nature. In 1964 the Supreme Court extended *Baker* by ruling in *Wesberry v. Sanders* (376 U.S. 1, 84 S. Ct. 526, 11 L. Ed. 2d 481) that legislative districts for the House of Representatives must be drawn so as to provide "equal representation for equal numbers of people," a concept often referred to as the one-person, one-vote standard. Later that same year, in lawsuits directly involving 15 states, the Supreme Court ruled in *Reynolds v. Sims* (377 U.S. 533, 84 S. Ct. 1362, 12 L. Ed. 2d 506) that districts for state legislatures must also be substantially equal in population. Further extending the principle, the Court ruled in *Avery v. Midland County* (390 U.S. 474, 88 S. Ct. 1114, 20 L. Ed. 2d 45 [1968]) that if county, city, and town governments elect their representatives from individual districts, the districts must be substantially equal in population.

Other individuals and states have subsequently challenged the method of apportionment used in the United States when that method has proved unfavorable for them. For example, in *Franklin v. Massachusetts* (505 U.S. 788, 112 S. Ct. 2767, 120 L. Ed. 2d 636 [1992]), Massachusetts and two of its registered voters filed an action against Secretary of Commerce Barbara B. Franklin, alleging, among other things, that the decision to allocate overseas employees was inconsistent with the Constitution. In June 1992 the Court reversed a federal district court decision in favor of Massachusetts, ruling that the allocation of overseas federal employees to their designated home states was consistent with the usual-residence standard used in early censuses and served the purpose of making representation in Congress more equal.

The state of Montana sued the U.S. COMMERCE DEPARTMENT, following the 1990 census, when it and 11 other states each lost one House seat. In seeking to keep the two seats it had held since 1910, Montana argued that the method of equal proportions was unconstitutional because it left the state with a single congressional district of 803,655 people—a number almost 40 percent larger than "ideal district size," which is a national average of 572,466 people. Montana also alleged that the variance between the single district's population and that of an ideal district could not be justified under the one-person, one-vote standard developed in *Wesberry*. The Montana case

was appealed to the U.S. Supreme Court, which in March 1992 unanimously upheld the method Congress uses to reallocate congressional seats among the states after a census (*United States DEPARTMENT OF COMMERCE v. Montana*, 503 U.S. 442, 112 S. Ct. 1415, 118 L. Ed. 2d 87).

The political impact of the census on congressional apportionment was made apparent when the Commerce Department proposed that statistical sampling be used for the 2000 census. (*Statistical sampling* is a method of surveying a subset of a larger population and applying the findings to the larger group.) Republicans in Congress reacted hostilely to this proposal from the Democratic administration of President BILL CLINTON, fearing that the proposed statistical sampling of hard-to-count persons (e.g., racial and ethnic minorities, poor persons, children, illegal aliens, renters) would favor large urban areas that were aligned with the DEMOCRATIC PARTY. Members of Congress filed suit to block the use of sampling and the Supreme Court agreed with their position in *Commerce Dept. v. U.S. House of Representatives* (525 U.S. 316, 119 S. Ct.765, 142 L.Ed.2d 797 [1999]). The Court held that the Census Act, which was first enacted in 1954 (and amended a number of times), expressly prohibited the use of sampling to determine populations for congressional apportionment purposes.

This ruling did not end the controversy over what constituted sampling. Following the 2000 census, the state of Utah filed suit against the Commerce Department, alleging that it should have increased its congressional representation from three seats to four. According to the census, the state had achieved a dramatic 30-percent population growth in ten years. Despite this growth, the number of representatives in the state did not increase. North Carolina, however, did pick up an additional seat through a statistical method called *imputation*. This method permits the Census Bureau to *impute*, or estimate, the number of members in a household after census takers repeatedly try to make direct contact. Comparing the numbers of imputed residents of Utah and North Carolina, Utah realized that if it could have these numbers thrown out by a federal court, the North Carolina seat would shift to Utah.

A three-judge panel rejected Utah's arguments that imputed numbers amounted to statistical sampling as prohibited by the 1999

Supreme Court decision. The panel concluded that it was common sense to realize that census takers would not be able to count every person and that reasonable alternatives needed to be employed to fill in the missing numbers. The actual enumeration required by the census clause did not mean that the court should reduce the number of persons imputed to households to zero. The imputation method was on the whole fair because it was adjusted for local neighborhood demographics and it was employed only after census takers failed on repeated attempts to contact the households in question. Therefore, the panel ruled that reducing the number to zero would be "inconsistent with the constitutional imperative of actual enumeration," for actual residents would not be counted.

In *Utah v. Evans* (536 U.S. 452, 122 S. Ct. 2191, 153 L.Ed.2d 453 [2002]), the Supreme Court affirmed the lower court ruling. The Court, in a 5–4 decision, rejected the idea that actual enumeration under the Census Clause was intended as a description of the only methodology for counting U.S. citizens. The Court pointed out that an interest in accuracy was favored by the Census Bureau, which used imputation as a LAST RESORT only after other methods had failed. The majority also decided that this method, used as a last resort, was not the same as sampling. Justice STEPHEN BREYER noted that "sampling seeks to extrapolate the features of a large population from a small one, but the Bureau's imputation process sought simply to fill in missing data as part of an effort to count individuals one by one." Moreover, the imputation method was not the equivalent of statistical sampling because the two methods were viewed as distinctly different when an amendment to the Census Act was passed in 1958.

The Commerce Department announced in 2009 that it would not use statistical sampling for the 2010 census.

FURTHER READINGS

Bestor, Arthur. "'Advice' from the Very Beginning, 'Consent' When the End Is Achieved." 1989. *American Journal of International Law* 83 (October).

Corpus Juris Secundum United States, vol. 91, secs. 11–12.

Cox, Gary W., and Jonathan N. Katz. 2002. *Elbridge Gerry's Salamander: The Electoral Consequences of the Reapportionment Revolution*. New York: Cambridge Univ. Press.

"Fair Representation: Meeting the Ideal of One Man, One Vote." 1984. *Michigan Law Review* 82 (February).

The Federalist Nos. 37, 38, 52, 54, 56, 57, 58, 62, and 63. 1787–88.

"Lies, Damn Lies and Statistics: Dispelling Some Myths Surrounding the United States Census." 1990. *Detroit College of Law Review* (spring).

"Montana's Lost Seats Begs Issue." 1992. *National Law Journal* (March 2).

"Politics and Purpose: Hide and Seek in the Gerrymandering Thicket after *Davis v. Bandmer*." 1987. *University of Pennsylvania Law Review* 136 (November).

"Reapportionment: The Supreme Court Searches for Standards." 1989. *Urban Law* 21 (fall).

Scher, Richard K. 1996. *Voting Rights and Democracy: The Law and Politics of Districting*. San Francisco: Wadsworth.

"The Thickest Thicket: Partisan Gerrymandering and Judicial Regulation of Politics." 1987. *Columbia Law Review* 87 (November).

"Understanding Dworkin." 1993. *George Mason Independent Law Review* 1 (spring).

Yates, Christopher St. John. "A House of Our Own or a House We've Outgrown? An Argument for Increasing the Size of the House of Representatives." 1992. *Columbia Journal of Law and Social Problems* 25.

Yarbrough, Tinsley E. 2002. *Race and Redistricting: The Shaw-Cromartie Cases*. Lawrence: Univ. Press of Kansas.

CROSS REFERENCES

Congress of the United States; Voting

APPRAISAL

A valuation or an approximation of value by impartial, properly qualified persons; the process of determining the value of an asset or liability, which entails expert opinion rather than express commercial transactions.

APPRAISER

A person selected or appointed by a competent authority or an interested party to evaluate the financial worth of property.

Appraisers are frequently appointed in probate and condemnation proceedings and are also used by banks and REAL ESTATE concerns to determine the MARKET VALUE of real property.

APPRECIATION

The fair and reasonable estimation of the value of an item. The increase in the financial worth of an asset as compared to its value at a particular earlier date as a result of inflation or greater market demand.

APPREHENSION

A reasonable belief of the possibility of imminent injury or death at the hands of another that justifies a person acting in self-defense against the potential attack.

An apprehension of attack is an element of the defense of SELF-DEFENSE that can be used in a criminal prosecution for ASSAULT AND BATTERY, MANSLAUGHTER, or MURDER. An individual who acts under apprehension of attack does not have to fear injury. It is sufficient that there is a likelihood of actual injury to justify the person's taking steps to protect himself or herself.

APPRENTICE

A person who agrees to work for a specified time in order to learn a trade, craft, or profession in which the employer, traditionally called the master, assents to instruct him or her.

Both minors and adults can be legally obligated under the terms of an apprenticeship contract, and any person who has the capacity to manage his or her own affairs may engage an apprentice. In some states, a minor may void a contract of apprenticeship, but in cases where the contract is beneficial to the minor, other jurisdictions do not permit the minor to void it. There must be strict compliance with statutes that govern a minor's actions concerning an apprenticeship.

An apprenticeship must arise from an agreement, sometimes labeled an indenture, which possesses all the requisites of a valid contract. If the contract cannot be performed within a year, it must be in writing, in order to satisfy the STATUTE OF FRAUDS, an old ENGLISH LAW adopted in the United States, which requires certain agreements to be in writing. The apprentice, the employer, and, if the apprentice is a minor, his or her parents or guardians must sign the apprenticeship agreement. Some jurisdictions require explicit consensual language in addition to the signature or signatures of one or both parents, depending upon the applicable statute. The contract must include the provisions required by law and drafted for the benefit of the minor such as those relating to his or her education and training. A breach of apprenticeship contract might justify an award of damages, and, unless authorized by statute, there can be no assignment, or transfer, of the contract of apprenticeship to another that would bind the apprentice to a new service.

A person who lures an apprentice from his or her employer may be sued by the employer, but the employer cannot recover unless the DEFENDANT knew of the apprentice relationship.

The apprenticeship may be concluded by either party for GOOD CAUSE, where no definite term of service is specified, by mutual consent, or by a dismissal of the apprentice. Automatic termination ensues from the expiration of the term of service, involuntary removal of the apprentice from the jurisdiction where he or she was bound, or service in the armed forces even though voluntary and without the consent of the employer. The death of either party terminates the relationship, as does the attainment of the AGE OF MAJORITY by the apprentice, in most instances. Courts may terminate such contracts when they violate statutes. The master's cruelty, immorality, interference with the apprentice's religious beliefs or duties, or other misconduct and the misbehavior of the apprentice also constitute grounds for termination.

APPROPRIATION

The designation by the government or an individual of the use to which a fund of money is to be applied. The selection and setting apart of privately owned land by the government for public use, such as a military reservation or public building. The diversion of water flowing on public domain from its natural course by means of a canal or ditch for a private beneficial use of the appropriator.

An *appropriation bill* is a proposal placed before the legislative branch of the government by one or a group of its members to earmark a particular portion of general revenue or treasury funds for use for a governmental objective. Federal appropriation bills can originate only in the House of Representatives as mandated by Article I, Section 7 of the Constitution. Once an appropriation law is enacted, a definite amount of money is set aside so that public officials can pay incurred or anticipated expenditures. When a law authorizes funds to be used for a particular purpose, it is known as a *specific appropriation.*

The appropriation of money by an individual occurs within the context of a debtor-creditor relationship. If a creditor is owed two separate debts by the same debtor who makes a payment without specifying the debt to which it is to be applied, the creditor can appropriate the payment to either debt.

Appropriation also refers to the physical taking and occupation of property by the government or its actual, substantial interference with the owner's right to use the land according to personal wishes by virtue of the government's power of EMINENT DOMAIN.

This right of an individual to use water that belongs to the public is embodied in the *prior appropriation doctrine* applied in arid western states where water supplies are not available in sufficient quantity to all who might need them. An individual landowner who first diverts water for personal benefit is entitled to its continued use as long as there is a reasonable need and the water is actually used.

CROSS REFERENCES

Federal Budget; Water Rights.

APPROVAL

The present confirmation, ratification, or assent to some action or thing done by another, which is submitted to an individual, group, or governmental body for judgment. The acceptance by a judge of a bond, security, or other document that is required by law to meet with the judge's satisfaction before it becomes legally effective.

APPURTENANCE

An accessory or adjunct that is attached and incidental to something that has greater importance or value. As applied to real property, an object attached to or a right to be used with land as an incidental benefit but which is necessary to the complete use and enjoyment of the property.

When a landowner has been given an easement for the passage of light and air over an adjoining lot, the easement is an appurtenance to the land. Other common appurtenances to land include barns, outhouses, fences, drainage and irrigation ditches, and rights of way.

ARBITER

[Latin, One who attends something to view it as a spectator or witness.] *Any person who is given an absolute power to judge and rule on a matter in dispute.*

An arbiter is usually chosen or appointed by parties or by a court on their behalf. The decision of an arbiter is made according to the rules of law and equity. The arbiter is distinguished from the arbitrator, who proceeds at his or her own discretion, so that the decision is made according to the judgment of a REASONABLE PERSON.

An arbiter may perform the same function as an umpire, a person who decides a controversy when arbitrators cannot agree.

CROSS REFERENCES

Alternative Dispute Resolution; Arbitration.

ARBITRAGE

The simultaneous purchase in one market and sale in another of a security or commodity in hope of making a profit on price differences in the different markets.

In its simplest form, arbitrage is "buying low and selling high." In this sense, any trader who buys something in one market—whether it is a commodity like grain, financial SECURITIES such as stock in a company, or a currency such as the Japanese yen—and sells it in another market at a higher price is engaged in arbitrage. That trader is called an arbitrageur. In economic theory, arbitrage is a necessary activity in any market, helping to reduce price disparities between different markets and to increase a market's liquidity (ability to buy and sell).

Arbitrage can be divided into the categories of riskless and risk. As an example of riskless arbitrage, imagine that the price of Microsoft Corporation COMMON STOCK on the Pacific Coast Stock Exchange is less than the price of the same stock on the New York Stock Exchange. A trader who buys Microsoft stock at the lower price on the Pacific Coast exchange and *simultaneously* sells it for a higher price on the New York exchange is engaging in an essentially riskless transaction. Aided by the speed of modern communications, the buying and selling occur at virtually the same time. This type of exchange occurs daily in the currency market, where a trader may buy French francs at a lower price in London and sell them at a higher price in Singapore.

Much arbitrage falls into the risk category. This type of arbitrage is not always completed with a sale at a higher price; it involves a risk that the price of the item being traded will fall before the trader can sell it. RISK ARBITRAGE came into prominence during the 1980s, when investors began to take advantage of a business atmosphere encompassing a large number of company MERGERS AND ACQUISITIONS. In a merger or acquisition, one company buys or takes over another company. When the management of the targeted company does not want to be acquired by a particular investor or group of investors, the merger is called a hostile takeover. Quite often, the aggressors in such takeovers are smaller in terms of assets than their targets. A hostile takeover is usually initiated when someone believes that the stock of a particular company is lower than its potential value, whether because of poor management or because of a lack of information about the true value of that company.

One way that hostile takeovers are initiated is through a device called the cash TENDER OFFER. The party attempting to initiate the takeover announces that it will pay cash for the target company's stock at a price well above the current MARKET VALUE. At this point, risk arbitrageurs become involved in the game. They buy stock from shareholders in the target company, then attempt to sell that stock at the higher price to the party attempting the takeover. If the takeover succeeds and the arbitrageurs receive a higher price for their stock, they profit; if the takeover fails or the arbitrageurs receive a lower price for their stock, they lose. Gauging the risk of a takeover's failure is therefore crucial to an arbitrageur's success.

An arbitrageur who purchases securities on the basis of inside information—that is, information about a pending takeover that is not available to the general public—violates the Securities Exchange Act of 1934 (§ 10[b], as amended, 15 U.S.C.A. § 78j[b]). However, purchasing securities on the basis of rumors about an imminent takeover is not illegal.

Ivan F. Boesky was one example of a risk arbitrageur who was found guilty of engaging in INSIDER TRADING. Boesky profited enormously from the many corporate takeovers of the mid-1980s. By 1985 he had become famous in financial circles and had published a book, *Merger Mania: Arbitrage: Wall Street's Best Kept Money-Making Secret,* that extolled the opportunities in risk arbitrage and the benefits the practice gave to the market. In 1986 only one year later, Boesky admitted that he had illegally traded on insider information obtained from Drexel Burnham Lambert, the securities firm that arranged the financing of many of the takeovers of the era. In return for a reduced sentence of three years in prison, Boesky agreed

to pay a $100 million penalty and to cooperate with the government's continuing investigation. Boesky named Drexel employee Michael R. Milken as a member of the insider trading network. In 1990 Boesky was released from prison after serving two years.

FURTHER READINGS

Boesky, Ivan. 1985. *Merger Mania.* New York: Holt, Rinehart and Winston.
"Complex Plan of Finance Successfully Navigates Arbitrage Rules." 2003. *Tax Management Memorandum* 44 (February 10).
Steuerle, C. Eugene. 2002. "Defining Tax Shelters and Tax Arbitrage." *Tax Analysts* (May 20).
Stokeld, Fred. 2001. "IRS on the Prowl for Illegal Arbitrage." *Tax Notes 92* (September 10).

CROSS REFERENCES

Corporations; Securities; Securities and Exchange Commission.

ARBITRARY

Irrational; capricious.

The term *arbitrary* describes a course of action or a decision that is not based on reason or judgment but on personal will or discretion without regard to rules or standards.

An arbitrary decision is one made without regard for the facts and circumstances presented, and it connotes a disregard of the evidence.

In many instances, the term implies an element of BAD FAITH, and it may be used synonymously with tyrannical or despotic.

The term *arbitrary* refers to the standard of review used by courts when reviewing a variety of decisions on appeal. For example, the *arbitrary and capricious* standard of review is the principle standard of review used by judicial courts hearing appeals that challenge decisions issued by administrative bodies.

At the federal level and in most states, administrative law is a body of law made by executive branch agencies that have been delegated power to promulgate rules, regulations, and orders, render decisions, and otherwise decide miscellaneous disputes. Non-elected officials in administrative agencies are delegated this authority in order to streamline the often lengthy and more deliberative process of legislative lawmaking that frequently grinds to a halt amid partisan gridlock. Although administrative agencies are generally designed to make lawmaking and regulation simpler, more direct, and less formal, they still must provide due process to affected parties. They must also comply with administrative procedures created by popularly elected state and federal legislatures.

One important right recognized in most administrative proceedings is the right of JUDICIAL REVIEW. Citizens aggrieved by the actions of an administrative body may typically ask a judicial court to review those actions for error. In establishing the standard by which judicial courts will review the actions of an administrative body, state and federal legislatures seek to provide agencies with enough freedom to do their work effectively and efficiently, while ensuring that individual rights are protected.

Congress tried to maintain this delicate balance in the Administrative Procedures Act (APA). The APA limits the scope of a reviewing court's authority to determining whether the agency acted arbitrarily and capriciously in exercising its discretion. 5 USCA § 701. In making this determination, the reviewing court will not find that the administrative body acted arbitrarily unless the agency failed to follow proper procedures or rendered a decision that is so clearly erroneous that it must be set aside to avoid doing an injustice to the parties.

Specifically, a reviewing court must determine whether the agency articulated a rational connection between the factual findings it made and the decision it rendered. The reviewing court must also examine the record to ensure that the agency decision was founded on a reasoned evaluation of the relevant factors. Although agencies are given wide latitude, reviewing courts must be careful not to rubber-stamp administrative decisions that they deem inconsistent with a statutory mandate or that frustrate the congressional policy underlying a statute.

Typically, reviewing courts look at the whole record in making this determination, take into account the agency's expertise on any particular matters, and accept any factual findings made by the agency. However, the reviewing court is free to determine how the law should apply to those facts. If the reviewing court concludes that the agency's actions were so arbitrary as to be outside any reasonable interpretation of the law, the court may overturn the agency's decision or remand the case back to the agency for further proceedings in accordance with the court's decision.

A reviewing court's determination that an agency acted in an arbitrary manner will often depend on the technical requirements of the governing law. For example, courts are often asked to determine whether a federal agency has acted arbitrarily under the National Environmental Policy Act (NEPA). Pub.L. 91-190, § 2, Jan. 1, 1970, 83 Stat. 852, as amended, 42 U.S.C. A. §§ 4321 et seq. In one case the Ninth Circuit ruled that the TRANSPORTATION DEPARTMENT acted arbitrarily under NEPA, when it failed to prepare an environmental impact statement, failed to consider whether its regulations would have violated air quality limits, and failed to perform localized analyses for areas most likely to be affected by increased truck traffic. *Public Citizen v. Department of Transportation*, 316 F. 3d 1002 (9th Cir. 2003).

CROSS REFERENCES

Administrative Procedure Act of 1946; Bad Faith; Due Process of Law; Judicial Review; Relevancy.

ARBITRATION

Arbitration is the submission of a dispute to an unbiased third person or persons designated by the parties to resolve the controversy; the arbitration award is the decision issued after a hearing at which both parties have an opportunity to be heard.

The two general types of arbitration are binding arbitration and non-binding arbitration. In binding arbitration, the arbitration award is usually final, and courts rarely reexamine it. In non-binding arbitration, the arbitration award is a recommendation, and the parties may choose whether to accept it. In either type of arbitration, the award is a decision issued after a hearing at which both parties have an opportunity to be heard.

Arbitration is a well-established and widely used means to end disputes. It is one of several kinds of ALTERNATIVE DISPUTE RESOLUTION, which provide parties to a controversy with a choice other than LITIGATION. Unlike litigation, arbitration takes place outside the court system, generally allowing less formal adherence to the rules of evidence and procedure and leading to a faster, less expensive resolution of a controversy. In the arbitration, the two sides select an impartial THIRD PARTY or parties, known as an

Arbitration Clause

Contractual Arbitration Clause

Standard Business

ARBITRATION. The Parties agree that any claim or dispute between them or against any agent, employee, successor, or assign of the other, whether related to this agreement or otherwise, and any claim or dispute related to this agreement or the relationship or duties contemplated under this contract, including the validity of this arbitration clause, shall be resolved by binding arbitration by the American Arbitration Association (or name other firm providing arbitration services, e.g., National Arbitration Forum), under the Arbitration Rules then in effect. Any award of the arbitrator(s) may be entered as a judgment in any court of competent jurisdiction.

A sample arbitration clause
ILLUSTRATION BY GGS CREATIVE RESOURCES. REPRODUCED BY PERMISSION OF GALE, A PART OF CENGAGE LEARNING.

arbitrator or an arbitration panel; they participate in a hearing at which both sides can present evidence and TESTIMONY; and they agree in advance whether they will be bound by the arbitration award. If the parties to a non-binding arbitration decline to adopt the award, they remain free to pursue their claims within the court system or to submit the dispute to another type of alternative dispute resolution.

Traditionally, labor and commerce were the two largest areas of arbitration. However, since the mid-1970s the technique has seen great expansion. Some states have mandated arbitration for certain disputes such as auto insurance claims, and court decisions have broadened into areas such as SECURITIES, antitrust, and even employment discrimination. International business issues are also frequently resolved using arbitration.

Arbitration in the United States dates back to the eighteenth century. Courts frowned on it, though, until attitudes started to change in 1920 with the passage of the first state arbitration law, in New York. This statute served as a model for other state and federal laws, including, in 1925, the U.S. Arbitration Act, later known as the Federal Arbitration Act (FAA) (9 U.S.C.A. § 1 et seq.). The FAA was intended to give arbitration equal status with litigation and, in effect, created a body of federal law. After WORLD WAR II, arbitration grew increasingly important to labor-management relations. Congress helped this growth with passage of the TAFT-HARTLEY ACT (29 U.S.C.A. § 141 et seq.) in 1947, and over the next decade the U.S. Supreme Court cemented arbitration as the favored means for resolving labor issues, by limiting the judiciary's role. In the 1970s arbitration began expanding into a wide range of issues that eventually included prisoners' rights, MEDICAL MALPRACTICE, and consumer rights. By 2003 all 50 states had modern arbitration statutes.

Arbitration can be voluntary or required. The traditional model is voluntary and closely linked to contract law: Parties often stipulate in contracts that they will arbitrate, rather than litigate, when disputes arise. For example, unions and employers almost always put an arbitration clause in their formal negotiations, known as COLLECTIVE BARGAINING agreements. By doing so, they agree to arbitrate any future employee grievances over wages, hours, working conditions, or job security; in essence, they agree not to sue if disagreements occur. Similarly, a purchaser and a provider of services who disagree over the result of a business deal may submit the problem to an arbitrator instead of a court. Mandatory arbitration was a later phenomenon. States such as Minnesota, New York, and New Jersey enacted statutes that force disputes over automobile insurance claims into this forum. In addition, courts sometimes order disputants into arbitration.

In theory, arbitration has many advantages over litigation. Efficiency is perhaps the greatest. Proponents say arbitration is easier, cheaper, and faster. Proponents also point to the greater flexibility with which parties in arbitration can fashion the terms and rules of the process. Furthermore, although arbitrators can be lawyers, they do not need to be. They are often selected for their expertise in a particular area of business and may be drawn from private practice or from organizations such as the American Arbitration Association (AAA), a national nonprofit group founded in 1926. Significantly, arbitrators are freer than judges to make decisions, because they do not have to abide by the principle of *stare decisis* (the policy of courts to follow principles established by legal precedent) and do not have to give reasons to support their awards (although they are expected to adhere to the Code of Ethics for Arbitrators in Commercial Disputes, established in 1977 by the AAA and the AMERICAN BAR ASSOCIATION).

These theoretical advantages do not always hold up in practice. Even when efficiency is achieved, some critics argue, the price is a lower quality of justice, and it can be made worse by the difficulty of appealing an award. The charge is frequently made that arbitration only results in "splitting the baby"—dividing awards evenly among the parties. The AAA roundly rejects this claim. Yet even arbitrators agree that as arbitration has become increasingly formal, it sometimes resembles litigation in its complexity. This may not be an inherent problem with the process as much as a result of flawed use of it. Parties may undermine arbitration by acting as lawyers do in a lawsuit: excessively demanding discovery (evidence from the other side), calling WITNESSES, and filing motions.

Ultimately, the decision to use arbitration cannot be made lightly. Most frequently, arbitration is binding, and courts in most jurisdictions enforce awards. Moreover, binding arbitration allows little or no option for appeal, expecting parties who arbitrate to assume the risks of the process. In addition, arbitration is subject to the legal doctrines of RES JUDICATA and COLLATERAL ESTOPPEL, which together strictly curtail the option of bringing suits based on issues that were or could have been raised initially.

Res judicata means that a final judgment on the merits is conclusive as to the rights of the parties and their privies, and, as to them, operates as an absolute bar to a subsequent action involving the same claim, demand, or CAUSE OF ACTION. *Collateral estoppel* means that when an issue of ultimate fact has been determined by a valid judgment, that issue cannot be relitigated between the same parties in future litigation. Thus, often the end is truly in sight at the conclusion of a binding arbitration hearing and the granting of an award.

The FAA gives only four grounds on which a court may vacate, or overturn, a binding arbitration award: (1) where the award is the result of corruption, FRAUD, or undue means; (2) where the arbitrators were evidently partial or corrupt; (3) where the arbitrators were guilty of

misconduct in refusing to postpone the hearing or hear pertinent evidence, or where their misbehavior prejudiced the rights of any party; and (4) where the arbitrators exceeded their powers or imperfectly executed them so that a mutual, final, and definite award was not made. In the 1953 case *Wilko v. Swan,* 346 U.S. 427, 74 S. Ct. 182, 98 L. Ed. 168, the U.S. Supreme Court suggested, in passing, that an otherwise-binding award may be set aside if it is in "manifest disregard of the law," and federal courts have sometimes followed this principle. PUBLIC POLICY can also be grounds for vacating a binding arbitration award, but this recourse is severely limited to well-defined policy based on legal precedent, a rule emphasized by the Supreme Court in the 1987 case *United Paperworkers International Union v. Misco* (484 U.S. 29, 108 S. Ct. 364, 98 L. Ed. 2d 286).

The growth of arbitration is taken as a healthy sign by many legal commentators. It eases the load on a constantly overworked judicial system, while providing disputants with a relatively informal, inexpensive means to solve their problems. One major boost to arbitration came from the U.S. Supreme Court, which held in 1991 that AGE DISCRIMINATION claims in employment are arbitrable (*Gilmer v. Interstate/Johnson Lane Corp.,* 500 U.S. 20, 111 S. Ct. 1647, 114 L. Ed. 2d 26). Writing for the majority, Justice BYRON R. WHITE concluded that arbitration is as effective as a trial for resolving employment disputes. *Gilmer* led several major employers to treat all employment claims through binding arbitration, sometimes as a condition of employment.

Arbitration clauses have become a standard feature of many employment contracts. This factor has led to conflicts concerning the applicability of these clauses when an employee seeks to sue an employer for a CIVIL RIGHTS violation under Title VII of the Civil Rights Act of 1964, as amended by the Civil Rights Act of 1991. A provision of this law addressed, for the first time, the arbitration of Title VII claims. Section 118 of the act states that the parties could, "where appropriate and to the extent authorized by law," choose to pursue alternative dispute resolution, including arbitration, to resolve their Title VII disputes. Since its enactment, the federal courts have been required to determine what this clause means in practice. For example, in the securities industry, disputes arose over whether employers could require their employees to WAIVE their right to bring a Title VII claim in court. The circuit courts of appeal have uniformly ruled that Congress did not mean to preclude compulsory arbitration of Title VII claims.

The EQUAL EMPLOYMENT OPPORTUNITY COMMISSION (EEOC) has contended that employment arbitration clauses do not prohibit the EEOC from filing an action against an employer for a civil rights violation. The Supreme Court agreed in *Equal Employment Opportunity Commission v. Waffle House, Inc.*, 534 U.S. 279, 122 S. Ct. 754, 151 L. Ed. 2d 755 (2002), holding that the EEOC could seek damages on behalf of an employee. The commission could also seek injunctive relief to change a company's discriminatory methods. In so ruling, the Court resolved an issue that had divided the circuit courts of appeal.

The employee in question was fired from his job at the Waffle House after he suffered a SEIZURE. He filed a claim with the EEOC, arguing that his rights under Title I of the Americans with Disabilities Act (ADA) had been violated. Under this act, the EEOC has the authority to bring its own enforcement actions against employers and to seek reinstatement, back pay, and compensatory and PUNITIVE DAMAGES on behalf of an employee. Moreover, the ADA makes no exception for arbitration agreements, nor does it even mention arbitration. Therefore the EEOC, which had not signed an arbitration agreement with the employer, was free to pursue its claims in court. The Court also concluded that the general policies surrounding the ADA, and the EEOC enforcement arm, justified the pursuit by the EEOC of victim-specific relief. It stated that punitive damages "may often have a greater impact on the behavior of other employers than the threat of an injunction."

The Supreme Court also has validated the enforceability of arbitration awards relating to collective bargaining agreements. In *Eastern Associated Coal Corporation v. United Mine Workers of American, District 17*, 531 U.S. 57, 121 S. Ct. 462, 148 L. Ed. 2d 354 (2000), the issue involved a labor arbitrator who ordered an employer to reinstate an employee who had twice tested positive for marijuana use. The employer filed a lawsuit in federal court seeking to have the arbitrator's decision vacated, arguing that the award contradicted a public policy

against the operation of dangerous machinery by workers who test positive for drugs.

The Court unanimously agreed that the employee should be reinstated. The Court made it clear that the question was not whether the employee's drug use itself violated public policy, but whether the agreement to reinstate him did so. However, the Court also pointed out that the public policy exception is a narrow one. Based on these principles, the Court ruled that the reinstatement did not violate public policy, as the award did not condone drug use or its impact on public safety. In addition, the arbitrator placed conditions on the employee's reinstatement, which included suspension of work for three months without pay, participation in a substance abuse program, and continued random drug testing. The fact that the employee was a recidivist did not tip the balance in favor of discharge.

In 2009 the Arbitration Fairness Act was introduced in Congress, limiting the scope of the FAA and declaring that no predispute arbitration agreement shall be valid or enforceable if it requires the arbitration of certain disputes. Such disputes include an employment, consumer, or franchise dispute, or a dispute arising under any statute intended to protect civil rights. The act, which would amend Chapter 1 of Title 9 of the United States Code with respect to arbitration, further requires that the validity or enforceability of an arbitration agreement shall be determined by a court under federal law. Arbitration provisions in collective bargaining agreements, however, are exempt under the act. Although early criticism of the Arbitration Fairness Act opines that it is anti-business, other assessments point out that it does not cover traditional disputes between sophisticated commercial parties; hence, its impact in the business realm may be minimal.

An April 3, 2009, decision from the Alaska Supreme Court supported a limitation on employment disputes, echoing the sentiment behind the Arbitration Fairness Act that perhaps the arbitration of such disputes gives employers an unfair advantage. In *Gibson v. NYE Frontier Ford*, Slip. Op. No. 6355 (Ala. S. Ct. Apr. 3, 2009), an employee ordered to arbitrate his wage and hour claim arising under state law consistent with the terms of an agreement governed by the FAA sought a declaration that the agreement was unconscionable. Among other factors, the agreement required him to pay substantial arbitration costs. In reviewing his claim and the agreement at issue, the Alaska court agreed with the employee, finding that arbitration may be required only if the employer agrees to pay the arbitration costs. Despite this decision, the trend still favors arbitration of disputes over litigation of such disputes within the court system.

FURTHER READINGS

Carbonneau, Thomas E. 2009. *Arbitration in a Nutshell.* 2d Ed. St. Paul, Minn.: West.

Coltri, Laurie S. 2010. *Alternative Dispute Resolution: A Conflict Diagnosis Approach.* Boston: Prentice Hall.

Crowley, Thomas. 1994. "The Art of Arbitration Advocacy." *Hawaii Bar Journal* (September).

Culiner, Helen. 1994. "Practical Guidelines for Lawyers Representing Clients in Arbitration Proceedings Today." *Dispute Resolution Journal* (September).

Deye, James, and Lesly Britton. 1994. "Arbitration by the American Arbitration Association." *North Dakota Law Review.*

Nolan-Haley, Jacqueline M. 2008. *Alternative Dispute Resolution in a Nutshell.* 3d ed. St. Paul: West Wadsworth.

Silverman, Peter 2009. "A Client's Guide to Mediation and Arbitration." *American Bar Association* (February).

Ware, Stephen J. 2001. *Alternative Dispute Resolution.* St. Paul: West Wadsworth.

CROSS REFERENCE

Alternative Dispute Resolution.

ARCHITECT

A person who prepares the plan and design of a building or other structure and sometimes supervises its construction.

A landscape architect is responsible for the arrangement of scenery over a tract of land for natural or aesthetic purposes in order to enhance or preserve the property.

Regulation

The practice of planning and designing a building requires the application of specialized skill and knowledge. Because the product of an architect's work is used by members of the general public, the legislature of a state may regulate the practice of those engaged in the profession. Regulatory statutes designed to protect public health and safety are created under the inherent authority of a state to protect the welfare of its citizens. As a general rule, regulatory statutes are valid, provided they are not unreasonable.

Statutes requiring that architects must be registered and licensed are based on PUBLIC POLICY aimed at protecting citizens from unqualified practitioners. In many states, statutes call for the revocation of a license for such conduct as fraud, dishonesty, recklessness, incompetence, or MISREPRESENTATION when an architect acts in his or her professional capacity.

The power to revoke a license is commonly given by the legislature to a state board of architects who must act in a manner prescribed by statute. Generally, an architect is entitled to notice and a hearing when the board seeks to revoke his or her license. The architect can appeal a revocation.

Qualifications

Statutes setting forth the requirements for obtaining a license or registration generally require that the applicants be of LEGAL AGE and of good moral character, have completed a certain course of study, and have a certain amount of practical experience. Many states have an additional requirement that applicants must pass an examination. A legislature may provide that certain persons who have practiced architecture for a period of time prior to legislation requiring an examination may register as architects without an examination. Such a statutory provision is called a GRANDFATHER CLAUSE.

Persons who present themselves to the public as architects must comply with the statutory registration and licensing requirements. The failure to do so is unlawful. In most states, persons who falsely hold themselves out as licensed architects are guilty of a misdemeanor, and contracts rendered by them with others are void and unenforceable.

Employment

The terms and conditions of an architect's employment are designated in a contract and are governed by general rules of contract law. Ordinarily, the person who employs the architect becomes the owner of the plans, unless the employment contract states otherwise. Customarily, the architect retains the plans after they have been paid for and the builder may possess and use them while constructing the building.

Authority and Powers

The power and authority of architects are determined by general rules of agency law. In most cases, unless the employment contract states otherwise, architects are held to be agents with limited authority. An employer is liable for acts of an architect when they are within the scope of the architect's agency, although the contracting parties may further restrict the powers if they so desire.

Architects have a duty to exercise their personal skill and judgment in the performance of their work, and they may not delegate this duty without express authority to do so. They may, however, delegate responsibility to subordinates while performing their duties as agents.

A supervising architect does not have implied authority to perform work that has been assigned to a contractor or to employ or discharge workers. The supervising architect does, however, have authority to make decisions concerning proper workmanship, fitness of materials, and the manner of work.

Duties and Liabilities

Although the duties of architects generally depend on what is designated in the employment contract, some duties are carried out as a matter of custom, such as the duty to supervise construction.

Architects are in a fiduciary relationship with their employers, and as such they must exercise GOOD FAITH and loyalty toward them. As professionals, they are held to a standard of reasonable and ordinary care and skill in applying their knowledge and must conform to accepted architectural practices. The failure to exercise reasonable care and skill can result in liability for damages and the loss of the right to recover compensation for their services.

Compensation

Architects have a right to compensation for their services unless there is an agreement that they shall work gratuitously. To be entitled to compensation, they must carry out their contract with reasonable skill and care and without any substantial omissions or imperfections in performance. The employment contract usually fixes the amount of compensation. A standard payment scale created by the American Institute of Architects is customarily used to determine the amount of compensation.

In the event that an architect is refused payment for services, he or she may sue for the amount of compensation agreed upon in the employment contract or, in the absence of an agreement, for the reasonable value of the services under the theory of QUANTUM MERUIT.

ARCHITECT OF THE CAPITOL

Established as a permanent office in 1876 (40 U.S.C.A. §§ 162, 163), the architect of the capitol oversees the mechanical and structural maintenance of the Capitol, the conservation and care of works of art in the building, the upkeep and improvement of the Capitol grounds, and the arrangement of inaugural and other ceremonies held in the building or on the grounds. In addition, the architect is responsible for the upkeep of all the congressional office buildings, the LIBRARY OF CONGRESS buildings, the U.S. Supreme Court building, the Federal Judiciary Building, the Capitol Power Plant, the Capitol Police headquarters, and the Robert A. Taft Memorial. The architect also serves as the acting director of the U.S. Botanic Garden.

The functions of the architect have become increasingly administrative, and the architectural or engineering dimensions less important. Special projects carried out by the architect include building renovation and restoration, including installation of broadcasting and security equipment in the Capitol.

Before 1989 the position of architect of the capitol was filled for an indefinite term by presidential appointment. Legislation enacted in 1989 (Pub. L. No. 101-163, 103 Stat. 1068 [codified at 40 U.S.C.A. § 162–1]) provided that the architect be appointed for a ten-year term by the president, with the ADVICE AND CONSENT of the Senate, from a list of three candidates recommended by a congressional commission. Upon confirmation by the Senate, the architect becomes an official of the legislative branch as an officer and agent of Congress and is eligible for reappointment after completion of a term.

FURTHER READINGS

Aikman, Lonnelle M.1991.We, the People: The Story of the United States Capitol, Its Past and Its Promise. Washington, D.C.: U.S. Capitol Historical Society.

The Architect of the Capitol Web site. Available online at http://www.aoc.gov/ (accessed August 28, 2009).

U.S. Government Printing Office Web site. Available online at http://www.gpoaccess.gov/gmanual; website home page: http://www.gpoaccess.gov/ (accessed July 4, 2009).

ARCHITECTURAL BARRIERS ACT OF 1968

See DISABILITY DISCRIMINATION.

ARCTIC, LEGAL STATUS OF

Establishment of territorial SOVEREIGNTY over portions of the Arctic and its seabed has become increasingly attractive to many nations for military purposes or as a source of minerals. Under INTERNATIONAL LAW, national claims of sovereignty over the Arctic traditionally were recognized only if accompanied by physical occupation. Consequently, two competing theories developed: (1) that no nation could achieve sovereignty over the Arctic (*res nullius*), and (2) that every nation shared in undivided sovereignty over the area (*res communes*). According to international law, sovereignty is considered to be a derivative of the exercise of government functions and of notoriety over new territory. Therefore, national claims of sovereignty over portions of the Arctic that are supported by such governmental activity have become more plausible. Many such claims have rested on the sector principle, a version of the doctrine of contiguity, to define the area included in the claim. The sector principle traces longitudinal parallels from borders of countries adjacent to the Arctic Circle to the North Pole, assigning the sectors so formed to the neighboring nations. Claims resting solely on the sector principle have been denied legal force by many nations, including the United States, and it appears that only those claims of sovereignty accompanied by government control may be eventually accepted under international law.

CROSS REFERENCES

Boundaries; Territory.

ARGUENDO

In the course of the argument.

When the phrase *in arguendo* is used by a judge during the course of a trial, it indicates that his or her comment is made as a matter of argument or illustration only. The statement does not bear directly upon the remainder of the discussion.

ARGUMENT

A form of expression consisting of a coherent set of reasons presenting or supporting a point of view; a series of reasons given for or against a matter under discussion that is intended to convince or persuade the listener.

For example, an argument by counsel consists of a presentation of the facts or evidence and the inferences that may be drawn therefrom, which are aimed at persuading a judge or jury to render a VERDICT in favor of the attorney's client.

An attorney may begin to develop an argument in the OPENING STATEMENT, the initial discussion of the case in which the facts and the pertinent law are stated. In most cases, however, an attorney sets forth the main points of an argument in the CLOSING ARGUMENT, which is the attorney's final opportunity to comment on the case before a judge or jury retires to begin deliberation on a verdict.

ARGUMENTATIVE

Controversial; subject to argument.

PLEADING, in which a point relied upon is not set out, but merely implied, is often labeled argumentative. Pleading that contains arguments that should be saved for trial, in addition to allegations establishing a CAUSE OF ACTION or defense, is also called argumentative.

❖ ARISTOTLE

Aristotle was born in 384 B.C., in Stagira, Greece. He achieved prominence as an eminent philosopher who greatly influenced the basic principles of philosophy and whose ideologies are still practiced in the early 2000.

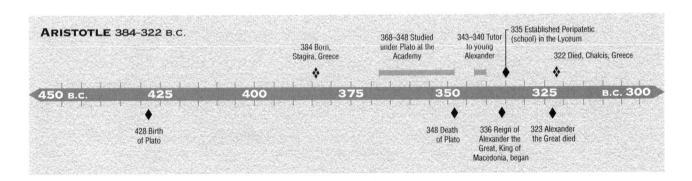

ARISTOTLE 384–322 B.C.

384 Born, Stagira, Greece

368–348 Studied under Plato at the Academy

343–340 Tutor to young Alexander

335 Established Peripatetic (school) in the Lyceum

322 Died, Chalcis, Greece

450 B.C. | 425 | 400 | 375 | 350 | 325 | B.C. 300

428 Birth of Plato

348 Death of Plato

336 Reign of Alexander the Great, King of Macedonia, began

323 Alexander the Great died

Aristotle was a student of the renowned philosopher Plato and tutored Alexander the Great, who became King of Macedonia in 336 B.C.

Aristotle established his own school in the Lyceum, near Athens, in 335 B.C. He often lectured his students in the portico, or walking place, of the Lyceum. The school was subsequently called Peripatetic, after the Greek word *peripatos* for "walking place."

In 323 B.C. the reign of Alexander ended with his death, and Aristotle sought refuge at Chalcis.

Aristotle formulated numerous beliefs about the reasoning power of humans and the essence of being. He stressed the importance of nature and instructed his pupils to closely study natural phenomena. When teaching science, he believed that all ideas must be supported by explanations based upon facts.

Concerning the realm of politics, Aristotle propounded that humans are inherently political and demonstrate an essential part of their humanity when participating in civic affairs.

Philosophy was a subject of great interest to Aristotle, and he theorized that philosophy was the foundation of the ability to understand the basic axioms that comprise knowledge. In order to study and question completely, Aristotle viewed logic as the basic means of reasoning. To think logically, one had to apply the syllogism, which was a form of thought comprised of two premises that led to a conclusion; Aristotle taught that this form can be applied to all logical reasoning.

To understand reality, Aristotle theorized that it must be categorized as substance, quality, quantity, relation, determination in time and space, action, passion or passivity, position, and condition. To know and understand the reality of an object required an explanation of its material cause, which is why it exists or its composition; its formal cause, or its design; its EFFICIENT CAUSE, or its creator; and its final cause, or its reason for being.

Aristotle agreed with his mentor, Plato, concerning the field of ethics. The goodness of a being depended upon the extent to which that being achieved its highest potential. For humans, the ultimate good is the continual use and development of their reasoning powers to fullest capacity. To effect fulfillment and contentment, humans must follow a life of contemplation, rather than pleasure.

Aristotle.
LIBRARY OF CONGRESS

MAN IS BY NATURE A
POLITICAL ANIMAL.
—ARISTOTLE

The fundamental source of Aristotle's theories were his lectures to his students, which were compiled into several volumes. They include *Organum,* which discusses logic; *Physics; Metaphysics; De Anima,* concerning the soul; *Rhetoric; Politics; Nichomachean Ethics and Eudemian Ethics,* involving principles of conduct; and *De Poetica,* or poetics.

He also wrote *Constitution of Athens,* a description of the foundations of the government of Athens. The work was discovered in the late nineteenth century.

Aristotle died in 322 B.C., in Chalcis, Greece.

ARMED SERVICES

The Constitution authorizes Congress to raise, support, and regulate armed services for the national defense. The PRESIDENT OF THE UNITED STATES is commander in chief of all the branches of the services and has ultimate control over most military matters.

The United States has always been wary of maintaining a strong military force. This concern was shown by the Framers of the Constitution when they finally allowed the creation of a standing army but at the same time limited the process by which money could

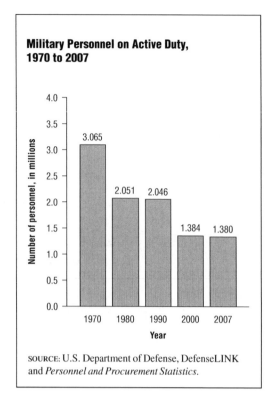

Military Personnel on Active Duty, 1970 to 2007

SOURCE: U.S. Department of Defense, DefenseLINK and *Personnel and Procurement Statistics.*

be raised to support the military; they required that Congress review the appropriations every two years. In this way, the Framers ensured that members of each new Congress had the opportunity to address their lingering concerns about domestic tyranny with a fresh perspective. Furthermore, the Framers ensured that the states could maintain their own militias and protect themselves from federal military domination, by recognizing "the right of the people to keep and bear Arms" (U.S. Const. amend. 2).

The various branches of the armed services were created at different times to serve different purposes. The earliest branch was the Army, instituted on July 14, 1775, followed closely by the Navy and the Marine Corps in the same year. All three were established to respond to the needs of the revolutionary forces fighting the British. The Navy and the Marine Corps were disbanded after the Revolutionary War but were reestablished in 1798. The Coast Guard traces its origins to 1790 but was officially created in 1915. Finally, the Air Force had its genesis in the Signal Corps of the Army and was formally established as the Army Air Service in 1920.

Military personnel are governed by a set of laws that is separate from and independent of CIVIL LAW. The UNIFORM CODE OF MILITARY JUSTICE (10 U.S.C.A. § 801 et seq.) outlines the basic laws and procedures governing members of the armed services. MILITARY LAW is mainly concerned with maintaining order and discipline within the ranks. It is unrelated to MARTIAL LAW, which is the temporary imposition of military rule during a national or regional crisis. Offenses committed by members of the armed services are tried by a COURT-MARTIAL, a special tribunal created specifically to hear a military case and then disbanded once judgment and punishment are pronounced.

The constitutionality of the military legal system has been challenged several times without success. In 1994 the Supreme Court reaffirmed the constitutionality of the system with a unanimous decision in *Weiss v. United States,* 510 U.S. 163, 114 S. Ct. 752, 127 L. Ed. 2d 1. At issue were the selection process and tenure of military judges, who are chosen by their branch's JUDGE ADVOCATE general. The plaintiffs claimed that because the judges could be removed at any time by the judge advocate general, they were biased toward the prosecution and could not be impartial. The Court held that sufficient safeguards were in place to protect against improper influence by the judge advocate general and that the defendants' FIFTH AMENDMENT due process rights had not been violated.

Major Events Affecting Armed Services

End of the Cold War With the breakup of the Soviet Union and the end of the COLD WAR, the U.S. government began the politically charged task of reducing military budgets and closing or -shrinking unnecessary military installations. The Defense Base Closure and Realignment Act (10 U.S.C.A. § 2687), passed by Congress in 1990, set off a firestorm of controversy over which bases should be closed and whether the country's military readiness was being compromised. The act created a presidential commission to decide which bases to close based on Pentagon recommendations. The commission's decisions are sent to the president, who accepts or rejects them in their entirety. If accepted, the recommendations are sent to Congress, which can only block the closings if both houses pass a resolution of disapproval within 45 days. Commissions meeting in 1988, 1991, and 1993 decided to close a total of 70 major installations.

The base closures came under immediate fire as senators and representatives tried to prevent bases in their home states or districts from being shut down. One group of elected officials, including the four senators from Pennsylvania and New Jersey, brought suit in federal court to challenge the procedures under the Defense Base Closure and Realignment Act and to block the closing of the Philadelphia Naval Shipyard, one of the region's biggest employers. The case never went to trial. Instead, the U. S. Supreme Court agreed to hear the Clinton administration's appeal on the question of whether the suit could be brought at all. The Court held that the government's choice of which bases to close under the act could not be challenged in federal court (*Dalton v. Specter*, 511 U.S. 462, 114 S. Ct. 1719, 128 L. Ed. 2d 497 [1994]).

At about the same time the *Dalton* decision was announced, the DEFENSE DEPARTMENT, concerned about the effect of base closings on surrounding communities, began planning to postpone the final round of shutdowns scheduled to follow the commission's 1995 meeting. A senior Pentagon official defended the delays, saying, "As the defense budget goes down and we close bases, the issue now is the pace of closures so people and communities can adjust." Some critics claimed that the delays were a political move designed to take pressure off the president and Congress until after the 1996 election.

The issue of cost and the shrinking military budget loomed large in the debate. The purpose of closing the bases was to eliminate unnecessary costs, but the process of preparing a base for nonmilitary use was itself expensive. Military bases are exempt from federal environmental regulations, but when they are converted to private use, all the stockpiled weaponry and toxic waste must be disposed of in order to avoid liability. The government had set aside $3 billion per year to cover environmental cleanup plus construction and repair of buildings and roads. Still, the projected savings by the end of the 1990s was $4.6 billion per year.

Foreign Policy after September 11 Terrorist Attacks The SEPTEMBER 11TH ATTACKS perpetrated on the United States in 2001 required the country to reevaluate its military policies. President GEORGE W. BUSH announced immediately that the U.S. would wage an unprecedented WAR ON TERRORISM and focused his attention initially on the Taliban regime of Afghanistan

Members of the Army, one of the branches of the armed services, train for urban warfare before the invasion of Iraq in March 2003.

AP IMAGES

for allegedly harboring Osama bin Laden, who led the terrorist organization al Qaida. Within months, the military began an aggressive operation in Afghanistan, which led quickly to the dismantling of the Taliban regime.

Following the fall of the Taliban, the United States quickly turned its attention to Iraq. On March 19, 2003, Operation Iraqi Freedom began, leading to the collapse of the regime of Saddam Hussein only weeks later. The United States captured Baghdad on April 9, 2003. Despite the early success, the IRAQ WAR continued for the remainder of the decade. The United States maintained a presence in Iraq, keeping between 100,000 and 200,000 troops in the country from 2003 through 2009. During that time, an estimated 4,296 U.S. troops were killed, while 31,102 were wounded.

Military operations against terrorist groups differ from those against foreign nations because the terrorist groups are, by their nature, mobile "armies." The United States has focused much of its attention on the use of military intelligence, as well as intelligence from such civil agencies as the CENTRAL INTELLIGENCE AGENCY. Accordingly, much of the deployment of military personnel in this war was covert in specific regions.

Military spending steadily increased under the Bush administration. In 2001 total military spending was $307.8 billion. By 2006 this number had increased to $535.9 billion, not including expenditures authorized specifically for the Iraq War. Although spending increased during the 2000s, military personnel numbers remained steady. As of December 31, 2002, the

The Branches of the Armed Services

The five branches of the U.S. armed services are staffed by volunteer enlisted men and women who hold various ranks. Military personnel are no longer conscripted, or drafted, into service.

Army

The Army was the first branch of the armed services established by Congress. The U.S. Army evolved from the Continental Army, created on July 14, 1775, by the Continental Congress to fight the Revolutionary War against the British.

The three segments of the Army are the Army Reserve, the Army National Guard, and the Active Army. The Army Reserve provides training and combat support to the Active Army in times of emergency. The Army National Guard, the oldest military force in the United States, began in the Massachusetts Bay Colony in 1636. During peacetime, the National Guard unit in each state is commanded by the state governor. The National Guard often assists in natural disasters, such as earthquakes or floods, or in civil unrest, such as riots. The president has the authority to call the Guard to federal duty when necessary. For example, President Dwight D. Eisenhower federalized the Arkansas National Guard in 1957 and assigned them to control angry mobs protesting the enrollment of African American students in a previously segregated Little Rock high school. Similarly, President George H.W. Bush assigned Guard units to duty with the Active Army during the Persian Gulf War of 1991.

The Army's many responsibilities include combat, combat support, and combat service support arms. The combat arms, including the infantry, armored divisions, air defense artillery, field artillery, and aviation, are directly involved in fighting. The combat support arms include the Corps of Engineers, the Signal Corps, the Military Police Corps, the Chemical Corps, and military intelligence. The combat service support arms provide logistical and administrative assistance to the other arms.

Women were originally restricted to the Women's Army Corps (WAC) but now serve alongside men in almost all capacities. Their roles have been gradually expanded, and they now serve in combat units, which gives them equal opportunities with men for higher pay and advancement in rank.

The U.S. Military Academy, the oldest of the service academies, was established at West Point, New York, in 1802. It was originally charged with training army engineers, but evolved into the training ground for those wishing to become officers in the Army. West Point has been coeducational since 1976.

Navy

The Navy traces its origins to 1775 and the American Revolution. A fleet established to fight the British was disbanded after the war, but the need for a naval force was again recognized in 1798, when Congress established the Navy Department. The Navy was a separate branch of the government until the National Security Act of 1947 (5 U.S.C.A. § 101 et seq., 10 U.S.C.A. § 101 et seq., 50 U.S.C.A. § 401 et seq.) created the Department of Defense with a cabinet-level secretary to oversee all branches of the military.

The Navy's forces are grouped into various fleets that serve in different areas of the world. Traditionally, odd-numbered fleets, such as the Third and Seventh Fleets, have served in the Pacific Ocean. Even-numbered fleets, such as the Second and Sixth Fleets, have served in the Atlantic Ocean. Over the years, U.S. Navy fleets have been disestablished (removed from service) and reconstituted (restored to service) as the distribution of military power throughout the world has changed.

military had a total of 1.411 million personnel. As of December 31, 2008, the number of personnel was 1.402 million.

Legal and Political Issues

Military Ban on Gay and Lesbian Behavior One controversial and divisive issue facing the military is the inclusion of gay and lesbian personnel. For more than 50 years, the U.S. armed services prohibited gay men and lesbians from serving in the military. In the past, members who disclosed that they were gay or lesbian were subject to immediate discharge. That policy was challenged in several prominent

A naval reserve force is made up of civilians who train regularly and stand ready to be called in times of need.

Although women originally could only join the Women Accepted for Voluntary Emergency Service (WAVES), they now serve alongside men, drawing equal pay and attaining equivalent rank.

The Naval Academy, at Annapolis, Maryland, was established in 1845 to train young men to be officers in the Navy and the Marine Corps. Women have been admitted since 1976.

Air Force

The Aeronautical Division of the Army Signal Corps, the precursor to the U.S. Air Force, was established on August 1, 1907. The First Aero Squadron was organized in 1914 and served with the Mexican Border Expedition in 1916. The Air Force remained a division of the Army until 1947.

The Air Force is responsible for domestic security in such areas as the Strategic Air Command (SAC), which plays a major role in deterring air and missile attacks as well as conducting space surveillance. Other responsibilities of the Air Force include maintaining a combat-ready mobile strike force and operating air bases in key areas around the world.

The Air Force's chief of staff, along with the chiefs of staff of the Army and the Navy, is a member of the Joint Chiefs of Staff, which advises the president and the secretary of defense.

The Air Force Academy, authorized in 1954 and located in Colorado Springs, Colorado, prepares college students to become officers in the Air Force. Women were admitted beginning in 1976.

Marine Corps

Steeped in history, tradition, and folklore, the Marine Corps, a self-contained amphibious combat force within the Department of the Navy, traces its roots to the Revolutionary War. During its two hundred-year history, the U.S. Marines has fulfilled its obligation to provide air, land, and sea support for naval forces, establish beachheads during war, and protect U.S. lives and interests at foreign embassies and legations.

The Marines maintain a large reserve unit, which, when mobilized in times of crisis, can increase the corps strength by 25 percent within weeks.

The Marine Corps Women's Reserve, established in 1942, provides support in the mainland United States and in Hawaii so that men are available for combat.

Marine Corps officers are trained mainly at the U.S. Naval Academy, at Annapolis.

Coast Guard

The U.S. Coast Guard was first established in 1790 as the U.S. Lighthouse Service under the Department of the Treasury. It later moved to the Department of Transportation, where it remained for 36 years. On February 25, 2003, the Coast Guard officially transferred to the Department of Homeland Security, where it comprises about one-fourth of the new department. The move was part of the largest government reorganization since the Defense Department was established in 1947.

The Coast Guard is charged with guarding the country's coasts against smuggling, enforcing customs laws, and responding to emergencies along the coasts. The move to the Department of Homeland Security did not change the Coast Guard's mission significantly, although it is now responsible for securing the nation's ports and has been prepared to be involved with international conflicts in the war on terrorism.

The Coast Guard provides officer training for college students at the Coast Guard Academy, at New London, Connecticut, which began admitting women in 1976.

CROSS REFERENCES

Homeland Security Department; Military Law.

cases during the late 1980s and early 1990s, and the Clinton administration addressed the issue with a new approach that ultimately led to more confusion and controversy.

The federal courts tackled the question of whether the military's automatic ouster of gay or lesbian personnel is constitutional, in *Meinhold v. United States DEPARTMENT OF DEFENSE*, 34 F.3d 1469 (9th Cir. 1994). The PLAINTIFF, Petty Officer Keith Meinhold of the Navy, announced on a national television broadcast in May 1992 that he is gay. As a result, discharge proceedings were begun against him. Meinhold was dismissed solely on the basis of his televised statement. He sued the

Navy and the Department of Defense, claiming that their policy was unconstitutional. The district court agreed, holding that the Navy's actions denied gay men and lesbians EQUAL PROTECTION under the law. In August 1994 the Court of Appeals for the Ninth Circuit agreed that Meinhold could not be discharged merely for stating that he was gay. However, the appeals court disagreed with the district court's finding that the military's policy was unconstitutional and instead found that by discharging Meinhold because of his status as gay and not because of any actions on his part, the Navy was equating status with prohibited conduct. The court conceded that the Navy could legally discharge someone who manifested a "fixed or expressed desire to commit a prohibited act," such as engaging in gay sex but found that Meinhold had not manifested any such desire and, therefore, must be reinstated. In November 1994 the Clinton administration announced it was dropping its efforts to bar Meinhold from serving and would not appeal the Ninth Circuit's ruling.

Another challenge to the military ban on gays and lesbians occurred in *Steffan v. Aspin,* 8 F.3d 57 (D.C. Cir. 1993). The plaintiff, Joseph Steffan, admitted to being gay just six weeks before his expected graduation from the U.S. Naval Academy, at Annapolis, Maryland, in 1987. Steffan was one of the top ten students in his class. He had consistently received outstanding marks for leadership and military performance. In his junior year he was named a battalion commander in charge of one-sixth of the academy's 4,500 students. After Steffan acknowledged his homosexuality to a classmate and a chaplain, he was brought before a disciplinary board that recommended he be discharged. Rather than face dismissal, he resigned. Sometime later, he asked to be reinstated. His request was denied, and he then sued for reinstatement to his commission, claiming that he was forced to resign because of his status as a gay, not because of any conduct—in violation of the Constitution's equal protection guarantee.

The district court granted SUMMARY JUDGMENT for the government (*Steffan v. Cheney,* 780 F. Supp. 1 [D.D.C. 1991]). A three-judge panel for the court of appeals reversed, stating that the dismissal policy had no rational basis and that it violated the Equal Protection Clause of the Fifth Amendment. The appeals court ordered the academy to award Steffan his diploma and reinstate him to his commission.

The government petitioned the court for a rehearing on whether the three-judge panel had exceeded its authority. The full court of appeals vacated the decision of the panel and ordered a rehearing before the full court on the constitutionality question. In November 1994, the full court reversed the decision of the three-judge panel and held that Steffan's dismissal did not violate the Constitution. The court said that the Navy's ban on homosexuals, like its height or eyesight requirements, did have a rational basis. The court also dismissed Steffan's argument that the ban punished status rather than conduct. Judge Laurence H. Silberman, writing for the majority, said, "Steffan's claim that the Government cannot rationally infer that one who states he or she is gay or lesbian is a practicing homosexual, or is at least likely to engage in homosexual acts, is so strained a constitutional argument as to amount to a basic attack on the policy itself" (*Steffan v. Perry,* 41 F.3d 677, 693 [D.C. Cir. 1994]). In an impassioned dissent, Judge PATRICIA M. WALD wrote, "In years to come, we will look back with dismay at these unconstitutional attempts to enforce silence upon individuals of homosexual orientation, in the military and out. Pragmatism should not be allowed to trump principle, or the soul of a nation will wither" (41 F.3d 677, 721).

In January 1995 Steffan announced that for tactical reasons he would not appeal the decision to the Supreme Court. Steffan's case was brought under the old policy, and he and his attorneys felt that the best case to have the Supreme Court address was one involving the new policy, which they believed was more vulnerable to constitutional attack. After his discharge from the naval academy, Steffan became a lawyer.

The case of Colonel Margarethe Cammermeyer further clouded official policy on homosexuals in the military (*Cammermeyer v. Aspin,* 850 F. Supp. 910 [W.D. Wash. 1994]). Cammermeyer was dismissed from the Washington State NATIONAL GUARD in June 1992 when she acknowledged in a security-clearance interview that she is a lesbian. Under the rules in effect at the time, her statement was grounds for dismissal, and Cammermeyer was given an honorable discharge. She was the highest-ranking officer to be discharged solely because of gay or lesbian orientation.

Cammermeyer, a highly respected nurse who was awarded the Bronze Star for her service with the Army in Vietnam, appealed the dismissal. In June 1994 Judge Thomas Zilly, of the Federal District Court for the District of Washington, ordered the military to reinstate Cammermeyer, holding that the policy in effect at the time of her dismissal violated the Equal Protection Clause. Zilly's decision dismantled the assumptions that formed the basis for both the old and the new government policies regarding gays and lesbians in the military. Zilly held that "there is no rational basis for the Government's underlying contention that gay or lesbian orientation equals desire or propensity to engage" in gay or lesbian conduct (850 F. Supp. at 920). The judge was direct and harsh in his criticism of the government's policy. He wrote, "The Government has discriminated against Colonel Cammermeyer solely on the basis of her status as a lesbian and has failed to demonstrate a rational basis for doing so" (850 F. Supp. at 926). Noting that military experts "conceded that their justifications for the policy are based on heterosexual members' fear and dislike of homosexuals," Zilly went on to say, "[m]ere negative attitudes, or fear, are constitutionally impermissible bases for discriminatory governmental policies" (850 F. Supp at 925).

The JUSTICE DEPARTMENT moved to delay Cammermeyer's reinstatement, but the U.S. Court of Appeals for the Ninth Circuit refused the request. Cammermeyer returned to her position as chief of nursing services for the 164th Mobile Army Surgical Hospital in July 1994.

At the same time that *Meinhold, Steffan,* and *Cammermeyer* were being decided, the Clinton administration was formulating and implementing a new policy that it hoped would deal with the issue of gays and lesbians in the military and put the controversies surrounding the old policy to rest. Before he was elected, BILL CLINTON had promised that as president, he would lift the ban on gay men and lesbians in the armed services. However, after taking office, Clinton faced strenuous opposition from the Joint Chiefs of Staff and the heads of the service branches, who argued that summarily eliminating the ban on gays and lesbians would lead to dissension among the troops and diminished military readiness. In December 1993 the Pentagon announced a compromise plan, which came to be known as the "don't ask, don't tell, don't pursue" policy (Policy Concerning Homosexuality in the Armed Forces, Pub. L. No. 103-160, 1993 H. R. 2401 § 571(a) [amending 10 U.S.C.A. § 654]). Under the

Col. Margarethe Cammermeyer was dismissed from the Washington State National Guard in 1992 after acknowledging that she was a lesbian. She was reinstated two years later and in 1997 retired with full military privileges.

AP IMAGES

new rules, gay men and lesbians could serve in the military as long as they kept their sexual orientation private and did not engage in gay or lesbian activity. The policy stated that sexual orientation is a "personal and private matter" about which recruits and members of the armed forces would no longer be required to answer questions. Criminal investigations and security checks conducted solely to determine sexual orientation would be eliminated. Sexual orientation alone would not be a bar to service. However, gay or lesbian conduct, which could take the form of "a homosexual act, a statement by the member that demonstrates a propensity or intent to engage in homosexual acts, or a homosexual MARRIAGE or attempted marriage" would subject the individual to dismissal. An acknowledgement of gay or lesbian orientation would not be sufficient grounds for expulsion but could be the basis for an investigation into whether the individual engaged in gay or lesbian acts.

Gay rights advocates immediately and vigorously criticized the new policy, saying it infringed on the free speech rights of gay service members and vowed to challenge it in court. In the months following implementation of the new rules, it became clear that, far from easing the plight of homosexual service members, "don't ask, don't tell, don't pursue" was actually making life worse for many of them. Some commanding officers were overly aggressive in implementing the new rules, and many critics felt that the policy further polarized attitudes among service members. Furthermore, the policy shifted the BURDEN OF PROOF to the individual to show that she or he had not engaged in homosexual acts.

The first legal challenge to the "don't ask, don't tell, don't pursue" policy was filed in March 1994 by the AMERICAN CIVIL LIBERTIES UNION and the Lambda Legal Defense and Education Fund. Six service members who had declared their homosexuality filed suit in the U.S. District Court for the Eastern District of New York, asking for injunctive relief and a declaration that the policy was unconstitutional. The case was heard by Judge Eugene H. Nickerson who issued orders on April 4, 1994, and June 3, 1994, enjoining the Army from pursuing discharge proceedings against the plaintiffs. Nickerson based his decision on the plaintiffs' showing that they would suffer irreparable harm if the injunction were not granted and that the case involved "sufficiently serious questions" that would warrant its going forward for a decision on its merits.

The U.S. Court of Appeals for the Second Circuit found that Nickerson had used an incorrect standard in determining whether the injunction should be granted. It held that in a case such as this, where an injunction is sought against a "government action taken in the PUBLIC INTEREST pursuant to a statutory or regulatory scheme," a more rigorous showing that the case has a "likelihood of success" must be made (*Able v. United States*, 44 F.3d 128 [1995] [per curiam]). The court allowed the injunctions to stand but remanded the case to the district court for a decision on the plaintiffs' constitutional claims within three months.

On March 30, 1995, Judge Nickerson delivered the decision the plaintiffs had hoped for. He held that the "don't ask, don't tell, don't pursue" policy violated the First and Fifth Amendments, and enjoined the government from enforcing the policy against the plaintiffs (*Able*, 880 F. Supp. 968 [E.D.N.Y.]). The court found that the FIRST AMENDMENT prohibits a restraint on the right of a serviceperson to declare his or her homosexuality. According to the court, "Plaintiffs have done no more than acknowledge who they are, that is, their status. The speech at issue in this case implicates the First Amendment value of promoting individual dignity and integrity and thus is protected by

the First Amendment from efforts to prohibit it because of its content." The court further found that to regulate speech content, even in the military context, the government must show a "compelling interest" and prove that it has chosen the "least restrictive means" to further that interest. Nickerson criticized the legal hairsplitting in the policy directives, which purported to differentiate between a homosexual "orientation" and a homosexual "propensity." Once a member of the armed services has admitted or acknowledged being a homosexual, he or she has only a hypothetical chance of escaping discharge. "Thus, the policy treats a statement of homosexual orientation as proof of the case," said Nickerson. "Once such a statement is made, the speaker is judged guilty until proven innocent of committing misconduct the government considers so threatening to the military mission that a member may be discharged for it. This seems to the court a rather draconian consequence of merely admitting to an orientation that Congress has determined to be innocuous."

Turning to the government's argument that the presence of openly gay or lesbian members would be detrimental to morale and troop cohesion, the court found that sufficient sanctions were available for dealing with "inappropriate behavior by a homosexual, whether in the closet or not." Nickerson further stated his belief that the policy may actually be detrimental to the military because "secrecy and deception invite suspicion, which in turn erodes trust, the rock on which cohesion is built." He noted that a 1993 study conducted by the RAND Corporation found that in countries that have nondiscrimination policies, "no serious problems were reported concerning the presence of homosexuals in the force."

Finally, on the Fifth Amendment equal protection question, the court found that the government had failed to show that the policy, which denied to gay and lesbian personnel the same free speech rights guaranteed to heterosexuals, was "tailored to serve a substantial governmental interest." The policy therefore violated the Fifth Amendment as well as the First, and the court enjoined the government from enforcing it.

The military policy of "don't ask, don't tell" has remained intact since 1993. Despite calls for repeal of the policy and return to the former policy of excluding gay and lesbian personnel from service, President George W. Bush did not change the policy, and EXECUTIVE BRANCH officials stated that the administration does not plan to change the policy. The controversy has nevertheless remained heated. Commentators have noted that the ban on gays and lesbians does not apply to such governmental agencies as the Central Intelligence Agency, which often engages in quasi-military activities. Moreover, evidence suggests that during times of war in the past, the military has allowed gays to remain in the service.

Legal challenges to the "don't ask, don't tell" policy continued in the 2000s. In *Witt v. Department of Air Force*, 527 F.3d 806 (9th Cir. 2008), an Air Force nurse named Margaret Witt challenged her suspension from the military due to discovery that she was engaged in a lesbian relationship. Witt argued that the military's action violated her equal protection and due process rights. Although the court concluded that the government's policy advanced an important governmental interest of managing the military, the court was not convinced that the policy significantly furthered the government's interest. The court remanded the case to a federal district court in Washington for further proceedings.

As a presidential candidate, BARACK OBAMA asserted that he would reverse the military's policy regarding gays and lesbians. Early in his administration, however, Obama decided not to address the policy until the *Witt* LITIGATION had been resolved.

Sexual Harassment in the Armed Services The inclusion of women in virtually all aspects of military life has changed the service from a male-dominated enterprise, strictly segregated by gender, into a microcosm of modern society. Although most men and women serve side by side without incident, charges of SEXUAL HARASSMENT in the military became increasingly numerous in the 1980s, 1990s, and 2000s.

Perhaps the most explosive and far-reaching incidence of this problem took place at the Tailhook Association convention in Las Vegas in September 1991. The Tailhook Association—named for the hook on a Navy jet that catches on the cables that stop it as it lands on an aircraft carrier—is a private group of active and retired Navy and Marine Corps pilots. After its 1991 meeting, Navy lieutenant Paula A. Coughlin charged that she and other women who unwittingly stumbled upon the Tailhook hospitality suites at the Las Vegas Hilton were forced to go through a "gauntlet" of drunken Navy and Marine officers who assaulted them, tore at their clothing, and grabbed at their bodies as they were propelled down the hallway. Coughlin's allegations launched an investigation that revealed drunken, lewd, and out-of-control behavior by the officers. In the ensuing months the Navy severed its ties to the Tailhook Association and submitted the names of more than 60 officers for possible disciplinary action. Nevertheless, a conspiracy of silence among the aviators hampered the investigation. In September 1992 the Pentagon's inspector general issued a report criticizing the Navy's inquiry into the incident and suggesting that top Navy officials deliberately undermined the investigation to avoid negative publicity. The commander of the Naval Investigative Service and the Navy's judge advocate general were relieved of their commands. The following April, the inspector general accused 140 aviators of indecent exposure, assault, and lying under oath in the incident. However, no one was ever court-martialed as a result of the charges, and those who were disciplined received only small fines or reprimands.

The Tailhook scandal set off a tidal wave within the upper echelons of the Navy. Navy Secretary H. Lawrence Garrett III resigned in June 1992, accepting full responsibility for the failure of leadership that allowed the incident to occur. In October 1993 his replacement, John H. Dalton, asked for the removal of Admiral Frank B. Kelso II, chief of naval operations, who was present at the convention but denied any knowledge of the debauchery. Dalton's request was overruled by Secretary of Defense Les Aspin. In February 1994 a military judge cited Kelso for using "unlawful command influence" to "manipulate the initial investigative process" and the Navy's disciplinary procedures "to shield his personal involvement" in Tailhook. Kelso, who was to retire on June 30, 1994, angrily denied any wrongdoing and declared that he would not resign early. In the end, however, he was persuaded to step down two months ahead of schedule in exchange for a tribute from Defense Secretary William J. Perry that would clear his name. After a bitter debate, the U.S. Senate voted 54 to 43 to allow Kelso, the Navy's top admiral and a 38-year veteran, to retire at his full four-star rank and with a full pension. The women in the Senate, along with many of their male colleagues, vehemently opposed the arrangement, but they were ultimately overruled.

Coughlin resigned from the Navy in February 1994, stating that the assault and "the covert attacks on me that followed have stripped me of my ability to serve." Coughlin was successful in a civil suit against the Tailhook Association, with whom she settled for an undisclosed amount. She also won a civil suit against the Hilton Hotels Corporation, parent company of the Las Vegas Hilton, which she accused of lax security; in October 1994 a jury awarded her $1.7 million in COMPENSATORY DAMAGES and an additional $5 million in PUNITIVE DAMAGES. Still suffering depression and post-traumatic stress from the incident, Coughlin expressed satisfaction with the award but uncertainty about her future, saying, "I'm hoping to slip into obscurity. I want to paint my house. I just want to go home."

Anxious to restore the Navy's tarnished image after the sordid series of events, top officials vowed to handle sexual harassment charges swiftly and sensitively. The Navy's new "zero-tolerance" policy on sexual harassment required automatic dismissal for aggravated sexual harassment or repeat offenses. Under the policy, about 90 officers and sailors had been dismissed by the end of 1994.

In spite of the publicity generated by Tailhook and other scandals, and the efforts of the military to clamp down on sexual harassment, charges continued to come to light. In one 1994 case that tested the resolve of Admiral Jeremy M. Boorda, Admiral Kelso's successor as chief of naval operations, two officers were reprimanded for failing to act properly on complaints by Lieutenant Darlene Simmons. Simmons charged that her commanding officer, Lieutenant Commander Arthur Catullo, had offered to advance her career in exchange for sexual favors. Catullo was censured. Simmons, who had an impeccable record before she brought the charges but received an "adverse" evaluation afterward, received an apology from Navy Secretary Dalton. Dalton also cleared her record and offered to extend her active-duty Navy service by two years.

Another egregious incident, again involving the Navy, occurred in 1994 when four male instructors were court-martialed and six others punished for sexually harassing 16 women students at the Naval Training Center in San Diego. The women, who were learning to operate the Navy's computer and telephone networks, claimed that the male instructors made unwanted verbal and physical advances. After a seven-month investigation, the Navy found all but one of the instructors guilty of the charges and imposed various sanctions, from a criminal conviction and $1,000 fine, to a loss in pay, required counseling, and inclusion of punitive letters in their files.

Sexual harassment was also found among the ranks at the U.S. Military Academy, at West Point, New York. In October 1994 female cadets complained that they had been groped at a pep rally by members of the West Point football team as the players ran past them in a regimental "spirit run." Lieutenant General Howard D. Graves, superintendent of West Point, launched an immediate investigation that resulted in three players being suspended from the team for the rest of the season, restricted to academy grounds for 90 days, and given 80 hours of marching discipline. Representative Patricia Schroeder (D-Colo.), a member of the House Armed Services Committee, criticized the punishment as too lenient, saying, "[I]t looks like [the incident] was treated as a prank and not as a serious violation of the code of conduct."

Despite the attention placed on the problem of sexual harassment in the military, incidents of sexual harassment have remained relatively common. According to a report released by the Pentagon in 2008, about one-third of military women polled said that they experienced sexual harassment in 2006.

Sexual misconduct by servicemen is not limited to sexual harassment. The Army acknowledged in 1992 that soldiers committed at least 34 sex crimes during the Gulf War in 1991, including RAPE and assault against fellow U.S. soldiers. One sergeant was charged with rape, indecent assault, and adultery after he allegedly raped several female soldiers in the port of Al Jubayl in Saudi Arabia in 1991. Some of the crimes reported by the Army at that time included consensual sexual activities, including adultery and gay and lesbian conduct. Army records disclosed few records regarding actions taken against the soldiers for their misconduct.

Four years later, three U.S. soldiers, two marines, and a sailor stationed near Japan, abducted and raped an 12-year-old Okinawa schoolgirl, in part prompting Okinawa citizens to call for the closing of U.S. military bases on the island. The incident likewise enraged citizens of Japan. According to a study of records in 1988, Navy and Marine bases in Japan held 169 courts martial for sexual assaults, far exceeding the number at any U.S. base elsewhere in the world. Statistics regarding Air Force courts martial likewise showed a significant number of assault charges on bases in Japan.

Prior to 2000, many criminal activities by military employees went unpunished because the host country in which the crime occurred failed to PROSECUTE the action or the military courts of the United States did not have jurisdiction to try the case. In 2000 Congress enacted the Military Extraterritorial Jurisdiction Act of 2000, Pub. L. No. 106-523, 114 Stat. 2488 (18 U.S.C.A. §§ 3261-3267), which extends federal criminal jurisdiction over crimes committed by military personnel and their dependents stationed abroad. The statute allows the U.S. Defense Department to order the arrest, detention, and removal of military employees for crimes that would constitute an offense punishable for more than one year if the conduct had been engaged in within the jurisdiction of the United States.

Several U.S. soldiers were convicted of some heinous criminal acts during the Iraq War. One of the worst incidents occurred in the Iraqi town of Al-Mahmudiyah in 2006. Five soldiers attacked the family of a 14-year-old girl, killing her father, mother, and younger sister before gang raping the girl. Four of the five soldiers stood trial by court martial, while a fifth was tried in a federal district court.

FURTHER READINGS

Bravin, Jess, and Laura Meckler. 2009. "Obama Avoids Test on Gays in Military." *Wall Street Journal.*
The Bulletin of the Atomic Scientists. 49, no. 4 (May 1993).
Shanor, Charles A., and L. Lynn Hogue. 1996. *Military Law in a Nutshell.* St. Paul, MN: West.
Winthrop, William. 2000. *Military Law and Precedents.* Buffalo, NY: William S. Hein.

CROSS REFERENCES

American Civil Liberties Union; Bias; Court-Martial; Defense Department; Equal Protection; Gay and Lesbian Rights; Judge Advocate; Military Law; National Guard; Sexual Harassment; Uniform Code of Military Justice; U.S. Court of Appeals for Veterans Claims; Veterans Affairs Department; War.

ARMISTICE

A suspending or cessation of hostilities between belligerent nations or forces for a considerable

time. An armistice differs from a mere "suspension of arms" in that the latter is concluded for very brief periods and for local military purposes only, whereas an armistice not only covers a longer period, but is agreed upon for political purposes. It is said to be general *if it relates to the whole area of the war, and* partial *if it relates to only a portion of that area. Partial armistices are sometimes called truces but there is no hard and fast distinction.*

Armistice Day originated as a day set aside by the United States, Great Britain, and France to commemorate the signing of the armistice on November 11, 1918, that brought an end to WORLD WAR I. After WORLD WAR II, it became a day for tribute to those who lost their lives in that

General Douglas MacArthur (top) signs the Japanese armistice documents on the USS Missouri on September 2, 1945. Mamoru Shigemitsu and General Yoshijiro Umezu, with delegation, witness.

(TOP) NATIONAL ARCHIVES AND RECORDS ADMINISTRATION (BOTTOM) LIBRARY OF CONGRESS

conflict as well. In Canada it became known as Remembrance Day, and in Britain the Sunday closest to November 11 was declared Remembrance Sunday to honor the dead of both world wars. In 1938 the day was made a federal holiday in the United States.

In 1954 after the KOREAN WAR, President DWIGHT D. EISENHOWER signed an act of Congress (5 U.S.C.A. § 6103 (a) [1995]) to change the name of the holiday to Veterans Day "to honor veterans on the eleventh day of November of each year . . . a day dedicated to world peace." Thus, Veterans Day now honors all U.S. veterans of all wars. From 1971 to 1977 the holiday was celebrated on the fourth Monday in October, but in 1978 the traditional date of November 11 was restored.

Veterans Day celebrations in towns and cities in the United States usually include parades, speeches, and floral tributes placed on soldiers' graves or memorials, with special services held at the Tomb of the Unknown Soldier in Arlington National Cemetery, in Arlington, Virginia, outside Washington, D.C. Group NATURALIZATION ceremonies, in which individuals are made citizens of the United States, have also become part of Veterans Day celebrations.

ARMS CONTROL AND DISARMAMENT

One of the major efforts to preserve international peace and security in the twenty-first century has been to control or limit the number of WEAPONS and the ways in which weapons can be used. Two different means to achieve this goal have been disarmament and arms control. *Disarmament* is the reduction of the number of weapons and troops maintained by a state. *Arms control* refers to treaties made between potential adversaries that reduce the likelihood and scope of war, usually imposing limitations on military capability. Although disarmament always involves the reduction of military forces or weapons, arms control does not. In fact, arms control agreements sometimes allow for the increase of weapons by one or more parties to a treaty.

History

Arms control developed both in theory and in practice during the COLD WAR, a period between the late 1940s and 1991 when the two military superpowers, the United States and the Union of Soviet Socialist Republics (USSR), dealt with one another from a position of mutual mistrust. Arms control was devised consciously during the postwar period as an alternative to disarmament, which for many had fallen into discredit as a means of reducing the likelihood of war. Germany had been forced to disarm following WORLD WAR I but became belligerent again during the 1930s, resulting in WORLD WAR II. Although Germany's weapons had been largely eliminated, the underlying causes of conflict had not. Germany's experience thus illustrated that no simple cause-and-effect relationship existed between the possession of weapons and a tendency to create war.

Following World War II, advocates of arms control as a new approach to limiting hostility between nations emphasized that military weapons and power would continue to remain a part of modern life. It was unrealistic and even dangerous, they felt, for a country to seek complete elimination of weapons, and it would not necessarily reduce the likelihood of war. Whereas disarmament had formerly been seen as an alternative to military strength, arms control was now viewed as an integral part of it. Arms control proponents sought to create a stable balance of power in which the forces that cause states to go to war could be controlled and regulated. The emphasis in arms control is thus upon overall stability rather than elimination of arms, and proponents recognize that an increase in weaponry is sometimes necessary to preserve a balance of power.

The development of arms control owes a great deal to the existence of NUCLEAR WEAPONS as well. By the 1950s, when both the United States and the Soviet Union possessed nuclear weapons, the superpowers became convinced that they could not safely disarm themselves of those weapons. In the absence of guaranteed verification—the process whereby participants in a treaty monitor each other's adherence to the agreement—neither side could disarm without making itself vulnerable to cheating by the other side. The goal of the superpowers and other nations possessing nuclear weapons therefore became not total elimination of those weapons, but control of them so that a stable nuclear deterrent might be maintained. According to the idea of *nuclear deterrence,* a state possessing nuclear weapons is deterred, or effectively prevented, from using them against another NUCLEAR POWER because of the threat of retaliation. No state is willing to attempt a first strike

because it cannot prevent the other side from striking back. Nuclear deterrence is therefore predicated upon a mutual abhorrence of the destructive power of nuclear weapons. This idea has come to be called *mutual assured destruction (MAD)*. Many experts see deterrence as the ultimate goal of nuclear arms control.

Because many civilians generally assume that arms control and disarmament are the same thing, there has often been public disappointment when treaties have resulted in an increase in the number or power of weapons. An advantage of arms control over disarmament, however, is that even states with a high degree of suspicion or hostility toward each other can still NEGOTIATE agreements. Disarmament agreements, on the other hand, require a high degree of trust, and their formation is unlikely between hostile nations.

Arms control is often used as a means to avoid an *arms race*—a competitive build-up of weapons between two or more powers. Such a race can be costly for both sides, and arms control treaties serve the useful purpose of

limiting weapons stockpiles to a level that preserves deterrence while conserving the economic and social resources of a state for other uses.

Modern Arms Control

Although disarmament and arms control agreements were forged prior to World War II (1939–45), the modern arms control effort began in earnest after the CUBAN MISSILE CRISIS of 1962. That situation erupted when the United States discovered that the Soviet Union was constructing launch sites for nuclear missiles on the island of Cuba, thereby threatening to put nuclear weapons very close to U.S. soil. President JOHN F. KENNEDY declared a naval blockade of the island, and for two weeks the United States and the USSR existed in a state of heightened tension. Finally, the USSR and the United States faced off in what became a white-hot international drama of brinksmanship, each side waiting to see who would blink first. With the United States' promise not to overthrow Fidel Castro's government in Cuba, the Soviets

U.S. President Jimmy Carter and Soviet President Leonid Brazhnev shake hands after signing SALT II in June 1979.
AP IMAGES

On December 13, 2001, former President George W. Bush, shown with General Richard Myers, Colin Powell, Donald Rumsfeld, and Condoleezza Rice, announced that the United States would withdraw from the Anti-Ballistic-Missile Treaty of 1972.

AP IMAGES

canceled plans to install the missiles. After the crisis, Kennedy wrote to Khrushchev, "I agree with you that we must devote urgent attention to the problem of disarmament. . . . Perhaps . . . we can together make real progress in this vital field."

Among the earliest arms control treaties were the LIMITED TEST BAN TREATY (LTBT), an agreement that prohibited nuclear test explosions in the atmosphere, under water, or in space, which was signed in 1963 by the United States, Britain, and the USSR, and the 1972 Biological Weapons Convention, a superpower treaty that banned biological weapons and provided for the destruction of existing stockpiles. The 1972 convention was the first and only example, since 1945, of true disarmament of an entire weapons category. Although negotiation on a comprehensive test ban—an agreement that would prohibit all nuclear testing—continued, this solution remained elusive. Nevertheless, in 1974 the superpowers signed the Threshold Test Ban Treaty (TTBT), which limits nuclear tests to explosive yields of less than 150 kilotons. (A kiloton represents the explosive force of one thousand tons of TNT.) But the TTBT did not prevent the superpowers from developing nuclear warheads (the bomb-carrying segments of a nuclear missile) with power exceeding 150 kilotons; warheads on the Soviet SS-17 missile possess as much as a 3.6-megaton capacity. (A megaton equals 1 million tons of TNT.) In 1976 the superpowers signed the Peaceful Nuclear Explosions Treaty (PNET), which banned so-called peaceful nuclear testing.

Numerous arms control agreements have been designed to improve communications between the superpowers. The first of these, coming just after the Cuban Missile Crisis, was the 1963 Hot Line Agreement, setting up a special telegraph line between Moscow and Washington. In 1978 the hot line was updated by a satellite link between the two superpowers. The United States and the USSR also sought to create protocols designed to prevent an accidental nuclear war. This effort led to the 1971 agreement, Measures to Reduce the Risk of Outbreak of Nuclear War, which required advance warning for any missile tests and immediate notification of any accidents or missile-warning alerts.

One highly celebrated arms control agreement is the 1968 Treaty on the Non-Proliferation of Nuclear Weapons, or Non-Proliferation Treaty, designed to prevent the spread of nuclear weapons to other countries. The agreement involves well over one hundred states. Under it, countries not possessing nuclear weapons give up their right to acquire such weapons, and countries with nuclear weapons waive their rights to export nuclear weapons technology to countries lacking that technology.

Another class of arms control treaties seeks to ban weapons from as-yet-unmilitarized areas. These include the 1959 Antarctic Treaty, which prohibits military bases, maneuvers, and tests on the Antarctic Continent; the 1967 Outer Space Treaty, a ban on the testing or deployment of "weapons of mass destruction" in Earth's orbit or on other bodies in the solar system; the 1967 Tlatelolco Treaty, prohibiting nuclear weapons in Latin America; and the 1971 Seabed Treaty, banning the placement of WEAPONS OF MASS DESTRUCTION on or below the seabed.

SALT I and After

The Strategic Arms Limitation Talks (SALT I and SALT II) were first undertaken in the era of détente in the early 1970s, when relations between the United States and the USSR became more amicable. SALT I led to two agreements: the ANTI-BALLISTIC-MISSILE TREATY OF 1972 (ABM Treaty), which eventually limited each superpower to one site for antiballistic missiles (ABMs), the missiles designed to intercept and destroy incoming missiles; and an "interim" arms agreement limiting the number of intercontinental ballistic missile (ICBM) launchers and submarine-launched ballistic missiles (SLBMs) to those already deployed by specific dates in 1972. It also required that any modernization and replacement of ICBMs and SLBMs be on a one-for-one basis and prohibited any development of new, more powerful ICBMs. The agreement was meant to set limits before a more definitive SALT II treaty could be negotiated. When the SALT II Treaty was signed in 1979, it set a limit of 2,400 strategic missiles and bombers for each side. Although the U.S. Senate did not ratify this treaty, the United States abided by it for several years.

The ABM Treaty of SALT I was much more successful than the interim ICBM-SLBM agreement. Because the SALT agreements limited only the number of ICBM launchers, or missiles, both superpowers went on in the 1970s to develop missiles with multiple warheads, called "multiple independently targetable reentry vehicles" (MIRVs). Launcher totals thus remained constant, but the number of warheads increased dramatically. Adding warheads to missiles also made nuclear deterrence more unpredictable; a superpower with MIRVs could have enough warheads to destroy the opponent's retaliatory capability, thereby making MAD ineffective. Both superpowers felt that their land-based missile forces had become vulnerable to a first strike from the other side.

Compliance with the SALT treaties became a contentious issue in the 1980s when the United States accused the USSR of violating treaty provisions on the development of new missiles. The administration of President RONALD REAGAN decided that alleged Soviet violations made it necessary to end U.S. compliance with the agreements. In 1986 the United States exceeded limits set by SALT II when a B-52 bomber equipped with cruise missiles (nuclear missiles that fly at a low altitude) entered active service. Another U.S. military proposal, the Strategic Defense Initiative (SDI), also complicated the ABM Treaty. In 1983 Reagan made a televised speech in which he announced plans to develop a space-based missile defense system. He presented SDI as an alternative to MAD. SDI would, he claimed, effectively shield the United States from a Soviet missile launch, including an accidental or third-party attack. SDI would also protect the land-based leg of the United States' nuclear triad, the other two legs of which are aircraft bombers and submarine-launched missiles. Many doubted whether such a missile defense system could actually be created, and others criticized SDI as a dangerous upset in the nuclear balance. A debate also arose as to whether SDI was in violation of the ABM Treaty.

Relations between the superpowers eventually warmed when Mikhail Gorbachev emerged as leader of the Soviet Union in the mid-1980s. Relatively young and dynamic compared with his predecessors, Gorbachev initiated reforms for increased openness in the Soviet Union that facilitated arms control agreements. In 1987 President Reagan and Soviet General Secretary Gorbachev signed the Intermediate-Range Nuclear Forces (INF) Treaty, another major step in arms control. The INF Treaty called for the elimination of an entire class of short- and intermediate-range (300- to 3,400-mile) nuclear missiles. These included 1,752 Soviet and 859 U. S. missiles. It was the first treaty to result in a reduction in the number of nuclear weapons. The agreement also involved the most complete verification procedures ever for an arms control treaty. These included data exchanges, on-site inspections, and monitoring by surveillance satellites.

After the INF Treaty, the superpowers continued to try to work out a strategic arms reduction treaty that would cut the number of long-range missiles by 50 percent. By that time, the superpowers each had nuclear arsenals that could destroy the other many times over, and a

50 percent reduction would still leave nuclear deterrence well intact.

A New World Order

Between 1989 and 1991 a number of significant events brought about the end of the Cold War. In 1989 Gorbachev surprised the world when he led the Soviet Union in its decision to give up its control over Eastern Europe. By the summer of 1991, not only had the Warsaw Pact—a unified group consisting of the Soviet Union and its allies in Eastern Europe—dissolved, but so had the Soviet Union itself. Soviet COMMUNISM, one-half of the superpower equation for over 40 years, had imploded.

During this time of increasingly warm relations between the superpowers, a number of major arms control treaties were created. On November 19, 1990, the United States, the USSR, and 20 other countries signed the CONVENTIONAL FORCES IN EUROPE TREATY (CFE Treaty), which President George H. W. Bush called "the farthest-reaching arms agreement in history," an accord that "signals the new world order that is emerging." The treaty grew out of a 1989 proposal by Bush that the superpowers each be limited to 275,000 troops in Europe. As events unfolded in Eastern Europe, however, and the countries of the former Eastern Bloc became independent from the USSR, that number of troops began to seem high. Under the CFE Treaty, each side was allowed to deploy, in the area between the Atlantic Ocean and the Ural Mountains, no more than 20,000 tanks, 30,000 armored troop carriers, 20,000 artillery pieces, 6,800 combat airplanes, and 2,000 attack helicopters. The treaty required the Soviet Union to disarm or destroy nearly 20,000 tanks, artillery pieces, and other weapons, to give a 27 percent reduction in Soviet armaments west of the Urals. That decrease was small, however, compared with the 59,000 weapons the USSR shipped east of the Urals to central Asia between 1989 and 1990 as it sought to realign its forces in response to world events. On the other side, the NORTH ATLANTIC TREATY ORGANIZATION (NATO) forces—the postwar alliance of Western European and North American states, including the United States—were required to destroy fewer than 3,000 pieces of military equipment. In May 1991 NATO decided to reduce its forces even further. The United States, for its part, reduced the 320,000 troops it had in Europe by at least 50 percent.

Arms agreements on nuclear weapons were also reached during this period. On July 31, 1991, Bush and Gorbachev signed the first Strategic Arms Reduction Treaty (START I). Negotiations on the technically complex accord had begun as early as 1982. The agreement required the USSR to reduce its nuclear arsenal by roughly 25 percent and the United States to reduce its arsenal by 15 percent, within seven years after ratification by both nations. Numerically speaking, the USSR would reduce its nuclear warheads from 10,841 to 8,040, and the United States would reduce its warheads from 12,081 to 10,395. These amounts would bring the nuclear arsenals of each nation roughly back to levels that existed in 1982, when START negotiations began. The agreement also limited the development of new missiles and required a number of verification procedures, including on-site inspections with spot checks, monitoring of missile production plants, and exchange of data tapes from missile tests.

Arms Control in the Post-Cold War Era

In June 1992 President George H. W. Bush met with Russian president Boris Yeltsin. In a "joint understanding," the two sides agreed to reductions of nuclear weapons beyond the levels provided for in the 1991 START agreement, with the ultimate goal of decreasing the total number of warheads on each side to between 3,000 and 3,500 by the year 2003. The two presidents also agreed to eliminate MIRVs by 2003. This agreement was signed, as START II, in early 1993.

The administration of President BILL CLINTON, who became PRESIDENT OF THE UNITED STATES in 1993, revived the debate surrounding missile defense systems—and created fears that a new arms race might begin—when it developed proposals for the Theater High-Altitude Area-Defense System (THAAD). THAAD would be an elaborate missile defense system aimed at protecting allied nations from short-range missile attacks launched by countries such as North Korea. Critics maintained that THAAD would violate the ABM provisions of SALT I, widely believed to be the most successful arms control provisions ever; upset the nuclear balance; and possibly lead to an arms race. Proponents of THAAD maintained that the ABM Treaty was a relic of the Cold War and that missile defenses could protect against accidental nuclear launches.

As for Europe, the new structure of power there would also create new challenges for arms control. Agreements such as the CFE were made when the Soviet Union still existed, and did not necessarily conform to current realities. As the war in the former Yugoslavia demonstrated during the early 1990s, a new political situation posed new risks. Would certain states become regional powers and upset the balance of power? Would agreements that were stabilizing for the Soviet Union turn out to be destabilizing for Russia and other states of the former USSR? Would nationalism rise as a destructive force, as it had before and during previous wars?

Some experts were proposing that the Conference on Security and Cooperation in Europe (CSCE) develop conventional arms control agreements to replace the CFE Treaty. The CSCE was formed in 1973 in an attempt to promote détente between the United States and the USSR. It includes 52 countries—50 European nations plus the United States and Canada. European leaders hoped the CSCE would play a greater role in determining a peaceful, stable future for Europe, with efforts in arms control being one of its major goals. Formally declaring this goal, European leaders signed the Pact of Paris in November 1990. Some leaders were proposing that the CSCE replace NATO as the chief military and political organization in Europe.

During the early 2000s, U.S. defense policy changed dramatically. The election of President GEORGE W. BUSH signaled the rise of neoconservative policy thinking about post-Cold War security, a framework that no longer prioritized defense against nuclear attack from Russia or the states of the former Soviet Union. Instead, TERRORISM and so-called rogue states were said to pose the greatest danger.

In a profound departure from the superpower analysis that had formed the basis of Cold War planning, the threat was now said to come from smaller, weaker nations. Defense planners identified potential THREATS from North Korea, Iraq, and Iran, which were said to be developing—or as in the case of Pakistan, had already developed—nuclear weapons. They pointed to the failure of international nonproliferation agreements as reasons for the United States to reconfigure its defenses and rethink its previous agreements.

Accordingly, the Bush administration moved swiftly on both fronts. In 1999 Bush had campaigned on the promise of reviving the Reagan-era SDI project to provide an antimissile defense system. In 2001 the president unilaterally withdrew from the ABM Treaty of 1972 in order to remove any legal hindrance from testing and development of missile defense.

The end of the ABM Treaty proved controversial. Advocates of preserving the treaty praised it for preserving strategic stability, allowing for easy verification of each side's nuclear capacity, and maintaining the concept of deterrence. Sharply critical of U.S. unilateral withdrawal, both the Russians and Chinese announced they would respond by increasing their nuclear arsenals. Downplaying this threat, critics of the ABM Treaty doubted that either nation could afford to do so.

Great uncertainties began to cloud the future of arms control. Following the September 11, 2001, terrorist attacks on the United States, the Bush administration announced its intention to change the policy led under previous administrations from a focus on independent arms control treaties and nonproliferation agreements to protecting the United States from global terror. Specifically, Bush's new doctrine was one of preemptive attack. Departing from historical tradition, the Bush administration declared its intention to attack enemy nations first. Accordingly, despite global objection to the doctrine, the Bush administration ordered the invasion of Iraq in 2003. In 2005 the Bush administration eliminated the nonproliferation and arms control bureaus in the United States DEPARTMENT OF STATE and reorganized them into a new Bureau for International Security and Nonproliferation. SECRETARY OF STATE under George W. Bush, Condoleezza Rice, stated that the purpose for such reorganization was to increase the role of the Department of State in "protecting America from weapons of mass destruction."

The risks of nuclear proliferation were starkly demonstrated in 2002 when Pakistan and India came to the brink of nuclear war, and again that year when North Korea, abrogating its nonproliferation agreement, defied the United States to stop it from developing nuclear weapons. By the end of the Bush administration, Iran was pursuing elements of a possible weapons program and was ignoring demands of suspending production of uranium. Additionally, North Korea had not only withdrawn from the Nuclear Non-Proliferation Treaty but had also tested two nuclear devices. With Washington laying out its largest defense spending in a quarter century, arms control and disarmament were clearly perceived to not be a priority of the Bush administration.

Under President BARACK OBAMA, the United States once again changed its focus back toward arms control and non-proliferation. In an April 2009 speech, Obama outlined a number of concrete steps that the United States was planning to take in order to address the threat of nuclear weapons. Specifically, the United States introduced a resolution on nuclear nonproliferation and disarmament during the UNITED NATIONS Security Council meeting chaired by President Obama on September 24, 2009. The Security Council unanimously approved Obama's resolution, which set forth a series of goals to eliminate nuclear weapons, ban the production of fissile material used to make such weapons, outlaw atomic tests and safeguard stockpiles of weapons. Additionally, the resolution advocated actions to be taken against nations that violate the International NUCLEAR NONPROLIFERATION TREATY by having their military use civilian nuclear technology. Obama's appearance at the United Nations Special Session of the Security Council was the first time any U.S. president had ever presided over a full-scale summit of the Security Council. This action sent a powerful signal to the world that the United States plans to reestablish being a leader on arms control. The United States is also planning on hosting a global nuclear security summit in Washington in April 2010, which will focus on raising the global standard for effective nuclear security.

FURTHER READINGS

Center for Arms Control and Non-Proliferation. 2009. "President Obama Making Good on Nuclear Weapons Promises." Press Release, September 23, 2009. Available online at http://www.armscontrolcenter.org/audience/media/092309_obama_good_on_nuclear_promises/ website home page: http://www.armscontrolcenter.org (accessed September 26, 2009).

Dunn, Lewis A., and Sharon A. Squassoni. 1993. *Arms Control: What Next?* Boulder, Colo.: Westview Press.

Laird, Melvin R. August 23, 2001. "Why Scrap the ABM Treaty?" *Washington Post,* A25.

Mufson, Steven. December 16, 2001. "ABM Treaty May Be History, But Deterrence Doctrine Lives." *Washington Post,* A37.

Parsons, Christi. September 25, 2009. "Security Council Backs Abolishing Nuclear Arms." latimes.com. Available online at http://www.latimes.com/news/nationworld/world/la-fg-obama-nuclear25-2009sep25,0,6589404. story website home page: http://www.latimes.com (accessed September 26, 2009).

"Project on Strengthening Arms Control and Nonproliferation." Center for Arms Control and non-Proliferation. Available online at http://www. armscontrolcenter.org/resources/strengthening_nonproliferation/ website home page: http://www.armscontrolcenter.org (accessed September 25, 2009).

Sheehan, Michael. 1988. *Arms Control: Theory and Practice.* Oxford: Blackwell.

Varner, Bill. September 25, 2009. "Obama Gets UN Nuclear Accord as U.K., France Put Heat on Iran." Bloomberg. com. Available online at http://www.bloomberg.com/apps/news?pid=20601087&sid=aiiuAu6px_Cw website home page: http://bloomberg.com(accessed September 26, 2009).

Weisman, Steven R. March 23, 2003. "A Nation at War: A New Doctrine, Pre-emption, Idea with a Lineage whose Time Has Come." *New York Times,* 1B.

CROSS REFERENCES

Anti-Ballistic-Missile Treaty of 1972; Blockade; Hot Line Agreement, 1971; Intermediate-Range Nuclear Forces Treaty; International Law; NATO; Nixon, Richard Milhous; Nuclear Nonproliferation Treaty; Nuclear Weapons; Terrorism; War.

ARRAIGNMENT

A criminal proceeding at which the defendant is officially called before a court of competent jurisdiction, informed of the offense charged in the complaint, information, indictment, or other charging document, and asked to enter a plea of guilty, not guilty, or as otherwise permitted by law. Depending on the jurisdiction, arraignment may also be the proceeding at which the court determines whether to set bail for the defendant or release the defendant on his or her own recognizance.

Although the initial appearance of the arrested person before a magistrate is sometimes referred to as an *arraignment,* it is not a true arraignment, which only comes after the DEFENDANT has been both arrested and formally charged. In all but extremely rare cases, arraignment also takes place before any suppression hearings and the trial itself. The interests at issue in an arraignment are the defendant's right to know of the charges against him or her and the defendant's right to have adequate information from which to prepare a defense. The state also has an interest in having the defendant make a PLEA so it can prepare accordingly.

The SIXTH AMENDMENT to U.S. Constitution guarantees that defendants shall "be informed of the nature and cause of the accusation against them." But the Sixth Amendment does not guarantee defendants the right to be informed of the charged offense at an arraignment. Although the Supreme Court has ruled that arraignments are a necessary pre-condition to trial under federal law, the Court has also ruled that failure to arraign a defendant is not a reversible error where the failure is inadvertent, the defendant knows that he is the accused, the defendant is apprised of the charged offense, the defendant is able to assist in preparing a defense, and the defendant is not otherwise prejudiced by the lack of an arraignment. Thus the importance and necessity of being arraigned before trial varies from case to case and from jurisdiction to jurisdiction. The law governing arraignment procedures is spelled out by statutes and court rules at both the state and federal levels.

The Federal Rules of CRIMINAL PROCEDURE provide that during the arraignment federal courts must read the indictment or information to the defendant or state the substance of the charge to the defendant and ask him or her to enter a plea thereto. FR Crim P, Rule 10. The defendant must also be given a copy of the indictment or information before he or she is called upon to plead. Generally speaking, the federal rules require defendants to be present at the arraignment. However, in prosecutions for offenses punishable by fine or imprisonment for not more than one year, the court, with the written consent of the defendant, may permit arraignment in the defendant's absence.

The court rules in some states only require that arraignments be held for felony-level charges, but not for misdemeanor-level offenses. Other states require arraignments for felonies, gross misdemeanors, and misdemeanors punishable by INCARCERATION or a fine greater than a certain amount. In addition to requiring that defendants be called before the court, informed of the charged offense, and asked to enter a plea, several state jurisdictions also require that defendants be informed of certain constitutional rights during arraignment, including the right to trial by jury, the right to assistance of counsel, and the right against SELF-INCRIMINATION. If the law of a particular state makes the arraignment a *critical stage* of the prosecution, such as when the court rules require the defendant to raise any defenses to the charged offense at the arraignment or WAIVE them, then the defendant must be afforded the RIGHT TO COUNSEL under the Sixth Amendment (*Hamilton v. Alabama*, 368 U.S. 52, 82 S. Ct. 157, 7 L.Ed.2d 114 [U.S.Ala. 1961]).

Defendants in both state and federal courts must be arraigned in a timely fashion. Ordinarily the accused must be arraigned before the impaneling of the jury or at least before the introduction of evidence. If an unreasonable delay occurs between the time a defendant is arrested and charged with an offense and the time the defendant is arraigned, state and federal courts will dismiss the criminal proceedings as having violated the defendant's Sixth Amendment right to a *speedy trial.*

Many jurisdictions require that defendants be arraigned within seventy-two hours of arrest. As a result, defendants arrested over the weekend are usually arraigned on Mondays, which can make for a packed courtroom. To speed up the arraignment process on busy days, defendants are often arraigned in groups, which is constitutionally permissible so long as each person being arraigned identifies himself or herself to the court and the court advises all defendants in attendance that the remarks of the court apply to each person individually. Courts conducting group arraignments must also ascertain on the record that each defendant was present throughout the entire course of the arraignment, heard the remarks, and understood them.

The right to be arraigned may ordinarily be waived, even when the charge is for a felony-level offense, provided the accused knows the nature of the charge offense and has a full opportunity to present a defense. The power to waive an arraignment must usually be exercised by the accused in person. Where the right of the accused to waive an arraignment is recognized, an express WAIVER in OPEN COURT is sufficient. An arraignment may also be waived in a less formal manner, such as by the voluntary entry of a plea, by failing to call the court's attention to a defect in the proceedings at the proper time, by announcing readiness for trial, by going to trial without objection, or by filing motions and obtaining rulings on issues of law in the case.

CROSS REFERENCES

Hearing; Incarceration; Sixth Amendment; Trial.

ARRAY

The entire group of jurors selected for a trial from which a smaller group is subsequently chosen to form a petit jury or a grand jury; the list of potential jurors.

Virtually all states have enacted statutes delineating requirements for jury service. In most states, convicted felons and insane persons cannot be jurors. Professional persons such as judicial and government officials, lawyers, ministers, and medical personnel may be exempted by statute from jury service.

As a general rule, a group of local officials acting within the statutory framework select the persons who will make up the array.

ARREARS

A sum of money that has not been paid or has only been paid in part at the time it is due.

A person who is "in arrears" is behind in payments due and thus has outstanding debts or liabilities. For example, a tenant who has not paid rent on the day it is due is in arrears. Arrears may also refer to the late distribution of the dividends of cumulative PREFERRED STOCK.

ARREST

A seizure or forcible restraint; an exercise of the power to deprive a person of his or her liberty; the taking or keeping of a person in custody by legal authority, especially, in response to a criminal charge.

The purpose of an arrest is to bring the arrestee before a court or otherwise secure the administration of the law. An arrest serves the function of notifying the community that an individual has been accused of a crime and also may admonish and deter the arrested individual from committing other crimes. Arrests can be made on both criminal charges and civil charges, although civil arrest is a drastic measure that is not looked upon with favor by the courts. The federal Constitution imposes limits on both civil and criminal arrests.

An arrest may occur (1) by the touching or putting hands on the arrestee; (2) by any act that indicates an intention to take the arrestee into custody and that subjects the arrestee to the actual control and will of the person making the arrest; or (3) by the consent of the person to be arrested. There is no arrest where there is no restraint, and the restraint must be under real or pretended legal authority. However, the detention of a person need not be accompanied by formal words of arrest or a station house booking to constitute an arrest.

The test used to determine whether an arrest took place in a particular case is objective, and it turns on whether a REASONABLE PERSON under these circumstances would believe he or she was restrained or free to go. A reasonable person is one who is not guilty of criminal conduct, overly apprehensive, or insensitive to the seriousness of the circumstances. Reasonableness is not determined in light of a defendant's subjective knowledge or fears. The subjective intent of the police is also normally irrelevant to a court's determination whether an arrest occurred, unless the officer makes that intent known. Thus, a defendant's presence at a police station by consent does not become an arrest solely by virtue of an officer's subjective view that the DEFENDANT is not free to leave, absent an act indicating an intention to take the defendant into custody.

An arrest constitutes a SEIZURE under the FOURTH AMENDMENT to the U.S. Constitution, and thus the procedures by which a person is arrested must comply with the protections guaranteed by the Fourth Amendment or the arrest will be invalidated and any evidence seized during the arrest or confessions made after the arrest will typically be suppressed. The U.S. Supreme Court has ruled that arrests made without a valid ARREST WARRANT based on PROBABLE CAUSE are presumptively invalid under the Fourth Amendment. Similarly, arrests made pursuant to a warrant that is later ruled defective may also be declared invalid, unless the officer in procuring the warrant and making the arrest acted in GOOD FAITH.

However, warrantless arrests do pass constitutional muster under some circumstances. The Supreme Court has ruled that warrantless arrests can be made when the circumstances make it reasonable to do so. For example, no warrant is required for a FELONY arrest in a public place, even if the arresting officer had ample time to procure a warrant, so long as the officer possessed probable cause that the suspect committed the crime. Felony arrests in places not open to the public generally do require a warrant, unless the officer is in HOT PURSUIT of a fleeing FELON. *Warden v. Hayden,* 387 U.S. 294,

87 S. Ct. 1642, 18 L.Ed.2d 782 (1967), The Fourth Amendment also allows warrantless arrests for misdemeanors committed in an officer's presence.

The exceptions to the Fourth Amendment's warrant requirement are based on the court's reluctance to unduly impede the job of law enforcement officials. Courts attempt to strike a balance between the practical realities of daily police work and the privacy and freedom interests of the public. Always requiring police officers to take the time to obtain an arrest warrant could result in the destruction of evidence, the disappearance of suspects, or both.

When an officer does seek an arrest warrant, the officer must present evidence to a neutral judge or magistrate sufficient to establish probable cause that a crime has been committed. The Supreme Court has said that probable cause exists when the facts within an officer's knowledge provide a reasonably trustworthy basis for a person of reasonable caution to believe that an offense has been committed or is about to be committed. Courts will deny requests when the warrant fails to describe in particularized detail the person to be arrested. The evidence upon which a warrant is based need not be ultimately ADMISSIBLE at trial, but it cannot be based on KNOWINGLY or intentionally false statements, or statements made in reckless disregard of the truth. However, inaccuracies found in a warrant due to ordinary NEGLIGENCE will not typically jeopardize a warrant's validity.

Police officers need no justification to stop someone on a public street and ask questions, and individuals are completely entitled to refuse to answer any such questions and go about their business. However, the Fourth Amendment prohibits police officers from detaining pedestrians and conducting any kind of search of their clothing without first possessing a reasonable and articulable SUSPICION that the pedestrians are engaged in criminal activity. TERRY V. OHIO, 392 U.S. 1, 88 S. Ct. 1868, 21 L. Ed. 889 (1968). Police may not even compel a pedestrian to produce identification without first meeting this standard. Similarly, police may not stop motorists without first having a reasonable and articulable suspicion that the driver has violated a traffic law. If a police officer has satisfied this standard in stopping a motorist, the officer may conduct a search of

An anti-war protester is arrested on charges of disorderly conduct and obstruction of government administration by a New York police officer. The procedures by which a person is arrested must comply with the protections guaranteed by the Fourth Amendment.

AP IMAGES

the vehicle's interior, including the glove compartment, but not the trunk, unless the officer has probable cause to believe that it contains CONTRABAND or the instruments for criminal activity.

Investigatory stops or detentions must be limited and temporary, lasting no longer than necessary to carry out the purpose of the stop or detention. An investigatory stop that lasts too long turns into a DE FACTO arrest that must comply with the warrant requirements of the Fourth Amendment. But no bright line exists for determining when an investigatory stop becomes a de facto arrest, as courts are reluctant to hamstring the flexibility and discretion of police officers by placing artificial time limitations on the fluid and dynamic nature of their investigations. Rather, the test is whether the detention is temporary and whether the police acted with reasonable dispatch to quickly confirm or dispel the suspicions that initially induced the investigative detention.

A sample arrest warrant

Arrest Warrant

F.C.A. §§153, 153-a

General Form 3
(Warrant of Arrest)

FAMILY COURT OF THE STATE OF NEW YORK
COUNTY OF

....

In the Matter of

Docket No. _____

WARRANT OF ARREST

Petitioner(s)

against

Respondent(s)

....
IN THE NAME OF THE PEOPLE OF THE STATE OF NEW YORK
TO ANY (POLICE)(PEACE) OFFICER IN THE STATE OF NEW YORK

A petition under Article _____ of the Family Court Act having been filed in this Court, a copy of which is annexed hereto, and it appearing that one of the grounds for issuance of a warrant as specified in the Family Court Act exists,

YOU ARE THEREFORE COMMANDED forthwith to arrest [specify name(s)]:

and bring said person(s) before this Court to be dealt with according to law.

YOU ARE FURTHER COMMANDED, under the Family Court Act, to bring before this Court the following child or children:

Name(s)   Date(s) of Birth

THIS WARRANT [check applicable box(es)]:

☐ may   ☐ may not be executed on Sunday.

☐ may   ☐ may not be executed at night.

☐ is subject to the following restriction(s) [specify]:

Dated: _____ , ____.

[continued]

Arrest Warrant

_____
FAMILY COURT JUDGE

BAIL IN THE SUM OF   **($)**   **DOLLARS IS RECOMMENDED.**

_____
FAMILY COURT JUDGE

NOTICE TO RESPONDENT PARENT(S) IN CHILD ABUSE OR NEGLECT CASES:
PLACEMENT OF YOUR CHILD IN FOSTER CARE MAY RESULT IN YOUR LOSS OF YOUR RIGHTS TO YOUR CHILD. IF YOUR CHILD STAYS IN FOSTER CARE FOR 15 OF THE MOST RECENT 22 MONTHS, THE AGENCY MAY BE REQUIRED BY LAW TO FILE A PETITION TO TERMINATE YOUR PARENTAL RIGHTS AND MAY FILE BEFORE THE END OF THE 15 MONTH PERIOD. IF SEVERE OR REPEATED ABUSE IS PROVEN BY CLEAR AND CONVINCING EVIDENCE, THIS FINDING MAY CONSTITUTE THE BASIS TO TERMINATE YOUR PARENTAL RIGHTS.

Family Court Act §155(1) provides that: " If an adult respondent is arrested under this act when the family court is not in session, he or she shall be taken to the most accessible magistrate and arraigned. The production of a warrant issued by the family court, a certificate of warrant, a copy or a certificate of the order of protection or temporary order of protection, an order of protection or temporary order of protection, or a record of such warrant or order from the statewide computer registry established pursuant to section 221-a of the executive law shall be evidence of the filing of an information, petition or sworn affidavit, as provided in section 154-d of this article. Upon consideration of the bail recommendation, if any, made by the family court and indicated on the warrant or certificate of warrant, the magistrate shall thereupon commit such respondent to the custody of the sheriff, as defined in subdivision 35 of section 1.20 of the criminal procedure law, admit to, fix or accept bail, or parole him or her for hearing before the family court, subject to the provisions of subdivision four of section 530.11 of the criminal procedure law concerning arrests upon a violation of an order of protection."

Family Court Act §155-a provides that: "A desk officer in charge at a police station, county jail or police headquarters, or any of his or her superior officers, may, in such place, take cash bail for his or her appearance before the appropriate court the next morning from any person arrested pursuant to a warrant issued by the family court; provided that such arrest occurs between eleven o'clock in the morning and eight o'clock the next morning, except that in the city of New York bail shall be taken between two o'clock in the afternoon and eight o'clock the next morning. The amount of such cash bail shall be the amount fixed in the warrant of arrest."

A sample arrest warrant (continued)
ILLUSTRATION BY GGS CREATIVE RESOURCES. REPRODUCED BY PERMISSION OF GALE, A PART OF CENGAGE LEARNING.

Not all arrests are made by members of law enforcement. Many jurisdictions permit private citizens to make arrests. Popularly known as _citizen's arrests,_ the circumstances under which private citizens may place each other under arrest are normally very limited. All jurisdictions that authorize citizen's arrests prohibit citizens from making arrests for unlawful acts committed outside their presence. Most jurisdictions that authorize citizen's arrests also allow citizens to make arrests only for serious crimes, such as felonies and gross misdemeanors, and then only when the arresting citizen has probable cause to believe the arrestee committed the serious crime. Witnessing the crime in person will normally establish probable cause for making an arrest.

Both private citizens and law enforcement officers may be held liable for the tort of FALSE ARREST in civil court. An ACTION for false arrest requires proof that the process used for the arrest was void on its face. In other words, one who confines another, while purporting to act by authority of law which does not in fact exist, makes a false arrest and may be required to pay money damages to the victim. To make out a claim for false arrest, the PLAINTIFF must show that the charges on which he or she was arrested ultimately lacked justification. That is, the plaintiff in a false arrest action must show that the arrest was made without probable cause and for an improper purpose.

CROSS REFERENCES

Accusation; Charge; Civil Procedure; Contraband; Criminal Action; Criminal Law; Criminal Procedure; De Facto; Evidence; Felony; Fourth Amendment; Hot Pursuit; Liability; Probable Cause; Seizure; Tort Law.

ARREST OF JUDGMENT

The postponement or stay of an official decision of a court, or the refusal to render such a determination, after a verdict has been reached in an action at law or a criminal prosecution, because some defect appears on the face of the record that, if a decision is made, would make it erroneous or reversible.

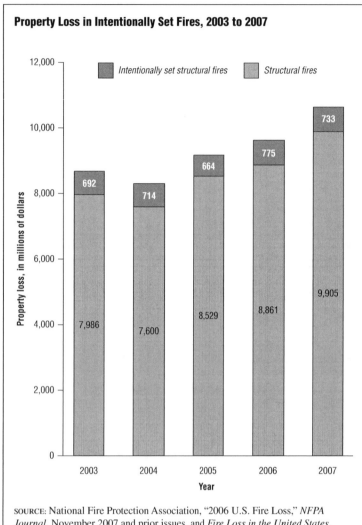

Property Loss in Intentionally Set Fires, 2003 to 2007

Legend: Intentionally set structural fires | Structural fires

Property loss, in millions of dollars

Year	Intentionally set structural fires	Structural fires
2003	692	7,986
2004	714	7,600
2005	664	8,529
2006	775	8,861
2007	733	9,905

SOURCE: National Fire Protection Association, "2006 U.S. Fire Loss," *NFPA Journal*, November 2007 and prior issues, and *Fire Loss in the United States*, August 2008.

ILLUSTRATION BY GGS CREATIVE RESOURCES. REPRODUCED BY PERMISSION OF GALE, A PART OF CENGAGE LEARNING.

Although the Federal Rules of CIVIL PROCEDURE make no such provision, state codes of civil procedure should be consulted concerning the issuance of an arrest of judgment in actions at law.

In criminal proceedings, a DEFENDANT must make a motion for an arrest of judgment when the indictment or information fails to charge the accused with an offense or if the court lacks jurisdiction over the offense charged. State and federal rules of CRIMINAL PROCEDURE govern an arrest of judgment in criminal prosecutions.

ARREST WARRANT

A written order issued by authority of the state and commanding the seizure of the person named.

An arrest warrant must be based on a complaint that alleges PROBABLE CAUSE that the person named has committed a specific offense, and it must be issued according to the formalities required by the rules of the court. The Federal Rules of CRIMINAL PROCEDURE specify that the warrant must be signed by the magistrate and must describe the offense charged. The DEFENDANT must be named or described in such a way that he or she can be identified with reasonable certainty. The warrant must also command that the defendant be arrested and brought before the nearest available magistrate.

ARROGATION

Claiming or seizing something without justification; claiming something on behalf of another. In civil law, the adoption of an adult who was legally capable of acting for himself or herself.

ARSON

At common law, the malicious burning or exploding of the dwelling house of another, or the burning of a building within the curtilage, the immediate surrounding space, of the dwelling of another.

Modern legislation has extended the definition of arson to include the burning or exploding of commercial and public buildings—such as restaurants and schools—and structures—such as bridges. In many states, the act of burning any insured dwelling, regardless of whether it belongs to another, constitutes arson if it is done with an intent to DEFRAUD the insurer. Finally, the common-law rule that the property burned must belong to another person has been completely eliminated by statute in some states.

Elements

The main elements necessary to prove arson are evidence of a burning and evidence that a criminal act caused the fire. The accused must intend to burn a building or other structure. Absent a statutory description of the conduct required for arson, the conduct must be malicious, and not accidental. Malice, however, does not mean ill will. Intentional or outrageously reckless conduct is sufficient to constitute malice. Motive, on the other hand, is not an essential element of arson.

Unless a statute extends the crime to other property, only a house used as a residence, or buildings immediately surrounding it, can be the subject of arson. If a house is vacated, is closed up, or becomes unfit for human habitation, its burning will not constitute arson. A temporary absence from a dwelling will not negate its character as a residence.

Generally, the actual presence of a person within a dwelling at the moment it is burned is not necessary. It may, however, be required for a particular degree of the crime. The fact, and not the knowledge, of human occupancy is what is essential. If a dwelling is burned under the impression that it is uninhabited when people actually live in it, the crime is committed.

Absent a statute to the contrary, a person is innocent of arson if that individual burns his or her own property while living there. The common exception to this rule is the burning of one's own property with an intent to defraud or prejudice the property insurer. In addition, under statutes that punish the burning of a dwelling house without expressly requiring it to be the property of another, a person who burns his or her own property might be guilty of arson. An owner, for purposes of arson, is the person who possesses the house and has the care, control, and management of it. In those states that have maintained the common-law rule that the property burned must belong to another person, an owner who burns his or her house while it is in the possession of a lawful tenant is guilty of arson.

Degrees

In many states arson is divided into degrees, depending sometimes on the value of the property but more commonly on its use and whether the crime was committed in the day or night. A typical statute might make the burning of an inhabited dwelling house at night first-degree arson, the burning of a building close enough to a dwelling so as to endanger it second-degree arson, and the burning of any structure with an intent to defraud an insurer thereof, third-degree arson. Many statutes vary the degree of the crime according to the criminal intent of the accused.

Punishment

Arson is a serious crime that was punishable by death under the COMMON LAW. Presently, it is classified as a FELONY under most statutes, punishable by either imprisonment or death. Many jurisdictions impose prison sentences commensurate with the seriousness of the

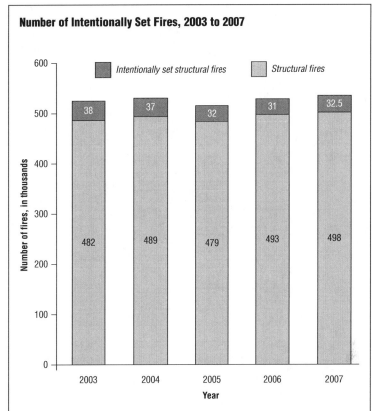

Number of Intentionally Set Fires, 2003 to 2007

SOURCE: National Fire Protection Association, "2006 U.S. Fire Loss," *NFPA Journal*, November 2007 and prior issues, and *Fire Loss in the United States*, August 2008.

ILLUSTRATION BY GGS CREATIVE RESOURCES. REPRODUCED BY PERMISSION OF GALE, A PART OF CENGAGE LEARNING.

criminal intent of the accused. A finding, therefore, that the offense was committed intentionally will result in a longer prison sentence than a finding that it was done recklessly. When a human life is endangered, the penalty is most severe.

ART LAW

The Framers of the Constitution acknowledged the importance of the arts when they wrote that Congress shall have the power "[t]o promote the Progress of Science and useful Arts, by securing for limited Times to Authors and Inventors the exclusive Right to their respective Writings and Discoveries" (Art. I, § 8). Despite this provision, or perhaps because of its very limited nature, the federal government offered little assistance to artists until the 1930s. Early unsuccessful attempts to aid the arts included an effort by President JAMES BUCHANAN to establish the National Commission of Fine Arts, a project that failed within a year when Congress did not appropriate funds. President

Lucile Lloyd puts the finishing touches on a new mural in the California State Building in Los Angeles in December 1936. The work was completed under the auspices of the Federal Art Project.

BETTMANN/CORBIS.

THEODORE ROOSEVELT also encountered a reluctant Congress half a century later when he proposed the Council of Fine Arts, but success came when his successor, WILLIAM HOWARD TAFT, persuaded Congress to create the National Commission of Fine Arts.

Even after the National Commission of Fine Arts was established, the federal government continued to play a minor role in funding the arts, but several municipal programs attempted to fill the void. In New York City the Civil Works Administration (CWA) sponsored paintings, murals, and art education. The primary goal of the CWA was to create employment for artists receiving government relief. With the only requirement for employment being an assertion that the applicant was an artist, the art produced under the CWA was often the work of unskilled amateurs.

Federal funding for the arts took off during the Great Depression with the creation of the Federal Art Project, a branch of the Works Progress Administration (WPA). The Federal Art Project was modeled on some of the earlier municipal attempts but avoided their problems by emphasizing the production of works of high technical competence, utilizing defined hiring guidelines, and encouraging creativity and experimentation. The Federal Art Project paid a *security wage,* an amount that was calculated to fall between the prevailing wage and the relief grants of the region involved and was graduated according to skill level. The WPA spent $35 million on the Federal Art Project and supported the production of approximately 1,500 murals, 18,800 sculptures, and 108,000 paintings as well as other works of art. The onset of WORLD WAR II effectively ended the WPA.

In the COLD WAR era following World War II, the federal government funded cultural exchanges to promote diplomatic ends. The major cultural institutions were located primarily in large cities, such as New York, Los Angeles, Chicago, and Boston. In 1965 only five state arts agencies existed. The quality of performances and exhibitions was inconsistent, and support for the best art depended on the discretion and charity of a few patrons. As a result, opportunities for artists were limited, and rural audiences had few chances to see the best productions or visit outstanding exhibitions.

In the mid-1990s, federal financial support for the arts and humanities was provided through several distinct agencies: the National Commission of Fine Arts, the National Endowment for the Arts (NEA), and the National Endowment for the Humanities (NEH). The Commission of Fine Arts, established in 1910, advises the president, Congress, and government department heads on matters of architecture, sculpture, painting, and other fine arts. The commission's primary function is to preserve and enhance the appearance of the nation's capital, Washington, D.C. (40 U.S.C.A. § 104 [1986]).

The National Foundation for the Arts and Humanities Act of 1965 (20 U.S.C.A. §§ 951–968 [West Supp. 1990]) established the NEA and the NEH. The NEA provides grants to, or contracts with, groups and individuals of exceptional talent, and state or regional organizations engaged in or concerned with the arts. NEA programs encourage individual and institutional development of the arts, preservation of the American artistic heritage, wider availability of the arts, leadership in the arts, and the stimulation of nonfederal sources of support for the nation's artistic activities. The goal of the NEA is not to provide employment, as the WPA did, but rather to make the arts more widely available to U.S. citizens, to preserve the nation's rich cultural heritage, and to encourage the creative development of the nation's finest artistic talent. By 2003 the NEA had made more than 120,000 grants for theater, dance, symphonic music, painting, and poetry.

As a major financier of the arts, the NEA has been a significant influence on much of the publicly exhibited art in the United States. For many years it led a quiet administrative existence, and although it was a force in the artistic community, the general public knew little about it. In late 1989, however, the organization became the center of controversy when some members of Congress questioned whether some works of art and performances funded by the NEA were OBSCENE. The NEA had provided funding for exhibits featuring the works of artists including Robert Mapplethorpe and Andres Serrano. Mapplethorpe's exhibit included sexually explicit photographs of men, and Serrano's exhibit included a jar of urine into which a photograph of a crucifix had been placed. The uproar from the public, and from members of Congress, was so strong that in 1990 Congress enacted a law that required the NEA to take into consideration "general standards of decency and respect for the diverse beliefs and values of the American public." This became known as the *decency test.*

Over the next several years other controversial grants were awarded and challenged, culminating in a case that went to the U.S. Supreme Court. The case, *National Endowment for the Arts v. Finley* 524 U.S. 569, 118 S. Ct. 2168, 141 L.Ed. 2d 500 (1998), was brought by four artists including Karen Finley. Finley became infamous for a performance art piece in which she would remove her clothing and smear chocolate on her body. The work, she explained, symbolized the way women were exploited in society. Finley and her fellow plaintiffs argued that the 1990 statute was unconstitutional and that the decency test was a violation of the rights of free speech and due process.

A district court agreed and the U.S. Court of Appeals upheld the district court's decision in 1996 100 F. 3d 671 (9th Cir.) In 1998 the Supreme Court ruled 8 to 1 that the law was constitutional, and that it violated no rights. Grant-seekers, the court noted, were required to submit their proposals to a panel representing diverse points of view; as such, the risk that an arbitrary ruling of indecency would be reached was minimal. In his dissent, however, Justice DAVID H. SOUTER warned that the law could force artists to censor their own work to ensure that it would not offend anyone in a position to approve a grant.

The NEH funds activities are designed to improve the quality of education and teaching in the humanities, strengthen the scholarly foundation for humanities study and research, and advance understanding of the humanities among general audiences. The NEH provides support through outright grants, matching grants, and a combination of the two. Schools, higher education institutions, libraries, museums, historical organizations, professional associations, other cultural institutions, and individuals are eligible to apply for NEH grants.

One avenue members of Congress use to support the arts is the Congressional Arts Caucus. This bipartisan group, composed of nearly 250 members of Congress who recognize and support the arts, acts as an information clearinghouse on arts issues. The caucus reports on legislation affecting artists and arts institutions, both commercial and nonprofit. It helps members of Congress prepare TESTIMONY and speeches on the arts.

The government also provides indirect aid designed to create a heightened public awareness of art and to provide artists with new outlets for their work. Among the effective means of indirect aid are the regulations adopted by many state and municipal governments, which require a percentage of the cost of building new government structures to be spent on art.

Federal, state, and local governments indirectly promote a heightened public awareness of the arts in the community through zoning. Zoning laws divide a city into districts and set forth the types of structural and architectural designs of buildings in those districts, and the uses that buildings may serve. Some zoning regulations and laws are designed to preserve the aesthetic features or values of an area. As of 2003, most state courts allowed the use of zoning laws for solely aesthetic purposes. These laws may, for example, restrict the placement of billboards or television satellite dishes or may require that junkyards be screened or fenced.

State and local governments have become involved in improving the appearance of publicly funded buildings, or any building built on public land, by requiring that new building designs and locations be approved by the local government. Local control over design was held constitutional in *Walnut & Quince Streets Corp. v. Mills,* 303 Pa. 25, 154 A. 29, *appeal dismissed,* 284 U.S. 573, 52 S. Ct. 16, 76 L. Ed 498 (1931). In *Walnut & Quince Streets,* a municipal arts panel refused to permit a theater owner to construct a large marquee extending over the sidewalk. The owner unsuccessfully argued that a local statute permitted the jury to act in an arbitrary fashion that deprived him of DUE PROCESS OF LAW and, furthermore, that the legislature did not have the authority to regulate aesthetics and thus could not delegate such authority to an "arts jury." The court upheld the statute as a legitimate legislative regulation of public property.

Many governments have enacted statutes and regulations prohibiting the destruction and alteration of historic landmarks. LANDMARK preservation laws indirectly aid the arts by increasing the public's awareness of the need for beautification and for preserving the work of past generations of artists. The earliest efforts to preserve the nation's heritage focused on particular buildings or national monuments. The application of historic preservation laws to limit a property owner's right to her or his property was declared constitutional in *Penn Central Transportation Co. v. New York City,* 438 U.S. 104, 98 S. Ct. 2646, 57 L. Ed. 2d 631 (1978). In *Penn Central,* the U.S. Supreme Court held that the New City Landmarks Preservation Commission's failure to approve plans for construction of a 50-story office building over Grand Central Terminal, a designated landmark, was not an unconstitutional taking of property.

Historic preservation law is an active and expansive area of zoning and planning law. According to the National Trust for Historic Preservation, more than 1,700 communities have enacted preservation laws. Federal efforts to encourage preservation include the enactment of laws providing some tax credits for the protection and restoration of old buildings (26 U.S.C.A. § 48 (g)(3)(A) [1986]) and for the protection of archaeological sites (16 U.S.C.A. § 461[1986]).

FURTHER READINGS

Brenson, Michael. 2001. *Visionaries and Outcasts: The NEA, Congress, and the Place of the Visual Artist in America.* New York: New Press.

Ellickson, Robert C., and Vicki L. Been. 1985. *Land-Use Controls: Cases and Materials.* Frederick, MD: Aspen.

Frohnmayer, John E. 1992. "A Litany of Taboo," *Kansas Journal of Law and Public Policy* 2 (spring).

Hulbert, Dan. 1998. "High Court Upholds NEA Decency Standards." *Atlanta Journal-Constitution* (June 26).

Rathkopf, Arden H., and Daren A. Rathkopf. 2005. *Rathkopf's The Law of Zoning and Planning.* 5th ed. St. Paul, MN: Thomson/West.

U.S. Congress. *Congressional Arts Caucus.* Serial 20515.

CROSS REFERENCES

Helms, Jesse Alexander, Jr.; Land-Use Control; Zoning.

✦ ARTHUR, CHESTER ALAN

Chester Alan Arthur was born October 5, 1830, in Fairfield, Vermont. He achieved prominence as a politician and as PRESIDENT OF THE UNITED STATES.

An 1848 graduate of Union College, Arthur was admitted to the New York City bar in 1851, and he established a legal practice in New York City that same year.

With the onset of the Civil War, Arthur served as quartermaster general and inspector general of New York. After the war, from 1871 to 1878, he performed the duties of collector for the Port of New York. Although Arthur was a believer in the spoils system, a practice that rewards loyal political party members with jobs that require official appointment, he served his office as an honest administrator. President RUTHERFORD B. HAYES was, however, an advocate of the CIVIL SERVICE system, which provided that qualified people receive employment fairly based upon their qualifications, and removed Arthur from the office of collector.

Arthur returned to politics with his election as VICE PRESIDENT of the United States in March of 1880. In September 1881, he assumed the duties of president, after the assassination of President JAMES GARFIELD.

As president, Arthur advocated the passage of the Pendleton Civil Service Reform Bill in 1883, adopting a view that was contrary to his previous support of the spoils system. He signed laws allowing for the modernization of the United States Navy and supported the prosecution of

Chester A. Arthur.
LIBRARY OF CONGRESS

the Star Route Trials, which exposed fraudulent activities in the United States Post Office Department. He also vetoed a Congressional bill, the Rivers and Harbours Bill of 1882, charging that the allotment of funds was too extravagant.

Arthur's presidential term ended in 1885; due to ill health, he did not seek renomination. He died November 18, 1886, in New York, New York.

MEN MAY DIE, BUT
THE FABRIC OF FREE
INSTITUTIONS
REMAINS UNSHAKEN.
—CHESTER ARTHUR

ARTICLES

Series or subdivisions of individual and distinct sections of a document, statute, or other writing, such as the Articles of Confederation. Codes or systems of rules created by written agreements of parties or by statute that establish standards of legally

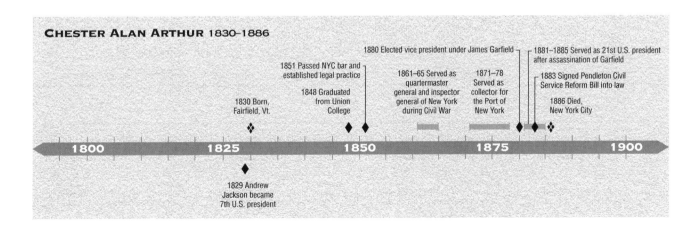

CHESTER ALAN ARTHUR 1830–1886

1880 Elected vice president under James Garfield
1881–1885 Served as 21st U.S. president after assassination of Garfield

1851 Passed NYC bar and established legal practice

1861–65 Served as quartermaster general and inspector general of New York during Civil War

1871–78 Served as collector for the Port of New York

1883 Signed Pendleton Civil Service Reform Bill into law

1848 Graduated from Union College

1830 Born, Fairfield, Vt.

1886 Died, New York City

1800   1825   1850   1875   1900

1829 Andrew Jackson became 7th U.S. president

acceptable behavior in a business relationship, such as articles of incorporation or articles of partnership. Writings that embody contractual terms of agreements between parties.

ARTICLES OF CONFEDERATION

The document that set forth the terms under which the original thirteen states agreed to participate in a centralized form of government, in addition to their self-rule, and that was in effect from March 1, 1781, to March 4, 1789, prior to the adoption of the Constitution.

The ARTICLES OF CONFEDERATION served as the first constitution of the newly formed United States. As it was originally drafted in 1776, the document provided for a strong central government. However, by the time it was ratified in 1781, advocates of states' rights had greatly weakened its provisions. Many of these advocates feared a centralization of power and wished to preserve a great degree of independence and SOVEREIGNTY for each state. Accordingly, the Articles as they were ratified provided only for a "firm league of friendship," in which, according to article II of the document, "[e]ach State retains its sovereignty, freedom and independence."

The Articles included provisions for military cooperation between the states, freedom of travel, EXTRADITION of criminal suspects, and equal PRIVILEGES AND IMMUNITIES for citizens. They also created a national legislature called the Congress. Each state had one vote in this body, that vote to be determined by a delegation of from two to seven representatives. The Articles called for Congress to conduct foreign relations, maintain a national army and navy, establish and maintain a postal service, and perform a number of other duties. The Articles did not create, as the Constitution later did, executive and judicial branches of government.

The Congress created by the Articles was successful on a number of fronts. In 1783 it negotiated with Great Britain a peace treaty that officially ended the Revolutionary War; it arranged to pay war debts; and it passed the NORTHWEST ORDINANCE, which allowed for settlement and statehood in new regions in the western part of the United States. However, with time, it became apparent that the Articles had created an unsatisfactory union of the states, chiefly because they established a weak central government. For example, under the Articles of Confederation, Congress did not have the power to tax or to effectively regulate commerce. The resulting national government did not prove competent at such tasks as raising a military or creating a stable currency. In addition, because amendments to the Articles required a unanimous vote of all thirteen states, the Articles proved to be too inflexible to last.

A series of incidents in the 1780s made it clear to many early U.S. leaders that the Articles of Confederation would not serve as an effective constitution. Among these incidents was Shays's Rebellion, in 1786–87, an insurrection in which economically depressed farmers demanded debt relief and closed courts of law in western Massachusetts. The Congress of the Confederation was not able to raise a force to respond to this civil unrest, which was later put down by a state MILITIA. GEORGE WASHINGTON and other leaders perceived this as a grievous failure. Therefore, when a constitutional convention assembled in 1787 to amend the Articles, it quickly decided to abandon them altogether in favor of a new constitution. By June 21, 1788, nine states had ratified the new U.S. Constitution and made it effective. It has survived as the basis of U.S. government for more than 200 years.

FURTHER READINGS

Harrigan, John J. 1996. *Politics and the American Future: Dilemmas of Democracy.* 4th ed. New York: McGraw-Hill.

Kesavan, Vasan. 2002. "When Did the Articles of Confederation Cease to Be Law?" *Notre Dame Law Review* 78 (December).

Levy, Michael B. 1988. *Political Thought in America: An Anthology.* 2d ed. Florence, KY: Brooks Cole.

CROSS REFERENCES

"Articles of Confederation" (Appendix, Primary Document); Constitution; Constitution of the United States; Federalism; Shays's Rebellion; Washington, George.

ARTICLES OF IMPEACHMENT

Formal written allegations of the causes that warrant the criminal trial of a public official before a quasi-political court.

In cases of IMPEACHMENT, involving the president, VICE PRESIDENT, or other federal officers, the House of Representatives prepares the ARTICLES OF IMPEACHMENT, because it is endowed with the "sole Power of Impeachment," under Article I, Section 2, Clause 5 of the Constitution.

The articles are sent to the Senate, which has the exclusive power to "try all Impeachments" by virtue of Article I, Section 3, Clause 6.

The use of articles of impeachment against state officials is governed by state constitutions and statutes. Articles of impeachment are analogous to an indictment that initiates criminal prosecutions of private persons.

Articles of Impeachment and the U.S. Presidency

Articles of impeachment have been drafted against three U.S presidents, ANDREW JOHNSON, RICHARD M. NIXON, and WILLIAM JEFFERSON CLINTON. Nixon resigned before the full House could vote to approve the articles of impeachment prepared by the judiciary committee, while Johnson and Clinton were both acquitted during Senate trials that were bitterly divided along party lines.

On February 24, 1868, the U.S House of Representatives voted to IMPEACH President Andrew Johnson. A week later the House approved 11 articles of impeachment, accusing the president of OBSTRUCTION OF JUSTICE, thwarting duly enacted federal laws, improperly removing military governors from the southern states, and attempting to bring into disgrace, ridicule, hatred, contempt, and reproach the CONGRESS OF THE UNITED STATES. Most historians consider all of the charges against Johnson to have been politically motivated, as the House of Representatives was controlled by radical Republicans who favored RECONSTRUCTION Era legislation that Johnson opposed.

In August 1867, Johnson tried to remove the last staunch Reconstructionist from his cabinet by dismissing Secretary of War EDWIN STANTON and replacing him with General ULYSSES S. GRANT. The Senate refused to approve the dismissal, so Johnson replaced Stanton with another general. One article of impeachment charged that Stanton's dismissal violated the TENURE OF OFFICE ACT, which prohibited the president from dismissing cabinet members without the Senate's approval.

Johnson's trial in the Senate commenced March 13, 1868, and lasted until May 26, 1868. Supreme Court Justice Salmon Chase presided. The Senate consisted of 45 Republicans and only nine Democrats. Thirty-six votes were required for conviction, so a party-line vote

would easily have removed Johnson. After voting on the first three articles of impeachment and failing to convict by a single vote on each of them (7 Republicans sided with 12 Democrats), the Senate adjourned without considering the other eight articles.

On July 27, 1974, the House Judiciary Committee approved three articles of impeachment against President Richard M. Nixon. The articles charged the president with obstruction of justice in trying to cover up the BURGLARY of DEMOCRATIC PARTY offices at the WATERGATE complex in Washington, D.C., ABUSE OF POWER for ordering the INTERNAL REVENUE SERVICE (IRS) to audit the taxes of political adversaries, and refusal to obey a SUBPOENA from the Judiciary Committee. A week later Nixon complied with a Supreme Court order compelling him to release the transcripts of three tape-recorded conversations of June 23, 1972, which demonstrated his involvement in, and knowledge of, the Watergate cover-up.

For example, the transcript of June 23, 1972, tape showed H. R. Haldeman, White House Chief of Staff, telling Nixon that campaign money had financed the Watergate burglary and Nixon telling Haldeman to use the CENTRAL INTELLIGENCE AGENCY (CIA) to curb a FEDERAL BUREAU OF INVESTIGATION (FBI) investigation of the money trail. This transcript was widely referred to as the "the smoking gun" tape because some Republicans had said they would not support impeachment until they found evidence of Nixon holding a "smoking gun" of guilt in his hand. With the public turning against Nixon and his approval rating hovering around twenty-five percent, Republican congressional leaders and some of the president's own aides put him under enormous pressure to resign. Three days after the tapes were released to the public, on August 8, 1974, President Nixon resigned. Nixon's resignation ended the impeachment inquiry, and following his resignation, President GERALD FORD pardoned Nixon for all crimes he may have committed as the nation's chief executive.

On December 19, 1998, the U.S. House of Representatives approved two articles of impeachment against Democratic president Clinton, accusing the president of having committed the crimes of PERJURY and obstruction of justice to conceal his relationship with former White-House intern Monica Lewinsky. The impeachment trial before the Senate began on January 7, 1999, and ended on February 12, 1999. Chief Justice WILLIAM REHNQUIST presided.

Like the impeachment trial of Andrew Johnson, the Clinton impeachment trial was also bitterly divided along party lines. The Senate was composed of 55 Republicans and 45 Democrats. However, several moderate Republicans privately questioned the propriety of impeaching a president whose job-approval ratings were at approximately 70 percent during a period when the STOCK MARKET was experiencing strong growth. Enough Republicans eventually joined all 45 Democrats in voting to ACQUIT the president on both articles of impeachment, neither article being supported by even a majority of votes, far short of the 67 votes required to convict.

FURTHER READINGS

Bowman, Frank O. III. 2001. "Falling Out of Love with America: The Clinton Impeachment and the Madisonian Constitution." *Maryland Law Review* 60.

Collier, Charles W., and Christopher Slobogin. 1999. "Terms of Endearment and Articles of Impeachment." *Florida Law Review* 51 (September).

Pious, Richard M. 1998. "The Constitutional and Popular Law of Presidential Impeachment." *Presidential Studies Quarterly* 28.

CROSS REFERENCES

Chase, Samuel, "The Samuel Chase Impeachment Trial" (Sidebar); Impeachment, "How Will the Trial of Bill Clinton Affect Future Impeachments?" (In Focus); Impeachment, "A Challenge to Impeachment" (Sidebar).

ARTICLES OF INCORPORATION

The document that must be filed with an appropriate government agency, commonly the office of the secretary of state, if the owners of a business want it to be given legal recognition as a corporation.

Articles of incorporation, sometimes called a certificate of incorporation, must set forth certain information as mandated by statute. Although laws vary from state to state, the purposes of the corporation and the rights and liabilities of shareholders and directors are typical provisions required in the document. Official forms are prescribed in many states.

Once the articles of incorporation are filed with the SECRETARY OF STATE, corporate existence begins. In some jurisdictions, a formal certificate of incorporation attached to a duplicate of the articles must be issued to the applicant before the business will be given legal status as a corporation.

ARTICLES OF ORGANIZATION

A document required to be filed with an appropriate state or local government agency, in order to establish legal recognition of a limited liability company (LLC). Articles of organization closely parallel articles of incorporation needed for legal creation and recognition of corporations.

Limited liability companies and corporations are creatures of statute. They do no exist, in the eyes of the law, until *articles of organization* or incorporation have been properly filed and accepted by the designated governmental agency—commonly the office of the SECRETARY OF STATE. A business owner is free to set up a LLC in any state; however, the state chosen becomes the state of *domicile* for such purposes as jurisdiction, employee and withholding taxes, and required annual filings.

Prior to filing articles of organization, a business owner must check with the state in which the articles will be filed to determine the availability of the chosen name for the new business entity. Most states do not require a specific format for the articles of organization. All states, however, do require specific minimum information to be contained within the articles. The required information includes the name of the new entity; the business form (e.g., LLC); a statement of general purpose; the name and address of an agent for SERVICE OF PROCESS; the form(s) of ownership interest (e.g., equitable and non-equitable ownership, voting and non-voting ownership, and other forms of ownership having different preferences. Limitations, rights, or duties); and the name(s) of initial owner(s) and manager(s). Standard forms are available in many states, which need only be completed and filed along with the corresponding administrative fee.

FURTHER READINGS

Max Filings, Inc. Web site. "Q&A: Limited Liability Companies (LLCs)." Available online at http://www.maxfilings.com/incorporation-knowledge-center/QA-limited-liability-companies-llc.php; website home page: http://www.maxfilings.com (accessed July 5, 2009).

Straub, Joseph T., and Raymond F. Attner. 1994. *Introduction to Business.* 5th ed. Belmont, CA: Wadsworth.

Toolkit Media Group Web site. 1995–2009. "Filing the Articles of Organization." Available online at http://www.toolkit.com/small_business_guide/sbg.aspx?nid=P12_6825; website home page: http://www.toolkit.com (accessed July 5, 2009).

Articles of Incorporation (For-Profit Corporation)

An example of for-profit articles of incorporation

ILLUSTRATION BY GGS CREATIVE RESOURCES. REPRODUCED BY PERMISSION OF GALE, A PART OF CENGAGE LEARNING.

INSTRUCTIONS:

STEP 1: CONTACT THE OFFICE OF THE SECRETARY OF STATE AT (334)242-5324 TO RESERVE A CORPORATE NAME.

STEP 2: TO INCORPORATE, FILE THE ORIGINAL, TWO COPIES OF THE ARTICLES OF INCORPORATION AND THE CERTIFICATE OF NAME RESERVATION IN THE COUNTY WHERE THE CORPORATION'S REGISTERED OFFICE IS LOCATED. THE SECRETARY OF STATE'S FILING FEE IS $40. PLEASE CONTACT THE JUDGE OF PROBATE TO VERIFY FILING FEES.

PURSUANT TO THE PROVISIONS OF THE ALABAMA BUSINESS CORPORATION ACT, THE UNDERSIGNED HEREBY ADOPTS THE FOLLOWING ARTICLES OF INCORPORATION.

ARTICLE I

The name of the corporation:

_____

ARTICLE II

The duration of the corporation is "perpetual" unless otherwise stated.

ARTICLE III

The corporation has been organized for the following purpose(s):

_____

_____

_____

ARTICLE IV

The number of shares which the corporation shall have the authority to issue is _____.

ARTICLE V

The **street address** (NO PO BOX) of the registered office: _____

_____ and the name of the registered agent at that office: _____

_____.

ARTICLE VI

The name(s) and address(es) of the Director(s):

_____

_____

_____.

ARTICLE VII

The name(s) and address(es) of the Incorporator(s):

_____

_____.

Any provision that is not inconsistent with the law for the regulation of the internal affairs of the corporation or for the restriction of the transfer of shares may be added.

IN WITNESS THEREOF, the undersigned incorporator executed these Articles of Incorporation

on this the _____ day of _____, 20____.

Printed Name and Business Address of Person Preparing this Document:

_____
Type or Print Name of Incorporator

_____
Signature of Incorporator

Rev. 7/03

CROSS REFERENCES

Articles of Incorporation; Jurisdiction.

ARTICLES OF PARTNERSHIP

A written compact by which parties agree to pool their money, labor, and/or skill to carry on a business for profit. The parties sign the compact with the understanding that they will share proportionally the losses and profits according to the provisions and conditions that they have mutually assented would govern their business relationship.

CROSS REFERENCE

Partnership.

ARTICLES OF WAR

Codes created to prescribe the manner in which the armed services of a nation are to be governed.

For example, the UNIFORM CODE OF MILITARY JUSTICE is an article of war applied to the Army, the Navy, the Coast Guard, and the Air Force of the United States.

CROSS REFERENCE

Military Law.

ARTIFICIAL INSEMINATION

The process by which a woman is medically impregnated using semen from her husband or from a third-party donor.

Artificial insemination is employed in cases of infertility or impotence, or as a means by which an unmarried woman may become pregnant. The procedure, which has been used since the 1940s, involves injecting collected semen into the woman's uterus and is performed under a physician's supervision.

Artificial insemination raises a number of legal concerns. Most states' laws provide that a child born as a result of artificial insemination using the husband's sperm, referred to as AIH, is presumed to be the husband's legal child. When a child is born after artificial insemination using the sperm of a third-party donor, referred to as AID, the law is less clear. Some states stipulate that the child is presumed to be the legal child of the mother and her husband, whereas others leave open the possibility that the child could be declared illegitimate.

Artificial insemination has grown in popularity as infertility becomes more prevalent and as more women opt to become single mothers. Eighty thousand such procedures using donor sperm are performed each year, resulting in the births of thirty thousand babies. By 1990 artificial insemination was a $164 million industry involving eleven thousand private physicians, four hundred sperm banks, and more than two hundred fertility centers.

The practice of artificial insemination is largely unregulated, and secrecy surrounding the identity of donors and recipients is the norm. Surveys of parents indicate that most do not plan to tell their children the circumstances of their births. This raises ethical questions about the right of an individual to be informed about his or her heritage. People who inadvertently discover they were conceived through artificial insemination often experience distress and feelings of confused identity. Many doctors compound the problem by failing to keep records on the identities and medical histories of donors.

The legal minefield created by artificial insemination continues to erupt with new and unprecedented issues. In 1990 Julia Skolnick sued a fertility clinic and a sperm bank for NEGLIGENCE and MEDICAL MALPRACTICE, charging that they mistakenly substituted another man's sperm for that of her late husband. The woman, who is white, gave birth to a child with African American features, and DNA analysis confirmed that her husband, who was also white, could not have been the child's father. In another case, Junior Lewis Davis sued to prevent his ex-wife, Mary Sue Davis Stowe, from using or donating fertilized embryos the couple had frozen for later use. The Tennessee Supreme Court held that individuals have "procreational autonomy" and have the right to choose whether to have a child (*Davis v. Davis*, 842 S.W.2d 588 (Tenn. June 1992). Arthur L. Caplan, former director of the Center for Biomedical Ethics at the University of Minnesota, commented, "In this case, the court said that a man cannot be made to become a parent against his will." The *Davis* case raises the question of the right of a sperm donor to prevent the use of his sperm by specific individuals.

Serious health questions also surround the issue of artificial insemination. AIDS, hepatitis, and other infectious diseases pose risks to women undergoing the procedure and their potential children. Although the American

Fertility Society recommends that donors be tested for infectious diseases, the guidelines are not binding. In fact, some doctors merely request that donors answer questions about their health history and sex life, and only a handful of states require testing. This casual approach to donor screening can lead to disaster. In 1994 Mary Orsak, of Downey, California, sued the Tyler Medical Clinic, in Westwood, California, for negligence when she discovered she was HIV-positive as a result of artificial insemination with donor sperm. In at least six other cases, HIV transmission through artificial insemination has been confirmed.

Other legal pitfalls open up as technology makes artificial insemination more sophisticated and more available. Because sperm can be frozen for future use, a woman can be impregnated at any time, even after her husband's death. In 1990 Nancy Hart and Edward Hart, of Covington, Louisiana, anticipating that Edward might not survive his bout with cancer and knowing that chemotherapy might leave him sterile, decided to place a sample of his sperm in a New Orleans sperm bank. Edward died in June 1990. Three months later Nancy underwent artificial insemination using his sperm, and on June 4, 1991, their daughter Judith was born. Under Louisiana law (L.S.A.-C.C. Art. 185), the state would not acknowledge Edward as the child's father because she had been born more than three hundred days after his death. As a result, Nancy was unable to receive SOCIAL SECURITY survivors benefits for her daughter. She sued both the state of Louisiana and the federal government. In June 1995 Administrative Law Judge Elving Torres ruled that the Social Security Administration (SSA) must pay Judith a $10,000 lump sum and $700 per month in survivor's benefits. According to Torres, the DNA EVIDENCE presented to him proved that Judith is Nancy and Edward Hart's child.

Medical technology enables recipients of artificial insemination to select the sex of their offspring, which raises still more ethical questions. Some religions condemn this practice as unnatural, although other theologians disagree. Some commentators have even suggested that it is unethical and exploitative to offer expensive, difficult, painful, and frustrating fertility procedures to desperate people when there may be little chance that a successful pregnancy will result.

The legal, ethical, and medical quagmires created by artificial insemination have not deterred thousands of couples and single women from seeking the procedure. Artificial insemination is sometimes the best, if not the only, solution for a person determined to achieve pregnancy.

FURTHER READINGS

Bernstein, Gaia. 2002. "The Socio-Legal Acceptance of New Technologies: A Close Look at Artificial Insemination." *Washington Law Review* 77 (October).

Goldstein, Karen L., and Caryn H. Okinaga. 2002. "Assisted Reproductive Technology." *Georgetown Journal of Gender and the Law* 3 (spring).

Gunning, Jennifer, and Helen Szoke, eds. 2003. *The Regulation of Assisted Reproductive Technology.* Aldershot, Hampshire, England: Ashgate.

Ross, Jane O. 1999. "A Legal Analysis of Parenthood by Choice, Not Chance." *Texas Journal of Women and the Law* 9 (fall).

CROSS REFERENCES

Family Law; Illegitimacy; Parent and Child; Reproduction.

ARTIFICIAL PERSON

A legal entity that is not a human being but for certain purposes is considered by virtue of statute to be a natural person.

A corporation is considered an ARTIFICIAL PERSON for SERVICE OF PROCESS.

AS IS

A term used to describe a sales transaction in which the seller offers goods in their present, existing condition to prospective buyers.

The term *as is* gives notice to buyers that they are taking a risk on the quality of the goods. The buyer is free to inspect the goods before purchase; but if any hidden defects are discovered after purchase, the buyer has no recourse against the seller. Any implied or express warranties that usually accompany goods for sale are excluded in an "as is" sale. Contract law and the UNIFORM COMMERCIAL CODE regulate "as is" sales.

AS PER

A phrase commonly recognized to mean "in accordance with the terms of" a particular document—such as a contract, deed, or affidavit— or "as authorized by the contract."

John Ashcroft.
GETTY IMAGES

❖ ASHCROFT, JOHN DAVID

In 25 years, JOHN ASHCROFT ascended from assistant state attorney general for the state of Missouri to U.S. attorney general. The political road to the JUSTICE DEPARTMENT was paved by this conservative right-wing Republican with his hard work and strong ethics.

JOHN DAVID ASHCROFT was born on May 9, 1942, in Chicago, Illinois. His family moved to rural Springfield, Missouri, when he was just a young boy. Springfield is the home of the Pentecostal Assembly of God Church, and because Ashcroft's father and grandfather were Pentecostal ministers, it seemed only natural that the family would make Springfield their home. Whereas the church forbids smoking, drinking, and dancing, it does promote gospel singing. Ashcroft took up playing the guitar and singing gospel when he was young, and it was a passion of his ever after.

After high school Ashcroft headed east to Yale where he received a degree in history in 1964. He then returned to the Midwest and studied at the University of Chicago Law School. There he met his later wife, Janet. They both graduated from the University of Chicago in 1967 and went on to teach business law at Southwest Missouri State University.

In 1972 Ashcroft decided to run for a spot in the U.S. House of Representatives. While he lost the race, he still found his way into politics when he was named assistant attorney general for the state of Missouri in 1975 under then-attorney general, John Danforth. While working there, Ashcroft met future U.S. Supreme Court Justice CLARENCE THOMAS.

In 1976 Danforth decided to run for the U.S. Senate, giving Ashcroft the opportunity to campaign for the soon-to-be vacated state attorney general position. Ashcroft won the election and, in this new role, established his conservative reputation when he vehemently opposed court-ordered SCHOOL DESEGREGATION in St. Louis and Kansas City. While he could not please everybody, he managed to please many, and he was elected for another term before then becoming the 50th governor of Missouri in 1984.

Ashcroft accomplished a great deal for the state of Missouri. He balanced budgets without increasing taxes. He also focused on WELFARE reform and education by imposing tougher testing requirements for student advancement. As a validation of these efforts, Ashcroft was

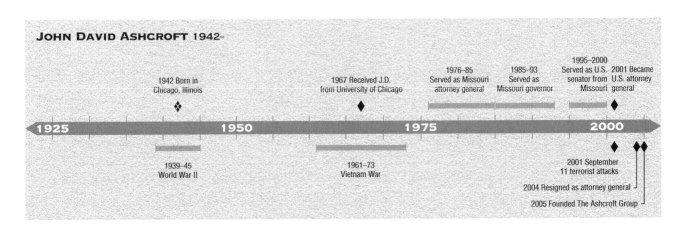

JOHN DAVID ASHCROFT 1942–

1942 Born in Chicago, Illinois

1967 Received J.D. from University of Chicago

1976–85 Served as Missouri attorney general

1985–93 Served as Missouri governor

1995–2000 Served as U.S. senator from Missouri

2001 Became U.S. attorney general

1925　　1950　　1975　　2000

1939–45 World War II

1961–73 Vietnam War

2001 September 11 terrorist attacks

2004 Resigned as attorney general

2005 Founded The Ashcroft Group

re-elected to a second term as governor with an impressive 65 percent of the vote. State law did not allow him to run for a third term.

In 1994 Ashcroft again followed in the footsteps of John Danforth, who was retiring from the Senate. Ashcroft was elected to the U.S. Senate and sworn in at the beginning of 1995. While in Congress, Ashcroft proposed and supported very conservative legislation, most of which did not become law. He was pro-life, against GUN CONTROL, and against AFFIRMATIVE ACTION. He sponsored the Human Life Amendment, which defined life to begin at conception and banned all abortions, including those involving incest or RAPE, except when needed to save the life of the mother. The legislation did not become law. He was also unsuccessful in his support for term limits for congressmen and prayer in schools. Ashcroft was, however, successful with his Charitable Choice provision, a component of the welfare reform legislation in 1996. The provision granted funding to religious organizations in order to provide social welfare programs.

In 1998 Ashcroft published a book, *Lessons from a Father to His Son,* about his father's preachings, his Christian faith, and how it influenced his life. Also in 1998 the Ronnie White confirmation hearings branded him by some as a racist. White was the first African American Missouri Supreme Court Justice. Then-president BILL CLINTON nominated him to the federal bench. During White's confirmation hearings, Ashcroft focused on a dissent that White made in a CAPITAL PUNISHMENT case and argued that White was soft on crime. Yet White had actually voted to uphold the death penalty in 41 of the 59 cases that he heard on the bench, and some argued that Ashcroft attacked White because of his race. Ultimately, the Senate voted down White, making him the first federal judicial nominee to be defeated since Robert Bork. That same year, Ashcroft seriously considered running for the REPUBLICAN PARTY nomination for U.S. president. After a short-lived campaign, however, he withdrew his name and supported GEORGE W. BUSH.

In 2000, Ashcroft ran once again for his Senate position, this time against Missouri governor Mel Carnahan. Carnahan died with his son in a plane crash three weeks *before* the election but still won the vote by a slim margin. Ashcroft was a gracious loser, and Carnahan's widow was appointed to replace her deceased husband in the Senate.

In 2001 Ashcroft was appointed by President Bush and confirmed by Congress for the position of U.S. attorney general, one of the most powerful positions in the country. As attorney general, Ashcroft became head of the Justice Department and would oversee many powerful segments of the federal government, including the DRUG ENFORCEMENT ADMINISTRATION, the FEDERAL BUREAU OF INVESTIGATION, and the U.S. Marshals.

The SEPTEMBER 11TH ATTACKS in 2001 caused an enormous change in the way Americans viewed the responsibilities of the nation's top law enforcement officials. In the aftermath of the attacks, Congress passed the Homeland Security Act and the USA Patriot Act, legislation that gave the Justice Department unprecedented latitude in dealing with suspected terrorists. In 2002 and early 2003, Ashcroft issued numerous regulations dealing with the issue of domestic security and the tracking of foreign nationals including orders that gave FBI agents and U.S. marshals permission to arrest such persons for IMMIGRATION violations when there was not sufficient evidence to hold them on criminal charges. The Justice Department stepped up its surveillance methods, including the issuance of "national security letters" that mandated businesses to turn over electronic records of finances and other information. Ashcroft also signed more than 170 classified "emergency foreign intelligence warrants," which allowed 72 hours of wiretaps and searches of persons viewed as national security THREATS before they needed to be reviewed and approved by the Foreign Intelligence Surveillance Court.

Groups representing Muslim immigrants, numerous civil liberties advocates, religious groups, and others protested much of the DOJ activity. One program that did not pass muster with Congress was the TERRORISM Information and Prevention System to be known by its acronym as "Operation TIPS." The program was planned to train millions of American workers including truck drivers, mail carriers, train conductors, and employees of utilities to look for and report any suspicious material or activity to a new FBI database.

Other Ashcroft initiatives that provoked controversy include the DOJ's challenge to an Oregon law that permits physician-assisted

OUR [ANTI-TERRORIST] EFFORTS HAVE BEEN CRAFTED CAREFULLY TO AVOID INFRINGING ON CONSTITUTIONAL RIGHTS, WHILE SAVING AMERICAN LIVES.
—JOHN ASHCROFT

SUICIDE and a California law that permits the possession of marijuana for medicinal use. In addition, Ashcroft filed a brief with the Supreme Court in support of ending the University of Michigan's affirmative action admission program. While in office, Ashcroft advocated protection for the rights of gun owners while pressing for more severe punishments of those who commited capital crimes using guns or other WEAPONS. Despite state moratoriums on capital punishment, exonerations of death row defendants in more than 100 cases, and Supreme Court decisions that banned the execution of mentally retarded inmates and overturned cases where judges rather than juries had imposed the death penalty, Ashcroft overruled U.S. attorneys who had decided not to seek the death penalty, and he approved death penalty prosecutions in nearly half of all federal cases where capital punishment might have been applicable.

Ashcroft resigned his position as attorney general in November of 2004. He was succeeded by ALBERTO GONZALES. On May 18, 2009, a lawsuit by Pakistani Muslim Javaid Iqbal against Ashcroft and FBI Director ROBERT S. MUELLER III charging abuse after the September 11th terrorist attacks was dismissed by the U.S. Supreme Court due to a lack of evidence. Four months later, however, the Ninth CIRCUIT COURT of Appeals ruled against Ashcroft in a similar case, giving Abdullah al-Kidd, a U.S. citizen, the right to sue Ashcroft for unlawful detainment.

As of late 2009, Ashcroft continues his work with the Kansas City (Missouri) law firm he founded, The Ashcroft Group.

FURTHER READINGS

Annual Accountability Report. 2002. Washington, DC: Department of Justice.

The Ashcroft Group. Available online at http://www.ashcroftgroupllc.com (accessed August 24, 2009).

Ashcroft, John. 1998. *Lessons from a Father to His Son.* Nashville: Thomas Nelson Publishers.

Branch-Brioso, Karen. March 5, 2003. "Ashcroft Reports Progress against Terrorism with Ridge and Mueller, He Tells Congress of Arrests, Better Information Sharing." *St. Louis Post-Dispatch.*

Cloud, John. 2001. "General on the March: John Ashcroft Wants to Mobilize the Justice Department to Fight Terror. Is He Going Too Far?" *Time.* (November 19).

Fechter, Michael. 2002. "Ashcroft Defends New Wiretap Powers." *The Tampa Tribune.* (November 21).

ASHWANDER RULES

A principle of constitutional law establishing judicial policy that courts should decide constitutional questions only when necessary and should decide the case on another basis if possible.

In *Ashwander v. Tennessee Valley Authority,* 297 U.S. 288, 56 S. Ct. 466, 80 L. Ed. 2d 688 (1936), Justice LOUIS BRANDEIS articulated a series of seven principles that apply to the Supreme Court's policy of deciding constitutional questions. These principles include the policy that the court: (1) should not decide a constitutional question in a FRIENDLY SUIT; (2) should not anticipate a question of CONSTITUTIONAL LAW; (3) should not create a rule of constitutional law that is broader than that called for by the facts of the case; (4) should not decide a constitutional issue if the case can be decided on another ground; (5) should not rule on the constitutionality of a statute unless the PLAINTIFF is harmed by the statute; (6) should not pass on the constitutionality if the plaintiff has accepted the benefits of the statute; and (7) should not rule on the constitutionality of an act of Congress without first analyzing whether the act can be fairly construed in a way that would avoid the constitutional question.

FURTHER READINGS

Farber, Daniel A. and Suzanna Sherry. 2009. *Judgment Calls: Principle and Politics in Constitutional Law.* New York: Oxford University Press.

Marks, Thomas C., Jr. 2008. "The Decline of American Culture: The Role of the Federal Judiciary." *Stetson Law Review.* 37 (spring).

CROSS REFERENCES

Constitutional Law; Jurisprudence

ASPORTATION

The removal of items from one place to another, such as carrying things away illegally.

Asportation is one of the elements required to establish the crime of LARCENY. In order to prove that asportation has occurred, it is not necessary to show that the goods were moved a substantial distance, but only that they were moved.

Asportation was one of the elements necessary to establish common-law KIDNAPPING, and in many states it remains as an element of statutory kidnapping.

ASSASSINATION

Assassination is murder committed by a perpetrator without the personal provocation of the victim, who is usually a government official.

First used in medieval times to describe the murders of prominent Christians by the Hashshashin, a secret Islamic sect, the word *assassination* is used in the twenty-first century to describe murders committed for political reasons, especially against government officials. Assassination may be used as a political weapon by a state as well as by an individual; it may be directed at the establishment or used by it.

The term *assassination* is generally applied only to political murders—in the United States, most commonly to attempts on the life of the president. However, the classification of any one incident as an assassination may be in part a matter of perception. The assassination of the outlaw Jesse James, in 1882, provides an example of the difficulties. Thomas T. Crittenden, governor of Missouri, assumed that being seen as responsible for the death of the notorious outlaw would be good for his political career. For this reason, Crittenden granted each of the killers a pardon in addition to a $10,000 reward. But the U.S. public spoke vehemently against James's killers, dubbing them assassins and his death an assassination. Crittenden was vilified by Americans, and his political career was destroyed.

It is not always easy to guess the motivations of those who attempt assassinations or to understand the historical and legal implications of their actions. The anti-constitutional nature of assassination has also made it a focal point for conspiracies and conspiracy theories. The first attempt at the assassination of a U.S. president was Richard Lawrence's attack on ANDREW JACKSON in 1835. Although a jury acquitted Lawrence on the ground of insanity, Jackson was convinced that the attack was part of a WHIG PARTY conspiracy.

The 1865 assassination of President ABRAHAM LINCOLN by John Wilkes Booth prompted its own set of theories. In a controversial decision, a military tribunal convicted nine people of conspiring in Lincoln's assassination. In the case of one of those hanged for the crime, Mary E. Surratt, all that could be proved was that she owned the rooming house in which the conspirators plotted. Nonetheless, high emotions at the end of the Civil War resulted in her execution. After sentiments cooled and talk of conspiracies calmed, the two surviving conspirators imprisoned for Lincoln's death gained pardons from President ANDREW JOHNSON.

President William McKinley was shot by Leon F. Czolgosz, on September 6, 1901, at the Pan-American Exposition in Buffalo, New York. McKinley died on September 14.
LIBRARY OF CONGRESS

Even greater controversy was caused when the public was deprived of the opportunity to see Lee Harvey Oswald tried for the assassination, in 1963, of President JOHN F. KENNEDY. Oswald's death at the hands of JACK RUBY sparked theories of conspiracy that ranged from Communist plots to Mafia hits to cover-ups by U.S. officials. President LYNDON B. JOHNSON appointed a group of national figures, led by Supreme Court Chief Justice EARL WARREN, to investigate the assassination and issue a report. The WARREN COMMISSION concluded that Oswald had acted alone.

Despite this conclusion, conspiracy theories remained widespread in books and in films such as Oliver Stone's *JFK: The Untold Story* (released in 1991). In an attempt to calm public suspicions surrounding the Kennedy assassination, the President John F. Kennedy Assassination Records Collection Act of 1992 (44 U.S.C.A. § 2107) was passed by Congress. The act released much of the Kennedy assassination material in government files. As of 2009, its effectiveness at stilling concern over a possible conspiracy remained to be seen.

It has become clear that the public demands a thorough investigation of any attempt on a president's life. Because it is a crime to advocate the assassination of any U.S. president, president-elect, VICE PRESIDENT, vice president-elect, or anyone legally acting as president (18 U.S.C. 1751), even THREATS are carefully investigated. In U.S. history, four presidents have lost their lives to assassins: Abraham Lincoln, JAMES GARFIELD, WILLIAM MCKINLEY, and John F. Kennedy.

Political Assassination by U.S Government Employees

In 1974 the Congress established a committee to investigate possible U.S. involvement in plots to assassinate foreign leaders deemed hostile to U.S. interests. Specifically, the committee investigated the alleged involvement of the CENTRAL INTELLIGENCE AGENCY (CIA) in plots to kill Patrice Lumumba of the Congo, Fidel Castro of Cuba, Rafael Trujillo of the Dominican Republic, Rene Schneider of Chile, and Ngo Dinh Diem of South Vietnam. The absence of a written record and the failing memories of principal WITNESSES prevented the committee from conclusively demonstrating that presidents Eisenhower, Kennedy, or Nixon personally authorized the assassination of any foreign leader. However, the evidence did show that between 1960 and 1970, the CIA was involved in several assassination plots.

The committee reported its findings in 1975 to a dismayed Congress. Public outcry was loud and immediate. At the urging of both the House of Representatives and the Senate, President GERALD R. FORD signed an EXECUTIVE ORDER banning all federal employees from committing assassination as a tool of U.S foreign policy or for any other reason (Exec. Order No. 11905). The order was extended by President RONALD REAGAN (who survived an assassination attempt) 15 years later to also preclude hired assassins. Title 18 U.S.C. §§ 2381 and 2385 (1976) prohibits the assassination of any officer of state or federal government.

Following the September 11, 2001, terrorist attacks in New York City and Washington, D.C., Congress and the White House revisited the propriety of political assassinations committed by members of the U.S. government. In December 2002, according to a *Globe and Mail* news story, President GEORGE W. BUSH gave the CIA written authority to kill about two dozen terrorist leaders if capturing them proved to be impractical and civilian casualties could not be minimized. The CIA relied on that authority in using a pilotless Predator aircraft to fire a Hellfire antitank missile at a car in Yemen carrying an al-Qaeda operative. The al-Qaeda operative and five other people died in the attack.

In July 2009 both the *New York Times* and *Wall Street Journal* published articles expounding on the CIA's sequential plans to target and kill identified terrorists. The plans were formally abandoned in mid-2009 by CIA director Leon Panetta after he advised congressional intelligence committees that he himself had just learned of the scope of the plans; they initially had been kept secret by the CIA's counterterrorism center under the order of former vice president Dick Cheney. According to the *Times* article, law professor Kenneth Anderson of American University noted that as far back as 1989 the United States had argued that killing terrorists did not violate federal law as it would constitute a legal act of SELF-DEFENSE under INTERNATIONAL LAW. Such killings would be premised on the condition that authorities in the country where the terrorist was located were either unable or unwilling to prevent the terrorist from proceeding. But international law experts rebutted Anderson's justification with their own concerns. They cited the potential for violating the SOVEREIGNTY of the country where the terrorist was killed, the differing legal status between the CIA and the uniformed military, and whether such a killing would fall under the purview of the law of war.

FURTHER READINGS

Allen Chair Symposium 2002. 2003. "Political Assassination as an Instrument of National Policy: An Inquiry into Operations, Expediency, Morality, and Law." *Univ. of Richmond Law Review* (March).

"C.I.A. Had Secret Al Qaeda Plan." 2009. *Wall Street Journal,* July 13.

Donoghue, Mary Agnes. 1975. *Assassination: Murder in Politics.* Chatsworth, Calif.: Major Books.

Edwards, William C., and Edward Steers. 2009. *The Lincoln Assassination: The Evidence.* Champaign, Ill.: Univ. of Illinois Press.

Harder, Tyler J. 2002. "Time to Repeal the Assassination Ban of Executive Order 12,333: A Small Step in Clarifying Current Law." *Military Law Review* 172 (June).

Mazetti, Mark, and Scott Shane. 2009. "C.I.A. Had Plan to Assassinate Qaeda Leaders." *New York Times,* July 14.

McKinley, James. 1977. *Assassination in America.* New York: Harper & Row.

Taylor, Stuart, Jr. 1998. "Assassination as Self-defense." *New York Law Journal* (November 30).

CROSS REFERENCE

Lincoln, Abraham, "Lincoln Assassination Conspiracy" (In Focus).

ASSAULT

At common law, an intentional act by one person that creates an apprehension in another of an imminent harmful or offensive contact.

An assault is carried out by a threat of bodily harm coupled with an apparent, present ability to cause the harm. It is both a crime and a tort and, therefore, may result in either criminal or civil liability. Generally, the COMMON LAW definition is the same in criminal and TORT LAW. There is, however, an additional CRIMINAL LAW category of assault consisting of an attempted but unsuccessful battery.

Statutory definitions of assault in the various jurisdictions throughout the United States are not substantially different from the common-law definition.

Elements

Generally, the essential elements of assault consist of an act intended to cause an apprehension of harmful or offensive contact that causes apprehension of such contact in the victim.

The act required for an assault must be overt. Although words alone are insufficient, they might create an assault when coupled with some action that indicates the ability to carry out the threat. A mere threat to harm is not an assault; however, a threat combined with a raised fist might be sufficient if it causes a reasonable apprehension of harm in the victim.

Intent is an essential element of assault. In tort law, it can be specific intent—if the assailant intends to cause the apprehension of harmful or offensive contact in the victim—or general intent—if he or she intends to do the act that causes such apprehension. In addition, the intent element is satisfied if it is substantially certain, to a REASONABLE PERSON, that the act will cause the result. A DEFENDANT who holds a gun to a victim's head possesses the requisite intent, because it is substantially certain that this act will produce an apprehension in the victim. In all cases, intent to kill or harm is irrelevant.

In criminal law, the attempted battery type of assault requires a SPECIFIC INTENT to commit battery. An intent to frighten will not suffice for this form of assault.

There can be no assault if the act does not produce a true apprehension of harm in the victim. There must be a reasonable fear of injury. The usual test applied is whether the act would induce such apprehension in the mind of a reasonable person. The status of the victim is taken into account. A threat made to a child might be sufficient to constitute an assault, while an identical threat made to an adult might not.

Virtually all jurisdictions agree that the victim must be aware of the danger. This element is not required, however, for the attempted battery type of assault. A defendant who throws a rock at a sleeping victim can only be guilty of the attempted battery assault, because the victim would not be aware of the possible harm.

Aggravated Assault

An AGGRAVATED ASSAULT, punishable in all states as a FELONY, is committed when a defendant intends to do more than merely frighten the victim. Common types of aggravated assaults are those accompanied by an intent to kill, rob, or RAPE. An assault with a dangerous weapon is

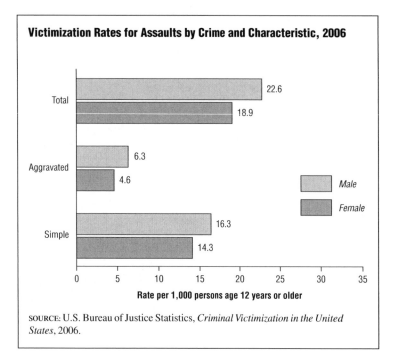

Victimization Rates for Assaults by Crime and Characteristic, 2006

Total: Male 22.6, Female 18.9

Aggravated: Male 6.3, Female 4.6

Simple: Male 16.3, Female 14.3

Rate per 1,000 persons age 12 years or older

Male
Female

SOURCE: U.S. Bureau of Justice Statistics, *Criminal Victimization in the United States*, 2006.

ILLUSTRATION BY GGS CREATIVE RESOURCES. REPRODUCED BY PERMISSION OF GALE, A PART OF CENGAGE LEARNING.

aggravated if there is an intent to cause serious harm. Pointing an unloaded gun at a victim to frighten the individual is not considered an aggravated assault.

Punishment

A defendant adjudged to have committed civil assault is liable for damages. The question of the amount that should be awarded to the victim is determined by a jury. COMPENSATORY DAMAGES, which are aimed at compensating the victim for the injury, are common. NOMINAL DAMAGES, a small sum awarded for the invasion of a right even though there has been no substantial injury, may be awarded. In some cases, courts allow PUNITIVE DAMAGES, which are designed to punish the defendant for the wrongful conduct.

The punishment for criminal assault is a fine, imprisonment, or both. Penalties are more severe when the assault is aggravated. Many states have statutes dividing criminal assault into various degrees. As in aggravated assault, the severity of the crime, the extent of violence and harm, and the criminal intent of the defendant are all factors considered in determining the sentence imposed.

FURTHER READINGS

Brewer, James. D. 1994. *The Danger from Strangers: Confronting the Threat of Assault.* New York: Insight Books.

Duhaime, Lloyd. "Assault." *Duhaime.org.* Available online at http://www.duhaime.org/LegalDictionary/A/Assault.aspx; website home page: http://www.duhaime.org (accessed August 28, 2009).

National Center for Victims of Crime Web site. "Assault Victimization." Washington, D.C.: Justice Department. Available online at http://www.ojp.usdoj.gov/ovc/publications/infores/help_series/pdftxt/assaultvictimization.pdf; website home page: http://www.ojp.usdoj.gov (accessed August 28, 2009).

ASSAULT AND BATTERY

Two separate offenses against the person that when used in one expression may be defined as any unlawful and unpermitted touching of another. Assault is an act that creates an apprehension in another of an imminent, harmful, or offensive contact. The act consists of a threat of harm accompanied by an apparent, present ability to carry out the threat. Battery is a harmful or offensive touching of another.

The main distinction between the two offenses is the existence or nonexistence of a touching or contact. While contact is an essential element of battery, there must be an absence of contact for assault. Sometimes assault is defined loosely to include battery.

Assault and battery are offenses in both criminal and TORT LAW; therefore, they can give rise to criminal or civil liability. In CRIMINAL LAW, an assault may additionally be defined as any attempt to commit a battery.

At COMMON LAW, both offenses were misdemeanors. As of the early 2000s, under virtually all criminal codes, they are either misdemeanors or felonies. They are characterized as FELONIOUS when accompanied by a criminal intent, such as an intent to kill, rob, or RAPE, or when they are committed with a dangerous weapon.

Intent

Intent is an essential element of both offenses. Generally, it is only necessary for the DEFENDANT to have an intent to do the act that causes the harm. In other words, the act must be done voluntarily. Although an intent to harm the victim is likely to exist, it is not a required element of either offense. There is an exception to this rule for the attempted battery type of criminal assault. If a defendant who commits this crime does not have an intent to harm the victim, the individual cannot be guilty of the offense.

Defenses Consent

In almost all states, consent is a defense to civil assault and battery. Some jurisdictions hold that in the case of mutual combat, consent will not suffice and either party may sue the other. Jurisdictions also differ on the question of whether consent is a defense to criminal assault and battery.

Consent must be given voluntarily in order to constitute a defense. If it is obtained by FRAUD or duress or is otherwise unlawful, it will not suffice. When an act exceeds the scope of the given consent, the defense is not available. A person who participates in a football game implies consent to a certain amount of physical contact; however, the individual is not deemed to consent to contact beyond what is commonly permitted in the sport.

Self-Defense Generally, a person may use whatever degree of force is reasonably necessary for protection from bodily harm. Whether this defense is valid is usually determined by a jury. A person who initiates a fight cannot claim SELF-DEFENSE unless the opponent responded with a greater and unforeseeable degree of force. When an aggressor retreats and is later attacked by the same opponent, the defense may be asserted.

The use of DEADLY FORCE in response may be justified if it is initially used by the aggressor. The situation must be such that a REASONABLE PERSON would be likely to fear for his or her life. In some states, a person must retreat prior to using deadly force if the individual can do so in complete safety. A majority of states, however, allow a person to stand his or her ground even though there is a means of safe escape.

Whether the degree of force used is reasonable depends upon the circumstances. The usual test applied involves determining whether a reasonable person in a similar circumstance would respond with a similar amount of force. Factors such as age, size, and strength of the parties are also considered.

Defense of Others Going to the aid of a person in distress is a valid defense, provided the defender is free from fault. In some states, the defender is treated as though he or she stands in the shoes of the person protected. The defender's right to claim defense of others depends upon whether the person protected had a justified claim of self-defense. In a minority of jurisdictions, the defense may be asserted if the defender reasonably believed the THIRD PARTY was in need of aid.

Defense of Property Individuals may use a reasonable amount of force to protect their property. The privilege to defend one's property is more limited than that of self-defense because society places a lesser value on property than on the integrity of human beings. Deadly force is usually not permitted. In most states, however, deadly force might be justified if it is used to prevent or stop a FELONY. An owner of real property or a person who rightfully possesses it, such as a tenant, may use force against a trespasser. Generally, a request to leave the property must be made before the application of force, unless the request would be futile. The amount of force used must be reasonable, and, unless it is necessary for self-defense, the infliction of bodily harm upon an intruder is improper. Courts have traditionally been more liberal in allowing the use of force to protect one's dwelling. Subsequent cases, however, indicated that there must be a threat to the personal safety of the occupants.

The states are divided on the question of whether a person who is legally entitled to property may use force to recover possession of it. In most jurisdictions, a landowner is not liable for assault and battery if the owner forcibly expels someone who is wrongfully on the property. The owner must not, however, use excessive force, and the fact that the person may not be held civilly liable does not relieve the owner of criminal liability. In some states, the use of force against a person wrongfully in possession of land is not permitted unless such person has tortiously dispossessed the actor or the actor's predecessor in title.

If possession of real or PERSONAL PROPERTY is in dispute, the universal rule is that force cannot be used. The dispute must be settled by a court.

With respect to personal property, the general view is that an owner may not commit an assault or battery upon the wrongdoer in order to recover property. A majority of jurisdictions recognize the right of an owner in HOT PURSUIT of stolen property to use a reasonable amount of force to retrieve it. In some states, stolen property may be taken back peaceably wherever it is found, even if it is necessary to enter another's premises. In all cases, the infliction of an unreasonable amount of harm will VITIATE the defense.

Performance of Duty and Authority A person may use REASONABLE FORCE when it becomes necessary in the course of performing a duty. A police officer, for example, may use force when apprehending a criminal. In some jurisdictions, private citizens may also use reasonable force to stop a crime being committed in their presence. Certain businesses, such as restaurants or nightclubs, are authorized to hire employees who may use reasonable force to remove persons who disturb other patrons. Court officers, such as judges, may order the removal of disruptive persons who interfere with their duties.

Persons with authority in certain relationships, such as parents or teachers, may use force as a disciplinary measure, provided they do not exceed the scope of their authority. Punishment may not be cruel or excessive.

Punishment

The law considers an assault and battery to be an invasion of the personal security of the victim for which the wrongdoer is required to pay for damages. The determination of the amount of damages to which a victim might be entitled if a defendant is found civilly liable is usually made by a jury. Generally, a PLAINTIFF is entitled to COMPENSATORY DAMAGES that compensate for injuries that are both directly and indirectly related to the wrong. Examples of compensatory damages include damages for pain and suffering, damages for medical expenses, and damages for lost earnings resulting from the victim's inability to work. NOMINAL DAMAGES, given although there is no harm at all, or merely a slight one, may also be awarded in an assault and battery action. Some jurisdictions allow the award of PUNITIVE DAMAGES. They are often given when the offense was committed wantonly or maliciously to punish the defendant for the wrongful act and to deter others from engaging in similar acts in the future. The defendant might additionally be subject to criminal liability.

If a defendant is found criminally liable, the punishment is imprisonment, a fine, or both. The amount of time a defendant must serve in prison depends upon the statute in the particular jurisdiction. When the offense is committed with an intent to MURDER or do serious harm, it is called AGGRAVATED ASSAULT and battery. An aggravated assault and battery is often committed with a dangerous weapon, and it is punishable as a felony in all states.

FURTHER READINGS

Brewer, J. D. 1994. *The Danger from Strangers: Confronting the Threat of Assault.* New York: Insight.

The Henry Law Firm (Philadelphia) Web site. 2009. "Assault & Battery." Available online at http://www.henryfirm.com/CM/FSDP/PracticeCenter/Criminal-Law/Assault.asp?focus=topic&id=1; website home page: http://www.henryfirm.com (accessed August 28, 2009).

Larson, Aaron. 2003. "Assault and Battery." *ExpertLaw Library.* Available online at http://www.expertlaw.com/library/personal_injury/assault_battery.html; website home page: http://www.expertlaw.com (accessed August 28, 2009).

CROSS REFERENCE

Hot Pursuit; Nominal Damages; Personal Property; Punitive Damages; Real Property.

ASSEMBLY

The congregation of a number of persons at the same location.

Popularly-elected political assemblies are those mandated by the Constitution and laws, such as the general assembly. The lower, or more populous, arm of the legislature in several states is also known as the *House of Assembly* or the *Assembly.*

Under the FIRST AMENDMENT to the United States Constitution, "Congress shall make no law ... abridging ... the right of the people peaceably to assemble." When a governmental unit sets aside property for the public use, the property is designed as a "public forum" for First Amendment purposes, and the governmental unit must properly allow the exercise by the public of constitutional rights, including freedom of assembly. Examples of public forums include sidewalks, parks, and libraries. The right to assemble includes the right to PROTEST, although rights of assembly are generally balanced with the need for public order. The Supreme Court has held that local governments may constitutionally require those participating in public parades first to obtain a permit to do so. However, the Court has held that an organizer of a parade cannot constitutionally examine the content of a message of a parade applicant in determining whether to grant to parade permit. *Forsyth County, Ga. v. Nationalist Movement,* 505 U.S. 123, 112 S. Ct. 2395, 120 L. Ed. 2d 101 (1992).

CROSS REFERENCES

First Amendment; Freedom of Speech; Public Lands.

ASSENT

An intentional approval of known facts that are offered by another for acceptance; agreement; consent.

Express assent is manifest confirmation of a position for approval. *Implied assent* is that which the law presumes to exist because the conduct of the parties demonstrates their intentions. *Mutual assent,* sometimes called the meeting of the minds of the parties, is the reciprocal agreement of each party to accept all the terms and conditions in a contract.

ASSESS

To determine financial worth. To ascertain the amount of damages. To fix and adjust the individual shares to be contributed by several persons toward a common beneficial objective in proportion to the benefit each person will receive. To tax by having qualified experts estimate the value of property by considering the nature of the property, its size, the value of other comparable property, and the proportionate share of services that is used by that property. To levy a charge on the owner of property that has been improved at the expense of the local government unit, such as when sewers or sidewalks are installed.

ASSESSED VALUATION

The financial worth assigned to property by taxing authorities that is used as a basis or factor against which the tax rate is applied.

A prescribed amount of the value of each unit must be paid as taxes in the future. In most cases, the assessed value is not representative of the FAIR MARKET VALUE of the property.

ASSESSMENT

The process by which the financial worth of property is determined. The amount at which an item is valued. A demand by the board of directors of a corporation for the payment of any money that is still owed on the purchase of capital stock. The determination of the amount of damages to be awarded to a plaintiff who has been successful in a lawsuit. The ascertainment of the pro rata share of taxes to be paid by members of a group of taxpayers who have directly benefited from a particular common goal or project according to the benefit conferred upon the individual or his or her property. This is known as a special assessment. The listing and valuation of property for purposes
of fixing a tax upon it for which its owner will be liable. The procedure by which the Internal Revenue Service, or other government department of taxation, declares that a taxpayer owes additional tax because, for example, the individual has understated personal gross income or has taken deductions to which he or she is not entitled. This process is also known as a *deficiency assessment.*

ASSET

Real or personal property, whether tangible or intangible, that has financial value and can be used for the payment of its owner's debts.

An *accrued asset* is one that arises from revenue earned but not yet due. For example, an accrued dividend is a share of the net earnings of a corporation that has been declared but has not yet been paid out to its shareholder(s).

In BANKRUPTCY, an asset is any form of property owned by a debtor who is insolvent that is not exempt from being used to repay debts.

For INCOME TAX purposes, a *capital asset* is property held by a taxpayer for personal enjoyment or investment, such as a home, furniture, stocks and bonds, or an automobile, but does not include inventory, commercial accounts, and notes receivable, depreciable property, commercial property, copyrights, and short-term government obligations. When a capital asset is sold, any gain received is given preferential tax treatment.

A *current, liquid,* or *quick asset* is an item that can be readily converted to cash, such as stocks and bonds.

A *fixed asset* is one of a permanent or long-term nature used in the operation of a business and not intended for sale.

A *frozen asset* is one that cannot be easily converted into cash, such as REAL ESTATE when there is no market, or that cannot be used because of a legal restriction, such as a SPENDTHRIFT TRUST.

An intangible asset is one to which an arbitrary dollar value is attached because it has no intrinsic MARKET VALUE but represents financial value, such as the GOOD WILL of a business, TRADEMARKS, or PATENTS.

ASSIGN

To transfer to another, as to assign one's right to receive rental income from property to another. To designate for a particular function, as to assign an attorney to defend an indigent in a criminal prosecution. To specify or point out, as to assign errors in a lower court proceeding on a writ of error that is submitted to request a court to reverse the judgment of the lower court.

ASSIGNED ACCOUNT

A type of secured transaction whereby an account receivable is pledged to a bank, factor, or other lender to secure the repayment of a loan.

It is common commercial practice for a manufacturer or wholesaler to sell inventory on OPEN ACCOUNT, a debt owed to the seller of inventory that is to be repaid by its buyer as the merchandise is sold. This arrangement creates an ACCOUNT RECEIVABLE that the seller uses as collateral for a loan.

ASSIGNED RISK

A danger or hazard of loss or injury that an insurer will not normally accept for coverage under a policy issued by the insurer, but that the insurance company is required by state law to offer protection against by participating in a pool of insurers who are also compelled to provide coverage.

ASSIGNED RISK PLAN

An insurance plan created and imposed by state statute under which persons who normally would be denied insurance coverage as bad risks are permitted to purchase insurance from a pool of insurers who must offer coverage to such individuals.

ASSIGNMENT

A transfer of rights in real property or personal property to another that gives the recipient—the transferee—the rights that the owner or holder of the property—the transferor—had prior to the transfer.

An *assignment of wages* is the transfer of the right to collect wages from the wage earner to his or her creditor. Statutes regulate the extent to which an assignment may be made.

ASSIGNMENT FOR BENEFIT OF CREDITORS

The voluntary transfer of all or most of a debtor's property to another person in trust so that he or she will collect any money that is owed to the debtor, sell the debtor's property, and apply the money received to the payment of the debts, returning any surplus to the debtor.

The debtor is the *assignor,* the transferor; and the person who takes LEGAL TITLE to the property is the *assignee.*

Types

There are three types of assignments that are categorized according to the limitations imposed upon the arrangement. A general assignment is one involving the transfer of all the debtor's property for the benefit of all his or her creditors. A partial assignment is one in which only part of a debtor's property is transferred to benefit all the creditors. When property is assigned to benefit only designated creditors, it is a special assignment.

The assignment results in the property being beyond the control of the debtor. It is different from agency arrangements, pledges, or mortgages.

Trust Law

Unless otherwise expressly provided, trust law governs assignments for the benefit of creditors. The assignee is considered a trustee and his or her duties and responsibilities to the debtor's creditors are the same as a trustee's to the beneficiaries of a trust. The document that embodies the terms of the assignment authorizes the assignee to liquidate the debtor's property in satisfaction of the creditors' claims against the debtor as quickly as possible. Under COMMON LAW, this was the assignee's chief function. Even if the assignment instrument does not expressly empower an assignee to sell the property, the assignee still has the power to do so in order to pay the creditors.

Creation

It is not necessary for a debtor to obtain the consent of creditors before making an assignment for their benefit. An owner of property has a right to transfer legal title to it by virtue of ownership. The limitation derived from common law that is placed upon its creation is that it cannot be done to dishonestly deprive a debtor's creditors of their rights to have property sold to repay debts. When an assignment for the benefit of creditors is intended by the debtor to place his or her property beyond the legal reach of creditors, it is called a FRAUDULENT CONVEYANCE. This type of assignment is void, or legally ineffective, under statutes that prohibit such arrangements. An assignment by which the assignor-debtor retains any interest, benefit, or advantage from the conveyance, such as keeping the right to revoke the assignment, made to DEFRAUD creditors is also a fraudulent conveyance, as is an assignment by which the assignee is required to delay liquidation of the assets.

In some jurisdictions, a partial assignment is considered a fraudulent conveyance because the creditors are hindered and delayed in receiving payment if they must seek payment from the debtor after first being referred to the assignee. Other jurisdictions treat any assignment by a solvent debtor as fraudulent on the theory that such an arrangement prevents the immediate sale of the property so that creditors are delayed and hindered.

Deficiency

A debtor is still liable to pay his or her creditors if the proceeds from the sale of personal and real property pursuant to an assignment for the benefit of creditors are not sufficient to completely repay the debts. When, however, creditors agree to accept the proceeds in satisfaction of the

debtor's obligations, such an agreement is called a COMPOSITION WITH CREDITORS. For this reason, assignments for the benefit of creditors are used by corporate, rather than individual, debtors.

Because preferences are permissible under common law, a common-law assignment for the benefit of creditors that provides for preferential payments to designated creditors is not a fraudulent conveyance. Most courts have held that debtors cannot use preferences to obtain discharges from creditors by conditioning preferences on their release from unpaid portions of their debts. To do so is considered a fraudulent conveyance, because a creditor would have to accept virtually any condition that the debtor decided upon if the creditor were to receive any money from the assignee.

Legality of Assignments

Most states have enacted statutes that regulate assignments for the benefit of creditors. Some states require that an assignment must comply with statutory requirements or be invalid, whereas in others the debtor may make a common-law assignment, which is regulated by

---

Assignment for the Benefit of Creditors

This agreement is made between _____ [*name of assignor*] ("Assignor"),

residing at _____ [*address*], and

_____ [*name of assignee(s)*] ("Assignee(s)"),

residing at _____ [*address*].

The Assignor is unable to pay in full and desires to assign all of [*his/her*] property to Assignee for the purpose of the payment of this debt. Therefore, the Assignor hereby assigns, conveys, grants, and transfers to Assignee all of Assignor's property and interests in property, whether real or personal, tangible or intangible (except property exempt by law from levy and sale under execution) wherever situated, in trust for the benefit of the Assignee.

[*Include description of the property and assets conveyed to the Assignee*]

DATED on _____ _____, 20_____ at:

_____
Assignor

ACCEPTED BY:

_____
Assignee

A sample assignment for the benefit of creditors

ILLUSTRATION BY GGS CREATIVE RESOURCES. REPRODUCED BY PERMISSION OF GALE, A PART OF CENGAGE LEARNING.

common law, or a statutory assignment, which is controlled by applicable statutes.

The state statutes require that the assignment be recorded, schedules of assets and liabilities be filed, notice be given to the creditors, the assignee be bonded, and the assignor be supervised by the court. Almost every jurisdiction prohibits the granting of a preference. All creditors except those with liens or statutorily created priorities are treated equally. Some statutes empower an assignee to set aside prior fraudulent conveyances, and others authorize the assignee to set aside preferences made before the assignment.

If a debtor has made substantial preferences, fraudulent conveyances, or allowed liens voidable in BANKRUPTCY to attach to his or her property, then creditors might be able to force the debtor into bankruptcy if they decide that the assignment does not adequately protect their rights. An efficiently handled assignment for benefit of creditors is frequently more advantageous to creditors than bankruptcy because it usually brings about better liquidation prices and its less rigid and formal structure saves time and money.

FURTHER READINGS

Buckley, Mike C., and Gregory Sterling. 2003. "What Banks Need to Know about ABCs." *Banking Law Journal* 120 (January).

Kupetz, David S. 2003. "Assignment for the Benefit of Creditors: Exit Vehicle of Choice for Many Dot-Com, Technology, and Other Troubled Enterprises." *Journal of Bankruptcy Law and Practice* 11 (November-December).

ASSIGNS

Individuals to whom property is, will, or may be transferred by conveyance, will, descent and distribution, or statute; assignees.

The term *assigns* is often found in deeds; for example, "heirs, administrators, and assigns to denote the assignable nature of the interest or right created."

ASSISTANCE, WRIT OF

A court order issued to enforce an existing judgment.

ASSISTED SUICIDE

Assisted suicide is the means by which an individual chooses to end his or her life via the help of another person, who may either share relevant medical knowledge or offer medical assistance. Forms of assisted suicide include active and passive euthanasia and physician-assisted suicide.

As a general matter, passive euthanasia is a generally accepted practice associated with an individual's right to refuse medical treatment. Conversely, active euthanasia and physician-assisted suicide have traditionally been proscribed throughout the United States, though movements in a small number of states have sought to allow terminally ill patients to hasten death through more active means. As of 2009, two states have enacted statutes allowing for assisted suicide, and the issue is being litigated and otherwise debated in other states.

Physicians abide by the Hippocratic Oath as a code of ethics. The oath is: "I will follow that method of treatment, which, according to my ability and judgment, I consider for the benefit of my patients, and abstain from whatever is deleterious and mischievous. I will give no deadly medicine to anyone if asked, nor suggest any such counsel." The American Medical Association takes a stance in line with this oath, strictly forbidding physicians from participating in assisted suicide because such a practice is "fundamentally incompatible with the physician's role as healer, would be difficult or impossible to control, and would pose serious societal risks."

The majority of states have outlawed assisted suicide through legislation, while courts in other states have determined that assisted suicide is a crime under common law. Since the 1990s, though, several states have considered proposals to allow terminally ill patients to self-administer lethal doses of medication prescribed by a doctor.

Jack Kevorkian

The activities of Dr. Jack Kevorkian brought the issue of assisted suicide to the forefront of public attention during the 1990s. Kevorkian assisted more than 40 people in committing suicide in Michigan. His first public assisted suicide took place in 1989, when he assisted in the suicide of Janet Adkins, who had been diagnosed with Alzheimer's disease. Kevorkian was charged with murder for his involvement in Adkins' death. However, because Michigan law did not specifically forbid a physician from assisting a patient in killing herself, the charges brought against Kevorkian were dismissed.

The Michigan Legislature in 1992 enacted an assisted-suicide bill that was designed specifically to prevent Kevorkian's activities. However, the bill's implementation was delayed due to questions of the legislation's constitutionality and other technical questions. Kevorkian was charged with murder several times, but prosecutors failed to bring about a judgment.

In 1998 Kevorkian took a more active role in the death of Thomas Youk, a 52-year-old Michigan man who had been diagnosed with amyotrophic lateral sclerosis (ALS). Kevorkian videotaped himself administering lethal medication that caused Youk's death. One week later CBS broadcast the tape on *60 Minutes*. Based on this evidence, authorities in Michigan charged Kevorkian with first-degree premeditated murder, criminal assistance of a suicide, and delivery of a controlled substance for administering legal medication to a terminally ill man. A jury in 1999 found Kevorkian guilty of second-degree murder in 1999. He was sent to prison and served eight years of a 10- to 25-year sentence. He was released in 2007.

Constitutionality of Assisted-Suicide Statutes

The Supreme Court issued two decisions that significantly affected the law governing assisted suicide. In *Washington v. Glucksberg* (521 U.S. 702, 117 S. Ct. 2258, 138 L. Ed. 2d 772 [1997]), the Court held that states have the right to prohibit assisted suicide. The case arose when three terminally ill patients brought an action against the State of Washington seeking a declaratory judgment that the state's ban on assisted suicide violated the patients' due process rights. A unanimous Supreme Court held that assisted suicide is not a fundamental liberty interest protected by the due process clause of the Fourteenth Amendment. Based on this conclusion, the state only had to prove that its assisted suicide bore a rational relationship to a legitimate government interest. The Court conclude that the state had met this standard.

In a second case, *Vacco v. Quill* (521 U.S. 793, 117 S. Ct. 2293, 138 L. Ed. 2d 834 [1997]), a group of physicians challenged a New York assisted suicide statute by arguing that the statute violated the equal protection clause. Based on its conclusion in the case of *Glucksberg*, the Court determined that New York needed to satisfy the rational basis standard. Because the state could show a rational relationship between the statute and the interests the state sought to protect, the Court ruled that the New York law was constitutional.

The Court in *Glucksberg* noted that if it struck down the Washington statute, the Court would also have to strike down policy choices in nearly every state. Though the Court allowed the statute to stand, the decision allowed states to review the issue to determine whether to lift or soften the bans on assisted suicide.

Oregon's Death with Dignity Act

In 1994 Oregon voters approved the state's Death with Dignity Act (Or. Rev. Stat. §§ 127.800 et seq.), which allows physicians to assist a terminally ill patient in committing suicide. Individuals wishing to employ the law must demonstrate that they are suffering from a terminal illness and have a life expectancy of six months or less. The patient must make two oral requests and one written for assisted suicide. Moreover, two physicians must be convinced that the patient is sincere and that the decision in voluntary. Although court challenges delayed the statute implementation, the statute took effect in October 1997. Between 1997 and 2008, a total of 401 patients took their own lives through assisted suicide method.

On November 6, 2001, former U.S. attorney general John Ashcroft issued a ruling that declared the use of controlled substances for the purpose of assisted suicide violated the Controlled Substances Act (CSA) (21 U.S.C. §§ 801 et seq.). This ruling, known as the *Ashcroft Directive*, reversed the position taken by former attorney general Janet Reno in 1998. Two days after the publication of the directive, the state of Oregon filed suit in federal court against Ashcroft and other federal officers and agencies. The U.S. District Court for the District of Oregon on November 8, 2001, enjoined the enforcement of the directive.

The CSA includes a schedule of controlled substances that are available only through written prescription. In 1971 attorney general John N. Mitchell issued a regulation that requires such a prescription to be used "for a legitimate medical purpose by an individual practitioner acting in the usual course of his professional practice" (21 C.F.R. § 1306.04

[2005]). Under the CSA, physicians are required to register with the attorney general, and the attorney general may deny, revoke, or suspend a registration when the registration would be "inconsistent with the public interest" (21 U.S.C. §§ 822, 824 [2000]).

In issuing the directive, Ashcroft determined that use of controlled substances for assisted suicide was not a "legitimate medical purpose." U.S. District Judge Robert E. Jones reviewed the CSA to determine whether Ashcroft had exceeded his authority in issuing the directive. According to Jones, Congress did not intend for the CSA to override a state's decision regarding what constitutes the practice of medicine. Since Ashcroft had acted pursuant to power that he did not possess, the court determined that his directive was invalid. Accordingly, the court entered a permanent injunction that prevented the directive from taking effect.

The federal government appealed the decision to the U.S. Court of Appeals for the Ninth Circuit. In an opinion issued on May 26, 2004, the Ninth Circuit upheld the district court's decision. According to Judge Richard C. Tallman, who wrote the opinion, not only had Ashcroft exceeded his authority in issuing the directive, but also the directive had exercised control over an area of law that was traditionally reserved to the states. Unless Congress is "unmistakably clear," a unit of federal government may not exercise this type of control. The Ninth Circuit thus let the injunction remain in force.

The U.S. Supreme Court granted certiorari in 2005 and rendered its decision on January 17, 2006. In an opinion written by Justice Anthony Kennedy, the majority affirmed the Ninth Circuit's decision. Kennedy wrote that Ashcroft's interpretation of the CSA was not entitled to deference by the Court because the CSA only extended limited power to the attorney general's office. Moreover, the Court noted that Ashcroft did not have sufficient expertise for his rule to be entitled to deference. According to Kennedy, "[t]he deference here is tempered by the Attorney General's lack of expertise in this area and the apparent absence of any consultation with anyone outside the Department of Justice who might aid in a reasoned judgment."

The federal government continued to argue that its power extended to this area through the provisions of the CSA. Kennedy disagreed entirely. "The Government, in the end, maintains that the prescription requirement delegates to a single Executive officer the power to effect a radical shift of authority from the States to the Federal Government to define general standards of medical practice in every locality," Kennedy wrote. "The text and structure of the CSA show that Congress did not have this far-reaching intent to alter the federal-state balance and the congressional role in maintaining it." Accordingly, the Court affirmed the Ninth Circuit's judgment (*Gonzales v. Oregon*, 546 U.S. 243, 126 S. Ct. 904, 163 L. Ed. 2d 748 [2006]).

According to statistics compiled by the Oregon Department of Human Services for 2008, the majority of those who took their own lives through assisted suicide were between the ages of 55 and 84, with a median age of 72. In previous years, the median age was slightly lower. About 80 percent of the patients had cancer. Smaller numbers of patients have other diseases such as ALS (also called Lou Gehrig's disease) or AIDS.

Other States Consider Assisted Suicide Proposals

Since the decision in *Gonzales v. Oregon*, six other states have considered proposals. On November 4, 2008, voters in the State of Washington approved a ballot measure that legalized assisted suicide. The statute is modeled on the Oregon statute. In 2008 a Montana trial court ruled that a terminally ill patient had the constitutional right to receive aid in dying. The Montana attorney general appealed the decision to the Montana Supreme Court. On December 31, 2009, the supreme court ruled that state law protects doctors from prosecution for helping terminally ill people die. In the 4-3 decision, the court did not rule on whether physician-assisted suicide is a right guaranteed under the Montana Constitution.

FURTHER READINGS

Behuniak, Susan M., and Arthur G. Svenson. 2003. *Physician-Assisted Suicide: The Anatomy of a Constitutional Law Issue.* Lanham: Rowman & Littlefield.

Mitchell, John B. 2007. *Understanding Assisted Suicide: Nine Issues to Consider.* Ann Arbor: Univ. of Michigan Press.

Wester-Mittan, Candle M. 2009. *Physician-Assisted Death: Four Views on the Issue of Legalizing PAD: A Legal Research Guide.* Buffalo, N.Y.: W.S. Hein.

CROSS REFERENCES

Euthanasia; Suicide

ASSIZE, OR ASSISE

A judicial procedure in early England whereby a certain number of men in a community were called together to hear and decide a dispute; a type of court. A type of writ, commanding the convening of such a tribunal in order to determine disputed rights to possess land. An edict or statute issued by an ancient assembly.

For example, the Assize of Clarendon was a statute, or ordinance, passed in the tenth year of the reign of King Henry II (1164). It proclaimed that those who were accused of a heinous crime and were unable to exonerate themselves had forty days to gather provisions from friends to provide for their sustenance before they were sent into exile.

The word *assize* comes from the Latin *assideo,* which describes the fact that the men taking action sat together. An assize could be a number of citizens, eventually settled at the number twelve, called to hear cases. They decided on the basis of information they had or could gather in the community. This group of neighbors was presumed to know the facts well enough to determine who was entitled to possession of disputed lands. A WRIT of assize could be issued on behalf of the king to commission this body of twelve to hear a dispute.

Eventually the writs gave birth to FORMS OF ACTION for lawsuits concerning real property. For example, the assize of novel disseisin was a form of action for the recovery of lands after the claimant had been wrongfully dispossessed (disseised). The assize of NUISANCE was proper to secure the ABATEMENT of a nuisance or for monetary damages to compensate for the harm done by the nuisance.

CROSS REFERENCES

Clarendon, Constitutions of; Henry II of England.

ASSOCIATE JUSTICE

The designation given to a judge who is not the chief or presiding justice of the court on which he or she sits.

An associate judge is usually a member of an appellate court.

ASSOCIATION, FREEDOM OF

See FREEDOM OF ASSOCIATION.

ASSOCIATION OF TRIAL LAWYERS OF AMERICA

See AMERICAN ASSOCIATION FOR JUSTICE.

ASSUMPSIT

[Latin, He undertook or he promised.] A promise by which someone assumes or undertakes an obligation to another person. The promise may be oral or in writing, but it is not under seal. It is express when the person making the promise puts it into distinct and specific language, but it may also be implied because the law sometimes imposes obligations based on the conduct of the parties or the circumstances of their dealings.

Assumpsit was one of the common-law FORMS OF ACTION. It determined the right to sue and the relief available for someone who claimed that a contract had been breached.

When the COMMON LAW was developing in England, there was no legal remedy for the breach of a contract. RANULF GLANVILL, a famous legal scholar, wrote just before the year 1200 that "[i]t is not the custom of the court of the lord king to protect private agreements, nor does it concern itself with such contracts as can be considered private agreements." Ordinary lawsuits could be heard in local courts, but the king was primarily interested in royal rights and the disputes of his noblemen. As commerce began to develop, the king's courts did allow two forms of action for breach of contract—the actions of COVENANT and debt. Covenant could be maintained only if the agreement had been made in writing and under seal and only if the action of debt was not available. One could sue on the debt only if the obligations in the contract had been fully performed and the breach was no more than a failure to pay a specific sum of money.

Finally, in 1370, a PLAINTIFF sought to sue a DEFENDANT who had undertaken to cure the plaintiff's horse but treated it so negligently that the horse died, and the action was allowed. In 1375 another man was permitted to sue a surgeon who had maimed him while trying to cure him. These cases showed a new willingness to permit a lawsuit for monetary damages arising directly from the failure to live up to an agreement. For the next hundred years the courts began to allow lawsuits for badly performed obligations but not for a complete failure to perform what was required by contract. Unexpectedly, this restriction was abandoned also, and a new form of action was recognized by the courts, an action in *special assumpsit* for breach of an express agreement.

Special assumpsit gave a new legal right to parties who could not sue on a debt. Gradually it became possible to sue in *assumpsit* if the defendant owed a debt and then violated a fresh promise to pay it. This action came to be known as *indebitatus assumpsit,* which means "being indebted, he promised."

As time passed, courts were willing to assume that the fresh promise had been made and to impose obligations as if it had. This allowed lawsuits for a whole range of contract breaches, not just those recognized by an action on the debt or in *special assumpsit.* If the plaintiff could claim that services had been performed or goods had been delivered to the defendant, then the law would assume that the defendant had promised to pay for them. Any failure to do so gave the plaintiff the right to sue in *assumpsit.* This development allowed such a wide range of lawsuits based on promises to private parties that it came to be known as *general assumpsit.*

Eventually the right to sue was extended even to situations where the defendant had no intention to pay but it was only fair that he or she be made to do so. This form was called *assumpsit on* QUANTUM MERUIT. *Special assumpsit, general assumpsit* (or *indebitatus assumpsit*), and *quantum meruit* are all *ex contractu,* arising out of a contract. Their development is the foundation of our modern law of contracts.

CROSS REFERENCE

Quantum Meruit.

ASSUMPTION

The undertaking of the repayment of a debt or the performance of an obligation owed by another.

When a purchaser of real property assumes the MORTGAGE of the seller, he or she agrees to adopt the mortgage debt, becoming personally liable for its full repayment in case of default. If a FORECLOSURE sale of the mortgaged property does not satisfy the debt, the purchaser remains financially responsible for the outstanding balance.

In contrast, a purchaser who takes subject to the seller's mortgage agrees to repay the mortgage debt, but that person's LIABILITY is limited only to the amount that the mortgaged property is sold for in the case of foreclosure. If the property is sold for less than the mortgage debt, the mortgagee must seek the remaining balance due from the seller, the original mortgagor.

ASSUMPTION OF RISK

A defense, facts offered by a party against whom proceedings have been instituted to diminish a plaintiff's cause of action or defeat recovery to an action in negligence, which entails proving that the plaintiff knew of a dangerous condition and voluntarily exposed himself or herself to it.

Under the federal rules of CIVIL PROCEDURE, assumption of the risk is an AFFIRMATIVE DEFENSE that the DEFENDANT in a NEGLIGENCE action must plead and prove. The doctrine of assumption of risk is also known as *volenti non fit injuria.*

Situations that encompass assumption of the risk have been classified in three broad categories. In its principal sense, assumption of the risk signifies that the PLAINTIFF, in advance, has consented to relieve the defendant of an obligation of conduct toward him or her and to take a chance of injury from a known risk ensuing from what the defendant is to do or leave undone. The consequence is that the defendant is unburdened of all legal duty to the plaintiff and, therefore, cannot be held liable in negligence.

A second situation occurs when the plaintiff voluntarily enters into some relation with the defendant, knowing that the defendant will not safeguard the plaintiff against the risk. The plaintiff can then be viewed as tacitly or implicitly consenting to the negligence, as in the case of riding in a car with knowledge that the steering apparatus is defective, which relieves the defendant of the duty that would ordinarily exist.

In the third type of situation, the plaintiff, cognizant of a risk previously created by the negligence of the defendant, proceeds voluntarily to confront it, as when he or she has been provided with an article that the plaintiff knows to be hazardous and continues to use after the danger has been detected. If this is a voluntary choice, the plaintiff is deemed to have accepted the situation and assented to free the defendant of all obligations.

In all three situations, the plaintiff might be acting in a reasonable manner and not be negligent in the venture, because the advantages of his or her conduct outweigh the peril. The plaintiff's decision might be correct, and he or she might even act with unusual circumspection because he or she is cognizant of the danger that will be encountered. If that is the case, the defense operates to refute the defendant's negligence by denying the duty of care that would invoke this LIABILITY, and the plaintiff does not recover because the defendant's conduct was not wrongful toward the plaintiff.

With respect to the second and third situations, however, the plaintiff's conduct in confronting a known risk might be in itself unreasonable, because the danger is disproportionate to the advantage the plaintiff is pursuing, as when, with other transportation available, the individual chooses to ride with an intoxicated driver. If this occurs, the plaintiff's conduct is a type of contributory negligence, an act or omission by the plaintiff that constitutes a deficiency in ordinary care, which concurs with the defendant's negligence to comprise the direct or PROXIMATE CAUSE of injury. In such cases, the defenses of assumption of risk and contributory negligence overlap.

In this area of intersection, the courts have held that the defendant can employ either defense or both. Because ordinarily either is sufficient to bar the action, the defenses have been distinguished on the theory that assumption of risk consists of awareness of the peril and intelligent submission to it, while contributory negligence entails some deviation from the standard of conduct of a REASONABLE PERSON, irrespective of any remonstration or unawareness displayed by the plaintiff. The two concepts can coexist when the plaintiff unreasonably decides to incur the risk or can exist independently of each other. The distinction, when one exists, is likely to be one between risks that were in fact known to the plaintiff and risks that the individual merely might have discovered by the exercise of ordinary care.

Express Agreement

The parties can enter into a written agreement absolving the defendant from any obligation of care for the benefit of the plaintiff and liability for the consequence of conduct that would otherwise constitute negligence. In the ordinary case, PUBLIC POLICY does not prevent the parties from contracting in regard to whether the plaintiff will be responsible for the maintenance

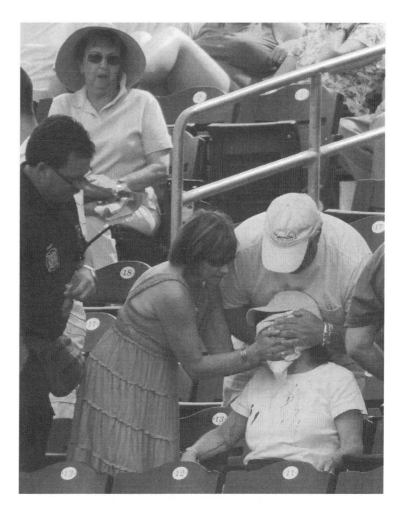

Visitors to professional sporting events assume the risk that they may be injured by competitors or game paraphernalia during the contest.

KEVORK DJANSEZIAN/ GETTY IMAGES

of personal safety. A person who enters into a lease or rents an animal or enters into a variety of similar relations entailing free and open bargaining between the parties can assent to relieving the defendant of the obligation to take precautions and thereby render the defendant free from liability for negligence.

The courts have refused to uphold such agreements, however, if one party possesses a PATENT disadvantage in bargaining power. For example, a contract exempting an employer from all liability for negligence toward employees is void as against public policy. A carrier transporting cargo or passengers for hire cannot evade its public responsibility in this manner, even though the agreement limits recovery to an amount less than the probable damages. The contract has been upheld, however, when it represents a realistic attempt to assess a value as liquidated or ascertained damages in advance, and the carrier graduates its rates in accordance with such value, so that complete protection would be available to the plaintiff upon paying a higher rate. The same principles apply to innkeepers, public warehousemen, and other professional bailees—such as garage, parking lot, and checkroom attendants—on the basis that the indispensable necessity for their services deprives the customer of all meaningful equal bargaining power.

An express agreement can relieve the defendant from liability for negligence only if the plaintiff comprehends its terms. If the plaintiff is not cognizant of the provision in his or her contract, and a reasonable person in the same position would not have known of it, it is not binding upon the individual, and the agreement fails for lack of mutual assent. The expressed terms of the agreement must apply to the particular misconduct of the defendant. Such contracts generally do not encompass gross, willful, WANTON, or reckless negligence or any conduct that constitutes an intentional tort.

Implied Acceptance of Risk

In a majority of cases, the consent to assume the risk is implied from the conduct of the plaintiff under the circumstances. The basis of the defense is not contract, but consent, and it is available in many cases in which no express agreement exists.

By entering voluntarily into any relationship or transaction in which the negligence of the defendant is evident, the plaintiff is deemed to accept and consent to it, to assume responsibility for personal safety, and to unburden the defendant of the obligation. Spectators at certain sports events assume all the known risks of injury from flying objects. Plaintiffs who enter business premises as invitees and detect dangerous conditions can be deemed to assume the risks when they continue voluntarily to encounter them.

Knowledge of Risk

The plaintiff will not normally be regarded as assuming any risk of either conditions or activities of which he or she has no knowledge. The plaintiff must not merely create the danger but must comprehend and appreciate the danger itself.

The applicable standard is basically subjective in nature, tailored to the particular plaintiff and his or her situation, as opposed to the objective standard of the reasonable person of ordinary prudence, which is employed in contributory negligence. If because of age, lack of information, or experience, the plaintiff does not comprehend the risk entailed in a known situation, the individual will not be regarded as consenting to assume it. Failure to exercise ordinary care to discover the danger is not encompassed within assumption of risk, but in the defense of contributory negligence.

An entirely subjective standard, however, allows the plaintiff considerable latitude in testifying that he or she did not know or comprehend the risk. To counteract the adverse effects of the application of this liberal standard, courts have interjected an objective element by holding that a plaintiff cannot evade responsibility by alleging that he or she did not comprehend a risk that must have been obvious.

A denial of cognizance of certain matters that are common knowledge in the community is not credible, unless a satisfactory explanation exists. As in the case of negligence itself, there are particular risks that any adult must appreciate, such as falling on ice, lifting heavy objects, and driving a defective vehicle. In addition, a plaintiff situated for a considerable length of time in the immediate vicinity of a hazardous condition is deemed to have detected and to comprehend the ordinary risks entailed in that situation. If the person completely understands the risk, the fact that he or she has temporarily forgotten it does not provide protection.

Even when there is knowledge and appreciation of a risk, the plaintiff might not be prohibited from recovery when the circumstances introduce a new factor. The fact that the plaintiff is totally cognizant of one risk, such as the speed of a vehicle, does not signify that he or she assumes another of which he or she is unaware, such as the intoxication of the driver.

Although knowledge and understanding of the risk incurred are encompassed within the concept of assumption of the risk, it is possible for the plaintiff to assume risks of whose specific existence he or she is unaware—to consent to venture into unknown conditions. In a majority of instances, the undertaking is express, although it can arise by implication in a few cases. A guest who accepts a gratuitous ride in an automobile has been regarded as assuming the risk of defects in the vehicle, unknown to the driver.

Voluntary Assumption

The doctrine of assumption of risk does not bar the plaintiff from recovery unless the individual's decision is free and voluntary. There must be some manifestation of consent to relieve the defendant of the obligation of reasonable conduct. A risk is not viewed as assumed if it appears from the plaintiff's words or from the circumstances, that he or she does not actually consent. If the plaintiff relinquishes his or her better judgment upon assurances that the situation is safe or that it will be remedied or upon a promise of protection, the plaintiff does not assume the risk, unless the danger is so patent and so extreme that there can be no reasonable reliance upon the assurance.

Even when the plaintiff does not protest, the risk is not assumed when the conduct of the defendant has provided the individual with no reasonable alternative, causing him or her to act under duress. When the defendant creates a peril, such as a burning building, those who dash into it to save their own property or the lives or property of others do not assume the risk when the alternative is to permit the threatened injury to occur. If, however, the danger is disproportionate to the value of the interest to be protected, the plaintiff might be charged with contributory negligence in regard to his or her own unreasonable conduct. When a reasonably safe alternative exists, the plaintiff's selection of the hazardous route is free and can constitute both contributory negligence and assumption of risk.

The defendant has a legal duty, which he or she is not at liberty to refuse to perform, to exercise reasonable care for the plaintiff's safety, so that the plaintiff has a parallel legal right to demand that care. The plaintiff does not assume the risk while using the defendant's services or facilities, notwithstanding knowledge of the peril, when he or she acts reasonably, and the defendant has provided no reasonable alternative other than to refrain completely from exercising the right. A COMMON CARRIER or other public utility which has negligently furnished a dangerously defective set of steps cannot assert assumption of risk against a patron who uses the steps as the sole convenient means of access to the company's premises. The same principle applies to a city maintaining a public roadway or sidewalk or other public area that the plaintiff has a right to use and premises onto which the plaintiff has a contractual right to enter. When a reasonable alternative is available, the plaintiff's recalcitrance in unreasonably encountering danger constitutes contributory negligence, as well as assumption of risk.

Violation of Statute

The plaintiff still assumes the risk where the defendant's negligence consists of the violation of a statute. A guest who accepts a nighttime ride in a vehicle with inoperative lights has been regarded as consenting to relieve the defendant of the duty of complying with the standard established by the statute for protection and cannot recover for injuries. Particular statutes, however, such as child labor acts and safety statutes for the benefit of employees, safeguard the plaintiff against personal inability to protect himself or herself due to improvident judgment or incapability to resist certain pressures. Since the basic objective of such statutes would be frustrated if the plaintiff were allowed to assume the risk, it is generally held that the plaintiff cannot do so, either expressly or impliedly.

Abolition of the Defense

Numerous states have abrogated the defense of assumption of risk in automobile cases through the enactment of no-fault insurance legislation or comparative negligence acts. The theories underlying its abolition are that it serves no purpose that is not completely disposed of by the other doctrines, it increases the likelihood of confusion, and it bars recovery in meritorious cases.

Assumption of risk is not a defense under state workers' compensation laws or in federal Employer's Liability Act actions. The workers' compensation laws abolished the defense in recognition of the severe economic pressure a threatened loss of employment exerted upon workers. A worker was deemed to have assumed the risk even when acting under a direct order that conveyed an explicit or implicit threat of discharge for insubordination.

The federal Employers' Liability Act (45 U.S. C.A. § 51 et seq. [1908]) was intended to furnish an equitable method of compensation for railroad workers injured within the scope of their employment. The act provides that an employee is not deemed to have assumed the risks of employment when injury or death ensued totally or partially from the negligence of the carrier's officers, agents, or employees, or from the carrier's violation of any statute enacted for the safety of employees, where the infraction contributed to the employee's injury or death. This doctrine was abolished because of the extreme hardship it imposed on workers in this dangerous line of employment.

FURTHER READINGS

Drago, Alexander J. 2002. "Assumption of Risk: An Age-Old Defense Still Viable in Sports and Recreation Cases." Fordham Intell. Prop. Media & *Ent. Law Journal* 12 (winter).

Gilles, Susan M. 2002. "From Baseball Parks to the Public Arena: Assumption of the Risk in Tort Law and Constitutional Libel Law." *Temple Law Review* 75 (summer).

Owen, Richard. 2000. *Essential Tort.* 3d ed. London: Cavendish, Ltd.

Rabin, Robert L. 2003. *Perspectives on Tort Law.* Frederick, MD: Aspen.

Simons, Kenneth W. 2002. "Reflections on Assumption of Risk." *UCLA Law Review* 50 (December).

CROSS REFERENCES

Cognizance; Consent; Insurance; Public Utilities; Reasonable Person.

ASSURED

A person protected by insurance coverage against loss or damage stipulated by the provisions of a policy purchased from an insurance company or an underwriter.

Assured is synonymous with INSURED.

ASYLUM

Protection granted to aliens who cannot return to their homeland.

Asylum is not to be confused with *refuge,* although the terms are sometimes used interchangeably. An alien who wishes to emigrate to another country is granted refugee status before leaving his or her native country. An asylum seeker (or *asylee*) seeks that status after arriving in the new country.

People who live in fear of being tortured or killed by their government often seek asylum, as do people who are persecuted for their religious or political beliefs. The United States has long been a haven for asylum seekers; in colonial days people came to America to escape religions persecution, and in later years people in danger of political torture have seen the United States as a place of hope and safety. In times of crisis, the United States has sometimes placed restrictions on who can enter the country. IMMIGRATION restrictions were enacted immediately after World Wars I and II. The September 11th terrorist attacks on New York City and Washington, D.C., likewise changed the picture for immigration. Nonetheless, the United States remains committed to providing a safe haven for people whose governments intend to do them harm.

Asylum in the United States is regulated under Section 208 of the Immigration and Nationality Act (INA), which was passed in 1952 and has been amended periodically afterward. Previously, asylum matters were handled by the Immigration and NATURALIZATION Service (INS). The Homeland Security Act of 2002 created three new agencies to handle all matters formerly handled by the INS. These new agencies, the Bureau of Citizenship and Immigration Services (BCIS); the Bureau of Customs and Border Protection; and the Bureau of Immigration and Customs Enforcement were made part of the HOMELAND SECURITY DEPARTMENT that became operational in March 2003. Although the BCIS was technically a new agency, it was to continue to conduct all business, including processing applications and requests, as the INS had.

Eligibility for Asylum

People who can prove that they will be persecuted if they are returned to their home country can apply for asylum in the United States. Much persecution is based on race, RELIGION, and politics, but there are other reasons as well. Students are frequently targeted for persecution, particularly if they choose to engage in social or political activism. Women in some countries may be subject to severe punishment (including execution) simply for having a baby out of wedlock. Homosexuals are persecuted in a number of countries, especially those in which religion is an integral part of the government.

People with a criminal record including *aggravated felonies* (i.e., serious crimes such as RAPE and MURDER) are generally not eligible for asylum, nor are those who have been found guilty of subversive activity against government agencies. Waivers are difficult to obtain; a person would need to provide substantive and irrefutable proof that he or she had been wrongfully or falsely charged by his or her government. Those who have communicable diseases or who have physical or mental disorders are ineligible for asylum unless they can provide proof that their condition is either cured or under control. Some people come to the United States to seek better job opportunities. Those people are not candidates for asylum; they are required to follow standard immigration procedures.

A person can seek asylum in the United States either through *affirmative asylum* or *defensive asylum*. In affirmative asylum, the person applying submits the proper paperwork (known as Form I-589) to the BCIS and is called to appear before an asylum officer for an interview. In defensive asylum, the person in question has been placed in removal proceedings by the Immigration Court and has to appear before an immigration judge from the Executive Office for Immigration Review (EOIR). Those who seek defensive asylum include undocumented ALIENS who have been caught entering the country illegally, but who also may be genuinely afraid of being persecuted if they are sent home. Asylum officers often refer undocumented aliens to EOIR for a defensive hearing if they feel that the fear of persecution is credible.

Article 3 of the UNITED NATIONS Convention Against Torture (1999) states that no asylum seeker can be returned home if the threat of torture is strong enough. The BCIS does have the option, however, of sending an unsuccessful asylum seeker to a third country in which there is no danger of torture or persecution.

Derivative Asylum

Often asylum seekers want protection not just for themselves but also for their families. Anyone seeking asylum may include a spouse and children under the age of 21 on the I-589 form. *Derivative asylum* is designed to give that same option to people who have already been granted asylum. Stepchildren are eligible if the applicant and spouse married before the child's 18th birthday; adopted children must have been adopted before their 16th birthday, and the applicant must have been a legal parent for at least two years. Asylum seekers have two years from the date they are granted asylum to apply for derivative asylum.

Temporary Protected Status

In some cases, an alien in the United States may choose to obtain "Temporary Protected Status" (TPS). Typically, TPS is granted by the DEPARTMENT OF JUSTICE to aliens whose home country is unsafe due to such causes as armed conflict or natural disaster. TPS generally lasts from six to 18 months; when TPS status terminates, the aliens generally return to the same immigration status they held before the status was granted.

The R-A Rule

In 1999 the Bureau of Immigration Affairs (BIA) ruled against an asylum seeker in *In re R-A-*, 22 I. & N. Dec. 906, Interim Decision (BIA) 3403, 2001 WL 1744475 (BIA, Jan 19, 2001). In the initial case, Ms. Rody Alvarado Pena was granted asylum by a San Francisco immigration judge in 1996 because she had suffered years of DOMESTIC VIOLENCE from her Guatemalan husband. In June 1999 the BIA reversed the immigration judge's decision and ordered Ms. Alvarado to be deported to Guatemala. The BIA ruled against granting asylum, in part because it saw domestic violence as a private matter within her own family, despite Ms. Alvarado's argument that she was, in fact, a member of a persecuted group. (She belonged to a support group for abused women.) The decision led to the denial of many women seeking asylum protection who were fleeing from a wide range of HUMAN RIGHTS violations, including trafficking for PROSTITUTION, honor killing, and domestic violence. In January 2001 Attorney General JANET RENO ordered the BIA to issue a new decision in Ms. Alvarado's case after the Department of Justice issued new regulations on the issue of gender asylum. The Department of Justice consulted with experts in domestic violence and noted its position that certain forms of domestic violence may indeed constitute persecution. For example, if a country's domestic violence laws were weak or ineffective against protecting abused spouses, that could be construed as a public issue, not merely a private one within individual families.

In 2005, during the GEORGE W. BUSH administration, Attorney General JOHN ASHCROFT reviewed the BIA's decision, vacated Reno's decision, and ordered that the parties involved in the case brief the case again (i.e., submit new legal arguments). The DEPARTMENT OF HOMELAND SECURITY at that time stated in its brief that it supported Ms. Alvarado's request for asylum and indicated that final regulations regarding the subject of gender asylum were under consideration. However, the regulations were never finalized. Accordingly, in September 2008 Attorney General MICHAEL MUKASEY ordered the BIA to reconsider the case, and removed the requirement that the BIA wait for the issuance of the proposed regulations. As of September 2009, the case was still pending a final decision.

FURTHER READINGS

"Documents and Information on Rody Alvarado's Claim for Asylum in the U.S." Center for Gender & Refugee Studies. Available online at http://cgrs.uchastings.edu/campaigns/Alvarado.php website home page: http://cgrs.uchastings.edu (accessed September 27, 2009).

Kimmel, Barbara Brooks, and Alan M. Lubiner. 2000. *Immigration Made Simple: An Easy-to-Read Guide to the U.S. Immigration Process.* Chester, N.J.: Next Decade.

Nicholson, Frances, and Patrick Twomey, eds. 1999. *Refugee Rights and Realities: Evolving International Concepts and Regimes.* Cambridge: Cambridge Univ. Press.

CROSS REFERENCES

Aggravation; Aliens; Homeland Security Department; Felony; Refugees

ASYLUMS

Establishments that exist for the aid and protection of individuals in need of assistance due to disability, such as insane persons, those who are physically handicapped, or persons who are unable to properly care for themselves, such as orphans.

The term *asylum* has been used, in constitutional and legislative provisions, to encompass all institutions that are established and supported by the general public.

An *insane asylum* is one in which custody and care is provided for people with mental problems. An orphanage is an asylum set up as a shelter or refuge for infants and children who do not have parents or guardians.

Establishment and Maintenance

In the absence of constitutional restrictions, the state is permitted to fulfill its OBLIGATION to aid or support individuals in need of care by contributions to care facilities established or maintained by political subdivisions and private charity. In addition, the state may inaugurate a state asylum, delegating the management responsibility thereof to a private corporation. Some authorities view contributions to asylums of religious organizations or private enterprises as violative of constitutional prohibitions of government aid to parochial institutions or individuals. Express exceptions can be made by state statute or constitution for the payment of funds for designated purposes to specific types of asylums. In situations that are embraced by such exceptions, the contribution that the state makes to the maintenance of the asylum is not regarded as a charity but as part of the state's duty to aid its citizens who cannot do so themselves.

Public Asylums Ownership and Status

An asylum founded and supported by the state has the status of a public institution. The state has the true ownership of the property that a state asylum occupies, and the character of the state's interest in such property is dependent upon the terms of the deed or contract under which it is held for the institution.

When a county conveys property to a board of directors of an insane asylum acting as trustees, title is not vested in the state to the extent that the power to reconvey the land to the county is restricted. In a situation in which property has been conveyed for a particular purpose connected to the operation of the asylum, it has been held that the trustees are permitted to reconvey the property to the county for the establishment of a general hospital.

Location and Support When no constitutional provision prescribing the location of public institutions exists, the state may designate a location or arrange for a place to be found by a specially appointed committee or commission.

A state asylum may be funded either by general state TAXATION or through an allocation of a portion or all of the costs among political subdivisions or to the inmates of the asylum.

Regulation Under the POLICE POWER of the state, the establishment and regulation of private asylums are subject to the state legislative authority. Such powers may be delegated to political subdivisions and administrative agencies. If legislative authority is delegated in such situations, guidelines and standards for regulatory enforcement must be present.

In order for a regulation to be valid, it must be reasonable, applied uniformly, and it must not infringe upon constitutional rights. A state or political subdivision cannot proscribe the lawful operation of an asylum or care facility or create or enforce unreasonable or arbitrary requirements regarding its construction or physical location. Similarly, it cannot make capricious requirements relating to the classification and nature of individuals to be admitted. Regulations and practices must comply with constitutional and statutory provisions.

The governing board of an asylum or institutional care facility is empowered to create all necessary rules and bylaws and is responsible for its policies and general administration. The courts will neither prescribe rules nor alter those created by the authorities, unless they are unreasonable or inappropriate.

Investigation and Inspection The legislature has the exclusive power to order an investigation of the management of an asylum or care facility. Private individuals may not conduct an investigation. When an investigation is initiated, the institution's governing board has the power to set forth regulations regarding relations with employees and patients and access to the records. A nursing home operator must make records kept pursuant to a public health statute available for inspection by authorized public officials. In addition, a private facility can be required to turn over annual fiscal reports to a regulatory agency.

Statutory requirements for the safety of individuals in institutions are imposed and must be observed. Similarly, standards concerning the type of personnel needed to care for the patients are usually set forth, but they must not be unreasonable.

Licenses Ordinarily, a license is required to operate an asylum or institutional care facility in order to ensure that minimal health and safety requirements imposed by law are observed. When a license is necessary, operation of a facility without one may be enjoined and, under certain statutes, a contract made by an unlicensed person is void, which would bar recovery for necessaries provided for individuals. The procedure for procuring a license is governed by statute, and the state licensing authorities have the discretion concerning whether it should be granted. When there is a final decision, determinations in licensing proceedings may be subject to JUDICIAL REVIEW. The proceedings on judicial review are generally regulated by statutory provisions that limit the proceedings to those initiated by aggrieved individuals. Under some statutes, before an institutional care facility can be built, a certificate of need, which establishes approval of its construction by a public agency, is required.

Officers and Employees

The rules that generally apply to public service employees govern the status of officers and

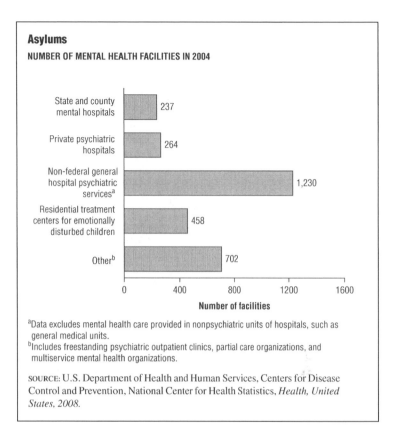

Asylums

NUMBER OF MENTAL HEALTH FACILITIES IN 2004

State and county mental hospitals: 237
Private psychiatric hospitals: 264
Non-federal general hospital psychiatric services[a]: 1,230
Residential treatment centers for emotionally disturbed children: 458
Other[b]: 702

Number of facilities

[a]Data excludes mental health care provided in nonpsychiatric units of hospitals, such as general medical units.
[b]Includes freestanding psychiatric outpatient clinics, partial care organizations, and multiservice mental health organizations.

SOURCE: U.S. Department of Health and Human Services, Centers for Disease Control and Prevention, National Center for Health Statistics, *Health, United States, 2008.*

ILLUSTRATION BY GGS CREATIVE RESOURCES. REPRODUCED BY PERMISSION OF GALE, A PART OF CENGAGE LEARNING.

employees of institutions. Statutory provisions may provide for the termination of such officers and employees.

Inmates, Patients, and Residents

Statutory provisions, administrative regulations, and discretion of its administrator govern the admission of inmates or patients to a public institution. When a public asylum is founded for the reception of a specific class of individuals, anyone in the designated class may be admitted.

A constitutional provision that requires the advancement and support of certain specified institutions does not mandate that the state incur the total cost of maintaining institutionalized individuals. The expedience of soliciting repayment from responsible people for the expense of care, support, and maintenance of a patient cannot be based exclusively upon whether the commitment is voluntary or involuntary. In addition, recovery might be permitted for services actually rendered.

The individual in charge of an asylum that stands IN LOCO PARENTIS to infants upon their admission has custody of the children who are committed to its care. Unless otherwise prohibited by statute, qualified people may examine the records of children in private institutions when so authorized by its administrators. When a statute exists that guarantees the adult residents of proprietary adult homes the right to manage their own financial affairs, their handling of such matters cannot be subject to judicial challenge. An institution may be mandated to meet the individual needs of its patients under rules that monitor the operation of private care facilities for the purpose of the MEDICAID program.

Appropriate regulations may govern the VISITATION RIGHTS of individuals in an asylum. An individual may be dismissed from the institution for conduct proscribed by the bylaws under penalty of expulsion, provided the person is first afforded notice and an opportunity to be heard.

Contracts for Care and Occupancy

The admission of an individual to a public institution for care can be the subject of a contract between the patient and the institution concerning the transfer of property to the institution. Even without an express agreement, however, the circumstances may bring about a QUASI CONTRACT to provide for services rendered. An individual may not rescind an occupancy agreement and regain an admission fee without proof of a breach of contract by the institution.

Management

The management of public institutions is usually entrusted to specific governing bodies or officers. The appropriate body can hire employees to operate the asylum but cannot relinquish its management responsibilities. Physicians who wish to visit patients in private nursing homes can be excluded. If an institution does not provide reasons at the time of the exclusion, it does not preclude the institution from excluding the physician, provided that valid reasons exist and are communicated upon request.

Generally, the governing body of an asylum has the power to decide how funds appropriated for its support shall be spent, in the absence of contrary legislative provision. Funds appropriated by a legislature for specific purposes cannot, however, be diverted, and the governing body of the asylum does not have the power to compel the state to provide funding for services other than those for which the money was appropriated. Similarly, they are not empowered to borrow money or incur debts beyond allotments made for the support of institutions.

It is proper procedure to make a provision that an asylum may only accept as many inmates for admission as the facilities can adequately accommodate. An institution may not initiate a visitation plan that limits a patient's right to allocate his or her visiting time among particular people, unless such limitation bears a rational relationship to the patient's treatment or security.

Liabilities

An asylum or institutional care facility has the obligation to exercise reasonable care toward patients and can be held liable for a breach of this duty of care. The care taken toward inmates should be in the light of their mental and physical condition.

Recovery for injuries precipitated by an institution's NEGLIGENCE can be barred or limited by the contributory negligence of the injured party. The defense of contributory negligence cannot, however, be used when an individual is physically or mentally incapable of self-care.

FURTHER READINGS

Goffman, Erving. 2007. *Asylums: Essays on the Social Situation of Mental Patients and Other Inmates.* New Brunswick, NJ: Aldine Transaction.

Jones, Kathleen. 1993. *Asylums and After: Revised History of the Mental Health Services from the Early 18th Century to the 1990s.* London: Athlone.

Rothman, David J. 2002. *The Discovery of the Asylum: Social Order and Disorder in the New Republic.* New York: Aldine de Gruyter.

CROSS REFERENCES

Disability Discrimination; Establishment Clause; Health Care Law; Patients' Rights.

AT ISSUE

A phrase that describes the status of parties in a lawsuit when they make contradictory statements about a point specified in their pleadings.

AT LARGE

Not limited to any place, person, or topic; for example, a representative at large is elected by the voters of the state as a whole rather than voters of a particular district. Free from control or restraint, such as a criminal at large.

AT LAW

According to law; by, for, or in the law, as in the professional title attorney at law. *Within or arising from the traditions of the common law as opposed to equity, the system of law that developed alongside the common law and emphasized fairness and justice rather than enforcement of technical rules.*

ATKINS V. VIRGINIA

In a landmark 6–3 ruling, the U.S. Supreme Court barred the execution of mentally retarded people, ruling that it constituted "cruel and unusual punishment" prohibited by the EIGHTH AMENDMENT. However, the Court left to the states to determine the definition of mental retardation. The decision affected as many as 300 mentally retarded death row inmates in 20 states.

The case involved Daryl Renard Atkins, who was convicted of capital MURDER and sentenced to death for abducting, robbing, and killing 21-year-old airman Eric Michael Nesbitt. The evidence introduced at trial showed that at approximately midnight on August 16, 1996, Atkins and William Jones, both armed with semiautomatic WEAPONS, abducted Nesbitt, robbed him, drove him to an automated teller machine, forced him to withdraw additional cash, and then took him to an isolated location where they shot him eight times at close range.

Initially, both Jones and Atkins were indicted for capital murder. The prosecution ultimately permitted Jones to plead guilty to first-degree murder in exchange for his TESTIMONY against Atkins. As a result of the PLEA, Jones became ineligible to receive the death penalty.

Jones and Atkins both testified in the guilt phase of Atkins's trial. Each confirmed most of the details in the other's account of the incident, except that each blamed the other for killing Nesbitt. Jones's testimony, which was both more coherent and credible than Atkins's testimony, was apparently credited by the jury in establishing Atkins's guilt. Highly damaging to the credibility of Atkins's testimony was its substantial inconsistency with the statement he gave to the police upon his arrest. Jones, in contrast, had declined to make an initial statement to the authorities.

At the penalty phase of the trial, the state introduced victim impact evidence and proved two aggravating circumstances: future dangerousness and "vileness of the offense." To prove future dangerousness, the state relied on Atkins's prior felony convictions as well as the testimony of four victims of earlier robberies and assaults. To prove the second aggravating circumstance, the prosecution relied upon pictures of the murdered man's body and the autopsy report.

The defense relied on one witness during the penalty phase, Dr. Evan Nelson, a forensic psychologist who had evaluated Atkins before trial and concluded that he was "mildly mentally retarded." His conclusion was based on interviews with people who knew Atkins, a review of school and court records, and the administration of a standard intelligence test, which indicated that Atkins had a full scale IQ of 59. Generally, IQs below 70 are considered in the retarded range. The state presented Dr. Stanton Samenow as an expert rebuttal witness. He testified that Atkins was not mentally retarded but rather was of "average intelligence, at least," and diagnosable as having antisocial personality disorder. A jury sentenced Atkins to death and the Virginia Supreme Court affirmed the sentence on appeal, saying it was "not willing to commute Atkins's sentence of death to life imprisonment merely because of his IQ score." *Atkins v. Commonwealth*, 260 Va. 375, 534 S.E.2d 312 (Va. 2000).

When the case was appealed, most observers expected the U.S. Supreme Court to affirm the sentence as well. In 1989 the Supreme Court had upheld the execution of a mentally retarded death row inmate, notwithstanding objections that such executions violate the Eighth Amendment's ban on CRUEL AND UNUSUAL PUNISHMENT. *Penry v. Lynaugh*, 492 U.S. 302, 109 S. Ct. 2934, 106 L.Ed.2d 256 (1989). But Justice JOHN PAUL STEVENS, writing for the majority in *Atkins*, concluded that times had changed in the 13 years since the *Penry* decision was handed down.

When *Penry* was decided, Stevens observed, only two of the 38 states allowing CAPITAL PUNISHMENT barred execution of mentally retarded inmates. However, at the time *Atkins* came before the Court, that number had risen to 18. Noting the "procession" of states in which executing the mentally retarded had been deemed illegal, Justice Stevens stated that it was not so much the number of states that was significant, but the consistency of the direction of change. "Given the well-known fact that anti-crime legislation is far more popular than legislation providing protections for persons guilty of violent crime," he stated, "the large number of states prohibiting the execution of mentally retarded persons (and the complete absence of states passing legislation reinstating the power to conduct such executions) provides powerful evidence that today our society views mentally retarded offenders as categorically less culpable than the average criminal." Thus, Stevens concluded that the Eighth Amendment now prohibited executing mentally retarded persons under the "evolving standards of decency" test by which punishments are evaluated to determine whether they are cruel and unusual.

Chief Justice WILLIAM REHNQUIST and Justices ANTONIN SCALIA and CLARENCE THOMAS dissented. Chief Justice Rehnquist criticized the majority for basing its decision on the fact that 18 states have laws barring execution of mentally retarded defendants, because the laws of 20 states would have otherwise continued to leave the question of proper punishment to the individuated consideration of SENTENCING judges or juries familiar with the particular offender and his or her crime. Chief Justice Rehnquist agreed with Justice Scalia's opinion that the majority's assessment of the current legislative judgment more resembled a post hoc rationalization for the majority's "subjectively preferred result" than "any objective effort to ascertain the content of an evolving standard of decency."

FURTHER READINGS

Dowling, Alexis Krulish. 2003. "Post-Atkins Problems with Enforcing the Supreme Court's Ban on Executing the Mentally Retarded." *Seton Hall Law Review* 33 (summer).

Henshaw, Jaime L. 2003. "Atkins v. Virginia: The Court's Failure to Recognize What Lies Beneath." *Univ. of Richmond Law Review* 37, vol. 4 (May).

"Implementing Atkins." 2003. *Harvard Law Review* 116 (June).

Velasquez, Eli. 2003. "The Shaping of an American Consensus against the Execution of Mentally Retarded Criminals." *Whittier Law Review* 24 (summer).

CROSS REFERENCES

Eighth Amendment; Felony; Forensic Science; Murder; Plea; Rebut; Victims of Crime.

ATTACHMENT

The legal process of seizing property to ensure satisfaction of a judgment.

The document by which a court orders such a SEIZURE may be called a WRIT of attachment or an order of attachment.

Originally, the main purpose of attachment was to coerce a DEFENDANT into appearing in court and answering the plaintiff's claim. The court's order pressured the sheriff to take the defendant's property into custody, depriving the individual of the right to use or sell it. If the defendant obstinately refused to appear, the property could be sold by the court to pay off any monetary judgment entered against him or her. In the early twenty-first century, the process of attachment has two functions, as a jurisdictional predicate and as a provisional remedy.

Attachment of property within reach of the court's jurisdiction gives the court authority over the defendant to the extent of that property's value even if the court cannot reach the defendant personally. For example, a court must have some connection with the defendant in order to require that person to appear and defend himself or herself in an action before that court.

A variety of different facts are sufficient to give the court jurisdiction over the defendant's person; for example, the defendant's residence within the state, the defendant's commission of a wrongful act within the state, or the defendant's doing business within the state.

If none of these kinds of facts exist to give the court jurisdiction over the defendant's person, the court may nevertheless assert its authority over property that the defendant owns within the state. In such a case, the PLAINTIFF cannot recover a monetary judgment for an amount larger than the value of the property nor can the individual reach the defendant's property outside the state, but this sort of jurisdiction, called jurisdiction in rem or quasi in rem, may be the best the plaintiff can get. Before the court can exercise jurisdiction over the property, the plaintiff must obtain a writ of attachment to bring it into custody of the court.

Attachment may also be a provisional remedy, that is, relief that temporarily offers the plaintiff some security while pursuing a final judgment in the lawsuit. For example, a plaintiff who has good reason to believe that the person he or she is suing is about to pack up and leave the state will want the court to prevent this until the plaintiff has a chance to win the action and collect on the judgment. The plaintiff can apply

A sample order of attachment

STATE OF NORTH CAROLINA

_____ County

File No. _____

Film No. _____

In The General Court Of Justice

☐ District ☐ Superior Court Division

Name Of Plaintiff	
	ORDER OF ATTACHMENT G.S. 1-440.12, 1-440.13
VERSUS	☐ *Alias and Pluries Order The Order originally issued against you was returned not served.
Name Of Defendant	
	Date Last Order Issued | *Disregard this section unless the block is checked.

To The Sheriff Of The County Named Below:

The above named plaintiff has applied for an attachment of the defendant's property in this action and has executed and delivered to the Court a satisfactory attachment bond. It appears to the satisfaction of the Court that the allegations in the plaintiff's affidavit are true.

You are commanded to attach and keep safely as much of the property of the defendant within your county which is subject to attachment, as is sufficient to satisfy the amount sought in the Affidavit in Attachment Proceeding, the costs of the action and expenses. You are further commanded to make return of this Order to this Court within the time allowed by law. The amount sufficient to satisfy the plaintiff's demand is shown below.

County In Which Order To Be Served	Date Issued
Amount Sufficient To Satisfy Plaintiff's Demand	Signature
$	☐ Assistant CSC ☐ Clerk Of Superior Court ☐ District Court Judge ☐ Superior Court Judge

AOC-CV-301, Rev. 1/98   Original-File   Copy-Each Defendant   Copy-Attorney/Plaintiff
©1998 Administrative Office of the Courts   (Over)

[continued]

STATE OF NORTH CAROLINA

	RETURN OF SERVICE	

I certify that pursuant to this Order I levied on the following described property of the defendant on the date set out below:

DATE OF LEVY	PROPERTY LEVIED ON

NOTE TO SHERIFF: *If you levy on real property and this Order Of Attachment was issued by a Clerk from a county other than your county, in addition to returning the order and return of service to the Clerk who issued it, you must give a copy of this order and return of service to the Clerk of Superior Court in your county. G.S. 1-440.17(a).*

NOTE TO CLERK: *If the return certifies that the sheriff levied on real property, note the levy on the judgment docket and index it.*

☐ No levy has been made within ten (10) days after the issuance of this Order Of Attachment for the following reasons:

Fee Paid $	Date Received	Name Of Sheriff
By	Date Served	County
	Date Returned	Deputy Sheriff Making Return

Judgment Docket Book And Page No. (If Real Property Attached)

AOC-CV-301, Side Two, Rev. 1/98
©1998 Administrative Office of the Courts

for an order of attachment that brings the property into the custody of the court and takes away the defendant's right to remove it or dispose of it.

Attachment is considered a very harsh remedy because it substantially interferes with the defendant's property rights before final resolution of the overall dispute. For this reason, there have been a number of challenges to the attachment procedures in different states, and the Supreme Court has established standards that are the least that due process requires. For example, for centuries attachment of a defendant's property was granted ex parte, that is, without first allowing the defendant to argue against it. The theory was that any defendant was likely to leave the state if he or she knew beforehand that his or her property was about to be attached. This collides with the individual's right to be free of interference with his or her rights unless the individual is given notice and an opportunity to be heard in the matter. States, therefore, now generally provide that notice must be given to the defendant before the seizure of property whenever practical, and the defendant must be given a hearing promptly after the seizure. Furthermore, a court cannot SANCTION a seizure that is made without a court order of attachment. To obtain the order, the plaintiff must swear to a set of facts that justify such a drastic interference with the defendant's property.

The process of attachment varies in detail from state to state, but it is not overly complicated. The plaintiff submits an application to the court describing the CAUSE OF ACTION against the defendant and the grounds for seeking an attachment. The plaintiff may have to include documents or other evidence to support the claim that he or she will probably win the lawsuit, and the individual usually is required to make the application under oath. States generally require that the plaintiff post a bond or undertaking in an amount sufficient to secure payment of damages to the defendant if it turns out that the plaintiff was not in fact entitled to the attachment.

The court issues a writ of attachment directing the sheriff or other law enforcement officer to serve a copy of the order on the defendant and to seize property equal in value to the sum specified in the writ. This is called a levy of attachment. The defendant then has a right to challenge the seizure or to post bond for the release of the property, in effect substituting the bond for the property in the court's custody. The order of attachment is effective only for a limited period, the time necessary to WIND UP the lawsuit between plaintiff and defendant or a specified period intended to permit resolution of the controversy. Provisions are usually made for special circumstances or extreme hardship.

Not every kind of property owned by the defendant is subject to attachment. The laws of a state may provide exemptions for certain household items, clothing, tools, and other essentials. The defendant's salary may be subject to attachment, but a certain amount is exempt in order to allow for personal support or for family support. Property belonging to the defendant but in the hands of someone else, such as salary owed or a debt not yet paid, may also be seized, but this procedure is usually called GARNISHMENT rather than attachment.

Courts always have the discretion to exempt more property than that specified in a statute or to deny the attachment altogether under the proper circumstances. This may be done, for example, when the court believes that the property sought to be attached is worth much more than any judgment the plaintiff could hope to win, or where the property is an ongoing business that would be destroyed by attachment.

FURTHER READINGS

Jasper, Margaret C. 2000. *The Law of Attachment and Garnishment.* Dobbs Ferry, NY: Oceana.

Lambert, Vicki. 1999. *Garnishment: A Practical Guide.* Chicago, IL: CCH.

Morganstern, Stanley. 1971. *Legal Protection in Garnishment and Attachment.* Dobbs Ferry, NY: Oceana

Siegel, Lee S., and Charlotte Biblow. 2000. "Attachment in Aid of Arbitration." *Banking Law Journal* 117, vol. 5 (September-October).

CROSS REFERENCE

Search and Seizure.

ATTAINDER

At COMMON LAW, that extinction of CIVIL RIGHTS and capacities that took place whenever a person who had committed TREASON or a felony received a sentence of death for the crime.

The effect of attainder upon a felon was, in general terms, that all estate, real and personal, was forfeited. In common law, attainder resulted in three ways: by confession, by verdict, and by process or outlawry. The first case was where the prisoner pleaded guilty at the bar, or having fled, confessed guilt and abjured the realm to save his or her life. The second was where the prisoner pleaded not guilty at the bar, and the jury brought in a verdict against him or her. The third, when the person accused made his or her escape and was outlawed.

In England, by statute 33 & 34 Vict. c. 23, attainder upon conviction, with consequent corruption of blood, FORFEITURE, *or* ESCHEAT, *was abolished. In the United States, the doctrine of attainder is now scarcely known, although during and shortly after the Revolution acts of attainder were passed by several of the states. The passage of such bills is expressly forbidden by the Constitution (Art. I, Sec. 9).*

Bills of attainder are special acts of the legislature that inflict capital punishments upon persons supposed to be guilty of high offenses, such as treason and felony, without any conviction in the ordinary course of judicial proceedings. If an act inflicts a milder degree of punishment than death, it is called a bill of pains and penalties, but both are included in the prohibition in the Constitution (Art. I, Sec. 9).

The term *attainder* is derived from *attincta,* Latin for stained or blackened. When attainder occurred, the condemned person was considered to bear a mark of infamy that corrupted his or her blood. Attainder was eventually abolished in England by statute.

In the United States, attainder is scarcely known today, although several states enacted acts of attainder during the Revolutionary War period. A few states consider the disqualification of a person impeached and convicted to hold any government office to be a type of attainder. Attainder is akin to the concept of CIVIL DEATH, the forefeiture of certain rights and privileges upon conviction of a serious crime.

ATTEMPT

An undertaking to do an act that entails more than mere preparation but does not result in the successful completion of the act.

In CRIMINAL LAW, an attempt to commit a crime is an offense when an accused makes a substantial but unsuccessful effort to commit a crime. The elements of attempt vary, although generally, there must be an intent to commit the crime, an OVERT ACT beyond mere preparation, and an apparent ability to complete the crime. Generally attempts are punishable by imprisonment, with sentence lengths that vary in time, depending upon the severity of the offense attempted.

ATTENUATE

To reduce the force or severity; to lessen a relationship or connection between two objects.

In CRIMINAL PROCEDURE, the relationship between an illegal search and a confession may be sufficiently attenuated as to remove the confession from the protection afforded by the FRUIT OF THE POISONOUS TREE doctrine, thereby making it admissible as evidence in a criminal prosecution depending upon the facts of the case.

ATTEST

To solemnly declare verbally or in writing that a particular document or testimony about an event is a true and accurate representation of the facts; to bear witness to. To formally certify by a signature that the signer has been present at the execution of a particular writing so as to rebut any potential challenges to its authenticity.

ATTESTATION

The act of attending the execution of a document and bearing witness to its authenticity, by signing one's name to it to affirm that it is genuine. The certification by a custodian of records that a copy of an original document is a true copy that is demonstrated by his or her signature on a certificate.

An attestation is a declaration by a witness that an instrument has been executed in his or her presence according to the formalities required by law. It is not the same as an acknowledgment, a statement by the maker of a document that verifies its authenticity.

An attestation clause is frequently found in legal documents that must be witnessed if they are to be valid, for example, a will or a deed. It states that the instrument has been completed in the manner required by law in the presence of the witness who places his or her signature in the designated space.

ATTICA PRISON RIOT

See PRISON "1971 Attica Prison Riot" (Sidebar).

ATTORN

To turn over money, rent, or goods to another. To assign to a specific function or service.

ATTORNEY-CLIENT PRIVILEGE

In the law of evidence, a client's privilege to refuse to disclose, and to prevent any other person from disclosing, confidential communications between the client and his or her attorney. Such privilege protects communications between attorney and client that are made for the purpose of furnishing or obtaining professional legal advice or assistance. That privilege that permits an attorney to refuse to testify as to communications from the client. It belongs to the client, not the attorney, and hence only the client may waive it. In federal courts, state law is applied with respect to such privilege.

The *attorney-client privilege* encourages clients to disclose to their attorneys all pertinent information in legal matters by protecting such disclosures from discovery at trial. The privileged information, held strictly between the ATTORNEY and the client, may remain private as long as a court does not force disclosure. The privilege does not apply to communications between an attorney and a client that are made in further-ance of a FRAUD or other crime. The responsibility for designating which information should re-main confidential rests with the client. In its most COMMON use, however, the attorney claims the privilege on behalf of the client in refusing to disclose to the court, or to any other party, requested information about the client's case.

As a basic construction in the judicial system, the privilege is an ancient device. It can be found even in Roman law—for example, Marcus Tullius Cicero, while prosecuting the governor of Sicily, could not call the governor's advocate as a witness, because if he were to have done so, the governor would have lost confi-dence in his own defender. Over the years, the close tie between attorney and client developed further with reforms in English COMMON LAW.

Because the attorney-client privilege often balances competing interests, it defies a rigid definition. However, one often-cited characteri-zation was set forth in *United States v. United Shoe Machinery Corp.,* 89 F. Supp. 357 (D. Mass. 1950). The court articulated five requirements: first, the person asserting the privilege must be a client, or must have sought to become a client at the time of disclosure; second, the person connected to the communication must be acting as a lawyer; third, the communication must be between the lawyer and the client exclusively—no non-clients may be included in the communication; fourth, the communication

must have occurred for the purpose of securing a legal opinion, legal services, or assistance in some legal proceeding, and not for the purpose of committing a crime; fifth, the privilege may be claimed or waived by the client only (usually, as stated above, through counsel).

Sometimes, even when all five of the *United Shoe* requirements have been met, courts will compel disclosure of the information sought. They base exceptions to the privilege on Rule 501 of the FEDERAL RULES OF EVIDENCE, which states that "the recognition of a privilege based on a confidential relationship ... should be determined on a case-by-case basis." Courts weigh the benefits to be gained by upholding the privilege (that is, preserv-ing the confidence between attorney and client) against the harms that might be caused if they deny it (that is, the loss of information that would be valuable to the opposing party).

Courts have declared that the fact of an attorney-client relationship itself need not always remain privileged information (*National Union Fire Insurance Co. of Pittsburgh v. Aetna Casualty & Surety Co.,* 384 F.2d 316 [5th Cir. 1967]); the privilege may be upheld, however, if the very existence of an attorney-client relationship could prove to be incriminating to the client (*In re Michaelson,* 511 F.2d 882 [9th Cir. 1975], *cert. denied,* 421 U.S. 978, 95 S. Ct. 1979, 44 L. Ed. 2d 469 [1975]). The attorney-client privilege does not always protect the client's name or the amount paid to an attorney (*Wirtz v. Fowler,* 372 F.2d 315 [5th Cir. 1966]). Further, the attorney's perception of the client's mental competency will not always be protected (*United States v. Kendrick,* 331 F.2d 110 [4th Cir. 1964] [holding that attorney's TESTIMONY that client was respon-sive, and logical in conversation and reasoning, and that he understood that the proceedings, did not address confidential matters]).

In general, exceptions to the attorney-client privilege can prove problematic to criminal defense attorneys, who try to keep a client's potentially incriminating disclosures confidential. One exception, however, is intended to protect attorneys: *Meyerhofer v. Empire Fire & Marine Insurance Co.,* 497 F.2d 1190 (2d Cir. 1974), *cert. denied,* 419 U.S. 998, 95 S. Ct. 314, 42 L. Ed. 2d 272 (1974), held that an attorney may circumvent the privilege if revealing information would relieve him or her of accusations of wrongdoing.

A client is not always a person; a corporation can be a client and can have a right to the attorney-client privilege. The U.S. Supreme Court's decision in *Upjohn Co. v. United States,* 449 U.S. 383, 101 S. Ct. 677, 66 L. Ed. 2d 584 (1981), ensured greater protection for confidential information between a corporation and its lawyers. In the mid-1970s Upjohn Company faced accusations of making questionable payments to officials of foreign governments in order to secure business from those governments. In response to those accusations, Upjohn authorized its corporate attorneys to conduct investigations of foreign payments. When the INTERNAL REVENUE SERVICE (IRS) issued a SUMMONS for the investigative documents that Upjohn had left to its lawyers, Upjohn refused to comply with the request. Upjohn argued that the documents were privileged. The U.S. Supreme Court ruled in favor of Upjohn, and this decision became the standard for determining the nature of services—either legal or business—provided by the corporate attorney.

By the early 1990s the attorney-client privilege was narrowed by federal guidelines that were intended to combat MONEY LAUNDERING. The federal government, in conjunction with President GEORGE H.W. BUSH's crackdown on drug trafficking, pressed an IRS policy that would deter drug dealers and other criminals from disguising profits. The law required attorneys to disclose to the government any cash payment in excess of $10,000, as well as the name of the client making the payment (26 U.S.C.A. § 6050 I).

In *United States v. Leventhal,* 961 F.2d 936 (11th Cir. 1992), Robert Leventhal, an attorney in Florida, refused to disclose to the IRS the names of clients who had paid him more than $10,000 in cash. Leventhal's clients had wished to remain anonymous, and Leventhal argued that the attorney-client privilege gave them that right. Leventhal cited the Florida Rules of Professional Conduct, which require disclosure of confidential client information only in rare circumstances. The federal government sued Leventhal. The court ruled that disclosing the clients' identities revealed only the existence of an attorney-client relationship, a simple factual matter that is not within the scope of the privilege. Therefore, Leventhal was compelled to reveal the sources of the payments.

The U.S. Court of Appeals for the Sixth Circuit followed *Leventhal* in *United States v. Ritchie,* 15 F.3d 592 (1994), *cert. denied,* 513 U.S. 868, 115 S. Ct. 188, 130 L. Ed. 2d 121 (1994).

Attorney Robert Ritchie had challenged the same IRS policy, but the court noted that Congress gave the IRS broad powers to ensure compliance with the tax code. Appeals court judge Alice M. Batchelder held that there was no "constitutionally protected liberty interest in spending large amounts of cash without having to account for it."

Attorneys have decried the federal government's position in such cases, but the attorney-client privilege remains useful as a defensive measure in more general circumstances. The privilege remains an exception to the general rule that individuals must TESTIFY to all facts within their knowledge. Rooted in ancient principles, it fosters trust within this important relationship and helps attorneys to develop fully their clients' cases by encouraging complete disclosure of relevant information.

The U.S. Supreme Court declined the opportunity to further narrow the attorney-client privilege in *Swidler & Berlin v. U.S., 524 U.S. 399, 118 S. Ct. 2081, 141 L.Ed.2d 379* (U.S. 1998), which raised the question of whether the attorney-client privilege survived the death of the client, and thus whether following the client's death the attorney could be compelled to disclose information that was protected as confidential while the client was still alive.

The dispute arose from the investigation conducted by the Office of the INDEPENDENT COUNSEL into the 1992 firing of several White House Travel Office employees, amid allegations of THEFT and kickbacks from air-charter companies. Deputy White House counsel Vincent Foster had met with a private attorney to seek LEGAL REPRESENTATION concerning the travel-office controversy, which the American press had since branded *Travelgate* The attorney took handwritten notes at the meeting. Nine days later, Foster committed SUICIDE.

Subsequently, a federal GRAND JURY, at the request of the Office of the Independent Counsel, issued subpoenas for the handwritten notes as part of a new investigation into whether crimes had been committed in obstructing the earlier investigations into the travel-office firings. Foster's attorneys moved to QUASH the SUBPOENA on the grounds that they were protected from disclosure by the attorney-client privilege.

The federal district court ruled that the notes were still protected by privilege, and it denied enforcement of the subpoenas. In reversing that ruling, the Court of Appeals recognized that most courts assume that the privilege survives death, but noted that such references usually occur in the context of the well-recognized TESTAMENTARY exception to the privilege allowing disclosure for disputes among the client's heirs. *In re Sealed Case*, 124 F.3d 230 (D.C. Cir. 1997). The court said that the risk of posthumous revelation, when confined to the criminal context, would have little or no chilling effect on client communication, but that the costs of protecting communications after death would be high. Concluding that the privilege is not absolute under such circumstances, and that a balancing test should apply instead, the appeals court recognized a posthumous exception to the attorney-client privilege for communications in which the relative importance to particular criminal LITIGATION is substantial.

The U.S. Supreme Court reversed, noting that courts generally presume that the attorney-client privilege extends beyond the death of the client, even in the criminal context, and that, at the very least, the burden was on the Office of the Independent Counsel to show that reason and experience required a departure from that rule. The Office of the Independent Counsel had failed to make a sufficient showing to overturn the common law rule that is embodied in the prevailing case law.

"Knowing that communications will remain confidential even after death encourages the client to communicate fully and frankly with counsel," the Court wrote. "While the fear of disclosure . . . may be reduced if disclosure is limited to posthumous disclosure in a criminal context," the Court continued, "it seems unreasonable to assume that it vanishes altogether." The Court emphasized that "[c]lients may be concerned about reputation, civil LIABILITY, or possible harm to friends or family," and thus "[p]osthumous disclosure of such communications may be as feared as disclosure during the client's lifetime."

FURTHER READINGS

Epstein, Edna Selan. 2007. *The Attorney-Client Privilege and the Work-Product Doctrine.* 5th ed. Chicago: American Bar Association.

Freedman, Monroe H. 2004. *Understanding Lawyers' Ethics.* 3d ed. New York: Bender.

Gillers, Stephen. 1979. *The Rights of Lawyers and Clients.* New York: Avon.

Lerman, Lisa G., and Philip G. Schrag. 2005. *Ethical Problems in the Practice of Law* (Casebook). Frederick, MD: Aspen.

Noona, John M., and Michael A. Knoerzer. 1989. "The Attorney-Client Privilege and Corporate Transactions: Counsel as Keeper of Corporate Secrets." In The Attorney-Client Privilege under Siege. *Tort and Insurance Practice.* Lake Buena Vista, FL, May 10–14.

Rice, Paul R. 2009. *Attorney-Client Privilege in the United States.* Eagan, MN: West.

Tinkham, Thomas, and William J. Wernz. 1993. *Attorney-Client Privilege, Confidentiality, and Work Product Doctrine in Minnesota.* Minneapolis: Dorsey & Whitney.

CROSS REFERENCES

Attorney Misconduct; Drugs and Narcotics; Ethics, Legal; Legal Representation; Model Rules of Professional Conduct.

ATTORNEY

A person admitted to practice law in at least one jurisdiction and authorized to perform criminal and civil legal functions on behalf of clients. These functions include providing legal counsel, drafting legal documents, and representing clients before courts, administrative agencies, and other tribunals.

Unless a contrary meaning is plainly indicated this term is synonymous with "attorney at law," "lawyer," or "counselor at law."

In order to become an attorney, a person must obtain a JURIS DOCTOR degree from an ACCREDITED LAW SCHOOL, although this requirement may vary in some states. Attendance at law school usually entails three years of full-time study, or four years of study in evening classes, where available. A bachelor's degree is generally a prerequisite to admission to law school.

With few exceptions, a person must pass the BAR EXAMINATION of that state in order to be admitted to practice law there. After passing a bar examination and practicing law for a specified period, a person may be admitted to the bars of other states, pursuant to their own court rules.

Although an attorney might be required by law to render some services PRO BONO (free of charge), the individual is ordinarily entitled to compensation for the reasonable value of services performed. He or she has a right, called an attorney's lien, to retain the property or money of a client until payment has been received for all services. An attorney must generally obtain court permission to discontinue representation of a client during the course of a trial or criminal proceedings.

Certain discourse between attorney and client is protected by the ATTORNEY-CLIENT PRIVILEGE. In the law of evidence, the client can refuse to

U.S. Attorneys General

Name	Term	President
Edmund Randolph	1789-1794	Washington
William Bradford	1794-1795	Washington
Charles Lee	1795-1801	Washington & John Adams
Levi Lincoln	1801-1805	Jefferson
John Breckenridge	1805-1806	Jefferson
Caesar A. Rodney	1807-1811	Jefferson & Madison
William Pinkney	1811-1814	Madison
Richard Rush	1814-1817	Madison
William Wirt	1817-1829	Monroe & John Q. Adams
John M. Berrien	1829-1831	Jackson
Roger B. Taney	1831-1833	Jackson
Benjamin F. Butler	1833-1838	Jackson & Van Buren
Felix Grundy	1838-1839	Van Buren
Henry D. Gilpin	1840-1841	Van Buren
John J. Crittenden	1841	Harrison & Tyler
Hugh S. Legare	1841-1843	Tyler
John Nelson	1843-1845	Tyler
John Y. Mason	1845-1846	Polk
Nathan Clifford	1846-1848	Polk
Issac Toucey	1848-1849	Polk
Reverdy Johnson	1849-1850	Taylor
John J. Crittenden	1850-1853	Fillmore
Caleb Cushing	1853-1857	Pierce
Jeremiah S. Black	1857-1860	Buchanan
Edwin M. Stanton	1860-1861	Buchanan
Edward Bates	1861-1864	Lincoln
James Speed	1864-1866	Lincoln & Johnson
Henry Stanberry	1866-1868	Johnson
William M. Evarts	1868-1869	Johnson
Ebenezer R. Hoar	1869-1870	Grant
Amos T. Akerman	1870-1872	Grant
George H. Williams	1871-1875	Grant
Edwards Pierrepont	1875-1876	Grant
Alphonso Taft	1876-1877	Grant
Charles Devens	1877-1881	Hayes
Wayne MacVeagh	1881	Garfield
Benjamin H. Brewster	1881-1885	Arthur
Augustus H. Garland	1885-1889	Cleveland
William H.H. Miller	1889-1893	Harrison
Richard Olney	1893-1895	Cleveland
Judson Harmon	1895-1897	Cleveland
Joseph McKenna	1897-1898	McKinley
John W. Griggs	1898-1901	McKinley
Philander C. Knox	1901-1904	McKinley
William H. Moody	1904-1906	Roosevelt
Charles J. Bonaparte	1906-1909	Roosevelt
George W. Wickersham	1909-1913	Taft
James C. McReynolds	1913-1914	Wilson
Thomas Watt Gregory	1914-1919	Wilson
A. Mitchell Palmer	1919-1921	Wilson
Harry M. Daugherty	1921-1924	Harding
Harlan Fiske Stone	1924-1925	Coolidge
John G. Sargent	1925-1929	Coolidge
William D. Mitchell	1929-1933	Hoover
Homer S. Cummings	1933-1939	Roosevelt
Frank Murphy	1939-1940	Roosevelt
Robert H. Jackson	1940-1941	Roosevelt
Francis Biddle	1941-1945	Roosevelt
Tom C. Clark	1945-1949	Truman
J. Howard McGrath	1949-1952	Truman
James P. McGranery	1952-1953	Truman
Herbert Brownell Jr.	1953-1957	Eisenhower
William P. Rogers	1957-1961	Eisenhower

[CONTINUED]

divulge and prohibit anyone else from disclosing confidential communications transmitted to and from the attorney. Notwithstanding, attorneys are permitted to make general (non-privileged) pre-trial statements to the press if there is a "reasonable likelihood" that the statements will not interfere with a fair trial or otherwise prejudice the due administration of justice (*In re Morrissey,* 168 F.3d 134 [4th Cir. 1999]).

CROSS REFERENCES

Attorney-Client Privilege; Attorney Misconduct; Continuing Legal Education; Legal Education; Legal Representation; Right to Counsel.

ATTORNEY GENERAL

The attorney general is the chief law enforcement officer of the United States or of a state government, typically serving in an executive branch position. The individual represents the government in litigation and serves as the principal advisor to government officials and agencies in legal matters.

The attorney general is head of the U.S. JUSTICE DEPARTMENT and chief law officer of the federal government. He or she represents the United States in legal matters generally and gives advice and opinions to the president and to other heads of executive departments as requested. In cases of exceptional gravity or special importance, the ATTORNEY general may appear in person before the U.S. Supreme Court to represent the interests of the government.

As head of the Justice Department, the U.S. attorney general is charged with enforcing federal laws, furnishing legal counsel in federal cases, construing the laws under which other executive departments act, supervising federal penal institutions, and investigating violations of federal laws. The attorney general also supervises and directs the activities of the U.S. attorneys and U.S. marshals in the various judicial districts. (U.S. attorneys PROSECUTE all offenses against the United States and prosecute or defend for the government all civil actions, suits, or proceedings in which the United States is concerned; U.S. marshals execute all lawful writs, processes, and orders issued under authority of the United States.)

The office of the attorney general was created by the First Congress in the JUDICIARY ACT OF 1789 (An Act to Establish the Judicial Courts of the United States, ch. 20, § 35, 1 Stat.

73, 92–93). The First Congress did not expect the attorney general—a part-time employee with scant pay, no staff, and little power—to play a major role in the emerging federal government. As the members of the First Congress established a system for the enforcement of federal laws, their primary concern was to protect state and individual freedoms and to avoid the creation of a central legal system that would allow the tyrannies they had experienced as American colonists under George III. Therefore, the Judiciary Act gave the attorney general just two principal duties: (1) to prosecute and conduct all suits in the SUPREME COURT OF THE UNITED STATES that concerned the United States and (2) to give an opinion on questions of law when asked to do so by the president or heads of other executive departments.

The early attorneys general spent little time arguing before the Supreme Court because few cases traveled through the nation's developing court system and even fewer warranted Supreme Court review. Together, the first three attorneys general—Edmund Randolph, WILLIAM BRADFORD, and Charles Lee—represented the United States in the Supreme Court only six times in their collective years in office.

Furthermore, early attorneys general were specifically restricted by the Judiciary Act from participating in lower-court actions. District attorneys (known in the early 2000s as U.S. attorneys) held the authority to represent the United States in district and circuit courts. Each DISTRICT ATTORNEY could independently decide which cases to pursue and on what grounds, a situation that soon resulted in a number of contradictory legal positions for the federal government. Because the attorney general had no power to direct district attorneys in their lower-court LITIGATION, the officeholder was often unaware of litigation that concerned the interests of the United States.

In a letter to President GEORGE WASHINGTON dated December 26, 1791, Attorney General Randolph expressed concern about the limitations of his office and complained specifically about the lack of a defined relationship with the district attorneys. Randolph was the first of many attorneys general to point out that their prescribed duties did not allow them to fully look after the interests of the United States, and he was the first to propose an expansion of the office's duties and jurisdiction.

U.S. Attorneys General

Name	Term	President
Robert F. Kennedy	1961–1964	Kennedy
Nicholas deB. Katzenbach	1965–1966	Johnson
Ramsey Clark	1967–1969	Johnson
John N. Mitchell	1969–1972	Nixon
Richard G. Kleindienst	1972–1973	Nixon
Elliot L. Richardson	1973	Nixon
William B. Saxbe	1974–1975	Nixon
Edward H. Levi	1975–1977	Ford
Griffin B. Bell	1977–1979	Carter
Benjamin R. Civiletti	1979–1981	Carter
William French Smith	1981–1985	Reagan
Edwin Meese III	1985–1988	Reagan
Richard Thornburgh	1988–1991	Reagan & George Bush
William Barr	1991–1993	George Bush
Janet Reno	1993–2001	Clinton
John Ashcroft	2001–2005	George W. Bush
Alberto R. Gonzales	2005–2007	George W. Bush
Michael B. Mukasey	2007–2009	George W. Bush
Eric H. Holder	2009–	Barack Obama

SOURCE: U.S. Department of Justice, "The Attorneys General of the United States," available online at http://www.usdoj.gov/ag/attygeneraldate.html (accessed on August 12, 2009).

ILLUSTRATION BY GGS CREATIVE RESOURCES. REPRODUCED BY PERMISSION OF GALE, A PART OF CENGAGE LEARNING.

Ignoring complaints and proposals, Congress remained reluctant to expand the duties of the attorney general and often passed legislation that assigned special legal functions to officials in other government departments. For example, in the early 1800s, Congress created a SOLICITOR of the treasury to handle all suits for the recovery of money or property in the United States, a move that further complicated the attorney general's efforts to fully look after the interests of the government.

With court appearances limited by the lack of both cases before the Supreme Court and jurisdiction to oversee lower-court cases, opinion writing consumed most of the time of early attorneys general. Together, Attorneys General Randolph, Bradford, and Lee wrote more than 40 formal opinions on such diverse issues as IMMUNITY for diplomats, applications for PATENTS, and the choice of directors for the nation's first federal bank. However, early attorneys general were not required to provide the government with written records of their opinions. When WILLIAM WIRT, the eleventh attorney general, took office in 1817, he found that his predecessors had provided no record of their past opinions to guide his deliberations. Understandably, early attorneys general, who received only a small stipend for their services and relied on the private PRACTICE OF LAW for their personal income, spent little money to hire clerks to transcribe and preserve their work. They simply relied on the recipients of their opinions to retain them for future reference. Still, legislative attempts to provide the attorney general with an office, a clerk, and supplies continually failed to win support.

The limited duties outlined for the attorney general by the First Congress, along with the lack of PERQUISITES for the office, made it difficult for presidents to attract qualified appointees and keep them in office. Even President Washington had difficulty convincing his personal attorney and long-time friend, Randolph, to take the job. Washington finally won Randolph over by pointing out that service as attorney general might enhance his earning opportunities in private practice. In fact, Randolph did not profit much from the prestige of the office during or after his tenure. Subsequent attorneys general did profit handsomely from the experience, but early officeholders often had difficulty balancing the dual commitments to private practice and public service.

The commitment to public service for early attorneys general was further complicated by institutional tensions between the executive, legislative, and judicial branches of government, which all claimed the officeholder's time, services, and allegiance. It has been said that the attorney general serves "three masters": the president, the Congress, and the courts (American Enterprise Institute for PUBLIC POLICY Research 1968). Although the attorney general advises the president, the basic authority of the office is derived from Congress and the functions of the office are subject to congressional control. In addition, the attorney general is a member of the bar and, therefore, an officer of the court subject to the directives of the judicial branch.

Although the First Congress defined the relationship between the attorney general and the president, it did not define the relationship between the attorney general and Congress. In addition, it was notably silent regarding who was ultimately to decide when and whether the interests of the United States were "concerned": nothing in the Judiciary Act of 1789 specified who should control the attorney general or to whom she or he should report. Early attorneys general took orders from the Congress as well as from the president and the heads of other executive departments. Attorneys general were often asked to deliver opinions to Congress on legislative proposals, and they came to be viewed as authorities on constitutional issues—much to the chagrin of both legislators, who frequently disagreed with their interpretations, and members of the judiciary, who assumed that they themselves were the final arbiters in constitutional matters.

The attorney general has also been said to straddle the legal and political worlds. When Congress created the executive departments, it did not specify who should or should not be members of the president's cabinet, and it could not predict the level of influence held by any one individual. In the early years, the attorney general did not have cabinet rank but served as counsel to those who did. However, as Washington's personal legal adviser, Randolph participated in cabinet meetings as early as 1792, establishing the PRECEDENT for attorneys general to have a hand in making policy as well as in interpreting and enforcing the laws. The attorney general's role in policy making soon brought into question the extent to which party lines and presidential preferences influenced his or her legal advice. Over time, some attorneys general handled the dilemma with more integrity and less partisanship than others.

The lack of centralized authority and the lack of basic institutional support for the office of the attorney general began to be remedied by Congress in the early nineteenth century. Subsequently, many of the issues caused or influenced by conflicting allegiances were dissolved or clarified through administrative policy and legislation.

In 1814, during the term of Attorney General RICHARD RUSH, President JAMES MADISON made the first move to expand formally the presence (if not the duties) of the attorney general, by proposing a requirement that the attorney general reside in or near Washington, D.C., while Congress was in session. The residency requirement had previously been resisted by some attorneys general. Although it made the officeholder available to the president and Congress when the attorney general was most needed, it also made the private practice of law more inconvenient to an attorney general who lived far from the Capitol.

Attorney General Wirt (1817–1829), under Presidents JAMES MONROE and JOHN QUINCY ADAMS, was the first to comprehend fully the officeholder's need for administrative structure. During his tenure, the attorney general was finally given government office space, a transcribing clerk, and a small fund for office supplies. The practice of providing opinions to Congress was also curtailed during this period, when Wirt presented a paper to President Monroe outlining the extent of his congressional workload and his objections. Wirt told the president that opinions had been provided to Congress in the past as a courtesy, not as a MATTER OF LAW. Wirt told the president the practice would not continue unless Congress revised the law and made it mandatory.

By 1853, when CALEB CUSHING became attorney general under President FRANKLIN PIERCE, the officeholder had four clerks and—for the first time—a salary comparable to those of other cabinet officers. Also in 1853, Cushing decided it was no longer appropriate to continue the private practice of law while in office. He was the nation's first full-time attorney general.

Recommendations that a department of law be created by Congress were discussed as early as 1830 and were championed by numerous presidents and attorneys general. A DEPARTMENT OF JUSTICE was first suggested in 1851 by Alex H. H. Stuart, secretary of the newly established DEPARTMENT OF THE INTERIOR.

No action was taken by Congress until February 25, 1870, when the Joint Committee on Retrenchments (appointed to find ways of reducing government expenditures) drafted a bill to consolidate legal functions and create a department of justice. The bill was made into law four months later, and the Justice Department officially came into existence on July 1, 1870 (An Act to Establish the Department of Justice, §17, 16 Stat. 162 [June 22, 1870]).

The June 22, 1870 law created a new position, that of SOLICITOR GENERAL, whose holder is in charge of representing the government in suits and appeals in the Supreme Court and in lower federal trial and appellate courts, in cases involving the interests of the United States. The law also provided for two assistant attorneys general. It gave the attorney general complete direction and control of the U.S. attorneys and all other counsel employed on behalf of the United States. Moreover, it gave the attorney general supervisory powers over the accounts of district attorneys, marshals, clerks, and other OFFICERS OF THE COURT involved in federal matters.

The first attorney general to head the new department was Amos T. Akerman of Georgia, appointed by President ULYSSES S. GRANT in 1870. So, 81 years after the creation of the office of the attorney general, the nation finally had a full-fledged organization to administer and enforce its laws. Evolution in the position of attorney general culminated in the formation of the Justice Department.

In the late twentieth and early twenty-first centuries, U.S. attorneys general, including JANET RENO and JOHN DAVID ASHCROFT, have been at the center of extensive media attention. Reno, for example, was the subject of intense scrutiny for her role in the deaths of about 80 members of the Branch Davidians, an armed religious sect, near Waco, Texas, in 1993. The deaths occurred when the FEDERAL BUREAU OF INVESTIGATION, following a long standoff, set fire to the group's compound during an attempted raid. Reno later took responsibility for the FBI actions. Subsequently, Reno was involved in the return to Cuba of a refugee child named Elian Gonzalez in April 2000. Reno ordered officers of the Immigration and NATURALIZATION Service to raid the home of the child's relatives in Miami in order to return the child to his father, who remained in Cuba. Ashcroft, a former U.S. senator and governor of Missouri, was at the center of attention throughout the investigation of terrorists following the September 11, 2001, attacks on the United States.

Still, perhaps the most controversial news regarding the Office of Attorney General involved the proposed IMPEACHMENT of ALBERTO GONZALES, appointed to the position by President GEORGE W. BUSH in 2001. He was the first Hispanic American to be appointed to that office and also the first U.S. attorney general to face impeachment. In September 2008, the Office of the Inspector General (OIG) within the U.S. Department of Justice (DOJ) released an investigation report clearly critical of his performance. the *Report of Investigation Regarding Allegations of Mishandling of Classified Documents by Attorney General Alberto Gonzales* ostensibly concerned itself with Gonzales's handling of documents containing classified information about the National Security Agency (NSA) sensitive surveillance program relating to national intelligence. However, during the course of the investigation, the OIG learned of other instances of potential mishandling of classified documents by Gonzales. The security compromise unequivocally violated Justice Department policies as well as the Federal

Criminal Code, which contains provisions relating to the improper handling of classified documents (e.g., 18 USC 1924). But Gonzales was not prosecuted, for he had already resigned a year prior (September 2007) amid a stormy controversy in Congress over his role in the firing of nine U.S. attorneys. He was about to face an impeachment inquiry by the House of Representatives at the time of his resignation.

The growth of the office of the attorney general from a part-time, one-person operation into a vast and complex law enforcement organization is an inseparable part of the story of the United States and the development of its institutions. As the role of government has expanded, so too has the role of the nation's attorney general. Moreover, though the attorney general's role continues to grow and evolve, the basic duties of the office and the structure of its supporting organization have been in place since the Civil War.

State Attorneys General

State attorneys general possess many of the same powers and responsibilities as their counterpart in the federal government. A state attorney general's office is typically a part of the EXECUTIVE BRANCH of the state government. He or she is generally entrusted with the duties of prosecuting suits and proceedings involving state government and advising the governor and other administrative officers of the state government. Many state statutes also establish the state attorney general as the official legal advisor or representative of various departments and agencies.

In some states, the power of the attorney general is limited to those specified by statute. The powers of most attorneys general are subject to the desires of the legislature, although powers in some states are prescribed by statute. In fulfilling the advisory function of the office, attorneys general are often requested to draft advisory opinions related to the application of the law to a particular agency or official. These opinions are generally not considered binding on the general public, though in some instances they may be binding upon the officials that request them.

FURTHER READINGS

American Enterprise Institute for Public Policy Research. 1968. *Roles of the Attorney General.* Washington: D.C.: American Enterprise Institute for Public Policy Research.

Baker, Nancy V. 1985. *Conflicting Loyalties: Law and Politics in the Attorney General's Office, 1789–1990.* Lawrence: Univ. Press of Kansas.

Justice Department. 1990. *200th Anniversary of the Office of Attorney General, 1789–1989.* Washington, D.C.: Justice Department.

Powell, H. Jefferson. 2002. *A Community Built on Needs: The Constitution in History and Politics.* Chicago, IL: Univ. of Chicago Press.

Justice Department. 2008. "Report of Investigation Regarding Allegations of Mishandling of Classified Documents by Attorney General Alberto Gonzales" Available at http://www.usdoj.gov/org/special/50809/final.pdf; website home page: http://www.usdoj.gov/org/ (accessed September 1, 2009)

CROSS REFERENCES

Justice Department; Officers of the Court; Supreme Court of the United States; Question of Law; Washington, George.

ATTORNEY MISCONDUCT

Behavior by an attorney that conflicts with established rules of professional conduct and is punishable by disciplinary measures.

More than any other profession, the legal profession is self-governing. That is, it is largely regulated by lawyers and judges themselves rather than by the government or outside agencies. In particular, the AMERICAN BAR ASSOCIATION (ABA), the largest professional association for attorneys, governs the PRACTICE OF LAW through its establishment of rules of conduct. These rules are then adopted, sometimes in a modified form, by state courts and enforced by court-appointed disciplinary committees or bar associations. Attorneys found to be in violation of professional standards are guilty of misconduct and subject to disciplinary procedures. Disciplinary action by a state BAR ASSOCIATION or other authority may include private reprimands; public censure; suspension of the ability to practice law; and, most severe of all, disbarment—permanent denial of the ability to practice law in that jurisdiction. The state supreme court is the final ARBITER in questions of professional conduct in most jurisdictions.

Since 1908 the ABA has been responsible for defining the standards of proper conduct for the legal profession. These standards, many of them established by the ABA Standing Committee on Ethics and PROFESSIONAL RESPONSIBILITY, are continuously evolving as society and the practice of law change over time. In 1969 the ABA passed its Model Code of Professional Responsibility, guidelines for proper legal conduct that were eventually adopted by all jurisdictions. The ABA modified the code by adopting the Model Rules of Professional Conduct in 1983. The model rules have been used by 40 states to create official guidelines for professional conduct; 11 states or jurisdictions, including Washington, D.C., and the Virgin Islands, have continued to base their ethical codes on the earlier model code. California has developed its own rules of professional conduct. Whatever their basis, these codes or rules define the lawyer's proper role and relationship to the client. It is essential that lawyers understand the ethical codes under which they must operate. Failure to do so may result in not only disciplinary action by the relevant professional authorities but also MALPRACTICE suits against the lawyer. A malpractice suit may result in loss of money or the ability to work with specific clients.

Rule 8.4 of the Model Rules of Professional Conduct contains the following statements on *attorney misconduct*:

It is professional misconduct for a lawyer to:

(a) Violate or attempt to violate the Rules of Professional Conduct, knowingly assist or induce another to do so, or do so through the acts of another;

(b) Commit a criminal act that reflects adversely on the lawyer's honesty, trustworthiness or fitness as a lawyer in other respects;

(c) Engage in conduct involving dishonesty, FRAUD, deceit or misrepresentation;

(d) Engage in conduct that is prejudicial to the administration of justice;

(e) State or imply an ability to influence improperly a government agency or official;

(f) Knowingly assist a judge or judicial officer in conduct that is a violation of applicable rules of judicial conduct or other law.

Besides issuing these general statements, the model rules set down many specific requirements for ATTORNEY conduct in different situations.

Because of an attorney's special relationship to the law, he or she is held to a special standard of conduct before the law, as the ABA asserts in its *Lawyers' Manual on Professional Conduct*:

As members of the bar and OFFICERS OF THE COURT, lawyers are beneficiaries of the privilege of the practice of law and also are subject to higher duties and responsibilities than are non-lawyers. A lawyer's fiduciary duties arise from his status as a member of the legal profession and are expressed, at least in part, by the applicable rules of professional conduct.

The word *fiduciary* in this quotation comes from the Latin word *fiducia*, meaning "trust"; as a fiduciary, then, the attorney acts as the trusted representative of the client. Trust is thus a defining element of the legal profession, and without it, the practice of law could not exist. For that reason, the legal profession has created strict rules of conduct regarding the attorney's relationship with the client.

Attorney-Client Relationship

The model rules set forth specific guidelines defining the attorney-client relationship. An attorney will be guilty of misconduct, for example, if she or he fails to provide competent representation to a client, to act with diligence and promptness regarding a client's legal concerns, or to keep a client informed of LEGAL PROCEEDINGS. Charging exorbitant fees or overbilling is also considered misconduct, as is counseling a client to commit a crime. For example, trial lawyer Harvey Myerson was suspended in 1992 from the practice of law by the New York Supreme Court after he was convicted of overbilling by millions of dollars (*In re Myerson*, 182 A.D. 2d 242, 588 N.Y.S.2d 142 [N.Y. App. Div. 1992]).

Many types of attorney misconduct involve a CONFLICT OF INTEREST on the part of the attorney. A conflict of interest arises when an attorney puts personal interests ahead of professional responsibilities to the client. The model rules specify the potential for conflict of interest in many different situations. Thus, for example, an attorney who by representing one client adversely affects another client has a conflict of interest and is guilty of misconduct. Conflict of interest rules also forbid an attorney to enter into a business transaction with a client unless the client is fully aware of how the transaction will affect his or her LEGAL REPRESENTATION and agrees to the transaction in writing. Similarly, an attorney is guilty of misconduct if he or she makes a deal with the client for acquisition of the book, film, or media rights to the client's story. Providing a client with financial assistance also introduces a conflict of interest into the attorney-client relationship.

If an attorney is related to another attorney as parent, child, sibling, or spouse, that attorney may not represent a client in opposition to the related attorney except when given consent to

Attorney-Client Sexual Relations

The American Bar Association (ABA) has recognized sexual relations between attorneys and their clients as a significant ethical problem for the legal profession. The ABA's Standing Committee on Ethics and Professional Responsibility addressed this issue in 1992 by issuing a formal opinion (no. 92-364). Although the opinion acknowledged that the Model Rules of Professional Conduct do not specifically address the issue of attorney-client sex, it argued that an attorney's sexual relationship with a current client "may involve unfair exploitation of the lawyer's fiduciary position and presents a significant danger that the lawyer's ability to represent the client adequately may be impaired, and that as a consequence the lawyer may violate both the Model Rules and the Model Code." Becoming sexually intimate with a client, the opinion adds, undermines the "objective detachment" necessary for legal representation because "[t]he roles of lover and lawyer are potentially conflicting ones." In addition, the opinion argued, attorney-client sex introduces a clear conflict of interest into a case, and it may also compromise attorney-client privilege, the principle that ensures the confidentiality of lawyer-client communication. Any secrets revealed to an attorney by a client outside of their legal relationship may not be protected by attorney-client privilege.

Proponents of professional rules against attorney-client sexual contact argue that the legal profession should follow the example of other professions such as psychology and psychiatry, and create strict sanctions against sex with clients. Legal clients, these proponents say, are often vulnerable when dealing with attorneys, particularly in such areas of legal practice as family law. A lawyer who becomes sexually involved with a client in a divorce proceeding can take advantage of the client undergoing emotional trauma. That lawyer may hinder any attempts at reconciliation between a couple and complicate matters for any children involved. Sexual relationships between lawyer and client may also affect custody and child visitation decisions in the case. The American Academy of Matrimonial Lawyers, in its Standards of Conduct in Family Law Litigation, specifically prohibits attorney-client sex: "An attorney should never have a sexual relationship with a client or opposing counsel during the time of the representation" (§ 2.16 [1991]).

Some attorneys object to such rules, arguing that they interfere with their First Amendment rights to freedom of association. They bristle at the notion of state bar associations regulating the private affairs of consenting adults. Nevertheless, attorneys are increasingly being disciplined for becoming sexually involved with clients, and state bar associations are drafting clearer and more stringent rules against attorney-client sexual contact. Wisconsin's Supreme Court, for example, in 1987, revoked the license of an attorney in part because he had sex with a client (*In re Hallows,* 136 Wis. 2d 72, 401 N.W.2d 557). The attorney, the court argued, was "placing his interests above" those of his client. In 1990 the same court for the first time suspended the license of a criminal lawyer who had sex with a client (*In re Ridgeway,* 158 Wis. 2d 452, 462 N.W.2d 671). Oregon and Minnesota have adopted outright bans on attorney-client sexual contact. Rule 1.8(k) of the Minnesota Rules of Professional Conduct, which became effective July 1, 1994, forbids attorney-client sexual contact during the conduct of a professional legal relationship. It allows exceptions to the rule only for relationships beginning before legal representation has commenced or after it has ended. In the case of clients that are organizations rather than individuals, an attorney may not have sexual contact with any member of the client organization directly overseeing the case.

FURTHER READINGS

Awad, Abed. 1998. "Attorney-Client Sexual Relations." *Journal of the Legal Profession* 22 (annual): 131–91.

Kane, Andrew W., et al. 1992. "Attorney Sexual Misconduct." *American Journal of Family Law* 6 (fall): 191–95.

Shirey, William K. 1999. "Dealing with the Profession's 'Dirty Little Secret': A Proposal for Regulating Attorney-Client Sexual Relations." *Georgetown Journal of Legal Ethics* 13 (fall): 131–60.

Struzzi, Melissa A. 1999. "Sex behind the Bar: Should Attorney-Client Sexual Relations be Prohibited?" *Duquesne Law Review* 37 (summer): 637–57.

do so by the client. This type of conflict of interest has become increasingly common as more women enter the legal profession and the number of marriages between attorneys grows. State bar associations, such as that of Michigan, have held that these guidelines also apply to lawyers who are living together or dating but are not married. The potential for conflict of interest when the opposing attorneys are married or romantically involved is clear. Imagine a woman representing a client in a PERSONAL INJURY lawsuit seeking millions of dollars worth of damages from a manufacturer, with her husband representing the manufacturer. As a couple, they have a monetary interest in gaining a large settlement from the manufacturer, thereby giving the husband an incentive to lose his case. Given this conflict of interest, the couple is obligated to reveal to their clients the fact that they are married. If the clients agree to go ahead with the case regardless of the conflict of interest, then the attorneys may decide to continue their representation.

Special examples of conflict of interest have arisen in cases involving indigent defendants who must use publicly provided defense attorneys. In many jurisdictions, it is considered misconduct for an attorney to refuse court appointment as a public service defender for a poor client, even when a spouse's legal associate or firm is involved on the opposing side of the case. Normally, for example, state bar associations allow a DISTRICT ATTORNEY to PROSECUTE persons defended by partners or associates of the district attorney's spouse as long as the client is notified of the situation; similarly, they will allow a district attorney's spouse to defend persons prosecuted by other members of the district attorney's staff. Nevertheless, in a 1992 case, *Haley v. Boles,* 824 S.W.2d 796, the Texas Court of Appeals found that a conflict of interest gave a court-appointed attorney grounds to refuse appointment as a PUBLIC DEFENDER for a poor client. The PROSECUTOR was married to the court-appointed counsel's law partner, creating a potential conflict of interest. According to the court's decision, a poor DEFENDANT who must rely on a public defender has fewer choices for legal representation than a defendant who can afford to employ her or his own attorney. Therefore, an attorney who has a conflict of interest must be able to refuse to represent a client as a public defender without being charged with misconduct, thereby ensuring that the client receives legal representation free of a conflict of interest.

Any breach of the trust by the attorney that underlies the relationship between that attorney and the client can be considered misconduct. For example, an attorney is often called upon to hold or transfer money for a client, and in this situation, the client places an extraordinary amount of trust in the lawyer. Any misuse of the client's money by the attorney—called misappropriation of client funds—constitutes a serious breach of trust and a gross example of misconduct. This offense includes stealing from the client, mingling the attorney's money with that of the client, and controlling client funds without authorization. The model rules require that funds given to a lawyer by a client be kept in an account separate from the lawyer's own account.

To encourage clients to inform their attorneys of all details relevant to a case, ethical codes also entrust attorneys with preserving the confidentiality of the information their clients give them; any failure to do so constitutes misconduct on the part of the attorney. The law protects attorney-client confidentiality with the principle of ATTORNEY-CLIENT PRIVILEGE, and under very few circumstances is it lawful to breach this privilege of confidentiality. The privilege may be revoked to prevent the client from "committing a criminal act that … is likely to result in imminent death or substantial bodily harm" (*Model Rules of Professional Conduct,* Rule 1.6 1983), or to respond to civil or criminal proceedings made by the client against the attorney. Except for these rare cases, only the client may WAIVE the attorney-client privilege of confidentiality.

Sexual contact between an attorney and a client is almost always considered a breach of conduct. Sexual contact represents a clear breach of attorney-client trust. It is also a clear conflict of interest because it can easily result in the attorney's placing his or her own needs above those of the client, and it makes it difficult for the attorney to argue the client's case dispassionately.

Other Types of Misconduct

As the model rules indicate, an attorney may be charged with misconduct if she or he commits a criminal act. However, not all violations of the law may result in professional censure. According to the ABA, a lawyer is professionally responsible "only for offenses that indicate lack of those characteristics relevant to law practice." These include violations involving "violence, dishonesty, breach of trust, or interference with the administration of justice" (*Model Rules of Professional Conduct*, Rule 3). Nevertheless, violations of the law may seriously impair an attorney's professional standing.

Ethical rules also govern the conduct of attorneys before courts. Thus, an attorney is guilty of misconduct toward the court if he or she brings a frivolous, or unnecessary, proceeding to court; makes false statements to the court; offers false evidence; or unlawfully obstructs another party's access to evidence. It is also considered misconduct if an attorney attempts to influence a judge or juror by illegal means, such as BRIBERY or intimidation, or states personal opinions regarding the justness of a cause or the credibility of a witness. Special rules govern trial publicity as well. These forbid an attorney to make statements outside of court that will influence a court proceeding. For example, an attorney may not make statements related to the character, credibility, guilt, or innocence of a suspect or witness in a court proceeding. Attorneys are forbidden to communicate directly or indirectly with a party represented by another lawyer in the same matter, unless they receive permission from the other attorney. This law is designed to protect laypersons involved in legal proceedings from possibly hurting their cases by speaking with the opposing lawyer.

Federal and state laws also define attorney misconduct and empower judges to discipline wayward attorneys. Rule 11 of the Federal Rules of Civil Procedure (28 U.S.C.A.), for example, requires sanctions for lawyers and clients who file frivolous or abusive claims in court. In a 1989 case, *Nasco, Inc. v. Calcasieu Television & Radio*, 124 F.R.D. 120 (W.D. La.), a federal district judge suspended two lawyers and disbarred another for "illegal and fraudulent schemes and conspiracies" designed to slow a case in court for the benefit of their client.

Beginning in the late 1980s, attorneys have been required to report the misconduct of other lawyers, with failure to do so considered to be misconduct in itself and resulting in serious disciplinary measures. A 1989 Illinois Supreme Court ruling, *In re Himmel*, 125 Ill. 2d 531, 533 N.E.2d 790, found that attorneys have a duty to report other lawyers' misconduct even when a client has instructed them not to do so. The Illinois Supreme Court suspended James H. Himmel from the practice of law for one year after he failed to report a misappropriation of client funds by another lawyer, a violation of rule 1-103(a) of the Illinois Code of Professional Responsibility. Himmel's failure to report, the court found, had allowed the offending attorney to bilk other clients as well. The attorney guilty of misappropriating funds was disbarred.

Lawyers have also been found guilty of misconduct with regard to the advertising of their services. It is legal and ethical for attorneys to advertise, but if that advertising is false, deceptive, or misleading, makes unsubstantiated comparisons to another lawyer's services, or proposes means contrary to rules of professional conduct, the attorney can be charged with misconduct. For example, an attorney was disbarred in Maryland for publishing misleading advertisements soliciting customers for "quickie" foreign divorces and misrepresenting his competence and knowledge of the law (*Attorney Grievance Committee v. McCloskey*, 306 Md. 677, 511 A.2d 56 [1986]).

FURTHER READINGS

American Bar Association (ABA) Web site. 2009. *Model Rules of Professional Conduct*. Chicago: ABA. Available online at http://www.abanet.org/cpr/mrpc/mrpc_toc. html; website home page: http://www.abanet.org (accessed July 5, 2009).

Andrews, Carol Rice. 2001. "Highway 101: Lessons in Legal Ethics That We Can Learn on the Road." *Georgetown Journal of Legal Ethics* 15 (fall).

Freedman, Monroe H. 2004. *Understanding Lawyers Ethics*. 3d ed. New York: Bender.

Hazard, Geoffrey C., Jr., and W. William Hodes. 2001. *The Law of Lawyering*. 2 vols. 3d ed. Frederick, MD: Aspen.

Heymann, Philip B., and Lance Liebman. 1988. *The Social Responsibilities of Lawyers: Case Studies*. Eagan, MN: West.

Lieberman, Hal R., and Ronald W. Meister. 1999. *Serving Clients Well: Avoiding Malpractice and Ethical Pitfalls in the Practice of Law*. New York: Practicing Law Institute.

Oldham, Lindsay M., and Christine M. Whitledge. 2002. "The Catch-22 of Model Rule 8.3." *Georgetown Journal of Legal Ethics* 15 (summer).

Powell, Sonya. 1993. "Intent as an Element of Attorney Misconduct." *Journal of the Legal Profession* 18.

Steinberg, Marc I. 2007. *Lawyering and Ethics for the Business Lawyer*. 2d ed. Florence, KY: Cengage Learning.

Wolfram, Charles W. 1986. *Hornbook on Modern Legal Ethics*. Eagan, MN: West.

CROSS REFERENCES

American Bar Association; Attorney-Client Privilege; Civil Procedure; Ethics, Legal; Legal Advertising; Legal Representation; Malpractice; Model Rules of Professional Conduct; Public Defender; Trial.

ATTORNEY'S FEES

Attorney's fees constitute payment to an attorney for legal services, which can be based on an hourly rate, a flat rate, or a percentage of a civil damages award.

The COMMON LAW rule in the United States, called the American Rule, requires each party to pay their own attorney's fees. The American Rule stands in contrast to the English rule, which requires a losing party to pay the prevailing party's attorney's fees. The Supreme Court, in *Alyeska Pipeline Service Co. v. Wilderness Society* (421 U.S. 240, 95 S. Ct. 1612, 44 L.Ed.2d 141 [1975]), reaffirmed the American Rule, yet there are many exceptions in federal law that require the losing party to pay.

Attorney's fees fall into three categories: fees based on an hourly rate, flat fees for certain legal services, and contingent fees, where the ATTORNEY is paid a percentage of a damages award but does not collect any money if the case is lost. Lawyers also perform *pro bono* legal services, which are unpaid and for the good of society.

Hourly Fees

Payment for legal services is usually based on a lawyer's hourly rate. This dollar amount is determined by the experience of the lawyer, the nature of the case, the estimated time it will take to handle the case, and the size of the law firm. Large law firms will charge much more because of overhead costs and their general reputation. In 2008, hourly rates ranged from $100 to over $1,000, with large corporate law firms charging around $500 per hour. In complex LITIGATION, several lawyers from a firm may be involved, and each of them will charge an hourly rate, which drives up the cost.

Most lawyers have their clients sign a retainer agreement, which sets out the hourly rates for the lawyer and a paralegal. The agreement discusses office expenses and filing fees that the client must pay; it also details how the fees will be billed. In many cases, the lawyer requires the client to pay a lump sum or retainer, which the lawyer then draws from as legal services are performed. Client funds must be deposited in a trust account and cannot be withdrawn unless the lawyer can demonstrate that services have been provided. Lawyers typically bill in tenths of an hour, which is six-minute periods. This is the minimum billing period, so a phone call or the drafting of a letter that only takes two or three minutes will be billed as one-tenth of an hour.

Keeping track of billable hours is important for the financial wellbeing of a lawyer and as documentation if a dispute arises over fees. Lawyers keep track of their time using paper forms and computer programs.

Flat Fees

Some legal services are so routine that lawyers set a flat rate. Drafting a simple will, a POWER OF ATTORNEY, or a simple contract can usually be set at a low flat fee, as lawyers have standard electronic template documents that can be populated with basic client information. These rates remain low because of the availability of off-the-shelf software and INTERNET forms that consumers can use to draft their own wills and simple legal documents. Some legal issues that require a lawyer to appear in court may also lend themselves to a flat fee, such as simple BANKRUPTCY. Another example is defending a person on a first offense for driving while under the influence of alcohol. Such cases usually end in a PLEA bargain instead of a trial. An additional example is an uncontested DIVORCE, where the drafting of the forms and the one court appearance can be accurately calculated by the lawyer. However, if the divorce turns into a contested proceeding, the lawyer is likely to require that his client begin paying an hourly rate.

Contingent Fees

Most PERSONAL INJURY, PRODUCT LIABILITY, MEDICAL MALPRACTICE, and CLASS ACTION lawsuits are handled under a CONTINGENT FEE arrangement. Plaintiffs rarely have the money in hand to litigate these types of cases, so lawyers agree to take cases in return for a percentage of a damages award that is recovered. If the lawyer fails to recover damages for the client, the client pays nothing. Because of the costs associated with litigating these types of cases, lawyers must carefully analyze the severity of the potential client's injuries; the degree of fault, if any, of the potential client; and the likelihood of recovery. Most recoveries are obtained through settlements with insurers rather than trials, so skilled plaintiffs' lawyers generally know what amount can be recovered.

If the lawyer believes the case is worth taking, a contingent fee agreement is signed by the lawyer and client, which sets a fee of between 25 and 40 per cent of the settlement, VERDICT, or award. Some agreements have a sliding scale. If the case is settled, the lawyer agrees to take 25 percent; if the case goes to trial, the fee rises to 40 percent to reflect the additional time invested by the lawyer. A key issue in contingent fee agreements is whether the percentage is based on the gross amount or net amount of the award. Most lawyers insist on using the gross amount. For example, if the lawyer recovers $100,000 in a settlement, a 25 percent fee will result in $25,000 for the lawyer. However, the client will not receive $75,000. The lawyer will first deduct from that amount costs associated with the case, which usually include filing fees, photocopying, process serving, postage, COURT REPORTER fees, and expert witness fees.

Exceptions to the American Rule

Congress has enacted many exceptions to the American Rule. A PREVAILING PARTY in a federal PATENT, trademark, or COPYRIGHT lawsuit may recover attorney's fees. The Civil Rights Attorney's Fees Awards Act of 1976 (2 U.S.C.A. § 1988), applies to all federal civil rights laws. It states that in "any action or proceeding to enforce a provision of sections 1981, 1983, 1985, and 1986 of this title … the Court, in its discretion, may allow the prevailing party, other than the United States, a reasonable attorney's fee as part of the costs." The Supreme Court has ruled that paralegal fees may be included as well as attorney's fees. However, if a PLAINTIFF only recovers NOMINAL DAMAGES of one dollar, there can be no recovery of attorney's fees. At the state level, a plaintiff who brings a frivolous action or act in bad faith may be required to pay the defendant's attorney's fees.

FURTHER READINGS

Biggs, Keith. 2009. *Lawyers Costs and Fees: Fees and Fixed Costs in Civil Actions*, 15th ed. London: Tottel.

Parker, Kristine. 2007. *Inside Lawyers' Ethics.* New York: Cambridge Univ. Press.

MacKinnon, F. B. 2008. *Contingent Fees for Legal Services: Professional Economics and Responsibilities.* Edison, N.J.: Aldine Transaction.

CROSS REFERENCE

Contingent Fee.

ATTORNEY'S LIEN

The right of a lawyer to hold a client's property or money until payment has been made for legal aid and advice given.

In general, a lien is a security interest used by a creditor to ensure payment by a debtor for money owed. Since an ATTORNEY is entitled to payment for services performed, the attorney has a claim on a client's property until compensation is duly made.

A *charging lien* is an attorney's right to a portion of the judgment that was won for the client through professional services. It is a specific lien and only covers a lawyer's claim on money obtained in a particular action.

A *retaining lien* is more general in its scope. It extends to all of a client's property that an attorney might come into POSSESSION of during the course of a lawsuit. Until an attorney is compensated for services, he or she has a claim or interest in such property.

AUCTIONS

A sale open to the general public and conducted by an auctioneer, a person empowered to conduct such a sale, at which property is sold to the highest bidder.

A *bid* is an offer by a *bidder,* a prospective purchaser, to pay a designated amount for the property on sale. A Dutch auction is a method of sale that entails the public offer of the property at a price in excess of its value, accompanied by a gradual reduction in price until the item is purchased.

According to the UNIFORM COMMERCIAL CODE (UCC), a body of law governing commercial transactions that has been adopted by the states, the auction sale of any item concludes with the fall of the hammer or in any other customary manner. Such a sale is "with reserve," which denotes that the goods can be withdrawn at any time, until the auctioneer announces the completion of the sale, unless the goods are explicitly put up "without reserve," which signifies that the article cannot be withdrawn after the call for bids unless no bid is made within a REASONABLE TIME. In both types of auctions, the bidder can withdraw a bid prior to the auctioneer's announcement that the sale has been completed.

Regulation

As a legitimate business enterprise, auctions cannot be proscribed. They are not above reasonable regulation by both state and local authorities. Some states subject auction sales to TAXATION.

In the absence of statutes, any person can act as an auctioneer, but a license, which usually restricts his or her authority to a certain region, is often required. Licensing officers can refuse to issue a license, but only if done reasonably, impartially, and to promote the interest of the community.

Agency of Auctioneer

An auctioneer serves as the agent of the seller who employs him or her, and the auctioneer must act in GOOD FAITH, advance the interest of the seller, and conduct the sale in accordance with the seller's instructions. If real property or goods priced at $500 or more are sold at auction, a written agreement is necessary to satisfy the STATUTE OF FRAUDS, an old ENGLISH LAW adopted in the United States that requires certain contracts to be in writing. The auctioneer is authorized to sign a memorandum of sale on behalf of both parties, but this authority is limited and expires shortly after the sale has been concluded. Both the buyer and the seller are bound by the announcement of the auctioneer concerning the identity of the property and the terms and conditions of the sale.

In the absence of a statutory provision requiring authority to be in writing, an agent, pursuant to oral authorization, can execute any contract required to be in writing. The statutory provisions vary, however, in regard to the execution of contracts to purchase real property.

Because of the trust and confidence the seller reposes in an auctioneer, the individual cannot delegate the power to sell without special authority from the seller. The delegation of insignificant duties, such as the striking of the hammer and the announcement of the sale, is allowable if conducted pursuant to the auctioneer's immediate supervision and direction.

An auctioneer's authority normally terminates upon the completion of the sale and the collection of the purchase price, but the seller can revoke the authority at any time prior to the sale. According to some authorities, the buyer or seller can end the auctioneer's authority to sign a memorandum on his or her behalf between the time of the fall of the hammer and the signing of the memorandum, but the prevailing view deems the auctioneer's authority to be irrevocable. Private sales by an auctioneer are generally impermissible.

Conduct and Validity of Sale

The owner of the property has the right to control the sale until its conclusion. Unless conditions are imposed by the seller, the auctioneer is free to conduct the sale in any manner chosen, in order to bar fraudulent bidders and to earn the confidence of honest purchasers. The auctioneer cannot amend the printed terms and conditions of the auction, but he or she is empowered to postpone the sale, if that is the desire. The

Paul Gaugin's Pont Aven Landscape was sold in an auction held by Christie's in May 1998.

auctioneer can modify the sale terms of goods advertised in a catalog at any time during the sale, if announced publicly and all of the bidders present are cognizant of it. The auctioneer may also retain the right to resell should there be an error or a dispute concerning the sale property. The description of the property in the catalog must be unambiguous. A significant error in a description might cause the cancellation of the sale, although trivial discrepancies between the property and the description are not problematic. The seller can withdraw property until the acceptance of a bid by an auctioneer.

A bid is an offer to purchase, and no obligations are imposed upon the seller until the bid is accepted. It can be made in any manner that demonstrates the bidder's willingness to pay a particular price for the auctioned property, whether orally, in writing, or through bodily movements, such as a wave of the hand. Secret signals between the bidder and the auctioneer militate against equality in bidding and are thereby prohibited. The auctioneer accepts a bid by the fall of the hammer or by any other perceptible method that advises the bidder that the property is his or hers upon tendering the amount of the bid in accordance with the terms of the sale. An auctioneer can reject a bid on various grounds, such as when it is combined with terms or conditions other than those of the sale, or is below the minimum price acceptable to the owner.

As a general rule, any act of the auctioneer, seller, or buyer that prevents an impartial, free, and open sale or that reduces competition in the bidding is contrary to PUBLIC POLICY. An agreement among prospective buyers not to bid has been held to void the sale to any buyer within this group. A purchase by a person who has not participated in the illegal agreement remains in effect. A *puffer* or *shill* is a person who has no intention of buying but is hired by the seller to place fictitious bids in order to raise the bidding of genuine purchasers. In general, if a purchaser at an auction can prove that a puffer was employed, he or she can void the sale. Some jurisdictions require the buyer to have been financially hurt by the puffer, but others permit an individual to void a sale even if no harm occurred. PUFFING and *by-bidding* are synonymous.

A deposit is not a PLEDGE but a partial payment of the purchase price, usually made payable to the auctioneer who retains it until the completion of the sale. The property of one person should not be commingled and sold with the property of another by the auctioneer unless notice is furnished to all interested parties, or it might constitute FRAUD.

An auctioneer is not entitled to bid on property that he or she has been hired to sell. The auctioneer can, however, bid a particular sum for a purchaser without violating any duties to the seller or even to other prospective bidders.

An auctioneer who does not have the required license but who executes a sale can be penalized, but the sale remains valid. An auction is void, however, when it is conducted without the owner's consent.

Rights and Liabilities of Buyer and Seller

In an unconditional sale, title passes to the bidder when the auctioneer's hammer falls. If conditions exist, title passes upon their fulfillment or through their WAIVER, the intentional relinquishment of a known right. The bidder is ordinarily entitled to POSSESSION when he or she pays the amount bid.

A person who bids on behalf of another is personally liable for the bid unless the person discloses this relationship to the auctioneer. Fraud, or a misrepresentation of a material fact on which the buyer detrimentally relied, or the seller's failure to provide good title furnishes a basis for setting aside the sale.

The seller has a lien, a security interest, on the property until the price is paid. If the purchaser fails to comply with the conditions of a sale, the seller can regard the sale as abandoned and sue for damages. Where a resale occurs, and the price is lower than the contract price, the defaulting buyer in some jurisdictions is liable to the seller for the difference between what he or she had agreed to pay and what the seller received on the resale. In general, whether a deposit or a partial payment must be repaid depends upon which party was responsible for the uncompleted sale. If the buyer is responsible, he or she cannot recover either the deposit or partial payment.

Compensation

The party employing the auctioneer pays a commission regardless of whether he or she procures a sale, unless the auctioneer is responsible for the failure of the sale. The auctioneer is entitled to a reasonable sum unless a statute or contract provision determines the amount.

Liabilities of Auctioneer

An auctioneer is usually liable to the seller for monetary losses attributable to his or her NEGLIGENCE in failing to follow the seller's instructions. The auctioneer can also be responsible to the buyer for fraud, conduct in excess of authority, and failure to deliver the goods. Because the auctioneer is a stakeholder, a THIRD PARTY designated by two or more persons to retain on deposit money or property that is the subject of a dispute, the auctioneer is liable to the buyer in those instances where the buyer is entitled to the return of the deposit. An auctioneer who sells property on behalf of one who does not own it and delivers the proceeds to that person is personally liable to the rightful owner even though the auctioneer acted in good faith and without knowledge of the absence of title. He or she can recover his or her losses from the person who received the proceeds in the form of damages that he or she was ordered to pay to the actual owner.

Online Auctions

With its ability to connect potential buyers and sellers from anywhere in the world, the INTERNET has become an increasingly important player in auctions. The first online auctions appeared on the Internet in 1995, and according to the FEDERAL TRADE COMMISSION (FTC) these auctions have become "perhaps the hottest phenomenon on the Web." Large organizations can participate in online auctions but so can individual sellers and small businesses.

The rules for online auctions are fairly straightforward. For a typical person-to-person site, the sellers will open an account and are assigned an on-screen name. They must pay a fee whenever they conduct an auction. The seller can set a time limit on the bidding, as well as a minimum price. If a buyer pits in a bid that the seller accepts, they complete the transaction, often via email, arranging for payment and delivery of the goods. Many sites allow buyers to pay by credit card (which protects the buyer in case merchandise is not delivered); some individual sellers require payment by cashier's check or money order (to protect against bounced checks). Some buyers and sellers conduct their money transactions through online payment or online escrow services, which serve as a secure site for sending and receiving payment information. These payment arrangements are more a matter of caution than lack of trust. In fact, auction sites usually offer some form of insurance or guarantees to ensure that merchandise is both paid for and delivered as agreed by the buyer and the seller.

Although online auctions are generally safe for both buyers and sellers, auction fraud does occur. Buyers who report online auction fraud to the FTC commonly complain that merchandise never arrives or that it arrives late or that the merchandise that does arrive is not what was advertised. There are other more problematic types of fraud. In "bid siphoning," a bidder is lured off a legitimate auction site by a phony seller who promises to sell the same item as that being auctioned for a lower price. The buyer sends money to this "seller," who offers no guarantees—and usually no merchandise. Fraudulent online sellers, like their "live" counterparts, may also employ puffers to bid up the price of an item, or they may engage in "bid shielding," in which extremely high bids are submitted and then retracted so that a preferred bidder can put in a lower bid and obtain the item.

Both buyers and sellers who engage in online auctions are advised to take common-sense precautions. First, people should deal with legitimate auction sites whose reputations are established. They should determine that terms of bidding, payment, and delivery are spelled out ahead of time. Also it is a good idea to check out online payment or escrow services, particularly if the buyer or seller insists on using a particular one whose reputation is not known. Buyers and sellers can contact their local branch of the Better Business Bureau to find out whether complaints have been lodged against a particular service or site.

FURTHER READINGS

Federal Trade Commission Web site. 2003. "Internet Auctions: A Guide for Buyers and Sellers." Available online at http://www.ftc.gov/bcp/edu/pubs/consumer/tech/tec07.shtm; website home page: http://www.ftc.gov (accessed August 5, 2009).

Gold, Sarah S., and Leon P. Gold. 2001. "Class Counsel Auctions Inconsistent with Reform Act." *New York Law Journal* 226 (October 10).

Hix, Nancy. 2001. *The Business Guide to Selling through Internet Auctions: A Proven Seven-Step Plan for Selling to Consumers and Other Businesses.* Gulf Breeze, FL: Maximum.

Ramberg, Christina Hultmark. 2003. *Internet Marketplace: The Law of Auctions and Exchanges Online.* New York: Oxford Univ. Press.

Rappaport, Bret, and Joni Green. 2002. "Calvinball Cannot be Played on this Court: The Sanctity of Auction Procedures in Bankruptcy." *Journal of Bankruptcy Law and Practice* 11 (March-April).

CROSS REFERENCES

Internet; Sales Law; Uniform Commercial Code.

AUDI ALTERAM PARTEM

[Latin, hear the other side.] It embodies the concept in criminal law that no person should be condemned unheard; it is akin to due process. The notion that an individual, whose life, liberty, or property are in legal jeopardy, has the right to confront the evidence against him or her in a fair hearing is one of the fundamental principles of constitutional law in the United States and England.

CROSS REFERENCE

Habeas Corpus.

AUDIT

A systematic examination of financial or accounting records by a specialized inspector, called an auditor, to verify their accuracy and truthfulness. A hearing during which financial data are investigated for purposes of authentication.

The INTERNAL REVENUE SERVICE (IRS) conducts two types of audits, called examination of taxpayer returns, and they are typically conducted using one of two types of procedures. The most common auditing procedure involves correspondence between the service and the taxpayer or interviews with the taxpayer in a local IRS office. A less common method involves field audits whereby IRS officials conduct the audit at the taxpayer's home or place of business. Treas. Reg. § 601.105(b)(1). The service determines which audit procedure should be followed in a particular case. During an audit, an IRS official may question the taxpayer about a particular transaction or transactions that appear on the taxpayer's return or may conduct a thorough investigation of the taxpayer's entire TAX RETURN.

Although many people fear audits by the IRS, the percentage of returns examined by the IRS is relatively low. For example, of 108,034,700 returns filed by taxpayers in 1997, the IRS examined 1,662,641, or about 1.5 percent of the total number of returns. Despite this low number, several stories surfaced in the 1980s and 1990s regarding abuses by IRS officials, many of which occurred during the audit process. Congress responded by enacting two "Taxpayer Bill of Rights," first in 1989 and again in 1996. The second act, the TAXPAYER BILL OF RIGHTS 2, Pub. L. No. 104-168, 110 Stat. 1452, established and delegated authority to the Office of Taxpayer Advocate. This office is responsible for assisting taxpayers in resolving problems with the IRS, identifying areas where taxpayers have had problems with the service, and identifying potential legislative and regulatory changes that could mitigate problems between the IRS and taxpayers.

FURTHER READINGS

Baran, Daniel J., Gerald F. Bernard, and James E. Brown. 1997. *IRS Audit Protection and Survival Guide: Attorneys.* Indianapolis: Wiley.

Merkel, Steven. 2009. "Surviving the IRS Audit." *Investopedia News and Articles.* Available online at http://www. investopedia.com/articles/pf/06/IRSAudit.asp?partner= answers&viewed=1; website home page: http://www. investopedia.com (accessed August 28, 2009).

Messier, William F., Jr. 1997. *Auditing: A Systematic Approach.* New York: McGraw-Hill.

CROSS REFERENCE

Internal Revenue Service.

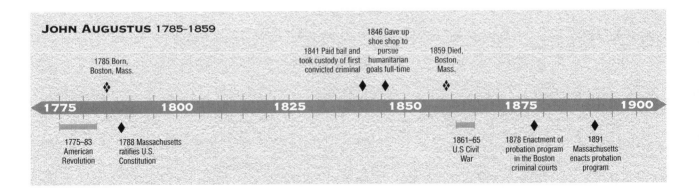

JOHN AUGUSTUS 1785–1859

1785 Born, Boston, Mass.

1841 Paid bail and took custody of first convicted criminal

1846 Gave up shoe shop to pursue humanitarian goals full-time

1859 Died, Boston, Mass.

1775–83 American Revolution

1788 Massachusetts ratifies U.S. Constitution

1861–65 U.S Civil War

1878 Enactment of probation program in the Boston criminal courts

1891 Massachusetts enacts probation program

❖ AUGUSTUS, JOHN

During the nineteenth century CRIMINAL LAW, in particular, was slowly evolving toward a more humanistic and equitable approach than had previously been taken. One man in Massachusetts, through an act of compassion, initiated a procedure that was the forerunner of the probation system.

John Augustus, born 1785, was a cobbler in Boston during the 1840s. He was interested in the legal process and often visited the criminal courts in Boston. In 1841 he was especially touched by the plight of a person convicted of public intoxication who begged the court not to incarcerate him and promised to give up alcohol in return for his freedom. Augustus, sensing hope for the man's rehabilitation, paid the man's bail; three weeks later, Augustus returned to court with his sober charge. The judge was favorably moved, and the man was allowed to go free.

After his initial success, John Augustus continued to take custody of convicted criminals. By the time he died in 1859, he had helped nearly 2,000 prisoners. He used his own money for bail or received financial aid from other residents of Boston who believed in his cause; several of these followers continued the program after his death.

Augustus's benevolence was made an official practice in 1878 when a law was enacted assigning a regular probation officer to the Boston criminal courts. In 1891 the commonwealth of Massachusetts adopted a similar program, and during the next nine years, other states began to provide for probationary programs based on the humanitarian actions of John Augustus.

Augustus died June 21, 1859, in Boston, Massachusetts.

❖ AUSTIN, JOHN

John Austin was a nineteenth-century legal theorist and reformer who achieved fame posthumously for his published work on *analytical* JURISPRUDENCE, the legal philosophy that separates positive law from moral principles.

According to Austin, positive law is a series of both explicit and implicit commands from a higher authority. The law reflects the sovereign's wishes and is based on the sovereign's power. Backed by sanctions and punishment, it is not the same as divine law or human-inspired moral precepts. Viewing the law in this way, Austin did not so much question what it ought to be but revealed it for what he thought it was. Analytical jurisprudence sought to consider law in the abstract, outside of its ethical or daily applications. In Austin's view, religious or moral principles should not affect the OPERATION OF LAW.

Austin was not as influential in his lifetime as his fellow Utilitarians JEREMY BENTHAM, James Mill, and JOHN STUART MILL. His intellectual output did not match his potential, owing in part to poor health and a self-defeating attitude. Yet Austin is regarded by legal historians as a significant figure in the development of modern English jurisprudence.

Austin was born in England in 1790, the son of a prosperous miller. After a stint in the army, he studied law but was not an enthusiastic or especially capable practitioner. Reflecting a keen, analytical mind, Austin's skills lay in writing and theory rather than in EQUITY pleadings. Austin gave up his law practice in 1825 and, in 1826, was named the first professor of jurisprudence at the University of London. To strengthen his academic credentials, Austin studied ROMAN LAW and German CIVIL LAW in Heidelberg and Bonn from 1827 to 1828.

> A LAW ... IN ITS LITERAL MEANING ... MAY BE SAID TO BE A RULE LAID DOWN FOR THE GUIDANCE OF AN INTELLIGENT BEING BY AN INTELLIGENT BEING HAVING POWER OVER HIM.
> —JOHN AUSTIN

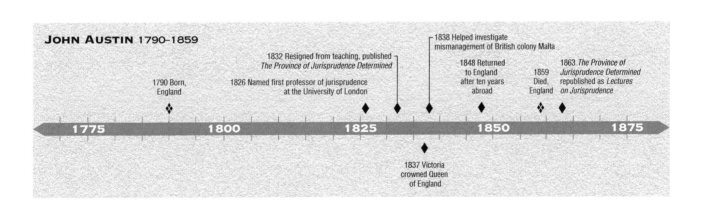

JOHN AUSTIN 1790–1859

1790 Born, England

1826 Named first professor of jurisprudence at the University of London

1832 Resigned from teaching, published *The Province of Jurisprudence Determined*

1837 Victoria crowned Queen of England

1838 Helped investigate mismanagement of British colony Malta

1848 Returned to England after ten years abroad

1859 Died, England

1863 *The Province of Jurisprudence Determined* republished as *Lectures on Jurisprudence*

1775   1800   1825   1850   1875

Austin's professional pursuits were undermined by his ill health and self-doubt. In 1832 he resigned from teaching because his lectures were poorly attended. During the same year, Austin published the barely noticed *The Province of Jurisprudence Determined*, a collection of his university lectures. Shortly thereafter, he accepted a post on the CRIMINAL LAW Commission, but he resigned from that when his suggestions were not followed. Austin's attempt, in 1834, to resume his legal lectures for the Society of the Inner Temple failed.

In 1838 Austin served on a commission investigating complaints about the management of Malta, a British colony. This time, his efforts were successful, as his work led to TARIFF reform and improvements in the Maltese government.

The following decade, Austin lived abroad with his wife, Sarah Taylor Austin. In 1848 the couple returned to England, where Austin died on December 1, 1859. In 1863 his widow republished *The Province of Jurisprudence Determined* under the new title *Lectures on Jurisprudence*. This single volume received the widespread acclaim that had eluded Austin during his lifetime.

Although critics of analytical jurisprudence do not accept Austin's SEPARATION of social and moral considerations from the law, they value his contributions to the discussion. Austin's writings influenced other prominent legal theorists, including U.S. Supreme Court justice Oliver Wendell Holmes Jr.

FURTHER READINGS

Hoeflich, M. H. 1985. "John Austin and Joseph Story: Two Nineteenth Century Perspectives on the Utility of the Civil Law for the Common Lawyer." *American Journal of Legal History* 29 (January): 36–77.

Merriam, Charles Edward. 1999. *History of the Theory of Sovereignty Since Rousseau.* Union, N.J.: Lawbook Exchange.

Rumble, Wilfrid E. 1996. "Austin in the Classroom: Why Were His Courses on Jurisprudence Unpopular?"*Journal of Legal History* 17 (April): 17–40.

CROSS REFERENCES

Jurisprudence; Utilitarianism.

AUTHENTICATION

The confirmation rendered by an officer of a court that a certified copy of a judgment is what it purports to be, an accurate duplicate of the original judgment. In the law of evidence, the act of establishing a statute, record, or other

document, or a certified copy of such an instrument as genuine and official so that it can be used in a lawsuit to prove an issue in dispute.

Self-authentication of particular categories of documents is provided by federal and state rules of evidence. A deed or conveyance that has been acknowledged by its signers before a NOTARY PUBLIC, a CERTIFIED COPY of a public record, or an official PUBLICATION of the government are examples of self-authenticating documents.

AUTHORITIES

Governmental entities that have been created and delegated with official responsibilities, such as a county highway authority. In legal research and citation, entities cited as sources of law, such as statutes, judicial decisions, and legal textbooks. Parties support their positions in a lawsuit by citing authorities in briefs, motions, and other documents submitted to the court.

Primary authorities are citations to statutes, court decisions, and government regulations that, if having the force of law, must be applied by the court to dispose of the issue in dispute if they are relevant to the matter. Secondary authorities are references to treatises, textbooks, or restatements that explain and review general principles of law that buttress a party's position in a lawsuit. Such authorities have no legal effect and can be disregarded by the court.

Authorities are also cited by scholars in legal treatises, hornbooks and restatements to establish the bases of the statements and conclusions contained in the works.

CROSS REFERENCES

Primary Authority; Secondary Authority.

AUTHORIZE

To empower another with the legal right to perform an action.

The Constitution authorizes Congress to regulate interstate commerce.

AUTOMATISM

An involuntary act such as sleepwalking that is performed in a state of unconsciousness. The subject does not act voluntarily and is not fully aware of his or her actions while in a state of automatism. Automatism has been used as a defense to show that a defendant lacked the requisite mental state for the commission of a crime. A defense based on automatism asserts that there was no act in the legal sense because at the time of the alleged crime, the defendant had no psychic awareness or volition. Some American jurisdictions have recognized automatism as a complete, affirmative defense to most criminal charges. An insanity defense, by comparison, asserts that the accused possessed psychic awareness or volition, but at the time of the offense, the accused possessed a mental disorder or defect that caused them to commit the offense or prevented them from understanding the wrongness of the offense.

AUTOMOBILE SEARCHES

The FOURTH AMENDMENT to the U.S. Constitution guarantees U.S. citizens freedom from "unreasonable searches and seizures." In *Katz v. United States,* 389 U.S. 347, 88 S. Ct. 507, 19 L. Ed. 2d 576 (1967), the U.S. Supreme Court established the principle that a WARRANT issued by a "neutral and detached magistrate" must be obtained before a government authority may breach the individual privacy that the Fourth Amendment secures. The *Katz* decision held that "searches that are conducted outside the judicial process, without prior approval by judge or MAGISTRATE,

are per se unreasonable under the Fourth Amendment—subject only to a few specifically established and well-delineated exceptions." Over the years the Court has recognized a number of exceptions to this rule that allow the police to conduct a legal search without a warrant in certain situations. One of these exceptions is for automobile searches.

Warrantless Searches

The automobile exception was first announced in *Carroll v. United States,* 267 U.S. 132, 45 S. Ct. 280, 69 L. Ed. 543 (1925), when the Court held that federal Prohibition agents had been justified in searching, without a warrant, an automobile that they had stopped on a public highway, because they had had probable cause to believe that it contained contraband. The Court found that the search had been justified by the exigency of the circumstances, noting that, unlike a dwelling, store, or other structure, an automobile can be "quickly moved out of the locality or jurisdiction in which the warrant must be sought."

After the *Carroll* decision, the Court embarked on a long, and often confusing, line of decisions that interpreted the automobile

A California highway patrolman searches a car allegedly used to sumggle drugs. In California v. Acevedo (1990), the U.S. Supreme Court held that police officers may search a car if there is probably cause to believe it contains evidence or contraband.
AP IMAGES

exception as it applied not only to automobiles but also to containers found in automobiles, to mobile homes, and to sobriety checkpoints. For several decades the Court rarely cited *Carroll* in vehicle-search cases. Instead, it relied on the "search-incident-to-arrest" doctrine, which allowed the police to search, without a warrant, the areas surrounding an arrest site. Originally the police could search areas that were outside the control of the arrested person. (See, e.g., *Harris v. Stephens,* 361 F.2d 888 [8th Cir. 1966], *cert. denied,* 386 U.S. 964 [1967], in which the Court let stand a ruling by the U.S. Court of Appeals for the Eighth Circuit that the search of a car parked in a driveway, while the suspect was arrested at the front door of his house, was valid.) However, the Court restricted the search-incident-to-arrest standard in *Chimel v. California,* 395 U.S. 752, 89 S. Ct. 2034, 23 L. Ed. 2d 685 (1969), which held that a warrantless search must be limited to the area within the immediate control of the arrestee.

After the *Chimel* decision, the Court abandoned this line of reasoning and returned to the "probable-cause-accompanied-by-exigent-circumstances" rationale in *Carroll.* In *Chambers v. Maroney,* 399 U.S. 42, 90 S. Ct. 1975, 26 L. Ed. 2d 419 (1970), the justices found that *Carroll* supported a warrantless search of an impounded car. They based this finding on the theory that had the search been conducted at the time of the arrest, it would have been valid because of the exigent circumstances that existed at that time. The fact that the car was impounded, and therefore immobile, by the time the search was conducted did not affect the Court's decision.

A year later, in *Coolidge v. New Hampshire,* 403 U.S. 443, 91 S. Ct. 2022, 29 L. Ed. 2d 564 (1971) (PLURALITY opinion), the Court held that a search conducted with a warrant that was later found to be invalid fell outside of the automobile exception. The Court stated that the police in *Coolidge* could not have legally conducted a warrantless search at the arrest scene, because no exigent circumstances existed: At the time of arrest, the arrestee had not had access to the car and therefore could not have moved it. The *Coolidge* decision firmly established that the police must show both PROBABLE CAUSE and exigent circumstances in order for a warrantless search to be valid.

The Court continued with this line of reasoning as recently as April 21, 2009, when it issued its decision in *Arizona v. Gant* 556

U.S. ___. In *Gant,* the respondent was arrested for driving on a suspended license. He was handcuffed and locked in a police car before the officers searched his car and found cocaine in one of his jacket pockets. The Supreme Court held that police officers may search the passenger compartment of a vehicle incident to an arrest only if it was reasonable to conclude that the individual may access the vehicle at the time of the search, or if the vehicle contains evidence of the offense of the arrest. In its decision, the Court rejected the broader holding of its previous decision in *New York v. Belton,* 453 U.S. 454 (1981), which permitted a vehicle search incident to an arrest even if no possibility existed that the arrestee could gain access to the vehicle at the time of the search. In *Gant,* the respondent was arrested for an offense in connection to which police officers could not have reasonably expected to find evidence in his car. Thus, the Court concluded that the search was unreasonable.

The Supreme Court added an alternative rationale to support automobile searches, with its decision in *Cardwell v. Lewis,* 417 U.S. 583, 94 S. Ct. 2464, 41 L. Ed. 2d 325 (1974) (plurality opinion). In *Cardwell,* the police had made an impression of the tires of the suspect's car and had taken paint samples from the car, without a warrant. The Court held that the search had been permissible because the police had had probable cause, and the search had been conducted in a reasonable manner. No exigency had existed in this case, but the Court found justification in the principle that individuals have a "lower expectation of privacy" in their automobiles. Writing for the plurality, Justice HARRY A. BLACKMUN stated, "One has a lesser expectation of privacy in a motor vehicle because its function is transportation and it seldom serves as one's residence or as the repository of personal effects."

The same rationale supported the Court's determination that police officers do not violate the Fourth Amendment when they search a passenger's personal belongings inside an automobile that they have probable cause to believe contains CONTRABAND. Officers with probable cause to search a car may inspect passengers' belongings that are capable of concealing the object of the search. If probable cause justifies the search of a lawfully stopped vehicle, including every part of the vehicle and its contents that may conceal the object of the search, then this rule extends to passengers' property as well, the Supreme Court wrote in *Wyoming v. Houghton,*

526 U.S. 295, 119 S. Ct. 1297, 143 L.Ed.2d 408 (U.S. 1999). The balancing of the relative interests weighs in favor of allowing searches of a passenger's belongings, because passengers, no less than drivers, possess a reduced expectation of privacy with regard to the property that they transport in cars.

This "lesser-expectation-of-privacy" rationale was not sufficient to support a warrantless search in *United States v. Chadwick,* 433 U.S. 1, 97 S. Ct. 2476, 53 L. Ed. 2d 538 (1977). In *Chadwick,* the defendants were arrested immediately after they had placed a footlocker in their trunk. Federal agents, who had probable cause to believe that the footlocker contained marijuana, impounded the car and opened the footlocker without a warrant. The Court found that although the agents did have probable cause to search the footlocker, they had not proved that they had had probable cause to search the car in order to find the footlocker. Because the car was impounded, no exigent circumstances existed. Furthermore, the Court held that the defendants had a greater expectation of privacy in the closed footlocker than in an automobile, which is open to public view. "The factors which diminish the privacy aspects of an automobile do not apply to the (defendants') footlocker," the Court concluded. Therefore, the lesser-expectation-of-privacy rationale did not support an extension of the automobile exception to the closed footlocker.

Armed with the *Carroll-Chambers* line of cases (the probable-cause-accompanied-by-exigent-circumstances rationale) and the *Chadwick* decision (the lower-expectation-of-privacy rationale), the Court tackled the question of whether a warrantless search of a suitcase found in the trunk of a taxi fell under either justification. In *Arkansas v. Sanders,* 442 U.S. 753, 99 S. Ct. 2586, 61 L. Ed. 2d 235 (1979), the police had probable cause to believe that a suitcase picked up by the DEFENDANT at an airport contained contraband. After the defendant placed the suitcase in the trunk of a taxi and left the airport, the police stopped the taxi, opened the trunk, and searched the suitcase, which contained the contraband that they expected to find. The Court evaluated the facts under each rationale and found that (a) once the taxi had been stopped, no exigency existed; and, (b) an individual's privacy expectations in a suitcase, which "serve[s] as a repository for personal items," are greater than his or her

privacy expectations in an automobile. For these reasons, the Court held that the search had violated the Fourth Amendment.

Later cases, however, extended the automobile exception to containers located in an automobile, where authorities have probable cause to search the automobile. For example, in *United States v. Ross,* 456 U.S. 798, 102 S. Ct. 2157, 72 L. Ed. 2d 572 (1982), the police stopped a car that they had probable cause to believe contained contraband. Without a warrant, they opened a closed paper bag that they found inside the car's trunk, and discovered heroin. The Court held that the search was valid, reasoning that if the police had probable cause to conduct a warrantless search of the vehicle, they also had justification to search the bag.

However, the Court retreated from this holding in *Knowles v. Iowa,* 525 U.S. 113, 119 S. Ct. 484, 142 L.Ed.2d 492 (U.S. 1998), where it held that a Fourth Amendment violation had occurred when a police officer had conducted a full search of a car, including the trunk, after the driver had been stopped for speeding. The officer had issued the driver a citation, rather than arresting him, although Iowa law would have permitted an arrest. The U.S. Supreme Court held that the search could not be sustained under the *search-incident-to-arrest* exception to the warrant requirement, as the underlying rationales for the exception, including the need to disarm the suspect and to preserve evidence, did not justify the search of the car's trunk. While the concern for officer safety in the context of a routine traffic stop might justify the minimal additional intrusion of ordering a driver and passengers out of the car, the Court said, it does not, by itself, justify the often considerably greater intrusion attending a full field-type search.

However the Supreme Court moved back toward its reasoning of *Ross* in the case of *Illinois v. Caballes* 543 U.S. 405 (2005). In that case, Caballes was stopped for speeding by an Illinois State Trooper. A second trooper arrived to the scene with his narcotics-detection dog and walked the dog around the car while the first trooper wrote Caballes a traffic ticket. The dog alerted the officers at Caballes' trunk. As a result, the officers searched the trunk, found marijuana and then arrested Caballes. The Supreme Court determined that a narcotics-detection dog sniff, which was conducted during a lawful traffic stop, and reveals no information other than the location of an unlawful substance, does not violate an individual's Fourth Amendment rights.

The automobile exception was also extended to searches of some mobile homes, in *California v. Carney*, 471 U.S. 386, 105 S. Ct. 2066, 85 L. Ed. 2d 406 (1985). In *Carney*, the police had searched a motor home that was parked in a public lot. The Court found the search to have been valid, stating that the mobile home was being used for transportation and that it therefore was as readily movable as an automobile. In addition, the Court noted a reduced expectation of privacy in a mobile home, as contrasted with an ordinary residence, as mobile homes, like cars, are regulated by the state. In this case, where the mobile home was parked in a public parking lot, rather than a mobile home park, and was not anchored in any way, it resembled a vehicle more than a residence. Therefore, the automobile exception applied. *Carney* established not only that the automobile exception applies to some mobile homes but also that it applies to parked vehicles.

Another extension of the automobile exception, called the "inventory exception," was recognized by the Court in *South Dakota v. Opperman*, 428 U.S. 364, 96 S. Ct. 3092, 49 L. Ed. 2d 1000 (1976). Donald Opperman's illegally parked vehicle was ticketed and towed to an impound lot, where the police inventoried its contents. In an unlocked glove compartment, they found marijuana. The Court held that once a vehicle has been legally impounded, its contents may be inventoried. Three justifications were given: protection of the owner's property while it is in police custody; protection of the police against claims; and protection of the police against danger. Likewise, in *Colorado v. Bertine*, 479 U.S. 367, 107 S. Ct. 738, 93 L. Ed. 2d 739 (1987), the Court found that marijuana discovered in a closed backpack during an inventory of an impounded vehicle had been legally seized because there was no showing that "the police, who had followed standardized procedures, had acted in bad faith or for the sole purpose of investigation." The Court concluded that "reasonable police regulations relating to inventory procedures administered in GOOD FAITH satisfy the Fourth Amendment."

This patchwork of decisions led many, including Justice Lewis F. Powell Jr., to conclude that "the law of SEARCH AND SEIZURE with respect to automobiles is intolerably confusing" (*Robbins v. California*, 453 U.S. 420, 101 S. Ct. 2841, 69 L. Ed. 2d 744 [1981] [Powell, J., concurring]). The Court attempted to put the confusion to rest with its decision in *California v. Acevedo*, 500 U.S. 565, 111 S. Ct. 1982, 114 L. Ed. 2d 619 (1991). In *Acevedo*, federal drug agents tracked a bag that they knew contained marijuana, as it was in transit to the defendant. They then notified police officers, who watched as the defendant put the bag into the trunk of a car and drove away. The police officers stopped the car, opened the trunk, and searched the bag, finding the marijuana. The Court held that the search had been legal, stating that it is not necessary for an officer to obtain a warrant before searching a container located in an automobile when the officer has probable cause to believe that the container holds contraband or evidence. After analyzing the long and ambiguous line of automobile exception cases, the Court decided that the distinction between the *Ross* situation (where the police had probable cause to search the car) and the *Sanders* situation (where the police had probable cause only to search the container) was not supported by the requirements of the Fourth Amendment. Discarding the reasoning in *Sanders* as unworkable and an unjustified impingement on legitimate police activity, the justices announced a new and unequivocal rule: "The police may search an automobile and the containers within it where they have probable cause to believe contraband or evidence is contained."

The *Acevedo* decision was met with harsh criticism by some legal analysts, who saw it as an excessive retreat from Fourth Amendment guarantees. Supporters, however, pointed out that the police still must establish that they have probable cause to conduct a warrantless search before such a search will be found valid. Probable cause can be shown in a variety of ways, but generally it follows from a chain of events that raise police suspicions from the level of mere conjecture to the level of reasonable grounds. For example, in *Acevedo*, federal drug enforcement agents had previously seized and inspected the package that was eventually delivered to the defendant, and they knew that it contained marijuana. In *Sanders*, a reliable informant had told the police that the defendant would arrive at the airport carrying a green suitcase containing marijuana. And in *Ross*, an informant had told the police that someone known as Bandit was selling drugs from the trunk of his car; when the police located the car described by the informant, they discovered through a computer check that the driver, the defendant, Albert Ross Jr., used the alias Bandit. From these cases, the Court has shown that arbitrary searches, or searches based on mere SUSPICION, will not be supported by a spurious claim of probable cause.

Warrantless Seizures of Automobile as Forfeitable Contraband

The Fourth Amendment does not require the police to obtain a warrant before seizing an automobile from a public place when they have probable cause to believe that it is forfeitable contraband. The U.S. Supreme Court thus reversed a decision in which the Supreme Court of Florida had held that the warrantless SEIZURE of an automobile, pursuant to the Florida Contraband Forfeiture Act, violated the Fourth Amendment in the absence of exigent circumstances. *Florida v. White*, 526 U.S. 559, 119 S. Ct. 1555, 143 L. Ed. 2d 748 (1999).

The case involved a defendant who had been convicted of POSSESSION of cocaine, which had been found during a police inventory search of his automobile following its warrantless seizure from a public parking lot pursuant to the Florida Contraband Forfeiture Act. Fla. Stat. 932.701. Although the police lacked probable cause to believe that the defendant's car contained contraband, they did have probable cause to believe that the vehicle itself was contraband under the Florida law.

Fourth Amendment JURISPRUDENCE recognizes the need to seize readily movable contraband before it is spirited away, and this need is equally weighty when the automobile, as distinguished from its contents, is the very contraband that the police seek to secure, the Court observed. In addition to the special considerations recognized in the context of movable items, the Court continued, Fourth Amendment jurisprudence has consistently afforded law enforcement officials greater latitude in exercising their duties in public places. Because the police had seized defendant's vehicle from a public area, the Court concluded that the warrantless seizure had not involved any invasion of the defendant's privacy.

Sobriety Checkpoints

During the 1980s and 1990s, the Court considered a new line of cases in which the automobile exception was been used to justify sobriety-checkpoint

programs. Under such programs, police stop motorists, typically along an interstate highway, for the purpose of apprehending drivers who are impaired by alcohol. One such program was challenged and found to be constitutional in *Michigan Department of State Police v. Sitz*, 496 U.S. 444, 110 S. Ct. 2481, 110 L. Ed. 2d 412 (1990). The Court applied a somewhat more stringent test than that used in automobile search cases, citing as relevant authority a line of cases involving highway checkpoints for discovering illegal ALIENS. (See, e.g., *United States v. Martinez*, 428 U.S. 543, 96 S. Ct. 3074, 49 L. Ed. 2d 1116 (1976); *Brown v. Texas*, 443 U.S. 47, 99 S. Ct. 2637, 61 L. Ed. 2d 357 (1979). *Brown* required "a weighing of the gravity of the public concerns served by the seizure, the degree to which the seizure advances the PUBLIC INTEREST, and the severity of the interference with individual liberty." Applying that balancing test, the majority in *Sitz* found that the intrusion on individual liberty imposed by Michigan's sobriety checkpoint program was outweighed by the advancement of the state's interest in preventing drunk driving. Therefore, it concluded that the program did not violate the Fourth Amendment.

Similar sobriety-checkpoint programs have been used in other states. Since the *Sitz* decision, all have passed constitutional muster. Less certain is the constitutionality of narcotics checkpoints. In 1992, Minnesota instituted a random narcotics checkpoint on an interstate highway's exit ramp. The police stopped every third or fourth car and asked several questions of the occupants. If the answers or demeanor of the occupants aroused suspicion, the car was diverted for further investigation. A number of individuals were cited when police found marijuana, either in plain view or after a consensual search of the vehicle.

The Minnesota scheme raised serious constitutional questions. Whereas the state has a legitimate interest in curbing the use of illegal drugs, it was not clear whether a narcotics-checkpoint program was a valid means of promoting this interest in light of the privacy interest that is violated by random questioning for investigation of drug possession or use. The Supreme Court addressed this issue in *City of Indianapolis v. Edmond* 531 U.S. 32 (2000). In that case, the City of Indianapolis conducted vehicle checkpoints in an effort to detect unlawful drugs. It established roadblocks where

AUTOMOBILE SEARCHES: IS THE FOURTH AMENDMENT IN JEOPARDY?

The right to move about freely without fear of governmental interference is one of the cornerstones of democracy in America. Likewise, freedom from governmental intrusions into personal privacy is a cherished U.S. right. Automobiles have come to symbolize these rights in the United States, but freedom and autonomy often conflict with law enforcement's interest in preserving domestic order.

The FOURTH AMENDMENT to the Constitution guarantees U.S. citizens freedom from "unreasonable searches and seizures." The Supreme Court, in *Katz v. United States,* 389 U.S. 347, 88 S. Ct. 507, 19 L. Ed. 2d 576 (1967), interpreted the Fourth Amendment to mean that a WARRANT issued by a "neutral and detached magistrate" must be obtained before police officers may lawfully search PERSONAL PROPERTY. The Court in *Katz* held that "searches conducted outside the judicial process, without prior approval by a judge or MAGISTRATE are *per se* unreasonable under the Fourth Amendment—subject only to a few specifically established and well-delineated exceptions."

In its struggle to balance the Fourth Amendment's personal privacy guarantees with the government's interest in effective law enforcement, the Court has allowed numerous exceptions to the warrant requirement, prompting debate over the amendment's continued viability. A particularly tricky area involves decisions regarding warrantless automobile searches.

Beginning with its decision in *Carroll v. United States,* 267 U.S. 132, 45 S. Ct. 280, 69 L. Ed. 543 (1925), the Court has granted law enforcement personnel substantial

latitude when searching automobiles and their contents. *Carroll* and its progeny established that automobiles constitute a distinct class of personal property that deserves less privacy protection than other types of property. The Court has consistently held that because a car and its contents are easily and quickly moved, police officers need not obtain a warrant to search them if they reasonably believe that doing so would result in lost evidence.

Since its decision in *Carroll,* the Supreme Court has articulated several rationales for allowing warrantless vehicle searches. First, the Court followed *Carroll* and held that a warrantless search of an automobile is valid because of the exigent circumstances involved (see, e.g., *Chambers v. Maroney,* 399 U.S. 42, 90 S. Ct. 1975, 26 L. Ed. 2d 419 [1970]). Next, the Court found that warrantless automobile searches are justified because individuals have a lower expectation of privacy in their automobiles than in their homes (see, e.g., *Cardwell v. Lewis,* 417 U.S. 583, 94 S. Ct. 2464, 41 L. Ed. 2d 325 [1974] [plurality opinion]). Finally, the Court extended the warrant exception to containers found inside a vehicle, reasoning that if the police could legally search an automobile, they could also legally search containers found in the automobile (see *United States v. Ross,* 456 U.S. 798, 102 S. Ct. 2157, 72 L. Ed. 2d 572 [1982]). However, the Court had previously ruled that where a vehicle search was illegal, a subsequent search of a suitcase found inside the trunk of the vehicle was also illegal (*Arkansas v. Sanders,* 442 U.S. 753, 99 S. Ct. 2586, 61 L. Ed. 2d 235 [1979]). The need to distinguish between a *Sanders* situation and a *Ross* situation caused some confusion, both for the police and for the

courts. This need was finally addressed by the Court in 1991.

Underlying all the exceptions to the warrant requirement is the need to assist law enforcement personnel without unduly trampling on the Constitution. However, some have argued that the pendulum has swung too far in favor of POLICE POWER. In 1991 the Court extended the permissible scope of the warrant exception with its decision in *California v. Acevedo,* 500 U.S. 565, 111 S. Ct. 1982, 114 L. Ed. 2d 619, which upheld the warrantless search of a bag found inside the defendant's vehicle. In an attempt to clarify the law regarding warrantless searches of containers found in automobiles, the justices announced that the Fourth Amendment does not require a distinction between PROBABLE CAUSE to search an entire vehicle, including containers found inside (as in *Ross*), and probable cause to search only a container found inside an automobile (as in *Sanders*). The Court announced a new and succinct rule regarding automobile searches: "The police may search an automobile and the containers within it where they have probable cause to believe contraband or evidence is contained."

The *Acevedo* decision provides what is known as a bright-line rule, that is, a RULE OF LAW that is clear and unequivocal. But bright-line rules can obscure the important nuances that surround an issue. The *Acevedo* decision left little doubt in the minds of law enforcement personnel that they could, with probable cause, search not only an automobile but also any containers found inside. But that clarity and the unfettered discretion it gives the police trouble some legal analysts. They assert that the ruling

one officer would conduct an open-view examination of the vehicle, while another walked around the vehicle with a narcotics-detection dog. Each stop that was conducted was without reasonable suspicion or probable

cause. In a 6–3 decision issued by Justice Sandra Day O'Connor, the Court held that, because the purpose of the checkpoint was indistinguishable from the general interest in crime control, the checkpoint violated the Fourth Amendment.

effectively guts the Fourth Amendment as it applies to automobile searches and, perhaps more disturbing, that its reasoning could and probably will be applied to searches of other types of personal property.

Justice JOHN PAUL STEVENS noted in his dissent to *Acevedo* that the majority's ruling creates the paradoxical situation in which a container, such as a briefcase, is not subject to a warrantless search when it is carried in full view on a public street but becomes subject to such a search upon being placed inside an automobile.

Critics of *Acevedo* also argue that it contradicts earlier rationales established to support exceptions to the warrant requirement. In *Acevedo,* the Court found no exigent circumstances to justify the search, as it had in *Carroll,* because the police could have legally seized the bag and obtained a warrant for a later search. Neither, assert critics, would the defendant's expectation of privacy in the bag be diminished by virtue of his placing it into the automobile.

Lacking both exigency and the lesser expectation of privacy justifications, the Court turned to policy considerations to support its decision in *Acevedo.* The majority stated that law enforcement personnel were unnecessarily impeded by the Court's previous rulings on this issue. The Court dismissed privacy concerns by stating that protection of privacy is minimal anyway, because in many automobile search cases the police may legally search a container under the "search-incident-to-arrest" justification. Critics respond that the policy underlying that exception is that the police should be able to secure the arrest site in order to protect their safety; it does not follow that the police should be allowed to search containers even when they are not in danger.

Critics assert that by giving the police the discretion to determine what is a reasonable search, the Court ignored

established PRECEDENT governing Fourth Amendment cases. Justice ROBERT H. JACKSON wrote in *Johnson v. United States,* 333 U.S. 10 (1948),

> The point of the Fourth Amendment, which is often not grasped by zealous officers, is not that it denies law enforcement the support of the usual inferences which reasonable men draw from evidence. Its protection consists in requiring that those inferences be drawn by a neutral and detached magistrate instead of being judged by the officer engaged in the often competitive enterprise of ferreting out crime.

According to Justice Stevens, the majority in *Acevedo* rejected this precedent without justification.

Justice ANTONIN SCALIA took a different approach. He suggested in his concurrence to *Acevedo* that the Fourth Amendment does not proscribe *warrantless* searches but rather prohibits *unreasonable* searches. Scalia argued that "the supposed 'general rule' that a warrant is always required does not appear to have any basis in the common law."

Lower federal courts and state courts of appeals have struggled with the question of whether *Acevedo* effectively expands law enforcement officers' ability to search automobiles without a warrant. For example, in *United States v. Brooks,* 838 F. Supp. 58 (W.D.N.Y. 1993), the U.S. district court for the Western District of New York upheld the conviction of an individual for distribution and conspiracy to distribute cocaine after officers conducted a warrantless search of the defendant's automobile. The officer, an undercover police agent, knew that a package contained cocaine, and the agent and other officers observed the DEFENDANT place the package in the front seat of the car. Noting Scalia's concurrence, the Court distinguished between a warrantless search and an unreasonable search. Because the officer knew

that the package contained cocaine, the search of the automobile for the package was reasonable.

Some state courts have invalidated warrantless searches notwithstanding the *Acevedo* decision, though even these courts have struggled with the application of the decision. In *Green v. Indiana,* 647 N.E.2d 694 (Ind. Ct. App. 1995), officers conducted surveillance of the defendant at his home in Indiana based upon reliable tips. The officers knew that the defendant and another individual planned to deliver cocaine from Texas to Indiana after making a trip to Texas. The officers anticipated that the defendant would return in two days and reestablished surveillance at a state highway in Indiana. The officers did not obtain a SEARCH WARRANT for the automobile, though they had discussed the idea. The officers stopped Green's car upon his return, arrested him, and conducted a warrantless search of his automobile. The officers discovered the cocaine during their search. The court held that though the officers had probable cause to conduct the search, it was not impracticable to secure a warrant. Relying in part on the *Acevedo* decision, the court held that though the officer had probable cause to conduct the search, it would not have been impracticable for them to secure a warrant, thus their failure to do so rendered the search illegal.

FURTHER READINGS

Dressler, Joshua. 2002. *Understanding Criminal Procedure.* Newark, N.J.: LexisNexis.

Gottlieb, Henry. 2002. "N.J. Joins Minority of States that Ban Freewheeling Consent Searches; Justices Invoke 'Reasonable and Articulable Suspicion' Standard." *New Jersey Law Journal* 167 (March 18).

Saltzburg, Stephen A., et al. 2003. *Basic Criminal Procedure.* St. Paul, Minn.: West Group.

CROSS REFERENCES

Privacy; Search and Seizure; Search Warrant.

The Court further noted that it could not SANCTION traffic stops that were justified only by the possibility that interrogation and inspection may reveal that any given motorist has

committed some type of crime. Although the *Sitz* and *Acevedo* decisions have been criticized as giving too much discretion to the police, the *Edmond* decision indicates that the Court is not allowing as much latitude to law enforcement officials in stopping and searching automobiles as it previously had.

FURTHER READINGS

Blade, Bryan S. 1991. "Fourth Amendment—The Constitutionality of a Sobriety Checkpoint Program." *Journal of Criminal Law and Criminology* 81 (winter).

Braeske, Chris. 1993. "The Drug War Comes to a Highway Near You: Police Power to Effectuate Highway 'Narcotics Checkpoints' under the Federal and State Constitutions." *Law and Inequality* 11 (June).

City of Indianapolis v. Edmond 531 U.S. 32 (2000).

Clancy, Thomas K. 2008. *The Fourth Amendment: Its History and Interpretation.* Durham, NC: Carolina Academic Press.

Fisanick, Christian A. 2002. *Vehicle Search Law Deskbook.* St. Paul, Minn.: Thomson/West.

Grant, Marguerite T., ed. 2003. *Motor Vehicle Stops: Update on the Law Governing Police Searches and Roadside Questioning.* Boston: Massachusetts Continuing Legal Education.

Illinois v. Caballes, 543 U.S. 405 (2005).

King, Lawrence T. 1988. "The Inventory Exception to the Fourth Amendment Warrant Requirement: Why the Last in Should Be the First Out—or, Putting *Opperman* and *Bertine* in Their Place." *American Journal of Trial Advocacy* 12 (fall).

Kole, Edward T. 1987. "Parked Motor Home Held to Be within Scope of Automobile Exception to Warrant Requirement—*California v. Carney*, 471 U.S. 386 (1985)." *Seton Hall Law Review* 17 (summer).

Lally, Nicole C. 2000. "Constitutional Law—Fourth Amendment Protection Against Unreasonable Searches and Seizures: Valid Automobile Search Includes a Passenger's Belongings." *Tennessee Law Review* 67 (winter): 455–73.

Logan, Wayne A. 2002. "Street Legal: The Court Affords Police Constitutional Carte Blanche." *Indiana Law Journal* 77 (summer): 419–67.

Soden, Steven D. 1992. "Expansion of the 'Automobile Exception' to the Warrant Requirement: Police Discretion Replaces the 'Neutral and Detached Magistrate.'" *Missouri Law Review* 57 (spring).

CROSS REFERENCES

Privacy; Drugs and Narcotics; Fourth Amendment; Probable Cause; Search and Seizure; Search Warrant.

AUTOMOBILES

The first automobile powered by an internal combustion engine was invented and designed in Germany during the 1880s. In 1903, Henry Ford founded the Ford Motor Company and started an era of U.S. leadership in auto production that lasted for most of the twentieth century. In 1908, Ford introduced the highly popular Model T, which by 1913 was being manufactured through assembly line techniques. Innovations by Ford, General Motors, and

other manufacturers near Detroit, Michigan, made that city the manufacturing center for the U.S. car industry. By the 1920s, General Motors had become the world's largest auto manufacturer, a distinction it still held by the mid-1990s. Over time, the auto industry in all countries became increasingly concentrated in the hands of a few companies, and by 1939, the Big Three—Ford, General Motors, and Chrysler Corporation—had 90 percent of the U.S. market.

No invention has so transformed the landscape of the United States as the automobile, and no other country has so thoroughly adopted the automobile as its favorite means of transportation. Automobiles are used both for pleasure and for commerce and are typically the most valuable type of PERSONAL PROPERTY owned by U.S. citizens. Because autos are expensive to acquire and maintain, heavily taxed, favorite targets of thieves, major causes of air and noise pollution, and capable of causing tremendous personal injuries and property damage, the body of law surrounding them is quite large. Automobile law covers the four general phases in the life cycle of an automobile: its manufacture, sale, operation, and disposal.

Brief History of the Automobile

In 1929 there were roughly 5 million autos in the United States. All of those cars required an infrastructure of roads, and by the end of WORLD WAR II, the federal government had begun aggressively to fund highway development. With the intention of improving the nation's ability to defend itself, Congress passed the Federal-Aid Highway Act of 1944 (58 Stat. 838). It authorized construction of a system of multiple-lane, limited-access freeways, officially called the National System of Interstate and Defense Highways, designed to connect 90 percent of all U.S. cities of 50,000 or more people. In 1956 the Federal-Aid Highway Act (23 U.S.C.A. § 103 [West 1995]) established the Federal Highway Trust Fund, which as of the early 2000s continued to provide 90 percent of the financing for interstate highways. By 1990 the interstate highway system was 99.2 percent complete and had cost $125 billion.

During the 1970s the U.S. auto industry began to lose ground to Japanese and European automakers, and U.S. citizens relied to an increasing degree on imported autos. Japan, for example, surpassed the United States in auto production in the 1970s. Oil shortages and embargoes during the 1970s caused the price of gasoline to rise and put a premium on smaller autos, most of which were produced by foreign companies. Foreign cars also earned a reputation for higher quality during this period. The share of foreign cars in the U.S. market rose from 7.6 percent in 1960 to 24.9 percent in 1984.

In the early 1980s the U.S. auto companies were suffering greatly, and the U.S. government bailed out the nearly bankrupt Chrysler Corporation. The U.S. government also negotiated a quota system with Japan that called for limits on Japanese autos imported into the United States, thereby raising the prices of Japanese cars. By the 1990s, the U.S. auto companies had regained much of the ground lost to foreign companies. In the mid-1990s, however, international manufacturing agreements meant that few cars, U.S. or foreign, were made entirely in one country.

Manufacture

Throughout the twentieth century, automakers were required to conform to ever stricter standards regarding the manufacture of their vehicles. These rules were designed to improve the safety, fuel consumption, and emissions of the auto.

Safety Standards As autos increased in number and became larger and faster, and people traveled more miles per year in them, the number of motor vehicle deaths and injuries rose. By 1965 some 50,000 people were being killed in motor vehicle accidents every year, making automobiles the leading cause of accidental death for all age groups and the overall leading cause of death for the population below age 44. Between 1945 and 1995, 2 million people died, and about 200 million were injured in auto accidents—many more than were wounded and injured in all the wars in the nation's history combined.

Beginning in the 1960s, consumer and automobile safety advocates began to press for federal safety standards for the manufacture of automobiles that would reduce such harrowing statistics. The most famous of these advocates was RALPH NADER, who published a 1965 book on the deficiencies of auto safety, called *Unsafe at Any Speed: The Designed-in Dangers of the American Automobile*. From 1965 to 1995, more than 50 safety standards were imposed on vehicle manufacturers, regulating the construction of windshields, safety belts, head restraints,

Ralph Nader celebrates the 40th anniversary of his 1965 book Unsafe at Any Speed, which documented the resistance of the automobile industry to the implementation of safety features.

AP IMAGES

brakes, tires, and lighting, as well as door strength, roof strength, and bumper strength.

In 1966 Congress passed the National Traffic and Motor Vehicle Act (15 U.S.C.A. § 1381 note, 1391 et seq. [1995]), which established a new federal regulatory agency, the National Highway Safety Bureau, later renamed the National Highway Traffic Safety Administration (NHTSA). NHTSA was given a mandate to establish and enforce rules that would force manufacturers to build vehicles that could better avoid and withstand accidents. It was also given the power to require manufacturers to recall and repair defects in their motor vehicles and the authority to coordinate state programs aimed at improving driver behavior. Also in 1966, Congress passed the Highway Safety Act (23 U.S.C.A. §§ 105, 303 note, et seq. [1995]), which provided for federal guidance and funding to states for the creation of highway safety programs.

As a result of these new laws, 19 federal safety regulations came into effect on January 1, 1968. The regulations specified accident-avoidance standards governing such vehicle features as brakes, tires, windshields, lights, and transmission controls. They also mandated more costly crash-protection standards. These included occupant-protection requirements for SEAT BELTS,

Unsafe at Any Speed

"For over half a century the automobile has brought death, injury, and the most inestimable sorrow and deprivation to millions of people." So Ralph Nader began his 1965 book *Unsafe at Any Speed: The Designed-in Dangers of the American Automobile,* a landmark in the history of U.S. consumer protection.

Nader's book recounts how U.S. automobile manufacturers resisted attempts to improve auto safety in the 1950s and 1960s. Even when makers of other vehicles such as planes, boats, and trains were forced to adhere to safety regulations, automakers were still largely uncontrolled in the area of safety. "The gap between existing design and attainable safety," Nader wrote, "has widened enormously in the post-war period."

Nader examined how auto companies lobbied against safety regulation and organized public relations campaigns that asserted over and over again that most injuries were the result of driver error. He argued that the best and most cost-effective way to reduce auto injuries is not to try to alter driver behavior—as honorable a goal as that might be—but to require automakers to design cars that better prevent accidents from occurring and better protect passengers if accidents do occur.

In telling his story, Nader cited sobering statistics on traffic injuries and fatalities, including the fact that auto accidents caused the deaths of 47,700 in 1964—"the extinguishment of about one and three-quarter million years of expected lifetimes," he noted—and one-third of all hospitalizations for injuries and 25 percent of all cases of partial and complete paralysis due to injury. Borrowing the zeal and spirit of the civil rights reform movement and the faith in technology of the space program, Nader looked at traffic fatalities as a public health issue that can be resolved through public action and technological innovation. Quoting Walt Whitman's epigram "If anything is sacred, the human body is sacred," Nader asserted that he was attempting to protect the "body rights" of U.S. citizens.

To protect those rights, Nader used his book to call for a number of different strategies to reduce traffic fatalities and injuries: federal safety standards; a federal facility for auto safety research, design, and testing; increased manufacturer research and development for safety technology; improved consumer information with regard to auto safety; better disclosure of auto manufacturers' safety engineering efforts; and the creation of a department of transportation. It is a mark of Nader's foresight and determination that all of those goals were achieved in the decades following the publishing of *Unsafe at Any Speed.*

CROSS REFERENCE

Nader, Ralph.

energy-absorbing steering wheels and bumpers, head restraints, padded instrument panels, and stronger side doors. These auto safety standards significantly reduced traffic fatalities. Between 1968 and 1979 the annual motor vehicle death rate decreased 35.2 percent, from 5.4 to 3.5 deaths per 100 million vehicle miles.

The seat belt requirement is usually considered the most important and effective safety standard. According to one study, seat belts that attach across both the lap and the shoulder reduce the probability of serious injury in an accident by 64 percent and of fatalities by 32 percent for front-seat occupants. However,

because people do not always use restraints that require their active participation, autos began to be required to have passive restraint systems such as automatic seat belts and air bags. Air bags pop out instantly in a crash and form a cushion that prevents the occupants from hitting the windshield or dashboard. These devices can substantially reduce the motor vehicle death rate. Cars made after 1990 must have either automatic seat belts or air bags, for front-seat occupants.

However, many auto safety experts point out that regulations on the manufacture of automobiles can only go so far in reducing injuries. Studies indicate that only 13 percent of auto accidents result from mechanical failure, and of those that do, most are caused by poor maintenance, not inadequate design or construction. Other analysts assert that safety regulations cause a phenomenon known as "offsetting behavior." According to this theory, people will drive more dangerously because they know their risk of injury is lower, putting themselves, their passengers, and other drivers, passengers, and pedestrians at greater risk and thereby offsetting the gain in safety caused by stricter manufacturing standards.

The NHTSA may also authorize recalls of cars on the road that it deems are safety hazards. In a recall, the federal government mandates that a manufacturer must repair all the vehicles that it has made that have a specific problem. Between 1976 and 1980 the NHTSA authorized the recall of more than 39 million vehicles. Recall is a controversial policy. One problem with it is that, typically, only 50 percent of auto owners respond to recall notices.

All of these manufacturing requirements, coupled with high labor costs and union demands, foreign imports, rising oil prices and a host of other excuses finally created the perfect storm, manifesting in the near-collapse of the U.S. auto industry in 2008. Almost all automakers lost money in 2008, though the so-called Big Three of General Motors, Ford, and Chrysler were hit hardest. When executives with these companies approached Congress for bailout money, the business strategies of these companies came into question. Though the government eventually agreed to provide the loans these companies requested, the loans came with a steep price: unprecedented government oversight of the automotive industry.

For years, the major American automakers had focused on larger vehicles such as trucks and SUVs. There were several reasons for this. First, demand for these types of vehicles remained fairly constant among U.S. consumers. Second, the cost of producing these types of vehicles was less than the cost of producing more fuel-efficient passenger cars. And third, because of the lower manufacturing costs, the profit margins of these larger vehicles were greater than the profit margins of typical passenger cars.

Each of the Big Three found themselves on the verge of BANKRUPTCY and began to lobby Congress for bailout loans that would help the companies survive the crisis. In September 2008 Congress and President GEORGE W. BUSH approved $25 billion in loans to the automakers. The plan for these loans had been in the works for some time, but the need became more pressing with the dire economic news. The terms included a generously low interest rate (estimated at about 4 percent) and no payments for five years.

Even with these loans, executives of the Big Three said that the corporations needed more assistance to survive. A collapse of any of these companies could result in the loss of some two million jobs, which would further drive the economy downward.

In December, Congress agreed to $17.4 billion in loans to the automakers that came out of a $700 billion bailout package authorized two months earlier. Despite the availability of money from these loans, Chrysler and General Motors continued to suffer. By the spring of 2009, however, Ford executives said that the company had enough credit that it may not need to take its part of the loans.

As the automakers continued to struggle, President BARACK OBAMA announced an alternative strategy to his original car czar proposal. In February 2009, he announced the formation of a task force that would oversee the bailout of Chrysler and General Motors and oversee any mergers, reorganizations, or manufacturing deals in an effort to save the industry from further collapse.

Emissions Standards Emissions standards are intended to reduce the amount of pollution coming from a car's exhaust system. Autos are major contributors to AIR POLLUTION. Some cities, such as Los Angeles, have notorious problems with smog, a situation that can cause serious health problems for those with respiratory problems such as asthma and bronchitis. Air pollution also damages plants, reduces crop yields, lowers visibility, and causes acid rain. In 1970, Congress passed the CLEAN AIR ACT Amendments (Pub. L. No. 91-604, 84 Stat. 1676–1713 [42 U.S.C.A. § 7403 et seq. (1995)]), which set an ambitious goal of eliminating, by 1975, 90 to 95 percent of the emissions of hydrocarbons, carbon monoxide, and oxides of nitrogen as measured in 1968 automobiles. Manufacturers did not meet the target date for achieving this goal, and the deadline was extended. Also, the new emissions standards caused problems because they reduced fuel economy and vehicle performance.

Congress modified emissions standards in the 1977 Clean Air Act Amendments (42 U.S.C.A. § 7401 et seq.) and in the Clean Air Act Amendments of 1990 (Pub. L. No. 101-549, 104 Stat. 2399 [42 U.S.C.A. § 7401 et seq. (1995)]). The modified standards, as defined and monitored by the ENVIRONMENTAL PROTECTION AGENCY (EPA), included new requirements for states with low air quality to implement inspection and maintenance programs for all cars. These inspections were designed to ensure that vehicle emissions systems were working properly. In 1992 the EPA implemented strict emissions testing requirements for 18 states and 33 cities with excessive levels of carbon monoxide and ozone.

California has been a leader in setting of air-quality standards. In 1989 it announced new guidelines that called for the phasing out gas-fueled cars in southern California by the year 2010.

Critics maintain that federal emissions regulations have been too costly and that regulators should focus on reducing the emissions of more significant polluters, such as power plants and factories.

Fuel Efficiency Standards In the 1975 Energy Policy and Conservation Act (Pub. L. No. 94–163, 89 Stat. 871 [codified as amended in scattered sections of 12 U.S.C.A., 15 U.S.C.A., and 42 U.S.C.A.]), Congress created a set of corporate average fuel economy (CAFE) standards for new cars manufactured in the United States. The secretary of transportation was empowered with overseeing these standards. The standards mandated that each car manufacturer achieve an average fuel economy of 27.5 miles per gallon (mpg) for its entire fleet of cars by 1985. Manufacturers that did not achieve these standards were to be fined. In 1980 an additional SALES TAX at purchase was placed upon "gas guzzlers" (cars that fail to achieve certain levels of fuel economy). The more a car's gas mileage is below a set standard—which was 22.5 mpg in 1986—the greater the tax. For example, a 1986 car that achieved less than 12.5 mpg was charged an additional sales tax of $3,850. Some members of Congress have lobbied for fuel-efficiency standards as high as a 40 mpg fleet average for auto manufacturers.

The fleet-average fuel efficiency of cars nearly doubled between 1973 and 1984. However, detractors of fuel efficiency standards maintain that the increase in efficiency was not entirely due to federal standards. They argue that fuel efficiency would have risen without regulation, in response to higher gas prices and consumer demand for more efficient cars.

But that did not happen soon enough, without legislative intervention. In December 2007 Congress passed the Energy Independence and Security Act of 2007 (P.L. 110–140), which mandates a CAFE of 35 mpg by 2020. Nearly concurrently, the EPA denied a Clean Air Act WAIVER for California to set its own proposed vehicle emissions standards (even though they would have required higher fuel efficiency than the new law) because they were made moot by the new energy law.

Import Quotas Faced with increasingly stiff competition from Japan and Europe, U.S. car manufacturers in the early 1980s pressed the federal government to limit the number of foreign cars imported into the United States. The administration of President RONALD REAGAN responded by negotiating quotas, or limits, on Japanese car imports from 1981 to 1985. The Japanese voluntarily continued quotas on their car exports through the late 1980s, and quotas on pickup trucks from Japan remained in effect through the mid-1990s.

Tort Law and Automobile Manufacturing Courts have established that manufacturers may be held liable and sued for property damage and personal suffering caused by the products they have manufactured. Automobile manufacturers, like all manufacturers, are thus subject to PRODUCT LIABILITY law. Anyone who suffers harm, injury, or property damage from an improperly made auto may sue for damages. Actions that involve a breach of the manufacturer's responsibility to provide a reasonably safe vehicle are a type of product liability suit.

Courts have found that auto manufacturers have a duty to reasonably design their vehicle against foreseeable accidents. The most important legal concept in this area is *crashworthiness*—a manufacturer's responsibility to make the car reasonably safe in the event of a crash. The standard of crashworthiness makes it possible to hold manufacturers liable for a defect that causes or enhances injuries suffered in a crash, even if that defect did not cause the crash itself. Auto injuries are often the result of a "second collision," when the occupant's body strikes the interior of the car or strikes an exterior object after being thrown from the vehicle. Second collisions can occur when the seat belt fails, for example. Other examples of failures in crashworthiness include instruments that protrude on a dashboard, or a fuel tank that explodes after impact. One landmark case in this area of manufacturer liability is *Larsen v. General Motors Corp.*, 391 F.2d 495 (8th Cir. 1968), in which an individual was compensated for injuries suffered when his head struck a steering wheel in an accident. In another significant case, *Grimshaw v. Ford Motor Co.*, 119 Cal. App. Ct. 3d 757, 174 Cal. Rptr. 348 (1981), a California jury required Ford Motor Company to pay $125 million in PUNITIVE DAMAGES (later lowered to $3.5 million) to a teenager who was severely burned in a fire that resulted when his Ford Pinto was rear-ended and the fuel tank exploded.

Automakers may also be held liable for failure to warn of a product's dangerous tendencies. Manufacturers have, for example, been sued for failing to warn drivers that certain vehicles had a tendency to roll over in some conditions.

One of the more high-profile cases involving defects in automobiles and their parts involved Ford Motor Company and the tire manufacturer Bridgestone/Firestone. On May 2, 2000, the NHTSA began an investigation involving Firestone tires. By that time, the agency had received 90 complaints from consumers who had suffered accidents because the tread on the tires of their Ford Explorers had allegedly caused their vehicles to roll over. These accidents had resulted in at least 27 injuries and four deaths. On August 9, 2000, Bridgestone/Firestone announced the recall of 6.5 million tires, many of which were standard equipment on Explorers.

Ford and Bridgestone/Firestone eventually faced more than 1,000 lawsuits in state and federal court. Many of these cases were settled, including several cases that had been followed closely by the national media. In one case, Marisa Rodriguez of Texas suffered permanent paralysis in 1998 when a faulty tire in the Ford Explorer in which she was riding caused the vehicle to roll over. Rodriguez sought damages of $1 billion when she brought suit in the U.S. district court for the Southern District of Texas, though she eventually settled the case for a reported $6 million.

By 2002 the total number of fatalities had increased to 271, with more than 1,000 injuries.

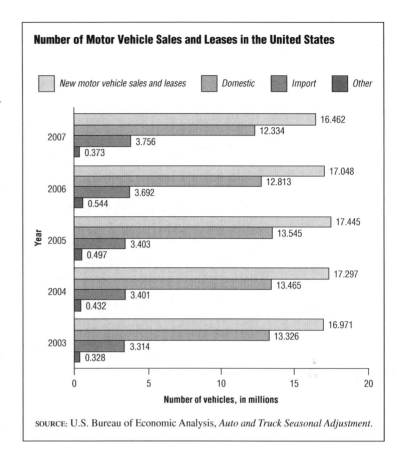

Number of Motor Vehicle Sales and Leases in the United States

Legend: New motor vehicle sales and leases · Domestic · Import · Other

Year		
2007	16.462 (New motor vehicle sales and leases)	
	12.334 (Domestic)	
	3.756 (Import)	
	0.373 (Other)	
2006	17.048	
	12.813	
	3.692	
	0.544	
2005	17.445	
	13.545	
	3.403	
	0.497	
2004	17.297	
	13.465	
	3.401	
	0.432	
2003	16.971	
	13.326	
	3.314	
	0.328	

Number of vehicles, in millions

SOURCE: U.S. Bureau of Economic Analysis, *Auto and Truck Seasonal Adjustment.*

By February 2003 several CLASS ACTION and other suits were pending against Bridgestone/Firestone. In 2001 Congress conducted a series of hearings investigating the Ford and Bridgestone/Firestone fiasco. Congress eventually enacted the Transportation Recall Enhancement, Accountability, and Documentation Act, Pub. L. No. 106-414, 114 Stat. 1800 (49 U.S.C. A. §§ 30101 et seq.). It provides criminal penalties for misleading the Secretary of Transportation with respect to vehicle and equipment-related safety defects. Although the provisions of the statute do not apply to the Firestone/Ford cases.

Sale, Lease, and Rental

When shopping for a car, consumers generally receive their first information through advertising. States regulate automobile ads in different ways. In some states, an ad must provide the number of advertised vehicles available for sale, the price, the dealer, and the factory-installed options and WARRANTY terms. Car buyers should beware of bait-and-switch advertising, in which a dealer advertises a specific car for sale without

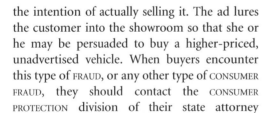

What to Do If You Are in an Auto Accident

Sooner or later, you are likely to have an accident. Fortunately, it will probably be a minor collision that damages only the vehicles involved. However, whether you are in a minor or major accident, behaving coolly, calmly, and properly after it occurs could save you a lot of money and trouble.

Some suggestions on what to do if you are in an auto accident:

1. If possible, move your car to the side of the road or out of the way of traffic.
2. Turn on your car flashers or set up flares to warn other motorists of the accident.
3. Do not make any statements concerning who was at fault, or assign blame to anyone involved.
4. Help any persons who are injured. Most states have laws requiring you to render aid to anyone injured in the accident. Call an ambulance if necessary.
5. Write down the name, address, license plate number, and driver's license number of the other driver and ask to see his or her vehicle registration certificate and proof of insurance. Write down the insurance company name and policy number of the other driver. If asked, do the same for the other driver. Do not reveal the amount of your insurance coverage.
6. Write down the names and addresses of all passengers involved and of any witnesses to the accident.
7. Notify the police, particularly if anyone is hurt or injured at the scene.
8. Write down the names and badge numbers of any police officers at the scene.
9. If possible, take a picture of the scene of the accident, including damage to cars and skid marks.
10. Draw a rough diagram of what happened in the accident, noting road conditions, weather, and lighting.
11. If you suspect you have any injuries, obtain medical care.
12. Talk to a lawyer if you intend to file a lawsuit regarding the accident.

All states require those involved in an accident to file a report with the police or bureau of motor vehicles if the accident involves a death, a personal injury, or property damage above a certain amount, such as $500. Some states require that the report be made immediately; others allow five to thirty days. Failure to file a report is a misdemeanor in most states and could result in the suspension of your driver's license.

Some insurance companies provide their policyholders with accident report forms. Such forms make it easier to obtain the necessary information if you are in an accident. If you have them, keep them handy in your vehicle.

---

the intention of actually selling it. The ad lures the customer into the showroom so that she or he may be persuaded to buy a higher-priced, unadvertised vehicle. When buyers encounter this type of FRAUD, or any other type of CONSUMER FRAUD, they should contact the CONSUMER PROTECTION division of their state attorney general's office.

The STATUTE OF FRAUDS of the UNIFORM COMMERCIAL CODE (UCC) governs the sale of autos in every state except Louisiana. According to the UCC, an auto contract must be in writing in order to be considered valid in court. The purchaser and an agent of the seller—an authorized salesperson,

supervisor, or manager—must sign the contract. Buyers should read all terms of the contract before signing. The contract should specify whether the car is new or used and include a description of the car, the car's vehicle identification number (VIN) (on the driver's side of the dashboard near the window), details of any trade-in, and the terms of financing, including the ANNUAL PERCENTAGE RATE.

In most states, the title for a new or used car passes to the buyer when the seller endorses the certificate of title. If the buyer does not maintain payments according to the finance agreement, the creditor can repossess the car as collateral for the

loan. The debtor has the right to buy back the car (redeem the collateral) and can do so by paying the entire balance due plus REPOSSESSION costs. Eventually, the creditor may sell the car to another party. If the profit from the sale does not satisfy the debt, the debtor is liable for the difference. If the profit from the sale is greater than the debt, the creditor must pay the difference to the debtor. In some states, the creditor is required by the UCC to notify the debtor of the time, place, and manner of any sale of the car.

All used-car dealers must attach a buyer's guide to the side window of any car they are selling. It must state whether the car comes with a warranty; outline the specific coverage of any warranty; recommend that an independent mechanic inspect the car; state that all promises should be put in writing; and provide a list of potential problems with the car. The buyer's guide becomes part of any contract with the seller. The seller must be truthful about the car and should provide the buyer with the car's complete service records and a signed, written statement of the odometer reading and its accuracy. If the car does not perform as promised, a breach of warranty may have occurred. If an individual pays more than $500 for a used car, he or she should have a written contract and a BILL OF SALE. The latter is required in many states to register a car and should include the date of sale; the year, make, and model of the car; the VIN; the odometer reading; the amount paid for the car and what

form it took; the buyer's and seller's names, addresses, and phone numbers; and the seller's signature.

The sale of new automobiles is subject to what are popularly called "lemon laws." *Lemon* is the slang term for a car that just does not work right. LEMON LAWS, in force in all states as of 2003, entitle a car buyer to a replacement car or a refund if the purchased car cannot be satisfactorily repaired by the dealer. States vary in their requirements for determining whether a car is a lemon. Most define a lemon as a vehicle that has been taken in at least four times for the same repair or is out of service for a total of 30 days during the coverage period. The coverage period is usually one year from delivery or the duration of the written warranty, whichever is shorter. The owner must keep careful records of repairs and submit a written notice to the manufacturer stating the problems with the car and an intention to declare it unfit for use. Many states require that the buyer and the manufacturer or dealer submit to private ARBITRATION, a system of negotiating differences out of court. Increasingly, states are passing lemon laws for used as well as new cars.

Leasing is a popular method of purchasing the use of a car. Leasing is essentially long-term rental. For persons who drive few miles per year, like to change cars often, or use their cars for business, leasing is an attractive option. A lease contract may or may not include other expenses such as sales tax, license fee, and

NO-FAULT AUTOMOBILE INSURANCE

Ever since the invention of automobiles, there have been automobile accidents. And with those accidents have come legal disputes about who was most at fault in causing them—and who should be forced to pay damages. The U.S. legal and political systems have struggled to determine the best way to handle the large number of legal disputes related to automobile accidents. Although the states vary in their procedures, two basic approaches have evolved. The first and older approach is the traditional LIABILITY LITIGATION system, which attempts to determine, usually through jury trials, who is more liable, or more at fault, and must pay damages. The second and more recent approach is no-fault insurance, which simply allows each party to be compensated, regardless of fault, by its own insurance company for accident damages. Both approaches have their advantages and disadvantages, and the debate about which is better continues.

The traditional liability litigation system developed out of the English COMMON LAW. Under this system, anyone who suffers an injury from a wrong or negligent act of another is free to sue the other party for damages. For example, someone who is paralyzed in an automobile accident and becomes confined to a wheelchair may sue the other driver or drivers involved in the accident. Whether or not the injured person receives payment for those damages is largely dependent on a determination of

who was more at fault in causing the accident. If, in a court of law, it is determined that the other driver is at fault, then the injured person may collect a large sum from the other driver or, if the other driver has liability insurance, from the other driver's insurance company; if it is determined that the other driver is not at fault, the injured person may not receive any payments beyond those from her or his own insurance company.

This system of resolving disputes is also called the tort litigation process. In relation to automobile accidents, a tort is a civil (as opposed to criminal) wrong that causes an accident—for example, failure to practice caution while driving, thus causing a collision with another car and injuries to its passengers.

As time passed and auto accidents became more frequent, some people began to point out problems in the liability litigation system for resolving accident disputes. They noted that, owing to the complicated nature of many automobile accidents, it often took a great deal of time to determine who was at fault. As a result, many accident victims had to wait a considerable period before they could receive adequate compensation for their injuries. Other victims who may have been unable to work because of injuries, frequently settled for smaller amounts or even waived their right to a trial, in order to receive faster payment from insurance companies.

Other critics of the liability litigation process claimed that the awards granted in auto accident cases varied greatly. Some people were overpaid, and others underpaid, for their damages. A better system, critics maintained, would make all drivers share in the cost of accidents. These critics began to press for a no-fault insurance system as an alternative to liability litigation.

As early as 1946, the Province of Saskatchewan, Canada, enacted no-fault auto insurance. Under a no-fault system, those involved in an accident are compensated for their physical injuries up to a certain limit; even the driver who causes the accident is paid for damages. In its purest form, no-fault automobile insurance does not allow those involved in an accident to sue each other, nor can any party recover damages for pain and suffering. However, no-fault plans are often combined with traditional liability systems to allow accident victims to sue when damages exceed a certain threshold. For example, in New York, it is possible to sue to recover for economic damages greater than $50,000 or for pain and suffering because of death or serious injury. No-fault insurance plans are always compulsory, and every driver who wishes to register a vehicle must obtain at least the minimum standard of no-fault insurance.

In the United States, no-fault automobile insurance was first enacted by Massachusetts in 1971 (Mass. Gen. Laws

insurance. In a closed-end, or "walkaway," lease contract, the car is returned at the end of the contract period, and the lessee is free to "walk away" regardless of the value of the car. In an open-end lease, the lessee gambles that the car will be worth a stated price at the end of the lease. If the car is worth more than that price, the lessee may owe nothing or may be refunded the difference; if the car is worth less, the lessee will pay some or all of the difference. Payments are usually higher

under a closed-end lease than under an open-end lease. Open-end leases more commonly have a purchase option at the end of the lease term.

To lease or rent an auto, an individual must show a valid driver's license and, usually, a major credit card. A rental business may require that a customer have a good driving record and be of a certain age, sometimes 25 years old or older. An auto rental, unlike a lease, may be as short as one day. A rental company may offer a

Ann. ch. 90 § 34A et seq. [West 1995]) in response to public dissatisfaction with long, drawn-out, and expensive court cases for compensation of losses suffered in traffic accidents. In the same year, Congress considered no-fault as a comprehensive national automobile insurance plan, but the proposal never became law. That unsuccessful bill evolved into the National Standards for No-Fault Insurance Plans Act, which would have set federal standards for state no-fault insurance laws. It too did not pass. Opponents of the bill claimed that the states should be allowed to experiment with this new approach before a national plan was adopted. By the mid-1990s, roughly half the states had enacted no-fault insurance plans.

In arguing for no-fault insurance, advocates pointed out a number of advantages, including faster benefits payment and more equal damages awards to accident victims. They claimed that no-fault insurance would reduce the number of traffic-related court cases, thereby freeing up the courts to consider other cases. No-fault, they argued, would also reduce the cost of car insurance premiums as the legal costs associated with settling auto-related cases decreased. Since the establishment of no-fault insurance in many states, no-fault advocates have bolstered their cause even more by pointing to statistics showing that no-fault plans increase the percentage of insurance benefits payments that go to victims rather than to lawyers and court costs. According to those statistics, in states without no-fault insurance, only forty-eight cents of each dollar spent for insurance premiums goes to those injured in accidents, whereas thirty-two cents goes to court costs and lawyers'

fees. However, under the no-fault system in force in Michigan, for example, seventy-three cents of each insurance premium dollar goes to accident victims and four cents goes to court costs and lawyers' fees (Carper 1992).

On the other side of the issue, critics make a number of different points against no-fault insurance. Many, including trial lawyers and some consumer advocates, object to no-fault insurance's elimination of or substantial restrictions on the right to sue for damages. Many states, for example, allow injured parties to sue for "pain and suffering" only if they have sustained specific injuries such as dismemberment, disfigurement, or fracture. Often, "soft-tissue" injuries such as whiplash are not allowed as adequate grounds for a lawsuit. Critics also maintain that no-fault insurance takes away the incentive to drive safely. Under the system of no-fault insurance, careless, negligent drivers are entitled to the same compensation in an accident as are careful, responsible drivers. In addition, critics of no-fault insurance cite evidence that the system has *not* reduced insurance premiums. Under no-fault plans, they argue, the number of persons receiving benefits payments has increased, thus offsetting the reduction in legal costs.

It remains to be seen whether no-fault insurance will continue to spread to other states. Nevada and Pennsylvania have tried no-fault insurance plans and repealed them, with Nevada returning to a financial responsibility law and mandatory liability and property damage insurance. California has considered no-fault insurance for many years but has never adopted it. Some states are looking at

compromise plans that preserve elements of both the traditional liability litigation system and the no-fault system. These plans, such as the one in New York, compensate all accident victims, regardless of fault, for basic economic losses—including medical and hospital expenses and lost wages or services—and in the process eliminate small cases where litigation is least cost-effective. At the same time, such plans preserve the right to sue for damages in cases of death or serious injury or when damages exceed a certain amount.

In the end, the question of how to handle auto accident disputes will be decided on the basis of which system—liability litigation, no-fault insurance, or a compromise between the two—is deemed better at limiting costs and at the same time preserving the value of fairness that underlies the U.S. system of justice.

FURTHER READINGS

Lascher, Edward L., Jr., and Michael R. Powers, eds. 2001. *The Economics and Politics of Choice No-Fault Insurance.* Boston: Kluwer Academic Publishers.

Liao, Y-Ping, and Michelle J. White. 2002. "No-Fault for Motor Vehicles: an Economic Analysis." *American Law and Economics Review* 4 (fall): 258–94.

Mandell, Mark S. 1999. "What's Wrong with Auto No-Fault: S. 625, the Auto-Choice Reform Act." *Trial Lawyers Quarterly* 29 (winter): 31–42.

Schwartz, Gary T. 2000. "Auto No-Fault and First-Party Insurance: Advantages and Problems." *Southern California Law Review* 73 (March): 611–75.

CROSS REFERENCES

Insurance; Tort Law.

collision damage waiver (CDW) option, which provides insurance coverage for damages to the rented car. The CDW option does not cover personal injuries or personal property damage.

Operation and Maintenance

The operation of an automobile on a public street or highway is a privilege that can be regulated by motor vehicle laws. The individual states derive authority to control traffic from

their POLICE POWER, but often they delegate this authority to a local police force. On the national level, Congress is empowered to regulate motor vehicles that are engaged in interstate commerce.

Automobile regulations are provided for the safety and protection of the public. The laws must be reasonable and should not impose an extraordinary burden on the owners or operators. Such laws also provide a means of identifying vehicles involved in an accident or a THEFT and of raising revenue for the state by fees imposed on the owner or operator.

Registration and Licensing Every state requires the owner of a vehicle to possess two documents: a certificate of ownership, or title, and a certificate of registration. Through registration, the owner's name, the type of vehicle, the vehicle's license plate number, and the VIN are all registered with the state in a central government office. On payment of a fee, a certificate of registration and license plates are given to the owner as evidence of compliance with the law. The operator is required to display the license plates appropriately on the car—one on the back of the vehicle and sometimes one on the front and the back—and have the certificate of registration and license in possession while driving and ready to display when in an accident or requested to do so by a police officer. If a driver moves to another state, he or she must register the vehicle in that state within a certain amount of time, either immediately or within 20 to 30 days.

A driver's license is also mandatory in every state. The age at which a state allows a person to drive varies, though it is usually 16. Other qualifications for a driver's license include physical and mental fitness, comprehension of traffic regulations, and ability to operate a vehicle competently. Most states require a person to pass a written examination, an eye test, and a driving test before being issued a license. States generally allow an individual with a learner's permit or temporary license to operate a vehicle when accompanied by a licensed driver. This arrangement enables a person to develop the driving skills needed to qualify for a license. A license can be revoked or suspended when the motorist disregards the safety of people and property, when a physical or mental disability impairs driving ability, or if the motorist fails to accurately disclose information on the license application. When the state revokes a person's license, it permanently denies that person the right to drive; when it suspends a license, it temporarily denies the right to drive.

Because teenaged drivers are more likely to cause traffic accidents, several states have adopted systems of graduated driver licensing (GDL). Under this system, teenaged drivers typically first receive a learner's permit for about six months, during which time all driving must be supervised by an adult. During the next stage, an intermediate level, teen drivers may drive at night without the supervision of an adult during the daytime but cannot drive without an adult until the age of 18, and cannot have more than one teenaged passenger in the car during unsupervised driving times. More than 30 states and the District of Columbia have adopted a GDL system.

Traffic Laws Dozens of laws are related to the operation of an automobile, a large number of which vary by state. Minor traffic offenses include parking and speeding violations. More serious traffic offenses are reckless driving, leaving the scene of an accident, and driving without a license. Most states require motorists to file reports with the proper authorities when they are involved in accidents.

Speed limits vary by state. In 1973, during the height of the energy crisis, Congress defined a national speed limit of 55 mph in order to reduce gasoline consumption; the 55-mph limit also had the unintended effect of lowering the traffic fatality rate. Since then, most states have returned to an upper limit of 70 mph. Two types of speed limits are imposed: fixed maximum and PRIMA FACIE. Under fixed maximum limits, it is unlawful to exceed the stated limit anywhere and at any time. Under prima facie limits, it is possible for a driver to prove in certain cases that a speed in excess of the limit was not unsafe and therefore not unlawful, given the condition of the highway, amount of traffic, and other circumstances.

All states require children riding in automobiles to be restrained using safety belts or safety seats. Most states require adults to wear belts as well, though some require belts only for adults in the front seat. Violation of such laws results in a fine. In 1984 New York became the first state to pass a law making seat belts mandatory for adults.

Driving under the Influence Driving under the influence of alcohol and other drugs is the major cause of traffic deaths in the United States. Drunk drivers kill an estimated 25,000 people per year. States use different terms to describe driving under the influence of mind-altering chemicals, or what is popularly known as "drunk driving." These include *driving under the influence (DUI), operating under the influence (OUI),* and *driving while intoxicated (DWI).* To arrest someone for drunk driving, the state must have proof that the person is under the influence of alcohol or other drugs, and the person must be in actual physical control of a vehicle and impaired in the ability to operate it safely.

Every state has "implied consent" laws that require those with a driver's license to submit to sobriety tests if a police officer suspects they are intoxicated. These tests may include a field sobriety test (a test at the scene, such as walking a straight line), or blood, breath, or urine tests, usually administered at a police station. Refusal to take a sobriety test can result in suspension of the driver's license. Most states have "per se" laws that prohibit persons from driving if they have a blood-alcohol reading above a certain level. Several states have lowered their per se blood-alcohol limits to 0.08 percent. Penalties vary by state but can be particularly severe for repeat offenders, often involving jail sentences and REVOCATION of driving privileges.

DRAMSHOP ACTS make those who sell liquor for consumption on their premises, such as bars and restaurants, liable for damages caused by an intoxicated patron's subsequent actions. In some states, individuals injured by a drunk driver have used such laws to sue bars and restaurants that served liquor to the driver. "Social host" statutes make hosts of parties who serve alcohol and other drugs liable for any damages or injuries caused by guests who subsequently drive while under the influence.

Several national organizations have been formed to combat drunk driving. These include MOTHERS AGAINST DRUNK DRIVING (MADD) and Students Against Drunk Driving (SADD). The legal drinking age has been raised to 21 in every state, largely in an attempt to reduce drunk driving. Most states also make it illegal to transport an open alcoholic beverage container in a vehicle. Alcohol-related deaths as a proportion of all traffic deaths decreased from about 56 percent in 1982 to 47 percent in 1991.

Other Crimes Criminals both target and use automobiles in a number of different types of crime. Cars have been a favorite object of theft ever since their invention. As early as 1919, the DYER ACT, or National Motor Vehicle Theft Act (18 U.S.C.A. § 2311 et seq.), imposed harsh sentences on those who transported stolen vehicles across state lines. Car theft remains a serious problem in many areas of the country and is a major contributor to high insurance

premiums in many urban areas. In 1994 Congress passed the Motor Vehicle Theft Prevention Act (18 U.S.C.A. § 511 et seq.; 42 U.S.C.A. § 13701 note, § 14171 [West 1995]), which established a program whereby owners can register their cars with the government, provide information on where their vehicles are usually driven, and affix a decal or marker to the cars. Owners who register their cars in the program authorize the police to stop the cars and question the occupants when the vehicles are out of their normal areas of operation.

Autos are also frequently used to commit crimes. Drivers whose NEGLIGENCE causes accidents that result in the death of other human beings may be found guilty of MANSLAUGHTER (the unlawful killing of another without MALICE AFORETHOUGHT, that is, without the intention of causing harm through an illegal act), including criminally negligent manslaughter, a crime punishable by imprisonment. Two types of crime that have received a great deal of public attention are drive-by shootings, in which occupants of a vehicle fire guns at pedestrians or at people in other cars, and car-jackings, in which criminals hijack, or take over, cars from their owners or operators, often robbing and sometimes killing the victims in the process. Because of the usually random nature of such crimes, the public has called for severe penalties for them. The VIOLENT CRIME CONTROL AND LAW ENFORCEMENT ACT OF 1994 (Pub. L. No. 103-322, 108 Stat. 1796) made killings caused by drive-by shootings or car-jackings punishable by death.

Insurance Most states require the owner to acquire auto insurance or deposit a bond before a vehicle can be properly registered. Insurance provides compensation for innocent people who suffer injuries resulting from the negligent operation of a vehicle. Other states have liability, or financial responsibility, statutes that require a motorist to pay for damages suffered in an accident resulting from his or her negligence and to furnish proof of financial capability to cover damages that he or she may cause in the future. These statutes do not necessarily require vehicle liability insurance.

About half of all states require that licensed drivers carry automobile insurance with liability, medical, and physical damage coverage. Liability insurance protects a vehicle owner against financial responsibility for damages caused by the negligence of the insured or other covered drivers. It consists of bodily injury, or personal liability protection and property damage protection. Medical payments insurance covers the insured's household for medical and funeral expenses that result from an auto accident. Physical damage insurance consists of collision coverage, which pays for damage to a car resulting from collision, regardless of fault, and comprehensive coverage, which pays for damage from theft, fire, or VANDALISM. More than 20 states also require that drivers carry coverage to protect against uninsured motorists. Such coverage allows insured drivers to receive payments from their own insurer should they suffer injuries caused by an uninsured driver. Most insurance policies offer a choice of deductible, which is the portion of an insurance claim that the insured must pay. The higher the deductible, the lower the annual insurance premium or payment.

Many states have laws requiring no-fault automobile insurance. Under no-fault insurance, each person's own insurance company pays for injury or damage in an auto accident, up to a certain limit, irrespective of whose fault the accident is. Each person is entitled to payment for loss of wages or salary, not exceeding a certain percentage of the value of such loss or a fixed weekly amount.

No-fault statutes provide that every person who receives PERSONAL INJURY benefits gives up the right to sue for damages. However, a person who is licensed to drive in a state that requires no-fault insurance may sue someone who has caused an accident and who is licensed in another state that does not require no-fault insurance. In some states, a person who has not obtained no-fault auto insurance is personally liable to pay damages. Some states do not abolish liability arising from the ownership, maintenance, or operation of a motor vehicle in certain circumstances, such as those in which the harm was intentionally caused, the injured person has suffered death or serious injuries, or medical expenses exceed a certain limit.

States that do not have compulsory automobile insurance typically have FINANCIAL RESPONSIBILITY ACTS. These laws are designed to ensure that negligent drivers who injure others will pay any resulting claims. They require a proof of financial responsibility from drivers involved in an accident. After reporting the accident to a state agency, drivers who do not have adequate insurance coverage must post a cash deposit or equivalent bond of up to $60,000, unless the other driver provides a written release from liability.

Disposal

The last stage in the life cycle of an automobile is its disposal and recycling. In the United States, between 10 and 12 million cars are disposed of each year. In most cases, the first stage of disposal is handled by a wrecking or salvage yard. Most states require the salvage yard to have the title to an auto before the vehicle can be destroyed and to contact a state agency regarding its destruction. This step helps to prevent the destruction of cars used in crimes. Salvage yards typically must be licensed with a state pollution control agency for hazardous waste disposal. Salvage yards remove parts and items of value that can be recycled from the vehicle, such as batteries and fluids. What is left of the automobile is then sold to a shredder, a business that breaks the car up into small parts and separates the metal from the nonmetal parts. Roughly 25 percent of the auto cannot be recycled and must be disposed of in a landfill. Auto residue to be disposed of in a landfill typically must be tested to see that it meets the standards for disposal of hazardous waste.

FURTHER READINGS

American Automobile Association. 1993. *Digest of Motor Laws.* Heathrow, Fla.: American Automobile Association.

"Automobiles." 1994. In *American Bar Association Family Legal Guide.* New York: Random House.

Carper, Donald L., et al. 1995. "Owning and Operating Motor Vehicles." In *Understanding the Law.* 2d ed. St. Paul, Minn.: West.

Crandall, Robert W., et al. 1986. *Regulating the Automobile.* Washington, D.C.: Brookings.

"Detroit Bailout is Set to Bring on More U.S. Oversight." *New York Times,* December 8, 2008.

Goodman, Richard M. 1983. *Automobile Design Liability.* 2d ed. Rochester, N.Y.: Lawyers Cooperative.

Haas, Carol. 1991. *Your Driving and the Law.* Bountiful, Utah: Horizon.

Kass, Stephen L., and Jean McCarroll. 2008 "Reforming U.S. Fuel Economy Standards."*New York Law Journal,* January 2, 2008.

Mashaw, Jerry L., and David L. Harfst. 1990. *The Struggle for Auto Safety.* Cambridge: Harvard University Press.

Nader, Ralph. 1965. *Unsafe at Any Speed.* New York: Grossman.

Research Institute of America, Inc. 2000. *Tax Consequences of Using Autos for Business.* New York: Research Institute of America.

Winston, Clifford, et al. 1987. *Blind Intersection? Policy and the Automobile Industry.* Washington, D.C.: Brookings.

CROSS REFERENCES

Alcohol; Automobile Searches; Collision; Consumer Protection; Environmental Law; Highway; Import Quotas;

Personal Property; Product Liability; Punitive Damages; Title; Transportation Department.

AUTOPSY

The dissection of a dead body by a medical examiner or physician authorized by law to do so in order to determine the cause and time of a death that appears to have resulted from other than natural causes.

This postmortem examination, required by law, is ordered by the local coroner when a person is suspected to have died by violent or unnatural means. The consent of the decedent's NEXT OF KIN is not necessary for an authorized autopsy to be held. The medical findings must be presented at an inquest and might be used as evidence in a police investigation and a subsequent criminal prosecution.

CROSS REFERENCE

Forensic Science.

AUXILIARY

Aiding; ancillary; subordinate; subsidiary.

Auxiliary or ANCILLARY ADMINISTRATION is the management and settlement of property belonging to a decedent that is not located where he or she was domiciled. It is subordinate to the principal or DOMICILIARY ADMINISTRATION of the decedent's property that occurs in the state where the individual was domiciled. Auxiliary administration ensures that any local creditors will be paid before the out-of-state property will be transferred for distribution under domiciliary administration.

CROSS REFERENCE

Estate.

AVER

To specifically allege certain facts or claims in a pleading.

AVERMENT

The allegation of facts or claims in a pleading.

The Federal Rules of Civil Procedure require that averments be simple, concise, and direct.

AVOIDABLE CONSEQUENCES

The doctrine that places the responsibility of minimizing damages upon the person who has been injured.

The major function of the doctrine is to reduce the damages brought about by the defendant's misconduct. Ordinarily, an individual cannot recover for losses that might have been prevented through reasonable effort by the person, particularly where the conduct causing the loss or injury is not willful, intentional, or perpetuated in bad faith. The rule of avoidable consequences applies to both contract and tort actions, but is not applicable in cases involving willful injury or where the PLAINTIFF could not possibly have circumvented any of the harm for which he or she claims damages.

The efforts that the person who has been injured must take to avoid the consequences of the misconduct are required to be reasonable, based upon the circumstances of the particular case, and subject to the rules of common sense and fair dealing. That which is reasonably required is contingent upon the extent of the potential injury as compared with the cost of rectifying the situation, and the realistic likelihood of success in the protective effort. A plaintiff who neglects to mitigate damages will not be entirely barred from recovering such damages that he or she might have circumvented through reasonable efforts.

Included in the effort that the law requires is the payment of reasonable expenditures. The injured party need not, however, make extraordinary payments to prevent the consequences of the wrongdoer's conduct. The plaintiff's inability to produce funds to meet the situation presented can excuse efforts to reduce the injury.

Breach of Contract

A party injured by the breach of contract generally must exercise reasonable efforts to lessen the damages. This rule has no application in an action on a contract for an agreed compensation. Upon the breach of a contract to supply PERSONAL SERVICE or the use of some type of specific equipment or instrumentality, the individual who agrees to furnish such service or items must attempt to acquire a replacement contract if one can reasonably be found. The DEFENDANT can then prove, in attempting to reduce damages, that the plaintiff has procured other employment as well as the amount he or she earned or might have earned by exercising reasonable care and diligence. The test of the applicability of this rule is whether the employment or services of the plaintiff were personal in nature. The rule is not applicable in contracts that do not require all, or a significant portion, of the plaintiff's time, or those that do not preclude the plaintiff from becoming engaged in simultaneous performance of other contracts.

Torts

A party who suffers a PERSONAL INJURY is required to exercise ordinary care and perseverance to find a cure, thereby reducing the damages to the most practicable extent. Such an individual should seek reasonable medical care if so required by the injury. It is not necessary for the person to undergo excessively painful treatment or that which involves a significant hazard of death or injury or offers a mere possibility of a cure. The pain inherent in the necessary medical care and treatment may be taken into consideration in assessing whether the plaintiff acted reasonably in declining to submit to it. Although submission to treatment is not a prerequisite to an award of damages, recovery cannot be obtained for increased damages that stem from the failure to submit to necessary medical treatment. Conversely, the mere fact that medical attention was not sought immediately, or at all, will not proscribe an award of damages where the circumstances did not reasonably indicate that medical aid and attention was necessary.

In addition, an injured party has no absolute duty to subscribe to a physician's advice to mitigate damages. The party might, however, under some circumstances, be under an OBLIGATION to exercise ordinary care in following such advice.

CROSS REFERENCE

Mitigation of Damages.

AVOIDANCE

An escape from the consequences of a specific course of action through the use of legally acceptable means. Cancellation; the act of rendering something useless or legally ineffective.

A taxpayer may take all legally recognized deductions in order to minimize the INCOME TAX LIABILITY. This conduct is called TAX AVOIDANCE and is legal. If, however, a taxpayer claims deductions to which he or she is not entitled so that the individual pays less income tax than is actually owed, then the taxpayer has committed TAX EVASION, a crime punishable by a fine, imprisonment, or both.

A PLEA in CONFESSION AND AVOIDANCE is one that admits the truth of allegations made in former PLEADING but presents new information that neutralizes or avoids the legal ramifications of those admitted facts.

AVOWAL

An open declaration by an attorney representing a party in a lawsuit, made after the jury has been removed from the courtroom, that requests the admission of particular testimony from a witness that would otherwise be inadmissible because it has been successfully objected to during the trial.

An avowal serves two purposes. It enables an ATTORNEY to have the court learn what a witness would have replied to a question had opposing counsel not made an objection to the question sustained by the court. It also provides the interrogator with an opportunity to offer evidence that contradicts the disputed TESTIMONY. If, upon appeal, an appellate court decides that a witness should have been allowed to respond to such questions before a jury, an avowal will be a record of the witness's response.

AVULSION

The immediate and noticeable addition to land caused by its removal from the property of another, by a sudden change in a water bed or in the course of a stream.

When a stream that is a boundary suddenly abandons its bed and seeks a new bed, the boundary line does not change. It remains in the center of the original bed even if water no longer flows through it. This is known as the *rule of avulsion.*

Avulsion is not the same as accretion or alluvion, the gradual and imperceptible buildup of land by the continuous activity of the sea, a river, or by other natural causes.

AWARD

To concede; to give by judicial determination; to rule in favor of after an evaluation of the facts, evidence, or merits. The decision made by a panel of arbitrators or commissioners, a jury, or other authorized individuals in a controversy that has been presented for resolution. A document that memorializes the determination reached in a dispute.

A jury awards damages; a MUNICIPAL CORPORATION awards a PUBLIC CONTRACT to a bidder.

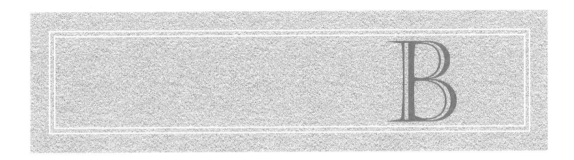

BABY M, IN RE

In 1988 the New Jersey Supreme Court declared surrogacy contracts void against state PUBLIC POLICY but then determined that the best interests of the child born to the surrogate mother required that custody of that child be awarded to the biological father and his wife, with liberal VISITATION RIGHTS later being granted to the biological mother. *In the Matter of Baby M*, 109 N.J. 396, 537 A.2d 1227 (N.J. 1988).

Mary Beth Whitehead entered into a contract with William Stern in which she agreed to be artificially inseminated with Stern's sperm. At the time, Mary Beth was married to Richard Whitehead, with whom she had two children. In the *Surrogate Parenting Agreement* Mary Beth agreed that after the baby was born she would relinquish the baby to Stern and his wife Elizabeth and would permit the termination of her parental rights so that the Sterns could adopt the baby. In return the Sterns would pay Whitehead the sum of $10,000, plus expenses. Elizabeth Stern was not a party to the contract.

Richard Whitehead did not object to the contract and acknowledged that his wife would be artificially inseminated by Stern's sperm. Prior to the *Baby M* case, surrogacy agreements had been most often used when the wife of the adopting couple was infertile. But in the *Baby M* case Elizabeth Stern was not infertile. Instead the Sterns decided not to have Elizabeth bear a child due to the possibility that being pregnant would exacerbate her multiple sclerosis.

Under the Surrogate Parenting Agreement, Mary Beth was not entitled to payment of her $10,000 fee until after the child was born, surrendered to the Sterns, and her parental rights had been terminated. The contract also provided that the Whiteheads would receive no compensation if the child was miscarried prior to the fifth month of pregnancy and would receive only $1,000 if the child was miscarried after that time. Additionally, Whitehead renounced her right to have an ABORTION, unless it was medically necessary.

Whitehead gave birth to a baby girl named Melissa on March 27, 1986. She turned custody of the child over to the Sterns on March 30, 1986, but immediately regretted doing so. Alarmed by Whitehead's anxieties and fearing that she might commit SUICIDE, the Sterns allowed her to have temporary custody of the child. After Whitehead refused to return the baby to the Sterns, William Stern filed an ex-parte application for an order to SHOW CAUSE why the Superior Court of New Jersey should not issue an order for SUMMARY JUDGMENT to enforce the surrogacy contract and a verified complaint seeking specific enforcement of the contract. The complaint sought injunctive relief to obtain custody, termination of Whitehead's parental rights, and an order allowing the Sterns to adopt Melissa.

The trial court issued a TEMPORARY RESTRAINING ORDER and an order requiring the Whiteheads to surrender Melissa to William Stern.

The Whiteheads refused to surrender the child, instead removing her from the state of New Jersey and taking her to Florida. While in Florida, Mary Beth Whitehead threatened to kill the child if Stern did not drop his case to enforce the surrogacy contract. She also threatened to accuse William Stern of sexually abusing Whitehead's other daughter. Melissa was later recovered by law enforcement officials in Florida and returned to New Jersey, where the Sterns assumed custody under the New Jersey court order.

The case then proceeded to a trial on the merits. During trial Mary Beth stressed the bond that had developed between her and Melissa, especially after the child's birth. Whitehead testified that she intended to turn over Melissa to the Sterns but that after the child was born she was emotionally unable to do so. She testified that she felt an obligation to the Sterns but said that the "the obligation [she] felt to [her] child was stronger." Whitehead also offered TESTIMONY by child development experts who testified as to the important and the unique role played by the biological mother in a child's early development and the harm that can result to both the child and the biological mother when the two are separated immediately after birth.

The EXPERT TESTIMONY offered by the Sterns at trial focused on the best interests of the child. For example, one doctor focused on the question of whether the Sterns or the Whiteheads would be better suited to meet the needs of the child, concluding that the Sterns would be able to make the child feel more wanted, provide more emotional stability for the child, provide more educational support, offer greater capacity to explain to the child what happened in the circumstances of her conception and birth, and better assist the child in reaching maturity. Another doctor testified that the Sterns could provide a stable and financially secure household, while the Whitehead household was dominated by Mary Beth Whitehead, who had established a pattern of dealing with her children by "inhibiting their development of independence."

The trial lasted 32 days and consisted of testimony from 23 lay WITNESSES and 15 expert witnesses. Ultimately, the trial judge declared the surrogacy contract valid and enforceable, awarded custody of Melissa to William and Elizabeth Stern, and terminated Mary Beth Whitehead's parental rights, although the judge permitted Mary Beth limited visitation rights pending her direct appeal to the New Jersey Supreme Court.

The New Jersey Supreme Court affirmed in part, reversed in part, and remanded the case to the trial court for further proceedings. Specifically, the state supreme court reversed the trial court's ruling that the surrogacy contract was valid and enforceable. The supreme court said the surrogacy contract was unlawful on two different bases: (1) it conflicted with existing New Jersey statutes and (2) it violated public policy.

The high court ruled that the surrogacy contract conflicted with state laws prohibiting the use of money in connection with adoptions, state laws requiring proof of parental unfitness or ABANDONMENT prior to the termination of parental rights, and state laws affording a parent the right to revoke a prior consent to ADOPTION. The contract also violated important principles of New Jersey public policy. Among these principles were the preference for retaining children with their natural parents; the equal status of mothers and fathers in custody determinations; the right of a parent to be fully informed prior to consenting to the relinquishment of a child; and the pre-eminence of the child's best interests in any custodial placement.

Once the surrogacy contract was declared illegal and unenforceable, the court said, the issue of custody over a child born pursuant to an invalid surrogate contract would be decided by determining the *best interests* of the child. In making this determination, the court said it was required to consider that Mary Beth had acted improvidently in violating the trial court's order by removing Melissa to Florida, threatening to kill Melissa, threatening to lodge phony sexual-abuse accusations against William Stern if he failed to drop his lawsuit, and her overall propensity to manipulate the system and use Melissa to achieve her own aims. The court also said it had to take into account the testimony of the expert witnesses who testified that stability in the Whitehead household was at best doubtful, while the Sterns were much more likely to provide Melissa with a strong foundation upon which to grow and thrive. Accordingly, the court ordered that custody of Melissa be awarded to William and Elizabeth Stern. The

New Jersey Supreme Court also ordered the trial court, on remand, to award Mary Beth Whitehead visitation rights as the trial court deemed appropriate. Following remand and after conducting a further hearing, the trial court granted Mary Beth Whitehead *unsupervised, uninterrupted, liberal visitation* with Melissa.

Baby M was the first case decided by a state court of final jurisdiction in which the lawfulness of a surrogacy contract was addressed. States responded to the *Baby M* decision by passing a flurry of legislation, which fell into four classes.

The first class of legislation declares all surrogacy agreements void and/or unenforceable in that jurisdiction. Such legislation has been enacted in Arizona, the District of Columbia, Indiana, Michigan, New York, North Dakota, and Utah. The second class of legislation prohibits only surrogacy agreements in which the surrogate is compensated with something of value over the expenses incurred as a result of the pregnancy. Such legislation has been adopted in Kentucky, Louisiana, Maryland, Nebraska, and Washington. A third class of legislation addresses one particular aspect of surrogacy contracts. For example, Alabama, Iowa, and West Virginia have exempted surrogacy agreements from statutory provisions making it a crime to sell babies.

The fourth class of legislation provides for the enforceability of surrogacy contracts but at the same time establishes significant safeguards for parties desiring to enter such contracts. For example, Illinois, Florida, Nevada, New Hampshire, and Virginia make surrogacy contracts enforceable so long as the parties to the contract (1) provide proof that the intended parents are medically unable to conceive or bear their own children; (2) obtain judicial preauthorization to enter the agreement; (3) participate in complete medical and psychological examinations; and (4) sign an INFORMED CONSENT notice acknowledging that they have entered the contract after having been apprised of all the risks in doing so.

In states that have not addressed the subject by statute, issues regarding the lawfulness and enforceability surrogacy contracts are resolved by courts in a manner similar to how the *Baby M* case was resolved, that is, by determining the best interests of the child and weighing any competing public policy concerns. However, disputes over the lawfulness and enforceability of surrogacy contracts would only come before the courts in these states if a dispute arose between the parties to the contract. According to some figures, as many as 1,000 babies are born each year to surrogate mothers without any judicial interference or oversight.

FURTHER READINGS

Boyer, Paul S. 2001. *Oxford Companion to United States History*. New York: Oxford Univ. Press.

NBC. January 25, 2002. *Today Show Transcripts.*

Richardson, Herbert, ed. 1987. *On The Problem of Surrogate Parenthood: Analyzing The Baby M Case.* Lewiston, NY: Mellen.

Robbins, Sara. 1988. *Baby M Case: The Complete Trial Transcripts.* Superior Court of New Jersey, Chancery Division, Family Part, Bergen County: Transcript of Proceedings. Buffalo, NY: Hein.

CROSS REFERENCES

Adoption; Artificial Insemination; Custody; Parent and Child; Surrogate Motherhood; Visitation Rights.

BACK PAY AWARD

A legally enforceable decree ordering an employer to pay to an employee retroactively a designated increase in his or her salary that occurred during a particular period of employment. A decision rendered by a judicial or quasi-judicial body that an employee has a legal right to collect accrued salary that has not been paid out to him or her.

Back pay awards ensue from LITIGATION involving employment discrimination and issues regarding labor-management relations. Federal CIVIL RIGHTS legislation provides for back pay awards to compensate the victim for economic losses suffered as a result of discrimination.

BACK TO WORK AGREEMENT

The accord reached between an employer and a union to which his or her employees belong that establishes the terms and conditions governing the return of striking employees to work.

Disputes involving back to work agreements are subject to applicable federal and state laws governing labor-management relations.

CROSS REFERENCES

Labor Union; Strike.

BACKDATING

Predating a document or instrument prior to the date it was actually drawn. The negotiability of an instrument is not affected by the fact that it is backdated.

❖ BACON, SIR FRANCIS

Sir FRANCIS BACON was an English lawyer and statesman whose philosophical theories and writings influenced the development of scientific and legal thought in Great Britain and the United States.

Bacon was born in 1561, the second son of Sir Nicholas Bacon, the lord keeper of the great seal, and Lady Ann, whose brother-in-law was Baron Burghley (William Cecil), the first minister to Queen Elizabeth I. Bacon, like his father, was educated at Trinity College, Cambridge, where he enrolled at the age of twelve. In 1576 he was admitted to Gray's Inn, one of the four INNS OF COURT in London, which were institutions established for LEGAL EDUCATION. He also spent time in France as a member of the English ambassador's staff, before his father's sudden death required him to return to England and resume his legal education so that he could support his family. After completing his studies, Bacon became a barrister in 1582 and then attained the posts of reader (lecturer at the Inn) and bencher (senior member of the Inn).

In 1584, at the age of twenty-three, Bacon was elected to the House of Commons, representing Taunton, Liverpool, the county of Middlesex, Southampton, Ipswich, and the University of Cambridge. In 1594 he argued his first major case, *Chudleigh's Case* (1 Co. Rep. 1136, 76 Eng. Rep. 261 [K.B. 1594]), which involved the interpretation of complex inheritance statutes. He also began writing about science and philosophy and started work on his first major volume, *Temporis Partus Maximus* (The greatest part of time), though the book, along with many of his earliest works, was never published and so disappeared.

Through his friendship with Robert Devereux, the Earl of Essex, Bacon became acquainted with Queen Elizabeth I and he eventually became her counsel around 1600. As counsel, Bacon later took part in the prosecution of Essex, from whom he had become estranged, for TREASON, and for these efforts Bacon was knighted in 1603. In 1605 he published his first book, *The Advancement of Learning,* a collection of essays on philosophy that he dedicated to King James I. Later the same year, he married Alice Barnham, the daughter of a wealthy London politician.

Bacon continued to curry the king's favor by assisting James in his plans to unite Scotland with England, and was named to the post of SOLICITOR GENERAL in 1607. He also continued to write, publishing in 1609 *The Wisdom of the Ancients,* in which he analyzed the meaning of ancient myths. Seeking promotion to attorney general, Bacon advised the king concerning affairs of state and the relationship between the Crown and Parliament. He successfully engineered the ouster of the chief justice of the COMMON PLEAS, SIR EDWARD COKE, a longtime rival who had earlier occupied SOLICITOR and ATTORNEY general posts that Bacon had sought. Bacon finally became attorney general in 1613, which enabled him to continue his feud with Coke. He eventually prosecuted Coke for his role in the case of Edmond Peacham, a clergyman charged with treason for advocating rebellion against OPPRESSION in an unpublished TREATISE, leading to Coke's dismissal in 1616. Bacon continued his

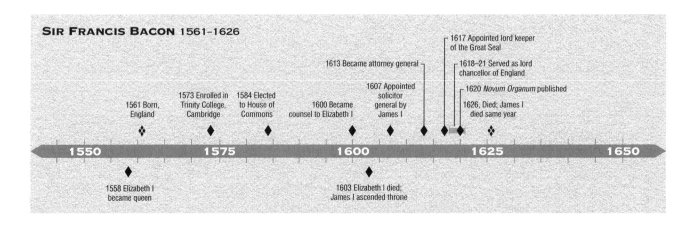

SIR FRANCIS BACON 1561–1626

1561 Born, England

1573 Enrolled in Trinity College, Cambridge

1584 Elected to House of Commons

1600 Became counsel to Elizabeth I

1607 Appointed solicitor general by James I

1613 Became attorney general

1617 Appointed lord keeper of the Great Seal

1618–21 Served as lord chancellor of England

1620 *Novum Organum* published

1626, Died; James I died same year

1550   1575   1600   1625   1650

1558 Elizabeth I became queen

1603 Elizabeth I died; James I ascended throne

service to the king and was appointed lord keeper of the great seal in 1617. A year later, he became lord chancellor of England, a post he held until 1621.

Bacon, a man of great intellect and energy, was often torn between his ambitions for higher office and his keen interest in science and philosophy. Though he was primarily concerned with his service to the Crown during most of his adult life, he did devote time to the study of philosophy. He was an early proponent of inductive reasoning, the theory that by analyzing observed facts, one can establish general laws or principles about how the world works. This theory is the opposite of deductive reasoning, which holds that one can draw specific conclusions by reasoning from more general premises. Bacon believed inductive reasoning to be more useful because it permitted the development of new theories that could be more generally and widely applied to a variety of situations. The legal systems of many countries, including the United States, were eventually grounded on the application of general laws derived from specific fact situations to govern conduct.

Bacon was likewise a strong believer in empiricism, the belief that experience is the most important source of knowledge. According to Bacon, scientists should try to learn about the world by using information gathered through the senses rather than by using reason or rules set forth by religious or political authority. Empiricism, like inductive reasoning, also influenced the development of later legal philosophies, in this case theories that viewed the law and justice as emerging from social life and experience.

Bacon was a prolific writer throughout his life, authoring a number of works expounding his theories. The *Novum Organum,* his most well known and widely read philosophical work, was published in 1620. The *Instauratio Magna* (Great instauration, from the Latin word *instaurare,* "to renew or begin afresh") was a comprehensive plan in which Bacon attempted to reorganize and redefine the sciences; it also contained his views concerning logic and scientific experimentation. In his philosophical writings, Bacon argued that the mind should be purged of what he termed idols, or tendencies to err. These idols, he maintained, arose from human nature, individual experience, and language. In addition, Bacon kept an extensive diary, which was discovered

Sir Francis Bacon.
LIBRARY OF CONGRESS.

after his death. The notebook, known as the *Commentarius Solutus* (Loose commentary), contained his notes about, among other things, his debts, his garden, and his health.

Later in his life, Bacon began to fall out of favor with the Crown. In 1618 the king criticized him for interfering in the MARRIAGE of Coke's daughter. In 1621 Bacon was charged with accepting a bribe concerning a grievance committee over which he had presided. Bacon admitted in a full confession that he had received gifts, but denied that they had influenced his judgment. Though he begged for mercy, Bacon found the king unsympathetic to his case and was forced to resign his office. Bacon was sentenced to a stiff fine (which was later suspended), imprisonment in the Tower of London (which actually lasted only four days), exclusion from holding any state office, and prohibition from coming within the vicinity of the Court of King's Bench.

Following his ouster from the court, Bacon returned to his large estate at Gorhambury, in rural England, to devote all of his energies to research and writing. He prepared digests of the laws and wrote a history of Great Britain and its monarchs. He planned to write six separate natural histories, but only two were completed: *Historia Ventorum* (History of the winds), which was published in 1622, and *Historia Vitae et Mortis* (History of life and death), which appeared the

> JUDGES MUST BE AWARE OF HARD CONSTRUCTIONS AND STRAINED INFERENCES, FOR THERE IS NO WORSE TORTURE THAN THE TORTURE OF LAWS.
> —SIR FRANCIS BACON

following year. He also wrote the *History of Henry VII,* published in 1622. In 1621 he enlarged his volume of *Essays,* which he had first published in 1597, and in 1627 he published *The New Atlantis.* He also corresponded with Italian philosophers and sent his work to them. Over the years, some writers have suggested that Bacon may have been the true author of William Shakespeare's plays, but because no concrete proof has been offered, the theory has been discounted by most scholars.

Sometime around 1623, Bacon, in ill health, was finally granted an audience with the king, but he was not granted a PARDON for his offenses. In London, on April 9, 1626, he died of bronchitis he contracted while conducting experiments on the effects of refrigeration on poultry.

FURTHER READINGS

Bowen, Catherine D. 1963. *Francis Bacon: The Temper of a Man.* Boston: Little, Brown.

Hogan, John C., and Mortimer D. Schwartz. 1985. "A Translation of Bacon's Maxims of the Common Law." *Law Library Journal* 77 (fall): 707–18.

Whitney, Charles. 1986. *Francis Bacon and Modernity.* New Haven, Conn.: Yale Univ. Press.

Zagorin, Perez. 1998. *Francis Bacon.* Princeton, N.J.: Princeton Univ. Press.

CROSS REFERENCES

Coke, Sir Edward; Inns of Court.

BAD FAITH

The fraudulent deception of another person; the intentional or malicious refusal to perform some duty or contractual obligation.

Bad faith is not the same as prior judgment or NEGLIGENCE. One can make an honest mistake about one's own rights and duties, but when the rights of someone else are intentionally or maliciously infringed upon, such conduct demonstrates bad faith.

The existence of bad faith can minimize or nullify any claims that a person alleges in a lawsuit. PUNITIVE DAMAGES, attorney's fees, or both, may be awarded to a party who must defend himself or herself in an action brought in bad faith.

Bad faith is a term commonly used in the law of contracts and other commercial dealings, such as COMMERCIAL PAPER, and in SECURED TRANSACTIONS. It is the opposite of GOOD FAITH, the observance of reasonable standards of fair dealings in trade that is required of every merchant. A government official who selectively enforces a nondiscriminatory law against the members of a particular group or race, thereby violating the CIVIL RIGHTS of those individuals, is acting in bad faith.

❖ BADGER, GEORGE EDMUND

George Edmund Badger was a lawyer, judge, and politician, and the subject of a U.S. Supreme Court confirmation battle in 1853.

The only son of a lawyer who died prematurely and a daughter of a Revolutionary War leader, Badger was born on April 17, 1795, in New Bern, North Carolina. He was first educated at a local academy and then attended Yale College. Because of poverty, he was forced to leave the college after only two years. He then returned home to North Carolina to study law. In 1814 he served for a short time as a major in a MILITIA called out to repel a threatened British invasion. A year later, he was admitted to the North Carolina bar. He quickly built a reputation as a brilliant and persuasive trial and appellate lawyer. In 1820, after four years of representing New Bern in the state house of commons, he was elected a judge of the

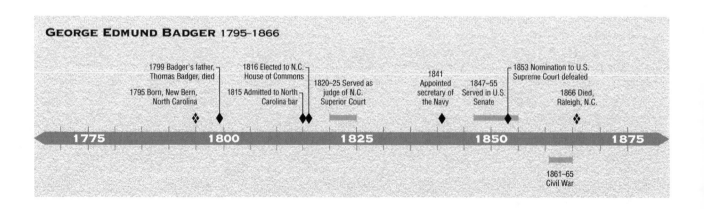

GEORGE EDMUND BADGER 1795–1866

1799 Badger's father, Thomas Badger, died

1795 Born, New Bern, North Carolina

1815 Admitted to North Carolina bar

1816 Elected to N.C. House of Commons

1820–25 Served as judge of N.C. Superior Court

1841 Appointed secretary of the Navy

1847–55 Served in U.S. Senate

1853 Nomination to U.S. Supreme Court defeated

1866 Died, Raleigh, N.C.

1861–65 Civil War

1775   1800   1825   1850   1875

superior court, where he served five years before resigning to practice law in Raleigh.

Initially a strong supporter of ANDREW JACKSON, Badger became a Whig in the mid-1830s and was appointed secretary of the Navy in 1841 by President WILLIAM H. HARRISON. He served for less than a year in this position and thus had little opportunity to have a lasting effect. However, during his tenure, he did recommend a home squadron to patrol the Caribbean and the Gulf of Mexico. He also authorized the construction of two steam vessels.

In 1846 Badger was elected to the U.S. Senate. As a senator, he strongly opposed the policies of the Polk administration. He also proposed reform of the Supreme Court's docket and advocated salary increases for the justices. In January 1853 President MILLARD FILLMORE, who had lost the 1852 election to FRANKLIN PIERCE, nominated Badger for a vacancy on the Court. Badger's nomination was met with widespread criticism from the Democratic papers of the South. Senators from Alabama, Louisiana, and Mississippi opposed his nomination because he resided outside the Fifth Circuit, where the vacancy on the Court arose. Even the Whig press, though it supported the proposed appointment, stated that "as a statesman, [Badger] is of no account, and as a politician detestable."

On previous occasions, the Senate had usually granted quick confirmation to a senator nominated for the Court, with little debate. But it postponed consideration of Badger's nomination until March 1853, so that Pierce could fill the vacancy with his own nominee—effectively defeating Badger's nomination. The same tactic would also be used to defeat later Supreme Court nominees.

Badger served in the Senate until 1855. After his retirement, he continued to practice law and took an active role in politics, helping to

organize the Constitutional Union party in 1861. This party was made up of conservative Whigs who had been alienated by the emergence of ABRAHAM LINCOLN as the leader of the Republican party during the presidential election of 1860. In its platform, the Constitutional Union party took no stand on the issue of SLAVERY and strongly advocated preservation of the Union. Badger was elected as a Union candidate, but a convention was never held.

Though he was widely known as a nationalist, when the Civil War broke out Badger was elected to the North Carolina SECESSION convention. At first he argued against secession, contending that it was unconstitutional. Instead he offered a DECLARATION OF INDEPENDENCE, which was rejected. As a result, he reluctantly voted for secession.

Badger continued to practice law in North Carolina until his death in 1866.

FURTHER READINGS

Congressional Quarterly. 2004. *Guide to the U.S. Supreme Court.* 4th ed. Washington, D.C.: Congressional Quarterly.

"George E. Badger (1795–1866). 2000. *Department of the Navy—Naval Historical Center.* Available online at http://www.history.navy.mil/photos/pers-us/uspers-b/g-badger.htm; website home page: http://www.history.navy.mil (accessed August 28, 2009).

Maisel, L. Sandy, ed. 1991. *Political Parties and Elections in the United States: An Encyclopedia.* New York: Garland.

CROSS REFERENCES

Fillmore, Millard; Slavery.

❖ BAER, GEORGE FREDERICK

George Frederick Baer was born September 26, 1842, near Lavansville, Pennsylvania. Baer was educated at Franklin and Marshall College, where he received an honorary master of arts degree in 1875 and a doctor of laws degree in 1886.

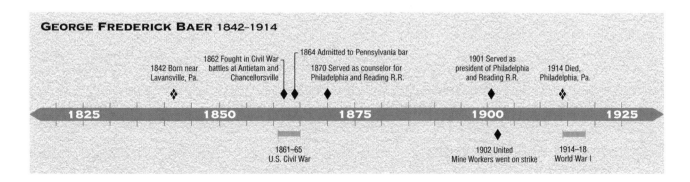

GEORGE FREDERICK BAER 1842–1914

1842 Born near Lavansville, Pa.

1862 Fought in Civil War battles at Antietam and Chancellorsville

1864 Admitted to Pennsylvania bar

1870 Served as counselor for Philadelphia and Reading R.R.

1901 Served as president of Philadelphia and Reading R.R.

1914 Died, Philadelphia, Pa.

1825   1850   1875   1900   1925

1861–65 U.S. Civil War

1902 United Mine Workers went on strike

1914–18 World War I

During the Civil War, Baer fought on the side of the Union at Bull Run, Antietam, Chancellorsville, and Fredericksburg.

He was admitted to the bar in 1864, moved to Reading, Pennsylvania, in 1868, and in 1870 performed the duties of counselor for the Philadelphia and Reading Railroad Company. He became a director of the railroad, acted as legal advisor to magnate J. P. Morgan, and was instrumental in the restructuring of the railroad in 1893. In 1901 he was president of the Philadelphia and Reading Railway Company, the Philadelphia and Reading Coal & Iron Company, and the Central Railroad Company of New Jersey.

When the United Mine Workers went on strike in Pennsylvania in 1902, Baer gained notoriety for his lack of sympathy for the plight of the miners.

Baer died April 26, 1914, in Philadelphia, Pennsylvania.

BAIL

The system that governs the status of individuals charged with committing crimes, from the time of their arrest to the time of their trial, and pending appeal, with the major purpose of ensuring their presence at trial.

In general, an individual accused of a crime must be held in the custody of the court until his or her guilt or innocence is determined. However, the court has the option of releasing the individual before that determination is made, and this option is called bail. Bail is set by the judge during the defendant's first appearance. For many misdemeanors, bail need not be set. For example, the DEFENDANT may be released on the issuance of a citation such as a ticket for a driving violation or when booked for a minor MISDEMEANOR at a police station or jail. But for major misdemeanors and felonies, the defendant must appear before a judge before bail is determined.

The courts have several methods available for releasing defendants on bail. The judge determines which of these methods is used. One alternative is for the defendant to post a BAIL BOND or PLEDGE of money. The bond can be signed by a professional surety holder, the accused, or the family and friends of the accused. Signing the bail bond is a promise that the defendant will appear in the specified criminal proceeding. The defendant's failure to appear will cause the signers of the bond to pay to the court the amount designated. The amount of bail is generally an amount determined in light of the seriousness of the alleged offense.

A defendant can also be released upon her or his own RECOGNIZANCE, which is the defendant's written, uninsured promise to return for trial. Such a release occurs only if the suspect has steady employment, stable family ties, and a history of residence in the community. Willful violation of the terms of a personal recognizance constitutes a crime.

Other conditions may also be set regarding the release of the defendant. The Bail Reform Act of 1984 (18 U.S.C.A. §§ 3141–3150) provided for many additional conditions that do not rely upon finances and that reflected current trends to move away from financial requirements for freedom. These conditions came about, in part, owing to concerns regarding the discriminatory nature of bail toward the poor. The Bail Reform Act allows for conditional releases dependent upon such circumstances as maintaining employment, meeting curfews, and receiving medical or psychiatric treatment.

Civil Actions

A defendant in a CIVIL ACTION can be arrested to ensure that he or she will appear in court to respond to the plaintiff's claims. Civil arrest prevents a defendant from leaving the jurisdiction to evade the LITIGATION, and from attempting to conceal or dispose of assets in order to keep the PLAINTIFF from collecting on the judgment if the plaintiff prevails. Because civil arrest is a drastic remedy, state laws must be consulted to determine when it may be used. The purpose of bail in a civil action is to ensure the presence of the defendant at trial and to guarantee the payment of a debt or the fulfillment of some civil duty, as ordered by the court.

The court sets the amount of bail, which is generally based on the probable amount of damage against the defendant. In some instances, if informed of changed circumstances, the court might increase or reduce bail. Cash, as opposed to a bail bond, may be deposited with the court only when authorized by statute. The purpose of the arrest and the statutory provisions determine whether this deposit may be used to pay the judgment awarded to the plaintiff.

Criminal Prosecutions

The objective of bail in criminal actions is to prevent the imprisonment of the accused prior to trial while ensuring her or his appearance at trial. Constitutional and statutory rights to bail prior to conviction exist for most offenses, but state constitutional provisions and statutes must be consulted to determine the offenses to which bail applies. The Bail Reform Act of 1984 governs bail in federal offenses. It provides the federal MAGISTRATE with alternatives to the incarceration of the defendant. If the charge is a noncapital offense (an offense not punishable by death), the defendant may be released on her or his own recognizance. If there is a reasonable likelihood that the defendant will not return for trial, the judge may impose bail. The judge may also release the defendant into the custody of a designated person or organization for supervision. Restricting the residence, extent of travel, and personal associations of the accused are other options.

Discretion of the Court

A court exercises its discretion with respect to the allowance of bail. In reaching its decision, it evaluates the circumstances of the particular case, including the existence of doubt as to the accused person's appearance at trial. Unreasonable

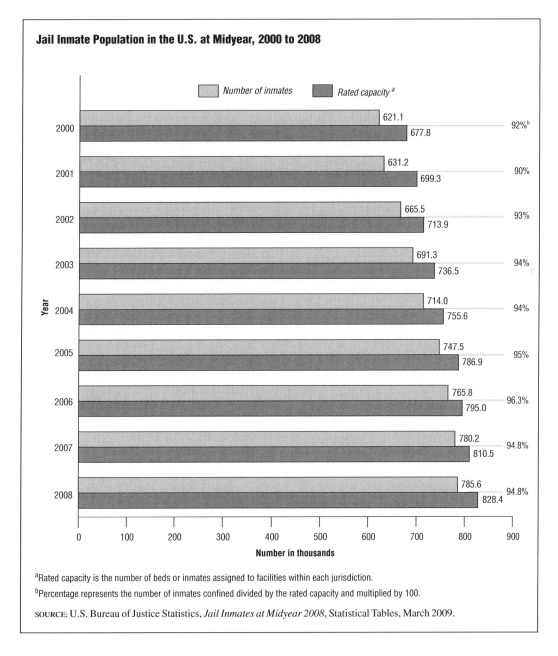

Jail Inmate Population in the U.S. at Midyear, 2000 to 2008

Number of inmates   Rated capacity [a]

Year	Number of inmates	Rated capacity	Percentage
2000	621.1	677.8	92%[b]
2001	631.2	699.3	90%
2002	665.5	713.9	93%
2003	691.3	736.5	94%
2004	714.0	755.6	94%
2005	747.5	786.9	95%
2006	765.8	795.0	96.3%
2007	780.2	810.5	94.8%
2008	785.6	828.4	94.8%

Number in thousands

[a]Rated capacity is the number of beds or inmates assigned to facilities within each jurisdiction.

[b]Percentage represents the number of inmates confined divided by the rated capacity and multiplied by 100.

SOURCE: U.S. Bureau of Justice Statistics, *Jail Inmates at Midyear 2008*, Statistical Tables, March 2009.

ILLUSTRATION BY GGS CREATIVE RESOURCES. REPRODUCED BY PERMISSION OF GALE, A PART OF CENGAGE LEARNING.

delay or postponement in the proceeding, which is not attributable to the accused, usually constitutes a ground for bail—in some jurisdictions, by absolute right; more frequently, at the discretion of the court.

In jurisdictions in which it is neither proscribed nor regarded as an absolute right, the grant of bail pending a motion for a new trial, a review, or an appeal is also discretionary. The grant of bail is then determined in light of the probability of reversal, the nature of the crime, the likelihood of the defendant's escape, and the character of the defendant.

The decision to grant or deny bail is reviewable, but the scope of the review is limited to whether the court abused its discretion in its determination.

The amount of bail set is within the discretion of the court. Once fixed, it should not be modified, except for GOOD CAUSE. An increase cannot be authorized when the ARREST WARRANT specifies the amount of the bail. An application for a change in bail is presented to the court by a motion based on an AFFIDAVIT (a voluntary written statement of facts) confirmed by the oath of the person making it. The affidavit must be taken before a person authorized to administer such an oath and must contain the facts justifying the change. The EIGHTH AMENDMENT to the Constitution and the provisions of most state constitutions prohibit excessive bail, meaning bail in an amount greater than that necessary to ensure the defendant's appearance at trial.

The Bail Reform Act of 1984 helped to set guidelines allowing courts to consider the danger a defendant might present if released on bail. This response to the problem of crimes committed by individuals who had been released on bail marked a significant departure from earlier philosophies surrounding bail. Bail laws took on a new importance; they would ensure the appearance of the defendant in proceedings, and they would see to the safety of the community into which the defendant was released.

Pursuant to the 1984 act, if the court deems that the accused may, in fact, pose a threat to the safety of the community, the accused may be held without bail. In 1987, *United States v. Salerno*, 481 U.S. 739, 107 S. Ct. 2095, 95 L. Ed. 2d 697, addressed the constitutionality of holding an individual without bail while awaiting criminal trial. The Supreme Court held that due process was not violated by the detention of individuals without bail.

Breach and Forfeiture

A breach of the bail bond occurs in both civil and criminal actions when the defendant "jumps bail" or "skips bail"—that is, deliberately fails to return to court on the specified date, thereby forfeiting the amount of the bond. The act of jumping bail is either a misdemeanor or a felony, depending upon statute. The mandatory appearance required in a bail arrangement consists not merely of responding to the charges but also of attendance by the defendant at the trial and SENTENCING by the court. Appearance by counsel ordinarily does not prevent a breach, although under some statutes, where the offense is a misdemeanor, such an appearance might be sufficient.

When a bond is breached, the court enters a judgment of FORFEITURE of the bail. In some jurisdictions, the judgment is appealable, but only if the failure to comply with the conditions of the bond was excusable and the state suffered no loss of rights against the defendant.

A final judgment normally cannot be entered on recognizance or bail bond without additional proceedings. Such proceedings are usually of a civil nature and follow the forfeiture of bail. These proceedings can be commenced by a WRIT (a court order) of *scire facias* (a judicial writ requiring the person against whom it is brought to SHOW CAUSE why the party bringing it should not have advantage of such record) or by an independent action.

FURTHER READINGS

Bredefeld, Nicole J. 2001. "The Bail Reform Act of 1984 and Felons who Possess Weapons: Discrepancy among the Federal Courts." *Seton Hall Legislative Journal* 26 (September).

Colbert, Douglas L., Ray Paternoster, and Shawn Bushway. 2002. "Do Attorneys Really Matter? The Empirical and Legal Case for the Right of Counsel at Bail." *Cardozo Law Review* 23 (May).

Goldfarb, Ronald. 1965. *Ransom: A Critique of the American Bail System.* New York: Harper & Row.

Israel, Jerold H., and Wayne R. LaFave, eds. 2006. *Criminal Procedure: Constitutional Limitations in a Nutshell.* 7th ed. Eagan, MN: West.

LaFave, Wayne R., Jerold H. Israel, and Nancy J. King, eds. 2007. *2006 Supplement to Modern Criminal Procedure and Advanced Criminal Procedure.* 11th ed. St. Paul, MN: Thomson West.

Sharma, R. 2002. *Human Rights and Bail.* New Delhi, India: APH.

Thomas, Wayne H. 1976. *Bail Reform in America.* Berkeley: Univ. of California Press.

U.S. House of Representatives. 2000. *Bounty Hunter Responsibility Act of 1999: Hearing before the Subcommittee on the Constitution of the Committee on the Judiciary, House of Representatives, One Hundred Sixth Congress, Second Session, on H.R. 2964, March 30, 2000.* Washington, D.C.: U.S. Government Printing Office. Available at http://commdocs.house.gov/committees/judiciary/hju65062.000/hju65062_0f.htm; website home page: http://commdocs.house.gov (accessed July 5, 2009).

CROSS REFERENCES

Due Process of Law; Eighth Amendment; Recognizance.

BAIL BOND

A written promise signed by a defendant or a surety (one who promises to act in place of another) to pay an amount fixed by a court should the defendant named in the document fail to appear in court for the designated criminal proceeding at the date and time specified.

A bail bond is one method used to obtain the release of a DEFENDANT awaiting trial upon criminal charges from the custody of law enforcement officials. The defendant, the defendant's family and friends, or a professional bail bond agent (or bail agent) executes a document that promises to forfeit the sum of money determined by the court to be commensurate with the gravity of the alleged offense if the defendant fails to return for the trial date.

Most defendants are financially unable to post their own bail, so they seek help from a bail agent, who, for a nonrefundable fee of 10 to 20 percent of the amount of the bail, posts bail. A bail agent becomes liable to the court for the full amount of bail if the defendant fails to appear for the court date. Before agreeing to assume the risk of posting bail, the bail agent requires collateral from the defendant, such as jewelry, SECURITIES, or written guaranties by creditworthy friends or relatives of the defendant. This collateral acts as security to ensure repayment for any losses the bail agent might incur. If the defendant appears to be a "poor risk," and unlikely to return to court for trial, the bail agent will refuse to post bail. A defendant who has a record of steady employment, has resided in the community for a reasonable length of time, and has no prior criminal record is considered to be a good risk.

The bail agent, the defendant, or another interested party posts bail in the form of the bail bond at the court where the defendant is required to return for the proceeding. The court clerk issues a bail ticket or similar document, which is sent to the police to notify them that bail has been met. The defendant is released from custody when the bail ticket is received by the police. LIABILITY under the bail bond ends when the defendant fulfills the conditions of the bond by appearing in court on the specified date, or if the terms of the bond become impossible to execute, such as by the death of the defendant or by his or her arrest, detention, or imprisonment on another offense in the same or different jurisdiction.

If a defendant fails to appear for trial on the date specified in the bail bond, the court will issue a WARRANT for the defendant's arrest for "jumping bail," and the amount of the bond will be forfeited to the court. The bail agent is generally authorized by statute to arrest the defendant and bring him or her back for criminal proceedings.

Kentucky, Illinois, Wisconsin, Nebraska, and Oregon have enacted laws making it illegal to post bail for profit, thereby outlawing the occupation of bail bond agent.

A bail bond may be similarly used in cases of civil arrest to prevent a defendant from fleeing a jurisdiction to avoid LITIGATION or fraudulently concealing or disposing of assets in order to become JUDGMENT PROOF (incapable of satisfying an award made against him or her if the PLAINTIFF is successful).

FURTHER READINGS

Berand, Laura, and Jean Montoya. 2002. *Criminal Litigation in Action.* Notre Dame, IN: National Institute for Trial Advocacy.

Marcus, Paul, and Jack Zimmerman. 2009. *Criminal Procedure in Practice.* 3d ed. Notre Dame, IN: National Institute for Trial Advocacy.

Simmons, Don, Jr. 2002. "Making a Living off Making Bail." Roanoke Times & *World News.*

CROSS REFERENCES

Asset; Collateral; Judgment Proof.

BAILEE

One to whom personal property is entrusted for a particular purpose by another, the bailor, according to the terms of an express or implied agreement.

CROSS REFERENCE

Bailment.

F. Lee Bailey.

❖ BAILEY, FRANCIS LEE

The career of ATTORNEY F. Lee Bailey is a celebrated one. Few criminal defense lawyers have earned as much success or notoriety as the tough-talking former Marine lieutenant, known for winning what have often been considered hopeless cases. Early in his career, Bailey built a reputation for fastidious attention to detail as an investigator who could ferret out the minutiae needed to acquit his clients. His CROSS-EXAMINATION style—long on hard-hitting machismo—earned him comparisons to some of the twentieth century's most noted lawyers. By his mid-30s, he had won a string of victories in shocking, nationally publicized cases, including an important U.S. Supreme Court ruling on

PRETRIAL PUBLICITY. His books on law became bestsellers, but controversy followed his criticisms of the legal system and his sometimes risky defense strategies. In 1994 he joined the defense team in the trial of O. J. SIMPSON for the MURDER of Nicole Brown Simpson and her friend Ronald Lyle Goldman.

Bailey might never have become a lawyer if he had not dropped out of college. Born in the Boston suburb of Waltham, Massachusetts, on June 10, 1933, he was the son of an advertising man and a schoolteacher who founded a large nursery school. In his teens, Bailey excelled at Kimball Union Academy, a prep school, and won a scholarship to attend Harvard in 1950. His goal was to study English. Yet academia could not hold him for long; he wanted adventure. Dropping out of Harvard at the end of his sophomore year, he enrolled in the Navy flight-training program and eventually joined the Marines, where he at first flew jet fighters. Soon Bailey had switched gears and was defending accused service members as part of the legal staff at the Cherry Point Marine Corps Air Station in North Carolina. Military life would leave its mark on him. More than 40 years later, he would write articles about jets for *Flying* magazine and, while defending Simpson, would say that he had spoken with a witness who was a veteran, as one Marine to another.

The experience of fighting courts-martial convinced Bailey to become a lawyer in civilian life. Leaving the service with the rank of second lieutenant, he entered Boston University Law School, which admitted him on the strength of his considerable MILITARY LAW practice. Once again, his ambition could scarcely be satisfied in books, and the precocious student founded a private detective agency. The firm did fieldwork

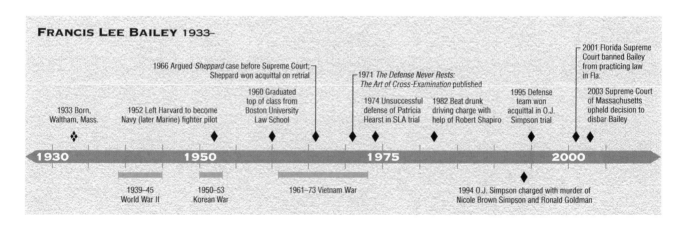

FRANCIS LEE BAILEY 1933–

1966 Argued *Sheppard* case before Supreme Court; Sheppard won acquittal on retrial

1971 *The Defense Never Rests: The Art of Cross-Examination* published

2001 Florida Supreme Court banned Bailey from practicing law in Fla.

1960 Graduated top of class from Boston University Law School

1974 Unsuccessful defense of Patricia Hearst in SLA trial

1982 Beat drunk driving charge with help of Robert Shapiro

1995 Defense team won acquittal in O.J. Simpson trial

2003 Supreme Court of Massachusetts upheld decision to disbar Bailey

1933 Born, Waltham, Mass.

1952 Left Harvard to become Navy (later Marine) fighter pilot

1930   **1950**   **1975**   **2000**

1939–45 World War II

1950–53 Korean War

1961–73 Vietnam War

1994 O.J. Simpson charged with murder of Nicole Brown Simpson and Ronald Goldman

to help attorneys prepare their cases, and Bailey claimed to devote sixty hours a week to this endeavor alone. It paid off: he handled some two thousand cases, honed his skills as an investigator, and later sold the agency. The long extracurricular hours did not stop him from finishing, in 1960, at the top of his class with the highest grade point average in the school's history.

Bailey next studied the lie detector at the Keeler POLYGRAPH Institute in Chicago, a tool much used in the courtrooms of the era. The skill he acquired there led to his first job, at age 27, as a polygraph expert hired by the defense in a highly publicized Boston trial, the *Torso Murder* case—so named because prosecutors charged the DEFENDANT, George Edgerly, with dismembering his wife and dumping the pieces of her body in the Merrimack River. Edgerly had failed a lie detector test, making the case difficult for the defense. Bailey was hired to help turn the case around. When the lead attorney suffered a heart attack, Bailey took over the case and won an acquittal for the defendant. His victory in the Edgerly case was the first of several in high profile cases over the next decade. Most notable was Bailey's role in the murder appeal of Dr. SAMUEL H. SHEPPARD, who had been convicted of second-degree murder in the bludgeoning death of his wife, Marilyn Sheppard. In 1966, Bailey helped convince the U.S. Supreme Court that the trial judge had erred in not shielding Sheppard from pretrial publicity, thus denying him a fair trial—establishing an important new standard for defendants' rights (*Sheppard v. Maxwell*, 384 U.S. 333, 86 S. Ct. 1507, 16 L. Ed. 2d 600). He subsequently cleared Sheppard.

The *Sheppard* case launched Bailey's career. Not only was he now proven in court, he was also attaining celebrity status. News magazines extolled his skills at cross-examination, with *Life Magazine* saying in 1967 that he was "methodical and relentless, boring in and tunneling under his prey like a determined badger." Frequently, comparisons to the fictional television character Perry Mason cropped up, which Bailey resented; just as often came comparisons to the great criminal defense lawyer CLARENCE DARROW, which he did nothing to discourage. Preparation and analysis were Bailey's most renowned legal skills, yet what brought him public attention was his talent for theatrics. His style was swaggering: he could thunderously tell

a courtroom that the charges against his client were "10 pounds of hogwash in a five-pound bag" or declare that he had just won a "thumping acquittal." He viewed LITIGATION as "the true substitute for gladiatorial combat." By the time the ABC television network gave him a slot in 1967 on the program *Good Company*, where he chatted up celebrities, he was himself a household name. His 1971 book, *The Defense Never Rests: The Art of Cross-Examination*, became a bestseller. Several legal, nonfiction, and fiction books followed.

For Bailey, fame was a double-edged sword that brought both attention and criticism. Often sought out by the news media for his opinions, he used their interviews as soapboxes from which to call for legal reforms. He argued that criminal defense attorneys needed several additional years of training; held that fewer frivolous lawsuits would tie up the courts if the U.S. legal system were to imitate the more rigorous British one; and, on the lecture circuit, even suggested that crime could be prevented by making it illegal for people to carry more than $500 at a time. He also simply liked the limelight: As the equally famous attorney Melvin M. Belli recalled, he and Bailey once stood at a bar betting each other $5 over who would be recognized first. Not all of Bailey's pronouncements met with praise; his outspokenness was sometimes seen as grandstanding. Ironically, for the attorney who had won *Sheppard*, he was criticized by the Massachusetts BAR ASSOCIATION for saying too much outside of court, and in 1971 the Supreme Court of New Jersey barred him for a year from practicing law there for similar reasons.

In 1974 Bailey faced his Waterloo when he unsuccessfully defended the publishing heiress PATRICIA HEARST. Hearst had stunned U.S. citizens when, after being kidnapped, she was photographed carrying an automatic weapon in a San Francisco bank heist. On trial for ROBBERY, she claimed to have been brainwashed by her abductors, a terrorist group known as the Symbionese Liberation Army (SLA). In orchestrating her defense, Bailey was widely criticized for the risky strategy of putting her on the WITNESS STAND, where she took the FIFTH AMENDMENT 42 times to avoid answering questions. Years after her conviction, Hearst herself blamed Bailey, arguing in a 1980 appeal that the attorney had been less interested in her defense than in writing a book about the case. The U.S.

THOSE WHO THINK THE INFORMATION BROUGHT OUT AT A CRIMINAL TRIAL IS THE TRUTH, THE WHOLE TRUTH, AND NOTHING BUT THE TRUTH ARE FOOLS.
—FRANCIS BAILEY

Ninth Circuit Court of Appeals ruled that "Bailey's potential CONFLICT OF INTEREST is virtually admitted," and granted Hearst a new hearing (*United States v. Hearst*, 638 F.2d 1190 [9th Cir. 1980]).

After the Hearst trial, Bailey disappeared from public view for a time. Nevertheless, his reputation as "flamboyant" and a "legend" persisted and he continued to win cases. In 1982 he attracted national attention again when he beat a drunk driving charge with LEGAL REPRESENTATION from his friend, ROBERT L. SHAPIRO. Bailey complained that the police had picked on him because he was famous. Soon he was campaigning publicly against what he saw as police harassment, warning, "The cops have decided to set some fierce public examples of their new hard line, probably to scare drivers into going easy on the booze." He promptly wrote a legal self-help book titled *How to Protect Yourself against Cops in California and Other Strange Places*, purporting to be a guide to avoiding unfair drunk driving convictions.

In 1994 the trial of Simpson returned Bailey to the spotlight when he and Shapiro were hired for the defense team. However, before the trial even began, the old friends engaged in a public feud. Shapiro accused Bailey of trying to destroy his credibility by leaking information to the press, comparing Bailey to a snake and demanding his removal from the case. In reply, Bailey criticized his colleague's "public outburst." According to *Newsweek*, Simpson admonished the two bickering attorneys, reminding them that his life was at stake. The spat died down, and in March of 1995 Bailey cross-examined a key prosecution witness, police detective Mark Fuhrman.

Surrounded by high expectations, the cross-examination was widely portrayed as a comeback attempt for the 62-year-old Bailey. He rose to the occasion with high expectations of his own, promising to "dismantle" Fuhrman. The defense had branded the detective a racist and alleged that he had planted a key piece of evidence at Simpson's estate: a bloody glove. Bailey's difficult job was to prove that Fuhrman had planted evidence and had once used the pejorative *nigger*; Fuhrman never conceded either point, despite several days of grilling on the stand. PROSECUTOR MARCIA CLARK attacked Bailey on several points, arguing that he had misrepresented what a Marine sergeant would TESTIFY to as to Fuhrman's language in the Marines and that he was manufacturing evidence with his conjecture that Fuhrman had

sneaked the bloody glove to the crime scene in a plastic bag in his sock.

After Bailey's questioning of Fuhrman, several prominent legal analysts argued that he had flopped. He defended his performance in *Time* magazine using a comparison that recalled the earliest praises of his career: "I'm not Perry Mason; nobody is. Other lawyers whom I respect told me that given what I had to work with, it was good. Norman Mailer called me and said it was flawless. So I feel good."

In March of 1996 Bailey himself became the subject of criminal prosecution after he and the United States government had a disagreement over who was entitled to millions of dollars of stock formerly held by Claude Duboc, a drug dealer and client of Bailey. The government demanded FORFEITURE of the stock, but Bailey said a plea bargain he had negotiated with the government on behalf of Duboc allowed Bailey to keep it. When Bailey refused to surrender 2.3 million dollars to the federal district court in Tallahassee, Florida, he was sentenced to six months in jail for CONTEMPT. In August of 2000 a federal judge held Bailey in contempt of court for failing to turn over the Duboc moneys. However, the judge declined to jail or fine Bailey on the grounds that federal prosecutors failed to properly trace the money or to recover assets from Bailey. In November of 2001 the Florida Supreme Court issued a decision based on Bailey's mishandling of the Duboc stock funds that ordered Bailey to be disbarred from practicing law in Florida. In April of 2003 the Supreme Judicial Court of Massachusetts issued a unanimous decision upholding the decision to disbar Bailey on the grounds that he deliberately broke ethics rules.

During the 2000s, Bailey has traveled the country giving lectures on his career and cases. He has appeared as a legal commentator on television shows such as *Larry King Live*, *Today*, and *Good Morning America*. He also writes fiction and non-fiction works.

FURTHER READINGS

Ash, Jim. August 31, 2001. "Bailey's Future as Lawyer Rests with State's High Court." *The Palm Beach Post*.

Bailey, F. Lee. 1971. *The Defense Never Rests*. New York: Stein and Day.

"Contempt Ruling for F. Lee Bailey: He's Spared Jail in Legal Fees Dispute." August 18, 2000. *Newsday*, A13.

CROSS REFERENCES

Hearst, Patty; Cochran, Johnnie L., Jr.; Simpson, O. J.

BAILIFF

An individual who is entrusted with some authority, care, guardianship, or jurisdiction over designated persons or property. One who acts in a managerial or ministerial capacity or takes care of land, goods, and chattels of another in order to make the best profit for the owner. A minor officer of a court serving primarily as a messenger or usher. A low-level court official or sheriff's deputy whose duty is to preserve and protect orderly conduct in court proceedings.

BAILMENT

The temporary placement of control over, or possession of, personal property by one person, the bailor, into the hands of another, the bailee, for a designated purpose upon which the parties have agreed.

The term *bailment* is derived from the French *bailor,* "to deliver." It is generally considered to be a contractual relationship because the bailor and bailee, either expressly or impliedly, bind themselves to act according to particular terms. The bailee receives only control or possession of the property while the bailor retains the ownership interests in it. During the specific period a bailment exists, the bailee's interest in the property is superior to that of all others, including the bailor, unless the bailee violates some term of the agreement. Once the purpose for which the property has been delivered has been accomplished, the property will be returned to the bailor or otherwise disposed of pursuant to the bailor's directions.

A bailment is not the same as a sale, which is an intentional transfer of ownership of PERSONAL PROPERTY in exchange for something of value. A bailment involves only a transfer of possession or custody, not of ownership. A rental or lease of personal property might be a bailment, depending upon the agreement of the parties. A bailment is created when a parking garage attendant, the bailee, is given the keys to a motor vehicle by its owner, the bailor. The owner, in addition to renting the space, has transferred possession and control of the vehicle by relinquishing its keys to the attendant. If the keys were not made available and the vehicle was locked, the arrangement would be strictly a rental or lease, because there was no transfer of possession. A gratuitous loan and the delivery of property for repair or safekeeping are also typical situations in which a bailment is created.

A library patron's use of library books and materials is an example of a bailment for the sole benefit of the bailee.

AP IMAGES

Categories

There are three types of bailments: (1) for the benefit of the bailor and bailee; (2) for the sole benefit of the bailor; and (3) for the sole benefit of the bailee.

A bailment for the mutual benefit of the parties is created when there is an exchange of performances between the parties. A bailment for the repair of an item is a bailment for mutual benefit when the bailee receives a fee in exchange for his or her work.

A bailor receives the sole benefit from a bailment when a bailee acts gratuitously—for example, if a restaurant, a bailee, provides an attended coatroom free of charge to its customers, the bailors. By virtue of the terms of the bailment, the bailee agrees to act without any expectation of compensation.

A bailment is created for the sole benefit of the bailee when both parties agree the property temporarily in the bailee's custody is to be used to his or her own advantage without giving anything to the bailor in return. The loan of a book from a library is a bailment for the sole benefit of the bailee.

Elements

Three elements are generally necessary for the existence of a bailment: delivery, acceptance, and consideration.

Actual possession of or control over property must be delivered to a bailee in order to create a bailment. The delivery of actual possession of an item allows the bailee to accomplish his or her duties toward the property without the interference of others. Control over property is not necessarily the same as physical custody of it but, rather, is a type of constructive delivery. The bailor gives the bailee the means of access to taking custody of it, without its actual delivery. The law construes such action as the equivalent of the physical transfer of the item. The delivery of the keys to a safe-deposit box is constructive delivery of its contents.

A requisite to the creation of a bailment is the express or implied acceptance of possession of or control over the property by the bailee. A person cannot unwittingly become a bailee. Because a bailment is a contract, knowledge and acceptance of its terms are essential to its enforcement.

Consideration, the exchange of something of value, must be present for a bailment to exist. Unlike the consideration required for most contracts, as long as one party gives up something of value, such action is regarded as good consideration. It is sufficient that the bailor suffer loss of use of the property by relinquishing its control to the bailee; the bailor has given up something of value—the immediate right to control the property.

Rights and Liabilities

The bailment contract embodying general principles of the law of bailments governs the rights and duties of the bailor and bailee. The duty of care that must be exercised by a bailee varies, depending on the type of bailment.

In a bailment for mutual benefit, the bailee must take reasonable care of the bailed property. A bailee who fails to do so may be held liable for any damages incurred from his or her NEGLIGENCE. When a bailor receives the sole benefit from the bailment, the bailee has a lesser duty to care for the property and is financially responsible only if he or she has been grossly negligent or has acted in bad faith in taking care of the property. In contrast, a bailee for whose sole benefit property has been bailed must exercise extraordinary care for the property. The bailee can use the property only in the manner authorized by the terms of the bailment. The bailee is liable for all injuries to the property from failure to properly care for or use it.

Once the purpose of the bailment has been completed, the bailee usually must return the property to the bailor, or account for it, depending upon the terms of the contract. If, through NO FAULT of his or her own, the return of the property is delayed or becomes impossible—

for example, when it is lost during the course of the bailment—the bailee will not be held liable for nondelivery on demand or when a hurricane blows the property into the ocean. In all other situations, however, the bailee will be responsible for the tort of conversion for unjustifiable failure to redeliver the property as well as its unauthorized use.

The provisions of the bailment contract may restrict the LIABILITY of a bailee for negligent care or unauthorized use of the property. Such terms may not, however, absolve the bailee from all liability for the consequences of his or her own FRAUD or negligence. The bailor must have notice of all such limitations on liability. The restrictions will be enforced in any action brought for damages as long as the contract does not violate the law or PUBLIC POLICY. Similarly, a bailee may extend his or her liability to the bailor by contract provision.

Termination

A bailment is ended when its purpose has been achieved, when the parties agree that it is terminated, or when the bailed property is destroyed. A bailment created for an indefinite period is terminable at will by either party, as long as the other party receives DUE NOTICE of the intended termination. Once a bailment ends, the bailee must return the property to the bailor or possibly be liable for conversion.

FURTHER READINGS

Cross, Frank B., et al. 2008. *West's Legal Environment of Business: Test Cases, Ethical, Global, and E-commerce Environments.* Florence, KY: South-Western.

Duhaime, Lloyd. "Bailment." *Duhaime.org.* Available online at http://www.duhaime.org/LegalDictionary/A/Bailment. aspx; website home page: http://www.duhaime.org (accessed August 28, 2009).

Hall, Kermit L. 1996. *A History of American Legal Culture: Cases and Materials.* 2d ed. New York: Oxford Univ. Press.

CROSS REFERENCES

Bad Faith; Conversion; Damages; Negligence.

BAILOR

One who places control over or possession of personal property in the hands of another, a bailee, for its care, safekeeping, or use, in accordance to the terms of a mutual agreement.

CROSS REFERENCE

Bailment.

BAILOUT
See ECONOMIC BAILOUT.

BAIT AND SWITCH
A deceptive sales technique that involves advertising a low-priced item to attract customers to a store, then persuading them to buy more expensive goods by failing to have a sufficient supply of the advertised item on hand or by disparaging its quality.

This practice is illegal in many states under their CONSUMER PROTECTION laws.

❖ BAKER, ELLA JOSEPHINE
Ella Josephine Baker helped found the U.S. CIVIL RIGHTS MOVEMENT and organize three national CIVIL RIGHTS organizations.

Baker was born in Norfolk, Virginia, on December 13, 1903, the second of three children of Georgianna Ross Baker and Blake Baker. Baker's mother insisted that her children do well in school, because she felt that they needed an education in order to live a full life. Baker was sent to a private boarding school from ninth grade to twelfth grade, after her mother decided that she and her siblings were not receiving high-quality instruction in the public school they had been attending. In 1918 Baker began studying at Shaw University, an all-black school in Raleigh, North Carolina, that offered high school and college-level instruction.

Baker graduated from Shaw University in 1927, ranked first in her class. However, she did

Ella Baker.
PHOTOGRAPH FROM/ BY THE NAACP COLLECTION, PRINTS AND PHOTOGRAPHS DIVISION, LIBRARY OF CONGRESS

not have enough money for further schooling to become either a medical missionary or a social worker, occupations to which she had aspired. Her college degree in hand, she went to New York City.

While living in New York, Baker wrote articles for Harlem newspapers, including the *West Indian Review.* Living and working in Harlem during the mid- to late 1920s, she became a part of the Harlem Renaissance, a

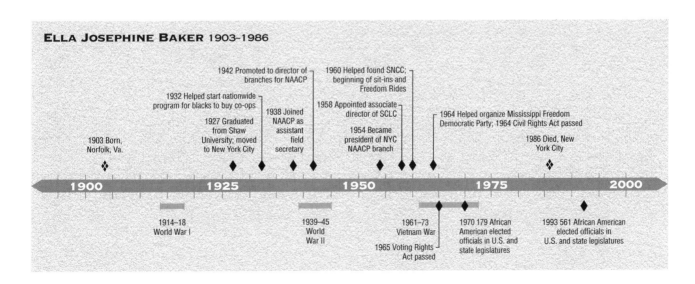

period of high artistic achievement and greater awareness of the possibilities for equality, justice, and true freedom. Baker participated in political discussions with many people, all over New York City. She later recalled, "Wherever there was a discussion, I'd go. It didn't matter if it was all men, and maybe I was the only woman … it didn't matter."

In the early days of the Great Depression, Baker was working for a Harlem newspaper along with George Samuel Schuyler, who was well known in the black community for his writing and who frequently railed against racial prejudice. In one article, Schuyler proposed that African Americans set up cooperatives to purchase goods in larger quantities, at lower prices than they could get otherwise. The response to this article was so positive that Schuyler decided to set up a cooperative on his own with Baker's help. Baker learned a great deal in this experience, and became an acknowledged expert on consumer affairs, a new idea that she helped introduce to the black community nationwide. In 1935 she was hired by the Works Progress Administration (WPA), a group of programs set up by President Franklin D. Roosevelt's NEW DEAL, to teach people living in Harlem how to purchase the most for the little money they had.

Baker worked for the WPA until 1938, when she left to become an assistant field secretary for the National Association for the Advancement of Colored People (NAACP), the first civil rights organization established in the United States. At that time the NAACP had fewer members in the South than in any other part of the United States, and most of its members were professionals—doctors, lawyers, and teachers. Baker believed that the organization had to reach the larger population of working people in order to accomplish its tasks. She targeted factory workers, household workers, and construction workers and tried to get them to support the NAACP. By 1941, thanks to Baker and the other NAACP field staffers, the NAACP's southern membership rolls had increased significantly.

In 1942 Baker was promoted to director of branches for the organization. In that position, she helped branch offices organize fund-raising and membership drives and encouraged them to become involved in local affairs to improve the lot of black people in their communities.

Through her contact with the branch offices, the organization became aware of court cases they could bring on behalf of blacks who were denied their civil rights, such as access to public institutions of higher education.

In 1954 Baker was named as president of the New York City branch of the NAACP. In May of that year, the U.S. Supreme Court issued its landmark decision in BROWN V. BOARD OF EDUCATION, 347 U.S. 483, 74 S. Ct. 686, 98 L. Ed. 873. The Court ruled in *Brown* that "separate but equal" schools for blacks and whites were unconstitutional. As a result, school districts in cities across the nation had to make sure they were not violating the law. Based on her experience raising her niece, Jackie, Baker believed that New York City schools were segregated, and she and other community leaders pressured city hall to examine the school system more closely for evidence of illegal SEGREGATION. The next year, the mayor of New York City asked Baker to join his newly created Commission on School Integration.

To present the commission's findings to parents of schoolchildren, Baker set up meetings around New York City. When she found that many parents were deeply concerned over the quality of their neighborhood schools, Baker encouraged them to petition the school board to allow their children to attend schools of their own choosing. In response to the petitions, New York developed one of the first open-enrollment plans for public schools. Open enrollment allowed public school students to attend schools outside their own neighborhoods, without requiring them to change their residency or pay extra tuition or transportation costs.

A new chapter in the civil rights movement began when ROSA PARKS refused to give up her seat on a Montgomery, Alabama, bus on December 1, 1955. In Montgomery black passengers could sit only in the back of the bus, behind the first ten rows of seats. Whites could sit in the black section of the bus, but when they did, a black person could not sit next to or in front of a white person. And black people could be forced to give up their seats if a white person had no place to sit.

Parks was an officer of the NAACP's Montgomery branch and had worked with Baker on the NAACP's Leadership Conference, a program designed to help local members

STRONG PEOPLE DON'T NEED STRONG LEADERS.
—ELLA BAKER

develop their leadership skills. In support of Parks, leaders of Montgomery's black community, including Dr. MARTIN LUTHER KING Jr., organized a boycott of the Montgomery bus system. The boycott lasted from December 1, 1955, until December 20, 1956, when blacks in Montgomery heard that the U.S. Supreme Court had ruled on December 17 that Montgomery's bus segregation laws were unconstitutional (*Gayle v. Browder,* 352 U.S. 903, 77 S. Ct. 145, 1 L. Ed. 2d 114 [Nov. 13, 1956], *reh'g denied,* 352 U.S. 950, 77 S. Ct. 323, 1 L. Ed. 2d 245).

After the success of the MONTGOMERY BUS BOYCOTT, Baker and others eventually convinced King to call a meeting of southern black leaders to plan to extend the battle. The meeting King called was to take place in Atlanta on January 11, 1957. The evening before, several locations in Montgomery were bombed, including homes of white and black supporters of the civil rights movement. King and the Rev. RALPH D. ABERNATHY, whose home was one of those bombed, left the meeting to investigate the incidents. Baker and an associate stayed in Atlanta to manage the conference with Coretta Scott King and the Rev. Fred L. Shuttlesworth. This meeting was the beginning of the SOUTHERN CHRISTIAN LEADERSHIP CONFERENCE (SCLC), an umbrella organization for groups fighting for civil rights.

One of the SCLC's first nationwide efforts was the Crusade for Citizenship, a voter registration program. By September 1959, when the organization had not motivated masses of African Americans to register, Baker proposed three changes that she believed would result in a stronger organization. The first suggestion was to create an overarching plan to coordinate the activities of SCLC member groups. The second was to actively develop the leadership skills of people in the member organizations who had demonstrated abilities in that area. The third was to organize black southerners to fight every form of discrimination by using mass action and nonviolent resistance.

One method of nonviolent resistance, the sit-in, was used as early as 1942 by a civil rights organization called the Congress of Racial Equality (CORE) to protest racial discrimination. Not until 1960, however, were sit-ins widely used as a form of protest. In February 1960, four black students sat at the lunch counter in a Woolworth's store in Greensboro, North Carolina. They were refused service, because it was a "whites-only" lunch counter, but remained seated until the store closed for the day. News of the incident spread quickly, and area high school and college students joined them in the following days. By the end of March, students had staged sit-ins in many other southern cities. Baker realized that although the sit-ins were generating publicity for the civil rights movement, their influence would be greater if they were better coordinated, so in April 1960 Baker organized a conference for student civil rights activists at Shaw University. More than 300 students attended the meeting, which was the genesis of the STUDENT NONVIOLENT COORDINATING COMMITTEE (SNCC). Among those attending were Marion Barry, future mayor and future city council member of Washington, D.C., and Julian Bond, future Georgia legislator.

Baker resigned from the SCLC and became SNCC's adviser and organized its main office. SNCC developed a unique, separate identity within the civil rights movement because of Baker's style of leadership. Baker believed that everyone in an organization should lead it, so she made sure that everyone in attendance at meetings stated an opinion, and that no other single civil rights leader or organization, including the NAACP and King, directed the activities of the committee. When SNCC nearly split apart over whether to pursue direct action (such as the Montgomery bus boycott and the Greensboro sit-ins) or voter registration, Baker suggested that the organization could do both, setting the stage for the 1961 Freedom Rides.

The Freedom Rides were begun in 1961 as a response to a 1960 ruling, *Boynton v. Virginia,* 364 U.S. 206, 81 S. Ct. 182, 5 L. Ed. 2d 206, in which the Supreme Court decided that interstate buses and trains, and the facilities in the terminals that served them, could not constitutionally remain segregated. The ruling was flagrantly ignored throughout the South. The Freedom Riders, who were both black and white, intended to stop the segregation by traveling together along the routes where segregated facilities were located. The Freedom Rides drew the attention of the Congress, which began debate on a civil rights bill in the summer of 1963. The 1964 Civil Rights Act, as the bill was called, was finally passed on July 2, 1964, guaranteeing African Americans EQUAL PROTECTION in the use of hotels, restaurants, and other public establishments; in job opportunities, raises, and promotions; and in the use of public schools (Pub. L. No. 88-352, 78 Stat. 241).

While the Freedom Riders traveled across the South, SNCC also pursued voter registration. In 1963 Baker went to Mississippi to help with the Freedom Vote, a project of CORE and SNCC. The Freedom Vote was a mock election intended to demonstrate that, contrary to the opinions held by many white southerners, blacks were interested in voting. Baker assisted the project by speaking at rallies, setting up polling places, and collecting and counting the ballots on voting day. The Freedom Vote was a big success: More than 80,000 of the 90,000 people who cast ballots that day were black, even though only around 20,000 blacks were registered for real elections. Two years later, in August 1965, the efforts of Baker and thousands of other activists bore fruit when the Voting Rights Act (Pub. L. No. 89-110, 79 Stat. 437) was passed. The Voting Rights Act nearly eliminated one of the last ways that had been used to prevent African Americans from voting—the literacy test—by prohibiting its use in states where fewer than 50 percent of eligible voters were registered.

In 1964 Baker again helped organize a civil rights group. The group was the Mississippi Freedom DEMOCRATIC PARTY (MFDP), begun in response to an established political party, the Mississippi Democratic party. The MFDP attempted to represent the state of Mississippi at the 1964 Democratic National Convention in Atlantic City, New Jersey, by claiming that, as an interracial group, it was better able to do so than the all-white Mississippi Democratic party. HUBERT H. HUMPHREY, vice PRESIDENT OF THE UNITED STATES, and Walter F. Mondale, Minnesota attorney general, suggested a compromise: Two MFDP members could be named as delegates to the convention, but would not be part of Mississippi's delegation. The MFDP refused this offer, but its request was the catalyst for a new rule passed by the national Democratic party, that all state delegations would have to be racially mixed.

After achieving notable successes in the U.S. civil rights movement, Baker continued to serve as SNCC's mentor as the organization became involved in protests against the VIETNAM WAR, and as an advocate for the free speech movement and women's rights. She also worked toward increased civil rights for blacks in other countries, including the former Southern Rhodesia, now Zimbabwe; South Africa; and Puerto Rico.

Baker died in New York City on December 13, 1986, her eighty-third birthday. By that time, some of the organizations she had been involved with no longer existed. SNCC fell apart after dissension developed over black power, or black independence from white America. The MFDP lasted through the 1967 elections, winning offices in local races, but was no longer needed after African Americans were allowed to join the state Democratic party. Baker's work, however, lives on in a generation of black U.S. leaders she nurtured and encouraged, who are able to carry on the struggle for civil and HUMAN RIGHTS worldwide.

FURTHER READINGS

Collins, Gail. 2007. "The Women behind the Men." *The New York Times* (September 22). Available online at http://www.nytimes.com/2007/09/22/opinion/22collins.html?_r=1&em&ex=1190606400&en=a20518e610336452&ei=5087%0A; website home page: http://www.nytimes.com (accessed August 28, 2009).

Dallard, Shyrlee, and Andrew Young. 1990. *Ella Baker: A Leader behind the Scenes.* Englewood Cliffs, NJ: Silver Burdett.

Ransby, Barbara. 2003. *Ella Baker and the Black Freedom Movement.* Chapel Hill: Univ. of North Carolina Press.

CROSS REFERENCES

School Desegregation; Voting.

BAKER V. CARR

The ideal of ONE PERSON, ONE VOTE motivated the founders of the United States of America to establish a census when they drafted the U.S. Constitution in 1787. Although that ideal has not yet been fully realized—because the census still undercounts racial and ethnic minorities, among others—the country took a giant step closer to equal representation for every citizen nearly two centuries later, during the era of the CIVIL RIGHTS MOVEMENT. On March 26, 1962, the U.S. Supreme Court ruled in the landmark case of *Baker v. Carr*, 369 U.S. 186, 82 S. Ct. 691, 7 L. Ed. 2d 663 (1962), that state legislative APPORTIONMENT cases could be reviewed by the federal courts. As a result, lawsuits challenging the constitutionality of the apportionment of legislative districts were filed in many states. In a ruling that Chief Justice EARL WARREN later called the most important of his tenure on the Court, Justice WILLIAM J. BRENNAN JR. wrote: "A citizen's right to vote free of arbitrary impairment by state action has been judicially recognized as a right secured by the Constitution."

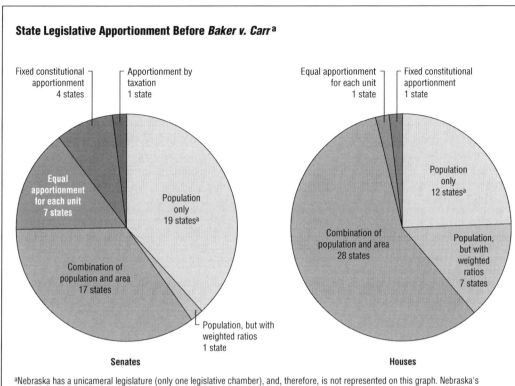

State Legislative Apportionment Before *Baker v. Carr* [a]

Fixed constitutional apportionment
4 states

Apportionment by taxation
1 state

Equal apportionment for each unit
7 states

Population only
19 states [a]

Combination of population and area
17 states

Population, but with weighted ratios
1 state

Senates

Equal apportionment for each unit
1 state

Fixed constitutional apportionment
1 state

Population only
12 states [a]

Combination of population and area
28 states

Population, but with weighted ratios
7 states

Houses

[a]Nebraska has a unicameral legislature (only one legislative chamber), and, therefore, is not represented on this graph. Nebraska's legislature was apportioned by population.

SOURCE: Gordon E. Baker, *State Constitutions: Reapportionment* (New York: National Municipal League, 1960), 5.

Also significant because it examined the notion of "political questions" and whether courts could address them, the *Baker v. Carr* case became a springboard for future apportionment lawsuits. In June 1964, the Supreme Court ruled on appeals from 15 states that had used *Baker* as a PRECEDENT, holding that both houses of a state legislature must be apportioned substantially on the basis of population. Within two years, every state had taken some type of apportionment action. By the late 1960s, congressional districts around the country had been redrawn to meet the Supreme Court's call for equal representation, and after the 1970 census, underrepresented urban areas were finally given an equal voice in Congress.

Every decade since 1790, U.S. citizens have complied with the Constitution and counted themselves. Whereas on its simplest level the census is a means to document historical changes in the U.S. population, it also determines how federal funds, power, political clout, and representation are divided, or apportioned, among the people of the United States. The notion of representation, more specifically equal representation, compelled Charles W. Baker

and other qualified voters in Tennessee to bring a lawsuit against Tennessee's SECRETARY OF STATE Joe C. Carr, on the grounds that the state's 1901 apportionment statute (Acts Tenn. 1901, c. 122) violated the FOURTEENTH AMENDMENT of the Constitution. The plaintiffs argued that Tennessee's method of unequally apportioning the members of the general assembly among the state's 95 counties unconstitutionally deprived people in the state of EQUAL PROTECTION of the laws and was obsolete because of a significant growth and population shift since 1900.

The plaintiffs' first round in court brought failure when a three-judge panel of the U.S. district court for the Middle District of Tennessee dismissed their complaint on December 21, 1959 (*Baker*, 179 F. Supp. 824). The panel dismissed the complaint on two grounds: (1) that the court lacked jurisdiction of the subject matter because it was a POLITICAL QUESTION and (2) that the complaint failed to state a claim upon which relief could be granted.

The plaintiffs appealed, and on November 21, 1964, the U.S. Supreme Court ruled that it had probable jurisdiction in the matter. This decision was significant because before the Supreme Court heard the *Baker* case, courts had abstained from addressing apportionment issues because they were considered political in nature. In the 1946 Supreme Court case *Colegrove v. Green,* 328 U.S. 549, 66 S. Ct. 1198, 90 L. Ed. 1432 (1946), Justice FELIX FRANKFURTER called apportionment a "political thicket" into which the judiciary should not venture. The subsequent ruling in *Baker* changed that interpretation, stating that federal courts possessed jurisdiction of the subject, that the citizens in Tennessee were entitled to relief, and that the federal district court in the state could settle the challenge to the apportionment statute of Tennessee.

In addressing the concern of some of his fellow Supreme Court justices who warned that the matter before them was a political question and therefore not appropriately dealt with in a court of law, Justice Brennan carefully wrote—and rewrote, ten times—his opinion in the 1962 decision. Brennan stated: "The mere fact that the suit seeks protection of a political right does not mean it presents a political question. Such an objection is little more than a play upon words." He added that the plaintiffs' complaint did present a JUSTICIABLE constitutional CAUSE OF ACTION and that the Fourteenth Amendment did provide judicial protection to the right asserted. Justices Frankfurter and JOHN MARSHALL HARLAN dissented, stating that Brennan should not inject the Court "into the clash of political forces and political settlements." The Court's 6-2 ruling in favor of the plaintiffs forced state legislatures to reapportion their seats to reflect population shifts before the elections that were to occur in the fall of 1962. It also decreed one person, one vote as part of the United States' constitutional heritage and opened the door to challenging state voting procedures and malapportionment on constitutional grounds.

In his book *Turning Point: A Candidate, a State, and a Nation Come of Age,* former president JIMMY CARTER described how revolutionary the *Baker* decision was in the 1960s and how it transformed state politics, especially southern politics. Carter wrote that the Georgia state government, like many others, proposed a number of stalling ploys, fake reapportionment plans, and other ways to avoid the shift in political power that the one-person, one-vote ruling had been designed to cause. "The

beneficiaries of the [old] system were the ones now charged with … changing it," he wrote. "At the same time, they would be reducing drastically the relative voting strength of their own constituents. It was understandable that [they] would do everything possible to circumvent or postpone the effect of the court's mandate." Federal judges rejected the bogus plans, however, and by late summer 1962, the state's political process had been thrown wide open. Incumbent politicians were suddenly without districts, and new seats had opened up. In these circumstances, a few weeks before the election, Carter decided to run for the Georgia State Senate.

FURTHER READINGS

Charles, Guy-Uriel E. 2002. "Constitutional Pluralism and Democratic Politics: Reflections on the Interpretive Approach of *Baker and Carr.*" *North Carolina Law Review* 80 (May).

"A Final Victory Marks the End of a Career." 1990. *National Law Journal* (August 13).

Fuentes-Rohwer, Luis. 2002. "Baker's Promise, Equal Protection, and the Modern Redistricting Revolution: A Plea for Rationality." *North Carolina Law Review* 80 (May).

"*Koohi v. United States.*" 1993. *Georgia Law Review* 28 (fall).

Pushaw, Robert J., Jr. 2001. "*Bush v. Gore*: Looking at *Baker v. Carr* in a Conservative Mirror." *Constitutional Commentary* 18 (summer).

Richie, Robert, and Steven Hill. 1999. *Reflecting All of Us: The Case of Proportional Representation.* Boston: Beacon.

Rush, Mark E. 1993. *Does Redistricting Make a Difference? Partisan Representation and Electoral Behavior.* Baltimore: Johns Hopkins Univ. Press.

"Some Implications of Arrow's Theorem for Voting Rights." 1995. *Stanford Law Review* 47 (January).

"*The Trustees of the Office of Hawaiian Affairs v. Yamasaki*: The Application of the Political Question Doctrine to Hawaii's Public Land Trust Dispute." 1988. *University of Hawaii Law Review* 10 (winter).

"*United States v. Alvarez-Machain*: Waltzing with the Political Question Doctrine." 1994. *Connecticut Law Review* 26 (winter).

"U.S. Supreme Court." 1990. *National Law Journal* (June 4).

"When Restraint Requires Activism." 1990. *Stanford Law Review* 42 (July).

CROSS REFERENCES

Apportionment; Brennan, William Joseph, Jr.; Equal Protection; Failure to State a Claim; Fourteenth Amendment; Frankfurter, Felix; Political Question; *Reynolds v. Sims*; Voting.

BAKKE AFFIRMATIVE ACTION CASE

SEE REGENTS OF THE UNIVERSITY OF CALIFORNIA V. BAKKE.

BALANCE SHEET

A comprehensive financial statement that is a summarized assessment of a company's accounts specifying its assets and liabilities. A report, usually prepared by independent auditors or accountants, which includes a full and complete statement of all receipts and disbursements of a particular business. A review that shows a general balance or summation of all accounts without showing the particular items that make up the several accounts.

BALANCING

A process sometimes used by state and federal courts in deciding between the competing interests represented in a case.

Used frequently to decide constitutional cases, balancing is one of two main legal decision-making methods, the other being categorization or STRICT CONSTRUCTION. Balancing involves weighing competing rights against each other and analyzing the relative strengths of many factors. A balancing decision is dependent upon the circumstances of each case. Therefore, the outcome is difficult to predict. By contrast, *categorization* is a classification and labeling process. It involves identifying a right and how it was infringed upon and analogizing these findings to a previously decided case or PRECE-DENT. Hence, the outcome is more predictable.

Balancing of Competing Interests in the U.S. Supreme Court

Balancing may take one of two forms in cases before the U.S. Supreme Court. In the first, the Court may measure competing interests against each other and determine which carries the most weight. For example, in *New York v. Ferber,* 458 U.S. 747, 102 S. Ct. 3348, 73 L. Ed. 2d 1113 (1982), the Court upheld a statute criminalizing distribution of CHILD PORNOGRAPHY because the evil eliminated by the statute far outweighed any infringement on free speech interests. In the second form of balancing, the Court attempts to "strike a balance" between competing interests. Thus, in *Tennessee v. Garner,* 471 U.S. 1, 105 S. Ct. 1694, 85 L. Ed. 2d 1 (1985), the Court held that a police officer may use DEADLY FORCE to stop a fleeing felon if the officer has PROBABLE CAUSE to believe that the suspect poses a threat of serious physical harm to others. In *Garner,* the Court did not find that one interest clearly outweighed the other.

Instead, both the state's interest in law enforcement and the individual's interest in being free from harm were weighed in the analysis and given due recognition.

Balancing was first used by the U.S. Supreme Court as one of its principal modes of judicial analysis in the late 1930s and early 1940s when the judiciary began to reject the rigid formalism and mechanical JURISPRUDENCE characteristic of the nineteenth and early twentieth centuries. Before the balancing era began in earnest with LOCHNER V. NEW YORK, 198 U.S. 45, 25 S. Ct. 539, 49 L. Ed. 937 (1905), the Court held that a New York statute setting maximum work hours was constitutional because such regulation was within the state's POLICE POWER. In reaching this decision, the Court did not attempt to balance the rights of the individuals against the state's interests, but it took a straightforward look at the language of the statute and found it valid. This earlier Court stated: "The purpose of a statute must be determined from the natural and legal effect of the language employed.... It seems to us that the real object and purpose [of the statute] were simply to regulate the hours of labor between the master and his employees."

Early proponents of balancing included such prominent Supreme Court justices as Oliver Wendell Holmes Jr., LOUIS D. BRANDEIS, and HARLAN F. STONE, all of whom sat on the Court in the early to middle 1900s. Holmes, sometimes called the patron saint of the anti-formalist movement, was one of the first to espouse the idea that the law is and should be an evolving product of social experience. He assailed the notion that rigid formulas could be applied to all situations before the Court. "[T]he law is a logical development, like everything else," he wrote. In a similar vein, Brandeis criticized the Court for ignoring contemporary social, political, and economic problems. He said, "[W]hether a measure relating to the public WELFARE is arbitrary or unreasonable ... should be based upon a consideration of relevant facts, actual or possible" (*Adams v. Tanner,* 244 U.S. 590, 37 S. Ct. 662, 61 L. Ed. 1336 [1917] [Brandeis, J., dissenting]). In another case, he wrote: "Whether a law enacted in the exercise of the police power is justly subject to the charge of being unreasonable or arbitrary can ordinarily be determined only by a consideration of the contemporary conditions, social, industrial, and political, of the community to be affected thereby. Resort to such facts is necessary, among other things, in order to appreciate the evils sought to be remedied and the possible effects of the remedy proposed" (*Truax v. Corrigan*, 257 U.S. 312, 42 S. Ct. 124, 66 L. Ed. 254 [1921] [Brandeis, J., dissenting]). Similarly, Stone forcefully advocated "consideration of all the facts and circumstances" in a case, including societal conditions that affected the parties, the controversy, and the outcome (*DiSanto v. Pennsylvania*, 273 U.S. 34, 47 S. Ct. 267, 71 L. Ed. 524 [1927] [Stone, J., dissenting]).

The Court uses a balancing approach most often to decide cases where constitutionally protected individual rights conflict with governmental interests. Many of the landmark constitutional cases of the 1960s, 1970s, and 1980s were decided in this manner, including ROE V. WADE, 410 U.S. 113, 93 S. Ct. 705, 35 L. Ed. 2d 47 (1973), which legalized ABORTION. In reaching its decision in *Roe*, the Court found that in the first trimester of pregnancy, a woman's right to privacy outweighed the state's interest in protecting health, but in the later stages of pregnancy, the state's interest gradually outweighed the woman's.

Contrary to popular belief, however, the Court has not used balancing as its primary method of deciding constitutional cases. In fact, some of the most important constitutional cases of the twentieth century were decided without any balancing of competing interests. For example, balancing was not used to decide BROWN V. BOARD OF EDUCATION, 347 U.S. 483, 74 S. Ct. 686, 98 L. Ed. 873 (1954) (outlawing segregated public schools); GIDEON V. WAINWRIGHT, 372 U.S. 335, 83 S. Ct. 792, 9 L. Ed. 2d 799 (1963) (guaranteeing indigent defendants appointed counsel in felony cases); and GRISWOLD V. CONNECTICUT, 381 U.S. 479, 85 S. Ct. 1678, 14 L. Ed. 2d 510 (1965) (outlawing state laws prohibiting contraceptives).

Balancing has always aroused controversy among legal scholars and judges. Critics contend that it gives too much discretion to judges and amounts to a USURPATION of the legislative function. They maintain that it is a vague and arbitrary method of measuring unequal interests against each other and that it results in unpredictable decision making. One vocal critic of balancing is Justice ANTONIN SCALIA. In his dissenting opinion in *Bendix Autolite Corp. v. Midwesco Enterprises*, 486 U.S. 888, 108 S. Ct.

2218, 100 L. Ed. 2d 896 (1988), he characterized the balancing of competing interests as an illusion. "[T]he scale analogy is not really appropriate," he wrote, "since the interests on both sides are incommensurate. It is more like judging whether a particular line is longer than a particular rock is heavy."

Scalia's frontal attack on balancing gained force in the 1990s when Scalia was joined on the Court by other justices who shared his philosophy that the Constitution should be construed strictly and literally. Evidence that Scalia's view was held by others on the Court can be found in the 1995 decision *Vernonia School District 47J v. Acton*, 515 U.S.646, 115 S. Ct. 2386, 132 L. Ed. 2d 564 (U.S. 1995), which held that schools could legally perform random drug tests on student athletes. The decision employed a straightforward analysis of the rationality of the school's policy to conduct random drug tests and dismissed concerns about infringement of the students' FOURTH AMENDMENT right to be free from unreasonable searches. Writing for the majority, Scalia stated: "The most significant element in this case is ... that the policy was undertaken in furtherance of the government's responsibilities, under a public school system, as guardian and tutor of children entrusted to its care." The Court held that the testing was a type of search that "a reasonable guardian and tutor might undertake."

Three justices disagreed vehemently. Writing for the dissent, Justice Sandra Day O'Connor emphasized her belief that the decision did not give due recognition to the students' constitutional rights and went too far in its broad approval of "intrusive, blanket searches of school children, most of whom are innocent, for evidence of serious wrongdoing." Under the ruling, she said, students no longer enjoyed "the Fourth Amendment's ... most basic ... protection: its strong preference for an individualized suspicion requirement."

Justice O'Connor's dissent in *Acton* echoed her strong approval of balancing competing interests and assessing a statute's intrusion on individual rights. O'Connor expressed her belief that balancing is an essential step in the Court's decision-making process, in *Employment Division, Department of Human Resources v. Smith*, 494 U.S. 872, 110 S. Ct. 1595, 108 L. Ed. 2d 876 (1990). The respondents in *Smith* were Native Americans who were fired from their jobs because they ingested peyote as part of a religious ceremony. The Court held that the state could deny them unemployment benefits without violating the Free Exercise Clause of the FIRST AMENDMENT. O'Connor concurred with the result but took issue with the majority's failure to consider the effect the disputed statute had on the free exercise of RELIGION. "To me," O'Connor wrote, "the sounder approach—the approach more consistent with our role as judges to decide each case on its individual merits—is to apply [a] test in each case to determine whether the burden on the specific plaintiffs before us is constitutionally significant and whether the particular ... interest asserted by the State before us is compelling."

Balancing of Competing Interests in Other State and Federal Courts

Although the U.S. Supreme Court generates close scrutiny of its decisions when it applies a balancing test to resolve high-profile or controversial issues before it, it is not the only court that resolves issues by balancing competing interests at stake in a legal dispute. Indeed, every day across the country state and federal courts are asked to balance the competing interests of litigants in determining the admissibility of evidence, the appropriateness of a sentence, or the viability of an appeal.

For example, state and FEDERAL RULES OF EVIDENCE call for the exclusion of relevant evidence when its probative value is substantially outweighed by the danger of unfair prejudice or by considerations of undue delay, waste of time, or the needless presentation of cumulative or confusing evidence. Consequently, before one party may introduce relevant evidence over another party's OBJECTION, the judge must balance the competing interests that would be served by excluding or admitting the evidence in question.

State and federal SENTENCING guidelines also generally require judges to balance the aggravating and MITIGATING CIRCUMSTANCES underlying a criminal offense before imposing a particular sentence on a DEFENDANT. Aggravating factors are those factors that justify a more severe punishment and are typically introduced by the prosecution, victim, or victim's family. Mitigating factors are those factors that justify a less severe sentence and are typically introduced by the defendant, the defendant's ATTORNEY, or WITNESSES speaking on behalf of the defendant.

Finally, appellate courts often ENGAGE in some form of balancing to review the lawfulness of a lower court decision. In addition, to the above examples from the U.S. Supreme Court, appellate courts employ a variety of standards of review by which they evaluate the record for error using some form of balancing analysis. For example, the *substantial* evidence standard of review requires appellate courts to determine if a lower court's decision was supported by sufficient evidence to avoid being overturned, meaning that the appellate court must weigh the evidence offered by the parties to some extent. Appellate courts applying the *arbitrary and capricious* standard of review must not only examine the gravity of the alleged arbitrary or capricious conduct in the lower court, but they must also take into consideration any evidence that makes the lower court's decision reasonable or justifiable.

FURTHER READINGS

Alexy, Robert. 2003. "Constitutional Rights, Balancing, and Rationality." *Ratio Juris* 16, vol. 2 (June).

Gottlieb, Stephen E., ed. 1993. *Public Values in Constitutional Law.* Ann Arbor, MI: Univ. of Michigan Press.

McKenna, George. 2007. *The Constitution: That Delicate Balance.* New York: Random House.

CROSS REFERENCES

Child Pornography; Deadly Force; Fourth Amendment; Judicial Review; Jurisprudence; Police Power; Precedent; Probable Cause; Strict Construction.

❖ BALDWIN, HENRY

Henry Baldwin was a prominent Pennsylvania ATTORNEY and politician who later became an ASSOCIATE JUSTICE of the U.S. Supreme Court, where he served for fourteen years.

Descended from an aristocratic British family dating back to the seventeenth century, Baldwin was born January 14, 1780, in New Haven, Connecticut. He grew up on a farm near New Haven and later moved to the city to attend Yale College. After graduating with honors in 1797, he studied law in Philadelphia with ALEXANDER J. DALLAS, a noted attorney. Admitted to the bar a short time later, Baldwin originally planned to establish a practice in Ohio, but instead settled in Pittsburgh. He then established a successful law firm with two other young attorneys. By his mid-20s, Baldwin had established a reputation as a legal scholar, in part because of his thorough and well-researched law briefs. He had also developed

WORDS ARE BUT THE EVIDENCE OF INTENTION; THEIR IMPORT IS THEIR MEANING, TO BE GATHERED FROM THE CONTEXT, AND THEIR CONNECTION WITH THE SUBJECT MATTER.
—HENRY BALDWIN

Henry Baldwin.
THOMAS SULLY,
COLLECTION OF THE
SUPREME COURT OF
THE UNITED STATES

an extensive personal law library, which contained a large collection of valuable English case reports and was among the finest and largest in the Northeast. Furthermore, Baldwin and his law partners were known for their political and civic leadership. The three published a newspaper, the *Tree of Liberty,* which supported the REPUBLICAN PARTY of western Pennsylvania. In addition to his political activities and his law practice, Baldwin found time for business, acting as part-owner of several mills in Pennsylvania and Ohio.

After the death of his first wife, Baldwin married Sally Ellicott, and they established a residence in Crawford County, Pennsylvania. In 1816 Baldwin was elected representative to the U.S. Congress for that area. As a congressman, Baldwin was active in trade issues and was a

strong advocate of TARIFF protection. He was also involved in mediating boundary disputes between northern and southern states and their representatives. He was twice reelected to the House. In 1822 he was forced to resign his seat because of illness. He returned home to Pennsylvania, where he once again practiced law and was active in local political affairs.

Baldwin soon became an avid supporter of ANDREW JACKSON and was a trusted adviser to Jackson concerning Pennsylvania politics. After Jackson was elected president in 1828, Baldwin hoped to become secretary of the treasury, but the appointment instead went to Samuel D. Ingham. The following year, after the death of Justice BUSHROD WASHINGTON, Jackson nominated Baldwin to the U.S. Supreme Court, against the wishes of his VICE PRESIDENT, JOHN C. CALHOUN, who preferred another candidate. Though Baldwin's protectionist views created some controversy, he was confirmed by the Senate with only two dissenting votes from southern senators who opposed his policies on tariffs.

On the bench, Baldwin was at first a strong supporter of the liberal views of Chief Justice JOHN MARSHALL but gradually moved toward a more moderate interpretation of the Constitution, favoring neither state sovereignty nor federal supremacy. In 1837 he published a pamphlet, *A General View of the Origin and Nature of the Constitution and Government of the United States,* in which he set forth what he termed his "peculiar views of the Constitution." In this work, he emphasized his position as a moderate on the Court, stating that he tended to take the Constitution "as it is, and to expound it by the accepted rules of interpretation." Baldwin also believed that the Court must

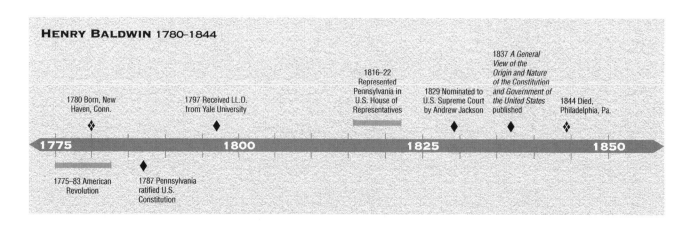

HENRY BALDWIN 1780–1844

1780 Born, New
Haven, Conn.

1797 Received LL.D.
from Yale University

1816–22
Represented
Pennsylvania in
U.S. House of
Representatives

1829 Nominated to
U.S. Supreme Court
by Andrew Jackson

1837 *A General
View of the
Origin and Nature
of the Constitution
and Government of
the United States*
published

1844 Died,
Philadelphia, Pa.

1775   1800   1825   1850

1775–83 American
Revolution

1787 Pennsylvania
ratified U.S.
Constitution

be politically sensitive when determining which powers belonged to the federal government and which remained with the states.

One of Baldwin's most influential majority opinions was *United States v. Arredondo,* 31 U.S. 691, 6 Pet. 691, 8 L. Ed. 547 (1832), in which the Court held that PUBLIC POLICY prevented the government from violating federal land treaties. With respect to the issue of SLAVERY, however, Baldwin's views were considered to be much more radical than those held by other members of the Court. In *Groves v. Slaughter,* 40 U.S. 449, 15 Pet. 449, 10 L. Ed. 800 (1841), the Court considered the constitutionality of a Mississippi provision that prevented the importation of slaves into the state. The Court ultimately struck down the statute on technical reasons, but Baldwin, in a separate opinion, argued that slaves were property as well as persons and viewed the prohibition as an obstruction of interstate commerce. He was the sole dissenter in *United States v. The Schooner Armistead,* 40 U.S. 518, 15 Pet. 518, 10 L. Ed. 826 (1841), in which the Court held that slaves who had mutinied and taken over the slave ship transporting them from Africa should be set free. Though he did not write an opinion, Baldwin had earlier maintained that the slaves should be returned to the custody of the slave traders.

As was the practice in the Court at the time, Baldwin traveled the circuit he represented, which included Pennsylvania and New Jersey, to hear cases. He heard important cases involving the construction of a will that made a bequest for charitable purposes and also presided over the trial of John F. Braddel, who in 1840 was accused of robbing the mails.

In his later years, Baldwin was plagued by financial and personal difficulties. He never fully recovered from losing a great deal of money during the depression of 1820. He also suffered from the failure of several speculative businesses, and he had to support some of his adult children when they got into financial trouble. He was eventually forced to sell his renowned personal law library to the LIBRARY OF CONGRESS to raise money. He also published and sold volumes of the opinions he decided while traveling the circuit.

At the same time, Baldwin's behavior became erratic and he was widely reported to be suffering from mental illness. While on the bench, he was often restless, inattentive, and abusive to litigants and his fellow justices. While on the circuit, he also exhibited bizarre behavior at times, often having coffee and cakes brought to him while he heard cases. Chief Justice ROGER B. TANEY was reported to be so concerned about Baldwin's unpredictable behavior that he advised President Jackson not to take action against the BANK OF THE UNITED STATES because Baldwin, as presiding judge over the case in Philadelphia, would be unreliable.

Baldwin's tenure on the Court ended on April 21, 1844, when he died of paralysis at the age of sixty-four. He was deeply in debt at the time of his death, and friends and family took up a collection to pay for his funeral expenses.

FURTHER READINGS

Congressional Quarterly. 1989. *Guide to the U.S. Supreme Court.* 2d ed. Washington, D.C.: Congressional Quarterly.

Elliott, Stephen P., ed. 1986. *A Reference Guide to the United States Supreme Court.* New York: Facts on File.

Swisher, Carl B. 1974. *The Taney Period, 1836–1864.* Vol. 5 of *History of the Supreme Court of the United States.* New York: Macmillan.

❖ BALDWIN, JOSEPH GLOVER

Joseph Glover Baldwin achieved prominence as a jurist and author despite his lack of formal education.

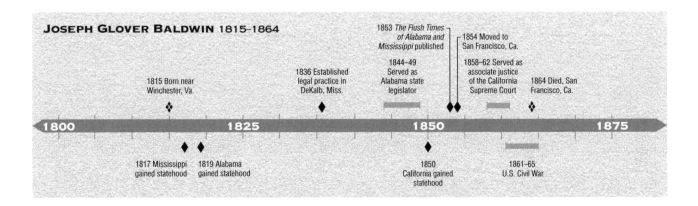

Baldwin was born in January, 1815, near Winchester, Virginia. After establishing a legal practice in 1836 in DeKalb, Mississippi, he relocated to Alabama and entered the legislature of the state in 1844, serving for five years.

In 1854 Baldwin moved again, this time to San Francisco. He maintained a successful practice and was involved in the formulation of the judicial system of San Francisco. He officially entered the judiciary in 1858, presiding as ASSOCIATE JUSTICE of the California Supreme Court until 1862.

As an author, Baldwin is famous for *The Flush Times of Alabama and Mississippi* (1853) and *Party Leaders* (1855). He died September 30, 1864, in San Francisco, California.

❖ BALDWIN, ROGER NASH

Roger Nash Baldwin spent his life crusading for CIVIL RIGHTS and liberties and was one of the principal founders of the AMERICAN CIVIL LIBERTIES UNION (ACLU).

Baldwin was born January 21, 1884, in Wellesley, Massachusetts, into a comfortably well-to-do Boston Brahmin family. His ancestral roots reached back to what he once referred to as "the inescapable Mayflower." His father, Frank Fenno Baldwin, was a conservative businessman. His mother, Lucy Cushing Nash, instilled in her children a love of art, literature, and music. Baldwin's parents raised their six children with all the privileges and advantages their wealth could provide, but they also emphasized service to others. The family attended the Unitarian Church, where an emphasis on helping others sowed in Baldwin the seeds of a social work career.

Baldwin was an unconventional boy who was not interested in competitive endeavors and shared his mother's interest in literature and art. He was a nonconformist who was influenced by Henry David Thoreau's philosophy of individualism and self-reliance. Although his parents were conservative, the young Baldwin was introduced to many progressive leaders at the home of his uncle and aunt, William Baldwin and Ruth Standish Bowles Baldwin. His uncle was president of the Long Island Railroad, director of the National Child Labor Committee, and a TRUSTEE of Tuskegee Institute. He also worked to end prostitution,. His aunt supported the fledgling labor movement and was a founder of the NATIONAL URBAN LEAGUE, a trustee of Smith College, and a member of the SOCIALIST PARTY. The couple often entertained the social reformers of the day, and Baldwin was influenced by his exposure to their somewhat radical ideas.

Baldwin was educated at Harvard, earning both a bachelor's degree and a master's degree there. In 1906 he left the East and headed for St. Louis to be a social worker. He directed a social settlement house for poor people and taught the first sociology courses offered at Washington University, in St. Louis. He became the chief probation officer of the St. Louis Juvenile Court in 1908. While in that position, he and Bernard Flexner coauthored the first textbook on the juvenile courts. Their book, *Juvenile Courts and Probation,* set out professional standards for juvenile practice and was the standard text in the field until the 1960s. In 1910 Baldwin became the secretary of the St. Louis Civic League, an urban reform agency supporting civic causes.

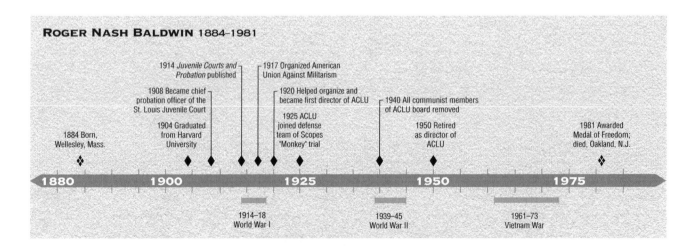

ROGER NASH BALDWIN 1884–1981

1914 *Juvenile Courts and Probation* published

1917 Organized American Union Against Militarism

1908 Became chief probation officer of the St. Louis Juvenile Court

1920 Helped organize and became first director of ACLU

1940 All communist members of ACLU board removed

1904 Graduated from Harvard University

1925 ACLU joined defense team of Scopes "Monkey" trial

1884 Born, Wellesley, Mass.

1950 Retired as director of ACLU

1981 Awarded Medal of Freedom; died, Oakland, N.J.

1880   1900   1925   1950   1975

1914–18 World War I

1939–45 World War II

1961–73 Vietnam War

While working in St. Louis, Baldwin met and became friends with the anarchist EMMA GOLDMAN. His first defense of free speech came in 1912 when he spoke in support of MARGARET SANGER, an early crusader for BIRTH CONTROL and reproductive rights, whose lecture was shut down by the police. Through the social work profession he was attracted to the reform movement and the labor movement. He organized the Division on Industrial and Economic Problems at the 1916 meeting of the National Conference of Social Work, and wrote a report calling for cooperative production and distribution systems to replace competitive labor systems.

In 1917, when the United States entered WORLD WAR I, Baldwin organized the American Union against Militarism (AUAM), which was later replaced by the National Civil Liberties Bureau (NCLB). In its early days, the AUAM was concerned with defending those who refused to be drafted to serve in the war. Baldwin was among the conscientious objectors opposed to the draft, and he was sentenced to a year in jail for his refusal to register. In a speech to the court before he was sentenced, he explained that his reason for opposing the draft was his "uncompromising opposition to the principle of CONSCRIPTION of life by the state for any purpose whatever, in time of war or peace."

After his release from prison, Baldwin worked as a common laborer around the Midwest and joined the radical International Workers of the World (IWW) union. He returned to New York in 1920 to help reorganize and reconstitute the NCLB with two conservative lawyers, Albert DeSilver and Walter Nelles, who shared his passion for championing the rights of the oppressed. Baldwin agreed to head the new organization, named the American Civil Liberties Union, and carry out its unique mission to impartially defend the civil liberties of all U.S. citizens, regardless of their affiliation or activities. Baldwin was launched in what would be a long and vigorous struggle to create "a society with a minimum of compulsion, a maximum of individual freedom and of voluntary association, and the abolition of exploitation and poverty."

Perhaps it was inevitable that Baldwin would become associated with leftist causes, because the people most in need of free speech protection during the 1920s and 1930s were often political liberals and radicals. He once told an interviewer that during this time he was heavily influenced by the Marxist theory that "the real center in society was the organized underdog in the trade unions," which he believed was true although only part of the whole picture.

Baldwin came to realize that the civil liberties of right-wing groups were just as likely to be infringed as those of left-wingers. Bewildered and frustrated by liberal groups who opposed the ACLU's support of free speech rights for the American Nazi party or the KU KLUX KLAN, Baldwin said, "[T]hese people can be just as great tyrants as the other side ... helping them get freedom didn't help the cause of freedom." Referring to the wide variety of causes the ACLU defended over the years, Baldwin said, "I always felt from the beginning that you had to defend people you disliked and feared as well as those you admired." Although not a member of any party, he supported the causes of Communists, Socialists, and other leftist organizations during the 1920s and 1930s. However, in 1940, when he began to realize that the *Communist* label was being used by totalitarian governments, he wrote a resolution that resulted in the removal of all the Communist members of the ACLU board. Ironically, Baldwin's resolution became the model for government loyalty oaths, which the ACLU later attacked in court.

Although he was a card-carrying *Wobbly*, as members of the IWW were called, Baldwin could not be categorized as liberal or conservative. He was active in the National Audubon Society, the American Political Science Association, and a number of other organizations on both ends of the political spectrum. The only label Baldwin accepted for himself was that of reformer: "I am dead certain that human progress depends on those heretics, rebels and dreamers who have been my kin in spirit and whose 'holy discontent' has challenged established authority and created the expanding visions mankind may yet realize."

During the years of Baldwin's leadership, the ACLU, using volunteer lawyers, was involved in a wide variety of civil liberties cases, especially involving free speech and assembly. One concerned a 1925 Tennessee law forbidding the teaching of evolution in public schools. The ACLU defended a science teacher, John Thomas Scopes, charged with violating the law (*Scopes v. State*, 152 Tenn. 424, 278 S.W. 57 [1925]; 154 Tenn. 105, 289 S.W. 363 [1927]). WILLIAM JENNINGS BRYAN, a three-time presidential candidate and well-known fundamentalist, helped the state attorney general PROSECUTE the case, and the

[OUR GOAL IS] A SOCIETY WITH A MINIMUM OF COMPULSION, A MAXIMUM OF INDIVIDUAL FREEDOM AND OF VOLUNTARY ASSOCIATION, AND THE ABOLITION OF EXPLOITATION AND POVERTY.
—ROGER NASH BALDWIN

notorious CLARENCE DARROW, a self-proclaimed atheist, defended Scopes. The trial ended with Scopes being convicted, although the VERDICT was later overturned because of a judicial error. The trial brought the issue of ACADEMIC FREEDOM to the public's attention and probably helped stunt the growth of the antievolution movement.

The ACLU was involved in the Sacco-Vanzetti MURDER case, in which it was widely believed that the two defendants, Nicolo Sacco and Bartolomeo Vanzetti, were scapegoated because they were Italian anarchists and draft resisters. Baldwin led the ACLU into the anticensorship arena in the fight to lift the importation ban on such books as James Joyce's *Ulysses*. In 1938 the ACLU obtained an INJUNCTION against Mayor Frank Hague of Jersey City, ordering him to cease antiunion activities. ACLU lawyers defended the free expression and free press rights of the Jehovah's WITNESSES, whose anti-Catholic rhetoric and aggressive canvassing tactics came under attack. They successfully argued that Henry Ford had a FIRST AMENDMENT right to express his antiunion views as long as he did not threaten workers. Possibly the most controversial cases accepted by the ACLU were those that challenged the free speech rights of unpopular groups such as the Ku Klux Klan, the German-American Bund, and the American Nazi party.

During WORLD WAR II Baldwin and the ACLU opposed the movement of Japanese Americans from their homes on the West Coast to relocation camps. After the war he helped General Douglas MacArthur set up a civil liberties policy for the occupation forces in Japan. He also consulted on civil liberties issues in the U.S. zone of occupied Germany.

Baldwin, always a nonconformist, lived an ascetic lifestyle, wearing the same ill-fitting suit

for years at a time and accepting a subsistence salary from the ACLU. He was married for fifteen years to Madeleine Z. Doty, a reformist lawyer. They divorced in 1934, and in 1936 he married another reformer, Evelyn Preston, whose two sons he adopted. The couple had one child, Helen Baldwin Mannoni.

Baldwin retired as head of the ACLU in 1950, but he never retired from the causes to which he was committed. He continued working until the day he died, August 26, 1981, at age 97. A few months before his death, President JIMMY CARTER awarded him the Medal of Freedom, the United States' highest civilian tribute. Reflecting on that honor, Baldwin expressed the philosophy he had lived by all his life: "Never yield your courage—your courage to live, your courage to fight, to resist, to develop your own lives, to be free." It is clear that Baldwin never yielded his courage, and that he remained to the end a dauntless crusader for freedom and liberty for all U.S. citizens.

FURTHER READINGS

Cottrell, Robert. 2000. *Roger Baldwin: Founder, American Civil Liberties Union.* New York: Columbia Univ. Press.

Lamson, Peggy. 1976. *Roger Baldwin: Founder of the American Civil Liberties Union.* Boston: Houghton Mifflin.

Walker, Samuel. 1999. *In Defense of American Liberties: A History of the ACLU.* Carbondale: Southern Illinois Univ. Press.

CROSS REFERENCES

Communism; First Amendment; Freedom of Speech; Japanese American Evacuation Cases; Sacco and Vanzetti; Scopes Monkey Trial.

❖ BALDWIN, SIMEON EBEN

Simeon Eben Baldwin was born February 5, 1840. He earned a bachelor of arts degree from Yale in 1861, received a master of arts degree in

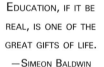

EDUCATION, IF IT BE REAL, IS ONE OF THE GREAT GIFTS OF LIFE.
—SIMEON BALDWIN

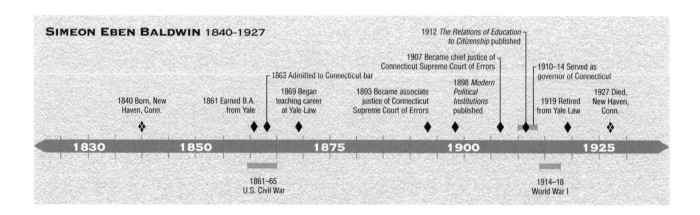

SIMEON EBEN BALDWIN 1840–1927

1912 *The Relations of Education to Citizenship* published

1907 Became chief justice of Connecticut Supreme Court of Errors

1863 Admitted to Connecticut bar

1910–14 Served as governor of Connecticut

1869 Began teaching career at Yale Law

1893 Became associate justice of Connecticut Supreme Court of Errors

1898 *Modern Political Institutions* published

1840 Born, New Haven, Conn.

1861 Earned B.A. from Yale

1919 Retired from Yale Law

1927 Died, New Haven, Conn.

1830   1850   1875   1900   1925

1861–65 U.S. Civil War

1914–18 World War I

1864, and then pursued legal studies at Yale and Harvard. Four honorary doctor of laws degrees were bestowed upon him: by Harvard in 1891; Columbia, in 1911; Wesleyan, in 1912; and Yale, in 1916.

Baldwin was admitted to the bar in 1863. In 1869 he returned to Yale to teach at the Yale Law School until 1919, when he became professor emeritus.

In 1893, Baldwin entered the judiciary, presiding as ASSOCIATE JUSTICE of the Supreme Court of Errors of Connecticut until 1907 and as chief justice until 1910. From 1910 to 1914, Baldwin was governor of Connecticut.

Baldwin contributed to the formulation of many areas of Connecticut law. He was instrumental in amending the general statutes of Connecticut as well as the system of TAXATION.

Baldwin wrote numerous publications, including *A Digest of All the Reported Cases of Connecticut* (1871–72); *Modern Political Institutions* (1898); *American Railroad Law* (1904); *The American Judiciary* (1905); *The Relations of Education to Citizenship* (1912); and *The Young Man and the Law* (1919).

He died January 30, 1927, in New Haven, Connecticut.

❖ BALLINGER, WILLIAM PITT

William Pitt Ballinger achieved prominence as a distinguished Texas lawyer, which earned him the name the "Nestor of the Texas bar."

Ballinger was born in 1825 in Barbourville, Kentucky. From 1840 to 1841 Ballinger attended St. Mary's College, then began to study law on his own. His father was clerk of the courts of Knox County and hired the young Ballinger to work as a deputy clerk and gain more legal background.

In 1843 Ballinger moved to Texas and resided with an uncle who was a practitioner. Ballinger acted as his uncle's apprentice before serving a tour of military duty in the Mexican War. After Texas was admitted to the Union in 1845, and Ballinger returned from the war in 1846, he was one of the first to be licensed to practice law in the new state.

Ballinger married into a prominent Texas family in 1850 and in 1854 formed a law firm in Galveston with his new brother-in-law, Thomas M. Jack. Their partnership, which ended in 1880, the year of Jack's death, was highly regarded throughout the South, particularly in cases dealing with land claims.

In 1854 Ballinger sought interstate business for his firm, and traveled to New York, Boston, and Philadelphia. The trip was successful, and the firm began to specialize and earn a reputation in corporate law.

As hostilities increased in the South during the pre–Civil War days, Ballinger proclaimed his support of the Union; he favored SLAVERY, but not SECESSION. When Texas seceded, however, Ballinger supported his state.

Ballinger served the CONFEDERACY as a lawyer as well as a receiver of enemy property. The SEQUESTRATION Act provided for the SEIZURE and sale of such property, the proceeds of which were deposited into a special Confederate treasury.

After the war Ballinger reached the peak of his success as an eminent corporate lawyer and was considered for a seat on the United States Supreme Court. He died January 20, 1888, in Galveston, Texas.

BALLOON PAYMENT

The final installment of a loan to be paid in an amount that is disproportionately larger than the regular installment.

THE NATIONAL GOVERNMENT MAY BE REESTABLISHED—THE POLITICAL UNION MAY BE PERPETUATED, BUT IF SO, IT WILL BE BY FORCE.
—WILLIAM BALLINGER

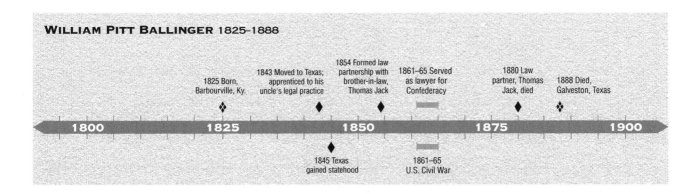

WILLIAM PITT BALLINGER 1825–1888

1825 Born, Barbourville, Ky.

1843 Moved to Texas; apprenticed to his uncle's legal practice

1854 Formed law partnership with brother-in-law, Thomas Jack

1861–65 Served as lawyer for Confederacy

1880 Law partner, Thomas Jack, died

1888 Died, Galveston, Texas

1800   1825   1850   1875   1900

1845 Texas gained statehood

1861–65 U.S. Civil War

When a loan is made, repayment of the principal, which is the amount of the loan, plus the interest that is owed on it, is divided into installments due at regular intervals—for example, every month. The earlier installments are usually payment of interest and a minimal amount of principal, while the later installments are primarily principal. When a BALLOON PAYMENT is provided in a loan agreement there are a number of installments for the same small amount prior to the balloon payment.

People with irregular or seasonal sources of income find a balloon payment provision in a loan useful for budgeting their expenses. This is not the case, however, for the average consumer. Frequently, a consumer is persuaded to enter a loan agreement providing a balloon payment that otherwise would be unwise for her or him. The consumer underestimates the full effect that the balloon payment will have on his or her budget by focusing on the small amounts to be repaid during the early stages of the loan. It is not uncommon for a consumer to be unable to pay the balloon payment when it is due. The consumer is presented with a dilemma: Either the consumer must return the item bought with the loan to the lender, thereby losing the MONEY PAID out in earlier installments, or the consumer can refinance by taking out an additional loan to use its proceeds to pay the balloon payment.

A balloon payment provision in a loan is not illegal per se. Federal and state legislatures have enacted various laws designed to protect consumers from being victimized by such a loan. The Federal TRUTH IN LENDING ACT (15 U.S.C.A. § 1601 et seq.) requires that a balloon payment—defined as an amount more than twice the size of a regularly scheduled equal installment—must be disclosed to the consumer. The consumer must be informed if refinancing is permitted and, if so, under what conditions. A creditor who fails to disclose such information can be held liable to the consumer for twice the amount of the finance charge, in addition to the costs incurred by the consumer in bringing a lawsuit. He or she can also be prosecuted and subject to a fine of up to $5,000, one year's imprisonment, or both.

Some states restrict the use of balloon payments to loans involving consumers with irregular or seasonal incomes. Those states that have enacted the provisions of the UNIFORM CONSUMER CREDIT CODE do not limit the use of balloon payments, but they give the consumer the right to refinance the amount of such payment without penalty at terms no more than those in the original loan agreement.

A *balloon note* is the name given to a PROMISSORY NOTE in which repayment involves a balloon payment. A *balloon mortgage* is a written instrument that exchanges real property as security for the repayment of a debt, the last installment of which is a balloon payment, frequently all the principal of the debt. Mortgages with balloon payment provisions are prohibited in some states.

CROSS REFERENCES

Consumer Credit Protection Act; Consumer Protection; Truth in Lending Act.

BANC

[French, Bench.] *The location where a court customarily or permanently sits.*

When a court is sitting in banc (or en banc), it means that a meeting or session of all the judges of a court is taking place. The usual purpose of sitting in banc is to hear arguments on demurrers or motions for a new trial.

BANISHMENT

Banishment is a form of punishment imposed on an individual, usually by a country or state, in which the individual is forced to remain outside of that country or state.

Although it is decidedly archaic in contemporary criminal justice systems, BANISHMENT enjoys continued existence and periodic resurgence in application. Its use is hard for legal scholars to track, but banishment is still employed in at least a handful of states, particularly in the South, as a viable alternative to incarceration.

Banishment—also known as exile or deportation—has its origins in Greek and Roman times and in worldwide histories of other kingdoms and countries such as China, Russia, and England. In ancient times, banishment was an effective punishment because it contemplated that offenders leaving a settled community would necessarily wander in the wilderness, shamed by their loved ones and unwelcome in other settlements. During England's colonial times, banishment and transportation were common forms of punishment. *Transportation* involved the relocation of criminals to one of the colonies. In colonial America, Englishmen who married African American or Native American women were banished from their colony.

In its original form, banishment had a two-fold efficacy. Not only was physical survival a challenge outside one's protected community, but the psychological and emotional damage from the scourge and condemnation of family, neighbors, and community was equally dreaded. However, as settlements and communities grew closer together, banishment meant the freedom to move to another location and perhaps to perpetrate the same crimes against an unknowing and unsuspecting community.

In contemporary populous societies, the effect is lost. One community's exile becomes the neighboring community's problem. In the 1980s California banished a parolee, giving him a one-way bus ticket to Florida, where he later murdered a woman. Cuba exiled much of its criminal prison population to the United States, where many of the exiles were imprisoned because of crimes committed there.

The U.S. Constitution does not prohibit banishment, as long as the punishment and SENTENCING meet the substantive and procedural requirements of DUE PROCESS OF LAW. Banishment is not considered CRUEL AND UNUSUAL PUNISHMENT. As recently as 2000, the Court of Appeals for the State of Mississippi addressed banishment in *Hamm v. Mississippi* (758 So. 2d 1042 [Miss App. 2000]), referring to it as an "outmoded form of punishment." Nevertheless, the court went on to address the limited circumstances under which the punishment may be used. The court insisted that the purpose of banishing someone must reasonably resemble the goals of probation—including that of rehabilitation of the offender—that both the person being sentenced and the general populace must be served and that the defendant's FIRST AMENDMENT, FIFTH AMENDMENT, and FOURTEENTH AMENDMENT rights not be violated.

Other states have been known to make at least limited use of the punishment in recent years. Section I of the BILL OF RIGHTS of the Constitution of the State of Georgia states that "Neither banishment beyond the limits of the state nor whipping shall be allowed as punishment for a crime." *Intrastate* banishment, by contrast, is permitted in Georgia. Georgia prosecutors find banishment particularly

effective in drug cases because it removes the offenders from the community that most likely contains their customers and suppliers. In 1974 the Georgia Supreme Court upheld prosecutors' use of banishment from seven Georgia counties against a woman who had challenged the punishment on constitutional grounds. In 2008, the same court upheld as constitutional the banishment of a felon to one county as a condition of his PAROLE and probation.

Kentucky and Arkansas also continue to use banishment for certain crimes. The Arkansas constitution prohibits banishment "from the state," but it allows intrastate banishment. In 2000 a Corbin, Kentucky, judge exiled from the entire state a person who had been convicted of DOMESTIC VIOLENCE. Florida judges have been known to address PROSTITUTION by meting out a five-year banishment sentence and buying the convicted prostitute a one-way ticket out of town.

Perhaps nowhere is the punishment of banishment still employed in the continental United States as much as on Indian reservations. Tribes administering their own justice to their own members often employ the use of banishment as the ultimate humiliation. When two teenagers robbed and beat a pizza delivery man with a baseball bat in the state of Washington, the Tlingit Nation banished them to separate islands for one year. In 1994 the Council of Chiefs of the Onondaga Nation in New York formally banished three members for gross violations of tribal laws. The men were formally stripped of their citizenship in the Onondaga Nation; were severed from their community and families; and had their rights, property, and protection under the ancient Iroquois Law of Onondaga territory extinguished. The Native Village of Venetie Tribal Government near Fairbanks, Alaska, punishes offenders who are caught drinking alcohol with a $50 fine. Repeat offenders are subject to banishment from the village.

An interesting case of tribal banishment occurred in 1998, in *Penn v. United States*. Margaret Penn, a non-Indian tribal PROSECUTOR and part-time grant writer on the Standing Rock Reservation of the Sioux Tribe in South Dakota, brought charges against a tribal court chief judge for UNETHICAL CONDUCT. She was terminated from her employment, and she then sued for wrongful termination. During the pendency of that suit, she was served an ex parte order from the tribal judge, banishing her from the reservation on false charges. She was given 45 minutes to gather her personal belongings and was escorted off the reservation within two hours.

Despite $17 million in 1998 federal funding for the tribal court, reservation, and tribal council, Penn was constrained in her ability to effectively sue the Standing Rock tribe by limited federal jurisdiction in the face of SOVEREIGN IMMUNITY. Relying on a HABEAS CORPUS remedy afforded by the Indian Civil Rights Act, she filed suit in U.S. district court, expressly requesting that the federal court find that it had jurisdiction to hear "any CAUSE OF ACTION arising out of … the banishment order."

The tribe responded by vacating the banishment order. In January 1999, the federal district court dismissed Penn's case as moot because the banishment order had been canceled. In March 2002, the court ruled on Penn's suit against the Bureau of Indian Affairs (BIA) and the county sheriff who has effected service of the facially invalid banishment order (*Penn v. United States*, Case No. A1–00–93). The court ruled in Penn's favor, defeating the defendants' claims of sovereign or qualified IMMUNITY. The two key issues involved were the "routine denial of fundamental constitutional rights by tribal governments and courts" and "holding the BIA and County Sheriff responsible for enforcing an [ex-parte] order that violated constitutional protections and issued by a [tribal] court with no jurisdiction over Maggie Penn."

The Eighth Circuit Court of Appeals reversed the trial court (335 F.3d 786 [2003]). The appeals court held that the judges could not be sued because they possessed absolute QUASI-JUDICIAL immunity.

FURTHER READINGS

Alloy, Jason S. 2002. "158-County Banishment in Georgia: Constitutional Implications under the State Constitution and the Federal Right to Travel." *Georgia Law Review* 36 (summer): 1083–1108.

Bleichmar, Javier. 1999. "Deportation as Punishment: A Historical Analysis of the British Practice of Banishment and Its Impact on Modern Constitutional Law." *Georgetown Immigration Law Journal* 14 (fall): 115–63.

Borrelli, Matthew D. 2003. "Banishment: The Constitutional and Public Policy Arguments against This Revived Ancient Punishment." *Suffolk University Law Review* 36 (winter): 469–86.

Smith, Stephanie. 2000. "Civil Banishment of Gang Members: Circumventing Criminal Due Process Requirements?" *University of Chicago Law Review* 67 (fall): 1461–87.

Snider, William Garth. 1998. "Banishment: The History of Its Use and a Proposal for Its Abolition under the First Amendment." *New England Journal on Criminal & Civil Confinement* 24 (summer): 455–509.

BANK FOR INTERNATIONAL SETTLEMENT

The BANK FOR INTERNATIONAL SETTLEMENT was established under the law of Switzerland. It also has legal capacity pursuant to the municipal law of each of its member states, but it lacks international legal capacity. It was denied a specific international personality. The bank is, therefore, solely in the control of its members.

BANK OF THE UNITED STATES

The American Revolutionary War resulted in the emergence of a new country faced with the task of establishing a fundamental basis for government embodying the principles of freedom for which the colonists had fought. The need for a sound financial system was most urgent, and this was remedied by the creation of the First Bank of the United States in 1791.

ALEXANDER HAMILTON, first U.S. secretary of the treasury, devised the original plan for the bank. It was argued that the Constitution did not empower Congress to institute such a bank, and that the bank was partial to commercial interests as opposed to those of farmers. Congress, nonetheless, endorsed the passage of the bank's charter.

The bank, located in Philadelphia, began with assets of $10 million, one-fifth of this money furnished by the federal government, the remainder provided by outside investors. Its affairs were administered by twenty-five directors. The bank's powers were limited to commercial enterprises, and loans were processed at six percent interest. The first bank performed well, but renewal of its charter in 1811 was thwarted by the argument against its constitutionality and by the opposition of agricultural workers. The First Bank of the United States closed for business in 1811 with a profit.

The need for a second national bank became apparent in 1816, after the WAR OF 1812 catapulted the country into a financial crisis. However, the constitutionality of such a bank was still in dispute. In *McCulloch v. Maryland*, the Supreme Court, in an opinion by Chief Justice JOHN MARSHALL, held that Congress possessed the authority to create a national bank and that the states lacked the power to tax it (17 U.S. [4 Wheat.] 316, 4 L. Ed. 579 [1819]).

The new bank began on a grander scale, with capital amounting to $35 million. For the first three years it tottered on the verge of disaster under the mismanagement of its chief administrator, William Jones. When Jones left the bank in 1819, Langdon Cheeves assumed his duties, and the bank became sound. By the time Nicholas Biddle became president in 1823, the bank was functioning efficiently, and it remained a reliable system of finance for the next ten years.

In 1832 Biddle requested renewal of the charter, which was due to expire in 1836. The bank again met opposition by those who believed it had become too powerful. President ANDREW JACKSON led the opposition, and the controversy became an issue in his presidential election campaign in 1832 against HENRY CLAY. Clay, an advocate of the bank, had encouraged Biddle to apply for the charter renewal earlier than necessary.

The reelection of Andrew Jackson sounded the death knell for the Second Bank of the United States. He rejected the renewal of the charter and in 1833 deposited federal monies into selected state banks, termed "pet banks." The loss of federal funds greatly crippled the effectiveness of the bank, and it closed in 1836, the year its charter expired.

FURTHER READINGS

Brown, Marion A. 1998. *The Second Bank of the United States and Ohio, 1803–1860: A Collision of Interests.* Lewiston, NY: Mellen.

Cowen, David Jack. 2000. *The Origins and Economic Impact of the First Bank of the United States, 1791–1797.* New York: Garland.

Markham, Jerry. 2001. *A Financial History of the United States.* Armonk, NY: Sharpe.

CROSS REFERENCE

Banks and Banking.

BANKER'S LIEN

An enforceable right of a bank to hold in its possession any money or property belonging to a customer and to apply it to the repayment of any outstanding debt owed to the bank, provided that, to the bank's knowledge, such property is not part of a trust fund or is not already burdened with other debts.

BANKRUPTCY

Bankruptcy is a federally authorized procedure by which a debtor (an individual, corporation, or municipality) is relieved of total liability for its debts by making court-approved arrangements for their partial repayment.

Once considered a shameful last resort, bankruptcy in the United States emerged as an acceptable method of resolving serious financial troubles. A record one million individuals filed for bankruptcy protection in the United States in the peak year of 1992, and between 1984 and 1994 the number of personal bankruptcy filings doubled. Despite congressional reforms, the number of bankruptcies has remained high. In 2008 a total of 1,074,225 individuals filed for bankruptcy, and bankruptcy courts saw a total of more than 1.1 million filings with businesses included.

The goal of modern bankruptcy is to allow the debtor to have a "fresh start," and the creditor to be repaid. Through bankruptcy, debtors liquidate their assets or restructure their finances to fund their debts. Bankruptcy law provides that individual debtors may keep certain exempt assets, such as a home, a car, and common household goods, thus maintaining a basic standard of living while working to repay creditors. Debtors are then better able to emerge as productive members of society, albeit with significantly flawed credit records.

History of U.S. Bankruptcy Laws

U.S. bankruptcy laws have their roots in English laws dating from the sixteenth century. Early English laws punished debtors who sought to avoid their financial responsibilities, usually by imprisonment. Beginning in the eighteenth century, changing attitudes inspired the development of debt discharge. Courts began to nullify debts as a reward for the debtor's cooperation in trying to reduce them. The public increasingly viewed debtors with pity, as well as with a realization that punishments such as imprisonment often were useless to creditors. Thus, a law that was first designed to punish the debtor evolved into a law that protected the debtor while encouraging the resolution of outstanding monetary obligations.

England's eighteenth-century insight did not find its way into the first U.S. bankruptcy statutes; instead, laws based largely on England's earlier punitive bankruptcy statutes governed U.S. colonies. After the signing of the DECLARATION OF

GAMBLING WITH BANKRUPTCY EXEMPTIONS

In bankruptcy cases, individual debtors have the privilege of retaining certain amounts or types of property that otherwise would be subject to LIQUIDATION or SEIZURE by creditors in order to satisfy debts. Laws protecting these forms of property are called exemptions.

Consistent with the goal of allowing the debtor a "fresh start," exemptions in bankruptcy cases help ensure that the debtor, upon emerging from bankruptcy, is not destitute. Exemption statutes generally permit the debtor to keep such things as a home, a car, and personal goods like clothes. Although exemptions inhibit the creditor's ability to collect debts, they relieve the state of the burden of providing the debtor's basic needs.

The bankruptcy code provides a list of uniform exemptions but also allows individual states to *opt out of* (override) these exemptions (11 U.S.C.A. § 522 [1993 & Supp. 2003]). Thus, the types and amounts of property exemptions differ greatly and depend upon the debtor's state of residence.

A debtor residing in a state that has not opted out is entitled to the exemptions described in the bankruptcy code. Examples of code exemptions are the debtor's aggregate interest of up to $15,000 in a home; up to $2,400 in a motor vehicle; up to $8,000 in household furnishings, household goods, clothes, appliances, books, animals, crops, and musical instruments; up to $1,000 in jewelry; up to $1,500 in professional books or tools of the debtor's trade; and certain unmatured life insurance policies owned by the debtor. The debtor also may claim an exemption for professionally prescribed health aids, such as electric wheel-chairs.

The majority of states have chosen to opt out of the uniform federal exemptions, replacing them with exemptions created by their own legislatures. *Homestead exemptions*, which excuse all or part of the value in the debtor's home, are the most common state-mandated exemptions. These are not uniform across states. For instance, Missouri mimics the federal government by placing a dollar limit on the exemption, but at $8,000, its cap is meager in comparison (Mo. Ann. Stat. § 513.475 [Vernon 2002]). The bordering state of Iowa limits the homestead exemption by acreage rather than dollar amount (Iowa Code Ann. §§ 561.1, 561.2 [West 1992]). Florida allows a homestead exemption without limits (Fla. Const. art. X, § 4(a) (1)). This lack of uniformity raises the question of fairness: bankruptcy laws are federal in nature, yet a debtor in Florida may have a significant financial advantage over a debtor in Missouri, owing to different exemption laws.

Despite the broad variance among states when it comes to bankruptcy exemptions, critics charge that even the uniform federal system can be grossly unfair. For example, assume two debtors, Arlene and Ben, each have estates valued at $28,000. Arlene, a dentist, has $15,000 of EQUITY in her home. She has $8,000 worth of furniture and household goods. Her car is worth $4,000, and she owns dental tools valued at $1,000.

Ben is an art lover. He owns no car, no furniture, and no house, having chosen instead to spend his money on paintings and sculptures that are now worth $26,000. His clothes, musical instruments, and other household goods are worth $2,000.

Arlene and Ben have states of equal value, but when the federal exemption statute is followed, Arlene can claim $27,200 in exemptions, whereas Ben can claim only $16,300. Arlene receives exemptions worth $15,000 for her homestead, $8,000 for her household goods, $2,400 for her car, and $1,000 for her dental tools, and an $800 general exemption for property not covered by other exemptions. Ben may claim an $8,000 exemption for his art and other household goods, as well as a general exemption worth $8,300, which replaces his unused homestead exemption.

Critics suggest that one problem with exemption laws is that legislators must determine the property that will best enable the average debtor to remain self-sufficient following a bankruptcy. Unconventional debtors, such as Ben, frequently are penalized as a result. In addition, laws that place monetary limits on exemptions often do nothing to help the debtor achieve a fresh start. When the value of certain property is worth more than the exemption, it is said to be only partially exempt and must be completely liquidated. Following liquidation, the debtor receives the value of the exemption in cash from the liquidation proceeds. Thus, in the case of Arlene's $4,000 car, the bankruptcy TRUSTEE would sell the car and from the sale proceeds give Arlene $2,400, the amount of the exemption. Arlene could then spend the money on a tropical vacation instead of a

---

INDEPENDENCE, individual states had their own laws addressing disputes between debtors and creditors, and these laws varied widely.

In 1789 the U.S. Constitution granted Congress the power to establish uniformity with a federal bankruptcy law, but more than a decade passed before Congress finally adopted the Bankruptcy Act of 1800. This act, like the early bankruptcy laws in England, emphasized creditor relief and did not allow debtors to file for relief

replacement car, rendering the vehicle exemption law virtually meaningless.

Debtors may also take advantage of exemption laws by transferring assets before filing for bankruptcy protection. For example, Ben could sell nonexempt artwork and, with the proceeds, purchase a small condominium. He could then file for bankruptcy and claim a homestead exemption, increasing by $7,500 his post-bankruptcy estate.

Congress actually supports this type of pre-bankruptcy planning, permitting the debtor "to make full use of the exemptions to which he is entitled under the law" (S. Rep. No. 989, 95th Cong., 2d Sess. [1978]). Still, courts view some pre-bankruptcy asset transfers as fraudulent, particularly when they involve large dollar amounts and there is evidence of intention to hinder, delay, or defraud creditors. Upon a finding of FRAUD, the bankruptcy court may deny discharge of the debtor's debts. But what constitutes a fraudulent transfer is often unclear and seemingly arbitrary.

Two bankruptcy cases from Minnesota exemplify the confusion surrounding fraudulent and nonfraudulent pre-bankruptcy transfers. The debtors in both cases were doctors who lost money in the same investment and who hired the same ATTORNEY to help them with their pre-bankruptcy planning. The outcomes of the cases differed significantly.

Before filing for bankruptcy, Omar Tveten liquidated most of his nonexempt assets, including his home. With the proceeds, he purchased life insurance and annuities valued at almost $700,000. Both the life insurance and the annuities were considered exempt under Minnesota law; however, the bankruptcy court held that the large amount converted was an indication of fraud and therefore refused to discharge Tveten's bankruptcy debts (*Norwest Bank Nebraska v. Tveten*, 848 F.2d 871 [8th Cir. 1988]).

Robert J. Johnson also transferred assets before filing for bankruptcy. Johnson converted nonexempt property into property exempt under Minnesota law: he purchased $8,000 in musical instruments, $4,000 in life insurance, and $250,000 in annuities from fraternal organizations, and he retired (paid off) $175,000 of the debt on his $285,000 home. The court focused on Johnson's claim for homestead exemption and in particular on the $175,000 MORTGAGE payment made just before filing for bankruptcy. As the court in *Tveten* demonstrated, an unusually large asset transfer can indicate fraud. But in *Johnson*, the court held that the homestead exemption was valid, stating that the value of an asset transfer to homestead property, unlike the value of an asset transfer to property in another exemption category, is of little relevance because "no exemption is more central to the legitimate aims of state lawmakers than a homestead exemption" (*Panuska v. Johnson*, 880 F.2d 78 [8th Cir. 1989]).

Legal commentators have criticized the *Tveten* and *Johnson* decisions as being arbitrary and as providing no clear lines to assist debtors in pre-bankruptcy planning. Critics charge that the different outcomes are simply a result of different judges presiding at the initial bankruptcy court level, because the facts of the cases were so similar. Bankruptcy attorneys are frustrated by a lack of uniformity among court decisions that apply similar principles but reach different results, and also a lack of uniformity in exemption laws among states.

Indeed, *forum shopping* (searching for the most advantageous jurisdiction in which to file bankruptcy) is prevalent because of the wide diversity of state exemption laws. *In re Coplan*, 156 B.R. 88 (Bankr. M.D. Fla. 1993), illustrates the problem. The debtors, Lee Coplan and Rebecca Coplan, incurred substantial debt in their home state of Wisconsin before moving to Florida. After residing in Florida for one year and purchasing a house for $228,000, they sought bankruptcy relief and a homestead exemption under Florida law (West's F.S.A. Const. Art. 10, § 4(a)(1)), which allows an exemption for the full value of the homestead. The court found that the Coplans had engaged in a systematic conversion of assets by selling their home in Wisconsin and paying cash for their new home in Florida. This action was conducted, according to the court, solely for the purpose of placing the assets out of the reach of creditors. As a result, the bankruptcy court in Florida allowed a homestead exemption of only $40,000, the extent provided by Wisconsin law (W.S.A. § 815.20(1)). Yet other bankruptcy decisions have held that a conversion of nonexempt property to exempt property for the purpose of placing such property out of reach of creditors will not alone deprive the debtor of the exemption (see, e.g., *In re Levine*, 139 B.R. 551 [Bankr. M.D. Fla. 1992]).

Exemption is an integral part of bankruptcy law but a difficult area to navigate. Courts and legislatures must constantly determine whether exemptions constitute fair and just vehicles by which debtors can achieve a fresh start without getting a head start at the expense of creditors. Unfortunately for attorneys, debtors, creditors, and trustees, the laws regarding exemptions are inconsistent. Attempting to maximize the benefits granted by bankruptcy exemptions can be more of a gamble than a science.

FURTHER READINGS

Epstein, David G. 2002. *Bankruptcy and Related Law in a Nutshell*. St. Paul, Minn.: West Group.

Resnick, Alan N. 2002. *Bankruptcy Law Manual*. Eagan, Minn.: Thompson West.

CROSS REFERENCE

Creditor.

voluntarily. Great public dissatisfaction prompted the act's repeal three years after its enactment.

Philosophical debates over whom bankruptcy laws should protect (i.e., debtor or creditor) had Congress struggling for the next 40 years to pass uniform federal bankruptcy legislation. The passage of the Bankruptcy Act of 1841 offered debtors greater protections and for the first time allowed them the option of voluntarily seeking bankruptcy relief. This act lasted

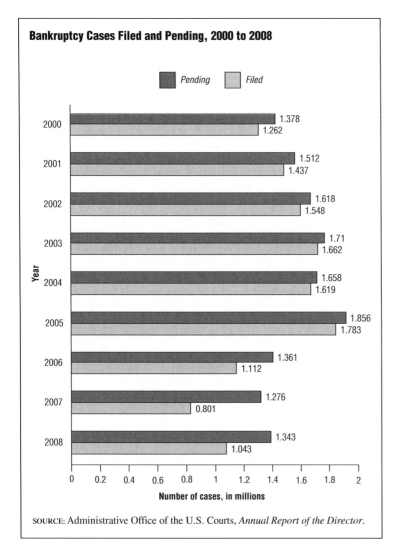

Bankruptcy Cases Filed and Pending, 2000 to 2008

Pending █ Filed ░

Year	Pending	Filed
2000	1.378	1.262
2001	1.512	1.437
2002	1.618	1.548
2003	1.71	1.662
2004	1.658	1.619
2005	1.856	1.783
2006	1.361	1.112
2007	1.276	0.801
2008	1.343	1.043

Number of cases, in millions

SOURCE: Administrative Office of the U.S. Courts, *Annual Report of the Director.*

ILLUSTRATION BY GGS CREATIVE RESOURCES. REPRODUCED BY PERMISSION OF GALE, A PART OF CENGAGE LEARNING.

eighteen months. A third bankruptcy act passed in 1867 and was repealed in 1878.

The Bankruptcy Act of 1898 endured for 80 years, thanks in part to numerous amendments, and became the basis for current bankruptcy laws. The 1898 act established bankruptcy courts and provided for bankruptcy trustees. Congress replaced this act with the Bankruptcy Reform Act of 1978 (11 U.S.C.A. § 101 et seq.), which, along with major amendments passed in 1984, 1986, 1994, and 2005, is known as the Bankruptcy Code.

Federal versus State Bankruptcy Laws

In general, state laws govern financial obligations such as those involving debts created by contracts—rental leases, telephone service, and medical bills, for example. But once a debtor or creditor seeks bankruptcy relief, federal law applies, overriding state law. This arrangement is dictated by the U.S. Constitution, which grants Congress the power to "establish ... uniform Laws on the subject of Bankruptcies throughout the United States" (U.S. Const. art. I, § 8). Federal bankruptcy power maintains uniformity among the states, encouraging interstate commerce and promoting the country's economic stability. States retain jurisdiction over certain debtor-creditor issues that do not conflict with, or are not addressed by, federal bankruptcy law.

Types of Federal Bankruptcy Proceedings

Federal bankruptcy law provides two distinct forms of relief: LIQUIDATION and rehabilitation (i.e., reorganization). The vast majority of bankruptcy filings in the United States involve liquidation, governed by Chapter 7 of the Bankruptcy Code. In a Chapter 7 liquidation case, a TRUSTEE collects the debtor's nonexempt assets and converts them into cash. The trustee then distributes the resulting fund to the creditors in order of priority described in the Bankruptcy Code. Creditors frequently receive only a portion, and sometimes none, of the money owed to them by the bankrupt debtor.

When the debtor is an individual, once the liquidation and distribution are complete, the bankruptcy court may discharge any remaining debt. When the debtor is a corporation, upon liquidation and distribution, the corporation becomes defunct. Remaining corporate debts are not formally discharged, as they are with individuals. Instead, creditors face the impossibility of pursuing debts against a corporation that no longer exists, making formal discharge unnecessary.

Rehabilitation, or reorganization, of debt is an option that courts usually favor because it provides creditors with a better opportunity to recoup what is owed to them. Rehabilitative bankruptcies are governed most often by Chapter 11 or Chapter 13 of the Bankruptcy Code. Chapter 11 typically applies to individuals with excessive or complex debts, or to large commercial entities such as corporations. Chapter 13 typically applies to individual consumers with smaller debts.

Until 2005, many debtors preferred to file Chapter 7 bankruptcy because this option allowed them to discharge most of their debts. Congress, however, made it more difficult to file a Chapter 7 bankruptcy through the enactment of the Bankruptcy Abuse and Prevention Act of 2005 (Pub. L. No. 109-8, 119 Stat. 23). Under this act, a debtor who has primarily incurred consumer debt must pass the so-called means test to file a Chapter 7 bankruptcy. Courts calculate the means test by comparing the debtor's average income for the previous six months to the median income for households of the same size in the same state as the debtor. If the debtor's income is greater than the state's median, then the Code presumes that the debtor is abusing the bankruptcy system. If the debtor cannot overcome this presumption by showing other facts related to his or her ability to pay (e.g., loss of employment), then the debtor cannot file a Chapter 7 bankruptcy. The goal of the law is the force more debtors to file Chapter 13 bankruptcies, because debts in a Chapter 13 are not discharged in the same manner as a Chapter 7 bankruptcy.

Unlike liquidation, rehabilitation provides the debtor with an opportunity to retain nonexempt assets. In return, the debtor must agree to pay debts in strict accordance with a REORGANIZATION PLAN approved by the bankruptcy court. During this repayment period, creditors are unable to pursue debts beyond the provisions of the reorganization plan. This arrangement gives the debtor the chance to restructure affairs in the effort to meet financial obligations.

To be eligible for rehabilitative bankruptcy, the debtor must have sufficient income to make a reorganization plan feasible. If the debtor fails to comply with the reorganization plan, the bankruptcy court may order liquidation. A debtor who successfully completes the reorganization plan is entitled to a discharge of remaining debts. In keeping with the general preference for bankruptcy rehabilitation rather than liquidation, the goal of this policy is to reward the conscientious debtor who works to help creditors by resolving his or her debts.

Farmers and municipalities may seek reorganization through the Bankruptcy Code's special chapters. Chapter 12 assists debt-ridden family farmers, who also may be entitled to relief under Chapters 11 or 13. When a local government seeks bankruptcy protection, it must turn to the debt reorganization provisions of Chapter 9.

Orange County Bankruptcy and Chapter 9
Seldom used, Chapter 9 attained notoriety in late 1994 following the bankruptcy of Orange County, California, in the largest municipal bankruptcy in U.S. history. A county of 2.6 million people with one of the highest per capita incomes in the United States, Orange County held an investment fund that was composed largely of derivatives that were based on speculation on the direction of interest rates. The problem was made worse because the county had borrowed the money it was investing. When interest rates began to climb in 1994, Orange County's leveraged investments drained the investment fund's value, prompting lenders to require additional collateral. The only way to raise the collateral was to sell the investments at the worst possible time. The result was a $1.7 billion loss. After consulting with finance experts and reviewing alternatives, county officials filed for Chapter 9 protection on December 6, 1994.

Residents of the affluent county faced immediate repercussions. Close to 10 percent of the 15,000 Orange County employees lost their jobs. School budgets were slashed, infrastructure improvements were put on hold, and experts predicted that property values in Orange County would decline. Legal fees involved in a bankruptcy of this complexity are extensive, and officials did not expect Orange County to emerge from bankruptcy for several years.

Critics of current bankruptcy law argue that irresponsible debtors too frequently receive protection at the expense of noncreditors, such as the residents of Orange County. Victims who allege corporate NEGLIGENCE and sue for injuries from dangerous products also become unwilling creditors when a corporation files for bankruptcy. But negligent or not, corporations battling multiple lawsuits often rely on the traditional rationale supporting bankruptcy: It offers an opportunity to pay debts that otherwise might go unpaid.

Dow Corning Corporation and Chapter 11
Dow Corning Corporation was a major manufacturer of silicone breast implants used in reconstructive and plastic surgeries. In 1991, after receiving thousands of complaints of health problems from women with silicone implants, the U.S. FOOD AND DRUG ADMINISTRATION banned the devices from widespread use. Women who had obtained the silicone implants in breast reconstruction or breast enlargement surgeries complained that the implants leaked, causing a variety of adverse conditions such as crippling pain, memory loss, lupus, and connective tissue

disease. Dow Corning soon became a DEFENDANT in a worldwide PRODUCT LIABILITY CLASS ACTION suit as well as at least 19,000 individual lawsuits.

Citing an inability to contribute $2 billion to a $4.2 billion settlement fund and pay for the defense of thousands of individual lawsuits, Dow Corning filed for Chapter 11 bankruptcy protection in May 1995. The bankruptcy move halted new lawsuits and enabled the company to consolidate existing claims while preserving business operations. As a result of the filing, Dow Corning stalled its obligation to contribute to the settlement fund.

The Dow Corning strategy was similar to that employed in the mid-1980s by A. H. Robins Company, distributor of the Dalkon Shield intrauterine device for BIRTH CONTROL. Like Dow Corning, A. H. Robins faced financial ruin owing to thousands of product LIABILITY lawsuits filed at the same time. Also like Dow Corning, A. H. Robins sought relief under Chapter 11 of the Bankruptcy Code, which allowed the company time to formulate a plan to pay the many outstanding claims. A reorganization plan approved by the courts involved the MERGER of A. H. Robins with American Home Products Corporation, which agreed to establish a $2.5 billion trust fund to pay outstanding product liability claims (*In re A.H. Robins Co.*, 880 F.2d 694 [4th Cir. 1989]).

On May 22, 1995, Dow Corning filed a request to stay all LITIGATION against its parent companies, Dow Chemical Company and Corning Incorporated, so that company lawyers could concentrate on the bankruptcy reorganization. That move further threatened the chance of recovery for the plaintiffs seeking compensation for injury.

Family Farmers and Chapter 12 In 1986, responding to an economic farm crisis in the United States, Congress designed Chapter 12 to apply to family farmers whose aggregate debts did not exceed $1.5 million. Congress passed the law to help farmers attain a financial fresh start through reorganization rather than liquidation. Before Chapter 12 existed, family farmers found it difficult to meet the prerequisites of bankruptcy reorganization under Chapters 11 or 13, often because they were unable to demonstrate sufficient income to make a reorganization plan feasible. Chapter 12 eased some requirements for qualifying farmers.

Congress created Chapter 12 as an experiment, and scheduled its automatic repeal for 1993. Determining that additional time was necessary to evaluate the effectiveness of the law, Congress in 1993 voted to extend it until 1998. Thereafter Chapter 12 was extended several times. It expired in 2004, and the Senate voted for it to be extended. As of 2005, Chapter 12 became a permanent part of the Bankruptcy Code.

Federal Bankruptcy Jurisdiction and Procedure

Regardless of the type of bankruptcy and the parties involved, basic key jurisdictional and procedural issues affect every bankruptcy case. Procedural uniformity makes bankruptcies more consistent, predictable, efficient, and fair.

Judges and Trustees Pursuant to federal statute, U.S. COURTS OF APPEALS appoint bankruptcy judges to preside over bankruptcy cases (28 U.S.C. § 152). Bankruptcy judges make up a unit of the federal district courts called bankruptcy court. Actual jurisdiction over bankruptcy matters lies with the district court judges, who then refer the matters to the bankruptcy court unit and to the bankruptcy judges.

A trustee is appointed to conduct an impartial administration of the bankrupt's nonexempt assets, known as the bankruptcy estate. The trustee represents the bankruptcy estate, which upon the filing of bankruptcy becomes a legal entity separate from the debtor. The trustee may sue or be sued on behalf of the estate. Other trustee powers vary depending on the type of bankruptcy and can include challenging transfers of estate assets, selling or liquidating assets, objecting to the claims of creditors, and objecting to the discharge of debts. All bankruptcy cases except Chapter 11 cases require trustees, who are most commonly private citizens elected by creditors or appointed by the U.S. trustee.

The Office of the U.S. Trustee, permanently established in 1986, is responsible for overseeing the administration of bankruptcy cases. The U.S. attorney general appoints a U.S. trustee to each bankruptcy region. It is the job of the U.S. trustee in some cases to appoint trustees and in all cases to ensure that trustees administer bankruptcy estates competently and honestly. U.S. trustees also monitor and report debtor abuse and FRAUD, and oversee certain debtor activity such as the filing of fees and reports.

Procedures As of the early 2000s, debtors file the vast majority of bankruptcy cases. A bankruptcy filing by a debtor is known as *voluntary bankruptcy*. The mere filing of a voluntary PETITION for bankruptcy operates as a judicial order for relief and allows the debtor immediate protection from creditors without the necessity of a hearing or other formal adjudication.

Chapters 7 and 11 of the Bankruptcy Code allow creditors the option of filing for relief against the debtor, also known as *involuntary bankruptcy*. The law requires that before a debtor can be subjected to involuntary bankruptcy, there must be a minimum number of creditors or a minimum amount of debt. Further protecting the debtor is the right to file a response, or answer, to the allegations in the creditors' petition for involuntary bankruptcy. Unlike voluntary bankruptcies, which allow relief immediately upon the filing of the petition, involuntary bankruptcies do not provide creditors with relief until the debtor has had an opportunity to respond and the court has determined that relief is appropriate.

When the debtor timely responds to an involuntary bankruptcy filing, the court will grant relief to the creditors and formally place the debtor in bankruptcy only under certain circumstances, such as when the debtor generally is failing to pay debts on time. When, after litigation, the court dismisses an involuntary bankruptcy filing, it may order the creditors to pay the debtor's ATTORNEY fees, compensatory damages for loss of property or loss of business, or PUNITIVE DAMAGES. This possibility reduces the likelihood that creditors will file involuntary bankruptcy petitions frivolously or abusively.

One of the most important rights that a debtor in bankruptcy receives is the automatic stay. The *automatic stay* essentially freezes all debt-collection activity, forcing creditors and other interested parties to wait for the bankruptcy court to resolve the case equitably and evenhandedly. The relief is automatic, taking effect as soon as a party files a bankruptcy petition. In a voluntary Chapter 7 case, the automatic stay gives the trustee time to collect and then distribute to creditors, property in the bankruptcy estate. In voluntary Chapter 11 and Chapter 13 cases, the automatic stay gives the debtor time to establish a plan of financial reorganization. In involuntary bankruptcy cases, the automatic stay gives the debtor time to respond to the petition. The automatic stay

terminates once the bankruptcy court dismisses, discharges, or otherwise terminates the bankruptcy case, but a *party in interest* (a party with a valid claim against the bankruptcy estate) may petition the court for relief from the automatic stay by showing GOOD CAUSE.

The Bankruptcy Code allows bankruptcy judges to dismiss bankruptcy cases when certain conditions exist. The debtor, the creditor, or another interested party may ask the court to dismiss the case. Petitioners—debtors in a voluntary case or creditors in an involuntary case—may seek to withdraw their petitions. In some types of bankruptcy cases, a petitioner's right to dismissal is absolute; other types of bankruptcy cases require a hearing and judicial approval before the case is dismissed. Particularly with voluntary bankruptcies, creditors, the court (or the U.S. trustee) has the power to terminate bankruptcy cases when the debtor engages in dilatory or uncooperative behavior or when the debtor substantially abuses the rights granted under bankruptcy laws.

Recent Developments in Federal Bankruptcy Law

Brought about by a surge in bankruptcy filings and public concern over inequities in the system, the Bankruptcy Reform Act of 1994 is one illustration of Congress's continuing effort to protect the rights of debtors and creditors. Consistent with Congress's goal of promoting reorganization over liquidation, the legislation made it easier for individual debtors to qualify for Chapter 13 reorganization. Previously, individuals with more than $450,000 in debt were not eligible to file under Chapter 13 and instead were forced to reorganize under the more complex and expensive Chapter 11 or to liquidate under Chapter 7. The 1994 amendments allow debtors with up to $1 million in outstanding financial obligations to reorganize under Chapter 13.

The new law helps creditors by prohibiting the discharge of credit card debts used to pay federal taxes or those exceeding $1,000 incurred within 60 days before the bankruptcy filing. In this way, the law deters debtors from shopping sprees and other abuses just before filing for bankruptcy. Creditors also benefit from new provisions that set forth additional grounds for obtaining relief from the automatic stay and require speedier adjudication of requests for relief from the stay.

It looked as though the bankruptcy system would see more reform with the introduction of

A sample involuntary petition for bankruptcy

Involuntary Petition for Bankruptcy

FORM 5. INVOLUNTARY PETITION

United States Bankruptcy Court _____ District of _____	INVOLUNTARY PETITION

IN RE (Name of Debtor – If Individual: Last, First, Middle)	ALL OTHER NAMES used by debtor in the last 8 years (Include married, maiden, and trade names.)
Last four digits of Social-Security or other Individual's Tax-I.D. No./ Complete EIN (If more than one, state all.):	

STREET ADDRESS OF DEBTOR (No. and street, city, state, and zip code)	MAILING ADDRESS OF DEBTOR (If different from street address)
COUNTY OF RESIDENCE OR PRINCIPAL PLACE OF BUSINESS	ZIP CODE

LOCATION OF PRINCIPAL ASSETS OF BUSINESS DEBTOR (If different from previously listed addresses)

CHAPTER OF BANKRUPTCY CODE UNDER WHICH PETITION IS FILED

☐ Chapter 7   ☐ Chapter 11

INFORMATION REGARDING DEBTOR (Check applicable boxes)

Nature of Debts (Check **one** box.)

Petitioners believe:

☐ Debts are primarily consumer debts
☐ Debts are primarily business debts

Type of Debtor (Form of Organization)

☐ Individual (Includes Joint Debtor)
☐ Corporation (Includes LLC and LLP)
☐ Partnership
☐ Other (If debtor is not one of the above entities, check this box and state type of entity below.)

_____

Nature of Business (Check **one** box.)

☐ Health Care Business
☐ Single Asset Real Estate as defined in 11 U.S.C. § 101(51)(B)
☐ Railroad
☐ Stockbroker
☐ Commodity Broker
☐ Clearing Bank
☐ Other

VENUE	FILING FEE (Check one box)
☐ Debtor has been domiciled or has had a residence, principal place of business, or principal assets in the District for 180 days immediately preceding the date of this petition or for a longer part of such 180 days than in any other District. ☐ A bankruptcy case concerning debtor's affiliate, general partner or partnership is pending in this District.	☐ Full Filing Fee attached ☐ Petitioner is a child support creditor or its representative, and the form specified in § 304(g) of the Bankruptcy Reform Act of 1994 is attached. *[If a child support creditor or its representative is a petitioner, and if the petitioner files the form specified in § 304(g) of the Bankruptcy Reform Act of 1994, no fee is required.]*

PENDING BANKRUPTCY CASE FILED BY OR AGAINST ANY PARTNER OR AFFILIATE OF THIS DEBTOR (Report information for any additional cases on attached sheets.)

Name of Debtor	Case Number	Date
Relationship	District	Judge

ALLEGATIONS (Check applicable boxes)	COURT USE ONLY
1. ☐ Petitioner(s) are eligible to file this petition pursuant to 11 U.S.C. § 303 (b). 2. ☐ The debtor is a person against whom an order for relief may be entered under title 11 of the United States Code. 3.a. ☐ The debtor is generally not paying such debtor's debts as they become due, unless such debts are the subject of a bona fide dispute as to liability or amount; or 3b. ☐ Within 120 days preceding the filing of this petition, a custodian, other than a trustee, receiver, or agent appointed or authorized to take charge of less than substantially all of the property of the debtor for the purpose of enforcing a lien against such property was appointed or took possession.	

B5 (Official Form 5) (12/07)

[continued]

Involuntary Petition for Bankruptcy

Name of Debtor _____

Case No. _____

(court use only)

TRANSFER OF CLAIM

☐ Check this box if there has been a transfer of any claim against the debtor by or to any petitioner. Attach all documents evidencing the transfer and any statements that are required under Bankruptcy Rule 1003(a).

REQUEST FOR RELIEF

Petitioner(s) request that an order for relief be entered against the debtor under the chapter of title 11, United States Code, specified in this petition.

Petitioner(s) declare under penalty of perjury that the foregoing is true and correct according to the best of their knowledge, information, and belief.

X_____
Signature of Petitioner or Representative (State title)

Name of Petitioner   Date Signed

Name & Mailing
Address of Individual   _____

Signing in Representative
Capacity

X_____
Signature of Attorney   Date

Name of Attorney Firm (If any)

Address

Telephone No.

X_____
Signature of Petitioner or Representative (State title)

Name of Petitioner   Date Signed

Name & Mailing
Address of Individual   _____

Signing in Representative
Capacity

X_____
Signature of Attorney   Date

Name of Attorney Firm (If any)

Address

Telephone No.

X_____
Signature of Petitioner or Representative (State title)

Name of Petitioner   Date Signed

Name & Mailing
Address of Individual   _____

Signing in Representative
Capacity

X_____
Signature of Attorney   Date

Name of Attorney Firm (If any)

Address

Telephone No.

PETITIONING CREDITORS

Name and Address of Petitioner	Nature of Claim	Amount of Claim
Name and Address of Petitioner	Nature of Claim	Amount of Claim
Name and Address of Petitioner	Nature of Claim	Amount of Claim
Note: If there are more than three petitioners, attach additional sheets with the statement under penalty of perjury, each petitioner's signature under the statement and the name of attorney and petitioning creditor information in the format above.	Total Amount of Petitioners' Claims	

B5 (Official Form 5) (12/07)   _____continuation sheets attached

A sample involuntary petition for bankruptcy (continued)

ILLUSTRATION BY GGS CREATIVE RESOURCES. REPRODUCED BY PERMISSION OF GALE, A PART OF CENGAGE LEARNING.

the Bankruptcy Reform Act of 1998. The act was a response to a report issued by the National Bankruptcy Review Commission, which recommended that the existing code be refined in order to provide incentives to debtors to file Chapter 13 reorganization and to increase debt repayment. The report was issued in response to concern that debtors were taking advantage of the bankruptcy system, evidenced by the fact that a record number of consumers filed for bankruptcy during a time of economic prosperity.

Between 1997 and 2005, Congress considered several bankruptcy reform bills. In several instances, bills passed the House of Representatives but failed in the Senate. With Republicans in control of Congress and President GEORGE W. BUSH in office, Congress finally passed the Bankruptcy Abuse and Prevention Act of 2005.

The main concern of the 2005 legislation was to make it more difficult for debtors to file for bankruptcy. The law had its desired effect. In calendar year 2003, a total of 1,625,208 individuals filed for bankruptcy, and 1,156,274 of these were Chapter 7 filings. In 2005, the year that the bankruptcy reform law was passed, a total of 2,039,214 non-businesses filed for bankruptcy. Of these, 1,631,011 were Chapter 7 bankruptcies. By 2007, two years after the bankruptcy law was passed, only 822,590 individuals filed for bankruptcy, with 500,613 filing under Chapter 7 and 321,359 filing under Chapter 13. However, bankruptcy rates increased in 2008 with the weakened economy.

Other provisions in the bankruptcy reform law included the addition of longer waiting periods between filings; requirements related to credit counseling before filing; expansion of exceptions to discharge; and limitations on the use of homestead exemptions.

While Congress was considering bankruptcy reform, the U.S. Supreme Court handed down two decisions that further defined the limits of bankruptcy law. In *Cohen v. De La Cruz* 523 U.S. 213, 118 S. Ct. 1212, 140 L. Ed. 2d 341, a unanimous Court held that where a debtor committed actual fraud and was assessed punitive damages, the debt would not be dischargeable because the Bankruptcy Code's prohibition against the discharge of fraudulently incurred debts is not restricted to the value of the money, property, or services received by the debtor. In *Young v. U.S.*, 535 U.S. 43, 122 S. Ct.

1036, 152 L. Ed. 2d 79, the Court held that the three-year lookback period allowing IRS to collect taxes against a debtor was tolled during pendency of a debtor's earlier Chapter 13 proceeding.

Apart from developments in the law, bankruptcy was much in the news during the opening years of the twenty-first century as an economic downturn forced many prominent U.S. companies into Chapter 11 bankruptcy. In 2001, the energy-trading firm Enron filed for the biggest corporate bankruptcy in history, with $64 billion in assets. Less than a year later, TELECOMMUNICATIONS firm WorldCom topped that record when it listed $104 billion in assets in its bankruptcy filing. Other prominent U.S. companies filing for bankruptcy included retailer K-Mart, financial services firm Conseco, and United Airlines PARENT COMPANY UAL.

The economic downturn in 2008 and 2009 also led to a new wave of high-profile bankruptcies. Probably the most stunning were bankruptcies filed in 2009 by Chrysler and General Motors, two of the so-called Big Three U.S. automakers.

FURTHER READINGS

Anderson, Nick. 2003. "House Passes Bankruptcy Reform Bill for the 7th Time." *Los Angeles Times* (March 20).

Hubler, James T. 2002. "The End Justifies the Means: The Legal, Social, and Economic Justifications for Means Testing under the Bankruptcy Reform Act of 2001." *American University Law Review* (October).

Jewell, Mark. 2002. "Conseco Bankruptcy Ranks Third in U.S." *Associated Press* (December 19).

Klee, Kenneth N. 2009. *Bankruptcy and the Supreme Court.* Newark, N.J.: LexisNexis.

Kuney, George W. 2008 *Mastering Bankruptcy.* Durham, N.C.: Carolina Academic Press.

CROSS REFERENCES

Debt; Debtor; Petition in Bankruptcy

BANKS AND BANKING

Banks are authorized financial institutions and banking is the business in which they engage, which encompasses the receipt of money for deposit, to be payable according to the terms of the account; collection of checks presented for payment; issuance of loans to individuals who meet certain requirements; discount of commercial paper; and other money-related functions.

Banks have existed since the founding of the United States, and their operation has been shaped and refined by major events in U.S.

history. Banking was a rocky and fickle enterprise, with periods of economic fortune and peril, between the 1830s and the early twentieth century. In the late nineteenth century, the restrained money policies of the U.S. TREASURY DEPARTMENT, namely an unwillingness to issue more bank notes to eastern-based national banks, contributed to a scarcity of cash in many Midwestern states. A few states went so far as to charter local banks and authorize them to print their own money. The collateral or capital that backed these local banks was often of only nominal value. By the 1890s, there was a full-fledged bank panic. Depositors rushed to banks to withdraw their money, only to find in many cases that the banks did not have the money on hand. This experience prompted insurance reforms that developed during the next fifty years. The lack of a regulated money supply led to the passage of the Federal Reserve Act in 1913 (in scattered sections of 12 U.S.C.A.), creating the Federal Reserve Bank System.

Even as the banks sometimes suffered, there were stories of economic gain and wealth made through their operation. Industrial enterprises were sweeping the country, and their need for financing was seized upon by men such as J. P. Morgan (1837–1913). Morgan made his fortune as a banker and financier of various projects. His House of Morgan was one of the most powerful financial institutions in the world. Morgan's holdings and interests included railroads, coal, steel, and steamships. His involvement in what we now consider commercial banking and SECURITIES would later raise concern over the appropriateness of mixing these two industries, especially after the STOCK MARKET crash of 1929 and the ensuing instability in banking. Between 1929 and 1933, thousands of banks failed. In 1933 President FRANKLIN D. ROOSEVELT temporarily closed all U.S. banks because of a widespread lack of confidence in the institutions. These events played a major role in the Great Depression and in the future reform of banking.

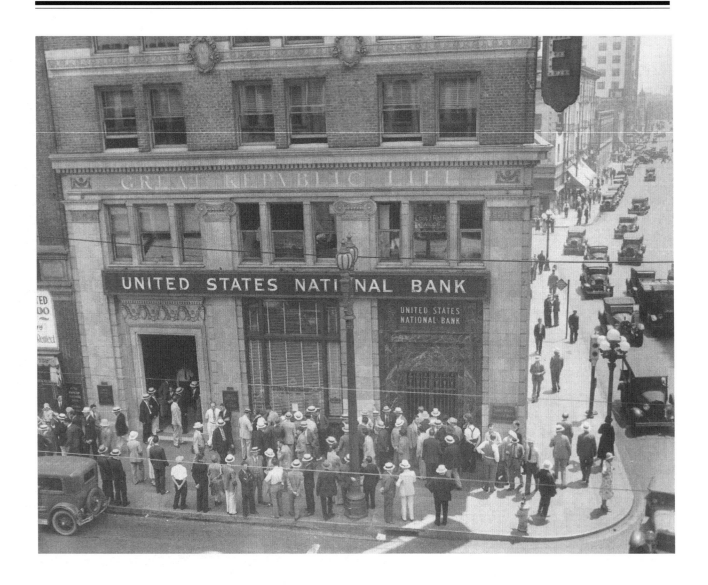

In 1933 Congress held hearings on the commingling of the banking and securities industries. Out of these hearings, a reform act that strictly separated commercial banking from securities banking was created (12 U.S.C.A. §§ 347a, 347b, 412). The act became known as the GLASS-STEAGALL ACT, after the two senators who sponsored it, CARTER GLASS (D-VA) and Henry B. Steagall (D-AL). The Glass-Steagall Act also created the FEDERAL DEPOSIT INSURANCE CORPORATION (FDIC), which insures money deposited at member banks against loss. Since its passage, Glass-Steagall has been the law of the land, with minor revision on several occasions.

Despite the Glass-Steagall reforms, periods of instability have continued to recur in the banking industry. Between 1982 and 1987, about 600 banks failed in the United States. More than one-third of the closures occurred in Texas. Many of the failed banks closed permanently, with their customers' deposits compensated by the FDIC; others were taken over by the FDIC and reorganized and eventually reopened.

In 1999 Congress addressed concerns of many involved in the financial industries with the passage of the Financial Services Modernization Act, Pub. L. No. 106-102, 113 Stat. 1338, also known as the Gramm-Leach Act. The act rewrote the banking laws from the 1930s and 1950s, including the Glass-Steagall Act, which had prevented commercial banks, securities firms, and insurance companies from merging their businesses. Under the act, banks, brokers, and insurance companies are able to combine and share consumer transaction records as well as other sensitive records. The act went into effect on November 12, 2000, though several of its provisions did not take effect until July 1,

2001. Seven federal agencies were responsible for rewriting regulations that implemented the new law.

Gramm-Leach goes beyond the repeal of the Glass-Steagall Act and similar laws. One section streamlines the supervision of banks. It directs the FEDERAL RESERVE BOARD to accept existing reports that a bank has filed with other federal and state regulators, thus reducing time and expenses for the bank. Moreover, the Federal Reserve Board may examine the insurance and brokerage subsidiaries of a bank only if reasonable cause exists to believe the subsidiary is engaged in activities posing a material risk to bank depositors. The new law contains many other similar provisions that restrict the ability of the Federal Reserve Board to regulate the new type of bank that the law contemplates. The Gramm-Leach Act also breaks down barriers of foreign banks wishing to operate in the United States by allowing foreign banks to purchase U.S. banks.

Since the mid-1980s, periods of instability have recurred in the banking industry. Beginning in 2006, the decline in U.S. housing prices and corresponding subprime MORTGAGE crisis were believed by many to be the cause of banks suffering major adverse consequences, including many bank failures. Government-issued bailout funds were provided to banks in conjunction with other measures designed to stimulate the weak economy and restore liquidity to the financial markets. As of May 2009, many referred to the period of economic instability as the worst financial crisis since the Great Depression.

Categories of Banks

There are two main categories of banks: federally chartered national banks and state-chartered banks.

A national bank is incorporated and operates under the laws of the United States, subject to the approval and oversight of the comptroller of the currency, an office established as a part of the Treasury Department in 1863 by the National Bank Act (12 U.S.C.A. §§ 21, 24, 38, 105, 121, 141 note).

All national banks are required to become members of the Federal Reserve System. The Federal Reserve, established in 1913, is a central bank with 12 regional district banks in the United States. The Federal Reserve creates and implements national fiscal policies affecting nearly every facet of banking. The system assists in the transfer of funds, handles government deposits and debt issues, and regulates member banks to achieve uniform commercial procedure. The Federal Reserve regulates the availability and cost of credit through the buying and selling of securities, mainly government bonds. It also issues Federal Reserve notes, which account for almost all the paper money in the United States.

A board of governors oversees the work of the Federal Reserve. This board was approved in 1935 and replaced the Federal Reserve Board. The seven-member board of governors is appointed to 14-year terms by the PRESIDENT OF THE UNITED STATES with Senate approval.

Each district reserve bank has a board of directors with nine members. Three nonbankers and three bankers are elected to each board of directors by the member bank, and three directors are named by the Federal Reserve Board of Governors.

A member bank must keep a reserve (a specific amount of funds) deposited with one of the district reserve banks. The reserve bank then issues Federal Reserve notes to the member bank or credits its account. Both methods provide stability in meeting customers' needs in the member bank.

One major benefit of belonging to the Federal Reserve System is that deposits in member banks are automatically insured by the FDIC. The FDIC protects each account in a member bank for up to $100,000 should the bank become insolvent. A state-chartered bank is granted authority by the state in which it operates and is under the regulation of an appropriate state agency. Many state-chartered banks also choose to belong to the Federal Reserve System, thus ensuring coverage by the FDIC. Banks that are not members of the Federal Reserve System can still be protected by the FDIC if they can meet certain requirements and if they submit an application.

The Interstate Banking and Branching Efficiency Act of 1994 (in scattered sections of 12 U.S.C.A.) elevated banking from a regional enterprise to a more national pursuit. Previously, a nationally chartered bank had to obtain a charter and set up a separate institution in each state where it wished to do business; the 1994 legislation removed this requirement. Also, throughout the 1980s and the early 1990s, a number of states passed laws that allowed for RECIPROCAL interstate banking. This trend resulted in a patchwork of regional compacts between various states, most heavily concentrated in New England.

Types of Banks

The term *bank* is generally used to refer to commercial banks; however, it can also be used to refer to savings institutions, savings and loan associations, and building and loan associations.

A commercial bank is authorized to receive demand deposits (payable on order) and time deposits (payable on a specific date), lend money, provide services for fiduciary funds, issue letters of credit, and accept and pay drafts. A commercial bank not only serves its depositors but also can offer installment loans, commercial long-term loans, and credit cards.

A savings bank does not offer as wide a range of services. Its primary goal is to serve its depositors through providing loans for purposes such as home improvement, mortgages, and education. By law, a savings bank can offer a higher interest rate to its depositors than can a commercial bank.

A SAVINGS AND LOAN ASSOCIATION (S&L) is similar to a savings bank in offering savings accounts. It traditionally restricts the loans it makes to housing-related purposes, including mortgages, home improvement, and construction, although some S&Ls have entered into educational loans for their customers. An S&L can be granted its charter by either a state or the federal government; in the case of a federal charter, the organization is known as a federal savings and loan. Federally chartered S&Ls have their own system, which functions in a manner similar to that of the Federal Reserve System, called the Federal Home Loan Banks System. Like the Federal Reserve System, the Federal Home Loan Banks System provides an insurance program of up to $100,000 for each account; this program is called the Federal Savings and Loan Insurance Corporation (FSLIC). The Federal Home Loan Banks System also provides membership options for state-chartered S&Ls and an option for just FSLIC coverage for S&Ls that can satisfy certain requirements.

A BUILDING AND LOAN ASSOCIATION is a special type of S&L that restricts its lending to home mortgages.

The distinctions between these financial organizations has become narrower as federal legislation has expanded the range of services that can be offered by each type of institution.

Bank Financial Structure

Banks are usually incorporated and, like any corporation, must be backed by a certain amount of capital (money or other assets). Banking laws specify that banks must maintain a certain minimum amount of capital. Banks acquire capital by selling CAPITAL STOCK to shareholders. The money that shareholders pay for the capital stock becomes the working capital of the bank. The working capital is put in a trust fund to protect the bank's depositors. In turn, shareholders receive certificates that prove their ownership of stock in the bank. The working capital of a bank cannot be diminished. Dividends to shareholders must be paid only from the profits or surplus of the bank.

Shareholders have their legal relationship with a bank defined by the terms outlined in the contract to purchase capital stock. With the investment in a bank comes certain rights such as the right to inspect the bank's books and records and the right to vote at shareholders' meetings. Shareholders may not personally sue a bank, but they can, under appropriate circumstances, bring a stockholder's derivative suit on behalf of the bank (sue a THIRD PARTY for injury done to the bank when the bank fails to sue on its own). Shareholders also are not usually personally liable for the debts and acts of a bank, because the corporate form limits their LIABILITY. However, if shareholders have consented to or accepted benefits of unauthorized banking practices or illegal acts of the board of directors, they are not immune from liability.

Bank Officials

The election and term of office of a bank's board of directors are governed by statute or by the charter of the bank. The liabilities and duties of bank officials are prescribed by statute, charter, bylaws, customary banking practices, and employment contracts. Directors and bank officers are both responsible for the conduct and honorable management of a bank's affairs, although their duties and liabilities are not the same.

Officers and directors are liable to a bank for losses it incurs as a result of their illegal, fraudulent, or wrongful conduct. Liability is imposed for embezzlement, illegal use of funds or other assets, false representation of the bank's condition made to deceive others, or fraudulent purchases or loans. The failure to exercise reasonable care in the execution of their duties also renders officials liable if such failure brings about bank losses. If such losses result from an error in judgment, liability will not be imposed so long as the officials acted in GOOD FAITH with reasonable skill and care. Officers and directors will not be held liable for the acts of their employees if they exercise caution in hiring qualified personnel and supervise them carefully. Civil actions against bank officials are maintained in the form of stockholders' derivative suits. Criminal statutes determine the liability of officers and directors for illegal acts against their bank.

Bank Duties

The powers and duties of a bank are determined by the terms of its charter and the legislation under which it was created (either federal or state regulations). A bank can enact reasonable rules and regulations for the efficient operation of its business through its governing board.

Deposits A deposit is a sum of money placed in an account to be held by a bank for the depositor. A customer can deposit money by cash or by a check or other document that represents cash. Deposits are how banks survive. The deposited money establishes a debtor and creditor relationship between the bank and the depositor. Most often, the bank pays the depositing customer interest for its use of the money until the customer withdraws the funds. The bank has the right to impose rules and regulations managing the deposit, such as restrictions governing the rate of interest the deposited money will earn and guidelines for its withdrawal.

Collections One primary function of a bank is to make collections of items such as checks and drafts deposited by customers. The bank acts as an agent for the customer. Collection occurs when the drawee bank (the bank ordered by the check to make payment) takes funds from the account of the drawer (its customer who has written the check) and presents it to the collecting bank.

Checks A check is a written order made by a drawer to her or his bank to pay a designated person or organization (the payee) the amount specified on the check. Payment pursuant to the check must be made in strict compliance with its terms. The drawer's account must be reduced by the amount specified on the check. A check is a demand instrument, which means it must be paid by the drawee bank on the demand of, or when presented by, the payee or the agent of the payee, the collecting bank.

A payee usually receives payment of a check upon endorsing it and presenting it to a bank in which the payee has an account. The bank can require the payee to present identification to prove a relationship with the bank, before cashing the check. It has no obligation to cash a check for a person who is not a depositor, since it can refuse payment to a stranger. However, it must honor (pay) a check if the payee has sufficient funds on deposit with the bank to cover the amount paid if the drawer of the check does not have adequate funds in his or her account to pay it.

A CERTIFIED CHECK is guaranteed by a bank, at the request of its drawer or endorser, to be cashable by the payee or succeeding holder. A bank is not obligated to certify a check, but it usually will do so for a customer who has sufficient funds to pay it, in exchange for a nominal fee. A certified check is considered the same as cash because any bank must honor it when the payee presents it for payment.

A drawer can revoke a check unless it has been certified or has been paid to the payee. The notice of REVOCATION is often called a STOP PAYMENT ORDER. A check is automatically revoked if the drawer dies before it is paid or certified, since the drawer's bank has no authority to complete the transaction under that circumstance. However, if the drawer's bank does not receive notice of the drawer's death, it is not held liable for the payment or certification of that drawer's checks.

Upon request, a bank must return to the drawer all the checks it has paid, so that the drawer can inspect the canceled checks to ensure that no forgeries or errors have occurred, in adjusting the balance of her or his checking account. This review of checks is usually completed through the monthly statement. If the drawer finds an error or forgery, it is her or his obligation to notify the bank promptly or to accept full responsibility for whatever loss has been incurred.

Bank Liabilities A bank has a duty to know a customer's signature and therefore is generally liable for charging the customer's account with a forged check. A bank can recover the loss from the forger but not from the person who in good faith and without knowledge of the crime gave something in exchange for the forged check. If the depositor's NEGLIGENCE was a factor in the forgery, the bank can be excused from the liability.

A bank is also responsible for determining the genuineness of the endorsement when a depositor presents a check for payment. A bank is liable if it pays a check that has been materially altered, unless the alteration was due to the drawer's fault or negligence. If a bank pays a check that has a forged endorsement, it is liable for the loss if it is promptly notified by the customer. In both cases, the bank is entitled to recover the amount of its loss from the thief or forger.

A drawee bank that is ordered to pay a check drawn on it is usually not entitled to recover payment it has made on a forged check. If, however, the drawee bank can demonstrate that the collecting bank was negligent in its collection duties, the drawee bank may be able to establish a right of recovery.

A bank can also be liable for the wrongful dishonor or refusal to pay of a check that it has certified, because by definition of certification it has agreed to become absolutely liable to the payee or holder of the check. If a bank has paid a check that has been properly revoked by its drawer, it must reimburse the drawer for the loss.

Drawer Liabilities A drawer who writes a check for an amount greater than the funds on deposit in his or her checking account is liable to the bank. Such a check, called an overdraft, sometimes results in a loan from the bank to the drawer's account for the amount by which the account is deficient, depending on the terms of the account. In this case, the drawer must repay the bank the amount lent plus interest. The bank can also decide not to provide the deficient funds and can refuse to pay the check, in which case the check is considered "bounced." The drawer then becomes liable to the bank for a handling fee for the check, as well as remaining liable to the payee or subsequent holder of the check for the amount due. Many times, the holder of a returned, or bounced, check will impose another fee on the drawer.

Loans and Discounts A major function of a bank is the issuance of loans to applicants who meet certain qualifications. In a loan transaction, the bank and the debtor execute a PROMISSORY NOTE and a separate agreement in which the terms and conditions of the loan are detailed. The interest charged on the amount lent can differ based on many variables. One variable is a benchmark interest rate established by the Federal Reserve Bank Board of Governors, also known as the prime rate, at the time the loan is made. Another variable is the length of repayment. The collateral provided to secure the loan, in case the borrower defaults, can also affect the interest rate. In any case, the interest rate must not exceed that permitted by law. The loan must be repaid according to the terms specified in the loan agreement. In case of default, the agreement determines the procedures to be followed.

Banks also purchase commercial papers, which are commercial loans, at a discount from creditors who have entered into long-term contracts with debtors. A creditor sells a COMMERCIAL PAPER to a bank for less than its face value because it seeks immediate payment. The bank profits from the difference between the discount price it paid and the face value of the bond, which it will receive when the debtor has finished repaying the loan. Types of commercial paper are educational loans and home mortgages.

Electronic Banking

Many banks are replacing traditional checks and deposit slips with electronic fund transfer (EFT) systems, which use sophisticated computer technology to facilitate banking and payment needs. Routine banking by means of EFT is considered safer, easier, and more convenient for customers.

Many types of EFT systems are available, including automated teller machines; pay-by-phone systems; automatic deposits of regularly received checks such as paychecks; automated payment of recurring bills; point-of-sale transfers or debit cards, where a customer gives a merchant a card and the amount is automatically transferred from the customer's account; and transfer and payment by customers' home computers.

When an EFT service is arranged, the customer receives an EFT card that activates the system and the bank is legally required to disclose the terms and conditions of the account. These terms and conditions include the customer's liability and the notification process to follow if an EFT card is lost or stolen; the type of transactions in which a customer can take part; the procedure for correction of errors; and the extent of information that can be disclosed to a third party without improper infringement on the customer's privacy. If a bank is planning to change the terms of an account—for example, by imposing a fee for transactions previously conducted free of charge—the customer must receive written notice before the change goes into effect.

Banks must send account statements for EFT transactions on a monthly basis. The statements must have the amount, date, and type of transaction; the customer's account number; the account's opening and closing balances; charges for the transfers or for continuation of the service; and an address and telephone number for referral of account questions or mistakes.

EFT transactions have become a highly competitive area of banking, with banks offering various bonuses such as no fee for the use of a card when the account holder meets certain provisions such as maintaining a minimum balance. Also, the rapid growth of personal and home office computing has increased pressure on banks to provide services online. Several computer software companies produce technology that can complete many routine banking services, such as automatic bill paying, at a customer's home.

Banks have a wide range of options available for notifying a customer that a check has been directly deposited into her or his account. If a customer has arranged for automatic payment of regularly recurring bills such as mortgage or utility bills, the customer has a limited period of time, usually up to three days before the payment is made, in which to order the bank to stop payment. When the amounts of such bills vary, as with utility bills, the bank must notify the customer of the payment date in sufficient time so that there is enough funds in the account to cover the debt.

If the customer discovers a mistake in an account, the bank must be notified orally or in writing after the erroneous statement is received. The bank must investigate the claim. Often, after several days, the customer's account will be temporarily recredited with the disputed amount. After the investigation is complete, the bank is required to notify the customer in writing if it concludes that no error occurred. It must provide copies of its decision and explain how it reached its findings. Then the customer must return the amount of the error if it was recredited to his or her account.

A customer is liable if an unauthorized transfer is made because an EFT card or other device is stolen, lost, or used without permission. This liability can be limited if the customer notifies the bank within two business days of the discovery of the misdeed; it is extended to $500 if the customer fails to comply with the notice requirement. A customer can assume unlimited liability if she or he fails to report any unauthorized charges to an account within a specified period after receiving the monthly statement.

A customer is entitled to sue a bank for COMPENSATORY DAMAGES caused by the bank's wrongful failure to perform the terms and conditions of an EFT account, such as refusing to pay a charge if the customer's account has more than adequate funds to do so. The customer can also recover a maximum penalty of $1,000, attorneys' fees, and costs in an action based upon violation of this law.

The expansion of the INTERNET in the mid-1990s allowed banks to offer many more electronic services to their customers. Although this form of business with banks is certainly convenient, it has caused a considerable concern regarding the security of transactions conducted in this manner. Although laws designed to prevent FRAUD in traditional banking also apply to electronic banking, identifying individuals engaged in fraud can be more difficult where electronic transactions are concerned. On the federal level, the Electronic Funds Transfers Act, 15 U.S.C.A. §§ 1693a et seq., provides protection to consumers who are the subject of an unauthorized electronic funds transfer.

The Gramm-Leach-Bliley Financial Modernization Act, PL 106-102 (S 900) November 12, 1999, also modified federal statutory provisions related to electronic banking. Under this act, banks must disclose the fees they charge for use of their automated teller machines. If the consumer is not provided with proper fee disclosure, an ATM operator cannot impose a service fee concerning any electronic fund transfer initiated by the consumer. Furthermore, the act requires that possible fees be disclosed to a consumer when an ATM card is issued.

Interstate Banking and Branching

In late 1994 the 103d Congress authorized significant reforms to interstate banking and branching law. The Interstate Banking Law (Pub. L. No. 103-328), also referred to as the Riegle-Neal Interstate Banking and Branching Efficiency Act of 1994, provided the banking

THE BANK BAILOUT PLAN OF 2008

Since the creation of the Federal Reserve System in 1913, the U.S. government has played a significant role in regulating banks and promoting the stability of the financial sector. Besides overseeing the activities of banks, the government created the FEDERAL DEPOSIT INSURANCE CORPORATION, which insures the money of depositors. However, the credit squeeze of 2008 and the accompanying collapse of major banks and other financial instructions led to what has been called "the bank bailout plan." Congress enacted and President GEORGE W. BUSH signed the Emergency Economic Stabilization Act of 2008 (EESA), Pub. L. 110-334. EESA established a program called the Troubled Asset Relief Program (TARP), which gave the TREASURY DEPARTMENT the authority to purchase or insure up to $700 billion of troubled assets. By the end of 2009, many of the affected banks had regained their financial footing and were paying back the TARPP funds to the Treasury. Despite this apparent success, critics of TARP argued that it had overpaid for the troubled assets. Moreover, the Obama administration had failed to make meaningful reforms of the financial industry.

The source of the 2008 financial meltdown, which government officials claimed almost brought the U.S. and world economies to collapse, was the decision by the FEDERAL RESERVE BOARD following September 11, 2001, to lower interest rates on the money it lends major banks. The U.S. economy had slipped into a mild recession following the terrorist attacks, and the Fed hoped to stimulate it by making money more

available. The Fed's hopes came true when the cheap money led to low home-mortgage rates. Low interest rates, combined with sub-prime, adjustable mortgages, allowed individuals who could never qualify for financing to own a home. Many individuals bought houses with little or no down payments and bought houses that were more than they could truly afford. The subprime mortgages in turn were packaged and "securitized" by investment banks; mortgage-backed SECURITIES became lucrative financial instruments, though the worth of them was tied to the ability of homeowners to make their payments.

The dramatic growth in the value of homes suggested to some economists that the United States was experiencing a REAL ESTATE bubble rather than a period of solid, sustained expansion. They feared that any type of economic contraction would lead to higher interest rates for subprime adjustable MORTGAGE holders and a high number of home foreclosures. As the economy started to tighten in 2006, the fears of these economists began to be realized. Many new homeowners could not pay skyrocketing monthly payments and foreclosures increased. Even long-time homeowners were affected because they had refinanced their homes for the low interest rates but took adjustable rate rather than fixed rate mortgages. Despite these signs, banks continued to sell these risky mortgages and financial products.

When investment bank Bear Stearns moved towards BANKRUPTCY in early 2008 because of the shrinking value of the mortgage-backed securities, the Federal Reserve stepped in, assumed $30 billion

of its debts and forced a sale of the bank to JPMorgan Chase for a price that was less than the value of the Bear Stearns' Manhattan skyscraper. In August the federally sponsored entities Freddie Mac and Fannie Mae raced towards insolvency. Freddie and Fannie were central to the U.S housing market, holding mortgages that diminished in value every day. On September 7, the Treasury Department took control of both entities.

The long-respected investment bank Lehman Brothers was next. Unlike Bear Stearns, the government refused to step in, forcing it into bankruptcy on September 12. On September 16, the American International Group (AIG), one of the world's largest insurance companies, revealed it was teetering on financial ruin. AIG had insured risky securities that were tied to securitized mortgages. The federal government feared that if AIG collapsed, it would produce a domino effect as banks that had insured its securitized mortgages would be left with toxic assets that had little value. The government essentially bought AIG for $85 billion. As these events unfolded, the STOCK MARKET dropped almost 500 points and individuals withdrew about $140 billion from their money-market funds, sparking fears that there would be a run on the banks.

On September 18, Treasury Secretary Henry Paulson, a former Wall Street investment banker, announced a three-page, $700 billion proposal to bail out the banks. He proposed that the government buy the toxic assets from the largest banks, which could stabilize their financial position. Members of Congress were skeptical, in part because the three-page

industry with major legislative changes. The Interstate Banking Act was expected to accelerate the trend of bank mergers. These mergers are a benefit to the nation's largest banks, which were expected to see savings of millions of dollars resulting from streamlining.

FURTHER READINGS

Adler, Joseph. 1995. "Banking without Glass-Steagall? Look Overseas." *American Banking Association Journal* (May).

Bunditz, Mark. 2006. *Consumer Banking and Payments Law.* Boston: National Computer Law Center.

proposal was scant on details and gave Paulson total, unreviewable control over how he spent the $700 billion. Because these events occurred during the 2008 presidential campaign, politics also factored into the debate on the proposal. On September 29, the House of Representatives voted down a modified version of Paulson's plan. The stock market lost nearly 9 percent of its value after the vote was taken, the worst decline since 1987. Congress took note of Wall Street's reaction and reached a compromise. The House passed the bill on October 3 and sent EESA to President Bush for signing. As the United States began to confront its problems, the banks of Europe and Asia were forced to deal with the crisis as it played out around the world.

The TARP program was set up to handle the disbursement of the $700 billion. The law defined "troubled assets" to include residential or commercial mortgages and any "securities, obligations, or other instruments that are based on or related to such mortgages" originated or issued before March 14, 2008. The securitized mortgages clearly were the prime "toxic assets" that burdened the balance sheets of the major banks. EESA released $250 billion to the Treasury immediately, with the president authorized to release $100 billion more. For the remaining $350 billion, the Treasury had to notify Congress of its intent to use the money. Congress had 15 days to pass a resolution denying the Treasury the authority to do so.

Paulson originally intended to hold AUCTIONS for the trouble assets but finally decided it would be better for the government to loan the money. TARP mandated that the Treasury receive non-voting stock from the banks in return for the TARP funds. Congress also was outraged at the enormous bonuses paid to bank executives for acquiring these toxic assets. The TARP contained language that banned

banks that accepted TARP money from offering incentives that encouraged "unnecessary and excessive risks" to its top executives. For senior executives hired in the future, the banks were banned from offering lucrative SEVERANCE packages.

TARP also was intended to help homeowners avoid FORECLOSURE. The Treasury was required to set up a program to achieve this objective but details were sketchy. Secretary Paulson had no interest in implementing this provision, telling Congress that TARP "was not intended to be an economic stimulus or an economic recovery package." Congress was concerned with how the Treasury would run TARP, so it established the Financial Stability Oversight Board and a Congressional Oversight Panel. A February 2009 report from the panel claimed that the government had greatly overpaid for the toxic assets. It had paid $254 billion for assets valued at $176 billon.

As TARP got off the ground, the U.S economy had taken a drubbing. It is estimated that $8 trillion of wealth was wiped out in the stock when measured from its highest point in the decade. Though TARP did stabilize the problem banks (nine banks took TARP money in return for stock), it was rumored that the incoming Obama administration might nationalize some of the troubled banks. That was not the case. Instead, Treasury secretary Timothy Geithner, who as head of the Federal Reserve Bank of New York played a key role in the fall 2008 with the bailout program, announced that it would perform "stress tests" on the 19 largest U.S. banks. The government wanted to know whether the banks were sufficiently capitalized to weather more declines in the economy. The results of the tests were promising. Ten of the 19 banks needed additional capital totaling $75 billion.

Starting in March 2009, some of the banks returned to profitability. Then in June, 10 banks were allowed to return their portion of the $700 billon TARP funds. They paid back to the government a total of $68 billion. The zeal with which the banks returned the money was primarily based on extricating them from government oversight and restrictions on executive pay. By September, Geithner reported to Congress that the TARP program was winding down and that more banks would likely repay their bailout funds. Though the bank bailout appeared to be successful in stabilizing the largest banks, financial reform regulation legislation was having a slow and difficult journey through Congress. Moreover, though the public came to the rescue of these private banks, credit remained tight in late 2009 for businesses and individuals alike.

FURTHER READINGS

Gasparino, Charles. 2009. *The Sellout: How Three Decades of Wall Street Greed and Government Mismanagement Destroyed the Global Financial System.* New York: HarperBusiness.

Goodman, Peter. 2008. "Taking Hard New Look at a Greenspan Legacy." *New York Times.* October 8.

Morris, Charles. 2009. *The Two Trillion Dollar Meltdown: Easy Money, High Rollers, and the Great Credit Crash.* New York: Public Affairs.

Phillips, Kevin. 2008. *Bad Money: Reckless Finance, Failed Politics, and the Global Crisis of American Capitalism.* New York: Viking.

Sorkin, Andrew Ross. 2009. *Too Big to Fail: The Inside Story of How Wall Street and Washington Fought to Save the Financial System and Themselves.* New York: Viking.

Varchaver, Nicholas, and Katie Benner. 2008. "The $55 Trillion Question." *Fortune.* September 30.

Carnell, Richard Scott, Jonathan R. Macey, and Geoffrey P. Miller. 2006. *The Law of Banking and Financial Institutions.* New York: Aspen.

Farrell, Cathlyn. 2008. *Law and Banking.* Washington, D.C.: American Bankers Association.

Lovett, William A. 2005. *Banking and Financial Institutions Law in a Nutshell.* St. Paul: West.

Timberlake, Richard H., Jr. 1993. *Monetary Policy in the United States: An Intellectual and Institutional History.* Chicago: University of Chicago Press.

CROSS REFERENCES

Bank of the United States; Federal Deposit Insurance Corporation; Federal Reserve Board; Glass-Steagall Act; Securities.

Dennis Banks.
AP PHOTOS.

❖ BANKS, DENNIS J.

Native American activist, organizer, and protest leader Dennis Banks (Nowacumig) helped found the influential AMERICAN INDIAN MOVEMENT (AIM). Under his passionate leadership in the late 1960s and early 1970s, AIM championed Native American self-sufficiency, traditions, and values. However, its demand for federal recognition of century-old treaty rights led to violent clashes with authorities, and the FEDERAL BUREAU OF INVESTIGATION (FBI) branded AIM an extremist group. In turn, illegal actions by the FBI led to Banks's acquittal on charges stemming from his role in AIM's occupation of Wounded Knee,

South Dakota, in 1973. While heightening national awareness of Native American issues, Banks faced prosecution several times. He spent nearly a decade as a criminal fugitive, receiving a form of political ASYLUM in California from then governor Jerry Brown before surrendering in 1984 and serving a shortened prison term. Since 1978, Banks has led a Native American spiritual organization in Kentucky called Sacred Run.

Banks was born April 12, 1937, in Leech Lake, Minnesota. His difficult early life began during one of many periods of upheaval in federal policy regarding Native Americans. Like many Anishinabe Ojibwa, or Chippewa, children, he was sent at the age of five to schools operated by the federal Bureau of Indian Affairs (BIA), and he spent part of his childhood being shuttled between boarding schools in North and South Dakota. The BIA managed such schools in accordance with a landmark change in federal policy known as the Indian Reorganization Act of 1934 (25 U.S.C.A. § 461 et seq.). Under the terms of this so-called NEW DEAL for Indians—a plan for tribal government that many traditional Native Americans had resisted—schools were to have been improved over those in previous decades that sought to Christianize or "civilize" their pupils. But the schools still deemphasized Native American culture by forbidding the speaking of the Ojibwa language, Lakota. Thus, like many of his generation, Banks lost his native tongue.

At the age of 16, Banks joined the U.S. Air Force and served in Japan. Discharged in the late 1950s, he returned to Minnesota, where he faced the same problems as young Native American men continued to face in the 1990s and the 2000s: alienation from his culture,

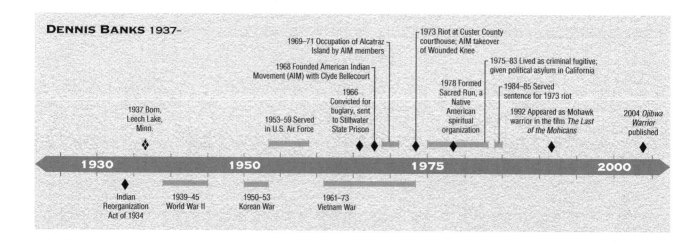

DENNIS BANKS 1937–

1969–71 Occupation of Alcatraz Island by AIM members

1968 Founded American Indian Movement (AIM) with Clyde Bellecourt

1973 Riot at Custer County courthouse; AIM takeover of Wounded Knee

1975–83 Lived as criminal fugitive; given political asylum in California

1966 Convicted for buglary, sent to Stillwater State Prison

1978 Formed Sacred Run, a Native American spiritual organization

1984–85 Served sentence for 1973 riot

1937 Born, Leech Lake, Minn.

1953–59 Served in U.S. Air Force

1992 Appeared as Mohawk warrior in the film *The Last of the Mohicans*

2004 *Ojibwa Warrior* published

1930   1950   1975   2000

Indian Reorganization Act of 1934

1939–45 World War II

1950–53 Korean War

1961–73 Vietnam War

unemployment, poverty, alcoholism, and crime. "I was heading down a road that was filled with wine, whiskey and booze," Banks later recalled. "Then I landed in prison." In 1966 he was convicted for burglarizing a grocery store and began serving 31 months of a three-and-a-half-year sentence in Stillwater State Penitentiary, in Minnesota. In prison, Banks met fellow convict Clyde Bellecourt, also an Ojibwa. The two men and others founded AIM in July 1968 with several goals in mind. They wanted to address the problems that beset their people and find solutions to basic needs such as housing and employment. To help Native Americans live successfully off reservations, they would start so-called survival schools. But fundamentally, they wanted to preserve their vanishing culture. AIM's emblem was an upside-down U.S. flag, what Banks called the international distress signal for people in trouble.

When the first AIM chapter started in Minneapolis in 1968, Banks would often use a police radio to guide him to the scene when officers were arresting Native Americans. Intending to prevent police abuses, he was frequently arrested on charges of interference. This kind of tough, streetwise advocacy helped spread the movement, making Banks, Bellecourt, and another AIM leader, Russell Means, heroes to many of their generation.

Over the next four years, the movement spread to all 50 states and to Canada. The organization's political message had widespread appeal for Native Americans who felt betrayed by the federal government's Indian Reorganization Act. Not only was this new deal perceived as no deal, but many believed that it opened the way for massive federal land grabs of Indian territory on which valuable minerals were located. Banks and his fellow leaders decided to reclaim former Indian territory, announcing that they would symbolically "retake the country from west to east" like the "wagon train in reverse."

The militancy of their claims was soon demonstrated. In its first act of protest, on November 4, 1969, AIM seized the abandoned federal prison on Alcatraz Island, in San Francisco Bay, California. Two hundred activists claimed the island as free Indian land and demanded that an educational and cultural center be established there. In ironic press statements, they announced the establishment

of a Bureau of Caucasian Affairs and offered to pay the U.S. government $24, in mockery of the 1626 purchase of Manhattan Island from Indians by Dutch settlers. The occupation, which lasted 19 months, stirred up considerable publicity. The U.S. House of Representatives passed a JOINT RESOLUTION directing President RICHARD M. NIXON to negotiate with the activists, but his administration's offer to build a park on the island was laughed off. U.S. marshals ultimately arrested the activists still on the island in June 1971.

In April 1971 Banks led several AIM members in a week-long takeover of the Fort Snelling Military Base, in St. Paul. Seizing an abandoned building, the group announced that it intended to start an Indian survival school there. Senator Walter F. Mondale agreed to negotiate with Banks, but before he could, a federal Special WEAPONS and Tactics (SWAT) unit arrested the protesters. Around the United States, other occupations of government property took place as AIM chapters demonstrated against broken treaties. As a white backlash against the protests began, several Indians were beaten or shot. Charges of MANSLAUGHTER brought against white attackers usually ended in acquittal, inflaming the Indian movement. It maintained that little or no help was forthcoming from the BIA or the FBI.

In response, car caravans converged on Washington, D.C., on November 2, 1972, in a protest rally dubbed the Trail of Broken Treaties. AIM presented a 20-point proposal demanding that the government revamp the BIA, recognize Indian sovereignty, restore the power of Indians to negotiate treaties, and create a review board to study treaty violations. A group of 400 protesters seized the BIA building; clashed with riot squads; and, renaming the facility the Native American Embassy, ransacked files that Banks said contained evidence of federal mistreatment of Indians. Banks told reporters, "We are trying to bring about some meaningful change for the Indian community. If this is the only action that will bring change, then you can count on demonstrations like this 365 days a year." On November 6, the Nixon White House agreed to negotiate. After two days, Banks's followers departed in return for the appointment of a special panel to investigate conditions on Indian reservations. But within a week after the takeover, federal funding was cut off for three of AIM's survival schools.

In early 1973, a turning point occurred in Banks's life and the direction of AIM. On

WHAT WE HAVE DONE, WE DID FOR THE SEVENTH GENERATION TO COME.... WE DID NOT DO THESE THINGS FOR OURSELVES ... [BUT] SO THAT THE SEVENTH GENERATION MAY BE BORN FREE.
—DENNIS BANKS

February 6, he led an AIM protest 200 strong in Custer, South Dakota, after a white man accused of killing an Indian in a barroom brawl was charged with INVOLUNTARY MANSLAUGHTER. Banks met with local officials, but when the slain man's mother, Sarah Bad Heart Bull, tried to enter the courthouse, she and other Native Americans were beaten by the police. A riot ensued, in which AIM members set fire to police cars and the chamber of commerce office. For his role in the Custer incident, Banks was charged with ARSON, BURGLARY, and malicious damage to a public building, all of which he denied. But his radicalization was complete. "We had reached a point in history where we could not tolerate the abuse any longer," Banks later explained, "where mothers could not tolerate the mistreatment that goes on on the reservations any longer, they could not see another Indian youngster die."

Three weeks later, Banks, Means, and other AIM members took over the town of Wounded Knee on the Pine Ridge Reservation in South Dakota. For Native Americans, the town has a bitter place in history: it is the site where, in 1890, 300 unarmed Sioux men, women, and children were massacred by the Seventh Cavalry of the U.S. Army. Banks and Means hoped to invoke this symbolism by seizing the town by armed force and issuing new demands. They wanted the federal government to investigate the BIA and to address treaty violations, and they denounced recent tribal elections as corrupt manipulations by white U.S. citizens. As national attention focused on the growing army of some three hundred FBI agents and U.S. marshals, and the armored personnel carriers surrounding the militants' fortifications, gunfire was frequently exchanged. Over 71 days, while the government ordered surrender without AMNESTY, the town was held. "We laid down our weapons at Wounded Knee," Banks told the press from within the stronghold, recalling the 1890 massacre. "Those weapons weren't just bows and guns, but also a sense of pride."

The takeover ended on May 9, 1973. Pentagon documents later revealed that the U.S. Army had readied a vast military arsenal to clear out AIM members, including more than 170,000 rounds of ammunition, grenade launchers, explosives, gas, helicopters, and jets. In the end, however, casualties were limited: two Native Americans were killed and several wounded; three members of the government forces were wounded, including one agent who was paralyzed. As a condition of surrendering, AIM was once again promised a federal investigation of its demands, but none was forthcoming.

Banks and Means were prosecuted on ten felony counts each in a dramatic eight-month trial in St. Paul, during which federal marshals used mace on courtroom spectators. The defendants alleged that their takeover of Wounded Knee was justified by the government's violations of the 1868 Treaty of Fort Laramie—a pact in which the Sioux Indians had been promised government protection for ending their armed resistance. But the case against Means and Banks foundered on revelations that the FBI had used illegal wiretaps and had changed documents, among other illegalities, in mounting its prosecution. On September 16, 1974, all charges were dismissed.

Although Banks acted as a negotiator during the mid-1970s, settling disputes between Native Americans and authorities, other aspects of his life soon changed for the worse. In July 1975 a South Dakota jury convicted him on charges of riot and assault with a deadly weapon for his role in the 1973 riot at the Custer County Courthouse. The conviction carried a maximum sentence of 15 years in prison. Before sentencing, Banks heard prison guards say he would not last 20 minutes in the South Dakota State Penitentiary. He fled, only to be arrested by FBI agents on January 23, 1976, in northern California. A massive petition movement supported by the actors Jane Fonda and Marlon Brando appealed to Governor Brown on Banks's behalf. Brown reduced Banks's bail, refused EXTRADITION requests from South Dakota, and informed authorities there that he was protecting Banks because of sworn statements that Banks's life would be endangered if he were imprisoned. Banks lived freely in California, serving as chancellor of the two-year Indian college Deganawidah-Quetzalcoatl University, until the 1983 inauguration of Republican governor George Deukmejian ended his asylum.

Banks then took sanctuary on the Onondaga Reservation in New York. Because reservations in the state are not under federal jurisdiction, the FBI chose not to arrest him as long as he remained there.

After nine years as a fugitive, Banks gave himself up to state authorities in South Dakota in fall 1984. His request for clemency was denied, and he was sentenced to three years in prison. After his PAROLE on December 9, 1985, he spent time on the Pine Ridge Reservation, where, through his success at persuading Honeywell and other companies to locate factories there, employment doubled. But his legal troubles continued. Banks had been charged with illegal POSSESSION of dynamite stemming from the 1975 arrest of his wife, Kamook Nichols. A lower court dismissed the charges in 1983 on the ground that Banks and three other defendants had been denied their SIXTH AMENDMENT right to a SPEEDY TRIAL, and a second federal court upheld the ruling. But on January 21, 1986, the members of the U.S. Supreme Court, in a 5–4 vote, held that their rights had not been violated, because they were free without bail and not under indictment during the 90-month delay in their prosecution. Banks pleaded guilty on March 8, 1988, and received five years' probation. Also in 1988, Banks's autobiography *Sacred Soul* was published.

In 1994 Banks led the four-month "Walk for Justice." The purpose of the trek from Alcatraz Island in San Francisco to Washington, D.C., was to publicize current issues regarding Native Americans.

Banks continued to serve as director of Sacred Run, an organization he founded in 1978 to address Native American spiritual concerns. Since then the Run has become an international, multicultural event that carries the message of the sacredness of life and of humankind's relationship to the earth. By 1996 Banks had led runners over 58,000 miles through the United States, Canada, Europe, Japan, Australia, and New Zealand.

Banks has had roles in movies including *War Party, The Last of the Mohicans,* and *Thunderheart.* A musical cassette, *Still Strong,* featuring Banks's original work as well as traditional Native American songs, was completed in 1993 and a music video with the same name was released in 1995.

As of 2009, Banks continues working toward the release of Leonard Peltier. Peltier, an Ojibwa whom Banks considers to be a political prisoner, was convicted in 1977 of the MURDER of two FBI agents during a gunfight in Oglala, North Dakota. In addition to supporting the Peltier defense and other issues concerning Native Americans, Banks sits on the board of directors for the Nowa Cumig Institute and travels and lectures in the United States and abroad.

FURTHER READINGS

Banks, Dennis J., with Richard Erdoes. 2004. *Ojibwa Warrior: Dennis Banks and the Rise of the American Indian Movement.* Norman, Oklahoma: University of Oklahoma Press.

Churchill, Ward. 1988. *Agents of Repression: The FBI's Secret Wars against the Black Panther Party and the American Indian Movement.* Boston: South End Press.

Sayer, John William. 1997. *Ghost Dancing the Law: The Wounded Knee Trials.* Cambridge: Harvard Univ. Press.

Smith, Paul, and Robert Warrior. 1997. *Like a Hurricane: The Indian Movement from Alcatraz to Wounded Knee.* New York: New Press.

Weyler, Rex. 1982. *Blood of the Land: The Government and Corporate War against the American Indian Movement.* New York: Everest House.

CROSS REFERENCE

Native American Rights.

BAR ASSOCIATION

An organization of lawyers established to promote professional competence, enforce standards of ethical conduct, and encourage a spirit of public service among members of the legal profession.

The mission of a bar association is frequently described in the words of ROSCOE POUND, legal scholar and dean of Harvard Law School from 1916 to 1936: "[To] promote and maintain the PRACTICE OF LAW as a profession, that is, as a learned art pursued in the spirit of a public service—in the spirit of a service of furthering the administration of justice through and according to law."

Bar associations accomplish these objectives by offering continuing education for lawyers in the form of publications and seminars. This education includes instruction on recent developments in the law and managing a law practice successfully as a business. Bar associations encourage members to offer PRO BONO legal services (to provide legal services at no cost to members of society who cannot afford them). The associations develop guidelines and rules relating to ethics and PROFESSIONAL RESPONSIBILITY and enforce sanctions for violation of rules governing lawyer conduct. They also offer attorneys the opportunity to meet socially to discuss employment prospects and legal theories.

The International Bar Association, based in London, is for lawyers and law firms involved in the practice of INTERNATIONAL LAW. In the United States, bar associations exist on the national, state, and local levels. Examples are the AMERICAN BAR ASSOCIATION (ABA) and the FEDERAL BAR

ASSOCIATION on the national level, the New Jersey State Bar Association and the Florida Bar Association on the state level, and the New York City Bar Association on the local level. Some law schools have student bar associations for the student body as a whole, and distinct, smaller bar associations for students with a common ethnic background or an interest in a specific area of practice.

In a majority of states, membership in the state bar association is mandatory for those licensed to practice law. When lawyers are required to join the bar in order to practice law, the bar is said to be integrated, or unified. Integration is generally accomplished by the enactment of a statute giving the highest court of the state the authority to integrate the bar, or by rule of that court in the exercise of its inherent power. In effect, lawyers are not free to resign from an INTEGRATED BAR, because by doing so, they lose the privilege to practice law.

The modern U.S. bar association traces its beginnings to the mid-nineteenth century. At that time, the practice of law was largely unregulated. People in need of legal services had no assurance that the lawyers they hired had had even minimum legal training. To address this situation, leaders of the legal profession began to organize self-governing bar associations to establish standards of education and of professional conduct. The first Code of Professional Ethics was formulated by the Alabama State Bar Association in 1887. The ABA Canons of Professional Ethics followed in 1908, and were subsequently adopted in whole or in part throughout the United States. These canons were revised and expanded in 1969, as the Model Code of Professional Responsibility, and again in 1983, as the Model Rules of Professional Conduct. The ABA amends the Model Rules periodically as necessary, and states are free to determine whether to adopt these amendments.

In addition to the rules, both the ABA and state bar associations issue ethics opinions, which are advisory statements regarding the application of an ethical rule. Although these opinions are not binding as law, they are often persuasive when reviewed by a court.

Major issues of concern to bar associations in the 2000s included:

- A perceived decline in professionalism among lawyers, manifested by a decline in civility and professional courtesy.

- The preservation of due process and other constitutional rights in light of the wave of international anti-terrorism sentiment.

- A conflict between lawyers' ethical responsibilities and their business interests. Critics within and outside the legal profession complain that some lawyers seek out clients using unethical methods, and engage in LITIGATION of questionable merit in the pursuit of personal profit rather than in the interests of justice.

- The politicization of bar associations and the preservation of judicial independence. On some occasions, bar associations have taken positions on hotly contested social and political issues. Critics argue that the conflict within the membership over these issues distracts bar associations from their primary duty of regulating the practice of law.

- Tort law reform. Bar associations continue to oppose any enactment of federal legislation that would preempt state tort law in such areas as PRODUCT LIABILITY, medical LIABILITY, and automobile liability, including federal initiatives aimed at creating maximum allowable damages in tort cases.

FURTHER READINGS

American Bar Association. Available online at https://www. abanet.org/home.html (accessed May 16, 2009).

Hamilton, Bruce. 1995. "What Makes a Great Bar Association." *Arizona Attorney* (January).

Martin, Peter A. 1989. "A Reassessment of Mandatory State Bar Membership in Light of *Levine v. Heffernan.*" *Marquette Law Review* 73 (fall).

Pound, Roscoe. 1953. *The Lawyer from Antiquity to Modern Times.* St. Paul, MN: West.

Warren, Kenneth J. 2003. "Multijurisdictional Practices Call for New Model Rules." *The Legal Intelligencer* (February 20).

Young, Don J., and Louise L. Hill. 1988. "Professionalism: The Necessity for Internal Control." *Temple Law Review* 61 (spring).

CROSS REFERENCE

Continuing Legal Education.

BAR EXAMINATION

The bar examination is a written test that an individual must pass before becoming licensed to practice law as an attorney. A license to practice law within a state or federal jurisdiction is generally premised upon admission to that jurisdiction's bar (a collective professional association of attorneys and counselors) by meeting its criteria, including passing that jurisdiction's bar examination.

Bar examinations are regulated by states, and their specific requirements vary from state to state. Generally, they cover numerous legal topics and consist of multiple-choice questions and/or essay questions; many jurisdictions additionally require a test designed to assess an examinee's fundamental lawyering skills in a hypothetical situation.

Each state has an interest in protecting its citizens by ensuring the quality and competency of lawyers who receive licenses to practice in the state. In addition to requiring bar candidates to pass a difficult and comprehensive test of substantive legal knowledge, most jurisdictions also require proof of graduation from an ACCREDITED LAW SCHOOL and successful completion of a character background review. With few exceptions, only people who satisfy these strict requirements and are licensed by a state bar may practice law in the licensing state. Critics of this system of ATTORNEY licensure argue that its true purpose is to reduce competition between lawyers by regulating the number of lawyers admitted to the bar.

Historically, lawyers have played an active role in determining who, and how many, would join their ranks as members of the bar. This tradition predates the U.S. Constitution by more than six centuries, when English courts governed who would be allowed to practice law. Courts have long relied on the rationale that the integrity and competency of practicing attorneys directly affect the quality of justice dispensed.

The U.S. legal system has adopted this rationale. Before 1828, states allowed practicing attorneys to determine the competency of prospective attorneys. Strict rules developed by lawyers at that time typically required an individual to obtain a college degree and work several years as an attorney's apprentice before being admitted to the PRACTICE OF LAW. Because attorneys controlled who would get apprenticeships, the general public perceived the system as catering to the elite.

A decline of elitist attitudes surrounding the election of President ANDREW JACKSON in 1828 prompted a change in the attorney licensing system. State legislatures divested the authority granted attorneys and reclaimed control of bar admission standards, which became far less stringent and far less exclusive. Apprenticeships remained the most common form of legal study, but by 1860, only nine states required any form of LEGAL EDUCATION for ADMISSION TO THE BAR. Written bar examinations, when required, were cursory.

By the late 1800s, a surge in formal law schools spurred a decline in legal apprenticeship programs. A new wave of interest in improving standards of legal education and bar admission prompted the founding of the AMERICAN BAR ASSOCIATION in 1878 and the American Association of Law Schools in 1900. These groups encouraged tougher bar admission standards, including the requirement that all bar candidates complete a written examination used to assess their fitness to practice law. In the early 2000s, every state offers a bar examination.

Administrative bodies established in each state generally govern the standards and particularities of the bar examination. In keeping with the tradition of attorney self-regulation, these boards usually are made up, at least in part, of licensed attorneys. The boards determine what legal topics will be covered; what types of questions will be asked; what grading methods will be applied; and the locations, dates, and times of examinations. Nearly every state requires, as one component of the examination, the Multistate Bar Examination.

The Multistate Bar Examination contains 200 multiple-choice questions covering six legal topics: contracts, CONSTITUTIONAL LAW, CRIMINAL LAW and procedure, evidence, real property, and torts. Examinees have six hours to complete the exam, or 1.8 minutes for each question. This computer-graded test is offered twice per year, usually in February and July. The test questions change each time the examination is given, and score results from the multistate examination taken in one state may be transferred to other states' bar admissions committees. According to the National Conference of Bar Examiners (NCBE), as of 2008, only Louisiana and Washington did not include the multistate examination as part of their respective bar examinations. The average raw score, according to the NCBE, has hovered between 125 and 130 out of 200.

Most states also require bar candidates to complete a test of their knowledge of state laws. Examinees usually take this portion of the exam on the day before or after the Multistate Bar Examination. This state-specific examination often contains essay questions or multiple-choice questions or a combination of the two.

It may cover a different range of legal topics than does the Multistate Bar Examination, although some topics are duplicated by the two tests.

In addition, as of 2007 all states except Maryland, Washington, and Wisconsin require a passing score on the Multistate PROFESSIONAL RESPONSIBILITY Examination (MPRE), a standardized multiple-choice test of legal and professional ethics. Bar applicants normally take this two-hour test several weeks before or after they take the bar examination. The Multistate Professional Responsibility Examination tests the applicants' knowledge of the American Bar Association's Model Rules of Professional Conduct. Topics include attorney-client confidentiality, conflicts of interest, and attorney advertising.

In 2008 a total of 34 jurisdictions incorporated the Multistate Performance Test (MPT) as part of their bar examinations. This test was designed to assess an examinee's ability to complete fundamental legal tasks that most beginning lawyers face in real life practice. The MPT assesses an examinee's ability to sort factual materials, separating relevant from irrelevant facts; analyze statutory, case, and administrative materials to extract the relevant principles of law; apply the relevant law to the presented facts in a manner that would resolve a client's legal problem; address all ethical concerns; and communicate the legal issue and solution effectively in writing. The MPT is a timed examination, and each jurisdiction determines the relative weight to give this part of the examination along with the other scores.

Finally, several states include a Multistate Essay Examination (MEE) as part of their overall bar examinations. The MEE consists of 30-minute essay questions on a more expansive array of legal topics than the standard six topics covered in the 200-question multistate examination. These additional areas of law include business associations, evidence, FAMILY LAW, federal CIVIL PROCEDURE, trusts and estates, and the UNIFORM COMMERCIAL CODE (UCC). Fewer than 20 states were testing the MEE in 2007.

A steady rise in the number of persons taking bar examinations keeps competition tight. According to the National Conference of Bar Examiners, 80,319 applicants took a bar examination in 2008; 70,172 of them were first-time takers. Overall, 71 percent, or 56,915 examinees, passed. However, among first-time takers from American Bar Association (ABA)-approved law schools, 85 percent passed, whereas repeat-takers had only a 43 percent pass rate. The examination can be taken more than once. In rare cases, an attorney who has been disbarred or suspended can take a special bar examination for reinstatement. In 2008, only 20 disbarred or suspended attorneys across the United States took a reinstatement exam (seven, or 35 percent, passed).

In a few states, an attorney may be licensed to practice law without taking the state's bar examination. Wisconsin permits graduates of accredited Wisconsin law schools to become licensed attorneys without taking any bar examination. Other states offer reciprocity, by accepting Multistate Bar Examination scores attained in other jurisdictions or by waiving the bar examination requirement for experienced attorneys licensed in other jurisdictions.

Jurisdictions also differ in their approach to legal education requirements. Most states require bar applicants to graduate from law schools accredited by the American Bar Association (ABA). Some states, such as California and Georgia, will admit bar candidates who received law degrees from unaccredited law schools under certain circumstances. California, Maine, New York, Vermont, Virginia, Washington, and Wyoming do not require law degrees at all, but alternatively require several years of legal study—also known as reading law—with a licensed attorney. According to the NCBE, in 2008, 56,357 persons were admitted to bars by examination; 7,888 by court motion, and 468 by diploma privilege. Whatever the legal education requirements, all members of the bar must pass the bar examination.

FURTHER READINGS

American Bar Association/Bureau of National Affairs. 1995. *ABA/BNA Lawyers' Manual on Professional Conduct.*

Bosse, Diane F., and Lawrence M. Grosberg. 2003. "The Bar Exam: Should the Test Continue in Its Current Form or Are Alternatives Needed?" *New York Law Journal Magazine* 2 (April): 12.

Curcio, Andrea A. 2002. "A Better Bar: Why and How the Existing Bar Exam Should Change." *Nebraska Law Review* 81 (winter): 363–423.

Curriden, Mark. 1995. "Lawyers Who Skip Law School." *American Bar Association Journal* 81 (February).

Darrow-Kleinhaus, Suzanne. 2009. *The Bar Exam in a Nutshell.* 2d ed. St. Paul, Minn.: West Group.

Garth, Bryant G. 1983. "Rethinking the Legal Profession's Approach to Collective Self-Improvement: Competence and the Consumer Perspective." *Wisconsin Law Review* 1983.

Getz, Malcolm, John Siegfried, and Terry Calvani. 1981. "Competition at the Bar: The Correlation between the Bar Examination Pass Rate and the Profitability of Practice." *Virginia Law Review* 67.

National Conference of Bar Examiners, 2009. "2008 Statistics." *The Bar Examiner*, May. Text available online at http://www.ncbex.org/fileadmin/mediafiles/downloads/Bar_Admissions/2008_Stats.pdf; website home page: http://www.ncbex.org/bar-admissions/stats/ (accessed August 5, 2009).

Pobjecky, Thomas A. "The Florida Board of Bar Examiners: The Constitutional Safeguard between Attorney Aspirants and the Public." *Nova Law Review* 18.

Rogers, W. Sherman. 1989. "Title VII Preemption of State Bar Examinations: Applicability of Title VII to State Occupational Licensing Tests." *Howard Law Journal* 32.

"Society of American Law Teachers Statement on the Bar Exam, July 2002." 2002. *Journal of Legal Education* 52 (September): 446–52.

Philip Barbour.
GETTY IMAGES

❖ BARBOUR, PHILIP PENDLETON

Philip Pendleton Barbour, an ASSOCIATE JUSTICE of the U.S. Supreme Court, was a strong advocate of states' rights and the STRICT CONSTRUCTION of the Constitution.

The son of a wealthy planter from one of Virginia's oldest families, Barbour was born May 25, 1783, in Orange County, Virginia. He was educated locally and excelled in languages and classical literature. At seventeen, he became an apprentice to an Orange County lawyer. After less than a year clerking and studying law, Barbour left Virginia for Kentucky, where he practiced law for a short time. In 1801 he returned to Virginia to attend the College of William and Mary, in Williamsburg, where he briefly studied law. A year later he established a law practice in Orange County, and quickly gained a reputation for his outstanding oratorical abilities in the courtroom. In 1804 he married Frances Johnson, the daughter of a local planter, with whom he had seven children.

Barbour's family was both socially prominent and politically active. His father, Thomas Barbour, was a member of the Virginia House of Burgesses for many years, and his older brother became a Virginia governor, U.S. senator, and secretary of war under President JOHN QUINCY ADAMS, whose administration Barbour would eventually oppose. Encouraged by his father's and brother's successes, in 1812 Barbour ran for and won a seat in the Virginia House of Delegates. Two years later he won a seat in the U.S. Congress and aligned himself with a group of older Republicans who favored strict construction of the Constitution and a limited federal government. Barbour served as

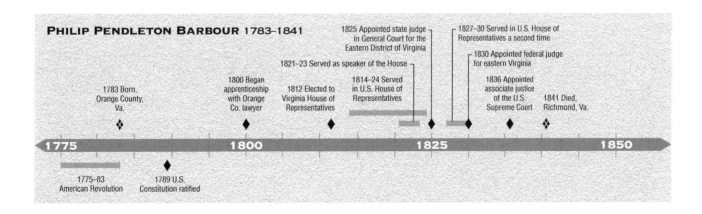

PHILIP PENDLETON BARBOUR 1783–1841

1775–83 American Revolution

1783 Born, Orange County, Va.

1789 U.S. Constitution ratified

1800 Began apprenticeship with Orange Co. lawyer

1812 Elected to Virginia House of Representatives

1814–24 Served in U.S. House of Representatives

1821–23 Served as speaker of the House

1825 Appointed state judge in General Court for the Eastern District of Virginia

1827–30 Served in U.S. House of Representatives a second time

1830 Appointed federal judge for eastern Virginia

1836 Appointed associate justice of the U.S. Supreme Court

1841 Died, Richmond, Va.

1775   1800   1825   1850

Speaker of the House from 1821 until 1823, when he was defeated by HENRY CLAY. In 1824 Barbour chose not to run for reelection to Congress, and returned to Virginia to resume his law practice.

During his career as a practicing ATTORNEY, Barbour was involved in a number of important cases. He argued the state's position before the U.S. Supreme Court in *Cohen v. Virginia*, 19 U.S. 264, 6 Wheat. 264, 5 L. Ed. 257 (1821), a landmark suit that helped to clarify the role of the federal courts in reviewing state court decisions. In *Cohen* the Court held that the federal judiciary could review cases arising in the state courts that involved constitutional issues. Though Barbour lost the case, his vigorous representation helped to further establish his reputation as a strong defender of the states against what he often saw as the growing encroachment of the federal government.

In 1825, after considering and then declining an offer from THOMAS JEFFERSON to join the law faculty at the University of Virginia, Barbour was appointed to the General Court for the Eastern District of Virginia, a state trial court, where he served for almost two years. In 1827, at the urging of his constituents, Barbour ran unopposed for Congress, though he lost the Speaker's race to fellow Virginian Andrew Stevenson. During his second stint in Congress, Barbour was a vocal opponent of President Adams, even though Barbour's brother James Barbour was a member of the Adams cabinet. Barbour objected to the administration's spending policies and to the imposition of a TARIFF in 1828. He also continued his relentless advocacy of states' rights and the narrow construction of the Constitution, introducing an unsuccessful bill in 1829 requiring that five of the seven justices on the U.S. Supreme Court concur in any decision involving a constitutional question.

In the late 1820s Barbour became a strong supporter of ANDREW JACKSON, who defeated the incumbent Adams in 1828. Barbour was considered for a position in the Jackson cabinet but was not appointed. In 1829 Barbour was chosen president of the Virginia Constitutional Convention, replacing the ailing JAMES MONROE. During the sometimes tumultuous convention, Barbour argued for APPORTIONMENT of representation based on both white population and property ownership, and argued that the latter should be a qualification for the right to vote. Barbour also sided with the conservative

WHAT IS SETTLED BY THE CONSTITUTION CANNOT BE ALTERED BY LAW.
—PHILIP BARBOUR

slaveholders in the eastern part of the state against citizens in the western part of the state who, opposed to SLAVERY, eventually formed a separate state, West Virginia.

Barbour's unwavering support of Jackson and his policies earned him an appointment as a federal judge for eastern Virginia in 1830. In 1832 he was briefly a candidate for VICE PRESIDENT against MARTIN VAN BUREN, even though Van Buren was Jackson's choice in his reelection bid. Barbour soon withdrew his candidacy to preserve party unity, and threw his support to Van Buren.

As early as 1831 Barbour was rumored to be next in line for a seat on the U.S. Supreme Court as soon as Jackson, now in his second term, had an opportunity to make an appointment. Nationalists, who disagreed with Barbour's states' rights and strict constructionist views, opposed Barbour as a possible candidate for the Court. In 1836 Barbour was nominated to succeed retiring justice Gabriel Duval, at the same time that ROGER B. TANEY was nominated as chief justice and confirmed to succeed JOHN MARSHALL, also retiring. As expected, Barbour's nomination drew criticism, but he was nevertheless confirmed by a vote of 30–11.

Barbour wrote only a dozen opinions for the Court. His most important majority opinion was in *City of New York v. Miln*, 36 U.S. 102, 11 Pet. 102, 9 L. Ed. 648 (1837). At issue in *Miln* was a New York state law requiring captains of vessels arriving at ports to provide harbor authorities with the names, ages, birthplaces, and occupations of arriving passengers. The Court considered whether the law was an unconstitutional invasion of the exclusive federal right to regulate interstate and international trade. The Court ruled that the law was a legitimate exercise of the state's "police power" to protect the health and welfare of its citizens. The decision provided the perfect opportunity for Barbour to expound upon his states' rights views. He wrote that the state not only had the right to impose such laws but also the "solemn duty . . . to advance the safety, happiness and prosperity of its people, and to provide for the GENERAL WELFARE, by any and every act of legislation, which it may deem to be conducive to these ends." The decision marked a significant departure from the philosophy of the previous Court, headed by Marshall, which had emphasized the importance of federal authority in matters that even indirectly involved interstate and international commerce. Though influential, *Miln* was criticized and limited by subsequent decisions of the Court.

In February 1841, at age 58, Barbour died suddenly of a heart attack. He thus served only five years on the Court, completing one of the shortest terms in its history.

FURTHER READINGS

Congressional Quarterly. 2004. *Guide to the U.S. Supreme Court.* 4th ed. Washington, D.C.: Congressional Quarterly.

Elliott, Stephen P., ed. 1986. *A Reference Guide to the United States Supreme Court.* New York: Facts on File.

Federal Judicial Center. Available online at http://www.fjc. gov (accessed August 28, 2009).

BARGAIN

A reciprocal understanding, contract, or agreement of any sort usually pertaining to the loan, sale, or exchange of property between two parties, one of whom wants to dispose of an item that the other wants to obtain. To work out the terms of an agreement; to negotiate in good faith for the purpose of entering into an agreement.

A union engages in COLLECTIVE BARGAINING on proposed contract terms.

BARGAINING AGENT

A union that possesses the sole authority to act on behalf of all the employees of a particular type in a company.

A bargaining agent is certified by the NATIONAL LABOR RELATIONS BOARD (NLRB) as the exclusive representative of a certain type of employee. The International Garment Workers Union, for example, might act as the bargaining agent for all seamstresses employed at a particular dress factory.

CROSS REFERENCES

Labor Law; Labor Union.

❖ BARLOW, FRANCIS CHANNING

Francis Channing Barlow achieved prominence as a lawyer and a soldier. Barlow was born October 19, 1834, in Brooklyn, New York. He graduated from Harvard in 1855, and was admitted to the New York bar in 1858. From 1859 to 1861, and also in 1866, Barlow practiced law.

At the onset of the Civil War in 1861, Barlow joined the Union Army and fought at various battles, including Fair Oaks, Antietam, Chancellorsville, and Spottsylvania. He was wounded at Gettysburg in 1863 but returned to service, and by the end of the war he had earned the rank of major general.

After the Civil War Barlow became SECRETARY OF STATE of New York, serving from 1865 to 1867, and 1869 to 1870. In 1869, he was U.S. marshal for the southern district of New York. He performed the duties of New York attorney general from 1871 to 1873, and was instrumental in the early proceedings concerning the prosecution of the Tweed Ring, a group of corrupt New York politicians.

Barlow returned to his law practice in 1874. In 1876 he participated in the investigation of the controversial Hayes-Tilden presidential election results. He died January 11, 1896, in New York City.

CROSS REFERENCE

Tammany Hall.

❖ BARR, WILLIAM PELHAM

William Pelham Barr served as attorney general of the United States from 1991 to 1993 under President GEORGE H.W. BUSH.

The son of Donald Barr and Mary Ahern Barr, WILLIAM BARR was born May 23, 1950, in

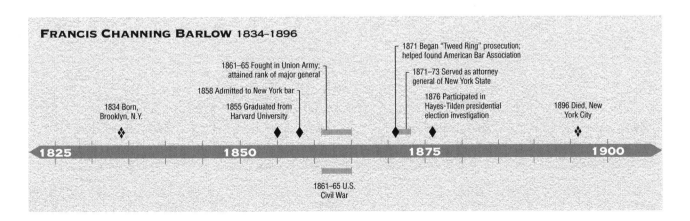

FRANCIS CHANNING BARLOW 1834–1896

1834 Born, Brooklyn, N.Y.

1855 Graduated from Harvard University

1858 Admitted to New York bar

1861–65 Fought in Union Army; attained rank of major general

1871 Began "Tweed Ring" prosecution; helped found American Bar Association

1871–73 Served as attorney general of New York State

1876 Participated in Hayes-Tilden presidential election investigation

1896 Died, New York City

1825   1850   1875   1900

1861–65 U.S. Civil War

William Pelham Barr.
AP IMAGES

New York City, and was schooled there. He completed an undergraduate degree at New York's Columbia University in 1971 and began a two-year master's program in Chinese studies. Armed with his graduate degree, he moved to Washington, D.C., in 1973 and went to work as a staff officer with the CENTRAL INTELLIGENCE AGENCY (CIA). He was accompanied by his wife, Christine Moynihan, to whom he was married on June 23, 1973.

While working at the CIA, Barr enrolled in the night program at George Washington University Law School. He earned his law degree in 1977, graduating second in his class.

After law school, he clerked for one year with the presiding judge of the District of Columbia Circuit Court. He was admitted to the Virginia bar in 1977 and to the District of Columbia bar in 1978. Also in 1978, Barr accepted an associate position at the Washington, D.C., law firm of Shaw, Pittman, Potts, and Trowbridge. There he concentrated on civil LITIGATION and federal administrative practice.

In 1982 Barr was named to President Ronald Reagan's Domestic Policy Council. During his two years of service, he became well known and respected by the administration and leaders in the REPUBLICAN PARTY. Barr returned to Shaw, Pittman in 1984, to resume his legal career. He was made a partner of the firm in 1985.

After several years in private practice, Barr reentered public service in 1989, when he was named assistant attorney general by the George H. W. Bush administration. He took over the Justice Department's Office of Legal Counsel, where his role was to advise the White House and the attorney general and other administration officials. Historically, the Office of Legal Counsel has been called upon to reassure presidents that their intended actions are within the law.

As assistant attorney general Barr authored two controversial advisory opinions that allowed President Bush to expand his war on drugs and to apprehend Panamanian drug lord Manuel Noriega. One opinion (13 U.S. Op. Off. Legal Counsel 387) held that U.S. military forces could be assigned to law enforcement operations abroad, and the other (13 U.S. Op. Off. Legal Counsel 195) that the president had authority to order the FEDERAL BUREAU OF INVESTIGATION (FBI) to arrest fugitives overseas without consent of the local government.

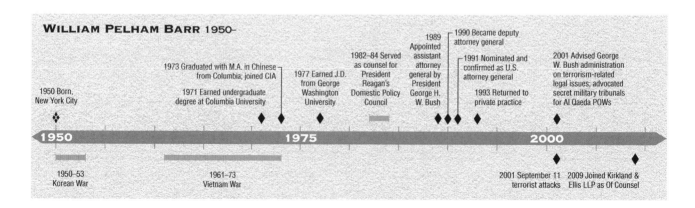

WILLIAM PELHAM BARR 1950–

1950 Born, New York City

1971 Earned undergraduate degree at Columbia University

1973 Graduated with M.A. in Chinese from Columbia; joined CIA

1977 Earned J.D. from George Washington University

1982–84 Served as counsel for President Reagan's Domestic Policy Council

1989 Appointed assistant attorney general by President George H. W. Bush

1990 Became deputy attorney general

1991 Nominated and confirmed as U.S. attorney general

1993 Returned to private practice

2001 Advised George W. Bush administration on terrorism-related legal issues; advocated secret military tribunals for Al Qaeda POWs

1950 ◆ 1975 ◆ 2000

1950–53 Korean War

1961–73 Vietnam War

2001 September 11 terrorist attacks

2009 Joined Kirkland & Ellis LLP as Of Counsel

Barr was named deputy attorney general in 1990. He became acting attorney general in June 1991 when RICHARD THORNBURGH resigned to enter the race for a U.S. Senate seat in Pennsylvania. Barr was nominated and confirmed as attorney general in the fall of 1991, becoming, at age forty-one, the youngest person to hold that post since Ramsey Clark, who was appointed in 1967.

After years of unpleasant and adversarial relationships with Attorneys General EDWIN MEESE III and Thornburgh, Congress welcomed Barr's appointment. Members of Congress praised his candor and cooperation, and they supported his decision to launch internal investigations into the Justice Department's handling of the Bank of Credit and Commerce International (BCCI) scandal and the Inslaw computer scandal. BCCI was shut down by bank regulators in 1991 for massive FRAUD, THEFT, MONEY LAUNDERING, and the financing of arms deals and terrorist activities. Depositors lost billions when the bank's assets were seized. Inslaw, Inc., accused the JUSTICE DEPARTMENT of conspiring to steal its proprietary software after the company's government contract had been revoked.

The AMERICAN BAR ASSOCIATION was encouraged by Barr's willingness to reconsider a Thornburgh decision that prevented local bar associations from interviewing judicial nominees, and an editorial in the November 25, 1991, issue of National Law Journal praised the department planned by the new attorney general as less political, more open, and more "inclined toward integrity" than the departments run by his immediate predecessors in the RONALD REAGAN and George H. W. Bush administrations.

However, Barr's honeymoon with the Democratic Congress and the nation's legal press did not last. Barr was soon criticized for his inability to obtain CIA cooperation in the BCCI and Banca Nationale del Lavoro (BNL) investigations and for delays in closing down the BCCI. A CIA investigation revealed that an Atlanta, Georgia, branch of the BNL had provided fraudulent loans to Iraq—loans that helped Saddam Hussein to build his military strength. Barr's internal investigation of the theft of an Inslaw-developed computer program by government officials was tagged a whitewash. He angered Japanese officials when he announced a

change in antitrust policy that allowed the Justice Department to bring cases against Japanese cartels that restricted U.S. exports. Moreover, Barr fought popular opinion and strong evidence of improprieties by the Justice Department when he continued to support the deportation of John Demjanjuk—wrongly accused of being the infamous Nazi death camp guard who was called Ivan the Terrible.

Finally, Barr took the unprecedented step of denying a congressional request for an independent investigation into the events known as Iraqgate. Barr said he and the Justice Department would conduct their own investigation to determine whether anyone in the Bush administration had committed a crime by giving aid to Saddam Hussein prior to the Iraqi invasion of Kuwait and the resulting Persian Gulf War.

Ongoing questions about the administration's knowledge of, and involvement in, Iraqgate contributed to Bush's defeat in the presidential election of 1992 and ended Barr's tenure as the nation's attorney general.

In spite of his bright beginning, Barr was unable to depart significantly from the agendas and operational styles of his predecessors and the presidents they served. According to the December 7, 1992 issue of National Law Journal, "Under Presidents Reagan and Bush and their Attorneys General Ed Meese, Dick Thornburgh and WILLIAM P. BARR, the nation witnessed the politicization of the JUSTICE DEPARTMENT beyond anything that has gone before".

In 1993 Barr returned to Shaw, Pittman and resumed the PRACTICE OF LAW. At the time, he was a member of the American Bar Association, the Virginia State Bar Association, and the District of Columbia Bar Association.

Barr later joined Verizon Communications, a provider of phone services, as head of its legal department. Under his leadership, the department developed a high percentage of minority and women attorneys and employees. The legal department of New York-based Verizon Communications was named the 2002 Northeast Region Employer of Choice by the Minority Corporate Counsel Association (MCCA).

In 2001, as the competition between local phone companies and other digital subscriber line (DSL) providers grew, Barr instituted a lawsuit against DSL provider Covad Communications.

I DON'T CARE HOW MUCH POLITICAL PRESSURE IS BROUGHT TO BEAR ... [OR THAT] THE OP-EDS [AND] JOURNALISTS ARE SAYING ... IT'S NOT FAST ENOUGH FOR THEM. THE STANDARD WILL STAY WHERE IT IS.
—WILLIAM BARR

The suit, which claimed that Covad employees had made false reports that Verizon had obstructed Covad's installation services, was dismissed by a federal district court judge in November 2002.

While working for Verizon, Barr lectured to groups such as the Federalist Society and offered advice to the administration of GEORGE W. BUSH concerning legal measures against TERRORISM.

Barr retired from Verizon Communications in late 2008, after serving as executive VICE PRESIDENT. While at Verizon, he led the legal, regulatory, and government affairs group. In early 2009 he joined Kirkland & Ellis LLP in an Of Counsel capacity, in its Washington, D.C., office.

FURTHER READINGS

Baker, Nancy V. 1992. *Conflicting Loyalties: Law and Politics in the Attorney General's Office, 1789-1990.* Lawrence: Univ. Press of Kansas.

Department of Justice. 1991. *200th Anniversary of the Office of the Attorney General, 1789-1989.* Washington, D.C.: Department of Justice, Office of Attorney General and Justice Management Division.

Fletcher, Martin. 2001. "Terror Leaders Could Die By Firing Squad." *London Times.* (November 16).

"Legal Job No. 1." 1992. *National Law Journal* 15 (December 7).

BARRATRY

In criminal law, the frequent incitement of lawsuits and quarrels that is a punishable offense.

Barratry is most commonly applied to an ATTORNEY who attempts to bring about a lawsuit that will be profitable to her or him. Barratry is an offense both at COMMON LAW and under some state statutes. The broader common-law crime has been limited by certain statutes. An attorney who is overly officious in instigating or encouraging prosecution of groundless LITIGATION might be guilty of common barratry under a particular statute. The requirement for the crime of barratry is that repeated or persistent acts of litigation are performed by the accused. Barratry is generally a MISDEMEANOR punishable by fine or imprisonment. In the case of an attorney, disbarment is the usual punishment. Because few cases have been prosecuted, barratry is considered by the legal community at large to be an archaic crime. This is particularly true today due to a highly litigious atmosphere.

In maritime law, barratry is the commission of an act by the master or mariners of a vessel for an unlawful or fraudulent purpose that is contrary to the duty owed to the owners, by which act the owners SUSTAIN injury.

A form of barratry is misconduct of the master of a ship in taking commodities on board that subject the ship to SEIZURE for SMUGGLING. It is essential in barratry that a criminal act or intent exist on the part of the master or mariners which inures to their own benefit and causes injury to the owners of the ship.

BARRISTER

In English law, an attorney who has an exclusive right of argument in all the superior courts.

A barrister is a counselor who is learned in law and who has been admitted to plead at the bar. A barrister drafts the pleadings in all cases, with the exception of the simplest ones. Distinguished from an ATTORNEY, which is an English lawyer who conducts matters out of court, a barrister engages in the actual argument of cases or the conduct of the trial.

BARRON V. BALTIMORE

In *Barron v. City of Baltimore*, 32 U.S. (7 Pet.) 243, 8 L.Ed. 672 (U.S. 1833), the U.S. Supreme Court ruled that the FIFTH AMENDMENT to the U.S. Constitution bound only the federal government and was thus inapplicable to actions taken by state and local governments. In 1868 the states ratified the FOURTEENTH AMENDMENT in part to nullify the Supreme Court's holding in *Barron v. Baltimore.* However, it was not until the twentieth century when the Supreme Court made most of the federal BILL OF RIGHTS applicable to the states.

The case arose when John Barron, owner of the largest and most profitable wharf in the eastern section of Baltimore, Maryland, sued the city for losses his wharf had allegedly suffered as a result of silting. When Barron had originally purchased the wharf, the wharf enjoyed the deepest waters in the area. However, in 1815 Baltimore had undertaken a major plan to renovate and modernize the city by building embankments, grading roads, and paving streets.

To facilitate this plan, the city began diverting water streams from a range of hills around the city into the wharf. In the seven years leading up to Barron's lawsuit, Baltimore experienced a number of violent rainstorms, causing the streams to fill with sand, mud, and earth from the newly graded roads and abutting embankments. The silt eventually poured into Barron's wharf, making the water so shallow that it was no longer accessible by larger ships. By 1822, the year Barron filed suit, the harbor had lost almost its entire value as a commercial wharf.

At trial in the Baltimore County Courthouse, Barron claimed that the city appropriated his private property for a public use without providing him JUST COMPENSATION, as he said was required by the Takings Clause of Fifth Amendment to the U.S. Constitution. The trial court agreed and awarded Barron $4,500 in damages. The city appealed, and a Maryland appellate court reversed. Barron then petitioned the U.S. Supreme Court by WRIT of error and review was granted. Chief Justice JOHN MARSHALL delivered the Court's unanimous opinion.

The sole issue before the Court was whether the Fifth Amendment to the federal Constitution applied to actions taken by state and local governmental entities. The federal Constitution "was ordained and established by the people of the United States for themselves, for their own government, and not for the government of the individual states," Marshall wrote. When the Founding Fathers made an exception to this rule in particular provisions of the U.S. Constitution, Marshall said, they made clear that those provisions were in fact applicable to the states. For example, Marshall observed that section 10 of Article I provides that "No State shall ... pass any Bill of Attainder." Yet none of the first Ten Amendments to the U.S. Constitution makes any similar reference to STATE ACTION, Marshall reasoned, evincing the Founding Fathers clear intent to make the Bill of Rights applicable only against the federal government.

"Each state established a constitution for itself, and in that constitution, provided such limitations and restrictions on the powers of its particular government, as its judgment dictated," the chief justice continued. If Barron's property interests were harmed by the city, then he was required to rely on state or local law to vindicate his rights. Neither the Fifth Amendment nor any other provision in the Bill of Rights was applicable to his lawsuit, Marshall concluded, and U.S. Supreme Court lacked jurisdiction to take any further action. Accordingly, Marshall dismissed the suit.

Barron v. Baltimore signaled a retreat from Marshall's earlier opinions that had expanded the scope and application of the federal Constitution, a change that reflected the growing states' rights movement over the issue of SLAVERY. Although *Barron v. Baltimore* was reaffirmed 12 years later in *Permoli v. New Orleans*, 44 U.S. (3 How.) 589, 11 L.Ed. 739 (1845), the Union's victory in the Civil War marked the beginning of the end for *Barron* as a valid and binding PRECEDENT.

In 1868 the states ratified the Fourteenth Amendment, which provides that no state shall "deprive any person of ... DUE PROCESS OF LAW ... [or] EQUAL PROTECTION of the laws." During the Congressional debates, JOHN BINGHAM, a Republican representative from Ohio and the primary architect of the Fourteenth Amendment, argued that enacting the Fourteenth Amendment was necessary to nullify the Supreme Court's holding in *Barron v. Baltimore.*

Despite Bingham's stated intentions, the Bill of Rights was not made applicable to the states through the doctrine of selective incorporation until the twentieth century. Under this doctrine, the Supreme Court has ruled that every protection contained in the Bill of Rights—except for the right to bear arms, the right to an indictment by a GRAND JURY, the right to trial by jury in civil cases, and the right against quartering soldiers—must be protected by state governments under the Equal Protection and Due Process Clauses of the Fourteenth Amendment.

The Supreme Court has explained that each of the incorporated rights is "deeply rooted in the nation's history," and is "fundamental" to the concept of "ordered liberty" embodied in the Due Process Clause. *Palko v. Connecticut*, 302 U.S. 319, 58 S. Ct. 149, 82 L.Ed. 288 (1937). Any state that denies one of these rights to its residents violates its duty to provide "equal protection of the laws" guaranteed to the residents of every state. States may provide their residents with more constitutional protection than is afforded by the U.S. Bill of Rights, but the Fourteenth Amendment prohibits any state from providing its residents with less protection.

FURTHER READINGS

Amar, Akhil Reed. 1992. "The Bill of Rights and the Fourteenth Amendment." *Yale Law Journal* 101.

Jenkins, Ray. 1987. "Amendable Constitution Allows for Corrections of Framer's Errors." *Los Angeles Daily Journal* (June 4).

Papenfuse, Edward C. 2006. *Outline, Notes and Documents Concerning Barron v. Baltimore, 32 U.S. 243*. Available online at http://mdhistory.net/msaref06/barron/index. html; website home page: http://mdhistory.net (accessed August 28, 2009).

BARTER

The exchange of goods or services without the use of money as currency.

Barter is a contract wherein parties trade goods or commodities for other goods, as opposed to sale or exchange of goods for money. Barter is not applicable to contracts involving land, but solely to contracts relating to goods and services. For example, when a tenant exchanges the performance of various maintenance tasks around a house for free room and board, a barter has taken place.

BASE FEE

An interest in real property that has the potential to last forever, provided a specific contingency does not occur.

For example, a grantee might be given an estate in blackacre, "provided the land is not used for illegal purposes."

This type of fee is also known as a *conditional, determinable,* or *qualified fee.*

BASE LINE

Survey line used in the government survey to establish township lines. Horizontal elevation line used as a centerline in a highway survey.

BASEBALL

Although certain laws have protected citizens for decades from various forms of monopolistic practices, the legal decisions surrounding "America's favorite pastime" have allowed it to be exempt from most forms of government intervention. Through the years, Major League Baseball (MLB) has escaped measures that would have ended its exclusive control over contracts and copyrights and its all-around monopoly on professional U.S. baseball. Meanwhile, as contracts and team expenditures have run well into the millions of dollars, many have come to see baseball as less of a sport and more of a business—and a business that should be regulated. Americans still revere baseball, but fans, players, and owners all hope that government decisions will save the game from labor strikes and a host of other ills. The federal government, however, has done little other than let baseball remain a special, nationally protected institution.

The growth of professional baseball—and some of its headaches—followed a natural economic progression. Much about the sport's origin is shrouded in myth, but the sport is thought to have begun sometime in the nineteenth century. The first organized contest probably took place on June 19, 1846, between two amateur teams: the New York Nine and the Knickerbockers. In 1869 the Cincinnati Red Stockings, a professional team, paved the way for other franchises to develop. In 1871 the National Association of Professional Base Ball Players was born. The National League of Professional Base Ball Clubs was formed in 1876, and baseball has been both a game and profitable enterprise ever since.

From baseball's early days, the courts have failed to see the game as posing a threat to business laws. The Sherman Antitrust Act of 1890 (15 U.S.C.A. § 1 et seq.)—a statute prohibiting monopolies—forbids undue RE-STRAINT OF TRADE on commerce between states. In 1920, an appeals court ruled that baseball is unobjectionable in part because it operates on an interstate level (*National League of Professional Baseball Clubs v. Federal Baseball Club of Baltimore,* 50 App. D.C. 165, 269 F. 681). It stated, in general reference to other forms of trade and commerce, that "the Sherman Antitrust Act . . . does not apply, unless the effect of the act complained of on interstate commerce is direct, not merely indirect or incidental." Baseball, the court found, did not pose a threat to the economy of the world of sports.

The *National League* case stemmed from allegations made by the Federal League's Baltimore Terrapins. In the early 1900s the struggling Federal League sought to be a venture of the major leagues and competed with other major league franchises. But the National and American Leagues bought out many of the Federal teams, sometimes player by player. The Terrapins, one of the last surviving teams in the Federal League, sued the National League. Representatives of the Terrapins argued that MLB owners had treated the Terrapins with scorn, offering the team only $50,000 in settlement for damages incurred by the buyouts. In court, the Terrapins argued that MLB had violated antitrust laws and had participated in monopolizing ventures.

The case made it all the way to the U.S. Supreme Court (*National League,* 259 U.S. 200,

42 S. Ct. 465, 66 L. Ed. 898 [1922]). In 1922, in an opinion written by Justice Oliver Wendell Holmes Jr., the Supreme Court declared baseball to be, first and foremost, a sport and not a business. In Holmes's words, baseball activities were "purely state affairs." The decision gave baseball the unique status of being the only official professional sports organization to be exempt from antimonopoly laws. In effect, the decision protected baseball as a national treasure.

The *National League* decision was reaffirmed in 1953 with *Toolson v. New York Yankees* (346 U.S. 356, 74 S. Ct. 78, 98 L. Ed. 64). In a brief statement, the Court ruled against the PLAINTIFF, minor league player George Toolson. Toolson's arguments were based on the complaint that baseball was a monopoly that offered him unfair contract deals. The Court said Congress alone had been given the right to exercise powers that could break up the structure of baseball's professional organization.

The controversial issue in *Toolson* was baseball's reserve clause, the earliest symbol of the sport's underlying business nature. The reserve clause stated that once a player had accepted a contract to play for a certain team, the player was bound to serve that team for one year and must enter into a new contract with the same team "for the succeeding season at a salary to be determined by the parties to such contract." It was agreed that if a player violated the reserve clause, he would be guilty of "contract jumping" and would be ineligible to serve in any club of the leagues until formally reinstated.

The reserve clause guaranteed players little more than an income. Players attacked it. In the 1970s, Curtis C. Flood, center fielder for the St. Louis Cardinals, brought charges against Bowie K. Kuhn, acting commissioner of baseball. The issue was a player's FREE AGENCY, which Flood had requested and Kuhn had denied. Free agency is the option to negotiate a contract with any team, basically a release from the reserve clause. Taking his case to the Supreme Court, Flood argued that the reserve clause unfairly prevented him from striking deals with other teams that would pay him more for his services. The Supreme Court decided on June 19, 1972, that it did not have the authority to act (*Flood v. Kuhn*, 407 U.S. 258, 92 S. Ct. 2099, 32 L. Ed. 2d 728). Only

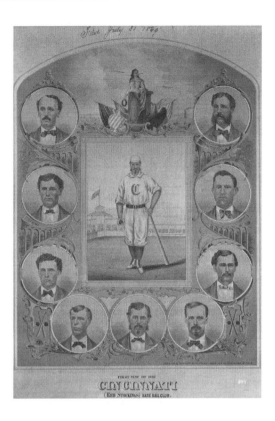

With a payroll of approximately $11,000, the 1869 Cincinnati Red Stockings were the first professional baseball team.

LIBRARY OF CONGRESS

baseball's acting commissioner could designate free agency.

Player discontent, as a reaction to the decision, set the stage for more free agency bids, and ARBITRATION between players and owners began in 1973. In January 1976, Andy Messersmith succeeded in obtaining free agency, which ushered in a new era of high stakes: Players could now dictate certain terms of employment, and the era of multimillion-dollar contracts began.

Money was also at issue in a case related to another aspect of the game. After more than a century of professional play, in 1986 televised broadcasts of baseball and the copyright laws surrounding them came into question. Players felt that the terms of their employment did not include their performances for television audiences. They insisted that the telecasts and the profits being derived from them were being made without their consent. In *Baltimore Orioles v. Major League Baseball Players Association*, 805 F.2d 663 (7th Cir. 1986), major league clubs sought a judgment that upheld their exclusive right to broadcast games. The major league players argued that their performances were not copyrightable works because they lacked sufficient artistic merit. Refusing to cut

Donald Fehr of the Major League Baseball Players Association addresses the findings of the Mitchell Report, which investigated steroid use in baseball.

AP IMAGES

into the control of MLB over the airwaves, the federal appellate court ruled that the telecasts were indeed copyrightable works and that clubs were entitled to the revenues derived from them.

As a result of these cases, economic decisions regarding baseball have been left to the players and owners. For this reason, baseball has been seen as an anomaly with regard to U.S. antitrust laws, and its exemption has been called "an aberration confined to baseball" (*Flood*). The push for congressional action to eliminate this exemption intensified with the baseball players' strike from 1994 to 1995. The strike left many in baseball, including fans, disenfranchised. Senator Howard M. Metzenbaum, an Ohio Democrat who headed the subcommittee on antitrust laws, led the fight to remove the antitrust exemption from baseball. However, the 234-day strike ended in an agreement between owners and players, in which owners promised to pay "luxury taxes" on clubs with high payrolls. Congress was spared the necessity of acting.

Local communities, however, faced the possibility of losing their MLB franchises as the economics of baseball changed dramatically in the late 1990s. Major market teams, many of them now owned by corporations rather than wealthy individuals, drove up player payrolls. This change hurt smaller market teams and teams owned by individuals who either lacked the resources or the desire to match salaries. The Minnesota Twins, unable to secure a new, publicly funded baseball stadium, threatened to move to another state in 1997. The state of Minnesota sought unsuccessfully to probe the team's finances and that of MLB, but in the end the Twins could not secure a sale or move for the team.

Unable to curb rising costs, the baseball league proposed contracting two teams before the 2002 season. Under contraction, MLB would buy out the owners and distribute the players to other teams through a draft. The league argued that contraction would strengthen the financial wellbeing of the sport. The owners, however, needed to move quickly if contraction was to happen before the 2002 season.

The Montreal Expos and the Minnesota Twins were rumored to be the teams selected for contraction. In Minnesota, the operators of the Metrodome, where the Twins play their home games, sued the Twins and MLB, asking a state court to order the Twins to play the 2002 season. They sought either to win on the merits or delay contraction for a year. The judge issued a PRELIMINARY INJUNCTION and the Twins appealed, arguing that the team did have an obligation to pay the rent for the season, but they could decide whether to play the season. The *Minnesota Court of Appeals, in Metropolitan Sports Facilities Commission v. Minnesota Twins Partnership,* 638 N.W.2d 214 (2002), upheld the injunction, which meant that contraction became impossible for the 2002 season. The baseball league later abandoned the concept of contraction, at least for the near future.

In addition to its ongoing financial troubles, baseball has faced other difficulties from incidence of steroid abuse. Baseball first began testing for performance-enhancing drugs during the 2003 season. The testing was a type of survey, designed to assess the number of players using steroids in the league. The tests were to be anonymous, and even those who tested positive would not be punished. In November 2003, MLB revealed that more than 5 percent of the tests conducted during the 2003 season were positive, prompting the first-ever mandatory testing and punishment for players who tested positive for performance-enhancing drugs.

In 2004 MLB faced increasing pressure from government to strengthen its drug policy or face legislative intervention. In 2005 MLB significantly increased the penalties for testing positive for performance-enhancing drugs. The more stringent standards required a 50-game suspension for the first offense, 100-game for the second offense, and a lifetime ban from baseball for the third offense.

In 2006 baseball commissioner Bud Selig appointed former U.S. Senator George Mitchell to investigate the use of performance-enhancing drugs in major league baseball. Senator Mitchell's investigation culminated with the delivery of the "Report to the Commissioner of Baseball of an Independent Investigation into the Illegal Use of Steroids and Other Performance Enhancing Substances By Players in Major League Baseball," also known as the "Mitchell Report." The Mitchell Report, issued in 2007, found that the use of performance-enhancing drugs had been pervasive for more than a decade, and it made recommendations for MLB for the future. As of 2009, the legal ramifications of the steroid investigation include government probes into drug distribution and indictments against major league players for PERJURY and OBSTRUCTION OF JUSTICE, related to allegedly false denials of steroid use.

FURTHER READINGS

Burk, Robert F. 1994. *Never Just a Game.* Chapel Hill: Univ. of North Carolina Press.

Helyar, John. 1994. *Lords of the Realm.* New York: Villard Books.

Kovaleff, Theodore P. 1994. *The Antitrust Impulse.* New York: Sharpe.

Laitner, Colin. 2006. "Steroids and Drug Enhancements in Sports: The Real Problem and the Real Solution."*De-Paul Journal of Sports Law and Contemporary Problems.* 3 (Summer).

Lewis, Michael. 2003. *Moneyball: The Art of Winning an Unfair Game.* New York: Norton.

Manfred, Robert D., Jr. 2008. "Federal Labor Law Obstacles to Achieving a Completely Independent Drug Program in Major League Baseball."*Marquette Sports Law Review.* 19 (Fall).

Radomski, Kirk. 2009. *Bases Loaded: The Inside Story of the Steroid Era in Baseball by the Central Figure in the Mitchell Report.* New York: Hudson Street Press.

Sands, Jack, and Peter Gammons. 1993. *Coming Apart at the Seams.* New York: Macmillan.

U.S. Congress Subcommittee on Economic and Commercial Law. 1993–94. *Baseball's Antitrust Exemption: Hearing before the Subcommittee on Economic and Commercial Law.* Washington, D.C.: U.S. Government Printing Office.

U.S. Congress Subcommittee on Oversight and Government. 2008. *The Mitchell Report: The Illegal Use of Steroids in Major League Baseball.* Washington, D.C.: U.S. Government Printing Office.

Zimbalist, Andrew S. 1992. *Baseball and Billions: A Probing Look Inside the Big Business of Our National Pastime.* New York: Basic Books.

Zimbalist, Andrew S., and Bob Costas. 2003. *May the Best Team Win: Baseball Economics and Public Policy.* Washington, D.C.: Brookings Institution.

CROSS REFERENCE

Sports Law.

BASIC BOOKS V. KINKO'S GRAPHICS CORP.

See COPYRIGHT "Copyright Law in Action" (Sidebar).

BASIS

The minimum, fundamental constituents, foundation, or support of a thing or a system without which the thing or system would cease to exist. In accounting, the value assigned to an asset that is sold or transferred so that it can be determined whether a gain or loss has resulted from the transaction. The amount that property is estimated to be worth at the time it is purchased, acquired, and received for tax purposes.

In a simple case, the basis of property for tax purposes under the INTERNAL REVENUE CODE is the purchase price of a piece of property. For example, if a taxpayer purchases a parcel of land for $500,000, and no deductions apply to that parcel of land, the taxpayer's basis is $500,000. If the taxpayer later sells the property for $550,000, the amount of gain realized by the transaction is the sale price ($550,000) less the adjusted basis ($500,000), or $50,000.

Where a taxpayer is allowed to depreciate property with a limited useful life, such as an automobile used primarily for business purposes, the taxpayer's adjusted basis is reduced. Assume a taxpayer purchases an automobile for $30,000, and then claims deductions for $5,000. The adjusted basis of the automobile is then reduced to $25,000. When the taxpayer sells the automobile for $26,000, the amount of gain realized is $1,000 (the sale price of $26,000 minus the adjusted basis of $25,000).

FURTHER READINGS

Bankman, Joseph, et al. *2008 Federal Income Tax: Examples and Explanations.* 5th ed. Frederick, MD: Wolters Kluwer Law & Business.

Hudson, David M., and Stephen A. Lind. 2007. *Federal Income Taxation.* Eagan, MN: West.

McEowen, Roger, and Neil Harl. 2008. *Estate Planning,* *PM–993.* Available online at http://www.calt.iastate. edu/basis.html; website home page: http://www.calt. iastate.edu (accessed August 28, 2009).

CROSS REFERENCES

Internal Revenue Code; Profit.

BASTARDY ACTION

An archaic name given to a court proceeding in which the paternity of an illegitimate child is determined in order to impose and enforce support obligations upon the father.

The term *bastardy action* is derived from the early common-law use of the word *bastard* to describe a child born out of wedlock. Modern legislation refers to such proceedings as filiation proceedings or paternity suits because of the derogatory connotation of the term *bastard.*

Although such proceedings are typically civil actions, a few states have established such actions as criminal proceedings.

CROSS REFERENCE

Illegitimacy.

❖ BATES, DAISY LEE GATSON

Daisy Lee Gatson Bates, a CIVIL RIGHTS activist and newspaper publisher, was a key figure in the integration of public schools in Little Rock, Arkansas, in the late 1950s. When a storm of violent public protest swept Little Rock, Bates orchestrated the strategies that would reverse 200 years of state-sanctioned segregation.

Bates was born in 1920 in Huttig, in the lumbering region of southeast Arkansas. When she was a baby, her mother was raped and murdered. No one was prosecuted for the crime, but suspicion in the town centered on three white men. After her mother's death, her father fled, leaving Bates with his best friends, Orlee Smith and Susie Smith, who adopted her and raised her as their only child. They were kind and indulgent parents and Bates grew to be a strong-willed and determined child. When she was eight, she learned of the circumstances of her birth and adoption. The painful knowledge of her parents' suffering and the harsh realities of life in the rural south became driving forces in Bates's life.

Although she grew up during difficult economic times, Bates's childhood was relatively comfortable. Her relationship with her adoptive parents was warm and loving, and she was especially close to her father. Nevertheless, Bates's childhood was not easy. Like other black children, she experienced the sting of racial discrimination from an early age. She attended a segregated public school, using worn textbooks handed down from the white children's school. Her school was little more than a room with a potbellied stove that gave so little heat she and her classmates often kept their coats on all day.

In 1941 Orlee Smith became gravely ill. When he knew he was going to die, he called his daughter to his side. He was aware of the anger and pain she carried because of her mother's death and her father's disappearance and because of the bigotry that was a part of their everyday life. He counseled her not to let hatred and hostility control her but rather to use her strong feelings as a catalyst to work for change. He said:

> Don't hate white people just because they're white. If you hate, make it count for

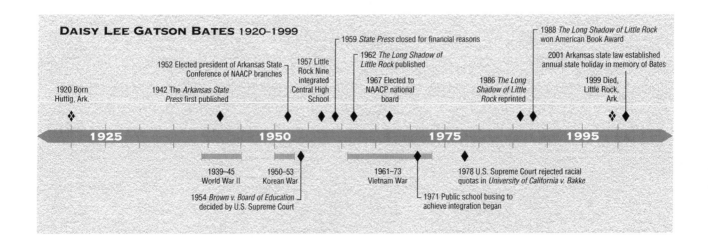

DAISY LEE GATSON BATES 1920–1999

1920 Born Huttig, Ark.

1942 The *Arkansas State Press* first published

1952 Elected president of Arkansas State Conference of NAACP branches

1957 Little Rock Nine integrated Central High School

1959 *State Press* closed for financial reasons

1962 *The Long Shadow of Little Rock* published

1967 Elected to NAACP national board

1986 *The Long Shadow of Little Rock* reprinted

1988 *The Long Shadow of Little Rock* won American Book Award

1999 Died, Little Rock, Ark.

2001 Arkansas state law established annual state holiday in memory of Bates

1925 1950 1975 1995

1939–45 World War II

1950–53 Korean War

1954 *Brown v. Board of Education* decided by U.S. Supreme Court

1961–73 Vietnam War

1971 Public school busing to achieve integration began

1978 U.S. Supreme Court rejected racial quotas in *University of California v. Bakke*

Daisy Bates.
AP IMAGES

something. Hate the humiliations we are living under in the South. Hate the discrimination that eats away at the soul of every black man and woman. Hate the insults hurled at us by white scum—then try to do something about it, or your hate won't spell a thing.

Smith's death became a kind of rebirth for Bates. She did not know it then, but his words would strengthen and sustain her resolve during the difficult struggles she was to face.

In 1942 Bates married Lucius Christopher Bates, an insurance agent and friend of her late father, and settled in Little Rock. Her husband had majored in journalism at Wilberforce College, in Ohio, and the young couple pooled their savings and began publishing the Arkansas *State Press*. While writing and publishing the fledgling paper, Bates also enrolled in business administration and public relations courses at Shorter College, in Rome, Georgia. The *State Press* quickly became the largest and most influential black paper in Arkansas.

With the entry of the United States into WORLD WAR II, Camp Robinson, near Little Rock, was reopened. The influx of soldiers, many of whom were black men from northern cities,

caused racial tensions to rise in the city. The *State Press* had gained a reputation as an independent "voice of the people" and regularly attacked police brutality, segregation, and inequities in the criminal justice system. When the paper reported a particularly gruesome incident in which a black soldier was killed by a white policeman, many advertisers who were wary of antagonizing their white patrons withdrew their support, and circulation of the paper dropped. However, the Bateses were able to stay afloat and eventually regain their advertisers and rebuild the paper's circulation. Their tenacity paid off in changes in working and living conditions for blacks in Arkansas. For example, as a result of their reporting on police brutality in black neighborhoods, black police officers were hired to patrol those areas.

From their earliest days in Little Rock, Bates and her husband were active in the local branch of the National Association for the Advancement of Colored People (NAACP). In 1952 Bates was elected president of the Arkansas State Conference of NAACP branches. In 1954 when the Supreme Court handed down its historic decision in BROWN V. BOARD OF EDUCATION 347 U.S. 483, 74 S. Ct. 686, 98 L. Ed. 873 (1954), declaring that segregated schools are "inherently unequal," she and her colleagues began pressing for implementation of the Court's mandate to desegregate the schools "with all deliberate speed" (*Brown v. Board of Education,* 349 U.S. 294 at 301, 75 S. Ct. 753 at 756, 99 L. Ed. 1083 [1955]). Because of her prominent position with the NAACP, Bates found herself a central character in the integration battle that soon erupted in Little Rock.

The Little Rock School Board chose nine black students to be the first to integrate Little Rock Central High School. Planning and coordination of the activities of the group, which came to be known as the Little Rock Nine, fell to Bates. By September 1, 1957, angry crowds had begun milling around Central High to protest and try to prevent the enrollment of the black students. On September 2, the day before school was to open, Governor Orval Faubus dispatched the Arkansas NATIONAL GUARD and ordered it to surround Central. Claiming that he was protecting Little Rock's citizens from possible mob violence, he declared that no black students would be allowed to enter the school and that "blood [would] run in the streets" if any attempted to do so.

NAACP lawyers Wiley Branton and THUR-GOOD MARSHALL (later a U.S. Supreme Court justice) promptly obtained an injunction against Faubus for his interference, but Faubus refused to withdraw the troops. Bates decided to have the students enter the school in a group. She contacted eight of them and told them to assemble at a designated intersection the morning of September 4 and travel to school together. The ninth student, Elizabeth Eckford, did not receive word of the plan. Unaware of the maelstrom awaiting her, Eckford arrived at Central High alone and was taunted, jeered, and accosted by hundreds of white people as reporters and photographers from around the world observed and recorded the scene. The National Guard did not attempt to help Eckford but instead blocked her entrance to the school. Neither she nor any of the other members of the Little Rock Nine—who arrived later in a group, as arranged—were allowed to pass through the line of Guard members surrounding the school.

The attempt by Bates and the nine students to enter Central set off a series of violent incidents that continued for 17 days. On September 20, attorneys Branton and Marshall obtained an injunction barring the use of the National Guard to interfere with integration at Central High. By this time, the Bateses' home had become the unofficial center of activity and communication for the integration effort. Reporters from all over the United States came and went, some staying days or weeks.

On September 23 all the Little Rock Nine met at the Bates home to try again to exercise their right to enter Central High. Traveling in two cars they drove to a side entrance of the building, away from the persistent throng, and were escorted into the school by police officers. Again mob violence spread through the city. Later in the day the students were secretly removed from the school through a delivery entrance, and the chief of police declared that Little Rock was under a reign of terror.

The next day the black students remained at home. The mayor and the chief of police appealed to the U.S. DEPARTMENT OF JUSTICE for assistance. In response, President DWIGHT D. EISENHOWER federalized the Arkansas National Guard and ordered Secretary of Defense Charles E. Wilson to enforce the integration order.

Wilson ordered 1,000 paratroopers from the 101st Airborne ("Screaming Eagles") Division of the 327th Infantry Regiment into Little Rock to restore order.

On September 25 the Little Rock Nine assembled again at the Bates home. Under the protection of the paratroopers they were taken to Central High, where they entered under the watchful eyes of hundreds of reporters, photographers, and news camera operators. The paratroopers remained at Central until September 30, when they withdrew to Camp Robinson, 12 miles away. The federalized Arkansas National Guard remained on patrol at Central until the end of the school year. Although it was not necessary to recall the paratroopers, and the number of minority students in Little Rock's formerly white schools steadily increased, violence, hatred, and acrimony continued to plague the city for many years.

Bates endured many attempts to harass and intimidate her, including rocks thrown through her window, gunshots fired at her house, dynamite exploded near her house, and crosses burned on her lawn. In late October 1957 she was arrested under a newly enacted ordinance that required officials of organizations to supply information regarding membership, donors, amounts of contributions, and expenditures. Although she was found guilty under the ordinance, the conviction was later overturned by the Supreme Court on grounds that the ordinance requirement interfered with the members' freedom of association (*Bates v. City of Little Rock*, 361 U.S. 516, 80 S. Ct. 412, 4 L. Ed. 480 [1960]). In 1959 Bates and her husband were forced to close the *State Press* for financial reasons.

Through all the harassment Bates remained determined to keep the wheels of the integration movement going forward. After closing the newspaper she traveled throughout the United States working on behalf of the Democratic National Committee and the Johnson administration's antipoverty programs. In 1965 she suffered a stroke and returned to Little Rock, but she continued to be active in the NAACP and in 1967 was elected to its national board. In 1968 she moved to Mitchellville, Arkansas, to organize the Mitchellville Office of Economic Opportunity Self-Help Project. The project was responsible for new water and sewer systems, paved streets, a community center, and a swimming pool.

WE'VE GOT TO DECIDE IF IT'S GOING TO BE THIS GENERATION OR NEVER.
—DAISY BATES

In 1984 Bates revived the *State Press* and was awarded honorary degrees by the University of Arkansas and Washington University. In 1986 the University of Arkansas Press published a reprint edition of her autobiography, *The Long Shadow of Little Rock,* and in 1988 the book received the American Book Award, the first reprint edition to be given that honor.

In 1987 Bates sold the *State Press* but she remained a consultant for the paper. In the same year Little Rock named a new facility the "Daisy Bates Elementary School". Bates continued her involvement in community activities until shortly before her death on November 4, 1999, in Little Rock. President BILL CLINTON honored her by allowing her body to lie in state at the Capitol.

FURTHER READINGS

Bates, Daisy. 2007. *The Long Shadow of Little Rock.* Fayetteville: Univ. of Arkansas Press.

Branch, Taylor. 1989. *Parting the Waters: America in the King Years, 1954–1963.* New York: Simon & Schuster.

Hine, Darlene C., Elsa B. Brown, Rosalyn Terborg-Penn, eds. 1993. *Black Women in America: An Historical Encyclopedia.* Bloomington: Indiana Univ. Press.

Jacoway, Elizabeth, and C. Fred Williams, eds. 1999. *Understanding the Little Rock Crisis: An Exercise in Remembrance and Reconciliation.* Fayetteville: Univ. of Arkansas.

Smith, Jessie C., ed. 2002. *Notable Black American Women.* Detroit: Gale Research.

CROSS REFERENCES

Brown v. Board of Education of Topeka, Kansas; Civil Rights Movement; NAACP; School Desegregation.

❖ BATES, EDWARD

Edward Bates served as U.S. attorney general in the cabinet of President ABRAHAM LINCOLN from 1861 to 1864.

Edward Bates.
LIBRARY OF CONGRESS

Bates was born September 4, 1793, in Belmont, Virginia. He left his native Virginia at the age of twenty-one and settled in Missouri, where he concentrated his career efforts.

Bates was admitted to the Missouri bar in 1816 and was attorney general from 1820 to 1822. He was also a member of the Missouri Constitutional Convention in 1820.

In 1822 Bates began the legislative phase of his career as a member of the Missouri House of

LIBERTY CANNOT EXIST EXCEPT UNDER GOVERNMENT OF LAW.
—EDWARD BATES

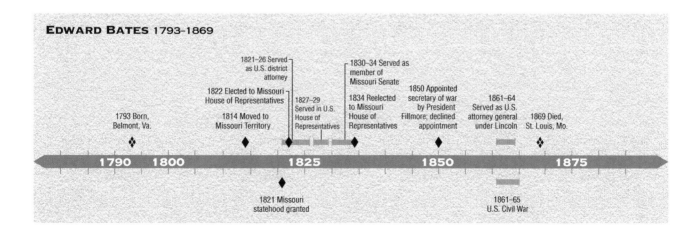

EDWARD BATES 1793–1869

1793 Born, Belmont, Va.

1814 Moved to Missouri Territory

1821 Missouri statehood granted

1821–26 Served as U.S. district attorney

1822 Elected to Missouri House of Representatives

1827–29 Served in U.S. House of Representatives

1830–34 Served as member of Missouri Senate

1834 Reelected to Missouri House of Representatives

1850 Appointed secretary of war by President Fillmore; declined appointment

1861–64 Served as U.S. attorney general under Lincoln

1861–65 U.S. Civil War

1869 Died, St. Louis, Mo.

1790   1800   1825   1850   1875

Representatives. In 1827 he became a representative for Missouri in the U.S. House of Representatives, serving for two years, and then returned to state government as a member of the Missouri Senate, serving from 1830 to 1834. In 1834 he became a member of the Missouri House of Representatives for a second time. Bates was also a U.S. DISTRICT ATTORNEY from 1821 to 1826.

Bates was an unsuccessful presidential nominee at the Republican National Convention of 1860. He died March 25, 1869, in St. Louis, Missouri.

BATTEL

Physical combat engaged in by an accuser and accused to resolve their differences, usually involving a serious crime or ownership of land. It was recognized by the English king from the eleventh to seventeenth centuries.

Trial by battel was introduced into England by William the Conqueror. It was based upon the belief that the winner of the battle, which was tried by God, was the party who was in the right in the dispute.

BATTERED CHILD/SPOUSE SYNDROME

A condition created by sustained physical, sexual, and/or emotional abuse, which creates a variety of physical and emotional symptoms.

Violence of any kind is traumatic to victims, and the thought that someone could exert extreme violence against a loved one or a child is repulsive. Battered-child syndrome and battered-spouse syndrome are both the result of repeated violence—beatings, choking, sexual ASSAULT, verbal abuse, or any combination. The resulting trauma leaves its victims with physical and emotional scars, which can show up in a variety of symptoms that can come on gradually or suddenly. Often the symptoms are similar to other, less dangerous conditions. Sometimes there are no visible symptoms. From a legal perspective, this makes both syndromes difficult to prove. The fact that there is heated disagreement about these syndromes, what they represent, and in fact whether they are true syndromes at all, only adds to the difficulty.

Although both syndromes stem from the same violent behavior (and in some cases, the same perpetrator), they need to be treated separately.

Battered-Child Syndrome

Children can be subjected to violence at the hands of any adult with whom they have contact. It could be a parent, an older sibling, a babysitter, a day-care provider, a family friend, a parent's romantic partner—in short, anyone. Some children are victimized by several people.

The victimization can come in the form of physical violence, SEXUAL ABUSE, or verbal abuse. If one of these factors is present, chances are that others are present as well. Physical abuse can go undetected for a long time. A child who suffers repeated falls or broken bones might be considered "clumsy", or the injuries might be brushed off as the kind of bumps and bruises all children get. Sexual abuse might have no outward signs, or the victim might be unusually forward or inappropriately flirtatious with adults.

Even infants are not immune to abuse. In *shaken-baby syndrome*, a baby is shaken so violently that brain injury can occur; repeated shaking episodes or even just one particularly severe episode can result in death.

A child suffering from battered child syndrome might be quiet and withdrawn, lethargic, depressed, or violent. Someone who does not know the particular child might not immediately spot emotional symptoms, but if the child displays unchildlike behavior, coupled with unexplained chronic physical bruising, chances are the child is a victim of abuse.

Those who investigate child-abuse crimes must be extremely thorough, especially if the child is very young and thus unable to corroborate what the evidence shows. Sometimes a physician will spot signs of abuse or battered-child syndrome when a child is brought into an emergency room for treatment of some injury. A full investigation requires interviews with anyone who has access to the child, including parents, siblings, other relatives, neighbors, day-care providers or babysitters, teachers, and doctors. Even those who are not involved in abuse might have valuable information to provide. Often, those who have committed the abuse will offer vague or conflicting information about what led to a particular injury. If warranted, a child could be placed in temporary PROTECTIVE CUSTODY while an investigation proceeds. Depending on the extent and severity of abuse, those who have committed the abuse might benefit from counseling or other forms of treatment (e.g., substance or they might face criminal charges and serve a prison sentence.

Battered-Spouse Syndrome

Battered-spouse syndrome is more commonly called "battered-women's syndrome" because most of the victims are women, either wives or girlfriends of the perpetrators. However, abused husbands and boyfriends have gained increased attention, as have same-sex abuse by gay and lesbian partners. With CHILD ABUSE, investigators are often at a loss because the child is too young to testify. In cases of battered-spouse syndrome, however, the problem is that often the victim refuses to testify. Guilt and shame are primary reasons, particularly for men who expect they will be ridiculed for being abused by a woman. Fear is an even stronger factor in abuse victims' silence.

Typical symptoms of a battered-spouse syndrome victim include the openly physical ones—bruises, black eyes, broken bones, cuts and scratches. The emotional symptoms include depression, lack of self-esteem, and hopelessness. Sufferers might be "hypervigilant" to any signs of conflict on the part of the spouse. Denial that a problem exists is a common response to questions from concerned friends, loved ones, or even medical professionals.

The phrase "battered-women's syndrome" was first used in the early 1980s; in ensuing years lawyers began using the "battered woman" defense in HOMICIDE cases in which women killed their husbands or boyfriends. Many women claimed SELF-DEFENSE, explaining that the MURDER victim had been physically abusive for years. As the concept of battered-spouse syndrome became more clearly articulated in the 1980s and 1990s, the syndrome as a self-defense argument gained strength. In fact, it played into the CLEMENCY decisions of several governors, beginning with Governor Richard Celeste of Ohio, who in 1990 granted clemency to 25 women who had murdered their spouses. Their trials had been unfair, he concluded, because testimony about their abuse had not been allowed as evidence. Other governors followed suit in the ensuing years, including Maryland governor Donald Schaefer, Massachusetts governor William Weld, and California governors Pete Wilson and Gray Davis. Experts in DOMESTIC VIOLENCE explained to skeptics the reason why many battered women did not simply leave their husbands, either to stay with friends or go to a women's shelter. In some cases, they said, these women had been so emotionally broken that they were too frightened to leave. Some had been abused for so long that they had actually come to believe that they were responsible for their own abuse.

In the 1990s a new movement emerged to point out that abuse can happen to men as well as women. The number of abused men was estimated at no higher than five percent of the abuse cases, and to a large extent it was not taken seriously. Advocacy groups for women claimed that for a man to claim that his wife or girlfriend physically terrorized him were absurd. Law enforcement officials often took abuse charges less seriously when the complainant was a man. Since the late twentieth century, statistical evidence about male abuse has been gaining credibility. Moreover, gay and lesbian partner abuse has also begun to be taken more seriously. In 1999 a Brooklyn, N.Y., Supreme Court judge ruled that a gay man who had stabbed his partner to death could invoke battered-spouse syndrome at his trial.

The bottom line from a legal standpoint is that battered-spouse syndrome, like battered-child syndrome, requires solid and substantive evidence if it is to be used as a defense in a murder trial. A woman who has no visible physical signs of abuse might have been abused, but simply claiming to have been abused with no evidence at all at least warrants a thorough investigation. Cases in which women—and men—have claimed that an estranged spouse has been violent, simply to gain custody of their children, are not uncommon. The issue of battered spouses may be clearer in the first years of the twenty-first century than it was in the 1970s and 1980s, but it continues to evolve.

FURTHER READINGS

Justice Department Web site. 2002. *Battered Child Syndrome: Investigating Physical Abuse and Homicide*. Washington, D.C.: U.S. Department of Justice. Available online at http://www.ncjrs.gov/pdffiles1/ojjdp/161406.pdf; website home page: http://www.ncjrs.gov (accessed July 6, 2009).

Parrish, Rob. 2009. *Abused Men: The Hidden Side of Domestic Violence*. Westport, CT: Greenwood.

Walker, Lenore E. 2009. *The Battered Woman Syndrome*. 3d ed. New York: Springer.

CROSS REFERENCES

Domestic Violence; Child Abuse; Women's Rights.

BATTERY

At common law, an intentional unpermitted act causing harmful or offensive contact with the "person" of another.

Battery is concerned with the right to have one's body left alone by others.

Both a tort and a crime, its essential element, harmful or offensive contact, is the same in both areas of the law. The main distinction between the two categories lies in the penalty imposed. A DEFENDANT sued for a tort is civilly liable to the PLAINTIFF for damages. The punishment for criminal battery is a fine, imprisonment, or both. Usually battery is prosecuted as a crime only in cases involving serious harm to the victim.

Elements

The following elements must be proven to establish a case for battery: (1) an act by a defendant; (2) an intent to cause harmful or offensive contact on the part of the defendant; and (3) harmful or offensive contact to the plaintiff.

The Act The act must result in one of two forms of contact. Causing any physical harm or injury to the victim—such as a cut, a burn, or a bullet wound—could constitute battery, but actual injury is not required. Even though there is no apparent bruise following harmful contact, the defendant can still be guilty of battery; occurrence of a physical illness subsequent to the contact may also be ACTIONABLE. The second type of contact that may constitute battery causes no actual physical harm but is, instead, offensive or insulting to the victim. Examples include spitting in someone's face or offensively touching someone against his or her will.

Touching the person of someone is defined as including not only contacts with the body, but also with anything closely connected with the body, such as clothing or an item carried in the person's hand. For example, a battery may be committed by intentionally knocking a hat off someone's head or knocking a glass out of someone's hand.

Intent Although the contact must be intended, there is no requirement that the defendant intend to harm or injure the victim. In TORT LAW, the intent must be either specific intent—the contact was specifically intended—or general intent—the defendant was substantially certain that the act would cause the contact. The intent element is satisfied in CRIMINAL LAW when the act is done with an intent to injure or with criminal negligence—failure to use care to avoid criminal consequences. The intent for criminal law is also present when the defendant's conduct is unlawful even though it does not amount to CRIMINAL NEGLIGENCE.

Intent is not negated if the aim of the contact was a joke. As with all torts, however, consent is a defense. Under certain circumstances consent to a battery is assumed. A person who walks in a crowded area impliedly consents to a degree of contact that is inevitable and reasonable. Consent may also be assumed if the parties had a prior relationship unless the victim gave the defendant a previous warning.

There is no requirement that the plaintiff be aware of a battery at the time it is committed. The gist of the action is the lack of consent to contact. It is no defense that the victim was sleeping or unconscious at the time.

Harmful or Offensive Conduct It is not necessary for the defendant's wrongful act to result in direct contact with the victim. It is sufficient if the act sets in motion a force that results in the contact. A defendant who whipped a horse on which a plaintiff was riding, causing the plaintiff to fall and be injured, was found guilty of battery. Provided all other elements of the offense are present, the offense may also be committed by causing the victim to harm himself. A defendant who fails to act when he or she has a duty to do so is guilty—as where a nurse fails to warn a blind patient that he is headed toward an open window, causing him to fall and injure himself.

Aggravated Battery

When a battery is committed with intent to do serious harm or MURDER, or when it is done with a dangerous weapon, it is described as aggravated. A weapon is considered dangerous whenever the purpose for using it is to cause death or serious harm. State statutes define aggravated battery in various ways—such as ASSAULT with intent to kill. Under such statutes, assault means both battery and assault. It is punishable as a felony in all states.

Punishment

In a CIVIL ACTION for tortious battery, the penalty is damages. A jury determines the amount to be awarded, which in most cases is based on the harm done to the plaintiff. Even though a plaintiff suffers no actual injury, NOMINAL DAMAGES (a small sum) may still be awarded on the theory that there has been an invasion of a right. Also, a court may award PUNITIVE DAMAGES aimed at punishing the defendant for the wrongful act.

Criminal battery is punishable by a fine, imprisonment, or both. If it is considered aggravated the penalties are greater.

❖ BAYLOR, ROBERT EMMETT BLEDSOE

Robert Emmett Bledsoe Baylor achieved prominence as a jurist, a Baptist preacher, and a law professor. He was instrumental in the founding of the first Baptist college in Texas, which was named Baylor University in his honor.

Baylor was born May 10, 1793, in Lincoln County, Kentucky. He began his political career in 1819 with service in the Kentucky legislature, moving to the Alabama legislature in 1824. He represented Alabama in the U.S. House of Representatives from 1829 to 1831.

In 1839 Baylor settled in Texas and began a judicial career. He was appointed to a Texas district court in 1841 and also served as associate judge of the Supreme Court of the Republic of Texas from 1841 to 1845. Following the annexation of Texas by the United States, he rendered decisions as a U.S. district judge from 1845 to 1861. He was also instrumental in the formation of the Texas state constitution in 1845.

As a Baptist preacher, Baylor helped to procure a charter for a Baptist college that would come to be named Baylor University. The university was originally located in Independence, Texas, but later moved to Waco in 1886, where it remained. Baylor began teaching courses in the science of law at the new university in 1849. In 1857, Baylor University established its original school of law, and Baylor served on the original faculty. With the exception of the period of the CIVIL WAR, when the school of law did not offer classes, Baylor taught courses in CONSTITUTIONAL LAW and jurisprudence until 1873. He died on December 30, 1873, in Washington County, Texas.

FURTHER READINGS

"1849 to 1883: The Early History." *Baylor Law School.* Available online at http://law.baylor.edu/history/ Time_Periods/early.htm; website home page: http:// law.baylor.edu (accessed July 6, 2009).

Baylor, Robert Emmett Bledsoe (1793–1874). *In Biographical Directory of the United States Congress 1774–Present.* Available online at http://bioguide.congress.gov/scripts/ biodisplay.pl?index=B000257; website home page: http:// bioguide.congress.gov (accessed August 28, 2009).

McSwain, Betty Ann McCartney. 1976. *The Bench and Bar of Waco and McLennan County, 1849–1976.* Waco, TX: Texian.

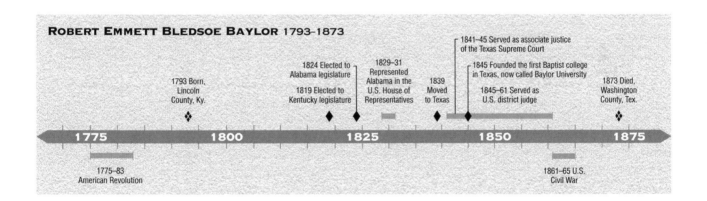

ROBERT EMMETT BLEDSOE BAYLOR 1793–1873

1793 Born, Lincoln County, Ky.

1824 Elected to Alabama legislature

1819 Elected to Kentucky legislature

1829–31 Represented Alabama in the U.S. House of Representatives

1839 Moved to Texas

1841–45 Served as associate justice of the Texas Supreme Court

1845 Founded the first Baptist college in Texas, now called Baylor University

1845–61 Served as U.S. district judge

1873 Died, Washington County, Tex.

1775   1800   1825   1850   1875

1775–83 American Revolution

1861–65 U.S. Civil War

A.	Atlantic Reporter	ACS	Agricultural Cooperative Service
A. 2d	Atlantic Reporter, Second Series	ACT	American College Test
AA	Alcoholics Anonymous	Act'g Legal Adv.	Acting Legal Advisor
AAA	American Arbitration Association; Agricultural Adjustment Act of 1933	ACUS	Administrative Conference of the United States
AALS	Association of American Law Schools	ACYF	Administration on Children, Youth, and Families
AAPRP	All African People's Revolutionary Party	A.D. 2d	Appellate Division, Second Series, N.Y.
AARP	American Association of Retired Persons	ADA	Americans with Disabilities Act of 1990
AAS	American Anti-Slavery Society	ADAMHA	Alcohol, Drug Abuse, and Mental Health Administration
ABA	American Bar Association; Architectural Barriers Act of 1968; American Bankers Association	ADC	Aid to Dependent Children
ABC	American Broadcasting Companies, Inc. (formerly American Broadcasting Corporation)	ADD	Administration on Developmental Disabilities
		ADEA	Age Discrimination in Employment Act of 1967
ABM	Antiballistic missile	ADL	Anti-Defamation League
ABM Treaty	Anti-Ballistic Missile Treaty of 1972	ADR	Alternative dispute resolution
ABVP	Anti-Biased Violence Project	AEC	Atomic Energy Commission
A/C	Account	AECB	Arms Export Control Board
A.C.	Appeal cases	AEDPA	Antiterrorism and Effective Death Penalty Act
ACAA	Air Carrier Access Act		
ACCA	Armed Career Criminal Act of 1984	A.E.R.	All England Law Reports
ACF	Administration for Children and Families	AFA	American Family Association; Alabama Freethought Association
ACLU	American Civil Liberties Union	AFB	American Farm Bureau
ACRS	Accelerated Cost Recovery System	AFBF	American Farm Bureau Federation

AFDC	Aid to Families with Dependent Children	Amer. St. Papers, For. Rels.	American State Papers, Legislative and Executive
aff'd per cur.	Affirmed by the court		Documents of the
AFIS	Automated fingerprint identification system		Congress of the U.S., Class I, Foreign Relations,
AFL	American Federation of Labor		1832–1859
AFL-CIO	American Federation of Labor and Congress of	AMS	Agricultural Marketing Service
	Industrial Organizations	AMVETS	American Veterans (of World War II)
AFRes	Air Force Reserve	ANA	Administration for
AFSC	American Friends Service Committee		Native Americans
AFSCME	American Federation of	Ann. Dig.	Annual Digest of Public International Law Cases
	State, County, and Municipal Employees	ANPA	American Newspaper Publishers Association
AGRICOLA	Agricultural Online Access	ANSCA	Alaska Native Claims Act
AIA	Association of Insurance Attorneys	ANZUS	Australia-New Zealand-United States Security
AIB	American Institute for Banking		Treaty Organization
AID	Artificial insemination	AOA	Administration on Aging
	using a third-party donor's	AOE	Arizonans for Official English
	sperm; Agency for International Development	AOL	America Online
AIDS	Acquired immune	AP	Associated Press
	deficiency syndrome	APA	Administrative Procedure Act of 1946
AIH	Artificial insemination	APHIS	Animal and Plant Health
	using the husband's sperm	App. Div.	Inspection Service Appellate Division
AIM	American Indian Movement		Reports, N.Y. Supreme Court
AIPAC	American Israel Public Affairs Committee	Arb. Trib., U.S.-British	Arbitration Tribunal, Claim Convention of 1853,
AIUSA	Amnesty International, U.S.A. Affiliate		United States and Great Britain Convention of 1853
AJS	American Judicature Society	Ardcor	American Roller Die Corporation
ALA	American Library Association	ARPA	Advanced Research Projects Agency
Alcoa	Aluminum Company of America	ARPANET	Advanced Research Projects Agency Network
ALEC	American Legislative Exchange Council	ARS	Advanced Record System
ALF	Animal Liberation Front	Art.	Article
ALI	American Law Institute	ARU	American Railway Union
ALJ	Administrative law judge	ASCME	American Federation of
All E.R.	All England Law Reports		State, County, and
ALO	Agency Liaison		Municipal Employees
A.L.R.	American Law Reports	ASCS	Agriculture Stabilization
ALY	*American Law Yearbook*		and Conservation Service
AMA	American Medical Association	ASM	Available Seatmile
AMAA	Agricultural Marketing Agreement Act	ASPCA	American Society for the Prevention of Cruelty to Animals
Am. Dec.	American Decisions	Asst. Att. Gen.	Assistant Attorney
amdt.	Amendment		General

AT&T	American Telephone and Telegraph	BOCA	Building Officials and Code Administrators International
ATF	Alcohol, Tobacco, Firearms and Explosives Bureau	BOP	Bureau of Prisons
		BPP	Black Panther Party for Self-defense
ATLA	Association of Trial Lawyers of America	Brit. and For.	British and Foreign State Papers
ATO	Alpha Tau Omega	BSA	Boy Scouts of America
ATTD	Alcohol and Tobacco Tax Division	BTP	Beta Theta Pi
ATU	Alcohol Tax Unit	Burr.	James Burrows, *Report of Cases Argued and Determined in the Court of King's Bench during the Time of Lord Mansfield* (1766–1780)
AUAM	American Union against Militarism		
AUM	Animal Unit Month		
AZT	Azidothymidine		
BAC	Blood alcohol concentration	BVA	Board of Veterans Appeals
BALSA	Black-American Law Student Association	c.	Chapter
		C³I	Command, Control, Communications, and Intelligence
BATF	Bureau of Alcohol, Tobacco and Firearms		
BBS	Bulletin Board System	C.A.	Court of Appeals
BCCI	Bank of Credit and Commerce International	CAA	Clean Air Act
		CAB	Civil Aeronautics Board; Corporation for American Banking
BEA	Bureau of Economic Analysis		
Bell's Cr. C.	Bell's English Crown Cases	CAFE	Corporate average fuel economy
Bevans	United States Treaties, etc. *Treaties and Other International Agreements of the United States of America, 1776–1949* (compiled under the direction of Charles I. Bevans, 1968–76)	Cal. 2d	California Reports, Second Series
		Cal. 3d	California Reports, Third Series
		CALR	Computer-assisted legal research
		Cal. Rptr.	California Reporter
		CAP	Common Agricultural Policy
BFOQ	Bona fide occupational qualification	CARA	Classification and Ratings Administration
BI	Bureau of Investigation		
BIA	Bureau of Indian Affairs; Board of Immigration Appeals	CATV	Community antenna television
		CBO	Congressional Budget Office
BID	Business improvement district	CBS	Columbia Broadcasting System
BJS	Bureau of Justice Statistics	CBOEC	Chicago Board of Election Commissioners
Black.	Black's United States Supreme Court Reports	CCC	Commodity Credit Corporation
Blatchf.	Blatchford's United States Circuit Court Reports	CCDBG	Child Care and Development Block Grant of 1990
BLM	Bureau of Land Management	C.C.D. Pa.	Circuit Court Decisions, Pennsylvania
BLS	Bureau of Labor Statistics	C.C.D. Va.	Circuit Court Decisions, Virginia
BMD	Ballistic missile defense	CCEA	Cabinet Council on Economic Affairs
BNA	Bureau of National Affairs		

CCP	Chinese Communist Party	CHINS	Children in need of supervision
CCR	Center for Constitutional Rights	CHIPS	Child in need of protective services
C.C.R.I.	Circuit Court, Rhode Island	Ch.N.Y.	Chancery Reports, New York
CD	Certificate of deposit; compact disc	Chr. Rob.	Christopher Robinson, *Reports of Cases Argued and*
CDA	Communications Decency Act		*Determined in the High*
CDBG	Community Development Block Grant Program		*Court of Admiralty (1801–1808)*
		CIA	Central Intelligence Agency
CDC	Centers for Disease Control and Prevention; Community Development Corporation	CID	Commercial Item Descriptions
		C.I.F.	Cost, insurance, and freight
CDF	Children's Defense Fund	CINCNORAD	Commander in Chief, North American Air Defense Command
CDL	Citizens for Decency through Law		
CD-ROM	Compact disc read-only memory	C.I.O.	Congress of Industrial Organizations
CDS	Community Dispute Services	CIPE	Center for International Private Enterprise
CDW	Collision damage waiver	C.J.	Chief justice
CENTO	Central Treaty Organization	CJIS	Criminal Justice Information Services
CEO	Chief executive officer	C.J.S.	Corpus Juris Secundum
CEQ	Council on Environmental Quality	Claims Arb. under Spec. Conv., Nielsen's Rept.	Frederick Kenelm Nielsen, *American and British Claims Arbitration*
CERCLA	Comprehensive Environmental Response, Compensation, and Liability Act of 1980		*under the Special Agreement Concluded between the United States and Great*
cert.	*Certiorari*		*Britain, August 18, 1910 (1926)*
CETA	Comprehensive Employment and Training Act	CLASP	Center for Law and Social Policy
C & F	Cost and freight	CLE	Center for Law and Education; Continuing Legal Education
CFC	Chlorofluorocarbon		
CFE Treaty	Conventional Forces in Europe Treaty of 1990	CLEO	Council on Legal Education Opportunity; Chief Law Enforcement Officer
C.F. & I.	Cost, freight, and insurance		
C.F.R	Code of Federal Regulations	CLP	Communist Labor Party of America
CFNP	Community Food and Nutrition Program	CLS	Christian Legal Society; critical legal studies (movement); Critical Legal Studies (membership organization)
CFTA	Canadian Free Trade Agreement		
CFTC	Commodity Futures Trading Commission		
Ch.	Chancery Division, English Law Reports	C.M.A.	Court of Military Appeals
CHAMPVA	Civilian Health and Medical Program at the Veterans Administration	CMEA	Council for Mutual Economic Assistance
		CMHS	Center for Mental Health Services
CHEP	Cuban/Haitian Entrant Program	C.M.R.	Court of Military Review

CNN	Cable News Network	CSA	Community Services Administration
CNO	Chief of Naval Operations	CSAP	Center for Substance Abuse Prevention
CNOL	Consolidated net operating loss	CSAT	Center for Substance Abuse Treatment
CNR	Chicago and Northwestern Railway	CSC	Civil Service Commission
CO	Conscientious Objector	CSCE	Conference on Security and Cooperation in Europe
C.O.D.	Cash on delivery		
COGP	Commission on Government Procurement	CSG	Council of State Governments
COINTELPRO	Counterintelligence Program	CSO	Community Service Organization
Coke Rep.	Coke's English King's Bench Reports	CSP	Center for the Study of the Presidency
COLA	Cost-of-living adjustment	C-SPAN	Cable-Satellite Public Affairs Network
COMCEN	Federal Communications Center	CSRS	Cooperative State Research Service
Comp.	Compilation	CSWPL	Center on Social Welfare Policy and Law
Conn.	Connecticut Reports		
CONTU	National Commission on New Technological Uses of Copyrighted Works	CTA	*Cum testamento annexo* (with the will attached)
Conv.	Convention	Ct. Ap. D.C.	Court of Appeals, District of Columbia
COPA	Child Online Protection Act (1998)	Ct. App. No. Ireland	Court of Appeals, Northern Ireland
COPS	Community Oriented Policing Services	Ct. Cl.	Court of Claims, United States
Corbin	Arthur L. Corbin, *Corbin on Contracts: A Comprehensive Treatise on the Rules of Contract Law* (1950)	Ct. Crim. Apps.	Court of Criminal Appeals (England)
		CTI	Consolidated taxable income
CORE	Congress on Racial Equality	Ct. of Sess., Scot.	Court of Sessions, Scotland
Cox's Crim. Cases	Cox's Criminal Cases (England)	CU	Credit union
COYOTE	Call Off Your Old Tired Ethics	CUNY	City University of New York
CPA	Certified public accountant	Cush.	Cushing's Massachusetts Reports
CPB	Corporation for Public Broadcasting, the	CWA	Civil Works Administration; Clean Water Act
CPI	Consumer Price Index		
CPPA	Child Pornography Prevention Act	DACORB	Department of the Army Conscientious Objector Review Board
CPSC	Consumer Product Safety Commission	Dall.	Dallas's Pennsylvania and United States Reports
Cranch	Cranch's United States Supreme Court Reports	DAR	Daughters of the American Revolution
CRF	Constitutional Rights Foundation	DARPA	Defense Advanced Research Projects Agency
CRR	Center for Constitutional Rights	DAVA	Defense Audiovisual Agency
CRS	Congressional Research Service; Community Relations Service	D.C.	United States District Court; District of Columbia
CRT	Critical race theory		

D.C. Del.	United States District Court, Delaware	DPT	Diphtheria, pertussis, and tetanus
D.C. Mass.	United States District Court, Massachusetts	DRI	Defense Research Institute
D.C. Md.	United States District Court, Maryland	DSAA	Defense Security Assistance Agency
D.C.N.D.Cal.	United States District Court, Northern District, California	DUI	Driving under the influence; driving under intoxication
D.C.N.Y.	United States District Court, New York	DVD	Digital versatile disc
		DWI	Driving while intoxicated
D.C.Pa.	United States District Court, Pennsylvania	EAHCA	Education for All Handicapped Children Act of 1975
DCS	Deputy Chiefs of Staff	EBT	Examination before trial
DCZ	District of the Canal Zone	E.coli	Escherichia coli
DDT	Dichlorodiphenyl-tricloroethane	ECPA	Electronic Communications Privacy Act of 1986
DEA	Drug Enforcement Administration	ECSC	Treaty of the European Coal and Steel Community
Decl. Lond.	Declaration of London, February 26, 1909	EDA	Economic Development Administration
Dev. & B.	Devereux & Battle's North Carolina Reports	EDF	Environmental Defense Fund
DFL	Minnesota Democratic-Farmer-Labor	E.D.N.Y.	Eastern District, New York
DFTA	Department for the Aging	EDP	Electronic data processing
DHS	Department of Homeland Security	E.D. Pa.	Eastern-District, Pennsylvania
Dig. U.S. Practice in Intl. Law	Digest of U.S. Practice in International Law	EDSC	Eastern District, South Carolina
Dist. Ct.	D.C. United States District Court, District of Columbia	EDT	Eastern daylight time
		E.D. Va.	Eastern District, Virginia
		EEC	European Economic Community; European Economic Community Treaty
D.L.R.	Dominion Law Reports (Canada)		
DMCA	Digital Millennium Copyright Act	EEOC	Equal Employment Opportunity Commission
DNA	Deoxyribonucleic acid		
Dnase	Deoxyribonuclease	EFF	Electronic Frontier Foundation
DNC	Democratic National Committee	EFT	Electronic funds transfer
DOC	Department of Commerce	Eliz.	Queen Elizabeth (Great Britain)
DOD	Department of Defense	Em. App.	Temporary Emergency Court of Appeals
DODEA	Department of Defense Education Activity	ENE	Early neutral evaluation
Dodson	Dodson's Reports, English Admiralty Courts	Eng. Rep.	English Reports
		EOP	Executive Office of the President
DOE	Department of Energy		
DOER	Department of Employee Relations	EPA	Environmental Protection Agency; Equal Pay Act of 1963
DOJ	Department of Justice		
DOL	Department of Labor	ERA	Equal Rights Amendment
DOMA	Defense of Marriage Act of 1996	ERDC	Energy Research and Development Commission
DOS	Disk operating system		
DOT	Department of Transportation	ERISA	Employee Retirement Income Security Act of 1974

ERS	Economic Research Service	FAS	Foreign Agricultural Service
ERTA	Economic Recovery Tax Act of 1981	FBA	Federal Bar Association
ESA	Endangered Species Act of 1973	FBI	Federal Bureau of Investigation
ESF	Emergency support function; Economic Support Fund	FCA	Farm Credit Administration
		F. Cas.	Federal Cases
ESRD	End-Stage Renal Disease Program	FCC	Federal Communications Commission
ETA	Employment and Training Administration	FCIA	Foreign Credit Insurance Association
ETS	Environmental tobacco smoke	FCIC	Federal Crop Insurance Corporation
et seq.	*Et sequentes* or *et sequentia* ("and the following")	FCLAA	Federal Cigarette Labeling and Advertising Act
EU	European Union	FCRA	Fair Credit Reporting Act
Euratom	European Atomic Energy Community	FCU	Federal credit unions
		FCUA	Federal Credit Union Act
Eur. Ct. H.R.	European Court of Human Rights	FCZ	Fishery Conservation Zone
Ex.	English Exchequer Reports, Welsby, Hurlstone & Gordon	FDA	Food and Drug Administration
Exch.	Exchequer Reports (Welsby, Hurlstone & Gordon)	FDIC	Federal Deposit Insurance Corporation
		FDPC	Federal Data Processing Center
Ex Com	Executive Committee of the National Security Council	FEC	Federal Election Commission
Eximbank	Export-Import Bank of the United States	FECA	Federal Election Campaign Act of 1971
F.	Federal Reporter	Fed. Cas.	Federal Cases
F. 2d	Federal Reporter, Second Series	FEHA	Fair Employment and Housing Act
FAA	Federal Aviation Administration; Federal Arbitration Act	FEHBA	Federal Employees Health Benefit Act
		FEMA	Federal Emergency Management Agency
FAAA	Federal Alcohol Administration Act	FERC	Federal Energy Regulatory Commission
FACE	Freedom of Access to Clinic Entrances Act of 1994	FFB	Federal Financing Bank
		FFDC	Federal Food, Drug, and Cosmetics Act
FACT	Feminist Anti-Censorship Task Force	FGIS	Federal Grain Inspection Service
FAIRA	Federal Agriculture Improvement and Reform Act of 1996	FHA	Federal Housing Administration
FAMLA	Family and Medical Leave Act of 1993	FHAA	Fair Housing Amendments Act of 1998
Fannie Mae	Federal National Mortgage Association	FHWA	Federal Highway Administration
FAO	Food and Agriculture Organization of the United Nations	FIA	Federal Insurance Administration
		FIC	Federal Information Centers; Federation of Insurance Counsel
FAR	Federal Acquisition Regulations		

FICA	Federal Insurance Contributions Act	FTA	U.S.-Canada Free Trade Agreement of 1988
FIFRA	Federal Insecticide, Fungicide, and Rodenticide Act	FTC	Federal Trade Commission
		FTCA	Federal Tort Claims Act
FIP	Forestry Incentives Program	FTS	Federal Telecommunications System
FIRREA	Financial Institutions Reform, Recovery, and Enforcement Act of 1989	FTS2000	Federal Telecommunications System 2000
FISA	Foreign Intelligence Surveillance Act of 1978	FUCA	Federal Unemployment Compensation Act of 1988
FISC	Foreign Intelligence Surveillance Court of Review	FUTA	Federal Unemployment Tax Act
FJC	Federal Judicial Center	FWPCA	Federal Water Pollution Control Act of 1948
FLSA	Fair Labor Standards Act		
FMC	Federal Maritime Commission	FWS	Fish and Wildlife Service
		GAL	Guardian ad litem
FMCS	Federal Mediation and Conciliation Service	GAO	General Accounting Office; Governmental Affairs Office
FmHA	Farmers Home Administration	GAOR	General Assembly Official Records, United Nations
FMLA	Family and Medical Leave Act of 1993		
FNMA	Federal National Mortgage Association, "Fannie Mae"	GAAP	Generally accepted accounting principles
		GA Res.	General Assembly Resolution (United Nations)
F.O.B.	Free on board		
FOIA	Freedom of Information Act	GATT	General Agreement on Tariffs and Trade
FOMC	Federal Open Market Committee	GCA	Gun Control Act
FPA	Federal Power Act of 1935	Gen. Cls. Comm.	General Claims Commission, United States and Panama; General Claims United States and Mexico
FPC	Federal Power Commission		
FPMR	Federal Property Management Regulations	Geo. II	King George II (Great Britain)
FPRS	Federal Property Resources Service	Geo. III	King George III (Great Britain)
FR	Federal Register		
FRA	Federal Railroad Administration	GHB	Gamma-hydroxybutrate
		GI	Government Issue
FRB	Federal Reserve Board	GID	General Intelligence Division
FRC	Federal Radio Commission		
		GM	General Motors
F.R.D.	Federal Rules Decisions	GNMA	Government National Mortgage Association, "Ginnie Mae"
FSA	Family Support Act		
FSB	Federal'naya Sluzhba Bezopasnosti (the Federal Security Service of Russia)		
		GNP	Gross national product
		GOP	Grand Old Party (Republican Party)
FSLIC	Federal Savings and Loan Insurance Corporation	GOPAC	Grand Old Party Action Committee
FSQS	Food Safety and Quality Service	GPA	Office of Governmental and Public Affairs
FSS	Federal Supply Service	GPO	Government Printing Office
F. Supp.	Federal Supplement		

GRAS	Generally recognized as safe	Hudson, Internatl. Legis.	Manley Ottmer Hudson, ed., *International Legislation: A Collection of the Texts of Multipartite International Instruments of General Interest Beginning with the Covenant of the League of Nations* (1931)
Gr. Br., Crim. Ct. App.	Great Britain, Court of Criminal Appeals		
GRNL	Gay Rights-National Lobby		
GSA	General Services Administration		
Hackworth	Green Haywood Hackworth, *Digest of International Law* (1940–1944)	Hudson, World Court Reps.	Manley Ottmer Hudson, ea., *World Court Reports* (1934–)
		Hun	Hun's New York Supreme Court Reports
Hay and Marriott	Great Britain. High Court of Admiralty, *Decisions in the High Court of Admiralty during the Time of Sir George Hay and of Sir James Marriott, Late Judges of That Court* (1801)	Hunt's Rept.	Bert L. Hunt, *Report of the American and Panamanian General Claims Arbitration* (1934)
		IAEA	International Atomic Energy Agency
		IALL	International Association of Law Libraries
H.B.	House Bill	IBA	International Bar Association
HBO	Home Box Office		
HCFA	Health Care Financing Administration	IBM	International Business Machines
H.Ct.	High Court	ICA	Interstate Commerce Act
HDS	Office of Human Development Services	ICBM	Intercontinental ballistic missile
Hen. & M.	Hening & Munford's Virginia Reports	ICC	Interstate Commerce Commission; International Criminal Court
HEW	Department of Health, Education, and Welfare		
HFCA	Health Care Financing Administration	ICJ	International Court of Justice
HGI	Handgun Control, Incorporated	ICM	Institute for Court Management
HHS	Department of Health and Human Services	IDEA	Individuals with Disabilities Education Act of 1975
Hill	Hill's New York Reports		
HIRE	Help through Industry Retraining and Employment	IDOP	International Dolphin Conservation Program
		IEP	Individualized educational program
HIV	Human immunodeficiency virus	IFC	International Finance Corporation
H.L.	House of Lords Cases (England)	IGRA	Indian Gaming Regulatory Act of 1988
H. Lords	House of Lords (England)	IJA	Institute of Judicial Administration
HMO	Health Maintenance Organization	IJC	International Joint Commission
HNIS	Human Nutrition Information Service	ILC	International Law Commission
Hong Kong L.R.	Hong Kong Law Reports	ILD	International Labor Defense
How.	Howard's United States Supreme Court Reports		
How. St. Trials	Howell's English State Trials	Ill. Dec.	Illinois Decisions
HUAC	House Un-American Activities Committee	ILO	International Labor Organization
HUD	Department of Housing and Urban Development	IMF	International Monetary Fund

INA	Immigration and Nationality Act	JCS	Joint Chiefs of Staff
IND	Investigational new drug	JDL	Jewish Defense League
INF Treaty	Intermediate-Range Nuclear Forces Treaty of 1987	JNOV	Judgment *non obstante veredicto* ("judgment nothing to recommend it" or "judgment notwithstanding the verdict")
INS	Immigration and Naturalization Service	JOBS	Jobs Opportunity and Basic Skills
INTELSAT	International Telecommunications Satellite Organization	John. Ch.	Johnson's New York Chancery Reports
Interpol	International Criminal Police Organization	Johns.	Johnson's Reports (New York)
Int'l. Law Reps.	International Law Reports	JP	Justice of the peace
Intl. Legal Mats.	International Legal Materials	K.B.	King's Bench Reports (England)
IOC	International Olympic Committee	KFC	Kentucky Fried Chicken
IPDC	International Program for the Development of Communication	KGB	Komitet Gosudarstvennoi Bezopasnosti (the State Security Committee for countries in the former Soviet Union)
IPO	Intellectual Property Owners	KKK	Ku Klux Klan
IPP	Independent power producer	KMT	Kuomintang (Chinese, "national people's party")
IQ	Intelligence quotient	LAD	Law Against Discrimination
I.R.	Irish Reports		
IRA	Individual retirement account; Irish Republican Army	LAPD	Los Angeles Police Department
IRC	Internal Revenue Code	LC	Library of Congress
IRCA	Immigration Reform and Control Act of 1986	LCHA	Longshoremen's and Harbor Workers Compensation Act of 1927
IRS	Internal Revenue Service	LD50	Lethal dose 50
ISO	Independent service organization	LDEF	Legal Defense and Education Fund (NOW)
ISP	Internet service provider	LDF	Legal Defense Fund, Legal Defense and Educational Fund of the NAACP
ISSN	International Standard Serial Numbers		
ITA	International Trade Administration	LEAA	Law Enforcement Assistance Administration
ITI	Information Technology Integration	L.Ed.	Lawyers' Edition Supreme Court Reports
ITO	International Trade Organization	LI	Letter of interpretation
ITS	Information Technology Service	LLC	Limited Liability Company
ITT	International Telephone and Telegraph Corporation	LLP	Limited Liability Partnership
ITU	International Telecommunication Union	LMSA	Labor-Management Services Administration
IUD	Intrauterine device	LNTS	League of Nations Treaty Series
IWC	International Whaling Commission	Lofft's Rep.	Lofft's English King's Bench Reports
IWW	Industrial Workers of the World	L.R.	Law Reports (English)
JAGC	Judge Advocate General's Corps	LSAC	Law School Admission Council

LSAS	Law School Admission Service	Miller	David Hunter Miller, ea., *Treaties and Other International Acts of the United States of America* (1931–1948)
LSAT	Law School Aptitude Test		
LSC	Legal Services Corporation; Legal Services for Children	Minn.	Minnesota Reports
		MINS	Minors in need of supervision
LSD	Lysergic acid diethylamide	MIRV	Multiple independently targetable reentry vehicle
LSDAS	Law School Data Assembly Service	MIRVed ICBM	Multiple independently targetable reentry vehicled intercontinental ballistic missile
LTBT	Limited Test Ban Treaty		
LTC	Long Term Care		
MAD	Mutual assured destruction	Misc.	Miscellaneous Reports, New York
MADD	Mothers against Drunk Driving	Mixed Claims Comm., Report of Decs	Mixed Claims Commission, United States and Germany, Report of Decisions
MALDEF	Mexican American Legal Defense and Educational Fund		
Malloy	William M. Malloy, ed., *Treaties, Conventions International Acts, Protocols, and Agreements between the United States of America and Other Powers* (1910–1938)	M.J.	Military Justice Reporter
		MLAP	Migrant Legal Action Program
		MLB	Major League Baseball
		MLDP	Mississippi Loyalist Democratic Party
		MMI	Moslem Mosque, Incorporated
Martens	Georg Friedrich von Martens, ea., *Noveau recueil général de traités et autres actes relatifs aux rapports de droit international* (Series I, 20 vols. [1843–1875]; Series II, 35 vols. [1876–1908]; Series III [1909–])	MMPA	Marine Mammal Protection Act of 1972
		Mo.	Missouri Reports
		MOD	Masters of Deception
		Mod.	Modern Reports, English King's Bench, etc.
		Moore, Dig. Intl. Law	John Bassett Moore, *A Digest of International Law*, 8 vols. (1906)
Mass.	Massachusetts Reports	Moore, Intl. Arbs.	John Bassett Moore, *History and Digest of the International Arbitrations to Which United States Has Been a Party*, 6 vols. (1898)
MCC	Metropolitan Correctional Center		
MCCA	Medicare Catastrophic Coverage Act of 1988		
MCH	Maternal and Child Health Bureau		
MCRA	Medical Care Recovery Act of 1962	Morison	William Maxwell Morison, *The Scots Revised Report: Morison's Dictionary of Decisions* (1908–09)
MDA	Medical Devices Amendments of 1976		
Md. App.	Maryland, Appeal Cases	M.P.	Member of Parliament
M.D. Ga.	Middle District, Georgia	MP3	MPEG Audio Layer 3
Mercy	Movement Ensuring the Right to Choose for Yourself	MPAA	Motion Picture Association of America
		MPAS	Michigan Protection and Advocacy Service
Metc.	Metcalf's Massachusetts Reports	MPEG	Motion Picture Experts Group
MFDP	Mississippi Freedom Democratic party	mpg	Miles per gallon
MGT	Management	MPPDA	Motion Picture Producers and Distributors of America
MHSS	Military Health Services System		

MPRSA	Marine Protection, Research, and Sanctuaries Act of 1972	NBS	National Bureau of Standards
M.R.	Master of the Rolls	NCA	Noise Control Act; National Command Authorities
MS-DOS	Microsoft Disk Operating System	NCAA	National Collegiate Athletic Association
MSHA	Mine Safety and Health Administration	NCAC	National Coalition against Censorship
MSPB	Merit Systems Protection Board	NCCB	National Consumer Cooperative Bank
MSSA	Military Selective Service Act	NCE	Northwest Community Exchange
N/A	Not Available	NCF	National Chamber Foundation
NAACP	National Association for the Advancement of Colored People	NCIP	National Crime Insurance Program
NAAQS	National Ambient Air Quality Standards	NCJA	National Criminal Justice Association
NAB	National Association of Broadcasters	NCLB	National Civil Liberties Bureau
NABSW	National Association of Black Social Workers	NCP	National contingency plan
NACDL	National Association of Criminal Defense Lawyers	NCSC	National Center for State Courts
NAFTA	North American Free Trade Agreement of 1993	NCUA	National Credit Union Administration
NAGHSR	National Association of Governors' Highway Safety Representatives	NDA	New drug application
		N.D. Ill.	Northern District, Illinois
NALA	National Association of Legal Assistants	NDU	National Defense University
NAM	National Association of Manufacturers	N.D. Wash.	Northern District, Washington
NAR	National Association of Realtors	N.E.	North Eastern Reporter
NARAL	National Abortion and Reproductive Rights Action League	N.E. 2d	North Eastern Reporter, Second Series
		NEA	National Endowment for the Arts; National Education Association
NARF	Native American Rights Fund		
NARS	National Archives and Record Service	NEH	National Endowment for the Humanities
NASA	National Aeronautics and Space Administration	NEPA	National Environmental Protection Act; National Endowment Policy Act
NASD	National Association of Securities Dealers		
NATO	North Atlantic Treaty Organization	NET Act	No Electronic Theft Act
NAVINFO	Navy Information Offices	NFIB	National Federation of Independent Businesses
NAWSA	National American Woman's Suffrage Association	NFIP	National Flood Insurance Program
		NFL	National Football League
NBA	National Bar Association; National Basketball Association	NFPA	National Federation of Paralegal Associations
		NGLTF	National Gay and Lesbian Task Force
NBC	National Broadcasting Company	NHL	National Hockey League
NBLSA	National Black Law Student Association	NHRA	Nursing Home Reform Act of 1987

NHTSA	National Highway Traffic Safety Administration	NPR	National Public Radio
		NPS	National Park Service
		NPT	Nuclear Non-Proliferation Treaty of 1970
Nielsen's Rept.	Frederick Kenelm Nielsen, *American and British Claims Arbitration under the Special Agreement Concluded between the United States and Great Britain, August 18, 1910* (1926)	NRA	National Rifle Association; National Recovery Act
		NRC	Nuclear Regulatory Commission
		NRLC	National Right to Life Committee
NIEO	New International Economic Order	NRTA	National Retired Teachers Association
NIGC	National Indian Gaming Commission	NSA	National Security Agency
NIH	National Institutes of Health	NSC	National Security Council
NIJ	National Institute of Justice	NSCLC	National Senior Citizens Law Center
NIRA	National Industrial Recovery Act of 1933; National Industrial Recovery Administration	NSF	National Science Foundation
		NSFNET	National Science Foundation Network
NIST	National Institute of Standards and Technology	NSI	Network Solutions, Inc.
N.J.	New Jersey Reports	NTIA	National Telecommunications and Information Administration
N.J. Super.	New Jersey Superior Court Reports		
NLEA	Nutrition Labeling and Education Act of 1990	NTID	National Technical Institute for the Deaf
NLRA	National Labor Relations Act	NTIS	National Technical Information Service
NLRB	National Labor Relations Board	NTS	Naval Telecommunications System
NMFS	National Marine Fisheries Service		
No.	Number	NTSB	National Transportation Safety Board
NOAA	National Oceanic and Atmospheric Administration	NVRA	National Voter Registration Act
NOC	National Olympic Committee	N.W.	North Western Reporter
		N.W. 2d	North Western Reporter, Second Series
NOI	Nation of Islam		
NOL	Net operating loss	NWSA	National Woman Suffrage Association
NORML	National Organization for the Reform of Marijuana Laws	N.Y.	New York Court of Appeals Reports
NOW	National Organization for Women	N.Y. 2d	New York Court of Appeals Reports, Second Series
NOW LDEF	National Organization for Women Legal Defense and Education Fund	N.Y.S.	New York Supplement Reporter
NOW/PAC	National Organization for Women Political Action Committee	N.Y.S. 2d	New York Supplement Reporter, Second Series
		NYSE	New York Stock Exchange
NPDES	National Pollutant Discharge Elimination System	NYSLA	New York State Liquor Authority
		N.Y. Sup.	New York Supreme Court Reports
NPL	National priorities list		

NYU	New York University	Ops. Comms.	Opinions of the
OAAU	Organization of Afro		Commissioners
	American Unity	OPSP	Office of Product
OAP	Office of Administrative		Standards Policy
	Procedure	O.R.	Ontario Reports
OAS	Organization of	OR	Official Records
	American States	OSHA	Occupational Safety and
OASDI	Old-age, Survivors, and		Health Act
	Disability Insurance	OSHRC	Occupational Safety and
	Benefits		Health Review
OASHDS	Office of the Assistant		Commission
	Secretary for Human	OSM	Office of Surface Mining
	Development Services	OSS	Office of Strategic
OCC	Office of Comptroller of		Services
	the Currency	OST	Office of the Secretary
OCED	Office of Comprehensive	OT	Office of Transportation
	Employment Development	OTA	Office of Technology
OCHAMPUS	Office of Civilian Health		Assessment
	and Medical Program	OTC	Over-the-counter
	of the Uniformed	OTS	Office of Thrift
	Services		Supervisors
OCSE	Office of Child Support	OUI	Operating under the
	Enforcement		influence
OEA	Organización de los	OVCI	Offshore Voluntary
	Estados Americanos		Compliance Initiative
OEM	Original Equipment	OWBPA	Older Workers Benefit
	Manufacturer		Protection Act
OFCCP	Office of Federal	OWRT	Office of Water Research
	Contract Compliance		and Technology
	Programs	P.	Pacific Reporter
OFPP	Office of Federal	P. 2d	Pacific Reporter, Second
	Procurement Policy		Series
OIC	Office of the	PAC	Political action
	Independent Counsel		committee
OICD	Office of International	Pa. Oyer	Pennsylvania Oyer and
	Cooperation and	and Terminer	Terminer Reports
	Development	PATCO	Professional Air
OIG	Office of the Inspector		Traffic Controllers
	General		Organization
OJARS	Office of Justice	PBGC	Pension Benefit
	Assistance, Research, and		Guaranty Corporation
	Statistics	PBS	Public Broadcasting
OMB	Office of Management		Service; Public Buildings
	and Budget		Service
OMPC	Office of Management,	P.C.	Privy Council (English
	Planning, and		Law Reports)
	Communications	PC	Personal computer;
ONP	Office of National		politically correct
	Programs	PCBs	Polychlorinated
OPD	Office of Policy		biphenyls
	Development	PCIJ	Permanent Court of
OPEC	Organization of		International Justice
	Petroleum Exporting		Series A-Judgments and
	Countries		Orders (1922–30)
OPIC	Overseas Private		Series B-Advisory
	Investment Corporation		Opinions (1922–30)
Ops. Atts. Gen.	Opinions of the		Series A/B-Judgments,
	Attorneys-General of the		Orders, and Advisory
	United States		Opinions (1931–40)

	Series C-Pleadings, Oral Statements, and Documents relating to Judgments and Advisory Opinions (1923–42)	PLO	Palestine Liberation Organization
		PLRA	Prison Litigation Reform Act of 1995
	Series D-Acts and Documents concerning the Organization of the World Court (1922 –47)	PNET	Peaceful Nuclear Explosions Treaty
		PONY	Prostitutes of New York
		POW-MIA	Prisoner of war-missing in action
	Series E-Annual Reports (1925–45)	Pratt	Frederic Thomas Pratt, *Law of Contraband of War, with a Selection of Cases from Papers of the Right Honourable Sir George Lee* (1856)
PCP	Phencyclidine		
P.D.	Probate Division, English Law Reports (1876–1890)		
PDA	Pregnancy Discrimination Act of 1978	PRIDE	Prostitution to Independence, Dignity, and Equality
PD & R	Policy Development and Research	Proc.	Proceedings
Pepco	Potomac Electric Power Company	PRP	Potentially responsible party
Perm. Ct. of Arb.	Permanent Court of Arbitration	PSRO	Professional Standards Review Organization
PES	Post-Enumeration Survey	PTO	Patents and Trademark Office
Pet.	Peters' United States Supreme Court Reports	PURPA	Public Utilities Regulatory Policies Act
PETA	People for the Ethical Treatment of Animals	PUSH	People United to Serve Humanity
PGA	Professional Golfers Association	PUSH-Excel	PUSH for Excellence
PGM	Program	PWA	Public Works Administration
PHA	Public Housing Agency	PWSA	Ports and Waterways Safety Act of 1972
Phila. Ct. of Oyer and Terminer	Philadelphia Court of Oyer and Terminer	Q.B.	Queen's Bench (England)
PhRMA	Pharmaceutical Research and Manufacturers of America	QTIP	Qualified Terminable Interest Property
PHS	Public Health Service	Ralston's Rept.	Jackson Harvey Ralston, ed., *Venezuelan Arbitrations of 1903* (1904)
PIC	Private Industry Council		
PICJ	Permanent International Court of Justice	RC	Regional Commissioner
Pick.	Pickering's Massachusetts Reports	RCRA	Resource Conservation and Recovery Act
PIK	Payment in Kind	RCWP	Rural Clean Water Program
PINS	Persons in need of supervision	RDA	Rural Development Administration
PIRG	Public Interest Research Group	REA	Rural Electrification Administration
P.L.	Public Laws		
PLAN	Pro-Life Action Network	Rec. des Decs. des Trib. Arb. Mixtes	G. Gidel, ed., *Recueil des décisions des tribunaux arbitraux mixtes, institués par les traités de paix* (1922–30)
PLC	Plaintiffs' Legal Committee		
PLE	Product liability expenses		
PLI	Practicing Law Institute	Redmond	Vol. 3 of Charles I. Bevans, *Treaties and Other International Agreements of the United States of*
PLL	Product liability loss		
PLLP	Professional Limited Liability Partnership		

	America, 1776–1949 (compiled by C. F. Redmond) (1969)	Sandf.	Sandford's New York Superior Court Reports
RESPA	Real Estate Settlement Procedure Act of 1974	S and L	Savings and loan
		SARA	Superfund Amendment and Reauthorization Act
RFC	Reconstruction Finance Corporation	SAT	Scholastic Aptitude Test
		Sawy.	Sawyer's United States Circuit Court Reports
RFRA	Religious Freedom Restoration Act of 1993	SBA	Small Business Administration
RIAA	Recording Industry Association of America	SBI	Small Business Institute
RICO	Racketeer Influenced and Corrupt Organizations	SCCC	South Central Correctional Center
RLUIPA	Religious Land Use and Institutionalized Persons Act	SCLC	Southern Christian Leadership Conference
		Scott's Repts.	James Brown Scott, ed., *The Hague Court Reports*, 2 vols. (1916–32)
RNC	Republican National Committee		
Roscoe	Edward Stanley Roscoe, ed., *Reports of Prize Cases Determined in the High Court Admiralty before the Lords Commissioners of Appeals in Prize Causes and before the judicial Committee of the Privy Council from 1745 to 1859* (1905)	SCS	Soil Conservation Service; Social Conservative Service
		SCSEP	Senior Community Service Employment Program
		S.Ct.	Supreme Court Reporter
		S.D. Cal.	Southern District, California
		S.D. Fla.	Southern District, Florida
		S.D. Ga.	Southern District, Georgia
ROTC	Reserve Officers' Training Corps		
		SDI	Strategic Defense Initiative
RPP	Representative Payee Program	S.D. Me.	Southern District, Maine
R.S.	Revised Statutes	S.D.N.Y.	Southern District, New York
RTC	Resolution Trust Corp.		
RUDs	Reservations, understandings, and declarations	SDS	Students for a Democratic Society
		S.E.	South Eastern Reporter
Ryan White CARE Act	Ryan White Comprehensive AIDS Research Emergency Act of 1990	S.E. 2d	South Eastern Reporter, Second Series
		SEA	Science and Education Administration
SAC	Strategic Air Command	SEATO	Southeast Asia Treaty Organization
SACB	Subversive Activities Control Board	SEC	Securities and Exchange Commission
SADD	Students against Drunk Driving	Sec.	Section
SAF	Student Activities Fund	SEEK	Search for Elevation, Education and Knowledge
SAIF	Savings Association Insurance Fund	SEOO	State Economic Opportunity Office
SALT	Strategic Arms Limitation Talks	SEP	Simplified employee pension plan
SALT I	Strategic Arms Limitation Talks of 1969–72	Ser.	Series
		Sess.	Session
SALT II	Strategic Arms Limitation Talks of 1979	SGLI	Servicemen's Group Life Insurance
SAMHSA	Substance Abuse and Mental Health Services Administration	SIP	State implementation plan
		SLA	Symbionese Liberation Army

SLAPPs	Strategic Lawsuits Against Public Participation	TNT	Trinitrotoluene
SLBM	Submarine-launched ballistic missile	TOP	Targeted Outreach Program
SNCC	Student Nonviolent Coordinating Committee	TPUS	Transportation and Public Utilities Service
So.	Southern Reporter	TQM	Total Quality Management
So. 2d	Southern Reporter, Second Series	Tripartite Claims Comm., Decs. and Ops.	Tripartite Claims Commission (United States, Austria, and Hungary), Decisions and
SPA	Software Publisher's Association		Opinions
Spec. Sess.	Special Session	TRI-TAC	Joint Tactical
SPLC	Southern Poverty Law Center		Communications
SRA	Sentencing Reform Act of 1984	TRO	Temporary restraining order
SS	Schutzstaffel (German, "Protection Echelon")	TS	Treaty Series, United States
SSA	Social Security Administration	TSCA	Toxic Substance Control Act
SSI	Supplemental Security Income	TSDs	Transporters, storers, and disposers
START I	Strategic Arms Reduction Treaty of 1991	TSU	Texas Southern University
START II	Strategic Arms Reduction Treaty of 1993	TTBT	Threshold Test Ban Treaty
Stat.	United States Statutes at Large	TV	Television
STS	Space Transportation Systems	TVA	Tennessee Valley Authority
St. Tr.	State Trials, English	TWA	Trans World Airlines
STURAA	Surface Transportation and Uniform Relocation Assistance Act of 1987	UAW	United Auto Workers; United Automobile, Aerospace, and Agricultural Implements Workers of America
Sup. Ct. of Justice, Mexico	Supreme Court of Justice, Mexico	U.C.C.	Uniform Commercial Code; Universal Copyright
Supp.	Supplement		Convention
S.W.	South Western Reporter	U.C.C.C.	Uniform Consumer Credit Code
S.W. 2d	South Western Reporter, Second Series	UCCJA	Uniform Child Custody Jurisdiction Act
SWAPO	South-West Africa People's Organization	UCMJ	Uniform Code of Military Justice
SWAT	Special Weapons and Tactics	UCPP	Urban Crime Prevention Program
SWP	Socialist Workers Party	UCS	United Counseling Service
TDP	Trade and Development Program	UDC	United Daughters of the Confederacy
Tex. Sup.	Texas Supreme Court Reports	UFW	United Farm Workers
THAAD	Theater High-Altitude Area Defense System	UHF	Ultrahigh frequency
THC	Tetrahydrocannabinol	UIFSA	Uniform Interstate Family Support Act
TI	Tobacco Institute	UIS	Unemployment Insurance Service
TIA	Trust Indenture Act of 1939	UMDA	Uniform Marriage and Divorce Act
TIAS	Treaties and Other International Acts Series (United States)		

UMTA	Urban Mass Transportation Administration	USCMA	United States Court of Military Appeals
U.N.	United Nations	USDA	U.S. Department of Agriculture
UNCITRAL	United Nations Commission on International Trade Law	USES	United States Employment Service
UNCTAD	United Nations Conference on Trade and Development	USFA	United States Fire Administration
		USFS	U.S. Forest Service
UN Doc.	United Nations Documents	USGA	United States Golf Association
UNDP	United Nations Development Program	USICA	International Communication Agency, United States
UNEF	United Nations Emergency Force	USMS	U.S. Marshals Service
UNESCO	United Nations Educational, Scientific, and Cultural Organization	USOC	U.S. Olympic Committee
		USSC	U.S. Sentencing Commission
UNICEF	United Nations Children's Fund (formerly United Nations International Children's Emergency Fund)	USSG	United States Sentencing Guidelines
		U.S.S.R.	Union of Soviet Socialist Republics
		UST	United States Treaties
UNIDO	United Nations Industrial and Development Organization	USTS	United States Travel Service
		v.	*Versus*
Unif. L. Ann.	Uniform Laws Annotated	VA	Department of Veterans Affairs
UN Repts. Intl. Arb. Awards	United Nations Reports of International Arbitral Awards	VAR	Veterans Affairs and Rehabilitation Commission
UNTS	United Nations Treaty Series	VAWA	Violence against Women Act
UPI	United Press International	VFW	Veterans of Foreign Wars
		VGLI	Veterans Group Life Insurance
URESA	Uniform Reciprocal Enforcement of Support Act	Vict.	Queen Victoria (Great Britain)
U.S.	United States	VIN	Vehicle identification number
U.S.A.	United States of America		
USAF	United States Air Force	VISTA	Volunteers in Service to America
USA PATRIOT Act	Uniting and Strengthening America by Providing Appropriate Tools Required to Intercept and Obstruct Terrorism Act	VJRA	Veterans Judicial Review Act of 1988
		V.L.A.	Volunteer Lawyers for the Arts
		VMI	Virginia Military Institute
U.S. App. D.C.	United States Court of Appeals for the District of Columbia	VMLI	Veterans Mortgage Life Insurance
U.S.C.	United States Code; University of Southern California	VOCAL	Victims of Child Abuse Laws
		VRA	Voting Rights Act
U.S.C.A.	United States Code Annotated	WAC	Women's Army Corps
		Wall.	Wallace's United States Supreme Court Reports
U.S.C.C.A.N.	United States Code Congressional and Administrative News	Wash. 2d	Washington Reports, Second Series

WAVES	Women Accepted for Volunteer Service	WIC	Women, Infants, and Children program
WCTU	Women's Christian Temperance Union	Will. and Mar.	King William and Queen Mary (Great Britain)
W.D. Wash.	Western District, Washington	WIN	WESTLAW Is Natural; Whip Inflation Now; Work Incentive Program
W.D. Wis.	Western District, Wisconsin	WIPO	World Intellectual Property Organization
WEAL	*West's Encyclopedia of American Law,* Women's Equity Action League	WIU	Workers' Industrial Union
Wend.	Wendell's New York Reports	W.L.R.	Weekly Law Reports, England
WFSE	Washington Federation of State Employees	WPA	Works Progress Administration
Wheat.	Wheaton's United States Supreme Court Reports	WPPDA	Welfare and Pension Plans Disclosure Act
Wheel. Cr. Cases	Wheeler's New York Criminal Cases	WTO	World Trade Organization
WHISPER	Women Hurt in Systems of Prostitution Engaged in Revolt	WWI	World War I
		WWII	World War II
Whiteman	Marjorie Millace Whiteman, *Digest of International Law,* 15 vols. (1963–73)	Yates Sel. Cas.	Yates's New York Select Cases
		YMCA	Young Men's Christian Association
WHO	World Health Organization	YWCA	Young Women's Christian Association